The Ultimate Guide to

U.S. Special Forces

Skills, Tactics, and Techniques

Edited by
Jay McCullough

Skyhorse Publishing

Skyhorse Publishing books may be purchased in bulk at special discounts for sales promotion, corporate gifts, fund-raising, or educational purposes. Special editions can also be created to specifications. For details, contact the Special Sales Department, Skyhorse Publishing, 307 West 36th Street, 11th Floor, New York, NY 10018 or info@skyhorsepublishing.com.

www.skyhorsepublishing.com

10 9 8 7 6 5 4 3 2 1

Library of Congress Cataloging-in-Publication Data is available on file.
ISBN: 978-1-61608-208-6

Printed in Canada

Contents

INTRODUCTION

This book is actually the third in a successful series, and they should be successful given that they are essentially compiled from materials written by some of the military's most articulate and well-versed writers, who unfortunately remain anonymous. The previous two tomes, *The Ultimate Guide to U.S. Army Skills, Tactics, and Techniques* and *The Ultimate Guide to U.S. Army Combat Skills, Tactics, and Techniques*, could cover interesting information of a more general nature. Dangerous snake species, survival tips in a post-nuclear environment, and hand-to-hand combat moves are somehow more finite, quantifiable, easily illustrated, and more able to be organized and put into a readable format. But this volume is necessarily specialized, and it stands to reason because although everybody goes through basic training, Special Forces have additional, specialized training.

An institution is only ever as good as the people who comprise it, and its continued success depends on how and whether those individuals can pass on their invaluable experience to new practitioners. I suspect that Special Forces training is more occult because much of it relies solely on experienced instructors, and because much of their wisdom will never be written down.

There are however aspects of that training that for one reason or another someone has seen fit to archive, and here is where you'll find some of the choicest selections, specifically written by or for the organizations within the Department of Defense that are recognized as being specifically "Special Forces." From a survey of everything I could acquire to consider for inclusion here, my understanding is that SF troops are assigned to unusual tasks, operations that cannot be accomplished by diplomacy or brute force. In other words, "Special" Operations. The impression left by the literature they use to train is that of the classic schlocky "Special Ops" movie, in that they concern themselves with insertion into a foreign land, observation, demolition or direct action of some sort, escape, and debriefing. And it is in that spirit that I have organized the sections and chapters here.

It's not every day you'll be navigating a zodiac by starlight, but you'll find that here. You may not take a donkey on your daily commute, but in some parts of the world it's one of the best ways of getting around. And you will likely never have to employ your sniper skills to stay still in a given place for days on end to observe someone or something with the degree of seriousness employed by someone whose life is on the line. But that's what makes these tasks unusual, worth cataloging, and the purview of an elite force within the military: In other words, Special Forces.

—Jay McCullough
January 2011
New Haven, Connecticut

PART I

Infiltration

One If By Sea: Special Forces Waterborne Operations

CHAPTER 1

Mission Planning

Special Forces operational detachments A (SFODAs) must conduct a detailed mission analysis to determine an appropriate method of infiltration. SF maritime operations are one of the many options available to a commander to infiltrate and exfiltrate a detachment into (or out of) a designated area of operations (AO) for the purpose of executing any of the SF missions. A thorough understanding of all factors impacting waterborne-related missions is essential due to the inherently higher levels of risk associated with even the most routine waterborne operations. The objective of this chapter is to outline mission, enemy, terrain and weather, troops and support available—time available and civil considerations (METT-TC) and planning considerations needed to successfully execute all types of waterborne operations.

PERSPECTIVE

1-1. Over five-eighths of the earth's surface is covered by water. SF units conduct waterborne operations to infiltrate a designated target area from these water-covered areas. Regardless of whether an AO has exposed coastlines, coastal river junctions, or harbors, many areas will have large rivers, lakes, canals, or other inland waterways located within their boundaries. These maritime or riverine features represent exploitable characteristics that special operations forces (SOF) can use to their advantage.

1-2. Throughout the world, military equipment sales programs by various countries have caused a proliferation of advanced radar technologies and coastal air defense systems. As local governments seek to exercise greater control over their indigenous territories, these facilities and the associated risks to SOF units' normal means of infiltration and exfiltration will continue to increase. Waterborne infiltrations and exfiltrations keep the high-value air, surface, or subsurface infiltration assets offshore and out of the detection and threat ranges of coastal defense installations.

1-3. Waterborne operations are a means to an end. Despite the increased use of sophisticated coastal surveillance systems and active surface and air interdiction efforts on the part of regional governments, local inhabitants continue to engage in various illicit activities; for example, smuggling and illegal fishing just as their forebears have for centuries. In many parts of the world, long coastlines, extensive waterways, and small undermanned and underpaid navies exacerbate these problems. The clandestine nature and high probability of success for these illicit operations mirrors SF unit's requirements for successful infiltrations into, or exfiltrations out of, potentially hostile areas of responsibility (AORs).

1-4. Personnel involved in waterborne operations require extensive knowledge of hydrography, meteorology, navigation, and maritime operations (MAROPS). They must be able to conduct realistic premission training, gather information, plan, rehearse, and use the appropriate waterborne operations technique to accomplish their assigned mission.

1-5. Commanders use sophisticated techniques and equipment to conduct waterborne operations. When used correctly, these factors give commanders another means to move teams and influence the battlefield. The skills and techniques used in waterborne operations are equally applicable to all SF missions, especially direct action (DA), special reconnaissance (SR), unconventional warfare (UW), and foreign internal defense (FID). Internal mission support taskings and humanitarian assistance (HA) missions may also require waterborne operations capability.

METT-TC

1-6. The successful execution of any operation is directly related to thorough and detailed planning. Mission planning begins with a detailed analysis of METT-TC questions (Table 1-1), with qualifiers pertaining to waterborne operations, that the SFODA must consider when selecting a method of infiltration.

Table 1-1. METT-TC analysis

Factors	Questions
Mission	• What is the specified mission? • What are the implied missions? • Is the objective within range of a coastline or waterway that a detachment can use as a route to infiltrate the AOR?
Enemy	• What are the ranges of enemy detection capabilities? • Does the enemy have the ability to detect or interdict conventional infiltration techniques; for example, static-line parachute, high-altitude low-opening (HALO) parachute technique, or air-mobile insertion? • Does the enemy have an extensive coastline or internal waterways that are vulnerable to a maritime or waterborne infiltration? • Is the enemy capable of detecting and interdicting U.S. maritime assets outside the range of the detachment's intermediate (or final) transport method?
Terrain and Weather	• Is the weather conducive to a maritime operation? • Are sea states within the operational limits of the detachment's chosen infiltration method? • Are any weather patterns expected in the AO that might cause unacceptable sea conditions? • What is the percentage of illumination? Can the detachment infiltrate during periods of limited visibility and illumination? • Are the tides and currents favorable during the desired infiltration window? • Are there suitable primary and alternate beach landing sites (BLSs) available to the detachment? • What are the surf conditions at the tentative BLS?
Troops and Support Available	• Does the detachment have the training and experience to successfully execute the selected infiltration method? Is additional training required? • Does the detachment have time to do the required training and rehearsals? • What equipment is required to execute the primary mission? • Does the detachment have the means to transport the required equipment? • Does the equipment require special waterproofing? Can it be submerged? • Does the equipment have special handling and storage requirements during the transit portion of the mission?

Time Available	• Is the mission time-critical?
	• Given the complexity of MAROPS and the extended transit times required, is time available for the detachment to plan, rehearse, and execute a long-range infiltration?
	• Is the mission flexible enough to allow time for a MAROPS infiltration window that is dependent on meteorological and oceanographic conditions?
	• How far is it from the BLS and enemy detection capabilities to an over-the-horizon (OTH) debarkation point?
	  ▪ Can the detachment make it from the debarkation point to the BLS and complete actions during the hours of darkness?
	  ▪ Will the detachment have the time and fuel to move to an alternate BLS if the primary site is unsuitable or compromised?

Table 1-1. METT-TC analysis (*Continued*)

Factors	Questions
Civil Considerations	• Can the operation be executed clandestinely so that the civilian populace is unaware of it? • If the operation is compromised, what will be the repercussions to the local populace? • If the detachment is receiving support from the locals, is there a risk of reprisals against them?

1-7. A thorough METT-TC analysis concentrating on the above questions will determine if water infiltration is appropriate. The detachment must then complete the remainder of the mission planning process.

PHASES OF WATERBORNE OPERATIONS

1-8. To aid the SFOD in planning and executing a maritime operation, waterborne operations are divided into seven phases. Figure 1-1 shows each phase and the following paragraphs provide the details for each.

PHASE I—PREINFILTRATION PREPARATION

1-9. Preinfiltration preparation starts with preparing an estimate of the situation. The SFOD uses the military decision-making process (MDMP) to identify critical nodes in the mission and to develop courses of action (COAs) to address them. During this phase, the detachment will plan the mission, prepare orders, conduct briefbacks and training, prepare equipment, and conduct inspections and rehearsals.

1-10. The key to the premission process is determining the infiltration method that the detachment will use from its home station to the debarkation point. The method may be aircraft, surface craft, submarine, or a combination of methods. The type of infiltration will determine the planning and preparations required during Phase I. The method selected depends upon the mission, time, and distance.

Aircraft

1-11. There is a wide variety of fixed- and rotary-wing aircraft that can deliver infiltrating detachments. Aircraft provide the most practical and rapid means of transporting infiltrating detachments to a debarkation point. They may be delivered by—

- Conventional static-line parachute techniques.
- Military free-fall parachute techniques.
- Water landing by amphibious aircraft..
- Helocast or free-drop from helicopter.

Surface Craft

1-12. Combat swimmers, divers, and boat teams may also use surface craft to reach the debarkation point. This method is generally considered the most efficient means of transporting infiltrating detachments. Surface craft can transport large quantities of supplies and are relatively unaffected by weather up to the point of debarkation. This method also allows the detachment to conduct operational planning and preparations en route to the debarkation point.

Submarine

1-13. The submarine is an excellent insertion vehicle. However, it requires extensive training and coordination to use effectively. SF commanders may prefer this method to insert combat divers, swimmers, or boat teams because it is a very effective means for a clandestine insertion or recovery. (Chapter 14 further explains submarine operations.)

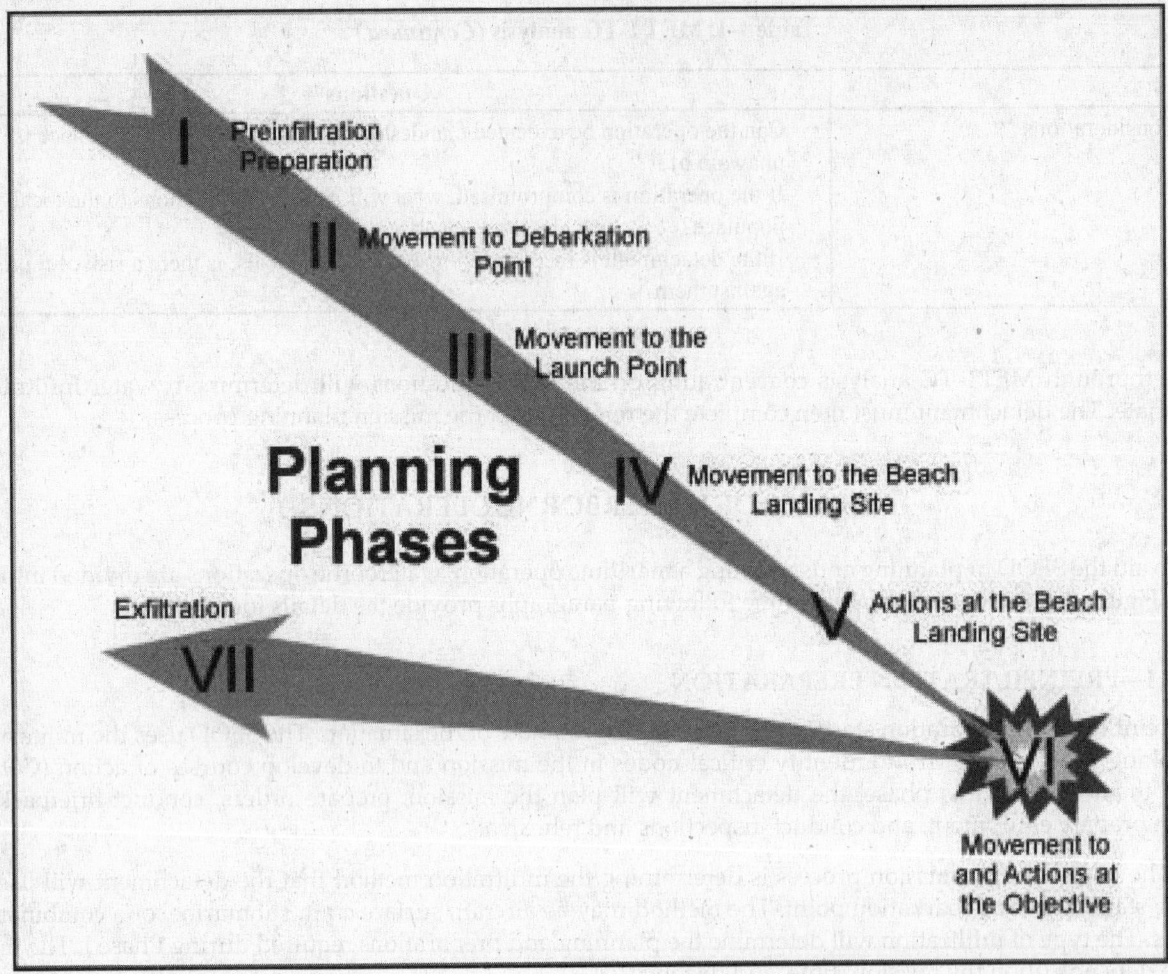

Figure 1-1. Waterborne operations planning phases

Combinations of Transport

1-14. In addition to aircraft, surface craft, and submarines, commanders may use various combinations of methods to deliver detachments. These combinations can enable commanders to create deception, increase the range of the mission, or decrease the time required for transport. To increase the range of the mission, operational elements may fly to a staging area and transfer to an aircraft carrier for transport to the debarkation point. Once there, carrier aircraft can transport the detachment to the next leg of the infiltration.

PHASE II—MOVEMENT TO DEBARKATION POINT

1-15. In Phase II of infiltration, the primary transport craft moves the swimmers to the selected debarkation point where they begin the initial transit to the BLS. All personnel should understand the following procedures while en route in the aircraft and surface craft.

Aircraft

1-16. During flight to the debarkation point, the pilot informs the troop commander of the aircraft's location and any changes in the infiltration plan. All personnel must know their relative position along the route in the event of a bail-out, an emergency abort, or enemy action. As the aircraft nears the debarkation point, the pilot provides preplanned time warnings for final personnel and equipment preparations. The infiltrating detachments arrive at the debarkation point by parachute operations, helocasting, or water landing.

1-17. In most situations, the delivery of swimmers by parachute during periods of limited or reduced visibility onto unmarked water drop zones (DZs) requires the use of the computed air release point (CARP). Parachutists exit the aircraft on the pilot's command at a point designated by the navigator, and attempt to group in the air as close as possible. Once in the water, they sink their air items and sterilize the DZ by sinking everything to ensure that nothing floats ashore. The detachment then begins movement to the BLS or launch point.

1-18. Enemy activity will usually prevent detachments parachuting within swimming range of a BLS. Normally a detachment will jump with inflatable boats, assemble on the boats, and motor the extended distances involved. When using inflatable assault boats, personnel should rig them for airdrop before loading the aircraft. At the command to exit the aircraft, personnel drop the rigged boatloads before they exit. Upon landing, predesignated personnel swim to the boats and begin derigging; they dispose of air items and prepare the boats for movement to the BLS. Remaining personnel link up with their buddy team members and rendezvous with the boats. (Chapters 6 and 7 discuss small-boat information).

Surface Craft

1-19. Designated personnel continue mission planning and preparations en route to the debarkation point. As they receive new or revised intelligence, they update the infiltration plan and inform all personnel of changes in the situation or mission. While en route, all personnel conduct rehearsals for each phase of the infiltration. The detachment should thoroughly rehearse debarkation procedures with those members of the crew assigned specific duties for the operation.

1-20. Upon arrival at the debarkation point, all personnel man their respective debarkation stations. The troop commander will be oriented in relation to the BLS and briefed on sea and surf conditions. Debarkation begins on orders from the vessel commander.

1-21. One of the simplest methods of debarkation is for swimmers to slip over the side of the vessel into the water; debarkation from large surface craft may require the use of landing nets. Once in the water, the swimmers link up with their swim buddies and begin movement to the BLS. Swimmers should only use this method when the hydrography and enemy situation permit debarkation within swimming range of the beach.

1-22. Swimmers can use a variation of this method when the situation requires debarkation beyond the swimmers' range. Here, the swimmers debark over the side of the surface craft and move by small watercraft to an intermediate transfer point. From there, the detachment uses inflatable assault boats to transport the swimmers to a launch point within swimming range of the beach.

PHASE III—MOVEMENT TO THE LAUNCH POINT

1-23. After the detachment reaches its debarkation point, it must conduct a transit to the launch point where it begins BLS procedures. The extended distances involved in any OTH operation require an intermediate transport system. The detachment normally uses inflatable assault boats and kayaks for this purpose. This equipment gives the detachment a planning range far greater than any combat swimmer operation and allows a larger mission equipment load. Inflatable assault boats or kayaks are especially useful when—

- Enemy air or coastal defense systems, hydrographic characteristics, or navigational errors prevent aircraft, surface craft, or submarines from delivering swimmers within range of the BLS.
- Tide, current, and wind conditions could cause swimmer fatigue.

1-24. Using boats requires detailed planning, extensive rehearsals, and consistent training that should take place in Phase I. Personnel must have a thorough knowledge of small-boat handling, dead reckoning or offset navigation techniques, and tide and current computations. They must maintain strict noise and light discipline throughout the operation, and adhere to the principles of patrolling as adapted from land operations, to include modifications of the movement formations.

1-25. The transit portion of the mission ends at the launch point. A launch point is the location where scout swimmers are released or combat divers and swimmers enter the water to begin the detachment's infiltration swim.

The enemy situation, hydrography, the type of equipment used, and the detachment's ability to swim the required distance determine how far the launch point should be from the BLS. The launch point can also be synonymous with the boat holding pool. Although well-conditioned personnel are capable of swimming extended distances, the maximum planning range for surface swimmers should not exceed 3,000 meters. Subsurface infiltrations should not exceed 1,500 meters (O/C) or 2,000 meters (C/C) unless diver propulsion vehicles (DPVs) are used.

1-26. Once at the launch point, the detachment sinks the inflatable boat, a designated member returns the boat to the primary surface transport vessel, or the detachment caches the boat at the BLS. Chapter 9 explains launch point procedures in detail.

PHASE IV—MOVEMENT TO THE BEACH LANDING SITE

1-27. After the infiltrating detachment enters the water at the launch point, its first action is to link up on a swim line and then swim along the predesignated azimuth toward the primary BLS. The equipment, enemy situation, and level of unit training determine whether they swim on the surface or subsurface. In some cases, a combination of surface and subsurface swimming techniques, commonly called turtle backing, can greatly extend the swimmers' range. However, it requires a closed-circuit underwater breathing apparatus (UBA), a special compass, and increased unit training.

1-28. As the detachment approaches the BLS, the commander signals swimmers to halt outside the surf and small arms fire zones. At this holding area a predesignated security team (scout swimmers) moves on the surface (or subsurface) to the BLS to determine the enemy situation. Once the scout swimmers determine that the site is clear of the enemy, they signal the remaining swimmers to come ashore. While waiting for the detachment, the scout swimmers establish left, right, and farside security (as appropriate) at the limits of visibility from the landing point. When the remaining swimmers reach the BLS, they sterilize it to obscure tracks, and remove equipment and debris to conceal evidence of the detachment's presence. The detachment then moves immediately to the assembly area or cache point.

1-29. In some situations, a reception committee may be present to assist with the infiltration by marking the BLS, providing guides, and transporting accompanying supplies. The detachment must coordinate the plan for initial contact with the reception committee before infiltration. The scout swimmers conducting the security check of the BLS make contact with the reception committee. Whenever the mission includes contact with unknown agencies, the detachment should make sure the communications plan includes a "duress" signal from the scout swimmers to the detachment and an abort contingency for the detachment.

PHASE V—ACTIONS AT THE BEACH LANDING SITE

1-30. At the BLS, the commander immediately accounts for his personnel and equipment. Infiltrating detachments are especially vulnerable to enemy action during this phase. To minimize the chances of detection the detachment must complete landing operations, clear the beach as rapidly as possible, and move directly inshore to the preselected assembly area. This area must provide cover and concealment and facilitate subsequent movement to the objective area. The swimmers cache equipment not required for the inland operation. If a reception committee is present, its leader coordinates personnel movement and provides current intelligence on the enemy situation. Finally, the detachment sterilizes the assembly area and begins moving to the objective area.

PHASE VI—MOVEMENT TO AND ACTIONS AT THE OBJECTIVE

1-31. Movement from the BLS to the objective area may require guides. If a reception committee is present, it provides guides to the area or mission support sites where additional equipment brought ashore may be cached. If guides are not available, the detachment follows the preselected route based on detailed intelligence and the patrolling plan developed during isolation. The route must take maximum advantage of cover and concealment, and must avoid enemy outposts, patrols, and installations. The detachment carries only mission-essential items (individual equipment, weapons, communications, and ammunition).

PHASE VII—EXFILTRATION

1-32. Exfiltration planning considerations for waterborne operations require the same preparations, tactics, and techniques as for infiltration. However, in exfiltration, the planners are primarily concerned with recovery methods. Distances involved in exfiltration usually require additional means of transport. Aircraft, surface craft, submarines, or various combinations of these three methods, can be used to recover infiltration swimmers. In addition, inflatable assault boats may be needed for seriously wounded personnel or for equipment.

BEACH LANDING SITE SELECTION CRITERIA

1-33. Before selecting a specific waterborne infiltration method, the SFODA examines the objective, the BLS, and the shipping and air assets available.

1-34. The BLS is of primary importance because it must facilitate and support the inland objective. The factors that determine the feasibility of a proposed BLS include hydrography, enemy situation, navaids, distance from the debarkation point to the BLS, beach vegetation and conditions, and routes of egress from the objective.

1-35. Hydrography deals with measuring and studying oceans and rivers along with their marginal land areas. Hydrographic conditions of interest to waterborne operations are ocean depth, beach depth, beach gradient, tide and surf conditions, and beach composition. Detailed hydrographic information can be obtained from a wide variety of sources, to include—

- Surf observation reports.
- BLS reports.
- Nautical charts.
- Tide and current data.
- Aerial photoreconnaissance.
- Hydrographic surveys.

Hydrographic surveys are the best and most accurate means of obtaining detailed and specific information concerning the BLS. However, these are normally prepared only for large-scale amphibious landings by U.S. Navy sea-air-land (SEAL) units or United States Marine Corps (USMC) reconnaissance (recon) units. It is not always possible to obtain as much detailed information on a BLS because of time limitations and the covert nature of the mission. Army terrain teams may also be able to supply applicable hydrographic information. Their duties include supplying information on coasts and beaches as well as inland waterway analysis. In these instances, up-to-date nautical charts, tide and current data, and photo reconnaissance provide the minimum data needed.

1-36. The enemy's situation and capabilities have a direct impact on the location of a proposed BLS. Ideally, a BLS would be located away from enemy observation and fields of fire. If this is not possible, the SFODA must consider the enemy's ability to locate and interdict the infiltration route based on—

- Location of coastal patrol boats.
- Coastal fortifications.
- Security outposts.
- Defensive obstacles.
- Artillery, mortar, and missile positions.
- Armor and mechanized units.
- Major communication and command posts.

1-37. Regardless of the hydrography or enemy situation, any SFODA must be skilled in basic navigation techniques when operating in oceans, large lakes, and rivers. Without basic skills, the infiltration detachment is severely limited and will not be able to apply the full range of techniques associated with waterborne operations. These skills include—

- Using dead-reckoning navigation.
- Reading nautical charts.

- Interpreting tidal data.
- Understanding international marine traffic buoys.
- Computing tidal current data for offset navigation.

1-38. The detachment determines what infiltration technique to use by the distance from the debarkation point to the BLS. For example, if the debarkation point from the primary vessel is 20 nautical miles offshore, the detachment uses a combat rubber raiding craft (CRRC) to bring them within range of the beach. Airdrops or helocasts can also deliver the detachment to a debarkation point. If the enemy situation permits, the same delivery systems could transport the detachment within swimming range of the BLS. Regardless of the combinations of delivery craft used, the distance should be no more than what the operational detachment can swim or travel by boat within the time available. The detachment should always use the simplest method possible to reduce potential equipment failures.

1-39. Hydrographic surveys, charts, photoreconnaissance, and tidal data outline the beach and vegetation conditions. The detachment should immediately determine the available cover and concealment once they arrive at the BLS. The BLS is the first danger area where combat swimmers are exposed to enemy observation and fire. The faster the detachment clears the beach of men and equipment, the less the chance of enemy detection. Therefore, the distance to the first covered and concealed location is extremely important. Personnel should also keep combat loads to an absolute minimum to make rapid movement off the beach easier.

1-40. Once the detachment completes infiltration, they move with the same stealth and secrecy inland to the target area. They can determine the suitability of a BLS by carefully analyzing the approach and withdrawal routes of the objective. The detachment should also examine all possible exfiltration points from the target area. Since the detachment has already transported the equipment ashore during infiltration, they can use this same equipment in exfiltration. Waterborne exfiltrations involve the same planning, preparation, and techniques required for infiltration. Offshore recoveries can be made by sea, air, or a combination of both.

SEQUENCE FOR CONDUCTING WATERBORNE OPERATIONS

1-41. Once planning considerations and shipping and air requirements have been determined, the means of conducting the waterborne operation become apparent. At this point, the commander divides the waterborne operation into four major phases: infiltration, movement to and from the objective, actions at the objective, and exfiltration. The most experienced personnel plan and develop the waterborne infiltration and exfiltration plan, and other designated personnel plan and develop land movements and actions at the objective. The detachment operations sergeant provides assignment taskings and ensures close coordination with all personnel.

1-42. To develop two separate plans that interconnect, the detachment should start at a common focal point. The easiest way to divide the operation is the transition point where the water meets the land. The focal point for both the waterborne infiltration and the land movement to the objective is at the BLS. Therefore, planning tasks for the waterborne infiltration end once the SFODA reaches the onshore assembly area. Consequently, the land movement to the objective starts once the detachment occupies the assembly area.

1-43. There are a few areas of waterborne planning that are vitally important for mission success. First, the infiltration should take place at night to provide the stealth and secrecy that the detachment needs. Second, the environmental factors produced by tides and currents must be suitable for successful infiltration. Therefore, the detachment must accurately plan the mission time to satisfy these two requirements. Personnel should use the reverse planning sequence to allow enough time for the most important phases of the operation to take place during the most favorable conditions. This sequence also enables the detachment to place emphasis on areas that are most critical to mission success. The following paragraphs explain each step of the reverse planning sequence.

BEACH SELECTION

1-44. The factors that form a suitable BLS have already been discussed. However, the SFODA also needs more detailed information to accurately plan for securing the BLS and for troop movement. These additional factors include—

- Offshore navigation conditions.
- Security precautions.
- Expected surf conditions.
- Distance from the launch point to the BLS.
- Access to the hinterland.

The detachment must also plan for an alternate BLS in case, upon arrival, the primary BLS is unsuitable or compromised. This adjustment may be the result of a delay in the operation, unexpected sea conditions, or a change in the enemy situation. The selection of an alternate BLS must meet the same mission requirements as the primary BLS. However, the alternate BLS should have a different azimuth orientation to counter any adverse weather effects on the primary BLS.

LAUNCH POINT

1-45. The launch point is the designated point where swimmers exit the boat within swimming range of the beach. In small-boat operations where the detachment will be taking CRRCs (or other watercraft) all the way onto the beach, the launch point is where designated scout swimmers exit the boat to survey and secure the BLS before the main element arrives. The launch point should be no farther than 2 nautical miles offshore to prevent unduly fatiguing the swimmers, and no closer than 500 yards (small arms range). Two nautical miles is the visible horizon for an observer six feet tall, standing on the beach. At this range, a CRRC with seated passengers is below the observer's line of sight. Additional factors limiting visibility such as percent of illumination, sea state, and weather conditions may allow the launch point to be moved much closer to the BLS. Personnel waiting offshore must also consider their ability to see features on shore so they can maintain position relative to the BLS in case the swimmers must return to the boats. Based on the tactical situation, swimmers can also designate the launch point as a noise abatement area in which they maintain strict noise and light discipline.

TRANSFER POINT

1-46. Commanders use a transfer point when the primary support vessel cannot deliver the SFODA within range of the beach due to hydrographic conditions or the danger of enemy detection. Depending upon the complexity of the infiltration plan, there may be several transfer points. These points are usually where the detachment transitions from the initial infiltration platform to an intermediate platform or to the detachment's organic assets, such as CRRCs, kayaks, or surface or subsurface swimming.

ROUTE SELECTION

1-47. The route selected by the SFODA depends primarily upon three elements: enemy situation, vessel capabilities, and vessel limitations. The detachment plans the route from the debarkation point to the BLS, taking advantage of all known navaids and checkpoints en route. After selecting the route, the detachment will prepare a navigation plan detailing time, distance, speed, course to steer, intended track, and navaids used to verify position. The SFODA should exercise caution when using navaids. During periods of conflict, they may be unavailable or even inaccurate and tampered with.

DEBARKATION POINT

1-48. The detachment's debarkation location is extremely important. It must start from a known location to execute dead-reckoning navigation. This method applies to surface craft as well as aircraft debarkation. En route to the debarkation point, the detachment members are assigned specific duties and stations. They rehearse debarkation procedures. At the debarkation point, the vessel commander orients the detachment to the BLS with a final update on weather and sea conditions. Once disembarked, the operational success will depend solely on the detachment's training and maritime skills.

1-49. Equally important as the reverse planning sequence is the ability to gather detailed information necessary to put together a highly accurate infiltration profile. The "typical beach profile" depicted in Figure 1-2 identifies portions of the ocean and marginal land areas of interest to waterborne operations. Any information that the detachment is lacking about one of these areas can be requested by name from the intelligence unit providing terrain analysis support. Once acquired, detachment personnel can use this information to update nautical charts. They also can use the identified changes in beach profile as checkpoints or phase lines when planning and coordinating troop movements. The terms used in identifying these areas of interest are standardized throughout military and civilian agencies, allowing for coordination between Joint and Sister Service commands.

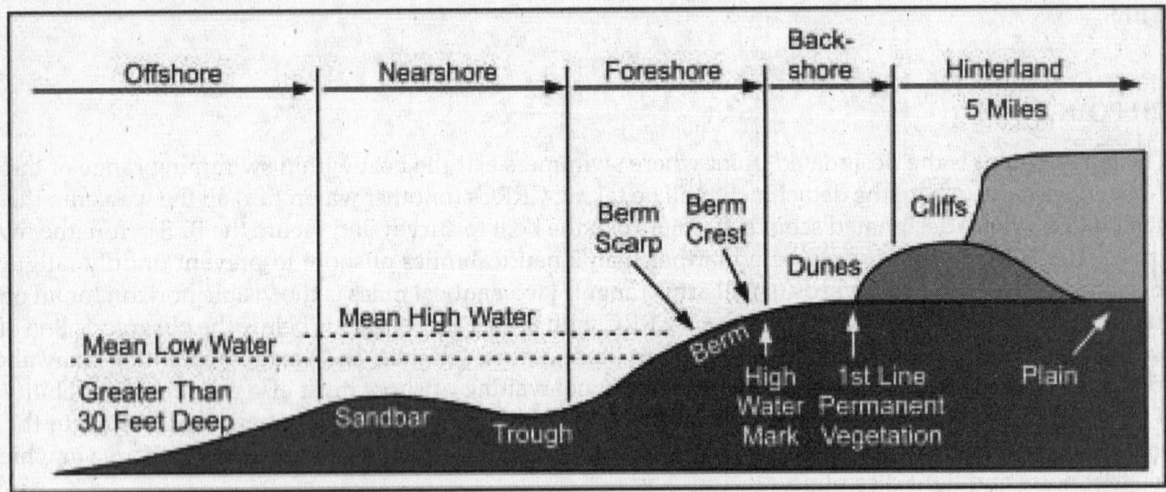

Figure 1-2. Typical beach profile

WATERBORNE EMPLOYMENT CONSIDERATIONS

1-50. If the detachment is fully trained, they can successfully execute the three methods of waterborne infiltration. Personnel must be able to calculate the time required to transit from release/launch/transfer point to the BLS for all types of infiltration methods. Figure 1-3 shows the nominal planning ranges. The time required can be calculated using the D = ST formula, where D equals the distance in nautical miles, S equals the speed in knots (kn), and T equals the time in hours.

1-51. If the detachment is fully trained, they can successfully execute the three methods of waterborne infiltration. Personnel must know how fast they can swim and how long it takes to swim a prescribed distance. This can be calculated using the D = ST formula, where D equals the distance in nautical miles, S equals the speed in knots (kn), and T equals the time in hours.

1-52. For infiltration planning purposes, the average swim speed for both surface and subsurface swimming is about 1 knot, equal to 1 nautical mile (NM) per hour on the surface of the water. Ideally, swims—especially underwater swims—are conducted at 3 minutes per 100 yards. This equals 2,000 yards per hour or about 1 NM per hour (1 NM = 2024.25 yards). This measure is true for both open- and closed-circuit swimming. This speed must not be exceeded when swimming closed-circuit due to the high probability of oxygen toxicity. Units should practice attaining this swim speed by using the 100-yard pace line. By using 1 knot as a planning speed, swimmers can easily apply calculations to nautical charts and other related maritime data.

1-53. Many special operations (SO) units are equipped with a closed-circuit UBA. Unlike open-circuit scuba, the closed-circuit UBA does not emit the diver's exhaust gases into the surrounding water. It uses pure oxygen as an air source. The diver rebreathes his own oxygen after his exhaust gas is recycled through a canister of carbon dioxide absorbent. By using closed-circuit UBA, the diver has a longer air supply duration and a more secure means of subsurface infiltration.

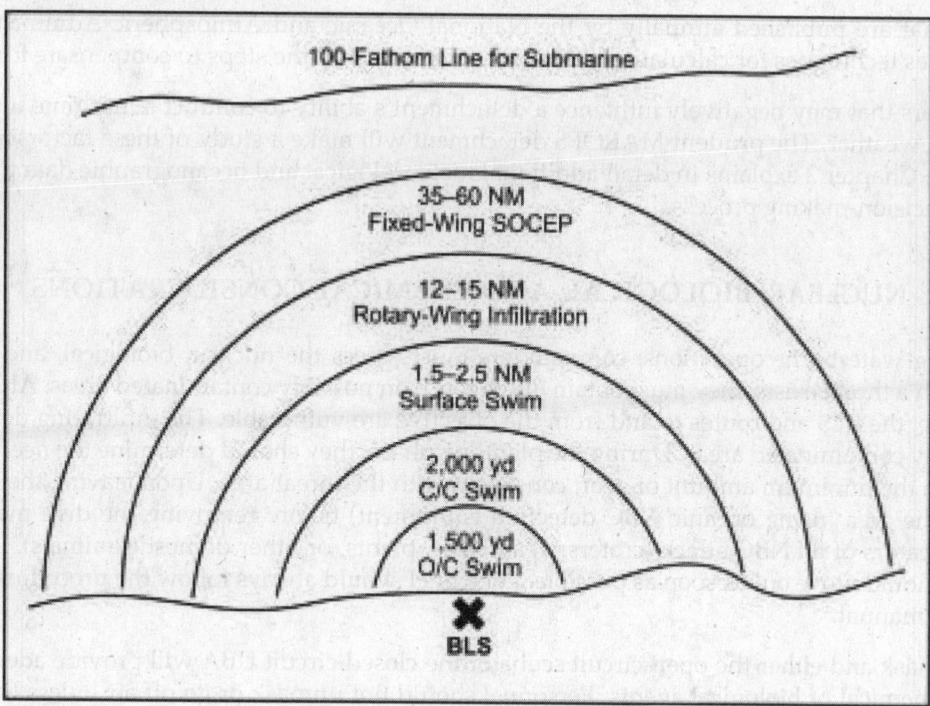

Figure 1-3. Nominal planning ranges

1-54. There is one major disadvantage in using closed-circuit UBAs. Most UBAs are pure oxygen rebreathers, and the effects of oxygen toxicity place limitations on the divers. To preclude the effects of oxygen toxicity, combat divers limit the depth of the dive, adhere to time limitations, and reduce physical exertion. The factors pertaining to oxygen toxicity and the most efficient oxygen consumption establish the diver's planning speed at about 1 knot when using a closed-circuit UBA.

1-55. In addition to planning the amount of time required for a combat swimmer or diver to travel from the launch point to the BLS, the detachment also plans for the amount of time required to travel from the debarkation point to the launch point. Personnel use the same formula (D = ST) to determine the travel time, regardless of the type of inflatable small boat and engine size. They can best determine this time during training, by running a measured nautical mile course over the ocean and recording the time. The small boat should be fully combat-loaded whenever checking for speed. Combat loads also include the total amount of fuel needed for the planned infiltration distance.

1-56. The detachment can establish a realistic mission capability once they determine the total travel time from the debarkation point to the BLS. The detachment can then execute an accurate, time-phased, and coordinated waterborne operation as long as they maintain a reasonable training sustainment program.

ENVIRONMENTAL CONSTRAINTS

1-57. The virtual all-weather capability of waterborne operations offers an increased advantage over other infiltration methods.

1-58. Environmental elements pose an immediate threat to the infiltration plan. The detachment must compensate for these to ensure successful completion of the operation. Two of the environmental elements that can impede or halt the conduct of waterborne operations are the height of the tide and the speed and direction of the tidal current. The detachment can predict both the tide height and tidal current with great accuracy by using Tide Tables and Tidal

Current Tables that are published annually by the National Oceanic and Atmospheric Administration (NOAA). Chapter 3 describes techniques for calculating tides, tidal currents, and the steps to compensate for their effects.

1-59. Other factors that may negatively influence a detachment's ability to conduct a maritime infiltration include wind, waves, and weather. The prudent MAROPS detachment will make a study of these factors as they pertain to basic seamanship. Chapter 2 explains in detail additional meteorological and oceanographic data that will influence a detachment's decision-making process.

NUCLEAR, BIOLOGICAL, AND CHEMICAL CONSIDERATIONS

1-60. In planning waterborne operations, commanders must assess the nuclear, biological, and chemical (NBC) threat. Where such a threat exists, they must obtain intelligence on possibly contaminated areas. Although risk in the water is negligible, the BLS and routes to and from the objective are vulnerable. The infiltrating detachment should carefully avoid any contaminated areas. During the planning phase, they should determine the need for NBC protective gear and take the minimum amount of gear, consistent with the threat area. Upon leaving the water, personnel should monitor the area (using organic NBC detection equipment) before removing the dive mask. They should also look for indicators of an NBC attack (craters; dead birds, plants, or other domestic animals). If the area is contaminated, they should move out as soon as possible. Personnel should always follow the procedures outlined in the appropriate NBC manual.

1-61. The dive mask and either the open-circuit scuba or the closed-circuit UBA will provide adequate respiratory protection from chemical or biological agents. Personnel should not unmask or go off air unless the area is clear or a protective mask can be donned within 9 seconds. Should the threat be such that protective equipment or clothing need to be carried, personnel must carry it in a waterproof container. Doing so will protect the equipment and clothing from the harmful effects of water and allow caching under water.

EXFILTRATION

1-62. The two main exfiltration methods used for waterborne exfiltration are small boats and surface swimming. Commanders generally use these methods to deliver the exfiltrating detachment from the beach departure site to a rendezvous point at sea. The most important part of exfiltration is the at-sea rendezvous (Chapter 13). The detachment is then either transferred to, or picked up by, one of the following secondary exfiltration methods:

- Submarine.
- Larger vessel.
- Rotary-wing aircraft.

1-63. In a submarine linkup, the boat teams or swimmers either do a subsurface lock-in or a surface load depending on tactical considerations. Although a surface recovery is simplest, a subsurface recovery is more secure. Submarine recovery procedures are complex and infrequent; therefore, the detachment must continuously sustain proficiency in submarine use. Boat teams or surface swimmers rendezvousing with larger vessels generally come aboard the vessels using cargo nets. Small boats can be recovered with a ship's hoist system, if necessary. When recovering swimmers or boat teams by helicopter, they are recovered by ladder or the boat may drive right up into the helicopter (depending on helicopter type).

CONSIDERATIONS

1-64. The detachment must thoroughly analyze tidal current data, offset navigation, and time distance criteria in infiltration methods as well as in exfiltration planning and execution. Personnel must direct detailed attention toward prearranged signals between the exfiltration detachment and the recovery systems.

1-65. Maritime operations are very equipment intensive. Detachments conducting waterborne exfiltrations must have assets available that are sufficient to exfiltrate the detachment, any casualties, and mission-essential equipment or personnel. Depending on the situation, the detachment may be able to use the same equipment it infiltrated with for its exfiltration. If using this COA, the detachment must ensure initial infiltration goes undetected because they will return to the same location to recover their cached equipment. In particular, personnel must ensure the BLS area is totally sanitized. Nothing must indicate the presence of infiltration swimmers or an equipment-cached area. Personnel can cache equipment either inland (using normal caching procedures) or subsurface. Other methods of supplying the detachment with the requisite equipment include pre-positioning and resupply.

CACHE

1-66. If a decision is made to emplace an underwater cache, the detachment should attempt to identify suitable areas of sea floor during premission planning. If adequate charts or hydrographic surveys of the AOR exist, it may be possible to identify ideal bottom conditions for emplacing underwater caches. Ideal conditions presuppose sufficient structures; for example, coral, rocky reefs, debris, or artificial constructs (pier or bridge pilings, docks) for the detachment to secure or anchor the cache so that it will not be disturbed. Flat, sandy bottoms that are exposed to the full effects of wave action make successful long-term caches almost impossible.

1-67. Underwater caches can be quite difficult to find and are normally not marked. Therefore, the detachment must use and record very accurate reference points and distances. In planning for the cache, personnel must consider how much weight will be required to make the cache negative-buoyant and ensure that it remains subsurface. To do so will require a tremendous amount of weight, perhaps more than the detachment can carry. The weights attached to the cache must be easy to jettison during recovery. The amount of weight must not only keep the cache negative buoyant, it must also be unaffected by currents. The detachment should attach lifting devices to the outside of the cache so that upon recovery the weights are jettisoned and the lifting devices inflated. This method will allow for rapid recovery and ease of movement out of the water.

1-68. In most cases, the detachment will have to plan for some type of anchor system. Caches placed in water shallow enough to recover by breath-hold diving are susceptible to wave action. If the cache is not anchored with all of the bundles interconnected, it is susceptible to being dispersed by wave action. This is especially true if severe weather causes an increased sea state with its attendant surge. Detachments must investigate available technologies to determine what will be most effective in their particular circumstances. Small craft anchors that can be wedged into bottom structures may present the most efficient solution. Personnel may also consider using mountaineering anchors (for example, "friends" or chocks) if suitable crevasses exist. Detachments must also determine how to protect the anchor ropes from chafing. Underwater structure becomes extremely abrasive over time and a frayed or broken line endangers the integrity of the cache.

1-69. Certain waterborne-related items are extremely sensitive to the environment. Personnel should completely seal buried items in airtight waterproof containers. Normally, heavy-duty plastic bags are adequate for small items. Large items, such as rubber boats, generally have their own heavy-duty rubber or canvas containers. Subsurface caching is much more time-consuming and difficult. Personnel must totally waterproof all sensitive items. The cache must be at a depth that can be reached by surface swimmers or divers. The detachment must also consider tide height and tidal current data when weighing where and at what depth to put the cache. The rise and fall of the tide will affect the depth. In any case, personnel should position the cache as close to the shore or beach as possible.

1-70. Because the detachment will return to its infiltration site, it should place the cache site under observation for a period before recovery execution to ensure the cache area is secure. To ensure the best possible execution of the operation, the detachment should always rehearse the recovery operation.

1-71. Another type of cache is pre-positioning. If the support mechanism in the AO allows it, personnel should pre-position the equipment for the exfiltration. This task will normally occur or be possible in waterborne scenarios with active auxiliary or underground forces. The caching element emplaces the cache and submits a cache report that is forwarded to the detachment. The detachment then establishes surveillance, emplaces security, and recovers the cache IAW the recovery plan.

RESUPPLY

1-72. A detachment may need to be resupplied with the equipment required to conduct a waterborne exfiltration. This additional support can be either a preplanned, on-call, or emergency resupply and is usually a contingency in case the primary exfiltration plan fails. It is very hard to conduct an airborne resupply since the equipment must, in most cases, be airdropped very close to the beach departure point or in the water near the shore. If the area to be exfiltrated has a coastal air defense system, this resupply method becomes extremely dangerous for the mission aircraft. However, if possible, one of the most effective means is to drop a "rubber duck" (or two). The aircraft can fly parallel to and just off the coast and put out a rubber duck packed with the needed equipment. The exfiltrating detachment then simply swims to the equipment, unpacks it, and exfiltrates.

1-73. If the equipment is not dropped in the water, it must be dropped very close to water because it may be hard to transport equipment overland. Because of the difficulties associated with airdropping resupplies, they will normally be delivered by sea or overland. Resupply by sea can be done by simply infiltrating the required equipment and caching it if the resupply takes place a long time before exfiltration. The personnel bringing in the resupply can secure the equipment and exfiltrate with the detachment. If possible, and if a support mechanism within the AO will allow it, resupply personnel can deliver the exfiltration equipment over land (by vehicle) to the beach departure point. Personnel can cache the equipment for later removal, or the detachment can begin the exfiltration as soon as the equipment arrives.

UNIT TRAINING AND CAPABILITIES

1-74. The ability of any unit to conduct a specified mission ultimately depends on its level of training and capabilities. The level of training is the responsibility of the unit commander. He ensures that his troops are prepared to carry out their wartime missions. A properly balanced training program must focus on the detachment as well as each individual to produce a reasonably proficient detachment.

1-75. The unit's capability to execute the mission is directly related to the amount and type of equipment available. Regardless of the amount or type of equipment, the unit should train to the utmost with the available assets to maintain a viable waterborne operations capability. Surface swimming, self-contained underwater breathing apparatus (scuba) techniques, submarine operations, small boat operations, and waterborne insertion or extraction techniques require special training programs to attain and maintain proficiency.

SUSTAINMENT TRAINING

1-76. The complexity of waterborne operations demands additional training, both for proficiency and for safety. At least one block of instruction in the detachment's weekly training schedule should focus on some aspect of maritime operations. Classes should range the entire spectrum of maritime operations to include infiltration and exfiltration tactics, means of delivery, equipment maintenance, and medical treatment of diving injuries. The detachment's senior diving supervisor should coordinate these classes.

1-77. The following paragraphs provide the B-team and C-team commanders an overview of the minimum training required to sustain their maritime operations detachments in a mission-ready status. It also provides the detachment a list of training requirements for developing their long-and short-range training plans. There are many techniques available to a detachment for use in a maritime environment to successfully infiltrate an operational area or to reach a specific target. Considerable training time is required to maintain the specialized MAROPS skills. To be fully mission-capable, the detachment must have the commander's support to allocate the required training time and resources. The training frequency matrix shows the minimum skills and topical areas to be covered during training. For each skill or area, there is a determination of how often training must be conducted. A description of each skill or area and details on what must be accomplished during the training periods follows. Finally, there is a listing of some of the critical tasks associated with waterborne operations. They may be used as aids for both training and evaluation.

TRAINING FREQUENCY MATRIX

1-78. This matrix (Table 1-2) identifies the subject areas that need to be covered during sustainment training. It also indicates how often this training must take place.

Table 1-2. Training frequency matrix

Subject Areas	Month	Quarter	6 Months	Year	2 Years
Perform Duties as a Combat Diver	X		X	X	
Operations and Infiltration Techniques	X			X	
Pool and Tower Training				X	
Open-Circuit Diving	X			X	
Closed-Circuit Diving	X				
Diving Physics					
U.S. Navy Diving Tables	X			X	
Individual Diving Equipment	X				
Diving Physiology				X	
Altitude Diving				X	
Submarine Operations (Train-Up)				X	
Submarine Operations (Mission)					X
Perform Duties as a Combat Diving Supervisor			X		
Plan and Supervise Combat Diving Operations			X		
Diving Operations	X		X	X	
Tides and Currents				X	
Diving Equipment	X				
Medical Aspects of Diving				X	
Recompression Chamber Operations				X	
Perform Duties as a Dive Medical Technician	X		X	X	
Medical Planning for Diving Operations	X		X	X	
Diagnosis and Treatment of Diving Injuries				X	
Dangerous Marine Life				X	
Conduct a Waterborne Infiltration			X	X	
Mission Planning			X		
Small Boat Operations		X			
Surface Infiltration		X			
Air Operations			X		
Nautical Charts and Navigation				X	
Kayak Operations				X	

Pay Dives

1-79. Divers are required to perform diving duties IAW AR 611-75 to maintain proficiency and draw special duty pay. As a minimum requirement, a combat diver must perform six qualifying dives within 6 months, one deep dive (70 to 130 FSW) within 12 months and be in a qualified status. The criterion for qualifying dives and status are listed in AR 611-75 and USASOC Reg 350-20. To maintain proficiency at infiltration swimming, detachments should conduct underwater compass swims monthly using open- or closed-circuit breathing apparatus. Swims should be done with properly waterproofed and neutrally buoyant rucksacks. Once each quarter, the team members waterproof and pack (according to the SOP) the team's equipment into their rucksacks. This operation should use the team swim concept—the detachment is linked together by a buddy line, if need be, and moves through the water and onto the shore as one unit.

Requalification

1-80. To maintain currency, all combat divers are required to perform certain diving tasks at least once annually. These tasks are outlined in AR 611-75. Divers who maintain their currency do not have a formal requirement to "requalify" annually. Divers who have allowed their qualifications to lapse or who have returned to diving duty after a period of inactivity must requalify for diving duty IAW AR 611-75.

1-81. Diving supervisors and DMTs are required to perform duties as a CDS or DMT at least once every 6 months and to attend a dive supervisor or dive medical technician training seminar every 2 years. DMTs supporting SO diving must also maintain all of their other medical qualifications IAW the applicable policies and procedures developed by the USASOC commander. The minimum required subjects for the CDS and DMT seminars are listed in USASOC Reg 350-20.

1-82. In addition to the above-stated annual requalification requirements, each combat diver must undergo a Type-B medical examination every 3 years with a minimum of a Type B update annually.

Operational Exercise

1-83. The goal of all sustainment training is for the detachment to be able to execute a full mission profile. To that end, the detachment must conduct a semiannual operational mission exercise that puts as many of their mission-ready skills to use at one time as can be realistically coordinated. This exercise can be conducted in conjunction with other training requirements mentioned above. Multiple delivery methods should be used, coupled with a surface swim, an underwater navigation team swim, or both. An example would be an airborne or airmobile OTH insertion with CRRCs with an offshore navigation to a drop-off point. This method would be followed by a turtle-back swim to a point 1,500 meters offshore, a closed-circuit underwater team compass swim with equipment to the BLS, and an over-the-beach infiltration. Following a UW or DA mission, the team would execute an over-the-beach exfiltration and some form of marine extraction. It may of course be impossible to include all of these phases in one tactical exercise. However, multiple phases must be conducted in each exercise. Realistic training challenges the detachment to excel and gives the commander an effective tool to assess mission capabilities.

1-84. Meeting these requirements does not guarantee an individual combat diver or combat diver detachment to be mission-ready. These are the minimum requirements which, when met, allow combat divers to engage in the training necessary to achieve a combat, mission-ready status.

CHAPTER 2

Environmental Factors

Weather and its effects on the friendly and enemy situations is a critical factor in mission planning and the safe execution of any operation. The maritime environment in which waterborne operations take place is always changing. Those changes have immediate and urgent effects on the types of small vessels available to an infiltrating or exfiltrating detachment. This chapter focuses on the effects weather has on the water, and the potential problems detachments face while operating small boats or conducting an infiltration swim.

Timely weather forecasts coupled with an understanding of the basic principles of weather patterns and their effects are a key element in the planning of waterborne operations. The environmental factors that have the greatest impact on waterborne operations include wind, storms, waves, surf, tides, and currents. This chapter examines the basic elements of weather, types of storm systems, storm propagation, and how to forecast weather from local observations. It also briefly explains how to read a weather map.

WIND

2-1. High winds are a genuine concern for personnel conducting waterborne operations. High winds can greatly impact on almost every type of waterborne operation. High seas are directly related to wind speed. The Beaufort Wind Scale is the internationally recognized guide to expected wave height and sea states under varying wind conditions (Table 2-1). When planning waterborne operations, planners should use this scale to define a particular state of wind and wave.

2-2. Without wind, weather would remain virtually unchanged. Wind is a physical manifestation of the movement of air masses. It is the result of horizontal differences in air pressure. Air flows from a high-pressure area to a low-pressure area producing winds. Solar radiation and the resultant uneven heating of the earth's surface is the

Table 2-1. The beaufort wind scale

Beaufort Wind Force	Wind Range (Knots)	Sea Indications	Wave Height (Feet)
0	Less than 1	Mirrorlike.	0
1	1–3	Ripples with appearance of scales.	0.25
2	4–6	Small wavelets; glassy appearance; no breaking.	0.5–1
3	7–10	Large wavelets; some crests begin to break; scattered whitecaps.	2–3
4	11–16	Small waves becoming longer; fairly frequent whitecaps.	3.5–5
5	17–21	Moderate waves; pronounced long form; many whitecaps.	6–8
6	22–27	Large waves begin to form; white foam crests are more extensive; some spray.	9.5–13
7	28–33	Sea heaps up; white foam from breaking waves begins to blow in streaks along the direction of the wind.	13.5–19
8	34–40	Moderately high waves of greater length; edges of crests break down into spindrift foam blown in well-marked streaks in the directions of the wind.	18–25

Table 2-1. The beaufort wind scale (*Continued*)

Beaufort Wind Force	Wind Range (Knots)	Sea Indications	Wave Height (Feet)
9	41–47	High waves; dense streaks of foam; sea begins to roll; visibility affected.	23–32
10	48–55	Very high waves with overhanging crests; foam in great patches blown in dense white streaks; whole surface of sea takes a white appearance; visibility affected.	29–41

driving force creating the pressure differentials that cause wind. The pressure gradient is shown on weather maps as a series of isobars or pressure contours connecting places of equal barometric pressure. The closer together the isobars appear, the steeper the pressure gradient and the higher the wind speed (Figure 2-1).

2-3. Wind direction is determined based on where it is coming from. If a person is looking north and the wind is in his face, it is a North wind. Wind speed is reported in knots and direction is reported in degrees true.

2-4. Major air masses move on a global scale. One of the modifiers for this movement is the Coriolis effect. The earth's rotation exerts an apparent force, which diverts air from a direct path between the high- and low-pressure areas. This diversion of air is toward the right in the Northern Hemisphere and toward the left in the Southern Hemisphere.

2-5. The uneven heating of the earth's surface results in differentially warmed air masses. Warm air expands and rises creating areas of lower air density and pressure. Cool denser air, with its greater pressure, flows in as wind to replace the rising warm air. These cells of high and low pressure have their own internal rotation influenced by

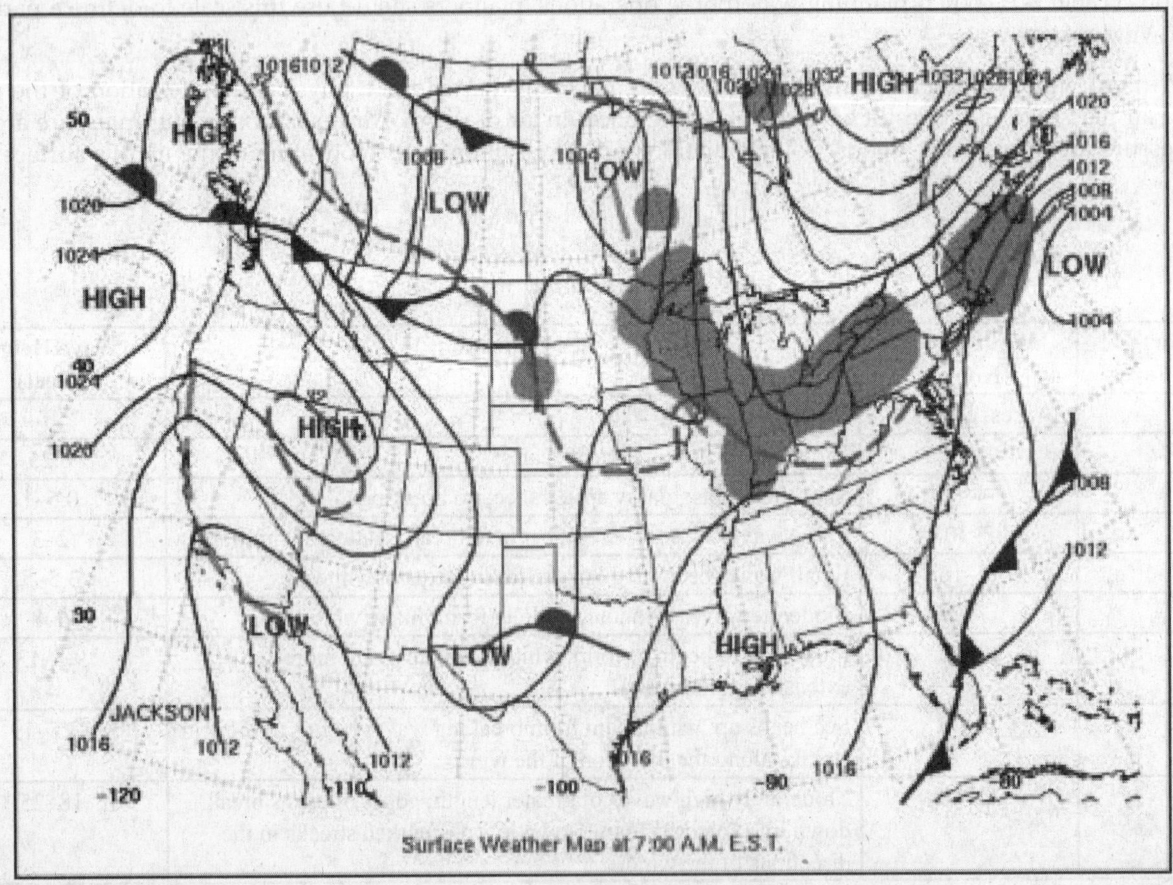

Figure 2-1. Synaptic weather chart

the global modifiers (Figure 2-2). High-pressure cells have clockwise rotating winds and are called anticyclones. Low-pressure cells have counterclockwise rotating winds and are called cyclones.

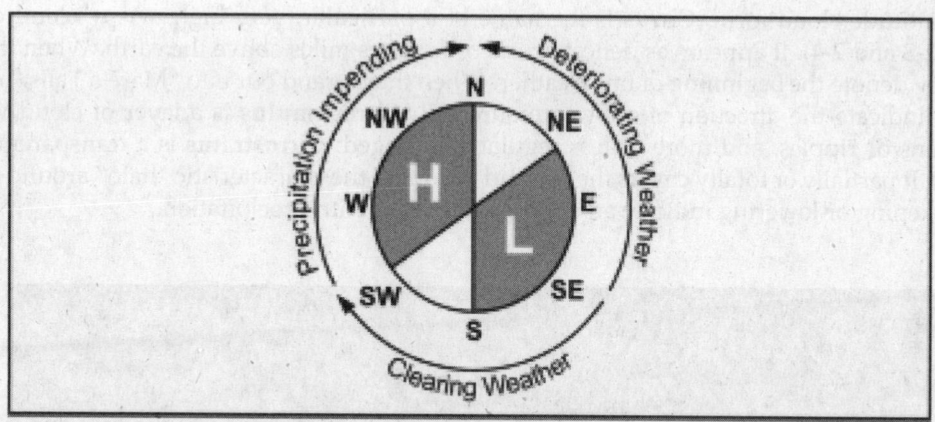

Figure 2-2. High and low pressure wind circulation

2-6. Local weather patterns are strongly affected by terrain and daily heating and cooling trends. Desert regions heat and cool rapidly; wooded or wet areas change temperature more slowly. Mountainous areas experience updrafts and downdrafts in direct proportion to the daily cycles. Coastal areas will experience onshore and offshore winds because of the differential solar heating and cooling of coastal land and adjoining water.

2-7. The advent of a high-pressure cell usually denotes fair weather. A high-pressure cell is evident to the observer when skies are relatively clear and winds are blowing from the southwest, west, northwest, and north. Low-pressure cells are the harbingers of unsettled weather. They are evident when clouds gather and winds blow from the northeast, east, southeast, and south. Winds that shift from the north toward the east or south signal deteriorating weather. Impending precipitation is signaled by winds (especially a north wind) shifting to the west and then to the south. Wind shifts from the east through south to west are an indicator of clearing weather. The approach of high- and low-pressure systems can also be tracked and anticipated with a barometer. Some wristwatches have an altimeter and barometer function. Barometers are most useful when monitoring trends. Normal barometric pressure is 29 inches of mercury (Hg). Planners should take readings at regular intervals and record changes. A drop in barometric pressure signals deteriorating weather (an approaching low-pressure system). A rise in barometric pressure indicates clearing weather (the approach of a high pressure system).

CLOUDS

2-8. Clouds are the most visible manifestation of weather. Cloud formations are valuable in determining weather conditions and trends. Clouds form when the moisture in rising warm air cools and condenses. They may or may not be accompanied by precipitation.

2-9. Naming conventions for cloud types are intended to convey crucial information about the altitude and type of cloud. Different cloud types have descriptive names that depend mainly on appearance, but also on the process of formation as seen by an observer. Cloud nomenclature that describes the cloud type is usually combined with prefixes or suffixes that describe the altitude of that cloud. Key descriptive terms are as follows:

- *Cumulo-cumulus.* Prefix and suffix that describes a vertical heaping of clouds. Castellated refers to a "turreted" cumulo-type cloud. These clouds grow vertically on summer afternoons to produce showers and thunderstorms.
- *Fracto-fractus.* Prefix and suffix that describes broken-up clouds.
- *Nimbo-nimbus.* Prefix and suffix that describes clouds that are full of rain or already have rain falling from them.

2-10. Despite an almost infinite variety of shapes and forms, it is still possible to define ten basic types. These types are grouped by altitude and are further divided into three levels: high, middle, and low.

2-11. High-altitude clouds have their bases at or above 18,000 feet and consists of ice crystals. **Cirro** is a prefix denoting a high-altitude cloud form. **Cirrus** is the name of a particular, very high, wispy cloud comprised of ice crystals (Figures 2-3 and 2-4). It appears as delicate curls or feathers miles above the earth. When these clouds form feathery curls, they denote the beginning of fair weather. When they strand out into "Mare's Tails," caused by strong winds aloft, they indicate the direction of a low-pressure cell. **Cirrocumulus** is a layer of cloud without shading, comprised of grains or ripples, and more or less regularly arranged. **Cirrostratus** is a transparent, whitish veil of cloud (Figure 2-4). It partially or totally covers the sky and produces the characteristic "halo" around the sun or moon. These clouds thickening or lowering indicate an approaching front with precipitation.

Figure 2-3. Cirrus clouds

Figure 2-4. Cirrus and cirrostratus clouds

2-12. Middle clouds have bases located between 7,000 and 18,000 feet. They consist of water droplets at lower levels of altitude and ice crystals at higher levels. **Alto** is the prefix describing middle zone clouds. Altocumulus is a layer of white, gray, or mixed white and gray clouds, generally with shading, and made up of round masses. Several layers of **altocumulus** clouds (Figure 2-5) indicate confused patterns of air currents, rising dew points, and impending rain and thunderstorms. Altocumulus clouds massing and thickening is a sign of coming thunderstorms. Altostratus is a grayish or bluish layer of cloud with a uniform appearance that partially or totally covers the sky. It may or may not be thick enough to obscure the sun. **Altostratus** clouds (Figure 2-6) indicate an oncoming warm front. Rain from thickening Altostratus clouds may evaporate before reaching the ground.

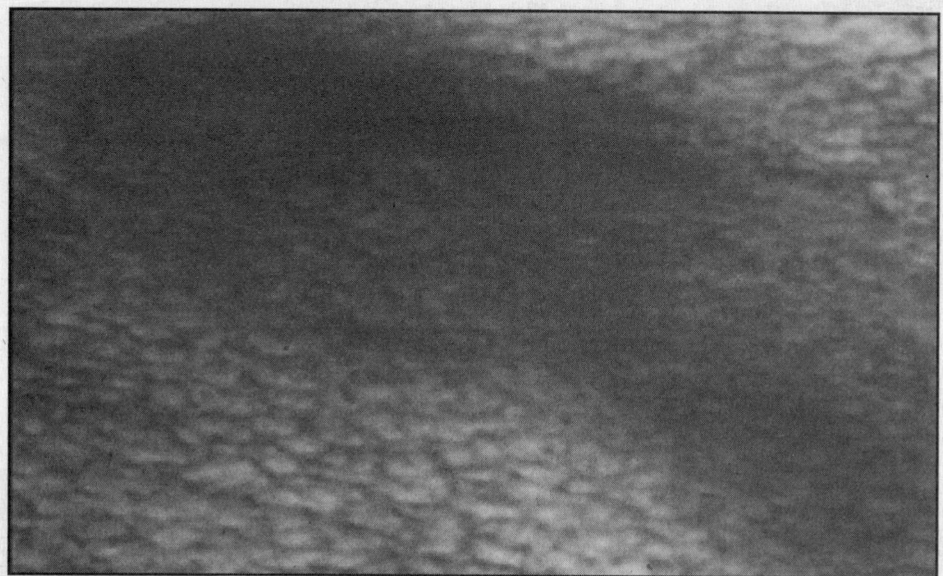

Figure 2-5. Altocumulus clouds

Figure 2-6. Altostratus clouds

2-13. Low clouds have bases below 7,000 feet. Low clouds consist mostly of water droplets; however, in colder climates, ice crystals may predominate. These clouds can develop into multilevel clouds and go through various phases of cloud formation. **Strato** is the prefix referring to the low part of the sky. When used as a suffix, **stratus** describes a spread-out cloud that looks sheetlike or layered. When used by itself, **stratus** is a complete name, describing a low-level cloud that is usually gray and covers a great portion of the sky. Other low-level clouds are **nimbostratus, stratocumulus** (Figure 2-7), **cumulus** (Figure 2-8), and **cumulonimbus**.

Figure 2-7. Stratocumulus clouds

Figure 2-8. Cumulus clouds

2-14. The cloud formation that signals conditions with the greatest risks to the detachment (or any maritime operator) is the **cumulonimbus** (Figure 2-9), which is the classic thundercloud. Thunderstorms are particularly dangerous not only because of lightning, but also because of the strong winds and the rough, confused seas that accompany them. On the ocean, a thunderstorm may manifest itself as a localized phenomenon or as a squall line of considerable length. Before a storm, the winds are generally from the south and west in the middle latitudes of the Northern Hemisphere, and the air is warm and humid. Sharp, intermittent static on the amplitude modulation (AM) radio is also an indicator of approaching thunderstorms. If the sky is not obscured by other clouds, an observer may determine the direction a thunderstorm will move; it will follow the direction the incus (the anvil-shaped top of the thunderhead) is pointing. The incus is the streamer blown forward from the top of the cumulonimbus cloud by high-altitude winds. The observer should not be deceived by surface winds. The strong updrafts inside the cloud that contribute to its vertical development will cause surface winds to blow in toward the base of the cloud. As the storm approaches, it may be preceded by the "calm before the storm," an apparent slackening of surface winds. Detachment personnel should always be alert to conditions that favor the development of thunderstorms. If possible, they should seek shelter; if not, they should batten down the hatches; it can be a rough ride.

Figure 2-9. Cumulonimbus clouds

LIGHTNING

2-15. Lightning is associated with some storms and is a potentially life-threatening event. It is caused by a buildup of dissimilar electrical charges within a vertically developing cumulonimbus cloud. Lightening occurs most often as a cloud-to-cloud strike. The lightening most likely to threaten mariners is the cloud-to-ground (water) strike. Thunder is caused by the explosive heating of the air as the lightning strike occurs. There are no guaranteed safeguards against lightning. It is very unpredictable and has immense power. Staying in port (assuming there are higher objects about) during thunderstorms can minimize the danger of having a boat struck. Personnel can also lessen the danger by installing a grounding system like those on buildings and other land structures. The grounding system provides lightning with a path to reach the ground without causing damage or injury.

2-16. A detachment member can judge his distance from a thunderstorm by knowing that light travels at about 186,000 miles per second and sound at about 1,100 feet per second (or about 1 mile in 5 seconds). If he times how long the sound of the thunder takes to reach him after he sees the lightning flash, he can roughly estimate the distance to the storm. (Counting ONE THOUSAND ONE, ONE THOUSAND TWO, ONE THOUSAND THREE will aid him in counting seconds.) Detachment personnel should reduce their exposure or risk of being struck by lightening by getting out of or off of the water and seeking shelter. If a detachment member is caught in a lightning strike area in a relatively unprotected boat (as in a CRRC), he should—

- Stay inside the boat, keep the crew centrally positioned and low down in the vessel, and stay dry.
- Avoid touching metal objects such as weapons, equipment, outboard motors, shift and throttle levers, and metal steering wheels.
- Avoid contact with the radio, lower and disconnect antennas, and unplug the antenna to save the radio in case lightning strikes.
- Quickly remove people from the water.
- If a lightning strike occurs, expect the compass to be inaccurate and to have extensive damage to onboard electronics.

FOG

2-17. Fog is a cloud in contact with the ground. It is composed of a multitude of minute water droplets suspended in the atmosphere. These are sufficiently numerous to scatter the light rays and thus reduce visibility.

2-18. The most troublesome type of fog to mariners is advection fog. Advection means horizontal movement. It is also the name given to fog produced by air in motion. This type of fog is formed when warm air is transported over colder land or water surfaces. The greater the difference between the air temperature and the ocean temperature, the deeper and denser the fog. Unlike radiation fog, advection fog is little affected by sunlight. It can and does occur during either the day or night. Advection fog is best dispersed by an increase in wind velocity or change in wind direction.

2-19. Fog awareness is a local knowledge item. Personnel should ask the local people questions such as, "Where does it usually occur? What time of day? What time of year?" If available, a dedicated staff weather officer (SWO) may be able to provide the desired information.

2-20. Unless small-boat operators have a compelling reason to go out in dense fog, they should not do so. If fog seems to be developing, they should try to run in ahead of it. The small boat operating on larger bodies of water or oceans should always maintain a running dead reckoning (DR) plot. If, for some reason, no plot has been maintained and fog rolls in, the boat operator should attempt to get a position-fix immediately. With an accurate heading to port and an accurate knowledge of speed over the bottom, it is possible to plot a course back home.

2-21. When in fog, the boat operator should slow down so he will have time to maneuver or stop if another vessel approaches. If the boat's size and configuration permit, an observer should stand lookout well forward and away from the engine sounds and lights to listen and look for other signals. The observer should also listen for surf in case the DR is incorrect. He should use all electronic aids available, but not depend upon them without reserve. Boat personnel should even consider anchoring to await better visibility, especially if their return to port includes transiting congested areas or narrow channels.

AIR MASSES AND FRONTS

2-22. Reading and understanding weather forecasts requires a basic knowledge of air masses and fronts. An air mass is another name for a high-pressure cell, which is a buildup of air descending from high-altitude global circulation. There is no corresponding term for the low-pressure equivalent. However, "air mass" refers to the volume of air and its physical mass, rather than its pressure characteristics. An air mass is capable of covering several hundred thousand square miles with conditions in which temperature and humidity are essentially the same in all directions horizontally.

2-23. Air masses derive their principal characteristics from the surface beneath them. They are characterized as continental or maritime, tropical or polar, and warmer or colder than the surface over which they are then moving. Maritime and continental air masses differ greatly. Maritime air masses tend to change less with the seasons. Oceans have less variation in their heating and cooling cycles, so maritime air masses moving over land tend to moderate conditions of excess heat and cold. Continental air masses are subject to large changes in humidity and temperature, which in turn, bring varying weather.

2-24. Cold air masses consist of unstable internal conditions as the air at the earth's surface attempts to warm and rise through the cooler air. Warm air masses are more stable as the air cooled by contact with the ground sinks and warm air above tends to stay there or rise. These changes cause strong, gusty winds in cold air masses, and weaker, steadier winds in warm air masses. Cumulus clouds usually mean cold air masses. As a cold air mass moves a warm air mass, these clouds may change to cumulonimbus clouds and produce thunderstorms. Warm air masses usually mean stratus clouds and extended drizzle.

2-25. Weather fronts are the boundaries between two different air masses. These bodies do not tend to mix but instead will move under, over, or around each other. The passage of a front brings a change in the weather.

COLD FRONT

2-26. An oncoming cold air mass will push under a warm air mass, forcing it upward (Figure 2-10). In the Northern Hemisphere, cold fronts are normally oriented along a northeast to southwest line and they advance toward the southeast at a rate of 400 to 500 miles per day—faster in winter, slower in summer. A strong, fast cold front will bring intense weather conditions that do not last long. A slow-moving front may pass over an area before precipitation starts. A weak cold front may not have any precipitation. An approaching cold front may have a squall line form in front of it. Winds will shift towards the south, then southwest, and barometric pressure will fall. Clouds will lower and build up; rain will start slowly but increase rapidly. As a cold front passes, skies will clear quickly and temperatures will drop. Barometric pressure will climb quickly. Winds will continue to veer towards the north and northeast. For a few days, at least, the weather will have the characteristics of a high.

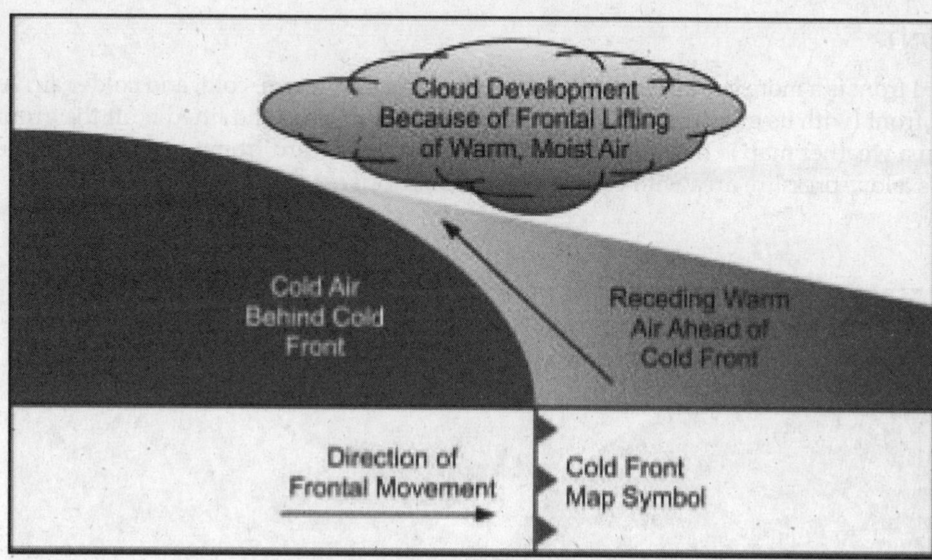

Figure 2-10. Cross-section of a cold front

WARM FRONT

2-27. An advancing warm air mass meets a colder mass and rides up over it (Figure 2-11). Warm fronts are generally oriented north to south, northwest to southeast, or east to west, and change their direction more often than cold fronts do. Warm fronts advance between 150 to 200 miles per day. Because of their slower speed, they are often overtaken by a following cold front. Approaching warm fronts signal milder weather than do cold fronts. Water fronts are

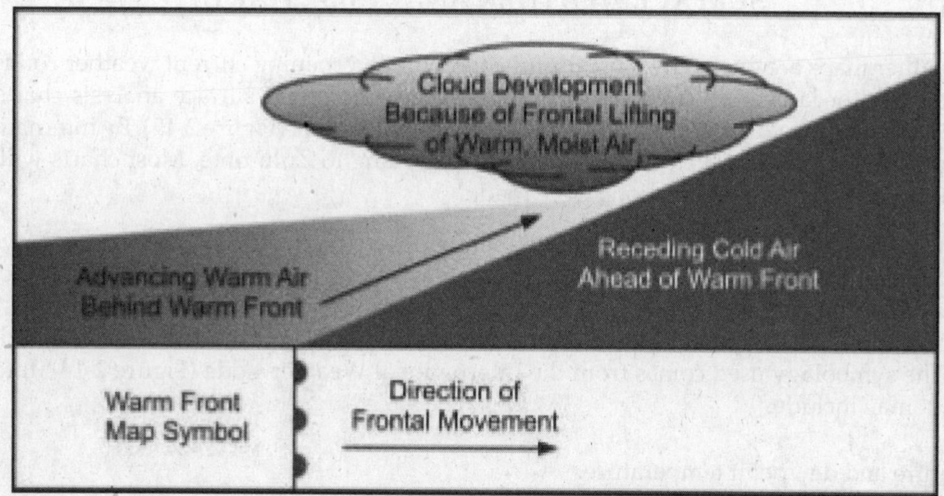

Figure 2-11. Cross-section of a warm front

preceded by low stratus cloud formations and moderate but extended rains. Another indicator of a warm front is a slowly falling barometer. As a warm front passes, cumulus clouds replace stratus clouds, and the temperature and barometer both rise.

2-28. A stationary front is a front that has slowed to a point where there is almost no forward movement. The neighboring air masses are holding their positions or moving parallel to one another. The result is clouds and rain similar to a warm front.

OCCLUDED FRONT

2-29. An occluded front is a more complicated situation where there is warm, cold, and colder air. An occluded front occurs after a cold front (with its greater speed) has overtaken a warm front and lifted it off the ground (Figure 2-12). The appearance on a weather map is that of a curled tail extending outward from the junction of the cold and warm fronts. This front is a low-pressure area with counterclockwise winds.

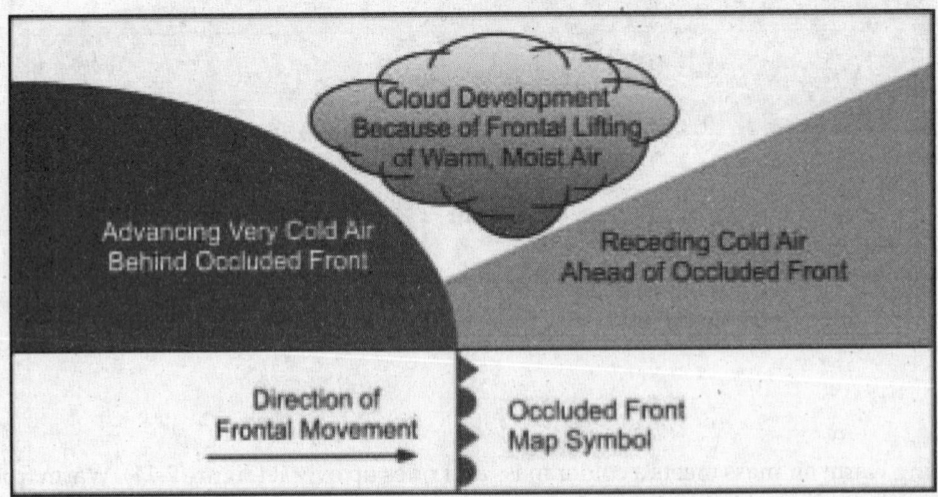

Figure 2-12. Cross-section of an occluded front

SURFACE WEATHER ANALYSIS CHARTS

2-30. Surface weather maps are one of the most useful charts for ascertaining current weather conditions just above the surface of the earth for large geographic regions. These maps are called surface analysis charts if they contain fronts and analyzed pressure fields, with the solid lines representing isobars (Figure 2-13). By international agreement, all meteorological observations are taken at the same time according to Zulu time. Most charts will list somewhere in the title the Zulu time when the observations were made.

2-31. Synoptic weather analysis requires the simultaneous observation of the weather at many widely located sites using standardized instruments and techniques. A display of this information would be difficult to make and interpret unless a uniform system of plotting were adopted. Weather data from each reporting station is plotted around the reporting station's symbol (a small circle on the base map) using a standardized methodology known as a station model. The symbology used comes from the International Weather Code (Figure 2-14). Information shown on a synoptic chart may include:

- Temperature and dewpoint temperature.
- Wind speed and direction.
- Barometric pressure.

- Weather (rain, snow).
- Precipitation intensities.
- Sky cover.

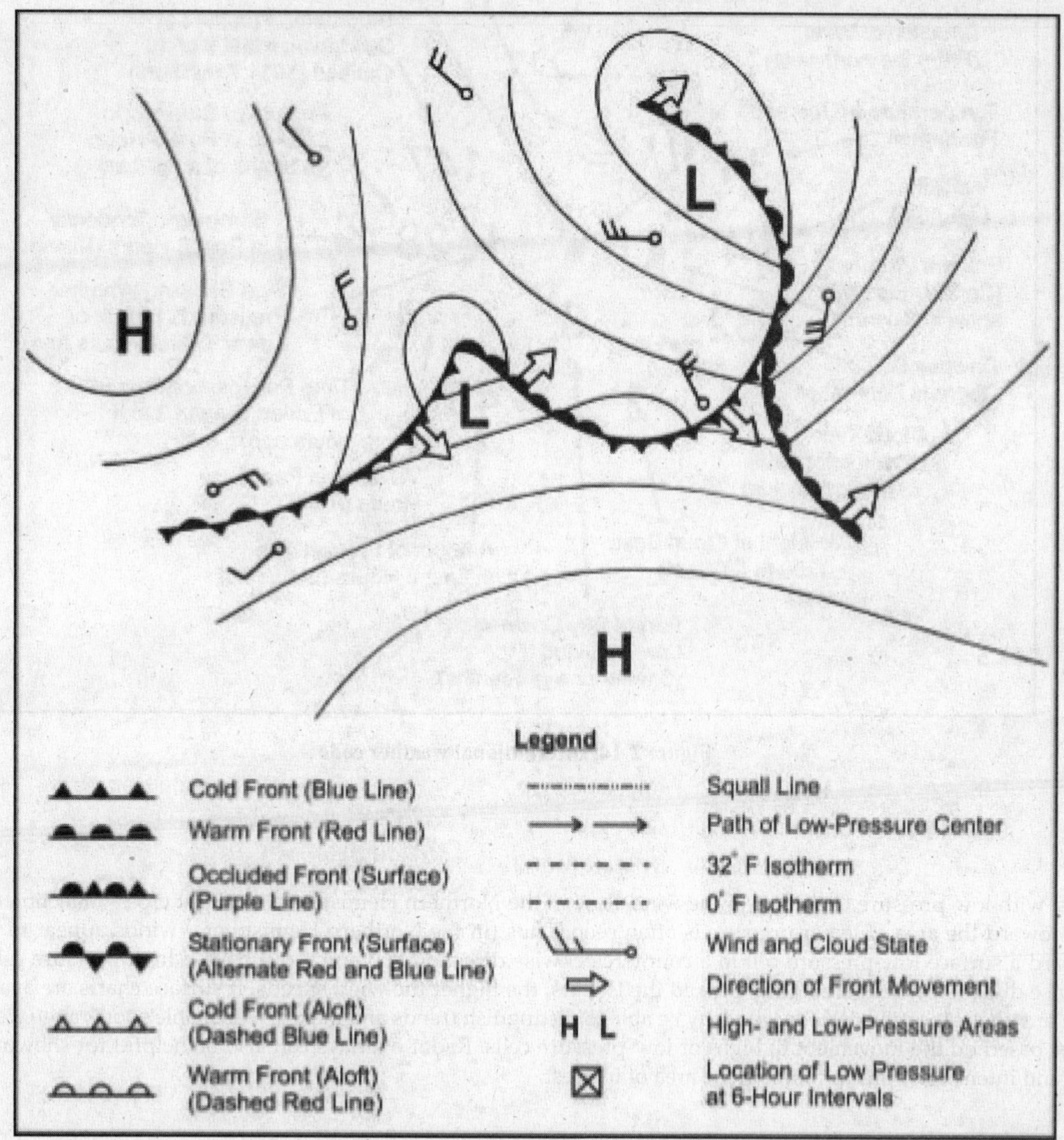

Figure 2-13. Sample weather chart

2-32. The surface analysis charts permit a person to identify and locate the large-scale features of the sea level pressure field and the surface fronts. Isobars with the lowest value will encircle the region with the lowest pressure, while closed isobars with the highest value will encircle the area with the highest pressure. How tightly the isobars are packed reveals the steepness of the pressure gradient between any two points. Wind flows tend to parallel the

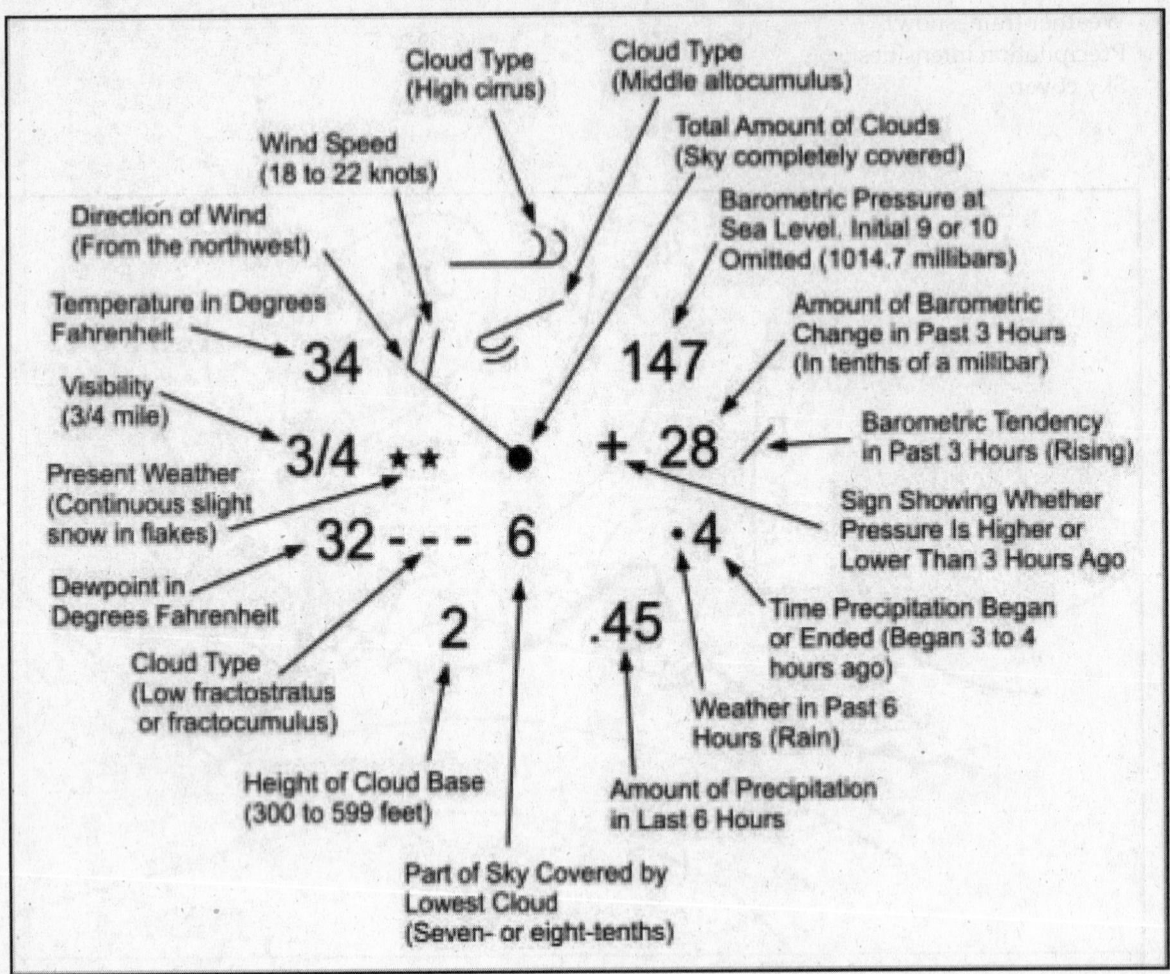

Figure 2-14. International weather code

isobars, with low pressure to the left of the wind flow in the Northern Hemisphere. A slight cross-deflection of the winds toward the area of lower pressure is often seen. Thus (in the Northern Hemisphere) winds appear to spiral in toward a surface low-pressure cell in a counterclockwise direction and spiral out from a high-pressure cell in a clockwise direction. The more tightly packed the isobars, the higher the wind speeds. If surface charts are available for the previous reporting periods, you may be able to distinguish trends and make a reasonable short-range weather forecast based on the movement of high- or low-pressure cells. Radar overlays can also be helpful for showing the extent and intensity of precipitation in the area of interest.

FORECASTING

2-33. Fifty years ago, U.S World War II fleet admirals had some of the best weather experts in this country on their staffs. Today the military can receive a better weather briefing than Admiral Halsey ever had. The satellite receiver-equipped TV weatherman and the National Weather Service's continuous very high frequency (VHF) weather briefings, coupled with local knowledge, should make personnel effective and safe weather-wise. But even experts are far from 100 percent correct concerning the weather. Figure 2-15 provides some generalizations that can indicate a change in the weather.

Indicators of Deteriorating Weather

- Clouds lower and thicken, ceiling lowers.
- Puffy clouds begin to develop vertically and darken.
- Sky darkens and looks threatening to the west.
- Clouds increase in numbers and move rapidly across the sky.
- Clouds move in different directions at different heights.
- Clouds move from east or northeast toward the south.
- Heavy rains occur at night.
- Barometer falls steadily or rapidly.
- Smoke from stacks lowers.
- Static develops on AM radio.
- North wind shifts east and possibly through east to south.
- A ring (halo) shows around the moon.
- If on land, leaves that grow according to prevailing winds turn over and show their backs.
- Strong wind or a red sky in the morning.
- Temperatures far above or below normal for the time of the year.

Indicators of Impending Strong Winds

- Light, scattered clouds alone in a clear sky.
- Sharp, clearly defined edges to clouds.
- A yellow sunset.
- Unusually bright stars.
- Major changes in temperature..

Indicators of Impending Precipitation

- Distant objects seem to stand above the horizon.
- Sounds are very clear and can be heard for great distances.
- Transparent, veil-like cirrus clouds thicken, ceiling lowers.
- Hazy and sticky air. (Rain can occur in 18 to 38 hours.)
- Halo shows around the sun or the moon.
- South wind increases with clouds moving from the west.
- North wind shifts to west and then to south.
- Barometer falls steadily.
- A pale sunset.
- A red sky to the west at dawn.
- No dew after a hot day.

Figure 2-15. Generalizations for weather forecasting

Indicators of Clearing Weather
• Cloud bases rise.
• Smoke from stacks rises.
• Wind shifts to west, especially from east through south.
• Barometer rises quickly.
• A cold front passes in the last 4 to 7 hours.
• A gray early morning sky that shows signs of clearing.
• A morning fog or dew.
• Rain stops and clouds break away at sunset.

Indicators of Continuing Fair Weather
• An early morning fog that clears.
• A gentle wind from west to northwest.
• Barometer steady or rising slightly.
• A red sky to the east with a clear sky to the west at sunset.
• A bright moon and a light breeze.
• A heavy dew or frost.
• A clear blue morning sky to the west.
• Clouds that dot the afternoon summer sky.
• Sounds do not carry; dull hearing.
• Clouds do not increase or actually decrease.
• Altitude of cloud bases near mountains increases.

Figure 2-15. Generalizations for weather forecasting (*Continued*)

NOTE

The observations discussed about weather phenomena and observational forecasting are regional in nature. The popular folk wisdoms mentioned in this manual are based on the global circulation patterns in the temperate zones of the Northern Hemisphere. Although the general observations are accurate, they may require modification when used outside the temperate regions and in the Southern Hemisphere.

WAVES

2-34. Wave formations and wave activity are extremely important in planning the successful execution of any waterborne operation. Waves impact on all surface-related activities, including boating or swimming. Waves can likewise affect the subsurface activities of the combat diver; therefore, divers must be totally familiar with the effects of waves.

2-35. Waves are a transfer of energy through water particles. Energy, not water, is what moves as waves pass. The actual water particles in a wave describe a circular orbit and return very nearly to their exact starting point at the end of a wave cycle. Like a cork bobbing freely, water particles in the open ocean move up and down in circular motion. There is very little lateral or horizontal movement.

2-36. When planners study waves, they break them into deep water waves and shallow water waves. In deep water waves, the orbit is intact or circular. In shallow water waves, the orbit reflects off the bottom and becomes elliptical. As the orbit becomes elliptical, the energy transfers and the breaking wave becomes surf. The following paragraphs discuss wave terms, the formation of waves, and types of waves.

TERMINOLOGY

2-37. Planners and operators must understand the basic wave activity and wave formation terminology (Figure 2-16). The common definitions that can assist personnel in understanding waves are as follows:

- *Crest* is the very top of the wave or the highest point in the wave.
- *Trough* is the lowest portion of the wave and is that point between two crests.
- *Wavelength* is the horizontal distance between a wave crest and the crest of the preceding wave. Wavelength can also be measured from trough to trough.
- *Wave height* is the total vertical distance from the crest of a wave to its trough.
- *Amplitude* is the height of a wave above or below sea level. Amplitude is equal to one-half of the wave height.
- *Wave period* is the time it takes, in seconds, for two consecutive wave crests to pass a fixed observation point.

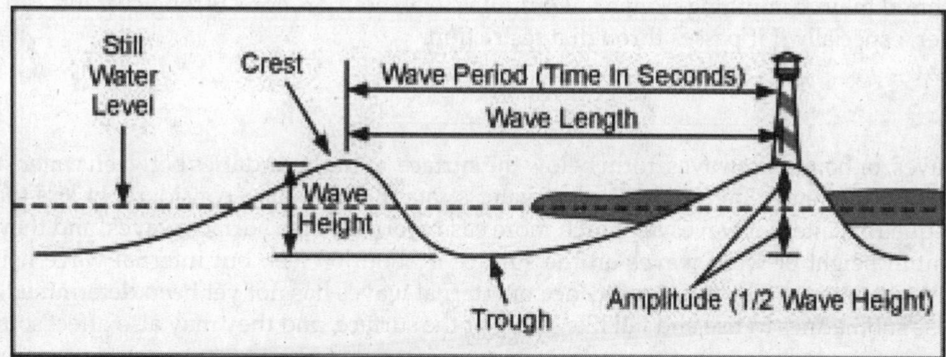

Figure 2-16. Wave characteristics

WAVE FORMATION

2-38. Planners and operators must also know how waves are formed. With this knowledge, the combat swimmer, when exposed to certain conditions, can anticipate what type of wave activity and wave action will most likely be prevalent. He must also know how waves react under certain conditions so that he can anticipate and react to sea conditions. Wave formation is primarily a wind function. As the wind blows across the waters of the ocean, it imparts energy onto the surface of the water, causing it to oscillate. Wave height depends on three factors: force, duration, and fetch. Force is the speed of the wind. Duration is how long the wind blows; it takes roughly 12 hours for fully developed waves to build. Fetch is the open distance over which the wind blows uninterrupted by land masses such as islands or reefs. As a rule of thumb, the maximum height of a wave will be equal to one-half of the wind velocity, providing the fetch is great and the duration is sustained.

2-39. Secondary causes of wave formation include geological disturbances such as earthquakes, landslides, volcanic action, or nuclear explosions. Any of these events can cause tsunamis (commonly referred to as tidal waves). Tsunamis may only be 1 meter high on the open ocean but can routinely reach heights of 60 feet as they approach shallow water. Other types of waves are storm surges, tidal bores, seiches, and internal waves.

Storm Surges

2-40. These surges always occur during bad weather. They result from the combination of tides and rising sea level. The low atmospheric pressure, coupled with the high winds and rising tides, forces large amounts of water inland, causing extensive flooding that can last through several tidal cycles. The worst storm surges normally occur with hurricanes, due to the extreme low pressure and high winds.

Tidal Bores

2-41. Tidal bores occur when land masses serve to restrict the flow of water. Normally, as in the Amazon Basin and the Bay of Fundi in Nova Scotia, the area is fed by a freshwater river. As the large amount of water is rapidly channelized, its speed increases dramatically. Large amounts of water are rapidly carried upstream due to the incoming tide, creating a wall of water. These occur throughout the tidal cycle, moving upstream during flood tides and downstream during ebb tides. Most tidal bores are found in Asia.

Seiche

2-42. This type of standing wave is normally found in lakes or semiclosed or confined bodies of water. It is a phenomenon where the entire body of water oscillates between fixed points without progression. Depending on the natural frequency of the body of water, these oscillations may be mononodal or multinodal. A seiche can be caused by changes in barometric pressure or strong winds of longer duration pushing the water in a lake to the opposite shore. When the wind diminishes, this buildup of water seeks to return to its normal level and the lake level will oscillate between the shores until it stabilizes. It is a long wave, usually having its crest on one shore and its trough on the other. Its period may be anything from a few minutes to an hour or more. Strong currents can accompany this movement of water, especially if it passes through a restriction.

Internal Waves

2-43. Internal waves, or boundary waves, form below the surface, at the boundaries between water strata of different densities. The density differences between adjacent water strata in the sea are considerably less than that between sea and air. Consequently, internal waves are much more easily formed than surface waves, and they are often much larger. The maximum height of wind waves on the surface is about 60 feet, but internal wave heights as great as 300 feet have been encountered. The full significance of internal waves has not yet been determined, but it is known that they may cause submarines to rise and fall like a ship at the surface, and they may also affect sound transmission in the sea.

BREAKING WAVES

2-44. Breaking waves (breakers) are another area of concern and interest. These waves form the different types of surf. Breaking waves can be spillers, plungers, or surgers (Figure 2-17). The actual type of breaker is normally dependent upon the bottom gradient.

2-45. If the slope of the bottom is very gentle or gradual, the breakers' force will be very gentle. Thus, the waves will create a spilling action or what is normally the white water at the crest of the wave. These breaking waves are called **spillers**.

2-46. If the slope of the bottom is steep, the breakers' force will be more pronounced. Thus the wave's crest, as it is unsupported, causes a plunging effect. These waves are called **plungers** and literally pound the beach.

2-47. With an extremely steep or near vertical slope, the wave literally surges onto shore all at once. These are **surging** waves and are very violent.

2-48. Knowing the types of breaking waves and what causes them is important for conducting any boat or swimmer operation in a surf area. Also, knowing the type of bottom (from a **chart** or survey) allows the swimmer to determine wave activity in his AO. From another standpoint, the swimmer can determine bottom slope by observing wave action in a surf zone. This information, when reported, could prove useful for future operations.

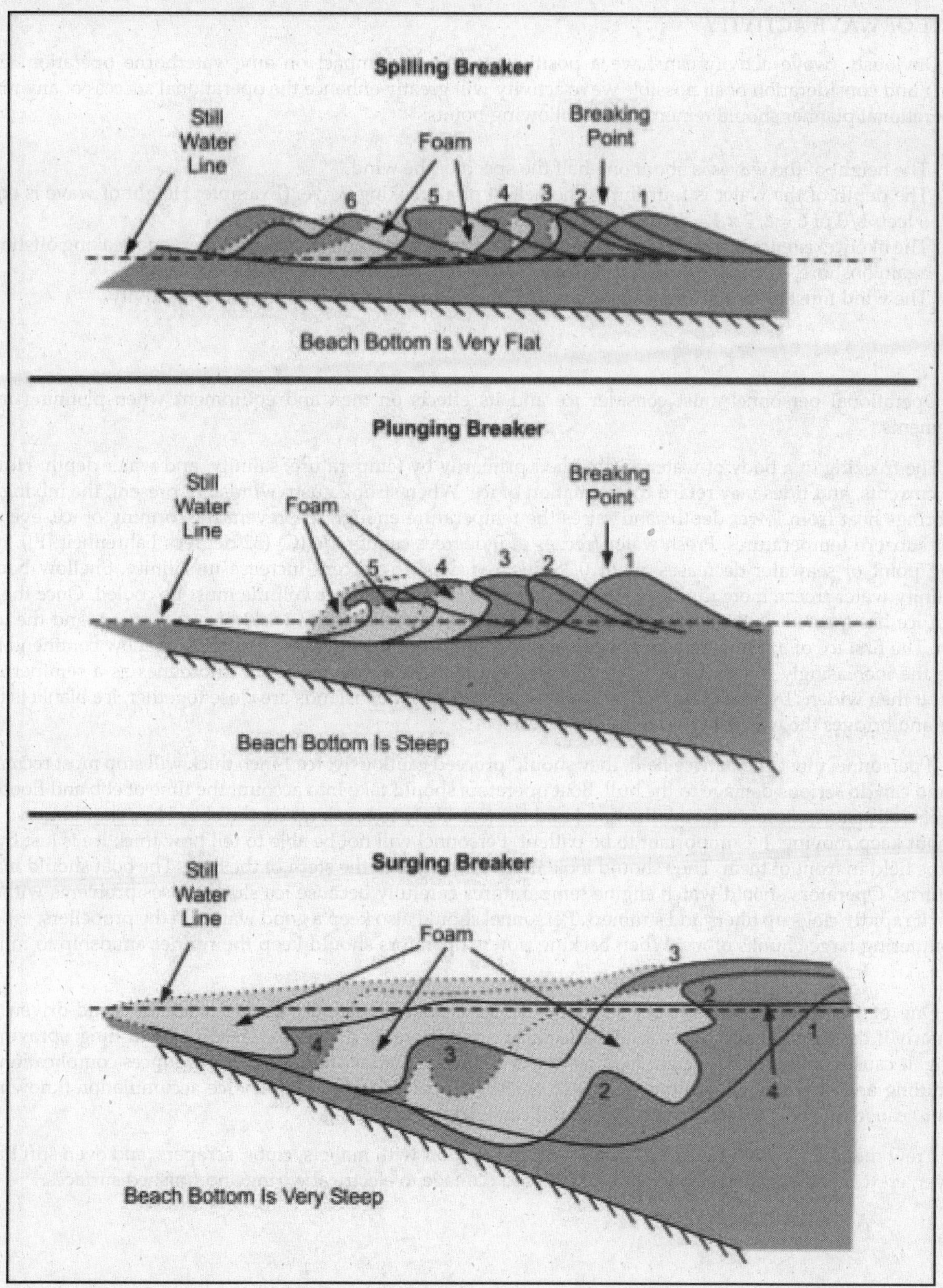

Figure 2-17. Types of breaking waves

IMPACT OF WAVE ACTIVITY

2-49. Obviously, wave activity can have a positive or negative impact on any waterborne operation. Careful planning and consideration of all possible wave activity will greatly enhance the operational success of any mission. The operational planner should remember the following points:

- The height of the waves is about one-half the speed of the wind.
- The depth of the water is four-thirds the height of a breaking wave. (Example: Height of wave is equal to 6 feet, 1/3 of 6 = 2, 2 × 4 = 8, depth of water is about 8 feet.)
- The likely existence of a sandbar or reef just under the water when waves are observed breaking offshore and again onshore.
- The wind must blow across the water about 12 hours to generate maximum wave activity.

ICE

2-50. Operational personnel must consider ice and its effects on men and equipment when planning mission requirements.

2-51. The freezing of a body of water is governed primarily by temperature, salinity, and water depth. However, winds, currents, and tides may retard the formation of ice. When strong gusty winds are present, the mixing of the water brings heat from lower depths and raises the temperature enough to prevent the forming of ice, even if the air is at subzero temperatures. Fresh water freezes at 0 degrees centigrade (C) (32 degrees Fahrenheit [F]), but the freezing point of seawater decreases about 0.28 degrees C per 5 percent increase in salinity. Shallow bodies of low-salinity water freeze more rapidly than deeper basins because a lesser volume must be cooled. Once the initial cover of ice has formed on the surface, no more mixing can take place from wind or wave action, and the ice will thicken. The first ice of autumn usually appears in the mouths of rivers that empty over a shallow continental shelf. During the increasingly longer and colder nights of autumn, ice forms along the shorelines as a semipermanent feature. It then widens by spreading into more exposed waters. When islands are close together, ice blankets the sea surface and bridges the waters between the land areas.

2-52. If personnel must enter an ice field, they should proceed cautiously. Ice 1 inch thick will stop most recreational boats and can do serious damage to the hull. Boat operators should take into account the time of ebb and flood tides; ice is generally more compact during the flood and is more likely to break up on the ebb. They should move at idle speed, but keep moving. It is important to be patient. Personnel will not be able to tell how thick ice is just by looking at the field in front of them. They should look at the broken ice at the stern of the boat. The boat should make no sharp turns. Operators should watch engine temperatures carefully because ice slush causes problems with water intakes; it rapidly clogs up filters and strainers. Personnel should also keep a good watch on the propellers, especially if encountering large chunks of ice. When backing down, operators should keep the rudder amidship to minimize damage.

2-53. One of the most serious effects of cold weather is that of topside icing, caused by wind-driven spray, particularly if the ice continues to accumulate. Ice grows considerably thicker as a result of splashing, spraying, and flooding. It causes an increased weight load on decks and masts (radar and radio). It introduces complications with the handling and operation of equipment. It also creates slippery deck conditions. Ice accumulation (known as ice accretion) causes the boat to become less stable and can lead to a capsizing.

2-54. Crew members should break ice away by chipping it off with mallets, clubs, scrapers, and even stiff brooms. However, crew members must be very careful to avoid damage to electrical wiring and finished surfaces.

CHAPTER 3

Tides and Tidal Currents

Successful amphibious landings are based on careful planning and a comprehensive knowledge of the environmental conditions that influence the landings. Weather, with its immediate effects on wind and waves, and the hydrography and topography of the BLS, are two of these environmental conditions. The third element is tide and tidal current data. Mistiming tides and tidal currents will have an immediate and obvious effect on the potential success or failure of a waterborne operation. History is full of invasion forces and raiding teams trapped and wiped out while crossing tidal flats at low tide. There were also many reconnaissance elements lost at sea or compromised by daylight because they could not make headway against contrary currents. Many of these operational disasters could have been avoided with proper prior planning.

Environmental conditions can affect every operation in a positive or negative manner. The height of the tide and the speed and direction of the tidal current can impede or halt a waterborne operation. These two elements require the detachment to properly conduct mission planning to ensure a positive impact. For operational teams to be successful, the height, direction, and speed of the tide must be compatible with the chosen infiltration method and must coincide with the hours of darkness. Adverse environmental elements can pose immediate threats to the detachment's infiltration plan. Therefore, compensating for these elements helps ensure successful completion of the mission.

After the detachment examines the environmental conditions and selects an infiltration time, it must develop viable contingency plans. To assist in developing contingency plans, the detachment should calculate the tide and tidal current data for at least 3 days before and 3 days after the desired time on target. For some missions, the environmental data may need to be computed for several weeks.

TIDES

3-1. Tide is the periodic rise and fall of the water accompanying the tidal phenomenon. A rising or incoming tide is called a flood tide, and a falling or outgoing tide is called an ebb tide. This variation in the ocean level is caused by the interaction of gravitational forces between the earth and the moon and, to a lesser extent, between the earth and the sun. Because the lunar day or tidal day is slightly longer than 24 hours (it averages 24 hours and 50 minutes), the time between successive high or low tides is normally a little more than 12 hours. When a high or low tide occurs just before midnight, the next high or low tide occurs approximately at noon on the following day; the next, just after the ensuing midnight, and so on.

3-2. The highest level reached by an ascending tide is called high water; the minimum level of a descending tide is called low water. The rate of rise and fall is not uniform. From low water, the tide begins to rise slowly at first but at an increasing rate until it is about halfway to high water. The rate of rise then decreases until high water is reached and the rise ceases. The detachment can then graphically plot the rate of rise and fall, as well as the speeds of the accompanying tidal currents, to determine optimal conditions for maritime operations. At high and low water, there is a brief period during which there is no change in the water level. This period is called stand.

3-3. The total rise or fall from low water to high, or vice versa, is called the range of the tide. The actual height of the water level at high and low water varies with phases of the moon, variations of wind force and direction, atmospheric pressure, and other local causes. The average height of high water, measured over an extended period, is called mean high water. The average height of low water, measured in the same way, is called mean low water. The plane midway between mean high and mean low water is called mean sea level (at sea) and called mean tide level near the coast and in inshore waters. Figure 3-1 shows each of these levels.

3-4. Spring tides occur near the time of full moon and new moon, when the sun and moon act together to produce tides higher and lower than average. When the moon is in its first or last quarter, it and the sun are opposed to each other, and neap tides of less than average range occur (Figure 3-2, page 40).

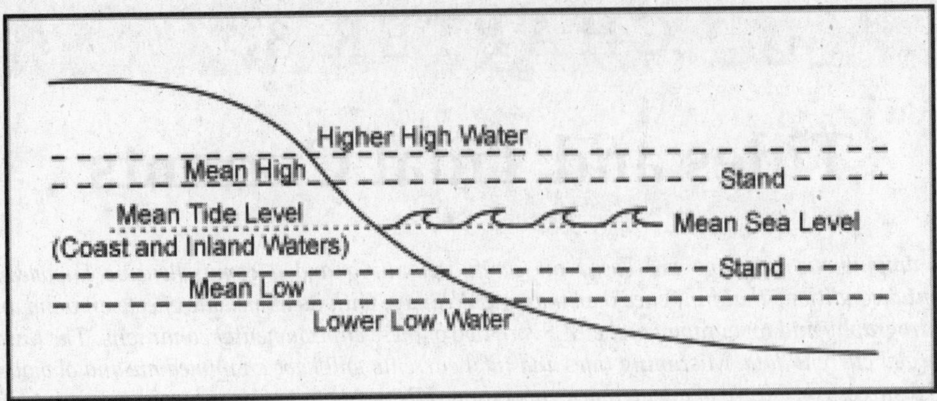

Figure 3-1. High and tow tides

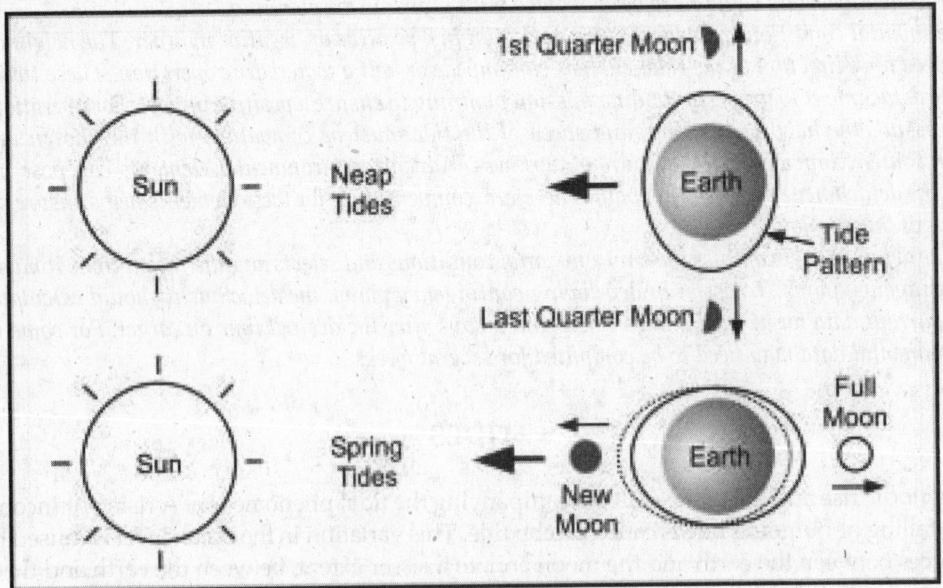

Figure 3-2. Neap and spring tides

3-5. Tides at a particular location are classified as one of three types: semidiurnal, diurnal, or mixed. In the semidiurnal tide, there are two high and two low waters each tidal day, with relatively small inequality in the high and low water heights. Tides on the Atlantic Coast of the United States are representative of the semidiurnal type.

3-6. In the diurnal tide, only one high and low tide (diurnal tide) occur each tidal day. These tides occur along the north coast of the Gulf of Mexico, in the Java Sea, in the Gulf of Tonkin (off the Vietnam-China coast), and in a few other localities.

3-7. In the mixed type of tide, the diurnal and semidiurnal oscillations are both important factors, and the tide is characterized by a large inequality in the high water heights, low water heights, or in both. There are usually two high and two low waters each day (semidiurnal), but occasionally the tide may become diurnal. Such tides are prevalent along the Pacific coast of the United States and in many other parts of the world. Where an inequality in the heights of high or low tides exists, the higher (or lower) of the two tides will be referred to as higher high water (or lower low water). Nautical charts in areas affected by mixed tides normally use this information to determine the depth or overhead obstruction datum.

3-8. A **tidal datum** is a level from which heights and depths are measured. Because water depths (soundings) measured during the initial charting of an area vary with tidal conditions, all soundings are converted to a common **chart sounding datum**. There are a number of such levels that are important to the mariner.

3-9. Detachment personnel should already be familiar with the tiny figures that indicate depth of water on a nautical chart. For example, a 6. Under the title on the chart, it says "Soundings in feet at mean low water." It is important to remember that mean low water is only an average of the various depths actually sounded in one particular area at low water during the survey. When working in shallow water areas, the navigator should know the minimum depth of water the vessel will pass through. Depth varies with stages of the tide. The actual water level at low water may be above or below mean low water at different times because of the height of tide. The charted depth, shown by one of the small figures on the chart, is an average. It does not indicate the lowest depth to be found at all times at that particular point.

3-10. The charted depth is the vertical distance from the reference plane, called datum, on which soundings are based (usually, but not always, mean low water), to the ocean bottom. As discussed earlier, the actual depth of water can be less than the charted depth or below the reference plane. This number is shown by a minus (–) sign placed before the height of tide in the tide tables. The depth of water is equal to the algebraic sum of the charted depth and the height of tide.

3-11. Frequently, operations take place near reefs, rocks, shallows, flats, sandbars, or shoals. Navigators should use the Tide Tables to determine the actual depth of the water at a particular time and place. As a further safety measure, a lead line is a valuable adjunct.

3-12. Currently, charts are being changed to use mean lower low water as datum. Mean lower low water is the average of the lowest of the low waters each day and can differ significantly from mean low water.

TIDE TABLES

3-13. Navigators can predict both the tide height and tidal current with great accuracy by using Tide Tables and Tidal Current Tables published annually by the NOAA.

3-14. The NOAA Tide Tables are divided into four volumes that provide worldwide coverage. Within each volume are six tables that provide specific information concerning tide calculations. The tables are as follows:

- Table 1-Daily Tide Predictions.
- Table 2-Tidal Differences.
- Table 3-Height of the Tide at Any Time.
- Table 4-Local Mean Time of Sunrise and Sunset.
- Table 5-Reduction of Local Mean Time to Standard Time.
- Table 6-Moonrise and Moonset.

3-15. Navigators need specific data from Tables 1 and 2. Table 3 may be useful in certain areas. Tables 4, 5, and 6 provide meteorological data useful to celestial navigators. The G-2 or S-2 that supports the operational team can supply the latter information.

3-16. Explanations are given for particular cases and particular tides. Tides are predicted specifically for a number of principal ports. These ports are referred to, for prediction purposes, as reference stations. The water level for each high and low tide and the time of each tide is listed for every day of the year for each reference station. Volume I, *East Coast of North and South America,* Table 1, lists only 48 reference stations. Figure 3-3 is an excerpt from Table 1 that shows daily tide predictions for Key West, Florida.

3-17. Navigators may want to predict tide levels and times at a greater number of locations than could possibly be listed in Table 1. Therefore, Table 2 (Figure 3-4) was devised to show the subordinate stations, or secondary points between the reference points listed in Table 1. It lists the time and height of the tide for the subordinate station as a correction to the times and heights of the tide at one of the reference stations (identified on each page of Table 2). Depending upon local conditions, the height of the tide at a subordinate station is found in several ways. If a difference for the height of high or low water is given, this is applied as the tables explain. The index and other explanations are provided to assist in finding the proper page of the table to use and to clarify any other unusual situations.

165

Key West, Florida, 2001

Times and Heights of High and Low Waters

April

Day	Time (h m)	Height (ft)	Height (cm)	Day	Time (h m)	Height (ft)	Height (cm)
1 Su	0420 0758 1445 2227	0.8 0.6 1.6 -0.2	24 18 49 -6	16 M	0539 0943 1604 2334	0.9 0.7 1.4 0.2	27 21 43 6
2 M	0547 0926 1615 2338	0.8 0.6 1.6 -0.2	24 18 49 -6	17 Tu	0832 1107 1728	1.0 0.6 1.4	30 18 43
3 Tu	0647 1057 1747	0.9 0.5 1.7	27 15 52	18 W	0024 0707 1212 1836	0.2 1.1 0.5 1.4	6 34 15 43
4 W	0036 0731 1213 1909	-0.2 1.1 0.3 1.7	-6 34 9 52	19 Th	0103 0736 1303 1929	0.1 1.2 0.3 1.4	3 37 9 43
5 Th	0124 0809 1317 2006	-0.2 1.3 0.1 1.7	-6 40 3 52	20 F	0136 0802 1348 2015	0.1 1.3 0.2 1.5	3 40 6 46
6 F	0206 0843 1414 2101	-0.2 1.5 -0.1 1.7	-6 46 -3 52	21 Sa	0204 0829 1425 2058	0.2 1.5 0.0 1.5	6 46 0 46
7 Sa	0243 0917 1506 2151	-0.1 1.6 -0.3 1.5	-3 49 -9 46	22 Su	0231 0856 1509 2140	0.2 1.6 -0.1 1.5	6 49 -3 46
8 Su	0320 0949 1556 2239	0.0 1.8 -0.4 1.5	0 55 -12 46	23 M	0250 0924 1541 2222	0.2 1.7 -0.3 1.4	6 52 -9 43
9 M	0356 1022 1644 2325	0.1 1.9 -0.5 1.4	3 58 -15 43	24 Tu	0327 0953 1621 2306	0.3 1.8 -0.4 1.3	9 55 -12 40
10 Tu	0430 1055 1731	0.2 1.9 -0.4	6 58 -12	25 W	0358 1024 1704 2350	0.3 1.9 -0.4 1.2	9 58 -12 37
11 W	0010 0505 1129 1821	1.2 0.3 1.9 -0.3	37 9 58 -9	26 Th	0431 1058 1751	0.4 1.9 -0.4	12 58 -12
12 Th	0057 0541 1206 1913	1.1 0.4 1.8 -0.2	34 12 55 -6	27 F	0043 0607 1138 1844	1.1 0.5 1.9 -0.3	34 15 58 -9
13 F	0148 0619 1248 2012	1.0 0.5 1.7 -0.1	30 15 52 -3	28 Sa	0141 0549 1225 1945	1.0 0.5 1.9 -0.3	30 15 58 -9
14 Sa	0250 0705 1336 2120	0.9 0.6 1.6 0.1	27 18 49 3	29 Su	0249 0643 1324 2054	0.9 0.6 1.8 -0.2	27 18 55 -6
15 Su	0413 0811 1442 2231	0.8 0.7 1.4 0.1	24 21 43 3	30 M	0405 0757 1439 2204	0.9 0.7 1.7 -0.1	27 21 52 -3

May

Day	Time (h m)	Height (ft)	Height (cm)	Day	Time (h m)	Height (ft)	Height (cm)
1 Tu	0515 0932 1610 2307	1.0 0.6 1.6 0.0	30 18 49 0	16 W	0519 1015 1633 2323	1.1 0.7 1.3 0.3	34 21 40 9
2 W	0610 1101 1741	1.2 0.5 1.5	37 15 46	17 Th	0601 1143 1750	1.2 0.5 1.3	37 15 40
3 Th	0000 0653 1215 1858	0.0 1.4 0.2 1.5	0 43 6 46	18 F	0002 0636 1236 1854	0.3 1.4 0.3 1.3	9 43 9 40
4 F	0046 0732 1317 2001	0.1 1.6 0.0 1.5	3 49 0 46	19 Sa	0037 0708 1322 1949	0.3 1.5 0.1 1.3	9 46 3 40
5 Sa	0126 0807 1411 2056	0.1 1.7 -0.2 1.5	3 52 -6 46	20 Su	0109 0740 1403 2039	0.3 1.7 -0.1 1.3	9 52 -3 40
6 Su	0205 0841 1500 2145	0.2 1.9 -0.3 1.4	6 58 -9 43	21 M	0140 0812 1443 2126	0.4 1.8 -0.2 1.3	12 55 -6 40
7 M	0241 0915 1546 2231	0.3 2.0 -0.4 1.3	9 61 -12 40	22 Tu	0213 0845 1524 2212	0.4 1.9 -0.4 1.3	12 58 -12 40
8 Tu	0318 0948 1630 2314	0.3 2.0 -0.4 1.2	9 61 -12 37	23 W	0248 0920 1608 2259	0.4 2.1 -0.5 1.2	12 64 -15 37
9 W	0354 1022 1714 2356	0.4 2.0 -0.4 1.2	12 61 -12 37	24 Th	0325 0959 1654 2347	0.4 2.1 -0.5 1.2	12 64 -15 37
10 Th	0430 1057 1800	0.5 2.0 -0.3	15 61 -9	25 F	0404 1041 1743	0.5 2.1 -0.5	15 64 -15
11 F	0039 0506 1135 1848	1.1 0.5 1.9 -0.2	34 15 58 -6	26 Sa	0038 0449 1128 1836	1.1 0.5 2.1 -0.4	34 15 64 -12
12 Sa	0124 0546 1217 1941	1.0 0.6 1.8 0.0	30 18 55 0	27 Su	0133 0540 1222 1933	1.1 0.5 2.0 -0.3	34 15 61 -9
13 Su	0218 0632 1306 2039	1.0 0.7 1.6 0.1	30 21 49 3	28 M	0232 0644 1324 2033	1.1 0.6 1.8 -0.2	34 18 55 -6
14 M	0318 0737 1404 2140	0.9 0.7 1.5 0.2	27 21 46 6	29 Tu	0333 0806 1437 2132	1.1 0.6 1.6 0.0	34 18 49 0
15 Tu	0424 0907 1514 2236	1.0 0.7 1.4 0.2	30 21 43 6	30 W	0432 0937 1604 2227	1.2 0.5 1.5 0.1	37 15 46 3
				31 Th	0525 1100 1734 2316	1.4 0.3 1.3 0.2	43 9 40 6

June

Day	Time (h m)	Height (ft)	Height (cm)	Day	Time (h m)	Height (ft)	Height (cm)
1 F	0612 1214 1852	1.6 0.1 1.3	49 3 40	16 Sa	0537 1202 1816 2333	1.5 0.3 1.1 0.4	46 9 34 12
2 Sa	0003 0654 1312 1957	0.3 1.8 -0.1 1.3	9 55 -3 40	17 Su	0612 1233 1925	1.6 0.1 1.1	49 3 34
3 Su	0046 0733 1405 2052	0.3 1.9 -0.2 1.2	9 58 -6 37	18 M	0013 0652 1339 2022	0.5 1.8 -0.1 1.1	15 55 -3 34
4 M	0127 0810 1451 2140	0.4 2.0 -0.3 1.2	12 61 -9 37	19 Tu	0053 0732 1424 2113	0.5 2.0 -0.3 1.2	15 61 -9 37
5 Tu	0207 0846 1535 2222	0.4 2.1 -0.4 1.2	12 64 -12 37	20 W	0134 0814 1509 2201	0.5 2.1 -0.4 1.2	15 64 -12 37
6 W	0245 0922 1617 2302	0.4 2.1 -0.4 1.1	12 64 -12 34	21 Th	0216 0859 1556 2247	0.5 2.2 -0.5 1.2	15 67 -15 37
7 Th	0324 0958 1658 2339	0.5 2.0 -0.3 1.1	15 61 -9 34	22 F	0301 0945 1643 2334	0.4 2.3 -0.5 1.1	12 70 -15 34
8 F	0401 1035 1740	0.5 2.0 -0.2	15 61 -6	23 Sa	0349 1034 1732	0.4 2.3 -0.5	12 70 -15
9 Sa	0017 0440 1114 1824	1.1 0.5 1.9 -0.1	34 15 58 -3	24 Su	0021 0441 1126 1831	1.1 0.4 2.2 -0.4	34 12 67 -12
10 Su	0056 0521 1156 1908	1.0 0.6 1.8 0.0	30 18 55 0	25 M	0109 0540 1222 1911	1.2 0.4 2.0 -0.2	37 12 61 -6
11 M	0139 0609 1241 1955	1.0 0.6 1.6 0.1	30 18 49 3	26 Tu	0159 0648 1323 2002	1.2 0.4 1.8 -0.1	37 12 55 -3
12 Tu	0226 0709 1332 2042	1.1 0.7 1.5 0.2	34 21 46 6	27 W	0251 0808 1439 2053	1.3 0.4 1.5 0.1	40 12 46 3
13 W	0316 0827 1431 2136	1.1 0.7 1.4 0.3	34 21 43 9	28 Th	0344 0934 1554 2143	1.5 0.3 1.3 0.2	46 9 40 6
14 Th	0406 0950 1542 2212	1.2 0.6 1.2 0.3	37 18 37 9	29 F	0438 1055 1724 2233	1.6 0.2 1.2 0.4	49 6 37 12
15 F	0450 1103 1701 2253	1.3 0.5 1.2 0.4	40 15 37 12	30 Sa	0529 1206 1846 2323	1.7 0.1 1.1 0.4	52 3 34 12

Time meridian 75° W. 0000 is midnight. 1200 is noon.
Heights are referred to mean lower low water which is the chart datum of soundings.

Figure 3-3. Table 1 excerpt, daily tide predictions (Key West, Florida)

305

TABLE 2 – TIDAL DIFFERENCES AND OTHER CONSTANTS

No.	PLACE	POSITION Latitude	POSITION Longitude	DIFFERENCES Time High Water	DIFFERENCES Time Low Water	DIFFERENCES Height High Water	DIFFERENCES Height Low Water	RANGES Mean	RANGES Spring	Mean Tide Level
		North	West	h m	h m	ft	ft	ft	ft	ft
	Florida Keys–cont. Time meridian, 75° W			on Key West, p.164						
4187	Sugarloaf Key, Pirates Cove	24° 39.2'	81° 30.8'	−0 46	+1 41	*0.58	*0.75	0.74	0.92	0.66
4189	Cudjoe Key, Cudjoe Bay	24° 39.6'	81° 29.5'	−0 28	+0 41	*0.87	*0.71	1.16	1.48	0.76
4191	Summerland Key, southwest side, Kemp Channel	24° 39.0'	81° 26.8'	−0 26	+0 50	*0.84	*0.54	1.12	1.40	0.69
4193	Cudjoe Key, Kemp Channel Bridge	24° 39.7'	81° 28.1'	---	---	*0.58	*0.50	0.79	0.99	0.52
4195	Cudjoe Key, northeast side, Kemp Channel	24° 41.2'	81° 29.0'	+3 45	---	---	---	--	--	--
4197	Cudjoe Key, north end, Kemp Channel	24° 42.0'	81° 30.6'	+3 32	+4 40	*1.63	*1.46	2.17	2.71	1.43
4199	Sugarloaf Key, northeast side, Bow Channel	24° 40.3'	81° 32.0'	+3 47	+3 24	*1.01	*0.71	1.40	1.75	0.87
4201	Cudjoe Key, Pirates Cove	24° 39.8'	81° 30.8'	+3 50	+2 55	*0.77	*0.79	1.01	1.26	0.69
4203	Sugarloaf Key, north end, Bow Channel	24° 41.6'	81° 33.3'	+3 37	+5 20	*1.29	*0.75	1.82	2.28	1.09
4205	Pumpkin Key, Bow Channel	24° 43.0'	81° 33.7'	+3 17	+4 39	*1.56	*1.17	2.14	2.68	1.35
4207	Sawyer Key, outside, Cudjoe Channel	24° 45.5'	81° 33.7'	+2 46	+5 24	*1.57	*0.50	2.32	2.90	1.29
4209	Sawyer Key, inside, Cudjoe Channel	24° 45.5'	81° 33.7'	+2 37	+5 19	*1.43	*0.50	2.10	2.62	1.17
4211	Johnston Key, southeast end, Turkey Basin	24° 42.6'	81° 35.6'	+3 26	+5 38	*1.19	*0.50	1.59	1.99	0.92
	Upper Sugarloaf Sound									
4213	Perky	24° 38.9'	81° 34.2'	+5 37	+8 25	*0.28	*0.06	0.42	0.52	0.23
4215	Park Channel Bridge	24° 39.3'	81° 32.4'	+5 47	+8 33	*0.26	*0.29	0.34	0.42	0.24
4217	North Harris Channel	24° 39.0'	81° 33.2'	+6 32	+8 04	*0.25	*0.25	0.33	0.41	0.22
4219	Sugarloaf Shores East <26>	24° 38.6'	81° 33.6'	---	---	---	---	--	--	--
4221	Tarpon Creek	24° 37.8'	81° 31.9'	−0 29	−0 17	*0.35	*0.38	0.46	0.58	0.32
	Lower Sugarloaf Sound <27>									
4223	Sugarloaf Shores <27>	24° 38.0'	81° 33.1'	---	---	---	---	--	--	--
4225	Sugarloaf Beach <27>	24° 36.4'	81° 34.0'	---	---	---	---	--	--	--
4227	Sugarloaf Shores North <27>	24° 38.4'	81° 34.2'	---	---	---	---	--	--	--
4229	Saddlebunch Keys, south end <27>	24° 36.1'	81° 34.9'	---	---	---	---	--	--	--
4231	Lower Sugarloaf Channel Bridge <27>	24° 38.0'	81° 35.2'	---	---	---	---	--	--	--
4233	Saddlebunch Keys, Channel No. 2 <27>	24° 37.6'	81° 35.9'	---	---	---	---	--	--	--
4235	Saddlebunch Keys <27>	24° 37.1'	81° 36.1'	---	---	---	---	--	--	--
4237	Snipe Keys, southeast end, inner Narrows	24° 39.6'	81° 38.8'	+3 25	+5 39	*1.28	*0.83	1.79	2.24	1.10
4239	Snipe Keys, Middle Narrows	24° 40.0'	81° 37.8'	+3 44	+5 34	*1.62	*0.87	1.42	1.78	0.87
4241	Snipe Keys, Snipe Point	24° 41.5'	81° 40.4'	+2 15	+3 33	*1.89	*1.29	2.31	2.88	1.47
4243	Waltz Key, Waltz Key Basin	24° 38.8'	81° 39.2'	+3 53	+5 33	*1.03	*0.86	1.36	1.75	0.91
4245	Duck Key Point, Duck Key, Waltz Key Basin	24° 37.4'	81° 41.1'	+3 27	+4 57	*1.18	*0.86	1.61	2.01	1.03
4247	O'Hara Key, north end, Waltz Key Basin	24° 37.0'	81° 38.7'	+3 53	+5 39	*1.03	*0.83	1.40	1.75	0.90
4249	Saddlebunch Keys, Channel No. 5	24° 36.7'	81° 37.5'	+4 22	+5 58	*0.66	*1.12	0.76	0.95	0.65
4251	Saddlebunch Keys, Channel No. 4	24° 36.9'	81° 37.9'	+4 35	+5 36	*0.54	*0.29	0.76	0.95	0.45
4253	Saddlebunch Keys, Channel No. 3	24° 37.4'	81° 36.2'	+1 44	−0 10	*0.43	*0.21	0.62	0.78	0.38
4255	Bird Key, Similar Sound	24° 35.3'	81° 36.3'	−0 21	+1 03	*0.58	*0.42	0.82	1.02	0.51
4257	Shark Key, southeast end, Similar Sound	24° 36.2'	81° 36.7'	+0 18	+1 51	*0.52	*0.46	0.70	0.88	0.46
4259	Saddlebunch Keys, Similar Sound	24° 36.0'	81° 37.2'	+0 39	+2 41	*0.37	*0.21	0.52	0.65	0.31
4261	Geiger Key, inside <26>	24° 35.0'	81° 39.3'	---	---	---	---	--	--	--
4263	Big Coppitt Key, northwest side, Waltz Key Basin	24° 36.1'	81° 39.3'	+4 21	+6 54	*0.84	*0.39	1.23	1.53	0.69
4265	Rockland Key, Rockland Channel Bridge	24° 35.6'	81° 40.1'	+5 02	+6 08	*0.76	*0.89	0.97	1.21	0.69
4267	Boca Chica Key, Long Point	24° 35.2'	81° 41.9'	+3 54	+5 22	*0.94	*0.71	1.28	1.60	0.81
4269	Channel Key, west side	24° 36.2'	81° 43.5'	+3 09	+3 07	*0.70	*0.71	0.91	1.14	0.62
4271	Boca Chica Channel Bridge	24° 34.6'	81° 43.2'	+1 23	+1 29	*0.57	*0.87	0.72	0.90	0.52
4273	Key Haven – Stock Island Channel	24° 34.8'	81° 44.3'	+2 25	+2 57	*0.73	*0.79	0.94	1.18	0.66
4275	Sigsbee Park, Garrison Bight Channel	24° 35.1'	81° 46.5'	+1 59	+2 06	*0.81	*0.88	1.04	1.30	0.73
4277	Key West, south side, Hawk Channel	24° 32.7'	81° 47.0'	−0 52	−0 30	*1.37	*0.92	1.44	1.80	0.94
4279	KEY WEST	24° 33.2'	81° 48.5'	Daily predictions				1.31	1.64	0.90
4281	Sand Key Lighthouse, Sand Key Channel	24° 27.2'	81° 52.6'	−1 02	−0 38	*0.84	*0.79	1.26	1.58	0.82
4283	Garden Key, Dry Tortugas	24° 37.6'	82° 52.3'	+0 29	+0 33	*0.84	*1.33	1.14	1.42	0.89
	Gulf Coast							Mean	Diurnal	
4285	Cape Sable, East Cape	25° 07'	81° 05'	+3 56	+4 43	*2.26	*2.20	2.9	3.8	2.0
4287	Shark River entrance	25° 21'	81° 08'	+3 20	+4 38	*2.71	*2.50	3.6	4.5	2.4
4289	Whitewater Bay	25° 18'	81° 02'	---	---	*0.38	*0.26	0.5	0.8	0.4
4291	Lostmans River entrance	25° 33'	81° 13'	+3 22	+4 42	*2.31	*2.31	3.0	3.9	2.1
4293	Onion Key, Lostmans River	25° 37'	81° 08'	+5 32	+7 46	*0.46	*0.46	0.6	0.8	0.4
4295	Chatham River entrance	25° 41'	81° 17'	+3 22	+4 46	*2.82	*2.50	3.3	4.2	2.1
				on St. Marks River Ent., p.172						
4297	Pavilion Key	25° 42'	81° 21'	−0 57	−0 43	*1.23	*0.71	3.5	4.3	2.2
4299	Chokoloskee	25° 49'	81° 22'	+0 14	+1 07	*0.92	*0.55	2.6	3.2	1.6
4301	Everglades City, Barron River	25° 52'	81° 23'	+0 23	+1 18	*0.82	*0.47	2.3	2.9	1.4
4303	Indian Key	25° 48'	81° 28'	−1 05	−0 48	*1.23	*0.83	3.4	4.3	2.3
4305	Round Key	25° 50'	81° 32'	−1 06	−0 55	*1.23	*0.81	3.4	4.3	2.3
4307	Pumpkin Bay	25° 55'	81° 33'	+0 39	+1 00	*0.77	*0.77	2.1	2.7	1.3
4309	Coon Key	25° 54'	81° 38'	−0 45	−0 36	*0.93	*0.86	2.6	3.5	1.3
4311	Cape Romano	25° 51'	81° 41'	−1 17	−1 03	*0.93	*1.02	2.6	3.5	1.9
4313	Marco, Big Marco River	25° 58'	81° 44'	−1 04	−1 08	*0.68	*0.68	1.7	2.6	1.2
4315	Naples, Naples Bay, north end	26° 08.2'	81° 47.3'	−1 17	−1 11	*0.80	*0.80	2.06	2.85	1.58
4317	Naples (outer coast)	26° 08'	81° 48'	−1 59	−2 04	*0.85	*0.85	2.1	2.8	1.6
				on St. Petersburg, p.168						
	Estero Bay									
4319	Little Hickory Island	26° 21'	81° 51'	−0 58	−1 05	*1.09	*1.09	--	2.5	1.3
4321	Coconut Point	26° 24'	81° 50'	−0 47	−0 40	*1.17	*1.17	--	2.7	1.3
4323	Carlos Point	26° 24'	81° 53'	−1 06	−1 28	*1.17	*1.17	--	2.7	1.4
4325	Matanzas Pass (fixed bridge) Estero Island	26° 27'	81° 57'	−1 10	−1 34	*1.22	*1.22	--	2.8	1.4
4327	Point Ybel, San Carlos Bay entrance	26° 27'	82° 01'	−1 50	−1 12	*1.21	*1.21	--	2.6	1.4
4329	Punta Rassa, San Carlos Bay	26° 29'	82° 01'	−1 01	−1 19	*1.04	*1.04	--	2.4	1.2

Endnotes can be found at the end of table 2.

Figure 3-4. Table 2 excerpt, tidal differences (Florida subordinate stations)

3-18. Detachment planners can better determine the optimum conditions if they can visualize the tide (and tidal current) during their proposed infiltration window. They can determine tide height at any point during the tidal cycle using the matrix (Table 3-1) or graphical methods (Figure 3-5). How-to instructions for each method are explained in the charts. Tide and current predictions are affected by meteorological conditions, and therefore may not be 100-percent accurate. Local knowledge is also important.

CURRENTS

3-19. As discussed earlier, tide is the vertical rise and fall of the ocean's water level caused by the attraction of the sun and moon. A tidal current is the result of a tide. Tidal current is the horizontal motion of water resulting from the vertical motion caused by a tide, distinguished them from ocean or river currents or from those created by the wind. Tidal currents are of particular concern in small-boat operations.

3-20. The horizontal motion of water toward the land caused by a rising tide is called flood current. The horizontal motion away from the land caused by a falling tide is known as ebb current. Between these two, while the current is changing direction, is a brief period when no horizontal motion is perceptible. This time is called slack water.

3-21. An outgoing or ebb current running across a bar builds up a more intense sea than the incoming or flood current. This sea results from the rush of water out against the incoming ground swell that slows the wave speed and steepens the wave prematurely.

3-22. Some currents run parallel to the shore and inside the breakers. The water the waves carry to the beach causes these currents. They are called longshore currents. A navigator should pay close attention to this type of current because it can cause his boat to broach (capsize), or cause an object that he is searching for to move farther than he would expect.

3-23. Currents affect boat speed. When going with the current, the boat's speed over the ground is faster than the speed or revolutions per minute (rpm) indication. The effect is the same as that experienced by an aircraft affected by head or tail winds. When going against the current, the boat's speed over the ground is slower than the speed or rpm indication.

Table 3-1. Constructing a tide table matrix

	High Tide		Low Tide	
	Time	**Height (Ft)**	**Time**	**Height (Ft)**
Reference Station	0148	1.0	0619	0.5
Subordinate Station 4275	+01:59	0.8	+02:06	0.88
Correction	**0347**	**1.81**	**0825**	**1.38**
	Time	**Height (Ft)**	**Time**	**Height (Ft)**
Reference Station	1248	1.7	2012	-0.1
Subordinate Station 4275	+01:59	0.81	+02:06	0.88
Correction	**1447**	**2.51**	**2218**	**0.78**

INSTRUCTIONS: Refer to Tables 1 and 2, NOAA Tide Tables. Data computed from Key West, Florida (Reference Station) and Sigsbee Park Florida (Subordinate Station 4275) on 13 April 2001.
Table 1 contains the predicted times and heights of the high and low waters for each day of the year at designated reference stations.
Table 2 lists tide predictions for many other places called subordinate stations. By applying the differences or ratios listed under the subordinate station to predictions listed at the reference station, the times and height of the tide can be corrected (Correction) nearest the desired location.
The height of the tide, referred to as the datum of the charts, is obtained by applying the correction of height differences or ratios to the charted depth.
NOTE: Nonapplicable low- or high-tide datum is ignored.

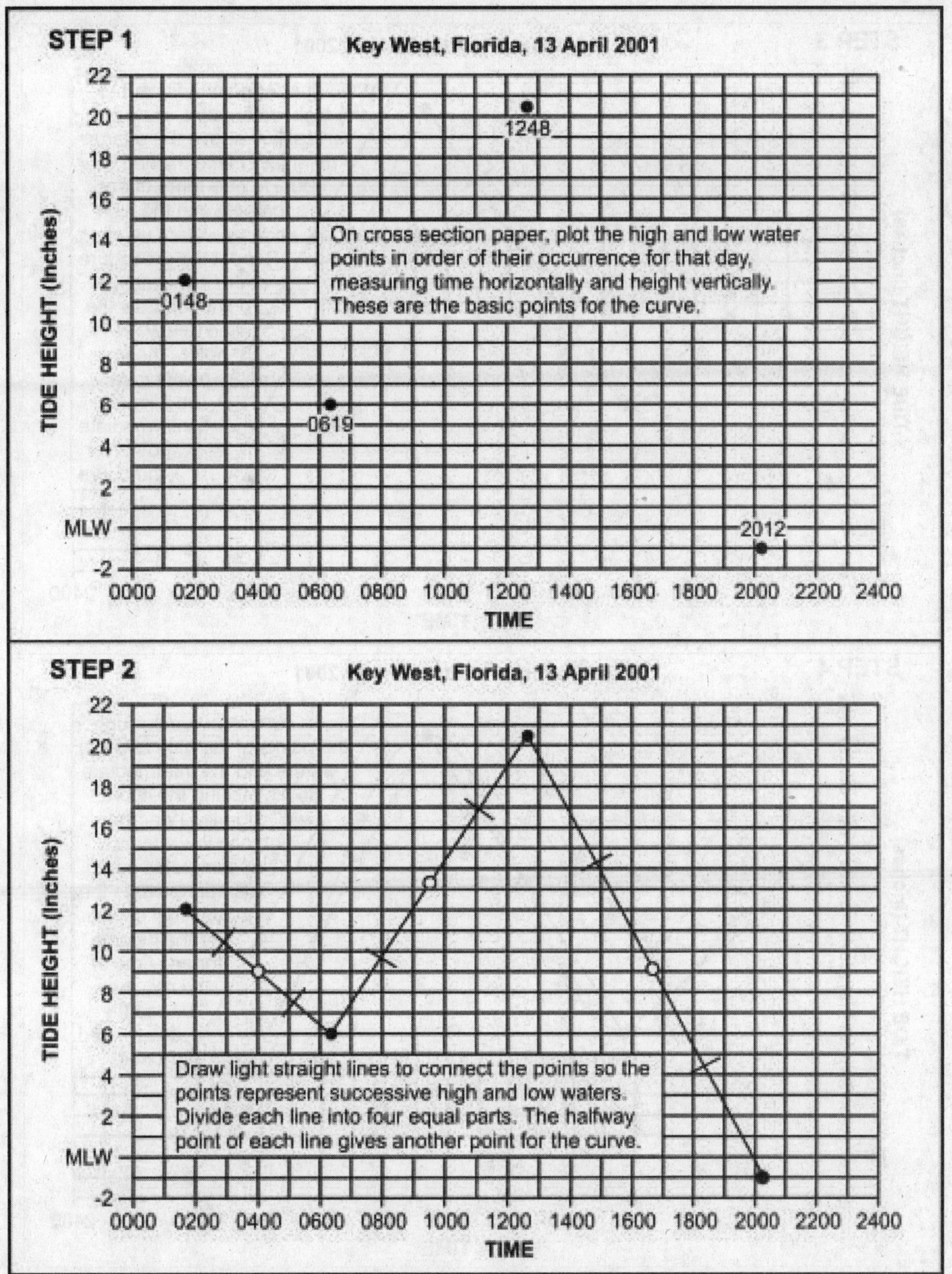

Figure 3-5. Plotting a tide curve

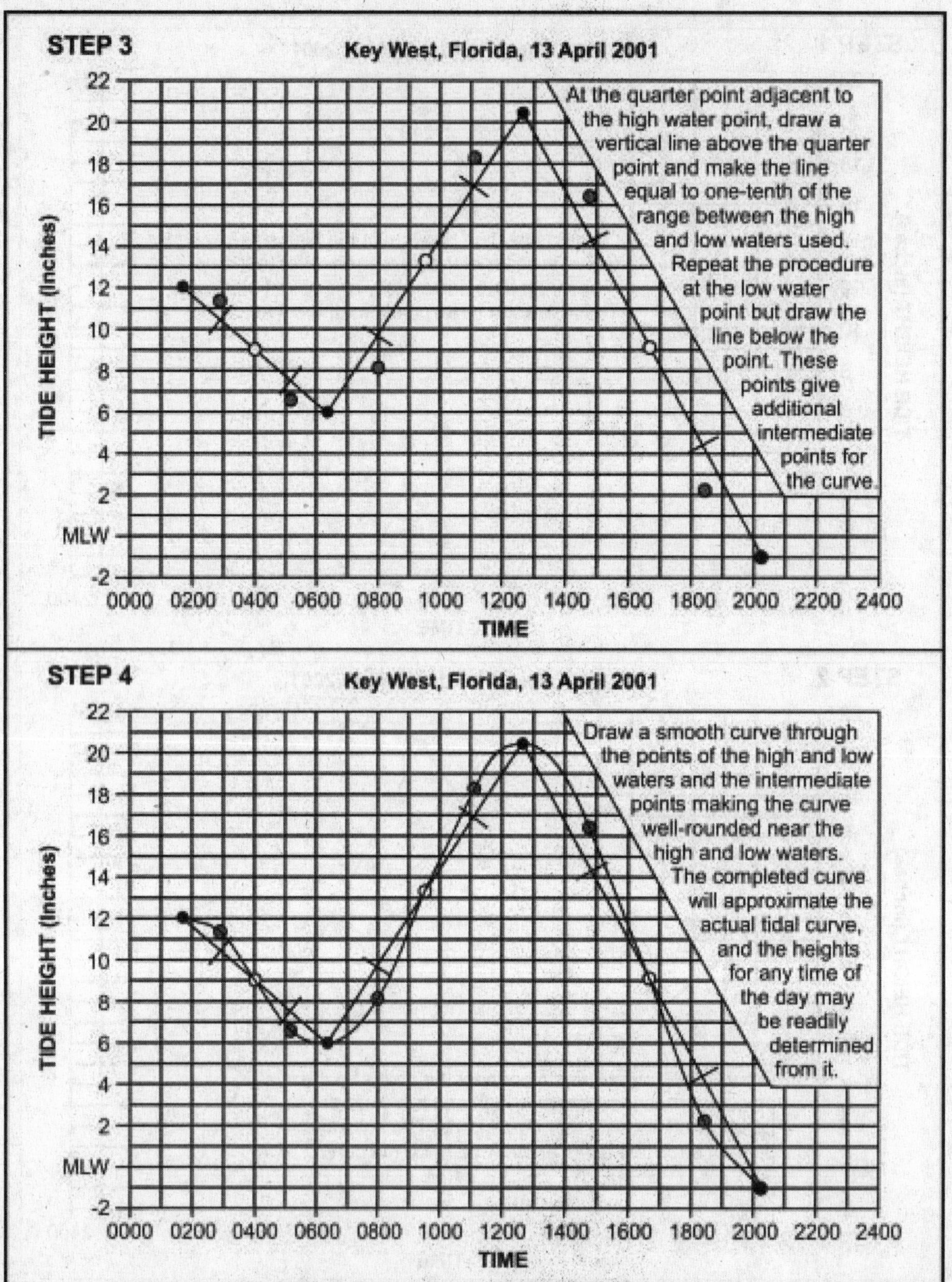

Figure 3-5. Plotting a tide curve (*Continued*)

3-24. Currents affect boat maneuverability. When working in current, the navigator must remember that the boat's maneuverability depends on its speed through the water. The boat may have significant speed in relation to fixed objects (a pier, for example), but because the current is carrying it, the boat may lack maneuverability if too little water is flowing past its rudder.

3-25. When crossing the current to compensate for the set, the navigator may have to put the boat in a "crab." That is, he must turn the bow slightly into the current or wind. As a result of this maneuver, the boat's heading and the actual course made good will be different. Therefore, the navigator must "play" the current or wind by either sighting on a fixed object, such as a range, or by marking bearing drift on some object as nearly in line with his destination as possible.

3-26. Eddy currents (eddies) are swirling currents, sometimes quite powerful, that occur downstream (down current) of obstructions (for example, islands, rocks, or piers) at channel bends, near points of land, and at places where the bottom is uneven. Eddies can be dangerous to small boats. Navigators should watch for and avoid them.

3-27. Wind affects current speed. A sustained wind in the same direction as the current increases current speed by a small amount. A wind in the opposite direction slows it down and may create a chop. A very strong wind blowing directly into the mouth of an inlet or bay can produce an unusually high tide by piling up the water. (Similarly, a very strong wind blowing out of a bay can cause an unusually low tide and change the time of the high or low tide.)

3-28. The time of a tidal current's change of direction does not coincide with the time of high or low tide. The current's change of direction always lags behind the tide's turning. This time interval varies according to the physical characteristics of the land around the body of tidewater. For instance, there is usually little difference between the times of high or low tide and the time of slack water along a relatively straight coast with only shallow indentions. But where a large body of water connects with the ocean through a narrow channel, the tide and the current may be out of phase by as much as several hours. In this case, the current in the channel may be running at its greatest speed during high or low tide.

3-29. Each navigator operating in tidal waters must know the set (direction toward) and drift (velocity or speed expressed in knots) of the tidal currents in the area. He can use the NOAA Tidal Current Tables to predict the force and direction of tidal currents in most oceans. The NOAA publishes these tables annually and organizes them in a manner similar to the Tide Tables. The Tidal Current Tables are also divided into four volumes. Each volume consists of five tables that provide specific information on tidal current characteristics. They are—

- Table 1–Daily Current Predictions.
- Table 2–Current Differences and Other Constants.
- Table 3–Velocity of the Current at Any Time.
- Table 4–Duration of Slack.
- Table 5–Rotary Tidal Currents.

3-30. Navigators need the specific data contained in Tables 1 and 2. Like the Tide Tables, they are divided into a table for reference stations and a table for subordinate stations. Table 1 lists predicted times of slack water and predicted times and speed of maximum flood and ebb at the reference stations for each day of the year.

3-31. Table 2 includes the latitude and longitude of each subordinate station (and reference stations), time and differences for slack water and maximum current, speed ratios for maximum flood and ebb, and direction and average speed for maximum flood and ebb currents. Figures 3-6 and 3-7 show examples of each table.

3-32. Winds, variations in stream discharges produced by heavy rain or snow and ice melt, and other weather factors frequently affect current direction and speed. When any of these occur, actual current conditions vary from those predicted. The ability to estimate the amount by which they vary can be acquired only through experience in a particular area.

3-33. Like the tidal difference in time, the time differences are applied to the slack and maximum current times at the reference station to obtain the corresponding times at the subordinate station. Maximum speed at the subordinate station is found by multiplying the maximum speed at the reference station by the appropriate flood or ebb ratio.

3-34. Flood direction is the approximate true direction toward which the flooding current flows. Ebb direction is generally close to the reciprocal of the flood direction. Average flood and ebb speeds are averages of all the flood and ebb currents. Tidal Current Table 3 is similar to Table 3 of the Tide Tables. It is used to find current speed at a specific time.

Key West, Florida, 2001

F–Flood, Dir. 020° True E–Ebb, Dir. 195° True

April

Day	Slack h m	Maximum h m	knots	Day	Slack h m	Maximum h m	knots
1 Su ◐	0408 1113 1509 2329	0047 0707 1255 1920	0.9F 1.2E 0.3F 1.7E	16 M	0449	0237 0818 1500 2021	0.5F 1.0E * 1.3E
2 M	0524 1233 1655	0230 0833 1444 2043	0.9F 1.3E 0.4F 1.7E	17 Tu	0036 0551 1329 1745	0341 0928 1603 2132	0.6F 1.2E 0.4F 1.4E
3 Tu	0242 0629 1325 1913	0351 0947 1607 2158	1.1F 1.5E 0.7F 1.9E	18 W	0129 0643 1400 1847	0430 1015 1644 2224	0.8F 1.3E 0.6F 1.6E
4 W	0144 0724 1415 1927	0449 1043 1705 2259	1.3F 1.8E 1.1F 2.1E	19 Th	0213 0727 1430 1938	0508 1051 1723 2308	0.9F 1.5E 0.8F 1.7E
5 Th	0237 0811 1459 2025	0536 1130 1753 2350	1.4F 2.0E 1.4F 2.3E	20 F	0251 0804 1459 2023	0540 1123 1759 2343	1.0F 1.7E 1.1F 1.8E
6 F	0325 0853 1538 2116	0618 1211 1836	1.5F 2.2E 1.6F	21 Sa	0326 0838 1529 2105	0608 1153 1817	1.0F 1.9E 1.3F
7 Sa ○	0408 0932 1615 2204	0036 0657 1249 1916	2.3E 1.5F 2.4E 1.7F	22 Su	0400 0908 1600 2145	0018 0630 1225 1846	2.0E 1.1F 2.1E 1.4F
8 Su	0451 1008 1656 2246	0117 0732 1326 1955	2.3E 1.4F 2.4E 1.7F	23 M ●	0435 0937 1634 2228	0054 0657 1255 1919	2.0E 1.1F 2.2E 1.5F
9 M	0532 1042 1740 2331	0156 0805 1402 2032	2.2E 1.2F 2.3E 1.6F	24 Tu	0510 1005 1710 2308	0131 0727 1335 1956	2.0E 1.0F 2.3E 1.6F
10 Tu	0613 1114 1822	0236 0837 1439 2109	2.0E 1.1F 2.2E 1.4F	25 W	0548 1036 1751 2352	0211 0802 1414 2036	2.0E 1.0F 2.3E 1.6F
11 W	0014 0656 1146 1907	0314 0910 1515 2149	1.8E 0.8F 2.0E 1.2F	26 Th	0631 1108 1838	0254 0841 1458 2121	1.8E 0.8F 2.2E 1.4F
12 Th	0057 0744 1217 1958	0356 0946 1600 2233	1.5E 0.6F 1.8E 0.9F	27 F	0041 0721 1146 1932	0341 0926 1547 2214	1.7E 0.7F 2.1E 1.3F
13 F	0144 0843 1249 2058	0443 1030 1649 2329	1.3E 0.4F 1.6E 0.7F	28 Sa	0136 0823 1235 2037	0436 1019 1643 2317	1.5E 0.6F 1.9E 1.1F
14 Sa	0236 2210	0539 1126 1747	1.1E * 1.4E	29 Su	0239 0937 1344 2152	0539 1126 1749	1.3E 0.4F 1.7E
15 Su ◐	0342 2327	0058 0650 1301 1858	0.5F 1.0E * 1.3E	30 M ◐	0348 1057 1520 2311	0036 0653 1257 1907	0.9F 1.3E 0.4F 1.6E

May

Day	Slack h m	Maximum h m	knots	Day	Slack h m	Maximum h m	knots
1 Tu	0456 1207 1654	0211 0812 1442 2030	0.9F 1.4E 0.6F 1.7E	16 W	0455 1229 1706	0235 0819 1505 2038	0.6F 1.2E 0.4F 1.3E
2 W	0024 0557 1303 1812	0326 0921 1554 2144	1.0F 1.6E 0.9F 1.8E	17 Th	0045 0547 1309 1812	0331 0913 1556 2137	0.6F 1.4E 0.7F 1.5E
3 Th	0127 0650 1351 1918	0424 1010 1650 2244	1.1F 1.8E 1.2F 1.9E	18 F	0131 0633 1345 1907	0414 0958 1637 2227	0.7F 1.6E 0.9F 1.6E
4 F	0220 0736 1435 2014	0512 1103 1737 2336	1.2F 2.1E 1.5F 2.0E	19 Sa	0214 0713 1420 1957	0449 1037 1713 2310	0.8F 1.8E 1.1F 1.7E
5 Sa	0306 0818 1516 2104	0554 1144 1820	1.2F 2.2E 1.6F	20 Su	0254 0750 1455 2043	0521 1114 1748 2351	0.9F 2.0E 1.2F 1.9E
6 Su	0351 0856 1556 2149	0019 0632 1221 1900	2.1E 1.2F 2.3E 1.7F	21 M	0332 0825 1531 2128	0552 1152 1823	0.9F 2.2E 1.5F
7 M ○	0432 0932 1636 2232	0059 0706 1258 1937	2.0E 1.1F 2.3E 1.6F	22 Tu ●	0410 0859 1610 2213	0031 0625 1231 1901	1.9E 1.0F 2.3E 1.6F
8 Tu	0512 1006 1716 2312	0136 0737 1334 2012	1.9E 1.0F 2.3E 1.5F	23 W	0450 0935 1651 2258	0112 0700 1312 1942	1.9E 1.0F 2.4E 1.7F
9 W	0552 1039 1758 2352	0213 0808 1410 2046	1.8E 0.9F 2.2E 1.4F	24 Th	0532 1013 1736 2345	0156 0743 1356 2026	1.9E 0.9F 2.4E 1.7F
10 Th	0634 1111 1840	0251 0841 1449 2123	1.6E 0.7F 2.0E 1.2F	25 F	0619 1056 1826	0241 0828 1443 2114	1.8E 0.9F 2.3E 1.5F
11 F	0033 0720 1143 1927	0331 0918 1531 2203	1.5E 0.6F 1.8E 1.0F	26 Sa	0034 0712 1145 1922	0331 0918 1535 2206	1.7E 0.8F 2.2E 1.4F
12 Sa	0116 0814 1220 2021	0416 1002 1619 2252	1.3E 0.4F 1.6E 0.8F	27 Su	0127 0813 1244 2025	0426 1016 1633 2309	1.6E 0.7F 2.0E 1.2F
13 Su	0204 0919 1307 2124	0507 1055 1713 2354	1.2E 0.3F 1.4E 0.6F	28 M	0223 0921 1358 2136	0526 1126 1738	1.5E 0.6F 1.8E
14 M	0258 2334	0607 1207 1817	1.1E * 1.3E	29 Tu ◐	0322 1031 1523 2246	0022 0634 1255 1853	1.0F 1.5E 0.6F 1.6E
15 Tu ◐	0357 1138 1548 2342	0116 0714 1348 1928	0.5F 1.1E 0.3F 1.3E	30 W	0422 1138 1646	0143 0744 1425 2012	0.9F 1.6E 0.8F 1.6E
				31 Th	0001 0518 1236 1759	0255 0849 1534 2126	0.9F 1.7E 1.0F 1.6E

June

Day	Slack h m	Maximum h m	knots	Day	Slack h m	Maximum h m	knots
1 F	0106 0610 1327 1903	0355 0945 1631 2227	0.9F 1.9E 1.2F 1.7E	16 Sa	0044 0532 1300 1835	0302 0904 1549 2145	0.8F 1.6E 0.9F 1.5E
2 Sa	0202 0658 1413 1959	0445 1034 1721 2318	0.9F 2.0E 1.4F 1.7E	17 Su	0135 0618 1342 1931	0352 0952 1637 2237	0.8F 1.8E 1.1F 1.6E
3 Su	0251 0741 1456 2049	0530 1117 1805	0.9F 2.1E 1.5F	18 M	0222 0703 1423 2023	0438 1039 1721 2325	0.7F 2.0E 1.4F 1.7E
4 M	0335 0822 1537 2133	0003 0609 1156 1848	1.8E 0.9F 2.2E 1.5F	19 Tu	0305 0747 1507 2112	0519 1124 1806	0.6F 2.2E 1.6F
5 Tu ○	0416 0900 1617 2215	0042 0644 1233 1922	1.7E 0.8F 2.2E 1.5F	20 W	0348 0831 1551 2200	0011 0602 1209 1848	1.8E 0.9F 2.4E 1.7F
6 W	0455 0936 1656 2254	0119 0716 1310 1958	1.7E 0.8F 2.1E 1.4F	21 Th ●	0432 0916 1637 2246	0057 0648 1255 1933	1.9E 0.9F 2.5E 1.7F
7 Th	0533 1011 1736 2332	0154 0746 1347 2029	1.6E 0.7F 2.1E 1.3F	22 F	0517 1004 1725 2330	0143 0732 1343 2019	1.9E 1.0F 2.5E 1.7F
8 F	0613 1046 1817	0230 0819 1426 2102	1.6E 0.7F 2.0E 1.2F	23 Sa	0606 1055 1816	0230 0821 1433 2107	1.9E 1.0F 2.4E 1.6F
9 Sa	0009 0656 1122 1901	0308 0856 1507 2138	1.5E 0.6F 1.8E 1.0F	24 Su	0020 0657 1150 1911	0319 0914 1525 2159	1.9E 0.9F 2.3E 1.4F
10 Su	0048 0744 1203 1949	0349 0938 1552 2220	1.4E 0.5F 1.7E 0.9F	25 M	0108 0754 1251 2010	0411 1012 1622 2254	1.8E 0.8F 2.0E 1.2F
11 M	0129 0838 1251 2042	0435 1027 1642 2307	1.3E 0.4F 1.5E 0.7F	26 Tu	0158 0855 1359 2114	0506 1118 1723 2356	1.7E 0.8F 1.8E 1.0F
12 Tu	0214 0934 1352 2142	0525 1124 1738	1.3E 0.4F 1.4E	27 W ◐	0249 1000 1513 2224	0605 1237 1832	1.7E 0.8F 1.6E
13 W ◐	0302 1032 1505 2245	0002 0620 1230 1839	0.8F 1.3E 0.4F 1.3E	28 Th	0342 1105 1629 2336	0106 0708 1359 1947	0.8F 1.7E 0.8F 1.6E
14 Th	0353 1126 1622 2347	0103 0716 1344 1944	0.8F 1.4E 0.5F 1.3E	29 F	0436 1207 1741	0218 0812 1511 2102	0.7F 1.7E 1.0F 1.4E
15 F	0443 1215 1732	0206 0812 1453 2047	0.9F 1.5E 0.7F 1.4E	30 Sa	0045 0529 1303 1846	0324 0912 1612 2208	0.7F 1.8E 1.2F 1.4E

Time meridian 75° W. 0000 is midnight. 1200 is noon.

* Current weak and variable.

Figure 3-6. Table 1 excerpt, tidal currents (Key West, Florida)

159

TABLE 2 – CURRENT DIFFERENCES AND OTHER CONSTANTS

No.	PLACE	Meter Depth	POSITION Latitude	POSITION Longitude	TIME DIFFERENCES Min. before Flood	TIME DIFFERENCES Flood	TIME DIFFERENCES Min. before Ebb	TIME DIFFERENCES Ebb	SPEED RATIOS Flood	SPEED RATIOS Ebb	Minimum before Flood knots	Minimum before Flood Dir.	Maximum Flood knots	Maximum Flood Dir.	Minimum before Ebb knots	Minimum before Ebb Dir.	Maximum Ebb knots	Maximum Ebb Dir.
		ft	North	West	h m	h m	h m	h m			knots	Dir.	knots	Dir.	knots	Dir.	knots	Dir.
	MIAMI HARBOR–cont. Time meridian, 75° W				on Miami Harbor Entrance, p.72													
	Fishermans Channel																	
8136	Fisher Is., 0.2 mi. NW of	15d	25° 45.87'	80° 09.08'	+0 14	+0 38	+0 17	+0 39	0.6	0.7	--	--	1.0	280°	0.1	014°	1.1	090°
8141	Lummus Is., 0.15 mi. off SW corner	15d	25° 45.89'	80° 09.69'	+0 20	-0 20	+0 10	+0 22	0.3	0.6	--	--	0.6	271°	--	--	0.9	095°
8146	West end, SW of Dodge Island	11d	25° 46.38'	80° 10.74'	-0 05	-0 32	-0 15	-0 21	0.1	0.2	0.1	002°	0.2	277°	--	--	0.3	089°
8151	Miami River entrance	10d	25° 46.21'	80° 11.23'	+0 15	-0 02	-0 01	+0 46	0.1	0.4	--	--	0.2	261°	--	--	0.8	071°
8156	Fowey Rocks Light, 1.5 miles SW of		25° 35'	80° 07'	See table 5.													
	FLORIDA REEFS to MIDNIGHT PASS				on Key West, p.76													
8161	Caesar Creek, Biscayne Bay		25° 23.2'	80° 13.6'	+0 07	-0 08	-0 14	-0 05	1.2	1.0	0.0	--	1.2	316°	0.0	--	1.8	123°
8166	Long Key, drawbridge east of		24° 50.4'	80° 46.2'	+0 58	+1 27	+2 21	+1 33	1.1	0.7	0.0	--	1.1	000°	0.0	--	1.3	202°
8171	Long Key Viaduct		24° 48.1'	80° 51.9'	+1 34	+1 28	+2 02	+1 57	0.9	0.7	0.0	--	0.9	349°	0.0	--	1.2	170°
8176	Moser Channel, swingbridge		24° 42.0'	81° 10.2'	+1 07	+1 30	+1 50	+1 47	1.4	1.0	0.0	--	1.4	338°	0.0	--	1.8	166°
8181	Bahia Honda Harbor, bridge		24° 39.4'	81° 17.3'	+1 01	+0 38	+1 53	+1 05	1.4	1.3	0.0	--	1.4	004°	0.0	--	2.1	182°
8186	No Name Key, northeast of		24° 42.3'	81° 18.8'	+0 55	+1 24	+1 20	+0 53	0.7	0.5	0.0	--	0.7	312°	0.0	--	0.9	142°
	Key West																	
8191	Main Ship Channel entrance		24° 28.4'	81° 48.1'	-0 44	-0 12	+0 10	+0 10	0.2	0.3	0.0	--	0.2	040°	0.0	--	0.4	178°
8196	Main Ship Channel <42>		24° 30.5'	81° 48.3'	---	---	---	+0 30	--	0.2	0.0	--	--	064°	0.0	--	0.4	133°
8201	KEY WEST, 0.3 mi. W of Ft. Taylor		24° 32.9'	81° 49.0'	*Daily predictions*						0.0	--	1.0	022°	0.0	--	1.7	194°
8206	Ft. Taylor, 0.6 mile N of		24° 33.5'	81° 48.5'	+0 20	+0 13	-0 11	+0 13	0.6	0.7	0.0	--	0.6	042°	0.0	--	1.2	202°
8211	Turning Basin		24° 34.0'	81° 48.35'	+0 43	+0 44	+0 29	+1 06	0.8	0.6	0.0	--	0.8	048°	0.0	--	1.1	216°
8216	Northwest Channel		24° 35.0'	81° 50.9'	-0 08	-0 03	-0 09	-0 07	1.2	0.8	0.0	--	1.2	353°	0.0	--	1.4	162°
8221	Northwest Channel		24° 37.3'	81° 52.8'	-0 28	-0 19	-0 20	-0 20	0.6	0.4	0.0	--	0.6	346°	0.0	--	0.6	166°
8226	Boca Grande Channel		24° 34'	82° 04'	-0 40	-0 45	-0 01	-0 06	1.1	0.8	0.0	--	1.1	353°	0.0	--	1.2	194°
8231	New Ground <43>		24° 30.0'	82° 25.0'	+1 36	+1 55	+1 28	+1 18	0.7	0.4	0.2	356°	0.7	008°	0.2	142°	0.7	244°
8236	Isaac Shoal		24° 33.5'	82° 32.3'	+1 00	+0 54	+1 52	+1 55	1.0	0.5	0.0	--	1.0	002°	0.0	--	0.8	181°
8241	Southeast Channel		24° 37.62'	82° 51.07'	-0 27	-0 06	+0 37	+0 36	0.6	0.4	0.0	--	0.6	004°	0.0	--	0.8	172°
8246	Southwest Channel		24° 36.92'	82° 54.70'	+0 45	+0 59	+1 26	+2 04	0.4	0.4	0.0	--	0.4	001°	0.0	--	0.6	229°
					on Tampa Bay Entrance, p.88													
8251	Point Ybel, 0.4 mile northwest of		26° 27.40'	82° 01.12'	-0 25	-0 52	+0 17	+0 35	0.8	0.7	0.0	--	1.0	259°	0.0	--	0.9	080°
8256	Captiva Pass <44>		26° 36.56'	82° 13.34'	-0 53	-1 29	-1 14	-0 23	1.4	0.9	0.0	--	1.8	067°	0.0	--	1.9	251°
8261	Boca Grande Pass, Charlotte Harbor		26° 42.86'	82° 15.40'	-0 15	-0 37	-0 15	+0 05	1.7	1.3	0.0	--	2.2	067°	0.0	--	1.8	251°
8266	Pine Island Sound		26° 40.60'	82° 11.87'	---	---	---	---	--	--	0.0	--	0.5	011°	0.0	--	0.5	191°
8271	Little Pine I. bridge, Matlacha Pass		26° 37.9'	82° 04.1'	---	-0 19	---	---	0.4	--	0.0	--	0.6	132°	0.0	--	--	--
8276	Cape Haze, 2.3 mi. S of, Charlotte Hbr		26° 44.7'	82° 09.1'	+0 30	+0 41	-0 20	+1 18	0.4	0.4	0.0	--	0.5	060°	0.0	--	0.5	268°
8281	Punta Gorda, Peace River Bridge		26° 56.7'	82° 03.4'	---	---	---	---	0.3	0.2	0.0	--	0.4	047°	0.0	--	0.3	230°
8286	Myakka River bridge <53>		26° 57.5'	82° 12.8'	+1 48	+1 58	+1 47	---	0.4	--	0.0	--	0.5	304°	0.0	--	--	--
8291	Gasparilla Pass		26° 48.74'	82° 16.86'	-1 15	-1 53	-0 35	-0 41	0.8	0.8	0.0	--	1.0	066°	0.0	--	1.1	238°
8296	Venice Inlet		27° 06.8'	82° 28.0'	-2 05	-2 08	-1 57	-1 59	0.8	0.7	0.0	--	1.1	087°	0.0	--	0.9	262°
8301	Blackburn Bay, south end, bridge		27° 07.4'	82° 28.2'	-0 55	-1 20	-1 28	-0 10	0.7	0.5	0.0	--	0.9	357°	0.0	--	0.7	180°
8306	Little Sarasota Bay, south end, bridge		27° 10.8'	82° 29.7'	-1 18	-0 56	-0 57	-0 06	1.1	0.5	0.0	--	1.4	167°	0.0	--	0.7	357°
8311	Midnight Pass entrance		27° 12.4'	82° 30.6'	-1 43	-1 59	-1 49	-1 13	1.4	1.1	0.0	--	1.8	061°	0.0	--	1.4	242°
	SARASOTA BAY																	
8316	Big Sarasota Pass		27° 18.0'	82° 33.8'	-1 54	-1 48	-1 34	-2 03	1.2	0.8	0.0	--	1.5	006°	0.0	--	1.0	183°
8321	Sarasota Bay, south end, bridge		27° 18.1'	82° 32.8'	-1 25	-1 39	-1 13	-0 32	0.2	0.2	0.0	--	0.3	196°	0.0	--	0.3	013°
8326	New Pass		27° 19.9'	82° 34.9'	-2 06	-2 48	-1 18	-1 25	1.2	0.8	0.0	--	1.6	046°	0.0	--	1.0	231°
8331	Golden Gate Point, off		27° 19.7'	82° 33.4'	-1 38	-1 57	-1 25	-1 19	0.3	0.2	0.0	--	0.4	344°	0.0	--	0.3	153°
8336	Longboat Pass		27° 26.5'	82° 41.4'	-2 32	-2 42	-1 51	-1 56	1.4	1.2	0.0	--	1.8	088°	0.0	--	1.6	267°
8341	Cortez, north of bridge		27° 28.2'	82° 41.6'	-1 47	-1 10	-0 25	-1 11	0.5	0.1	0.0	--	0.8	346°	0.0	--	0.1	162°

Endnotes can be found at the end of table 2.

Figure 3-7. Table 2 excerpt, tidal currents (Florida subordinate stations)

3-35. Actual conditions often vary considerably from those predicted in the Tide Tables and the Tidal Current Tables. Changes in wind force and direction or in atmospheric pressure produce changes in ocean water level, especially the high-water height. For instance, the hurricane that struck the New England coast in September 1938 piled up a huge wall of water in Narragansett Bay. This wall of water increased to such a point that it became a huge storm wave when it struck the city of Providence. Generally, with an onshore wind or a low barometer, the high-water and low-water heights are higher than the predicted heights. With a high barometer or offshore wind, those heights are usually lower than predicted.

3-36. When working with the tidal current tables, the navigator should always remember that the actual times of slack or strength of current may sometimes differ from the predicted times by as much as 1/2 hour. On rare occasions, the difference may be as much as 1 hour. However, comparison between predicted and observed slack times shows that more than 90 percent of slack water predictions are accurate to within 1/2 hour. Thus, to fully take advantage of a favorable current or slack water, the navigator should plan to reach an entrance or strait at least 1/2 hour before the predicted time.

3-37. Tidal current calculations are by far the most critical factor pertaining to environmental conditions. The entire waterborne operation can be jeopardized without precise knowledge of the speed and direction of the tidal current. For example, a 1-knot ebb tidal current will halt any forward movement of a combat swimmer in the water. Even a 0.5-knot current will cause excessive fatigue on a combat swimmer.

CAUTION

Precise knowledge of speed and direction of a tidal current is essential to the success of a waterborne operation. Any current against the infiltration direction will slow down or even stop the forward progress of a combat swimmer.

Table 3-2. Constructing a tidal current matrix

	Slack	Maximum	Speed (kn)
Reference Station	0144	0443	1.3 ebb
Subordinate Station 8211	+00:29	+1:06	0.6
Correction	**0213**	**0549**	**0.78 ebb**
Reference Station	0843	1030	0.4 flood
Subordinate Station 8211	+00:43	+00:44	0.8
Correction	**0926**	**1114**	**0.32 flood**
Reference Station	1249	1649	1.6 ebb
Subordinate Station 8211	+00:29	+1:06	0.6
Correction	**1318**	**1755**	**0.96 ebb**
Reference Station	2058	2329	0.7 flood
Subordinate Station 8211	+00:43	+00:44	0.8
Correction	**2141**	**0013**	**0.56 flood**

INSTRUCTIONS: Refer to NOAA Tidal Current Tables 1 and 2. This data was computed from Key West, Florida (Reference Station) on 13 April 2001, and Key West, Turning Basin (Subordinate Station 8211).

Table 1 contains the list of reference stations for the predicted times of slack water and the predicted times and velocities of maximum current—flood and ebb—for each day of the year.

Table 2 enables the navigator to determine the approximate times of minimum currents (slack water) and the times and speeds of maximum currents at numerous subordinate stations.

By applying specific data given in Table 2 to the times and speeds of the current at the reference station, the navigator can compile reasonable approximations (Correction) of the current of the subordinate station.

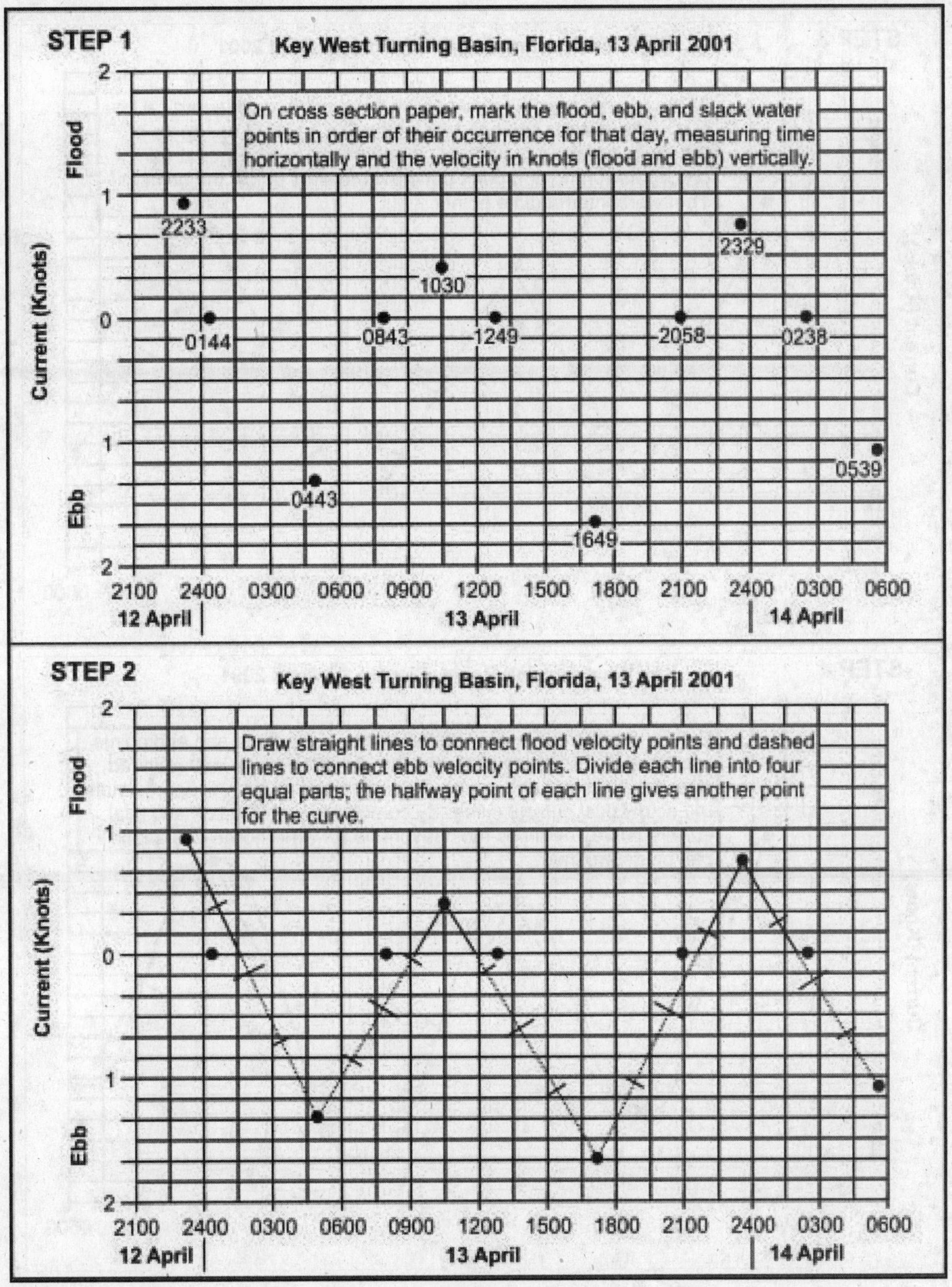

Figure 3-8. Plotting an approximate tidal current curve

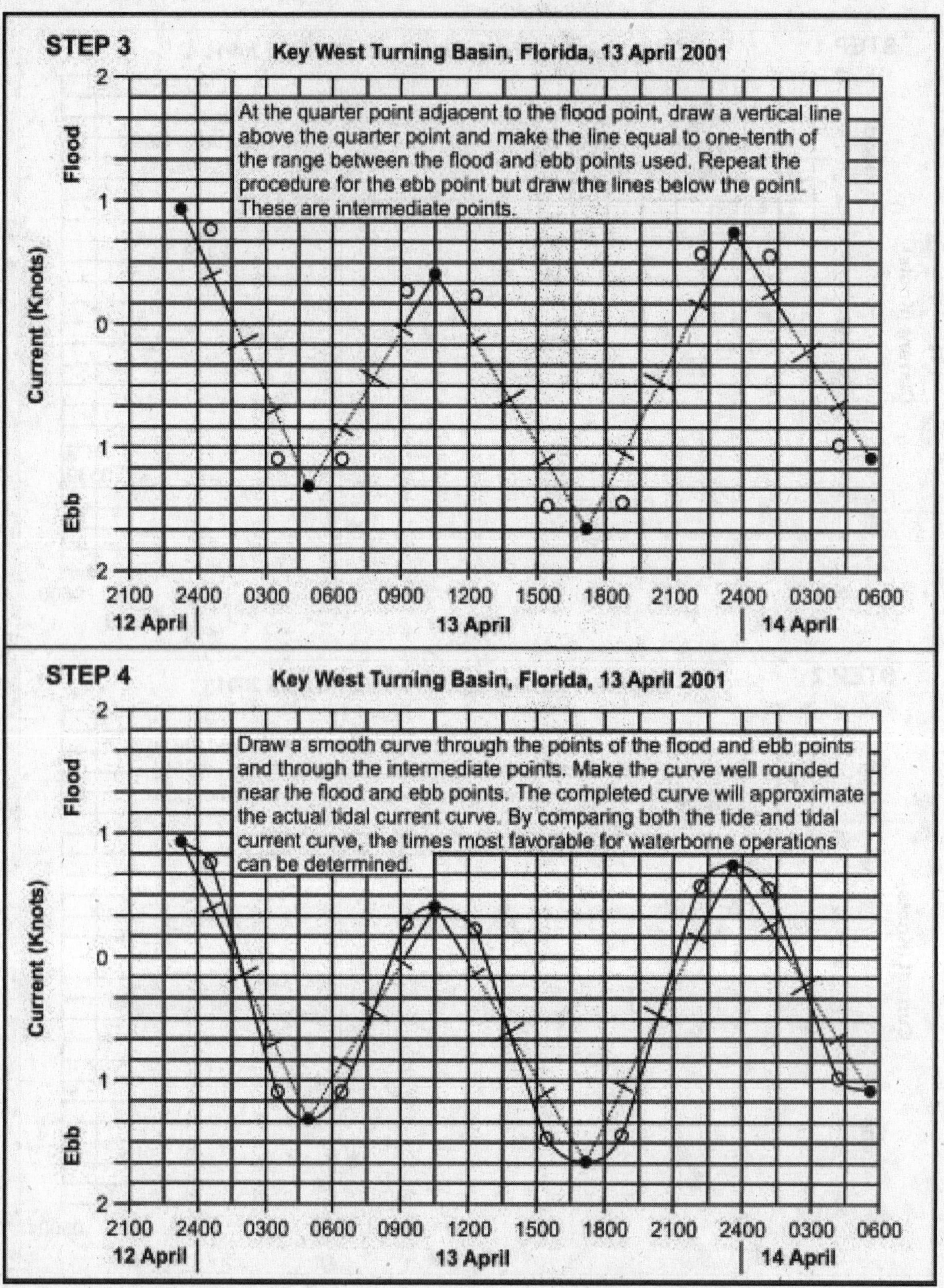

Figure 3-8. Plotting an approximate tidal current curve (*Continued*)

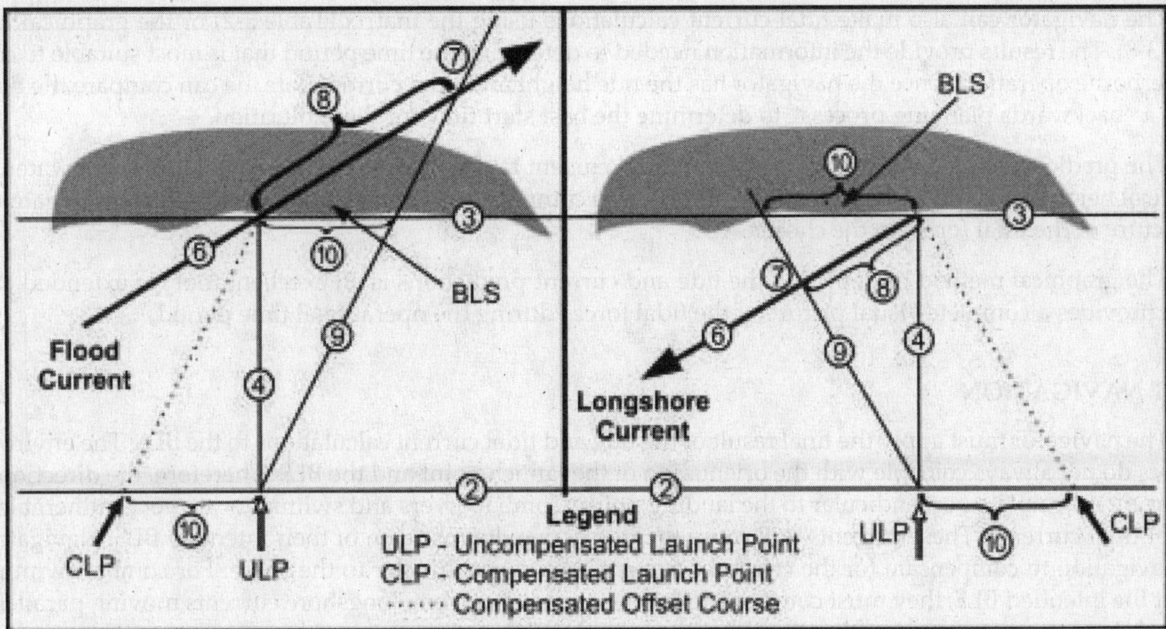

INSTRUCTIONS: From Tables 1, 2, and 3 of the NOAA current tables, compute the set and drift of the tidal current for the planned launch time at the subordinate station nearest to the launch point.

1) On the chart or map that includes the BLS, project a line parallel to the coastline. This line represents the track of the transporting vessel.
   A) The track is normally 2 miles offshore (the limit of horizontal visibility for an observer 3 feet above the surface of the water).
   B) The distance from the shoreline must be measured to scale.

2) Project a second line (BLS line) parallel along the coastline through the BLS.

3) Extend a perpendicular line from the BLS to the track. This line represents the course of the boat or swimmer unaffected by a current. The intersection of this line and the track is called the ULP.

4) Calculate the time required for passage from the ULP to the landing point: **T** (time) = $\frac{\textbf{D (distance)}}{\textbf{S (speed)}}$

5) From the BLS, protract a line (azimuth) representing the set of the current. The direction of set of the current is listed as degrees **true** as listed in Table 2 of the current tables.

6) Compute the effect of current: duration of passage (Step 4) multiplied by the drift (speed) of the current.

7) Measure this value (effect on the current) along the set line (Step 5) using the same scale used in Step 1.

8) Draw a line connecting the ULP through the set of the current value on the set line to the BLS parallel line. This represents the course determined by the exposure to the current.

9) Compensate for the effect of the current on the BLS line by offsetting an equal value on the **upcurrent** side of the track. This produces a **minimum offset** from the derived CLP.

Figure 3-9. Offset navigation techniques

3-38. The navigator can also make tidal current calculations using the matrix (Table 3-2) or the graphical method (Figure 3-8). The results provide the information needed to determine the time period that is most suitable to conduct the waterborne operation. Once the navigator has the tide height and tidal current data, he can compare the data and execute a "backwards planning process" to determine the best start time for the infiltration.

3-39. The predicted slacks and strengths given in tidal current tables refer to the horizontal motion of water, not to the vertical height of the tide. Therefore, it is important to compute both tide height and tidal current to gain a complete picture of the tidal forces in the chosen AO.

3-40. The graphical method of depicting the tide and current predictions is an excellent tool for extended calculations. It provides a complete visual picture of the tidal forces during the operational time period.

OFFSET NAVIGATION

3-41. The navigator must apply the final result of the tide and tidal current calculations to the BLS. The environmental factors do not always coincide with the orientation of the launch point and the BLS. Therefore, the direction of the tidal current may not be perpendicular to the landing point. Combat divers and swimmers are very vulnerable to the effects of tidal currents. These currents will cause them to arrive downstream of their intended BLS. Navigators use offset navigation to compensate for the effects of currents not perpendicular to the shore. For combat swimmers to arrive at the intended BLS, they must compensate for two types of current: longshore currents moving parallel to the shore and flood currents that are other than 90 degrees to the BLS.

3-42. The determination to use offset navigation is based on the criticality of the currents. Criticality is determined based on the current's projected effect on swimmers. Because the swimmers need the most time to traverse any given distance, the farther away from shore the launch point is, and the longer the period of time that the swimmer is exposed to it, the more effect the current will have. For launches within 460 meters of the beach, currents of 0.5 knot or greater are considered critical. For launches in excess of 460 meters, a 0.2 knot current is considered critical.

3-43. Figure 3-9 illustrates the construction of a tidal current offset used to compensate for longshore and flood currents that may or may not be perpendicular to the shore.

CHAPTER 4

Nautical Charts and Publications

Charts and publications are the navigator's library. This chapter introduces the detachment to some of the reference materials available for planning and executing maritime operations. The mission planner must learn as much as possible about his designated AO to improve the chances of mission success.

Without accurate, updated charts, mission planning and safe navigation are virtually impossible. These resources contain a wealth of invaluable information, and reflect channels, water depths, buoys, lights, lighthouses, prominent landmarks, rocks, reefs, sandbars, and much more information to aid in navigation. A thorough and complete understanding of the nautical chart is absolutely essential in ensuring the safe and successful navigation of a vessel.

Publications are the supplemental tools of the navigator's trade. They are the supporting reference materials that explain, amplify, update, or correct charts. They also provide important information, such as tides and current data, that cannot be depicted on a chart.

This chapter will provide the SF maritime operator with a basic understanding of nautical charts and publications. To do mission planning and safe navigation, operators must be able to identify the required chart, order it, update (correct) it, interpret the information contained on it, and use it to plan and execute maritime movements.

NAUTICAL CHARTS

4-1. Charts, like maps, provide a graphic representation of features on the earth's surface. Unlike most maps, charts are primarily concerned with hydrography: the measurement and description of the physical features of the oceans, seas, lakes, rivers, and their adjoining coastal areas, with particular reference to their use for navigation.

4-2. Nautical charts are the mariner's most useful and widely used navigation aid. They are maps of waterways specifically designed for nautical navigation. They are a graphic depiction of a portion of the earth's surface, emphasizing natural and man-made features of particular interest to a navigator. Nautical charts cover an area that is primarily water, and include such information as the depth of water, bottom contours and composition, dangers and obstructions, the location and type of aids to navigation, coastline features, currents, magnetic variation, and prominent landmarks.

4-3. Charts are essential for plotting and determining mission position whether operating in familiar or unfamiliar waters. Navigators can order charts from the National Imagery and Mapping Agency (NIMA) Catalog of Hydrographic Products, 10th Edition, April 2000. Waterborne units can order all charts from the Defense Mapping Agency (DMA). The other publications are available from the National Ocean Survey, a part of the NOAA, the Defense Mapping Agency Hydrographic and Topographic Center (DMAHTC), and the United States Coast Guard (USCG).

4-4. DMA Catalog, Part 2, contains 12 volumes. It is used to locate and order charts. Volumes 1 through 9 list the charts for the 9 regions of the world, Volume 10 contains the numbers for special purpose charts, Volume 11 lists classified charts, and Volume 12 details the ordering procedures. Commercial telephone access is available at 1-800-826-0342. Defense Switched Network (DSN) access is available at DSN 695-6500 callers should press 2 after connection. Maritime operators should never get underway without the appropriate charts. They should also always ensure that their charts are corrected, up-to-date, and adequately prepared.

4-5. Basic chart information is contained in a number of places on a nautical chart. The general information block (Figure 4-1) contains the following items:

- The chart title, which is usually the name of the prominent navigable body of water within the area covered in the chart.
- A statement of the type of projection and the scale.
- The depth measurement unit (feet, meters, or fathoms).

4-6. Nautical charts contain a great deal of information. Throughout the next few paragraphs, specific information and parts of the charts will be explained.

CHART CLASSIFICATION AND SCALE

4-7. The scale of a nautical chart is the ratio between the distance (measurement unit) on the chart and the actual distance on the surface of the earth. Since this is a ratio, such as 1:2,500,000, it does not matter what size the unit is or in what system it was measured (inch, foot, meter). For example, the scale of 1:5,000,000 means that one unit of measurement on the chart is equal to 5,000,000 units of measurement on the earth's surface. Therefore, one inch on the chart would equal 5,000,000 inches on the earth's surface. This would be a small-scale chart, since the fraction 1/5,000,000 is a very small number. The scale of 1:2,500 (1 inch on the chart equals 2,500 inches on the earth's surface) is a much larger number and is referred to as a large-scale chart. This concept is confusing at first since a large-scale chart actually represents an area smaller than one-half that of a small-scale chart. There is no firm definition for the terms large scale and small scale; the two terms are only relative to each other. It is easier just to remember "large scale = small area, and small scale = large area."

4-8. The primary charts used in small-boat navigation are classified into "series" according to their scale. Charts are made in many different scales, ranging from about 1:2,500 to 1:14,000,000 (and even smaller for some world maps). Navigators should always use the largest scale chart available for navigation. The types of nautical charts that U.S. navigators commonly use are discussed below.

4-9. **Sailing Charts.** These charts are produced at scales of 1:6,000,000 and smaller. They are the smallest-scale charts used for planning a long voyage. The mariner uses them to fix his position, to approach the coast from the open ocean, or to sail between distant coastal ports. On such charts, the shoreline and topography are generalized. Saling charts show only offshore soundings, the principal lights, outer buoys, and landmarks visible at considerable distances. Charts of this series are also useful for plotting the track of major tropical storms.

4-10. **General Charts.** They are produced at scales between 1:150,000 and 1:600,000. They are used for coastal navigation outside of outlying reefs and shoals, when a vessel is generally within sight of land or aids to navigation, and its course can be directed by piloting techniques.

4-11. **Coast Charts.** These charts are produced at scales between 1:50,000 and 1:150,000. They are intended for inshore coastal navigation where the course may lie inside outlying reefs and shoals. Navigators also use them for entering large bays and harbors or navigating intracoastal waterways.

4-12. **Harbor Charts.** Navigators usually use these charts for navigation and anchorage in harbors and small waterways. The scale is generally larger than 1:50,000.

4-13. **Small-Craft Charts.** These are produced at scales of 1:40,000 and larger. They are special charts of inland waters, including the intracoastal waterways. Special editions of conventional charts called small-craft charts are printed on lighter-weight paper and folded. These charts contain additional information of interest to small-craft operators, such as data on facilities, tide predictions, and weather broadcast information.

4-14. **Approach Charts.** These are NIMA charts that incorporate the features of coast and harbor charts in one. They are smaller than about 1:150,000 and are especially useful for planning reconnaissance operations.

4-15. **Combat Charts.** These charts are special topographic and hydrographic products that contain all of the information of both charts and maps. They are prepared to support combined and joint operations.

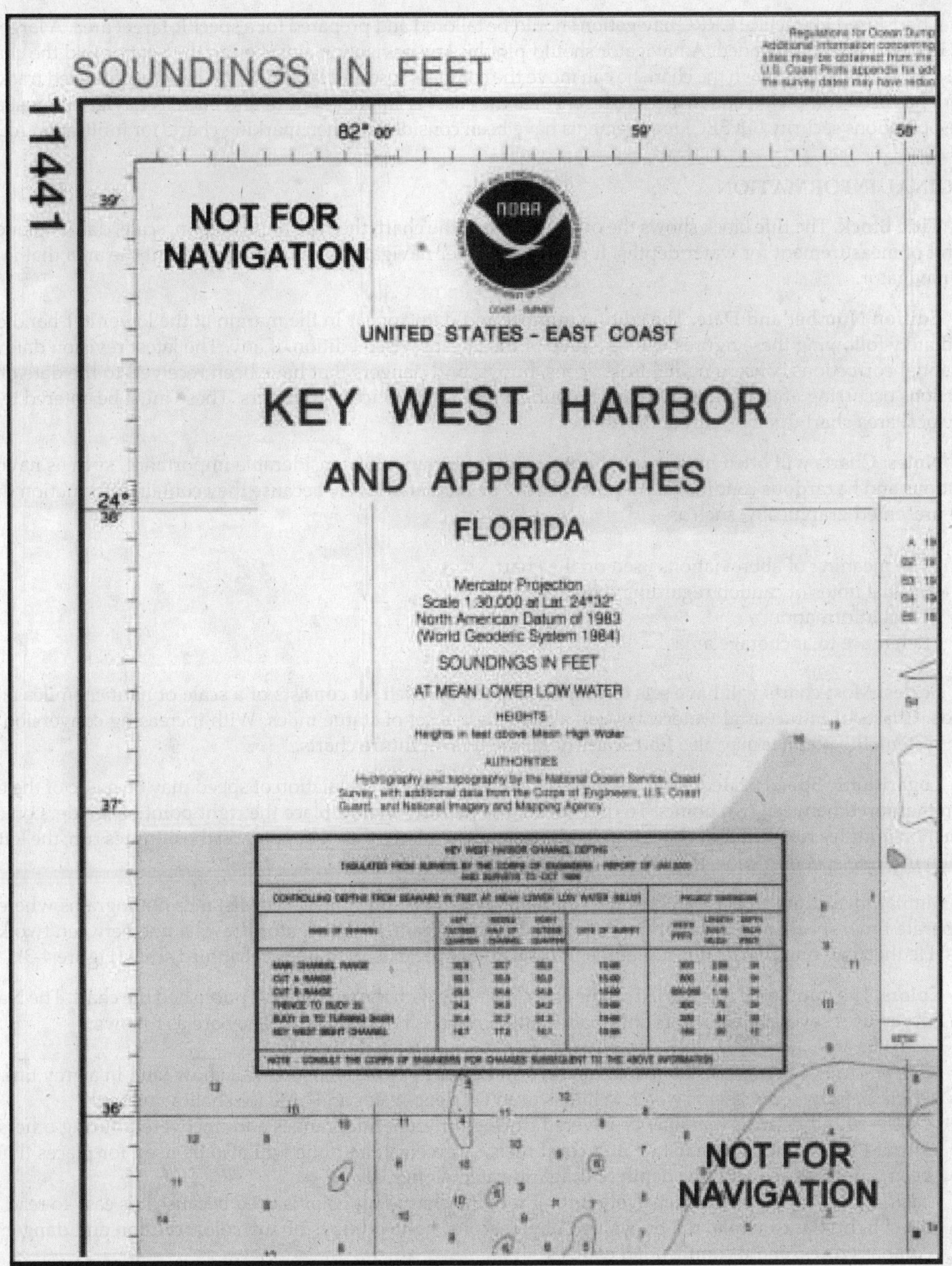

Figure 4-1. Example of nautical chart information

4-16. Charts used for tactical CRRC navigation should be tailored and prepared for a specific target area. A larger-scale chart (1:50,000) is recommended. A navigator should plot his key navigation aids; he can then cut or fold the chart to a usable size. After cutting down the chart, he can move the compass rose and latitude scale near the intended track. After all work has been completed and inspected, he ensures the chart is laminated front and back. A navigator must always ensure operations security (OPSEC) requirements have been considered when marking charts for infiltration routes.

MARGINAL INFORMATION

4-17. **Title Block.** The title block shows the official name of the chart, the type of projection, scale, datum plane used, and unit of measurement for water depths. It may show other navigational information about the area that is useful to the navigator.

4-18. **Edition Number and Date.** The edition number and date appear in the margin at the lower left-hand corner. Immediately following these figures will be a date of the latest revised edition, if any. The latest revision date shows all essential corrections concerning lights, beacons, buoys, and dangers that have been received to the date of issue. Corrections occurring after the date of issue are published in the Notice to Mariners. These must be entered by hand on the local area chart upon receipt of the notice.

4-19. **Notes.** Charts will often have printed notes with information of considerable importance, such as navigation regulations and hazardous conditions. All notes should be read attentively because they contain information that can not be presented graphically, such as—

- The meaning of abbreviations used on the chart.
- Special notes of caution regarding danger.
- Tidal information.
- Reference to anchorage areas.

4-20. **Scales.** Most charts will have sets of graphic bar scales. Each set consists of a scale of nautical miles and one of yards. Charts of intracoastal waterways will also include a set of statue miles. With increasing conversion to the metric system, the planner may also find scales of kilometers on future charts.

4-21. **Logarithmic Speed Scale.** This is a scale from which a graphic calculation of speed may be made of the time of the run measured between two points. To find speed, the planner should place the right point of dividers on 60 and the other on minutes run. Without changing divider spread, he places the right point on the minutes run; the left point will then indicate speed in knots (Figure 4-2).

4-22. Similar logarithmic scales can be found on maneuvering board time-speed-distance nomograms where there are separate time, speed, and distance lines. To use the nomogram, the navigator draws a line between two known factors. He then can find the third factor at the intersection of the extended line at the third scale (Figure 4-3).

4-23. **Colors.** The number of colors used on the chart will vary with the agency that published the chart. The National Ocean Survey uses several basic colors and shades of them on its regular charts. They are as follows:

- *Buff or Yellow*—represents land areas, except on DMAHTC charts, which will show land in a gray tint.
- *White and Blue*—represents water. White is used for deep water and blue for shallow water.
- *Green*—signifies areas that may be covered during different tidal ranges and uncovered during others, such as mud flats, sandbars, marshes, and coral reefs. A greenish halftone will also be used for places that have been wire-dragged with the depth of drag indicated alongside.
- *Nautical Purple*—appears extensively throughout the chart. This color is used because it is easy to read under a red light. For example, red buoys, red day beacons, lighted buoys of any color, caution and danger areas, compass roses, and recommended courses.
- *Black*—represents most symbols and printed information.
- *Gray*—shows land masses on some charts.

4-24. **Lettering.** Vertical lettering (nonslanted) is used for features that are dry at high water and are not affected by the movement of water. Slanted lettering is used for water, under water, and floating features with the exception of depth figures.

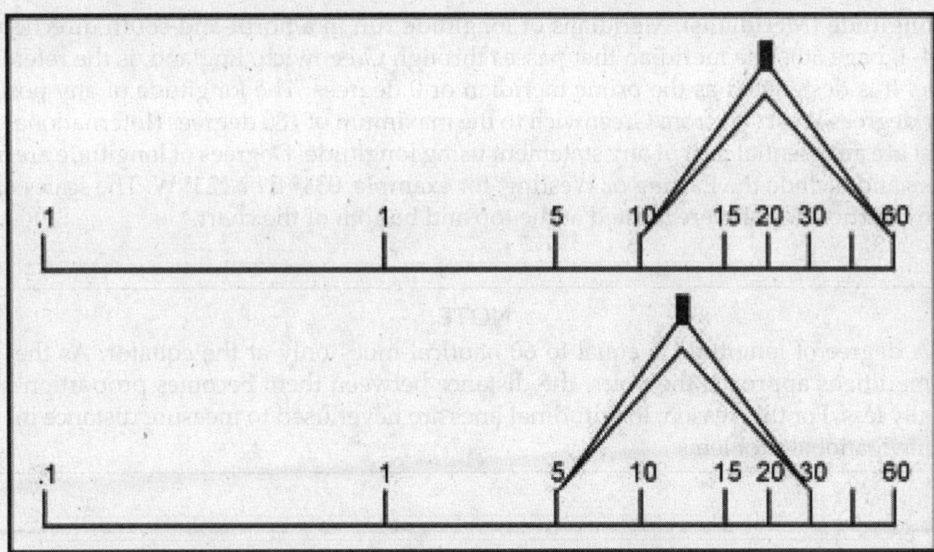

Figure 4-2. Example of a logarithmic speed scale

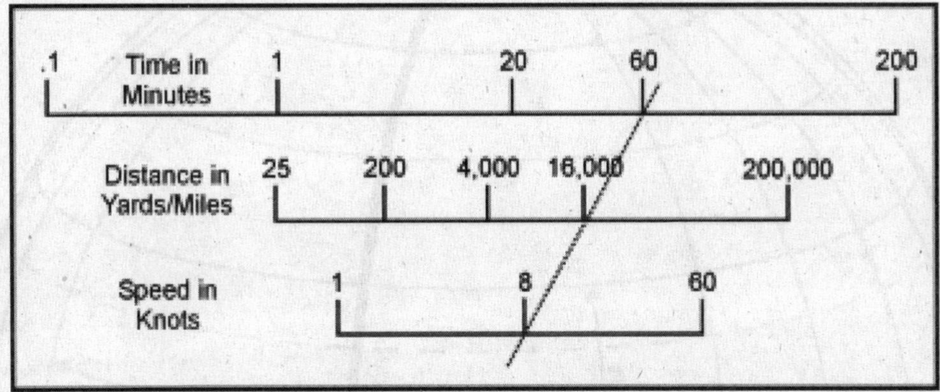

Figure 4-3. Example of a time-speed-distance logarithmic scale

4-25. **Bottom Composition.** This data can be abbreviated and be in slanted lettering. For example, GRS, HRD, and S. See Figure 4-10 for a complete list of bottom characteristics with approved abbreviations.

4-26. **Fathom Curves.** These are connecting lines of equal depths usually shown as 1, 2, 3, 5, 10, and multiples of ten (1 fathom = 6 feet).

4-27. **Depths.** These figures indicate the depth in feet or fathoms. Some charts will use feet for shallow water and fathoms for deep water, but this practice is usually rare. Some newer charts will use meters and decimeters.

GEOGRAPHIC COORDINATES

4-28. Nautical charts are oriented with north at the top. The frame of reference for all chart construction is the system of parallels of latitude and longitude. Any location on a chart can be expressed in terms of latitude and longitude. The latitude scale runs along both sides of the chart, while the longitude scale runs across the top and bottom of the chart.

4-29. Navigators use the latitude and longitude scales to pinpoint objects on the chart just as six- and eight-digit grid coordinates are used on a military map. There are scales on the top and bottom for longitude and on each side for latitude. Each scale is broken down in degrees, minutes, and seconds; the size of the scale will vary according to the scale of the chart. A navigator should always use the scale from his AOR.

4-30. **Lines of Longitude (Meridians).** Meridians of longitude run in a north-and-south direction and intersect at the poles (Figure 4-4, page 60). The meridian that passes through Greenwich, England, is the reference for measurements of longitude. It is designated as the prime meridian or 0 degrees. The longitude of any position is related to degrees East (E) or degrees West (W) from Greenwich to the maximum of 180 degrees (International Date Line) either way. East and West are an essential part of any statement using longitude. Degrees of longitude are always written as three-digit numbers and include the Easting or Westing, for example, 034° E or 123° W. The scales used to determine the longitude of any particular point are located at the top and bottom of the chart.

> **NOTE**
> A degree of longitude is equal to 60 nautical miles only at the equator. As the meridians approach the poles, the distance between them becomes proportionally less. For this reason, longitudinal lines are never used to measure distance in navigational problems.

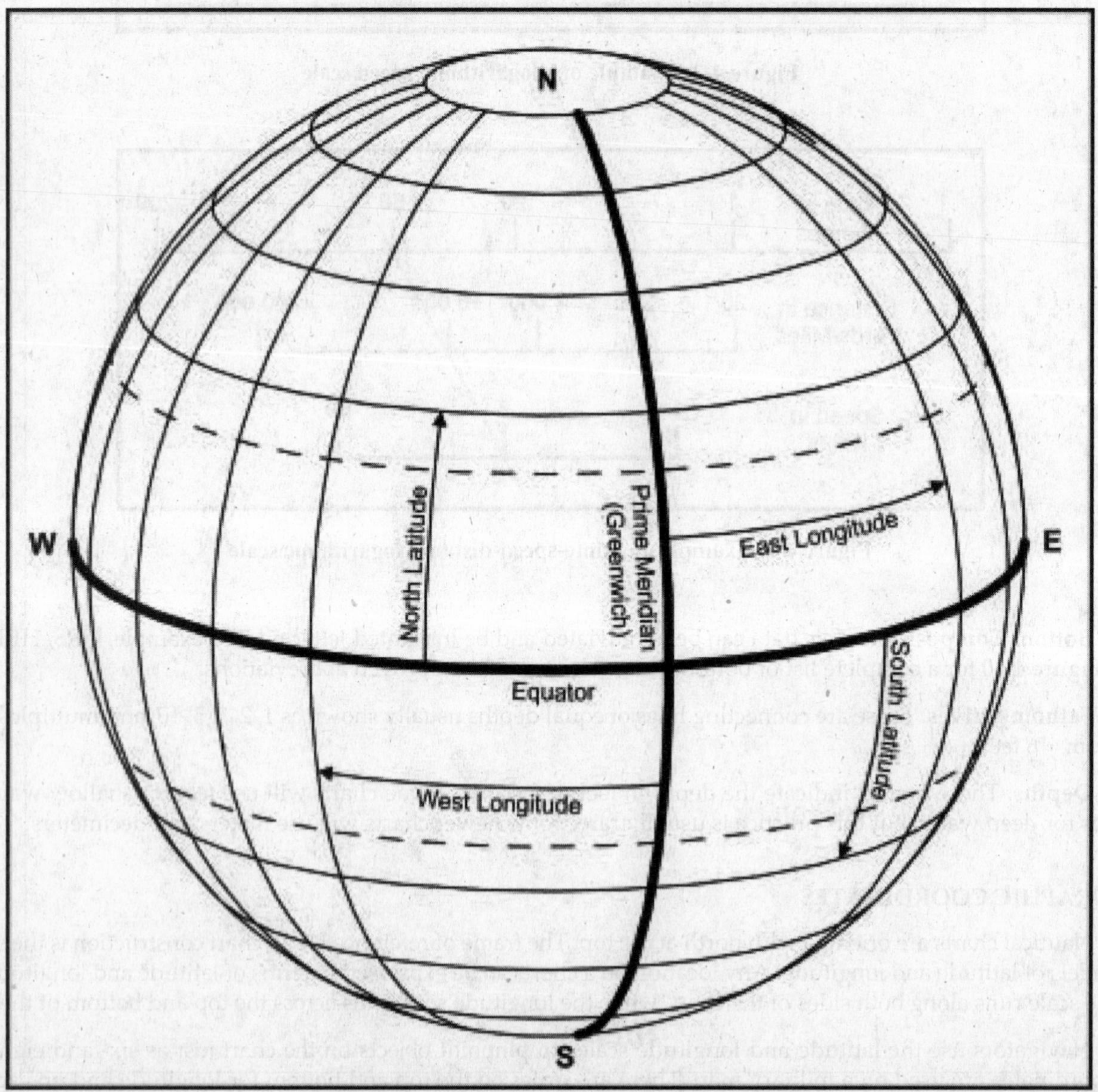

Figure 4-4. Global latitude and longitude lines

4-31. **Lines of Latitude (Parallels).** Parallels of latitude run in an east-and-west direction. They are measured from the equator starting at 0 degrees and increasing to 90 degrees at each pole (Figure 4-4, page 60). Navigators should put N for North or S for South when using parallels of latitude. Lines running from side-to-side indicate the latitude parallels on a nautical chart; the latitude scales are indicated along the side margins by divisions along the black and white border. One degree of latitude (arc) is equal to 60 nautical miles on the surface of the earth.

4-32. When navigators use latitude and longitude to locate necessary objects, they should keep the following points in mind:

- For greater precision in position, degrees are subdivided into minutes (60 minutes equals 1 degree) and seconds (60 seconds equals 1 minute).
- When moving closer to the poles, the meridians of longitude get closer together due to the elliptical shape of the earth; therefore, there is no set distance between them.
- For all practical purposes, parallels of latitude are essentially equally spaced and the distance is basically the same. One degree of latitude equals 60 nautical miles, 1 minute of latitude equals 1 nautical mile, and 1 second of latitude equals 100 feet.

Conversion Factors

4-33. A proper geographic coordinate should read: 32° 40′ N 117° 14′ W. The following conversion factors will help navigators interpret data and apply it to nautical charts (Figure 4-5).

1 second (″) = 100 feet (ft)
60 seconds = 1 minute of latitude
1 minute (′) = 1 nautical mile (NM)
60 minutes = 1 degree (°)
6,076.10 feet = 1 NM
2,024.5 yards = 1 NM
1.85 km = 1 NM
1 km = 0.539 NM
5,280 feet = 1 statute mile
1,760 yards = 1 statue mile
0.868 NM = 1 statute mile

Figure 4-5. Conversion factors

Plotting a Geographic Coordinate

4-34. Plotting a position when latitude and longitude are known is a simple procedure. Navigators should—

- Mark the given latitude on a convenient latitude scale along the meridian bar.
- Place a straightedge at this point running parallel to the latitude line.
- Hold the straightedge in place, and set a pair of dividers to the desired longitude using a convenient longitude scale.
- Place one point on the meridian at the edge of the straightedge moving in the direction of the given longitude, making sure not to change the spread of the dividers.
- Lightly mark the chart at this point.

4-35. The navigator can then determine the coordinates of a point on the chart. He should—

- Place a straightedge at the given point and parallel to a line of latitude.
- Determine the latitude where the straightedge crosses a meridian.

- Hold the straightedge in place, and set one point of the dividers at the given point and the other at the nearest interior meridians on longitude.
- Place the dividers on a longitude scale and read the longitude from this point, making sure not to change the spread.

DETERMINING DIRECTION

4-36. Direction is measured clockwise from 000 degrees to 360 degrees. When speaking of degrees in giving a course or heading, navigators should always use three digits; for example, "270 degrees" or "057 degrees." Directions can be in true degrees, magnetic degrees, or compass degrees. True direction uses the North Pole as a reference point. Magnetic direction uses the magnetic north. There are important differences between true and magnetic compass directions. True direction differs from magnetic direction by variation.

4-37. The compass rose is the primary means of determining direction. Nautical charts usually have one or more compass roses printed on them. These are similar in appearance to the compass card and are oriented with north at the top. A compass rose consists of two or three concentric circles several inches in diameter and accurately subdivided. Personnel use these circles to measure true and magnetic directions on the chart. True direction is printed around the outer circle with zero at true north; this is emphasized with a star. Magnetic direction is printed around the inside of the compass rose with an arrow pointing to magnetic north. Variation for the particular area covered by the chart is printed in the middle of the compass rose (as well as any annual change). The middle circle, if there are three, is magnetic direction expressed in degrees, with an arrow printed over the zero point to indicate magnetic north. The innermost circle is also magnetic direction, but is listed in terms of "points." There are 32 points at intervals of 11 1/4 degrees, further divided into half and quarter points. Stating the names of the points is called boxing the compass (Figure 4-6).

4-38. Each chart will have several compass roses printed on it at convenient locations where they will not conflict with navigational information. Roses printed on land areas may cause the elimination of typographical features in these regions.

4-39. Several cautions are necessary when measuring directions on charts. When large areas are covered, it is possible for the magnetic variation to differ for various portions of the chart. Navigators should check each chart before using it to be sure to always use the compass rose nearest the area for which they are plotting. Depending upon the type and scale of the chart, graduations on the compass rose circles may be for intervals of 1, 2, or 5 degrees. Navigators can use the following procedure for determining direction from point to point:

- Place parallel rulers so that the edge intersects both points.
- "Walk" rulers across the chart to the compass rose, without changing the angle of the rulers.
- Read degrees in the direction that the boat is heading (magnetic or true).

4-40. In summary, a navigator can express direction in three ways. He can refer to it as—

- *True*–when using the true (geographic) meridian. (True differs from magnetic by *variation*.)
- *Magnetic*–when using the magnetic meridian. (Magnetic differs from compass by *deviation*.)
- *Compass*–when using the axis of the compass card. (Compass differs from true by *compass error*, the algebraic sum of deviation and variation.)

DETERMINING DISTANCE

4-41. The latitude bar is the primary scale used to measure distance. One degree of latitude is equal to 1 nautical mile. Latitude bars are located on the right and left side of the chart. The longitude scales are not used to measure distance due to the distortion of the Mercator projection. On large-scale charts, navigators should use the bar scale provided. The tool used to measure distance is the dividers. There are two different methods that can be used.

4-42. On large-scale charts, the navigator simply spreads the dividers and places the points on the distance to be measured. He then (without spreading the dividers further) places them on the bar scale provided in the upper and lower margin.

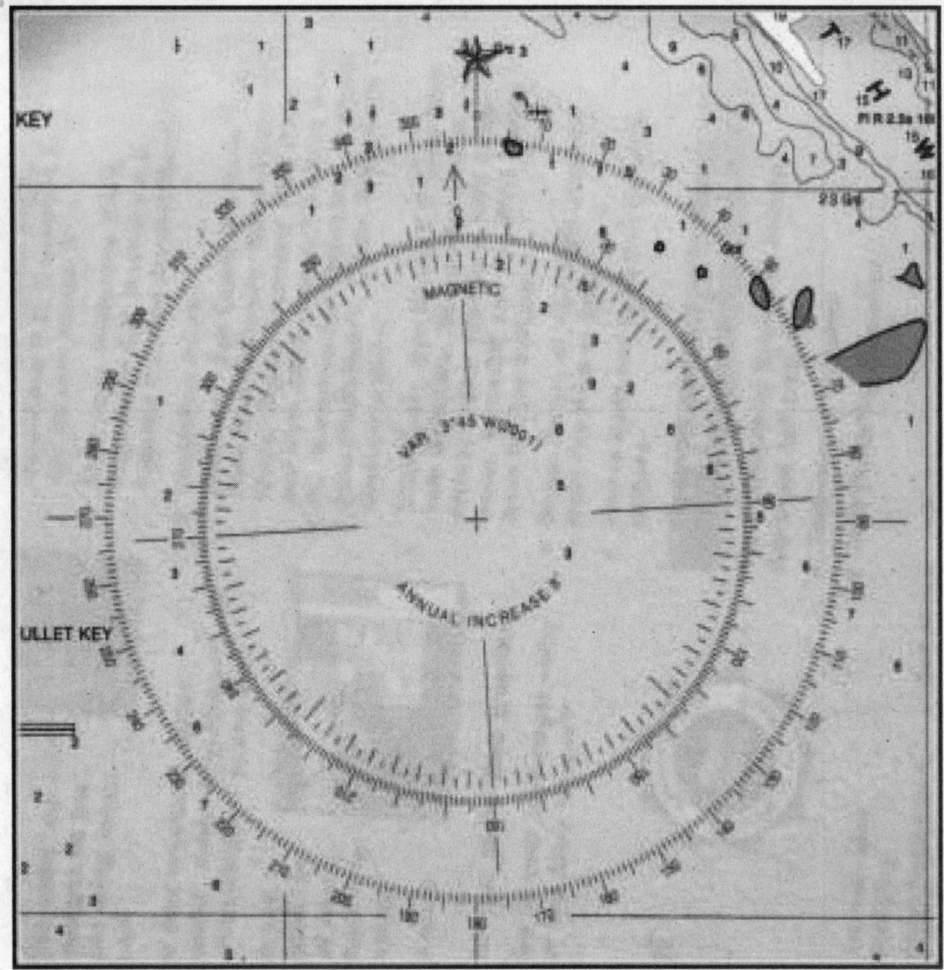

Figure 4-6. The compass rose

4-43. On small-scale charts, the navigator first measures off 5 to 10 nautical miles on the latitude bar. Next, he places one point of the dividers on the desired point of origin. From this point, he walks the dividers along the plotted vessel track (counting the turns as he walks the dividers) to the end. If there is any distance left at the end of the track, he closes the dividers to the end of the vessel track and measures the remainder on the latitude scale (bar), adding this measurement to his distance (Figure 4-7).

SOUNDINGS

4-44. Another important type of information that the navigator can learn from using the nautical chart is the bottom characteristics in the water. The chart provides this data by using a combination of numbers, color codes, underwater contour lines, and a system of standardized symbols and abbreviations.

4-45. Most of the numbers on the chart represent water depth soundings at mean low tide. Datum refers to the baseline from which a chart's vertical measurements are made. On the East and Gulf coasts, the tidal datum is mean low water (the average low tide). The tidal cycle on the East and Gulf coasts produces tides approximately equal in highness and lowness. Since the greatest danger to navigation is during low tide, a number of low tide depths are averaged to produce the average low tide. On the Pacific coast, the datum is the mean lower low-water mark. The reason for using the mean lower of the two low tides for the West coast tidal datum is because the cycle of low tides may differ by several feet, thus making one lower than the other. In the interest of navigation safety, the mean or average of the lower of the two tides in the tidal cycles is used for soundings.

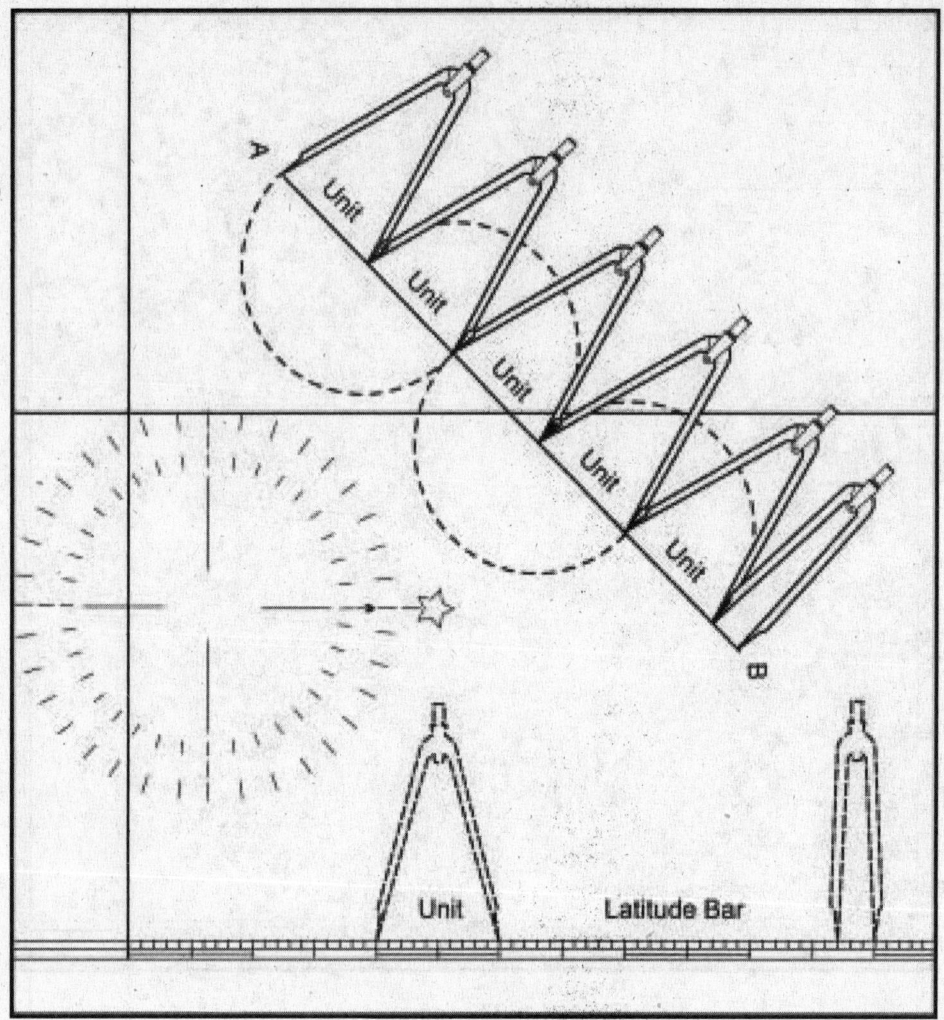

Figure 4-7. Determining distance on charts

4-46. Contour lines, also called fathom curves, connect points of roughly equal depth and provide a profile of the bottom. These lines are either numbered or coded according to depth using particular combinations of dots and dashes. Generally, the shallow water is tinted darker blue on a chart, while deeper water is tinted light blue or white. Water depth may either be in feet, meters, or fathoms (a fathom equals 6 feet). The chart's legend will indicate which unit (feet, meters, or fathoms) is used. The nautical chart's water depth is measured downward from sea level at low water (soundings); heights or landmarks are given in feet above sea level.

SYMBOLS AND ABBREVIATIONS

4-47. Symbols and abbreviations appear in Chart No. 1 published jointly by the DMAHTC and the NOAA. They indicate the physical characteristics of the charted area, and details of the available aids to navigation. They are uniform and standardized, but are subject to variation, depending on the chart's scale or chart series. Generally speaking, man-made features will be shown in detail where they will reflect directly to waterborne traffic, such as piers, bridges, and power cables. Built-up areas will be determined or identified by their usefulness to navigation. Prominent isolated objects like tanks and stacks will be shown accurately so that they may be used for taking bearings. The following paragraphs explain these symbols and abbreviations.

4-48. **Color.** Nearly all charts employ color to distinguish various categories of information, such as shoal water, deep water, and land areas. Color is also used with aids to navigation to make them easier to locate and interpret.

Nautical purple ink (magenta) is used for most information, as it is more easily read under red nighttime illumination normally used in the pilothouse of a small boat or bridge of a ship to avoid interference with night vision.

4-49. **Lettering.** Lettering on a chart provides valuable information. For example, slanted Roman lettering is used to label all information that is affected by tidal changes or current (with the exception of bottom soundings). All descriptive lettering for floating navaids is found in slanted lettering. Vertical Roman lettering is used to label all information that is not affected by tidal changes or current. Fixed aids such as lighthouses and ranges are indicated by vertical lettering.

4-50. **Lighthouses and Other Fixed Lights.** The basic symbol for these lights is a black dot with a magenta flare that looks like a large exclamation mark (Figure 4-8). Major lights are named and described; minor lights are described only.

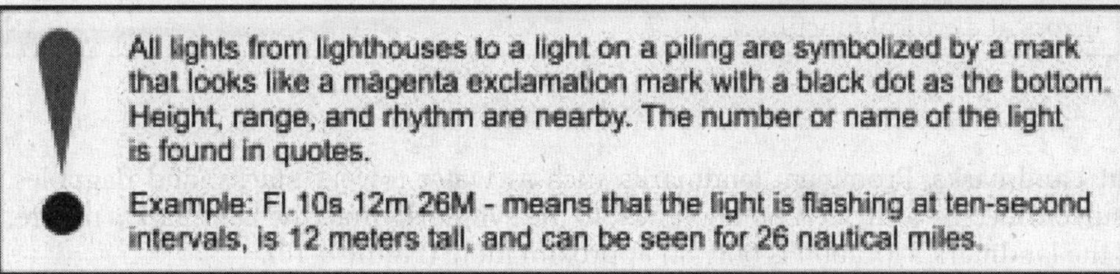

Figure 4-8. Symbols for lighthouses and other fixed lights

4-51. **Ranges and Day Beacons.** Ranges are indicated on charts by symbols for the lights (if lighted) and a dashed line indicating the direction of the range. Day beacons are indicated by small triangles, which may be colored to match the aid. Day beacons, also commonly called day marks, are always fixed aids (that is, they are on a structure secured to the bottom or on the shore). They have many different shapes (Figure 4-9).

4-52. Ranges are two man-made structures or natural features that are placed in a line to facilitate rapidly determining a line of position (LOP) when piloting a vessel in restricted waters. In port, ranges are set corresponding

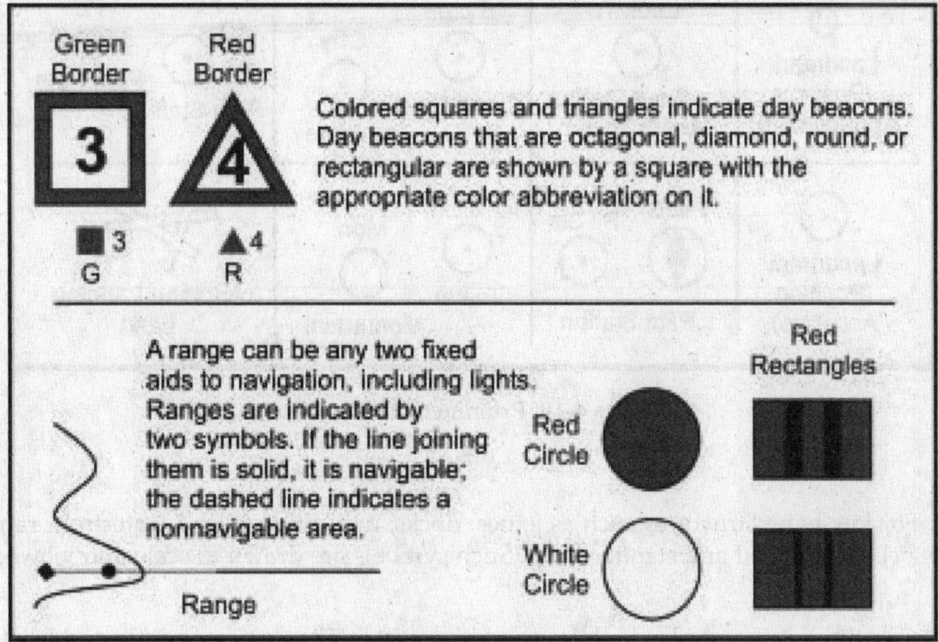

Figure 4-9. Symbols for ranges and day beacons

to the exact midchannel course, or turning points for course changes, to ensure safe navigation. Ranges may be either on the shore or in the water. The closest range mark will be shorter or lower than the far range mark. Ranges may use white, red, or green lights and will display various characteristics to differentiate from surrounding lights. As a general rule, the back range is higher than all other lights and is steady. The front is lower and usually a flashing light.

> **NOTE**
> Navigators should exercise caution during conditions of poor visibility, especially at night. If the observer is too close to the near range, his visual angle may make the near range appear to be higher than the far range. This perception is most likely in small craft, such as CRRCs. This confusion could result in navigational errors at a critical juncture.

4-53. **Prominent Landmarks.** Prominent landmarks such as water towers, stacks, and flagpoles are shown by a symbol of a dot surrounded by a circle. A notation next to the symbol defines the landmark's nature. The omission of the dot indicates the landmark's location is only an approximation. (Figure 4-10).

4-54. **Wrecks, Rocks, and Reefs.** These features are marked with standardized symbols (Figure 4-11). For example, a sunken wreck may be shown either by a symbol or by an abbreviation plus a number that gives the wreck's depth at mean low or lower low water. A dotted line around any symbol calls special attention to its hazardous nature.

4-55. **Bottom** Characteristics. A system of abbreviations, used alone or in combination, describes the composition of the bottom, providing information for the navigator to select the best holding ground for anchoring (Figure 4-12, page 67).

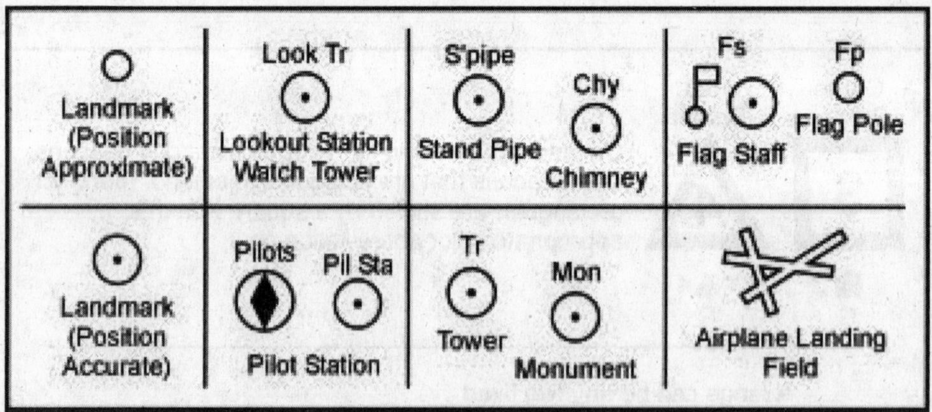

Figure 4-10. Prominent landmarks

4-56. **Structures.** For low-lying structures such as jetties, docks, drawbridges, and waterfront ramps, a shorthand representation has been developed and standardized. Such symbols are drawn to scale and viewed from overhead (Figure 4-13).

4-57. **Coastlines.** Coastlines are viewed at both low and high water. The navigator notes and labels any landmarks that may help him obtain a fix on his position (Figure 4-14).

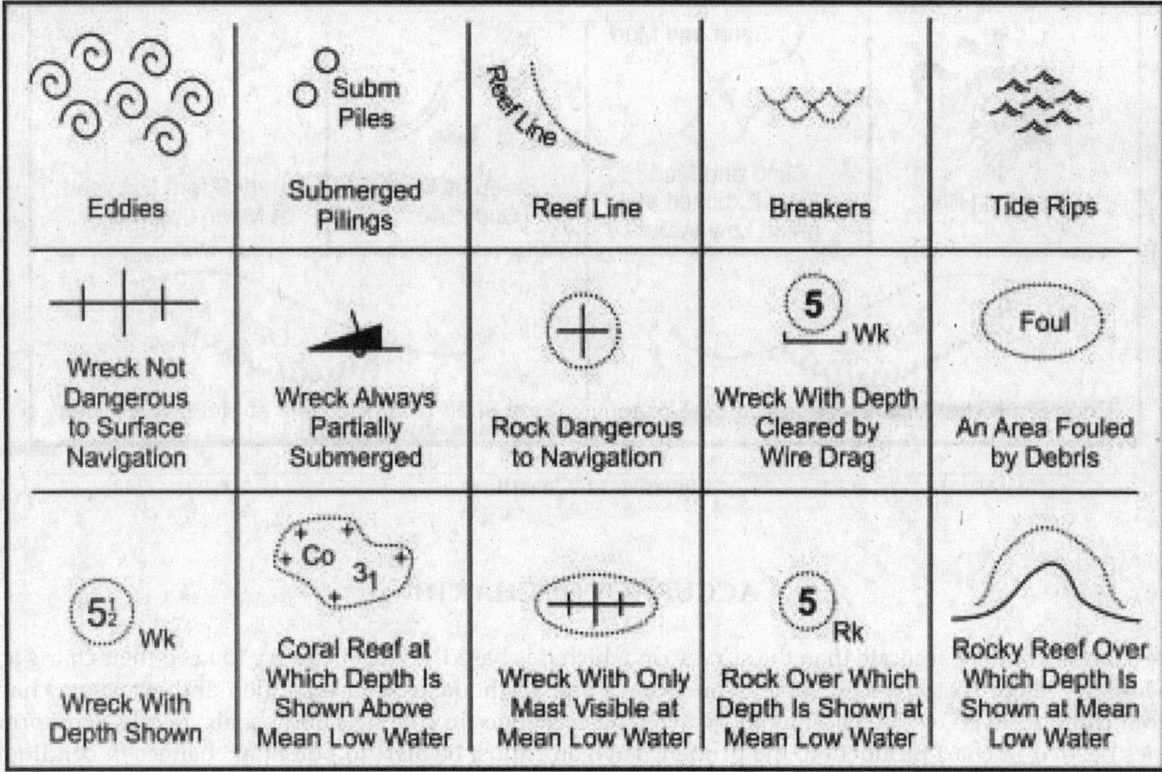

Figure 4-11. Symbols for wrecks, rocks, and reefs

Hrd	Hard	*S*	Sand	*M*	Mud; Muddy	*Wd*	Seaweed
Sft	Soft	*Co; Cr*	Coral	*G*	Gravel	*Grs*	Grass
Cy; Cl	Clay	*Co Hd*	Coral Head	*Br*	Brown	*Oys*	Oysters
St	Stone	*Sh*	Shells	*Gy*	Gray	*Stk*	Sticky

Figure 4-12. Bottom characteristics

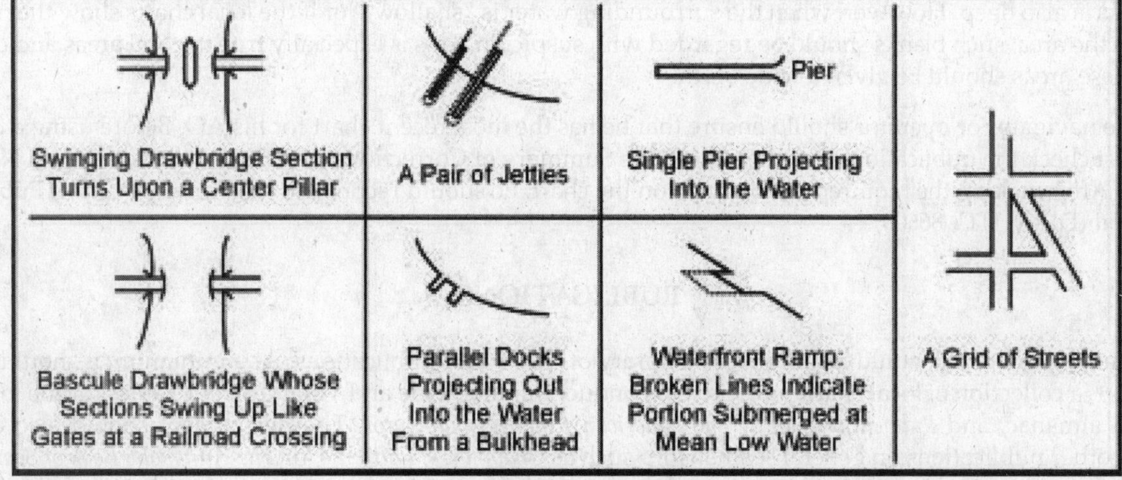

Figure 4-13. Structures

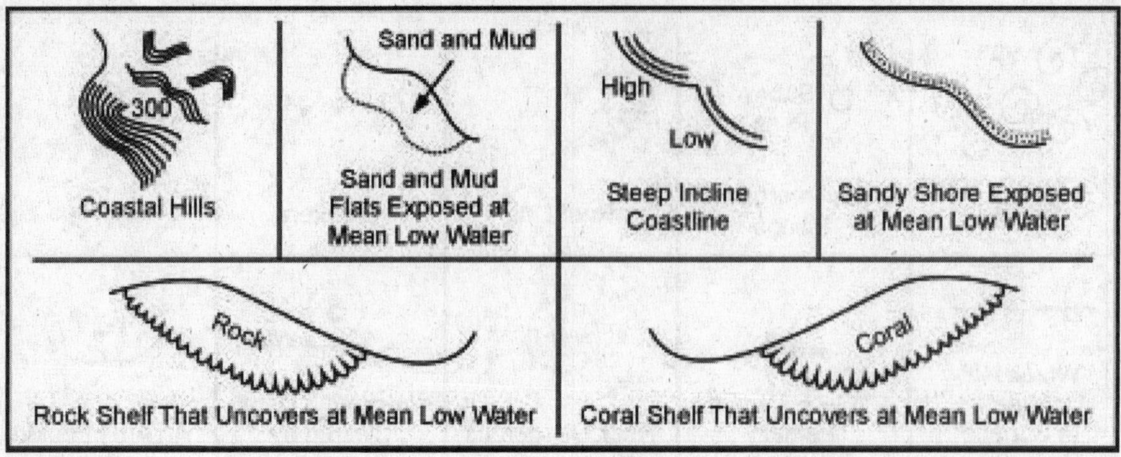

Figure 4-14. Coastlines

ACCURACY OF CHARTS

4-58. A chart is no more accurate than the survey on which it is based. Ail agencies try to keep their charts accurate and up-to-date. Major disturbances, such as hurricanes and earthquakes, cause sudden and extensive changes in the bottom contour. Even everyday wind and waves cause changes in channels and shoals. Because compromise is sometimes needed in chart production, the prudent navigator must be alert to potential changes in conditions and inaccuracies of charted information. Any information presented must be understood with ease and certainty. Various factors may prevent the presentation of all collected data for a given area. The navigator should always consider the following points to judge the accuracy and completeness of a survey.

4-59. The source and date of the chart are generally given in the title along with the changes that have taken place since the date of the survey. The earlier surveys often were made under circumstances that precluded great accuracy of detail. Until a chart based on such a survey is tested, it should be viewed with caution. Except in well-frequented waters, few surveys have been so thorough as to make certain that all dangers have been found.

4-60. Noting the fullness or scantiness of the soundings is another method of estimating the completeness of the survey. However, the navigator should remember that the chart seldom shows all soundings that were obtained. If the soundings are sparse or unevenly distributed, it should be taken for granted, as a precautionary measure, that the survey was not in great detail. Large or irregular blank spaces among soundings mean that no soundings were obtained in those areas. Where the nearby soundings are "deep," it may logically be assumed that the water in the blank areas is also deep. However, when the surrounding water is "shallow," or if the local charts show that reefs are present in the area, such blanks should be regarded with suspicion. This is especially true in coral areas and off rocky coasts. These areas should be given a wide berth.

4-61. The navigator or operator should ensure that he has the most recent chart for his AO. Before using a chart, he should first check the publication date, then check the Summary of Corrections, and finally check the local Notice for Mariners. After making the required annotations on the chart, he should record the changes on a Chart/Pub Correction Record (DMAHTC- 86609).

PUBLICATIONS

4-62. Every detachment should acquire a basic library of charts and publications. At a minimum, it should include Chart No. 1, a collection of local charts sufficient to conduct training, Tide and Tidal Current Tables for the local area, a nautical almanac, and *Publication No. 9; The American Practical Navigator*. The detachment should also consider obtaining other publications on general seamanship such as *Chapman's, Dutton's*, or *The Annapolis Book of Seamanship*. These references can be of considerable value when conducting training or missions, especially in areas where the detachment might encounter commercial marine traffic and aids to navigation. Because most publications are broken down by geographic region, it is only necessary to acquire those volumes pertinent to designated training and operational areas. Some of these publications will require periodic updates; the detachment should replace or update them as required to ensure their continued use and safety of navigation.

SUGGESTED REFERENCES

4-63. **Chart No. 1.** This reference is also titled the *United States of America Nautical Chart Symbols, Abbreviations, and Terms* but is usually referred to as Chart No. 1. It is the only book that contains all symbols and abbreviations approved for use on nautical charts published by the United States. It is generally used worldwide. Chart No. 1 is divided into an introduction and five sections: general, topography, hydrography, aids and services, and alphabetical indexes. The table of contents is located on the back cover.

4-64. **Tide Tables.** Tide tables give daily predictions of the height of water at almost any place at any given time. They are published annually in the following volumes:

- Volume I. Europe and West Coast of Africa (including the Mediterranean Sea).
- Volume II. East Coast of North and South America (including Greenland).
- Volume III. West Coast of North and South America (including the Hawaiian Islands).
- Volume IV. Central and Western Pacific Ocean and Indian Ocean.

4-65. **Tidal Current Tables.** These tables provide the times of flood and ebb currents and times of the two slack waters when current direction reverses. They also tell the predicted strength of the current in knots. The time of slack water does not correspond to times of high and low tides; therefore, the navigator is unable to use the tide tables to predict current situations. These tables are published as follows:

- Volume I. Tidal Current Tables, Atlantic Coast.
- Volume II. Tidal Current Tables, Pacific Coast.

4-66. **Coast Pilots.** Available space and the system of symbols used limit the amount of information that can be printed on a nautical chart. Additional information is often needed for safe and convenient navigation. The NOAA publishes such information in the Coast Pilots. These are printed in book form covering the coastline and the Great Lakes in nine separate volumes. Each Coast Pilot contains sailing directions between points in its respective area including recommended courses and distances. It describes channels, their controlling depths, and all dangers and obstructions. Harbors and anchorages are listed with information on those points at which facilities are available for boat supplies and marine repairs. Information on canals, bridges, and docks is also included.

4-67. **Sailing Directions.** The Sailing Directions provide the same type of information as the Coast Pilots, except the Sailing Directions pertain to foreign coasts and coastal waters. They consist of geographically grouped volumes, which are as follows.

4-68. *Planning Guide.* This guide consists of eight volumes and is printed annually. The volumes are divided into ocean basins that provide information about countries adjacent to that particular ocean basin. Contents are listed as follows:

- Chapter 1. Countries.
  - Government Regulations.
  - Search and Rescue.
  - Communications.
  - Signals.
- Chapter 2. Ocean Basin.
  - Oceanography.
  - Environment.
  - Magnetic Disturbances.
  - Climatology.

- Chapter 3. Warning Areas.
  - Operating Areas.
  - Firing Areas.
  - Reference Guide to Warnings and Cautions.
- Chapter 4. Ocean Routes.
  - Route Chart and Text Traffic.
  - Separation Schemes.
- Chapter 5. Navigation Aids.
  - Systems.
  - Electronic Navigation Systems.
  - Systems of Lights and Buoys.

4-69. *En Route.* This guide consists of 37 volumes and is printed annually. It is divided into subgeographical sectors that include detailed coastal and approach information. Each part contains the following information:

- Pilotage.
- Appearance of coastline (mountains, landmarks, visible foliage).
- Navigation aids in general.
- Local weather conditions.
- Tides and currents.
- Local rules of the road, if any.
- Bridges, type and clearance.
- Anchorage facilities.
- Repair facilities.
- Availability of fuel and provisions.
- Transportation service ashore.
- Industries.

4-70. **Light Lists.** Light Lists provide more information about navigation aids than can be shown on charts. However, they are not intended to replace charts for navigation. Light Lists are published in five volumes. The List of Lights provides the same information for non-U.S. waters.

- Volume I. Atlantic Coast from St. River, Maine to Little River, South Carolina.
- Volume II. Atlantic and Gulf Coasts from Little River, South Carolina to Rio Grande, Texas.
- Volume III. Pacific Coast and Pacific Islands.
- Volume IV. Great Lakes.
- Volume V. Mississippi River System.

4-71. **List of Lights**. This is an annual publication (7 volumes) with similar information found in Light Lists but pertaining to foreign coastal areas.

4-72. **Notice to Mariners**. The DMAHTC publications already mentioned are published at more or less widely separated intervals. As a result, provisions must be made for keeping mariners informed of changes in hydrographic conditions as soon as possible after they occur. The Notice to Mariners is the principal medium for distributing corrections to charts, light lists, and other DMAHTC publications. Each notice is divided into the following sections:

- Section I. Chart Corrections.
- Section II. Light List Corrections.
- Section III. Broadcast Warnings and Miscellaneous Information.

4-73. **Local Notices to Mariners**. The local Coast Guard district publishes this information weekly. The notice provides corrections to nautical charts, coast pilots, and light lists. It also issues marine information particular to that district.

4-74. **Summary of Corrections.** Every 6 months, DMAHTC publishes this summary in two volumes. Volume I covers the Atlantic, Arctic, and Mediterranean areas. Volume II covers the Pacific and Indian Oceans and the Antarctic. These volumes cover the full list of all changes to charts, Coast Pilots, and Sailing Directions. The navigator uses the Summary of Corrections to supplement—not replace—the Notice to Mariners.

4-75. **Fleet Guides.** DMAHTC publishes Publication No. 940 (Atlantic) and Publication No. 941 (Pacific). Similar to the Sailing Directions and Coast Pilots, they are prepared to provide important command, navigational, repair, and logistic information for naval vessels. Both publications are restricted. They are a valuable source when conducting aid-to-navigation and harbor destruction missions.

AIDS TO NAVIGATION

4-76. Navigation aids assist the navigator in making landfalls when approaching from seaward positions overseas. They mark isolated dangers, make it possible for vessels to follow the natural and improved channels, and provide a continuous chain of charted marks for coastal piloting. All aids to navigation serve the same general purpose, and they differ only to meet the conditions and requirements for a certain location.

4-77. The prudent MAROPS detachment will prepare its navigation plan so that (as much as possible) it does not rely on artificial aids to navigation; for example, lights, buoys, or daymarkers. During periods of hostility, these aids may not be present, accurately located, properly maintained, or lighted during periods of darkness. They are also most commonly emplaced in areas with concentrations of marine traffic. Detachments should seek to avoid these areas whenever possible.

INTERNATIONAL ASSOCIATION OF LIGHTHOUSES AUTHORITIES (IALA)

4-78. The IALA is a nongovernmental body that exchanges information and recommends improvements to aids to navigation. At present there are two systems termed IALA Maritime Buoyage System "A" Combined Cardinal and Lateral System (Red to Port) and IALA Maritime Buoyage System "B" Lateral System Only (Red to Starboard). Most European countries, including the countries of the former Soviet Union, have or will adopt System A. System B is still being developed. The United States uses the lateral system of buoyage (similar but not the same as System B) recommended by the International Marine Conference of 1889. A graphic depiction of the different marking schemes as discussed below can be found in Chart No. 1.

BUOYS

4-79. The basic symbol for a buoy is a diamond and small circle. Older charts will show a dot instead of the circle. The diamond may be above, below, or alongside the circle or dot. The small circle or dot denotes the approximate position of the buoy mooring. Some charts will use the diamond to draw attention to the position of the circle or dot and to describe the aid. The various types of buoys are as follows:

- *Nun Buoys.* These are conical in shape, painted solid red, and mark the right side of the channel when one is entering from seaward.
- *Can Buoys.* These are cylindrical in shape and are painted solid green or black. They indicate the left side of the channel when one is entering from seaward (green) and mark the left side of rivers and intracoastal waterways (black).
- *Sound Buoys.* The four basic types are as follows:
  - **Bell** is sounded by the motion of sea.
  - **Gong** is similar to bell buoy but with sets of gongs that sound dissimilar tones.
  - **Whistle** is a tube mechanism that sounds by the rising and falling motion of the buoy at sea, making a loud, moaning sound.
  - **Horn** has an electrically sounded horn at regular intervals.

4-80. Additional features on buoys include sound signals, radar reflectors, numbers or letters, or any combination of these features. Bells and horns are spelled out; radar reflectors are abbreviated (Ra Ref); whistles are abbreviated (WHIS); and numbers or letters painted on buoys are shown in quotation marks ("8").

Buoy Symbols

4-81. Nautical charts will show the buoy type by the initials of its shape. For example, nun buoys (N) and can buoys (C) (Figure 4-15). A mooring (anchor) buoy is the only one that is not indicated by the diamond and circle or dot. This symbol is a trapezoid (a figure having two parallel and two nonparallel sides) and a circle.

4-82. If the aid is painted red, the diamond will usually be indicated in red on the chart; if the aid is painted black, the diamond will be black. There are five other color patterns used on buoys (Chart No. 1). These buoys have no lateral significance; that is they do not mark port or starboard. Although the buoys may not be numbered, they may be lettered (Figure 4-15).

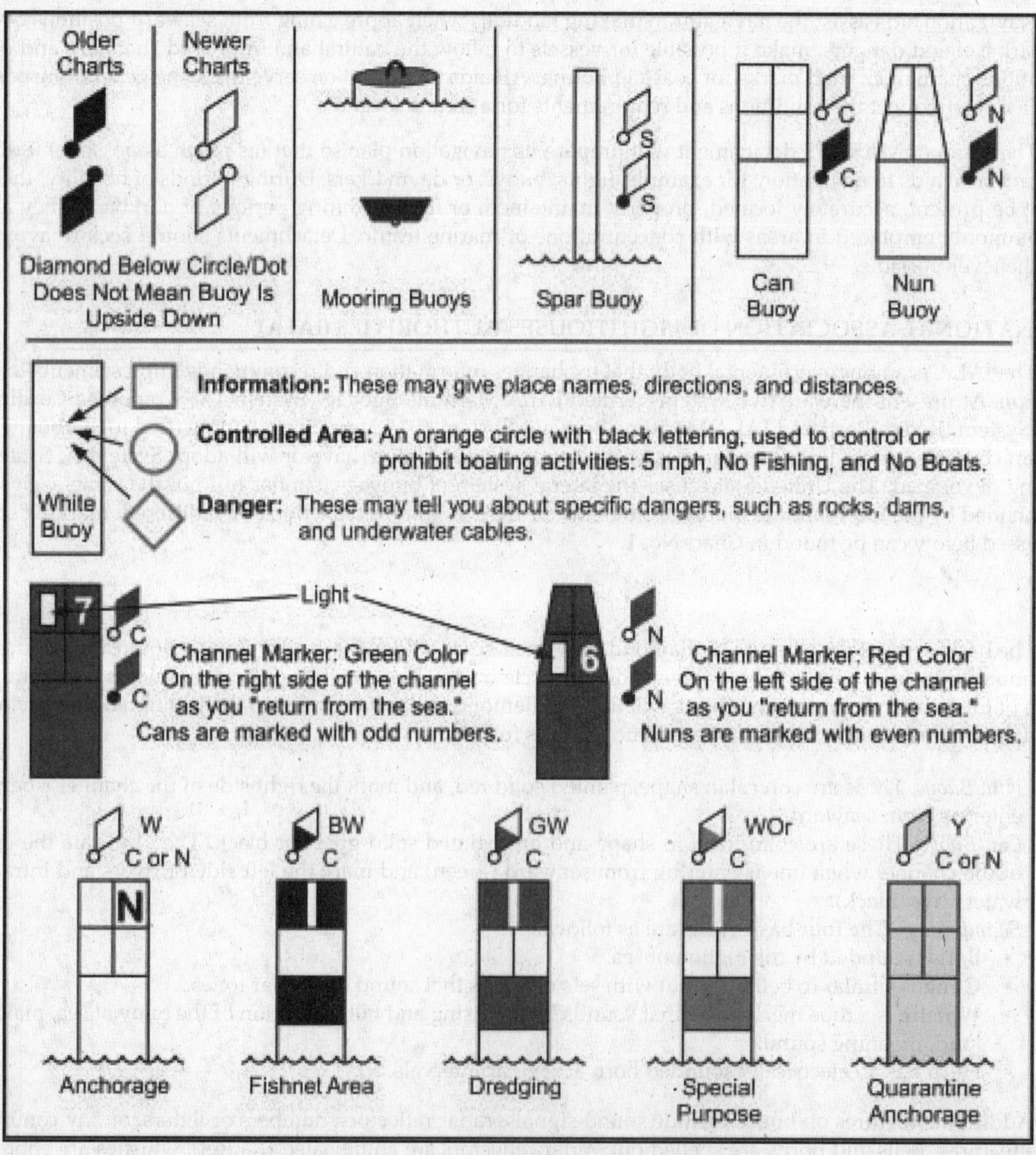

Figure 4-15. Buoys

4-83. The primary function of buoys is to warn the navigator of some danger, obstruction, or change in the bottom. A navigator may also use buoys to help mark his location on a chart, which aids in establishing his position. However, he should not rely solely on buoys or other floating objects for fixes because they are not immovable objects.

Buoy Lights

4-84. If a buoy is lighted, a magenta (nautical purple) disc will be overprinted on the circle. The characteristic of the light and its color will be indicated on the chart. Buoy lights can be either red, green, or white. The letters R or G are used for red and green lights. The absence of a letter indicates a white light (Figure 4-15). The light phase characteristics and the meanings of abbreviations used to describe them are detailed in Chart No. 1 as shown in Figure 4-16. Each color is used as follows:

- *Red lights* appear on red aids (nun buoys) or red and black horizontally banded aids with the topmost band red.
- *Green lights* appear on black aids (can buoys) or red and black horizontally banded aids with the topmost band black.
- *White lights* appear on any color buoy. The purpose of the aid being indicated by its color, number, or light-phase characteristic.

Abbreviations	Class of Light	Description	Illustration
F	Fixed	A continuous, nonblinking light.	
F. Fl.	Fixed and Flashing	A continuous light, varied at regular intervals by flashes of greater brilliance.	
F. Gp. Fl.	Fixed and Group Flashing	A continuous light, varied by groups of two or more flashes.	
Fl.	Flashing	A light that flashes at regular intervals of **not** less than 2 seconds and whose period of darkness **exceeds** the period of light.	
Gp. Fl.	Group Flashing	A light that sends out groups of two or more flashes at regular intervals.	
Gp. Fl. (1+2)	Composite Group Flashing	A flashing light in which the flashes are combined in alternating groups of different numbers.	
Mo. (A)	Morse Code	A flashing light which blinks signal letters in Morse Code. The letter "A" in Morse Code: (one short and one long flash).	
Qk. Fl.	Quick Flashing	A light that flashes 60 times or more a minute, used only on buoys and beacons.	
I. Qk. Fl	Interrupted Quick Flashing	A light in which 5 seconds of quick flashes is followed by 5 seconds of darkness.	
E. Int.	Equal Interval	A light with equal periods of light and darkness.	
Occ.	Occulting	A light that is eclipsed at regular intervals, but whose period of light is **always** greater than the duration of darkness.	
Gp. Occ.	Group Occulting	A light with regular spaced groups of two or more occultations.	
Gp. Occ (2+3)	Composite Group Occulting	A light whose combinations combine in alternate groups of different numbers.	

Figure 4-16. Light characteristics

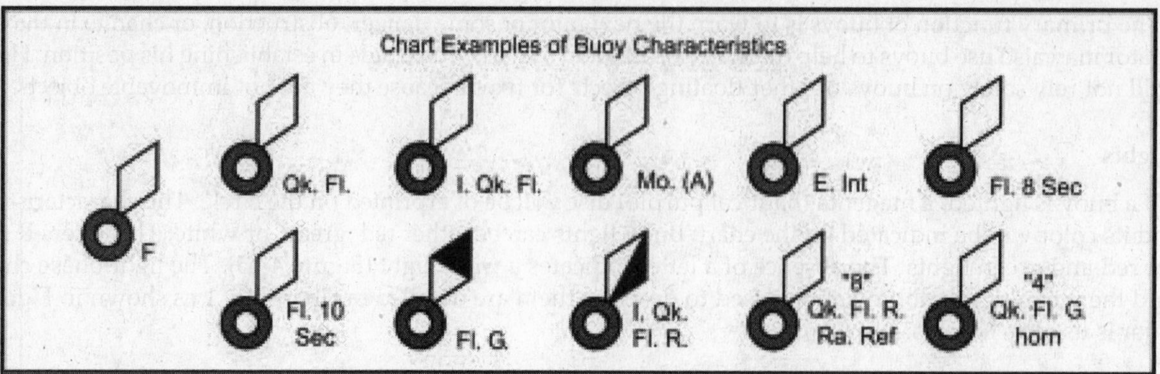

Figure 4-16. Light characteristics (*Continued*)

Distance of Visibility of Lights

4-85. Distance of visibility is dependent on many factors. For all objects, the atmospheric conditions are the most important factors. The height of an object increases the distance from which it can be seen. Similarly, if one increases the height of one's view, one will increase the distance an object can be seen. Figure 4-17 explains the types of ranges that a navigator must consider when conducting small-boat operations.

FOG SIGNALS

4-86. All lighthouses and light platforms or large naval buoys are equipped with fog signals that are operated by mechanical or electrical means and that are sounded on definite time schedules during periods of low visibility. For a fog signal to be an effective aid, the navigator must be able to identify the characteristic sound as coming from a certain point. This information is found on the chart and in the Light List. The characteristics of mechanized signals are varied blasts and silent periods. A definite time period is required for a complete signal. Various types

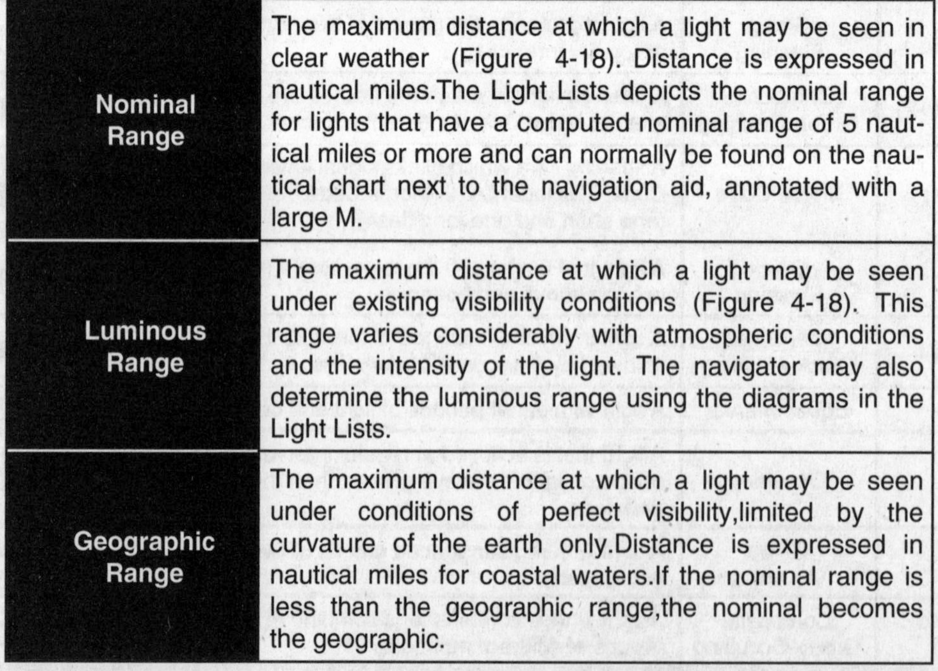

Nominal Range	The maximum distance at which a light may be seen in clear weather (Figure 4-18). Distance is expressed in nautical miles.The Light Lists depicts the nominal range for lights that have a computed nominal range of 5 nautical miles or more and can normally be found on the nautical chart next to the navigation aid, annotated with a large M.
Luminous Range	The maximum distance at which a light may be seen under existing visibility conditions (Figure 4-18). This range varies considerably with atmospheric conditions and the intensity of the light. The navigator may also determine the luminous range using the diagrams in the Light Lists.
Geographic Range	The maximum distance at which a light may be seen under conditions of perfect visibility,limited by the curvature of the earth only.Distance is expressed in nautical miles for coastal waters.If the nominal range is less than the geographic range,the nominal becomes the geographic.

Figure 4-17. Types of ranges

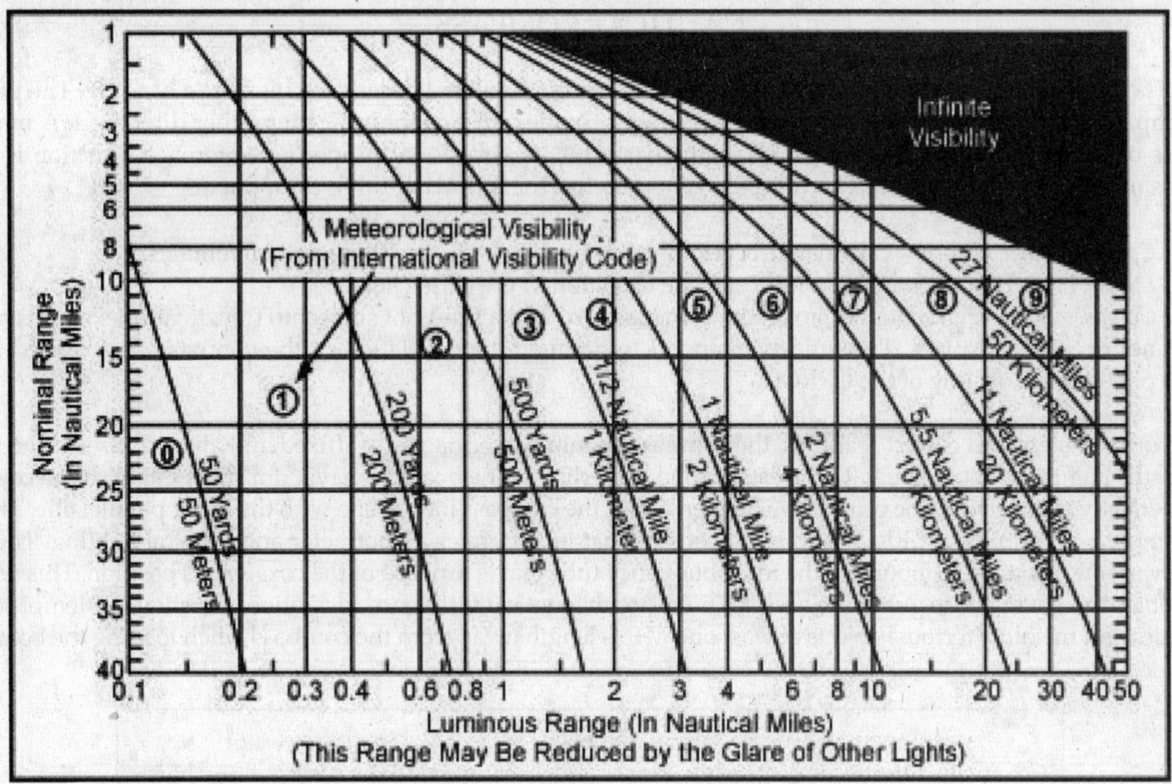

Figure 4-18. Nominal and luminous ranges

of fog signals also differ in tone, which facilitates recognition of the respective stations. The various mechanisms are as follows:

- *Diaphones* produce sound by compressed air. They produce two tones of varied pitch.
- *Diaphragm disc* vibrates by air or electricity.
- *Sirens* are disc-shaped rotors that are activated by compressed air, steam, or electricity.
- *Whistles* are compressed air emitted through a circular slot into a cylindrical bell chamber.
- *Bells* are sounded by means of a hammer actuated by a descending weight, compressed gas, or electricity.

4-87. To determine geographic range, the navigator first checks Table 12, page 673, Publication Number 9, *Bowditch* (Example 1), which is the distance to the horizon table. He will see that Table 12 is divided into four different columns—height in feet (of the navaid), nautical miles (seen from seaward), statute miles, and height in meters. The navigator first checks his nautical chart and finds the height of his navaid. In this case, the navigator uses the Point Loma Light that is 88 feet. He moves down the height column until he finds the height closest to his navaid's height (he should always round down; 88 feet = 85 feet on Table 12). The navigator then moves to the nautical miles column and the figure there (10.8) will be the basic geographic range. He determines his height in feet and moves down the first column. For this height, he uses 4 feet, the height of a man sitting on a gunwale tube. The figure in the nautical miles column for 4 feet is 2.3. The navigator then adds the range of the navaid to the range of his height (10.8 + 2.3 = 13.1), which results in his geographic range. He then plots a range ring on his course.

4-88. To determine luminous range, the navigator first checks the luminous range diagram in the Light List. The luminous range diagram is a graph that depicts nominal range on the bottom, visibility scale on the right side, and the luminous range on the left. The navigator requires two factors: an estimate of visibility and the nominal range of his navaid. He looks along the bottom of the diagram until he comes to his nominal range. He then looks up the scale to the center of the visibility tube that corresponds to his estimated condition. The navigator draws a straight line to the left side of the diagram and reads the luminous range for his navaid.

NAUTICAL COMPASS

4-89. The magnetic compass is the navigator's most important tool in determining his boat's heading. The purpose of a compass is to locate a reference direction and then provide a means for indicating other directions. A magnetic compass depends upon the magnetic fields of the earth for its directional properties; reference direction is called compass north or magnetic north. The compass generally has the following three components:

- *Compass Card.* It shows cardinal directions and degrees in 1-, 5-, or 10- degree increments.
- *Lubber Line.* This reference line indicates the direction of the ship's head.
- *Compass Bowl.* This container holds the compass card and a fluid not subject to freezing, for example, methanol or mineral spirits. The fluid is intended to dampen the oscillation of the compass card caused by the pitching and rolling of the CRRC.

4-90. For consistent and correct readings, the compass should be permanently affixed and aligned level to the vessel. To align the compass lubber line with the established centerline of the boat, the navigator must establish a second line that is perfectly parallel with the centerline. He then aligns the compass lubber line with the offset parallel line. The best way to mount a compass in CRRCs is to use a console that incorporates a knotmeter and integral lighting. There are current variants designed to mount on the main buoyancy tube that is forward of the coxswain's position. This position best enables the navigator to guide the vessel. To reduce magnetic interference (deviation), he should attempt to keep electronics and metallic (ferrous) objects at least one M16's length away from the compass when loading the boat.

NOTE

Coxswain fatigue and steering errors are best avoided by using only hard-mounting compasses of sufficient size that are designed for marine use.

4-91. A prudent user will check the accuracy of the compass frequently. The magnetic compass is influenced not only by the earth's magnetic field, but also by fields radiating from magnetic materials aboard the boat. These two effects are referred to as "variation" and "deviation." A compass is also subject to unanticipated error resulting from violent movement as might be met in heavy weather and surf operations (Figure 4-19).

VARIATION

4-92. Variation is the angular difference between the magnetic and geographic meridians. It is measured as the difference in degrees between the directions of the magnetic and true North Poles. The amount of variation changes from one point to the next on the earth's surface. However, it will always be expressed in degrees in either an easterly or westerly direction.

4-93. A navigator can find the amount of variation for a given location on the compass rose of any chart for that area. Increases in variation may continue for many years (sometimes reaching large values), may remain nearly the same for a few years, and then may reverse (decrease). Navigators should use predictions of the changes for short-term planning, such as a few years.

4-94. Applying variation is similar to using a declination diagram on a topographical map. On a nautical chart, variation and its annual change can be found in the center of the compass rose. The navigator should always use the compass rose closest to the desired area, as variation changes from one area or compass rose to another. Not all charts will have a compass rose. Because variation changes daily (diurnal) and yearly (secular), the navigator should refer to DMA Chart 42 to find the correct variation in the intended objective area, especially if his chart is very old.

4-95. Navigators should always use the latest charts available. Normally, the compass rose will show the amount of predicted change. To determine the annual variation increase or decrease, the navigator should—

- Locate the compass rose nearest to the AO on the chart.
- Read the variation and annual increase or decrease from the center of the compass rose.

- Locate the year for which the information is given from the center of the compass rose.
- Subtract the year indicated in the compass rose from the present year.
- Multiply the number of years difference by the annual increase or decrease.
- Add or subtract the sum of the previous step to the variation within the compass rose.

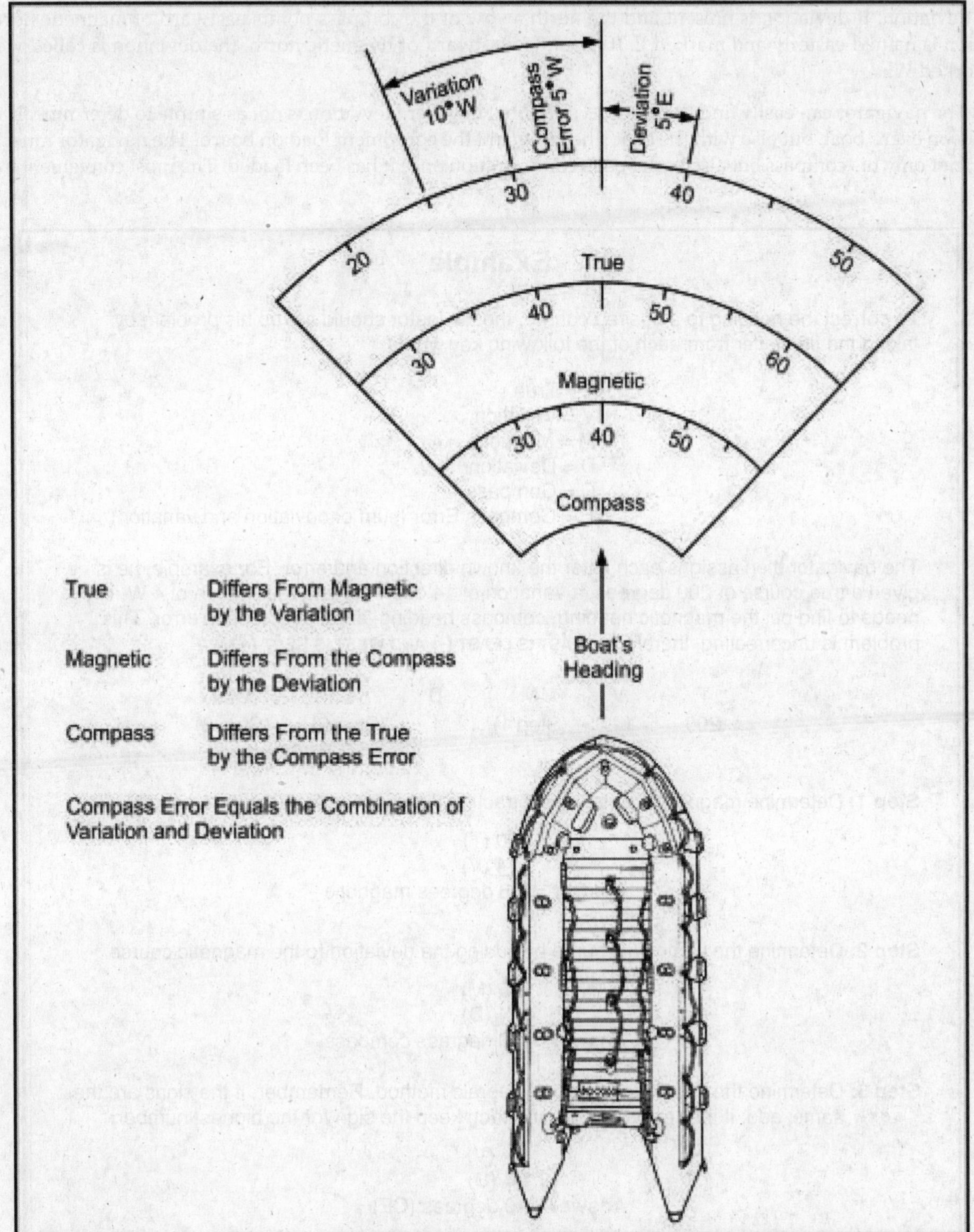

Figure 4-19. Compass direction

DEVIATION

4-96. Magnetic compasses function because of their tendency to align themselves with the earth's magnetic field. Unfortunately, the compass is subject to the magnetic influences of other metallic or electronic objects. The presence of these outside magnetic influences—for example, machineguns or radios—tends to deflect the compass from the magnetic meridian. This difference between the north-south axis of the compass card and the magnetic meridian is called deviation. If deviation is present and the north arrow of the compass points eastward of magnetic north, the deviation is named easterly and marked E. If it points westward of magnetic north, the deviation is called westerly and marked W.

4-97. The navigator can easily find the correct variation. However, deviation is not as simple to determine. It varies, not only on every boat, but also with the boat's heading and the equipment load on board. The navigator must swing (check) not only his compass but also each boat's configuration once it has been loaded. The most convenient method

Example

To correct the heading to a desired course, the navigator should set up his problem by taking the first letter from each of the following key words:

T = True
V = Variation
M = Magnetic
D = Deviation
C = Compass
CE = Compass Error (sum of deviation and variation)

The navigator then assigns each letter the known direction and error. For example, he is given a true course of 200 degrees, a variation of 14 degrees, and a deviation of 4 W. He needs to find out the magnetic heading, compass heading, and the compass error. This problem is uncorrecting, therefore—**EAST IS LEAST (-) AND WEST IS BEST (+).**

T	V	M	D	C	CE
200	14	(Step 1)	4	(Step 2)	(Step 3)

Step 1: Determine magnetic course by subtracting the variation from the true course.

200 (T)
- 14 (V)
Answer 186 degrees magnetic

Step 2: Determine the compass course by adding the deviation to the magnetic course.

186 (M)
+ 4 (D)
Answer 190 degrees compass

Step 3: Determine the compass error by algebraic method. Remember, if the signs are the same, add; if they are different, subtract; keep the sign for the highest number.

-14 (V)
(-) + 4 (D)
Answer 10 degrees (CE)

Figure 4-20. Determining variation and deviation

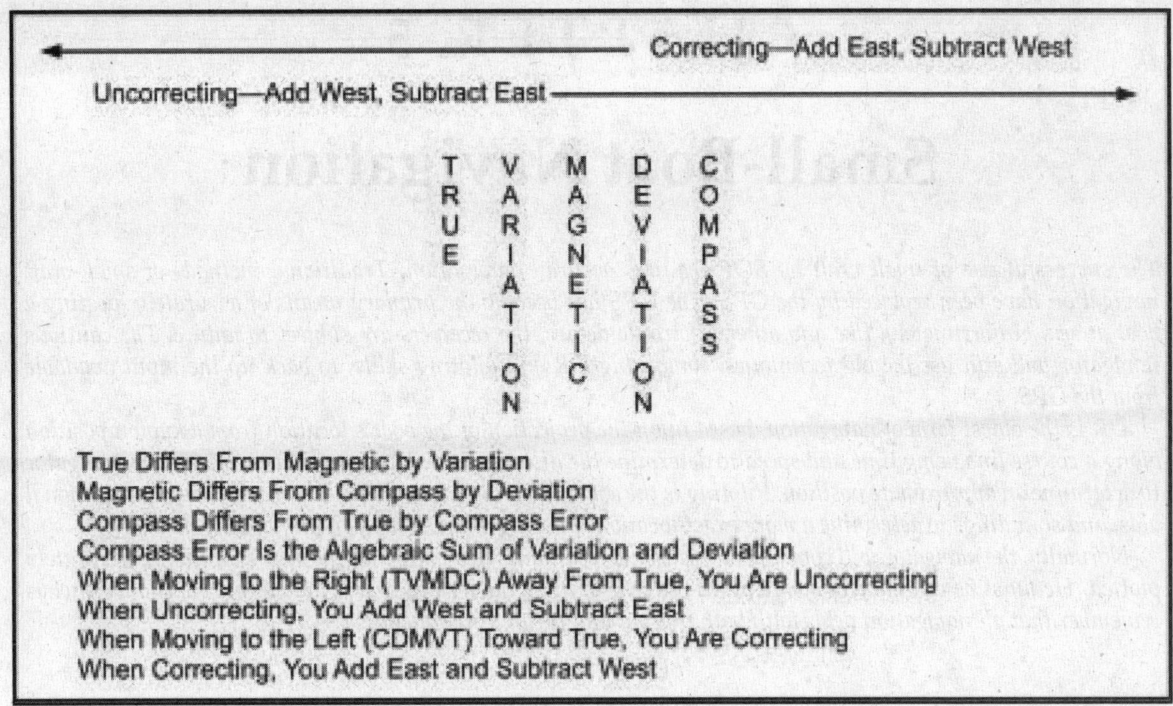

Figure 4-21. Guide to applying variation and deviation

for small craft (CRRCs and kayaks) is to check the boat's compass every 15 degrees on a compass rose. Larger vessels use a process called "swinging the ship" that is outside the scope of this manual.

4-98. Most naval air stations or air bases will have a compass rose laid out on the ground. It is "surveyed" so that accurate and repeatable measurements of the compass deviation caused by differences in equipment loading or configuration are possible. To record the deviation for his magnetic compass, the navigator should—

- Center the loaded boat with its mounted compass on the compass rose.
- Rotate the boat on the compass rose, stopping every 15 degrees.
- As he moves through the headings, compare the compass bearing with the surveyed bearing of the compass rose and record the number of degrees the compass is off on a deviation card. He should label it west if it is high and east if it is low.
- Apply the deviation when he actually conducts movement, if a magnetic heading is taken off the chart.

4-99. When compass error (the sum of variation and deviation) is removed, the correct true direction remains. Hence, the process of converting a compass direction to a magnetic or true direction, or of converting a magnetic direction to a true direction, is one of "correcting" or removing errors. The opposite of correcting is "uncorrecting," or the process of applying errors. The following rules apply:

- When correcting, easterly errors are additive and westerly errors are subtractive.
- When uncorrecting, easterly errors are subtractive and westerly errors are additive.

4-100. To plot a course properly, the navigator must apply variation and deviation. Figures 4-20 and 4-21 explain how to apply both of these differences.

CHAPTER 5

Small-Boat Navigation

The successful use of small craft by SOF requires accurate navigation. Traditional methods of small-craft navigation have been replaced by the GPS. The GPS has become the primary means of accurately locating a boat at sea. Unfortunately, like any other electronic device, the receivers are subject to failure. The cautious navigator will still use the old techniques, combining DR and piloting skills, to back up the input available from the GPS.

DR is the oldest form of navigation, based upon the projection of the boat's location from a known position along a course line using time and speed to determine the distance run. This information allows the navigator to determine an approximate position. Piloting is the art of directing a boat using landmarks, other navigational aids, and soundings to determine a more exact location. Piloting and DR are complimentary skills.

Normally, the navigator will combine navigational techniques to ensure that the boat's location is accurately plotted. He must be consciously aware of his current location, as well as where he will be. He should always remember that all navigation deals with both present and future consequences.

NAVIGATION

5-1. Navigation is the process of directing the movement of a boat from one point to another. Both art and science are involved in navigating a boat accurately to a BLS or rendezvous site at sea. Art is involved in the proficient use of all available aids and methods and the interpretation of the resulting data with good judgement to determine (or fix) a position. Science includes the mathematical computation for various navigational problems and the use of tables, almanacs, and publications intended to increase the accuracy of an intended route. Great progress has been made in advancing the science of navigation, but such progress is in vain if the navigator is not skilled in his trade.

THE NAVIGATION TEAM

5-2. Accuracy in navigation demands that a number of events take place simultaneously and in a timely manner. One man, of course, cannot perform all of the duties required. Consequently, a division of labor is necessary.

5-3. The piloting team consists of three individuals: the navigator, the assistant navigator, and the coxswain. All three should be well-versed in small-boat navigation and must become intimately involved in the research and development of the navigation plan. Once underway, the piloting team members perform the following duties:

- *Navigator.* The navigator orders course and speed to the coxswain and keeps total time of passage. He operates the plotting board by plotting bearings, currents, and DR plots. He notifies the assistant navigator when to take bearings and speed checks. The navigator oversees the entire navigation plan and is in charge of the safe piloting of the boat.
- *Assistant Navigator.* The assistant navigator renders aid to the navigator as directed and shoots bearings, measures speed, and keeps time between legs. The assistant navigator must be alert and observant of sea conditions, aids to navigation, and land features.
- *Coxswain.* The coxswain maintains the ordered speed and course and must not allow any deviation.

TYPES OF NAVIGATION

5-4. There are four types or methods of navigation used today. They are piloting, DR, celestial navigation, and electronic or radio navigation. Each method is explained below.

Piloting

5-5. Piloting is the process for obtaining constant fixes (positions) by using geographical features, lines of position, and electronic devices. It involves the frequent (or continuous) determination of position (or lines of position) relative to the charted geographical position. Navigators most commonly use piloting near land or in harbors where they can see and use charted geographic features for reference. Piloting is usually done by shooting bearings at fixed land positions and using those bearings to fix the boat's position. This process is very similar to resection as used in land navigation. Piloting requires the greatest amount of area study and premission planning before launching.

Dead Reckoning

5-6. DR enables the navigator to determine a boat's approximate position by moving the boat's position on a chart from a known point, using the course steered and the speed through the water. As long as the navigator can measure time, speed, and direction, he can always plot a DR position. This position is approximate but it is the only method by which a basic fix can always be determined. It does not take into account the effects of wind, waves, currents, or poor steering. Because DR gives only an approximate position, the navigator uses it as a reference to locate his true position.

Celestial Navigation

5-7. Nautical astronomy is the oldest of sciences. It uses the sun, moon, planets, designated stars, and their angular relationship to the observer's position to determine terrestrial coordinates. It is widely used by navigators on larger boats. Celestial navigation is not practical in smaller boats such as CRRCs because it requires the use of publications for reference and a stable platform to use the sextant. However, a basic knowledge of the relationships between celestial objects can be useful to the small-craft navigator. When conducting an OTH transit, the navigator can still use prominent stars and planets as steering guides until he can see onshore features. When using celestial bodies as steering guides, it is critical to cross-check with the boat's compass at regular intervals because of the way the stars move throughout the night.

Electronic or Radio Navigation

5-8. In some circumstances, highly accurate electronic means and radio waves may be available to provide an exact location or fix. This method includes such equipment as radar, radio direction finder, Doppler and inertial systems, long-range aid to navigation-C (LORAN-C), and the GPS. These systems are generally unaffected by environmental conditions or tidal current data. They are capable of greatly enhancing navigation accuracy. Therefore, their availability should be considered in the planning phase of the mission. Most of these systems are available on large boats. Detachments conducting infiltrations from a "mother craft" should access all onboard navigation systems during mission planning and directly before debarkation to accurately fix their movement point.

5-9. The most viable form of electronic navigation for detachments to use in small craft is satellite navigation. The primary satellite navigation system is the NAVSTAR GPS. This system is an all-weather, worldwide system that will give pinpoint positioning through three-dimensional fixes. Given the advances in recreational, commercial, and military receivers since the introduction of the service, accuracy results routinely exceed 5 meters. Accuracy results have been enhanced by the implementation of the Wide Area Augmentation System (WAAS) and the Differential Global Positioning System (DGPS)—two commercial GPS supplement systems normally available on newer civilian GPS receivers. These systems use ground stations to augment the satellite signal and further refine the positional accuracy. They are not available in all areas. During periods of conflict, it is still possible for the U.S. Government to encrypt or "dither" the GPS signal to reduce its accuracy and subsequent use to unauthorized users.

NOTE

GPS should be considered a backup navigation system for small-craft operations. It is critical that detachments realize it is not a substitute for a good chart and competent navigation skills.

5-10. The drawbacks of using electronic or radio navigation should be readily apparent. Despite the sophistication of electronic aids, they may become ineffective due to loss of power, propagation difficulties, and equipment malfunction. They are also subject to being jammed by the enemy. Therefore, it is necessary that navigators become skilled in and practice the older, but still reliable, piloting and DR techniques.

NAVIGATION TERMS

5-11. Navigation is a "scientific" art with its own specialized vocabulary to ensure precision when communicating navigational information. The detachment should thoroughly understand the following terms and definitions if conducting maritime operations.

5-12. **Bearing** is the horizontal direction of one terrestrial (earthbound) point from another (the direction to an object from a position). It is expressed as the angular distance (degrees) from a reference direction (a direction used as a basis for comparison of other directions). A bearing is usually measured clockwise from 0 degrees through 360 degrees at the reference direction: true north, magnetic north, compass north, or relative to the boat's centerline.

5-13. **Course** is the intended horizontal direction of travel (the direction one intends to go) expressed as angular distance from a reference direction clockwise through 360 degrees. For marine navigation, the term applies to the direction to be steered. The course is often designated as true, magnetic, compass, or grid depending on the reference direction. A course can either be an accomplished or anticipated direction of travel. Small boats normally use magnetic or compass; large boats use true. A navigator should always mark his course as to what it is.

5-14. **Heading** is the actual direction the boat's bow is pointing at any given time. It is not necessarily the same direction as the boat's intended course.

5-15. **Course line** is the graphic representation of a ship's course, normally used in the construction of a DR plot.

5-16. **Current sailing** is a method that allows for current when determining the course made good, or determining the effect of a current on the direction or motion of a boat.

5-17. **Dead reckoning** is the determination of approximate position by advancing a previous position using course and distance only, without regard to other factors such as wind, sea conditions, and current.

5-18. **DR plot** is the graphic representation on the nautical chart of the line or series of lines showing the vectors of the ordered true courses. Distances run on these courses at the ordered speeds, proceeding from a fixed point. The DR plot originates at a fix or running fix; it is suitably leveled as to courses, speeds, and times of various DR positions. DR plots are made and confirmed every 15 minutes, and when changing course or speed.

5-19. **Position** refers to the actual geographic location of a boat. It may be expressed as coordinates of latitude and longitude or as the bearing and distance from an object whose position is known.

5-20. **DR position** is a boat's location, determined by plotting a single or a series of consecutive course lines (vectors) using only the direction (course) and distance from the last fix, without consideration of current, wind, or other external forces acting on the boat.

5-21. **Estimated position** is the most probable location of a boat, determined from incomplete data or data of questionable accuracy. This point is also a DR position modified by additional information that in itself is insufficient to establish a fix.

5-22. **Estimated time of arrival (ETA)** is the best estimate of the predicted arrival time at a specified location IAW a scheduled movement.

5-23. **Estimated time of departure (ETD)** is the planned time of departure from a specified location IAW a schedule for movement.

5-24. **Time of passage (TOP)** is the time estimated for the CRRC to motor between specified points.

5-25. **Fix** is an exact position determined at a given time from terrestrial, electronic, or celestial data or two or more lines of position from geographic navigational aids.

5-26. **Running** fix **(R. FIX)** is a position determined by crossing LOPs obtained at different times.

5-27. **Line of position** is a line of bearing to a known object along which a boat is presumed to be. The intersection of two or more LOPs can result in a fix.

5-28. **Coast piloting** refers to directing the movements of a boat near a coast or in harbors where the navigator can see charted geographic features for use as a reference. It involves the frequent (or continuous) determination of position (or lines of position) relative to the charted geographical position. It is usually done by shooting bearings at fixed land positions and using those bearings to fix the boat's position in a process that is very similar to resection as used in land navigation. This technique requires the greatest amount of area study and premission planning before launching.

5-29. **Range** refers to two types that are used in piloting. A range can be two or more man-made structures or natural features, plotted on the appropriate charts, placed in a line. A range is used as an aid to piloting—to determine bearings, distance off, or course to steer. When two plotted objects line up to provide a bearing along which the boat's position can be estimated, these objects are said to be "in range."

5-30. Ranges are also distance measured in a single direction or along a great circle. Distance ranges are measured by means of radar, range finders, or visually with a sextant. In small crafts, ranges can also be determined by using binoculars with a mil scale—measuring the angular height (or width) of an object of known size and using the formula (distance = height in yards × 1000/mil scale points). This procedure (albeit somewhat less precise) is also used with the sextant; it is simply modified for the equipment available on a small boat. This type of range when plotted on charts as a range circle or arc is useful for determining distance off and visible ranges of navaids. Ranges are particularly useful in determining an estimated position (EP) when combined with a bearing to the ranged object.

5-31. **Speed** is the rate measured in knots that a boat travels through the water. A knot is a unit of speed equal to 1 nautical mph. A nautical mile is 2,025.4 yards (2,000 yards for rough calculations over short distances) or 1 minute of latitude. External forces (for example, wind or current) acting on the boat cause the difference between the estimated average speed and the actual average speed.

5-32. **Speed made good (SMG)** is the vessel's speed over the surface of the earth. It differs from the vessel's speed through the water by the influence of any currents acting on the vessel. The effect of any currents is calculated by constructing a vector diagram. This data is then used to determine how the current influences the vessel's speed, which is sometimes called speed over ground (SOG).

5-33. **Speed of advance (SOA)** is the average speed in knots that must be maintained to arrive at a destination at a preplanned time. The rounded speed in knots is plotted on the intended track.

5-34. **Track** is the rhumb line or lines describing the path of a boat actually made good relative to the earth (sometimes referred to as course over ground [COG]). The direction may be designated true or magnetic.

5-35. **Intended track (ITR)** is the anticipated path of a boat relative to the earth. The ITR is plotted during mission planning as part of course determination.

5-36. **Set** is the direction toward which a current is flowing, expressed in degrees true.

5-37. **Drift** is the speed of a current, usually stated in knots.

5-38. **Course made good (CMG)** is the actual track of the boat over the ground. It is the resultant direction of movements from one point to another.

5-39. **Estimated current** is a prediction derived by the use of publications. It is also used for planning.

5-40. **Actual current** is determined by measuring the displacement of a boat from a DR position to a fix.

5-41. **Current triangle** is a graphic vector diagram with one side representing intended track, another the set and drift of the current, and the third the course to steer (CTS). It is the heading to be taken to cause the boat to actually follow the intended track.

5-42. **Rendezvous point (RV)** is the linkup point at sea.

5-43. **Beach landing site** is the area designated on shore where the boat is intended to land.

5-44. **Insert point (IP)** is where the mother ship or intermediate boat launches the CRRC or kayaks.

BASIC NAVIGATION EQUIPMENT

5-45. In determining position and safely conducting a boat from one position to another, the navigator uses a variety of piloting instruments. The navigator must be skilled in using these instruments and experienced at interpreting the information obtained from them. Piloting instruments must provide considerable accuracy.

5-46. One of the best-known navigational instruments is the magnetic compass, which is used for the measurement of direction. Aside from the compass, piloting equipment falls under the categories discussed below.

5-47. Most of these instruments are readily available at battalion or group level as components of the diving equipment set.

BEARING-TAKING DEVICES

5-48. **Compass**. The magnetic boat compass is used to reference direction for accurate steering over a long track. It is the most important tool for quickly determining a boat's heading relative to the direction of magnetic north. A compass can also be incorporated into a navigation console that may include a knotmeter and some type of illumination system. A compass should be hard-mounted parallel to the centerline of the boat and have a light system for navigation in low-visibility conditions. The glow should be shielded from the view of all but the coxswain. Chemlights are the preferred method of illuminating the compass because of the potential problems with electrical systems in small craft.

5-49. The compass gives a constant report on the boat's heading. Users must make corrections for deviation and variance. A compass may also be used as a sighting instrument to determine bearings. A mark, called a "lubber line," is fixed to the inner surface of the compass housing. Similar marks, called 90-degree lubber lines, are usually mounted at 90-degree intervals around the compass card. The navigator can use these intervals to determine when an object is bearing directly abeam or astern. Centered on the compass card is a pin (longer than the lubber line pins) that enables the navigator to determine a position by taking bearings on visible objects.

5-50. **Hand-Bearing Compass**. The hand-bearing compass is a hand-held, battery-powered (illuminated) compass that has transparent forward and rear sight vanes with yellow cursor lines. The navigator uses this compass to determine relative bearings to navigational aids. It can also be an invaluable aid to piloting. Users must correct for the boat's heading by cross-referencing the bearing obtained from the hand compass with the boat's primary compass. A lensatic compass can be substituted if a hand-bearing compass is not available.

SPEED-MEASURING DEVICES

5-51. **Knotmeters**. These are speedometers for boats. They are usually incorporated into a navigation console that will also include the primary magnetic compass and some type of illumination system (preferably chemlight). The navigator can use either of the following knotmeters to accurately measure the speed of a small boat.

5-52. The *impeller-type knotmeter* measures speed by the use of an impeller (a rotating paddlewheel or propeller) mounted underneath or behind the boat. The knotmeter measures the boat's speed by counting the impeller's revolutions as the boat moves through the water. This measurement can be made with a direct mechanical connection to the gauge or indirectly using optical or magnetic sensors. Some systems may require a through-hull penetration.

5-53. The *pitot tube-type knotmeter* measures speed using an open-ended tube mounted to the stern or underneath the boat. The pitot tube is attached to the knotmeter at one end and submerged in the boat's slipstream at the other end. As the boat moves through the water, the open end of the tube creates a venturi effect, and draws a vacuum relative to the boat's speed that registers on the knotmeter as indicated speed.

5-54. Of the two types, the impeller is more accurate than the pitot tube. However, it is also at greater risk of being damaged, especially when beaching the boat. This risk increases significantly in a surf zone. Pitot tubes are mechanically simpler but are not as accurate as impellers. The tube is prone to being blocked by sand, debris, and algae. Damage from beaching is less likely to render the pitot tube useless, provided the mount is not destroyed and the navigator checks for blockages.

5-55. **Speed Wand (Tube)**. The speed wand measures speed through the water. It is a hollow, handheld tube with graduated markings that designate boat speed. Speed tubes are available in two types (speed ranges) 1.0 to 7 knots and 2.5 to 35 knots. Boat speed is measured by testing the pressure of the water mass against the moving tube. To use the speed wand, the navigator holds the large end and submerges the small end into the water with the inlet hole facing in the direction of travel. He lifts it out after 4 or 5 seconds (the metal ball will trap a specific volume of water in the tube). Speed is determined by comparing the trapped water level with the graduated lines on the tube. The navigator can then read the miles per hour (mph) and translate it into knots from the top of the tube.

5-56. **Stopwatch or Timepiece**. An accurate, reliable timepiece for clocking transit times between two points or at specified speeds is essential. A stopwatch or navigational timer that can be started and stopped at will is very useful. The navigator can use it for D/ST calculations when running a speed check. He can also use it to identify the lighted period or interval of a navigational aid, such as a flashing light. A waterproof digital watch works well for this requirement. A handheld stopwatch (NSN 6645-01-106-4302, PN: TM0016, CAGE: 52870) is available as part of the diving equipment set.

NOTE

Most GPS receivers are capable of showing "speed made good" or speed over ground. This function is a byproduct of the continuous position update (fix) available from the GPS. It is most useful for projecting time of transit and fuel consumption when the boat's indicated (knotmeter) speed is being affected by the set and drift of an unknown current.

NOTE

A motorized boat's speed may also be closely estimated by premarking throttle settings. This method is known as a timed-distance run and consists of noting the time needed to cover a known distance at different throttle settings. For this technique to be accurate, it is essential that the timed-run duplicate mission requirements or boat configuration and sea state conditions as closely as possible.

DEPTH-MEASURING DEVICES

5-57. **Hand-Held Lead Line**. This is a line, graduated with attached marks and fastened to a sounding lead, used for determining the depth of water when making soundings by hand. The leadsman takes a sounding from the bow of the boat by casting the lead (sounding weight) forward, allowing it to sink as the boat passes over the site. He then reads the graduated marking as the line comes taut. The leadsman usually uses the lead line in depths of less than 25 fathoms. An improvised lead line is most commonly used by swimmers to determine the bottom profile when conducting hydrographic surveys.

5-58. **Type Fathometer or Echo Sounder**. The diver-held, sonar system (NSN 4220-01-439-8217, PN: DS-1, CAGE: 61257) is available as part of the diving equipment set. This is a handheld (flashlight-sized), waterproof sonar system designed to measure depth or distance to submerged objects.

PLOTTING INSTRUMENTS

5-59. Pencils. The most basic of plotting instruments is the pencil, preferably a quality mechanical pencil with a 0.5 mm lead. During the mission-planning phase, it is best to use a fine-line mechanical pencil to maintain accuracy. As an alternative, the planner can use a No. 2 or No. 3 pencil, sharpening it regularly. He should keep all lines short, and print legibly and lightly for easy erasure. Art gum erasers are normally used for erasure since art gum is less destructive to chart surfaces than India red rubber erasers. Again, the planner should keep his pencils sharp; a dull pencil can cause considerable error in plotting a course due to the width of the lead. A grease pencil will be necessary during the transit for marking on the PBC plotter, chart case, or acetated chart.

5-60. **Navigation Set.** There are two navigation sets available in the diving equipment set. The sets are complimentary and their components are designed to be used interchangeably. The navigator can use either of the following:

- NSN 6605-01-363-6346, PN: 00331, CAGE: 0CJM9 consists of an instruction book and the following parts:
  - A sextant.
  - An artificial horizon (for training with sextant).
  - A parallel rule.
  - A time-speed-distance computer (nautical slide rule).
  - A three-arm protractor.
  - Dividers.
- NSN 6605-01-362-6327, PN: 00792, CAGE: 0CJM9 consists of an instruction book and the following parts:
  - A one-arm protractor.
  - A course plotter.
  - A protractor triangle.
  - A parallel rule.
  - Professional dividers.
  - A pencil.

5-61. **Divider/Drafting Compass.** Dividers are two hinged legs with pointed ends. They are used to measure distance on a chart. The drafting compass is an instrument similar to dividers. However, one leg has a pencil attached. The planner uses this tool for swinging arcs or circles when plotting coordinates and marking arcs of distance on the chart.

5-62. **Flat Divider.** This improvised scale is usually constructed by transferring distance increments (a latitude scale) from the chart being used onto a tongue depressor. The planner uses it to measure distances on laminated charts and plotting boards.

5-63. **Nautical Slide Rule**. A navigator uses the nautical slide rule to determine speed, time, and distance problems. Using the slide rule provides greater speed and less chance of error than multiplication and division, especially during open boat transits at night. There are several makes of nautical slide rules, but all operate on the same basic principle. The nautical slide rule has three clearly labeled scales: speed, time, and distance. By setting any two of the values on the opposite scales, the third is read from the appropriate index. More specifically, it consists of two dials on a base plate. These dials will turn together or independently. A nautical slide rule (NSN 6605-00-391-1110, PN: S2407-533638, CAGE: 80064) is available as part of the diving equipment set.

5-64. **Plotting Board.** The position, bearing, course (PBC) plotting board is a precision navigation instrument designed to accommodate small-boat navigation (Figure 5-1). The plotting board is a flat plastic board with an overlay containing a rotating wheel and a variation offset device that serves as a mount for the nautical chart. It enables the navigator to quickly convert bearings to line of position (LOP). The plotting board permits instant navigation in true or magnetic direction without protractors or parallel rules.

5-65. To set up the plotter, the planner places an appropriately sized map (folded or cut) on the plotter's base sheet with the map's longitude lines as nearly vertical as possible. He reassembles the rest of the plotter on top of the map and snaps or clips the assembly together. He orients the plotter to the map by turning the plotter's red grid to true north on the underlying map (he aligns a meridian of longitude on the map with the red lines on the plotter). To obtain magnetic variation (the preferred method), he then determines local variation and sets it by rotating the plotter's compass rose (adjustable azimuth ring) until the correct number of degrees of variation line up with the index line, and locks it in place with the setscrew.

5-66. A planner can use the plotter to obtain LOP and fixes by taking bearings of visible navaids with binoculars (integrated compass) or hand-bearing compasses. He can plot these magnetic bearings by turning the red pointer to

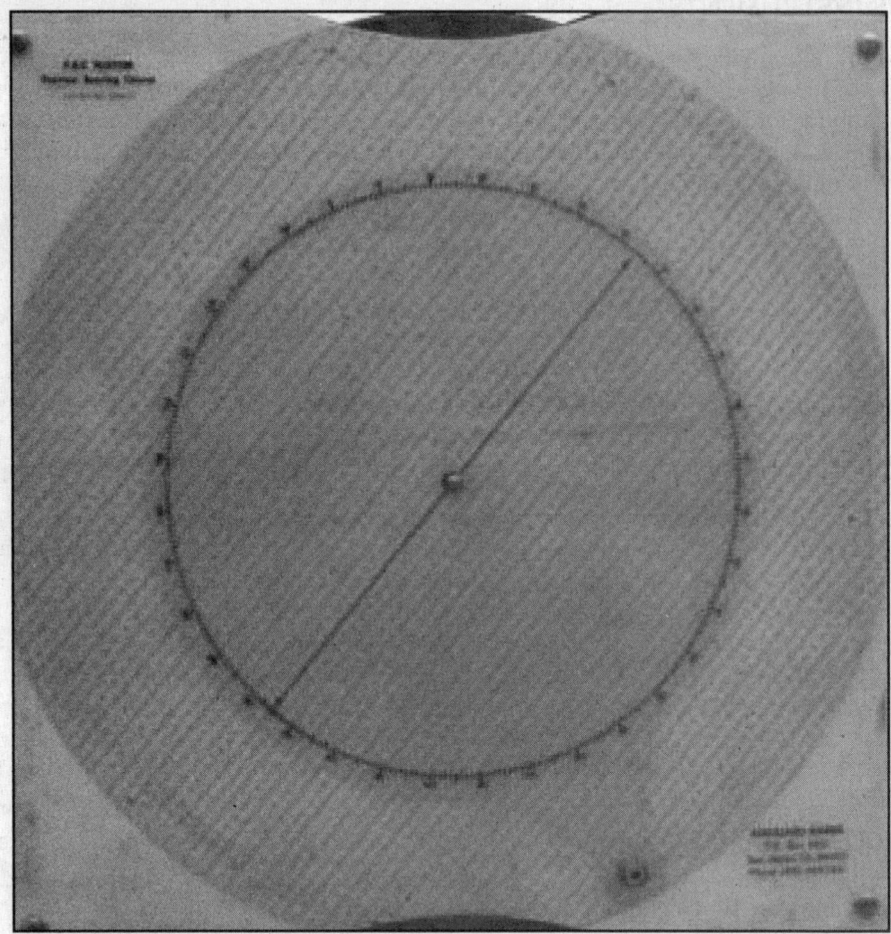

Figure 5-1. Plotting board

the measured bearing (it is not necessary to calculate back azimuths as in resection). He then traces a grease pencil line parallel to the red lines starting at the navaid and extending **backward** through his probable position. He repeats this process with another navaid or does a running fix using the original navaid. If one of the red lines does not fall directly on top of both the start and finish points, he will have to interpolate. The planner simply rotates the dial until the red line is equidistant from (and on the same side of) the desired points. The intersection of the two LOPs represents a fix. His next course from any fix is determined by turning the red pointer so that the red parallel line connects (interpolates) both his position and his intended destination.

5-67. A plotting board, coordinate converter (NSN 5895-01-362-6329, PN: S10154, CAGE: 0H9W2) is available as part of the diving equipment set. It is not initially issued as a component of the SKO; however, it may be requisitioned "as required" when authorized by the commanding officer. (The PBC plotting board is not currently in commercial production. Detachment members will have to search aggressively to find one.)

5-68. **Parallel Rules.** These are simple devices for plotting direction. The rules consist of two parallel bars with parallel cross braces of equal length, which form equal opposite angles. The rules are laid on the compass rose (direction reference of a chart) with the leading edge aligning the center of the rose and the desired direction on the periphery of the rose. Holding first one bar and moving the second, then holding the second and moving the first, parallel motion is ensured. Firm pressure is required on one leg of the ruler while the other is being moved to prevent them from slipping off course. Lines representing direction may be plotted as desired on the chart. The primary use of the rulers is to transfer the direction of the boat's course line to the compass rose and vice versa.

MISCELLANEOUS INSTRUMENTS

5-69. **Binoculars.** High quality waterproof binoculars are extremely useful in waterborne operations. 7 × 50 (magnification × diameter of the objective lens) has been found to be the best compromise between light-gathering ability, magnification, and stability of the visual image. Some binoculars are equipped with an illuminated magnetic compass and a mil scale calibrated at 10 mils per index mark. These can be used to determine a magnetic bearing, measure the height/breadth, or determine range or height of any object.

> **NOTE**
> Distance = Height in Yards × 1000/Mil Scale Points

5-70. **Radar Reflector**. This type of reflector is used for linkup at sea with a mother craft. Small rubber boats generally have no discernable signal or signature in the water. By using the reflector on a telescopic pole, it will aid the mother craft in locating its position and assist in guiding the craft to the linkup point.

5-71. Additional tools and expendable supplies of value to the navigator include:

- Grease pencils (preferably mechanical).
- Masking tape.
- Acetate roll (self-stick).
- Binder clips.

RECOMMENDED NAVIGATION EQUIPMENT

5-72. To assist in mission planning and execution, the navigation tools listed below and shown in Figure 5-2 are recommended. Additional tools may be procured and used based on the navigator's personal preferences.

- A–Binoculars (mil scale reticule, integral compass).
- B–H and-bearing compass (hockey puck).
- C–Stop watch.
- D–Parallel rule.
- E–Divider.
- F–Nautical slide rule.
- G–Compass.
- H–Depth finder.
- I–Pencil.
- J–3-legged protractor.

DEAD RECKONING

5-73. The small boat team, given the required resources, must be able to plan and execute the navigation required to conduct an accurate beach landing or rendezvous at sea at the appointed time after a minimum transit of 20 nautical miles. Ideally, the team meets this requirement using a combination of all of the tools and techniques available to it. Small-craft navigation will frequently be centered on the use of a GPS. However, because no single system is fail-safe, DR and piloting navigation skills are essential to back up the GPS. DR enables the navigator to determine a boat's position at sea, any time, by advancing the last known position using speed, time, and distance computations. The navigator also uses DR to determine an intended course during premission planning.

5-74. Dead reckoning is assessing something dead in the water (a previously fixed position) and hence applying it to courses and speeds through the water. The navigator always starts from a known position and does not consider the effects of current in determining a DR position. (Speed over water or speed made good is when the combined effects of all the forces acting on the boat are taken into account.) Due to leeway caused by wind, inaccurate

Figure 5-2. Navigation tools

allowances for compass error, imperfect steering, or error in measuring speed, the actual motion through the water is seldom determined with complete accuracy. Because of this leeway, detachments must remember that a DR position is only an approximate position. It must be corrected (with piloting or electronic input) as the opportunity presents itself.

MEASUREMENTS

5-75. Navigators keep their DR by plotting directly on the chart, drawing lines to represent the direction and distance of travel, and indicating DR positions and estimated positions from time to time. The key elements of DR are discussed below.

Direction

5-76. Magnetic courses are used to determine a DR position. Direction is the relationship of a point (known as the reference point) to another point. Direction, generally referred to as bearing, is measured in degrees from 000 through 360. The usual reference point is 000 degrees. The relationships between the reference points and reference directions are listed below:

- Measurement is always done from the closest compass rose to the individual's position. Compass roses for both true and magnetic directions may be given, but they must be labeled magnetic or true.
- The plotting board is a useful alternative to the compass rose. It can be oriented to any reference direction and can account for local variation, thereby enabling the navigator to always plot true or magnetic direction.

Distance

5-77. The distances run are obtained by multiplying a boat's speed in knots by an anticipated time or an accomplished time (D = S × T). Once the distance run has been calculated, it must be transferred to the chart. The length of a line on a chart is usually measured in NMs to the nearest 0.1 mile. For this reason, navigators should use the latitude scale on a chart (1 minute of latitude = 1 NM). Navigators measure distance by marking it off with dividers and comparing the span of the dividers to the chart's scale or the closest latitude line. When the distance to be measured is greater than the span of the dividers, the dividers can be set at a minute or number of minutes of latitude from the scale and then "stepped off" between the points to be measured. The last span, if not equal to that setting on the dividers, must be measured separately. To do this, the navigator then steps the dividers once more, closing them to fit the distance. He measures this distance on the scale and adds it to the sum of the other measurements. He should use the latitude scale nearest the middle of the line to be measured. (The longitude scale is never used for measuring distance.) To measure short distances on a chart, the dividers can be opened to a span of a given distance, then compared to the NM or yard scale.

Time

5-78. Time is usually expressed in four figures denoting the 24-hour clock basis. When using the D = S × T formula, most individuals will find it easier to calculate times if they convert hours and minutes to straight minutes before they perform any calculations. A time expressed in decimal form may be converted to minutes by multiplying the decimal time by 60. Time expressed in minutes may be converted into decimal form by dividing the minutes by 60.

5-79. Besides providing a means for continuously establishing an approximate position, DR also has key applications in—

- Determining the availability of electronic aids to navigation.
- Predicting times of making landfall or sighting lights.
- Estimating time of arrival.
- Evaluating the reliability and accuracy of position-determining information.

5-80. As previously discussed, the navigator cannot totally rely upon electronic systems and, even if they are available, he must still be able to navigate to the intended destination from a known (fixed) location. In DR, course and speed are generally computed without allowance for wind or current. The necessary components of DR are—

- *Course.* A course must be known and an exact heading maintained.
- *Speed.* The boat must maintain a consistent speed that is verified on a regular basis.
- *Distance.* The navigator must preplan the course distance (always plotted in NMs) that he intends to travel.
- *Time.* Total time must be kept from each fixed position. DR will be used in planning the intended course before infiltration and then used to locate the CRRC's geographic position at sea, using speed, time, and distance. During the mission-planning phase, the navigator will plot an intended DR track. Using all of the information available, he will determine the potential BLS and IP. He will then plot a minimum-risk route between the IP and BLS, taking into account hazards to navigation and potential enemy threats. Once the detachment is inserted and underway, the navigator will track the detachment's position from the IP, as confirmed by the navigator of the delivery craft. The detachment is dependent on DR for its approximate position along the ITR until it reaches a point where navaids are available for determining LOPs.

COMPUTATIONS

5-81. Calculating time, distance, and speed requires a single basic mathematical formula. An easy way to remember how the formula works is to use the phrase "D street" or in mathematical terms, D/ST.

5-82. In the course of piloting the boat, both coxswain and crew members will make numerous calculations for time (minutes), speed (knots), and distance (NMs). For these computations, speed is expressed to the nearest tenth of a knot, distance to the nearest tenth of a NM, and time to the nearest minute. There are three basic equations for speed, time, and distance. In each case, two elements are known and used to find the third, which is unknown. When solving problems involving time, individuals should change time into hours and tenths of an hour. For example, 1:15 minutes = 1.25 tenths. Figure 5-3 shows the basic equations for making the necessary calculations.

T (time) = $\frac{60 \times D}{S}$	S (speed) = $\frac{60 \times D}{T}$	D (distance) = $\frac{S \times T}{60}$

Figure 5-3. Basic equations

> **NOTE**
> The nautical slide rule is made to solve speed, time, and distance problems. It provides greater speed and less chance of error than multiplication and division, especially during open boat transits at night. The slide rule has three clearly labeled scales—one each for speed, time, and distance. By setting any two of the values on the opposite scales, the third is read from the appropriate index. Figure 5-4 provides examples of using the D/ST formula.

NAVIGATION PLANNING

5-83. There are many factors to consider during the initial planning phase for insertion and extraction. Because time is top priority, the first step is to have all reference material at hand, to include pilot charts, sailing directions, light lists, and the latest nautical chart editions for the area (updated from the Summary of Corrections and the Notice to Mariners).

5-84. The navigator should conduct liaison with the following staff sections, agencies, and personnel for information:

- *S2/G2.* The navigator should obtain weather and enemy situation information particular to the type of waterborne operation being conducted.
- *Weather.* The navigator should determine tide, current, wind, visibility due to natural phenomenon, sea state, wave height, and astronomical data.
- *Enemy Situation.* The navigator should obtain the visual and auditory threshold of detection; radar, satellite and hydrophone detection capabilities; and the effects of sea state and weather upon these thresholds. He should determine particular areas to avoid due to patrol boats, weapons, or natural hazards.
- *Insert/RVBoat.* The navigator should coordinate with the craft's master and quartermaster to determine boat capabilities; for example, speed, ETD from ship, ETA to IP, and methods of fixing insert position. He should consult the ship's quartermaster for any additional navigational and landing area information.

5-85. After the navigator collects all the information possible, he should make a detailed chart or map for navaids that will assist in positioning himself once he is in piloting waters. Some navaids to look for are—

- Land forms (profiles).
- Towers.
- Lights.
- Buoys.
- Horns.

5-86. The navigation plan is a point-by-point detailing of the ITR. It should include all of the variables that could affect navigating the boat. The plan should include, but not be limited to, the following:

- Intended track (complete with labels).
- Current vector (included in ITR).
- Magnetic bearings to navaids.
- Range rings of luminous distances of lights.
- Geographic distance rings of other navaids.
- Danger bearings for course restrictions and arcs of detection.

5-87. When preparing the navigation plan, the navigator should not depend upon navaids to fix his position. Navaids are not always as depicted on the charts. They are continuously updated to reflect changes in hydrography and traffic patterns. Lights (lighthouses, range markers, and lighted buoys) are subject to being turned off during periods of hostilities. These changes are usually reflected in the Notice to Mariners, Sailing Directions, or other publications for navigators. However, these documents may not be available to the detachment during mission planning.

5-88. The navigator should use tides and currents to his advantage. However, he must also fully understand the effects of tides and their ranges (for example, some places have a 9-meter tidal range).

Determining Distance When Speed and Time Are Known

A person is running at 10 knots. How far will he travel in 20 minutes?

Step 1. $D = \frac{S \times T}{60}$

Step 2. $D = \frac{10 \times 20}{60}$

Step 3. $D = \frac{200}{60} = 3.3$ nautical miles

Determining Distance When Speed and Time Are Known

A person can travel from his station to the shipping channel in 3 hours and 45 minutes moving at a speed of 10 knots. What is the distance to the shipping channel?

Step 1. Use minutes to solve the time, distance, and speed equation. Convert the 3 hours to minutes (3 hours x 60 minutes = 180 minutes). Add the 45 minutes; time equals 225 minutes.

Step 2. Use the distance equation: $D = \frac{S \times T}{60}$

Step 3. Compute information opposite the appropriate letter.

$$D = \frac{10 \text{ knots} \times 225 \text{ minutes}}{60}$$

Step 4. $D = \frac{2{,}250}{60} = 37.5$ nautical miles (nearest tenth)

Determining Speed When Time and Distance Are Known

A person assumes it will take 40 minutes to travel 12 nautical miles. What is his speed?

Step 1. $S = \frac{60 \times D}{T}$

Step 2. $S = \frac{60 \times 12}{40}$

Step 3. $S = \frac{720}{40} = 18$ knots

Figure 5-4. D/ST formula examples

Determining Speed When Time and Distance Are Known

A person's departure time is 2030. The distance to his destination is 30 nautical miles and his wants to arrive at 2400. What is the speed that he must maintain?

Step 1. Find the time interval between 2030 and 2400. Remember to subtract "hours and minutes" from "hours and minutes." Determine the time interval as follows:

23 hours 60 minutes (23 hrs/60 min equals 24 hrs 00 min)
–20 hours 30 minutes
3 hours 30 minutes

Step 2. REMEMBER to use minutes to solve the time, distance, and speed equation. Convert the 3 hours to minutes (3 hours x 60 minutes = 180 minutes). Add the 30 minutes remaining from Step 1. Time (T) is 210 minutes.

Step 3. Write down the speed equation: $S = \frac{60 \times D}{T}$

Step 4. Compute the information in the equation:

$$S = \frac{60 \times 30 \text{ miles}}{210 \text{ minutes}}$$

Step 5. $S = \frac{1{,}800}{210} = 8.6$ knots (nearest tenth)

Determining Time When Speed and Distance Are Known

A person is cruising at 15 knots and has 12 nautical miles to cover before arriving on station. How long will it take before he arrives at his destination?

Step 1. $T = \frac{60 \times D}{T}$ D = 12 miles, S = 15 kn

Step 2. $T = \frac{60 \times 12}{15}$

Step 3. $T = \frac{720}{15}$

Step 4. T = 48 minutes

Figure 5-4. D/ST formula examples (*Continued*)

LAYING THE COURSE

5-89. The navigator must follow specific steps to lay a course. He should—

- Draw a straight line from his departure point to the intended destination. This fix is his course line.
- Consider all navigational aids and other information presented on the chart along the course line.
- Lay one edge of his parallel rules along the course line. Walk the rules to the nearest compass rose on the chart, moving one rule while holding the other in place. He must ensure that the rules do not slip. If they do, the original line of direction will be lost.
- Walk the rules until one edge intersects the small plus (+) that marks the compass rose center. From the inside degree circle, he should read the course where the rule's edge intersects the center of the compass rose in the direction he is heading. This fix is his magnetic course.

PLOTTING AND LABELING COURSE LINES AND POSITIONS

5-90. All lines and points plotted on a chart must be labeled. Figure 5-5 shows the standardized symbols commonly used in marine navigation.

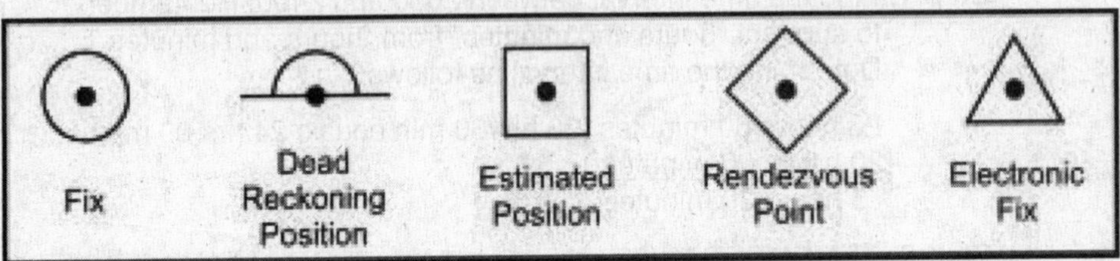

Figure 5-5. Standardized plotting symbols

CONSTRUCTING A DEAD-RECKONING PLOT

5-91. The following steps explain how to construct a DR plot. The navigator should—

- Plot the starting point and label it with A and the starting time.
- Plot the remaining turn points and the finish point, and label them B, C, D, and so on.
- Attach a rhumb line from A to B, B to C, and so on.
- Find the heading in degrees magnetic for each leg of the transit.
- Measure distance of each leg using the latitude scale.
- Place speed of the transit for each leg below the distance for that leg.
- Calculate the time of transit for each of the legs using the D/ST formula.
- Label the arrival time at the beginning of each leg next to the letter designator.
- Calculate the distance between DR positions using the D/ST formula.
- Use the dividers to mark the DR position on the rhumb line. Label the DR positions with the proper symbol and with the time of arrival.
- Plot the DR positions (as nearly possible)—
  - At least every half hour.
  - At the time of every course change.
  - At the time of every speed change.

LABELING A DEAD-RECKONING PLOT

5-92. The DR plot starts with the last known position (usually a fix). The navigator labels a DR plot using the steps below. He should label the—

- DR positions with a two-digit arrival time (minutes).
- First plot of a new hour with a four-digit time.
- Course with a three-digit heading and the letter M (magnetic) above the course line and as close to the departure point for each.
- Departure and arrival time in four digits rounded to the nearest minute. If the time falls exactly on a half minute, he should round to the nearest even minute.
- Distance rounded to the nearest tenth of an NM and placed below the course line as close to the departure point for each leg.
- Speed rounded to the nearest knot and placed below the distance for each leg (Figure 5-6).

5-93. There are various ways to label a DR plot; however, it is important that all involved can readily understand the method the navigator uses.

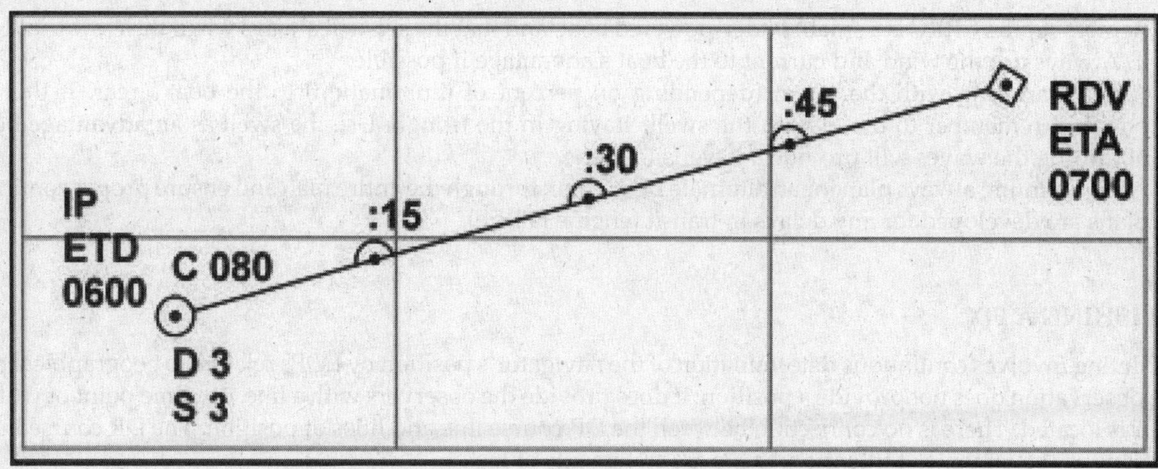

Figure 5-6. Example of labeling a dead-reckoning plot

5-94. After plotting the ITR and the above information, the navigator writes the plan on a chart or plotting board in a noncritical area using the format shown in Table 5-1.

Table 5-1. Example of a navigation plan

Leg	Course (mag)	Distance (NM)	Time/Speed (min/kn)	Bearing to Navaid
IP–B	090	5.0	30/6	lighthouse 290 mag
B–C	171	6.75	40/6	
C–D	085	1.0	10/6	lighthouse 300 mag
D–C	265	1.0	10/6	
C–B	359	6.75	40/6	
B-IP/RDV	270	5.0	30/6	lighthouse 110 mag

5-95. At least two pilot team members should inspect and validate all information. Once inspection is complete and final coordination is made, the navigator cuts the chart to a workable size to fit the plotting board. He also makes sure the portion of chart that remains includes the following features:

- Latitude and longitude bars.
- Logarithmic speed scale.
- Compass rose.

5-96. The last step is to trace the ITR and navigation plan in black, highlight navaids, and laminate the chart front and back.

5-97. To ensure the navigation plan is thorough and complete, the navigator should consider the following planning hints:

- Include all members of the piloting team in planning and have them double-check all computations.
- Be careful and methodical during plotting and inspecting. Remember, one miscalculation will throw all of the plans awry.
- Check with every weather service and cross-reference their forecasts on a constant basis until departure.

- Remember the CRRC is a small, under-powered boat, and that the sea will always win if the crew tries to fight it. Always use the wind and current to the boat's advantage if possible.
- Avoid transiting with the moon (depending on percent of illumination) to the boat's rear. If this is not possible, remember to travel with the swell, staying in the trough. Use the swell as an advantage because not riding the waves will provide a lower silhouette.
- At a minimum, always plan for an alternate BLS. Think through the entire plan and ensure proper contingency plans are developed for any delays in transit (engine failure).

ESTABLISHING A FIX

5-98. Piloting involves continuous determination of the navigator's position by LOPs relative to geographical points. A single observation does not provide a position; it does provide the observers with a line, on some point of which the navigator is located. There is no connection between the DR course line and lines of position. The DR course line and DR positions are statements of intention; LOPs are statements of fact.

5-99. The simplest and most accurate LOP is determined by observing a range. If two fixed objects of known position appear to the observer to be in line, then at that instant, the boat's location is somewhere on the line passing through the objects.

5-100. It is not always possible to find two fixed objects in line at the time the navigator wishes to make an observation. Consequently, the LOP is usually obtained by plotting a bearing on a chart. The observer sights his hand-bearing compass or military binoculars (with integral compass) toward a fixed, known object and thus determines the direction of the LOS to the object. This point is called the bearing of the object. There are an infinite number of possible positions on any single LOP. To fix the boat's position, the navigator must therefore plot at least two LOPs that intersect (no more than three), preferably at angles as near to 90 degrees as possible. This method is exactly like a resection in land navigation; however, the process is easier due to the functions of the plotting board. The ideal angle is 90 degrees. If the angle is small, a slight error in measuring or plotting either line results in a large error in position. Fixes less than 30 degrees should be regarded with caution. Closer navaids are preferable to those of considerable distance because the linear (distance) error resulting from an angular error increases with distance.

NOTE

Rule of sixty—the offset of the plotted bearing line from the observer's actual position is 1/6th the distance to the object observed for each degree of error. Therefore, a 1-degree error represents about 100 feet at a 1-mile distance and about 1,000 feet at 10 miles distance.

5-101. **Running Fix.** When the navigator cannot obtain two simultaneous observations, he must resort to a running fix. This point results by using two LOPs that are obtained by observations at different times. To plot a running fix, the navigator must make allowance for the exact time elapsed between the first observation and the second. He then advances the earlier LOP to the time of the second observation. The navigator assumes that, for the limited period between observations, the ship makes good via the ground a definite distance in a definite direction. He then plots this point by moving the earlier LOP, parallel to itself, to this advanced position. The new advanced line now represents the possible positions of the ship at the time of the second observation. A new DR is started from a running fix.

5-102. **Danger Bearing.** The navigator uses this factor to keep his boat clear of an outlying danger area, zone of detection, or other threats. He establishes a danger bearing between two fixed objects or a fixed object and a projected zone of danger.

5-103. If a distance to an object is known, the boat must lie somewhere on the perimeter of a circle centered on the object, with the known distance as the radius. This distance is called a distance circle of position. Distance may be determined by binoculars and mil scale for the purpose of CRRC navigation (formula follows), or by observation of a precalculated threshold (range rings). Plotting concentric circles of position of various distances before entering piloting waters is recommended, rather than attempting computation while underway (as discussed in aids to navigation).

$$\textbf{D} = \text{Height in Yds} \times 1000/\text{Mil Scale Points}$$

$$\textbf{MSP} = \text{Yds} \times 1000/\text{Distance}$$

CURRENT SAILING

5-104. Current sailing is the art of determining course and speed through the water, making due allowance for the effect of a predicted or estimated current, so that, upon the completion of travel, the ITR and the actual track will coincide. Current sailing may also include the determination of an existing current as measured by the displacement of the boat from its ITR. In essence, current sailing is applying the best information to the ITR to determine the course and speed to steer.

5-105. The difference between the DR position and an accurate fix is the result of the action of various forces on a boat, plus any errors introduced when laying out course and speed. A boat is set off course by wind and current. The distance it is displaced results from the combination of set and drift, as well as steering error. The results can be disastrous if not corrected.

5-106. The direction in which the current is moving, the direction a boat is moved by current and winds, or the combination of both is called set. When referring to the boat's movement, the term commonly used is leeway. This movement is the leeward (downwind or down current) motion of a boat caused by wind and sea action. The direction of set is usually expressed in degrees (true). The speed of the current and the speed at which a boat is being set is called drift, which is expressed in knots.

5-107. As previously discussed, a DR position represents the actual position of a boat only if the direction is accurate, the speed is accurate, and if no external forces have acted upon the craft. In navigation, many factors can cause a boat to depart from its intended course. However, all of the currents that can affect a CRRC can be preplanned or estimated from several publications. Table 5-2 describes types and effects of currents that can cause navigational error and how to preplan for them.

Table 5-2. Current types, effects, and corrections for navigational errors

Type	Effect	Estimating Correction
Ocean Current	Is a well-defined current that extends over a considerable ocean area.	Is best planned for from the Pilot Chart, Coast Pilot, and Sailing Directions. If planning onboard a ship, ocean current updates are usually available from the quartermasters and navigators onboard.
Tidal Current	Is caused by tidal action. Effect is often seen in harbors or estuaries. Most often occurs along the coastline.	Is computed from the tidal current tables. Tidal current is not computed with ocean current.
Wind Current	Is limited to an area affected by a strong wind blowing 12 hours or more. The force of the earth's rotation will cause the current to set to the right the Northern Hemisphere and to the left in the Southern Hemisphere.	Is most often described in the Coast Pilot, Pilot Chart, and the bimonthly Mariners Weather Log. Local air or naval weather stations will also issue updated information about wind and weather.
Murphy's Current	Is the displacement of the boat from the ITR caused by human errors such as inaccurate steering, unknown compass error, DR errors (speed determination, time calculation), and sudden weather changes.	Unfortunately, this current can only be corrected while at sea. Even so, navigators should study all available navaids since no one publication is intended to be used alone. The more information the navigator has about the AO and the average conditions encountered, the better he can adjust his ITR.

5-108. The combined effects of these factors can cause a boat to depart from its intended course. Hence, the term **current** has two meanings—the horizontal movement of water due to ocean and wind currents, or the combined effect of all errors listed above.

5-109. There are also terms that navigators and crew members use that further explain current sailing and enable each person to thoroughly understand what functions or actions may occur. A clear understanding of the following terms is essential when conducting waterborne operations (Figure 5-7).

CURRENT EFFECTS/VECTOR

5-110. If a navigator can determine the effects of set and drift, a better position can be obtained by applying the correction to the intended track. For example, from point (A) a CRRC is bearing 90 degrees for 10 NM at a speed of advance of 5 knots. Assuming that 90 degrees is steered for 1 hour with a set of 180 degrees and drift of 2 knots, the boat will crab to point D, 2 miles south. To make good his course, the navigator must allow for current and steer to a point 2 miles north (C) at a slightly greater speed to crab to point (B) in 1 hour's time.

5-111. In working problems to correct for set and drift, the navigator must allow for current and compensate for its effect using a vector diagram called a "current triangle." From this diagram, the navigator can find the course and speed his boat will make good when running a given course at a given speed, the course he must steer, and the speed at which he must run to make good a safe, desired course and itinerary. He may solve the set and drift problem by constructing a current vector (or triangle) (Figure 5-8) to provide a graphic solution. He can construct the vector directly on the chart's compass rose, or set up with a protractor. Vector diagrams are most commonly constructed to determine course to steer (estimated current) and course made good (actual current). Information obtained from these vector diagrams will allow the navigator to anticipate course corrections so that he can adhere as closely as possible to his ITR. A discussion of both types of problems follows.

Constructing an Estimated Current Triangle

5-112. The following steps explain how to construct an estimated current triangle (Figure 5-9):

- Plot the intended track (DR plot), complete with labeled information.
- Estimate the set and drift of the current using the applicable publications. Examples of the required publications include Tidal Current Tables, Pilot Charts, and Coast Pilot Sailing Directions.

Term	Definition
Estimated Current	Determined by estimating all the known forces that will contribute to the sum total of current effects in a given area.
Actual Current	Determined by the displacement of the boat from the DR position to a fix. This point can be determined when an accurate position can be obtained once underway. The difference is direction and distance between the fix and the DR position, for the time of the fix establishes the actual current.
Set	The direction toward which the current flows; expressed in degrees true.
Drift	Current velocity expressed in knots.
Estimated Position	The most probable position of a boat determined from all available data when a fix or running fix is unobtainable. The EP includes the effects of any estimated currents.
Current Triangle	A graphic vector diagram in which one side represents set and drift of the current, and the third side represents the track of the craft. If any two sides are known, the third can be determined by measurement.

Figure 5-7. Terms used in current sailing

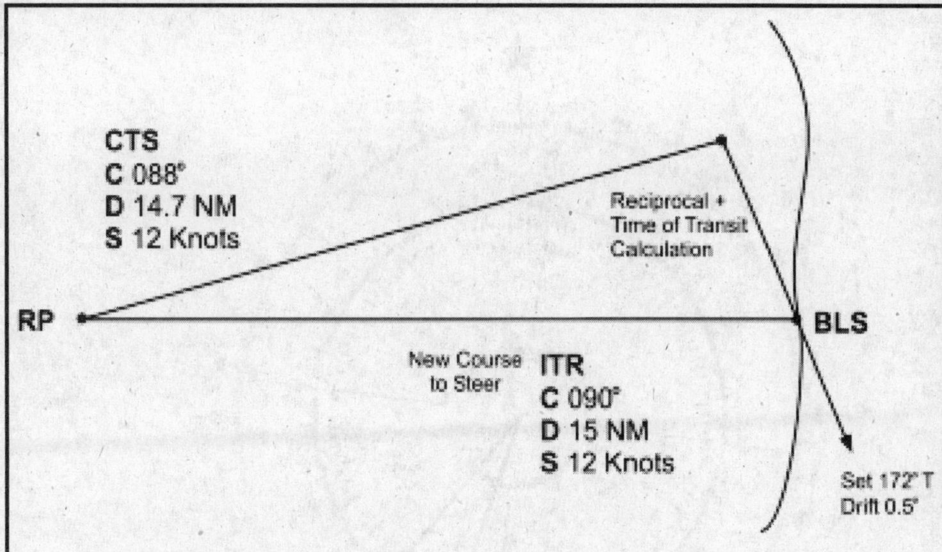

1. The navigator has an intended track of 15 NM, speed to make good of 12 knots, a course to make good of 90 degrees mag, and a time of passage of 1:15 minutes (1.25).
2. From the pilot chart, he determines an anticipated set of 172 degrees and a drift of 0.5 kn.
3. From the BLS, the reciprocal course of 352 degrees T is plotted: 172°T + 180°T.

NOTE: Remember, if the set is less than 180 degrees, add 180; if it is more, subtract 180.

4. Multiply the drift of 0.5 by the time of passage of 1.25: 1.25 x 0.5 = 0.625 (round down to 0.6).

NOTE: A distance of 0.6 NM is plotted on the reciprocal current line.

5. After plotting the current vector, a course to steer of 88 degrees mag is measured, and a distance of 14.7 NM is measured.
6. Time of passage of 1.25 is divided into the vector distance of 14.7 NM.

NOTE: Example of speed is rounded to the tenth place; therefore, the speed remains at 12 knots.

Figure 5-8. Steps required to prepare a vector diagram

- Plot a line parallel to the set of the current, through the arrival point at the end of the leg of the transit. Draw an arrow on this line to indicate the direction of set.
- Label the setline with the three-digit set and the letter T (true) above the line, and the drift below the setline on the downstream side.
- Calculate the distance the drift will move the craft during the time of passage for the leg using the D/ST formula. This indicates the offset necessary to arrive at the intended arrival point.
- Plot a point upstream of (into) the current on the set line from the arrival point equal to the distance the current will move the craft during the transit for that leg.
- Connect a line from the departure point to the point upstream of the arrival point. This is the "course to steer" line. Determine the course to steer (magnetic) with the parallel rules. Erase the old heading (on the intended track line) and replace it with the new "course to steer" heading.

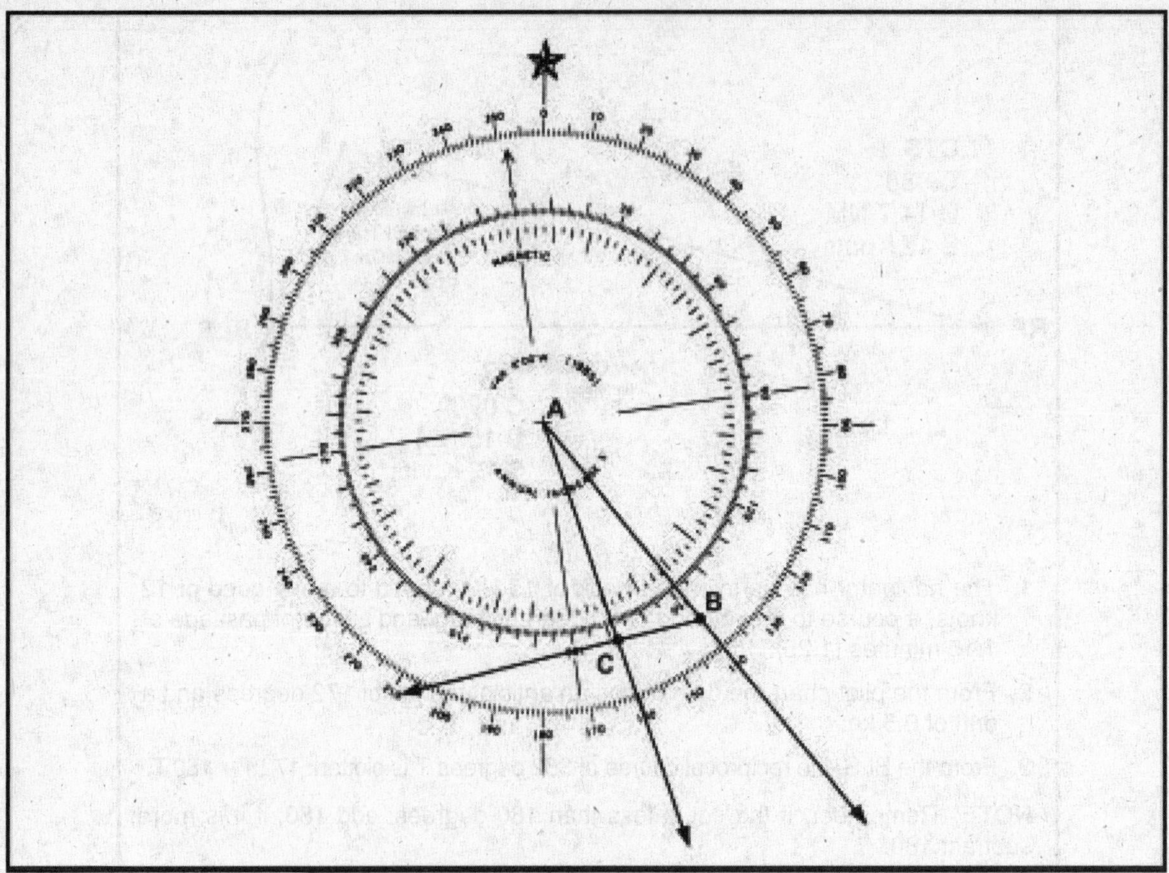

Figure 5-9. Example of an estimated current triangle with labeling

- Using the parallel rule, transfer the DR positions to the course to steer line. Leave the old DR positions in place and place tick marks on the course to steer line labeled with corresponding times.
- Measure the distance of the new course to steer line and use the D/ST formula to determine if the current planning speed will enable the boat to reach the arrival point within the planning period. If not, adjust either the planning speed, starting point, starting time, or the arrival point or time. Mission requirements and proper planning will dictate the best course of action. Adjust one of these variables and relabel the plot with the new information.

> **NOTE**
> All bearings must be annotated on the chart using either true or magnetic. All speeds must be in knots and all times in minutes.

> **NOTE**
> If the navigator adjusts times or distances, his time of passage will have changed and the problem will have to be recomputed to ensure accuracy.

Actual Current

5-113. Upon fixing a boat's position and finding that it does not correspond to the correct DR position on the DR plot, the navigator can compute and compensate for the effects of actual currents and forces being applied to the boat to push the boat off course. In short, he can fix the boat's position and compare his actual position to his preplanned position at any given time.

Constructing an Actual Current Triangle

5-114. The following steps explain how to construct an actual current triangle (Figure 5-10). The navigator—

- Plots the actual position of the craft.
- Draws a line through the actual position of the craft and the intended position. The intended position is along the DR track or the course to steer track if an estimated current triangle is in use.
- Determines the direction in degrees true from the intended position to the actual position using the parallel rules. This path is his set. He draws a line parallel to the set through the arrival point. He places the set above this line on the downstream side of the arrival point.
- Determines the drift using the D/ST formula. He measures the distance the craft drifted (the distance from the craft's actual position to the craft's intended position). The drift is equal to the distance the craft has drifted divided by the time it took to drift that far. He places the value of the drift under the set line at the arrival point on the downstream side.
- Calculates the distance the craft, will drift for the remaining portion of the transit leg using the D/ST formula. Drift is equal to the speed of the current times the time remaining to reach the arrival point.
- Plots a point on the upstream side of the arrival point the same distance that the craft will drift along the set line.
- Draws a line from the craft's actual position to this point. This line is the new course to steer line. He writes the course to steer above the line.
- Calculates the new speed using the D/ST formula. The speed is equal to the distance of the new course to steer line divided by the time remaining in the transit. He writes this value below the new course to steer line.

COMBINED CURRENTS

5-115. The small-craft navigator operating close inshore is likely to encounter multiple currents. The combined effects of all of the currents will have to be calculated to determine their impact on the boat's ITR.

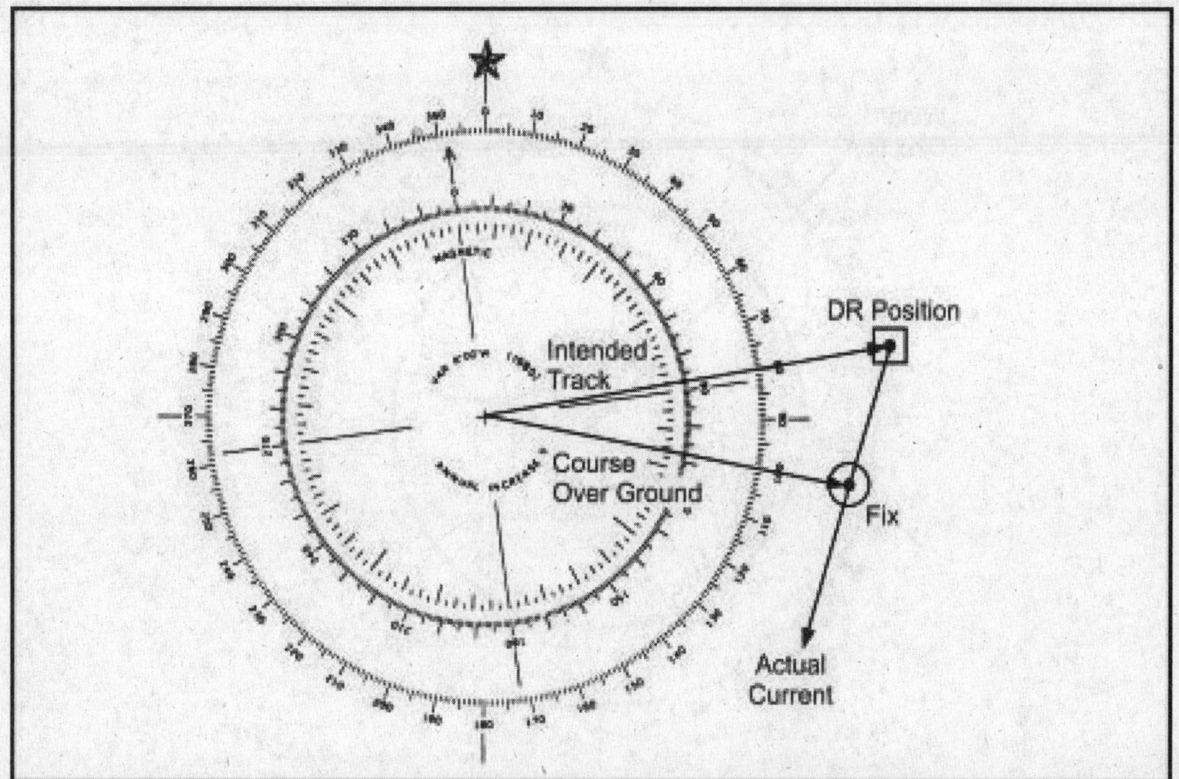

Figure 5-10. Example of actual current triangle with labeling

Currents in the Same Direction

5-116. When two or more currents set in the same direction, it is a simple matter to combine them. The resultant current will have a speed that is equal to the sum of all the currents, and it will set in the same direction. For example, a boat is near the former location of the Sand Key Light at a time when the tidal current is setting 345 degrees with a speed of 0.5 knots, and at the same time a wind of 50 mph is blowing from 150 M. The current that the boat will be subjected to is computed as follows. Since a wind of 50 miles from 150 degrees will give rise to a current setting about 345' with a speed of 0.7 knots, the combined tidal and wind currents will set in the same direction (345 degrees) with a speed of 0.5 + 0.7 = 1.2 knots.

Currents in Opposite Directions

5-117. The combination of currents setting in opposite directions is likewise a simple matter. The speed of the smaller current is subtracted from the speed of the greater current, which gives the speed of the resultant current. The direction of the resultant current is the same as that of the greater current (Figure 5-11).

5-118. As an example, suppose the navigator is required to determine the speed of the current at the former location of the San Francisco Lightship when the tidal current is setting 331 degrees with a speed of 0.5 knots and with a wind of 45 mph blowing from the northwest. The current produced by a wind of 45 mph from northwest would set 151 degrees with a speed of 0.6 knots. Therefore, the tidal and wind currents set in opposite directions, the wind current being the stronger. Hence, the resultant current will set in the direction of the wind current (151 degrees) with a speed of 0.6 knots minus 0.5 knots or 0.1 knots.

Currents in Different Directions

5-119. The combination of two or more currents setting neither in the same nor in opposite directions, while not as simple as in the previous cases, is, nevertheless, not difficult. The best solution is a graphic one (Figure 5-12). The

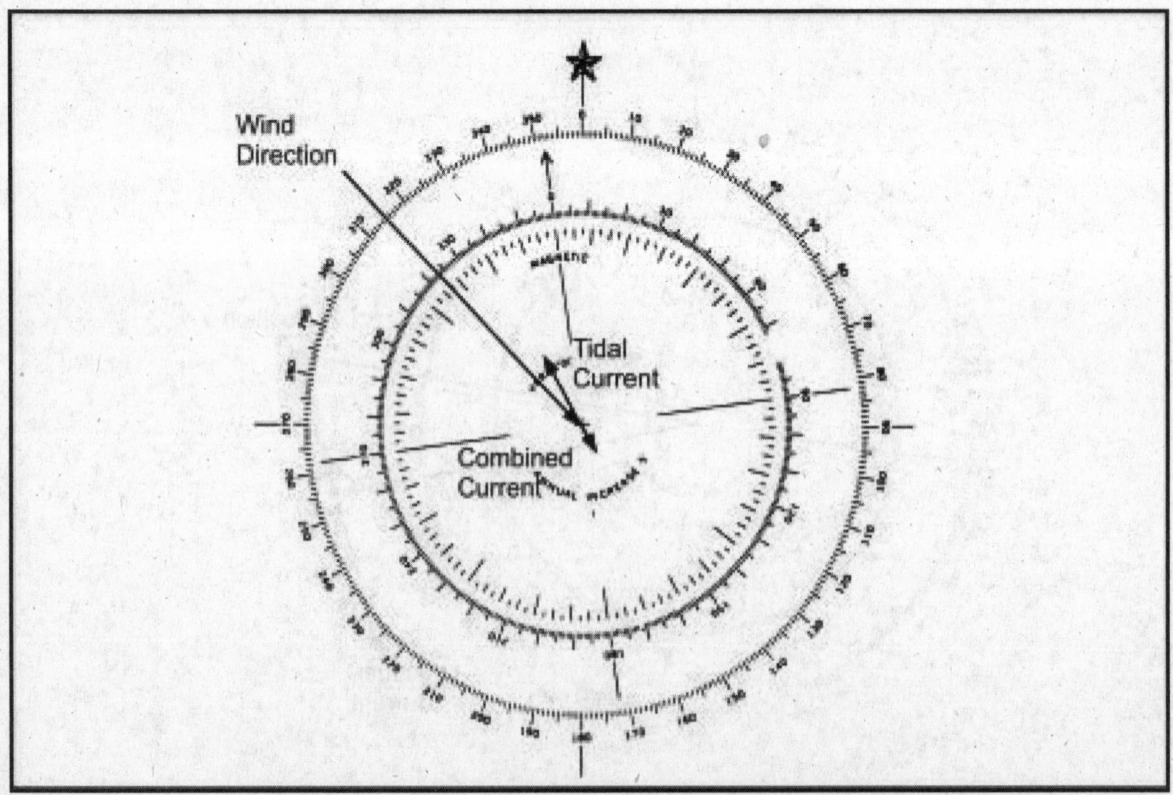

Figure 5-11. Opposing currents

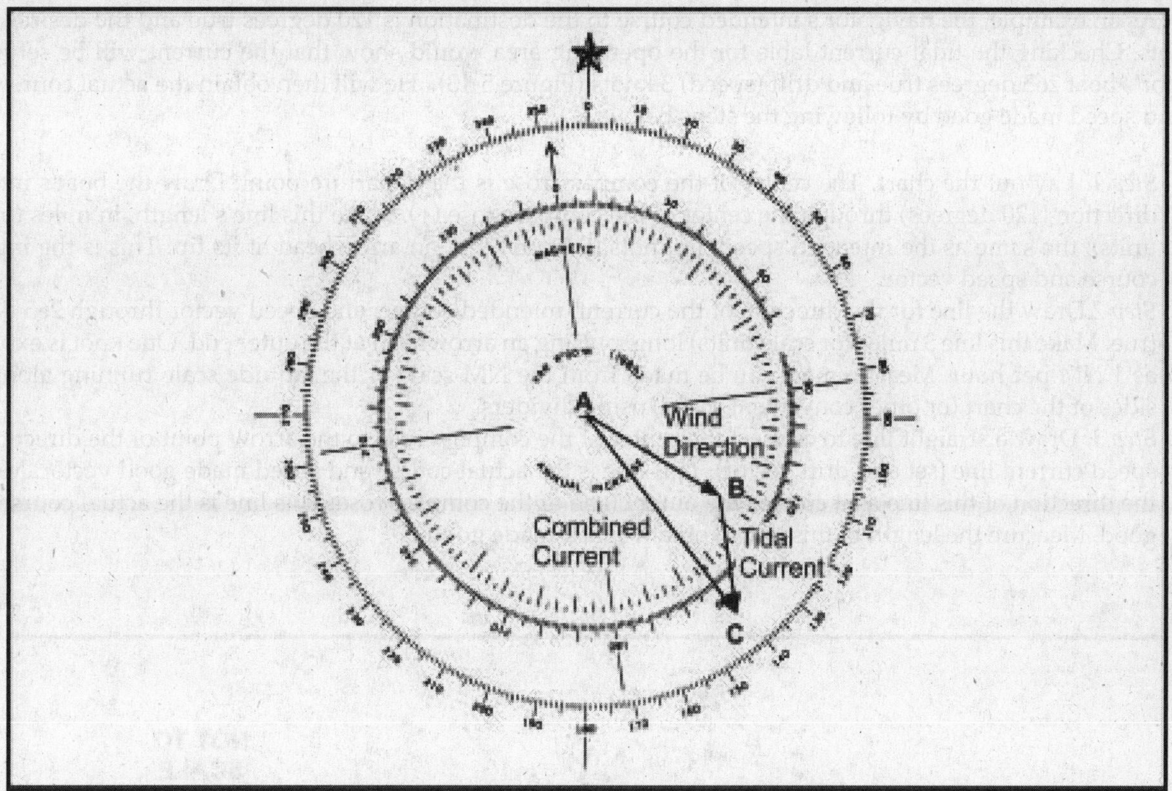

Figure 5-12. Currents in different directions

navigator draws a line from the cross reference of the compass rose in the direction of one of the currents to be combined and whose length represents the speed of the current from the latitude bar scale. From the end of this line, he draws another line in the direction and the length of which represents the other current to be combined. By joining the two lines together (the origin with the end of the second line), the navigator determines the direction and speed of the resultant current.

5-120. As an example, the location of the Smith Shoals Lighthouse at a specified time indicates the tidal current is setting 0.4 knots at 315 degrees with the wind blowing from 273 degrees at 50 mph. The wind current would therefore be 0.9 knots setting at 093 degrees. Using the latitude scale, the navigator measures 0.4 of a NM, draws from point A a line 0.4 NM in the direction of 315 degrees to represent the tidal current. From point B, he then draws a line BC 0.9 NM on a line of 093 degrees to represent the wind current. The line AC represents the resultant current of 0.7 NM in length directed 062 degrees. The resulting current sets 062 degrees with a speed of 0.7 knots.

DETERMINATION OF ACTUAL COURSE AND SPEED MADE GOOD

5-121. This current triangle is a graphic vector diagram in which the direction of the first line drawn from the center of the compass rose indicates the boat's intended direction, course length in miles (or other convenient scale unit on the chart), and speed. The navigator draws a second line down from the end of the intended direction (first line) and along the set (direction) of the current. The length of this line in miles (or in the same units used to draw the intended course line) will be the current's drift (speed) in knots. He draws a third line from the center of the compass rose to the tip of the second line that provides the course the boat is actually making good. Its length in miles (or the units used to draw the first two lines) is the actual speed made good.

5-122. The navigator should show the current direction in degrees relative to true north as noted in the tidal current tables. He should also always plot the current using the compass rose outer circle (true direction).

5-123. As an example, the navigator's intended course to the destination is 120 degrees true and the desired speed is 5 knots. Checking the tidal current table for the operating area would show that the current will be setting the navigator's boat 265 degrees true and drift (speed) 3 knots (Figure 5-13). He will then obtain the actual course made good and speed made good by following the steps below:

- *Step 1.* Lay out the chart. The center of the compass rose is the departure point. Draw the boat's intended direction (120 degrees) through the center of the compass rose (+). Make this line's length, in miles (or scale units), the same as the intended speed, in knots (5 knots). Put an arrowhead at its tip. This is the intended course and speed vector.
- *Step 2.*Draw the line for the direction of the current, intended course, and speed vector through 265 degrees true. Make this line 3 miles (or scale units) long, putting an arrowhead at the outer end. One knot is expressed as 1 NM per hour. Measurement can be made from the NM scale or the latitude scale running along both sides of the chart (or other convenient scale), using dividers.
- *Step 3.* Draw a straight line to connect the center of the compass rose to the arrow point of the direction and speed current line (set and drift vector). This line is the actual course and speed made good vector. Measure the direction of this line as it crosses the outer circle of the compass rose. This line is the actual course made good. Measure the length of this line to obtain speed made good.

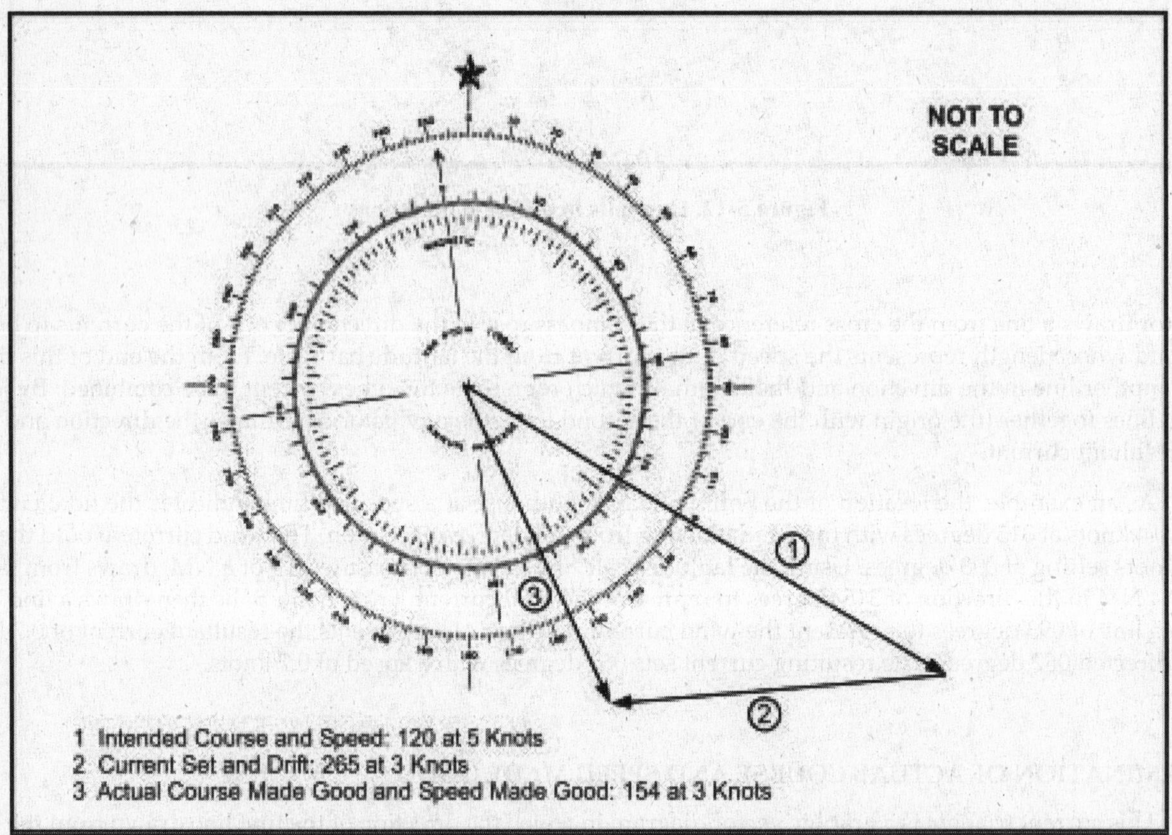

Figure 5-13. Determination of actual course and speed made good

DETERMINATION OF COURSE TO STEER AND SPEED TO RUN FOR ACCOMPLISHING INTENDED COURSE AND SPEED

5-124. This current triangle is a graphic vector diagram in which the navigator once again draws the first line from the center of the compass rose in the direction intended to be run. He draws its length in miles (or scale units) for the speed (knots) intended to be run. This line is the intended course and speed vector. The navigator puts an arrowhead at its end. Next, he lays out the current vector with its set from the center of the compass rose outward, to a length in miles equal to its drift and puts an arrowhead at its tip. Then, he draws the actual course and speed vector from the tip of the current vector to the tip of the intended course and speed vector. He puts an arrowhead at this tip. The length of this line is the actual speed to run. The direction of the line is the actual course to steer (Figure 5-14).

DETERMINATION OF COURSE TO STEER AND ACTUAL SPEED MADE GOOD USING INTENDED BOAT'S SPEED

5-125. The navigator intends to run at least 6 knots. He uses the graphic vector diagram and draws the first line from the center of the compass rose, which is the course he intends to run. At this time, he draws a line of indeterminate length.

5-126. Next, from the center of the compass rose, the navigator draws the current vector with its direction outward in the direction of the set and its length (in miles) that of the drift (knots). He puts an arrowhead at its tip. Using his drawing compass, he lays down a circle with its center at the end tip of the current vector and its radius (in miles) equal to the intended speed of his boat (6 kn). Where this circle crosses the first line (the intended course line), he makes a mark. He then draws a line from the tip of the current vector to this mark. The direction of this line is the course to steer at 6 knots. The length now established by the mark on his intended course line will be the actual speed he will make good. He should then use this speed made good to calculate his estimated time en route (Figure 5-15).

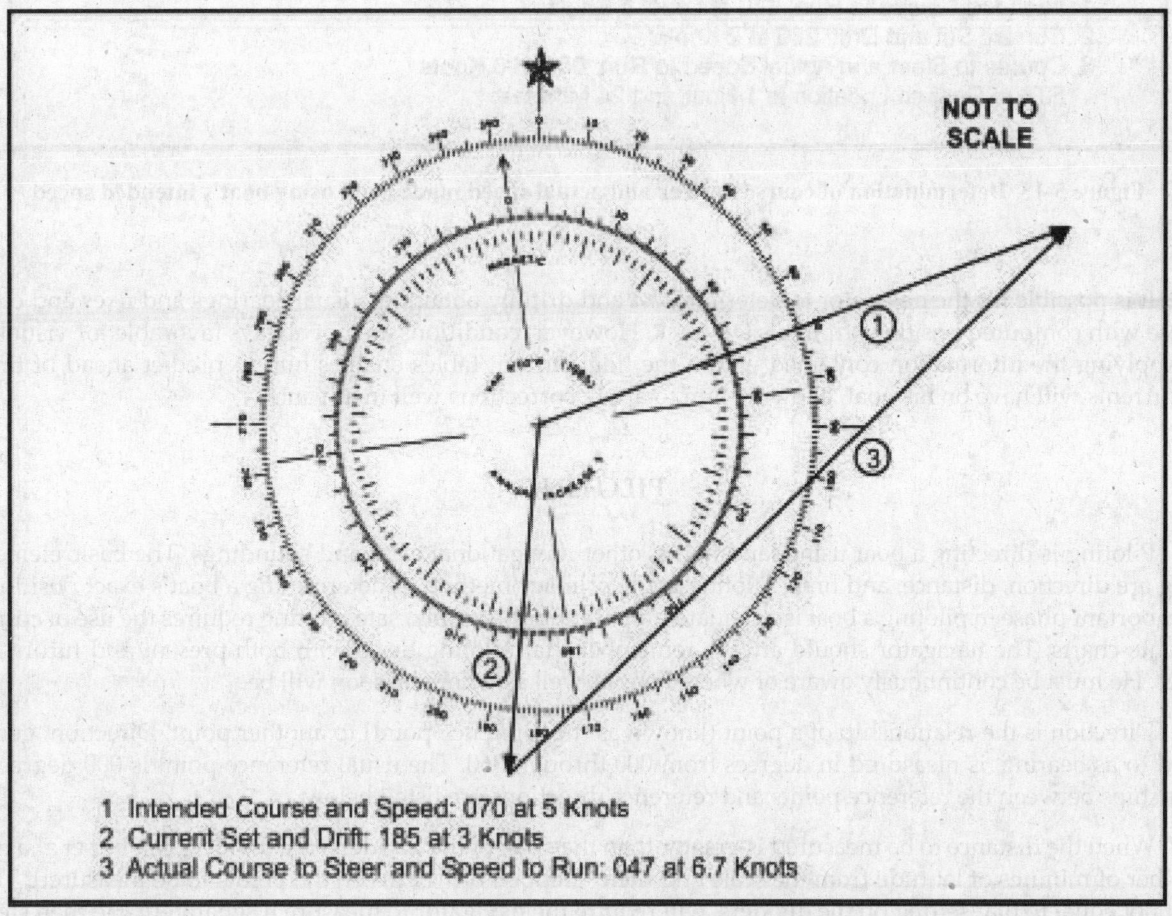

Figure 5-14. Determination of course to steer and speed to run

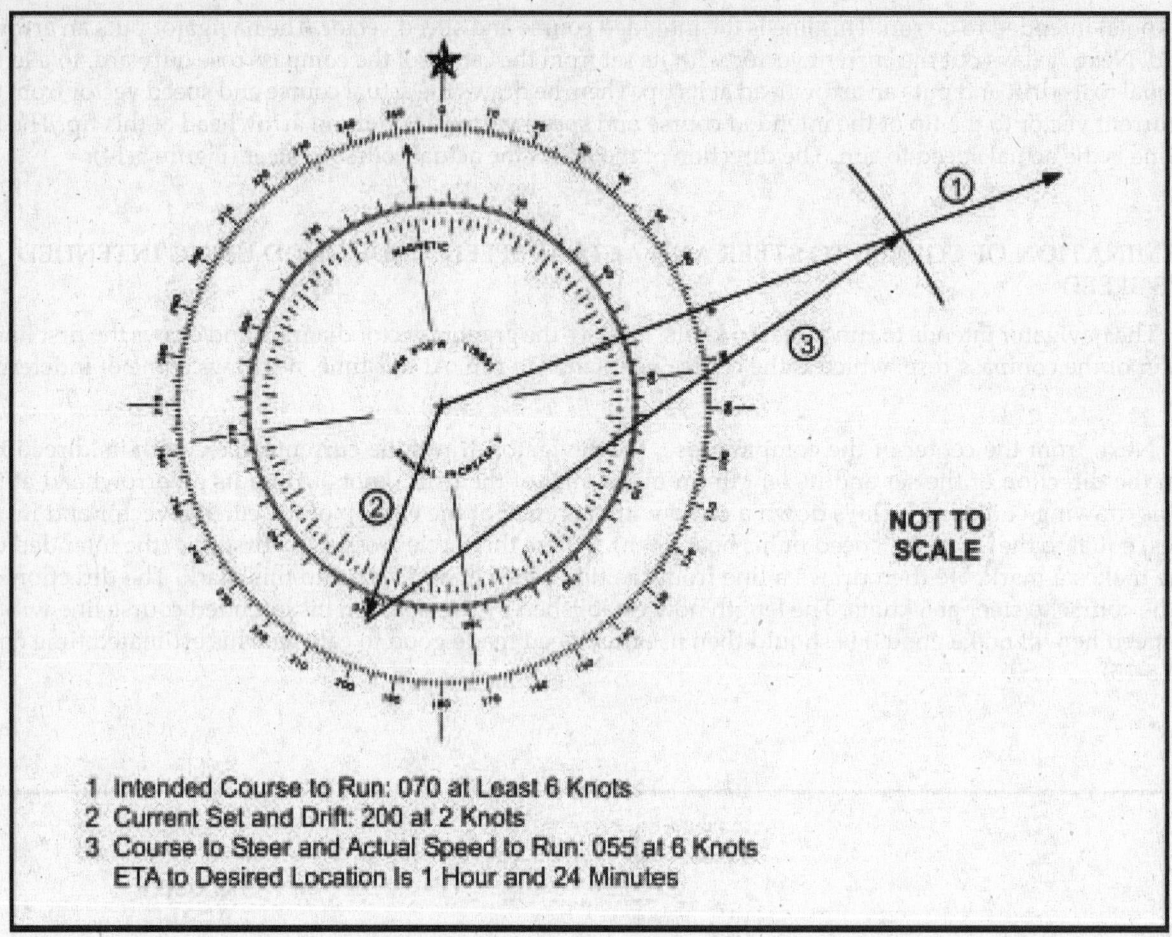

Figure 5-15. Determination of course to steer and actual speed made good using boat's intended speed

5-127. It is possible for the navigator to determine set and drift by obtaining visual bearings and fixes and comparing these with computed positions from his DR track. However, conditions are not always favorable for visual sightings. Applying the information contained within the tidal current tables enables him to predict ahead of time the effect currents will have on his boat, allowing him to apply corrections well in advance.

PILOTING

5-128. Piloting is directing a boat using landmarks, other navigational aids, and soundings. The basic elements of piloting are direction, distance, and time. Piloting is the primary method of determining a boat's exact position. The most important phase in piloting a boat is adequate preparation. Naturally, safe piloting requires the use of corrected, up-to-date charts. The navigator should always remember that piloting deals with both present and future consequences. He must be continuously aware of where he is as well as where he soon will be.

5-129. Direction is the relationship of a point (known as the reference point) to another point. Direction, generally referred to as bearing, is measured in degrees from 000 through 360. The usual reference point is 000 degrees. The relationships between the reference points and reference directions are listed below.

5-130. When the distance to be measured is greater than the span of the dividers, the dividers can be set at a minute or number of minutes of latitude from the scale and then "stepped off" between the points to be measured. The last span, if not equal to that setting on the dividers, will require the navigator to measure it separately. He then steps the dividers once more, closing them to fit the distance. He measures this distance on the scale and adds it to the sum of the other measurements. He should use the latitude scale nearest the middle of the line to be measured. (The longitude scale is never used for measuring distance.) To measure short distances on a chart, the navigator can open the dividers to a span of a given distance, then compare them to the NM or yard scale.

5-131. Time is the third basic element of piloting. Time, distance, and speed are related. Therefore, if any two of the three quantities are known, the third can be found. The basic equations, the speed curve, the nautical slide rule, and their uses have been discussed earlier.

PLOTTING BOARD

5-132. Upon sighting the shoreline or the offshore navigational aids system, the navigator of a boat may make a transition from DR methods to piloting by using a plotting board and basic tools of navigation. Information gathered from the navigator's field of view can be quickly depicted graphically on the nautical chart. This data allows the navigator to frequently and more precisely determine his position in relation to geographic features.

5-133. The navigator follows a step-by-step procedure for setting up the plotting board. He should—

- Prepare the chart for the plotting board. He ensures that all plotting (DR plot, distance rings, corrections, enemy positions, preplanned LOPs) is completed.
- Laminate the chart and fold it to the size of the plotting board.
- Orient the plotting board to the chart. He—
  - Aligns the plotting board meridians to true north.
  - Sets the variation using the thumbscrew.
  - Follows all directions on the back of the board for setting up and using ABC MARK III plotting boards.

> **NOTE**
> The plotting techniques discussed below can be used without a plotting board. However, applying these techniques on the water would be considerably more difficult and time consuming, likely resulting in less-accurate piloting.

FIXING A POSITION

5-134. Techniques for fixing a boat's position on the water include LOPs, distance rings, ranges, running fixes, or various combinations of these techniques.

5-135. **Lines of Position.** An LOP is a bearing (azimuth) to an object depicted graphically on a chart. Simply stated, once the navigator's bearing to an object is drawn on the chart, he knows that his position lies somewhere along that LOP. Bearings must be to a known fixed position and converted to back azimuths before depicted on the chart (resection).

5-136. **Distance Rings.** Distance from an object can be determined if the height of that object is known by using the mil scale displayed in some binoculars. The navigator should—

- Locate a fully visible object of known height (found on the chart).
- Place the horizontal reticle line at the base of the object.
- Read the height of the object in mil scale points, 1 on the scale is equal to 10 mil scale points.
- Use the distance = height (in yards)/1000 mil scale points formula.
- With the bow compass, draw a circle (ring) around the object, using the determined distance as the radius.

The boat's position lies somewhere along the circle (ring) this distance from the object.

5-137. **Range.** A range is achieved when two objects of known position appear along a straight line of sight. The boat's position lies somewhere along this line. The three types of ranges are as follows:

- *Natural range* has two natural objects such as the edges of two islands.
- *Man-made range* has two man-made objects such as two lights.
- *Combination range* has both natural and man-made objects.

> **NOTE**
> When this line is drawn on the chart it becomes an LOP.

5-138. Fixes. A position fix can be determined by various methods as illustrated in Figure 5-16. The navigator can determine a fix by—

- Range and LOP—using the intersection of a range line and LOP, which is considered very reliable.
- Range and distance—using the distance/mil scale rings from a fixed object of known height.
- Distance and LOP—using the distance and LOP from the same object of known height.
- Two distances—where distance rings obtained from two different objects intersect.
- Two or more LOPs—using a minimum of two and a maximum of five LOPs, which gives a fairly accurate position.

5-139. **Running Fix.** The navigator uses a running fix technique when only one navigational aid is available. He—

- Determines an LOP to an object and marks the DR plot accordingly. He notes the time.
- Takes a second LOP from the same object after a specific period of time. He plots it and notes the time.
- Calculates the distance run between the two LOPs.
- Advances the first LOP on the DR track. He draws a line parallel to the first LOP "advanced" along the ITR by the distance run since establishing the first LOP.

Where the advanced LOP intersects the second LOP is the running fix position. Constant speed and accurate time are necessary for a running fix.

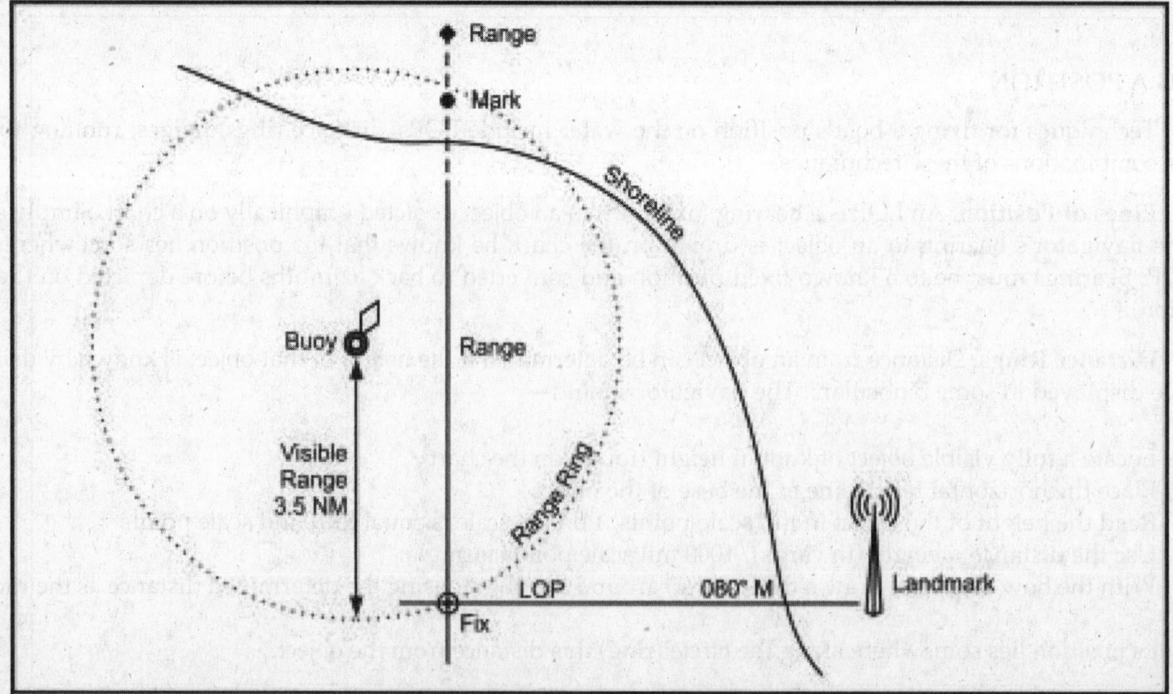

Figure 5-16. Determining a fix

CHAPTER 6

Combat Rubber Raiding Craft Operations

This chapter specifically addresses CRRC operations. It is intended to ensure interoperability among all U.S. special operations commands and to promote operational readiness and safety through uniform execution of policy and training. For the purposes of this chapter, CRRCs are noncommissioned, inflatable rubber boats, powered by outboard motors and capable of limited independent operations. They are not designated as service craft.

MARITIME PROPONENCY

6-1. The United States Special Operations Command (USSOCOM) Directive 10-1, *Terms of Reference*, gives the Commander, Naval Special Warfare Command (NAVSPECWARCOM) proponency for SO maritime (including underwater operations), riverine, and coastal operations. As such, NAVSPECWARCOM serves as USSOCOM's senior advisor on all matters pertaining to SF maritime, riverine, and coastal operations; training and doctrine; safety; equipment; and interoperability for USSOCOM's Active and Reserve forces. Accordingly, NAVSPECWARCOM shall—

- Standardize maritime, riverine, and coastal operations, training, techniques, and procedures, to include basic skill qualifications for all USSOCOM components.
- Validate programs of instruction at all USSOCOM-component maritime, riverine, and coastal operations schools and training facilities.
- Test, validate, and standardize maritime, riverine, and coastal operations equipment.
- Develop, publish, and distribute safety messages, equipment bulletins, and quality deficiency reports.

RESPONSIBILITIES

6-2. This section describes the minimum duties of key personnel in the planning, preparation, and execution of CRRC operations by the following USSOCOM components.

UNIT COMMANDERS AND COMMANDING OFFICERS

6-3. Unit commanders and commanding officers implement and administer CRRC safety and training policies. Individual commands may issue supplementary regulations and instructions for the safe operations of assigned CRRC. In addition, commanders will—

- Ensure personnel involved in CRRC handling or operations are properly qualified and follow approved procedures.
- Ensure that all CRRCs are equipped with the required safety equipment.
- Develop and implement NAVSPECWARCOM-approved training plans to ensure adequate training of appropriate personnel in CRRC mission areas. Requalification and training will be documented in individual service records, as appropriate, and in command training files.
- Ensure accidents and mishaps resulting in death, lost time (24 hours or more), personnel injury, or significant material damage are reported IAW Service directives. Ensure that NAVSPECWARCOM is an "INFO ADDEE" on all CRRC accident reports.

OFFICER IN CHARGE

6-4. All SF evolutions require a designated individual in charge. The officer in charge (OIC) will plan the assigned evolution using the CRRC officer, as appropriate, to supervise the CRRC portion of the operation. The OIC and the

CRRC officer may be one and the same if the OIC is a qualified CRRC officer. The OIC is not required to remain in the CRRC during the entire mission.

CRRC OFFICER

6-5. A competent, qualified, and reliable E-5 or above will be designated as the CRRC officer. He is in charge of the operation and handling of the CRRC during the mission. Each CRRC officer should be experienced in underway operations, rules of the road, prudent seamanship, navigation, CRRC handling characteristics, sea-state limitations, surf-zone procedures, and communications with the chain of command. The CRRC officer—

- Should be the coxswain.
- Will assist the OIC in coordinating and planning all aspects of the CRRC operation, identify safety hazards, and develop emergency procedures during the planning phase of the mission. He should use checklists and guidance developed by his unit or provided in this manual.
- Will advise the operations OIC on all matters pertaining to the planning, execution, and safety of the CRRC portion of the mission.

THE NAVIGATION TEAM

6-6. The navigation (or piloting) team consists of the navigator and coxswain. Long-range transits and OTH operations would benefit from the assignment of an assistant navigator. All team members should be well-versed in small-boat navigation and be intimately involved in the development of the navigation plan (NAVPLAN). Development of the NAVPLAN should include input from indigenous sources, if available, familiar with the waters being navigated. Once underway, the duties of the navigation team are as follows:

- *Navigator.* He orders course and speed to the coxswain; keeps total time of passage; and operates the plotting board by plotting bearings, currents, and DR plots. He notifies the assistant navigator when to take bearings and speed checks. He oversees the entire NAVPLAN and safe piloting of the CRRC.
- *Assistant Navigator.* He renders aid to the navigator as directed and shoots bearings, measures speed, and keeps time between legs. He must be alert and observant of sea conditions, aids to navigation, and land features.
- *Coxswain.* He maintains the ordered course and speed.

6-7. All personnel who embark in the CRRC will wear the equipment and clothing directed by the OIC or CRRC officer. They will be aware of the unit SOPs and the particular contingency plans associated with the mission or training evolution.

TRAINING

6-8. To ensure safe and successful operations, all personnel who participate in CRRC operations must be skilled and proficient. This section provides guidance on SF CRRC training, to include initial training qualification and the integration of CRRC training into unit training plans.

INITIAL CRRC TRAINING QUALIFICATION

6-9. Training for CRRC operations occurs primarily at the unit level. However, the Naval Special Warfare Center, Coronado, California; the Naval Special Warfare Center, Detachment Little Creek, Norfolk, Virginia; and the John F. Kennedy Special Warfare Center and School, Fort Bragg, North Carolina, and its School in Key West, Florida, have offered formal courses in long-range maritime operations and waterborne infiltration. USMC reconnaissance forces and assigned raid forces receive their initial training and familiarization in CRRC operations at one of the following sites: The Basic Reconnaissance Course (selected reconnaissance personnel only), EWTGLANT, EWTGPAC, or 1st, 2d, or 3d Special Operations Training Groups. Follow-on training and advanced OTH skills may be taught at a formal school or the unit level with oversight by the S-3 training sections. Initial training for all services consists of classroom lectures, conferences, and practical exercises.

Classroom Lectures and Conferences

6-10. The lectures and conferences should familiarize personnel with—

- Unit SOPs.
- CRRC safety regulations.
- CRRC operating characteristics.
- Proper waterproofing of equipment and stowage procedures.
- Boat and engine maintenance requirements.
- Navigation techniques.
- Rules of the road.
- First aid.

Practical Exercises

6-11. Practical exercises (PEs) are conducted under the supervision of experienced personnel. PEs are designed to introduce trainees to the various aspects of CRRC operations. Areas covered in these exercises include the following:

- Practical navigation.
- Basic seamanship.
- Launch and recovery techniques from various host platforms.
- OTH operations.
- Surf passage.
- At-sea rendezvous techniques.
- Over-the-beach operations.
- Chart study and publications.
- Tides and currents.
- Planning navigation routes.
- Repair and maintenance of the CRRC and outboard motor (OBM).

SUSTAINMENT AND UNIT TRAINING

6-12. After initial qualification, it is necessary to sustain and build upon the skills acquired during initial training. Personnel should perform refresher and advanced training on a continuous basis to maintain proficiency.

Refresher or Sustainment Training

6-13. Training will consist of practical training and classroom instruction. Units should maintain lesson plans and review or update them annually. Regular command training for all personnel who participate in CRRC operations should include, but not be limited to, the following:

- Classroom instruction, to include the following:
  - General safety precautions.
  - Equipment maintenance.
  - Waterproofing techniques.
  - First aid.
  - Cardiopulmonary resuscitation.
  - Navigation techniques.
  - Rules of the road.
  - Unit SOPs.
- Practical work, to include the following:
  - Practical navigation.
  - Repair and maintenance of the CRRC and OBM.
  - In-water emergency procedures.
  - Launch and recovery techniques from various host platforms.

- OTH operations.
- Surf passage.
- At-sea rendezvous techniques.
- Over-the-beach operations.

6-14. Commanding officers, after completion of a unit-level CRRC/RHIB refresher training package or SOTG small-boat refresher package, may approve and issue licenses that may be required by higher commands for forces to be properly designated to operate small boats.

Mission-Essential Task List Focus

6-15. Unit CRRC training will be METL-focused to the maximum extent possible. CRRC training plans will be unit-specific. Training will be progressive to attain or maintain the skills required to conduct CRRC operations in support of assigned missions in projected operational environments. Collective CRRC training will be integrated with other METL-focused training as much as possible. The use of realistic field training exercises (FTXs), based on full mission profiles (FMPs), to train and evaluate the unit's CRRC capability should be the norm rather than the exception. Standards for various CRRC evolutions (for example, CRRC OTH navigation, CRRC paradrop insertion, and at-sea rendezvous) are delineated in FXP-6, *Naval Special Warfare Exercises*, with specific lesson guides contained in NAVSPECWARCOM INST 3502.1, *Lesson Planning Guide Database.*

Advanced Training and Qualifications

6-16. Additional training and certification is necessary to perform certain technical and supervisory functions required in the conduct of SF-CRRC operations. The functions and training are discussed below.

6-17. **OBM Technician.** Advanced training is offered at factory schools to train mechanics in the proper maintenance and repair of outboard motors. On-the-job (OJT) training must also be available at the command level. Personnel who have demonstrated a mechanical aptitude can learn maintenance and repair techniques and procedures under the tutelage of experienced OBM technicians. Motor maintenance skills are critical to ensure mission completion.

6-18. **CRRC Officer.** Training that leads to written certification of individuals as CRRC officers is provided by the unit commander and must include detailed knowledge of the following subjects:

- *Navigation.* Personnel must demonstrate their abilities in the following areas:
  - Charts and publications, which includes how to interpret, plot, use, order, and correct nautical charts.
  - Magnetic compass, which involves determining deviation, variation, and true direction.
  - Tide tables, which tests the computation of the tides' state.
  - Current sailing, which applies the proper course corrections for currents of various speeds.
  - Tidal current sailing, which involves computing tidal currents and applying appropriate course corrections.
  - Tools of navigation, which involves using the GPS, a hand-bearing compass, a plotting board, and a sextant.
  - Navigation planning, which includes laying out a track with the turn bearings, waypoints, and ranges.
  - Piloting, which involves navigating from one location to another.
  - Dead reckoning, which involves determining position without using navigational aids.
  - Electronic navigation, which involves using the GPS.
- *Seamanship.* Personnel must show proficiency in the following areas:
  - Rules of the road.
  - Small-boat safety regulations.
  - CRRC handling characteristics.
  - Sea-state limitations.
  - Surf-zone procedures.
- *Operational Planning.* Personnel must be well-versed in the following:
  - SF planning procedures.
  - Planning for CRRC operations.
  - Communications planning.

OPERATIONS AND PLANNING

6-19. A unit can conduct CRRC operations as infiltration and exfiltration operations. The organization for a particular operation is dependent on the nature of the mission and the unit's SOPs. When organizing for the mission, unit and individual qualifications or experience should be matched to the specific requirements of the mission or training event. Unit integrity is an important consideration when conducting CRRC operations; however, there are times when unit attachments may be necessary to fulfill the mission. In such cases, all participants must be briefed regarding the unit's tactical SOPs to be followed in an emergency.

6-20. Without preliminary planning, the entire operation may fail and, in extreme cases, lives may be endangered. The following information provides planning guidelines for a safe and successful CRRC operation. This information is not a guide to tactical mission planning. Specific mission planning factors to CRRC operations are discussed below.

TACTICAL LOADS

6-21. As a rule, the mission OIC should not load the CRRC to its maximum capacity when preparing for a mission. In a crowded CRRC, personnel in the forward positions are subjected to a greater degree of physical discomfort owing to the turbulence created by the effect of swell and wave activity. This concern is especially significant during long-transit periods. Increased physical stress may diminish an individual's ability to perform once he has arrived at the objective site. Furthermore, the OIC must take into account the possibility of prisoners, casualties, and the evacuation of friendly forces. Thus, it is always wise to have sufficient additional boat space for unforeseen contingencies. For example, although the F470 CRRC with a 55 hp engine is capable of transporting ten personnel, no more than six personnel should be embarked. The optimum weight ceiling for the F470 CRRC is 2,000 pounds. Any weight above this ceiling significantly reduces the CRRC's efficiency. Experience has shown that six personnel, with mission-essential equipment, on average, come closest to this weight ceiling. In marginal sea states or when there are extended distances to be covered, consideration should be given to limiting embarked personnel to four.

COMMAND RELATIONSHIPS

6-22. The SF mission or unit OIC is responsible for every phase of the CRRC tactical mission. He conducts planning and coordinates any external support required to execute the mission. However, SF elements will frequently be tactically transported aboard host ships or aircraft. SF elements may also have personnel from other units attached. The following paragraphs provide additional guidance for these circumstances.

6-23. The ship or submarine commanding officer is generally the officer in tactical command (OTC) and the SF OIC is embarked under his command. Although the ship's commanding officer is in a supporting role to the SF OIC, he has ultimate responsibility for the safety of his ship and crew. Thus, his authority is absolute until the CRRC mission is launched. At the point of launch, tactical command of the mission shifts to the SF OIC. It is essential that the OIC coordinate every aspect of the operation with the host ship's commanding officer and discuss with him every phase of the mission that requires his participation.

> **NOTE**
> The above guidelines also apply when being transported aboard host aircraft.

6-24. After launch, the authority of the SF mission commander is absolute during the conduct of the mission. He is solely responsible for the successful execution of the mission, as well as the safety and well-being of assigned personnel. Any attached personnel, civilian or military, regardless of rank or position, cannot override the decision-making authority of the SF mission OIC. Any variance to this policy must be clearly addressed in the operation plan (OPLAN), with guidelines as to who is in tactical command at each phase of the operation.

6-25. The CRRC officer, generally the coxswain, will follow the directions of the SF mission commander. It is his responsibility to keep the mission commander informed as to location and status of the CRRC.

6-26. When planning an OTH CRRC operation, the SF OIC must be the focal point from the outset. The planning sequence must depict continuous parallel, concurrent, and detailed planning. Planning support and information will be needed from all sources. In addition, planning requires close cooperation and teamwork between the supported and supporting elements. As the plan develops, all aspects should be briefed, reviewed, and understood by planners and decision makers before becoming finalized.

6-27. As with the planning of any operation, provisions must be made to deal with uncertainty. Plans should be developed to address contingencies and emergencies during CRRC transits to include—

- *OBM Breakdown.* Unit should have a trained technician and bring tools and spare parts or spare motor, if space and time permit.
- *Navigational Error.* Unit should study permanent geographical features and known tides, currents, and winds, take into account the sea state, and intentionally steer left or right of the target BLS so once landfall is reached, a direction to target is already established. (When using the GPS, the CRRC should aim directly at the BLS; it should not offset left or right of target. Proper use of the GPS will take the CRRC directly and accurately to the BLS.)
- *Low Fuel or Empty.* Unit should run trials with a fully loaded CRRC in various sea states to calculate fuel consumption rates. The CRRC should take enough fuel for a worst-case scenario.
- *Emergency MEDEVAC Procedures.* Unit should know location of nearest medical treatment facility and develop primary and alternative plan for evacuating casualties.
- *CRRC Puncture.* Unit should carry expedient plugs.

OPERATIONAL CONTINGENCIES

6-28. Many other contingencies may arise during the conduct of CRRC operations. They may be caused by a wide variety of factors or events, and can occur at any time. When CRRCs operate with host platforms, operational contingencies fall into four general categories.

Mission Abort

6-29. This action occurs when a decision is made not to continue the mission as scheduled. It may lead to the cancellation of the mission or to a delay. Mission abort may result from a system or equipment failure that severely impacts performance, adverse weather conditions, or a changing tactical situation that jeopardizes mission success. The abort decision should be made after evaluating all the circumstances and their impact on the mission. Mission-abort criteria should be defined before the mission gets underway. Should the SF OIC decide to abort the mission while underway, he should communicate his decision to the supporting craft as soon as tactically feasible to initiate rendezvous, recovery, or casualty assistance operations. The decision to abort the mission is normally controlled by the on-scene tactical commander, or may be dictated by the operational chain of command.

Rendezvous Point Interference

6-30. In CRRC operations, the rendezvous point (RP) is vulnerable to interference because other craft are in the area. Detailed rules of engagement must be developed to respond to both hostile and civilian interference at the primary and alternate RPs. The presence of hostile forces in the rendezvous areas may indicate compromise of the mission. Whatever the interference, a decision must be made to proceed with the rendezvous as planned or shift to an alternate RP.

Missed Rendezvous

6-31. A rendezvous is missed when the allotted time window has expired. The time window will vary depending on each mission. Mission planners define the time window and include it in the OPLAN. Generally, the time window will be approximately 1 hour. If late arrival is anticipated and emission control (EMCON) conditions permit, the CRRC should attempt to communicate with the host platform and coordinate an adjusted rendezvous time.

In most cases, unless notified by the CRRC of a delay, the host platform will not remain in the rendezvous area longer than the scheduled time window. If the initial scheduled rendezvous and recovery do not succeed, subsequent efforts will be more difficult because—

- The CRRC crew will have extended exposure to the elements.
- Endurance (fuel) will be nearing exhaustion.
- The enemy will have a longer time to react.

6-32. Many factors can cause a missed rendezvous. For example, the CRRC may not make the rendezvous point on time. An equipment casualty, such as loss of motor propulsion or CRRC damage can prevent the CRRC from reaching the rendezvous point. Also, cumulative navigation error of the CRRC and the host platform can exceed the range of capability of the rendezvous locating system. This problem may not be obvious at the time. The navigation error may go unrecognized until the CRRC has exhausted its fuel. Bad weather can seriously reduce the range of the rendezvous locating systems or a failure of the rendezvous locating system may occur.

Search Considerations

6-33. Four items should be considered before starting a search for a CRRC after a missed rendezvous. Each should be carefully evaluated during planning and thoroughly briefed to the support personnel and host platform crew so they can make informed decisions as the tactical situation changes. The four questions are—

- How much time will be available to conduct a search, and what size search area can be covered before departing the rendezvous area?
- How much fuel will be expended during the search and how will it affect the host platform's ability to return to its base or host ship?
- Will the search effort increase the probability of detection?
- How long can the CRRC wait for the searching host platform?

6-34. The SF mission OIC will be faced with a "time-to-leave" decision based on endurance (fuel), remaining hours of darkness, and alternate COAs—for example, lay up ashore or return to sea for a CSAR or other preplanned E&E procedures. If communications with the operational unit fail and a search is initiated, the search will continue at the discretion of the host platform's commander as preplanned E&E procedures are initiated. If the host platform is in positive communications with the operational element, the search will continue until the element is recovered or as long as feasible to prevent detection of the host platform or operational element.

SEA CONDITIONS

6-35. The reference for understanding and judging sea conditions is *The American Practical Navigator (Bowditch)*, Chapter 37. The sea-keeping characteristics of the CRRC permits operations in Sea State 4, although rough weather greatly increases the fuel consumption and risks associated with launch or recovery of the CRRC. The maximum sea state for CRRC launch or recovery and ocean transits during training evolutions is Sea State 4. The high winds generally associated with higher sea states will adversely affect the maneuverability of the CRRC. High sea states and corresponding winds force slower CRRC speeds and result in longer transit times. An advantage offered by operating in higher sea states is a reduced vulnerability to detection. High seas degrade the detection range and effectiveness of electronic sensors and contribute to tactical surprise. Sea conditions can fluctuate rapidly. During the planning phase for an OTH operation, the navigator must consider the forecasted meteorological factors that could adversely affect the sea state during all mission times. For example, if the navigator anticipates that conditions at launch will be Sea State 3, he should, during the planning phase, determine if any forecasted meteorological factors exist that could cause the sea state to go to 4 or 5 during the operational window. Also, a low sea state does not mean a benign surf zone; sea and surf zone conditions must be considered independently.

DISTANCE

6-36. The optimum CRRC launch occurs at least 20 NM from shore, but usually no more than 60 NM. In determining the actual distance to execute a launch, the navigator must consider the sea state, weather, transit times, and enemy electronic-detection capabilities. The objective is to keep the host platform undetected while minimizing the CRRC transit distance, thereby reducing the physical demands caused by long open-ocean transits.

NAVIGATION

6-37. Dead reckoning and coastal piloting are the primary methods of navigation for the CRRC. Passive electronic methods of navigation (for example, GPS) are a useful complement. However, electronics should not be totally relied upon due to problems in propagation, signals interruption in adverse weather conditions, and the general unreliability of electronic instruments in a saltwater environment.

> **NOTE**
> GPS is faster and much more accurate than dead reckoning. By naval convention, GPS should be considered the secondary navigation method. Militarized GPS receivers are extremely rugged instruments—not fragile. GPS was designed to minimize signal propagation problems due to adverse weather conditions.

6-38. Celestial navigation in CRRCs is normally impractical because of the extensive publications required, and the unstable nature of the CRRC as a platform from which to use a sextant. Whenever possible, development of the NAVPLAN should include input from indigenous sources familiar with the waters being navigated.

THE SURF ZONE

6-39. A key planning consideration for a CRRC operation is the characteristics of the surf zone near the BLS. The navigator will analyze key elements, planning and execution factors, and surf limits for inclusion in the NAVPLAN. Detailed information on the surf zone can be found in COMNAVSURFPAC/COMNAVSURFLANT Instruction 3840. IB, *Joint Surf Manual*, Chapters 4 and 5. Other-the-beach operations should always include scout swimmers to verify or monitor surf conditions, especially if the conditions are marginal or likely to change during the operation.

> **NOTE**
> SUROBS is an 8-line report; the North Atlantic Treaty Organization (NATO) format surf report (SURFREP) is a 10-line report, the first two lines being unit of measure and date-time group (DTG), the last eight lines corresponding to the 8-line SUROBS.

Key Elements

6-40. The critical considerations for CRRC surf zone operations are the SIGNIFICANT WAVE HEIGHT (height of the highest one-third of the breakers observed), the PERIOD (the time interval between waves measured to the nearest half-second), and the BREAKER TYPE (spilling, plunging, or surging). The danger factor in CRRC surf zone operations increases as wave height increases, the period between waves lessens, and waves begin plunging or surging. These critical factors must be considered, both individually and in combination, and their effect on CRRC operations carefully and prudently evaluated, especially in light of boat or engine maintenance conditions and coxswain or boat crew experience level. Personnel trained and experienced in CRRC operations—for example, designated CRRC officers—should conduct this evaluation. Although these three elements represent the most critical considerations, other information contained in the SUROBS is important for navigation and planning for negotiating the surf zone.

Planning and Execution

6-41. Surf conditions are critical in making the final determination to launch or not launch the CRRC. Once the CRRC is launched and arrives outside the surf zone at the BLS, the CRRC officer will advise the OIC regarding the final beaching decision. If prelaunch SUROBS, visual sighting, or mission necessity warrant further surf evaluation, the OIC may use scout swimmers for this purpose. He must consider the surf conditions as they exist at the time, his mission and command guidance, boat or engine maintenance conditions, and coxswain or boat crew safety. Further surf conditions, like sea states, can change rapidly. During planning, the forecasted meteorological factors that could adversely affect surf conditions should be evaluated. Swimmer scouts should always be used during over-the-beach operations.

Surf Limits

6-42. The recommended CRRC surf passage table in Figure 6-1, page 117, outlines recommended operating limits for CRRC surf zone operations. The table plots breaker height versus breaker period, and is applicable to both spilling and plunging waves. Plunging breakers are more dangerous to CRRC operations than spilling breakers, and greater care and judgment must be exercised as the percentage of plunging breakers increases. Surging breakers are not included in the table. The recommended surf limits are provided as a guide and are not intended to usurp the judgment of officers exercising command.

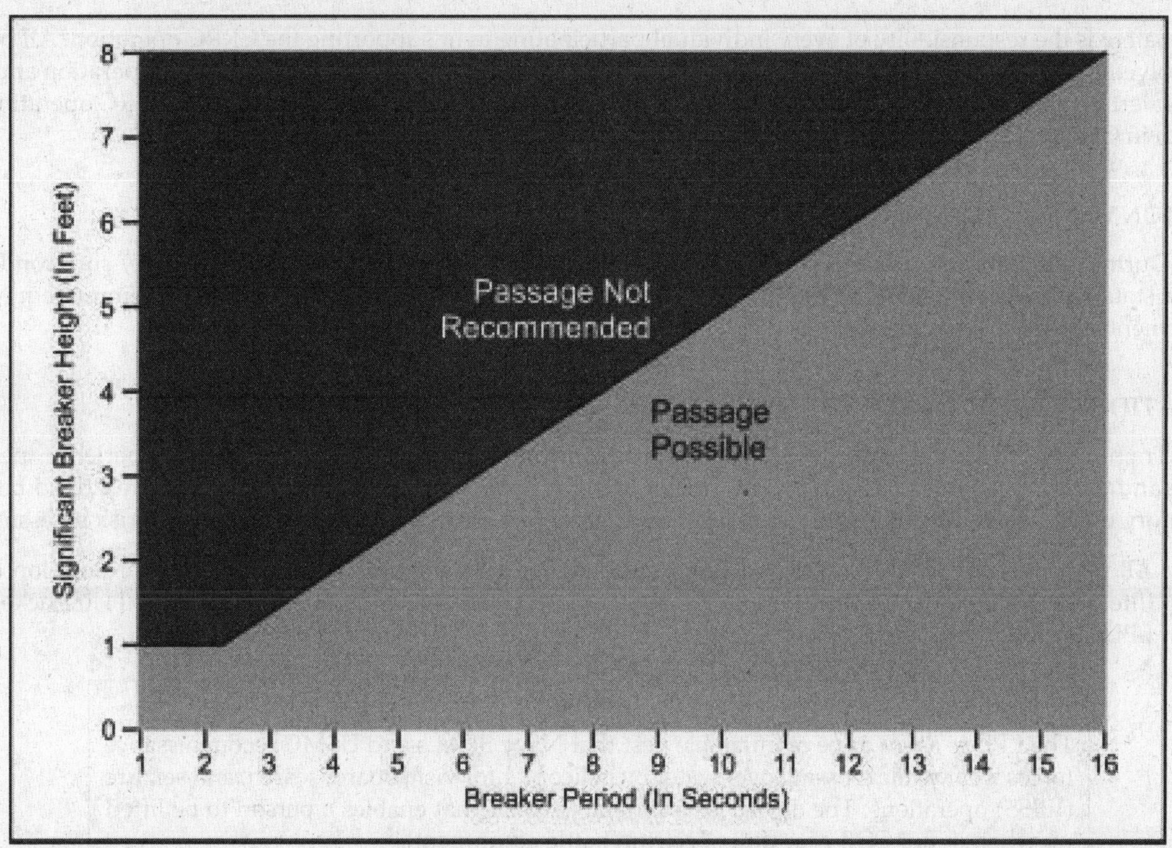

Figure 6-1. CRRC surf passage table

MISSION REHEARSALS

6-43. Rehearsals should be conducted for all phases of the CRRC operation, if time and the tactical situation permits. Rehearsals are as important for the crew of the host or supporting platform as they are the SF element. This practice occurs because supporting personnel may not be familiar with the support requirements for SF missions. Host platform crews should be given every chance to rehearse their portion of the mission with the SF unit they are to support. If embarked on a host ship, time may be available while in transit or during an in-port period. Special attention should be given to the time-critical elements in each phase and to the completion time for each task. Performance conditions and standards for success or failure should be determined to allow modification of the plan or training. Planners must balance the advantages of rehearsal experience against possible equipment degradation and personnel fatigue. As a minimum, rehearsal events for CRRC operations should include the following:

- Launch procedures.
- Rendezvous procedures.
- Recovery procedures.
- Communications procedures.
- Contingency plans.
- Over-the-beach insertion procedures.
- Insertion and extraction procedures.

6-44. All maritime operations have inherent risks. Proper training and in-depth preparation and planning will reduce the potential for accidents. Safety considerations will be fully addressed during planning and integrated into all CRRC training. Unit commanders will perform risk assessments before conducting the "crawl-walk-run" manner of training.

6-45. Safety is the responsibility of every individual participating in or supporting the CRRC operation. All personnel involved in a particular evolution must be constantly aware of the nature and progress of the operation and must remain alert for possible danger. Specific, individual responsibilities for the safe conduct of SF CRRC operations are set forth in Chapter 2.

ENVIRONMENTAL PERSONNEL LIMITATIONS

6-46. During the planning process, consideration must be given to how weather, temperature, surf conditions, and sea state will effect the safety of the CRRC evolution. These planning considerations and minimum equipment requirements are discussed below.

OPERATIONAL PROCEDURES

6-47. Training and operations must be planned with consideration to individual and unit experience, personal fatigue and exposure factors, and equipment capabilities. Observance of the safety regulations prescribed below is mandatory unless waived by the appropriate level of command as determined by the operational risk assessment.

- All personnel involved in CRRC operations should wear an inherently buoyant personal flotation device (life jacket) or an inflatable life preserver, for example, an underwater demolition team (UDT) life jacket or an LPU.

> **NOTE**
> The LPU is a new type of inflatable vest that Navy SEALs and USMC reconnaissance forces wear while crossing over water by helicopter for visit, board, search, and seizure (VBSS) operations. The device is an inflatable collar that enables a person to be lifted up when in full CQB gear (full-spectrum battle equipment).

- During CRRC training evolutions, personnel will not be bound in any manner (for example, handcuffs, flex-cuffs, or zip ties). Fatalities have occurred in the past when bound personnel were inadvertently thrown from the craft.
- For single CRRC operations, a minimum of two persons are required to be in the craft (towed craft are considered single-craft operations). For multiple CRRC operations, one person or coxswain per boat is acceptable, and one CRRC officer is sufficient for all boats. The SF OIC should be in the same CRRC as the CRRC officer. For administrative movement under good conditions and within confined, protected or sheltered waters, it is acceptable to operate a CRRC with only one person in the craft, and a CRRC officer is not required.
- Before getting underway, the CRRC coxswain will—
  - Make certain that the CRRC is equipped with the required safety equipment.
  - Verify adequacy of boat fuel.

- Establish and maintain positive communications as directed in the OPLAN or training plan.
- Warm up the outboard engines at idle speed for 5 minutes.

- CRRC launch and recovery from underway platforms will not be routinely conducted in Sea State 4 or greater during training evolutions.
- CRRC transits should also not be conducted in Sea State 4 or equivalent sea conditions for routine training evolutions.
- CRRC will not be operated in surf zones with breaker heights greater than 8 feet. In this situation, the recommendation of the CRRC officer and judgment of the OIC will dictate alternate options for transiting the surf zone.
- Every CRRC will be equipped with a radio. Positive radio communications will be established before getting underway. Communications will be maintained with the parent command or operational commander as provided for in the training plan or the signal operating instructions (SOI).
- CRRC operations will be cleared with the immediate operational commander. He will approve intended and alternate navigation tracks.
- The CRRCs will be operated within the limits of the designated specifications for weight or personnel on board. (Chapter 7 provides information on the F470 CRRC and the CRRC [small]).
- Equipment will be secured in the CRRCs so as not to impede egress of personnel in emergency situations.
- Commanders or commanding officers and their appointed safety officers must ensure their personnel, particularly those directly involved with CRRC operations, are fully aware of the potential hazards inherent in all waterborne activity. The safety regulations and operating guidelines are not intended to usurp the judgment of officers exercising command.

NOTE

Minimum equipment requirements have been established. They are listed in the equipment section of this chapter and are considered essential for conducting safe CRRC operations.

EMERGENCY PROCEDURES

6-48. Emergency procedures are key collective skills that support the mission-essential task list (METL) of all combat units. Planning and rehearsing these skills should be an integral part of all unit training. Unit standing operating procedures (SOPs) should be developed to deal with anticipated emergencies that could arise during CRRC operations. An emergency action plan should be established and coordinated with supporting commands or units, as appropriate. At a minimum, the plan should include considerations for towing, capsized CRRC, loss of contact, man overboard, engine failure, and low fuel.

Towing Operations

6-49. All CRRCs must be rigged and equipped for tow or to-be-towed operations. When a CRRC fails, personnel should—

- Immediately prepare the craft for towing. Towlines should be long enough to sag under its own weight. Taunt towlines result in accidents.
- Cross-deck a technician to repair the OBM.
- Cross-deck personnel to alternate craft to lighten the load, if towing is required.
- Tow the inoperable CRRC with only the coxswain and technician onboard.
- Ensure the principles below are followed while towing. CRRC personnel should—
  - Tow at a slower speed than the CRRCs normally travel.
  - Not make quick turns.
  - Assign a lookout in the towing craft to observe the towed CRRC.
  - Not stop suddenly.
  - Maintain steering control of the towed CRRC. If the towing craft stops suddenly, the towed CRRC must be able to steer clear without ramming the towing boat.
  - Raise the engine on the towed craft.

Capsized CRRC

6-50. If a CRRC begins to capsize, the coxswain should warn the craft's occupants and attempt to stop the engine. When the passengers and coxswain are in the water, they should protect their heads with their arms. Actions taken after capsizing include the following:

- All personnel should inflate life jackets, orally if possible, when clear of the CRRC.
- The senior man or coxswain should conduct a head count.
- All personnel should swim to the seaward side of the craft to keep it from being pushed by swells over the top of them. They should remain in a group.
- Personnel should attempt to right the craft. If unable to do so, they should stay with the CRRC. If capsized in the surf zone, the CRRC will be pushed ashore. If in the near-shore area but outside the surf zone, personnel should try to swim the CRRC to shore. If at sea, it is easier for CSAR efforts to spot a capsized CRRC than individual swimmers.

Loss of Contact

6-51. If contact is lost between crafts when conducting operations involving multiple CRRCs, the usual procedure is for the lead craft to wait a preplanned period of time for the missing CRRC to catch up. Every attempt must be made to reestablish contact as soon as possible. Factors to consider include the following:

- CRRCs are most likely to lose contact at night and in reduced visibility (fog, rain, and heavy seas). To reduce the likelihood of lost contact, the following measures should be followed:
  - Formations are kept tight and the coxswain maintains visual contact with the other craft.
  - Other passengers in the CRRC are assigned to assist the coxswain in his duty.
- If a CRRC falls behind the formation or stops, the other craft will stop to render assistance. In the event that a CRRC cannot maintain the formation speed, the CRRCs will travel at the slow craft's best possible speed.
- If contact is lost, the lead CRRC should stop and wait for the lost craft to catch up. If after a short period, the lost craft does not catch up, the lead CRRC should follow a reciprocal bearing until contact is made. Contingency plans include the following:
  - If contact is not made along the track, the lead CRRC will proceed to a predesignated rally point and wait until the lost craft arrives.
  - The coxswain of the lost craft should attempt to reestablish contact. If contact is not swiftly made, the coxswain should move to the predesignated rally point to await the rest of the force.
  - The OIC shall decide if the mission or the lost craft takes precedence, taking into account the time available for the mission and the preplanned abort criteria.

Man Overboard

6-52. If a man falls overboard, the coxswain or his designee will alert the OIC and other craft in the area using voice, radio, or visual signals. To facilitate recovery, each person will have a chemlight or strobe (these may be IR depending on the tactical situation) attached to his life jacket. It will be activated upon falling overboard.

6-53. Unless the CRRC is in a dangerous surf zone, where stopping would endanger the entire CRRC crew, the coxswain will maneuver to avoid the man and shift the engine into neutral until past the man to prevent the propellers from striking him.

6-54. Depending on the tactical situation, a man overboard in the surf zone will either return to the beach where a designated boat will recover him, or he will swim through the surf zone and be recovered.

6-55. To recover a man overboard into the CRRC, the following steps must be performed in sequence:

- Observe the man in the water. Make a rapid turn toward the man, ensuring the propellers do not hit him. Keep the man in sight until he is recovered. Recover the man on the coxswain side to maintain visual contact by the coxswain throughout the evolution. Before reaching the man overboard, reduce speed and cut the engine off.

- Approach the man facing into the current or wind, whichever is the stronger of the two. (By steering into the elements, the coxswain will maintain steerageway even at slow speed and can use the elements to slow and stop the CRRC.)
- When close to the man, the coxswain will indicate to the crew whether he will recover him to port or starboard.
- When the man is within reach, a line or paddle will be extended to assist him back into the CRRC. Only as a last resort should a crew member attempt a swimming rescue.

6-56. The CRRC from which the man fell will normally perform the recovery. If it cannot, the coxswain will request assistance from another craft and direct it to the vicinity of the man.

EQUIPMENT

6-57. For the purpose of this chapter, a CRRC is a noncommissioned inflatable rubber boat. It is powered by an OBM and capable of limited independent operations. CRRCs are not designated as service craft. Tables 7-1 through 7-4 outline the characteristics of CRRCs, associated OBMs, and fuel containers currently used by SF.

6-58. Equipment will be used IAW applicable Service regulations, instructions, and appropriate technical manuals. Information on the characteristics of specific craft and fuel consumption data is provided in Chapter 7 along with further guidance for preparing the CRRC and OBM for an operation.

6-59. A dangerous oversimplification exists when relying on any general minimum equipment list. The requirements of each operation will dictate the equipment necessary. The OIC and CRRC officer must take all facets of the mission profile into consideration before issuing the equipment list for a particular CRRC operation. The OIC must consider the following items for each operation:

- *Inherently Buoyant Personal Flotation Device (or UDT life jacket).* One device is required for each embarked member. A personal flotation device must be worn by each individual in the CRRC and must have sufficient lift to support the individual and his combat load. Each individual should conduct "float tests" to ensure that he has adequate flotation before the CRRC mission or training evolution. For flotation devices that use gas bladders for buoyancy, the activation mechanism (for example, gas cartridges and activators) should be inspected for proper functioning and ease of access while soldiers are in full combat dress.
- *Radio Transceiver.* A compatible radio transceiver, with sufficient spare batteries, will be carried in each CRRC.
- *Navigation Equipment.* Passive electronic methods of navigation such as GPS are recommended. However, they should not be totally relied upon due to problems in propagation, signal interruption in adverse weather conditions, and the delicacy of electronic instruments. As a minimum, the following navigation equipment is recommended:
  - Binoculars (waterproof).
  - Hand-bearing compass.
  - Speed-measuring devices.
  - Navigation chart of the AO.
  - Nautical slide rule (speed wheel).
  - Plotting board.
  - Flat dividers.
  - Boat compass.
- *Flares.* Only approved military flares will be used IAW current directives. Personnel should carry a minimum of four flares.
- *Paddles.* A sufficient number of paddles should be transported to provide propulsion and steering for the CRRC in case of OBM failure.
- *Repair Kit.* This kit should contain provisions for the CRRC and OBM.
- *Foot Pump.*
- *Strobe Light.*
- *Bow and Stern Lines.* They should be at least 15 feet long.
- *Towing Bridle.*

- *Protective Clothing*. Generally, protective clothing will be worn at the discretion of the OIC and CRRC officer as dictated by water and atmospheric temperatures. The planners should consider the desires of the individual crew. Planners should remember that crew members can suffer hypothermia during prolonged exposure to sea spray and wind even in relatively mild air temperatures.
- *Identification Friendly or Foe (IFF)*. This transponder is similar to those used on aircraft, ships, and armored vehicles. It transmits its identification in response to a query by U.S. targeting systems.

6-60. When planning for maritime operations, the "submariners rule" should be applied when practical. It is a rule of thumb that provides an operational guide to equipment redundancy requirements when operating isolated from support facilities. This guideline is intended to foster the mindset that preparedness with redundant equipment is the only way to ensure mission success in case a critical piece of equipment fails. The submariner's rule states that three of any required item is actually only two that can be counted on, two is one, and one is none. For example, when conducting an OTH infiltration using a SOCEP with two F-470s, prudent planning requires three OBMs.

CHAPTER 7

Inflatable Boats

This chapter provides information of value to detachments desiring introductory training on inflatable boats. Information is provided to familiarize personnel with boat team composition, organization, and duties. Basic boat-handling drills and emergency procedures are discussed. These procedures explain how to safely operate a CRRC in all conditions, with or without a motor. This chapter also provides information about CRRCs in general and the Zodiac F-470 in particular. The F-470 is the CRRC that detachments are most likely to use. It is the baseline by which all other CRRCs are judged.

NOTE

When coordinating with sister services, detachments must be aware that the term CRRC only applies to the F-470.

Historically, inflatable boat training has been based on the inflatable boat, small (IBS)—a small (7-man) inflatable landing boat that personnel paddle onto the beach and cache or abandon. Much of today's team organization and duties, as well as the handling techniques, are still based on this craft even though SF now uses vastly improved, motorized CRRCs to conduct our MAROPS.

BASIC BOAT-HANDLING SKILLS

7-1. The extended distances that MAROPS teams must travel to avoid detection have made motors a necessity. Unfortunately, this need has resulted in a general degradation of basic seamanship and boat-handling skills. Motors can fail leaving the unprepared detachment at the mercy of an unforgiving ocean. Therefore, basic seamanship skills are still of great value.

BOAT TEAM COMPOSITION

7-2. A boat team consists of the crew and passengers. The number of crew and passengers will be dictated by the rated capacity of the boat and motor, the mission load, the distance to be traversed, the sea state, and the required speed over the water. Obviously, the more restrictive the qualifiers, the smaller the mission load and the fewer the number of personnel that can be transported in the boat.

7-3. During training, the boat team of an inflatable landing boat will normally consist of seven men—a coxswain and six paddlers. Three paddlers are located along each gunwale, and the coxswain is located in the stern.

7-4. There are two methods of numbering paddlers: the long count and the short count. When the numbering of the boat team is by pairs, it is known as the short count; when the numbering of the boat team is by individuals, it is known as the long count. When using the long count, starboard (right side) paddlers are numbered 1, 3, and 5; port (left side) paddlers are numbered 2, 4, and 6 counting from bow to stern. The coxswain is team member Number 7.

7-5. When using a short count, paddlers are numbered in pairs from bow to stern. If passengers are carried, they are numbered consecutively from bow to stern starting with Number 8. The coxswain will issue commands to all boat team members using their respective number. As an example, when the coxswain issues a command to an individual paddler, he will use that team member's number. When addressing a pair of paddlers, he will use the short count terms, "ones," "twos," or "threes," indicating team member Numbers 1 and 2, 3 and 4, and 5 and 6, respectively. When addressing either side of the boat, he will use the terms starboard side or port side.

BOAT TEAM ORGANIZATION

7-6. The coxswain forms the boat team by commanding, "Team, fall in." The boat team forms facing the coxswain in a column of twos. The team members assume the relative positions they will occupy in the boat, hereinafter referred to as boat stations. Passengers form at the rear of the two columns by number—even numbers in the left column and odd numbers in the right. After the team has formed, the coxswain commands, "Team, count off." All hands sound off with their position numbers in order, including the coxswain who is Number 7.

TEAM MEMBER RESPONSIBILITIES

7-7. The tactics and techniques used in boat handling are similar and generally apply to most operations. However, to operate efficiently, each boat team member must perform the following specific duties:

- *Number 1.* The stroke sets the rate of paddling and maintains the paddling rhythm as directed by the coxswain. He assists the coxswain in keeping the boat perpendicular to the breaker line when beaching or launching the boat. He assists the coxswain in avoiding obstacles in the water.
- *Number 2.* He also assists the coxswain in keeping the boat perpendicular to the breaker line and in avoiding obstacles. He handles the towline and quick-release line during towing operations.
- *Numbers 3 and 4.* They lash and unload equipment in the boat. They are used as scout swimmers during tactical boat landings if scout swimmers are not carried as passengers.
- *Numbers 5 and 6.* They assist in lashing and unloading equipment in the after section of the boat. They also assist the coxswain in maneuvering in swift currents, and rigging and handling the sea anchor.
- *Number 7.* The coxswain oversees the team's performance, the handling of the boat, and the distribution of equipment and passengers in the boat. He issues all commands to team members, maintains course and speed, and operates the outboard motor if it is used.

7-8. During boat training, all team members will not display the same aptitude for boat handling, nor do all members need to acquire the same degree of boat-handling proficiency. When a boat team is formed for an operation, as opposed to a boat training exercise, the man chosen as coxswain should be the one with the greatest ability as a boat handler. The one chosen as the stroke should be selected for his strength and ability to maintain a steady rhythm.

BOAT TEAM SETUP

7-9. Additional duties of the boat team members will be determined by the mission requirements. Factors that must be considered are as follows:

- The individual overall responsible for the mission should consider being the primary navigator located in the lead boat. Each boat will have its own coxswain whose only duties are driving and following a bearing.
- Each boat will also have its own navigator who independently navigates that boat. Navigators should cross-check with the lead navigator or command craft. The assistant navigator (or bearing taker) takes bearings for the navigator and assists him as required.
- The boat watch monitors communications if applicable and observes the other boats to avoid separation and breaks in contact. Only the coxswain should sit on the buoyancy tubes. The remainder of the boat team sits inside the craft to reduce their exposure to the elements or enemy observation.

INDIVIDUAL EQUIPMENT

7-10. The unit leader specifies the uniform and equipment carried by each boat team member. There are some general rules, the most important being to ensure that all personnel wear an approved life preserver. All boat team members must wear adequate flotation, either rigid or inflatable life jackets. Every man wears a knife and a distress light or marker on his life jacket during night operations. Inflatable flotation must have CO_2 cylinders for pull-type inflation. Inflatable life preservers are usually more comfortable and less restrictive. Unfortunately, they require additional maintenance, are more susceptible to damage that would render them useless, and require activation before they will provide flotation. The detachment must perform an "in-water" float test to determine if the life preserver provides enough flotation to support the swimmer and his combat load; for example, weapon, load-carrying equipment (LCE), and any additional exposure protection. This need will be particularly important when operating in a riverine environment where the team may be in close proximity to hostile forces and jettisoning the equipment may not be an option.

7-11. When team members wear LCE in the boat, they should prepare it as for any waterborne operation and ensure it is easy to jettison if the wearer falls overboard. They should sling the weapon diagonally across the back, muzzle up and pointing outboard. If the operator falls overboard and cannot remain afloat with the rifle, he must be able to quickly jettison it.

7-12. For cold-weather operations, personnel should wear suitable exposure protection. This cover may include neoprene wet suits or dry suits, either of which will provide considerable warmth and buoyancy while in the water. These suits somewhat restrict paddlers' movements and may cause chafing in the armpits. Personnel should wear rubber tennis shoes for foot protection. Each man should carry a field uniform and boots to be worn during extended operations after the landing.

RIGGING THE CRRC AND STOWING ORGANIZATIONAL EQUIPMENT

7-13. After inflating the CRRC, crew members must prepare it for operations by rigging towing bridles, capsize lines, lifting slings (if required), equipment tie down lines, and setting up the navigation console.

Towing Bridles

7-14. Accident, combat damage, or mechanical failure can render a CRRC immobile in the water. Continuing with a mission or extracting a damaged vessel to a place of safety requires it to immediately be placed under tow. The detachment does this by pre-rigging the boat for towing, so that a tow can be initiated quickly. There are two types of towing rigs used with the CRRC.

7-15. **The first type** is the factory-supplied Zodiac towing harness consisting of two 15-foot nylon ropes with eye-splices and shackles on each end. This rig is primarily used under relatively calm conditions and when towing short distances. To use it, the crew member attaches the ends of the ropes to the towed boat's bow towing D-rings with the included shackles. He then passes the ropes forward to the towing vessel and attaches to that boat's opposite stern towing D-rings (port bow to starboard stern, starboard bow to port stern). The ropes should cross (X-fashion) between the bow of the towed vessel and the stern of the towing vessel.

7-16. **The second type** is an expedient harness, permanently tied onto each vessel during mission preparation. This is the preferred towing rig for operational use. It distributes the tow stresses over the entire structure of the CRRC allowing towing at higher speeds, over extended distances, and in rougher sea states. (Figure 7-1).

7-17. The expedient harness is made using approximately 60 feet of 7/16th climbing rope or 1-inch tubular nylon webbing. Two CRRCs can be rigged from one 120-foot rope. To tie the harness, the crew member cuts the 120-foot rope in half, one half per boat. For each boat, he doubles the rope and ties a figure-8 loop on the bight. He places the loop in front of the bow and extends one "leg" of the harness down each side of the CRRC. Working from the bow to the stern on each side of the CRRC, he threads the rope on that side straight through the bow towing D-ring and back through each carrying handle. The crew member passes the rope from the top of the carrying handle through the bottom, continuing through all handles to and through the rear towing D-ring. He takes the extreme end of the rope and ties a snug bowline around the tail cone of the main buoyancy tube immediately behind the rear towing D-ring. He secures the bowline onto the main buoyancy tube by tying it to the transom on the inboard side with a piece of suspension line (this keeps it from slipping off the tail cone if the harness should become slack). The crew member works any slack in the harness forward towards the bow, extends the figure-8 loop to the front of the CRRC, and ensures it is centered on the bow. If necessary, he adjusts the loop's position and fastens a snap link into it. He secures the excess harness by daisy chaining or coiling, and correctly stows it in the bow for rapid deployment without tangling.

7-18. The crew member prepares the towing component by tying (or splicing) small loops into the ends of a sling rope. He ensures the sling rope is long enough to pass around the rear of the CRRCs OBM without interfering with its

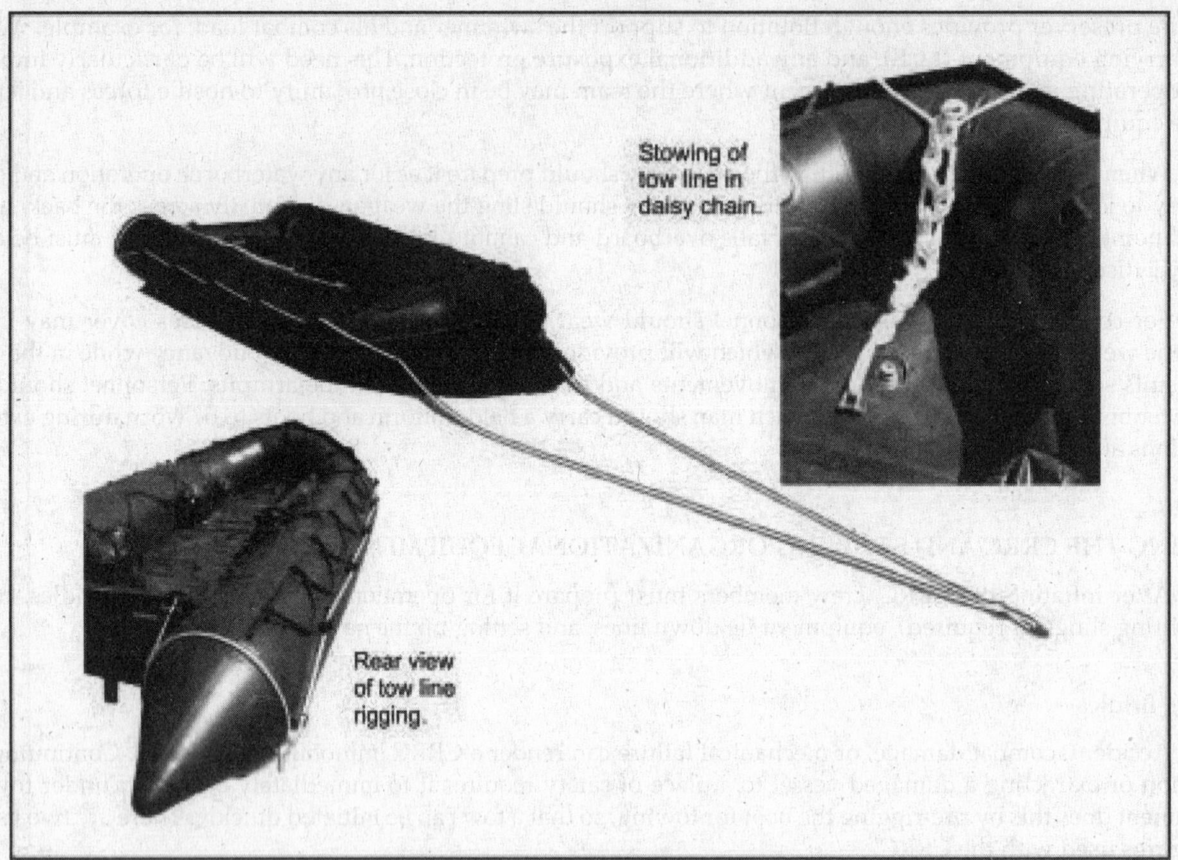

Figure 7-1. Expedient harness

operation. He puts a snap link into each loop and clips the snap links to the transom lifting rings. This bridle can be left in place by flipping it forward over the OBM and securing it with retaining bands on the inside of the transom. It also can be stowed in the towing vessel and emplaced only when required.

7-19. To initiate a tow, a crew member has the towing vessel back down on the bow of the towed vessel. He clips the snap link on the towed vessel's harness to the towing bridle on the towing vessel. As the towing vessel pulls away, the bow man on the towed vessel controls the deployment of the harness's slack to prevent entanglement. Throughout the tow, crew members in both vessels monitor the towing line to ensure that any slack is controlled before it can become entangled in the towing vessel's propeller. If the sea state requires extending the tow, crew members can easily add additional line (rope) between the towing harness and the towing bridle.

Capsize Lines

7-20. If the CRRC capsizes, crew members must right it as quickly as possible. To help right the boat, crew members must rig the capsize lines. These lines help apply the leverage required to right an upside-down boat. There are two common methods of rigging capsize lines (Figure 7-2).

7-21. The preferred method is to attach a 20-foot line (rope or 1-inch tubular nylon) to the foremost and aftmost equipment lashing (50 mm) D-rings on the starboard main buoyancy tube. The crew member can either tie on or secure this line with snap links or shackles. He zigzags the slack between the two D-rings and secures it with retaining bands. When used, a crew member pulls the capsize line loose from the retaining bands and passes it across the bottom of the boat to the other crew members assigned to right the boat.

7-22. The alternate method is to attach sling ropes, one to each of three equipment tie-down (50 mm) D-rings, usually on the starboard side of the CRRC. The crew member stows the sling ropes by coiling and securing them with

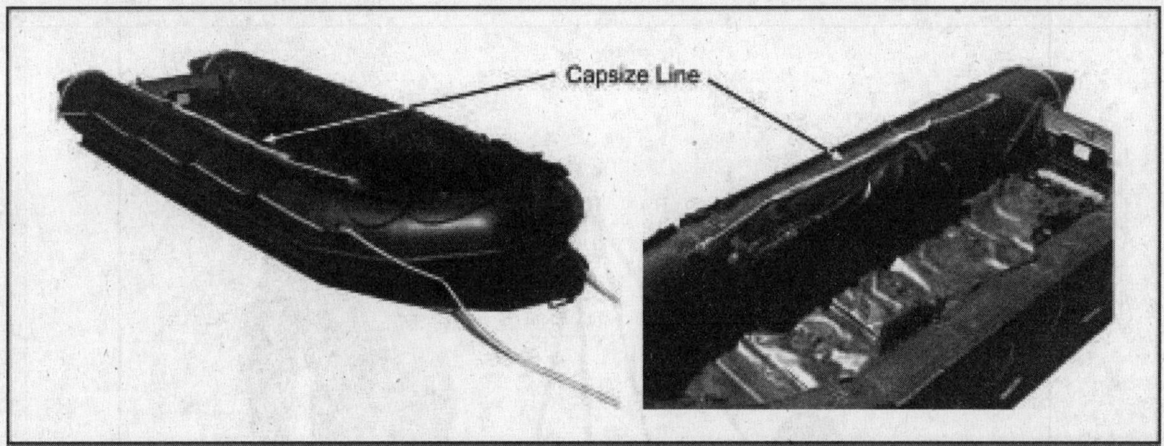

Figure 7-2. Capsize line

retaining bands. To use, the crew member pulls the ropes free of the retaining bands and tosses each capsize line across the bottom of the CRRC to a crew member waiting on the other side.

Lifting Slings

7-23. The Zodiac F-470 comes from the factory with an accessory lifting kit consisting of lifting points (eye bolts on the bow thrust board and lifting rings through-bolted on the transom) and a lifting harness (a center ring with a pair of long lines and a pair of short lines—all terminated in eye splices with shackles for attachment to the lifting points) (Figure 7-3). The lifting kit allows detachments engaged in mothership operations to launch and recover fully rigged (but not loaded) CRRCs from the deck of a mothership equipped with a deck crane or hoist. If the mothership has the capability, hoisting the CRRC into or out of the water provides significant advantages, greatly increasing the safety and security of the operation and significantly reducing the physical exertion required.

7-24. In use, the CRRC is completely rigged with OBM mounted, fuel bladders attached and secured, and all operating equipment stowed. Individual and team equipment is staged on the deck of the mothership. The lifting harness is attached to the CRRC with the short legs of the lifting harness shackled to the bow lifting points and the long legs to the stern. This ensures that when the CRRC is lowered over the side of the mothership, the stern hits first causing the bow to "weathervane" and point into the waves and current.

7-25. To hoist the CRRC, the crew member places the center ring of the lifting harness in the hoist's hook. The mothership's crew operates the hoist to launch or retrieve the CRRC. Crew members maneuver the CRRC using its bow and stern lines to maintain control throughout the hoisting operation. Once the CRRC is in the water, it is secured to the mothership with the handling (bow and stern) lines, the lifting harness is disconnected from the hoist, and individual or detachment equipment is loaded and secured.

Equipment Tie Downs

7-26. All individual and detachment equipment that is not worn by crew members must be secured inside the CRRC. Crew members should place all organizational equipment that is not worn by the boat team, such as machine guns, radios, and demolitions, in waterproof bags (as required) or rucksacks. They should pad sharp corners and projections on equipment to prevent damage to the boat. They should also stow and lash the bags or rucksacks securely in the boat before launching.

7-27. There are numerous equipment tie-down procedures available to crew members. The most common ones include securing each bundle or rucksack to a fixed D-ring with snap links, and rigging a series of individual equipment tie-down lines athwartships between opposing D-rings to secure the bundles or rucksacks to these lines with snap links. When using the accessory rigid floorboard, crew members can rig equipment attachment loops by running

Figure 7-3. Lifting sling

lengths of 1/2-inch tubular nylon through holes drilled in the floorboards. This modification is required when rigging the CRRC for airdrop.

7-28. An alternate method that offers some advantages if the boat capsizes is for a crew member to rig a single equipment line from the lifting ring on the transom, forward to a D-ring on the opposite bow. He then ties a loop near the bow end of the line and snap links a rucksack (stopper) into the loop. He snap links the remainder of the bundles or rucksacks into the equipment line between the stopper and the transom. The equipment should be free to slide the length of the equipment line and to be retained on the line by the stopper. If the CRRC capsizes, the crew member releases the bow end of the line and allows the cargo to float free (secured at the transom), while the CRRC is righted. This method removes a significant portion of the weight from the CRRC and makes it easier to right the boat. Personnel can then recover the equipment over the stern (or towed, if the situation requires).

7-29. An alternative to individually securing each piece of equipment is to secure the entire load with a cargo net. Netting the cargo allows detachments to rapidly secure odd-shaped bundles or large quantities of smaller items, a characteristic that is especially useful when CRRCs are used for logistics support missions. Purpose-built nets designed for the F-470 and similar craft are available through the GSA catalog (NSN# 3940-01-477-7081) from suppliers such as Loadtamer®.

Navigation Console

7-30. CRRCs designated as navigation platforms should have a navigation console secured on the gunwale tube forward of the coxswain. The manufactured consoles consist of a boat compass (for example, Ritchie compass) and a marine knotmeter (for example, OMC speedometer) mounted in a molded housing contoured to fit on the main buoyancy tube (Figure 7-4). Instrument lighting is provided by a chemlight. This equipment allows the coxswain to maintain course and monitor speed.

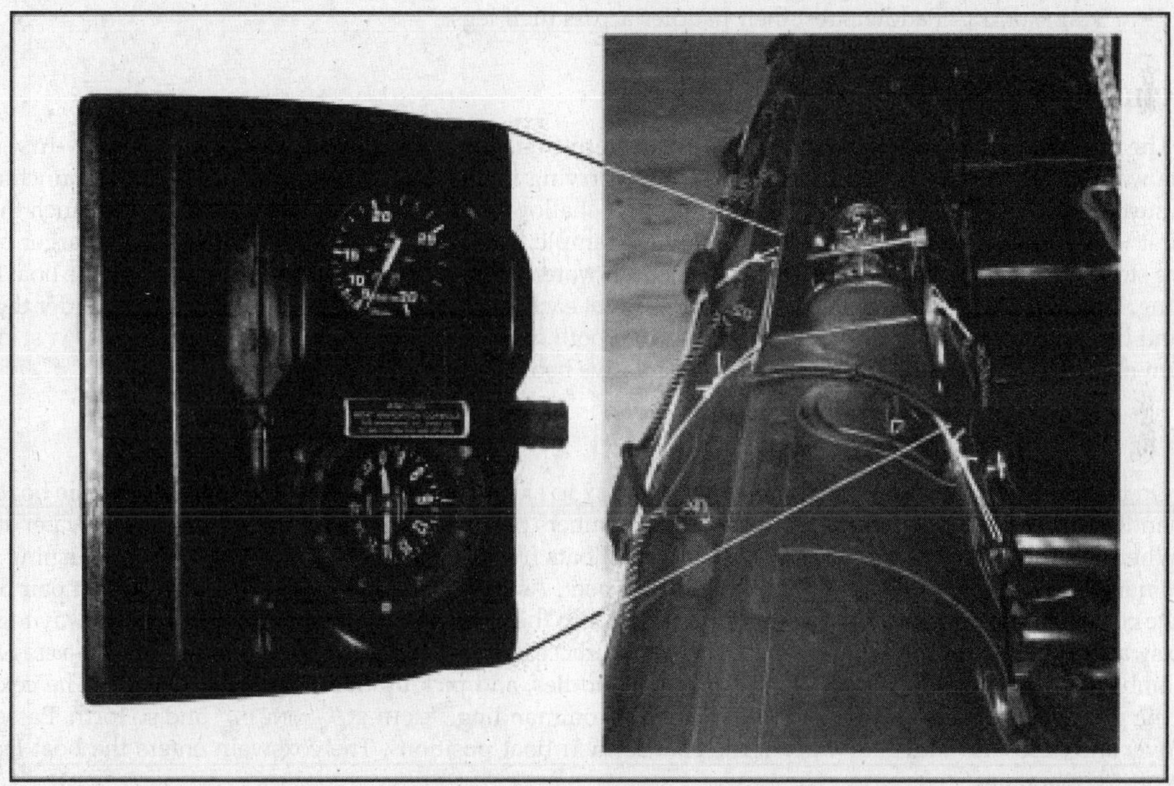

Figure 7-4. Boat navigation console

7-31. The console is strapped or tied to attachment points (D-rings, carrying handles) with 550 cord or straps laced through cutouts in the console. Care must be taken when routing the vacuum tube for the knotmeter to ensure that it is not cut or kinked. Running the hose to the inside, under the swell of the main buoyancy tube, and taping it in place with duct tape will maximize the available protection.

7-32. The boat must also be "swung" to account for deviation. This allows the navigator to account for compass errors caused by the magnetic field of the boat or any embarked equipment. In use, crew members ensure that large metal objects and electronics are kept far enough from the console so they do not affect the compass.

INFLATABLE BOAT COMMANDS

7-33. All boat personnel should be knowledgeable of operational terms to ensure they respond or react appropriately. The specific commands used when handling inflatable boats are as follows:

- *Preparatory Commands.* The coxswain issues preparatory commands to indicate who will execute the command to follow. In some instances the preparatory command includes the expression "STAND BY TO...."
- *Boat Handling Commands.* These commands should be understood by all boat team members:
  - "LOW CARRY." Team members form up at boat stations and face the bow of the boat. On command, they lift the boat by the carrying handles to about knee height.
  - "HIGH CARRY." Team members form up at boat stations and face the stern of the boat. On command, they lift the boat to shoulder height while simultaneously rotating their bodies under the boat so that they face forward with the boat resting on their inboard shoulders. Team members maintain their grip on the carrying handle with the outboard hand.
  - "GIVE WAY TOGETHER." Paddlers stroke in unison, following the rhythm set by Number 1.
  - "HOLD WATER." Paddlers hold their paddles motionless in the water with the blade perpendicular to the direction of motion.
  - "BACK WATER." Paddlers paddle backward in unison with Number 1.
  - "REST PADDLES." Paddlers rest their paddles across their legs.

LAUNCHING THE BOAT

7-34. The boat team may launch the boat bow-first or stern-first. Personnel should launch the boat bow-first whenever the water is shallow enough for them to wade-in carrying the boat at low carry. An example is launching the boat in surf or from the shore of any body of water that is shallow at its banks. The boat team should launch the boat stern-first when the water is too deep for wading; for example, launching the boat over the side of a larger boat or from the steeply sloping bank of a river. Personnel should waterproof, stow, and lash all equipment in the boat before launching. They should distribute the paddles in the boat at each boat station with the blades wedged under the cross tubes and the handles forward and slightly outboard. In both cases, the coxswain commands, "CREW, BOAT STATIONS," and team members form alongside the boat in their relative boat positions facing forward.

Launching the Boat Bow-First

7-35. On the coxswain's preparatory command, "STAND BY TO LAUNCH BOAT," the team members grasp the boat's carrying handles. On the command, "LAUNCH BOAT," team members perform a low carry and move into the water at a fast walk. When the depth of the water is such that the boat floats free of the bottom, all hands continue pushing it seaward remaining in their relative positions alongside the boat. As the water reaches the knees of the first pair of paddlers, the coxswain commands, "ONES IN." The ones climb into the boat, unstow their paddles, and give way together. The coxswain orders each pair of paddlers into the boat in succession by commanding, "TWOS IN," and "THREES IN." The pairs climb into the boat on command, break out their paddles, and pick up the stroke of Number 1. The coxswain orders the passengers into the boat after the paddlers by commanding, "EIGHT IN," "NINE IN," and so forth. Passengers board over the stern and move forward in the boat to their boat positions. The coxswain enters the boat last and sounds off, "COXSWAIN IN."

Launching the Boat Stern-First

7-36. On the coxswain's preparatory command "STAND BY TO LAUNCH BOAT," the team members grasp the boat's carrying handles. On the command, "LAUNCH BOAT," team members perform a low carry and carry the boat stern first to the water's edge. They launch the boat by passing it back along the line of team members. When Number 2 can no longer aid in passing the boat back, he moves to the bow of the boat and handles the bowline. Other team members follow suit, taking their places along the bowline between Number 2 and the boat. When the boat is in the water, the coxswain enters the boat and takes his boat station. The coxswain then commands the boat team to load by the long count; that is, "SIX IN," "FIVE IN," "FOUR IN," "THREE IN," and "ONE IN." Passengers are loaded next: "NINE IN," "EIGHT IN." When the coxswain is ready to cast off, he commands "TWO IN." Number 2 casts off and climbs into the boat and takes his boat position.

Paddling Rate

7-37. A paddling cadence of 30 strokes per minute is maintained for open-water paddling. A faster rate is necessary when launching a boat through surf; a slower rate for long distances. The coxswain may order a cadence of 10 to 20 strokes per minute by commanding, "REST STROKE." The stroke decreases to about half of normal cadence and each paddler comes to the position of rest paddle between strokes. Well-conditioned paddlers can maintain a rest stroke cadence for hours.

Maintaining Course

7-38. Inflatable boats should be kept perpendicular to the waves in rough seas but may take waves off the bow or stern in a calm sea. Thus, the course may have to be maintained by tacking. Strong winds and currents may require the coxswain to steer a compensated course.

Turning the Boat Rapidly

7-39. The coxswain steers the boat with his paddle, called the sweep. If he wants to turn the boat rapidly, he orders the paddlers on one side to back water while those on the other side give way together. Thus, a rapid turn to starboard is executed by commanding, "STARBOARD, BACKWATER, PORT, GIVE WAY TOGETHER."

TRANSIT FORMATIONS

7-40. Transit formations are used to control several boats operating together. Formations are determined based on the distance to be transited, the sea state, and the enemy situation. Mission commanders should select the formation that provides the greatest control while still ensuring the flexibility and mutual support necessary to react to enemy contact. Detachments should use prearranged hand signals to change formations (if required) without using communications. The mission planner should review the NAVPLAN and enemy situation to anticipate formation changes en route. The navigator uses the following formations when encountering the conditions described:

- File:
  - Tight areas.
  - When expecting contacts from flanks.
- Wedge:
  - Very dark and low visibility.
  - All-around defense.
  - Can move to more of a diamond with four boats.
- Echelon (left or right):
  - Open areas.
  - High visibility.
  - Flexible response.
  - All-around defense.
  - Formed away from sea obstacles.

LANDING THE BOAT

7-41. The manner in which the coxswain orders the boat team to unload the boat when landing depends on the depth of the water at the landing point. Each depth and its differences are discussed below.

Shallow Water

7-42. As the boat nears the shore, the coxswain sounds with his sweep and orders the team to disembark when the water is waist deep, using the command "BEACH BOAT." On this order, die team stows their paddles and disembarks. The team members grasp the carrying handles and push the boat as far as it will float, then they carry it at low carry thereafter.

Deep Water

7-43. When the boat is landed in deep water, such as when tying up to a submarine, the coxswain uses the following procedure to unload and land the boat. As the boat comes alongside the landing platform, the coxswain orders, "TWO OUT." Number 2 stows his paddle and, with bowline in hand, gets out of the boat onto the landing platform and pulls the boat up close to the landing. The other team members either stow their paddles in the boat or pass them up to personnel on the landing platform. The coxswain commands, "ONE OUT," and Number 1 climbs out of the boat followed in order by the passengers and Numbers 3, 4, 5, and 6. The coxswain is the last to leave the boat. As the team members climb out over the bow of the boat, they take their places along the bowline corresponding to their boat positions. After the coxswain gets out of the boat, the team pulls the boat out of the water and onto the landing platform. As the boat is pulled up, team members leave the bowline and move to positions where they can handle the boat by its carrying handles and pass it up between them. When boat team members get into or out of the boat, they maintain a low silhouette to prevent being thrown off balance overboard.

BEACHING THE BOAT IN SURF

7-44. The coxswain beaches his boat during one of the recurring periods of relatively light breakers that exist between series of heavy breakers. Before entering the surf zone, the coxswain orders all hands to shift aft to put as much weight as possible in the stern. Even small breakers will capsize a boat if they can raise the stern out of the water.

7-45. As the boat enters the surf zone, the coxswain keeps the boat perpendicular to the surf line, assisted by the ones who may back paddle as necessary. The paddlers take advantage of each wave's momentum by paddling faster as the wave raises the boat. The coxswain periodically observes the sea astern of the boat, but paddlers never look astern since they must concentrate on maintaining the cadence.

7-46. The coxswain sounds with his sweep and orders the team to disembark when the water is waist deep. The team grasps the carrying handles and pushes the boat as far as it will float, carrying it at low carry thereafter. The coxswain may order the boat overturned at the water's edge to empty it of water.

7-47. The greatest chance of capsizing or swamping exists just before a boat is beached. The turbulence caused by incoming waves meeting the backrush of water from the beach makes it hard to keep the boat perpendicular to the surf.

LAUNCHING THE BOAT IN SURF

7-48. The coxswain launches the boat in surf during a period of relatively light breakers. He takes advantage of rip currents if they are present. As each pair of paddlers embarks, they shift forward in the boat to put as much weight as possible in the bow. Number 1 sets a fast, strong cadence without waiting for orders from the coxswain. In moderate or heavy surf, the boat team has little chance of successfully transiting the surf zone if the boat is not through before the next series of relatively heavy breakers arrives.

OVERTURNING AND RIGHTING THE BOAT IN THE WATER

7-49. A coxswain may have to right a capsized boat or empty a swamped boat by overturning it and righting it in the water. A boat is overturned (broached or capsized) and righted by the same procedure. All but three members of the boat team and the coxswain (who holds all the paddles) stay in the water during the overturning or righting. Prerigged capsize lines attached on one side of the boat are passed across to the opposite side where they are grasped by the three remaining paddlers. These paddlers stand on the gunwale or main buoyancy tube and fall backward into the water, pulling the boat after them and overturning it. They are assisted as necessary by the three paddlers in the water. The command, "BROACH BOAT," is used in training to cause the boat team to overturn the boat in water.

TACTICAL BOAT LANDINGS AND WITHDRAWALS

7-50. Boat teams conduct minor tactical exercises during training to demonstrate and improve their boat-handling ability under operational conditions. All members of the team are trained to perform the duties of all other members during these exercises.

Landings

7-51. As the boat approaches the surf zone, the team leader orders the coxswain to lie outside the surf zone and maintain position relative to the beach. The team leader then orders the coxswain to send in his scout swimmers. The coxswain commands, "TWOS OUT," and Numbers 3 and 4 enter the water and swim to the beach.

7-52. Scout swimmers must avoid splitting a breaker line or foam line because doing so results in them being silhouetted against a white foam background. The scout swimmers determine the presence or absence of enemy in the landing area. They usually move singly about 50 yards in opposite directions after reaching the beach.

7-53. When the scout swimmers have determined that the landing area is free of enemy personnel, they advise the boat team using a predetermined signal that will be clearly visible and unmistakable to the detachment waiting at the boat pool. The selected signaling method must also take into consideration the threat of detection by the enemy. One method is for the scout swimmers to use a filtered (infrared), hooded flashlight with a prearranged light signal. The scout swimmers give the signal from the point on the beach that they have selected as the most suitable for landing. After signaling the boat, the scout swimmers move in opposite directions from the landing point to listening and observation positions. These security positions are at the limit of visibility from the landing point.

7-54. When the boat team receives the scout swimmers' signal, the team leader orders the coxswain to beach his boat at the point from which the signal originated. After the boat is beached, the team leader orders it hidden and camouflaged as previously covered in his fragmentary patrol order.

Withdrawals

7-55. The detachment conducts a security halt short of the withdrawal area or cache site. The team leader then orders a pair of scouts forward to determine if the withdrawal area is clear of enemy personnel. These scouts reconnoiter the cache to see if it has been disturbed and observe the beach for the presence of enemy personnel.

7-56. After the scouts report that the area is clear, the team leader orders the coxswain to prepare the boat for withdrawal. In some cases, the boat may have to be inflated from air bottles or hand and foot pumps. During this preparation, the team leader posts security just short of the limit of visibility from the cache to warn that the enemy is approaching. One observer is usually posted at each flank of the withdrawal area, while the team leader observes the route previously taken by the boat team on their way to the cache.

7-57. When the boat is prepared for withdrawal, the coxswain informs the team leader, who then orders the coxswain to launch the boat. Just before the boat enters the water, the team leader calls his security observers to the boat where they take their boat team positions usually as twos. The coxswain then assumes control of all hands for the launching.

ZODIAC F-470 INFLATABLE BOAT

7-58. The Zodiac Marine Commando F-470 is the most frequently used assault boat (Figure 7-5) for all SOF. The MARS (OMC) 35-horsepower engine is issued for use with the Zodiac F-470 inflatable boat (Figure 7-6). However, with minor modifications, the Zodiac F-470 can accommodate other engine packages, such as the 55-HP OBM, that will enhance performance.

7-59. The USMC's Small Craft Propulsion System (SCPS) is an optional power plant for the CRRC. It was developed and adopted to replace the USMC's OTH configuration that used twin 35-HP OBMs. The SCPS is a 55-HP submersible OBM. The principle difference between the SCPS and a standard 55-HP OBM is a replacement bottom-end that exchanges the standard propeller for a pump jet. The pump jet is a fully enclosed (shrouded) impeller. It provides an added degree of safety by reducing the possibility of a prop-strike. When compared to the twin 35-HP OTH configuration, the SCPS offers significant advantages for the USMC.

7-60. SF units will find that the SCPS offers detachments some limited safety advantages when operating in the vicinity of swimmers, in debris-laden waters, shallow-draft, or in case of a capsize (for example, heavy surf zones). The disadvantages of this system for SF units (when compared to the propeller-driven, 55-HP OBM) include a

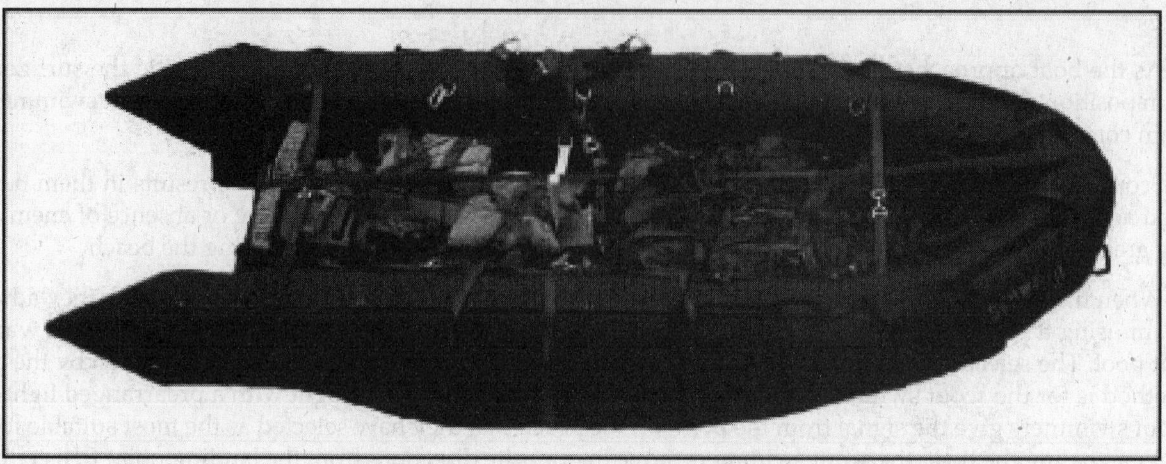

Figure 7-5. Zodiac F-470 Inflatable boat

Figure 7-6. MARS engine

weight increase, reduced top speed, increased fuel consumption, increased mechanical complexity, and more expensive to purchase.

CHARACTERISTICS

7-61. The Zodiac is a squad-sized inflatable craft capable of amphibious small-boat operations. The F-470 is made of neoprene-coated, tear-resistant nylon cloth. When fully inflated (240 millibars [mb], or 3.5 pounds, per square inch gauge [psig]), the F-470 weighs approximately 280 pounds without the engine. The maximum payload is 1,230 kilograms (kg) (2,710 pounds). The overall length of the craft is 4.70 meters, or 15 feet and 5 inches. The overall width of the craft is 1.90 meters, or 6 feet and 3 inches. The F-470 should be loaded to a weight ceiling of 2,000 pounds to allow the craft to perform at its optimum. F-470s outfitted with aluminum decking ensure a higher rate of speed, mobility, and maneuverability. The aluminum deck is composed of four lightweight, self-locking aluminum sections and two aluminum stringers. Table 7-1 lists the F-470 specifications.

Table 7-1. Zodiac F-470 specifications

Feature	Size/Weight/Dimension
Overall length	4.70 m or 15 ft, 5 in.
Overall width	1.90 m or 6 ft, 3 in.
Inside length	3.30 m or 10 ft, 10 in.
Inside width	0.90 m or 3 ft
Tube diameter	0.50 m or 20 in.
Maximum number of passengers	10
Maximum payload	1,230 kg or 2,710 pounds
Maximum HP with standard 40 HP	40 HP matted floor, short shaft
Maximum HP with optional 65 HP	65 HP aluminum floor, short shaft
Dimensions in bag	1.50 × 0.75 m or 59 in. × 29.5 in.
Weight with standard matted floor	120 kg or 280 pounds
Weight with optional aluminum floor	120 kg or 280 pounds
Number of airtight chambers	8
Weight of CO2 charged bottle with manifold (U.S. DOT-approved)	20.45 kg or 45 pounds

7-62. Detachments working with other Services may encounter additional types of small craft that fill the same operational niche as the Zodiac F-470. Knowing what is available is important, especially when requesting insertion or extraction by a Sister Service, for example, a USMC raid or reconnaissance force. Table 7-2 shows different types and characteristics of inflatables used by other agencies.

Table 7-2. CRRC characteristics (inflatables)

Item		Weight (pounds)	Length (feet)
Avon		450	15
Avon		460	15
Avon		520	17
Z-Bird		400	15
IBS		120	13
Zodiac F-470		280	15
OBMs Used With CRRCs		**Gas Bladder**	**Gas Can**
55 HP 35HP 15 HP	202 pounds 118 pounds 78 pounds	18 gallons (13.5 gallons maximum allowed on aircraft)	6 gallons (4.5 gallons maximum allowed on aircraft)

7-63. The F-470 is the CRRC in the Marine Corps supply inventory. The USMC uses it for both reconnaissance forces and MEU(SOC) raid force operations. Marines also use the CRRC-LR and rigid hull inflatable boats (RHIBs). The CRRC-LR is a long-range, rigid hull version of the CRRC that can be taken apart and stored in nearly the same space as a CRRC. The RHIB is a one-piece rigid hull with an inflatable flotation collar (equivalent to the main buoyancy tube of the CRRC). Both of these boats have handling and load-carrying characteristics that are superior to the F-470, especially when operating in marginal sea states. They can also use more powerful OBMs.

7-64. The Zodiac offers numerous advantages when conducting waterborne infiltrations or exfiltrations. The Zodiac—

- Offers mobility and speed that surpasses scout swimming and scuba methods.
- Enables personnel to reach the BLS rested, dry, and ready to conduct the mission.
- Can be launched from submarine, aircraft, or mothercraft.
- Has five compartments that are separately inflatable.
- Cannot be overinflated because of overpressure relief values.
- Has an inflatable keel that offers a smoother and more stable ride.
- Can oftentimes avoid radar detection due to its fabric construction.
- Has accessory rigid floorboards that prevent buckling and pitching with heavy loads during operations.
- Can adequately accommodate six men with equipment.

COMPONENTS

7-65. The Zodiac consists of the following components:

- Five airtight chambers in the hull.
- Two separate airtight chambers (speed skegs) under the main buoyancy tube.
- Overpressure relief valves.
- A plank-reinforced, roll-up floorboard that can be left installed when packing the boat.
- An accessory rigid floor that has four reinforced aluminum antislip floorboards.
- An inflatable keel.
- Eight carrying handles.
- A reinforced transom.
- Stainless steel towing rings.
- Lifeline and bow grab lines.
- Bow pouches with foot pumps, hoses, and a field repair kit.

7-66. The Zodiac F-470 (SW) CRRC variant for USMC use has a full-height transom modification designed specifically to accommodate a 55-HP OBM. New or replacement F-470s acquired for USASOC units will also conform to the USMC specifications. F-470s with the full-height transom require the use of long-shaft OBMs. Short-shaft engines will cavitate.

ASSEMBLY

7-67. Personnel follow specific steps to assemble the Zodiac. They should—

- Roll out the Zodiac and inspect it for serviceability.
- Turn the valves to the inflate position and remove the valve caps.
- Place the accessory rigid aluminum floorboards in the boat (1 through 4) and interlock them.
- Attach hoses with foot pumps to each valve and inflate the boat.
- Place stringers (short ones in front, long ones in the rear) on each side of the floorboards and lock them in place.
- Check the inflation pressure by placing a pressure gauge in a valve for the recommended (240 mb) reading when the boat is fully inflated.
- Turn all valves to the navigation position, thereby closing the valve and isolating the five separate air chambers in the main buoyancy tube.
- Secure the clamps on the connecting tubes between the main buoyancy tube and the speed skegs.
- Inflate the keel to the prescribed (220 mb) reading.

GENERAL MAINTENANCE

7-68. Personnel should follow the recommendations outlined below for the use and care of the Zodiac. They should—

- Never run the Zodiac underinflated.
- Wash down the Zodiac with fresh water after every use.
- Avoid dragging the Zodiac on rocky beaches, rough surfaces, coral reefs, and so forth.
- Ensure the Zodiac is thoroughly dry and free of grit and sand before deflating it and placing it in a carrying bag.
- Never lift the Zodiac by the lifeline.

EMERGENCY REPAIR AT OPERATOR LEVEL

7-69. CRRCs are extremely vulnerable. In any exchange of fire, it is probable that the CRRC will sustain damage. Punctures will cause the boat to deflate rapidly! Air pressure gives the boat its rigidity and, depending on the quantity and severity of the punctures, the detachment may only have seconds before the CRRC has lost enough air that it will fold up when the engine is used. The first priority of the team members is to clear the kill or danger zone. Then attempt to patch the CRRC (and any wounded). If the CRRC has lost a significant amount of air, it may be easier and safer to tow it to a safer location rather than risk collapsing the boat by trying to motor to safety. To this end, CRRCs must always be rigged to facilitate rapid towing.

7-70. Detachment SOPs should specify quantities, types, and locations of emergency repair materials. The most effective emergency repairs are made with "lifeboat patches." There are two types available. The first is a series (graduated by size) of plugs resembling threaded cones that can be either plastic or wood. The team member should screw the plugs into the puncture until it is sealed. The second emergency patch is the "clamshell" type. It is a two-piece, gasketed, elliptical metal patch joined by a stud with a retained wing nut. The team member should separate the halves and insert the back half (point-first) through the hole, enlarging as required. He then rotates the patch to align its long axis with the hole and screws the two halves together. Both types of patch should be contained in easily accessible repair kits, strategically placed, throughout the boat. The CRRC has pouches for repair kits and pumps located fore and aft on the main buoyancy tube. Second echelon maintenance facilities can add extra pouches if desired.

7-71. After plugging any holes in the boat, personnel must reinflate it before continuing with or aborting the mission. The fastest, easiest method for reinflating is to use the CRRC's CO2 inflation system. It is a single-point, pressurized inflation system consisting of a CO2 bottle (original issue) or a 100-ft^3 (updated to meet USN requirements) air cylinder with a low-pressure manifold attached to valves in the CRRC. To inflate the boat using this system, the team member should first open the interconnecting (I/C) valves by rotating them from "navigate" to "inflate," and open the cylinder valve. He controls the rate of inflation by manipulating the cylinder valve to prevent blown baffles or overinflation. He only adds enough air to the CRRC to enable it to maintain its shape and resist the force of the outboard motor. The emergency repairs performed with the lifeboat patches are not secure enough to resist the full inflation pressure (240 mb in the main tube). The repairs will still leak, even at a reduced pressure. Any gas (air/CO2) remaining in the cylinder will be needed to top off the CRRC at regular intervals. To conserve the available gas, it may be possible to top off the CRRC using the foot pumps. These measures will allow the detachment to continue using a damaged CRRC until it can be patched using the emergency repair kit issued with the boat.

7-72. Once the detachment reaches an area of relative safety, personnel make temporary repairs that will allow them to use the CRRC. When repairing the CRRC, the team member should—

- Clean the patch and the area to be repaired with methyl ethyl ketone (MEK) and allow it to dry before application. The objective is to remove all contaminants such as oil, grease, or salt and to chemically prepare the surface for gluing.

NOTE

Alcohol or water may be used if MEK is not available, but the patch will not adhere as well.

- Cut patch material so that it extends a 1-inch minimum on all sides of the tear.
- Use the pumice stone included in the repair kit to rough up the surface of the material on the patch and on the boat.

- Apply a thin, even coat of the Zodiac glue to both the patch and the boat, making a total of 3 applications to each.
- Wait approximately 10 minutes between each application to allow the glue to set up.
- Carefully apply the patch, rolling it on evenly and smoothly to guard against wrinkles.
- Vigorously rub the patch over its entire surface with the boning tool (stainless steel spatula) included in the repair kit to ensure positive contact between the patch and the boat.
- Let the repair dry (cure) for 12 to 24 hours before inflating the boat to full pressure (if the situation permits).

> **NOTE**
> Detachments should seek additional training in the use of the emergency repair kit from qualified technical personnel.

FUEL CONSUMPTION DATA

7-73. To plan a maritime infiltration using any small craft, detachments must be able to accurately calculate the amount of fuel required to execute a transit from the debarkation point to the BLS. The prudent planner will then add in allowances for exfiltration and possible contingencies such as the requirement to move to an alternate BLS. He then uses this data as a baseline to determine an appropriate safety margin (at least 15 to 20 percent additional fuel) to allow for increased fuel consumption caused by wind, waves, currents, and variations in the boat's calculated fuel usage. These combined factors will help define the total amount of fuel required to safely conduct the mission. The planner also considers the following variables when determining overall fuel use:

- Type of boat.
- Speed maintained.
- Displacement and weight of personnel and cargo.
- Type of motor and propeller.
- Engine throttle setting.
- Wind speed and direction.
- Current, set, and drift.
- Sea state.

7-74. Fuel consumption is a critical element when planning mission requirements. The detachment computes fuel consumption to provide to the planner for inclusion in the NAVPLAN. Team members perform the following:

- Ensure fuel tanks are topped off.
- Measure and record total gallons in fuel tanks.
- Start engines and record the time.
- Set desired rpm for engines or throttle setting, and record.
- Record set rpm/throttle.
- Stop engines and record the time.
- Measure and record total gallons of fuel in tanks.
- Subtract total gallons in tanks after running 1 hour from total gallons recorded on boat at beginning of underway period.
- Record the difference.
- Measure the distance traveled, and record.
- Compute boat speed, and record.
- Apply the formula—time (T) × gallon per hour (GPH) = total fuel consumption (TFC).
- Recompute GPH after changing rpm or throttle setting and follow the procedures "record set rpm/throttle" through "apply the formula."

7-75. The following data was assembled from test runs conducted by the Naval Special Warfare Center (NSWC) (Table 7-3 and Figure 7-7). It is presented for information only. To accurately calculate fuel usage for their CRRCs, detachments must conduct their own sea trials with mission loads and sea states as nearly identical to mission conditions as possible.

Table 7-3. Sample fuel usage for CRRCs

Payload (pounds)	Maximum Speed (knots)	NM Per Gallon
Configuration 1: Zodiac F-470, 35 HP Evinrude OBM, 11″ × 13″ Propeller		
1,800	6.5	2.5
1,600	6.7	2.8
1,400	8.2	4.1
1,200	16.4	4.3
Configuration 2: Zodiac F-470, Twin 35 HP Evinrude OBM, 11″ × 13″ Propeller		
2,200	7.9	3.9
2,000	17.7	6.5
1,800	18.8	6.7
Configuration 3: Zodiac F-470, 55 HP Evinrude OBM, 13 1/4″ × 17″ Propeller		
1,800	7.5	2.5
1,600	20.3	3.4
1,400	17.3	3.4
1,200	18.5	3.4
1,000	18.8	3.4
800	20.0	3.4
Configuration 4: Zodiac F-470, 55 HP Evinrude OBM, 13 3/4″ × 15″ Propeller		
2,200	8.8	1.7
2,100	18.8	3.1
2,000	18.9	3.1
1,800	19.3	4.2

- Navigation Equipment:
  - Nautical Slide Rule
  - Hand-Held Compass
  - Steiner Binoculars
  - GPS
- Plotting Board:
  - Laminated
  - Bar Scale
  - 2 Grease Pencils
  - Flat Divider With Laminated Scale
- Cache Gear:
  - Camouflage Netting
  - Shovels
  - Rakes
- COMM Gear:
  - Radios
  - Signal Mirror
  - Strobe With Directional Shield/IR Cover
  - Para Flares: 3 White, 3 Red, 2 Green
  - Smoke Grenades (Floatable)
  - Hand-Held Flares
  - Pencil Flares
- Poncho for Tactical Plotting
- Boat Equipment
- Bow Line (Not to Reach Prop If Overboard)
- Spare Water (Minimum of 5 Gallons/ 1 Gerry Can)
- Boat Pumps/Hose
- Floor Boards With Tie-Down Loops Through Boards
- Gear Tie-Down Straps
- Towing Line/Capsize Lines
- Paddles
- Gas Cans or Bladders
- Stern Line
- Boat Compass and Lighting System
- Lifting Slings (For Pickup by Hoist)
- CO2 Bottles and Inflation Fittings
- Night Vision Equipment/Radios

Figure 7-7. Maritime operations gear

7-76. The SCPS's carrying capability and speed estimates are slightly different from propeller-driven, 55-HP OBMs. It is rated by the USMC to carry a pay load of 2,018 pounds, obtaining an average speed of 19 knots per hour at wide open throttle (WOT) in Sea State 1. It has a fuel consumption of 3.0 gallons per hour or 4.5 NM per gallon.

7-77. The following notes and recommendations are derived from the operational experience of units using the CRRC:

- Solid 7-foot stringers, as used by the USMC for their OTH configuration, provide extra deck plate rigidly to handle the increased weight and HP of the 55-HP OBM with or without a pump jet.
- The Zodiac 6-gallon (NSN 2910-01-365-2694) and 18-gallon (NSN 2910-01-447-4893) fuel bladders are certified by the USAF at Wright Patterson AFB for use aboard all USAF aircraft. This certification alleviates what has been a hazardous material shipping problem.

7-78. The use of Zodiac (PN N45451) heavy-duty fuel lines with dripless connections will further minimize fuel line dripping and the attendant fumes aboard aircraft and naval vessels.

CHAPTER 8

Over-the-Beach Operations

The planning and execution that takes place during the initial phases of a waterborne operation are intended to move a detachment from home station to the debarkation point. Once the detachment has been "dropped off" at the debarkation point, they are committed to the mission and are essentially on their own. Aircraft making a static-line parachute drop cannot recover a detachment in trouble. Helicopters, surface vessels, and submarines have a limited loiter or recovery capability in the event the mission must be aborted.

Assembly on the water after delivery by aircraft, surface vessel, or submarine marks the start of the transit phase of the mission. At that point, the detachment's survival and mission success depend upon reaching land safely (seamanship and navigation) and without compromise. The transit plan must include a link-up plan in case there is a break in contact during the transit. Once the detachment comes within sight of land, the tactical portion of the mission commences. Getting the detachment ashore and inland is the most technically difficult aspect of a maritime operation. This chapter outlines how to aid a detachment in identifying requirements, formulating a plan or SOPs, and conducting training to prepare for the unique mission challenges.

BEACH LANDING SITE PROCEDURES

8-1. As the SFOD nears land, the transit portion of the mission is ending. General navigation (dead reckoning) gives way to the requirement for precision navigation (piloting). The detachment must place itself in the vicinity of the BLS and hold-up offshore in a "boat pool" to prepare for the landing operation. Although the use of a GPS receiver will ensure precision navigation, the detachment must have an alternate (independent) means of confirming its location. The preparation of a horizon sketch or profile during mission planning, with bearings to prominent terrain features, allows the detachment to confirm the BLS from the boat pool.

8-2. The boat pool is an assembly area or rallying point for the CRRCs, analogous to the last covered and concealed position before crossing the line of departure (LOD). The boat pool is located far enough offshore that the CRRC formation is reasonably protected from observation and direct fire, but still close enough for scout swimmers to reach the shore and perform beach reconnaissance in a reasonable amount of time. This distance will vary depending on meteorological (light, weather, and sea state) conditions. Actions to be accomplished in the boat pool mirror the actions taken in an objective rallying point (ORP) before and during a leader's reconnaissance of an objective.

8-3. The SFOD will assemble all of the CRRCs at the boat pool. When the boats assemble, personnel should be prepared to pass bow and stern lines if such action is required or desired to raft the CRRCs. If seas are not calm, bungee cords are an ideal substitute. CRRCs may be anchored to prevent or control drift while waiting in the boat pool. Whenever using an anchor, personnel should always secure it with a quick-release. In an emergency, it is easier to release the anchor than it is to recover it. A quick-release is also safer than attempting to cut an anchor line in adverse conditions.

8-4. The OIC should take time while in the boat pool to give last-minute orders, confirm signals, and review the rendezvous plan with the scout swimmers. If the boats are not rafted or anchored, the coxswains must work together to maintain the boats' positions and keep the boats' engines away from shore. This practice redirects and minimizes the exhaust noise signature. All personnel should have their equipment on but unbuckled, with weapons ready. Swimmers should be ready to enter the water. Everyone must keep a low profile to reduce the boats' outlines. The lower the boats' profiles, the closer the visual horizon of an individual standing on the beach and the less likely the detachment is to be compromised. After the OIC launches the scout swimmers, the detachment should motor (or paddle) the boats to a position that allows them to provide cover for the scout swimmers. This position should be left or right of the intended track of the swimmers so that any required covering fire does not endanger the swimmers. If necessary, the boats can be anchored to maintain this position without using the motors.

8-5. Whenever the SFOD elects to use scout swimmers, they should be a senior person (chief warrant officer [CWO], team sergeant) and the point man or rear security. Contingency plans will identify the revised chain of command on the affected boats. After the scout swimmers have negotiated the surf zone, they will conduct reconnaissance of the BLS, establish security, and conduct a surf observation report (SUROBSREP) to determine the wave sets. It will be the scout swimmer's call whether or not the boats can be brought in. If required, the scout swimmers will set up transit lights to mark and guide the boats in on a selected route that avoids obstacles.

SURF PASSAGE

8-6. After the scout swimmers signal the boats, the detachment begins an orderly movement to the BLS. The first obstacle that the detachment is likely to encounter will be a surf zone. The planning criterion and operational restrictions for negotiating a surf zone are contained in Chapter 12.

8-7. The conduct of a safe and efficient CRRC surf passage is a critical part of any maritime operation. Surf passages place the detachment in a very vulnerable position. The chances of injury, loss of gear, or damage to the boats and motors are greatest in the surf zone. Because the detachment members are concentrating on safely passing through the surf zone, they become more vulnerable to enemy action.

8-8. The coxswain is in charge of the boat and crew during the surf passage. If the surf is expected to be high, the most experienced coxswains should take charge of the boats. They must ensure that all gear is securely stowed and tied into the boat. Gear also includes the motor, repair kits, gas cans, and crew-served weapons. Everything must be secured but ready to use. Detachments may also want to secure the engine cover with tape to prevent its possible loss if the boat capsizes. Whenever possible, personnel should conduct a surf observation to determine the high and low set. Finally, they check to make sure the engine kill switch works correctly.

8-9. If the surf is moderate to severe, the boats should execute their surf passages one at a time. This type of movement keeps the detachment from having all of its assets committed at the same time, and allows the uncommitted boats to provide cover or assistance as required. While advancing from the boat pool towards the surf zone, the coxswain will ensure the outboard motor is on tilt (unlocked) and that the crew members have their paddles ready. The coxswain must time high and low series and observe sets of waves in the surf zone. He should inch his way to the impact zone and position the CRRC behind a breaking wave. The CRRC should ride behind the white water as long as possible, watching for overtaking and double waves. Concern for follow-on waves depends on the height of the white water.

8-10. Personnel should remember the saying, "Be bold; he who hesitates is lost!" An outboard motor can outrun any wave unless the operator has placed himself in the wrong position. The objective is to position the CRRC on the backside of a wave and ride it all the way through to the beach. The key is to manipulate the throttle to follow the wave as closely as possible without overtaking it, or allowing the next wave to catch up. Following as closely behind a wave as possible keeps the greatest amount of water under the boat, keeps the boat concealed as long as possible, and is the easiest way to maintain control of the boat. Under no circumstances should the coxswain attempt to "surf" or ride a wave with a zodiac. A zodiac that gets ahead of a wave is in danger of broaching (getting sideways to the wave and being rolled), pitch-poling (catching the bow in the trough of the wave and flipping end over end), grounding out, or being overrun by the following wave. Once the entire detachment is ashore and the BLS procedures are complete, the detachment reorganizes and continues with the primary mission.

8-11. Surf zones are two-way obstacles. When the time comes for the detachment to exfiltrate, it must be prepared to negotiate the surf zone in reverse. The objective is to select a route having the smallest breakers and timing the passage so that the CRRCs are moving through the lowest-possible set. If conducting the surf passage following an over-the-beach (OTB) exfiltration, the coxswain should begin surf observations as soon as possible. The surf observations allow him to determine the timing of the wave sets. High, medium, and low sets are usually present. Depending on the length of the surf zone, it may be desirable to start the passage at the end of a high set so that the CRRCs are not caught in the middle of the surf zone as the sets change. If the coxswain can determine the location of a riptide, it makes an excellent exfiltration route through the surf zone. The waves are usually lower, the risk of grounding on a sandbar (or meeting breaking waves on the bar) is minimized, and the outflowing current will assist.

8-12. Before embarkation, detachment members must ensure that the paddles are accessible and ready for use and that all gear is stowed and tied down. They should walk the CRRC into the water until it is deep enough to allow the coxswain to start the motor (if the detachment is not going to paddle out). After the motor is started, they maintain only the minimum number of people in the water to control the boat. At the coxswain's signal all personnel will get into the boat and start to go.

8-13. When the CRRC is breaching a wave, the coxswain should let the bow of the boat power through the wave before he lets up on the throttle. This maneuver will allow the bow of the boat to come down easily, and the weight of the bow will actually pull the rest of the boat through the wave.

8-14. The detachment should avoid overloading the bow of the boat to prevent plowing through the waves. If the boat does plow through a wave, everyone should attempt to stay in the boat. If it capsizes, they should attempt to return to and stay with the boat (to prevent possible separation at night). Wave action will carry it back to the beach. The boat OIC should assess the situation, carry out the necessary actions, and inform the detachment OIC ASAP of the situation. All craft should rendezvous at the back of the surf zone, then continue with the mission. The detachment OIC should always explain capsizing actions in detail within the patrol order.

BEACH LANDING

8-15. **All Going Well.** If the BLS is secure and it is safe to bring in the detachment, the scout swimmers will signal from the shore. The boats will cast off from each other and line up for the surf passage. All personnel will sit on the main buoyancy tube and maintain a low profile with one leg over the side. This routine will allow for a rapid, controlled exit when the boat has penetrated the surf line. The boats will move in one at a time adjusting their tactics (drive or paddle) depending on the characteristics of the surf zone. If using the outboard motor, the coxswain should not run it aground; however, he should keep it running as long as possible. He should make sure the motor tilt lock is released so that the motor can kick up to prevent damage if it does run aground. Everyone except the coxswain should exit the boat as soon as the water is shallow enough to wade. Designated members of the boat crew will move to augment BLS security. The remainder of the crew will act as gear pullers and move each CRRC and its components to the cache site individually to facilitate recovery after the mission. As each boat clears the beach, it should signal the next boat in. Care must be taken to prevent boats and equipment from piling up on the beach. A good point to remember is to "always think of security versus speed."

8-16. **All Not Going Well**. The detachment waiting in the boat pool depends upon the skills and judgment of the scout swimmers to determine if the BLS is suitable and safe. If the scout swimmers encounter unfavorable conditions (hydrography, topography, or enemy situation), they make the decision to abort the landing. They will signal out to the boats and activate the withdrawal plan. Personnel waiting in the boats must be prepared for contact or compromise. While the scouts are swimming back to the boat pool, the flank boats hold position and provide cover. The OIC or lead boat prepares to pick up the scout swimmers if required. The objective is to avoid compromise, move to the alternate BLS, and continue the mission.

8-17. **Enemy Contact.** If the boat pool or the scout swimmers are compromised from the shore before the detachment is committed to the landing operation, it may be safer to retreat out to sea. Unfortunately, this situation leaves the detachment separated with a requirement to recover, or cover the withdrawal of, the scout swimmers. The swimmers can either return to the CRRCs, get picked up by the CRRCs, or—if they have not been compromised—move to the shore and rendezvous with the detachment later. If the swimmers have been compromised, the boats must cover their withdrawal the best way possible. If a decision is made to recover the swimmers, the flank boats provide covering fires, and the center boat (normally the OIC) runs in to extract them. If possible, swimmers should attempt to get out past the surf line to make a pickup easier and safer.

8-18. The most difficult aspect of the problem is determining a method of marking the swimmers to facilitate recovery and protect them from friendly fire. The chosen method must mark the swimmer's location and aid in vectoring a recovery vessel to them without contributing to the risk of compromise or aiding the enemy's fire direction. The detachment must research available marking technologies and select one that will be visible in adverse conditions, that can be activated by a disabled swimmer in the water, and that does not have an overly bright (compromising) signature. Most infrared (IR) beacons, to include chemlights, will meet these requirements provided the detachment has adequate NVGs available.

8-19. If there is contact, the detachment's primary objective is to break off the engagement and withdraw. As soon as it is safe to do so, the mission commander must assess the situation and make a determination whether or not to continue the mission. If it is possible to continue, the detachment will regroup and move to the alternate BLS. If the contact resulted from a chance encounter with coastal patrol boats or aircraft, the detachment may be required to immediately get off of the water. Detachments can quickly find themselves outgunned with nowhere to hide. The only option is to evade to the nearest land and disperse until something can be done to salvage the mission or initiate an emergency recovery plan.

8-20. Detachments must have a sound rendezvous or linkup plan in case they have to split up to avoid contact or compromise. If there is enemy contact, the detachment should observe the same basic principles as a mounted detachment in land warfare—the coxswain (driver) doesn't shoot, he just drives; the remainder of the detachment works to gain superior firepower as soon as possible. If possible, the detachment will break contact and attempt to screen the withdrawal with smoke (bubble-wrapped or floating), then exit the area. The OIC must then assess the situation and take relevant action to continue or abort the mission.

8-21. Detachment members must maintain muzzle awareness and discipline. During an ocean infiltration, consideration should be given to having weapons without rounds in the chamber until just before the formation reaches the boat pool. The extended visual detection ranges make chance contacts unlikely. The same is not true for riverine or estuarine movement. Once contact has been initiated, it is important to consider the increased risk of fratricide caused by the unstable firing platform and the rapid changes in relative position during evasive maneuvers. After the engagement, detachment members must also be aware of the risks of a cookoff and the danger of a hot barrel making chance contact with the boat and puncturing it.

SCOUT SWIMMERS

8-22. Scout swimmers are surface or subsurface swimmers used in conjunction with small boat, combat swimmer, and combat diver infiltrations. They reconnoiter and secure the BLS before committing the entire team to the beach landing. Scout swimmers normally work in pairs. In addition to locating a suitable BLS, scout swimmers must also locate an assembly area, look for suitable cache sites, and select a location from which to signal the team. They may be used to confirm that the enemy does not occupy a proposed landing site, that a landing site is suitable and surf is passable, or to rendezvous with a beach reception party if one is present.

8-23. Scout swimmers are equipped with fins, flotation devices, exposure suits, and weights as needed. If the selected infiltration technique includes diving, the scout swimmers will require appropriate diving gear (open circuit [O/C] and closed circuit [C/C]). Additionally, they carry LCE, an individual weapon, and the prearranged signaling device to be used to pass signals to the team from the BLS. Scout swimmers should be neutrally buoyant and armed with automatic rifles, pistols (sometimes suppressed), and grenades. Scout swimmers must be prepared to remain ashore if an unforeseen problem occurs. They must be able to survive for a reasonable amount of time if there is enemy contact, compromise, or any other separation where they cannot rejoin the main body. Experience has shown that a vest is the best way to carry the following equipment:

- Ammunition.
- Evasion and escape kit.
- Rations and water for 24 hours.
- Flashlight and signaling devices (and backup devices).
- Knife.
- Compass.
- Communications (for example, short-range COMM to main body or survival radio if required).

8-24. Scout swimmers should be selected during the planning phase to allow detailed plans to be formulated and drills rehearsed. Backup swimmers should be nominated in case of seasickness or loss. The composition of the team will depend on the situation, but may include a scout and the OIC, assistant officer in charge (AOIC), or noncommissioned officer in charge (NCOIC). Sometimes the swimmers may have to take in an agent, foreign national, or someone else who might be a weak swimmer. Contact drills, casualty recovery, and rendezvous drills must be rehearsed. A detailed and sound briefing must occur before the scouts are deployed. All contingencies must be covered and briefbacks conducted so there are no misunderstandings. When using scouts, a finite time must be placed on them to achieve their goals and "actions on" if that time limit is exceeded.

8-25. Scout swimmer deployment procedures begin on arrival in the vicinity of the BLS. The CRRC members form a boat pool a tactical distance from the shoreline and conduct a visual reconnaissance. The CRRC transporting the swimmers moves to the swimmer release point (SRP), fixes its position, and takes a bearing on an obvious shore identification point. The swimmers should move in and out on that bearing.

8-26. Before leaving the main body, the scout swimmers receive last minute instructions or adjustments to the original plan based on observations made during the infiltration thus far. Scout swimmers should leave their rucksacks with the main body. Normally, the main body halts in a holding area outside the surf zone and small arms fire (about 500 yards) from the beach.

8-27. Because the tactical (or hydrographic) situation may require the swimmers to return to the CRRCs, the current and drift at the SRP must be tested. Depending on the drift, the coxswain will decide whether to anchor or try to maintain position by paddling. The outboard motor can be left at idle to prevent the extra noise of trying to restart the motor. If the night is very still and quiet with no surf, paddles may be a better choice than the engine.

8-28. The swimmers, once released, should swim on a bearing to a previously identified point. To keep their direction, they use a dive compass or guide on prominent terrain features or lights on the beach. The raiding craft should be prepared to act as fire support to cover the swimmers if they are contacted. The swimmers should count the number of kicks and the time it takes to swim in. Most of the time it is impractical to do this through the surf zone. However, the swimmers should know how many kicks it will take them to get from the back of the surf zone to the RP or boat pool. Surface swimmers should swim and maintain 360 degrees visual observation around them. They can have this view by using the sidestroke. While approaching the surf zone or general vicinity of the BLS, swimmers should face each other and observe the area beyond the other swimmer.

8-29. As the scout swimmers reach the surf zone or when they get fairly close to the BLS, they use the breaststroke so they can observe the beach. It is imperative that the scout swimmers use stealth and caution while approaching the beach. They must keep a low profile in the water as well as when on the beach. The use of a camouflage head net is ideally suited for concealing scout swimmers as they approach the beach.

8-30. Swimmers should conduct a short security halt to look and listen before they commit to a surf zone passage. Once they reach waist-deep water and perform another stop, look, and listen, the swimmers decide whether to take off and secure their fins (while still keeping them accessible) while keeping as low as possible in the water. Depending on the beach gradient, there are two methods:

- If the water offshore is still relatively deep, one scout pulls security by observing the BLS, while the other scout removes and stows his own fins.
- If the water just offshore is relatively shallow and gently sloping up to the beach, one scout can low crawl to a position in front of the other. The man in front pulls security while the rear man removes the front man's fins for him. The scouts then change places and repeat the procedure. This method is much quieter in shallow water.

Before the swimmers leave the water, they should conduct a good visual reconnaissance to select the place they will cross the beach to ensure that the least amount of sign or tracks are left. Swimmers should not be hasty at this stage, there may be something on the beach that cannot be seen. They should use maximum stealth when approaching the BLS and leaving the water.

8-31. The swimmers should then move onto the beach maintaining as low a profile as possible. If the task is to clear the beach, the pair should stay together and use silent covered movement to conduct a reconnaissance of the landing site. They should be working to a set time. The two methods of moving across the beach, conducting reconnaissance, and securing the BLS are as follows:

- If the wood line (hinterland) can be seen easily from the waterline, one scout remains in the water just at the waterline and covers the other as he moves quickly across the beach. Once the inland scout has moved to the edge of the wood line, he covers his partner while he moves across the beach to the same position.
- If the beach topography is such that the hinterland cannot easily be observed from the waterline, the above method can be modified to include successive bounds, or both scouts can move quickly across the beach together. If both scouts move together, they must observe the beach area thoroughly before moving. It may be necessary to observe the beach from a certain distance offshore from the waterline to properly observe the hinterland.

8-32. Once both scout swimmers have moved inland, they conduct a reconnaissance and establish security. There are three techniques (cloverleaf, box, and modified box) used to reconnoiter and secure the BLS. The terrain, time, size of landing party and vegetation (cover and concealment available) will determine which method the scout swimmers use. The scouts agree on a suitable assembly and cache site when they finish their reconnaissance. One scout then positions himself at the edge of the hinterland (or backshore, if suitable cover and concealment are available) to provide security for the main body's landing and from which he can guide the main body to the assembly area. The other scout positions himself where he can signal the main body. He must ensure that the signal is not masked by the waves and can be seen by the main body. As soon as he sees the main body, he moves to the waterline.

8-33. When the main body reaches the BLS, the scout at the waterline directs them to the other scout who guides them to the assembly area. After the last man has passed him, the scout at the waterline disguises any tracks left in the sand and then rejoins the main body.

8-34. If at all possible, scouts should not use an assembly area as a cache site. If the enemy discovers and follows the tracks or trail from the beach to the assembly area, he can easily determine the number of personnel involved in the operation by counting the swim gear. Also, the cached equipment may be needed to support exfiltration at another location.

8-35. If the swimmers are to return to the boats, they swim out from the previously identified point using the back bearing of their approach for the specified distance (set time and number of kicks). Divers should conduct a tactical peek after swimming a predetermined distance. They then signal over the agreed sector using red-lensed flashlights (or other appropriate mid-range signaling device) for identification and position location. The problem with this method is that flashlights offer very limited peripheral coverage and there is an increased risk of compromise.

8-36. If the swimmers are far enough offshore, the boats should move to the swimmers to effect a rendezvous. Having the boats move to the swimmers speeds the recovery and conserves the diver's strength. If the signal equipment fails and no pickup occurs, the swimmers should not swim about vaguely but return to the beach and try to fix the problem. If the time window has closed, the swimmers should move to the alternate swimmer recovery point. If they cannot, then they should carry out their rendezvous procedure as detailed in their OPORD.

8-37. If the swimmers make contact or are compromised, they must decide whether to move back through the water to the boat pool (swimmer recovery rendezvous) or across land to a land rendezvous (maybe the alternate BLS). If the swimmers are in contact, they should try to use grenades rather than rifle fire. Grenades cause confusion at night and do not pinpoint the swimmer's position. Illumination is a bad call in this situation; it will just compromise the boat pool and the swimmers. The use of darkness should be an advantage.

8-38. The swimmers require a means to identify their position tactically, so that if the raiding craft is in a position to provide fire support, the crew will know where the swimmers are to minimize risk to the swimmers. The CRRCs need to stay in visual distance of each other while loitering in the boat pool. The left and right flank boats need to be prepared to move out wide to provide fire support if required. The center boat may have to recover the swimmers while the OIC's boat is level with or forward providing fire support. Firing from the water is inaccurate. Boats located behind the swimmers may only be able to provide indirect fire with weapons like the M-203 or some other type of high trajectory fire support. Boats to the flanks need to be out far enough so that they can fire small arms or light machine guns into the beach to support or assist the swimmers in making a clean break and withdrawing.

8-39. Actions on contact must be covered in-depth in the OPORD. The risk of fratricide is high. Any decision to compromise the boats and their location by providing fire support to the scout swimmers is a tactical decision that can only be made by the on-scene commander at that time. The other boats or crews must not give away their presence or position until the command to initiate fire support is given.

SIGNALS

8-40. Signals should be well thought-out, rehearsed, and coordinated with all necessary agencies. Personnel should plan for all possible contingencies. The various signaling devices, methods, and types are discussed below.

SIGNALING DEVICES

8-41. Personnel can use numerous signaling devices during waterborne operations. The capabilities, limitations, and uses of these signaling devices are as follows:

8-42. **Infrared Signaling Devices**. IR emitting devices are probably the most secure and versatile signaling devices available. A good IR signaling device must possess the capability to send Morse code signals. Night vision devices (scopes or goggles) are a secure and available method of detecting IR signals.

8-43. **Flashlights**. When IR devices are not available, personnel can use flashlights. Personnel should always waterproof the flashlights and fit them with a directional cone to aid in limiting their signature. Personnel should consider using filters because white light will usually be too bright and attract undue attention. They should also avoid red and green filters where possible because these colors can easily be mistaken for red or green buoy lights that abound along coastlines of the world. Flashlights are the most commonly used signaling devices because of their availability and the fact that they can be used to send Morse code.

8-44. **Lightsticks (Chemlights)**. When nothing else is available, a lightstick can be used for signaling. For correct use, fit it with a directional cone. Morse signals can then be sent by passing the hand back and forth over the cone. The primary drawbacks to using light sticks are that they are overly bright, cannot be turned off, and are difficult to adapt for directional and Morse code signals. Also, they float and can compromise the BLS if misplaced.

8-45. **Strobe Lights**. Strobe lights and other pulse-type devices are the least desirable signaling devices. Even when used in conjunction with IR filters or a directional cone, a strobe light's signal cannot be varied and Morse code cannot be used. Thus, only one signal can be sent as opposed to several: danger, abort, or delay. Personnel should use strobe lights as an absolute last resort only. However, a strobe fitted with an IR filter could serve as a good danger signal if another IR source were available to send other signals.

MISSION SIGNALS

8-46. The detachment should, as a minimum, plan for and coordinate the signals that will be used during the mission. All detachment members must understand and remember the signals that are established in the mission planning phase. Types of signals may include the following:

8-47. **Safe Signal**. The scout swimmers send this signal to the main body upon completing their reconnaissance and determining the BLS area is clear. This signal should be a Morse code letter that does not consist of either all dots or dashes. This type message makes it readily distinguishable out at sea.

8-48. **Delay Signal**. The scout swimmers send this signal to the main body to indicate that a temporary situation exists that requires the main body to delay its movement to the BLS. This signal can be sent before or after the safe signal has been given. It also could be given due to unanticipated activity on the beach. The signal should be Morse code and readily distinguishable from the safe signal.

8-49. **Abort Signal**. This is a signal from the scout swimmers to the main body to indicate a dangerous situation exists that will compromise the mission if the main body attempts to land. This signal is sent only if the scout swimmers can send it without compromising themselves. Although a Morse code letter can be used, it is best to use a quickly and easily sent signal such as a rapid series of either dots or dashes.

8-50. **Absence of Signal**. This signal is again from the scout swimmers to the main body. The absence of a signal indicates a condition exists on the beach that precludes safe landing. This is a time-driven signal. When none of the above signals are received within a certain time after releasing the scout swimmers, the main body uses a contingency plan that calls for meeting the scout swimmers at another location. The detachment must remember that the time required for scout swimmers to swim in, properly reconnoiter, and secure the BLS is extensive and must be stated in the contingency plans. For planning purposes, the detachment should allow 60 to 90 minutes before going to any contingency plans. The absence of a signal can also be used in conjunction with a delay signal. The OIC should activate a contingency plan if no other signal is seen for a specified time after receiving the delay signal.

8-51. **Signals Used With Pickup Craft**. When using an amphibious aircraft or surface craft for exfiltration or pickup, signals are normally exchanged in order for both parties to ensure that they are dealing with the correct people. Normally, the team initiates one signal and the pickup craft comes back with another. The team initiates because the pickup craft is considered more vulnerable and valuable at that point. Also, the team is generally signaling out to sea. The team—

- Heads out to sea on a specific azimuth.
- Sends a Morse signal after a specific time along that azimuth.
- Repeats this signal at a predetermined interval until a return signal is received from the pickup craft.

8-52. It is important to send the signals at an unhurried rate. The recommended rate is 1 second for a dot and 2 seconds for a dash with 1 second between dots and dashes. If signals are sent too quickly, the Morse letter that is intended may not be recognized and be misinterpreted as an abort or delay signal or as the wrong signal.

SIGNALING METHODS

8-53. Scout swimmers use specific signaling methods that are predesignated during mission planning. They normally use the one-lamp or two-lamp system.

8-54. **One-Lamp System**. The scout at the waterline positions himself on the beach where he can shine his light onto the water clear of the breakers. The scout should use the following procedures to ensure the main body sees the signal, whatever its angle of approach. He first sends the agreed upon signal at the proper time and interval—two times straight out to sea at the expected approach azimuth. After that, he sends—

- Two times at an angle of 010 degrees to the left of the approach azimuth.
- Two times at an angle of 010 degrees to the right of the approach azimuth.

8-55. **Two-Lamp System**. A reception committee normally uses this system. Personnel first position two weak white lights (different colors can be used as a positive identification technique) on the beach. Then they align the lights (exactly like a Range Mark) to provide a line of approach for the main body and to indicate the BLS. The committee will—

- Position the lower light as in the one-lamp system and use it in the same manner. Hold this light about 1.5 meters above the sea. In a variation of the system, stake it in place at that height.
- Secure the second light (which normally remains switched on continuously) to a stake. Position it 6 meters behind the lower light and 1 meter above it. Normally, this is a weak light that can be a different color from the lower one.

NOTE

If the distance between the two lights is more than 6 meters, ensure the gradient between the lights is as close to 1:6 as possible.

DETACHMENT INFILTRATION SWIMMING

8-56. Detachments may occasionally encounter circumstances that preclude landing on the beach with CRRCs or kayaks. In case the detachment cannot land, they must be prepared to swim from the launch point to the beach. Detachment infiltration swimming should only occur as a last resort. Infiltration swimming requires allowing additional transit time, higher physical exertion levels, greater environmental exposure, and reduced quantities of mission-essential equipment. It is the least favorable infiltration technique.

8-57. To maintain team integrity, combat diver and combat surface swims are conducted using a swim line. Once the infiltration team has arrived at the launch point, it is recommended that all swimmers hook up on a swim line before beginning the swim. This practice is a control measure designed to maintain unit integrity. An advantage of the swim line is that even if the environment adversely affects the team, the entire team and its equipment will remain together. There are many varieties of swim lines, each offering advantages and disadvantages. The most common techniques are discussed below.

SWIM LINES

8-58. There are generally two types of swim lines for infiltration swimming—on-line or column variation. The column method can also be conducted in two ways (Figure 8-1, page 149). The swim line can be constructed of climbing rope, tubular nylon, suspension line, or any other strong material. Tubular nylon is preferred because it is light but strong and is far less bulky than climbing rope. Swimmers should remember never to use climbing rope for actual climbing or rappelling after it has been exposed to salt water.

8-59. **Column (Offset)**. This method is one of many variations of the standard in-line column formation. Its major advantage is that the length of the line can be reduced to half the normal size while still allowing 10 feet between swim teams on the same side of the line. Swimmers primarily use this formation for underwater swims because it eases control of the swim team underwater.

8-60. **Column (In-Line)**. This formation is used for combat surface or subsurface swimming. The line can be a solid straight rope with loops placed about every 10 feet. It can also be 10-foot sections of line with end loop splices at each

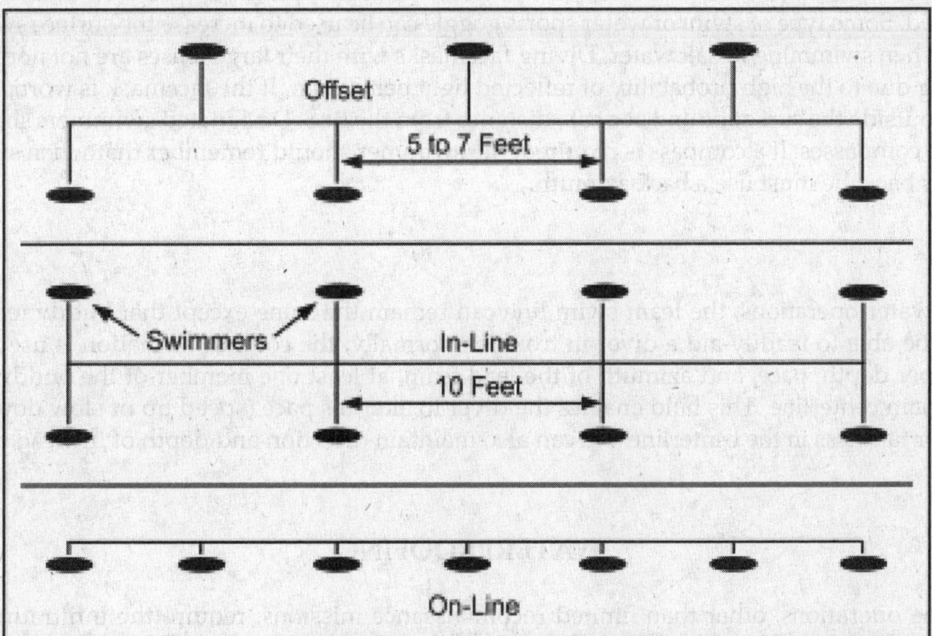

Figure 8-1. Swim line formations

end, then fastened together with snap links. The swim team buddy lines are then routed through the loops or snap links on the centerline. All swimmers then follow the azimuth and pace of the lead swim team.

8-61. **On-Line**. Swimmers most frequently use the on-line swimming formation for combat surface swimming. The actual line is formed by using a solid straight rope with hand loops placed 5 to 7 feet apart. Each team member positions himself at a hand loop location. The team then swims on-line toward its target area.

SURFACE SWIMMING

8-62. Regardless of the swim formation that the team uses, certain surface swimming concepts remain constant. The team members swim on their backs or sides using the flutter kick. They wear enough weights to ensure their flutter kick remains subsurface, thereby maintaining a low profile and minimizing surface disturbances. Alternating the swimmers on a swim line or when swimming in two-man teams, allows each team member to observe across the other's back area and to the front. Swimmers can switch sides during the swim for partial physical recovery, because one leg tends to work harder than the other. This gives the body a partial rest when sides are switched and allows maintaining a steady swim pace. Equipment bundles are towed on lines held by the swimmers. The lines must be long enough not to interfere with the swimmer's flutter kick.

8-63. An alternative swimming style incorporating the use of the swimmer's arms is the combat sidestroke with fins method. WW II Amphibious Recon Platoons sent in from Subs to recon islands in the South Pacific originally developed the technique. It consists of swimming with fins on feet, while executing the sidestroke. While on your side with arm extended out in front, one side down as a normal sidestroke, the arms are pulled into the body's center, meeting at the chest. Then they can be extended back out in an underwater recovery stroke method as to not disturb the water, while the feet fin in a normal flutter kick fashion maintaining position with one side down. Sprint speeds in excess of 1 knot are achievable by an individual who is proficient in the technique. This speed aids in overcoming littoral currents that often run parallel or diagonal to the beach.

8-64. Swimmers waterproof and buoyancy test any bundles to make sure they are neutral buoyant and likewise maintain a low profile in the water. They can wear LCE in the normal manner and their individual weapons are heavily lubed and slung across the chest with an over-the-shoulder sling. Very small rucksacks or equipment bags can be worn over the chest with the arms through the shoulder straps. If the swimmer desires, he can carry his weapon by attaching it to the rucksack; however, this is not recommended.

8-65. All individual swimmers must wear flotation devices, fins, appropriate exposure suits, knife with flares, and weights as required. Some type of swim or water sports goggle can be used to increase the surface swimmer's comfort level, especially when swimming in salt water. Diving facemasks with their large lenses are not normally worn when surface swimming due to the high probability of reflected light being seen. If the facemask is worn, it must definitely be removed well outside the surf zone and at a safe distance from the BLS. Designated swimmers should be equipped with watches and compasses. If a compass is required, the swimmer should remember that when swimming beyond the horizon on his back, he must use a back azimuth.

DIVING

8-66. For underwater operations, the team swim line can remain the same except that buddy teams must remain close together to be able to readily aid a diver in trouble. Normally, the column formation is used (Figure 8-1). To maintain the proper depth, pace, and azimuth of the lead team, at least one member of the buddy team must keep his hand on the main centerline. This hold enables the diver to alter his pace (speed up or slow down) by feeling the amount of slack or tautness in the centerline. He can also maintain direction and depth of the lead team.

WATERPROOFING

8-67. Waterborne operations, other than limited reconnaissance missions, require the infiltrating detachment or swimmer to transport equipment to and from the objective. Depending on the mission, this equipment will vary from light and compact to bulky. In every case, equipment must be limited to the absolute minimum necessary to accomplish the mission.

PROCEDURES

8-68. The size, weight, and quantity of bundles are dependent on the size of the team, distance to swim, and method of insertion into the objective area. Swimmers should use the following guidelines:

- *Size.* Bundle size should be limited to a cube no larger than 14" × 30" × 18". This enhances diver comfort, reduces drag in the water, allows easy handling, and presents minimal problems for the swimmer if held correctly. Whatever container the equipment is transported in, must also be carried on land to the ultimate inland objective or cached.
- *Weight.* Before swimming the bundle, the swimmer will adjust its buoyancy by either adding weight or putting floatation devices on it to make it neutral or slightly positive. Each bundle must be man-portable.
- *Quantity.* The number of bundles will be determined by dividing the mission-essential equipment into the size and weight restrictions previously identified.

PRINCIPLES

8-69. Waterproofing is necessary to ensure items will operate once they are used on the objective. Electronic equipment is particularly susceptible to water damage. Using the following principles when waterproofing equipment will make sure it functions reliably when needed:

- Do not waterproof anything that does not require it.
- Cushion all sharp edges of equipment in a bundle to prevent punctures.
- Try to use waterproof plastic or rubber sacks. Place item in it, withdraw all air, and seal.
- Disassemble equipment into component parts. Small items are easier to waterproof.
- Identify all items with tags or tape on the outside of the bag to aid in quick assembly.
- Waterproof items more than once. (Triple-consecutive containment is recommended.)
- Swim at shallow depths to minimize pressure and reduce potential water infiltration.
- Maintain equipment integrity within the bundle to facilitate putting the equipment into service once on shore.

8-70. Waterproofing of materials and equipment is an essential task when preparing for waterborne operations. The procedures discussed herein are not all inclusive; however, they do provide a basis from which to develop additional techniques peculiar to unit operations. All items of individual and TOE equipment are waterproofed basically in the same manner.

8-71. Waterproofing materials are divided into two groups: improvised and issued. Improvised items can be any type of plastic bag, ammunition can, tape, wax, or prophylactics. Issued items include commercial off-the-shelf or purpose-built items and waterproof bags available through the GSA Catalog from vendors such as Diving Unlimited International, Inc. and USIA Underwater Equipment Sales Corporation. Examples include rucksack or daypack liners (NSN:8465-01-487-3183), transport and shoot-through weapons bags, radio bags, and general purpose kit bags. They are superior in all ways to improvised systems based on the OD waterproof bags (issued with the rucksack) or waterproof bags issued with magazines, radio battery bags, mortar round canisters, and the waterproof bag for medical gear. These bags also offer simplicity of use and durability over improvised waterproofing systems.

8-72. Personnel should remove waterproofing one layer at a time. They should check to ensure that no water has leaked in any of the layers. If fresh water has leaked in, it should be wiped off and all metal parts should be oiled. If salt water has leaked in, it should be rinsed off with fresh water as soon as possible and should then be dried and oiled. If fresh water is not available, the article should be oiled well and checked for rust. If ropes or clothing are wet from salt water, they must be washed with fresh water as soon as possible. Salt water will cause material to rot relatively quickly and the dried salt cuts into rope fibers.

RADIOS

8-73. To waterproof a radio, a swimmer first identifies all sharp edges. He removes the rubber boot from the handset plugs and checks to make sure the radio is operational. He should always install new batteries. The swimmer pads all sharp edges using the clothing in the rucksack; he does not use separate padding material unless absolutely necessary. This reduces the sterilization problem once in the assembly area. He leaves enough room so that the controls can be reached and used. Once he ties or tapes the padding in place, the radio is then put into the first waterproof bag with the controls and antenna or handset plugs in the bottom of the bag. The swimmer removes all air by either sucking it out by mouth or by using a small boat pump in the suction mode. Once the air is removed, he twists the remainder of the bag into a gooseneck, bends it back on itself, and ties it securely. He makes sure there is enough room at the bottom of the bag to turn the radio on and off with the switch between preset frequencies without breaking the bag. He repeats the same steps with the second and third waterproof bags. For best results, the first two bags should be heavy-duty plastic bags and the last one should be an issue bag so that the strongest and most durable bag is on the outside. The third bag provides abrasion and puncture protection for the first two bags. The swimmer then waterproofs the handset by placing it inside a small waterproof bag such as a plastic battery bag or a plastic sandwich bag and repeats the steps outlined above.

WEAPONS

8-74. The individual weapon must be waterproofed so that it is functional. The primary reason for waterproofing weapons is to keep sand and salt out of the working parts (a significant problem when swimming through heavy surf), not necessarily to keep water out. There are two primary techniques that can be modified for crew-served weapons:

8-75. The simplest method is to place the weapon in a purpose-built weapons bag. There are two types: a shoot-through bag designed for individual weapons and a transport bag designed for crew-served or special-purpose weapons. These are available through the supply system or the GSA Catalog. The swimmer pads the weapon as required to protect the weapon and the bag. If the weapon is going into a shoot-through bag, he makes sure the weapon functioning is not compromised and the operator can still manipulate the weapon's controls.

8-76. If weapons bags are not available, then the swimmer must protect the weapon with improvised packaging. He tapes the muzzle or tapes a muzzle cap in place and places the weapon into a waterproof plastic bag. He then twists the bag into a gooseneck and ties it off as described above. He tapes the bag to the weapon so that it conforms essentially to the shape of the weapon, but allows the moving parts to function. If the weapon must be fired, the swimmer pushes his index finger through the bag and manipulates the selector switch from the outside. He fires the weapon through the bag. When taping the bag to the weapon, the swimmer leaves enough space around the ejection port so that ejection can occur and no stoppages are caused.

8-77. If the swimmer decides not to waterproof the weapon, he must still make sure it can resist the infiltration of sand into the mechanism. He tapes a muzzle cap in place or tapes the muzzle itself to prevent water from entering the barrel. He wraps plastic bag material around the receiver group allowing room for the charging handle selector switch and trigger to operate. He also leaves room for expended rounds to eject.

BUNDLE TRANSPORTING

8-78. It is recommended that the bundle be towed or carried in the swimmer's hands. It should not be attached to his body except in parascuba operations and then only for the duration of the jump. As a safety precaution, the swimmer should be able to quickly jettison heavy bundles that would hinder a safe ascent to the surface in an emergency situation. An attack board should be used when swimming bundles underwater.

CHAPTER 9

Combat Diving and Swimming Operations

This chapter addresses duties and safety for personnel and units conducting combat swimming and diving operations. Its purpose is to ensure interoperability among all USSOCOM elements and to promote operational readiness and safety through a uniform execution of policy and training.

> **NOTE**
> The U.S. Army, Air Force, and Marine Corps use the terms combat diving and combat divers to describe the diving requirements of SOF personnel primarily engaged in infiltration swimming. The U.S. Navy uses the terms combat swimming and combat swimmer.

ORGANIZATION AND DUTIES

9-1. Every SF individual involved in combat swimmer and diving operations must attain and maintain a high state of mental and physical alertness and readiness for the safe and successful execution of each operation. This chapter outlines the minimum duties of key personnel in the planning, preparation, and execution of combat swimmer and diving operations by USSOCOM components.

THE NAVY DIVING ORGANIZATION

9-2. Combat diving is fundamental to all SF diving. The Navy trains the majority of military personnel in combat diving skills and has therefore been assigned proponency for diving throughout DOD. Accordingly, USSOCOM assigned proponency for combat diving operations to the NAVSPECWARCOM in USSOCOM Directive 10-1, *Terms of Reference.* Because combat diving is an inherently maritime activity, clear understanding of certain Navy instructions (the Navy uses "instructions" rather than regulations or orders) and organization is the key to full joint integration and standardization of combat diving within SF. The following paragraphs outline the manner by which the Navy has assigned duties with regard to the planning and conduct of diving operations.

Commander, Naval Special Warfare Command

9-3. The NAVSPECWARCOM is located in Coronado, California, and is the naval component of USSOCOM. The USSOCOM commander has designated the Commander, NAVSPECWARCOM as the proponent for maritime SO.

Supervisor of Diving

9-4. The Navy supervisor of diving (SUPDIVE) is located in Arlington, Virginia, and works for the Director of Ocean Engineering within the Naval Sea Systems Command. This is the primary Navy office that is concerned with diving operations and publishes the Navy Diving Manual.

Naval Sea Systems Command

9-5. The Naval Sea (NAVSEA) Systems Command is located in Arlington, Virginia, and is the major Navy organization (called a Systems Command) which oversees all naval diving matters ashore and afloat except for shore-based diving facilities (for example, hyperbaric chambers). The NAVSEA command certifies dive systems that are used afloat. The SUPDIVE is an office of the NAVSEA command.

Naval Facilities Engineering Command

9-6. The Naval Facilities (NAVFAC) Engineering Command is the major Navy organization responsible for design, construction, and maintenance of naval shore facilities. NAVFAC certifies dive systems that are used ashore (for example, shore located hyperbaric chambers).

Naval Special Warfare Center

9-7. The NAVSPECWARCEN is located in Coronado, California, and is the Navy's school for special operations. Among other courses of instruction, it teaches the Basic Underwater Demolition/SEAL (BUD/S) course. The NAVSPECWARCOM commander has designated NAVSPECWARCEN as the executive agent for SF open- and closed-circuit diving issues. These duties are comprehensive and include issues such as open-, closed-, and semi-closed circuit diving; combat diver operations; diving equipment; dive policies; dive planning; diving mobile training teams; and diving systems certification as directed by NAVSPECWARCOM Memorandum, 8 February 1993, Subject: *Naval Special Warfare [NSW] Executive Agent for Special Operations and Closed Circuit Diving.*

Naval Safety Center

9-8. The naval safety center (NAVSAFECEN) is located in Norfolk, Virginia, and works closely with the NAVSPEC-WARCEN concerning safety aspects of combat diving and certification procedures for all SO diving equipment. The NAVSAFECEN conducts comprehensive safety inspections of USSOCOM Divers Life Support Maintenance Facilities (DLSMFs).

Navy Experimental Diving Unit

9-9. The Navy experimental diving unit (NEDU) is located in Panama City, Florida. Before recommending that diving equipment be approved as Authorized for Navy Use (ANU), the Navy SUPDIVE refers the request to the NEDU for testing and recommendations.

SPECIFIC DUTIES

9-10. The NAVSPECWARCOM commander is designated as the proponent for USSOCOM combat swimmer and diving matters. As such, NAVSPECWARCOM develops USSOCOM policy as it relates to combat swimming and diving matters and serves as the SOC's focal point for these issues. The personnel who participate in these operations are explained below.

Unit Commanders and Commanding Officers

9-11. The commanders and commanding officers of USSOCOM subordinate commands that participate in diving operations will—

- Ensure all diver life support systems, support equipment, and diving life support maintenance facilities are maintained IAW Chief of Naval Operations Instruction (OPNAVINST) 4790.4C, *Ship's Maintenance Material Management (3-M) Manual*, and adhere to Navy certification standards.
- Ensure that divers use only systems and equipment that have been certified or ANU, unless a waiver has been obtained through the Chief of Naval Operations. Naval Sea Instruction (NAVSEAINST) 10560 Ser OOC/3112, *Diving Equipment Authorized for Navy Use*, provides a listing of ANU equipment.
- Maintain diving system certification IAW NAVSEAINST 3151.01, *Diving and Manned Hyperbaric System Safety Certification Program.*
- Ensure that diving is conducted only by qualified personnel following approved procedures.

- Ensure all assigned diving personnel meet the physical standards set forth in appropriate Service directives, regulations, and instructions.
- Develop and implement command training plans to ensure adequate training of divers in all unit diving mission areas. Requalification and training will be appropriately documented in individual service records, as appropriate, and in unit training files.
- Ensure a Dive Log (DD Form 2544) is maintained for all dives conducted by the command. This log is an official record and will be retained for three years. Ensure the dive log is completed for all dives and submitted to the NAVSAFECEN IAW OPNAVINST 3150.2B / 9940.2B, *A Diving Log Accident/Injury Report*, and applicable supplemental instructions. In addition, individual divers will maintain a personal dive log.
- Ensure diving mishaps resulting in death, lost time (24 hours or more), personnel injury, recompression treatment, or significant material damage are reported within 24 hours to the NAVSAFECEN IAW OPNAVINST 5102.1C, *Mishap Investigation and Reporting*. The appropriate USSOCOM component command will also be notified as soon as possible following the incident via telephone and followed by a written report, as required.
- Establish procedures to ensure that diving equipment (which may have contributed to an accident) is secured, not tampered with, and shipped by the fastest traceable means to the NEDU for analysis. This procedure should specify that the equipment shall not be dismantled, cleaned, or altered in any way before shipment.
- Conduct annual operational, administrative, and material inspections of diving units or elements to verify compliance with this directive and other appropriate diving regulations or instructions.
- Designate, in writing, diving officers, supervisors, and other personnel as required by appropriate regulations or instructions.

Diving Officer

9-12. The commander or commanding officer designates the diving officer to oversee the safe and efficient conduct of diving operations. In addition to his duties outlined in the USN Diving Manual and amplifying Service directives, regulations, and instructions, the diving officer will—

- Monitor diving operations to ensure compliance with established policies and procedures. Be responsible for the safe conduct of all diving operations.
- Ensure that the qualifications of all personnel participating in diving operations remain current IAW Service directives.
- Establish a dive training program. Monitor lesson plans and lectures to ensure correct and proper information is being disseminated.
- Ensure, by observation and routine inspection, that safe operation and maintenance procedures are performed on all diver life support systems, maintenance facilities, and associated equipment.
- Ensure that diving supervisors complete all diving forms, logs, and checklists, as required by OPNAVINST 3150.2B, the USN Diving Manual, technical manuals for the type of diving equipment used, this manual, and amplifying regulations or instructions.

Diving Medical Officer

9-13. The diving medical officer (DMO) is a physician or physician assistant trained at the Diving Medical Officer School at Panama City, Florida, who maintains currency IAW appropriate Service directives. The DMO will—

- Review all diving physicals and determine if individuals are physically qualified to perform diving duties.
- Be present during buoyant ascents, free ascents, submarine lockout and lock-in training, and pressure and oxygen tolerance testing.

Officer-in-Charge and Noncommissioned Officer-in-Charge

9-14. All diving evolutions require a designated individual in charge. An E-7 or above normally oversees SF operations that include diving as part of a larger operation, exercise, or training. The OIC or NCOIC will plan the evolution using the assigned diving supervisor to supervise the actual diving portion of the operation. The OIC or NCOIC and the diving supervisor may be the same individual if the OIC or NCOIC is a qualified diving supervisor. The divers will receive all commands and direction from the diving supervisor during his period of responsibility. The OIC or NCOIC may relieve the diving supervisor of his duties if the OIC or NCOIC is himself a qualified diving supervisor or if another qualified diving supervisor is immediately available. The OIC or NCOIC is not required to remain on the surface.

Diving Supervisor

9-15. The diving supervisor must be an E-5 or above who is thoroughly familiar with the equipment, conditions, safety precautions, and hazards inherent to diving operations. Diving supervisors will be designated in writing by his commander or commanding officer. He will be a qualified diver and have successfully completed an approved NAVSPECWARCEN or USAJFKSWCS diving supervisor course. Waivers to the above qualifications must be approved by the appropriate USSOCOM component commander after policy coordination with the NAVSPECWARCOM commander. The diving supervisor will perform the duties outlined in the USN Diving Manual and amplifying Service directives, regulations, and instructions. The diving supervisor will—

- Be responsible to the diving officer for the safe and efficient conduct of diving evolutions. He will be in charge of the actual diving operation; no diving operations will be conducted in his absence and he will remain on-scene until all divers are out of the water.
- Coordinate and plan all aspects of the diving operation, ensure proper clearance is obtained from appropriate higher authority, identify safety hazards, and develop emergency procedures during the planning phase to ensure safety and the success of the mission. When planning the dive, the diving supervisor will use the diving safety checklist, emergency assistance checklist, diving boat safety checklist, and the ship repair safety checklist for diving found in the USN Diving Manual. Other derivative and locally prepared checklists may be used.
- Advise the OIC or NCOIC of the operation on all matters pertaining to the planning, execution, and safety of the dive.
- Conduct the dive brief.
- Assess the physical readiness and qualifications of the divers with the assistance of the DMO and the DMT, as available. All divers will have current diving physicals as prescribed by appropriate Service directives.
- Ensure that support personnel are present for all briefings and are adequate to support the dive. Inspect all support and special equipment to ensure that it is in proper working condition and able to perform its intended function.
- Personally supervise the set up and testing of all diving equipment.
- Ensure all divers receive a diving supervisor check before entering the water.
- Know the location and operational condition of the nearest recompression chamber and status of the chamber crew, for example, chamber supervisor, outside tender, inside tender, and log keeper. Ensure that arrangements have been made for expeditious transportation of any casualties and for contacting a diving medical officer.
- Have the requisite equipment needed to perform his duties and responsibilities, to include meeting any likely emergency situation.
- Assign one or more assistant diving supervisors to perform his duties, as directed, when the nature of the operation requires more than one diving platform, for example, launch and recovery from different locations or a large number of divers.
- Ensure proper diving signals (day or night) are displayed when dive training operations are in progress.
- Ensure that divers maintain a safe distance from energized sonar IAW NAVSEAINST C9597.3A, *Safe Diving Distances from Transmitting Sonar*, and that sonars that present a potential hazard are tagged-out and in the passive mode.
- On repetitive dives, check each diver's remaining air and oxygen supply and residual nitrogen times before divers leave the surface. When diving closed-circuit scuba (for example, MK 25), ensure the C02 absorbent is changed per Navy and manufacturer's technical manuals and NAVSEA directives.
- Be the single point of contact during any diving emergency.
- Supervise postdive cleaning and storage of all dive and support equipment.
- Ensure that all dive logs are properly completed, signed, and submitted to the diving officer.

Assistant Diving Supervisor

9-16. When assigned, the assistant diving supervisor will—

- Be a qualified diving supervisor, or a member who has completed an approved diving supervisor course and is under the supervision of a qualified diving supervisor for training purposes.
- Perform those functions directed by the diving supervisor.

Diving Medical Technician

9-17. The diving medical technician (DMT) must be a graduate of a recognized course of instruction for qualification as a DMT or SOT. He will—

- Be present for all mixed gas and closed-circuit dives. His presence during open-circuit dives will be at the discretion of the diving supervisor, unless otherwise required by amplifying Service directive.
- Provide medical care and treatment to divers on a routine basis or in case of a diving emergency. Accompany any injured party to the treatment facility, if additional treatment is necessary.
- Have the proper equipment, as prescribed in the USN Diving Manual to resuscitate a diver and provide first aid.

Standby or Safety Diver

9-18. The standby or safety diver will be a fully qualified diver whose functions are to provide emergency assistance to divers and to perform the duties outlined in the USN Diving Manual. Additional duties require him to be—

- Present during the dive briefing and operation. The standby or safety diver should be qualified in the type of scuba being used by the divers in the mission or training evolution.
- Knowledgeable of the rescue procedures for the type of scuba equipment being used by the divers.

> **NOTE**
> The standby diver will wear open-circuit scuba equipment regardless of what equipment the divers are using, unless directed otherwise by the diving supervisor. The USN Diving Manual outlines the minimum equipment required for scuba diving.

- Positioned as best possible to render assistance in the event of an emergency. Be fully dressed for immediate entry into the water after receiving instructions to do so from the diving supervisor. (The regulations or instructions of the USSOCOM component commanders may authorize the standby diver to be fully dressed with the exception of scuba, fins, and face mask, which will be staged and ready for quick donning).

> **NOTE**
> Single standby divers or safety divers will be tended by a surface crew with a tending line.

Divers

9-19. A diver is qualified for the type of scuba to be used during the dive. Basic qualifications and physical standards are described in the USN Diving Manual. He also will—

- Be present at the dive brief.
- Be physically and mentally prepared for each dive.

- Have personal equipment prepared for each dive.
- Properly set up scuba equipment, using appropriate check sheets.
- Promptly obey all diving signals and instructions received from the diving supervisor.
- Promptly report equipment malfunction or damage to the diving supervisor.
- Observe the buddy system as outlined in the USN Diving Manual and oversee the safety and welfare of his buddy.

Ship Safety Observer

9-20. A ship safety observer is assigned for simulated combat diver ship attacks. He ensures the target ship is safe to dive underand completes the Ship Safety Checklist (found in the USN Diving Manual). He acts as liaison between the target ship and the diving supervisor and informs—

- The diving supervisor of any discrepancies in the Ship Safety Checklist.
- Other ships and craft nested with or along the same pier as the target ship of the dive plan.
- Ships on adjacent piers and pier sentries of the dive plan.
- All ship participants when the operation is secured.

TRAINING

9-21. To ensure safe diving operations, all divers must be skilled and proficient. This section provides broad guidance on the conduct of SF diving training to include initial training and qualification and the integration of diver training into unit training plans.

INITIAL TRAINING AND QUALIFICATION

9-22. Details concerning qualification standards and requirements are contained in the appropriate Service directives. Each level of training is discussed below.

Diver

9-23. A diver must be a graduate from a formal military dive course. Service divers who are not designated as combat divers will not normally participate in SF diving training or operations. Exceptions will be authorized by the appropriate USSOCOM component commander for the purpose of rendering specialized support (for example, dry deck shelter [DDS] operation), documentation of training (for example, combat camera teams), or observing SF diving operations. A member is qualified as a combat swimmer or diver by completing one of the following:

- Graduate from the USAJFKSWCS Combat Diver Qualification Course.
- Graduate from the BUD/S Course.
- Graduate from a recognized military dive course and subsequent attendance at NAVSPECWARCEN or USAJFKSWCS Combat Diver Course for training on the Draeger MK 25 scuba.

Sustainment Training or Unit Training

9-24. After initial qualification, it is necessary to sustain and build upon the skills acquired as individuals during diver qualification courses. Additional training is as follows:

9-25. **Refresher and Sustainment Training.** Training will consist of practical training, lectures, and classroom instruction. Units should maintain lessons plans and review or update them annually (Appendix B). Regular command training for all divers should include, but not be limited to the following:

- Lecture. Information covered includes the following:
  - Underwater physics.
  - Underwater physiology.

  - Basic diving procedures for scuba.
  - Diving air decompression tables.
  - Diving hazards.
  - General safety precautions.
  - Reports and logs.
  - Standard diving equipment.
  - Open-circuit scuba.
  - Closed-circuit scuba.
  - First aid.
  - Cardiopulmonary resuscitation.
  - High-pressure air compressor (stationary and portable).
  - Air sampling program.
  - System certification procedures.
  - Hyperbaric chamber operation.
  - Hyperbaric treatment tables.
  - Decompression sickness (Type I and II).
- Practical Work. Tasks include the following:
  - Maintenance and repair of all types of scuba used by the unit.
  - Repair and maintenance of diving air compressors.
  - Demonstrate working knowledge of decompression tables and, where appropriate, combat swimmer multilevel diving procedures.
- Diving. Operations might include the following:
  - Subsurface infiltrations and exfiltrations using open- or closed-circuit systems during day and night.
  - Underwater search and recovery operations.
  - In-water emergency procedures.

9-26. **Diver Requalification**. Details concerning requalification standards and requirements are contained in AR 611-75, *Management of Army Divers*. A brief summary follows:

- Each Service prescribes the type, number, and periodicity of dives required to maintain currency.
- If a diver's currency has lapsed for 6 months or less, he may regain currency by fulfilling the requirements prescribed for requalification. Dive pay stops the date currency lapses; it restarts the date the diver becomes current again.
- If a diver's currency has lapsed for longer than 6 months, he must be retrained and recertified IAW established Service procedures.

MISSION-ESSENTIAL TASK LIST FOCUS

9-27. Unit dive training will be METL-focused to the maximum extent possible. Dive training plans will be unit-specific. Training will be progressive to attain and maintain the skills required to conduct dive operations in support of assigned missions in projected operational environments. Collective dive training will be integrated with other METL-focused training as much as possible. The use of realistic field training exercises (FTXs) based on full mission profiles (FMPs) to train and evaluate the unit's divers should be the norm rather than the exception. Standards for various dive evolutions are delineated in FXP-6, *Naval Special Warfare Exercises (U)*.

ADVANCED TRAINING QUALIFICATIONS

9-28. Additional training and certification is necessary to perform certain supervisory and medical support functions required to conduct SF diving operations. The training and qualifications for these positions are prescribed by appropriate Service directives. The positions are as follows:

- *Diving Supervisor*. He must be an E-5 or above who is thoroughly familiar with the equipment, conditions, safety precautions, and hazards inherent to SO diving. He will be a qualified diver and have successfully completed an approved NAVSPECWARCEN or USAJFKSWCS Diving Supervisor course.

- *Diving Medical Technician.* He will be a qualified diver and a graduate of a recognized course of instruction for qualification as a DMT or SO technician.

OPERATIONS

9-29. SF diving, with the exception of specific missions assigned to NSW forces, can be described as an insertion or exfiltration technique. U.S. Army and Air Force SOF divers use diving as a means of clandestine infiltration and exfiltration and, as such, treat diving as a phase of a larger operation. Naval Special Warfare forces also use diving as an infiltration and exfiltration technique; however, as USSOCOM's maritime component, they are tasked with a myriad of maritime missions that require more sophisticated diving skills. Other NSW diving operations include the following:

- Combat swimmer ship attack (Limpeteer attack).
- Underwater demolition raids.
- Harbor reconnaissance.
- Submerged hydrographic reconnaissance.
- Underwater obstacle demolition or mine countermeasures.

ORGANIZATION

9-30. The organization for a particular operation is dependent on the nature of the mission, the type of diving to be conducted, and the unit's SOPs. The minimum supervisory and support personnel required by the USN Diving Manual will be present for all SF diving operations. When organizing for the dive, it is important to match unit and individual qualifications and experience to the specific requirements of the operation or mission. Unit integrity is an important consideration when conducting diving operations. However, there are times when attachments to a unit may be necessary to fulfill its mission. In such cases, it is imperative to fully brief all participants in the operation regarding unit SOPs to ensure that everyone knows what procedures to follow in the event of an emergency.

PLANNING

9-31. Preliminary planning, as outlined in the USN Diving Manual, is vital for a successful dive. Without adequate planning, the entire operation may fail and, in extreme cases, the lives of the divers may be endangered. The following information describes plans for a safe and successful dive operation and is appropriate for training as well. It is not a guide to tactical mission planning. The planning phase of a diving operation consists of the following tasks:

- *Surveying the Problem.* The first step is to study all aspects of the diving operation to be conducted and how it fits into the broader plan for the entire mission. After framing the entire diving operation and defining the objectives, select an approach to the problem.
- *Choosing Diving Equipment.* Planners should consider the requirements to solve the problem—range, depth, thermal protection, communication, decompression, and similar needs. Factors that must be considered before making a decision are—
  - Underwater visibility.
  - Tides and currents.
  - Water temperature.
  - Water contamination.
  - Bioluminescence.
  - Surface conditions (wave or surf action, air temperature, and visibility).
  - Qualifications and experience level of divers.
  - Available diving equipment (safety boats, recompression chamber, resuscitator, personal flotation devices).
  - Adequate diving platform (can the divers enter or return aboard without difficulty?).
  - Ability to recover a diver in distress.
  - The necessary items to mark the location of a missing diver.
  - Any other conditions that are required to safely support the particular diving operation.

- *Selecting Equipment.* Equipment selection depends on the type of evolution to be undertaken and the availability of specific equipment. A Diving Equipment Checklist is provided in the USN Diving Manual.
- *Establishing Safety Precautions.* The applicable safety precautions must be determined by considering the—
  - General precautions for scuba diving.
  - Specific precautions for the particular type of scuba to be used, to include hazardous materials such as oxygen and O2 absorbents (soda lime).
  - Safety precautions particular to the operation.

> **NOTE**
> If time and the nature of the operation permits, a local Notice to Mariners should be issued. Furthermore, when routine diving operations are to be conducted in the vicinity of other ships, they must be properly notified by message.

- *Briefing the Divers.* A thorough briefing will be given for each dive evolution. All proper precautions against foreseeable contingencies should be thoroughly covered in the briefing. It must be remembered that a great percentage of the work involved in a diving operation should be completed topside through proper planning. Inadequate briefings and supervision can, and have, caused fatal accidents.

DIVING

9-32. SF combat diving will be conducted IAW the guidance provided in the USN Diving Manual and the safety considerations listed in USASOC Reg 350-20. Additional guidance for specific diving techniques and types of operations can be found in Chapter 10.

SAFETY

9-33. Diving operations are inherently hazardous. Proper training and in-depth preparation and planning will reduce the potential for accidents. Safety considerations will be fully addressed during planning and integrated into all dive training. Unit commanders will conduct risk assessments before training and training will be conducted in a progressive crawl-walk-run manner. Specific guidance for conducting risk assessments is contained in FM 100-14, *Risk Management.* USASOC units must also reference USASOC Reg 385-1, *Safety, Accident Prevention and Reporting.* The arbiter of safety questions is the USASOC Safety Office.

RESPONSIBILITIES

9-34. Safety is every individual's duty if participating in or supporting the diving operation. All personnel involved in a particular dive evolution, operator and support personnel alike, must be constantly aware of the nature and progress of the operation, and must remain alert for possible danger. Chapter 2 outlines the specific individual duties for safely conducting SF diving operations.

ENVIRONMENTAL PERSONNEL LIMITATIONS

9-35. During the planning process, consideration must be given to how weather, temperature, surf conditions, and sea state will effect the safety of the dive evolution. Chapter 6 outlines the minimum equipment requirements. Environmental limitations on divers and equipment are found in the USN Diving Manual.

OPERATIONAL PROCEDURES

9-36. The element of danger is always present during SF diving operations. Training and operations must be planned with consideration given to individual and unit experience, swimmer fatigue factors, and repetitive diving times. General dive procedures are provided below as guidelines for the safe conduct of SF dive operations. (Specific guidance for operations such as combat swimmer ship attack, hull searches, turtlebacking and tactical purge procedures, and diving with foreign units is provided in USSOCOM Reg 350-4.) Adherence to these safety procedures will enhance the probability of success during combat operations and reduce the incident of diving casualties.

- All diving conducted by USSOCOM forces will follow the procedures of the USN Diving Manual and the amplifying guidance set forth in AR 611-75 and USASOC Reg 350-20, without exception.
- Only equipment that is certified or ANU IAW NAVSEAINST 10560 Ser OOC/3112 will be used during diving operations, unless a waiver has been granted by the appropriate authority.
- Every dive will be preceded by a dive brief to be attended by all personnel involved in the dive. If key support personnel are unavailable to attend the dive brief, then the diving supervisor will ensure they are briefed separately.
- It is mandatory-that each diver use the appropriate predive check sheets for setting up his scuba. Each diver will sign the check sheet and ensure that his check sheet is signed by the diving supervisor. Sample check sheets are provided in USASOC Reg 350-20.
- A standby diver is mandatory for any diving operation. He need not wear the same scuba as the divers, but he must have the same depth capabilities and be able to enter the water immediately after being briefed by the diving supervisor. He should be qualified to dive the scuba being used by the divers in the mission or training evolution.
- No dives will be conducted through a surf zone if the surf zone contains more than three lines of waves with a wave height of more than three feet, unless otherwise directed by the unit commander. Dives conducted through plunging surf of any size require careful consideration of diver safety.
- A diver recall device is mandatory equipment for all dives. Approved recall devices are listed in NAVSEAINST 10560 Ser OOC/3112.
- A buddy line will be used between divers as required by the USN Diving Manual, unless otherwise authorized by the unit commander.
- A marking float should be used whenever possible to mark the location of divers in the water. At the discretion of the diving supervisor, a light source may be attached for easier location during night dives.
- A life jacket with a whistle attached to the oral inflation hose and the proper CO2 cartridges or air bottles in place will be worn during all diving operations. There will be no quick releases in the body straps of the life jacket. CO2 cartridges will weigh no less than 3 grams below their original weight and will be weighed before each use.
- All scuba cylinders used during diving operations will be charged to at least 75 percent of the working pressure. The diving supervisor will ensure that sufficient diver's breathing medium remains to conduct any repetitive dive.
- Both individuals in a dive pair will use the same type of scuba.
- The diving supervisor and corpsman must have flashlights or diving light when conducting diving operations between sunset and sunrise. Chemlites, dive lights, or flares are mandatory for each diver.
- Radio communications will be maintained on the scene between all safety boats, the diving supervisor, ship safety observer, if designated, and the parent command for immediate notification in case of emergency.
- Before allowing divers to enter the water in the vicinity of or beneath surface vessels or submarines, the diving supervisor shall make contact with, and obtain clearance from, the ship safety observer aboard the vessel.
- Free swimming ascent (FSA) and buoyant ascent (BA) are considered to be emergency procedures and should not be included in a diving evolution, unless—
  - The sole purpose is to train divers in FSA and BA.
  - Properly trained instructors are on station and in control of the divers situation from air source to the surface.
  - A certified recompression chamber is on station and immediately available for use.
  - A DMO is on scene and can be summoned to the recompression chamber within 5 minutes.
  - Divers are checked by a DMT or SOT immediately upon surfacing.
- Divers should not exceed the normal rate of descent (75 feet per minute [fpm]) or ascent (30 fpm).
- If a diver senses any adverse physiological symptoms or mechanical malfunctions, he should surface immediately. Never force continuation of a dive during training evolutions.

- A weighted ascent or descent line is required for all dives deeper than 100 feet. The following procedures will apply:
  - When at depth, remain within visual sight of the descending line unless using a circling line, then contact must be maintained with the circling line. In case the current is in excess of 0.5 knots, contact will be maintained with the descending or ascending line.
  - If the descending or circling line is lost, surface and report to the diving supervisor.
- Divers should breathe normally and continuously at all times to avoid lung-over pressurization or CO2 buildup.
- Supervisor should not turn off the main control valve for the breathing medium until the diver is out of the water.
- Diving training operations will be suspended for any of the following reasons:
  - Small craft warnings, when sea state makes it difficult to recover divers, thunderstorm conditions, or similar warnings.
  - When, in the opinion of the diving supervisor, the current or tides present an unsafe diving condition.
  - Restricted surface visibility of less than 500 yards, due to rain, snow, fog, or other meteorological conditions.

NOTE

Use judgment considering lost diver procedures and the possible hazard of unseen ship or boat traffic.

  - Any unsafe condition exists (for example, environmental problems, water pollution, red tide, civilian agencies closing water areas, unexpected or unresolved operational concerns).
  - Any circumstance that requires one of the mandatory dive supervisory or support personnel to leave the diving scene.

EMERGENCY PROCEDURES

9-37. Emergency procedures are key collective skills that support the METL of all combat dive units. Planning and rehearsing these skills will be an integral part of all unit dive training. Units should establish SOPs to deal with any anticipated diving emergencies. The following procedures apply with each type of emergency:

- *Separation From a Dive Partner.* If the divers become separated and lose visual contact, each should—
  - Stop, look (look up, down, and 360 degrees around; in poor visibility extend an arm in the direction you are looking), and listen—then surface immediately.
  - If the dive buddy is on the surface, regroup, connect buddy line, and descend to continue the dive.
  - If the buddy is not on the surface after a reasonable wait, signal the safety boat (signal by waving your arms during the day or a chemlite at night; if there is not an immediate response from the safety boat, use smoke during the day or a flare at night) and wait for assistance.
- *Diver in Need of Assistance.* Functions should include the following:
  - In an emergency, render assistance to the swim partner by inflating his flotation device, dropping his weight belt if necessary, and bringing him to the surface. Use particular caution when surfacing from under a ship, floating pier, or other overhead obstruction. The diver rendering assistance should come off dive status, for example, remove his regulator mouthpiece only after the man in distress is safely aboard the safety boat or if required to administer first aid or CPR on the surface.

CAUTION

If diving the MK 25, drop the weight belt only as a last resort.

  - In an emergency, ignite a flare or signal with your flashlight in a circular motion at night. During the day, ignite smoke or wave one or both hands over your head. For nonemergency assistance, shine a flashlight

toward the safety boat at night; during the day, hold one arm out of the water, palm toward the safety boat.
    - Render first-aid, CPR, or mouth-to-mouth resuscitation as appropriate.
- *Loss of a Diver*. Functions should include the following:
    - Initiate diver recall immediately upon determining that a diver is lost.
    - Mark the last known location of a diver with a buoy.
    - Contact the parent command via radio. **At no time will the name of any lost diver be passed over the radio**! Reference may be made to the dive pair's number if appropriate. Pass the word that a diver is missing and that a search is being initiated.
    - Organize divers on hand and decide if there is adequate bottom time to conduct a search. If so, commence a search of the immediate area using the standby diver or other available divers. Use the buoy as the center of the search area. **Do not move the buoy**! If no bottom time is available with divers on hand or if it is suggested that available bottom time is inadequate for the task at hand, contact the unit for additional resources.

EQUIPMENT

9-38. All equipment used for any type of diving operation must be approved by the Navy. The U.S. Navy publishes an ANU list that contains all Navy-approved diving equipment. The procurement and use of unauthorized scuba and associated equipment as well as unauthorized modification of approved equipment is expressly prohibited. Equipment will be used IAW the USN Diving Manual, applicable Service regulations and instructions, and appropriate technical manuals.

MINIMUM EQUIPMENT

9-39. The USN Diving Manual lists the minimum equipment for open- and closed-circuit scuba diving. Equipment that does not appear on the approved Navy diving equipment list normally will not be used except for authorized research, development, test, and evaluation (RDT&E) purposes. However, a dangerous oversimplification exists when relying on any general minimum equipment list.

Diver Equipment

9-40. The requirements of each dive will dictate the equipment necessary. The diving supervisor must take all facets of the dive profile into consideration before issuing the equipment list for a particular dive. Specific items of consideration are discussed below:

- *Personal Flotation Device.* The Navy-approved personal flotation devices used by SF units are as follows:
    - The MK-4 flotation device is suitable for open circuit, MK 16, and MK 16 scuba.
    - The Secumar TSK 2/42 flotation device is suitable for all dives using the MK 25 Draeger scuba.

NOTE

Past experience has shown that CO2 cylinders can lose their charge due to faulty manufacture. All unexpended CO2 cylinders shall be weighed individually before the start of each dive and per appropriate Preventative Maintenance System schedules. Quick releases will not be used on flotation devices. CO2 cylinders will weigh no less than 3 grams below their original weight.

- *Knife.* Carrying a knife is a safety requirement. The knife will be attached to the diver's web belt or the leg or body strap of the flotation device, but never to the weight belt. The knife will be kept sharp and free from rust. The dive buddy will be aware of the location of his partner's knife.
- *Depth Gauge.* A depth gauge will be worn on the arm or on the attack board of the diver.

- *Wristwatch.* A wristwatch will be worn by each diver.
- *Compass.* Compasses will be used at the discretion of the OIC or NCOIC of the dive, depending upon the type of evolution planned. For compass accuracy dives, at least one compass will be carried by each pair of divers. Whenever possible, an attack board with compass, depth gauge, and wristwatch will be used for those dive profiles requiring compass accuracy (for example, infiltration, exfiltration, and ship attacks). The attack board with the compass is to be attached to the diver's wrist or flotation device by a lanyard.
- *Signal Flare.* Only approved flares will be used IAW current directives.
- *Light Sources.* Chemlights or dive lights are mandatory for each diver when diving between the hours of sunset and sunrise.
- *Diver's Slate.* A slate will be worn when directed by the OIC or NCOIC and is used for recording information or for diver-to-diver communication.
- *Life Lines.* The two types are—
  - *Buddy lines.* The buddy line will be 6 to 10 feet long. It will be used to connect dive pairs at night or in other conditions of poor visibility and for all closed-circuit or semiclosed-circuit dives. It should be strong and have a neutral or slightly positive buoyancy. Nylon, Dacron, and manila are suitable materials.
  - *Tending lines.* If only one diver is available, he will be tended by a surface crew with a line. The line is to be of sufficient strength to support the diver's weight while pulling him to the surface and clear of the water. However, it should not be so heavy as to interfere with the diver's ability to perform his assigned duties. The line will be tended IAW procedures set forth in the USN Diving Manual.
- *Protective Clothing.* Generally, protective clothing will be worn at the discretion of the diving supervisor or the OIC or NCOIC as dictated by the water and atmospheric temperatures. Protective clothing also offers protection against scrapes and cuts from underwater obstacles. The desires of the individual diver should be considered by the dive planners. Even in warm water, a diver can suffer hypothermia during prolonged exposure.
- *Weight Belt.* A weight belt with an approved quick-release mechanism will be worn as required by each diver. It must be worn outside of all equipment so that it can be ditched in case of emergency.
- *Whistle.* One whistle per diver is required for all diving operations and should be attached to the oral inflation tube of the flotation device.
- *Dive Buoys.* A dive buoy for each swim pair may be used at the discretion of the OIC or NCOIC and diving supervisor. A light source (light or chemlite) may be attached to the buoy for easier location during night dives.

Breathing Apparatus

9-41. SF elements use three types of scuba units—open circuit, closed circuit (MK 25), and semiclosed circuit (MK 15 and MK 16). All scuba cylinders used during diving operations will be charged to at least 75 percent of their working pressure. The diving supervisor will ensure that sufficient breathing medium remains to conduct any repetitive dives. Equipment checklists for each of the three types of scuba can be found in USSOCOM Reg 350-4.

SUPPORT EQUIPMENT

9-42. Divers require specific support equipment for conducting all diving operations. The following reflects the minimum support equipment that is used by SF units:

9-43. **Safety Boat.** Personnel use a power boat during all administrative and training dives and for picking up divers in case of an emergency. They may use a safety boat on operational dives as circumstances permit. A safety boat is mandatory for any training dive conducted in open water. It must be highly maneuverable and must be ready to rapidly render assistance to a diver in distress. If the probability exists that divers will become widely dispersed (such as on dives or swims of 2 or 3,000 yards, around a point of land, or with inexperienced personnel), two or more safety boats should be used as deemed necessary by the OIC or NCOIC and the diving supervisor. The following minimum equipment will be on board each safety boat:

- *High Intensity Light.* Divers should use a high intensity light during all night dives.
- *First Aid Kit and an AMBU-Type Resuscitator.* A DMT will have in his possession the proper equipment, as prescribed in the USN Diving Manual to resuscitate a diver and provide first aid.

- *Diving Safety Boat Checklist.* A sample checklist can be found in the USN Diving Manual.
- *Diving Flag or Diving Navigational Lights.* Navigation rules require the following visual be displayed when diving evolutions are conducted:
  - *Daytime.* The international signal Code pennant and the Alpha flag.
  - *Night.* In addition to the normal running lights, three 360-degree lights in a vertical line (red over white over red) will be displayed.

9-44. **Light Sources.** A flashlight or diving light is required for the diving supervisor and DMT or SOT during all night dives.

9-45. **Diver Recall Device.** A diver recall device is mandatory equipment for all dives. Approved recall devices are listed in NAVSEAINST 10560 Ser OOC/3112.

9-46. **Communications Equipment.** Radio communications will be maintained on the scene between all safety boats, the diving supervisor, safety observer (if assigned), the parent unit, and other units as required (for example, harbor patrol) for immediate notification in the event of an emergency.

SPECIFIC MANNING REQUIREMENTS

9-47. The minimum manning requirements for conducting dive operations are specified in AR 611-75. The dive supervisor oversees the safe conduct of SF diving operations. To assist the diving supervisor and render emergency medical support in case of a diving accident, the minimum requirements for on-scene medical support would be a DMO and a DMT or SOT.

- *Diving Medical Officer.* The DMO is required to be present during buoyant ascents, free ascents, submarine lock-out and lock-in training, and pressure and oxygen tolerance testing. The DMO is responsible for developing a medical plan to monitor all divers who are involved in the diving evolutions listed above. He has the responsibility to recommend that a diver not participate in an evolution due to adverse health or physical condition. He personally monitors diving operations in progress and stands ready to provide medical treatment if necessary.
- *Diving Medical Technician or Special Operations Technician.* He is required to be present for all mixed gas and closed-circuit dives. His presence during open-circuit dives will be at the discretion of the diving supervisor, unless otherwise required by amplifying Service directive. The DMT or SOT should be positioned where he can best monitor the progress of the dive and provide medical care and treatment to divers on a routine basis or in case of a diving emergency. He will have in his possession the proper equipment, as prescribed in the USN Diving Manual to resuscitate a diver and provide first aid. He will accompany any injured party to the treatment facility, if additional treatment is necessary.

CHAPTER 10

Open-Circuit Diving

Combat swimming and diving operations are a small piece of the total spectrum of SF waterborne capabilities. Combat diving operations are highly decentralized in both the planning and execution phases. It is because diving operations are specialized and require advanced training of all personnel involved. These skills are rarely required; however, when they are—no other skill set will meet mission requirements. To ensure combat divers are successful in their operations, the team must become involved early in the planning phase to ensure mission requirements and proper safety considerations are met.

The objective of this chapter is to provide the dive supervisor, dive detachments, commanders, and staffs with essential information necessary to identify planning considerations required to conduct and supervise horizontal dives, vertical dives, search and rescue dives, contaminated water dives, cold water or ice dives, and limited-visibility dives. In support of this objective, this chapter contains excerpts from relevant reference material. Where appropriate, that material has been expanded to emphasize key elements peculiar to SF diving. The definitive material that is required to actually conduct diving operations is contained in the following references:

- AR 611-75, *Management of Army Divers.*
- FM 20-11, *United States Navy Diving Manual.*
- USASOC Reg 350-20, *USASOC Dive Program.*

NOTE

Detachments conducting diving operations are required to have these references on-hand throughout the operation.

OPEN-CIRCUIT DIVE OPERATIONS

10-1. Open-circuit diving is an ideal medium for training and support. It is the simplest method to get underwater and stay there long enough to do useful work. It may be used for any operation not requiring secrecy or when underwater detection capabilities are very limited. Planning ranges for infiltration swims are approximately 1,500 yards depending on equipment loads and diver conditioning.

NOTE

When conducting combat diving operations, the planning considerations need to be calculated in U.S. standards of measure. Dive planners use a 1-knot swim speed as the goal. This establishes a time/distance standard for planning purposes of 100 yards per 3 minutes. If using the metric system, distances covered would be less than planned (if using the 1-knot standard or 30.8209 meters per minute, after 3 minutes the diver will travel 92.4627 meters vice 101.118 yards in the same time) causing the combat divers to surface early or miss the intended navigation point if using time.

10-2. SF teams are most likely to use open-circuit diving for initial diver training, detachment training and training support, underwater reconnaissance in a permissive environment, ship bottom search, and underwater search and recovery. It must be used whenever the operational depth exceeds the capabilities of the closed-circuit (O2) rebreathers (20 feet of seawater [FSW] with excursions to 50 FSW). Depth limits for open-circuit (diving) are 130 FSW in training and 190 FSW (IAW regulatory guidance) in exceptional circumstances. Complete guidance for operational depths may be found in NAVSEAINST 10560 Ser OOC/3112.

DIVE PLAN AND BRIEFING

10-3. All diving operations require meticulous planning. The designated primary diving supervisor will prepare the dive plan and present the dive briefing.

10-4. The combat dive supervisor (CDS) prepares a dive plan to ensure the proper and timely execution of all required support functions. The plan is prepared in the normal five-paragraph operation order (OPORD) format and serves to notify commanders and staff of the impending operation. It is required to ensure that all diving operations are coordinated, controlled, and conducted safely. Detachments will find that major portions of these formats do not change from dive to dive. They should be incorporated as a permanent part of the detachment's diving SOP.

10-5. A dive briefing precedes all combat diving operations. Dive briefings are a compact synopsis of the overall dive plan that is tailored to include only the information necessary for the completion of the dive. It is given to the participants (divers and support personnel) as close to the time of the dive as possible. Each dive briefing is different.

STANDARDS FOR COMPRESSED AIR

10-6. Internal training, external training (FID), mission support, and combat diving operations all require that a dive detachment be capable of filling and refilling diving tanks. SFODs have the option of deploying with organic portable air compressors or obtaining air from host nation or commercial sources. Air purity standards and testing procedures are detailed in the USN Diving Manual. SFODs conducting diving operations must, as a minimum, adhere to the published Navy standards.v

10-7. The quality of compressed air is critically important and must be strictly monitored and controlled. The air used in diving operations must meet the standards of purity as established by the Commander of the Naval Medicine Command. This standard applies to all sources of air or methods used for charging the cylinders. Table 10-1, page 168, outlines the required minimum standards.

Table 10-1. Minimum standards of compressed air

U.S. Military Diver's Compressed Air Breathing Purity Requirements for ANU-Approved or Certified Sources	
Constituent	**Specification**
Oxygen concentration	20 to 22 percent by volume
Carbon dioxide	1,000 parts per million (ppm) maximum
Carbon monoxide	20 ppm maximum
Total hydrocarbons	25 ppm other than methane
Particulates and oil mist	5 mg/m^3 maximum
Odor and taste	Not objectionable
Oxygen concentration	20 to 22 percent by volume
Carbon dioxide	500 ppm maximum

Table 10-1. Minimum standards of compressed air (*Continued*)

Diver's Compressed Air Breathing Requirements if From a Commercial Source	
Constituent	**Specification**
Carbon monoxide	10 ppm maximum
Total hydrocarbons as methane (CH_4) by volume	25 ppm maximum
Particulates and oil mist	.005 mg/l maximum
Odor and taste	Not objectionable
Separated water	None
Total water	0.02 mg/l maximum
Halogenated compounds (by volume): solvents	0.2 ppm maximum

Reference: FED SPEC BB-A-1034 A and B

10-8. Contamination of divers' air can cause illness, unconsciousness, or even death. The NAVSEA Systems Command requires that an air sample be taken semiannually from each operational air source. The Naval Coastal Center in Panama City, Florida, is the central authority to schedule the sampling of divers' air sources. All field units should coordinate air sampling requirements through that center. The Navy provides this service, semiannually, for each registered air source at no cost to the unit. Alternatively, diving detachments may use a commercial sampling service provided by a certified laboratory.

10-9. Detachments deploying with organic assets that have been maintained and tested IAW USN standards can be assured that their equipment and the air supply it produces meets or exceeds the minimum standards. Detachments that are forced to obtain air from other sources must exercise reasonable precautions such as examining the facility's physical plant (compressors, air banks, distribution panel) and the air analysis certificate to ensure that it meets the minimum standards. Diver's air procured from commercial sources shall be certified in writing by the vendor as meeting the purity standards of FED SPEC BB-A-1034 Grade A Source I (pressurized container) or Source II (compressor) air. When examining a commercial air analysis certificate, detachments should verify that the certificate is current (within previous 6 months) and the tested sample met or exceeded Grade E.

10-10. Units deploying to locations without certified air sources must be prepared to conduct their own tests of breathing gas purity before using air from unknown sources. Air quality test kits using disposable chemical test strips or test vials are available through the supply system, the GSA catalog, or issued as a component of the unit's portable compressors. Personnel should ensure the kit's chemicals are fresh and they will not expire during the mission. Procedures vary between the types of test kits. Detachments must review the operating instructions whenever they conduct air quality sampling.

DIVING INJURIES AND MEDICINE

10-11. The USN Diving Manual contains detailed information about anatomy and physiology as it relates to diving. It also contains an extremely detailed presentation of diving injuries and the required medical treatment, including recompression therapy.

ACCIDENT MANAGEMENT

10-12. Tables 10-2 through 10-4 are extracts from the NOAA Diving Manual. They serve as an excellent guide for preparing and executing a diving accident management plan. The importance of evacuation planning cannot be overemphasized. Planning must be thorough and complete, keeping in mind that it will involve several modes of transportation (for example, boat, truck, aircraft, and ambulance) and communications (for example, voice, radio, and telephone).

Table 10-2. Injuries during descent

Type Injury	Cause	Symptoms	Treatment	Prevention
Sinus Squeeze	1. Blocked sinus opening. 2. Too rapid a descent.	1. Pain in facial sinus area. 2. Bleeding from nose in severe cases. 3. Blood in nasal mucous discharge in all cases.	1. Provided there are no complications, time is the only treatment required.	1. Do not dive with head cold. 2. Valsalva maneuver. 3. Bounce dive. 4. Use nasal spray and drops.
Ear Squeeze	1. Blocked eustachian tube or external ear canal preventing pressure equalization. 2. Too rapid a descent.	1. Pain, increasing with depth. 2. Rupture of tympanic membrane, relief from pain. 3. Blood from ear, nose, or throat.	1. Valsalva maneuver or bounce dive. 2. With bleeding severe pain see medical doctor.	1. Do not dive with head cold. 2. Valsalva maneuver or bounce dive. 3. Use nose drops or spray. 4. Do not dive with tight-fitting hoods. 5. Stop dive if pain persists.
Lung Squeeze	1. Breath-holding while diving to a depth where lungs collapse. 2. Underwater explosions.	1. Pain, usually quite severe in chest. 2. Difficulty in breathing when diver returns to surface.	1. Artificial respiration if breathing has stopped. 2. Possible surgical drainage may be required. 3. If no complications, allow time for tissues in lungs to heal. 4. In all cases consult the medical officer.	1. Breathe normally during descent. 2. Do not make breath-hold dive to a depth sufficient to compress the lungs below their residual volume.
Minor Squeezes (Face, Intestine, and Tooth)	1. Unequal pressure to some part of the body. 2. Failure or inability to equalize.	1. Pain, sometimes severe. 2. Swelling, redness of tissues, bleeding in severe cases.	1. Equalize pressure. 2. Cold packs. 3. In case of tooth, report to a dental officer.	1. Equalize pressure in mask. 2. Proper dental hygiene.

Table 10-3. Injuries during ascent

Type Injury	Cause	Symptoms	Treatment	Prevention
Mediastinal Emphysema (Rupture of Lung, Overexpansion and Air Escaping into the Mediatinal Space)	Holding breath on ascent produces overexpansion.	1. Slight pain under breastbone. 2. Possible shortness of breath or fainting. 3. Possible slight blueness of lips and face.	Usually none. Dis-sipates with time.	Do not hold breath on ascent.
Subcutaneous Emphysema	1. Holding breath on ascent. 2. Possible from air embolism, pneumo-thorax, or mediastinal emphysema.	1. Swelling of neck tissues. 2. Change in voice. 3. Crepitation.	Usually none. Dissipates with time.	Do not hold breath on ascent.

Table 10-3. Injuries during ascent (*Continued*)

Pneumothorax (Air Escaping the Lungs and Entering the Pleural Space Between the Lung Lining and Chest Wall)	1. Holding breath on ascent. 2. Weak pleura.	1. Severe chest pain made worse by deep breathing. 2. Sudden shortness of breath. 3. Irregular pulse. 4. Possible shock or cyanosis.	1. See medical doctor ASAP. 2. Air may have to be surgically removed from the pleural cavity.	Do not hold breath on ascent.
Air Gas Embolism (AGE)	Holding breath on ascent.	1. Sudden onset of bloody, frothy sputum. 2. Dizziness. 3. Paralysis. 4. Visual disturbances. 5. Unconsciousness (normally within 15 surfacing). **NOTE:** If a diver sustains an AGE, he most likely will also have the other injuries on this table.	1. Immediate recompression. 2. Administer 100 percent oxygen. 3. Contact a DMO ASAP.	Do not hold breath on ascent.

Table 10-4. Injuries caused by indirect effects of pressure

Type Injury	Cause	Symptoms	Treatment	Prevention
Decompression Sickness (Bends or Caisson Disease, N_2 Bubbles in Blood)	1. Inadequate decompression. 2. Overstaying bottom time. 3. Ascending too fast. 4. Exceeding planned depth. 5. Flying after diving.	1. Brain or spinal cord involvement. • Unconsciousness • Convulsions. • Inability to speak. • Muscular paralysis. • Nausea, vomiting, visual problems. • Dizziness, vertigo. • Paralysis of lower body. • Loss of bladder and bowel control. 2. Lung involvement (chokes). • Shortness of breath. • Coughing and shallow breathing. 3. Pain only. • Muscle and joint area bubbles. • Severe pain in joints. • Localized pain anywhere. • Swelling (associated with pain). • Skin bends. • Red itching rash. • Skin welts.	Immediate recompression.	1. Adhere to dive plan. 2. Do not fly for 12 hours after diving. 3. Good physical condition. 4. Avoid overexertion.

Table 10-4. Injuries caused by indirect effects of pressure (*Continued*)

Oxygen Toxicity	Generally unknown but normally caused by breathing 100-percent oxygen at 33 feet or greater.	Use letters VENTIDC: V – Visual problem (tunnel vision) E – Ringing in ears N – Nausea T – Twitching/tingling I – Irritability D – Dizziness C – Convulsions	1. Surface. 2. Remove oxygen source.	1. Know symptoms. 2. Observe operational limits. 3. Use buddy system.
Nitrogen Narcosis	Partial pressure of nitrogen gas has a narcotic effect at 99 feet (4 atmosphere absolute)	1. Disorientation. 2. Confusion. 3. Unusual behavior. 4. Loss of skill. 5. Lack of concern. 6. Drunkenness.	Controlled ascent.	1. Recognize symptoms. 2. Use buddy system. 3. Avoid deep dives.

BLAST PRESSURE

10-13. Combat divers or swimmers may be exposed to the effects of underwater explosions in the course of their missions. Blast overpressure is the sudden increase in pressure, above the normal pressure, caused by an explosion. Because water is 800 times denser than air, it transmits this increased pressure very efficiently in the form of a shock wave. Ideally, swimmers should be out of the water whenever underwater explosives are detonated. Divers or swimmers exposed to blast pressure risk serious injury or death. An overpressure of 50 psig or greater may cause injury to organs and body cavities containing air. An overpressure of 300 psig may cause severe injury to a fully submerged diver, and 500 psig may cause death.

10-14. When divers cannot exit the water, detachments must calculate a minimum safe distance so as to reduce the effect of the blast overpressure on the divers. The objective is to ensure that they are not exposed to a blast pressure in excess of 50 psig. The detachment uses the following formula to determine the pressure exerted at a given distance by an underwater explosion of tetryl or TNT.

$$\text{Pressure (P)} = \frac{13{,}000 \times \sqrt[3]{\text{Weight of Explosive}}}{\text{Distance in Feet}}$$

WARNING

The above formula is for TNT. It is not applicable to other explosives.

10-15. To compute a minimum safe distance in feet from an underwater explosion, modify the above blast pressure formula to the following:

$$\text{Minimum Safe Distance in Feet} = \frac{13{,}000 \times \sqrt[3]{\text{Weight of Explosive}}}{\text{50 psig}}$$

10-16. Distance from the explosion is the primary factor serving to mitigate the effects of blast pressure. Once a safe distance has been computed, planners must calculate the amount of time the divers will require to reach it. Planners should use the D × S = T formula to determine the fuzing requirements of the charge.

MINIMIZING THE EFFECTS OF AN EXPLOSION

10-17. When expecting an underwater blast, the diver should get out of the water and out of range of the blast whenever possible. If he has to be in the water, it is prudent to limit the pressure he experiences from the explosion to less than

50 pounds per square inch. To minimize the effects, the diver can position himself with feet pointing toward and head directly away from the explosion. The head and upper section of the body should be out of the water or the diver should float on his back with his head out of the water. Divers should be aware of bottom topography, composition, underwater structures, and how these factors may influence the shock waves through reflection, refraction, and absorption. Generally, high brisance (REF) explosives generate a high-level shock wave of short duration over a limited area. Low brisance (high power) explosives create a less intense shock and pressure wave of long duration over a greater area.

DIVE TABLES

10-18. The USN is the proponent agency for all matters concerning military diving. The USN decompression tables are special tables and rules that have been developed to prevent decompression sickness and enhance the diver's safety. These tables and rules take into consideration the amount of nitrogen absorbed for any given depth and time period, and allow for the elimination of the inert gases through normal processes. With rapid changes and advances in diving medicine, the most current USN Diving Manual should always be available at the dive site for reference.

NOTE

The tables must be rigidly followed to ensure maximum safety. Combat diving operations will normally be performed within the no-decompression limits IAW AR 611-75.

AIR DECOMPRESSION TABLES

10-19. To properly use USN air decompression tables, divers must understand specific terms. Each term is explained below.

- *Depth.* This term indicates the depth of a dive. Divers should always use the maximum depth attained during the dive. Depth is always measured in feet.
- *Bottom Time.* This term refers to the total elapsed time from where the diver leaves the surface until he begins his ascent. This time is rounded up to the next whole minute. It is always expressed in minutes.
- *Decompression Schedule.* It is the specific decompression procedure for a given combination of depth and bottom time. It is indicated in feet and minutes.
- *Single Dive.* This dive is conducted at least 12 hours after the most recent previous dive.
- *Repetitive Dive.* This dive is conducted 10 minutes after and within 12 hours of a previous dive.
- *Decompression Stop.* This stop occurs at a specified depth where the diver remains for a specified time to eliminate inert gases from body tissues.
- *Surface Interval.* The diver spends this amount of time on the surface following a dive. It begins as soon as the diver surfaces and ends as soon as he begins his next descent.
- *Residual Nitrogen.* This term refers to excess nitrogen gas that is still present in the diver's tissues from a previous dive.
- *Repetitive Group Designation.* This letter designation relates directly to the amount of residual nitrogen in a diver's body.
- *Residual Nitrogen Time.* This amount of time must be added to the bottom time of a repetitive dive to compensate for the nitrogen still in solution following a previous dive.
- *Equivalent Single Dive Time.* This term refers to the sum of residual nitrogen time and bottom time of the repetitive dive. It is measured in minutes and used to select the decompression schedule and repetitive group designator on a repetitive dive.

Selection of Decompression Schedule

10-20. There are four USN decompression tables. They are as follows:

- USN Standard Air Decompression Table.
- No-Decompression Limits and Repetitive Group Designation Table.

- Surface Decompression Table Using Oxygen.
- Surface Decompression Table Using Air.

> **NOTE**
> Scuba or combat divers do not use the surface decompression tables, therefore their use will not be discussed. They are mentioned for information purposes only.

10-21. Divers should select the appropriate decompression table based on the dive's parameters. These factors are depth and duration of the dive, availability of a recompression chamber, availability of an oxygen breathing system within the chamber, and the specific environmental conditions (sea state, water temperature).

10-22. All USN decompression schedules have general guidelines that divers must follow to account for slight differences in the actual dive and the manner in which the decompression schedules of all tables are arranged. Above all, the decompression schedules provide for maximum safety of the diver. Divers should consider the following principles when selecting a decompression schedule:

- Schedules for all tables are given in 10-foot depth increments.
- Bottom times for all schedules are usually in 10-minute increments.
- Depth and total bottom time combinations form actual dives.
- Always select exact or next greater depth.
- Always select exact or next greater time.
- Do not interpolate between decompression schedules.
- Do not alter or modify decompression schedules without prior approval of a DMO.
- Diver's chest should be located as close as possible to the stop depth.
- Decompression stop times begin when the diver reaches the stop depth.
- Do not include ascent time as part of stop time.
- If the diver is delayed in reaching the decompression stop, the delay time is added to the bottom time and the dive is recomputed for the longer bottom time.
- If the diver was exceptionally cold, showed signs of extreme fatigue during the dive, or if his workload was relatively strenuous, the next longer decompression schedule should be selected.

Unlimited/No-Decompression Limits and Repetitive Group Designation
Table for Unlimited/No Decompression Air Dives

10-23. SF divers use this table most often. This table outlines the maximum amount of time that a diver may remain at a given depth without incurring a decompression obligation. Each depth listed has corresponding no-decompression time limits given in minutes. Should a diver need to make a repetitive dive, this table provides the group designator for no-decompression dives (Table 10-5).

REPETITIVE DIVES

10-24. Any dive performed within 12 hours of a previous dive is a repetitive dive. The period between dives is known as the surface interval (SI). During the SI, divers are off-gassing, or reducing through normal respiration, the level of nitrogen absorbed into their bodies during previous dives. Keeping track of their SI allows divers to recalculate their residual nitrogen group to take advantage of the reduction (over time) of the absorbed nitrogen in their bodies.

10-25. Surface interval times are expressed in hours and minutes and range from a minimum of 10 minutes to a maximum of 12 hours. Any surface interval of less than 10 minutes is ignored and the bottom times of the two dives are combined and treated as one continuous dive. It is only necessary to track SI for 12 hours. After 12 hours, the diver is considered desaturated (no remaining residual nitrogen from the previous dive) and any further dives start from scratch.

Table 10-5. Unlimited/No-decompression limits and repetitive group designation table for unlimited/no decompression air dives

Depth (feet)	No-Decomp Limits (min)	Group Designation														
		A	B	C	D	E	F	G	H	I	J	K	L	M	N	O
10	Unlimited	60	120	210	300	797	*									
15	Unlimited	35	70	110	160	225	350	452	*							
20	Unlimited	25	50	75	100	135	180	240	325	390	917	*				
25	595	20	35	55	75	100	125	160	195	245	315	361	540	595		
30	405	15	30	45	60	75	95	120	145	170	205	250	310	344	405	
35	310	5	15	25	40	50	60	80	100	120	140	160	190	220	270	310
40	200	5	15	25	30	40	50	70	80	100	110	130	150	170	200	
50	100		10	15	25	30	40	50	60	70	80	90	100			
60	60		10	15	20	25	30	40	50	55	60					
70	50		5	10	15	20	30	35	40	45	50					
80	40		5	10	15	20	25	30	35	40						
90	30		5	10	12	15	20	25	30							
100	25		5	7	10	15	20	22	25							
110	20			5	10	13	15	20								
120	15			5	10	12	15									
130	10			5	8	10										
140	10			5	7	10										
150	5			5												
160	5				5											
170	5				5											
180	5				5											
190	5				5											

10-26. The residual nitrogen timetable for repetitive air dives provides information relating to the planning of repetitive dives. Divers should follow the steps below when using the timetable (Figure 10-1):

- Refer to the repetitive group designator (RGD) from the previous dive assigned by either the standard air or no-decompression table.
- Determine the residual nitrogen time by using the residual nitrogen timetable for repetitive air dives.
- Enter the SI table horizontally to select the appropriate surface interval.
- From the appropriate SI, read down to the bottom of the table to obtain the new repetitive group letter.
- Determine the equivalent single dive time. Add the residual nitrogen time and the total bottom time to get the equivalent single dive time.
- Obtain the residual nitrogen time corresponding to the planned depth of the repetitive dive as follows:
  - Read down from the repetitive group letter to the row that represents the depth of the repetitive dive.
  - Add the time shown at the intersection (the residual nitrogen time in minutes) to the repetitive dive to obtain total nitrogen time for the repetitive dive.
- Select the decompression schedule according to the new equivalent single dive time.
- Use the equivalent single dive time from the preceding repetitive dive to determine the proper schedule, if additional dives are needed.

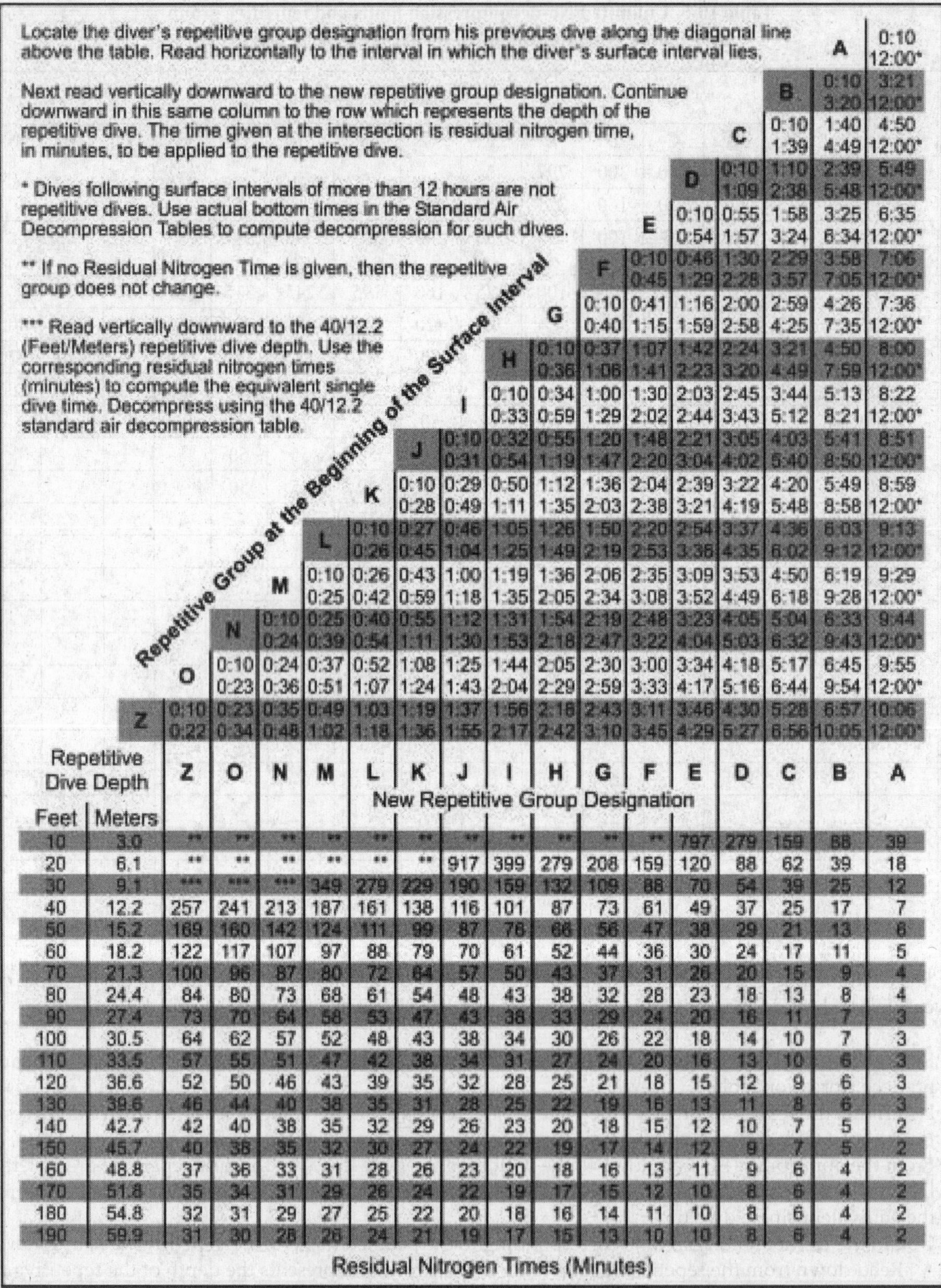

Locate the diver's repetitive group designation from his previous dive along the diagonal line above the table. Read horizontally to the interval in which the diver's surface interval lies.

Next read vertically downward to the new repetitive group designation. Continue downward in this same column to the row which represents the depth of the repetitive dive. The time given at the intersection is residual nitrogen time, in minutes, to be applied to the repetitive dive.

* Dives following surface intervals of more than 12 hours are not repetitive dives. Use actual bottom times in the Standard Air Decompression Tables to compute decompression for such dives.

** If no Residual Nitrogen Time is given, then the repetitive group does not change.

*** Read vertically downward to the 40/12.2 (Feet/Meters) repetitive dive depth. Use the corresponding residual nitrogen times (minutes) to compute the equivalent single dive time. Decompress using the 40/12.2 standard air decompression table.

Repetitive Group at the Beginning of the Surface Interval

Repetitive Group	Z	O	N	M	L	K	J	I	H	G	F	E	D	C	B	A
A																0:10 12:00*
B															0:10 3:20	3:21 12:00*
C														0:10 1:39	1:40 4:49	4:50 12:00*
D													0:10 1:09	1:10 2:38	2:39 5:48	5:49 12:00*
E												0:10 0:54	0:55 1:57	1:58 3:24	3:25 6:34	6:35 12:00*
F											0:10 0:45	0:46 1:29	1:30 2:28	2:29 3:57	3:58 7:05	7:06 12:00*
G										0:10 0:40	0:41 1:15	1:16 1:59	2:00 2:58	2:59 4:25	4:26 7:35	7:36 12:00*
H									0:10 0:36	0:37 1:06	1:07 1:41	1:42 2:23	2:24 3:20	3:21 4:49	4:50 7:59	8:00 12:00*
I								0:10 0:33	0:34 0:59	1:00 1:29	1:30 2:02	2:03 2:44	2:45 3:43	3:44 5:12	5:13 8:21	8:22 12:00*
J							0:10 0:31	0:32 0:54	0:55 1:19	1:20 1:47	1:48 2:20	2:21 3:04	3:05 4:02	4:03 5:40	5:41 8:50	8:51 12:00*
K						0:10 0:28	0:29 0:49	0:50 1:11	1:12 1:35	1:36 2:03	2:04 2:38	2:39 3:21	3:22 4:19	4:20 5:48	5:49 8:58	8:59 12:00*
L					0:10 0:26	0:27 0:45	0:46 1:04	1:05 1:25	1:26 1:49	1:50 2:19	2:20 2:53	2:54 3:36	3:37 4:35	4:36 6:02	6:03 9:12	9:13 12:00*
M				0:10 0:25	0:26 0:42	0:43 0:59	1:00 1:18	1:19 1:35	1:36 2:05	2:06 2:34	2:35 3:08	3:09 3:52	3:53 4:49	4:50 6:18	6:19 9:28	9:29 12:00*
N			0:10 0:24	0:25 0:39	0:40 0:54	0:55 1:11	1:12 1:30	1:31 1:53	1:54 2:18	2:19 2:47	2:48 3:22	3:23 4:04	4:05 5:03	5:04 6:32	6:33 9:43	9:44 12:00*
O		0:10 0:23	0:24 0:36	0:37 0:51	0:52 1:07	1:08 1:24	1:25 1:43	1:44 2:04	2:05 2:29	2:30 2:59	3:00 3:33	3:34 4:17	4:18 5:16	5:17 6:44	6:45 9:54	9:55 12:00*
Z	0:10 0:22	0:23 0:34	0:35 0:48	0:49 1:02	1:03 1:18	1:19 1:36	1:37 1:55	1:56 2:17	2:18 2:42	2:43 3:10	3:11 3:45	3:46 4:29	4:30 5:27	5:28 6:56	6:57 10:05	10:06 12:00*

New Repetitive Group Designation

Repetitive Dive Depth Feet	Meters	Z	O	N	M	L	K	J	I	H	G	F	E	D	C	B	A
10	3.0	**	**	**	**	**	**	**	**	**	**	**	797	279	159	88	39
20	6.1	**	**	**	**	**	**	917	399	279	208	159	120	88	62	39	18
30	9.1	***	***	***	349	279	229	190	159	132	109	88	70	54	39	25	12
40	12.2	257	241	213	187	161	138	116	101	87	73	61	49	37	25	17	7
50	15.2	169	160	142	124	111	99	87	76	66	56	47	38	29	21	13	6
60	18.2	122	117	107	97	88	79	70	61	52	44	36	30	24	17	11	5
70	21.3	100	96	87	80	72	64	57	50	43	37	31	26	20	15	9	4
80	24.4	84	80	73	68	61	54	48	43	38	32	28	23	18	13	8	4
90	27.4	73	70	64	58	53	47	43	38	33	29	24	20	16	11	7	3
100	30.5	64	62	57	52	48	43	38	34	30	26	22	18	14	10	7	3
110	33.5	57	55	51	47	42	38	34	31	27	24	20	16	13	10	6	3
120	36.6	52	50	46	43	39	35	32	28	25	21	18	15	12	9	6	3
130	39.6	46	44	40	38	35	31	28	25	22	19	16	13	11	8	6	3
140	42.7	42	40	38	35	32	29	26	23	20	18	15	12	10	7	5	2
150	45.7	40	38	35	32	30	27	24	22	19	17	14	12	9	7	5	2
160	48.8	37	36	33	31	28	26	23	20	18	16	13	11	9	6	4	2
170	51.8	35	34	31	29	26	24	22	19	17	15	12	10	8	6	4	2
180	54.8	32	31	29	27	25	22	20	18	16	14	11	10	8	6	4	2
190	59.9	31	30	28	26	24	21	19	17	15	13	10	10	8	6	4	2

Residual Nitrogen Times (Minutes)

Figure 10-1. Residual nitrogen timetable

> **NOTE**
> There is one exception to this table. In some instances, when the repetitive dive is to the same or greater depth than the previous dive, the residual nitrogen time may exceed the actual bottom time of the previous dive. In this case, the diver should use the actual total bottom time of the previous dive as the residual nitrogen time in determining equivalent single dive time.

10-27. The principles outlined above are illustrated in the repetitive dive flowchart (Figure 10-2). The flowchart converts into the repetitive dive profile shown in Figure 10-3.

AIR DIVING TABLES

10-28. These tables consist of the USN standard air decompression table and the exceptional exposure table. SF divers are usually limited to 130 feet and a no-decompression profile. For this reason, they normally do not use these tables. The type of diving that does require their use is outside the scope of this manual. If the SFOD has a requirement to conduct decompression dives, it must seek and obtain the appropriate waivers and ensure that only personnel trained in decompression procedures participate in the dives. Detachments must strictly adhere to the procedures laid out in the USN Dive Manual.

> **NOTE**
> Normally, combat diving operations do not involve decompression stops. Sometimes they are unavoidable, for example, when an entanglement inadvertently extends bottom time. If decompression stops are required, the diver must be prepared to safely execute them using the USN standard air decompression table.

EQUIPMENT AND BASIC TECHNIQUES

10-29. The types of equipment available to SF divers are changing and improving rapidly as more equipment is tested and approved by the USN. The ANU list available from NAVSEA specifies the equipment that units and divers are allowed to purchase or use. SF units can use this list to tailor their equipment purchases to more closely satisfy requirements unique to their particular environment or mission. Because diving places extra stress on the human body, the one-size-fits-all approach to equipment acquisition cannot adequately meet all the unique requirements of SF divers and missions.

WEARING OF EQUIPMENT

10-30. The variety of equipment available to SF divers as well as the diver's personal preferences can result in a number of different equipment configurations. Units must establish an SOP that specifies how critical items of equipment should be worn. Examples would include the placement of an alternate air source, emergency signaling devices, depth gauges, watches, or the fastening of a weight belt. Other items may be left to diver preference for comfort and efficiency. Examples include determining the degree of exposure protection worn and placement of dive tools, lights, and nonessential accessories. Individual divers should rig and precheck their own and their buddy's gear before reporting to the CDS for the formal predive inspection. Individual divers should—

- Gauge their own cylinders and record pressure.
- Attach the regulator to the manifold keeping saltwater off the filter.
- Check for air leaks, check high-pressure gauge reading, and ensure the regulator is functioning properly.
- Adjust the harness for proper fit.
- Ensure the reserve lever is in the up position.

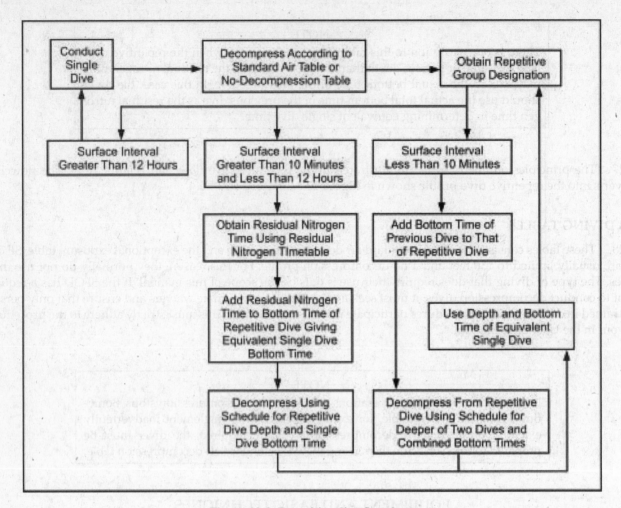

Conduct Single Dive

Decompress According to Standard Air Table or No-Decompression Table

Obtain Repetitive Group Designation

Surface Interval Greater Than 12 Hours

Surface Interval Greater Than 10 Minutes and Less Than 12 Hours

Surface Interval Less Than 10 Minutes

Obtain Residual Nitrogen Time Using Residual Nitrogen Timetable

Add Bottom Time of Previous Dive to That of Repetitive Dive

Add Residual Nitrogen Time to Bottom Time of Repetitive Dive Giving Equivalent Single Dive Bottom Time

Use Depth and Bottom Time of Equivalent Single Dive

Decompress Using Schedule for Repetitive Dive Depth and Single Dive Bottom Time

Decompress From Repetitive Dive Using Schedule for Deeper of Two Dives and Combined Bottom Times

Figure 10-2. Repetitive dive flowchart

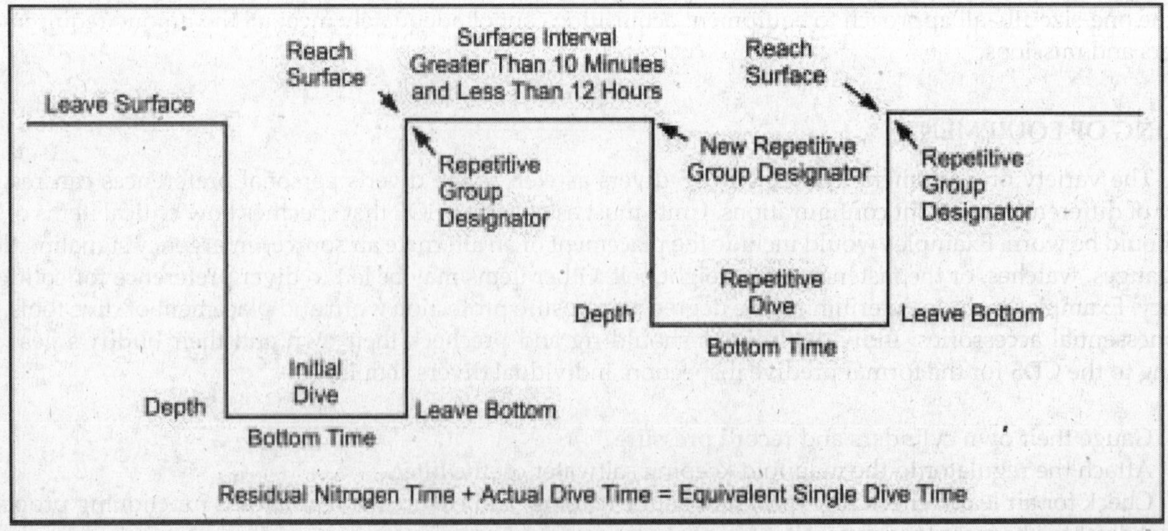

Figure 10-3. Repetitive dive profile

10-31. Before entering the water, all divers must be given a predive inspection by a diving supervisor. The CDS will inspect each diver for safety and ensure the diver meets mission requirements. Dive supervisors receive specialized training in performing predive personnel inspections as part of their initial diving supervisor training. They must ensure that every diver participating in the operation is properly equipped and correctly rigged before entering the water. The CDS is the final determiner of a diver's readiness to enter the water. Points of inspection include the following:

- Air cylinders are worn so that the manifold will not strike the diver's head during the dive. They must be positioned so that the diver can manipulate the on/off valve while submerged and activate the reserve lever when needed.
- The primary regulator hose is routed over the diver's right shoulder.
- The alternate (octopus) regulator (if worn) must be routed to the front of the diver's body and secured so that it is visible and accessible to the diver and his dive partner. Units must establish an SOP that specifies how the octopus is to be routed and secured.
- The low-pressure inflator is routed (depending on the equipment configuration) over or under the diver's arm and firmly attached to the buoyancy compensator military (BCM) inflation device.
- The submersible pressure gauge is routed under the diver's arm (as desired) for easy access.
- All hoses and accessories are secured so as not to present an entanglement hazard.
- A shirt or protective dress (for example, wet suit, dry suit, or mission uniform) is worn for environmental protection.

EQUIPMENT USE AND MAINTENANCE

10-32. Military diving places our soldiers in a potentially hazardous environment. The hazards found in diving are made safe through personnel selection, training, safety guidelines, supervision, and properly maintained equipment. The equipment provided to combat divers is extremely reliable and safe if properly maintained and used. Specific maintenance requirements for each piece of equipment are identified on that equipment's maintenance requirements card (MRC). These requirements derive from the USN's maintenance procedures. US Army Special Forces divers are required to follow them. Most of them apply only to the servicing DLSMF. The maintenance allocation charts (MAC), coupled with the manufacturer's instructions, provide the framework to properly maintain equipment. For certain types of equipment additional formalized training needs to be given to certain individuals. For example, servicing compressors or regulators involves working on life support systems that must be maintained by qualified individuals. Appendix C contains an outline of mandatory maintenance procedures.

PREDIVE PREPARATION

10-33. **Cylinder Inspection.** Before filling the diving cylinders with high-pressure air, divers must—

- Check the O-ring and manifold.
- Inspect the general condition of the cylinders. Ensure they have not been exposed to extreme heat, as it weakens the metal significantly. If heat exposure has occurred, ensure the cylinders undergo a hydrostatic test.
- Check for the Department of Transportation (DOT) or Interstate Commerce Committee (ICC) regulation stamp that indicates the type and grade of metal and working pressure of the cylinders.
- Check to ensure the hydrostatic test date has not expired. Cylinders must be hydrostatically tested every 5 years and visually inspected annually IAW the MRC.
- Ensure the reserve handle is down so that cylinders are filled completely.
- Check for proper strap adjustments and that straps are not missing, frayed, or torn.
- Check for proper band position and tightness.
- Check for air leaks with soapy solution or underwater.

NOTE

Divers should not fill cylinders faster than 400 psig per minute. This will prevent heat buildup and loss of psig when the cylinder cools down. **Do not overfill!**

10-34. **Regulators.** Military divers currently use the single-hose, two-stage regulator fitted with an additional low-pressure hose for inflating the buoyancy compensator and a submersible pressure gauge to monitor the quantity of air remaining in the diver's cylinders. Divers use this type of regulator for training and it adequately fits most mission profiles. Safety divers should be equipped with an additional second stage regulator (octopus) on a longer hose so they can provide an alternate air source to a distressed diver. Navy guidance currently allows commanders to decide if all divers within their commands should be equipped with octopus regulators.

10-35. **Regulator Inspection.** Specific functions must be checked before use. The diver must—

- Ensure that hoses, plugs, and the mouthpiece are all correctly attached and serviceable.
- Inspect hoses for tears or breaks.
- Inspect the sintered filter on the 1st stage for corrosion.
- Attach regulator to manifold and turn air on. Inspect for air leakage and free flow.
- Check purge flow by pushing purge button and ensure that regulator functions correctly by taking at least three normal breaths.

10-36. **Postdive Regulator Maintenance.** Divers must also check the regulator after each use. They should—

- Rinse regulators with fresh water after each dive. Periodically wash off with warm water and mild germicidal solution. *Never purge the second stage while washing the regulator.*
- Allow regulators to dry and store in cool, dry area out of direct sunlight. Store regulator with dust cap assembly firmly in place. If possible, regulators should be stored flat with hoses loosely coiled.
- Periodically, lightly lubricate neoprene parts with breathable silicone lubricant.
- Inspect and maintain regulator body and internal parts at least once a year. Repair and adjust as stated in manufacturer's repair manuals. Adjust intermediate pressures as required.

DIVER COMMUNICATIONS

10-37. Safety and the efficient management of divers and diving operations require reliable communications. There are three types of diving signals— standard, emergency, and special. These may be either visual, audible, or by physical contact. All dive plans must include a subparagraph that details the designated communications methods.

10-38. Visual signals are the primary means of communications between submerged divers. Divers also use visual signals for longer distance surface communications. The simplest visual signals are hand-and-arm signals. The USN Diving Manual depicts the standardized signals. Additional hand-and-arm signals are easily adapted from detachment SOPs to meet mission requirements. Other visual signals are more appropriate to long-distance signaling. They include smoke or handheld flares commonly worn attached to the dive tool, the safety sausage (a surface marker buoy), and the United States Air Force (USAF) survival mirror. All of these can be invaluable when attempting to locate and recover separated and distressed divers, especially at night in open water.

10-39. Audible signals are most valuable when communicating instructions from the surface to submerged divers. The diver recall system (DRS), a component part of the Support Set B, is the primary audible signaling device. It consists of a splash-proof, battery-operated surface unit with a microphone and a transducer that is suspended in the water. It is most effective when used in the tone mode. The dive supervisor can toggle continuous or intermittent tones (similar to a sonar pulse) and communicate with the divers using a prearranged code. The surface unit can also be used to give verbal instructions. Unfortunately, the unit has considerable distortion and limited effective range when used in the voice mode. Surface personnel must make sure to enunciate clearly, speak slowly, and keep instructions simple.

10-40. The simplest method of communicating with submerged divers is to bang two metal objects together. The clanking noise produced by the metal-to-metal contact is distinct from any other sound found in nature and it propagates well. This technique is especially useful when rendezvousing with a submarine at sea. Other acoustic signaling devices include the whistle attached to each diver's BCM, the sonic alert (an air-powered horn attached between the low-pressure inflator hose and the BCM), and the USN's pyrotechnic diver recall device.

10-41. Physical contact usually refers to line-pull signals. These signals are particularly useful when conducting surface tended search operations. They are also useful between buddy pairs when swimming in limited visibility water.

The USN Diving Manual gives a list of standard signals. Special signals may be devised between the CDS and the diver to meet particular mission requirements. When a diver uses line-pull signals, he should first remove all slack from the tending line, then give a series of sharp distinct pulls. Even hand signals can become a contact sport when diving in limited visibility conditions. By exaggerating the movements and feeling the partner's hand as the signal is being formed, it is possible to communicate in blackout conditions with reasonable accuracy. Signals are acknowledged by repeating them as received. All signals must be answered promptly. Failure of a diver or partner to respond to a signal should be considered an emergency.

10-42. Underwater communications systems are the most precise means of communicating for divers and support personnel. These systems require special equipment and training to use and maintain. They include hard-wired and wireless systems. Hard-wired systems consist of a surface unit, a helmet or full facemask for the diver, and a communications wire that is embedded in the diver's umbilical. Wireless systems are AM or SSB transceivers, usually mounted in a full-face mask, that allow three-way communications from the surface, to the surface, and between divers. All of these systems allow a greater degree of control, especially when the diver is engaged in extremely precise operations underwater. This factor is especially useful in search and recovery operations. Before any through-water communications system is used, planners should consult the ANU list to ensure that it is approved.

FREE SWIMMING ASCENT

10-43. The free-swimming ascent (FSA) is a controlled ascent, from any given depth to the surface, by a diver that has been breathing compressed gas at ambient (depth) pressure. The diver executes the ascent by starting a controlled exhalation and swimming upwards from his start depth. The diver must exhale continuously until after his head breaks the surface. The entire ascent is completed without breathing additional compressed gas.

10-44. FSAs are commonly executed in training, or operationally, when practicing the ditching and donning of dive equipment, or when executing an underwater cache and recovery of diving equipment. During initial dive training, FSAs are normally conducted in a controlled environment (50-foot FSA tower) and the students only use facemasks. Later, training is conducted using surface swim gear. If the training is focused on "ditch and don" or underwater cache and recovery, the weight belt and diving equipment will be ditched before the ascent.

10-45. Because of the potential threat of a lung over-expansion injury, FSAs are considered a high-risk training event. Actual procedures for conducting FSA training in a training tower are detailed in NAVSPECWARCEN Instruction 1540.5C. This instruction has the force of regulation and must be adhered to by USSOCOM units conducting this type of training. In addition to the above instruction, trainers must review and adhere to the additional regulatory requirements in the USN Diving Manual, AR 611-75, and USASOC Reg. 350-20.

10-46. Combat divers receive FSA training during their initial dive course. Because of the risks, this initial training is required to be conducted in a controlled environment under the direct supervision of certified instructors. It should be repeated or refreshed before any operation requiring a deliberate FSA evolution, for example, submarine lock-out/lock-in (LO/LI) training. NSWC and USAJFKSWCS maintain training towers and adequate cadre to support units requiring this type of training, provided the units make timely coordination so as not to interfere with the schools' primary mission. An FSA supervisor should oversee FSAs conducted operationally.

10-47. The ideal rate of ascent for a planned FSA is no faster than the ascent rate of the diver's smallest exhaled bubbles (a vertical flow of bubbles must be visible above the student's face mask). This practice results in an ascent that is faster than normal (normal = 30 fpm); however, the bubbles are a readily identifiable reference that the diver can use to gauge his ascent rate under almost all conditions. To reduce the risk of a lung overexpansion injury, the diver must exhale continuously as he ascends while looking to the surface, with a hand extended over his head. The diver may fin slowly to reach the surface. He must not activate the life jacket firing mechanisms. If the ascent results from an out-of-air emergency, the diver should retain the weight belt until he surfaces if possible. (Dropping the weight belt unnecessarily will result in an uncontrolled ascent.)

10-48. If an FSA is required as the result of an out-of-air emergency, the diver should keep the dive gear until he surfaces. If he has difficulty reaching the surface, then he should ditch the weight belt and inflate the buoyancy compensator (execute a buoyant ascent). Once the diver has surfaced, a decision can be made whether or not to jettison the dive equipment.

BUOYANT ASCENT

10-49. Buoyant ascent training is no longer conducted at the initial entry level in combat diving. Buoyant ascents are an emergency procedure performed by ditching the diver's weight belt and inflating the buoyancy compensator. This movement results in an uncontrolled ascent to the surface. The diver is at significant risk of suffering a lung overexpansion injury and possible decompression sickness (DCS). Divers forced to execute a buoyant ascent should start the procedure with a forceful exhalation and make a conscious effort to continue exhaling all the way to the surface.

WARNING

This method is an emergency procedure; present doctrine precludes practicing it in training!

10-50. Accidental buoyant ascents are normally the result of a loss of buoyancy control. These are usually caused by inattention, the loss of a weight belt, accidental activation of the buoyancy compensator, or problems with a dry suit. All diver training must include techniques for dealing with a loss of buoyancy control. Divers must also be aware of the dangers presented by overhead obstacles when deciding to execute a buoyant ascent. A fully inflated buoyancy compensator (BC) (or dry suit) is capable of pinning a diver to the underside of an overhead obstacle and holding him there immobile so he must be recovered by outside assistance.

DITCHING AND DONNING SCUBA EQUIPMENT

10-51. Scout swimmers or entire detachments approaching a BLS have the option of removing and caching their dive equipment in the water or wearing it across the beach. The MK 25 with its smaller, lighter case is usually worn until the detachment occupies the assembly area where it can be cached. Open-circuit equipment because it is heavier and bulkier is more likely to impede the movement of the detachment as it crosses the beach. Consideration should be given to caching it in the swimmer holding area behind the surf line. The technique for removing and replacing the equipment is referred to as "ditching and donning."

DIVING CONSIDERATIONS

10-52. This section discusses some of the more important considerations and training requirements associated with combat diving. Information is provided concerning air consumption, underwater navigation techniques, and limited-visibility operations.

DURATION OF AIR

10-53. All combat diver missions require planning for the diver's air supply. Duration of air depends upon the diver's consumption rate, depth of the dive, and capacity of the cylinders. No mission can be effectively accomplished if the diver runs out of air prematurely. The diver must compute his air consumption rate. There is a standard formula that must be applied; the USN Diving Manual explains this formula. The formula is quite simple; however, it requires gathering actual "in-water" air consumption information. That information is then used to calculate expected consumption requirements at any given depth and exertion rate.

10-54. The CDS must designate a "turnaround pressure" for each dive. Turnaround pressure is that which remains in the dive tanks when the dive must stop and a return to the surface begins. This amount is especially important when conducting a dive where there is an "overhead environment" and the diver cannot ascend directly to the surface. An overhead environment can occur by an obstruction (ship bottom search), physiology (decompression obligation), or the threat of enemy activity (observation or fire). Rules to plan turnaround are based on an expected reserve requirement such as having enough air to return to the start point and still react to emergencies. The most common rules from most to least conservative are as follows:

- Thirds: 1/3 in, 1/3 out, and 1/3 for contingencies.
- 1/2 + (x) psig – 1/2 of total tank pressure plus a designated reserve (usually 200 psig).
- Designated minimum remaining pressure (usually 300 to 500 psig at end of dive).

WARNING

Diving in a true overhead environment involving penetration into an enclosed space is beyond the scope of activity for combat divers. It is extremely hazardous and requires specialized training and equipment that is not normally available to SF divers.

UNDERWATER NAVIGATION

10-55. The success of any type of infiltration is directly dependent upon the unit's ability to arrive at its objective. Underwater operations are no different. Underwater navigation poses additional challenges because of the limited opportunities for terrain association. These problems are compounded if the infiltration route is complicated by "doglegs" or course changes en route. The most reliable navigation technique is dead reckoning with a magnetic compass.

10-56. Dead reckoning requires an accurate determination of distance and direction. The accuracy of this method increases as divers gain experience conducting practice swims. Accurate distance calculations are especially critical if the dive mission includes "doglegs" or other precision navigation requirements. Divers determine distance using two methods—pace (or kick) count and timed distance runs. Both methods require the diver to swim a measured course a number of times so that a valid average can be determined. It is imperative that the swim be conducted with the equipment load that will be worn on the mission so the equipment's drag can be factored in. If the divers are swimming a relatively short distance, the pace count method will be marginally more accurate. For longer distances, the timed method will prove more useful. Neither one of these methods allow for the effects of contrary currents. These must be taken into account for whenever calculating pace/time required to cover a given distance.

10-57. A good operational swimming speed (goal) for slick divers is 100 yards every 3 minutes. This pace was determined based on the requirements for swimming the C/C MK 25 UBA. Well-conditioned divers swimming O/C equipment slick (without extra equipment causing drag) may find this pace to be slower than optimal. This pace must be practiced repeatedly using a measured course until the swim teams develop a consistent speed. Divers burdened with mission equipment will have to conduct numerous practice swims to determine their actual (sustainable) swim speed.

Compasses

10-58. Directional information or control is provided by the compass. There are two basic types of compasses—those designed to be worn around the wrist or handheld and those ball-type compasses that are secured to some type of board.

10-59. **Wrist Compass.** The compass consists of a fluid-filled capsule containing a stationary lubber line and a north-seeking arrow. Two stadia lines on a rotating bezel enable the user to maintain alignment of the north-seeking arrow with the course bearing. The azimuth may be referenced by 5-degree graduations marked on the rotating bezel surrounding the capsule. All features are luminous to enable the diver to operate the compass in limited visibility. The compass is most frequently worn on the wrist but can also be handheld or strapped to an improvised tactical (TAC) board or to the rucksack frame. To use the compass, a diver simply points the compass' lubber line toward the target. He then turns the bezel ring until the two stadia lines straddle the north-seeking arrow. As long as the diver swims keeping the compass level and the north-seeking arrow between the stadia lines, he will arrive on target. It is important that a diver ensure that the north-seeking arrow does not get stuck or frozen as may happen if the compass is held at an angle.

10-60. **Other Compasses.** There are ball-type compasses similar to ship-mounted binnacle compasses that are of a much higher quality than the aforementioned wrist compass. They are usually more accurate, easier to read, and easier to use. The diver should point the compass at the target, observe the desired azimuth, and swim the desired azimuth to the target, as it is read or set. It is best to use these compasses in a TAC board-mounted role. The TAC board is highly recommended for all operations. It is a form of console usually set up with the compass center-mounted, with watch and depth gauge mounted above. Field-expedient TAC boards can be made of wood or Plexiglas and are normally held in the diver's hands. It is recommended that units use the TAC board in the console mode, as it keeps essential instrumentation organized and readily visible to the diver.

Other Techniques

10-61. If pinpoint accuracy is absolutely essential, the tactical peek should be incorporated into the swim. Under these circumstances, one diver, on azimuth, exhales all his air and very slowly breaks the surface, just to the point where he can see the objective and verify his position. He then returns subsurface as quickly as possible without unduly disturbing the surface of the water. His dive partner stands by underneath him, ready to pull the surface diver back underwater if he loses buoyancy control and rises too high out of the water. This method requires extensive buddy team practice.

10-62. Underwater navigation can also be facilitated with acoustic beacons. Beacons consist of two parts—a sending unit (the beacon) placed in the water at the objective and a receiver unit used by the divers to hone in on the beacon. They are a component of the Diver's Support Set B. Beacons work like a sonar direction-finder, indicating signal strength and bearing, usually by a series of light emitting diodes (LEDs) that illuminate sequentially as signal strength and receiver alignment improve. Obviously this is only viable when returning to (or going towards) a previously emplaced beacon. This is especially useful when returning to a cache, a work/search site, or an extraction point. Unfortunately the sending units have limited range, are susceptible to enemy intercept, and require prior emplacement of the sending unit.

10-63. Research and development is underway to provide SO divers with other effective methods of underwater navigation. These efforts include handheld inertial or Doppler navigation systems and submersible GPSs. Obviously underwater navigation is a critically important skill that all combat divers must practice frequently.

LIMITED-VISIBILITY DIVING OPERATIONS

10-64. Planners define limited visibility as diving under conditions where a diver cannot distinguish objects at a distance of 10 feet or less. Limited-visibility is caused by particles suspended in the water or a lack of ambient light. Turbidity is the description or measurement of the amount of suspended particles in the water and their effect on visibility. Turbidity is caused or exacerbated by surface runoff, high winds, a rolling surf, upwellings, and extreme tidal changes. Divers can expect better visibility at high tide than at low tide; they should use tide tables in dive planning. A minus tide (a low tide lower than the mean low tide) will greatly reduce visibility. Rivers and their outflows, harbors, bays, and other near-shore areas within the littoral zone are all subject to increased siltation and other conditions that contribute to reduced visibility.

10-65. Training for diving under limited-visibility conditions is especially important. Diving in these conditions can be very disorienting to an unprepared diver. The lack of visual references exacerbates latent tendencies to claustrophobia, which may manifest themselves as significant psychological stumbling blocks. Ideally, dive teams should have considerable experience under good conditions before they begin limited-visibility operations. Maintaining contact between dive buddies and maintaining precise navigation are much more difficult. Practicing in a pool at night with the lights out, or with masks blacked out, will improve skills.

10-66. Equipment that should be available and used on limited-visibility dives includes the following:

- Buddy lines.
- Diving lights.
- Diving knives.
- UDT vest or BC.
- One compass per dive team.
- Heavy gloves regardless of temperature.
- Descending lines, safety lines, and surface floats if the tactical situation permits and the mission so requires.

10-67. Procedures for limited-visibility diving operations are simple common sense. If possible, the diver should make the first dive in a new area when visibility conditions are good (before diver's actions silt up the site). He then should work upstream facing the current and allowing the current to wash silt downstream away from the work area. He must proceed slowly and cautiously when visibility is poor. Unseen debris on the bottom (or in the water column) can cause impalements, punctures, cuts, lacerations, and entanglements. If the diver becomes entangled, he should work slowly and carefully to clear the entanglement. He should attempt to back out, the direction of entry is probably clear. He should dive in dirty water with one hand extended in the direction of movement. When swimming parallel to the bottom, the diver should keep one hand held underneath his body slightly touching the bottom to assist in maintaining a reference. He must always be conscious of surge and currents to avoid being carried into unseen rocks.

10-68. A diver should verify direction frequently. He should make an effort to maintain a definite course or swim pattern and to know his position at all times. If not attached by a buddy line, he should check his swim buddy more often than usual and maintain close contact. If possible, he should use an anchor line or descent line for reference to assist in maintaining orientation. Judging the rate of ascent may be difficult. A diver should always use the watch and depth gauge in combination and maintain buddy contact.

10-69. Underwater searches in limited visibility require strict control measures to ensure diver safety and adequate coverage of the search area. The smaller the object to be found or recovered the greater the degree of control required. Tended line or jack stay searches are the most effective. All must be practiced dry before divers are committed to the water. When conducting working dives (for example, search or recovery), the detachment should consider using a single diver on a tether, tended from shore or a boat. The safety diver (also tended on a tether) would then be able to clip into the stricken diver's tether and follow it directly to him without concern for visibility issues.

10-70. In coastal areas, limited visibility in water may be caused by man-made pollution. Divers should pay particular attention to disinfecting their ears and ensuring that any cuts or abrasions are treated to prevent infection.

CONTAMINATED WATER DIVING

10-71. River mouths, estuaries, harbors, and bays located along an enemy coastline are areas of military interest where SFODs may find themselves operating. These areas are usually economically important and have a high probability of human activity that would result in significant pollution. Special characteristics of the local topography and hydrography may combine to further concentrate existing pollutants. In addition to tactical requirements, SFODs performing other missions may occasionally be called upon to dive in the vicinity of harbors, sewers, or industrial outlets that discharge contaminated waters.

10-72. The most common pollutants are sewage, surface or agricultural runoff, chemical or manufacturing wastes, and petrochemicals (usually as a result of spills or military operations). They present special problems when viewed from a military operations perspective. Working in or around these pollutants will expose detachments to disease or chemical hazards. Either threat has the potential to incapacitate personnel and destroy mission-essential equipment. MAROPS detachments must be prepared to deal with the event of operating in contaminated waters.

10-73. Divers conducting operations in polluted water are especially vulnerable to skin irritations and ear infections. Other more virulent pathogens (for example, hepatitis, E. Coli, salmonella) pose serious, potentially life-threatening risks to unprepared or unprotected divers. When planning a dive operation in waters that are known to be polluted, protective clothing must be used and appropriate preventive medicine procedures taken. The most effective medical protective measures are an active vaccination program with emphasis on blood and waterborne pathogens and a rigorously performed postdive decontamination program.

10-74. Physical protection is only afforded by a complete barrier system, usually a suitable commercial-grade, vulcanized rubber or polyurethane-coated, hooded dry suit with a full-face mask. Wet suits do not provide adequate protection for diving in contaminated waters. Full-face masks are essential to prevent the accidental ingestion of polluted water. A diver who gets polluted materials into his mouth may have both physiological and psychological problems.

10-75. Divers wearing full body protection (usually dry suits) or diving in waters with an elevated temperature are subject to hyperthermia—an elevated body core temperature (Figure 10-4).

10-76. Toxic materials or volatile fuels leaking from barges or tanks can irritate a diver's skin and damage his equipment. Oil leaking from underwater wellheads or damaged fuel tanks can cause fouling of equipment. Aviation fuel is particularly damaging to dive equipment. It (and most other petrochemical-based pollutants) will actually dissolve rubber or neoprene components. Before diving in polluted water, all dive team members must be thoroughly briefed on the possible hazards.

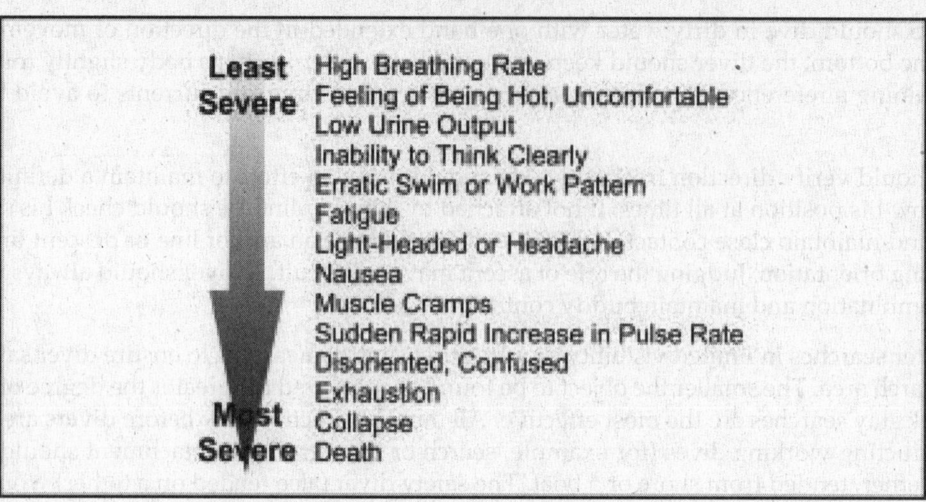

Figure 10-4. Hyperthermia symptoms

10-77. Physical decontamination of the diver and his equipment is essential. All decontamination procedures should start with the diver still encapsulated in his gear and breathing compressed air. Personnel should not break the seal on the diver's gear until an initial decontamination is completed. The best and most thorough decontamination method is to adopt procedures similar to those used in a full-blown chemical decontamination. Obviously, this method works best in a nontactical environment where sufficient logistics support is available. Operating in the field (nontactical) without a dedicated decontamination team requires some improvisation. The safest, simplest decontamination method is to use multiple washes with a strong detergent (emulsifies petrochemicals and provides a degree of sterilization), and multiple rinses preferably using hot water. Equipment that cannot be decontaminated should be bagged for disposal. If in an environmentally sensitive area, personnel should make sure that runoff from the decontamination process does not further contaminate the affected waterway.

10-78. When operating in a tactical environment, options are more limited. Divers should at least attempt a freshwater rinse before removing their dry suit and equipment. They should carefully remove the equipment while attempting to avoid unnecessary contact with contaminated surfaces, bag the equipment for disposal, and then wash exposed skin with a disinfectant and dry. They should always be prepared to discard contaminated equipment, especially if it has been exposed to petrochemicals or solvents. The deterioration of the materials in the dive gear cannot be reversed and it may render the equipment unsafe for further use.

10-79. Accidental exposure to nuclear radiation may occur due to proximity to weapons systems, or occasionally, substances in the natural state. Exposure to radiation can result in serious damage to the body and its systems. Safe tolerance levels are outlined in NAVSEA No. 0389-LP-015-3000, *U.S. Navy Radiological Control Manual*. Before diving on a vessel with nuclear capability, the SFOD leader must consult the radiological control officer. All divers will wear a thermoluminescence dosimeter (TLD) or similar device and should be made aware of the locations of possible exposure. The detachment must collect and process TLDs postdive IAW the supported vessel's SOPs, so that diver exposure can be accurately monitored.

ALTITUDE DIVING

10-80. The USN Diving Manual contains the most recent information pertaining to altitude diving. The following information provides general guidance to SFODs and commanders required to conduct or supervise high altitude (>999 feet above sea level) diving operations. This information is intended to inform divers of the limitations imposed by the increased altitude. Any unit engaged in high-altitude diving must have a copy of the USN Diving Manual on hand whenever conducting operations.

10-81. Because of the reduced atmospheric pressure, dives conducted at altitude require more decompression than identical dives conducted at sea level. Standard air decompression tables, therefore, cannot be used as written. Some organizations calculate specific decompression tables for use at altitude. An alternative approach is to correct the altitude dive to obtain an equivalent sea-level dive, and then determine the decompression requirement using standard tables. This procedure is commonly known as the cross correction technique and always yields a sea-level dive that is deeper than the actual dive at altitude. A deeper sea-level equivalent dive provides the extra decompression needed to offset effects of diving at altitude.

10-82. No correction is required for dives conducted at altitudes between sea level and 300 feet. The additional risk associated with these dives is minimal. At altitudes between 300 and 1,000 feet, correction is required for dives deeper than 145 fsw (actual depth). At altitudes above 1,000 feet, correction is required for all dives.

10-83. To simplify calculations, the USN Diving Manual, Table 8-3, gives corrected sea-level equivalent depths and equivalent stop depths for dives from 10 to 190 feet and for altitudes from 1,000 to 10,000 feet in 1,000-foot increments..

10-84. Upon ascent to altitude, two things happen. The body off-gasses excess nitrogen to come into equilibrium with the lower partial pressure of nitrogen in the atmosphere. It also begins a series of complicated adjustments to the lower partial pressure of oxygen. The first is called equilibration; the second is called acclimatization. Twelve hours at altitude is required for equilibration. A longer period is required for full acclimatization.

10-85. If a diver begins a dive at altitude within 12 hours of arrival, the residual nitrogen left over from sea level must be taken into account. In effect, the initial dive at altitude can be considered a repetitive dive, with the first dive being the ascent from sea level to altitude. The USN Diving Manual, Table 8-4, gives the repetitive group associated with an initial ascent to altitude. Using this group and the time at altitude before diving, the diver must check the Residual Nitrogen Timetable (USN Diving Manual, Table 8-7) to determine a new repetitive group designator associated with that period of equilibration. He determines sea-level equivalent depth for his planned dive using the USN Diving Manual, Table 8-3. From his new repetitive group and sea-level equivalent depth, the diver determines the residual nitrogen time associated with the dive. He then adds this time to the actual bottom time of the dive.

WARNING

Altitudes above 10,000 feet can impose serious stress on the body resulting in significant medical problems while the acclimatization process takes place. Ascents to these altitudes must be slow to allow acclimatization to occur and prophylactic drugs may be required. These exposures should always be planned in consultation with a DMO. Commands conducting diving operations above 10,000 feet may obtain the appropriate decompression procedures from NAVSEA Command.

10-86. The exact procedures for altitude diving, to include work sheets and tables, are in the USN Diving Manual. SFODs should not conduct altitude dives without referencing it.

COLD WEATHER DIVING

10-87. SF divers rarely have the luxury of diving in tropical environments, and mission requirements usually don't allow the detachment to wait until the water is warmer. The SF diver that finds himself forced to dive in cold water must be aware of the potential risks and knowledgeable in the techniques and equipment available to mitigate those risks and accomplish the assigned mission.

10-88. Water conducts heat 25 times faster than air. Because of its greater conductivity, water does not have to be extremely cold for it to adversely affect the diver's ability to conduct his mission. Even relatively warm (70 degrees F) water will eventually cause the unprotected diver to suffer hypothermia (Figure 10-5). The major effect of cold water diving is body heat loss or hypothermia. Other and sometimes related effects include cramps, increased fatigue, loss of strength, increased air consumption, and frequent urination. More serious effects are the loss of ability to recall information and to concentrate, increased stress, increased susceptibility to bends, occasional loss of muscle control, and symptoms similar to those of nitrogen narcosis.

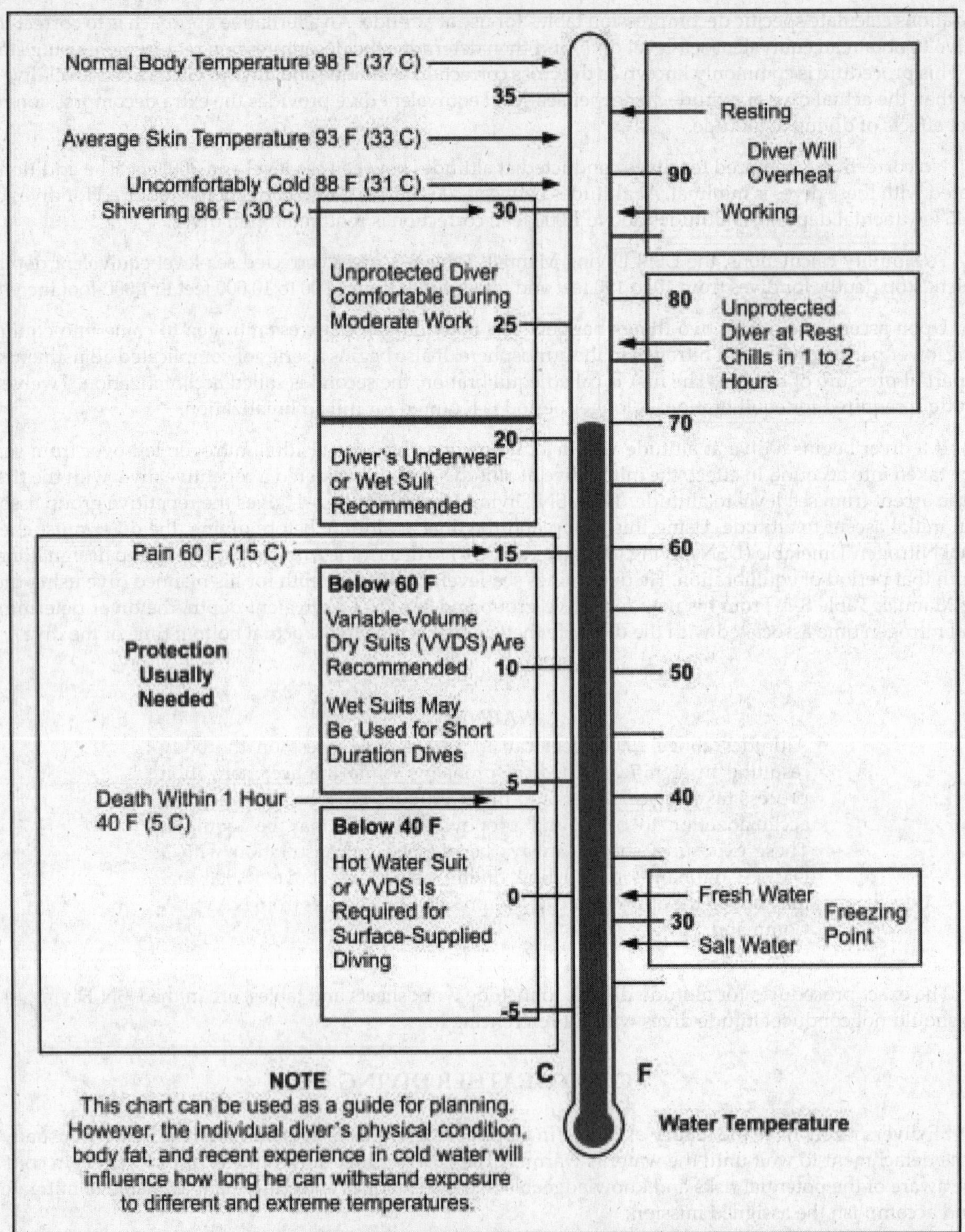

Figure 10-5. Water temperature protection chart

SHORT-DURATION DIVING IN EXTREMELY COLD WATER

10-89. This section provides general guidelines to assist dive personnel in planning and conducting short-duration diving operations in cold water situations where the surface water temperature is 37 degrees F and below. Typical missions may include search or reconnaissance dives; inspecting ice conditions for cracks, pressure ridges, or thin spots before crossing by vehicles; and supporting amphibious operations.

10-90. Ice diving normally is not required of SF divers. SFODs that may find it necessary to conduct ice dives should refer to the specialized procedures outlined in the USN Diving Manual. They must conduct internal (detachment) training to ensure that all personnel are adequately prepared to perform both the diving and the support tasks required to conduct a safe operation. The dive supervisor should keep the following general rules in mind when planning extreme cold weather diving operations:

- Divers should have protected areas for dressing and undressing. After suiting up, a diver should not delay his water entry. Time on surface must be kept to a minimum.
- A chilled diver should never go into the water. He must be completely rewarmed before reentering the water. A diver should not remain in the water after he begins to shiver.
- A diver should make sure that equipment does not restrict circulation.
- Mittens should be large enough for protection, but not so large as to decrease dexterity. Upon surfacing, a diver should not remove his mittens until he is able to dry his hands and put on warm gloves.

10-91. The primary concern is to dive warm. A diver should start warm and stay warm. Cold divers start with a heat deficit that cannot be recovered from. This deficit only gets worse as diving operations continue. Factors that should be considered are the general state of the divers' health, physical and psychological conditioning, and the degree of training for the specific environment. Divers should be well rested and fed; they should generally consume a high protein meal 2 hours before the dive. The protein will supply energy gradually over a long period of time. Consuming simple sugars shortly before diving and between dives to provide quick energy also helps. Energy can be conserved and thus warmth retained by keeping warm before diving. Wearing a jacket and staying out of the wind en route to the dive site are simple but often overlooked precautions. Physical protection from the cold is achieved through the use of a wet or dry suit during the dive.

GENERAL EQUIPMENT CONSIDERATIONS

10-92. When selecting equipment for a cold weather diving operation, divers should use only equipment with proven cold weather reliability. They also should consider the specific climatic conditions of the dive site, the probable lack of facilities to support the operation, the lack of communications, and the distance over which support must be provided.

10-93. The selection of the regulator must be made very carefully for cold weather diving operations. The ANU list specifies which regulators have been found suitable for use in water temperatures less than 37 degrees F. This cutoff is used because at that temperature the expansion of compressed air inside the regulator can result in sufficient cooling to cause icing in the first stage and a potential free-flow.

10-94. Physical protection from the cold is provided by wet or dry suits. They protect the diver by providing an insulating layer between the diver and the surrounding water. Figure 10-6, depicts the differences in wet and dry suit functions.

WET SUIT CHARACTERISTICS

10-95. A wet suit works by restricting the flow of water into the suit and preventing the exchange of water inside the suit (warm) with water outside the suit (cold). Any water that infiltrates the suit should remain trapped in a thin layer next to the diver's body where it is warmed by body heat. Good seals at the wrists, neck, and ankles and a sealing surface behind the zipper and on any of the suit's mating surfaces help to prevent or restrict this exchange of water. These features coupled with quality neoprene formulations make for wet suits that are better insulators, have better recovery from compression, are more flexible and durable, and conform to the diver's body (fit) more readily.

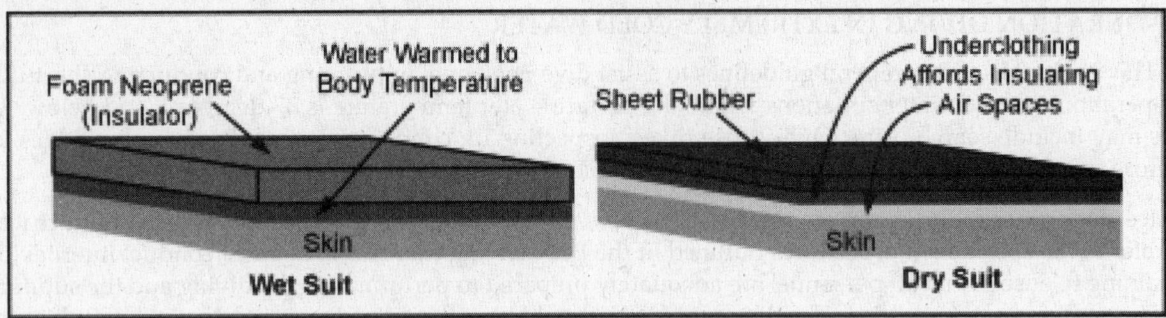

Figure 10-6. Wet and dry suits

10-96. How a wetsuit fits the diver is its most important characteristic. A thin suit that has been properly fitted will provide far more protection for the diver than a thicker suit that does not fit properly. An excessively tight suit restricts circulation, especially in the extremities and contributes to the loss of body heat. However, there should not be any areas where the suit does not contact the diver's body. A properly fitted suit is one that envelops the diver snuggly without restricting movement or circulation. Any place where a gap exists between the diver and his wet suit is a potential point of water circulation or exchange. Each inhalation and exhalation, kick, or arm movement serves to pump warm water out of the wet suit and siphon cold water into it. The diver will rapidly become chilled or hypothermic as his body struggles to warm the cold water that is continuously flooding his suit.

10-97. The wet suit has been satisfactorily used in extremely cold water. However, it compresses at depth and greatly reduces its insulating capability. In the thicker suits, a diver's movement is restricted and the additional buoyancy becomes problematic. Other problems include the diver chilling after leaving the water and difficulty in drying the suit. In addition to the advantages of availability and simplicity, wet suits are unlikely to have material failure, allowing sudden flooding as may happen with all dry suits. Generally, for short- duration dives of limited depth, the wet suit is satisfactory, even in water temperatures below 32 degrees F. A wet suit consisting of the following items has been satisfactorily used in water at a temperature of 30 to 32 degrees F:

- Pants—5-mm neoprene.
- Jacket—5-mm neoprene.
- Hood—5-mm neoprene.
- Vest or hood combination—3-mm neoprene.
- Gauntlet type mitten—5-mm neoprene.
- Inner sock—3-mm neoprene.
- Booties—5-mm neoprene

THE DIVER AND WET SUIT USE

10-98. To be effective, each diver should have an assigned wet suit that has been individually measured and fitted. His most effective dress consists of the various pieces identified in the previous paragraph. They allow the diver the flexibility to choose the appropriate level of protection based on the water temperature, the expected level of exertion, and personal comfort. Semicustom wet suits are the preferred solution because generic sizing does not provide an adequate range of sizes to fit and protect all divers in extremely cold water. To meet this requirement, commands may purchase off-the-shelf suits from reputable manufacturers or commercial sources IAW the guidance promulgated in the ANU list. After the suit has been sized and issued to the diver, he is responsible for its use and maintenance. Because of issues like individual sizing and personal hygiene, suits should not be swapped off between divers.

10-99. When divers are using wet suits, they should consider the following points:

- It is especially important to insulate the head when diving in cold water. The unprotected head can account for more than 50 percent of the body's entire heat loss. The use of cold water hoods with chin cups, neoprene booties, and mittens or gloves will also help prevent heat loss at the extremities. A diver should not cut ear holes in the hood, for that will cause an unnecessary loss of body heat. He should also glue shut all small holes in the suit.

- A one-piece suit helps conserve heat. An attached hood adds more protection. Both features serve to restrict water exchange in the suit. Pullover jackets without zippers are much warmer than jackets with front and cuff zippers, but they are less convenient. Hooded vests worn under conventional zipped jackets are a good compromise between convenience and warmth.
- Custom or semicustom suit modifications can add significantly to warmth. A diver can increase his warmth by adding a spine pad down the back to reduce water seepage and putting a backing flap behind zippers. Wrist and ankle cuffs of smooth neoprene that seal against the skin significantly reduce water circulation to help keep the body warm. Eliminating the nylon lining at the cuffs prevents wicking cold water into the suit.
- A diver should not exercise in an attempt to get warm. He will stimulate circulation to the extremities where heat loss is greatest. He should keep the breathing rate down if possible. Heating cold air inhaled from the tank requires a great deal of energy. If a diver begins to shiver uncontrollably, it is time to terminate the dive.
- A diver should preheat the suit by filling it with warm (not hot) water immediately before diving in cold water. He should avoid a high entry into cold water, particularly on repetitive dives. If he eases into the water, any warm water in the suit can be retained. Boots should be worn inside the pant legs. If worn outside, each kick will pump warm water out of the boot and suck cold water in.
- The SFOD should provide a sheltered area protected from the wind (heated if possible) for divers to reduce evaporative cooling from wet wet suits.

DRY SUIT CHARACTERISTICS

10-100. Dry suits are the other option for protecting divers in extremely cold water. They provide superior thermal protection both in and out of the water. Modern dry suits are generally one piece with attached boots and a hood. Entry into the suits is usually through a zippered opening. They function by encapsulating the diver in a dry microenvironment that is maintained by watertight seals at the wrist, neck, and zipper.

10-101. Dry suits can be worn with a variety of clothing underneath. Depending on water temperature and expected exertion levels, the diver can wear various types and amounts of long thermal underwear to keep warm. Underwear specifically designed for use with the suit is best. The type used will vary with the mission and individual preference. Too much underwear will be bulky and can cause the diver to overheat before entering the water, thus perspiring and later chilling. For scout swimming purposes, dry suits proved satisfactory when used with a standard military uniform underneath. Used this way, they can greatly reduce the time required on the beach after infiltration and before entering the land phase of the operation.

10-102. Dry suits are available in various weights and constructions. While all suits work on the same basic principle, they differ greatly in design and quality. Dry suits appropriate for diving are usually of the variable volume type. Nondiving applications can use the somewhat simpler nonvariable volume suits.

10-103. The three suit materials or construction methods most commonly encountered are vulcanized rubber, trilaminate, and neoprene. The most durable are the vulcanized rubber suits. However, they are heavier and less flexible. Divers required to perform heavy work, diving in contaminated waters, or diving where there are significant risks of entanglement and snagging or tearing the dry suit should consider using the commercial weights of vulcanized rubber suit. They are extremely durable, easily repaired by trained personnel, resistant to many chemical or biological contaminants, and readily decontaminated.

10-104. Trilaminate suits are lighter weight and more flexible, but they are not as durable. They are constructed of multiple (usually three) layers of material that have been laminated (bonded) together; normally an outer wear layer, a middle waterproof membrane, and an inner wear layer. Their flexibility and relative comfort make them more acceptable when the diver is expected to be extremely active such as during an infiltration swim. Trilaminates also make ideal exposure suits for personnel conducting surface support operations or CRRC infiltrations. Unfortunately, most trilaminate suits are not as puncture resistant as the other types.

10-105. Neoprene suits are constructed of the same material as wet suits. Because the neoprene is itself an insulating material, neoprene suits do not necessarily require additional insulating undergarments. However, because it is constructed of neoprene, the suit is subject to the same compression at depth as wet suits. This factor will reduce its insulating properties somewhat. A neoprene suit that floods-out (looses its integrity and fills with water) will still provide some thermal protection. Newer models take advantage of neoprene's stretchiness with closer tailoring to make a suit that conforms more closely to the diver. Older models were often very bulky. Neoprene suits, because of their inherent buoyancy also require more weight to make the diver neutrally buoyant. Neoprene suits are not as readily decontaminated as the other types of dry suit nor are they as resistant to some pollutants.

VARIABLE-VOLUME DRY SUITS

10-106. VVDS have been adapted for diving by the addition of a low-pressure inflator and various exhaust valves. As the diver descends, the suit material is subjected to normal compression. In a variable-volume suit, introducing additional air into the suit through the low-pressure inflator equalizes pressure to counteract the effects of suit squeeze. A diver must take care to prevent the suit from becoming overly buoyant, especially on ascent.

NOTE

Divers must receive proper training in and be thoroughly familiar with the dry suit before they attempt to use it operationally. Any diver planning to use a VVDS in any water, especially while diving under ice, should be thoroughly familiar with the functioning of the suit and the manufacturer's operational literature. Divers should have experience with the suit before deployment to the dive site. In addition to gaining experience using the suit, the diver should get a thorough checkout on the proper method of donning and doffing, suit care, and maintenance. Three dives to increasing depths are normally sufficient for an experienced diver to become familiar with the suit.

10-107. The two greatest risks to the diver using a dry suit are floodout and blowup. Floodout is the sudden compromise of the suit's watertight integrity usually caused by a tear or the failure of one of the watertight seals. When the suit fills with (cold) water, it suddenly looses its buoyancy and quickly becomes very negative. The diver may also experience thermal shock caused by the sudden exposure to the very cold water. Blowup is the sudden loss of buoyancy control caused by the rapid expansion of air trapped inside the suit. It is most commonly caused by an inadvertent ascent without venting the suit, a stuck (often frozen) low-pressure inflator, or a closed or jammed exhaust valve. Proper training prepares the diver to deal effectively with these emergencies. Cause of death for untrained divers is usually drowning, air embolism, DCS, or a combination of these factors.

10-108. The VVDS should not be subjected to an ambient outside temperature below 32 degrees F before a dive. Such exposure can result in super cooling of the inlet and exhaust valves and can cause icing on immersion. If it is necessary to expose the suit to extreme temperatures before diving, the diver should lubricate the valves with silicone. He should attempt to re-warm the valves before entering the water.

10-109. Nonvariable-volume dry suits (usually trilaminate construction) are satisfactory for surface swimmers. They provide exceptional exposure protection for detachments conducting long-range surface transits in CRRCs. They also can be used for underwater swimming if precautions are taken to prevent suit squeeze.

10-110. Use of dry suits is limited by the following:

- Horizontal swims may be fatiguing due to suit bulk.
- If the diver is horizontal or head down, air can migrate into the foot area and become trapped there causing the diver to lose attitudinal control. Because there are no exhaust valves in the legs, the diver may find himself ascending feet first and out of control. The expanding air in the legs can cause overinflation, loss of buoyancy

control, and a rapid uncontrolled ascent. The expanding air trapped in the feet may also cause the diver's fins to pop off.

- Inlet and exhaust valves can malfunction on variable-volume suits.
- A collapsing or parting seam or zipper or a rip in the suit can result in sudden and drastic loss of buoyancy and in thermal shock.
- With variable-volume suits, extra weight is required to achieve neutral buoyancy. It is generally best to use oversized weights.

10-111. The SFOD should keep the following spare parts and repair items on hand for suit maintenance and repair:

- Sharp, heavy-duty scissors for cutting neoprene.
- Needle and thread for seam repairs (15-pound test nylon fishing line works well).
- Neoprene rubber cement.
- Extra neoprene material for cuff, face seal, and suit repair.
- Spare exhaust and inlet valves for variable-volume suits.
- Spare low-pressure inflator hoses for variable-volume suits.
- Large amount of assorted O-rings, silicone spray, and zipper wax.

SAFETY CONSIDERATIONS

10-112. Personnel taking part in cold or ice water diving operations should know the emergency procedures for the following situations:

- *Surface Personnel Falling Into the Water.* Prevention is the key. Buddy teams should work around the entry hole and keep unnecessary personnel away from the hole.
- *Stricken Diver.* The buddy diver should get the stricken diver to the surface as soon as possible.
- *Breathing System Failure.* Diver should switch to backup system, notify partner, and surface together.
- *Suit Failure.* Diver should surface immediately.
- *Uncontrolled Ascent.* Diver should exhale continuously during ascent, relax against the ice, and relieve pressure from the suit. If applicable, he should signal on the tether and proceed to the entry hole or wait for assistance from his buddy diver.
- *Lost Diver.* Diver should ascend to the surface immediately, relax as much as possible, and attempt to return to the entry hole or wait for assistance.

DIVE OPERATIONS PLANNING

10-113. For convenience, the planning of SF dive operations is normally divided into vertical and horizontal dives. Vertical dives are usually open-circuit such as working dives that range from annual requalification to reconnaissance or search and recovery dives. Horizontal dives are normally closed-circuit infiltration or exfiltration and training dives. Each type of dive has its own unique requirements. Pertinent information is included in the Dive Safety and Planning Checklist, USN Diving Manual.

10-114. Personnel should follow specific steps for conducting a vertical (deep) training dive. They should—

- Prepare the dive site.
- Update the situation.
- Conduct the dive supervisor personnel inspection.
- Supervise the entry of the dive team into the water.
- Get an OK from all divers. Get an OK from the group leader when his team is at the dive buoy and is prepared to descend.
- Begin the dive time as soon as the first diver's head leaves the surface of the water.
- Record all times and maintain elapsed times.
- Ensure normal descent procedures are followed. The entire group will maintain contact with the ascent or descent line and will descend no faster than 75 fpm.

- Ensure that the total time of the dive does not exceed the no-decompression limits.
- Record the total time of the dive. The dive is complete when the last diver's head breaks the surface of the water. Receive the total time of the dive and the maximum depth reached from the group leader.
- Supervise the water exit.
- Ensure that all personnel are accounted for before leaving the dive site.

10-115. Special equipment required for deep or vertical dives includes the following:

- An ascent and descent line.
- A safety line from the surface craft to the dive buoy.
- A safety line from the dive buoy to the safety boat.
- A safety line from the dive platform for divers.
- A securing line for the ladder.
- An inflatable safety buoy or pumpkin.
- Snap links.
- Lead weights or anchor system (weight clump sufficient to keep the bottom of the descent line at the desired depth).
- Small lift bag (50 to 100 pounds to facilitate the recovery of the weight clump).
- Backup regulators.
- A dive flag.
- A safety boat.
- Extra equipment.
- A diver recall system.

10-116. Personnel should follow specific steps for conducting horizontal dives. The steps are as follows:

- Before loading the boat with divers and equipment, the dive supervisor will inspect the boat. The USN Diving Manual contains a diving boat safety checklist.
- Divers will enter the boat when instructed to do so by the dive supervisor. They will maintain three points of contact when entering the boat without stepping on the gunwale. The buddy team will assist each other.
- Seating will be arranged with equal weight distribution in mind and with the buddy teams seated facing each other. Divers will don their fins.
- All boats will be under the control of the dive supervisor from the loading point to the dive site. While en route, the dive supervisor will initiate purge procedures when using a closed-circuit UBA. Upon reaching the dive site, the divers will signal the dive supervisor that they are ready to enter the water.
- The dive supervisor will command, "PREPARE TO MOUNT THE GUNWALE," at which time each diver will don his mask and place his regulator in his mouth. (Closed-circuit divers will stay alert for the next command.)
- On the command, "MOUNT THE GUNWALE," the divers will carefully sit on the gunwale and direct their attention to the dive supervisor.
- The dive supervisor will direct the boat driver to "BACK IT DOWN" (the driver will place the boat in slow reverse). Then, from bow to stern, the CDS will dispatch the divers into the water with the commands "PREPARE TO ENTER THE WATER" (buoy man tosses the buoy rearward, and each diver looks right or left over his shoulders to ensure his water entry point is clear) and "ENTER THE WATER" (each diver executes a proper backroll into the water).
- After entering the water and executing a proper ascent, each diver will exchange the OK signal with the dive supervisor. Divers will exchange the descend signal with the dive supervisor who will record the time the divers go subsurface. He will monitor the dive until all divers are safely ashore.
- The dive supervisor will ensure that he has proper accountability of all personnel and equipment. He will then supervise postdive operations, which include debriefing, maintenance of equipment, and record posting.

10-117. Special equipment for horizontal dives might include the following:

- Buoys.
- Buddy lines.
- Team swim lines.
- Snap links.
- Chemlites.
- A diver recall system.
- Extra equipment.
- Spotlights.
- Communications.
- A vehicle at the beach landing site.

10-118. The preceding guidelines are not intended to be all-inclusive. They should be seen as tools to aid the CDS in planning and executing his assigned duties. Obviously, requirements will change based on the mission and the situation. The prudent dive supervisor will conduct a thorough risk analysis and incorporate all of the pertinent information when he prepares and presents his dive plan and brief.

CHAPTER 11

Closed-Circuit Diving

The U.S. Army, as well as the USN, has adopted the MK 25 UBA for use by SOF. The MK 25 UBA is light, easy to operate, and eminently suited for the conduct of maritime special operations. The information presented in this chapter is for the most part an extract of the USN Diving Manual and NAVSEA SS-600-A3-MMA-010/53833, Technical Manual for the MK 25 MOD 2 UBA. *NAVSEA 3151 Ser 00C34/3160, 27 September 2001 (Confidential) supersedes NAVSEA 10560 Ser 00C35/3215, 22 April 1996. The procedures outlined must be followed, as they constitute the official doctrine concerning use of the MK 25 UBA.*

SAFETY CONSIDERATIONS

11-1. Divers must make sure they adhere to and follow the data provided below. Diving safety and successful operations of the MK 25 UBA depend upon the following:

- Competence and performance of operation.
- Operations planning.
- Adherence to approved operating, emergency, and maintenance procedures.

11-2. The safety guidelines stated in Figure 11-1 apply to operation and maintenance procedures. Personnel must thoroughly understand and comply with them to ensure the MK 25 UBA operates safely and efficiently.

DESCRIPTION

11-3. The general description of the system provides an overview of the UBA and its principal components. The gas flow pattern, adding oxygen to the breathing bag, and operational duration of the MK 25 UBA are also addressed.

11-4. In addition to standard predive guidelines, planners must consider mission requirements for using the MK 25 UBA. SF, USMC reconnaissance units, and U.S. Navy SEALS use the MK 25 UBA in shallow water operations. They must also use it in conjunction with an approved life preserver. Personnel should only use MK 25 UBA-approved life preservers, as cited in NAVSEA 10560 Ser 00C/3112, *Diving Equipment Authorized for U.S. Navy Use,* 15 May 1997.

General Warnings

- Monitor the gas supply for the MK 25 UBA because it has no positive reserve. Use the pressure gauge that is provided for this check.
- Monitor the MK 25 UBA breathing bag because it does not have a dump valve and overinflation may occur. Recharge the breathing bag at minimum possible depth. Do not overcharge.
- Stay aware that the MK 25 UBA pressure reducer has an operating range of 10 to 207 bar (145 to 3,000 psig).
- Do not charge oxygen cylinder above 207 bar (3,000 psig).
- Do not exceed fill rate of 14 bar (200 psig) per minute.

Figure 11-1. Safety guidelines

Canister and Scrubber Warnings

- Use only NAVSEA-authorized carbon dioxide absorbents with the MK 25 UBA. Use of other hydroxide chemicals is not currently authorized.
- Thoroughly settle bed of carbon dioxide-absorbent granules. If improperly filled, channels that permit gas to bypass the absorbent may form, causing elevated levels of carbon dioxide in the breathing loop. Do not overfill canister past fill mark.
- Fill the canister outdoors (or in a well-ventilated space) over a container suitable for disposal of the absorbent.
- Do not mix different brands of absorbent in the same canister. Granules could pulverize, leading to channeling of the absorbent.
- Avoid contact with carbon dioxide absorbent dust; it will irritate the eyes, throat, and skin. Take appropriate precautions to avoid breathing absorbent dust or getting it into your eyes or on your skin. Do not stand downwind of canister while filling or emptying.
- Do not use the last 1 inch of carbon dioxide absorbent in the container because absorbent dust accumulates in the bottom of the container.
- Do not overfill the canister. Overfilling can lead to canister flooding.
- Comply with hazardous material regulations for the appropriate state.
- Refer to NAVSEA 3151 Ser 00C34/3160 (Confidential) for MK 25 UBA 0/1/2 canister duration limits.

Oxygen Handling Warnings

- Ensure the cylinder valve on the oxygen cylinder is shut. Before working on pneumatic components, vent pressure from the pneumatic subsystem.
- Never mix different brands of MIL-G-27617, Type III greases. Ensure all old grease is removed before applying new grease.
- Do not allow oil, grease, or any other foreign material to come in contact with high-pressure oxygen. Such material exposed to oxygen under high pressure may explode or ignite.
- Keep sparks and flames away from oxygen systems. Secure electrical equipment in the immediate area during maintenance of oxygen systems.
- Purge cylinders by pressuring with oxygen to 60 to 120 psig because empty cylinders may contain residual nitrogen. Relieve pressure, purge again, then charge the cylinder.
- Check the one-way valves in both hoses before each operation.
- Install cylinder valve cap and reducer plug to prevent dirt or water from entering the reducer. This practice will prevent the potential for an oxygen fire and possibly degrading performance of the oxygen reducer.

Figure 11-1. Safety guidelines (*Continued*)

Maintenance Warnings
• Do not install expired components. • Ensure poloxamer-iodine cleansing solutions are carefully diluted. Use of solutions with greater concentrations of iodine will cause degradation of the rubber components of this equipment. Failure to thoroughly rinse all poloxamer-iodine solution from the equipment may result in lung irritation or long-term degradation of the equipment's rubber components. • Wear goggles to prevent chemicals from splashing in eyes. If sanitizing agent splashes in eyes, rinse with large amounts of water and consult medical personnel. • Open cylinder valve slowly to avoid heat generation that may burn the lower spindle seat. • Always assume pneumatic subsystem is pressurized. Before assembly or disassembly, vent pneumatic subsystem by depressing manual bypass button on the front of the unit.
General Cautions
• Ensure only qualified MK 25 UBA technicians perform maintenance. However, qualified divers may perform premission, predive, and postdive actions under the guidance of a technician. • Do not interchange the rotary valve (barrel) and housing. If either part needs repair, replace the entire mouthpiece valve. • When inspecting breathing bag connecting pieces for secure attachment, do not lift or pull bag material from glued seams or use fingernails to pry connecting pieces from the breathing bag. • To avoid damaging canister lid seal, do not overtighten canister lid to canister housing. • Do not soak the urethane canister housing, lid, or associated soft goods in a vinegar-water solution. • Attach breathing bag to demand valve with care; connecting piece cap nut can be easily cross-threaded. • Do not overcharge the breathing bag. Damage to the system may occur. The breathing bag should be firm, but not stretched. • While rinsing the canister components, keep them separate from the other UBA components. When mixed with water, the absorbent produces a caustic base mixture that can damage rubber and plastic components. • Before proceeding, read and understand the purpose and precautions of the purge procedures. • Make sure all MK 25 UBA components are completely dry before reassembly and storage to prevent mildew formation, bacteria growth, and material rot. • Ensure proper handling of valve body to avoid leakage. Handle carefully to avoid scratching body. • Use extreme care not to damage thread on gauge line or connecting line while removing reducer. • Do not allow pressure to exceed 200 psig while testing relief valve. • Do not use sharp tools on the boot.

Figure 11-1. Safety guidelines (*Continued*)

DANGER

Omission of any operating procedures may result in equipment failure and possible injury or death to operating personnel.

11-5. The MK 25 UBA is worn in the front of the swimmer and is attached with two harness straps (neck and waist). The mouthpiece is held in place with a head strap. All system components are attached to or contained in an equipment housing. The oxygen cylinder is secured in place at the bottom of the equipment housing with two straps and is connected through a cylinder valve to a reducer, which reduces cylinder gas pressure. Gas flows from the reducer to the demand valve assembly. This valve controls oxygen flow into a single breathing bag. The swimmer receives breathing on demand from the breathing bag through the inhalation hose and the mouthpiece. The mouthpiece contains a rotary valve that, in the dive (up) position, supplies the breathing gas and, in the SURFACE (down) position, isolates the gas flow loop from the ambient atmosphere or water conditions. The exhalation hose also connects to the mouthpiece and takes exhaled gas to the soda lime canister (carbon dioxide scrubber). Both the inhalation and exhalation hoses are fitted with one-way valves (discs) to ensure the correct flow path of the gas. The canister contains a soda lime material (hydroxide chemical) that absorbs carbon dioxide. Gas flows from the canister to the breathing bag, completing the loop.

11-6. Additional oxygen is metered into the breathing bag from the oxygen cylinder by the demand valve assembly as required. A pressure gauge mounted on the top of the equipment housing indicates the amount of oxygen remaining. On the front of the equipment housing is a bypass button which permits the operator to bypass the (automatic) demand valve and manually add oxygen to the breathing bag. The MK 25 UBA is equipped with a removable canister insulator package. When installed, the insulator package helps retain heat inside the canister, extending the duration of the carbon dioxide absorbent in cold water (below 60 degrees F). Using the insulator in warm water (60 degrees F and above) may decrease canister absorbent duration. When the canister insulator is used, the diver must fit weight pouches around the demand valve to counter the buoyancy effects of the insulator. The weight pouches fit into pockets installed at the demand valve and weigh a total of 3.18 pounds.

FUNCTION

11-7. Table 11-1 and Figure 11-2 depict the functional description of the MK 25 UBA. From the oxygen cylinder (15), high-pressure oxygen passes through the cylinder valve (14) to the reducer (11), where the high-pressure gas is reduced to an average intermediate working pressure of 3.3 to 3.7 bar (47.8 to 53.6 psig) over ambient pressure. The gas is then piped through the low (intermediate) pressure line (12) to the demand valve assembly (10), which is adjustable for an actuation pressure of 8.5 ± 1.5 inches of water (0.31 ± 0.05 psig). High-pressure gas is also piped through the high pressure line (13) to the 0 to 350 bar (0 to 5,075 psig) pressure gauge (9) located on top of the equipment housing (16). The demand valve assembly (10), secured to the equipment housing (16) and fitted to the breathing bag (7), functions each time the bag is emptied on inhalation and a negative pressure occurs. On inhalation, the one-way valve (disc) (5), located in the inhalation hose (6), opens and the diver receives gas from the breathing bag (7). If not enough gas is available, the demand valve actuates due to negative pressure, adding more oxygen to the system. As the diver exhales, the exhalation one-way valve (disc) (2) opens, the inhalation one-way valve (disc) (5) closes, and the exhaled gas flows through the exhalation hose (1) to the soda lime canister (carbon dioxide scrubber) (8). The gas then filters through the soda lime canister with the next inhalation. During descent or to purge the unit, the diver depresses the demand bypass button located in the front center of the equipment housing (10) to manually add oxygen to the system.

COMPONENTS

11-8. The MK 25 UBA has three major subsystems—the recirculation subsystem, the pneumatic subsystem, and the equipment housing and UBA harness. Each is described in the following paragraphs.

Table 11-1. MK 25 UBA Components list

	Recirculation Subsystem
1	Exhalation Hose
2	One-Way Exhaust Valve (Disc Valve)
3	Mouthpiece Valve Assembly (with Rotary Valve)
4	Head Strap
5	One-Way Inhalation Valve (Disc Valve)
6	Inhalation Hose
7	**Breathing Bag Assembly**
7A	Connecting Piece, Inhalation
7B	Connecting Piece, Demand Valve
7C	Connecting Piece, Canister
8	**Soda Lime Canister**
8A	Canister Intake Port
8B	Canister Outlet Port
8C	Canister Lid
	Pneumatic Subsystem
9	Pressure Gauge
10	Demand Valve/Bypass Knob (reverse, not shown)
11	**Reducer**
11A	Reducer Handwheel/Hand Grip (rubber ring)
11B	Safety Valve Assembly
12	Connecting Line (Low-Pressure)
13	Pressure Gauge Line (High-Pressure)
14	**Oxygen Cylinder Valve**
14A	Oxygen Cylinder Valve Safety Burst Disc Oxygen Cylinder
15	Oxygen Cylinder
	Equipment Housing and UBA Harness
16	**Equipment Housing**
16A	Exhalation Hose Slotted Indent
16B	Inhalation Hose Slotted Indent
17	Cylinder/Canister Harness
18	Positioning Strap
19	Waist Harness
20	Neck Harness
21	Triglide
22	Lead Shot Pouch Kit
23	Canister Insulator

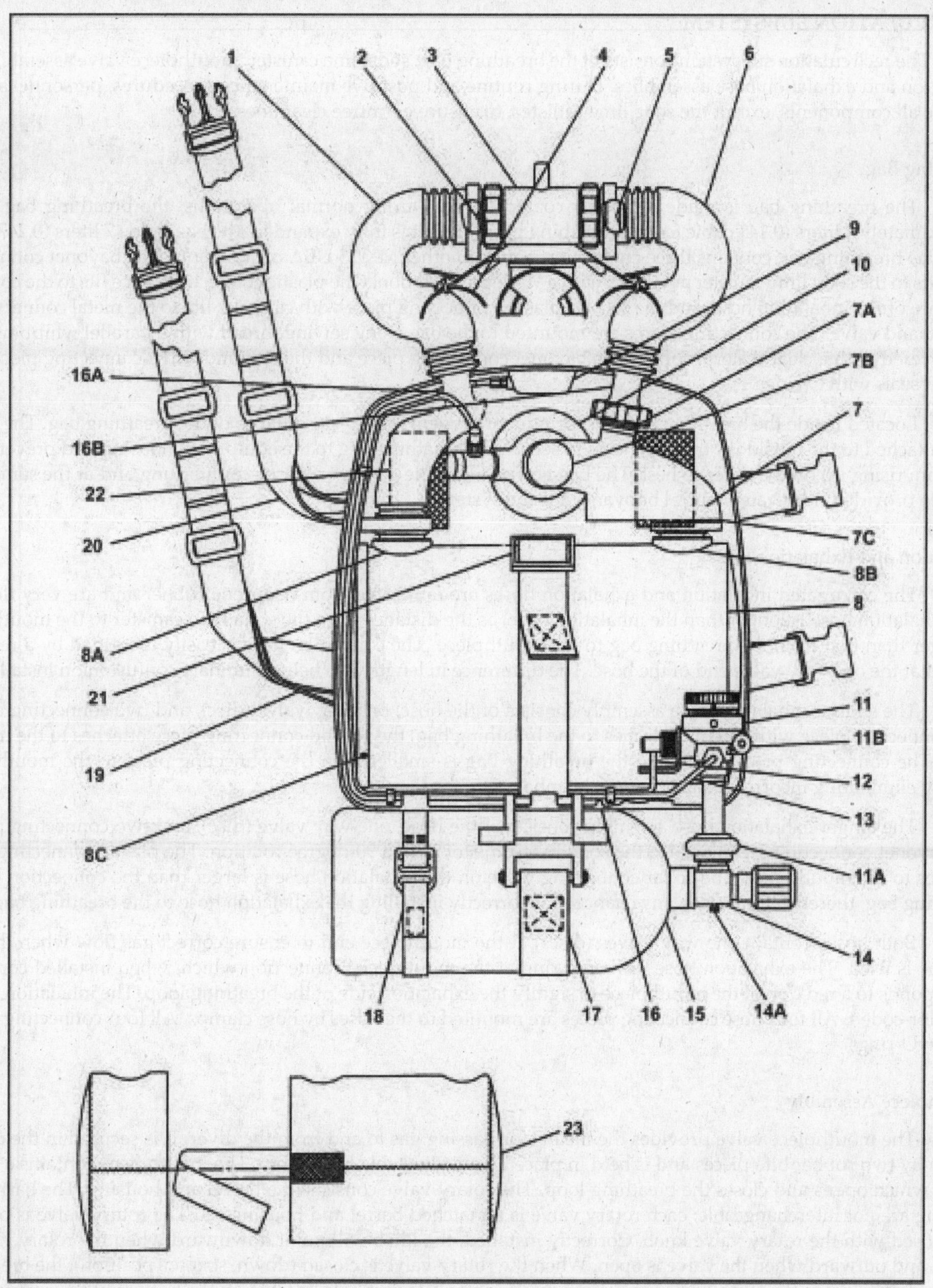

Figure 11-2. MK 25 UBA Component locations (As Worn)

RECIRCULATION SUBSYSTEM

11-9. The recirculation subsystem consists of the breathing bag, soda lime canister, mouthpiece valve assembly, and inhalation and exhalation hose assemblies. During routine and postdive maintenance procedures, personnel should sanitize all components, except the soda lime canister, to ensure germfree cleanliness.

Breathing Bag

11-10. The breathing bag is made of rubber-coated fabric. During normal operations, the breathing bag holds approximately 4 liters (0.141 cubic feet) of breathing gas. When it is fully expanded, the bag holds 7 liters (0.247 cubic feet). The breathing bag contains three connection points to other MK 25 UBA components. The bayonet connecting piece fits to the soda lime canister and locks with a 90-degree rotation. One plastic connecting piece fits to the connecting piece of the inhalation hose, and the second plastic connecting piece with cap nuts fits to the metal connection of the demand valve. The connecting pieces are mounted to the bag using sewing thread with a parallel whipping knot and covered with a clear waterproofing. The bayonet connecting piece and the demand valve-connecting piece with cap nut seals with O-rings.

11-11. Located inside the breathing bag is a spring that prevents complete collapse of the breathing bag. The safety cord, attached to the outside of the bag, helps to secure the breathing bag to the equipment housing and prevents the bag from rising up on the diver's chest. The bag acts as a flexible gas reservoir or counterlung and at the same time helps to provide underwater neutral buoyancy for the system.

Inhalation and Exhalation Hoses

11-12. The corrugated inhalation and exhalation hoses are fabricated from neoprene rubber and are very flexible. The exhalation hose is longer than the inhalation hose, as the distance from the soda lime canister to the mouthpiece is longer than that from the breathing bag to the mouthpiece. The exhalation hose is easily identified by a red ring located at the one-way valve end of the hose. The difference in length also helps eliminate confusion on installation.

11-13. The shorter inhalation hose assembly consists of the hose, one-way valve (disc), and two connecting pieces. The connecting piece with cap nut attaches to the breathing bag; the second connecting piece attaches to the mouthpiece. The connecting piece that fits to the breathing bag is smaller than the connecting piece to the mouthpiece, thereby eliminating incorrect installation of the inhalation hose.

11-14. The longer exhalation hose assembly consists of the hose, one-way valve (disc), and two connecting pieces. The bayonet connecting piece locks to the soda lime canister with a 90-degree rotation. The plastic connecting piece attaches to the mouthpiece. The collar connecting piece on the exhalation hose is larger than the connection on the breathing bag, thereby eliminating any chance of incorrectly installing the exhalation hose to the breathing bag.

11-15. Both hoses contain one-way valves (discs) at the mouthpiece end to ensure correct gas flow when the MK 25 UBA is used. The exhalation hose has a red ring at the mouthpiece connection which, when installed correctly, corresponds to a red dot on the mouthpiece to signify the exhalation side of the breathing loop. The inhalation side is not color-coded. All four hose connecting pieces are mounted to the hoses by hose clamps. All four connecting pieces contain O-rings.

Mouthpiece Assembly

11-16. The mouthpiece valve provides the means for passing gas to and from the diver. It is secured in the diver's mouth by two rubber bite pieces and is held in place by an adjustable head strap. The mouthpiece contains a rotary valve, which opens and closes the breathing loop. The rotary valve consists of a barrel and housing. The barrel and housing are not interchangeable; each rotary valve is a matched barrel and housing set. The rotary valve is opened and closed with the rotary-valve knob. Correctly installed, the knob will point downward when the rotary valve is closed and outward when the valve is open. When the rotary valve is closed (down, SURFACE position), the breathing loop is isolated from the surrounding environment. A water blowout hole, located on the bottom of the rotary-valve housing, permits the diver to clear the mouthpiece of water before opening the valve. When the rotary valve is open (up, dive position), the MK 25 UBA is ready for breathing. The mouthpiece bite pieces are mounted onto the rotary-valve housing using monofilament cord with a parallel whipping knot. The rotary-valve knob contains one O-ring.

Soda Lime Canister (Carbon Dioxide Scrubber)

11-17. The soda lime canister removes both moisture and carbon dioxide from the gas in the breathing loop. The canister is molded from urethane or fiberglass and contains two separate chambers. (The fiberglass canister is still in use and requires a different type of absorbent as described in NAVSEA 3151 Ser 00C34/3160.) Gas flows from the exhalation hose into the first chamber, which contains carbon dioxide absorbent, and then into a smaller second chamber, which acts as a moisture trap. The absorbent chamber holds approximately 5.75 pounds of absorbent. The moisture trap can hold up to 200 cubic centimeters (cc) of liquid before any liquid will enter the absorbent material. After the carbon dioxide and moisture are removed, the gas flows into the breathing bag. The soda lime canister has two ports, both of which are bayonet couplings and contain spiral waves to ensure a snug fit. The port closest to the canister lid connects to the exhalation hose fitting; the second port connects to the breathing bag. The port for the breathing bag connecting piece is slightly larger than the port for the hose-connecting piece, which eliminates the possibility of incorrect installation. When the bayonet connecting pieces are locked to the canister, a snug fit results with no play in the connections.

11-18. The components of the canister can be completely disassembled. Should carbon dioxide absorbent residue clog the screens and canister rod threads, these components may be soaked in a solution of vinegar-water, scrubbed lightly with a nylon bristle brush to remove grit, and then rinsed with fresh water.

11-19. The canister lid seal should be inspected often for wear and tear. It is not lubricated. The soda lime canister contains two O-rings, one on the lid pin and the other on the nut at the opposite end of the canister rod.

PNEUMATIC SUBSYSTEM

11-20. The pneumatic subsystem of the MK 25 UBA consists of the oxygen cylinder and cylinder valve, reducer, demand valve, pressure gauge, and pressure lines. Each component of the pneumatic subsystem, except the pressure gauge, when disassembled for any reason, must be cleaned using NAVSEA-approved oxygen-safe cleaning procedures before reassembly. With the exception of the cylinder valve to reducer connection, any entry into the pneumatic subsystem requires that reentry control (REC) procedures be followed to maintain system certification.

Oxygen Cylinder

11-21. The MK 25 UBA oxygen cylinder is made of aluminum alloy 6061-T6. The cylinder has a basic internal volume of 1.9 liters (0.067 cubic feet) and may be charged to 207 bar (3,000 psig). When fully charged, the cylinder holds 410 liters (14.49 cubic feet) of oxygen at standard conditions. The cylinder has an average weight of 6.6 pounds (without the cylinder valve). The oxygen cylinder mouth has internal, straight threads to accept the oxygen cylinder valve. The cylinder is held in place on the equipment housing with two straps, a self-tensioning cylinder or canister strap (harness), and a polypropylene Velcro positioning strap. The oxygen bottle connects to the oxygen reducer with hard piping and is equipped with a supply (on/off) valve. The MK 25 UBA 3AL aluminum oxygen cylinder is DOT approved. Regulatory guidance mandates that the cylinder undergo visual inspection annually and hydrostatic testing every 5 years.

Cylinder Valve

11-22. The cylinder valve is connected to the oxygen cylinder with a straight thread connection and is sealed with an O-ring. The outlet connection of the valve is a CGTA 540 connection that assembles directly to the reducer. The cylinder valve has a rated service pressure of 207 bar (3,000 psig), and is equipped with a burst disc that eliminates hazardous overpressurization of the cylinder. The burst disc ruptures when the cylinder pressure exceeds 5,000 (nominal) psig.

11-23. The cylinder valve has two O-rings. The O-ring between the valve and the oxygen cylinder is always replaced during the annual inspection of the cylinder or as required. The internal O-ring is replaced during the 5-year overhaul of the cylinder valve.

Reducer

11-24. This reducer regulates the cylinder gas pressure to 3.3 to 3.7 bar (47.8 to 53.6 psig) over ambient pressure. The reducer is designed to operate with an oxygen supply pressure of 10 to 207 bar (145 to 3,000 psig). The reducer contains two outlet ports. The high-pressure outlet port is connected by hard piping to the pressure gauge. The seal between the high-pressure outlet port and the piping is a ridged, metal sealing ring. The intermediate pressure outlet port is connected hard piping to the demand valve. The connection is sealed with an O-ring.

11-25. The reducer has two safety features. The velocity reducer, located in the high-pressure inlet of the reducer, slows the high flow rate of incoming oxygen. Excessive oxygen flow rate increases the potential for combustion of any foreign particles inside the reducer. The second safety feature is the safety valve assembly, connected to the reducer body. The safety valve precludes over pressurization of the reducer's inner chamber that may result from a high-pressure oxygen leak. Excessive intermediate pressure from the reducer will cause an increase in back pressure in the demand valve and increased breathing resistance. The safety valve is set to vent a 9 to 13 bar (130 to 190 psig). The safety valve reseats at 8 bar (116 psig).

11-26. The MK 25 UBA reducer is an unbalanced pressure regulator. It means the actual pressure provided to the demand valve is dependent on oxygen cylinder pressure. As the cylinder pressure decreases, the intermediate pressure supplied to the demand valve increases the breathing necessary to actuate the demand valve increases. For this reason, the reducer intermediate pressure must be set a 3.3 to 3.7 bar (47.8 to 53.6 psig) using a supply pressure of 100 ± 5 bar (1450 ± 72 psig). The intermediate pressure output of the reducer must be checked annually. The reducer must be overhauled every 6 years or when flooded, whichever comes first.

Demand Valve Assembly

11-27. The demand valve assembly meters the oxygen supply into the breathing bag. This demand valve is located below the breathing bag and is attached to the equipment housing. The demand valve receives low (intermediate) pressure oxygen from the reducer via hard piping. The connection is sealed with an O-ring. The breathing bag plastic connecting piece with cap nut attaches to the demand valve's metal housing.

11-28. Negative pressure inside the breathing bag actuates the demand valve rocker, which allows oxygen to flow into the breathing bag. As negative pressure inside the breathing bag decreases, the valve rocker reseats, shutting off the flow of oxygen. The demand valve actuation point is set to 8.5 ± 1.5 inches of water (0.31 ± 0.05 psig).

11-29. A manual bypass button is located on the front of the demand valve. This button is used by the diver to override the automatic metering of the demand valve to add oxygen to the breathing bag. The bypass button allows oxygen to enter the breathing bag at a rate of 60 liters per minute. Adjustments to the demand valve actuation point must be in the range of 8.5 ± 1.5 inches of water (0.31 ± 0.05 psig). However, low actuation points may result in free-flow of the demand valve due to depth or diving attitude changes. Adjustments must be made with the correct reducer intermediate pressure output using a 100 ± 5 bar (1450 ± 72 psig) oxygen supply. Increased intermediate supply pressure, either by incorrect intermediate pressure setting or depletion of oxygen in the cylinder, will increase the actuation point of the demand valve. The demand valve actuation point must be checked annually and must be checked using correct output pressure from the reducer. The demand valve must be overhauled every 2 years.

Pressure Gauge

11-30. The pressure gauge, the diver's only indicator on the MK 25 UBA, displays oxygen cylinder pressure. The gauge fits within a boot in the top of the equipment housing. When the MK 25 UBA is donned, the diver can see the gauge by glancing downward. The pressure gauge is connected to the reducer via hard piping. The connection at the gauge is sealed with a metal sealing ring. This flat sealing ring should not be confused with the ridged sealing ring connecting the piping to the reducer. The pressure gauge has a range of 0 to 350 bar (0 to 5,075 psig) and is graduated in bar; conversion to psig may be made by multiplying the gauge reading (in bar) by 14.5. The gauge must be tested for accuracy every 18 months.

Pressure Lines

11-31. Two pressure lines are used in the MK 25 UBA to carry oxygen. Both lines are made of chrome-plated copper tubing. The pressure-gauge line assembly provides oxygen cylinder pressure to the pressure gauge from the high-pressure port of the reducer. Connection seals on both ends are made by metal sealing rings. (The ridged sealing ring is used in the reducer port; the flat sealing ring is used in the gauge connection.) These sealing rings are replaced every time the connections are broken. The connecting line assembly carries low-pressure oxygen (3.3 to 3.7 bar/47.8

to 53.6 psig) to the demand valve from the low-pressure port of the reducer. Seals on both ends of this line are made with O-rings. These connections are hand-tightened.

EQUIPMENT HOUSING AND UBA HARNESSES

11-32. This subsystem consists of the equipment housing, associated hardware, and harness assemblies. These components need only be cleaned with soapy water when necessary.

Equipment Housing

11-33. The equipment housing is made up of a single unit from reinforced fiberglass and provides an attachment point for all components of the MK 25 UBA. Slots are provided for the exhalation and inhalation hoses, reducer, and harness and strap assemblies. Circular holes are provided in the housing for the demand valve and the pressure gauge. The housing is fitted to the diver by two harnesses. Two retaining straps are incorporated into the housing. The cylinder or canister strap (harness) that holds both the oxygen cylinder and canister in place is made of 1 1/2-inch, polypropylene or neoprene, self-tensioning material. It attaches to the housing via a plate retainer (located under the canister) and hooks to the bottom of the housing, after passing over the canister and encircling the oxygen cylinder, by means of a retaining hook. A triglide, located at the canister end of the strap, allows for adjustment. A positioning strap, made of 1-inch polypropylene webbing containing hook and pile (Velcro) tabs and a ladder buckle, passes through the bottom of the housing (passing under the pressure lines) and encircles the oxygen cylinder, acting as a second securing strap. The positioning strap may be tightened using the ladder buckle and Velcro tabs. The equipment housing also provides an attachment point for the reducer. The equipment housing holder secures the reducer in place; the holder is attached to the housing with two screws. Three sets of retaining clamps secure the pressure lines to the equipment housing.

Harnesses

11-34. The MK 25 UBA is fitted to the diver using two harnesses. The neck and waist harnesses are made of 1 1/2-inch polypropylene webbing that is fitted with quick-release side buckles. Adjustments in the harnesses are made with the incorporated triglide adjusters. When donned properly, the MK 25 UBA fits over the lung area of the chest, with the top of the UBA 7 to 10 inches below the chin. The waist strap fits loosely to allow expansion room for the breathing bag.

CANISTER INSULATOR PACKAGE

11-35. The MK 25 UBA canister is equipped with a removable neoprene insulator package that may be used in cold water (below 60 degrees F) to extend the duration of the carbon dioxide absorbent. The insulator has two components. The larger insulator slides onto the canister housing. After aligning the insulator holes with the canister ports, the insulator is held in place by a Velcro strap that fits over the canister lid. The smaller insulator fits on to the canister lid. The hole in the small insulator must align with the exhalation hose port in the canister. When installed, the insulation may be lifted to check for leaks and release any trapped air. To offset the positive buoyancy effects created by the canister insulator, a set of two lead-shot weight pouches are included in the equipment housing. The lead shot pouches are loaded with 1.59 pounds of lead shot each (3.18 pounds total) and are inserted into pockets that surround the demand valve. These weights are used only if the canister insulator package is installed.

GAS FLOW PATH

11-36. The gas is exhaled by the diver and directed by the mouthpiece one-way valves into the exhalation hose. The gas then enters the carbon dioxide-absorbent canister, which is packed with a NAVSEA-approved carbon dioxide-absorbent material. The carbon dioxide is removed by passing through the CO2-absorbent bed and chemically combining with the CO2-absorbent material in the canister. Upon leaving the canister, the used oxygen enters the breathing bag. When the diver inhales, the gas is drawn from the breathing bag through the inhalation hose and back to the diver's lungs. The gas flow described is entirely breath-activated. As the diver exhales, the gas in the UBA is pushed forward by the exhaled gas, and upon inhalation the one-way valves in the hoses allow fresh gas to be pulled into the diver's lungs from the breathing bag (Figure 11-3, page 206).

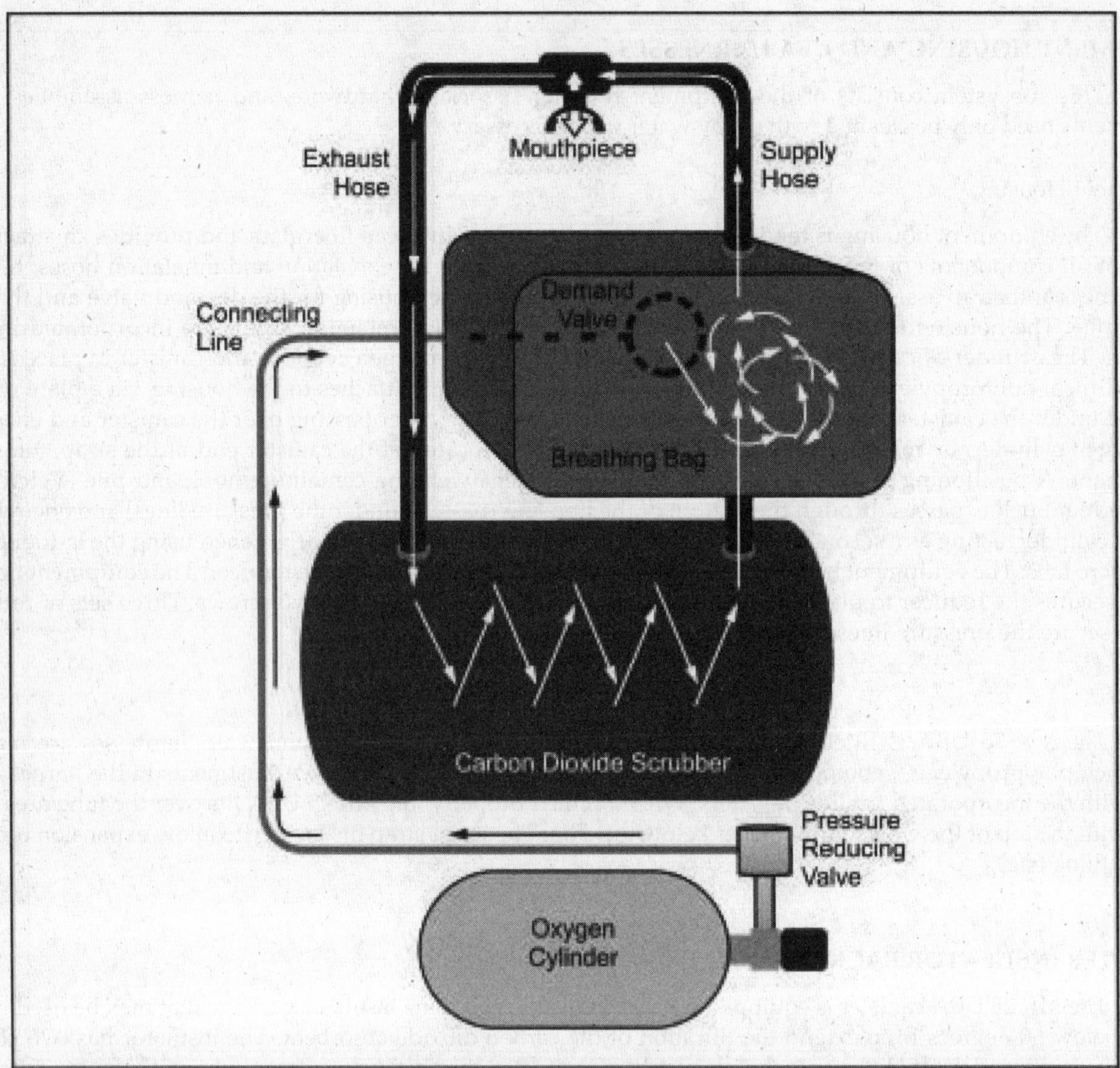

Figure 11-3. Gas flow path

BREATHING LOOP

11-37. The demand valve adds oxygen to the breathing bag of the UBA from the oxygen cylinder only when the diver empties the bag on inhalation. The demand valve also contains a manual bypass button to allow for manual filling of the breathing bag during rig setup and as required. There is no constant flow of fresh oxygen to the diver.

CHARACTERISTICS

11-38. The MK 25 UBA has significant specifications that distinguish it from other models. They are as follows:

- *Weight*—27 pounds (with full canister and charged O2 bottle, no insulation package). Neutral in water with approximately 2 liters of oxygen in the breathing bag..

- *Dimensions*—Length: 18.25 inches, width: 13.25 inches, height: 7 inches.
- *Operating Time*—4 hours based upon canister duration limits and an oxygen cylinder charged to full capacity.
- *Diving Depth*—0–50 FSW.
- *Temperature*—Diving: 35 to 90 degrees F/Transport: −22 to 120 degrees F.
- *Oxygen Cylinder*—1.9-liter volume, charged to 207 bars (3,000 psig) with 99.5 percent pure aviator's oxygen.
- *Reducer*—Reduces cylinder pressure to 3.3–3.7 bars (47.8–53.6 psig).
- *Demand Valve*—Adds oxygen to breathing bag only when bag is emptied on inhalation or when the manual bypass button is manually bypassed. Opening pressure is adjustable from 9.0 to 11.5 inches H2O.
- *CO2 Scrubber Canister*—Volume of 0.09 cubic feet (2.55 liters) with approved carbon dioxide absorbent.
- *Breathing Bag*—Maximum volume is approximately 7.0 liters. Maximum volume, when UBA is donned by diver, is approximately 4 liters.
- *Manual Bypass Valve*—Allows oxygen to be added manually to the breathing bag via the demand valve.
- *Equipment Housing*—Material made of fiberglass. Lead-shot weight pouches (3.18 pounds) at demand valve that offsets neoprene insulation.

OPERATIONAL DURATION OF THE MK 25 UBA

11-39. The operational duration of the MK 25 UBA may be limited by either the oxygen supply or the canister duration. These two constraining factors are discussed below.

OXYGEN SUPPLY

11-40. The MK 25 UBA oxygen bottle is charged to 207 bars (3,000 psig). The oxygen supply may be depleted in two ways—by the diver's metabolic consumption or by the loss of gas from the UBA. A key factor in maximizing the duration of the oxygen supply is for the diver to swim at a relaxed, comfortable pace. A diver swimming at a high exercise rate may have oxygen consumption of 2 liters per minute (oxygen supply duration = 205 minutes) whereas one swimming at a relaxed pace may have an oxygen consumption of 1 liter per minute (oxygen supply duration = 410 minutes). Figure 11-4, page 208, illustrates oxygen consumption rates from which the diver can estimate his cylinder duration.

CANISTER DURATION

11-41. The canister duration is dependent on the water temperature, exercise rate, and the mesh size of the NAVSEA-approved carbon dioxide absorbent. Typically, absorbent duration will increase as water temperatures decrease. The MK 25 UBA is equipped with a removable canister insulator package for use in water temperatures below 60 degrees F. Use of the insulator increases the duration of the canister in colder waters by holding heat within the absorbent material. However, use of the canister insulator in water temperatures above 60 degrees F can actually decrease canister duration. Divers should refer to NAVSEA 3151 Ser 00C34/3160 and applicable diving advisories for authorized canister duration for the MK 25 UBA. Exceeding authorized canister duration limits for given temperatures can result in very high levels of carbon dioxide in the breathing gas. The canister will function adequately for the time period as long as the UBA has been properly set up.

PREDIVE PROCEDURES

11-42. The MK 25 UBA is set up using the predive checklist (Appendix D). The diver should pay special attention to the following details:

- Gauge oxygen bottle for minimum operating pressure. The normal operating minimum is 207 bars (3,000 psig).
- Inspect and fill scrubber canister with absorbent (Figure 11-5, page 209). Use only approved C02 absorbent. Check upper and lower screens for clogging. If screens are clogged, refer to MRC R-4. Fill canister to scribe

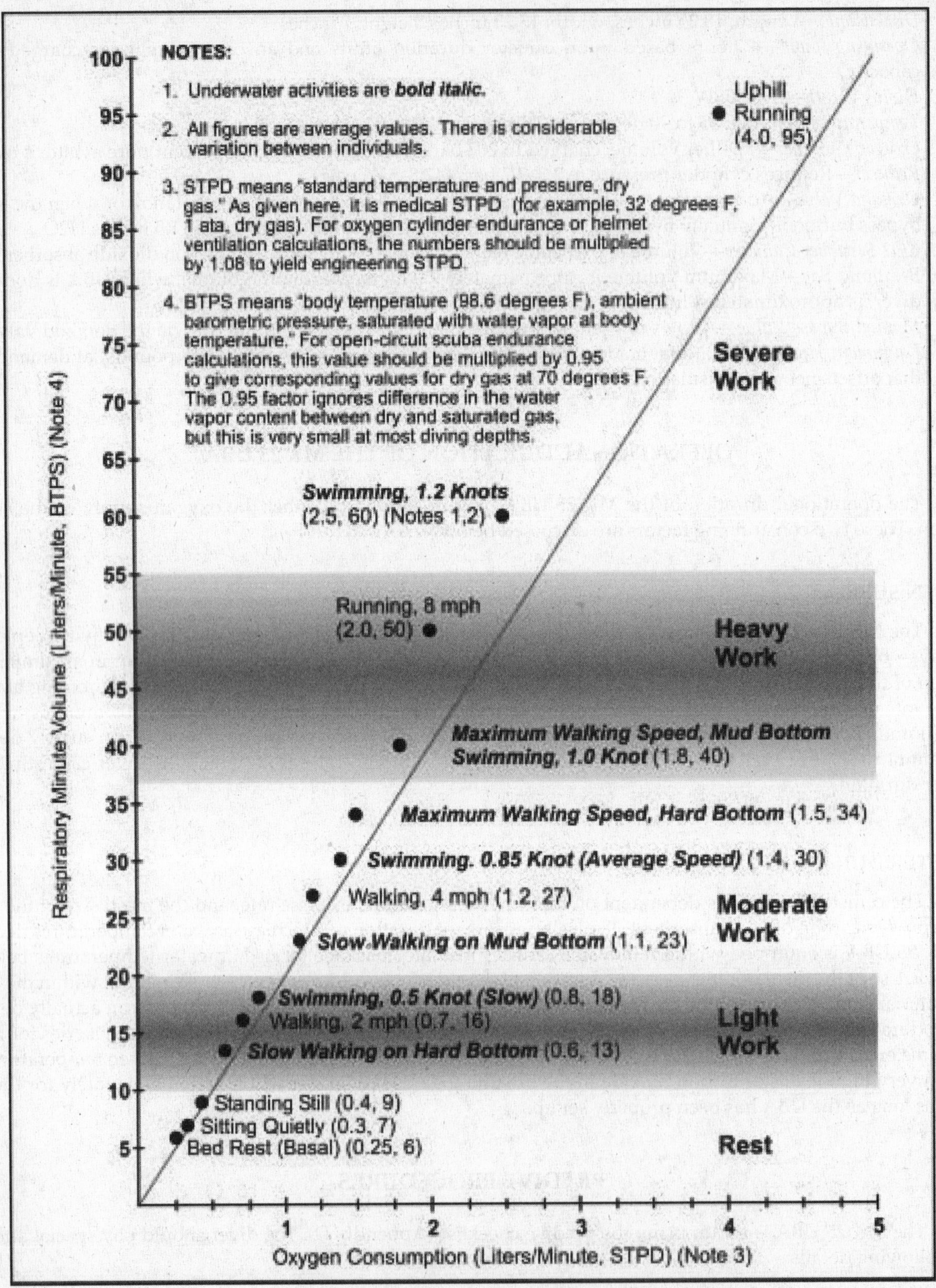

Figure 11-4. Oxygen consumption rates

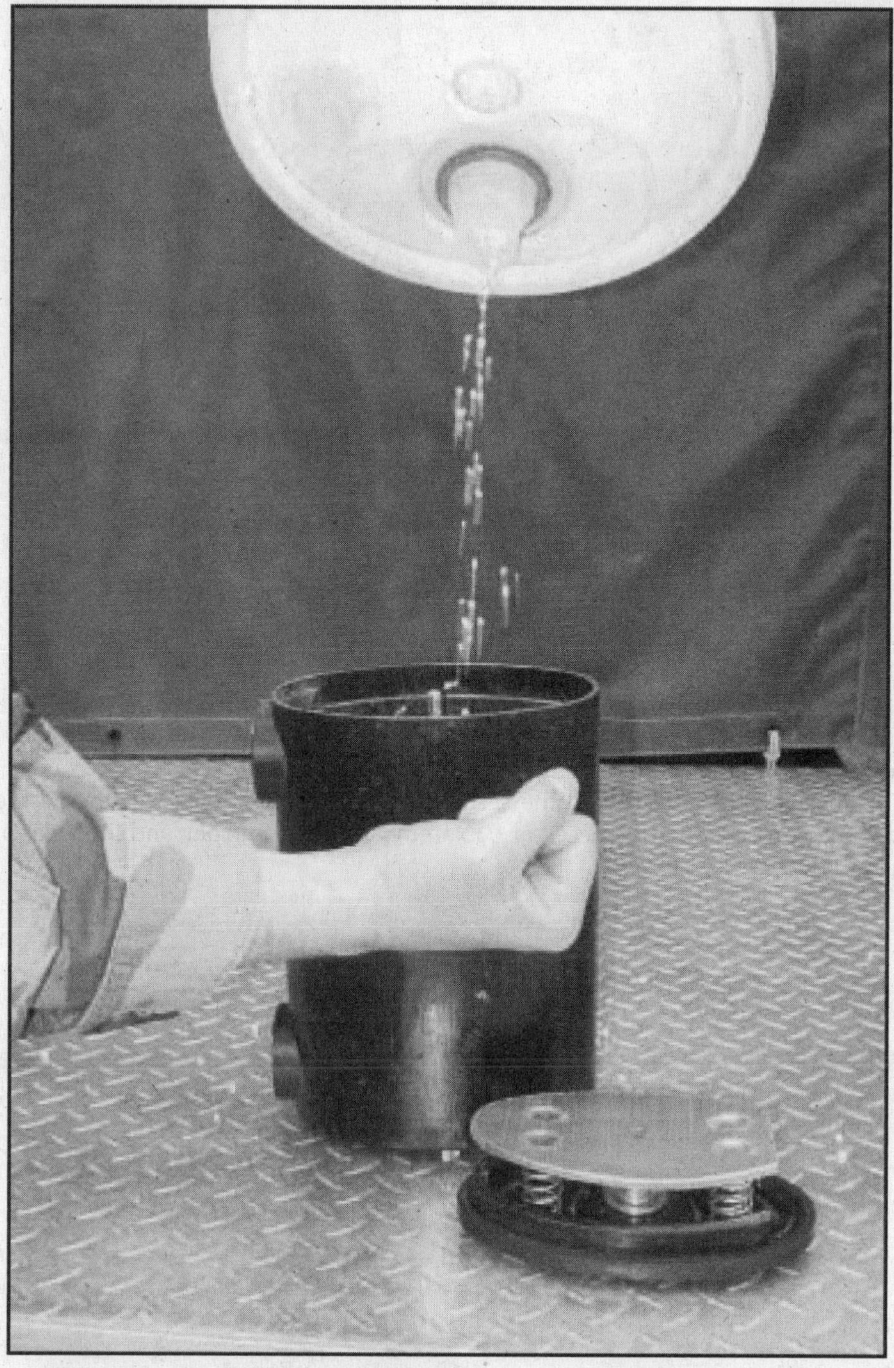

Figure 11-5. Filling canister with absorbent

line. Do not overfill. Inspect bayonet connector circle springs, ensuring they are free to move in their grooves and that no deformity is present. When installing top cover, do not overtighten. Overtightening may cause the support rod to rip from the fiberglass housing or to crack the bottom of the canister.

- Inspect and check the operation of the one-way check valves in the inhalation and exhalation hoses. Don't confuse the supply and exhaust hoses. Check the O-rings on the hose connectors; replace or lubricate if necessary.

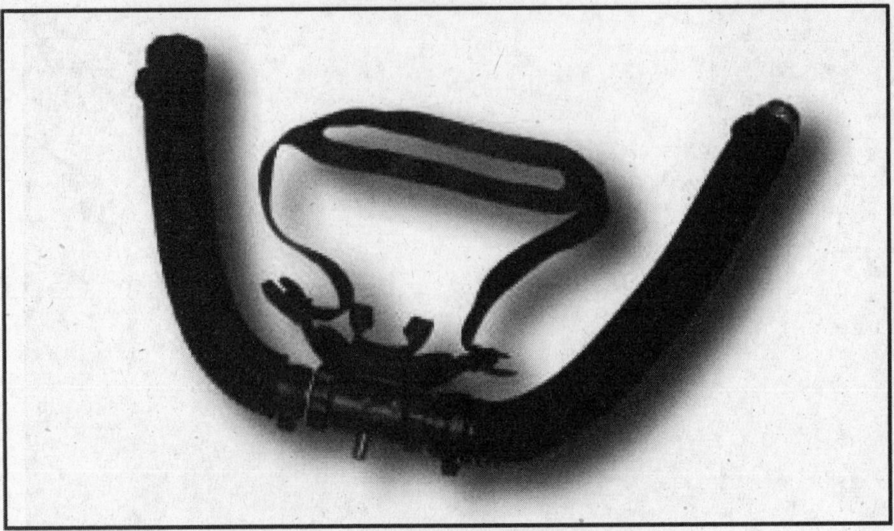

Figure 11-6. Inhalation and exhalation hoses

- Inspect and attach the inhalation and exhalation hoses to the mouthpiece (Figure 11-6). Close the dive-surface valve.
- Attach the supply hose to the breathing bag.
- Inspect and attach the breathing bag to the scrubber canister (Figure 11-7). Examine the O-rings on the breathing bag. Lubricate or replace if necessary. Examine the breathing bag and the breathing bag muffs for signs of puncture or wear.

Figure 11-7. Breathing bag attached to scrubber canister

- Install the scrubber canister in the proper orientation. Secure with the retainer strap. Ensure that the canister lid is to the left and correctly oriented.
- Attach the breathing bag to the demand valve (Figure 11-8). To prevent stripping, use extreme care when threading the plastic breathing bag coupling to the metal demand valve.

Figure 11-8. Breathing bag attached to demand valve

POSTDIVE PROCEDURES

11-43. The diver checks the MK 25 UBA using the postdive checklist (Appendix D).

MALFUNCTION PROCEDURES

11-44. Some of the common equipment problems encountered with the MK 25 UBA are listed, and the appropriate actions to be taken by the diver are described below.

CNS OXYGEN TOXICITY

11-45. **Symptoms.** Divers must be aware of the possibilities of the central nervous system (CNS) when breathing pure oxygen under pressure. The most hazardous is a sudden convulsion that can result in drowning or arterial gas embolism. The symptoms of CNS oxygen toxicity may occur suddenly and dramatically, or they may have a gradual, almost imperceptible onset. The letters V, E, N, T, I, D, C are a helpful reminder of these common symptoms:

- *Visual*—Tunnel vision, a decrease in the diver's peripheral vision, and other symptoms, such as blurred vision, may occur.
- *Ear*—Tinnitus is any sound perceived by the ears but not resulting from an external stimulus. The sound may resemble bells ringing, roaring, or a machinery-like pulsing sound.
- *Nausea or Spasmodic Vomiting*—These symptoms may be intermittent.
- *Twitching and Tingling*—Any of the small facial muscles, lips, or muscles of the extremities may be affected. These are the most frequent and clearest symptoms.
- *Irritability*—Any change in the diver's mental status; including confusion, agitation, and anxiety.
- *Dizziness*—Symptoms include clumsiness, incoordination, and unusual fatigue.
- *Convulsions*—The first sign of CNS oxygen toxicity may be a convulsion that occurs with little or no warning. These symptoms may occur singly or together. They occur in no particular order and there is no one symptom which could be considered more serious than another, or which is a better warning of an impending convulsion.

11-46. **Actions**. Diver notifies dive buddy and makes a controlled ascent to the surface while exhaling through the nose to prevent embolism. When on the surface, he inflates the life preserver, **shuts** the oxygen valve, closes the mouthpiece rotary valve, removes the mouthpiece from his mouth, and signals for assistance.

SYSTEM FLOODING

11-47. Symptoms. Symptoms include increased breathing resistance, a gurgling sound, a bitter taste in the mouth (caustic cocktail), and possibly gas escaping from the system.

11-48. **Actions.** The diver immediately attains a vertical position to keep the mouthpiece higher than the scrubber canister, and activates the demand valve bypass button. He notifies his dive buddy and makes a controlled ascent to the surface while breathing in the open-circuit mode (breath in from mouthpiece, exhale through nose). The diver maintains a vertical position while ascending and activates the bypass button as necessary. When on the surface, he inflates the life preserver, closes the mouthpiece rotary valve, removes the mouthpiece from his mouth, and signals for assistance.

CAUTION
Do NOT shut the oxygen cylinder valve.

NOTE
If the canister insulator is used, condensation may occur in the demand valve, causing a gurgling sound when the demand valve is activated.

BYPASS OR DEMAND VALVE STUCK OPEN

11-49. **Symptoms.** Symptoms include increased exhalation resistance and an overabundance of gas accompanied by the sound of oxygen being added to the breathing bag. When the bypass valve is stuck open, the flow rate is approximately one liter / second.

11-50. **Actions.** Diver notifies dive buddy and makes a controlled ascent to the surface while exhaling through the nose to prevent embolism. He must **NOT** hold his breath. When on the surface, he inflates the life preserver, shuts the oxygen cylinder valve, closes the mouthpiece rotary valve, removes the mouthpiece from his mouth, and signals for assistance.

BREATHING GAS PRESSURE DEFICIENCY

11-51. **Symptoms.** Breathing gas pressure deficiency occurs when the rig is not supplying an adequate amount of pressurized oxygen into the breathing loop to sustain the diver's need. Symptoms include increased breathing resistance and deflation of the breathing bag. Probable causes range from low cylinder pressure to a malfunction in the oxygen cylinder valve, reducer, demand valve, or breathing loop.

11-52. **Actions.** Diver notifies dive buddy and makes a controlled ascent to the surface while exhaling through the nose to prevent embolism. When on the surface, he inflates the life preserver, closes the mouthpiece rotary valve, removes the mouthpiece from his mouth, and signals for assistance.

CAUTION
Do NOT shut the oxygen cylinder valve.

DEMAND VALVE FAILURE (AUTOMATIC OR MANUAL)

11-53. **Symptoms.** Symptoms include demand valve failure to supply oxygen in either mode of operation.

11-54. **Actions.** Diver notifies dive buddy and makes a controlled ascent to the surface while exhaling through the nose to prevent embolism. When on the surface, he inflates the life preserver, closes the mouthpiece rotary valve, removes the mouthpiece from his mouth, and signals for assistance.

CAUTION
Do NOT shut the oxygen cylinder valve.

CLOSED-CIRCUIT OXYGEN EXPOSURE LIMITS

11-55. The USN closed-circuit oxygen exposure limits have been extended and revised to allow greater flexibility in closed-circuit oxygen diving operations. The revised limits are divided into the following categories:

TRANSIT-WITH-EXCURSION LIMITS

11-56. The transit-with-excursion limits (Table 11-2) call for a maximum dive depth of 20 FSW or shallower for the majority of the dive, but allow the diver to make a brief excursion to depths as great as 50 FSW. The transit-with-excursion limits is normally the preferred mode of operation because maintaining a depth of 20 FSW or shallower

Table 11-2. Transit with excursion limits table

Depth	Maximum Time
21 to 40 FSW	15 minutes
41 to 50 FSW	5 minutes

minimizes the possibility of CNS oxygen toxicity during the majority of the dive yet allows a brief downward excursion if needed. **Only a single excursion is allowed.**

11-57. A transit with one excursion, if necessary, will be the preferred option in most combat swimmer operations. When operational considerations necessitate a descent deeper than 20 FSW for longer than allowed by the excursion limits, the appropriate single-depth limit should be used. Figure 11-9, page 214, depicts the following transit definitions:

- *Transit*—That part of the dive spent at 20 FSW or shallower.
- *Excursion*—The portion of the dive deeper than 20 FSW.
- *Excursion Time*—Is the time between the diver's initial descent below 20 FSW and his return to 20 FSW or shallower at the end of the excursion.
- *Oxygen Time*—Is calculated as the time interval between when the diver begins breathing from the closed-circuit oxygen UBA (on-oxygen time) to the time when he discontinues breathing from the closed-circuit oxygen UBA (off-oxygen time).

11-58. A diver who has maintained a transit depth of 20 FSW or shallower may make one brief excursion as long as he observes the following rules:

- Maximum total time of dive (oxygen time) should not exceed 240 minutes.
- A single excursion may be taken at any time during the dive.
- The diver must have returned to 20 FSW or shallower by the end of the prescribed excursion limit.
- The time limit for the excursion is determined by the maximum depth attained during the excursion (Table 11-2). The diver should remember that the excursion limits are different from the single-depth limits.

EXAMPLE 1

A dive mission calls for a swim pair to transit at 20 FSW for 45 minutes, descend to 36 FSW, and complete their objective. As long as the divers do not exceed a maximum depth of 40 FSW, they may use the 40 FSW excursion limit of 15 minutes. The time at which they initially descend below 20 FSW to the time at which they finish the excursion must be 15 minutes or less.

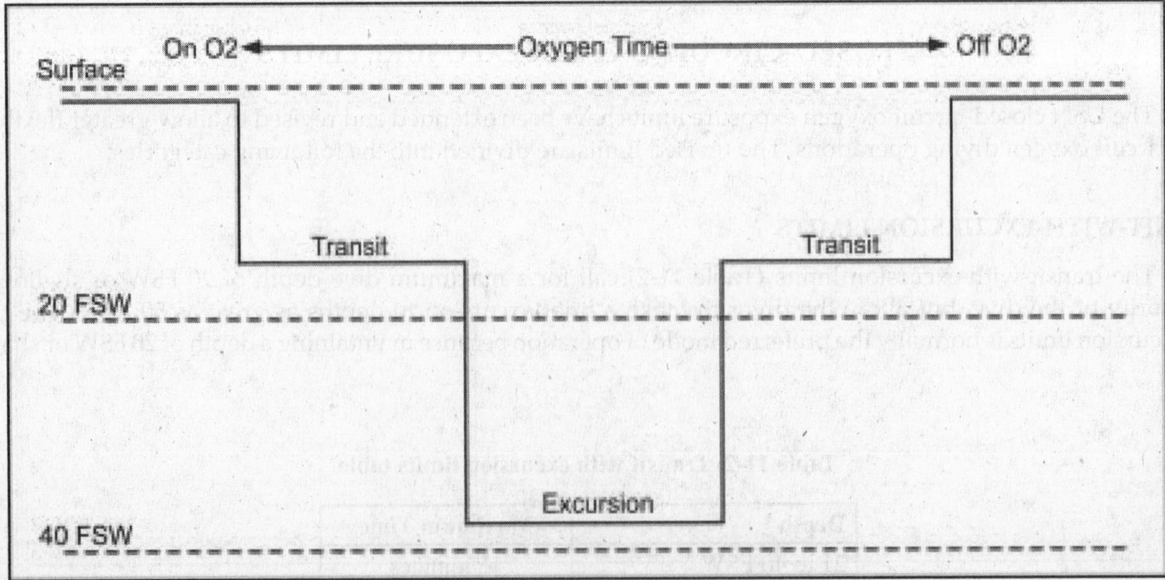

Figure 11-9. Transit with excursion limits

11-59. If an inadvertent excursion should occur, one of the following situations will apply:

- If the depth or time of the excursion exceeds the limits in the previous paragraph or if an excursion has been taken previously, the dive must be aborted and the diver must return to the surface.
- If the excursion was within the allowed excursion limits, the dive may be continued to the maximum allowed oxygen dive time, but no additional excursions deeper than 20 FSW may be taken.
- The dive may be treated as a single-depth dive applying the maximum depth and the total oxygen time to the single-depth limits shown in Table 11-3.

EXAMPLE 1

A dive pair is having difficulty with a malfunctioning compass. They have been on oxygen (oxygen time) for 35 minutes when they notice that their depth gauge reads 55 FSW. Because this exceeds the maximum allowed oxygen exposure depth, the dive must be aborted and the divers must return to the surface.

EXAMPLE 2

A diver on a compass swim notes that his depth gauge reads 32 FSW. He recalls checking his watch 5 minutes earlier and that time his depth gauge read 18 FSW. As his excursion time is less than 15 minutes, he has not exceeded the excursion limit for 40 FSW. He may continue the dive, but he must maintain his depth at 20 FSW or less and make no additional excursions. NOTE: If the diver is unsure how long he was below 25 FSW, the dive must be aborted.

SINGLE-DEPTH LIMITS

11-60. The single-depth limits (Table 11-3) allow maximum exposure at the greatest depth, but have a shorter overall exposure time. Single-depth limits may, however, be useful when maximum bottom time is needed deeper than 20 FSW. Depths greater than 20 FSW do not allow for an excursion. They may, however, be useful in certain diving situations. Although the limits described in this section have been thoroughly tested and are safe for the vast majority of individuals, occasional episodes of oxygen toxicity up to and including convulsions may occur. This is the basis for requiring buddy lines on closed-circuit oxygen diving operations. These limits have been tested extensively over the entire depth range and are acceptable for routine diving operations. They are not considered exceptional exposure. Specific operational considerations are addressed below.

Table 11-3. Single-depth oxygen exposure limits

Depth	Maximum Oxygen Time
25 FSW	240 minutes
30 FSW	80 minutes
35 FSW	25 minutes
40 FSW	15 minutes
50 FSW	10 minutes

11-61. The term single-depth limits does not mean that the entire dive must be spent at one depth, but refers to the time limit applied to the dive based on the maximum depth attained during the dive.

11-62. The following definitions apply when using the single-depth limits:

- *Oxygen Time*—Calculated as the time interval between when the diver begins breathing from the closed-circuit oxygen UBA (on-oxygen time) to the time when he discontinues breathing from the closed-circuit UBA (off-oxygen time). Time of transit with excursion limits, above.
- *Depth*—Used to determine the allowable exposure time that is determined by the maximum depth attained during the dive. For intermediate depth, the next deeper depth limit will be used.
- *Depth or Time Limits*—Provided in Table 11-3. No excursions are allowed when using these limits.

EXAMPLE 1

22 minutes (oxygen time) into a compass swim, a dive pair descends to 28 FSW to avoid the propeller of a passing boat. They remain at this depth for 8 minutes. They now have the following choices for calculating their allowed oxygen time:

1. They may return to 20 FSW or shallower and use the time below 20 FSW as an excursion, allowing them to continue their dive on the transit with excursion limits to a maximum time of 240 minutes.
2. They may elect to remain at 28 FSW and use the 30-FSW single-depth limits to a maximum dive time of 80 minutes.

Exposure Limits for Successive Oxygen Dives

11-63. If an oxygen dive is conducted after a previous closed-circuit oxygen exposure, the effect of the previous dive on the exposure limit for the subsequent dive is dependent on the off-oxygen interval.

Definitions for Successive Oxygen Dives

11-64. The following definitions apply when using oxygen exposure limits for successive oxygen dives:

- *Off-Oxygen Interval.* The interval between off-oxygen time and on-oxygen time is defined as the time from when the diver discontinues breathing from his closed-circuit oxygen UBA on one dive until he begins breathing from the UBA on the next dive.
- *Successive Oxygen Dive.* A successive oxygen dive is one that follows a previous oxygen dive after an off-oxygen interval of more than 10 minutes but less than 2 hours.

Off-Oxygen Exposure Limit Adjustments

11-65. If an oxygen dive is a successive oxygen dive, the oxygen exposure limit for the dive must be adjusted as shown in Table 11-4. If the off-oxygen interval is 2 hours or greater, no adjustment is required for the subsequent dive. An oxygen dive undertaken after an off-oxygen interval of more than 2 hours is considered to be the same as an initial oxygen exposure. If a negative number is obtained when adjusting the single-depth exposure limits, a 2-hour off-oxygen interval must be taken before the next oxygen dive.

NOTE

A maximum of 4 hours of oxygen time is permitted within a 24-hour period.

Table 11-4. Adjusted oxygen exposure limits for successive oxygen dives

Type	Adjusted Maximum Oxygen Time	Excursion
Transit With Excursion Limits	Subtract oxygen time on previous dives from 240 minutes.	Allowed if none taken on previous dives.
Single-Depth Limits	1. Determine maximum oxygen time for deepest exposure. 2. Subtract oxygen time on previous dives from maximum oxygen time in Step 1.	No excursion allowed when using single-depth limits to compute remaining oxygen time.

- *Maximum Allowable Oxygen Time.* Divers should not accumulate more than 4 hours of oxygen time in a 24-hour period.
- *Exposure Limits for Oxygen Dives Following Mixed-Gas or Air Dives.* When a subsequent dive must be conducted and the previous exposure was an air or MK-16 dive, the exposure limits for the subsequent oxygen dive require no adjustment. If diving mixed-gas in conjunction with oxygen, the diver should refer to the USN Diving Manual for further guidance.

OXYGEN DIVING AT ALTITUDE

11-66. The oxygen exposure limits and procedures set forth in the preceding paragraphs may be used without adjustment for closed-circuit oxygen diving at altitudes above sea level.

FLYING AFTER OXYGEN DIVING

11-67. Flying is permitted immediately after oxygen diving unless the oxygen dive has been part of a multiple-UBA dive profile in which the diver was also breathing another breathing mixture (air or N202, He02). In this case, the rules found in the USN Diving Manual apply.

COMBAT OPERATIONS

11-68. The oxygen exposure limits in this chapter are the only limits approved for use by the USN and should not be exceeded in a training or exercise scenario. Should combat operations require a more severe oxygen exposure, an estimate of the increased risk of CNS oxygen toxicity may be obtained from a DMO or the Navy experimental diving unit (NAVXDIVINGU). The advice of a DMO is essential in such situations and should be obtained whenever possible.

EXAMPLE 1

90 minutes after completing a previous oxygen dive with an oxygen time of 75 minutes (maximum dive depth 19 FSW), a dive pair will be making a second dive using the transit with excursion limits. Calculate the amount of oxygen time for the second dive, and determine whether an excursion is allowed.

SOLUTION

The second dive is considered a successive oxygen dive because the off-oxygen interval was less than 2 hours. The allowed exposure time must be adjusted. The adjusted maximum oxygen time is 165 minutes (240 minutes minus 75 minutes previous oxygen time). A single excursion may be taken because the maximum depth of the previous dive was 19 FSW.

EXAMPLE 2

70 minutes after completing a previous oxygen dive (maximum depth 28 FSW) with an oxygen time of 60 minutes, a dive pair will be making a second oxygen dive. The maximum depth of the second dive is expected to be 25 FSW. Calculate the amount of oxygen time for the second dive, and determine whether an excursion is allowed.

SOLUTION

The diver first computes the adjusted maximum oxygen time. This is determined by the single-depth limits for the deeper of the two exposures (30 FSW for 80 minutes) minus the oxygen time from the previous dive. The adjusted maximum oxygen time for the second dive is 20 minutes (80 minutes minus 60 minutes previous oxygen time). No excursion is permitted using the single-depth limits.

WATER ENTRY AND DESCENT

11-69. The diver is required to perform a purge procedure before or during any dive in which closed-circuit oxygen UBA is to be used. The purge procedure is designed to eliminate the nitrogen from the UBA and the diver's lungs as soon as he begins breathing from the rig. The procedure prevents the possibility of hypoxia as a result of excessive nitrogen in the breathing loop. The gas volume from which this excess nitrogen must be eliminated is comprised of more than just the UBA breathing bag. The carbon dioxide-absorbent canister, inhalation and exhalation hoses, and diver's lungs must also be purged of nitrogen.

PURGE PROCEDURE

11-70. Immediately before entering the water, the divers should carry out the appropriate purge procedure. It is both difficult and unnecessary to eliminate nitrogen completely from the breathing loop. The purge procedure need only raise the fraction of oxygen in the breathing loop to a level high enough to prevent the diver from becoming hypoxic. For the MK 25 UBA, this value has been determined to be 45 percent. The purge procedure for the MK 25 UBA, (Figure 11-10) is taken from NAVY 22600-A3-MMA-010/53833, *Operations and Maintenance Instructions for the MK 25 MOD 2 UBA,* 16 October 1998. This procedure produces an average oxygen fraction of approximately 75 percent in the breathing loop.

11-71. If the dive is part of a tactical scenario that requires a turtleback phase, the purge must be done in the water after the surface swim, before submerging. If the tactical scenario requires an underwater purge procedure, the diver will complete it while submerged after an initial subsurface transit on open-circuit scuba or other UBA. When the purge is done in either manner, the diver must be thoroughly familiar with the purge procedure and execute it carefully with attention to detail so that it may be accomplished correctly in this less-favorable environment.

TURTLEBACK EMERGENCY DESCENT PURGE PROCEDURE

11-72. This procedure is approved for turtleback emergency descents. The diver should—

- Open oxygen supply.
- Exhale completely, clearing the mouthpiece with the dive or surface valve in the surface position.
- Put the dive or surface valve in the DIVE position and make the emergency descent.
- Immediately upon reaching depth, perform purging under pressure (pressurized phase) IAW the appropriate MK 25 UBA technical manual.

1. Don the apparatus by attaching the neck and waist straps. The upper surface of the UBA should be approximately at the level of the diver's lower chest.

NOTE: The waist strap should fit loosely to permit complete filling of the breathing bag.

2. Ensure that the oxygen supply valve is closed. Blow all air out of the lungs and insert mouthpiece. Open the dive-surface valve. (The dive-surface valve is left open for the remainder of the procedure.)
3. Empty air out of the breathing bag by inhaling from the mouthpiece and exhaling into the atmosphere (through the nose). Continue until the bag is completely empty.

NOTE: Be sure **not** to exhale into the mouthpiece (breathing bag) during the emptying process in Step 3 or 5.

4. Open the oxygen supply valve and fill the breathing bag by depressing the bypass valve completely for approximately 6 seconds. (The oxygen supply valve is left open for the remainder of the procedure.)
5. Empty the breathing bag once more as in Step 3.
6. Fill the breathing bag to a comfortable volume for swimming by depressing the bypass valve completely for approximately 4 seconds. Begin normal breathing.
7. The MK 25 UBA is now ready for diving.
8. If the purge procedure is interrupted at any point, the procedure should be repeated starting with Step 2. It should also be repeated any time the mouthpiece is removed and air is breathed.

NOTE: Additional purging during the dive is not necessary and should **not** be performed.

Figure 11-10. Predive purge procedures

AVOIDING PURGE PROCEDURE ERRORS

11-73. The following errors may result in a dangerously low percentage of oxygen in the UBA and should be avoided. The diver should avoid—

- Exhaling back into the bag with the last breath rather than into atmosphere while emptying the breathing bag.
- Underinflating the bag during the fill segment of the fill/empty cycle.
- Adjusting the waist strap of the UBA or adjustment straps of the life jacket too tightly. Lack of room for bag expansion may result in underinflation of the bag and inadequate purging.
- Breathing gas volume deficiency caused by failure to turn on the oxygen-supply valve before underwater purge procedures.

UNDERWATER PROCEDURES

11-74. During the dive, personnel should adhere to the following guidelines:

- Know and observe the oxygen exposure limits.
- Check each other carefully for leaks at the onset of the dive. Perform this check in the water after purging, but before descending to a transit depth.
- Swim at a relaxed, comfortable pace as established by the slower swimmer of the pair (100 yards per 3 minutes is the objective swim speed).
- Be alert for any symptoms suggestive of a medical disorder (CNS oxygen toxicity, carbon dioxide buildup).
- Observe the UBA canister limit for the expected water temperature.
- Use minimum surface checks consistent with operational necessity.
- Minimize gas loss from the UBA (keep good depth control; avoid leaks and excessive mask clearing).

- Use proper amount of weights for the thermal protection worn and for equipment carried.
- Use tides and currents to maximum advantage.
- Swim at 20 FSW or shallower unless operational requirements dictate otherwise.
- Maintain frequent visual or touch checks with buddy.
- Wear the appropriate thermal protection.
- Do not use the UBA breathing bag as a buoyancy compensation device.
- Wear a depth gauge to allow precise depth control. The depth for the pair of divers is the greatest depth attained by either diver.
- Do not perform additional purges during the dive unless the mouthpiece is removed and air is breathed.
- Ensure the diver not using the compass carefully notes the starting and ending time if an excursion occurs.
- Provide at least one depth gauge per pair. Because of the importance of maintaining accurate depth control on oxygen swims, both divers in a swim pair should carry a depth gauge whenever possible.

UBA MALFUNCTION PROCEDURES

11-75. The diver shall be thoroughly familiar with the malfunction procedures unique to his UBA. The following procedures are described in the appropriate MK 25 UBA operational and maintenance manual:

- *Ascent Procedures.* The ascent rate shall never exceed 30 fpm.
- *Postdive Procedures and Dive Documentation.* UBA postdive procedures should be accomplished using the appropriate checklist (Appendix D). Document all dives performed by submitting a combined diving log.

TRANSPORT AND STORAGE OF PREPARED UBA

11-76. Once the MK 25 UBA predive checklist has been completed, the UBA is ready to dive. At this point, the UBA may be stored for up to 14 days before diving. If stored in excess of 14 days, the carbon dioxide absorbent in the canister must be changed. Before storing, the diver should shut the oxygen cylinder valve and depress the demand valve bypass button to vent the pneumatics subsystem. He should deplete the breathing bag and place the mouthpiece rotary valve in the SURFACE (closed) position. In this configuration, the UBA is airtight and the carbon dioxide absorbent in the canister is protected from moisture that can impair carbon dioxide absorption. He then puts a laminated or hard copy of the completed predive checklist (Appendix D) with the stored UBA.

11-77. High temperatures during transport and storage should not adversely affect carbon dioxide absorbents; however, storage temperatures below freezing may decrease performance and should be avoided. The diver should check the manufacturer's recommendations regarding storage temperatures.

11-78. If an operation calls for an oxygen dive followed by a surface interval and a second oxygen dive, the MK 25 UBA shall be sealed during the surface interval as described above (mouthpiece rotary valve in SURFACE position, oxygen supply valve shut). It is not necessary to change the carbon dioxide absorbent before the second dive as long as the combined canister durations of all subsequent dives do not exceed the canister duration limits specified.

11-79. For certain immediate-use missions, the MK 25 UBA must be shipped with a fully charged oxygen cylinder. The MK 25 UBA oxygen cylinder, composed of aluminum alloy 6061-T6, is manufactured and certified to DOT 3AL specifications. No certificate of equivalency is required when transporting a charged MK 25 UBA oxygen cylinder by any civilian or military means.

CHAPTER 12

Surface Infiltration

A surface vessel can be the primary means of infiltration, an intermediate transport platform, or one of a series of vessels used in a complex infiltration chain. Surface assets include any seagoing vessel from aircraft carriers to Coast Guard cutters, from merchant vessels to charter fishing boats, including CRRCs and kayaks. Selection criteria and planning considerations vary according to the mission requirements and the assets available. This chapter will examine the characteristics of different surface infiltration assets and explain the planning aspects of a CRRC (or other small craft) infiltration and exfiltration.

MOTHER SHIP OPERATIONS

12-1. Missions using large surface vessels are commonly referred to as "mother ship" operations. The term mother ship implies using a large ship as a mission support craft. The mother ship's primary mission is to transport an SFODA from a staging base to a launch point within range of the detachment's organic infiltration assets; for example, CRRCs or kayaks. Vessels suitable for use as a mother ship are generally divided into military and commercial types.

MILITARY SHIPPING

12-2. Military shipping is usually available from U.S. (joint) or Allied (combined) navies. Navies have always been the lead elements of "gunboat diplomacy." Because governments have a need to influence situations outside their borders, some assets, often as large as a task force, are often already deployed within range of a potential "hot spot." Regional instabilities mean that friendly naval assets are sometimes the only secure staging base available to a detachment seeking entry into a potentially hostile area. Military shipping has several advantages and disadvantages to other methods of deployment (Figure 12-1).

12-3. Detachments can be assigned or attached to naval task forces as part of a contingency operations package. Special operations command and control elements (SOCCEs) may be required for liaison with the fleet commander and his staff. Higher headquarters may task detachments to use military shipping during contingency operations. Detachments desiring to train with naval assets can take advantage of this by making coordination at the Joint headquarters level.

12-4. The U.S. Navy's mobility can be used to extend the range of both fixed-and rotary-wing aircraft into many areas of the world where land-based support is denied. Aircraft carriers normally have at least one cargo aircraft capable of being configured for airdropping a limited number of personnel and a limited amount of equipment. Heliborne operations are not restricted to aircraft carriers; most large naval ships have landing decks that will accommodate one or more helicopters. Available vessels include landing craft, troop transports, aircraft carriers, and a wide variety of other surface craft presently in the USN and Army inventory.

COMMERCIAL SHIPPING

12-5. Commercial or civilian shipping includes any vessel that is not a "flagged" military vessel. These may include civilian pleasure craft, charter or commercial fishing vessels, or merchant shipping. Detachments select commercial shipping as an alternative to military shipping based on mission requirements. Factors may include a lack of available military shipping or a desire to reduce or conceal the military signature associated with naval vessels. Civilian shipping also has several advantages and disadvantages to other methods (Figure 12-2).

12-6. If the mission requires concealment of the sponsor's identity, commercial shipping becomes a very viable means of infiltration. It requires less training and coordination than submarine infiltration and can be used when an

Advantages	Disadvantages
• Coordination can be made through joint headquarters. • Sophisticated communications and navigation support is available to the SFOD throughout the embarked phase. • Precise navigation can be maintained to the debarkation point. • Weather, tide, and current updates are available. • Additional planning and training can be conducted en route. • Large quantities of supplies can be transported. • Relatively unaffected by weather. • Provides long-range delivery and simplicity during debarkation. • Exfiltration can be planned in conjunction with infiltration using the same assets. • Close air support and naval gunfire can be coordinated and requested.	• Sponsor identification cannot be concealed. • Training with Navy shipping assets is more difficult. Army personnel do not conduct enough joint operations with the Navy. • Surface craft require more transit time to make long-distance transits. This factor may not meet the mission's time constraints. • Hydrographic characteristics of the area and enemy shore defenses may force larger vessels to remain further offshore. • An intermediate transport vessel such as a CRRC or kayak is usually required to transport the team to the BLS or a final debarkation point.

Figure 12-1. Military shipping considerations

Advantages	Disadvantages
• Sponsor ID is concealed. • Civilian shipping blends in with local boat traffic. • The detachment has more control of the route. • Civilian crew members may be able to provide the detachment with invaluable "local knowledge." • Commercial shipping may be more responsive to the detachment's requirements.	• Lack of fire support. • Sophisticated communications and navigation support may not be available. • Operational security may be difficult to achieve and maintain. • Exfiltration support may be limited or nonexistent. • Suitable vessels/crew may be difficult or impossible to obtain.

Figure 12-2. Civilian shipping considerations

OTH airdrop is not possible. If a detachment has the requisite ship handling skills, or if it can be augmented with suitable crew, it is possible to conduct a "stand-alone" infiltration. If not, external assets are required to support the detachment's infiltration plan.

12-7. Small craft can be purchased outright, rented, leased or otherwise acquired with or without a crew. Larger vessels will probably require a professional crew and are therefore beyond the capability of most detachments. Detachments must select an appropriate vessel, ensuring that it is seaworthy, has adequate facilities to support the detachment while embarked, and will not draw undue attention to itself due to being "out-of-place." Figure 12-3 lists the characteristics that a detachment should consider when choosing a craft.

- Vessel-type common in the area of operations, low visual signature.
- Viable reason for being in the area.
- Reasonable cruising speed.
- Adequate fuel supply and sufficient range, including contingencies.
- Sufficient space for equipment, personnel, and mission preparation.
- Adequate navigation and communications equipment (augment with detachment assets as backup).
- Redundancy and reliability (twin engines required, preferably diesel inboards).

Figure 12-3. Desirable characteristics for choosing a craft

ACTIONS EN ROUTE TO THE DEBARKATION POINT

12-8. Upon assignment of a transport vessel, detachment personnel should become familiar with the ship's characteristics, including exact troop locations and dimensions of storage areas. Learning the ship is best done by coordinating with the vessel commander. Personnel then prepare and package the equipment according to the dimensions and weights compatible with the assigned craft. All equipment must be waterproofed and marked for easy identification.

12-9. Planning for the debarkation of swimmers is the most important consideration when using surface craft. Some large vessels cannot deliver the operational elements within swimming range of the BLS because of hydrographic characteristics of the area or danger of enemy detection. This situation requires additional planning, preparation, and coordination for intermediate transport from the point of debarkation to the launch point in the vicinity of the BLS.

12-10. Once the SFOD selects the debarkation method, it designates specific duties and stations and conducts rehearsals. The detachment should continue debarkation rehearsals en route with all personnel involved in the operation.

CRRC MISSION PLANNING FACTORS

12-11. Once the detachment is safely embarked on its mother ship, it can finalize mission planning and conduct rehearsals to the extent allowed by the support vessel. At this time, the detachment will formalize the infiltration plan from the debarkation point to the swimmer launch point using internal assets. These assets are usually CRRCs or kayaks. Because many of the planning considerations for kayaks are similar or less complicated, this portion of the chapter will concentrate on CRRCs.

TACTICAL LOADS

12-12. While the CRRC is capable of transporting up to ten personnel, it is highly recommended that no more than six personnel be embarked. The weight ceiling for the CRRC is 2,000 pounds. Any weight above this amount significantly reduces the CRRC's efficiency. Experience has shown that six personnel, with mission-essential equipment, on average, comes closest to this weight ceiling. (This data pertains to the F-470/55HP engine combination.) For extended transits or marginal sea conditions, the mission commander should consider reducing this maximum load to four persons. In a crowded CRRC, those personnel in the forward positions are subjected to a greater degree of physical pounding from the effect of swell and wave activity on the bow. This beating is especially significant during long transit periods; the increased physical stress may diminish operator ability to perform after arrival at the objective. The detachment commander must also take into account the possibility of prisoners, casualties, and the evacuation of friendly forces. It is prudent to allow sufficient boat space to contend with contingencies.

COMMAND RELATIONSHIPS

12-13. SFOD can be called upon to operate CRRCs from a variety of platforms. If CRRCs are embarked on a USN ship, that ship's commanding officer or other officer in tactical command (if so assigned) must ensure CRRC operations are safely conducted. If not embarked, this task rests with the commander of the detachment.

PLANNING RESPONSIBILITIES

12-14. When planning an OTH CRRC operation, the detachment operations sergeant is normally the focal point because of his knowledge and experience. The planning sequence must consist of continuous parallel, concurrent, and detailed planning. Planning support and information will be required from a variety of sources. Planning must be characterized by teamwork between the supported and supporting elements. As the plan develops and is completed, all aspects should be briefed, reviewed, and understood by planners and decision makers. The CRRC mission planning checklist provides a planning sequence guide that can be modified as required (Figure 12-4).

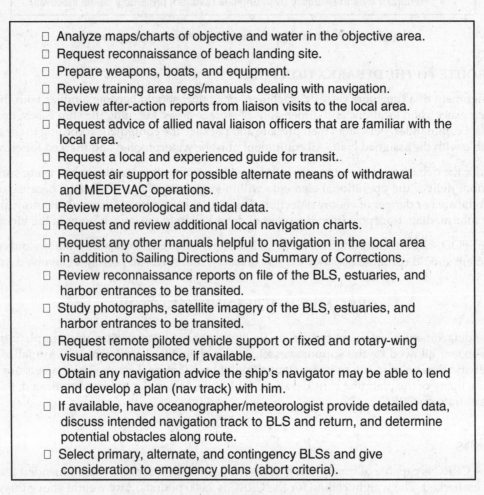

- ☐ Analyze maps/charts of objective and water in the objective area.
- ☐ Request reconnaissance of beach landing site.
- ☐ Prepare weapons, boats, and equipment.
- ☐ Review training area regs/manuals dealing with navigation.
- ☐ Review after-action reports from liaison visits to the local area.
- ☐ Request advice of allied naval liaison officers that are familiar with the local area.
- ☐ Request a local and experienced guide for transit.
- ☐ Request air support for possible alternate means of withdrawal and MEDEVAC operations.
- ☐ Review meteorological and tidal data.
- ☐ Request and review additional local navigation charts.
- ☐ Request any other manuals helpful to navigation in the local area in addition to Sailing Directions and Summary of Corrections.
- ☐ Review reconnaissance reports on file of the BLS, estuaries, and harbor entrances to be transited.
- ☐ Study photographs, satellite imagery of the BLS, estuaries, and harbor entrances to be transited.
- ☐ Request remote piloted vehicle support or fixed and rotary-wing visual reconnaissance, if available.
- ☐ Obtain any navigation advice the ship's navigator may be able to lend and develop a plan (nav track) with him.
- ☐ If available, have oceanographer/meteorologist provide detailed data, discuss intended navigation track to BLS and return, and determine potential obstacles along route.
- ☐ Select primary, alternate, and contingency BLSs and give consideration to emergency plans (abort criteria).

Figure 12-4. CRRC mission planning checklist

CRRC LAUNCH AND RECOVERY OPERATIONS

12-15. Personnel must perform launch and recovery operations in a specific manner. The following general guidelines apply.

12-16. Ship Handling. The ship's stability is of prime importance for launch and recovery evolutions. An appropriate heading must be found to minimize pitch and roll to achieve the best launch and recovery condition. In addition, winds may cause a cross swell; consequently, close coordination between the bridge and the launch and recovery control station is required. Minimizing roll of the ship is the major concern. Handling, launching, and recovering CRRC can become extremely difficult as seas increase to Sea State 3. If possible, ship course and speed changes should be avoided during CRRC launch and recovery operations. This avoidance reduces the possibility of cross-wave action across the stern gate or sill.

12-17. Command, Control, and Communications (C3). Hand-held portable radio and sound-powered phone communications should be established between the bridge and launch or recovery control stations. When the CRRC is ready to launch, the control station will request the bridge to maneuver the ship into the launch heading. Also, the control station establishes communications with the CRRC through hand signals or voice via portable bullhorn or ship's well-deck public address (PA) system. Before the scheduled launch time, the CRRC officer should make a "go" or "no-go" recommendation based on the prevailing sea state to the ship's commanding officer through the control station. The ship's commanding officer has the ultimate responsibility and authority to launch and recover CRRC.

12-18. The mobility and versatility of the CRRC allows it to be launched and recovered from a variety of platforms. They are—

- Fixed-wing aircraft (launch only).
- Rotary-wing aircraft.
- Surface ship (either wet-well or over-the-side).
- Combatant craft.
- Submarine (submerged or surfaced).

12-19. Specific techniques for CRRC launch and recovery operations are addressed in the following:

- Naval Special Warfare Air Operations Manual.
- NWP 79-0-4, *Submarine Special Operations Manual-Unconventional Warfare.*
- NSW Combatant Craft TACMEMO (XL-2080-2-89).
- Dry-Deck Shelter TACMEMO (XL-2080-4-89).
- Mass Swimmer LO/LI SOP (DDS Technical Manual, Vol III).

SEA STATES

12-20. The reference for understanding and judging sea conditions is the American Practical Navigator Bowditch, Volume I. The sea-keeping characteristics of the CRRC permits operations up to Sea State 4. It is important to understand that rough weather greatly increases the risks associated with launch and recovery of CRRCs, as well as increases fuel consumption and transit times. Another important consideration is that high winds associated with higher sea states adversely affect the maneuverability of the CRRC. Higher sea states and corresponding winds will result in slower speeds and longer transit times. CRRC launch, recovery, and transits will not be routinely conducted in Sea State 4 or greater.

12-21. The mission commander must carefully weigh the tradeoffs when he decides whether operating in marginal sea conditions is feasible or advisable. The advantage offered by operating in higher sea states is a reduced vulnerability to detection by visual means and enemy electronic sensors. Higher sea states will degrade the ranges at which electronic sensors are effective, enhancing the clandestine nature of the operation and contributing to tactical surprise.

12-22. It is also important to understand that sea conditions can fluctuate rapidly. During the planning phase of an OTH operation, the commander must consider the forecasted meteorological factors that could affect the sea state during the operation. If it is likely that sea conditions at launch time will be Sea State 3, the commander should ask, "Are there any forecasted meteorological factors that may cause the sea state to go to 4 or 5 during the operation?"

12-23. Another important consideration is that sea states and surf conditions are not necessarily related to one another. A low sea state does not mean a benign surf zone; sea state conditions and surf zone conditions must be considered independent of one another.

THE SURF ZONE

12-24. A key planning consideration for a CRRC insertion will be the characteristics of the surf zone at the BLS. CRRC will not be operated in surf zones with significant breaker heights greater than 8 feet. If significant breaker heights develop above 8 feet, the judgment of the designated CRRC officer will dictate alternate options for transiting the surf zone. Significant breaker heights are determined per reference.

12-25. Detailed information on surf zone characteristics can be found in Chapters 4 and 5. Surf zone conditions are reported by a SUROB as discussed earlier.

SUROB KEY ELEMENTS

12-26. The critical considerations for CRRC surf zone operations are the significant wave height (height of the highest one-third of the breakers observed), the period (the time interval between waves measured to the nearest half-second), and the breaker type (spilling, plunging, or surging). The higher the significant wave height, the shorter the period, the greater the percentage of plunging or surging waves, and the greater the danger to CRRC surf zone operations. These critical factors must be considered both individually and in combination. The commander should also carefully evaluate the effect on CRRC operations, especially in light of boat or engine maintenance conditions and coxswain or boat-crew experience level. Trained and experienced CRRC personnel should conduct this evaluation. It should also be understood that, although these three elements are the most critical considerations, the other information contained in the SUROB is important for navigation and surf zone negotiation planning.

PLANNING AND EXECUTION CONSIDERATIONS

12-27. Surf conditions are critical in making the final determination to launch or not launch the CRRC. Once a CRRC is launched and arrives outside the surf zone at the BLS, the mission or boat commander must make the final beaching decision. If prelaunch SUROBS, visual sightings, and mission necessity warrant further surf evaluation, the mission commander may use his own scout swimmers for this purpose. The commander must consider the surf conditions as they exist at the time, his mission and command guidance, boat or engine maintenance conditions, and coxswain or boat crew training and experience level. As the CRRC officer of the boat crew and the on-scene commander trained in this capability, he is best qualified to make the final beaching decision. It's also important to understand that surf conditions, like sea states, can change rapidly. During the planning phase, the commander should routinely evaluate the forecasted meteorological factors that could adversely affect surf conditions.

SURF LIMITS

12-28. Figure 6-1, page 117, sets forth recommended operating limits for CRRC surf zone operations. The table plots breaker height versus breaker period, and is applicable to both spilling and plunging waves, or combinations of both. As already noted, plunging breakers are more dangerous to CRRC operations than spilling breakers, and greater care and judgment must be exercised as the percentage of plunging breakers increases. Surging breakers are not included in the table. These recommended surf limits are set-forth as a guide; they are not intended to usurp the judgment of officers exercising command.

DISTANCE

12-29. The point at which the CRRC is launched for OTH operations is required to be at least 20 NM from shore, but usually no more than 60 NM (normally, 35 miles is sufficient). In determining the actual distance to execute a launch, the sea state, weather, transit times, and enemy electronic detection capabilities should be considered. The commander should keep the launch platform protected and far enough away to prevent operational compromise, while minimizing the distance for the raid force.

CONTINGENCY PLANNING

12-30. A commander must include provisions for the unexpected when planning any operation. Plans must address the following contingencies and how to effectively resolve them:

- *OBM Breakdown*. Bring tools and spare parts or a spare motor, if space and time permit. Make sure a trained mechanic is available. Ensure spare parts include extra plugs and fuel filters.
- *Navigational Error*. Study permanent geographical features and known tides, currents, and winds; take into account sea state; and establish en route checkpoints. Intentionally steer to the left or right of the target so, once landfall is reached, a direction to the target is already established.

- *Low on Fuel or out of Fuel.* Run trials with a fully loaded boat in various sea states to get exact fuel consumption figures. Take enough fuel for a worst-case scenario. Carry one extra full fuel bladder.
- *Emergency MEDEVAC Procedures.* Know location of nearest medical facility. Develop primary and alternate plans for evacuating casualties.

PLANNING FOR A RENDEZVOUS AT SEA

12-31. The most critical aspect of exfiltration operations is the rendezvous at sea. An OTH rendezvous is the most difficult because of the precision navigation required to effect linkup. These difficulties are compounded when coupled with the limited navigational equipment available in small craft. A GPS and good communications can make an at-sea rendezvous relatively easy; however, these items are electronic. They are subject to shock and water damage, power failure, propagation problems, and enemy interference. These are serious problems and are frequently encountered during maritime operations. Chances are, one or all of the systems could fail at the crucial moment. At a minimum, the waterborne detachment must have access to a GPS, a compass to shoot bearings with, and a compass to steer the CRRC. To avoid a long swim home, it is a good idea to make the designated rendezvous.

12-32. The most crucial portion of any rendezvous procedure is prior planning, which begins with a NAVPLAN. The commander should start with the worst-case scenario and try to cover all contingencies. The NAVPLAN must include primary and alternate plans that are well developed, realistic, and achievable. Every attempt should be made to adhere to it as closely as possible. Both primary and contingency plans must be complete with built-in fudge factors to allow for variances in time of transit and actual fuel consumption. All plans must include primary and alternate rendezvous locations, each with its own signal plan. The signal plan should encompass audible and visual recognitions—challenge and reply, time windows, and radio frequencies with a method of changing from primary to alternate. Plans must be thoroughly briefed for all possible contingencies and backup plans. Figure 11-5 provides a sample rendezvous plan.

12-33. On occasion, the CRRC formation will still be out of position and the mother ship will have to (if possible) vector the detachment to the rendezvous, or move from the designated rendezvous point to the detachment to effect the linkup (depending on the capabilities of the mother ship).

RAIDING CRAFT DETECTABILITY AND CLASSIFICATION COUNTERMEASURES

12-34. Ideally, SFODs conducting a waterborne infiltration will have done a complete area assessment and selected a minimum-risk route (MRR) for their infiltration. MRRs will seek to avoid known or suspected enemy detection and surveillance facilities or capabilities. Information on enemy capabilities can be obtained from the N-2, S-2, or the JIC. All of these sources can provide an analysis of enemy detection facilities in the vicinity of the target and their respective capabilities. If mission requirements dictate an infiltration or exfiltration route that will pass within detection range of an enemy installation, consideration must be given to detection countermeasures.

12-35. Detection threats are determined by the ranges of the detection systems, the expertise of the operators, and the amount of time that the detachment spends inside the threat system's detection range. The most common enemy detection systems include active and passive sonar arrays and shore-based shipboard and airborne radar systems. Other technical assets include forward-looking infrared (FLIR) or thermal imaging systems and night vision goggles (NVGs) or optics. These are most likely to be encountered in conjunction with coastal patrol craft, coast watchers, and informants such as "loyal citizens" reporting unusual activities to the authorities. Any one of these can be defeated by deception, distraction, or bypassing. The detachment's goal is to prevent the CRRC formation from being detected and identified or classified as a threat. Unfortunately, the better integrated and more sophisticated the enemy's "defense in-depth" is, the more difficult it will be to defeat.

12-36. The easiest way to defeat a detection system is to avoid it. Detachment personnel should locate the enemy radar positions and establish fans of coverage. They should take these fans and the level of operator proficiency into consideration during mission planning. They should make sure to select routes and destinations outside the system's detection range. If the system cannot be avoided, personnel should select a route that will take advantage of terrain masking. The detachment may be able to find a corridor or gap in the coverage that will allow it to bypass the threat,

1. Pick up sites:
   a. Primary Rendezvous: 3245 34n 11734 23w 0100-0130 13 Jan 94.
   b. Alternate Rendezvous: 3237 30n 11729 30w 0230-0300 13 Jan 94.
2. VHF primary: 32.90 MHz; HF primary ______; UHF primary________
   alternate: 36.50 MHz; alternate ______; alternate ________
3. Call signs:
   a. Detachment—Frogman.
   b. USS Shoe Factory—Paint Chipper.
4. Signal:
   a. Visual:

	Signal	Reply
Primary:	IR strobe	three red
Alternate:	directional white strobe	three red

NOTE: Think of direction flashed or shone and the possibility of compromise by the enemy.

   b. Audible:
      Primary: pinger vector by ship/visual signal.
      Alternate: M 80s vector by ship/visual signal.
   c. Challenge and reply signal:
      Primary time and place: approach primary visual signal.
      Direction: then primary signal.
      Alternate communications: code words.
5. Procedure:
   a. Navigate to rendezvous site and check navigation by all means available.
   b. Initiate primary signal at beginning of window.
   c. If ship is visible, wait for proper visual reply.
   d. Proceed to mother ship and begin recovery procedures.
6. Contingency plans to cover at least the following cases:
   a. Unable to make primary rendezvous due to time; move directly to alternate rendezvous.
   b. Threat at or near primary rendezvous; move to alternate.
   c. Ship is not visible at rendezvous point:
      (1) Recheck navigation and confirm position.
      (2) Carry out rendezvous procedure
      (3) At end of rendezvous time window, move to alternate rendezvous and carry out rendezvous procedure.
   d. Mother ship not at alternate rendezvous or threat at alternate rendezvous:
      (1) Move back to shore.
      (2) Cache.
      (3) Carry out secondary night rendezvous procedure.

NOTE: Think of emergency pickup or hot extraction plan and fire support plan. Plan and brief thoroughly and when conducting operation, never rely fully on GPS. Always crosscheck navigation with speed, time, and distance.

Figure 12-5. Sample rendezvous plan

or a natural obstruction that will shield the detachment from detection. This method is particularly useful with shore-based and shipboard (low-altitude) radar systems, as well as active visual observation methods such as coast watchers. Some high-altitude radars may have a blind spot immediately under them that can be exploited by a detachment posing as commercial shipping that would be able to launch from a mother ship close enough to get under the radar's minimum detection range. Unfortunately, the greatly increased detection ranges of airborne radars may cancel any air operation even if the infiltration aircraft is able to imitate civilian traffic.

12-37. Detachments facing a surface radar threat have to consider the strength of the radar signal versus the quantity and quality of local traffic. The greater the signal strength, the greater the range or the better the target discrimination. Because CRRCs have such a small signature, it is possible to lose them in the "clutter" of false returns in congested areas. Specific techniques for confusing enemy radars to avoid detection or classification include the following:

- Coordinate with Naval assets for EA-6B air support for the mission. These aircraft may be able to jam enemy radar in or near the detachment's vicinity, the vicinity of the target, or the BLS.
- Launch the CRRCs from the support vessel at greater intervals with each craft traveling in pairs to a RV point off of the BLS (or at the BLS) where the entire force converges. With greater separation, the craft are less vulnerable to detection. GPS navigation and a foolproof linkup plan will simplify the operation.
- Move at slower speeds to reduce the wake size and thus the radar signature.
- If the detachment is infiltrating in the vicinity of commercial shipping lanes, it can take advantage of merchant traffic to mask the movement of the CRRC formation. A good technique is to place a larger vessel (commercial or fishing) between the detachment and any threat radars. Traveling in the wake or to the flank of the larger vessel will keep the detachment masked by the ship's structure, wake, or waves. This technique carries its own risks of compromise by the same merchant traffic that the detachment is using to screen its movement.
- Group the CRRCs together to provide a radar return similar to a commercial or fishing vessel. Move at the same speeds as indigenous vessels and other harbor or local traffic simulating their radar return.

12-38. If traffic in the area is tightly controlled by the enemy, sonar arrays, when present, may prevent the use of CRRCs. The detachment should seek S-2, N-2, or JIC assistance to determine if the enemy possesses this capability and the locations where it is used. It should avoid these locations wherever possible. Methods to reduce the risks presented by sonar include the following:

- Take advantage of the presence of large commercial vessels that tend to wipe out sonar's ability to detect OBMs due to the increased background noises.
- Paddle the CRRCs into the BLS from a designated point outside of sonar range.
- Coordinate with naval assets to increase underwater noise by whatever means available; for example, high-speed coastal ships and hydrophones.
- Small fishing vessels often use OBMs for propulsion. Determine the types, times, and locations where they are active and, if possible, plan the operation to coincide with their activity.

12-39. Detachment personnel should seek S-2, N-2, or JIC assistance to determine if the enemy possesses a FLIR or other thermal-imaging capability and the locations where it is used. Again, these locations should be avoided wherever possible. Methods to reduce the risks presented by FLIR include the following:

- Ensure that the CRRCs are kept as close to the operating water temperature as possible.
- Use covers made of insulating material to place over the OBM cover when pursued, when within range of a possible FLIR or thermal imager, or when within range of thermal devices on the BLS.

12-40. To reduce the possibility of compromise by other visual imaging techniques such as NVGs or optics, the detachment should plan operations during rain, fog, or other inclement weather. Smoke pots or smoke grenades can be used to conceal movement by floating or dragging them behind the CRRC during withdrawal, contact, or pursuit. Wherever possible, minimize the risks by avoiding known patrolled areas.

Two If By Land: Special Forces Use of Pack Animals

Preface

This field manual (FM) is a guide for Special Forces (SF) personnel to use when conducting training or combat situations using pack animals. It is not a substitute for training with pack animals in the field. This manual provides the techniques of animal pack transport and for organizing and operating pack animal units. It captures some of the expertise and techniques that have been lost in the United States (U.S.) Army over the last 50 years. Care, feeding, and veterinary medicine constitute a considerable portion of the manual; however, this material is not intended as a substitute for veterinary expertise nor will it make a veterinarian out of the reader. SF personnel must have a basic knowledge of anatomy and physiology, common injuries, diseases (particularly of the feet), feeding, watering, and packing loads to properly care for the animals and to avoid abusing them from overloading or overworking.

Though many types of beasts of burden may be used for pack transportation, this manual focuses on horses, mules, donkeys, and a few other animals. One cannot learn how to pack an animal by reading; there is no substitute for having a horse or mule while practicing how to load a packsaddle for military operations. However, the manual is useful for anyone going into an environment where these skills are applicable.

The most common measurements used in pack animal operations are expressed throughout the text and in many cases are U.S. standard terms rather than metric.

CHAPTER 1

Military Pack Animal Operations

Since the deactivation of the pack transport units after the Korean Conflict, the Army has relied on air and ground mobility for transporting personnel and equipment. Today and throughout the operational continuum, SF may find themselves involved in operations in rural or remote environments, such as Operations UPHOLD DEMOCRACY or ENDURING FREEDOM, using pack animals.

SF personnel must conduct a detailed mission analysis to determine the need for pack animals in support of their mission. Military pack animal operations are one of the options available to a commander to move personnel and equipment into or within a designated area of operations (AO). Pack animal operations are ideally suited for, but not limited to, conducting various missions in high mountain terrain, deserts, and dense jungle terrain.

Personnel must have a thorough understanding of all the factors that can impact military pack animal operations. The objective of this chapter is to familiarize the reader with military pack animal operations and to outline the planning considerations needed to successfully execute them.

CHARACTERISTICS

1-1. Commanders use military pack animal operations when the AO restricts normal methods of transport or resupply. Animal transport systems can greatly increase mission success when hostile elements and conditions require the movement of combat troops and equipment by foot.

1-2. The weight bearing capacity of pack animals allows ground elements to travel longer distances with less personnel fatigue. The pack train can move effectively and efficiently in the most difficult of environments with conditioned animals, proper/modern equipment, and personnel with a moderate amount of training in handling packs. The pack detachment, without trail preparation, can traverse steep grades and heavily wooded areas, and can maintain acceptable speeds over terrain that is not mountainous, carrying 35 percent of their body maximum (150 to 300 pounds [1b]). This amount should be decreased for loads that are prone to excessive rocking as the animal walks (for example, top-heavy loads and bulky loads). This capability continues indefinitely as long as the animals receive proper care and feed. In mountainous terrain, with no reduction in payload, the mule or horse can travel from 20 to 30 miles per day.

1-3. The success of pack operations, under extreme weather and terrain conditions, depends on the selection and training of personnel and animals. Personnel involved in pack animal operations require extensive knowledge of pack animal organization and movement, animal management, animal health care, pack equipment, and load planning. Planning the use of pack animals is not a simple task, nor is it always a satisfactory solution to a transportation problem.

1-4. When used correctly, pack animal operations give commanders another means to move Special Forces operational detachments (SFODs) and influence the battlefield. The skills and techniques used in pack animal operations are applicable to all SF missions.

PLANNING CONSIDERATIONS

1-5. Successful pack animal operations depend on thorough mission planning, preparation, coordination, and rehearsals. Initial mission planning should include a mission, enemy, terrain and weather, troops and support available—time available and civil considerations (METT-TC) analysis to assist in determining whether or not to use pack animals in a mission. Analyzing the METT-TC questions (Table 1-1) will enable the executing element to consider all factors involved when using pack animals in their mission profile.

Table 1-1. METT-TC analysis

Factors	Questions
Mission	• What is the duration of the mission? • What type of terrain does the operational area comprise and at what altitude is it located? • Does the mission profile require a lot of movement? Is the projected rate of foot movement feasible? • Is the operational area conducive to pack animal use? Is the mission time-critical?
Enemy	• How will the enemy threat, capabilities, disposition, and security measures affect the mission? • Does the enemy use pack animals? • Does the enemy have a similar capability to detect or interdict conventional infiltration methods?
Terrain and Weather	• Is the terrain conducive to pack animal operations? • Does altitude prohibit or restrict pack animal operations? • Does seasonal bad weather prohibit or restrict pack animal use? • Does the detachment have experience navigating pack animals in limited visibility conditions?
Troops and Support Available	• Does the detachment have the training and experience to successfully execute pack animal operations? • Are pack animals available for training and rehearsals? • What types of pack animals are available in the operational area? • What special equipment is required to conduct pack animal operations? • What is the anticipated duration of the operation? • Are there areas for the animal to graze or forage? • Does the detachment have the means to infiltrate the required equipment into the AO? • Does the equipment require special rigging? Does it have special handling and storage requirements? • Is the detachment going to use the local pack equipment? Does the detachment know about local pack equipment? • Does the detachment need to hire a local handler to pack the animals? Will the handler travel far from home?
Time Available	• Is time available for the detachment to plan and rehearse pack animal use before mission execution? • Will time be available on the ground for the detachment to rehearse packing the animals? • Will there be time to acquire local equipment and feed, and to inspect animals if needed?
Civil Considerations	• Can the operation be executed clandestinely so that the civilian populace is unaware of it? • If the operation is compromised, what will be the repercussions to the local populace? • If the detachment is receiving support from the locals, is there a risk of reprisals against them?

1-6. A thorough METT-TC analysis concentrating on the above questions pertaining to pack animal operations will determine if pack animal use is appropriate. The detachment must then complete the remainder of the mission planning process.

CHAPTER 2

Animal Management

The survivability of a pack animal detachment and its ability to successfully complete a mission depend on the animals and their management. Historically, animals of all types and sizes have been successfully used for pack transportation throughout the world. Animals indigenous to the AO are usually more effective than imported animals. Although native animals may be smaller and not ideally proportioned, they are acclimated to the environment, generally immune to local afflictions, and accustomed to the native forage. Nevertheless, any animal locally procured needs to be thoroughly inspected for disease and physical soundness. Animal management entails selection, feed, and feeding along with stable management. Employing an untrained pack master, making poor animal selections, and improperly feeding the pack animals could prove disastrous for the detachment.

MULE CHARACTERISTICS

2-1. Mules are the hybrid product of a male donkey and a female horse (Figure 2-1). Male mules are called Johns and female mules are called mollies or mare mules. Mollies are a cross between male donkeys and Belgium horse mares. Mollies generally have a gentler disposition than Johns. Intelligence, agility, and stamina are all characteristics of mules. These qualities make mules excellent pack animals. Unlike horses, which carry about 65 percent of their weight on their front legs, mules carry 55 percent on their front legs. This trait makes them very well balanced and surefooted in rugged terrain.

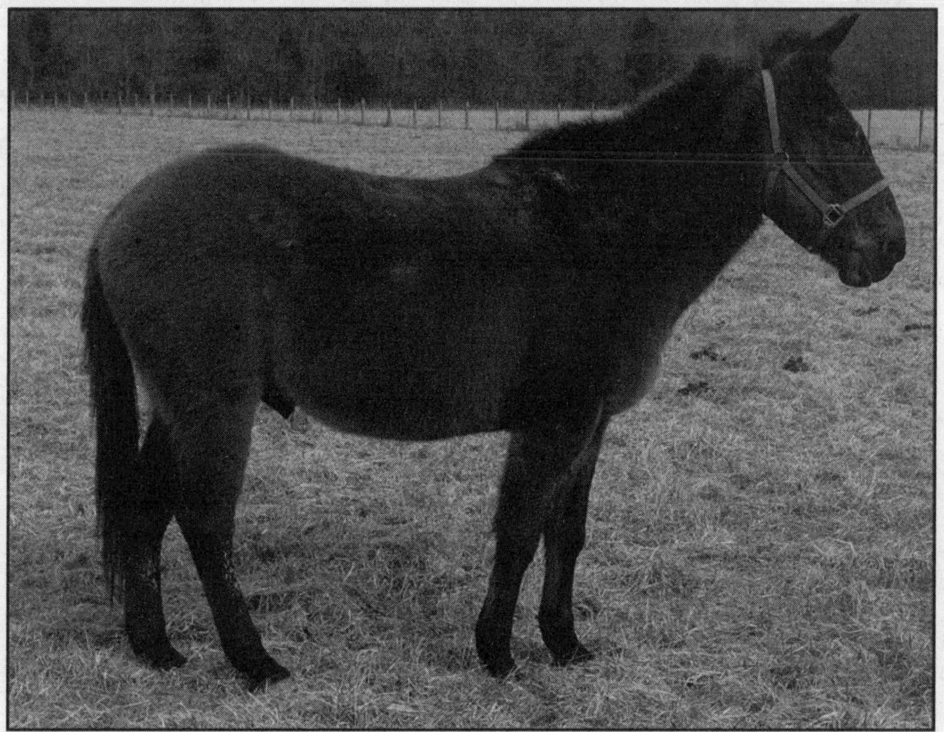

Figure 2-1. Mule

2-2. Some people think stubbornness is a mule characteristic—stubborn as a mule! Mules are intelligent and possess a strong sense of self-preservation. A packer cannot make a mule do something if the mule thinks it will get hurt, no matter how much persuasion is used. Therefore, many people confuse this trait with stubbornness. Mules form close bonds with horses, especially mares. The bond is so close that mules willingly follow a mare. That is why a mare will usually be wearing a bell leading a string of mules. A wrangler, or mule skinner, can usually control an entire pack string simply by controlling the bell mare. At night in the backcountry, mule skinners can picket the bell mare and turn the mules loose. The mules will disperse and graze freely, yet remain close to the mare. Environmental impacts are reduced and the mules are easy to gather in the morning.

2-3. Young mules are naturally and easily startled but if treated with great patience and kindness can easily be broken in. All harsh treatment of any kind must be avoided or could prove to be fatal to successful training.

DONKEY CHARACTERISTICS

2-4. The first thing a person thinks of when a donkey comes to mind is what? Big ears? Or maybe a short whisk broom tail? Figure 2-2 shows the donkey's features, which help him succeed and survive in a harsh environment. Donkeys vary in size and provide different levels of transport. A detachment can use any of the following-sized donkeys:

- Miniature: up to 36 inches.
- Small standard: 36 to 40 inches.
- Standard: 41 to 48 inches.
- Large standard: 48 to 56 inches.
- Mammoth jack stock: 54 inches and up for jennets (females); 56 inches and up for jacks (males).

2-5. Donkeys evolved in the desert. Because food was usually scarce, high concentrations of donkeys in one area were not possible. Donkeys still have to drink water daily, but due to desert adaptations, their bodies do not waste or lose moisture as readily as does a horse. The donkey's body extracts most of the moisture from his own feces and

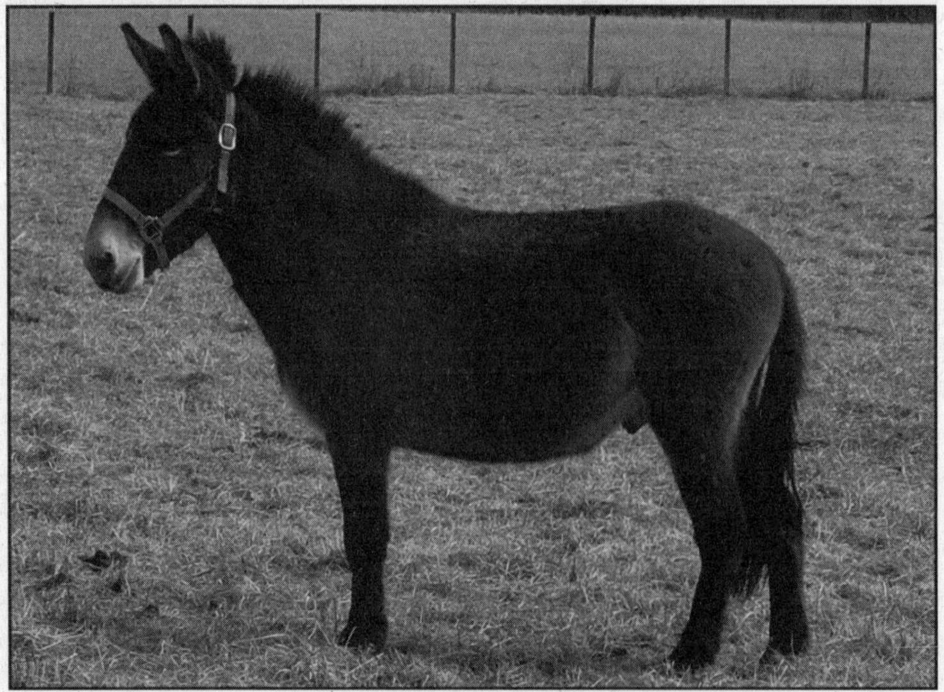

Figure 2-2. Donkey

does not need to sweat as much as a horse would (a donkey does not have large muscle mass to always have to keep cool), which makes him a better water conservationist.

2-6. The donkey's mighty bray allowed even widely spaced donkeys to keep in contact or define their territories. Their big funnel-shaped ears could catch the distant calls and maybe help dissipate some hot desert heat. Their ears also serve as a visual communication system, telegraphing danger or asinine moods. They punctuate their "ear-ial" code messages with tail swishes, body language, and of course, grunts and moans.

2-7. Other special characteristics of donkeys are tough, compact hooves that can handle sand and rock, woolly hair to insulate from desert heat and cold, and a lean body mass that is fuel-efficient and easily cooled, yet very strong and enduring. They also have a digestive system that can break down almost inedible roughage while at the same time extracting and saving moisture in an arid environment. Donkeys have only five lumbar vertebrae compared to most horses, which have six. They also generally have upright, sparse, spiky manes with no forelock.

2-8. Donkeys come in various colors, but the most common (for standards and miniatures) is the mouse gray called gray dun. There are spotted donkeys, white donkeys, various shades of brown that breeders refer to as "chocolate," black donkeys, sorrel donkeys, and even pink donkeys, which have light, red hair mixed with a gray dun coat giving the illusion of pink. There are also various roan and frost patterns. Donkeys come with or without a cross, leg stripes, or collar buttons. Most have white muzzles, eye rings, and light bellies. Mammoth jack stock tend to not have crosses and usually are seen as black, red, red roan, blue, blue roan, and spotted combinations, to name a few.

2-9. Regardless of the packaging and through the ages, different countries bred the donkey in whatever form they needed (the donkey had many uses then, as it still does today—riding, packing, draft work, creating mules), so donkeys now come in any size (from 64-inch-plus mammoths to 28-inch-or- less miniatures), shape, coat color, and length of hair. But inside all is the same gentle, calm, and slightly mischievous soul.

2-10. Donkeys are cautious of changes in their environment. Donkeys have a strong sense of survival. If they deem something as dangerous, they will not do it. It is not stubbornness—it is Mother Nature, and they are smart enough to know when they cannot handle something. A handler should never lose his temper or use brute force to accomplish a task because the donkey will then fear his handler for life. Yet, with trust and confidence in their handlers, donkeys will go along with what tasks are necessary and accomplish the mission.

2-11. Donkeys, because of the rugged terrain that they evolved in, could not just run away from danger in absolute panic. Running without caution simply placed them in further peril. Natural selection weeded out the less intelligent, so that now donkeys generally will freeze when frightened or run a little way then stop to look at what startled them. (This instinct to freeze rather than flee is what is so desired in the mule, along with the donkey's stamina and intelligence.) Donkeys will also naturally attack canines to protect themselves and their young (or if properly conditioned, a donkey will also protect sheep and goats).

2-12. This strong, calm, intelligent worker that does not tend to run away in terror after being spooked and has a natural inclination to like people adds up to an animal that is easy to take care of and easy to work.

2-13. Table 2-1 explains the differences in the makeup of the equine family.

Table 2-1. Equine comparisons

Features	Donkey	Mule	Horse
Ears	Long.	Medium (depends).	Short.
Muzzle	Normally white.	Normally tan.	Usually same color as entire face; bare in the summer.
Eye Rings	White.	Lacking, though shape of orbital eye sockets usually distinctive in the mule.	Lacking.
Chest	Smooth muscling over chest, not divided.	Smooth muscling over chest, normally not divided.	Divided breast muscles over thickly muscled chest.

Table 2-1. Equine comparisons (*Continued*)

Features	Donkey	Mule	Horse
Belly	Usually white.	Color same as body.	Color same as body.
Vertebrae	Usually has 5 lumbar vertebrae.	Not documented; usually depends on genetics from parents.	Normally has 6 lumbar vertebrae (some barbs and mustangs have only 5).
Head	Wide between eyes and crown with a much bigger jaw.	Usually intermediate, but normally larger than a horse's; has a wider brow and jaw.	Usually petite in comparison to long-eared counterparts.
Withers	Usually lacking distinctive horse withers; can make the back appear even longer.	Usually lacking withers in comparison to the horse.	Average horse has a 2- to 4-inch prominence above and forward of the back line.
Hip and Hindquarters	Normally steeper than a horse; croup can be somewhat peaked.	Varies depending on bloodlines; normally reflects the smooth muscling of the donkey but with a larger muscle mass. Top lines can reflect either parent.	Normally more muscled than mules and donkeys; muscle groups are defined depending on breed.
Chestnuts	Have only front, which are flat, soft, and leathery.	Can follow either parent or be a mixture of the two.	Normally one on each leg; thick, horny protrusions that grow and sometimes require trimming.
Tail	Has longer coarse tail hairs on the bottom third, short hairs at the top third.	Normally tailed like a horse, though often not as full in body, with stiffer hairs.	Normally full and long, depending upon breed.
Hooves	Normally steeper and more boxy than mules and horses; frog is more developed with a thicker sole. Hoof angles average about 65 degrees.	Usually steeper than a horse and boxier rather than oval.	Normally quite oval with walls that spread out; frog is less developed; hoof size is larger in comparison to body size than the donkey. Hoof angles average around 55 degrees.
Gestation	Average 365 days.	Not applicable.	Average 342 days.

SELECTION

2-14. Mobility and effectiveness of the pack animal detachment depend largely on the selection and training of the pack animals. The pack animal, regardless of its color, breed, or size, should have a friendly disposition, a gentle nature, and no fear of man. It should be willing to travel under a load and be sure-footed. Large, draft-type horses usually are not agile and do not make good pack animals. The ideal pack animal should be 56 to 64 inches (14 to 16 hands) tall. (Since one hand equals about 10 centimeters [cm], the metric equivalent is 140 cm to 160 cm.) It must be tough, compact, sturdy, and well-formed. Figure 2-3 shows specific parts of an ideal pack animal (horse). For additional information and a more detailed illustration of the pack animal, see *Care and Feeding of the Horse*, Lon D. Lewis, ISBN 0-68-304967-4.

ANIMAL CONFORMATION

2-15. Conformation is a term used to describe what a good pack animal should look like with regard to size, shape, height, weight, and dimensions. The single most important conformation factor is good body condition. Thin animals are poor candidates for many reasons. They should be avoided if they do not gain weight after being given adequate

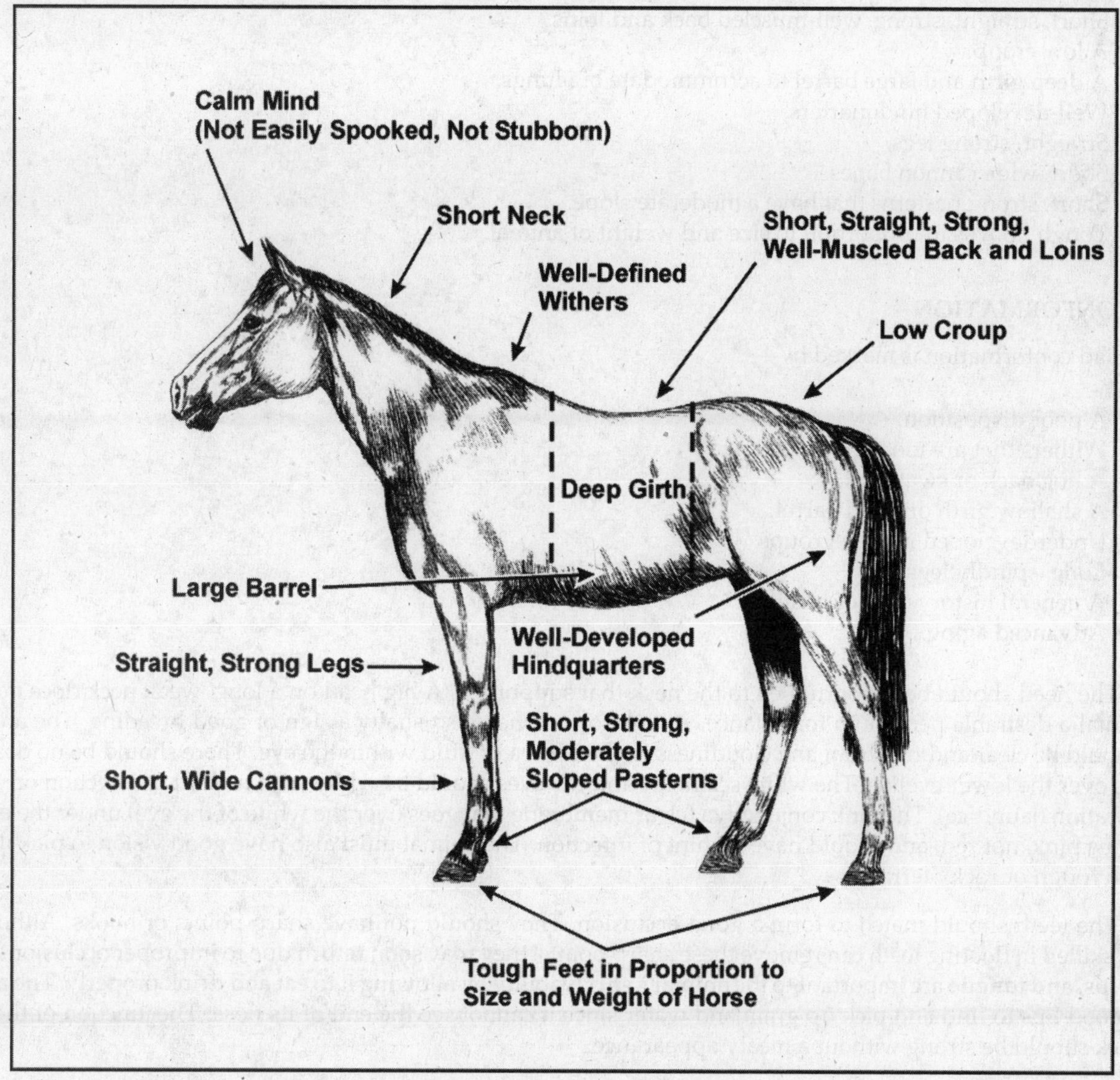

Figure 2-3. Animal conformation

nutrition. Thin animals do not tolerate the rigors of long pack trips since they have little time to eat or graze. They easily develop saddle or pack sores on their backs because of the prominence of bones. The lack of body condition may be due only to poor nutrition. However, it may be due to more serious problems such as bad teeth or chronic infection. A pack animal should be calm and not easily spooked, easy to work around and not stubborn, and should be able to socialize well with other pack animals so that it is not too timid or too aggressive.

GOOD CONFORMATION

2-16. Good conformation is marked by—

- A steady, intelligent mind.
- A short, strong neck.
- Well-defined withers that are not too high or too low.
- A large muscular chest.

- Short, straight, strong, well-muscled back and loins.
- A low croup.
- A deep girth and large barrel to accommodate big lungs.
- Well-developed hindquarters.
- Straight, strong legs.
- Short, wide cannon bones.
- Short, strong pasterns that have a moderate slope.
- Tough hooves in proportion to size and weight of animal.

BAD CONFORMATION

2-17. Bad conformation is marked by—

- A poor disposition.
- Withers that are too high or too low.
- A hog back or swayback.
- A shallow girth or small barrel.
- Underdeveloped muscle groups.
- Long, spindly legs.
- A general history of poor health.
- Advanced aging.

2-18. The head should be proportioned to the neck that supports it. A big head on a long, weak neck does not give the animal a desirable pendulum for balance. A well-formed head is usually a sign of good breeding. The animal's eyes should be clear and free from any cloudiness in the cornea or fluid within the eye. There should be no drainage of tears over the lower eyelids. The white sclera around the eyes should be white with no hint of infection or yellow discoloration (jaundice). The pink conjunctiva (clear membrane that goes over the white of the eye) under the eyelids should be pink, not red, and should have no hint of infection. The animal must also have good vision to pick its way through rough or rocky terrain.

2-19. The teeth should match to form a good occlusion. They should not have sharp points or hooks. Although a person skilled in floating teeth can remove these sharp points, they may soon return due to improper occlusion. **Good teeth, lips, and tongue** are important to the animal's survivability by allowing it to eat and drink properly. The animal needs good lips to find and pick up grain and water since it cannot see the end of its nose. The junction of the head and neck should be strong without a meaty appearance.

2-20. The neck should be proportioned to the animal's body and not too long. The animal needs strength in the neck to use its head as a pendulum and keep its balance in adverse terrain.

2-21. On a pack animal, the withers should be prominent, but not so high the packsaddle will rub or ride on it. Flat, rounded, or mutton (flat and thick) withers should be avoided because the packsaddle will not ride well on the animal. Attention is given to the height of the withers in relation to the height of the croup. An animal with withers lower than the croup has greater difficulty carrying a load because the load will constantly ride forward causing greater strain on the shoulders and forelegs. In contrast, an animal with extremely high withers and a low croup has difficulty with the load sliding back into the hip, leaving the possibility of the breast collar impeding movement and breathing.

2-22. The **shoulders** of a pack animal should be long, deep, and sloping to provide a larger surface for bearing the weight of a pack load when the animal is ascending hilly terrain. The **chest** should be muscular and deep but not too broad.

2-23. The legs should be straight, well-muscled, and free of any bulging joint capsules. The detachment should avoid animals that have any of the following characteristics on any legs or hooves:

- Club feet (foot and pastern axis of 60 degrees or more).
- Long, sloping pasterns (foot and pastern axis less than 45 degrees in front or less than 50 degrees in back).

- Short, upright pastern (foot and pastern axis more than 55 degrees in front or more than 60 degrees in back).
- Thin hoof walls.
- Thin sole.
- Buttress foot (swelling on the dorsal surface of the hoof wall at the coronary band).
- Bull-nosed foot (dubbed toe); unilateral contracted foot.
- Toed-in (pigeon-toed) or toed-out. (Normal animals will toe-in or toe-out if not trimmed correctly. The detachment should avoid animals that continue to toe-in or toe-out after trimming to ensure the bottom of the hoof [inside heel to outside heel] is perpendicular to the median plane of the body.)
- Any hoof **that** is sensitive to moderate pressure applied by a hoof tester to the toes, sole, frog, or across the heels.

2-24. There are also specific defects that pertain only to the front and back legs of the animal. The detachment should avoid animals with the following defects:

- Front legs:
  - Open-knees (enlargement of the distal growth plate of the radius and corresponding enlargement in the knee).
  - Calf-knees (backward deviation of knees).
  - Buck-knees (forward deviation of knees).
  - Offset knees or bench knees (knee sits too far medially over lower leg rather than sitting centered over lower leg).
- Rear legs:
  - Cow hooks (knock-knees).
  - Sickle leg (excessive angle of the hock).

2-25. The feet are a critical factor in the animal's ability to perform, stay physically sound, and endure the hardships of packing. Ideally, the horse should stand with its feet at a 45- to 50-degree angle to the ground. The size of the foot should be in proportion to the size of the animal. Small feet are often brittle and do not have the base to support a heavy load or absorb concussion. Large feet could cause the animal to be clumsy and awkward. Mules have a tendency to have smaller feet, but this fact does not present a problem. The sole should be slightly concave and the frog prominent, flexible, and tough. Again, when viewed from the front, an animal that is toed-out should be avoided.

2-26. The **girth** should be deep from the withers to the floor of the body, and the body should be wide and flat. This size indicates ample space for vital organs, such as the heart and lungs. The barrel should be large. A large barrel shows a good spread of the ribs that, in turn, give a good load-bearing surface on top.

2-27. The **back** should be short, strong, and well-muscled. A short back is better equipped to carry a load without sagging. Horses with one less vertebra than others would be good selections. The backbone should be prominent. A pack animal with a rounded back and ill-defined backbone is difficult to pack so that the load rides properly. Chances are good the load will slip or roll, and the detachment will waste valuable time repacking the load during movement.

2-28. The **loin** should be of moderate length, well-muscled, and broad. A long loin will cause weakness at that point. The **croup** should be low and of moderate width and slope. The hindquarters should be strong and well-developed to provide power to the animal.

CONFORMATION DEFECTS

2-29. In the selection of a pack animal, the above criteria are ideal, but many serviceable pack animals have defects in their conformation and still perform well. Nevertheless, it is better in the long run to avoid animals with many defects. Personnel should try to ensure that the larger animals carry the heaviest loads, and the gentle, experienced animals carry the fragile, easily breakable items. The smaller animals or animals with certain conformation defects should be tasked with carrying the light and not-so-fragile loads, such as food for animals and Soldiers. Bigger (size and weight) is not necessarily better. A load of 100 to 150 pounds is big enough for most packers. Heavier loads risk injury to an animal unless it is exceptionally well proportioned. The detachment probably cannot use the extra capacity anyway. The pack handler will have to lift the load in the field, and a 100-pound load is usually about as much as a person can properly lift and position by hand on a packsaddle. Between fourteen and fifteen hands (4 feet 7 inches to 5 feet 2 inches) is a good range for pack stock. (**Note:** One hand equals 10.2 cm or 4 inches.) Even men more than 6 feet tall can have difficulty loading animals that are higher.

HEALTH AND WELFARE

2-30. The health and welfare of the pack animal is a major concern of animal handlers in garrison and in the field. Each individual provides for the welfare of pack animals. Whole pack trains can be lost and missions compromised because of poor animal care. Implementing animal care will be distinctly different for field and garrison conditions even though the requirements and desired end points are the same.

FIELD MANAGEMENT

2-31. Rarely will a packer have the luxury of shelter or even corrals to hold animals in when packing. If fencing or corrals are not available, some means of limiting movement is necessary. The packer can limit movement by tying long "stake-out" lines to trees, using the high line or by using auger devices secured into the ground. These methods permit animals to graze in defined areas and provide windbreaks during cold winds. However, there are some disadvantages. The animals must be moved every few hours as they graze the available forage. Sometimes they become entangled in the stake-out lines or entangle the line in brush or rocks. Some animals panic at loud noises (for example, thunder) and snap the line or pull the auger out.

2-32. The packers can hobble the animals by tying their front legs together with just enough space between their legs to take small steps but not run. They can secure the hobbles around the pastern or above the knees. Pastern hobbles (American hobbles) are easier to apply and maintain but can cause some animals to become entangled in brush or rock. Hobbles above the knees (Australian hobbles) are more difficult to apply and maintain but prevent entanglement with brush and rocks. Packers must slowly acclimate animals to hobbles in garrison before using the hobbles for an extended time on pack trips. Figure 2-4 shows two types of hobbles that the handler can use for various purposes.

2-33. The animals must have as much access to good forage as possible. This need means that packers should include probable grazing areas in their movement schedules. Even with optimal grazing, pack animal detachments take additional supplemental feed (in the form of grain) because the animals do not have enough time to graze and rest after carrying packs for much of the day. Also, the grazing is often less than optimal and the animals have to range over considerable distances to obtain adequate nutrition.

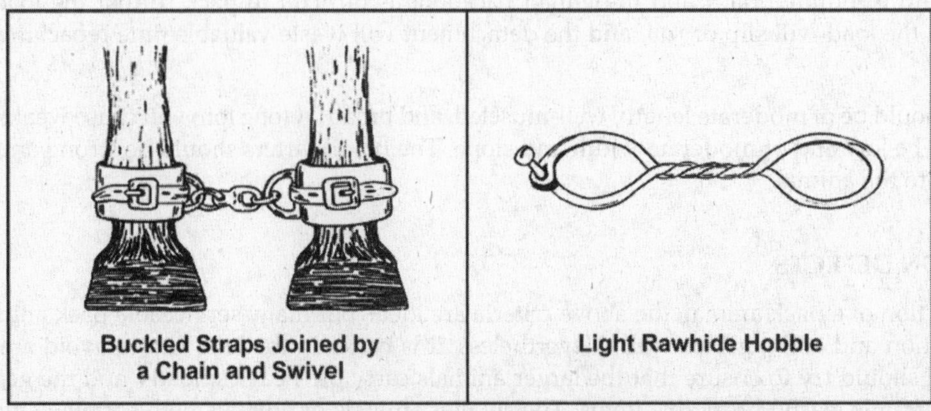

Figure 2-4. Two types of hobbles

> **NOTE**
> Pack animal detachments can also consider using portable electric fencing. However, a few animals are not deterred under normal conditions, and most animals are not deterred if spooked by thunder and lightning.

SHELTERED HOUSING FACILITY (STABLE BUILDING)

2-34. In an unconventional warfare (UW) scenario, the pack animal detachment will probably not have the luxury of a permanent or semipermanent stable facility. However, most of the field routines may be applied in stables by support personnel before the mission or after the unit has completed their operation.

2-35. The detachment commander has command responsibility for stable management and the training of his Soldiers. However, subordinate leaders are directly responsible for stable management and the stable routine.

2-36. Stable management includes the supervision and maintenance of the stables and other facilities. The subordinate leaders will ensure the grounds and buildings in the stable area are kept as clean and sanitary as available time and labor will allow and that the grounds are reasonably level and well drained. They will also ensure the animals are well-groomed, properly shod, and free of injuries and diseases. Since a large number of animals may be involved in a pack animal detachment, subordinate leaders should keep records at the stables on all the assigned animals.

2-37. The design and construction of a stable facility may be limited to the materials at hand. Regardless of the materials used, the stable should provide adequate shelter, good ventilation, and few maintenance requirements. The stable building should provide ready access to the corrals and storage for feed and packing equipment.

STALLS

2-38. Stalls vary in size depending on the average size of the animals, amount of time the animals are expected to spend in the stall, and available space. A 12- by 12-foot stall allows freedom for a large horse or mule to maintain fair physical condition during long periods of idleness while confined to stables. Stalls of this size are normally used for recuperation, foaling of mares, and protection in extreme climates. A 10- by 10-foot stall is normally satisfactory when animals are in stables only for feeding and rest. To reduce waste in feeding hay and grain, the stalls should be equipped with hayracks and feed boxes. Stall walls must be free of sharp or rough projections and unfinished woodwork. A major concern when dealing with animal care is the construction and maintenance of stall floors. The floor should be level and have good drainage. It should also be resilient to help maintain a healthy condition of the animals' feet and legs. The floor should also be nonabsorptive for cleanliness and sanitation. Earthen floors composed of clay are satisfactory but require continual work to clean, level, and smooth. Rough-finished concrete provides the best type of floor because it is sanitary, is easy to clean, and requires little maintenance. However, a concrete floor having little resilience must be covered with a bedding of straw or hay for cushion. Wooden floors, even if impregnated, are not desirable since they are slippery and unsanitary. Because of their porosity, they cannot be adequately disinfected such as would be necessary during a Salmonella outbreak. Regardless of the floor chosen, a good bed contributes to the comfort and efficiency of the animals. A clean, comfortable bed will induce the animal to lie down and get better rest. It provides a soft surface that will prevent bruising or abrasion of elbows, hocks, and other body parts. It also provides insulation for the body and a comfortable surface for the animal to stand.

2-39. Horses and mules are herd animals and do not thrive in stalls. This confinement can lead to behavioral problems that would not be experienced when the animals are kept in a field environment.

STORAGE

2-40. Storage facilities provide protection and security for feed and tack. They should also be convenient to the stables and corral. Feed storage should provide protection from rodents, water, and any loose animals that may overeat. When possible, personnel should stack feed on pallets (best), plastic sheets (second best), or boards so that it is not in direct contact with the ground. Feed should be stacked at least 6 inches from walls to discourage rodents.

Rodents prefer narrow spaces to avoid predators, and the extra distance decreases the frequency of rodent visits. When covering feed outside, there should be no pinpoint holes in the cover because they are just enough to cause spoilage if it rains. The detachment should also arrange to minimize time and personnel necessary for feeding. A tack room should be planned for each stable and partitioned from the stall area. It should have facilities for inspection, cleaning, preserving, repair, and storage of all pack and riding saddles, bridles, halters, panniers, and accessories for the detachment.

CORRALS

2-41. The pack animal detachment should provide corrals for the animals to move freely and exercise when they are not in use or in the stalls. The corrals should be close and easily accessible to the stables, be well drained, and provide good footing. Personnel should fill and level, as much as possible, any depressions and heavily traveled areas where water can collect. They should set fences at a sufficient height and strength to ensure the safekeeping of the animals. Fences and gates should be of a height above the base of the horse's neck to prevent escape or injury in attempts to escape. The fence should be free of sharp or rough projections, exposed nails, and edges prone to splintering with pressure or rubbing. The animals should have water troughs or tanks to allow them free access to water. The containers should be large enough to allow the watering of several animals without congestion. Individual feed boxes or buckets are much better than shared bunks to control contagious diseases and minimize fighting. If feed bunks are used, they should provide at least 3 feet of bunk space per animal with no more than four animals per bunk to decrease fighting over feed and to prevent one dominant animal from eating more feed than the others. Handlers should establish hitching posts or a picket line to groom or pack the animals. The footing at the picket line must be strong enough to sustain heavy use. The line should be established on high ground so water (even if dry season), urine, and feces do not accumulate around the picket line. Also useful is a foundation of stone cover with coarse (but smooth) gravel or sand. Personnel should try to avoid fine gravel or coarse gravel with rough edges as these can lodge in the frog or sulcus. If there is no natural shelter from the sun and bad weather, the handler should provide shelter for the animal's protection.

SOCIAL DOMINANCE

2-42. Horses (and mules) develop a social hierarchy or "pecking order." All animals in the herd respect this hierarchy. Fighting and injury prevail until the hierarchy is established. Once the hierarchy is established, fighting decreases. The hierarchy can change as new animals are introduced or as dominant animals age or become debilitated.

2-43. The handler should let the animals establish their hierarchy but manage it so as to minimize the injuries as the hierarchy forms. Introducing new animals to the herd with a wooden fence (or other similar barrier) separating them will help in managing the herd. This method decreases the chances of kick and bite injuries as subordinate animals try to escape.

2-44. The hierarchy can be very helpful if understood and used. The dominant animals fight to be at the front of the pack line and fight to eat first. Handlers should identify the dominant and subordinate animals and place them in the pack line according to the hierarchy. Likewise, the animals should be fed in the same order to reinforce the existing hierarchy. Attempting to alter the hierarchy will likely result in an even greater effort of the horses or mules to reestablish the hierarchy, leading to fighting and injury.

SANITATION

2-45. Sanitizing at the stables and in the field is a continuous process for maintaining the health of animals and personnel. Stables and corrals must be kept clean to reduce the breeding of flies, which is one of the most serious sanitation problems that lead to disease and infection. The most effective countermeasure to reduce flies is to reduce moisture and harborage. Good drainage and the removal of wet or soiled bedding help control moisture. Eliminating areas favorable to fly breeding and hatching—that is, moist, dark areas with organic material—controls fly harborage. Personnel should also brush out all feed boxes daily and scrub them monthly. Individual watering buckets or troughs are preferred. If this is not possible, the water trough should be drained and cleaned weekly. Only the animals belonging to the detachment should drink from these troughs. Most importantly, personnel should ensure birds cannot defecate in the troughs, and rodents cannot swim in them. Any animals suffering from a communicable disease should be watered from a bucket that is thoroughly cleaned and disinfected after each use and not shared with other animals.

FEED AND WATER

2-46. The health, condition, and effectiveness of a pack animal directly relate to the type and amount of food being consumed. The animal handler determines the amount and type of food by the amount and type of work to be performed. The working animal needs more concentrates (proteins, minerals) in its diet to supply fuel for energy, replacement of tissue, and maintenance of condition. An idle animal does not require as many nutrients in its diet. Personnel in the pack animal detachment need to have a basic knowledge of feed grains and roughage, their characteristics, and their geographical availability. This information is also critical for operational planning.

FEED REQUIREMENTS

2-47. The body requires food for growth, repair of body tissue, and energy for movement. The body also needs food to maintain temperature and energy for such vital functions as circulation, respiration, and digestion. Protein from feeds such as oats, barley, corn, and bran provide for body growth and repair of tissue. Minerals from feeds such as grass, hay, bran, and bone meal are needed for healthy bones. Carbohydrates and fats from feed such as corn, wheat, rye, and oats produce heat and energy or are stored as fat and sugar as an energy food reserve. Bulk feeds such as hay, grass, bran, and oats are necessary for digestion. Most foods, with the exception of hay or good forage, do not contain all the necessary nutrients for horses and mules; therefore, foods are combined to obtain the desired nutritional value. Oats are the best grain feed for stabled animals. For animals on pasture, natural grasses come closest to providing all required nutrients. The nutritional value of feed is measured in terms of the amount and proportions of digestible nutrients it supplies.

2-48. A ration is the feed allowed one animal for 24 hours, usually fed in two portions, morning and evening. The components of a ration depend upon the class and condition of the animals, the work being done, the variety of available foods, the kind of shelter provided, the climate, and the season. Feed must be selected and combined, proportionately, to form a balanced ration that consists of proteins, carbohydrates, fats, minerals, and vitamins. Pack animals cannot thrive on concentrated foods alone. They need both forage and concentrates, but the ratios need to be controlled as explained below. Quantities of feed in one ration vary depending on the amount of idle time the animals have, the work being performed, and the availability of the feed. Insufficient feed—particularly bulky feed—causes loss of conditioning, general weakness, and predisposes an animal to disease. Too much feed can be wasteful and cause an animal to be overweight. An animal that is too heavy will tire prematurely, suffer heat stress, and possibly develop laminitis (lameness caused by swelling of the feet).

GUIDELINES FOR FEEDING

2-49. All pack animal handlers should adhere to specific principles for optimal feeding. The following paragraphs explain each of these principles.

2-50. **Feed to Maintain a Body Condition Score (BCS)** of 5. Table 2-2 clarifies the differences seen with different BCSs. It is important for animals to maintain a BCS of 5 for several reasons. If animals are too thin, they will—

- Be prone to saddle sores because the bones (especially the withers) will protrude.
- Have less energy and be sluggish.
- Have less body reserve to sustain them if rations are unavailable.
- Be more susceptible to infections and contagious diseases.

2-51. Handlers must also be aware of the opposite effect. If animals become too heavy, they will—

- Be wasting feed that may be needed later.
- Be predisposed to heat stress.
- Be predisposed to premature exhaustion.
- Cause their packs not to fit well.
- Be prone to laminitis and other problems of lameness.

Table 2-2. Horse's appearance associated with dietary energy intake

BCS	Descriptions
2–Very Thin	Animal emaciated; slight fat covers base of spinous process; transverse processes of lumbar vertebrae feel rounded; spinous processes, ribs, tailhead, tuber coxae, and tuber ischii prominent; withers, shoulders, and neck structure faintly discernible.
3–Thin	Fat buildup about halfway on spinous process; transverse process cannot be felt; slight fat cover over ribs; spinous processes and ribs easily discernible; tailhead prominent, but individual vertebra cannot be identified visually; tuber coxae appear rounded but easily discernible; tuber ischii not distinguishable; withers, shoulders, and neck not obviously thin.
4–Moderately Thin	Slight ridge along back; faint outline of ribs discernible; tailhead prominence depends on conformation, but fat can be felt around it; tuber coxae not discernible; withers, shoulders, and neck not obviously thin.
5–Moderate	Back is flat (no crease or ridge); ribs not visually distinguishable but easily felt. Fat around tailhead slightly spongy; withers appear rounded over spinous process; shoulders and neck blend smoothly into body.
6–Moderately Fleshy	May have slight crease down back; fat over ribs spongy, fat around tailhead soft; fat beginning to be deposited along the side of withers, behind the shoulder, and along the side of the neck.
7–Fleshy	May have crease down back; individual ribs can be felt, but there is a noticeable filling between ribs with fat; fat around tailhead soft; fat deposits along withers, behind shoulders, and along the neck.
8–Fat	Crease down back; difficult to feel ribs; fat around tailhead very soft; area along withers filled with fat; area behind shoulders filled with fat; noticeable thickening of neck; fat deposits along inner thighs.

Sources: *Care and Feeding of the Horse.* Lon D. Lewis. 2d Ed., Williams and Wilkins, 1996. *Nutrient Requirements of Horses.* National Academy Press, 5th Ed., Washington, DC, 1989.

NOTE

A BCS of 5 indicates the proper amount of dietary energy intake; 3 or less indicates inadequate energy intake; and 7 or greater indicates excess energy intake.

2-52. **Feed According to the Animal's Feeding Weight.** Dietary intake is best determined by adjusting the ration first to the animal's feeding weight (not necessarily current weight). Although accurate scales may not be readily available, the animal's weight can be reasonably estimated by measuring around the animal at the girth line. A tape measure is placed around the thorax just behind the withers and follows underneath the animal in the same manner as using a cinch strap. Measurements are taken following respiratory expiration. Personnel should hold the tape snug through several respiration cycles and note the smallest number.

2-53. This measurement is then converted to an estimated weight shown in Table 2-3. If the animal is not at BCS 5 at the time of measurement, the handler should add or subtract 200 pounds per BCS difference. For example, if the BCS was 3, he should add 400 pounds to the girth-measured estimated weight to arrive at a new feeding weight. This extra feed is needed to increase the animal's body. If the BCS is 4, the handler adds 200 pounds. Additional rations may need to be added for compensatory weight gain.

Table 2-3. Estimating a horse's weight from girth measurements

Girth Length (in)	Weight (lb)
55	500
60	650
62	720
64	790
66	860

Table 2-3. Estimating a horse's weight from girth measurements (*Continued*)

Girth Length (in)	Weight (lb)
68	930
70	1,000
72	1,070
74	1,140
76	1,210
78	1,290
80	1,370

Source: *Care and Feeding of the Horse.* Lon D. Lewis. 2d Ed., Williams and Wilkins, 1996.

2-54. **Increase Feed for Work Over Maintenance Level.** Animals should be fed two rations—one for idle (not working) and one for working. The inactive ration is calculated to maintain body condition but not to allow for increased weight. The idle ration can be predominantly forage. A small amount of grain is beneficial to ensure protein, amino acids, and trace mineral requirements are met. The idle ration should be of low enough energy content to preclude "typing-up" once the animal resumes strenuous work. It is best to feed fat, grain with high fat content, or soluble carbohydrates if they are accessible.

2-55. Working rations need to have increased amounts of high energy feed. The animals need this increase for the following reasons:

- Working animals have less time to forage and rest if working long hours. Even on optimal pastures, pack animals need 4 to 5 hours of grazing to meet their nutritional requirement.
- Working animals have an increased demand for energy.
- Grain and oil are easier to transport than forages.
- Small amounts of grain or oiled grain can easily be fed in nose bags (feed bags) during short halts.

2-56. Dietary components directly affect performance and onset of fatigue. High fat diets often enhance aerobic and anaerobic performance and delay fatigue. Fats or oil are preferred over either soluble carbohydrates or proteins. Likewise, soluble carbohydrates are preferred over protein. However, it is more difficult to balance the ration. Using regular grain is simpler, but not as beneficial. Table 2-4 shows amounts of forage and grain to feed for idle and working pack animals.

Table 2-4. Idle and working rations

Feeding Weight (lb)	Forage (lb)	Grain (lb)
800	14	7
1,000	15	10
1,200	16	13

Additional grain (or oil) increment for working is as follows:

One pound of high-quality grain per hour worked up to a maximum of 40 percent grain in the total ration. Over 40 percent will cause some animals to founder (lameness) or colic. Therefore, if more energy is needed, personnel should add oil to the grain and forage (for example, vegetable oil, corn oil, soy oil, or animal fat) in the diet. One pint of oil per 5 pounds of grain results in 20 percent added fat in the grain.

Example: An 800-pound pack animal working for 8 hours would need an additional 80 ounces (8 hours × 10 ounces) or 5 pounds.

NOTE: These are general guidelines that are suitable for most conditions. More precise rations can be formulated using the references cited at the end of this manual.

2-57. **Feed Animals as Individuals.** Some animals will require more feed for the same work even though they may appear to be of similar size, age, and temperament. These guidelines to feeding should only be considered as a starting point. Rations will have to be adjusted for the animal, weather, terrain, and altitude. In some cases as described below, the ration may need to be increased 50 percent or even more.

2-58. **Adjust as Needed to Maintain Ideal Body Weight.** Once the animal achieves a BCS of 5, the ration should be adjusted to maintain that BCS. Animals should be taped around the girth line regularly to track changes in body weight. Most people are too subjective and variable in their visual appraisals of weight and often will not detect weight change until the animal gains or loses 100 pounds. The ration will also have to be adjusted for work, weather, and altitude.

2-59. **Adjust Rations to Cold Weather, Hot Humid Weather, and Very High Altitude.** Horses and mules with a long, thick coat of hair can tolerate cold weather well if they remain dry and out of the wind. The energy requirement increases only about 1 percent for each degree Fahrenheit (F) below 18 degrees F. However, if the animals become wet and are subject to wind, the energy requirement can increase 20 percent.

2-60. Hot humid weather can decrease the animal's appetite. Therefore, it may be necessary to increase the palatability of the grain mix by adding molasses or other sweet-tasting feed. It may also be necessary to feed a high-grain and low-forage diet. Very high altitude can also decrease the animal's appetite. Likewise, it may be necessary to increase palatability of the ration.

2-61. **Change Forages Slowly**. The handler should change forages gradually over 5 days. If introducing animals to a new pasture, the handler should limit grazing to 1 hour the first day and increase by 1 hour for the following 4 days. The animal should be fed hay before turning out to graze to preclude overeating on new lush pastures.

TYPES OF RATIONS

2-62. There are three basic types of rations: garrison, field, and emergency. All three can be altered in quantities and substance depending on conditioning and training taking place, type and health of the animals, season, and combat situation. Table 2-5 shows a recommended allowance for garrison and field rations. The types of horses discussed in Table 2-5 fall in the following categories: small horses are usually found in overseas areas; light horses weigh less than 1,150 pounds; and heavy horses weigh more than 1,150 pounds.

Garrison Rations

2-63. The detachment uses these provisions at permanent or semipermanent operational bases where the pack animals are fairly idle. These rations contain a standard feed allowance of approximately 10 pounds of grain (8 for mules), 14 pounds of hay, and 5 pounds of bedding. Again, this ration can be increased slightly depending on the animal's condition or the training taking place. Idle horses can often be maintained on good quality hay or pasture without grain supplements.

Field Rations

2-64. While the detachment is deployed, the animals receive these rations so they can maintain condition and strength during heavy work. The field rations contain an allowance of about 12 pounds of grain (10 for mules), 14 pounds of hay, and no bedding. Such quantities and combinations of feed could cause a logistic problem in a combat situation and may be altered. If the situation permits, consider pre-positioning or caching the feed. Another way to prevent having to carry all the feed is to consider aerial delivery.

Emergency Rations

2-65. The detachment uses these temporary rations for a short time when the combat situation or environment prohibits the use of field rations. An emergency ration is a modification of a field ration for reasons such as logistic problems or the lack of forage in the operational area. This ration can vary greatly depending on the situation.

Table 2-5. Recommended ration allowances

Garrison Rations			
	Grain (lb)	**Hay (lb)**	**Bedding (straw/sawdust) (lb)**
Horses: Small	7	14	5
Light	10	14	5
Heavy	12.5	15	5
Mules	8	14	5
Field Rations			
	Grain (lb)	**Hay (lb)**	**Bedding (straw/sawdust) (lb)**
Horses: Small	9	14	None
Light	12	14	None
Heavy	14	16	None
Mules	10	14	None

NOTES:

1. Bran may be substituted in amounts not to exceed 3 pounds for a like amount of grain. One-half pound of linseed meal may be substituted for 1 pound of grain.
2. The substitution of barley, rice, copra meal, or any other local product can be made for the grain ration.
3. The substitution of native grasses, bamboo shoots, or banana stalks can be made for the hay ration.
4. Fifteen pounds of corn fodder or grain sorghum is considered the equivalent of 10 pounds of hay.

FEED COMPONENTS

2-66. Types of grains and hay or combinations of available grains and hay will depend on the geographic location of the detachment. It is important, however, to come as close as possible to meeting all the nutritional requirements of the pack animals. Some of the grains, hay, and other items that may constitute a ration are described below.

2-67. Oats are the safest and most commonly used of all grains for the pack animal. Usually all other grains are combined with oats or regarded as substitutes. Oats may be safely fed in quantities up to 10 pounds per day but no more than 6 pounds when the animals are idle. Oats may be fed whole or crushed; however, crushing ensures more thorough chewing and digestion. Oats can be steamed or boiled for ill animals but new oats should not be fed until a month after thrashing.

2-68. Corn is best combined with oats and hay for feeding during the colder months since it has a tendency to produce heat and fat. When feeding ear corn, 6 to 12 ears are recommended depending on the amount of work being performed and the individual animal. If substituting corn for oats, the handler should make the change gradually because corn is considered a "hot" feed. That means it contains greater than 16 percent protein. If the change is made too quickly or the animal is fed too much, he could develop colic or founder. The handler can substitute about 2 pounds of corn for an equal quantity of oats weekly.

2-69. Barley is used extensively in Asia, Southeast Asia, and parts of Europe. It is considered a good grain and may be safely substituted for oats and fed in the same quantities. The change from oats to barley should be made gradually over an extended period, substituting 2 pounds of barley for an equal amount of oats weekly. Barley is very hard and should be crushed or soaked in water for 2 to 3 hours before feeding, but it may be fed whole. Barley is also a "hot" feed and the same care should be taken as with corn.

2-70. Rye is not regarded as a very good feed for horses and mules. If other feeds are scarce, it may be mixed with other feed such as oats or bran when necessary. Rye is very hard and should be rolled or crushed before feeding.

2-71. Wheat alone is not a safe feed for horses. It should be rolled and combined with a bulky grain or mixed with chaff or hay before feeding. One or two pounds should be given at first and the amount gradually increased to a maximum of 6 pounds per day.

2-72. Bran is the seed husk of grains such as wheat, rye, and oats, separated from the flour by sifting. It is an excellent food for the pack animal. Bran, having a mild laxative effect, is most useful as a supplement to a ration consisting largely of grains. It helps in building bone and muscle, has no tendency to fatten, and adds to the general tone and condition of animals. To supply the desired laxative and tonic effect, the handler can add necessary bulk and stimulate more thorough chewing. He should feed about 2 pounds of dry bran mixed with oats or other grain every day.

2-73. Rice—that is, rough rice, when rolled, crushed, or coarsely ground—may be fed in quantities up to one-half the grain ration. In an emergency, it may be fed in quantities up to 8 pounds daily.

2-74. Grain sorghum has a general food value of slightly less than that of corn. The handler should feed the pack animal the same amount of grain sorghum as he would feed corn, and under the same circumstances. Grain sorghum is less fattening than corn and has higher protein content.

2-75. Salt is essential to the health and well-being of all animals. The pack animal's need for salt is greatly influenced by the amount and type of work he is performing, since a considerable amount is excreted in his sweat. A supply of salt, adequate to replace that lost through sweating, is an important factor in preventing heat exhaustion during hot weather. Salt (8 to 10 ounces per day) should be available free-choice in a salt block. The handler should add no more than 4 ounces to the daily grain ration. If animals sweat excessively, they will need up to 12 ounces per day. Prolonged sweating depletes the body's store of potassium, which causes muscle weakness and early onset of fatigue. Potassium can be replaced with "lite salt" that is one-half sodium chloride and one-half potassium chloride. The handler can add 3 ounces lite salt per day in grain and add molasses to increase palatability and bind the salt to the grain. Otherwise, the salt will settle out of the grain as the animal eats. If salt blocks are used, they should contain trace minerals. Trace minerals are vitally important. Availability in forages and grains varies by region. Animals must receive supplements of trace minerals unless the rations are analyzed and guaranteed to be adequate. Trace minerals can be conveniently supplemented by providing trace-mineralized salt, either as a loose form or in block. The trace mineral mix should include zinc, manganese, iron, copper, cobalt, and iodine as a minimum. If the region is deficient or marginally variable in selenium, then it also should be added. Areas in which forages contain excessive selenium (over 5 parts per million of the total ration), including selenium in trace minerals, will cause both selenium poisoning and impaired use of other trace minerals. Selenium poisoning causes abnormal hair and hoof growth. The availability of a salt block eliminates the requirement to add salt to the feed except when lite salt needs to be used to counter potassium depletion.

2-76. Hay is the basic element of the ration that provides the bulk necessary for the proper performance of the digestive system. The pack animal should not be deprived of hay or something with similar bulk, such as straw, for any considerable length of time. Animals will suffer more on a ration of grain than on one of hay alone. Should the supply of hay normally required for the daily rations be diminished, the animals should be grazed or fed such roughage as can be gathered or produced locally. Oat straw is one of the best substitutes for hay if the oat heads are still on it. Otherwise, it is not a good substitute. Any straw, not spoiled, may be used, but barley and rye straw are not recommended. The handler should never feed moldy hay to horses and mules; cows can eat it without suffering ill effects, but horses and mules cannot. If bulky feed is unavailable, he can give the animals green or dried weeds or leaves as substitute roughage. All hays, except for the legumes, have nearly equal feeding values. Some of the more common hays are alfalfa, timothy, oat hay, and prairie grass. Alfalfa is protein-rich roughage of high nutritive value that more closely approximates that of grains than the common roughage. Alfalfa is an excellent source of calcium and vitamins. Being high in protein, alfalfa combines well with corn to create a laxative effect. If changing to an alfalfa ration, the handler should give about 2 or 3 pounds daily. The ration should compose not more than one-half of the hay allowance.

2-77. Timothy is usually considered the standard hay, although it is not particularly rich in digestible nutrients. Timothy mixed with clover gives a higher nutritive value and a better supply and balance of minerals and vitamins. However, the clover content should not exceed 50 percent. This mixture is common in areas where timothy is available, as timothy and clover are frequently seeded together.

2-78. Prairie hay, or wild hay, is produced from the natural grass growing on prairie land. Upland prairie hay, its feeding value being slightly higher than timothy, makes excellent hay when properly cured. Midland prairie hay, which is produced from coarser wild grasses growing on low land, is of lower feeding value and is not considered desirable.

2-79. Oat hay is oat straw before removing the oat grain from the head of the plant. It is cured in the same manner as other hay. It has a nutrient value about equal to that of timothy but is richer in protein.

GRAZING

2-80. Grazing alone can maintain idle animals satisfactorily. It provides good feed and exercise for the animals. As with any change in feed components, grazing periods should increase gradually over 5 days to condition the animal's digestive system. Grazing is an important source of roughage and should be used at every opportunity to reduce the consumption of hay, which may be difficult to obtain or be of questionable quality. Grazing also allows the detachment to carry less. Grazing on wet or frosted alfalfa or clover should be avoided to prevent gas colic. Except in an emergency, Johnson grass and grain sorghum should not be grazed.

PELLET FEED

2-81. This type of feed has several advantages over conventional hay or grain rations. Storage requirements are decreased, it is easily deliverable by air, and nutritious by-products can be included. Total feed intake is usually increased when pellets are fed. One disadvantage is that the cost is higher than conventional feeding. The contents of pelletal feed should be selected according to the type of roughage being fed. Alfalfa, for example, provides more protein and calcium than grasses such as timothy and orchard. Consequently, the protein and calcium content of the pellet should be lower.

WATER

2-82. Drinking water as a feed component is of utmost importance. The nutrients of the feed must be in a solution before they can be absorbed. During work, sweating and other physiological functions greatly deplete the water content of the body's tissues. To compensate for this loss, the body draws from the digestive tract. A deficiency of water in the digestive tract not only affects digestion but also may affect the general health of the animal by causing such problems as impaction colic and debility. An animal can survive for a considerable time without food but succumbs in a few days if deprived of water. Table 2-6 contains the chart for watering working animals.

Table 2-6. Average daily water requirements for working animals

Species	Liters Per Day
Horse	30–50
Mule	15–30
Donkey	10–20
Buffalo	45
Ox	20–35
Camel, Dromedary and Bactrian	20–30
Llama	4
Caribou (Domesticated Reindeer)	Not Established
Dog	4
Goat	4
Elephant	169

FEEDING IN GARRISON

2-83. The times of feeding and watering while in the operational base or rear area should be fixed and regular. Feeding and watering, both as to time and amount, are based on the training, conditioning, and work being performed.

WATERING THE ANIMALS

2-84. It is important to offer the animals water and give them plenty of time to drink before feeding time. Normally, a pack animal requires about 8 gallons of water per day. However, the temperature and amount of work being performed will determine water requirements (Table 2-7). The animals should be watered three times per day under normal conditions and four times per day when operating in an extremely warm climate. Under ideal conditions, water should be available to the animals at all times when they are not being used. Feed should not be distributed while the animals are being watered because they will not water properly when they have feed available.

Table 2-7. Heat conditions and countermeasures (increasing severity)

Heat Condition Color Code	WBGT Index Degrees F	Water Intake Liters	Work/Rest Cycle Minutes Per Hour
Green	82–84	0.5	50/10
Yellow	85–87	1.0–1.5	45/15
Red	88–89	1.5–2.0	30/30
Black	90 and Up	2.5 and Up	Stop Work

QUANTITY AND FREQUENCY OF FEEDING

2-85. The stomach of the horse and mule is small and is unable to function properly while holding large quantities of food. Once the stomach is two-thirds full, the feed will pass through the stomach at the rate it is taken into the mouth. Therefore, the stomach functions properly when it is two-thirds full. If the animal is fed too much at one time, the stomach may become excessively distended and feed will be wasted by not being properly digested. A 3- to 4-pound feed of grain represents the approximate amount an average animal should be fed at a single meal. This feeding may be followed by a long and slow consumption of hay. Under these conditions the gradual passage of food into the intestines then takes place under favorable conditions. If the total amount of grain is increased, it is better to increase the number of feeds rather than to increase the size of the ration at each meal.

WORKING AFTER FEEDING

2-86. Working an animal hard after a full feed interferes with its ability to work and with its ability to digest the feed properly. The animal's ability to work is hampered by difficulty in breathing, which is caused by the swelling of the stomach and bowels against the diaphragm and lungs. Digestion is also accompanied by an increased flow of blood and secretions and increased muscular activity in the bowels. Hard work diverts blood to other parts of the body, tires the intestinal muscles, and reduces secretions needed to aid digestion. As a result, the animal suffers a loss of nourishment from the feed, may develop serious disorders of the digestive tract, and may die. The animals may be worked safely 1 hour after feeding.

FEEDING AFTER WORKING

2-87. The digestive organs of a tired animal are just as fatigued as the rest of the body. Therefore, a tired animal should not be fed a full ration. Most of the blood supply is still in the muscles, the muscles of the digestive tract are tired, and the glands used to secrete digestive fluids are not ready to function properly. The animal must be cooled and rested before feeding. The handler should give the animal small amounts of water at frequent intervals and permit him to eat long hay. After about 30 minutes of rest, he can give the animal a small portion of grain followed by the balance, a little at a time, after an hour or more. Failure to take these precautions frequently results in colic, laminitis, or both. The method of feeding just mentioned is time-consuming. If it is not possible to use this method, the handler should feed the animals once after waiting 1 to 2 hours after work.

FEEDING PROCEDURES

2-88. Feeding a small amount of hay before feeding grain stimulates an increased flow of saliva and gastric juices, takes the edge off the appetite, and quiets the nervous animal. In the morning, it is not necessary to feed hay first because the animal has probably been eating hay all night. An ideal way to feed hay is to keep it before the animal continuously by replenishing the supply frequently with small quantities. Feeding chaff with the grain adds bulk and forces the animal to eat more slowly, ensuring more thorough mastication.

FEEDING IN THE FIELD

2-89. Feeding pack animals away from garrison in a field or combat environment presents problems that are not present in garrison. The greatest problem is setting a regular schedule of feeding times. The hours that animals work in the field or under combat conditions are seldom the same every day. Therefore, to adhere to the principles outlined above, the animals must be fed smaller rations at more frequent intervals. It is very important to ensure every animal is fed a full ration every day to maintain the strength required to work in the field.

2-90. Due to logistic constraints, there may not be enough hay available to ensure the animal receives the required roughage. In this case, the animal must be allowed to graze at every opportunity to obtain sufficient roughage. Grazing should be allowed while at a bivouac location and at halts while on the march. A halt of an hour or more to feed grain should be planned if the duration of the movement will exceed 5 hours. Important points to consider when feeding in the field are covered below.

WATERING ON THE MARCH

2-91. Watering on the march should be done whenever possible, especially on hot days. When watering a string of animals on the move, such as at a stream crossing, the handler should allow the entire string to get in the water before letting any of the animals drink. Otherwise, the lead animals will drink and then try to move down the trail before the rest of the animals in the string have a chance to drink. The handler must watch to ensure all animals have a chance to drink before moving the string. He should angle the string upstream so the animals ahead do not foul the water. The handler should give the animals ample time to drink their fill and not be led away the first time they raise their heads. After watering, he should keep the animals at a walk for 10 to 15 minutes before increasing the gait or coming to a long halt. This action will prevent digestive disturbances.

FEEDING HALTS

2-92. The handler should try to plan the place for a feeding halt 2 or 3 miles past a watering point. He should give the animals a little hay after arriving at the feeding point and tying them to the high line. This procedure will help relax the animals and start the secretion of the gastric fluids.

FEEDING AT BIVOUAC

2-93. When it is necessary to feed and water at a bivouac location, the handler should wait at least 45 minutes after arrival to water the animals. He removes the bits if a full watering will be allowed. When watering at the bivouac location, the handler should lead the animals to the water on foot. He should lead no more than two animals at a time. When they drink, he should stand between the animals so they do not crowd each other. As stated before, the animals should receive ample time to drink and should not be led away from the water the first time they raise their heads. The animals should go to the water and leave the water together. Handlers should closely watch that the animals do not start pawing the water or lie down in it after being watered, as they often do. These actions will stir sediment on the bottom and make the water unfit to drink by other animals.

FEEDING OFF THE GROUND

2-94. Whenever possible, the handler should keep animals from feeding off the ground. As they eat off the ground, they pick up dirt and sand. The sand or dirt will accumulate in the colon. With time the animals will develop colic due to obstruction or they will develop diarrhea due to irritation. Feeding off the ground also causes premature wear of their teeth. For animals that are predisposed to forming sharp points and hooks, this will accelerate their development and subsequently degrade the animal's ability to eat.

WATER SHORTAGES

2-95. When water is scarce, its consumption will have to be regulated. If the bits are removed, animals can drink from a very shallow container. A small quantity will let an animal keep moving if he is given the water by the swallow instead of allowing him to take one long draft.

FEEDING HAY

2-96. When the animals are on a high line, the handler should break the hay from the bales and distribute it along the high line. The hay should be given in small quantities and replenished frequently. This procedure is especially important in damp climates or while it is raining. Moldy hay should never be given. As mentioned before, cattle can eat moldy hay without problems, but horses and mules cannot. The handler should break the bales of hay apart and distribute only as needed. Personnel should ensure the animals do not work the hay beneath them where they cannot get to it. The handler should place the hay flakes directly under the animal's head at the point where the animal's lead line is attached to the high line.

FEEDING GRAIN

2-97. When feeding grain in the field, the handler should feed the animals from a feed bag and ensure the feed bags fit properly. If they are too loose, the animals will toss their heads trying to get to the feed, and grain will be spilled and wasted. Personnel should watch the animals while they are feeding from a feed bag, and should never allow the animals access to water until they have finished eating and the feed bags are removed. While attempting to drink, the animals could get the feed bag filled with water and drown. Any leftover feed should be spread on a cloth to dry. The feed can then be used for the next feed. Grain should not be spread on the ground for the animals to eat. When the animals eat the grain, they also ingest dirt that can lead to colic. Any grain spilled on the ground in front of the animals should be swept. Figure 2-5 shows another method of feeding grain and commercial alfalfa cubes to the animal. If the handler is not using a feed bag, he can place about a 3-inch flake of hay on the ground with the grain placed on top of the flake. This method will keep the grain off the ground and keep the animals from ingesting dirt.

Figure 2-5. Grain on flaked hay

FEEDING ALFALFA CUBES

2-98. Foraged cubes are gaining popularity as an alternative to feeding long-stem hay (Figure 2-6). The cubes available may be 100-percent alfalfa, a mixture of alfalfa and grasses, or a mixture of alfalfa and whole corn plant. Alfalfa cubes can be used in feeding programs to replace a portion or all of the forage that animal handlers would feed their animals. They have high nutrient values for energy, protein, calcium, and vitamins. As with any feedstuff, there are advantages and disadvantages that the handler must consider when making the decision to use alfalfa cubes in his feeding program (Figure 2-7).

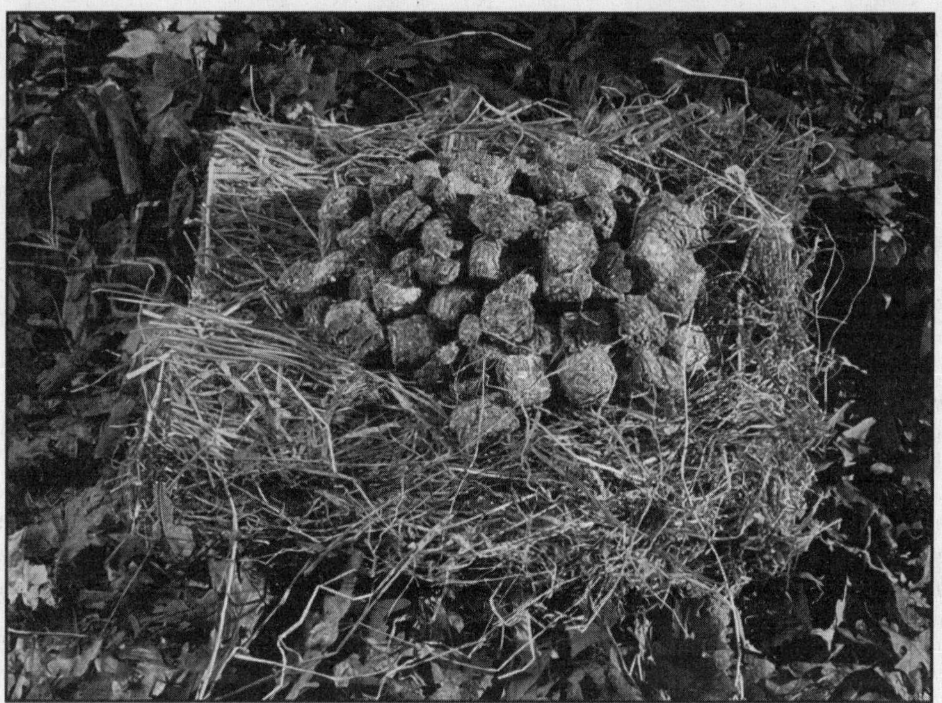

Figure 2-6. Commercial alfalfa cubes

Advantages
• **Reduced feed waste.** Horses fed long-stem hay can separate the leaves from the stems and consume the parts they prefer; this does not happen with cubes.
• **Controlled feed intake.** It is easier for the animal handler to monitor and regulate the daily intake of cubed forage than long-stem hay.
• **Consistent nutrient content.** The nutrient levels found in cubes tend to be more consistent than hay.
• **Reduced dust.** Cubes have little dust and are therefore a good alternative to hay for animals with certain respiratory problems.
• **Reduced storage requirements.** Cubes can be mechanically handled in bulk and are denser than hay; therefore, they require less storage space.
• **Reduced transportation costs.** Cubes take up less space and are easy to transport on pack animals. The density of cubes allows trucks or planes to be loaded to their full legal capacity.

Figure 2-7. Considerations for using alfalfa cubes

Disadvantages
• **Excessive feed intake.** The handler must feed cubes in a controlled manner to avoid overweight animals and, more importantly, to avoid serious digestive upsets. • **Handling.** As with hay, alfalfa cubes require a storage area that provides protection from the weather to prevent spoilage caused by excessive moisture. • **Cost.** Processing adds to the cost of the feed, and there may be additional costs associated with shipping. The major sources for cubed alfalfa are the western United States, western Canada, and Ontario.

Figure 2-7. Considerations for using alfalfa cubes (*Continued*)

CARE OF FORAGE

2-99. The care of forage is extremely important to the health of the herd. Feeding damp or moldy hay can cause colic and could disable a large portion of the herd at once. The handler should inspect the forage at the time of delivery to ensure the quality of it. In garrison, shelters are available to keep the forage dry. In the field, the unit should make every attempt to keep it dry. When the feed is packed on animals for transportation, it should be covered with a manta. This precaution will protect the feed from the elements and keep the animals from getting into it during the movement. During temporary storage, the unit should raise the forage off the ground by timbers or whatever else is available. This technique will keep the forage from getting wet and keep loose or stray animals from getting into it.

CHAPTER 3

Animal Care and Training

The proper care and training of pack animals is essential to the health of the animals and their performance in the field. Without proper care, the animal's health and the unit's ability to complete its mission will suffer. Without proper training, the unit cannot rely upon the animal to behave in a manner that ensures mission accomplishment.

GROOMING

3-1. Grooming is essential to the general health, condition, and appearance of animals. It promotes good health practice and allows the handlers to bond with the animals. Animals in a herd bond by grooming each other; this action can be duplicated by the handler grooming the animal. In the wild, horses groom each other as well as rolling at will and rubbing against trees to maintain healthy skin. Domesticated horses must rely on humans to provide the opportunity for skin care. Grooming, no matter who does it (humans or horses), increases the circulation to the skin and releases the oils that provide luster to the animal's coat. It also provides an excellent time to inspect them for injuries. When grooming before movement, the handler should check the animals for injuries. He should also check the condition of past injuries, if any, at this time. When grooming after movement, the handler should check the animals for injuries sustained on the trail and for any evidence the saddle or harness may have chafed the animal. These precautions permit treatment of any problems before they get to the point of incapacitating the animal. The value of grooming depends on how thorough the handler does it. The animal handler obtains efficient grooming when he takes pride in the appearance of his animals.

WHEN TO GROOM

3-2. The animal handler should groom every animal thoroughly, at least once each day. He should always groom the animal before it leaves the stable area for work or exercise. Before saddling the animal, the handler should make sure the areas where the saddle pad, cinch, breast collar or strap, quarter straps, and britching ride are free of dirt and foreign objects. Failure to clean these areas will result in sores and could cause the animal to be unusable. On return from work or exercise, the handler should remove, clean, and put away any equipment. A heated, wet, or sweating animal should be cooled before grooming it. The handler should give the animal a brisk rubbing with a cloth to partially dry the coat, then blanket the animal (if a blanket is not available, he should leave the saddle pad on) and walk it until it is cool. The handler should check for injuries that may have occurred during movement. After removing the saddle and the animal is released, it will usually roll on the ground. The handler should hold off grooming until the animal has finished this process or all the effort that is put into grooming the animal will be a waste of time.

EQUIPMENT

3-3. Each individual responsible for the care of animals should have a grooming kit. The basic kit consists of a currycomb, horse or body brush, hoof pick, and a grooming cloth (Figure 3-1).

Currycomb

3-4. The handler can use this circular metal device with sawtooth-like edges to remove caked mud, to loosen matted or dried skin and dirt in the hair, and to clean the body brush while grooming. He should never use it on the legs below the knees or hocks and never use it about the head. These areas are mostly skin and bone and the animal could be injured.

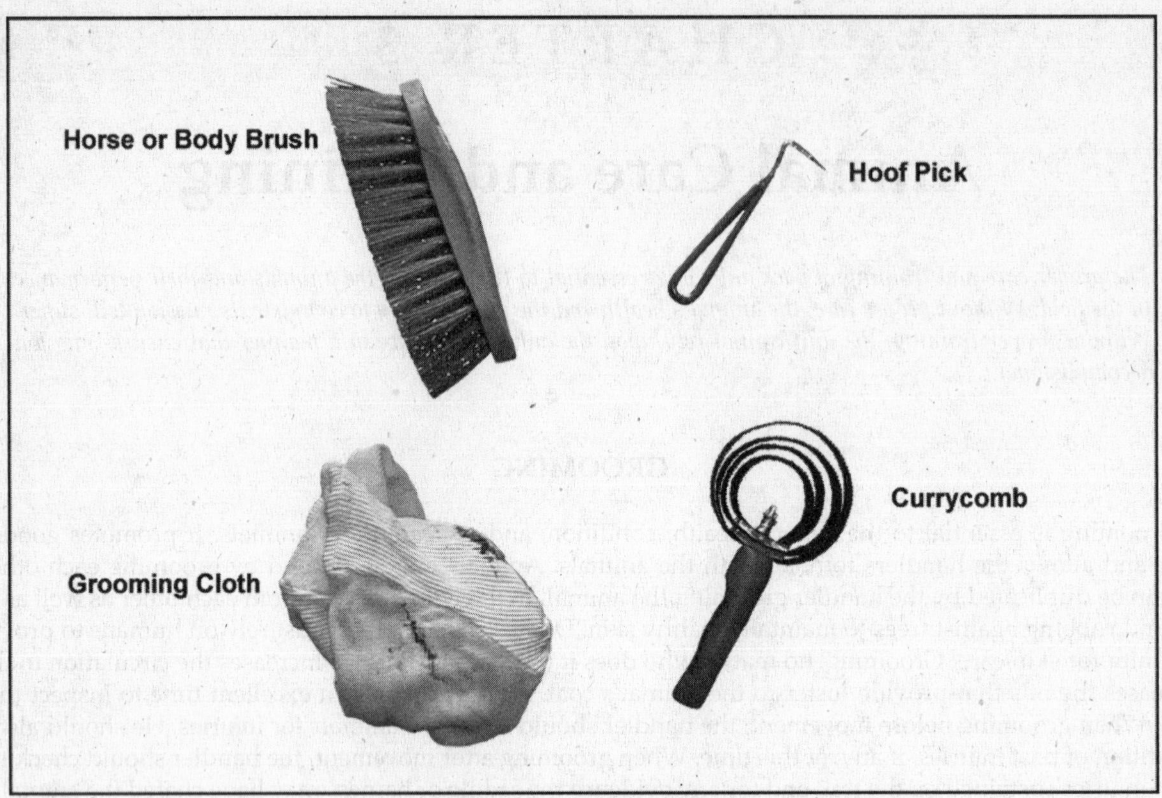

Figure 3-1. Grooming equipment

Horse or Body Brush

3-5. This brush is the main tool used in grooming. When used properly, the bristles of the brush penetrate through the hair of the coat and remove dirt and flaked skin from the hide as well as from the hair. Various brushes are available. Generally, it is better to use a stiffer bristle to better penetrate the hair on the coat.

Hoof Pick

3-6. Hooves should be cleaned daily and trimmed or reshod every 4 to 6 weeks. This small metal pick allows the handler to clean rocks and packed dirt from the hooves. The handler should always use the hoof pick in a downward motion toward the toe.

Grooming Cloth

3-7. The handler uses the grooming cloth to clean the body orifices and to give a final polish to the coat. He can make a grooming cloth, about 2-feet square, from old toweling or any other type of soft cloth.

GROOMING SEQUENCE

3-8. A prescribed sequence of grooming will enable the animal handler to groom effectively and thoroughly. The following paragraphs explain the recommended sequence.

3-9. The handler should first check the animal for any signs of lameness or abnormalities as the animal walks to the grooming area. If any exist, he should thoroughly clean the hoof of the affected leg with the hoof pick and look for rocks or other debris causing the problem. The handler should clean each hoof every day in working animals. One school of thought is that the soft dirt and debris packed in the hoof gives the animal extra cushion to walk on in rough terrain. Whether cleaned daily or not, the handler should check the animal's feet for thrush, torn frog, loose or missing shoes, and cracks. He should report defects at once to the medic or veterinarian.

3-10. The handler should use the currycomb in the right hand and the brush in the left. Beginning at the neck, he should brush over the left side of the animal with the currycomb. The handler continues down to the breast, withers, shoulders, foreleg, and knee; then smoothly transitions to the back, side, belly, croup, and hind leg to the hock. He should strike the currycomb frequently against his heel or side of the brush to free the accumulated dirt and dried skin. The handler should make sure the currycomb follows the natural lay of the hair.

NOTE
The handler should never use the currycomb on the animal's face or below the knees; these areas are tender and are made up of mostly bone.

3-11. The handler should brush the entire left side of the animal in the same order as above except brush the legs down to the hoofs. After a few strokes, he should clean the brush with the currycomb. The handler should stand well away from the animal when using the brush, keeping his arm stiff, and throwing the weight of his body behind the brush. A twist of the wrist at the end of each stroke will flick the dirt away from the hair. This use of the brush is not necessarily a separate activity from currying; the handler can do both at the same time with a brush stroke following each currycomb stroke. He should pass to the right side of the animal, change hands with the brush and currycomb, and groom the right side in the same order as above.

3-12. The head, mane, and tail are the last grooming features. In cleaning the mane and tail, the handler should begin brushing at the ends of the hair and gradually to the roots, separating the locks with his fingers to remove dried skin and dirt. He then wipes the eyes, nostrils, and lips and rubs the head, ears, and muzzle with the grooming cloth. The handler cleans the dock (fleshy part of the tail) and gives a final polish to the coat.

NOTE
To prevent the spread of skin diseases, the handler should wash grooming equipment and drying cloths with soap and water once a week.

ANIMAL INSPECTION

3-13. The handlers should inspect the animals, as indicated above, while grooming them. Good grooming offers the opportunity for close examination of the animal and the discovery of injuries or defects that otherwise might pass unnoticed. Correcting or treating these defects or injuries greatly reduces the number of noneffective animals in a unit. Along with wounds or other injuries present, there are others that are not immediately visible to the naked eye. For example, the animal handler can detect some joint and ligament injuries by inflammation or swelling. These injuries are often very slight and subtle, and the handler can best detect them by knowing precisely what is normal. The handler can establish an experience base by running his hands along the animal's body **daily** paying particular attention to the legs. If the animal flinches when touched in the area just to the rear of where the saddle rides, it is a sign that the animal's kidneys are sore. This pain might result from poor saddle placement or improper riding position.

GROOMING SICK ANIMALS

3-14. Handlers should never groom animals that are sick, weak, or depressed. These animals should be hand-rubbed at least once a day. The handler should wipe the animal's eyes and nostrils out with a damp sponge or soft cloth and clean the feet. This cloth should be left near that animal, not placed near other animals' equipment or feed, and not used on any other animal. The handler should groom animals with minor ailments in the usual manner. He should never clean or disturb animals with tetanus in any manner at all.

WARNING
Under no circumstances should an untrained Soldier attempt to shoe an animal. Improper shoeing or quicking of an animal will result in long-term damage to the animal and Soldier.

FARRIER SCIENCE

3-15. While not farriers, Soldiers must be able to replace, at least, a loose or missing shoe when a farrier is not available. The usefulness of a pack animal depends on the health and condition of its feet. The use of a "hoof boot" should be the first course of action when an animal loses a shoe. This item is part of the pack animal first-aid kit. The feet of a normal animal, due to their structure, require very little care or protection while on free pasture or even under light working conditions. At moderate work levels on good footing, an animal may require no more than cleaning and periodic rasping to trim and level its feet. The hind feet need only moderate care since they receive less shock. The front feet carry 60 to 65 percent of the load. As the workload increases or the terrain becomes more difficult, the animal's feet require additional care and protection. Shoeing protects the feet from excessive wear and enhances balance, support, and traction.

BASIC SHOEING

3-16. Shoes should be selected to suit the activity of the horse. Normally, shoes are for protecting the feet and supporting the limbs. The most common error made by the inexperienced horseshoer is to use shoes that are too small. The shoe should be as light as practical, but wide enough to offer sufficient protection to the bottom of the foot. The fit should be exactly to the perimeter of the foot at the toe and quarters. The shoe should fit slightly wider than the foot near the heels (approximately 1-1/2 inches of the heel of the shoe). This expansion can range from 1/16 to 3/16 inch.

3-17. Hoof growth, shoe wear, and the work required of the animal govern the frequency of shoeing. On the average, shoes may remain on the animal without change or adjustment for 1 to 2 months, though 3 to 4 months wear is occasionally possible. A farrier does the routine refitting. However, all handlers should have a basic understanding of the shoeing process. Several personnel in each unit should be able to replace or refit a lost or outgrown shoe.

FARRIER TOOLS

3-18. The farrier's kit should contain pincers, a pritchel, clinch cutter, hoof knife, hoof nipper, hoof rasp, blacksmith and driving hammers, clincher, fencing pliers, and assorted shoes and nails (Figure 3-2).

RAISING AND HOLDING THE FRONT AND HIND FEET

3-19. An individual should know how to properly raise and hold an animal's foot before doing any grooming or farrier work so he can control the animal and have both hands free to work. Working with the front and hind legs is slightly different.

3-20. On front feet, the shoe should at least be large enough to cover the buttress of the heels. On horses with underrun heels, the shoe may need to extend past the buttress of the heels as much as 1/2 inch. This extension provides additional support to the flexor tendons and suspensory ligament.

3-21. The animal's leg should be held at a comfortable height for the animal, not a comfortable height for the handler. The handler stands with his feet apart, bends his legs, and keeps his back straight. This posture will free the handler to work with both hands (Figure 3-3). While the handler is working on the animal's leg, he should be alert to things around him so that he can predict the animal's intentions. Unless suddenly startled, an animal is quite predictable about wanting its feet on the ground. When an animal is getting tired and wants the front leg down, it will jerk its leg a few times to test the handler's grasp. If the animal is going to hop on its other foot to get away, it will move forward slightly with both hind feet in preparation for this move.

3-22. The farrier or groomer should not let an animal take its leg away every time it tries. The groomer should be considerate of the animal, but should not let the animal be the boss. If he does, the animal will soon get the idea that it can set its foot down whenever, which can be dangerous.

3-23. On most hind feet, the fit will be the same as the front feet except that it is desirable for the heels of the shoes to extend beyond the buttress of the heels 1/8 to 1/4 inch. This extension provides support and protection to the bulbs of the heels while the animal is stopping and turning. Figure 3-4, page 265, explains the procedures on raising the hind feet.

Tool	Description
Pincers	Used to remove the shoe from the hoof, cut off excess length of clinches, or remove improperly driven nails.
Pritchel	Used to enlarge the nail holes on shoes or to assist in extracting reusable nails from shoes.
Clinch Cutter	Used to cut or straighten the nail clinch before removing the shoe. The handler uses the blade end for that purpose. He can use the other end as a pritchel.
Hoof Knife	Used for cutting excess horn from the sole of the hoof and for trimming the frog, if necessary. It is available in right- and left-handed models.
Hoof Nipper	Used to remove the excess growth of wall from the hoof when preparing to replace or refit a shoe.
Hoof Rasp	Used to remove excess hoof wall and to level the bottom surface of the hoof. The rough rasp is a hoof rasp that has become dulled. The handler can use it to remove the burr under the clinches and to smooth the clinch after the shoe has been replaced. He can also use the rough rasp to file away the clinches when removing a shoe.
Blacksmith Hammer	Used to shape the shoes to the animal's feet.
Driving Hammer	Used for driving the nails that secure the shoe to the hoof and for forming the clinches.
Clincher	Useful in finishing the clinches, especially when working on young or lame horses that object to having their feet struck with the hammer.
Fencing Pliers	Have several uses in the kit. They can be used as a hammer or for cutting nails and many other functions in caring for animals' feet. Can also be used to repair saddles and harnesses.

Figure 3-2. Farrier tools

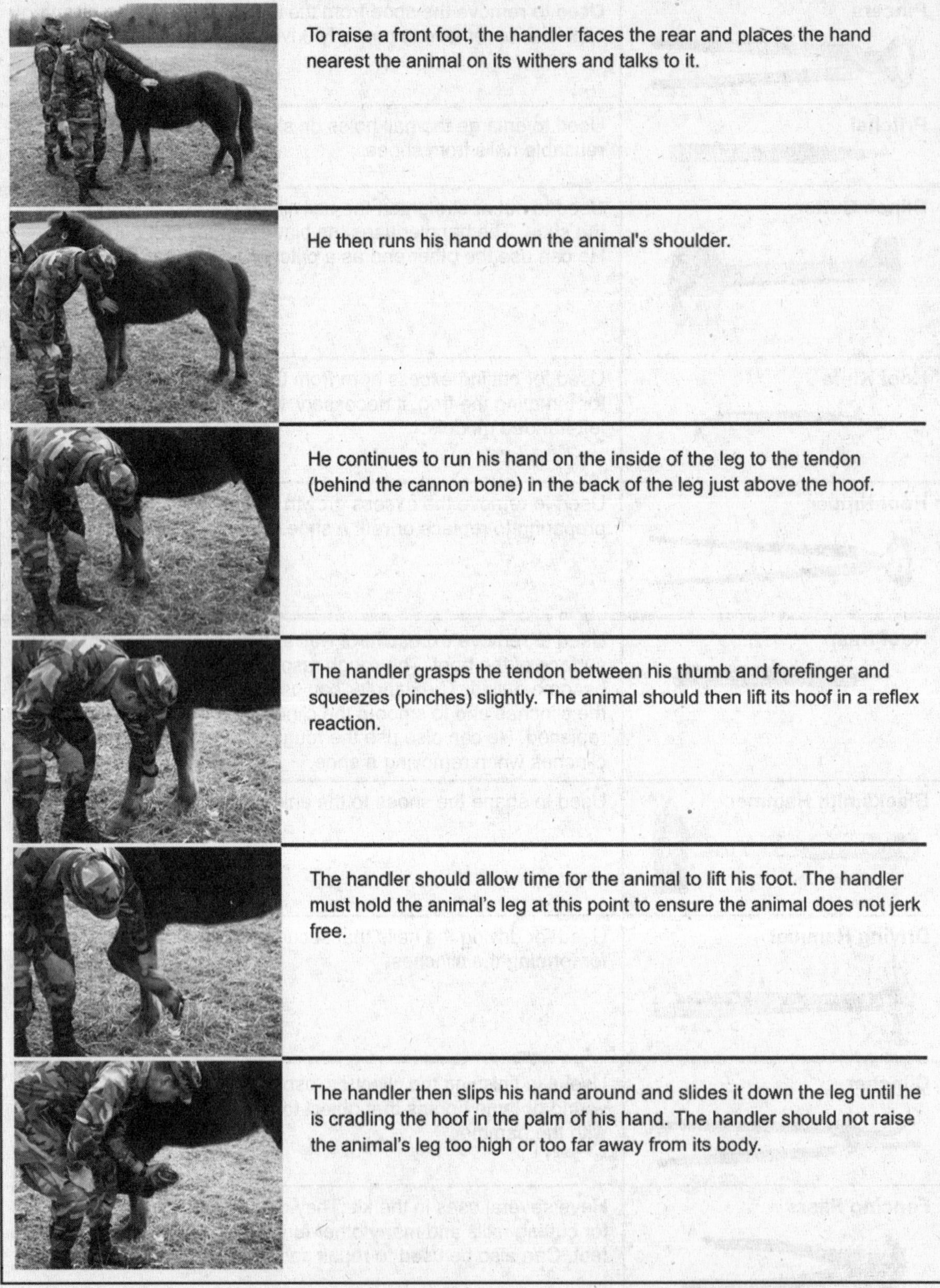

Figure 3-3. Raising the front foot

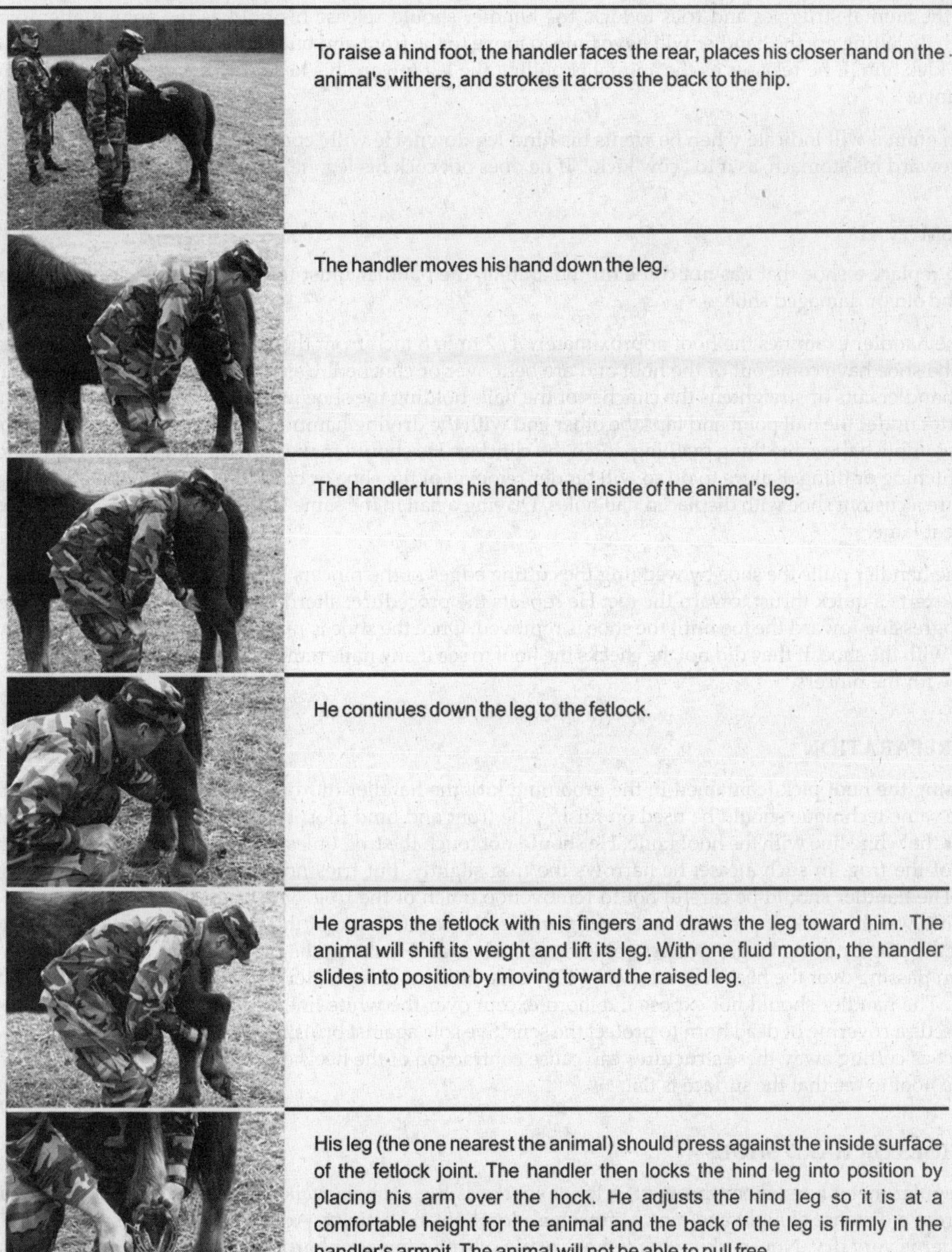

Figure 3-4. Raising the hind foot

3-24. If the animal struggles and tries to kick, the handler should release his hold as the animal attempts to kick backward. By letting go, the handler will have time to move to the front and out to the side before the animal can pull back and kick him. If he releases as the animal is pulling the leg toward his head, the handler will not have enough time to move.

3-25. An animal will indicate when he wants his hind leg down. He will "cock" his leg by drawing it forward and upward toward his stomach, as if to "cow kick." If he does not cock his leg, he cannot kick with any force.

SHOE REMOVAL

3-26. To replace a shoe that has not come off the animal, the handler must follow a specific sequence to correctly remove the old or damaged shoe.

3-27. The handler examines the hoof approximately 1/2 to 5/8 inch from the shoe. He should see where the nails holding the shoe have come out of the hoof and are bent over or clinched. Using the clinch cutter and driving hammer, the handler cuts or straightens the clinches of the nails holding the shoe in place. He places the blade end of the clinch cutter under the nail point and taps the other end with the driving hammer. The handler can also use the rough rasp to accomplish the same thing by filing down the clinches. He should make sure the clinches are completely gone by straightening or filing. Failure to do so will hinder removal of the shoe or crack the outer hoof wall. This outcome will require a custom shoe with displaced nail holes. Driving a nail in the same location will likely "quick" the animal and make it lame.

3-28. The handler pulls the shoe by wedging the cutting edges of the pincers between the shoe and hoof at the heel and then exerts a quick thrust toward the toe. He repeats the procedure, alternating from one side of the shoe to the other, progressing toward the toe until the shoe is removed. Once the shoe is removed, he checks to see if all the nails came out with the shoe. If they did not, he checks the hoof to see if any nails remain. The handler removes any remaining nails with the pincers.

HOOF PREPARATION

3-29. Using the hoof pick (contained in the grooming kit), the handler thoroughly cleans dirt and debris from the hoof. The same technique should be used on raising the front and hind foot. The handler then pares away the dead horn over the white line with the hoof knife. He should not touch the frog unless he cannot insert a hoof pick between the bars of the frog. In such a case, he narrows the frog slightly, but tries not to involve the surface touching the ground. The handler should be careful not to remove too much of the frog. The frog must be touching the ground and bearing weight. Lack of pressure on the frog will lead to contraction of the heels. The handler should level the foot with the rasp by using long, smooth strokes from heel to toe. He should be careful not to use too much rasp pressure when passing over the heel. He can always take off a little more heel later, but he cannot replace what has been removed. The handler should not expose live horn except over the white line and the outer border of the sole; the animal needs a covering of dead horn to protect the sensitive sole against bruising. He should also be sure to leave the bars intact as cutting away these structures can cause contraction of the heels and quarters. The handler then checks across the hoof to see that the surface is flat.

SOFT SHOES OR HARD SHOES

3-30. Regular metal horseshoes throw off a lot of sparks as the animals walk over rocky ground. These can easily be seen from a distance at night and may compromise location and activity. Additionally, these sparks can start fires if the tinder is very dry. Nonsparking horseshoes made of softer metal or hard plastic avoid these problems, but do wear out faster.

SHOE REPLACEMENT

3-31. The handler should fit the shoe to the hoof by holding it so that he can see the white line through the nail holes. He checks to make sure the shoe lies flat on the hoof surface without rocking. He eliminates any wobble between the shoe and hoof by rasping the high spot on the hoof. The handler may have to bend or shape the shoe as needed since it may have become deformed if it was worn loose for a time. An excess hoof wall in front of the toe of the shoe is not critical because it will be rasped away later in the shoeing process.

3-32. For most activities, six nails should be sufficient to attach the shoe to the foot. The handler may use eight nails on horses that travel in rough terrain or are troublesome about keeping shoes on. Height of the nails should be no lower than 3/4 inch above the shoes and no higher than 1 inch.

3-33. Before driving nails, the handler positions the shoe over the hoof and makes absolutely sure all nail holes are outside the white line. The white line measures approximately 1 millimeter wide and forms the juncture between the fleshy sensitive lamella (attached to the bone inside the hoof) and the hard insensitive lamella (attached to the hoof wall). Driving a nail into the white line can make the pack animal lame.

3-34. The handler secures the shoe to the hoof with nails and the driving hammer. He slightly bends the horseshoe nails near the point so they will turn out of the hoof when pounded into it. The other side of the nail is flat. The handler should always place the flat side of the nail so that it faces the outer edge of the hoof. He can be sure the nail is facing the right way by looking at its head; there is checkering on one side of the nail head. The checkering should always face the inside of the hoof. The handler grasps the nail between his thumb and forefinger and makes sure the flat side of the nail faces the outer surface of the hoof. He places the point of the first nail through the third nail hole on one side of the shoe, pointing parallel to the horn fibers of the hoof. He then taps the nail lightly several times to start it into the hoof wall.

3-35. To force the point of the nail through the outer surface of the wall at the desired spot, the handler continues to apply light blows until the nail is driven approximately 2/3 the required distance. He should then apply one sharp heavy blow on the head of the nail to force the point through the wall. The bevel on the point of the nail is effective only when driven rapidly through the horn. If the animal twitches or jerks away at any time during the nailing, the handler pulls the nail and checks for moisture or blood on it. The nail should exit approximately 3/4 of an inch above the ground surface of the foot to sufficiently hold the shoe. If there are old nail holes in the wall, the new nails should emerge at least 3/8 of an inch from the old holes. This length puts the new nails in hoof fibers strong enough to properly hold the nail. After the point emerges and the handler drives the nail head solidly into the crease of the shoe, he should immediately remove the point of the nail. The handler must do this quickly to avoid serious injury to himself should the animal decide to pull his leg away suddenly. To remove the point of the nail, he points the claws of the hammer toward the toe of the hoof. The handler places the claws onto the nail point as deep as possible and close to the hoof wall, bends the nail straight out from the wall, and rotates the hammer. This procedure will wring off the point and excess length of the nail. The handler then repeats the process with the same hole on the opposite side of the shoe.

3-36. After driving in two nails, the handler checks the shoe to ensure it still fits properly. He can adjust the fit by tapping lightly with the hammer to move it into place. He then puts the remaining nails in the shoe. It may be easier to start the first nail on each side of the shoe before driving either of them all of the way. The handler then sets the nails by striking the heads sharply with the driving hammer. He should make sure to hold a solid metal object (such as the flat side of the pincers) firmly against the end of the nail that protrudes through the hoof when he strikes. Some farriers think that the order in which clinches are set is very important. The recommended sequence is to set the two nails nearest the toe on the opposite side, then the quarter and heel nail on the first side, followed by the remaining heel nail. The handler cuts off the nail points with the pincers, leaving enough length for a proper clinch. The clinch should be approximately 1/8 of an inch long. A clinch that is too long can cause the wall to break should the shoe become caught on something and pulled off. The wall fibers of the hoof will break when the nail emerges. The handler removes the resulting burr under the seated clinch with the file side of the rough rasp. He should be careful to file away only the burr. The groove around the hoof should only be large enough to contain the clinch. The handler then uses the clincher to bend the clinches down into the groove.

3-37. Once again, the handler takes the pincers and the hammer to finish forming the clinch. He holds the pincer jaws against the head of the nail and strikes the end of the nail to seat it even with the wall surface. He should bend the nail abruptly at the hoof wall, ensuring the hammer travels parallel and as close to the hoof wall as possible. He can use the clincher for this step if one is available. The clinches are now finished. Using the file side of the rough rasp, the handler smoothes the nails leaving no sharp edges on the wall of the hoof. He then rasps and shapes the hoof to the shape of the shoe. Most of this rasping will take place in the area of the toe and anterior quarter. He must be careful not to rasp too much and rasp away the clinches. Clinches should be square in shape, embedded in the wall and smooth to the touch. The outer hoof wall should be smooth to the touch and free from coarse rasp marks. The periople at the hairline should be undisturbed.

FARRIER'S OBJECTIVE

3-38. The shoeing process will become clearer when it has been demonstrated. The intent of this section is only to enable the handler to replace a loose or missing shoe. If possible, he should fit each animal with an extra front and hind shoe. These shoes, their nails, extra nails, and farrier tools should be part of the standard equipment packed whenever the handler takes the animals out. The best way to prevent losing shoes is to catch loose ones early. The handler should check the shoes frequently by tapping them with a hoof pick. Shoes that are loosening will often sound different. The frequency to check them depends on the terrain. Loose shoes may not be lost from a pastured animal for several days. However, loose shoes in rocky terrain can be lost in a few hours. If a shoe becomes loose on the trail, the handler should remove it, if possible, to avoid its loss or injury to the animal. It would be ideal to replace lost or loosened shoes immediately, in garrison or on the trail. However, there will be times in the field when it is impossible to replace a shoe before 2 or more days have elapsed. This delay is typical and may have little or no adverse results. If this situation occurs, the handler can reduce the load of the pack animal or have a rider spend more time walking than riding his mount if it is a riding animal. Finally, there is the polyurethane boot that is tough, durable, and fits securely to the animal's foot. This boot slips over the hoof and clamps tight with a ski-boot buckle. These boots are easy to use and are remarkably durable. They are also a safe solution to the problem of mules who will not stand to be shoed. Animal handlers can use the easy boots (Figure 3-5, page 268) as replacements to shoes, to add traction or to soak an injured hoof. These boots are also used in correcting and treating hoof disease. These boots were designed to provide hoof protection for occasional and long-distance riding and to give traction on rocks, pavement, snow, and ice. The boot can be worn over iron shoes, in place of iron shoes, or only when needed. The adaptable inside strap can be adjusted, reversed, trimmed, or removed. To size, the handler must measure the animal's trimmed hoof across the bottom at the widest point. Easy boots can be ordered in the following shoe sizes: 00 (3 7/8 to 4 1/4), 0 (4 1/4 to 4 5/8), 1 (4 1/2 to 4 7/8), 2 (4 7/8 to 5 1/4), and 3 (5 1/4 to 5 3/4).

Figure 3-5. Easy boots

FIELD TRAINING

3-39. A pack animal detachment will not always be able to work with animals that are trained and conditioned to pack. Even if the animals are trained to pack, they may need retraining or conditioning. In such cases, the handler should know some of the basics of training and conditioning animals. This section should provide enough information to evaluate the animals' current level of training and to train and condition them as necessary for pack operations.

TRAINERS

3-40. The attitude of personnel training pack animals is extremely important. A person assigned to train animals must have a better than average knowledge of animals. He must also have patience, tact, firmness, and a liking and aptitude for animal management. Experienced and knowledgeable trainers seldom need much in the way of restraint. They work confidently, orderly, and efficiently around the animals. As a result, the animals are cooperative, more productive, and sustain few injuries. Inexperienced trainers tend to use more restraint then necessary; are less confident and orderly; and consequently less efficient. Likewise, the animals buck more, are less productive, and sustain more injuries. A person who is afraid of animals or who will become frustrated easily with them will not do well. Above all, the trainer must not take out his frustrations on the animal by beating, kicking, or using excessive restraint on the animal. A good animal trainer combines an intelligent respect for animals with a lack of fear. An ideal pack animal trainer should be—

- Systematic.
- Patient.
- Tactful and resourceful.
- Moderate.
- Observant.
- Exacting.
- Logical.
- Tenacious.
- Consistent.

REQUIREMENTS

3-41. Previous experience and current abilities will determine the training needs of animals. Along with their physical conditioning, trainers must evaluate the animals on their level of proficiency in leading, packing, riding, picketing, standing, gaiting, swimming, balance, and conditioning to the sights, sounds, and smells of battle. Untrained animals never used for pack purposes will require a complete training and conditioning program.

EXERCISE

3-42. Exercise must be regular, graduated, and always within the capabilities of the animal. Working tired or unfit animals can cause accidents. If an animal is idle for a considerable time, the handler must repeat its process of conditioning. The minimum period of exercise necessary to maintain an animal in working condition is 2 hours daily. Animals need not be maintained in peak condition for field duty at all times. However, they should remain in such condition that a relatively short period of carefully scheduled work will put them in fit condition for anticipated duty. The kind and amount of exercise given to animals depend on the type of work they are to perform, their current condition, and the number of individuals available to exercise them. Although the most satisfactory exercise is gained by assigning one or two animals to an individual, pack units (with limited manpower) will normally have to adopt other methods. The trainer should begin any period of exercise with 10 to 15 minutes of walking to ensure good circulation, particularly in the feet. Instead of hard surface roads, the trainer should try to select dirt roads for exercise because they are easier on the animals' feet and legs. He can also work the animals on trails or cross-country to maintain their fit condition. If exercising two animals, he should try to always ride one out and the other in and lead each alternately on his right and left. This habit will get the animals used to being both led and ridden. The trainer should end each exercise period with a 10-minute walk to return the animals to the stables dry and breathing normally. The walk is the prime-conditioning gait. Walking develops muscle, trotting improves balance, and galloping develops wind. If the trainer uses either of the faster gaits in excess, the animal will lose rather than gain condition. He can determine the length of trot periods by the condition of the animals, but in no case exceed 7 minutes. The routes for exercise from day to day should vary so that the animals will not recognize the route and try to hurry back to the stables. Also, using different routes relieves monotony. The training and conditioning program should be set up according to the amount of time available and the level of proficiency of the animals and handlers.

CONDITIONING

3-43. An animal requires good conditioning to perform the work demanded of it without injury to its body and muscular organs. The handler can acquire and maintain good conditioning through a progressive program of proper exercise and feeding. Objectives of the program are endurance, stamina, a good state of flesh, and resistance to disease. The handler can attain these objectives only by proper feeding and long periods of conditioning that work at the slower gaits, mostly the walk. He must condition both pack and riding animals to carry the weights required in field operations.

3-44. Equine, as well as human, physiology naturally but gradually compensates and strengthens (shapes up) during times when more work is needed. But like humans, horses can quickly lose conditioning or "get out of shape" during long periods of rest. That is, a strenuous mountain ride would not be an appropriate activity just after 3 months of pasture or stall rest. These factors include cardiovascular fitness, respiratory fitness, thermoregulation, muscle fatigue, and skeletal fatigue.

Cardiovascular Fitness

3-45. The resting heart rate of horses is approximately 35 beats per minute (bpm) and can reach up to 250 bpm during extreme high-intensity exercise. Each beat can pump between 0.8 and 1.2 liters of blood. Therefore, a horse exercising at maximum intensity can pump enough blood to fill a 55-gallon drum in 1 minute! As a horse becomes more fit, the stroke volume increases permitting sufficient oxygen transport with fewer beats. Conditioning exercise will improve blood circulation through muscles. As blood circulates more efficiently through muscle, more oxygen is made available, and more heat can be removed.

Respiratory Fitness

3-46. Respiration is, of course, how oxygen is introduced to the horse's blood. Limiting factors can influence the amount of available oxygen. These include the volume of the lungs, the diameter of the airway from the nostrils through the windpipe, and their gait (since horses breathe in rhythm to their stride). One reason horses breathe faster during hard work is directly related to the pH of the blood. The more acidic the blood (from carbon dioxide and lactic acid), the harder the horse will breathe to get rid of excess carbon dioxide, as well as to take in sufficient amounts of oxygen.

Dissipation of Heat

3-47. Working muscles produce heat. Horses have two ways to remove it. One is through breathing heavily. Horse's lungs are very large and the expiration of hot air and inspiration of cool air help to reduce the temperature of the body, especially the area around the heart. The second is, of course, through sweating. As a horse overheats, blood vessels in the skin become dilated so that they can hold more blood. Then evaporation and transpiration of sweat helps to cool the horse much like a swamp cooler can cool a house. The sweating mechanism works best in cool, dry air. Warm or humid conditions may cause many horses to have more difficulty in keeping cool.

3-48. Fat horses and horses with heavy muscling are not able to eliminate heat as efficiently as leaner and lighter muscled animals. Safety becomes a concern when overheated horses become lethargic and uncoordinated. Conditioning exercise (particularly walking and trotting) in balance with proper feeding will remove body fat and improve the horse's ability to dissipate heat. Also, as blood circulation through muscles improves, the horse's heat can be more efficiently carried to the skin for cooling.

Muscle Fatigue

3-49. Working muscles need fuel. During normal (aerobic) exercise (walking or trotting on level ground), fuel stored in muscles is combined with oxygen from the blood to produce energy and motion.

3-50. During intense exercise (exercise that causes the heart rate to exceed 150 bpm), oxygen is depleted more quickly than it can be supplied. Many of the cells in the muscles then switch to an energy system that does not require oxygen. The main problem with this anaerobic system is that it requires over ten times the amount of fuel to produce the same amount of energy. This system also produces lactic acid as metabolic waste. If too much lactic acid accumulates in one area of the muscle, inflammation and soreness result. With a proper conditioning regimen, the horse will gradually improve his ability to both take up oxygen and deliver oxygen to working muscles. Conditioning will also improve his ability to rid muscle tissue of metabolic wastes before they can build up and cause any damage.

3-51. One good way to help ensure that the horse's muscles remain healthy after a high-intensity work effort is to allow 30 minutes or so of walking and light work to allow the horse to "cool out" before going back into a trailer or stall. During this cool out period, lightly active muscles allow blood and lymph fluids to circulate and rid muscular tissues of metabolic waste and heat much better than if the muscles were not moving.

Skeletal Fatigue

3-52. The skeletal system includes the horse's bones, joints, tendons, and ligaments. If overstressed, skeletal failure can cause abrupt and serious injury to both the horse and rider. Overworked horses are more likely to suffer sprains and strains when at a crucial moment in the horse's stride a particular muscle fails to contract, resulting in a momentary and sometimes repeated malpositioning of a related joint or ligaments.

3-53. During exercise, the horse's bones, joints, and ligaments are constantly changing to adapt and compensate for activity changes and to the rider's added weight. How they compensate is specific to the type of work performed. For example, roping, cutting, or barrel-racing horses will not necessarily be prepared for a strenuous day of climbing steep grades on a long mountain ride.

3-54. One big problem with skeletal conditioning is that compensatory changes occur much slower than circulatory, respiratory, and muscular conditioning. It takes approximately 60 days of 5-day/week riding for the density of a horse's cannon bones to adapt to more strenuous activity and to carrying the added weight of a rider. Therefore, while the horses may feel fit, the vast majority of personnel (weekend riders) do not ride enough to cause any significant changes in skeletal fitness. Unconditioned bones, joints, and ligaments are especially susceptible to shock, twists, and torsion. For this reason, riders should always be careful to slow horses to a walk on surfaces that are hard, slippery, uneven, or deep.

3-55. To sum up, before the handler can expect the horse to perform a new type of activity, he must consider how well the horse's varied systems have been prepared. To avoid problems, the handler should always introduce high-intensity work gradually, allow plenty of time after a high-intensity work effort for the horse to cool off before returning to a stall, and understand that physical limits vary with weather conditions or between horses and that fatigue may set in sooner than expected.

3-56. Factors that can cause lameness on the trail for an out-of-shape horse include the following:

- Work intensity exceeds oxygen supply to working muscles.
- Aerobic function is limited.
- Anaerobic function is increased.
- Rider fails to recognize symptoms of anaerobic onset.
- Lactic acid production increases.
- Circulation is inadequate to remove lactic acid.
- Fuel in individual muscles is depleted.
- Fatigue and soreness cause changes in movement.
- Changes in movement cause forces to be distributed differently on supportive ligaments, joints, and bones.
- A bad step causes a fall or injury.

3-57. Signs that indicate the horse is approaching his limitations are as follows:

- Panting or blowing respirations.
- Heart rate more than 150 bpm.
- Profuse sweating.

NOTE

If the above symptoms occur, the handler should do the following:

- Stop and rest.
- If the horse is still breathing heavily or the heart rate has not gone below 100 bpm after 5 minutes of rest, discontinue its exposure to intense work for a few days. For instance, if trail riding, it would be best to dismount and walk until the horse is rested, then choose less strenuous routes on subsequent rides until its conditioning improves.
- If the horse continues to blow and sweat after several minutes of rest, it may have been overworked. Immediately discontinue riding, cool out the horse, and consider it off limits for at least a week.

PROGRAM DEVELOPMENT

3-58. At the beginning of training, animals may be in poor physical condition and unaccustomed to hard work. To properly condition animals, yet avoid injury, the handler should ensure operations are long in duration but mild in character. According to the training principles mentioned above, each animal should receive advanced training that includes gentling, leading, riding, standing, packing, gaiting, swimming, and seasoning to battle conditions. The handler should use actual field movements, progressive in length, throughout the training period to build up endurance. He can conduct a part of such field movements and other phases of training at night to prepare the animals for night operations. The handler should pay close attention to the animals during night training to determine if any are night blind. If so, he can supplement their diet with Vitamin A. Personnel who train animals should know how to use restraining devices for controlling animals. Such devices include the twitch, cross tie, and blinds. Personnel should exercise great care when using such devices. It is best to use the mildest and least dangerous method of restraint necessary to achieve the desired results. Oftentimes, kindness, perseverance, and tact will accomplish the desired purpose without using restraints.

3-59. The 21-Day Pack Training Plan is based on a system developed by the United States Army Artillery (Pack). This plan was developed for use with mules and may need to be adapted for use with other species. Because of the length of this training plan, time may not be available to conduct all of the training for the animals and ARSOF personnel, but the plan will provide guidelines and techniques for planning training.

3-60. During the training period, the animals have been made acquainted with many of the things to be encountered in open country, mountainous terrain, and jungles, including objects (tractors, newspapers, helmets, cans), strange noises (vehicle exhausts, gun shots, locomotive whistles), and odors (iodine, ether, smoke). These things should be presented in such a way that the animals do not associate them with harm or pain to themselves.

3-61. Obstacles should include loading ramps, steps cut in banks, small ditches, corduroy roads to cross swamps or bogs, and narrow bridges such as grease racks for cars and trucks. (The handler can simulate narrow bridges by constructing a walk, six-tenths of a meter wide and not over one-third of a meter high, over a pool of water; later, he can narrow the bridge and make it higher. He can also cut and place trees over a small stream, and with the top of the tree squared off, make a practical field bridge.) The handler should tie loads that rattle (a #10 can with stones in it) during the training. He should select narrow trails and make the animal do a considerable amount of climbing. He should have the animals go down slides, and walk up and down banks. The handler should load and unload the animals into trucks and, if appropriate, rail cars. He should always keep the animals coming along slowly and try to keep them in BCS 3.

RESTRAINING ANIMALS

3-62. Many ingenious devices have been developed over the years for restraining animals. Some have proven useful and humane and have helped to quiet and train animals. Others, although they could temporarily quiet and subdue an animal, make its attitude worse than it was originally. The handler should use restraints only when needed and use the least amount of restraint needed.

Blinding

3-63. This method is the easiest way to restrain an animal. The handler makes sure to tie the animal securely to a tree or post. Then he takes a piece of cloth (a gunnysack or jacket), or anything else that can be placed over the eyes, and ties it around the back of the animal's head. When blinded, an animal will seldom try to move. Once the animal responds to the restraint, the handler can vary the amount and use the least amount of restraint necessary. Animals should always be rewarded for good behavior. By responding with less restraint to the animal when he behaves correctly, the handler will gain his trust and respect. The animal in turn will be more productive and easier to manage.

NOTE

Under no circumstances should an animal be moved while it is blinded.

Twitches

3-64. An animal handler uses twitches because they are the handiest and most common method of restraint. Because the twitch shuts off circulation in the lip, the handler should never use it continuously for an extended time and never with greater force than is necessary. The handler makes a twitch by running a small piece of rope or chain through a hole in the end of a rounded piece of wood 2 to 5 feet long, such as a pick handle, and ties it in a short loop (Figure 3-6). He passes the loop of the twitch over the upper lip, which he seizes by hand and draws forward, taking care to turn the edges of the lip in to prevent injury to the mucous membranes. The handler tightens so the twisting points up over the outside of the upper lip. If the twitch is twisted down toward the end of the upper lip, it will easily slide off as the animal shakes its head or pulls away. He then tightens the loop by twisting the stick until he obtains sufficient pressure. Light changes in pressure with increases against resistance and decreases as the reward for obedience will help keep the animal's mind off the reason for the restraint and reduce the need for severity. These changes also help in training the animal to be more controllable. The handler should seldom use the twitch as a restraint while saddling or packing animals. He should use the twitch mostly when restraining for medical treatment or shoeing.

Figure 3-6. Twitch

CAUTION

Any long-handle twitch can be very dangerous. If the animal is successful in pulling free, the twitch becomes a high-velocity, high-energy object that can fly 50 meters or more. Fractious horses and mules can eventually pull these twitches free from even the strongest and most determined handler. Other twitches are safer. One is the pincher style that can be clipped to the halter.

3-65. A handler also uses a type of twitch made from a 16-inch piece of cord, such as parachute cord, and a horseshoe. He ties the cord with a square knot to form a continuous loop. He then twists it and folds to form two smaller double loops. He places the double loops over the upper lip in the same manner as a long-handle twitch. The handler inserts one-quarter of the horseshoe into the loop so that the cord will tighten against the side (quarter) of the horseshoe. He turns the horseshoe to tighten the loops in the same manner as tightening a tourniquet with a stick. The handler should tighten so the twisting points up over the outside of the upper lip. If the twitch is twisted down toward the end of the upper lip, it will easily slide off as the animal shakes its head. The handler then inserts the opposite quarter of the horseshoe into the ring on the halter. If this twitch is applied properly, it will not come off as the horse or mule pulls back and shakes its head. If the animal tries, the handler should let him. After a few failing attempts, the animal will cease fighting and the handler can proceed.

Cross Tie

3-66. Trainers often use the cross tie as a mild form of restraint. It consists of securing the animal's head in a normal raised position by two tie ropes extending from the ring in the halter to opposite sides of the stall or between two trees (Figure 3-7). When the cross tie is properly adjusted, the trainer may use it to his advantage while grooming, saddling, or doing any work around the animal. The cross tie also prevents an animal from chewing a wound and from lying down when he needs to be standing.

Distractions

3-67. Often a distraction rather than a restraint will enable the handler to accomplish what task needs to be completed. Three forms of distraction are as follows:

- Rubbing the lower eyelid.
- Tapping over the nasal sinuses.
- Hand twitches to the point of the shoulder.

3-68. The handler can distract the animal to complete short procedures merely by rubbing the animal's lower eyelid with his index finger. He places the palm of the hand on the side of the face so that the hand will move as the head moves. Failure to maintain contact with the palm against the face will often result in inadvertently touching the eye as the animal moves its head. The handler then rubs the lower eyelid with light to moderate pressure, but ensures the index finger does not slip into the eye. Lightly tapping over the nasal sinuses will also distract

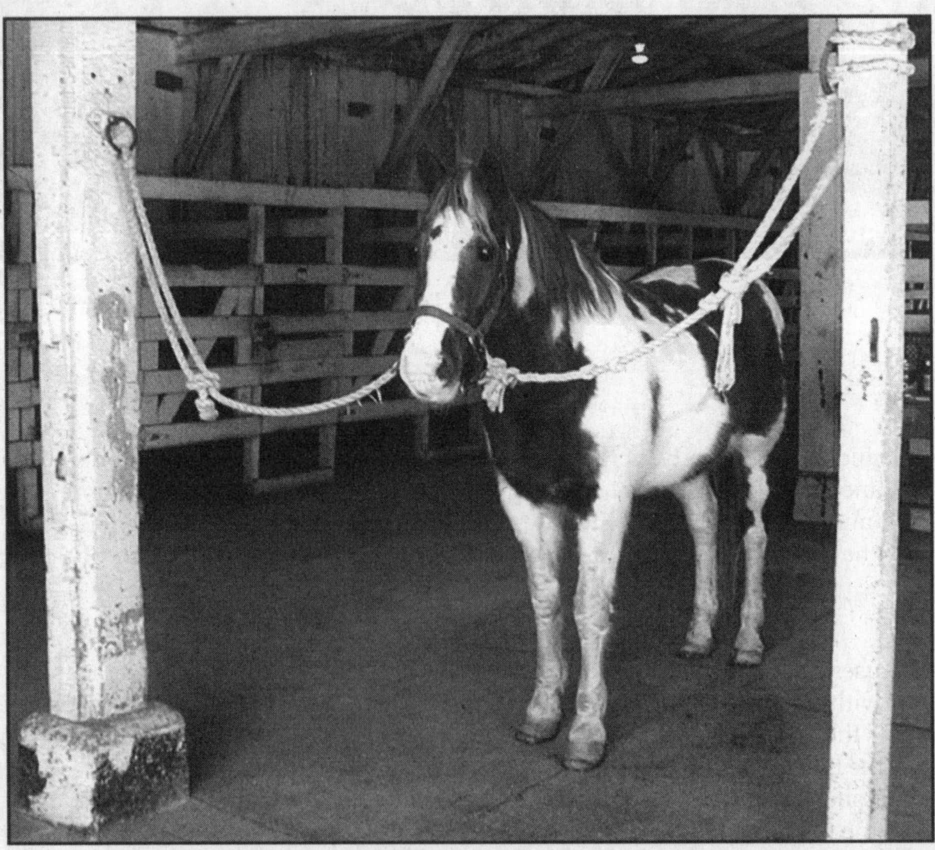

Figure 3-7. Cross tie

the animal enough to complete short procedures. The handler taps the fingers over the nasal sinuses with light to moderate pressure.

Other Restraints

3-69. Trainers use additional types of restraints when treating an animal whose condition is such that complete immobilization of the part to be treated is required. They use these methods only under normal conditions. Giving tranquilizers makes the more severe restraints unnecessary and reduces the danger to the animal from abuse at the hands of the ignorant or inexperienced. Other restraints include the—

- Side stick.
- Muzzle.
- Knee strap.
- Casting rope.
- Side line.
- Running "W." (Both front legs are restricted by rope and can be pulled out from under the horse. This restraint should only be done on soft ground to prevent injuring the horse's knees.)

CALMING AN ANIMAL

3-70. Fear is one of the animal's strongest instincts. If fear is allowed to remain a dominant instinct, the animal cannot be trained satisfactorily to do the work demanded of it. The goal of the trainer throughout the training period should be to gain and maintain the confidence of the animal. Horses and mules have a remarkable memory and tend to remember the unpleasant experiences longer than the pleasant ones. Retraining thus becomes more difficult than initial training, especially with a young, impressionable animal. Rewards for accomplishment are extremely valuable in the gentling process. Patting the neck, rubbing the head, and hand-feeding are good aids in gaining the confidence of the animal. The unwarranted use of whips, switches, or other devices to inflict pain or restraint should not be allowed in training. A willing, confident animal will work to the extent of its physical ability, but the scared, reluctant animal will expend less productive energy than its trainer.

CATCHING AN ANIMAL

3-71. The most convenient method of catching loose stock is by just walking up to the animal either in a corral or in the field. However, the handler must first have gained its trust. Only through love and kindness to the animal will the handler gain trust and respect for his presence at the animal's neck. Once the handler starts to catch a loose animal, he should not give up just because the animal walks off or spooks. The handler should not leave to go to another animal. If the handler is not firm, he will soon have an animal that is impossible to catch without either roping or cornering it in a corral. The handler will have taught the animal to avoid him by letting go at the first sign of resistance. The handler should maintain eye-to-eye contact while he tries to catch a loose animal. The animal often communicates his intentions through his eyes. The handler should also watch the animal's ears. If they point backwards or cock to one side, he does not have the animal's complete attention, and he must have it to catch it. The animal must respect the handler above all animals in the immediate area. The head of an animal being caught is not always the first thing a person should touch. Often the middle of the neck or the back area is the best area. Rubbing the animal about the withers and back will enable the handler to step in close to it and then hook his arm over the animal's neck. Some animals will try to pull away at this point. If the animal pulls away from the handler more than once, he should slip the halter rope over the animal's neck when it starts to scratch or fondle him. The handler will then have a loop to hold it. When the animal starts to move away, the handler can stop it firmly. The animal should immediately be rewarded for his obedience with a few reassuring pats and caresses. The handler must never knock the animal around for responding to the halter rope around its neck. If he does, the next time he wants to catch this animal, he may not be able to get near it. Last, but not least, a little grain in a bucket or feed bag will usually let the handler catch most animals that are used to being grained. If the animals get used to being grained immediately after being caught, their anticipation of the grain will make them very easy to catch. Having an apple or carrot to give the animals after catching them is another way to ensure their cooperation, but the handler should be sure to always give it to them. The handler should never tease the animals with a treat just to coax them into getting close enough to catch, then not give it to them. As mentioned before, horses and mules—especially mules—have good memories and will not forget such an insult.

BREAKING TO PICKET

3-72. Picket breaking is an important thing to teach animals to ensure against halter pulling. If the handler picket-breaks an animal before attempting to saddle or pack it, the impression of secure fastening will never leave the animal. It will feel that any strain put on the halter or halter shank is useless. Trainers have used the following method for picket breaking successfully for many years. It saves time and labor, since the animal does most of the work, and seldom has to be repeated. The handler catches the animal and puts a strong halter with a large halter ring around its neck. He should use a good, strong, soft rope, 1 inch or more in diameter. The handler runs one end through the halter ring and ties a fairly snug bowline around the animal's neck. He ties the other end securely to the middle of a smoothly trimmed log approximately 12 inches in diameter and approximately 20 feet long. The handler then places the log in the middle of a smooth, open piece of ground where the animal will not be able to become entangled with anything except the above-mentioned equipment. If no logs are available, he can use something like a large truck or tractor tire. The animal may pull, tug, and jerk on the log and try everything it can think of to get away from the log but without success and without harm. Soon the animal will learn that it cannot go anywhere and that a halter and rope mean escape is impossible.

3-73. The handler should teach an animal to stand still when the lead rope is hanging. Trainers call this kind of restraint a "ground hitch." Breaking to a ground hitch will prevent an animal from straying or running away if it comes loose from the pack string. One way to train an animal to stand with the lead rope hanging down is to run the lead rope through a ring attached to a spike in the ground. The handler places a set of hobbles on the animal and runs the lead rope through the ring and then ties it to the hobbles. When the animal tries to move, he will not be able to. The animal soon learns to stand still when the lead rope is hanging. During the training period, the handler makes sure to observe the animal from a distance to ensure no harm comes to it.

LEADING

3-74. The handler must teach all animals to lead. He first teaches them to lead next to a dismounted packer. Then he teaches them to lead alongside well-broken animals. Leading should be at the walk, as daily exercise, until the new animals lead quietly and have improved sufficiently in condition to allow them to start their instruction under saddle.

RIDING

3-75. The handler should break all animals to riding and ride with regularity during training before initial work under the pack. Since the mouths of young or untrained animals are tender, the handler should not use bits during the initial riding periods. He can attach the reins to the halter or use a hackamore (a bridle with a loop capable of being tightened about the nose in place of a bit).

PACKING

3-76. After the animal has been ridden for about 10 days, the handler can mount a packsaddle on him. For the first few days, the animal's packsaddle should not be loaded. The handler should ensure the animal is thoroughly familiar with the method of saddling and unsaddling. He should also make sure the animal stands quietly while packers are working before he places any load on the saddle.

3-77. Training under load should be progressive. Initial loads should be light, single-side loads, such as sacks of oats. The handler should not attempt to condition the animal for top loads until it is completely conditioned for full side loads. When the animal is comfortable with this weight, the handler can add top loads to the side loads. He should gradually increase the load from day to day until the animal is carrying his full payload of 200 to 250 pounds. After the handler trains the animal to stand, he should train it to stand while being saddled and packed. If at first the animal does not stand quietly, the handler may need to use the blind. As mentioned before, the blind is an exceptional aid and should only be used when the animal clearly indicates the need. An animal should never be moved a single step while blinded.

GAITING

3-78. Animals individually led by dismounted drivers maintain a rate of march from 3 1/2 to 4 miles per hour and seldom move at a gait faster than a walk. Those led by mounted drivers may be required to take any gait demanded by the situation. The walk and amble are the most satisfactory gaits for mules. The animals can maintain the walk for long periods at 4 miles per hour (a natural gait for the animal) and tend to disturb the load less than at any other gait. The amble is an acquired gait, easily acquired by the mule, that increases the rate of march to slightly more than 5 miles per hour. This gait is also easy on the load and hitches and, due to the increased rate of march, is favored over the walk on fairly level ground. Trainers teach the amble to pack mules by increasing the rate of march gradually during the training period. In hurrying to keep up with the column, mules will first break into the amble for a few steps. These periods at the amble will gradually increase until they become confirmed in this gait.

SWIMMING

3-79. A handler must teach pack animals to swim boldly and freely. Although they are naturally good swimmers, some animals are initially afraid of the water and will resist entering it. When they do go into the water, such animals fight their environment and swim very poorly. The handler should introduce the animals to the water quietly, coax them to wade through shallow water at first, and then lead them into increasing depths gradually until they must swim. Known good swimmers should accompany the green swimmers during this phase of training to give confidence to the novices. Chapter 8 explains water crossing.

BATTLE INDOCTRINATION

3-80. The handler should try to mentally condition his pack animals to as many of the sights, sounds, and smells of combat as possible. Once the animals become accustomed to these sensations, he can feel assured about their docility and good conduct in the field. The handler must conduct this mental conditioning or battle indoctrination so that animals will not associate the sight, sounds, or smells with harm or pain to themselves. Following are some tips:

- Conduct a portion of the training in marching, packing, and unpacking close to motor parks. The animal will then be subjected to the—
  - Sounds of motors being started and warmed up.
  - Pounding of metal on metal and an occasional backfire.
  - Smells of exhaust fumes and raw fuel.
  - Sight of many types of vehicles, both moving and at rest.
- Lead the animals as close to active firing ranges as safety will allow, near rail yards and crossings, and in areas near operating airfields. These areas get them used to loud, sharp sounds and the sight of flying aircraft. Another way to accustom the animal to gunfire is to crack a bullwhip near it.
- Place cans containing pebbles, boxes of tin cans, or other noisy cargo on the loads so that creaks, rattles, and unusual noises generated on the load will not spook the animal.
- Subject the animals to such odors as iodine, ether, smoke, gasoline, disintegrating flesh, and rotting vegetation.

TRAINING FOR BALANCE

3-81. Units normally use pack animals when crossing over terrain that is impassable by any type of motor vehicle. Traversing such ground requires a well-developed sense of balance. The mule naturally has a fine sense of balance. However, saddle and load will interfere with natural balance unless the animal has some training under load over difficult terrain and learns to adjust to the actions of this dead weight on its back. The handler should train the animal on terrain that is as similar as possible to the terrain in the operational area. He should make the animal cross extremely narrow bridges, fallen trees, and ditches. The handler should work the animal on steep, narrow trails; on corduroy roads; over swamps and boggy areas; and along rocky slopes where it must select safe footing among loose stones. The handler should use judgment in handling pack animals on difficult terrain, and should avoid interfering with the animal's natural balance. The mule usually shows better judgment than the average handler. Therefore, the handler should let the mule pick its way through the very difficult terrain.

CHAPTER 4

Animal Health Management

Evaluation of the general state of any animal's health is an ongoing process accomplished through daily observation of behavior and routine examination of specific areas of the animal's anatomy. A rudimentary understanding of anatomy and physiology, a few simple examination techniques, and a familiarity with the behavioral patterns of the healthy animal form the foundation of veterinary science. Aided by materials contained in the basic first-aid kit, handlers can treat pack animals suffering from minor injury or disease.

Soldiers performing veterinary care on animals in underdeveloped areas need to keep local cultural practices and economy in mind. An injured or debilitated animal may be of no use to the local people except as a significant source of food. It may be more practical for them to humanely destroy the animal and salvage the meat for food, rather than provide the animal with long-term care. Administration of medications may render the meat inedible. Before initiating any type of medical care involving medications, sedation, or other drugs, the Soldier needs to ascertain whether the animal may be used as a food source; if so, treatment in the form of drugs should be withheld pending the animal's immediate, humane destruction.

ANIMAL BEHAVIOR

4-1. Animals exhibit behavior patterns that resemble human emotion and well-being. They express anger, fear, and boredom with characteristic mannerisms. They also express pain and disability. Regardless of the individual personality traits developed by each animal, general behavioral patterns are common to the species and are useful as tools to evaluate physical status.

HEALTHY ANIMAL BEHAVIOR

4-2. The behavior a well animal exhibits is the benchmark. The handler must become familiar with its behavior patterns and be alert to changes in emotional or physical well-being. The healthy animal looks and acts well, reflecting mannerisms associated with humans. Emotions run the full spectrum from sadness to happiness. Behavior patterns become especially apparent when animals are observed in groups.

4-3. An animal shows its **happiness** by an initial dropping of the head, followed by lifting the muzzle in a circular manner. The upper lip may curl, displaying the teeth in a classic "horse smile." Prancing and lifting the tail usually accompanies this behavior. The well animal, pleased with its activities, may also prance with its ears pointed forward, nostrils flared, tail up, and neck arched with head pointed down.

4-4. Intense absorption, where the nose, eyes, and ears are all intently focused on the item or surroundings, indicates **curiosity**. Even the stance brings the body into line. The animal will sway its head to better see an object directly to the front.

4-5. Circling, pawing or stamping, head shaking, and sideward dancing characterize **frustration**. As frustration continues, the animal's activity results in sweating and unruliness. This behavior also typifies nervousness.

SICK ANIMAL BEHAVIOR

4-6. The sick animal, whether its illness is emotional or physical in nature, exhibits behavior indicative of its condition. An unhappy animal that is otherwise healthy will bring illness on itself. A sick animal will exhibit mannerisms that aid in early awareness of injury and disease.

4-7. Signs of intense interest characterize **fright**. The animal will shift its head from side to side, allowing better vision. It holds its head high and makes audible sniffing sounds. Dancing and shying, often in a circular motion, shivering, and tail swishing accompany increasing nervousness. Its ears will be mobile, seeking the source of threat when it is unapparent. As anxiety increases, profuse sweating occurs. The animal will attempt to flee and, if restrained, may buck and kick. Under extreme conditions, its eyes will roll, showing the whites. Ultimately, the animal becomes terror-stricken. At this point it will scream and, if loose, will attempt to run through any obstruction until it collapses in shock.

4-8. A more common problem is **boredom**. Unchecked, it leads to behavioral problems that will remain a part of its personality. Chewing on wood such as stall doors (cribbing), drawing air into its stomach (wind sucking), and rocking side to side (weaving) are common traits adopted by a bored animal.

4-9. A horse demonstrates **irritation** by laying back its ears and swishing or lashing its tail, often exaggerating the motion on one side. The animal will tense its front or hindquarters and lift a hoof in preparation for kicking. It can glare threateningly and bite or kick with surprising swiftness and ferocity.

4-10. **Pain** elicits reaction according to location (internal or external) and severity. With mild pain (fly bites, chafing, or early arthritis) and hoof pain (such as a pebble caught in the shoe), the animal will shrug, shiver, or kick in an effort to dislodge or soothe the area. It may flick its tail and nip at the afflicted area as a means of removing the irritant. Overall activity is fairly continuous, be it biting and bumping against an object or head tossing in distraction. Head shaking and ear twitching may also represent a head injury or uncomfortable bit.

4-11. **An internal injury** may exist when the animal shows signs of generalized listlessness, melancholia, increased distraction, and flagging (pointing the head) toward the affected side. The animal may lay its ears back and nip or rub its side. It lifts its hind legs alternately and hunches its abdomen in attempts to relieve the discomfort. Vocalizations such as groans are common. If pain, such as colic pain, continues, the groaning deepens and the animal will bite itself on the side and roll on the ground, worsening the condition.

4-12. An animal shifting its weight to the unaffected side and limping or refusing to move indicates leg **pain**. The animal will also "point" or extend the affected leg to try to relax it. The head will bob or swing to the side in an effort to bring the afflicted side forward.

4-13. Signs of **illness** may include a dulling of the coat, decrease in appetite, or such obvious symptoms as discharges from the eyes or nose, running sores, or diarrhea. The animal will carry its head down and show blankness in its eyes. The legs tend to splay outward while standing and the ears point outward in a splayed fashion also. Progressive illness leads to increased severity in symptoms. Leg splaying, head drooping, eye and coat dullness, fever, shivering, sweating, swaying, and staggering are all manifested to varying degrees.

OVERALL BEHAVIOR PATTERNS

4-14. Through examination of healthy animals and familiarity with their behavior in natural surroundings, handlers gain early recognition of the sick or injured animal. Neglecting small changes in behavior, coupled with ignorance of common maladies, may result in delay of movement or loss of an animal.

PHYSICAL EXAMINATION

4-15. The physical examination of an animal proceeds in the same overall manner as any physical exam. Certain precautions and allowances for the animal's natural fears and curiosity must be exercised. The examiner should enlist help in controlling the animal and constantly remain alert for signs of bolting, biting, and kicking. He should never assume a position between an animal and a fixed object. By leaning or shying sideways or forward, the animal can pin and injure the examiner or helper.

4-16. The animal should be examined when it is quiet and rested. Excitement and heavy exertion will drastically alter the animal's temperature, respiration, and pulse. When the physical examination is combined with routine grooming, the animal will receive it with more cooperation. Also, during every rest period and bivouac, the handler should examine every animal briefly for common maladies.

4-17. The handler should follow an orderly sequence during each examination to preclude overlooking any area. The handler should keep a record of the animal's feeding habits, bowel and bladder habits, general demeanor, and any cough or discharges. He should record results of physical examinations in chart form and include all immunizations. The handler should also maintain an extract version with the animal.

EQUIPMENT

4-18. A general examination may be performed without the use of any medical equipment. However, when available, the handler should use the following items:

- Watch with second hand or second indicator.
- Veterinary rectal thermometer (flexible, digital).
- Petroleum jelly or substitute.
- Stethoscope.
- Penlight or ophthalmoscope.
- Equine dental float (file).
- Rubber gloves.
- Several pieces of cloth or gauze.
- Twitch or hobbles for uncooperative animals.

PROCEDURE

4-19. The examiner begins the examination with an overall look at the animal, noting general demeanor, carriage, and gait. When unfamiliar with the particular animal, he should ask the handler about changes in diet and elimination. Also, he should ask about problems encountered during previous examinations, such as biting or kicking, medical conditions, and injuries. The examiner then checks specific areas of the animal. Many examiners refer to the head, ears, eyes, nose, and throat as **HEENT**.

Head

4-20. The examiner looks for signs of chafe from the halter, such as lesions and areas of hair loss. He notes how the animal carries its head and if it shakes or rubs it. Encephalitis or concussion and distemper (lockjaw) are detectable by confusion and loss of coordination.

Ears

4-21. The animal's ears should be checked gently because they are sensitive. The examiner looks for halter chafe, lesions (external and internal), and discharge. He notes how the animal carries its ears and watches to see if it shakes its head or rubs its ears. Ear mites, ear flies, and ticks are the main problems encountered.

Eyes

4-22. The examiner performs the eye examination in two parts. First, he does an overall examination of the eye, its orbit, and the lids with available light. He checks for lesions, foreign matter, and discharges. The examiner notes the color of the conjunctiva and the third eyelid—a whitish membrane that closes to cleanse the eye of particles. Communicable eye infections, biting flies, and gnats pose significant problems. Corneal abrasions and ulceration are common, especially in dusty or sandy environments. These minor problems can become serious if not treated properly, leading to blindness or loss of the entire eye. Occasionally, lesions (tumors) will grow on the inner eyelid, requiring surgery. When an animal exhibits photosensitivity by squinting or partially closing an eye, it may be suffering from conjunctivitis or other problems, such as snow blindness. Next, the examiner uses a light source, such as a flashlight, ophthalmoscope, or candle, and working in shade, examines the cornea. By shining the light from an angle, he looks for opacities and surface irregularities. Shining the light from the front, he observes the quality and clarity of the reflected image in the eye. To see if the animal is blind, the examiner moves his open hand in and out toward the animal's eye. If the animal has no reaction to this procedure or does not blink, the animal is most likely blind. The examiner performs the same procedure with the other eye.

Nose

4-23. The nostrils are sensitive and may be moist or dry, according to the environment. Nasal discharge presents a draining moistness, which increases in profusion when the animal's head is down, as in grazing. Discharge is usually accompanied by noise, such as snorting or sneezing, and licking or rubbing to clean the lip and nostrils. Sores are minimal unless inflicted by branches or the lead rope. Animals recovering from pneumonia, strangles, or milder respiratory infections may develop sinus infections. These infections are characterized by drainage, which increases when the head is down. The examiner should tap lightly with a knuckle on the bone just below each eye. Pain will be elicited in an animal with infection.

Oral Cavity

4-24. This examination includes the mouth, lips, gums, teeth, and tongue. The lips may contain splinters or pieces of burrs. The examiner checks for areas of abrasion around the mouth where the coat is rubbed away. Such abrasions may indicate an ill-fitting halter or bit. Malocclusions of the teeth, such as severe overbite or underbite, may interfere with grazing. The examiner checks the teeth for uneven wear, which occurs naturally but is also a common sign of cribbing (gnawing). Normal wear causes uneven, sharp slopes of the molars, whereas cribbing causes uneven wear on the incisors. The examiner checks the inner edges of the lower molars (lingual) and the tongue. When the molars become sharp, the tongue is often ulcerated by contact. He also examines the outer edges (buccal) of the upper teeth. Sharp edges here will ulcerate the inner cheek. In either case, the examiner uses a tooth float (rasp) to smooth the sharp surfaces. Lesions on the tongue can be traumatic and may be caused by ill-fitting bits or plant awns (bristle-like fibers, as on the heads of barley, oats, or wheat). Certain systemic illnesses, such as kidney disease and certain other infectious diseases, can cause ulceration of the tongue and oral mucosa.

Neck and Mane

4-25. The examiner checks the neck and mane for lesions and signs of chafe from contact with tack items. Ticks and mites are frequent in this area because the animal has difficulty dislodging them. Lymph glands located below the jaw can become enlarged from inflammation. Inflammation is somewhat difficult to detect in the glands except in the case of strangles. The examiner takes the pulse using the artery that runs along the inside of the jaw (mandible) on both sides of the head. The pulse will vary from 36–40 bpm during normal rest to 80–100 bpm after exertion, especially at higher elevations. Blood samples can be taken easily from the jugular veins on either side of the neck.

Chest and Shoulders

4-26. The animal's chest and shoulders are examined primarily for lesions caused by foliage and saddle rigging. The examiner notes the carriage, which is the distribution of the weight on the forelegs. He steps back and records the respirations by observing the rise and fall of the chest from the side. The animal must be rested and acclimatized. Normal rates will vary according to species and altitude. The normal rate at sea level is 8 to 16 breaths a minute. After exertion, a rate of 30 to 40 breaths a minute is normal. An animal that coughs or has noisy or staggered breathing requires an examination of the chest (lung fields) with a stethoscope. The examiner listens for gurgling, grating or rustling, or an absence of sound.

Flanks and Abdomen

4-27. The flanks and abdomen receive the heaviest amount of wear from the saddle and the associated rigging and loads. The examiner should thoroughly check for signs of chafe and loss of hair. A lesion in this area will rapidly become worse and possibly become infected without early management. Cysts and boils will require lancing and antibiotic dressings. Relief from further irritation is essential. An animal with an ulcerated area should not be put back under blanket or harness until fully healed and showing hair regrowth. An animal exhibits internal pain, such as colic, the same way a human does, with drawing-up and obvious attention to the afflicted region. The examiner should always know the animal's recent history of appetite and thirst. Loss of appetite is a sure sign of disorder or malady. When colic is suspected, the examiner uses a stethoscope to examine the abdominal region (if colic is present, there will be an absence of normal stomach noises) and supplements with a rectal exam.

Forelegs and Hooves

4-28. The animal's forelegs and hooves can be examined by lifting the lower leg rearward. The examiner supports the leg in one hand and examines the leg from sole upward. He pays particular attention to the entire hoof and each joint of the leg. To check the hoof, the examiner may need a hoof pick or similar device to clean the sole before the examination. All unit members should be familiar with specific injuries common to the legs and hooves. They should also be knowledgeable of specific hoof and bone deformities.

Hind Legs

4-29. The hind legs are best examined from slightly to the side, never directly to the rear. The examiner lifts the leg rearward and checks the hoof. He returns the hoof to the ground and examines the leg from the bottom up. Pulling the tail down and to the side will encourage the animal to stand with both hooves firmly on the ground. Injuries and conformation problems are less common than on the forelegs.

TEMPERATURE

4-30. While holding the tail down and to the side, the examiner takes a rectal temperature, ensuring the thermometer is well inserted and remains in place for at least 1 minute. Alternatively, digital thermometers should remain in place until the thermometer signals that the reading is complete (about 1 minute). Normal temperature for a horse is 99 to 101 degrees Fahrenheit (F). Normal temperature for a mule is 100 to 101.5 degrees F for a mule.

4-31. The proper way to take a rectal temperature is as follows:

- Shake the thermometer down if it is analog (mercury).
- Wipe it clean with alcohol.
- Cover it with petroleum jelly.
- Tie a cord to the thermometer if it has a ring at the end of it.
- Hold on to the cord or tie it to the animal's tail after inserting the thermometer into the animal's rectum.
- Keep the thermometer in for at least 1 minute.
- After withdrawing the thermometer and reading it, clean it with soap and water.

NOTE

If using a digital thermometer, the examiner should follow the manufacturer's directions.

OVERALL OBJECTIVES

4-32. Grooming is an essential part of animal care. The daily grooming period is the ideal time to perform a routine examination, excluding temperature, pulse, and respiration. These are checked only when illness is suspected. Early detection and correction of problems, such as chafe, is essential in the prevention of more serious disorders and possible loss of the animal. The examiner should never overestimate the durability of the animal. A mule is more durable than a horse. However, all animals are vulnerable to a wide variety of problems caused by both the environment and infection passed from animal to animal. Despite great size and strength, these animals are among the most susceptible to injury and disease. Constant vigilance must be exercised to maintain health and effectiveness of animals during sustained operations.

FIRST-AID SUPPLIES

4-33. A basic first-aid set should be carried specifically for use on the animals because standard bandages are too small for most purposes. The handler should put supplies in a weatherproof container in sufficient quantity to care for 10 percent of the animals. As with all critical items, duplication is suggested.

4-34. Figure 4-1, pages 283 and 284, lists the minimum supplies and equipment needed for treatment of a wounded animal. They include dressing changes since bandaging supplies (tape, cotton, gauze) will be expended rapidly and will require restocking or supplementing.

4-35. The examiner should include and apply heavyweight sutures with the same considerations as in humans. More sophisticated procedures require additional supplies. In most instances, the same equipment carried for treatment of humans is applicable to treatment of animals. Antibiotics and steroidal anti-inflammatory medicines are a notable exception. With these agents, it is either sensitivity to the drug or altered prescribing principles that pose the exception. A veterinarian must approve all medications before including them in the kit. Because replenishment of veterinary supplies may be difficult, the handler should include possible substitute or expedient materials, resupplies, and caches in mission planning.

Item	Quantity
Providine iodine solution	500 milliliter
Chlorhexidine solution	500 milliliter
Providine iodine or chlorhexidine surgical scrub brushes	2 each
Sterile saline for irrigation (0.9%), 500 milliliter	1 each
Lidocaine 2%, injectable 100 milliliter	1 each
Triple antibiotic ointment, 15-milliliter tube	1 each
Xylazine, injectable, 100 milligram/milliliter	100 milliliter
Trimethoprim sulfa, 960-milligram tablets	200 tablets
Duct tape, 100-mph tape	1 roll
Gauze, 4- x 4-inch, nonsterile	1 package
Vetwrap/Coban, 4-inch roll	6 rolls
Cotton, 12-inch roll	1 roll
Elastic bandage (Elastikon), 4-inch roll	2 each
Brown gauze, 6-inch roll	4 each
Conforming gauze bandage, 6-inch roll (for example, Kerlex)	3 rolls per animal
White bandage tape, 2-inch roll	2 rolls
Gloves, latex, exam, nonsterile	100 pairs
Gloves, latex, surgical, size 7 1/2	4 pairs
Stethoscope	1 each
Penlight	1 each
Scalpel blades, #10	6 each
Scalpel handle, #10	1 each
(Alternate to above 2 items: Disposable #10 scalpels with handle)	10 each
Scissors, surgical (Mayo or Metzenbaum)	1 each
Forceps: Brown Adson or Allis tissue forceps	1 each
Large needle holders with scissor blade	1 each
Hemostats, curved	4 each

Figure 4-1. Supplies and equipment needed to treat a wounded animal

Item	Quantity
Surgical towels	3 each
Gauze pads, 4- x 4-inch, sterile	10 pads
Gauze pads, 24 to 30 inches, sterile	3 sheets
Vetwrap/Coban, 4-inch roll	1 roll
(Package this kit together and autoclave.)	
Leg Bandage Kit	
Sheet cotton, 26- x 30-inch	3 sheets
Vetwrap/Coban, 4-inch roll	3 rolls
Brown gauze, 6-inch roll	1 roll
(Package this kit together in a plastic bag and compress with food vacuum preserver. The kit will compress down to a very compact size. This kit has essential items for one lower limb bandage. For full limb, two kits are used.)	

Figure 4-1. Supplies and equipment needed to treat a wounded animal (*Continued*)

FIRST-AID TREATMENT

4-36. Most principles of care in the administration of first aid directly parallel the treatment of humans; the major differences are in anatomical structure. Ethics will play a lesser role in treatment in the field: It is more likely animals will be destroyed in the field even though they could have been saved under normal circumstances by performing a radical procedure. Otherwise, the time involved for an animal to recover from lameness or the debilitation that occurs as a result of a serious injury could hamper the unit's ability to accomplish its mission.

OPEN WOUNDS

4-37. Bleeding, infection, and tissue loss are the main concerns in wounds resulting from external trauma. The examiner should give particular attention to any open wound on the hoof or hind leg. These wounds pose the highest threat of contamination and subsequent infection from bacteria contained in feces. Horses and mules are very susceptible to tetanus. The examiner should supplement treatment of open wounds, especially punctures, with a tetanus booster. Wounds directly over or close to joints may actually penetrate into the joint. Severe lameness or arthritis can result from joint infection, and these wounds need to be treated aggressively with systemic antibiotics.

LACERATIONS

4-38. These wounds, caused by a tearing of the skin, usually result in slight to moderate bleeding. The vessels contract and limit the flow of blood to the affected area. The examiner inspects the injury to determine the severity, depth of penetration, and degree of damage to underlying structures. He cleans it with soap and water to remove all foreign material. When the wound is small and the edges will remain closed, he applies an antibiotic ointment and covers the wound with a clean dressing. The examiner closes the larger wounds, and those where the edges gape open, with sutures, butterfly bandages, or surgical staples, if available. If closing the skin will leave a large pocket or cavity under the skin where tissues are damaged, it is better to leave the wound open than to suture the skin. Large cavities under the skin tend to accumulate blood and body fluids and can promote infection. The examiner applies antibiotic ointment and a clean dressing. He keeps the area dry and changes the dressing daily.

INCISIONS

4-39. Incised wounds tend to bleed freely. The first priority is to **STOP THE BLEEDING.** The examiner should use direct pressure, pressure dressings, tourniquets, and ligation with the same indications and precautions as on humans. Circulation to the lower leg is mainly superficial. Direct pressure is usually sufficient to stop bleeding in the extremities. Consequently, the examiner uses a tourniquet only when absolutely necessary and releases it every 15 minutes. Ligation should be accomplished as soon as practical to restore circulation to the limb. When the wound is dirty, the examiner places a constricting band above it to reduce bleeding and quickly, but thoroughly, cleans the wound before closing it with a dressing. The examiner uses sutures to close large or gaping incisions. When available, he gives a tetanus booster.

PUNCTURE WOUNDS

4-40. The causative agent may remain in the wound or be withdrawn. In all cases, the first step is to **STOP THE BLEEDING**. The examiner evaluates the severity of the wound and continues to control the bleeding. Puncture wounds are either low or high velocity. Low-velocity wounds impact only on the actual tissue penetrated and tend to bleed freely. High-velocity wounds impact on the actual tissue penetrated and impart a shock wave into surrounding tissue. This concussion tends to cause contraction of ruptured vessels, temporarily reducing the immediate blood loss. Packing the wound with gauze will aid in stopping blood loss when done in conjunction with standard pressure dressings. Impaled objects can also aid in stopping blood loss and may be left in place for a short period after being trimmed off flush and supported with a dressing. However, if the object impedes joint function, it must be removed. A topical antibiotic should never be put into a puncture wound; such an action causes systemic absorption of a topical medicine. The examiner irrigates the wound thoroughly with saline or water, sterile if possible. He cleans and dresses the wound. He then administers a tetanus booster, if available, especially in cases where punctures could allow direct access of pathogens into the bloodstream.

4-41. Animal handlers should follow specific steps when dressing wounds. The procedure for applying routine dressings is as follows:

- Inspect the wound and take appropriate measures to stop the bleeding.
- Cleanse the wound and surrounding area with clean, warm water and a nonirritating antibacterial soap. Typically, the area surrounding the wound should be shaved during cleansing.
- Apply a triple antibiotic ointment or other antibiotic topically.
- Cover the wound with gauze.
- Cover the gauze dressing with cotton padding.
- Wrap the area with roll gauze and secure with tape.

4-42. Animals will tear off the dressing if it is loosely applied. There are roll tapes specifically intended for use with animals. This tape (Vetwrap, similar to Coban bandage for humans) sticks only to itself, diminishing the trauma of dressing changes. Also, the handler should be careful of overtightening the dressing, creating a tourniquet.

CLOSED WOUNDS

4-43. Closed wounds result from external mechanisms such as overuse, hyperextension (straightening past the normal locking point of the joint), or hyperflexion (bending beyond the normal range of motion). Injuries include bruising, stretching, or tearing of connective tissue; joint dislocation; bursal inflammation or rupture; cartilage damage; and various degrees of bone fracture. Symptoms of these injuries are swelling, stiffness, and a partial or complete loss of function.

4-44. Major partial- and full-thickness burns and displaced and open fractures require specialized, lengthy treatment and recuperation. Destroying the animal becomes a matter of operational necessity when conducting a mission.

ALLERGIC REACTIONS

4-45. Allergy or anaphylaxis (severe allergic reaction) stems from a variety of causes. Most common are bites, stings, and skin absorption. Less common, but more serious, are reactions caused by substances eaten by the animal and entering the bloodstream. Horses, donkeys, and mules can also have allergic reactions to certain medications and vaccinations. Signs range from mild urticaria (hives) to anaphylaxis.

Bites and Stings

4-46. Allergic reactions to insect bites and stings result in small blistered areas (wheals) or generalized swelling (edema). The extent of swelling is dependent on the number of bites or the toxicity of the venom injected. A single fly bite will result in a wheal, whereas multiple bee stings will result in generalized swelling. Snakebites and scorpion stings produce similar reactions. Treatment is symptomatic. The handler applies ice to the affected area to reduce swelling and slow the spread of venom. Generally, large animals tolerate venom better than humans. However, antihistamines increase the effect of snake venom and **SHOULD NOT** be administered. The handler gives tetanus antitoxin and broad-spectrum antibiotics to counteract bacterial infection associated with snakebites. Emergency tracheotomy has been successfully used in cases of respiratory distress. Constricting bands will slow dissemination while increasing local necrosis and circulatory obstruction. Treatment for shock is indicated in moderate to severe cases.

Urticaria (Hives)

4-47. Stinging nettle, poison ivy, and chemical irritants result in blistering or rash formation. These rashes progress rapidly from localized to generalized when an animal becomes sensitized from repeated or heavy exposure to the irritant. Cold soaks and antihistamines will reduce the reaction, especially when respiratory distress develops. Ingestion of a large amount of protein will produce a similar effect. Gorging on food concentrates, spoiled hay, and a variety of other ingested substances will result in an allergic reaction (anaphylaxis). To treat the symptoms, the handler passes a tube to remove the stomach contents and gives laxatives and antihistamines.

BURNS

4-48. Burns are extremely painful injuries for animals and are difficult to manage if severe. With full-thickness burns over more than 30 percent of the animal's body, or over the head and face, prognosis is poor and euthanasia should be considered.

Superficial Burns (First-Degree Burns)

4-49. These burns are characterized by reddening of the skin. Vesicle (blister) formation is uncommon. Localized tenderness will necessitate refitting of tack or shifting loads until the animal tolerates pressure on the afflicted area. No other treatment is necessary.

Partial-Thickness Burns (Second-Degree Burns)

4-50. Tissue damage from these burns is limited to superficial layers of the skin. Vesicle formation occurs, resulting in the peeling away of dead skin after the fluid has drained and the blister dried. Pain lasting several hours after initial injury subsides to localized tenderness. Treatment of the burn consists of trimming the coat over the afflicted area and examining the wound. The handler applies an appropriate topical medication (such as silvidene ointment). He covers the area for 3 days with a clean, dry dressing to prevent vesicle rupture. Additional padding is required under harness straps when the animal must be harnessed. The handler drains all vesicles on the fourth day and allows drying for 5 days. He continues to protect the wound during this time to prevent infection. He trims away the dried skin on the tenth day after initial injury. The handler then places padding under tack until healing is completed.

Full-Thickness Burns (Third-Degree Burns)

4-51. These burns are characterized by charring of the flesh and coat. Severe tissue damage extending into underlying layers occurs. Moderate to severe pain, dehydration, and shock are symptoms. Treatment, when small areas are involved, is generally successful. However, severe burns covering a large percentage of the animal require clinical attention or destruction. The handler treats in the same way as for second-degree burns, encouraging fluid intake, adequate rest, and a restricted diet. Topical burn preparations will lessen pain; however, novocaine (lidocaine) nerve blocks may be required for the first days. The handler observes for signs of dehydration, infection, and shock.

LAMENESS

4-52. This general term describes many types of injury and conformation faults. Basically, lameness is caused by pain in one or more legs. Conformation faults, arthritis, and a variety of joint and tendon malfunctions result in lameness. Often in these cases, first-aid treatment is not applicable. Consequently, only lameness resulting from injury will be covered in this section.

4-53. The handler examines the animal in motion to isolate the limbs involved. The animal will step quickly off a painful leg and swing toward its good side. The handler observes for stiffened joints, reduced range of motion, nodding, limping, or swaying gait. He examines suspect limbs from the sole upwards and always looks for a hoof injury first. He does the examination in three parts—inspecting the sole, tapping the hoof, and flexing the individual joints, watching for evidence of pain. The handler walks the animal after each examination. If the gait is affected, he focuses on the last area examined. This procedure is time-consuming but is the only practical method for field use.

Hoof Lameness

4-54. The hoof is vulnerable to a variety of injuries and infection. An unshod, untrimmed hoof will develop cracks. Injuries from overtrimming and improper nailing occur during routine trimming and shoeing. An animal can develop corns if it goes too long without reshoeing. While moving, impact forces cause stress on the bones, suspensory ligaments, and tendons. Rocks and a multitude of sharp objects bruise and pierce the sole or lodge under the shoe. These are injuries for the farrier's or the veterinarian's care. Exceptions are thrush and cracked heels as explained below.

4-55. Routine care of the hoof consists of regular trimming and shoeing. During halts, the handler inspects the sole and removes any objects that have lodged there, especially in rocky terrain. Painting the wall (outside) of the hoof with hoof oil may reduce cracking.

4-56. **Thrush** is caused by bacteria infecting the frog. It is characterized by a dark, foul-smelling discharge from between the frog and the sole. Most common among stabled animals, it is caused by standing in wet and unsanitary conditions, or from untrimmed hooves where the frog has become overgrown. Treatment consists of proper hoof trimming, thorough cleansing supplemented by application of iodine, copper sulfate, or a diluted bleach solution to the infected area around the frog only.

4-57. **Cracked heel** is actually a skin condition affecting the pastern above the heel of the hoof. Caused by continued incomplete drying of this area, it is seen in animals pastured in wet or muddy fields. The skin develops dry scaling that degenerates into cracking, as in athlete's foot. Treatment consists of cleansing and thorough drying. The handler applies an ointment or petroleum jelly. The problem is a result of dryness and chafing. The animal should never be treated with an agent that will cause further drying of the area.

Lower Leg Lameness

4-58. Any injury below the knee is potentially very serious. There is little muscle tissue in this area, the blood supply is limited, and the area is in continual motion, which tends to aggravate injuries. Furthermore, the chance of infection is greater in areas close to the ground because they are hard to keep clean.

4-59. Injury to the lower leg is a result of either stress, caused by a misstep or prolonged travel on a hard surface, or trauma from hoof strikes inflicted by other animals or self-inflicted. Isolated occurrences result in temporary lameness. Repeated or prolonged injury generally results in formation of calluses or calcium deposits in the area. Treatment of isolated occurrences is successful when time for adequate rest is allowed. Formation of calluses and calcium deposits require care by a veterinarian and protracted periods of rest.

4-60. When, as the result of an inflammation, synovial fluid collects around a joint or tendon, the condition is termed synovitis. Synovial fluid is produced as a lubricant for joint motion. Inflammation will cause an overproduction of this fluid, which is then trapped in and around the joint. Reabsorption occurs naturally over time in most cases, provided inflammation is reduced. Needle aspiration and cortisone injections are stopgap measures and may result in the eventual destruction of the joint. With early diagnosis and prompt treatment, these conditions need not result in lameness. Treatment consists of rest, ice packs, or cold soaks and reduction of load or variations in surface traveled. Some of these cases will result in permanent deformity in the form of an enlarged joint capsule.

4-61. Sprains of the flexor tendons or suspensory ligament occur during running or jumping but may be seen when tripping occurs on a wedged hoof. A sprain is a stretching, tearing, or complete rupture of the affected tendon or ligament. A common name for these conditions is "bowed tendon." Symptoms consist of lameness, which is often severe, and pain and swelling over the injured region. Inflammation will generate warmth, detectable to the touch. In severe cases (rupture of the tendon), loss of support occurs in the joint during weight bearing. Length of recovery depends on the extent of the stretch or tear.

4-62. Treatment consists of complete rest, ice packs (at least twice daily), or cold soaks, supplemented by supportive wrapping or casting of the leg. Recovery from a moderate tear or complete rupture requires surgical repair. Needle aspiration and cortisone injections have promoted healing in some cases.

PARASITIC INFESTATION

4-63. Parasites are classified according to location of residence: external (ectoparasites) or internal (endoparasites). Of the two, internal parasites are more debilitating, though it is external parasites that carry the most infectious disease and present the greatest nuisance. There are large numbers of different parasites. Of these, some affect only a specific host. Others afflict any warm-blooded animal, including man.

ECTOPARASITES

4-64. External parasites that reside on or just under the surface of the skin by burrowing include insects such as flies, fleas, lice, mosquitoes, mites, and ticks. The area around the eyes, ears, neck, and anus are the most common sites of infestation because they are areas of secretion, and the skin in these regions offers the easiest penetration.

4-65. Depending on the type of parasite, symptoms range from rashes and blistered areas to patches of hair loss (alopecia). Animals displaying excessive itching, hair loss, or rough, thickened skin should be suspected of hosting parasites. Closer examination will reveal blisters or burrows, dried blood, or the insect itself.

4-66. The handler treats for parasites by applying topical insecticides. This treatment works best on those parasites that remain on the host, such as mites. It is less effective on flying insects because the brief feeding period reduces total dosage absorbed. Insect repellents provide relief from these pests and are the only practical solution in a field environment.

ENDOPARASITES

4-67. Internal parasites generally live within the intestinal tract. They remain there throughout their life cycle or migrate out the anus as larva to spend their adult cycle outside the host. Less common are the endoparasites that live in other internal organs or surrounding muscle tissue. Regardless of residence, the mouth is the most frequent point of entry.

4-68. Symptoms are subtle, except for the dramatic appearance of the parasite exiting the anus or contained in manure deposited on the ground. Evidence of unexplained weight loss, chronic tiredness, or dullness of coat is frequently the result of parasites. These anemic-like symptoms result from the loss of nutrients to the parasite, especially a large colony of parasites. Untreated, these colonies debilitate the host, often causing blockages and colic.

4-69. Treatment of internal parasites is more successful than treatment of external parasites because a more consistent dosage of antiparasitic is absorbed by the invading parasites. Preventive administration of antiparasitics is a common practice and is the most convenient method. Many anthelmintic medications are available for horses, donkeys, and mules, including ivermectin, fenbendazole, oxibendazole, and moxidectin. They are available in an easy-to-administer oral paste form. When treating animals that have not been dewormed regularly throughout their life, the first treatment should be given as half the normal dose, 2 weeks apart. With extremely heavy parasite load, rapid die-off of large numbers of parasites can cause intestinal impaction, diarrhea, or other adverse reactions.

DISEASES

4-70. Zoonosis are diseases that usually affect only animals but can be transferred from animals to humans under natural conditions. Anthrax (cattle fever) and rabies are excellent examples. People working with animals are at particularly high risk for zoonotic diseases.

4-71. Currently, there are immunizations for most major infectious diseases affecting horses, mules, and similar animals. The key to disease management is to follow a schedule of routine inoculation and parasite control. Additionally, proper sanitation and hygiene must be maintained.

4-72. New and ill animals should be quarantined to prevent the spread of disease among the healthy animals. Frequently, animals will develop flu-like symptoms after being transported or stressed by changes in environment. This syndrome is referred to as "shipping fever." Disease pathogens congregate in food, bedding, and tack. Therefore, personnel should ensure that these items remain clean and are not transferred from animal to animal without some form of disinfection.

STRANGLES

4-73. Strangles is an infection of the lymph nodes caused by the bacteria *Streptococcus equid.* This condition is highly infectious between horses and is usually seen as an outbreak within a herd or stable.

4-74. Occurrence is most frequent among young animals but will occur in any equine not previously exposed or immunized. The infectious period is approximately 4 weeks. The incubation period is 3 to 6 days, with flu-like symptoms. Fever with temperatures as high as 106 degrees F may occur. Few infections in horses cause as significant fevers as with *Streptococcus equid* infection. If a fever over 103.5 degrees F is observed, strangles or equine influenza should be suspected. A nasal discharge follows rapidly and is quite heavy. As inflammation of the lymph nodes in the throat and neck continues, abscesses form. Abscesses can also form in any lymph nodes of the body, especially in the mesenteric lymph nodes along the intestines. The animal may also have a foul smell about it. These are classic symptoms of the disease. The lymph tracts, which run the length of the neck and trunk bilaterally, become so swollen that they appear rope-like under the skin. Central nervous system (CNS) damage occurs in some cases. However, pneumonia is the greatest cause of death.

4-75. Treatment is largely symptomatic. The focus of treatment should be on draining abscesses and controlling fever. Although *Streptococcus equid* responds well to penicillin antibiotics, use of antibiotics to treat the disease may result in prolonging the problem. Antibiotics are indicated if secondary pneumonia develops during the course of the disease. Otherwise, with good drainage and nursing care, horses will often completely recover within 4 to 6 weeks.

4-76. Using hot packs to bring the abscess to maturity is more appropriate. Next, the handler should incise and drain (I&D) these mature abscesses using proper techniques to prevent the invasion of other pathogens into the lymphatics. Vaccinations are available to help prevent the disease. Due to the short incubation period (3 to 6 days), once one animal in a herd or stable is affected, it may be too late for vaccination of the other exposed horses to be effective.

4-77. If adequate drainage of abscesses is obtained and fever is controlled, animals can recover completely. However, complications can occur in severe or untreated cases including laminitis, severe myopathy (muscle damage), pneumonia, or airway obstruction. Because of the location of affected lymph nodes in the throat area, the airway can become obstructed in severe cases. Emergency tracheotomy may be necessary in these cases.

TETANUS

4-78. An acute infectious disease, tetanus is caused by an introduction of contaminated soil into tissue and the bloodstream and affects the CNS. This anaerobic neurotoxin is normally inactive and lives in a spore state. Usually introduced through a wound, the disease causes tissue decay, which provides the anaerobic environment required for reproduction. After reproduction, the bacteria rupture, resulting in the release of the neurotoxin, which migrates along the nerves to the spinal cord.

4-79. Symptoms of tetanus, either ascending (motor nerve to spinal cord) or descending (lymphatic to CNS), consist of a characteristic muscle spasm after even mild stimulation and localized stiffness increases to generalized rigidity. Especially prone to spasms are the muscles in the jaw and neck, giving rise to the common name of lockjaw. Symptomatic progression leads to rigidity of the ears, spine, and legs. The stance widens (sawhorse) and the nostrils dilate. Closing (prolapse) of the third eyelid, profuse sweating, continued excitation spasms, rapid respiration, cardiac irritability, and arrhythmia are present in the latter stages.

4-80. Treatment is begun by preventive immunization of all animals, followed by routine booster injection (tetanus toxoid). After an animal is wounded, it should receive good wound care, consisting of thorough cleansing and disinfecting of the wound site, followed by a tetanus booster. In animals that have contracted the disease, treatment consists of drainage and disinfection of the wound, removal of all dead tissue, and an injection of tetanus toxoid and tetanus antitoxin (100 to 200 units per kilogram [kg] intramuscular [IM]) in different injection sites. Treatment with sedatives (acepromazine 0.05 milligrams [mg]/kg IM every [q] 6 hours [hr]) or phenobarbital (6 to 12 mg/kg intravenous [IV], initially followed by the same dose orally q12 hr) has succeeded in moderately severe cases. Procaine penicillin G should be administered (22,000 to 44,000 mg/kg IM q12 hr for 7 days). The handler supplements treatment by keeping the animal in a darkened, quiet stall. He should avoid any incidence of startling the animal. The handler elevates food and water since the animal has difficulty lowering its head. Recovery periods average 2 to 6 weeks.

EQUINE INFECTIOUS ANEMIA

4-81. Commonly known as swamp fever, equine infectious anemia is a viral disease very common among horses worldwide. Transmission occurs from blood-to-blood interaction such as in the use of contaminated syringes or scalpels. It can reach epidemic proportions when transmitted by bloodsucking flies.

4-82. The disease is characterized by flu-like, low-grade fevers, yellowing of the gums, depression of appetite and demeanor, weight loss, and obvious signs of anemia during microscopic blood examination. Continued weight loss, enlarged spleen, swelling of the infected area, debilitation, and death follow if the disease is untreated. Diagnosis through the use of a serological test (Coggins test) is done in the clinical environment. This test shows the presence of antibodies in the blood of an infected animal. Vaccines exist although their effectiveness is questionable. Quarantine of any suspect or new animal and symptomatic treatment is the only therapy. Control of vectors, by use of insect repellents and insecticides, plus proper sterilization of medical instruments will minimize the impact of this disease on the herd.

COLIC

4-83. Colic is a term used to denote pain in the abdomen from a variety of different causes. Colic is often caused by distention of the bowel resulting from excessive gas production (flatulent colic), impaction of feces or bowel obstruction from colonies of intestinal parasites (obstructive colic), twisted intestine (torsional colic), or gorging or overfeeding. Colic may also result from circulatory problems due to the inactivity of bowel segments. Colic from intestinal impaction often occurs when horses do not drink sufficient water. This often occurs at the change of seasons when the temperature suddenly becomes cold or hot, or when horses are moved to an area with a different source of water unfamiliar to them.

4-84. Regardless of the type of colic and its cause, the animal exhibits a sudden loss of appetite, depression, and frank attention to the abdominal region. Bowel sounds frequently diminish or alter. Rectal examination may locate the obstructed region. Marked distention of the flanks may be present, especially in young animals or in severe stages.

4-85. Treatment is largely symptomatic. It includes administering analgesic agents and making sure the animal is sufficiently hydrated. The handler should keep the animal on its feet to reduce the chance of complications, but if the animal is violently painful to the point of hurting itself or humans, it is best to try to allow it to lay down in a soft, open area, such as on sand or grass, with no fences or other objects nearby. A painful horse can throw itself down quite suddenly, resulting in severe injury of its handlers. All nonessential personnel should stay away from the animal. The handler passes a bloat tube (nasogastric) to relieve gastric distention. If the animal does not reflux a net amount of gastric contents through the nasogastric tube (more flowing out than amount of water pumped in) and has no obvious signs of complete obstruction, mineral oil (2 to 4 liters) can be given by stomach tube to disperse impactions.

The handler may supplement the mineral oil by administering an osmotic laxative (magnesium sulfate) or an irritant (neostigmine). Passage of the tube and administration of any material through the tube should only be performed by personnel well trained in this procedure. Accidental passage of the tube into the trachea instead of the esophagus can result in death of the animal. Analgesics, to prevent self-injury, may be indicated. Flunixin meglumine (Banamine) is recommended at 1.1 mg/kg IV or IM q12 nr. Flunixin meglumine is very effective at relieving mild to moderate pain and reducing fever and inflammation associated with irritation in the intestine. If flunixin is not available, phenylbutazone can be used instead, also at 1.1 mg/kg q12 hr. Butorphanol can be used for severe pain at 0.01mg/kg q1—2 hr IV as needed to control pain. Due to possible excitatory reactions, morphine is not generally used in horses, mules, or donkeys. Decompression through the use of a large-bore needle (trocharization) inserted into the upper flank is sometimes effective in relief of severe distention as a last-ditch effort. Severe cases of colic, such as with intestinal torsion, require surgery to correct the problem. If complete obstruction occurs, pressure from buildup of gas, fluid, and fecal material will eventually cause rupture of the stomach or intestine. If this occurs, the animal will often suddenly become significantly more comfortable for a short time. However, within 30 minutes to an hour, signs of shock, such as trembling, diffuse sweating, staggering, or collapse, will occur and the animal will die soon after. This condition is essentially untreatable and the animal should be humanely destroyed. Prevention, through proper diet, dental care, and parasite control, is the most effective method of dealing with colic.

HYPOTHERMIA

4-86. Hypothermia will kill livestock as well as humans. Shivering is one of the first signs of cold stress. The symptoms progress through listlessness and loss of feeling in the limbs until death occurs.

4-87. Hypothermia is a lowering of the body's temperature. At a rectal temperature of less than 28 degrees Celsius (C) (82 degrees F), the ability to regain normal temperature naturally is lost, but the animal will continue to survive if external heat is applied and the temperature returns to normal. It is important to observe and measure the vital signs—pulse, breathing, mental status, and rectal temperature.

4-88. Knowing the severity of hypothermia is valuable to decide the rewarming techniques to be used for treatment. On the basis of body temperature, hypothermia can be classified as mild—30 to 32 degrees C or 86 to 89 degrees F, moderate—22 to 25 degrees C or 71 to 77 degrees F, and severe— 0 to 8 degrees C or 32 to 46.5 degrees F. There is tremendous variability in physiological responses at specific temperatures among individuals and species (Table 4-1). The simplest way to determine whether the patient is hypothermic or not is to assess body temperature by placing a bare hand against the skin (preferably in axilla or groin region) of the patient. If the skin feels warm, hypothermia is unlikely. Patients with cold skin should have rectal temperatures taken with a low-reading thermometer.

Table 4-1. Temperature ranges for work species

Species	Low Dangerous Range (C)	Normal Range (C)	High Dangerous Range (C)	Quit Work (C)
Horse	30–32	37.5–38.5	39.5–40.0	40.5
Donkey	30–32	37.5–38.0	39.5–40.0	40.5
Mule	30–32	37.5–38.0	39.5–40.0	40.5
Ox	31–33	38.0–39.0	39.5–39.8	40.0
Camel	29–33	36.5–42.0	42.5–43.5	44.0
Llama	30–32	37.2–38.9	39.2–40.0	41.0
Elephant	Not Available	36.0–37.0	38.0–38.2	38.3
Reindeer	Not Available	38.0–39.0	39.2–39.4	39.5
Dog	31–33	38.9–39.9	40.9–41.9	42.3
Goat	Not Available	38.6–39.6	40.6–41.6	42.0

EXAMINATION FOR HYPOTHERMIA

4-89. To examine a hypothermia animal, the handler should make sure that the animal has an open airway, is breathing, is within the normal pulse and respiration range (Table 4-2), and has a normal rectal temperature. These factors are commonly known as the ABCs. The handler should also perform a—

- Brief history (for example, duration of exposure regarding circumstances in which animal is found).
- Brief physical examination, to include the following:
  - Feel-of-body temperature.
  - Level of consciousness and neurological examination.
  - Cardiopulmonary examination.
  - Associated trauma.
  - Weight of animal. Depending upon the availability of staff and equipment, chest X ray, urinalysis, complete blood work, and arterial blood gases are also recommended.

Table 4-2. Pulse and respiration ranges for work species

Species	Normal Pulse (per minute)	Normal Respiration (per minute)
Horse	23–70	12–14
Donkey	40–56	14–16
Mule	35–67	13–15
Ox	60–70	30–32
Camel	40–51	10–13
Llama	60–90	10–30
Elephant	24–40	6–15
Reindeer (Summer)	20–40	20–50
Reindeer (Winter)	40–70	8–16
Dog	70–120	18–34
Goat	70–80	16–34

MANAGEMENT OF HYPOTHERMIC ANIMALS

4-90. Once it is established that an animal is hypothermic, the primary goal in the treatment and handling of the animal is to keep the animal alive by warming, avoid any further exposure to cold, and then transport the animal to a site of complete veterinary care if possible. The severity of hypothermia will determine the rewarming technique to be used for treatment.

HYPOTHERMIC REWARMING TECHNIQUES

4-91. There are three rewarming techniques—passive external, active external, and active internal—which should be used according to severity of hypothermia. To treat the hypothermic animal appropriately, the handler should first know that the animal is in fact hypothermic. Once the severity is determined, the handler has to decide the rewarming technique to be used for treatment.

Passive External

4-92. The animal's own metabolic process continues to produce heat spontaneously, so no external heat is required. Shivering is an example of thermogenesis. This method is the simplest and slowest but is sufficient for mild hypothermic animals.

Active External

4-93. This method includes warm baths, hot water bottles, blankets, heating pads, and radiant heaters. This type of rewarming is safe only for mild hypothermia because externally applied heat stimulates peripheral circulation.

> **NOTE**
> The handler should avoid direct application of hot objects or excessive pressure (for example, uninsulated hot water bottles or tourniquets). He should ensure that items such as oxygen and fluids coming into contact with the animals are warmed. A severely hypothermic animal should not be put in a shower or bath.

Active Internal

4-94. These rewarming methods are usually more complex and need to be carried out by professionals (veterinarians or animal health technicians). These include inhalation rewarming (ventilation of patient with heated, humidified air or oxygen), circulation of heated fluids (40.5–43.5 C) in body cavities (gastric, thoracic, and peritoneal lavage), and heated intravenous solutions, preferably dextrose, as these provide energy to meet increased metabolic demands but contribute little heat due to vasoconstriction in cold extremities.

> **NOTE**
> Inhalation rewarming is the only method that can be used by a layman and does not require much training (mouth-to-mouth breathing). Inhalation of warm, saturated air delivers heat directly to the lungs and heart. The brain is also warmed from this blood flow and from conductive heat flow from the respiratory and nasal cavities. This method also assists in rehydration as an added benefit.

HEAT AND SUN STRESS

4-95. The range of temperature in which heat distress will be noted is similar to that for humans. If the handlers and other detachment members are showing signs of severe discomfort, the animals may be in distress as well. Direct sun all day long not only overheats animals in most environments, but it can also lead to sunburn. In severe cases, heat exhaustion or sunstroke can result. The handler can use any piece of shade that is available. Livestock should always be placed where a breeze will help with the cooling process. Portable shade can be obtained by putting straw hats on animals' heads.

4-96. The danger signs of heat distress, in all species except camels, are tremors, "drawn" expression, heavy perspiration, panting, frothing at the mouth, and dark yellow urine with a strong smell. Heat injuries begin with "thumps," progress to heat cramps, and advance to heat exhaustion.

- *Thumps* is characterized by panting, widely dilated nostrils, heavy sweating, and a deep thumping sound from the lower lungs and flanks.
- *Heat cramps* occur due to loss of salts, especially potassium. The animal then becomes stiff in the large muscles, such as the hind legs. The animal may cry in pain and try to either stand still or roll on the ground.
- *Heat exhaustion* is shown by large amounts of sweat, tremors of the limbs, and profuse amounts of sweat. If the animal stops sweating, sunstroke is underway.

4-97. In all heat injuries, the animal should be cooled as quickly as possible by pouring cool water over the head and back. Alcohol will cool even faster and should be applied if available. All heat injuries require prompt attention, but sunstroke is a true emergency and requires immediate action or the animal will die.

4-98. Rehydration should be attempted if the animal can drink. If available, citrus-based electrolyte solutions such as a mixture of water, a small amount of sodium salt, and an equal amount of potassium salt flavored with sugar will suffice. This amount is enough to give a slight taste of salt and a stronger taste of sugar. A quick sample of the solution will tell the handler if it is correct. Honey and water with a little salt can also be used. The handler can also add potassium salt if possible.

4-99. Once the animal's body temperature has begun to drop (according to the rectal thermometer), chills must be avoided. The animal should be given a gentle massage to help move blood to the skin. A dry blanket should be applied and secured with a strap. Once this crisis has passed, rest is best under the watchful eye of a veterinary nurse or first-aid provider. If chills set in, the handler should add more blankets and continue to massage the animal. A hot or recovering animal should not be fed grain. It can be given forage and free access to water.

IMMUNIZATION SCHEDULE

4-100. The following paragraphs list several diseases that plague animals, and also provide a suggested immunization schedule. For primary immunization, an initial vaccination is required, followed by a repeat dose in 3 to 4 weeks. Table 4-3 is a handy reference guide for scheduling immunizations.

Table 4-3. Immunization schedule

Type	Frequency Profile
Tetanus	All horses; foals at 2–4 months; annually thereafter. Brood mares at 4–6 weeks before foaling.
Encephalomyelitis (WEE, EEE)	All horses; foals at 2–4 months; annually in spring thereafter. Brood mares at 4–6 weeks before foaling. *Note: Vaccinate for Venezuelan Equine Encephalomyelitis (VEE) in endemic areas only.*
Influenza	Most horses; foals at 3–6 months, then every 6 months. Traveling horses that will contact other "outside" horses, every 6 months. Brood mares biannually, plus booster 4–6 weeks prefoaling.
Rhinopneumonitis	Foals at 2–4 months and younger horses in training. Repeat at 2- to 3-month intervals. All brood mares at least during 5th, 7th, and 9th months of gestation.
Rabies	Foals at 2–4 months; annually thereafter.
Strangles	Foals at 8–12 weeks; biannually for high-risk horses. Brood mares biannually with one dose 4–6 weeks prefoaling. Some adverse reactions are associated with this vaccination. *Note: Vaccinate only in situations where infection is likely.*
Potomac Horse Fever	Foals at 2–4 months; biannually for older horses. Brood mares biannually with one dose at 4-6 weeks prefoaling. *Note: Vaccinate in endemic areas only.*
West Nile Virus	Initial vaccination, booster in 2–4 weeks, then annually. *Note: Vaccinate only in areas where infection is likely.*

MEDICAL SUPPLY LIST

4-101. In addition to the supplies contained in the veterinary first-aid kit, Table 4-4 lists items that are consolidated into a single kit for use in more definitive care.

Table 4-4. Consolidated list of items used for definitive care

Item	NSN
Kit, minor, surgical	NSN 6545-00-957-7650
Float, dental, veterinary	NSN 6515-00-938-4301
Needle, hypodermic 20-gram (g), 1 1/2-inch	NSN 6515-01-003-2368
Needle, hypodermic 18g, 1 1/2-inch	NSN 6515-00-754-2834
Needle, hypodermic 25g, 1-inch	NSN 6515-01-037-5590
Basic IV drip set, 10 or 15 drops/milliliters (ml)	NSN 6515-01-332-1276
Pump, injection and suction, veterinary	NSN 6515-00-938-4718
Suture, nonabsorbable size 3-0, with cutting needle	NSN 6515-00-054-7444
Suture, nonabsorbable size 0, with cutting needle	NSN 6515-01-195-7701
Twitch, chain	NSN 3770-00-191-8055
Clipper, hair	NSN 3770-00-804-4700
Stethoscope, bell/diaphragm	NSN 6515-01-304-1027
Thermometer, digital, flexible	NSN 6685-00-444-6500
Tube, nasogastric, veterinary	NSN 6515-01-153-5387
Gloves, examination, veterinary	NSN 8415-01-359-7935
The Merck Veterinary Manual	ISBN 0911910557
Orsini and Divers Manual of Equine Emergencies	ISBN 0712624251
Syringes, 3-ml, 5-ml, 10-ml, and 60-ml Luer tips	Varies per Size

PHARMACOLOGICAL LISTING

4-102. Table 4-5 lists antibiotics, antiparasitics, and antifungals used to treat pack animals. It also lists the recommended drugs, dosages, and routes of each item used.

Table 4-5. Pharmacological listing

Drug Class: Antibiotics	Drug	Route and Dosage
Penicillins	Sodium	pcn G, IV, 10,000–20,000 immunizing units (IU)/kg, q6 hr
	Potassium	pcn G, po 25,000 IU/kg, q6 hr
	Procaine	pcn G, IM, subcutaneously, 22,000–44,000 IU/kg, q12 hr
Cephalosporins	Cefazolin	IV, IM 20–25 mg/kg, q6 to 8 hr
Aminoglycosides	Gentamicin	IM, 4 mg/kg, q24 hr
Tetracyclines	Oxytetracycline	IV, 5 mg/kg, q12 to 24 hr
Sulfonamides	Trimethoprimsulfa	20 mg/kg q12 hr

Table 4-5. Pharmacological listing (*Continued*)

Drug Class: Antiparasitics	Drug	Route and Dosage
Anthelmintics	Thiabendazole	po 44 mg/kg, q24 hr or 22 mg/kg, q12hr
	Ivermectin	0.2 mg/kg po once
	Fenbendazole	10 mg/kg po once
	Pyrantel Pamoate	6.6 mg/kg po once
	Oxibendazole	15 mg/kg po once
Drug Class: Antifungals	**Drug**	**Route and Dosage**
	lodine	Topical
	Copper Sulfate	Topical
	Tolnaftate	Topical
	Miconazole	Topical

EUTHANASIA

4-103. Euthanasia refers to the ending of a life, in a humane manner, to relieve suffering from illness or injury. While caring for animals during combat conditions, the handler may find that serious illness or injury will necessitate the destruction of an animal that is beyond the scope of available medical treatment. Euthanasia under field conditions is frequently a rather brutal affair, without the poisonous gases and injectable venoms used in the clinic. Despite this lack of "civilized" methods of destruction, every effort should be taken to effect euthanasia as rapidly and painlessly as possible. In addition, any personnel near the animal must exercise caution to avoid injury to themselves should the animal be grievously wounded but not immediately killed. The thrashing of these powerful animals will result in injury to bystanders and could create panic among other animals stationed nearby. The handler should keep other animals as far away from the site as possible.

4-104. Equines, despite their immense size and strength, are fairly fragile animals. Nearly any injury resulting in a fracture of the legs will necessitate destruction of the animal. If the animal was otherwise healthy, the meat of the animal may be used as food. The unit should avoid eating animals that were ill or infested with internal parasites, or that were recently treated with medications. Medications have specific meat and milk withdrawal times that specify how long after their use one must wait to consume the animal or its by-products (for example, milk) as food. These withdrawal times are listed in veterinary drug reference books.

4-105. When a veterinarian is not available to the pack animal detachment in the field, the detachment medic (18D) should receive medical training in the use of euthanasic drugs from a large animal veterinarian for a rapid, humane, and silent manner of euthanasia. A variety of methods are available for field euthanasia. Of these, most are impractical because they require a very advanced degree of anatomical expertise or require dosages of common drugs in amounts larger than would logically be available. Consequently, simple mechanical methods of destruction are all that will be available to the average soldier. Personnel should always remember that an animal euthanized with these agents cannot be used for food.

CHAPTER 5

Packing Equipment

This chapter explains some of the most commonly used packing equipment, how it should be maintained, and how it should be fitted to the animal. There are variations in equipment; however, the principles for using it remain the same.

> **NOTE**
> Most injuries and wounds to pack animals result from poorly adjusted equipment, such as the saddles, pack frames, thickness of pack pads, and harnesses.

SELECTION OF EQUIPMENT

5-1. Before departing, the detachment should try to determine the size of the animals with which they will be working. Locally available packsaddles, bridles, halters, harnesses, or any other forms of equipment are not always necessarily the best available. The detachment leader should research carefully the species he intends to use, the method he intends to use them with, and how he proposes to get from point A to point B. If buying overseas, the detachment leader can bargain for equipment but should never "buy cheap." Bad equipment will cause difficulties continuously, especially if it breaks down because it was insufficient to begin with. The detachment should be conservative with its funds and invest in quality. If the size of the animals can be determined, the detachment will have an idea of what size to buy. When in doubt of an animal's size, the detachment should get the equipment a little larger and punch some extra holes for adjustment. Equipment that can be adjusted should always be the preferred option. Having equipment that will not fit the animals and cannot be sold or bartered for suitable gear is useless. If local equipment is purchased, the detachment should make sure it fits and, if possible, should always use the same well-fitted equipment on the same animal.

PACKSADDLES

5-2. The type and variety of packsaddles available are extremely wide and are controlled by the type of animals being used and their relative sizes. The types of packsaddles discussed in this chapter are the sawbuck (or crosstree), the Bradshaw, the Decker, and the new hybrid-version sawbuck and Decker saddles. They are all very adaptable to different types of loads and, therefore, are the best type to use in carrying cargo of different weights and sizes. These saddles can carry side loads, top loads, or a combination of the two. All of these saddles can accommodate standard packing hitches with a minimum requirement for tying and threading lash ropes to secure a load. They can be quickly and easily packed and unpacked.

SAWBUCK SADDLE

5-3. The sawbuck saddle is one of the oldest types of packsaddles still in use throughout the world. It is the simplest and most easily constructed. The sawbuck saddle (Figure 5-1) consists of two sidebars connected at the front and rear by crosspieces (bucks) forming an "X" over the spine. The two sidebars are called "humane bars" if they are curved to fit the shape of the animal's body. The humane bars allow the saddle to fit the animal better and make carrying the load more comfortable. Most sawbuck saddles produced today have humane bars. Cargo is carried on the saddle in panniers, pannier bags, mantees, or boxes that are hung from the bucks or carried by hitches and slings.

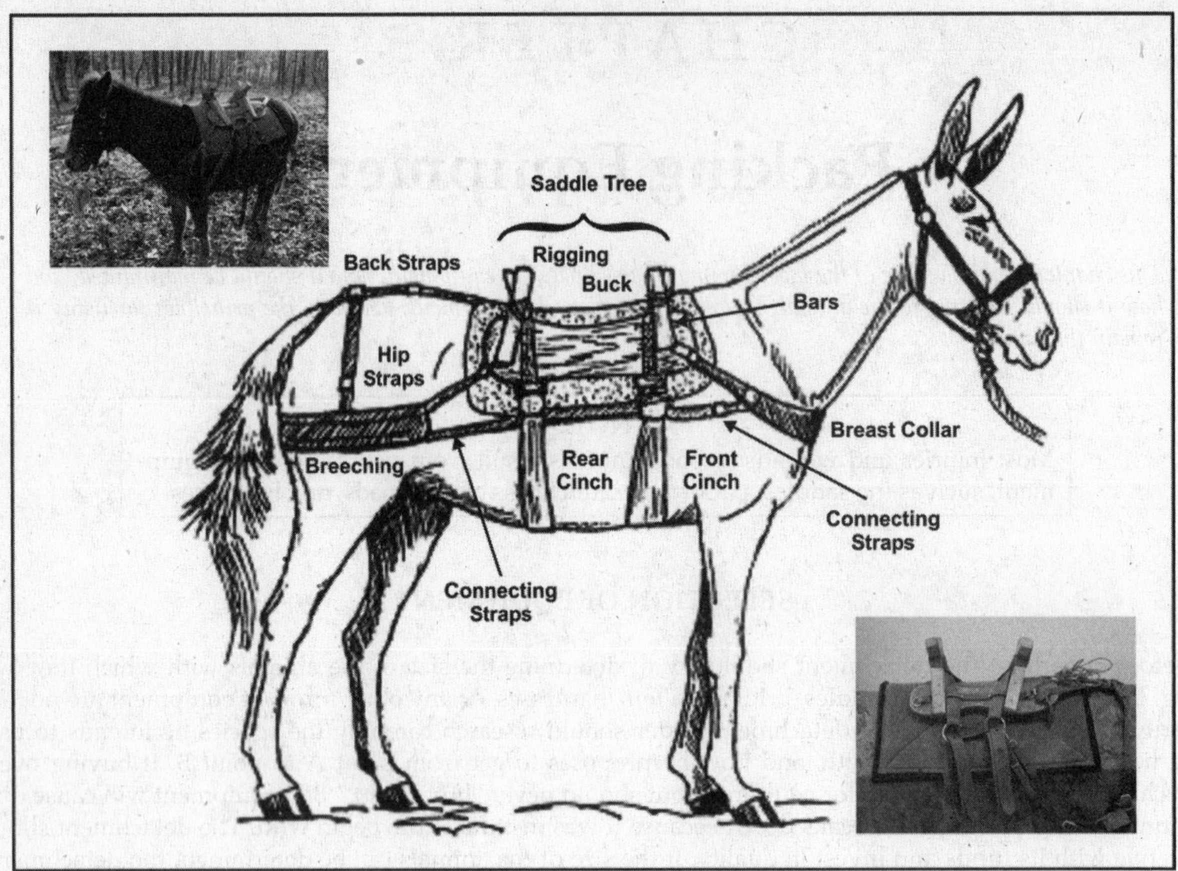

Figure 5-1. Sawbuck saddle on a mule

BRADSHAW SADDLE

5-4. The Bradshaw saddle is only slightly different from the sawbuck saddle. The Bradshaw in Figure 5-2 has extended wood crosspieces and a steel bar near the bottom, connecting them on both sides. The extended crosspieces give more protection to the animal's flanks from bigger loads, reducing the weight that is applied directly to the animal.

DECKER SADDLE

5-5. The Decker saddle is made basically the same way as the sawbuck. The difference is that it has metal hoops (arches) instead of cross bucks holding the humane bars together (Figure 5-3). Some packers prefer the Decker saddle to the sawbuck saddle because the humane bars on the Decker saddle can be adjusted by bending the metal hoops to fit the animal better. The animal carries cargo in nearly the same manner as on the sawbuck. The difference with the Decker saddle is that the panniers are hung over the metal hoops instead of the cross bucks. Decker saddles have "ears" welded to the metal hoops to keep the panniers from slipping off or to run the sling rope around when using one. The ears are pieces of metal stock approximately 2 inches long and 1/2 inch in diameter and are welded to the metal hoops near the top on either side. Panniers with adjustable straps are sometimes secured to the Decker saddle by running the strap under the metal hoops and then fastening the buckle.

HYBRID VERSION SADDLES

5-6. The hybrid-version sawbuck and Decker saddles in Figure 5-4 have fully floating plastic composite humane bars with fully adjusting crosspieces (Bucks) made of aluminum. This system was designed to greatly reduce back sores and provide more energy to the pack animal. This system weighs less than half of the standard sawbuck packsaddle and is rigged the same as the more conventional sawbuck and Decker packsaddles.

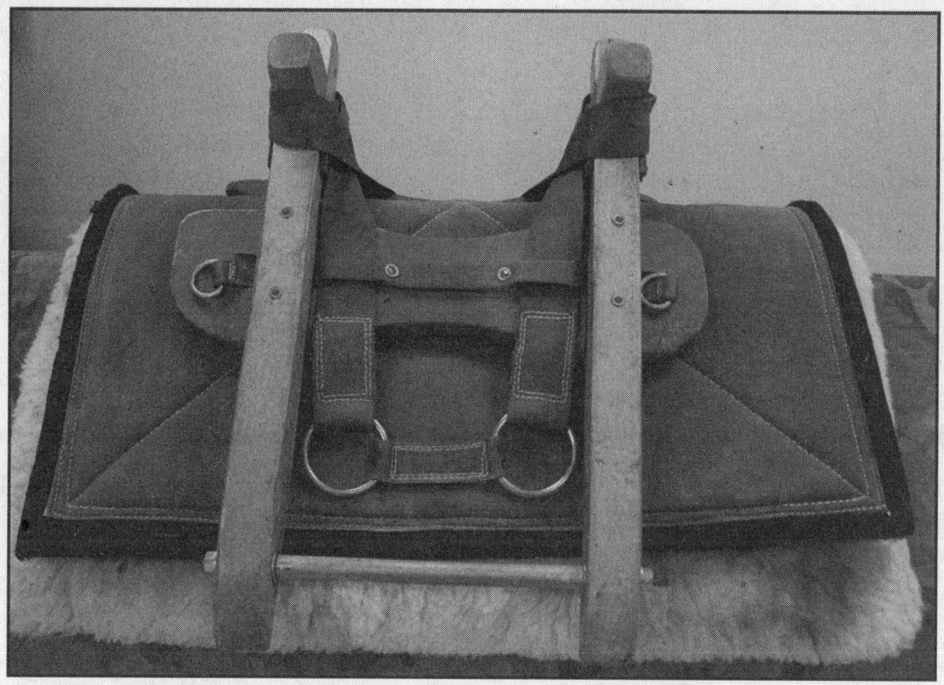

Figure 5-2. Bradshaw saddle

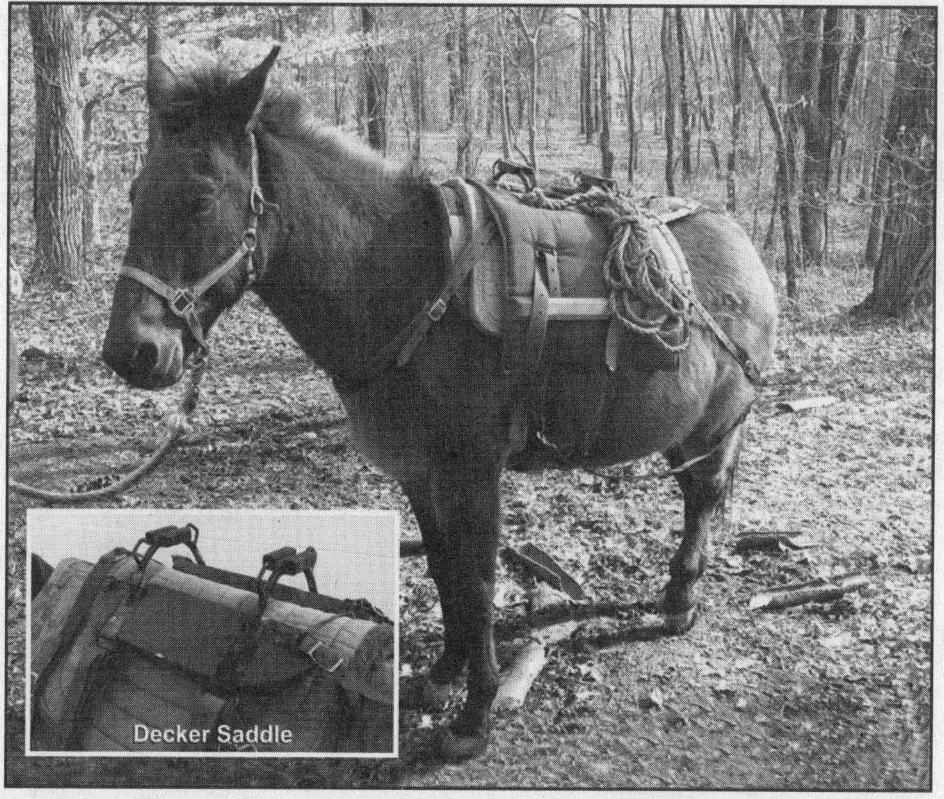

Figure 5-3. Decker saddle with half-breed saddle cover

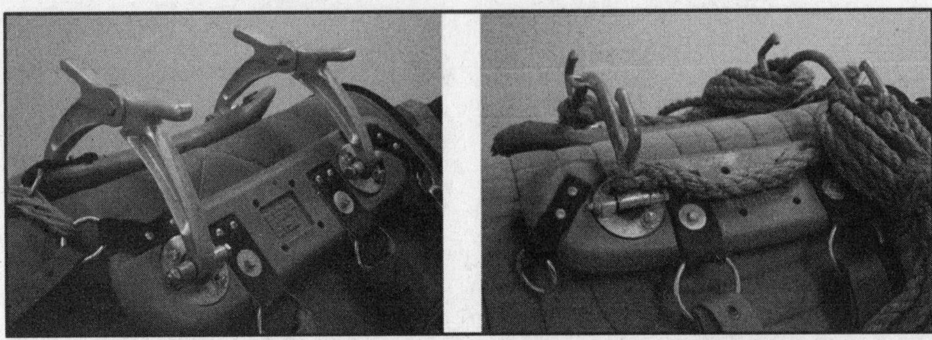

Figure 5-4. Hybrid saddles

SADDLE HARNESS

5-7. A variety of different straps form the harness. It holds and stabilizes the saddle to the animal. The main components of the harness are the cinches, breast collar, breeching, and crupper. The packer secures all of the straps either directly to the saddle or to the rigging.

Rigging

5-8. The rigging is a leather strap that wraps around the cross bucks on the sawbuck and around the metal hoops on a Decker saddle. The packer secures it to the humane bars with screws and allows the ends to hang below the bars. He attaches the rigging rings to the ends of the straps. He then secures the latigos (which are used to secure the cinches) and the connecting straps (which help hold the breeching and breast collar in place) to the rigging rings.

Cinches

5-9. Cinches are the part of the harness that hold the saddle to the animal and provide stability to the saddle once it is packed. Most packsaddles have two cinches, one in front and one in the rear. They fit around the belly or barrel of the animal. The packer secures the cinches to the rigging rings by the latigos.

Breast Collar

5-10. The breast collar provides stability to the saddle while the animal is traveling uphill. It keeps the saddle from moving rearward over the animal's kidneys and rump. The breast collar is usually made of leather or cotton duck material and is approximately 4 inches wide. Two connecting straps from the front of the humane bars secure the breast strap, which is usually made of wool or tail and mane hair.

Breeching

5-11. The breeching fits around the animal's hips and keeps the saddle from moving forward over its withers while traveling downhill. The breeching is made of leather or cotton duck material and is approximately 4 inches wide. It is held in place by connecting straps, back straps, quarter straps, and hip straps. The connecting straps run from the rigging rings to the ends of the breeching. The back straps run from the rear of the humane bars to a metal ring (called a spider) that rests on the animal's rump. The hip straps run from the metal ring to the breeching.

Crupper

5-12. The crupper is a leather strap that runs under the animal's tail and attaches to the metal ring. It keeps the saddle from slipping forward. Cruppers serve the same purpose as the breeching but are not widely used. They can be used in place of, or with, the breeching.

HALTER AND PACKING EQUIPMENT

5-13. A halter is a control device that fits around an animal's head and must be placed on the animal before packing it. By controlling the animal's head, a person can control the animal. The halter is used mainly for leading rather than riding an animal. Without one it would be next to impossible to maintain control of an animal for any length of time. Halters are simple devices constructed generally of nylon webbing or rope. Another essential item for controlling an animal is the lead line or lead rope. A lead line is a piece of rope usually 1/2 or 3/4 inch in diameter, made of pliable material, usually cotton or nylon, and approximately 10 feet long. The line attaches to the chin ring on the halter under the animal's chin. It can be permanently spliced into the chin ring or attached by means of a snap (Figure 5-5).

NOTE
A person should never wrap the lead line around his hand. If the animal is frightened, the person could be entangled in the rope. A person should S-fold the rope and place it in the center of his hand.

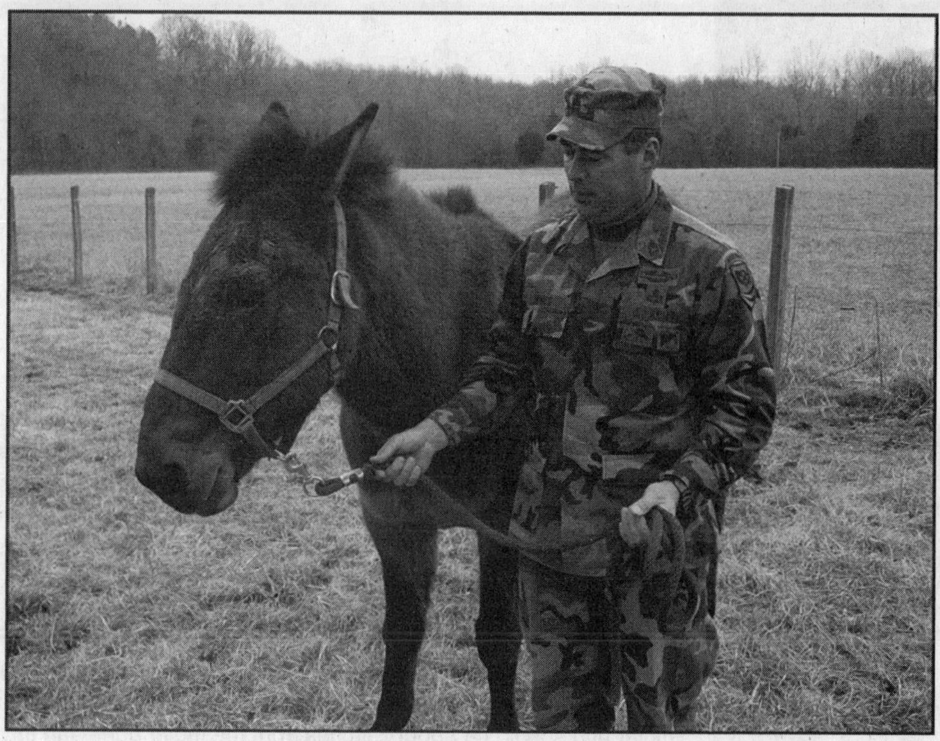

Figure 5-5. Halter with lead line

HALTER PLACEMENT

5-14. To place a halter on an animal, the handler should first gain control of the animal (Figure 5-6). He places the halter and lead line over his left shoulder so the animal does not become familiar with seeing him walking into the pasture with the lead line in hand. He approaches the animal talking to it or by offering the animal grain.

SADDLE PACK PAD

5-15. The saddle pack pad provides the only protection between the loaded saddle and the animal's hide. Pack pads are usually thicker than riding pads because a pack animal carries "dead" weight. A riding animal carries "live" weight, which means that a rider will shift his weight as the animal traverses different types of terrain. A pack load is dead weight, which means it will not move with the animal. It is important that the saddle pack pad be made of a material that will stay soft and not compress and get hard during use. Pack pads are usually 30 × 30 inches, and made of fiber, fleece, felt, or hair with a canvas portion on one side to protect the animal's back from the bars and equipment on the packsaddle.

Once the handler determines the animal is calm, he reaches around the animal's neck with his left hand holding the end of the lead line.

The handler then grabs the lead line with his right hand. He should now have control of the animal and the animal should follow his commands.

He holds the halter with the lead line ring down, with the closed end to the front of the animal's nose, and the open end to the rear of the animal's head.

The handler slips the closed end over the nose, brings the running end of the open end over the back of the animal's head behind the ears, and attaches it. He keeps control of the lead line during this process by holding the lead line with one hand or by placing one foot on the running end of the lead line to prevent the animal from pulling the halter away as he puts it on.

The handler now checks to see if there are any twists in the halter straps and that the halter is properly adjusted. If the halter is properly adjusted, the molar ring should be about 2 inches from the molar bone, the throat latch should be a hands width between the animal's jaw and throat latch, and the noseband should be two fingers' width from the animal's nose.

Figure 5-6. Placement of halter on animal

NOTE

The handler should not connect the lead line to the molar or cheek ring. It should only be connected to the chin ring.

5-16. Some packers use what is called a cheater pad on animals that have high withers or very thin backs, or for extra protection. These small pads are usually 30 × 30 inches, and made of fiber, fleece, felt, wool, or hair (Figure 5-7). The cheaters can be placed between two regular pack pads in the withers area to raise the front of the packsaddle off the

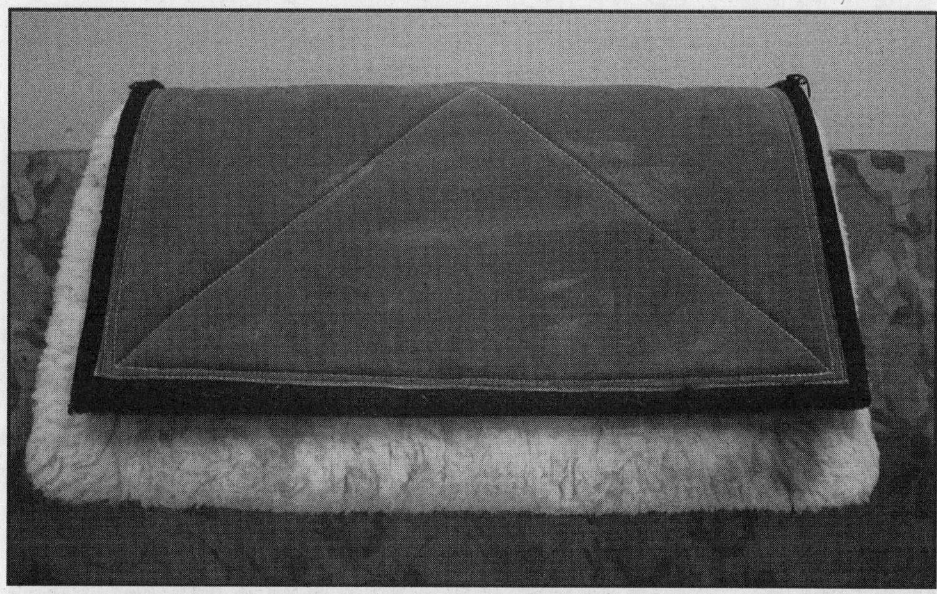

Figure 5-7. Pack pad with cheater pad

withers and yet have the saddle sit evenly on the pack animal's back. It is important that the cheater pad is the first pad placed on the animal's back. Not all animals will need this extra padding.

SADDLE COVER

5-17. The saddle cover, sometimes called a half-breed, is used when it is necessary to protect the animal's flanks from the load or the saddle rigging. The saddle cover is commonly made of two pieces of canvas sewn together with slots cut in it so that it will fit over the cross bucks or metal hoops. The saddle cover can have padding sewn into it or it can have stuffing slits so that the user can fill it with as much padding as is necessary for the load. It usually has sideboards made of wood, 2 to 4 inches wide, attached near the bottom to provide further protection to the animal's flanks. The saddle cover can be placed over the saddle once it is on the animal, or it can be placed over the humane bars and under the rigging (Figure 5-8).

MANTEE

5-18. A mantee is a tarp usually made of canvas that is lashed over the top load secured on a packsaddle or used to wrap up cargo that is to be placed or slung on a packsaddle. A mantee protects the load from trees, bushes, rocks, or anything else the animal may brush against while it is moving. It also helps protect the load from rain and snow. The size is generally 8 × 8 feet. Each mantee has an assigned cargo rope that goes with it. Mantees are folded four to a bundle with ropes located in the center. However, a packer can use any size that will protect the load.

LASH ROPE AND CINCH

5-19. The lash rope and cinch (Figure 5-9) secure the load and mantee to the animal by means of different types of packing hitches. The lash rope is usually 36 feet long, 1/2 to 5/8 inch in diameter, and made of manila or nylon. The lash cinch is usually made of heavy cotton duck material with a ring at one end and a hook at the other. The lash rope is spliced to the cinch at the end with the ring.

SLING ROPE

5-20. The sling rope fastens to the front cross buck on a sawbuck saddle or the front and rear arch on a Decker saddle. It secures loads that will not fit in panniers or secures panniers that do not have straps. A sling rope is normally 36 feet long, 1/2 inch in diameter, and made of hemp, nylon, or polyester.

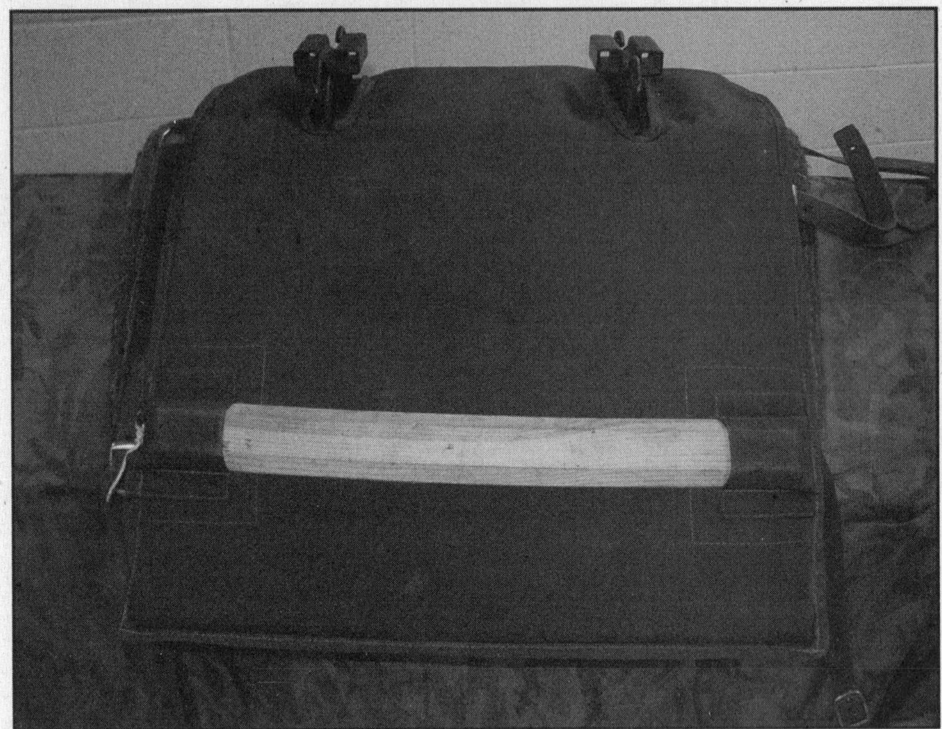

Figure 5-8. Saddle cover

Figure 5-9. Lash rope and cinch

PANNIERS

5-21. Panniers are cargo containers that hang from the cross bucks on a sawbuck or the metal hoops on a Decker saddle (Figure 5-10). Some panniers do not have straps to hold them to the saddle. If they do not have straps, the packer can use the sling rope to hold the panniers in place. The dimensions of most commercially made panniers are approximately 26 inches long, 19 inches high, and 12 inches deep. Panniers are made of many different types of materials. Some of the most popular are canvas, aluminum, hard plastic, plywood covered with fiberglass, or a wood frame covered with cowhide.

Figure 5-10. Two types of panniers

CARE OF EQUIPMENT

5-22. The packer has the primary responsibility for the care and preservation of the packsaddle and equipment. The packer should perform the routine cleaning, preservation, and daily inspection for the packing equipment to ensure mission readiness.

5-23. The packer checks saddles daily to ensure there are no cracked, broken, or loose parts. He checks the cross bucks or hoops, humane bars, rigging, and latigos. He tightens any loose items and repairs or replaces cracked or broken parts. The packer cleans any mud or other debris from the saddles that may have collected during the day's movement. He should check all parts of the harness for signs of wear, breaks, cleanliness, and serviceability (Figure 5-11).

Cinches	• Check cinches for any broken strands. • Check the cinch rings for any signs of cracking or metal fatigue. • Repair or replace any damaged pieces.
Breast Collar	• Check the breast collar and connecting straps for any signs of wear or debris collected during the day's movement. • Check the fastening devices to ensure serviceability. Repair or replace items as necessary.
Breeching	• Check the breeching and all associated straps for cleanliness and serviceability. • Pay close attention to all fastening devices. • Repair or replace items as necessary.
Crupper	• Check the crupper (if used) for cleanliness and serviceability.

Figure 5-11. Checks for harness parts

5-24. The packer brushes or shakes out the saddle pads after he removes them from the animal. He checks them thoroughly for any foreign objects that can come in contact with the animal's hide. The packer then lays the saddle pads where they can air out and dry.

5-25. The saddle cover should be treated in the same manner as the saddle pad. In addition, the packer checks the wooden bars for serviceability. He checks the padding to see if some should be added or taken out. He also checks the mantee for rips, holes, and general serviceability.

5-26. The lash and sling rope should be checked for signs of wear. The packer replaces or repairs them immediately if there are signs of excessive wear. Breaking a lash or sling rope on the trail could cause a wreck. The ropes should be kept as dry as possible, especially if the rope is made of hemp. Wet weather causes hemp ropes to become hard to manage. Wet hemp ropes will dry and stretch out, leaving the pack loose or uneven. The packer should never throw the ropes on the wet ground while packing or unpacking an animal. They should be hung on a tree limb or laid on a tarp or any dry surface until ready for use.

5-27. The packer checks the lash cinch often for signs of the material fraying. Badly frayed material can tear on the trail and cause a load to come loose. Frayed material can also rub on the animal's belly and cause a sore. The packer also checks the cinch ring for signs of wear and metal fatigue, replacing or repairing items as necessary.

5-28. The packer cleans panniers and checks them for overall serviceability. Most importantly, he checks the straps and fasteners on the straps that hold them to the saddle.

5-29. All leather items should be kept clean and free of grit and dirt. In cleaning off mud or excessive dirt, the packer uses a grooming brush or a blunt piece of wood and a sponge, lukewarm water, and saddle soap. After cleaning, the packer applies neat's-foot oil to the leather for both protection and appearance. He also cleans all metal parts as well.

5-30. Equipment made from canvas and duck material should always be kept free of dirt and mildew. A frequent brushing will remove dirt. The best remedy for mildew is air and sunlight.

FITTING AND ADJUSTING THE SADDLE

5-31. The proper positioning of the saddle and correct cinch adjustment are very important factors. Improper adjustment may cause injury to the animal or may affect the time and distance the animal can carry its load. Before placing anything on the animal's back, it is important to be sure that the animal feels comfortable about it. Many will get skittish if they are unfamiliar with the equipment. A good way to get the animal accustomed to the equipment is to hold it in front of the animal and let him see it and smell it. The animal should be saddled with the packer standing on its left (onside). When making adjustments to the saddle or harness, the packer will have to move to the right (offside) of the animal. The packer should always move around the rear of the animal when moving from one side to the other while saddling. To do this, he gets close to the animal and maintains contact with it by keeping a hand on its rump. If the animal should kick while he is moving around it, receiving a kick from a short distance is much better than from a long distance after the full force of the kick has been generated.

GROOMING

5-32. The handler should always groom the pack animal before saddling. While grooming, the handler removes any debris from the animal that may cause saddle sores. He also checks for any sores from the previous movement or sores that may have occurred during the night. The handler treats the sores as necessary or asks the medic or vet for assistance. If there is any question as to the ability of the animal to carry a load, the handler should ask the medic or vet to make a determination. The animal should not aggravate existing sores.

PAD PLACEMENT

5-33. The handler checks the saddle pad thoroughly for any foreign objects before placing it on the animal. He places the saddle pad square on the animal's back, forward of where it needs to rest, and then slides it rearward into position. Sliding the pad rearward will make the hair lie naturally and prevent sores. The forward portion of the pad should be over the withers with its forward edge about a hand's breadth in front of the rear edge of the shoulder blade.

5-34. The animal may need more than one pack pad or cheater pad depending on the shape of its back. The best way to determine how many pads the animal needs is to set the packsaddle on him, and then check the clearance between the saddle and his withers. The handler should allow for the saddle settling down on the pads after the animal is loaded. If there is any chance of the saddle forks coming in contact with the top of the withers, the handler can put another pack pad under the saddle. He should be careful not to get too much padding on the withers so the packsaddle is pinching the withers from the pads being too thick. The purpose of putting extra padding on a high-withered animal is to raise the packsaddle off the tops of the withers. If the pads being used are the same thickness throughout, the handler will not gain much. The pad must be thicker over the withers and thinner toward the rear of the animal. A cheater pad sits on the withers only and that is why it is usually the best thing to use for a high-withered animal. Also, pads always have a tendency to slip to the rear of the animal.

SADDLE PLACEMENT

5-35. The handler places the saddle square on the pack pads allowing 4 to 6 inches of padding to be exposed in the front and rear of the saddle. The forward edge of the saddle will be approximately 2 to 3 inches to the rear of the shoulder blades. It is important to ensure there is adequate saddle pad forward of the saddle to protect the animal's back from the leading edge of the saddle.

5-36. The handler fastens the cinches, the front one first, making sure there are no twists in the offside latigos or the cinches themselves. The front cinch should be a hand's breadth to the rear of the front leg.

5-37. The cinches should be tightened just enough to hold the saddle in place until the breast collar and breeching are adjusted. These adjustments are explained in detail below.

BREAST COLLAR

5-38. The breast collar should ride just above the point of the animal's shoulder and go around the breast below the animal's neck. It should not be tight; its only function is to keep the saddle from slipping back. The handler adjusts the breast collar so that it is snug when a front leg is fully extended. He makes sure the two connecting straps are adjusted to the same length so that the breast collar rides evenly.

BREECHING

5-39. Once the saddle is in place and cinched lightly, the handler adjusts the breeching. The handler—

- Places the spider on the animal's rump and adjusts the back straps so that it rests on the highest point of the animal's shoulder. The handler ensures that both straps are the same length so the ring will stay centered.
- Adjusts the hip straps so the breeching rides approximately halfway between the base of the tail and the bottom of the hindquarters. He adjusts the straps on both sides to the same length to ensure the breeching rides level.
- Attaches the crupper if used. He lifts the animal's tail and slides the crupper under it. He must always be very careful when working around the animal's hind end. Some animals will try to kick.

NOTE

The best thing for the handler to do is stay very close to the animal with his side touching the animal's flank. The animal will telegraph any intention to kick by tightening its muscles. The handler should watch the animal's ears. If it intends to kick, it will lay its ears back.

- Talks to the animal reassuringly while lifting the tail to slide the crupper under it. The crupper should be snug, but not tight, against the base of the tail but not tight. The handler ensures both connecting straps on the crupper are the same length for even riding.

- Adjusts the connecting straps. A good rule of thumb to follow for adjusting the connecting straps is to make sure that, when the animal is walking and one hind leg reaches its rearmost position in the stride, the breech strap is firmly against the animal's rump. The breeching should not be so tight as to hinder the animal's natural gait. However, if it is too loose, it is useless.
- Connects the quarter straps to the front cinch ring. The handler adjusts them snugly to keep the front cinch from moving forward while the animal is moving. He makes sure the upper quarter strap is snug and the lower quarter strap has a 1-inch sag to it.
- Completes initial adjustment of the breeching and then pulls the animal's tail out from under the breeching. The crupper adjustment discussed above explains the best method.

5-40. The breeching is now adjusted approximately to where it should be. The handler walks the animal around to check how the breeching is riding on the animal and makes adjustments as necessary. When traveling down long steep slopes, it may be necessary to tighten the back and connecting straps some to keep the saddle from slipping over the withers and shoulders.

CINCHING

5-41. Proper cinching is essential because the packsaddle covers so great an area of moving surface. Excessive binding of the front cinch may injure the back and sides, interfere with breathing, or cause cinch sores. The handler uses the front cinch to secure the saddle in place and makes sure it is tighter than the rear cinch. The rear cinch keeps the saddle from rocking front to rear as the animal is walking; therefore, the rear cinch does not need to be as tight as the front cinch. Since the hind legs are the propelling members, the hindquarters move from side to side and up and down. These movements should not be restricted by cinch pressure. There must be no interference with the animal's locomotion. Only experience can teach a person how to determine the exact amount of cinch pressure needed. A safe rule to follow is to give the front cinch sufficient pressure to hold the saddle in place. Usually, one finger should pass easily between the front cinch and the animal's chest.

5-42. The rear cinch should be tight enough to limit the rocking motions of the saddle and help prevent the saddle from slipping forward. The rear cinch should not be so tight that the whole hand cannot be slipped under it. In testing cinch pressure, the handler should be able to insert a finger from the rear to the front so that, when it is withdrawn, the hair does not ruffle. Ruffled hair may cause sores. Excessive binding of the rear cinch will cause a pack animal to tire quickly. It is very important to center the cinch on the animal's belly. The cinch rings on either side of the cinch should be the same distance from the rigging when the cinch is pulled tight. This type of fit is called a ring-to-ring check. An uneven cinch could cause cinch sores or cause the saddle to slip. The latigos should be secured on both sides of the saddle with a quick-release knot. This knot is important because it allows the load to be released quickly from an animal if the load should fall onto its side or upside down. With other knots it is necessary to cut the load away from the animal. Having to cut the load may cause injury to the animal and will ruin the latigos or cinches on the saddle.

5-43. To fasten the cinch on the animal, the handler runs the latigo through the cinch ring (the end of the latigo is run through the cinch ring so that it comes through the ring toward the packer) and back up through the rigging ring (the end of the latigo is run through the rigging ring so that it goes through the ring toward the animal). If the latigos are long, or the animal has a small barrel, they may have to be wrapped more than once to take up the excess length of the latigo. The knot used is a "half-Windsor." To form this knot, the handler brings the running end of the latigo around the portion of the latigo running through the rigging ring, up through the rear of the rigging ring, and down through the loop just formed. He forms the quick release by passing the running end of the latigo up through the knot just formed (Figure 5-12).

FINAL ADJUSTMENTS

5-44. When the saddle is in the right position on the animal and the breast collar, breeching, and cinches are snug, it is time to "untrack" the animal before packing it. Many times an animal will force air into its lungs and belly when it realizes that it is going to be saddled. The animal does this to make the saddle fit more comfortably. Once the animal starts moving, it will expel the air and the saddle will fit more loosely. If the animal is packed without untracking it, the saddle could slip shortly after movement begins and the whole load will have to be repacked. To untrack an

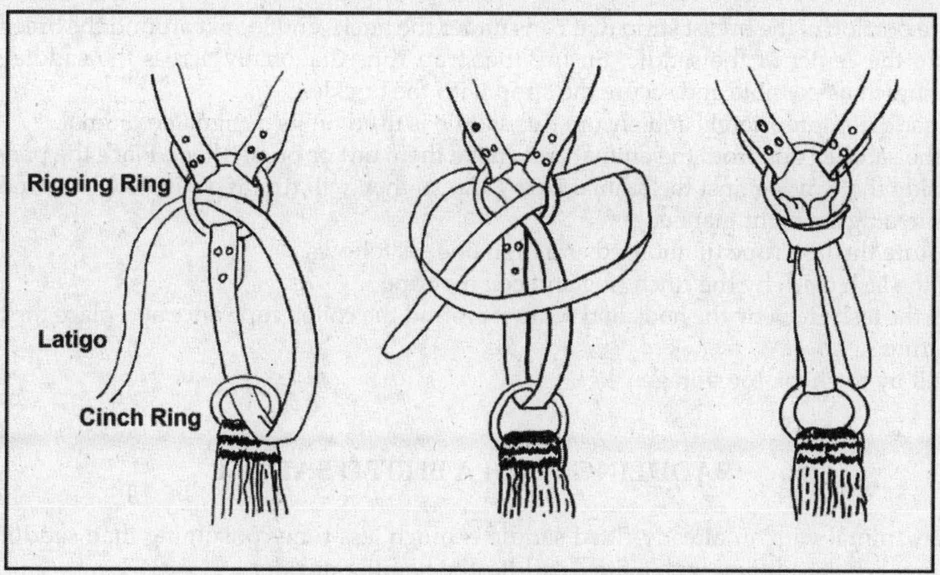

Figure 5-12. Latigos fasten the cinches to the rigging ring

animal, the handler takes the animal from the place it was saddled and walks it around for approximately 30 seconds. He ties the animal up and tightens the cinches again if needed. The animal is now ready to be packed.

MARKING SADDLES

5-45. After fitting the saddle to the pack animal, the handler marks it with the animal's name or number and uses it with the same animal throughout the movement. The same saddle pads and, if needed, cheater pads should be kept with the animal so the saddle fits the same every time. This technique will save time refitting the packsaddles every time the unit prepares to move.

UNSADDLING THE ANIMAL

5-46. The animal should be unsaddled in the opposite sequence that it is saddled. By following this sequence, the saddle will be stored in a manner that will make saddling the animal quick and easy the next time it is needed. Since the breast strap, breeching, and cinches were adjusted properly when the animal was saddled, the rider can maintain a proper fit if he loosens only the quarter straps, cinches, and breast collar (onside strap and the strap going to the hobble ring). To properly unsaddle an animal, the handler or rider should—

- Unfasten the breast collar strap from the front hobble ring on the front cinch and from the onside connection. Take the breast collar strap from around the neck of the animal and run the onside breast collar strap under the bucks from the rear to the front leaving the buckle visible at the rear of the saddle.
- Lay the excess strap on the animal's neck and fold the excess breast collar into the center of the saddle between the bucks.
- Unfasten the quarter straps and hook them onto the rear rigging rings and unfasten the rear cinch.
- Put the running end of the latigo through the rigging ring twice and bring the running end around the latigo, up through the rear of the rigging ring and down through the loop just formed. He should repeat the procedure for the front cinch.
- Slide the saddle rearward to loosen the breeching. If a crupper is used, unfasten the onside strap and lift the animal's tail to remove the breeching.
- Lift the breeching over the rump and place the spider and crupper, if used, between the bucks. Lay the breeching across the saddle between the bucks. Fold the excess straps into the center of the saddle between the bucks and fold the cinches into the center of the saddle on top of the breeching.

- Take in the portion of the breast strap that runs under the bucks and loop it around the breeching and cinches folded into the center of the saddle. Ensure the strap runs diagonally across the saddle so the strap will tighten as much as possible and secure the strap with the buckle.
- Store the saddle appropriately and ensure this saddle is used on its designated animal.
- Remove the saddle pads from the animal and shake them out or brush them. Place the pads over the saddle with the side that was against the animal facing out so they will dry. If a sling rope is used, wrap it around the bucks in a figure-eight manner.
- Roll and store the lash rope (if not used as a high line) as follows:
  - Hold the lash cinch by the cinch ring and coil the rope.
  - Grasp the lash cinch by the hook and wrap it around the coiled rope once and place the hook through the cinch ring.
  - Hang it by the hook for storage.

SADDLING WITH A FITTED SADDLE

5-47. Saddling an animal with an already-fitted saddle is much less time-consuming than saddling and having to adjust the breeching. When saddling with a fitted saddle, the handler or rider—

- Properly grooms the animal.
- Places the saddle pad on the animal.
- Places the saddle on the animal correctly.
- Loosens the strap holding the cinches and rigging together between the bucks.
- Lets the cinches fall to the offside of the animal.
- Pulls the breeching from the stowed position and fits it around the rump of the animal.
- Ensures the saddle is in its proper position.
- Attaches the front cinch loosely.
- Attaches the rear cinch.
- Attaches the quarter straps to the front cinch ring.
- Attaches the crupper, if used.
- Attaches the breast collar.
- Tightens the front cinch.

Since the saddle has already been adjusted to the animal, it should fit properly without further adjustment. However, the handler or rider should check the fit of the saddle and all the rigging to make sure it does fit properly.

CHAPTER 6

Horsemanship

This chapter discusses horsemanship and should help guide unfamiliar personnel. In many cases, authorities vary on how to perform many functions of good horsemanship, even when presented with the same task. Tactical, environmental, social, and other factors influence how animals are used in a combat environment. The descriptions of equipment and techniques are based on the American-Western style of riding. This style of riding is most familiar to U.S. Soldiers and the most easily adaptable to sustained combat operations.

The emphasis on American-Western style is one of functionality and stability, but as in any style of riding, success is dependent on rider performance. As in most cases, any basic flaws in technique can most likely magnify during combat operations. A pack animal unit will have to improvise equipment or adapt to indigenous equipment in many cases. A basic knowledge of animals, equipment design and function, and tactics should be sufficient for a detachment to perform their mission given any set of circumstances. Reading this chapter is in no way any substitute for experience.

EQUIPMENT

6-1. The following equipment descriptions and instructions for use come from the American-Western style of equipment. In the horse industry, these items are known as tack. Variations of these items are commonplace, but the principles of their design and use remain constant.

BRIDLE AND REINS

6-2. The rider uses the bridle to control the animal when he rides. The bridle consists of various lengths of leather or nylon that the rider can adjust to fit the animal (Figure 6-1). The bridle's basic components include the following:

- The **bit** rests against the back of an animal's mouth and controls the animal by transferring pressure from the reins to the animal's mouth. The rider uses the reins or steering lines to command the animal. They are generally leather, approximately 72 to 84 inches long, and can be either split reins (not joined at the ends) or joined at the end. They are attached to the bit at the side rings. The curb chain or strap gives the animal pressure on the bottom of the jawbone when the reins are pulled and assists in stopping the animal. Cheek straps run the length of the bridle. Their purpose is to join the bit and the headpiece.
- The **headpiece** runs behind the ears and gives long axis anchor to the bridle. The **browband** runs across the forehead and holds the headpiece in place. The **throatlash** runs from the junction of the headpiece and the browband on each side and under the animal's throat. It further anchors the headpiece. The **noseband** fits around the animal's nose several inches behind the mouth. It keeps the animal from opening its mouth too wide and also provides stability for the bridle.

BRIDLE AND REINS INSPECTION

6-3. The rider checks all the leather in the bridle, using the same flexing and twisting technique that he used on the billets and stirrup leathers. He pays extra attention to areas of strain, such as where the rein wraps around the bit. Any cracking or separation in that area is a danger signal telling the rider that it is time to invest in a new set of reins.

6-4. The rider should also check all the stitching, especially on the reins. If he has the tools, he may be able to make simple repairs himself. When in doubt, the rider can consult the local saddler for repair work.

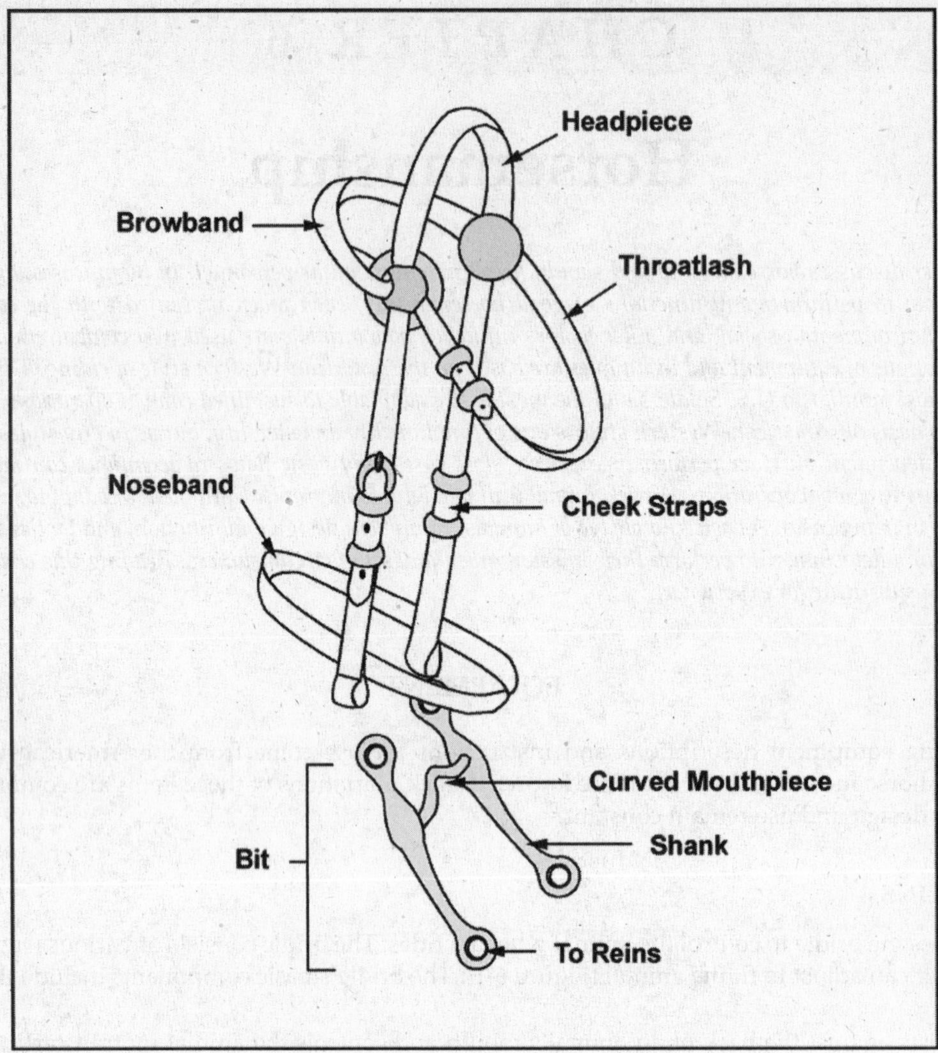

Figure 6-1. Typical horse bridle and standard bit

6-5. The bit should be checked for rough edges that will damage the horse's delicate lips. The rider replaces any bit that shows signs of roughness and wear immediately.

6-6. As the rider goes over the bridle, he checks the buckles to make sure they are not rusting through and that the tongues are not bent. Bent tongues may allow the buckle to work undone in use.

> **NOTE**
>
> The same safety checks that a rider makes on his bridle should be made on any other equipment that he uses, be it martingales, breastplates, or a complete harness for driving horses. Keeping the leatherwork clean and in good shape will lengthen its useful life span and will be more comfortable for the horse.

6-7. There are many types of bridles. The components identified are not necessarily present on all bridles. Placing the bridle on the animal requires the rider to perform sequential steps (Figure 6-2).

1. Stand on the onside of the animal, untie the animal, and remove the halter. Place the reins behind the animal's head and drape them over its neck or the rider's arm.
2. Unbuckle the throatlash.
3. Hold the headpiece in the right hand.
4. Hold the bit in the left hand with the thumb pointed up the axis of the animal's head.
5. Place the right hand on the animal's head between the ears to keep it down.
6. With the left hand, open the animal's mouth at the corner by putting a thumb between its canine and back teeth (the taste of the rider's thumb will cause the animal to open its mouth). Then slide the bit in by pulling with the headpiece in the right hand.
7. Slide the headpiece behind the ears, and place the browband on the forehead.
8. Buckle the throatlash loosely.
9. The bit should be adjusted so that the back of the animal's mouth is drawn up into a slight "smile."
10. Pull loose any restricted mane that is caught under the bridle straps.

Figure 6-2. Steps for putting the bridle on the animal

SADDLE PAD

6-8. Riding pads are generally the same as the pads used on packing animals. The average size is 30 × 30 inches. Chapter 5 explains the use and care of saddle pads.

CHEATER PADS

6-9. Cheater pads can be used on riding animals as on packing animals. Chapter 5, page 303, also explains using cheater pads.

WESTERN AND MCCLELLAN SADDLES

6-10. There are a number of saddles on the market today specifically designed for endurance and rough riding. So which one is best for the mission? There is no easy answer. First of all the saddle must fit the horse, and every horse is different. Weight might or might not be an important consideration for the rider, but no packer's saddle should weigh over 30 pounds.

WESTERN SADDLE

6-11. The modem Western saddle is a direct descendant of the deep-seat saddle brought to the Americas by the Spanish Conquistadors in the sixteenth century. It is heavy, and most western saddles put the rider's weight too far to the rear, leading to early fatigue and soreness. Western saddles are designed to keep the rider in place while working cattle, not to provide balance and comfort for miles and miles of rough, mountainous terrain riding. Another flaw of the western saddle is that the rigging is too far forward, contributing to girth soreness or galls. The stiff fenders and stirrup leathers of the western saddle might wear like iron, but can rub a rider's legs raw. Among the characteristics common to Western saddles are the deep seat, saddle horn, long stirrups, and high cantle (Figure 6-3). It also comes with a complement of tie-down straps to secure personal equipment to the saddle.

6-12. Western saddles are constructed of wood or synthetics for the tree (frame) and stirrups and covered in leather. If the manufacturer has placed padding in the bars of the saddle, the rider still needs a saddle pad.

6-13. The typical Western saddle will have one cinch to secure the saddle to the animal and may or may not have a flank cinch. Figure 6-4 explains the steps for saddling the animal.

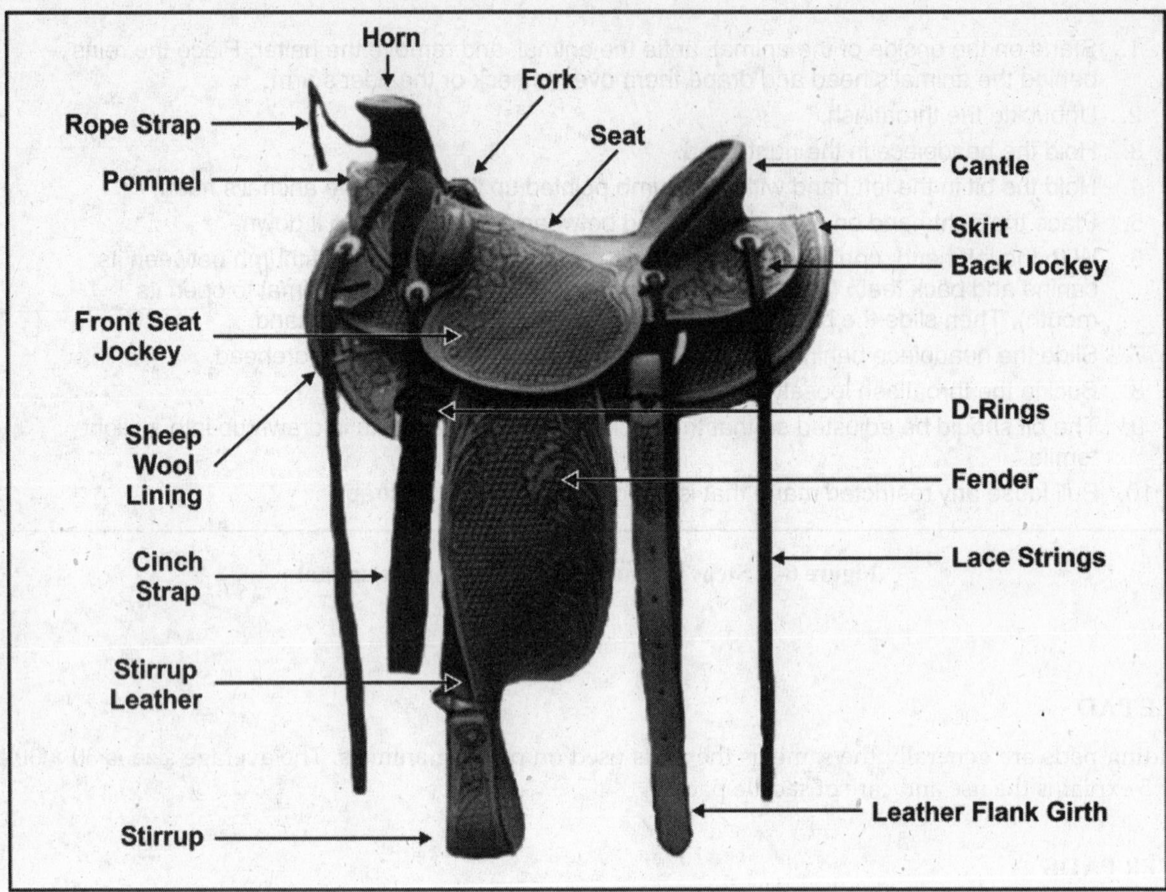

Figure 6-3. Western saddle

1. Ensure the animal is properly groomed.
2. Place the saddle pad on the animal.
3. Ensure the saddle is properly "rolled" for placement on the animal. Being rolled means that the cinch, offside stirrup, and any tie-down straps are pulled over the seat of the saddle.
4. Grasp the saddle by the front center under the horn and the rear center.
   NOTE: If the animal is skittish, or if it does not know the handler, allow it to see and smell the saddle at this time. Make sure the animal is never surprised.
5. From the onside, set the saddle on the animal's back. The front edge of the saddle should be 1 to 2 inches from the front edge of the pad and above the rear of the withers. Grasp the front edge of the pad, and lift it up into the tree to allow space for air to circulate under the pad.
6. Pull down the cinch and connect. Initially, snug the cinch tight enough to secure it to the animal.
7. Connect the flank (rear) cinch, if one is present. It should rest just against the animal's flank and be secured snugly. Connect it to the front cinch in the center with the connecting strap.
8. Lower the stirrups into place. Never drop them against the animal's side.
9. Ensure that no saddle strings or any other objects are between the saddle and the animal.
10. Walk the animal around for a short distance and then adjust the cinches again. The main cinch should be tight enough that three fingers can slide underneath it without much effort.
11. After riding or waiting for a time, recheck the cinches. Exertion or excitement may cause the animal's girth size to change.

Figure 6-4. Steps for saddling the animal

MCCLELLAN SADDLE

6-14. The McClellan saddle (Figure 6-5) was adopted by the U.S. War Department in 1859. It was an excellent saddle and remained the standard issue with slight improvements for the remaining history of the horse cavalry. McClellan saddles have a lot to offer the distance rider, but comfort is not one of them. This saddle was used by the cavalry, and was designed to be good for the horse with no compromises toward rider comfort. If a rider finds this saddle satisfactory for his body, he might not find a better saddle for keeping himself in good condition on long rides.

6-15. The typical McClellan saddle features an open, metal-reinforced wooden tree. Saddle skirts of harness leather are screwed to the sidebars. Stirrups are hickory or oak.

6-16. The McClellan saddle can also be used as a packsaddle with no modifications. The McClellan saddle can be rigged in the same configuration as the sawbuck saddle or Decker saddle by using a sling rope to construct a barrel hitch or basket hitch.

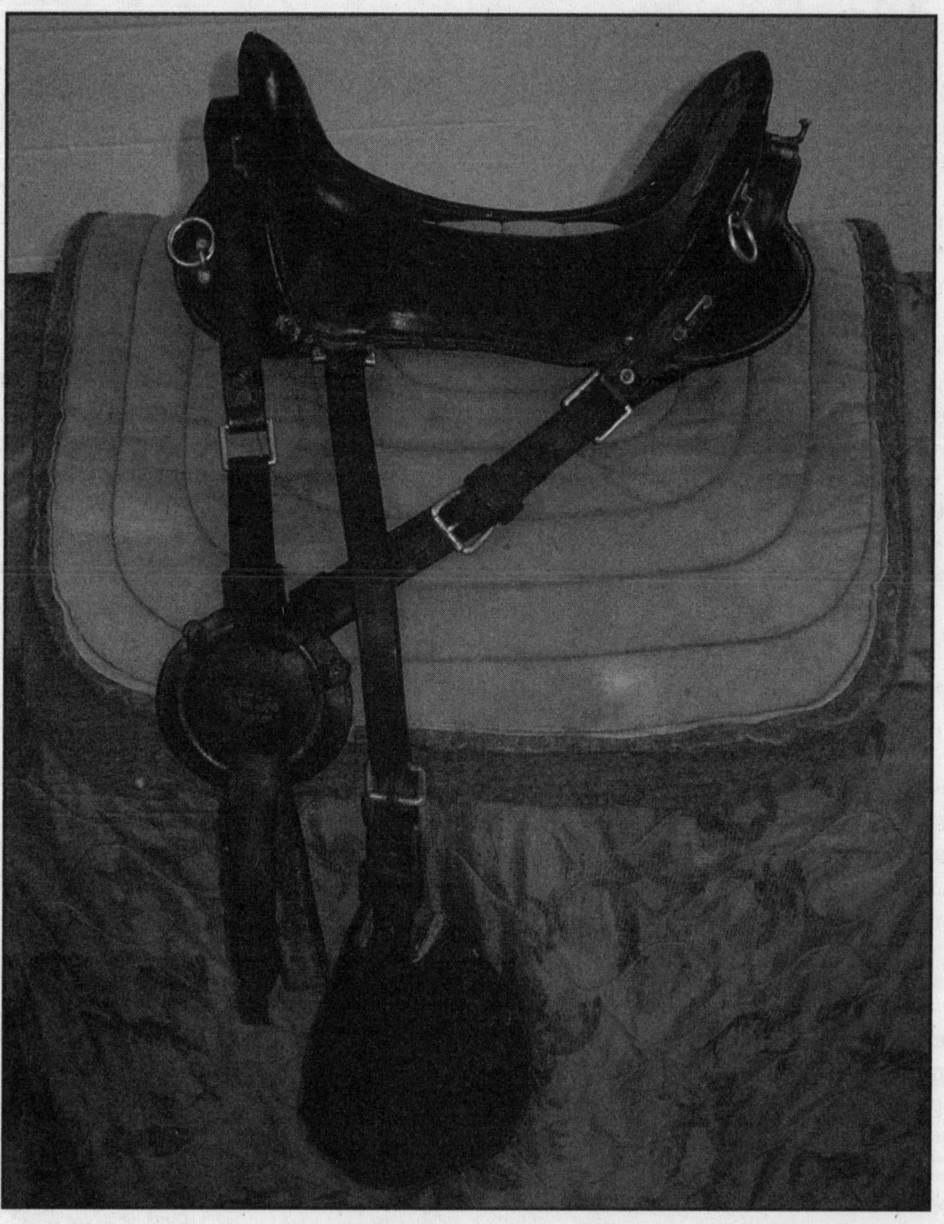

Figure 6-5. McClellan saddle

6-17. English saddles are lighter and put the rider's weight more forward than Western saddles. They offer closer contact with the horse than Western saddles, but riders sometimes feel less secure in them. The biggest shortcoming of English tack is a lack of distribution of the rider's weight over a large enough area of the horse's back.

RIDER'S EQUIPMENT

6-18. The problem encountered with equipping a U.S. Soldier for mounted operations is that no consideration has been given to the requirements for this type of operation in quite some time. This time lapse can pose various challenges in each mission.

6-19. Many items that are critical for dismounted use are critical to use while mounted as well, but may not perform suitably in both situations. Boots are a prime example. Boots suited for dismounted operations may be detrimental to mounted operations. The very nature of combat operations demands interoperability. This section will address such difficulties. The commander who assigns a unit to perform mounted operations should properly equip those units.

Boots

6-20. Their leather construction, pull-on design, high one-piece uppers, smooth sole, pointed toes, and high heels characterize boots ("cowboy boots") normally associated with American-Western style riding. Boots normally associated with dismounted operations have treated multipiece leather uppers, a lace-up design, lug soles, broad toes, short heels, and are generally shorter than riding boots. Soles that provide traction and footing on the ground can be dangerous when trying to dismount a horse. Lug soles tend to catch on stirrups. Boots with buckles or those with hooks used for speed lacing are not good because the buckles or hooks can catch on the saddle. Boots designed for riding are totally unsuitable for carrying loads over any irregular terrain while walking or for walking any appreciable distance. Riding boots are more difficult to fit and break in as well. Standard military boots, in most cases, will not accept spurs. Standard riding boots will not accept mountaineering equipment (for example, crampons, snowshoes, and skis). Modifying stirrups is not advisable or simple to accomplish. The more suitable approach would be to use military boots with the minimum amount of lug required, shaving down the edges of the soles to prevent the stirrups from becoming wedged into the lug. The widest stirrups available should be used. When using military boots, the rider should exercise care when removing the foot from the stirrup and pay particular attention to how a low heel will affect his ability to maintain the correct seat.

Spurs

6-21. Spurs are removable metal devices that attach to the heel of a rider's boots and assist in the use of his legs as riding aids. There are hundreds of variations of spurs but two basic designs. The classic or cavalry type is a short one-piece spur. The Western style is the star or wheel shape that rotates on a pin. Spurs are not essential for tiding but can be useful in controlling an animal. Experience, tactical considerations, the animal's training, and availability of spurs will influence the choice of using them or not. Inexperienced riders may tend to use spurs improperly, which can cause more problems than are corrected. Inexperienced animals may not understand what the rider is asking of them when spurs are applied. When using spurs, the rider should never poke an animal with their points. The spurs' purpose is to enable the horse to better feel the commands of the rider's legs. When applying spurs to the animal's flanks, the rider uses the side of the spur and rolls it upward. A Soldier must remember that spurs may not be usable with his boots and will impair him when dismounted.

Chaps

6-22. Chaps are leather leggings worn to protect the legs while riding. Chaps are not required for riding but do provide considerable protection against chafing from the friction between the legs and the stirrup fenders. They also protect the leg against foliage, limbs, and other such items the rider can brush against while riding. Chaps come in two basic designs: shotgun chaps, which are narrow and zip up the side, and open or bat-wing chaps that connect by ties at the side. The shotgun type, if not too tight, provides the best compromise between tactical use considerations and horse-related work. Shotgun chaps are quieter and will not snag as easily when the rider dismounts. When doing farrier-type work, open or bat-wing chaps are preferred if a farrier's apron is unavailable.

Uniform

6-23. Other than the items already addressed, the requirements for a suitable uniform are the same as for conventional dismounted operations. Some additional factors for the rider to remember are as follows:

- Wear leather gloves when leading pack animals. A rider may find it necessary to take the gloves off during saddling, unsaddling, and tasks such as tying knots.
- Wear a hat to protect the head from low limbs. It should not restrict hearing or vision (particularly peripheral). A chinstrap is helpful since wind and obstructions may cause the hat to be lost and recovery from horseback is impossible. A good choice is the jungle hat or watch cap.
- Carry nothing in the rear trouser pockets.

Necessary Bag

6-24. A necessary bag is a small kit carried by a rider to make field repairs to tack or other equipment. It is normally carried in a saddlebag. There is no specific item list, but typical contents are as follows:

- Leather punch or sharp awl.
- Assorted leather or sail maker's needles.
- Beeswax.
- Waxed sail maker's thread.
- Sewing palm.
- Rivets (for leather).
- Leather bootlaces.
- Small bits and pieces of leather.

Saddlebags

6-25. Saddlebags are of particular importance to the Soldier. There are many different styles of saddlebags. Construction is usually of nylon, canvas, or leather. For military uses, heavy nylon is preferable because it is rot-resistant, abrasion-resistant, and easily repaired. Saddlebags are attached to the rear of the saddle and tied down with the saddle strings located to the rear of the cantle. Locally fabricated models can be designed to work with issued load-carrying equipment (LCE), perhaps attaching to the rider's back. Typical dimensions of saddlebags are 11 × 11 inches × 5 inches thick. When used, as with pack loads, saddlebags must be balanced and sharp contents packed away from the animal.

RIDING TECHNIQUES

6-26. As stated previously, this manual discusses the American-Western style of riding. Riding basics for combat applications are no different from those for pleasure riding. What makes a difference is the skill level required of the rider. Combat conditions force the mounted Soldier to be a master of the basic skills of riding if he is expected to accomplish his mission. Riders must conduct actual training and practice on a regular basis for the skills of a mounted Soldier to remain of high enough caliber to conduct combat operations.

PREPARING TO MOUNT

6-27. Once a rider's animal has been prepared to ride (for example, it is properly groomed and all tack is on and properly adjusted), the rider must ensure that he is ready to ride. All equipment he wishes to carry must already be in place on the animal and himself.

MOUNTING

6-28. The rider unties the animal from its hitch and holds both reins in the left hand before mounting. From the onside, he stands just in front of the saddle, faces to the animal's rear, and turns the stirrup around so he can place his left foot into it. With the rider's left foot in the stirrup, he places his right hand on the saddle horn and left hand on top of the animal's neck. He then swings his right leg over the animal's back. He places his right foot in the stirrup when seated.

NOTE

Only when seated properly in the saddle can the stirrup length be judged to be proper or not. If proper, the knee will have a slight bend in it (approximately 20 degrees) and the rider should just be able to see the tip of the toe over the knee. Another way for the rider to tell if he is seated properly is to stand in the stirrups. There should be enough room to place two fingers between the saddle and his crotch. The rider ensures that the stirrup adjustment hardware is secure after making adjustments.

PROPER SEAT AND AIDS

6-29. The proper seat, or how the rider positions himself in the saddle, is very important to proper riding. If the rider does not sit correctly, the animal will become confused with the commands the rider gives and will not have the proper stability it needs to traverse difficult terrain.

6-30. The position of the rider in the saddle and the way he uses that position is referred to as the "aids." Mastering the aids is the single most important function of riding in control (assuming, of course, that the animal has been properly trained). When in the saddle, the position of the rider's body is very important and relates specific functions to the animal.

6-31. The rider uses his legs to create and control the forward motion of the animal and to assist in steering. When at the normal position, the legs should lie against the animal's side with the heel resting just behind the girth. The feet are placed in the stirrup with the rider's weight resting on the balls of his feet. This position remains the same unless the rider must give the animal a kick. The variance comes from the pressure delivered to the side of the animal by squeezing the leg muscles. To increase forward motion, the rider squeezes more in equal amounts to both sides. When turning, he keeps the inside leg at the girth, and the outside leg back. When halting, he applies light pressure with both legs. When applying any aid, the rider ceases the pressure when the animal responds.

6-32. The primary objective of how the rider distributes his **weight** is to remain in contact with the animal and feel its movements so he can move with the animal. The majority of the rider's weight will be in the stirrups; thus the saying, "standing tall in the saddle." The spine should be straight but not stiff. The remaining weight should be distributed evenly in the seat. If the rider is about to change pace, he should press down in the seat with his pelvis momentarily, without leaning forward, to warn the animal. When riding uphill, the rider must lean forward slightly, and when riding downhill, lean slightly to the rear. In either case, the rider must not exaggerate the movement but keep the weight in the seat. These adjustments are made to assist the animal when it must change its center of gravity.

6-33. The primary function of the **hands** as an aid is to control the reins. Western-style riding (and horses trained Western-style) refers to the technique known as "neck-reining." This style allows the reins to be controlled with only one hand. The reins are held in the dominant hand slightly above the saddle horn. The reins should be held with slight pressure, just enough to maintain light contact with the animal's mouth and low on the neck. To turn the animal, the rider simply moves the rein hand in the direction he wishes to turn and should never over-rein. The rider provides just enough pressure so the animal will understand what is expected. Some experts insist that the animal responds to the pressure created by the reins on the neck, while others maintain that it is a combination of the movements that makes the animal react. In any case, all aids (legs, weight, and hands) must be applied simultaneously and with only enough pressure to achieve the desired effect.

PACES

6-34. As with anything, a rider must "learn to walk before he runs." When training a new rider, it must be done in a controlled environment, such as a corral. The rider starts with the easiest pace first and progresses only when he is comfortable with the level at which he is working.

6-35. The rider gets the horse to **start** moving by making light contact with the horse's side by squeezing his legs. The rider must maintain the proper seat and balance. Riding one hour a week, bareback, will improve a rider's balance rapidly. The rider must not allow his weight or rein hand to come too far forward, as is often the tendency.

He should keep the shoulders square to the animal always. A rider may hold the saddle horn if he needs to steady himself at first but should never use the reins for any purpose other than controlling his mount.

6-36. Unless the animal has been started in a violent manner, he should assume a **walk** when given the command to start out. The rider maintains all aids as described above when riding at the walk. Also, he should be on the lookout for anything that may be affecting the animal, such as a piece of saddle string under the pad. The rider must remember to "stand" in the stirrups, keeping approximately two-thirds of his weight on the balls of his feet.

6-37. **To halt** the horse, the rider closes the lower legs against the animal's side and lightly tightens, not pulls, the reins. When the animal responds, he releases the pressure but not the control. It will take a rider a little time to determine how responsive any given animal is to this or any other command.

6-38. **The jog and lope** paces are two different paces, but are closely related. The aids are the same as for any pace except that the rider's weight shifts slightly forward. In the jog, the horse will bounce quite a bit, and the rider must learn to move with the animal. To initiate the jog from a walk, the rider repeats the steps used to start the animal from a halt into a walk. The lope is a more relaxing pace for the rider. The animal will tend to bounce less, and it will be easier for the rider to maintain the proper balance. The lope is slightly faster than the jog and is initiated from the jog.

6-39. The **gallop** is the fastest pace of a ridden animal and the most dangerous. It is very easy for a rider to lose control of an animal at the gallop if the animal becomes overexcited, which is often the case when an animal is ordered to gallop. When at the gallop, the rider maintains control with the aids as previously described. The rider must transfer his weight from the seat to the stirrups and the knees. Contact should be maintained on the reins.

6-40. The rider uses the **rein back** to make the animal move straight back. It should not be used over any distance. It is always performed from the halt. The rider performs the rein back by using an "elastic" and staggered pull on the reins and positions his weight slightly forward of center.

LEADING A PACK STRING

6-41. When stringing pack animals together, there are many things to consider: which animals get along with each other, which ones will be easy to lead, which ones will be harder to lead, which ones are more experienced than others, and which ones are carrying the heaviest loads. One of the principal advantages of using animals in the era of modern combat is that mounted elements can move large quantities of material in areas not suitable for conventional transport. When using pack animals, it is often preferable to lead them from horseback to take advantage of the animal's speed. Leading pack animals from horseback is not difficult but the rider must observe the following rules:

- It is best for inexperienced packers to start by leading only one pack animal first. As the rider's confidence and experience level grows, he can add more stock to his string.
- In general, the rider puts the pack animals with the heaviest loads toward the front of the string. The farther back the animals are in the string, the more they have to work to keep up.
- The rider places the pack animal that is easiest to lead up front so the animals do not pull on the rider as he heads up the trail. The pack animals that are a little harder to lead can be tied into the sawbuck saddle or Decker saddle by using a small piece of baling twine (40 to 60 pounds) tied in a pigtail knot (Figure 6-6) as a breakaway from the pack animal ahead. If the rider has an animal that continues to break the pigtail, he should double or triple the pigtails being used. For animals that are not equipped with packsaddles, the rider can use a tail knot (Figure 6-7, page 320), that is connected to the lead animal's tail with the lead line of the trailing animal.
- For the safety of the rider and animal, there are two ways to tie a pack string together during movement. The choice of tying the animals together is up to the rider and what he is familiar with. The techniques that most mule handlers use are the pigtail and tail knot.
- A pack string should **never** be tied to the lead (ridden) animal. If an accident occurs or the pack string becomes frightened, the rider is in certain danger if he cannot release the string. This point also applies to leading a single animal. The lead line should always be held in one hand. The rider forms a bight, if needed, over the saddle

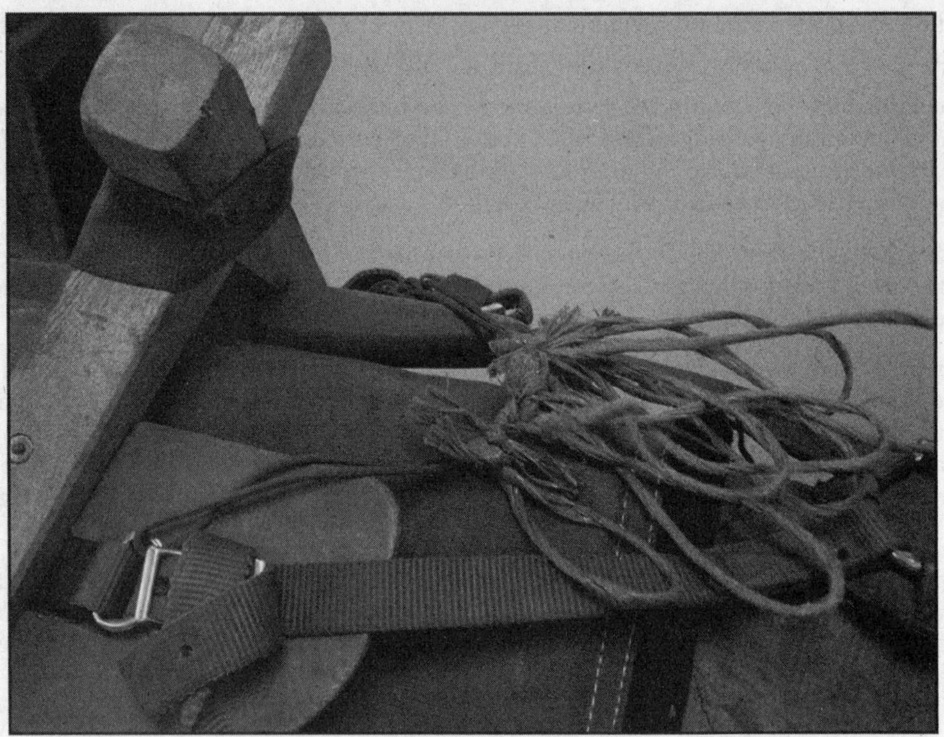

Figure 6-6. Pigtails on sawbuck saddle

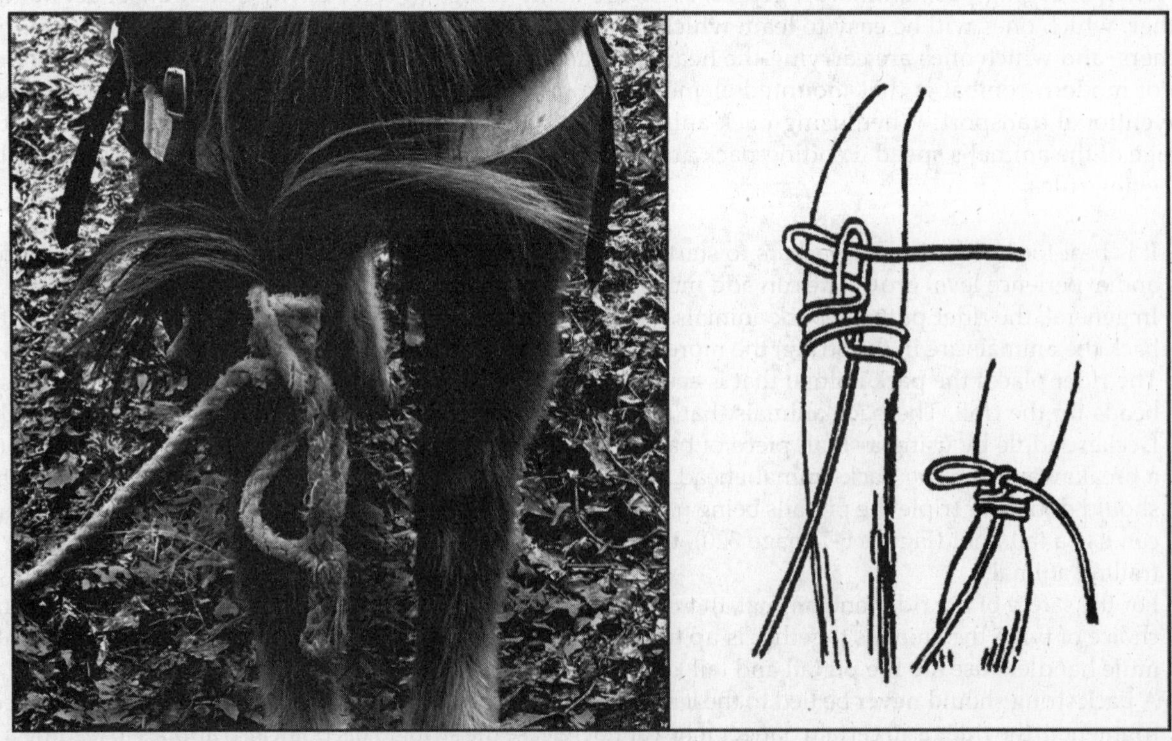

Figure 6-7. Tail knot

horn, but he must be sure that the lead line can be jettisoned immediately, if required. Likewise, there should be no loose loops in the lead rope because of the danger of getting a hand or foot caught and being dragged.

- The rider should **never** move a pack string faster than the animals in it can comfortably navigate obstacles or difficult terrain. He should also keep in mind that the pack animals are carrying dead weight and, often, heavy loads. It is often preferable to give the string more slack when traversing an obstacle so the animals can pick their own way.
- It is preferable to have **two riders** per pack string—a puller and a drag man. The puller observes the trail to the front to anticipate problems. More important, the drag man observes the pack string and assists with any problems that may arise, such as a shifted load.
- If a rider is alone and does not have someone to watch the string for him, he can ride in a figure 8 to get a good look at the string.
- The rider should **always** be wary at halts. The majority of accidents occur at halts when the animals have the freedom to mill about and can become entangled. The rider should **never** allow a lead line to run under the tail of any animal, pack or ridden.
- If negotiating dense terrain (timber or rocks) and the pack animals choose a different route than the lead animal, it is better to **drop** the lead line and **recatch** the string than it is to become entangled in an obstacle with the string.
- The rider should never allow the pack string to get in front of him because if the string should become startled, the rider could get caught up in them.
- The normal distance between the lead pack animal and the rider's animal varies according to terrain and the animals' training and experience. A rule of thumb is the lead pack animal's **nose** should be even with the back of the rider's **flank** while traveling over easy terrain.

COMBAT CONSIDERATIONS

6-42. There are too many types of missions and units that could be assigned to mounted duty to allow this manual to encompass all aspects of military riding. Weapons, climatic conditions, and table of organization and equipment (TOE) will vary too greatly for this chapter to provide specific standing operating procedures (SOPs) and doctrine capable of covering all applications. This document will assist the user in formulating his procedures with general guidance.

WEAPONS

6-43. Individual weapons are as important to the mounted Soldier, regardless of his duty, as they are to the foot Soldier. They must be ready to be brought into action at all times. Achieving this state of readiness from horseback poses certain difficulties. A Soldier normally will carry his weapon in his hands when in a high state of readiness. While mounted, a Soldier's hands are often occupied. Also, there is the problem of keeping the weapon free of the animal and the equipment surrounding the rider. For a rider, there is also the ever-present danger of being separated from his animal. So a primary weapon cannot be kept attached to an animal.

Side Arms

6-44. There is a very real requirement for all mounted personnel to be issued a side arm. The preferred method of carry is the shoulder holster. The holster serves two functions: one—the weapon will be out of the way of tack and lines, always making it instantly accessible; two—the weapon will always be with the Soldier. Due to the large number of duties that mounted Soldiers must perform with their hands (to include tactical movement), a side arm, because of its ever-present availability, becomes a necessity.

Personal Weapons

6-45. Although the use of animals provides a commander a valuable asset for getting individuals and equipment to a battle, fighting from horseback is not considered a primary function of mounted Soldiers today. However, when a unit is in a hostile environment, it must be ready to fight at any time. For a mounted unit, this responsibility includes while on the move. As stated, side arms are a requirement for mounted Soldiers but they are insufficient as a primary weapon.

6-46. The standard weapons of the U.S. military (M16A2, M60, M240 MG, M203, and M249 squad automatic weapon [SAW]) have a serious defect in their size for mounted operations. It is difficult to handle the reins of a horse and a lead line while holding a large rifle. These weapons also demand a certain degree of accuracy that is next to impossible to achieve from horseback. To compromise between effective firepower and effective size, carbines are recommended. U.S. M16 variants such as the M4 are acceptable or, if operations were conducted in a UW environment, an AK folding stock variant would be acceptable. The ability of a submachine gun to lay a heavy base of fire from an unstable position makes it a valuable choice. A selective fire weapon with a folding stock, extended for accuracy when required, is the ideal choice. A very good choice of immediate suppression weapon for the mounted unit is the U.S. M79 grenade launcher. It is much shorter and lighter than the M203 and can be maneuvered with one hand. The launcher's compact size allows it to be placed in a scabbard and still be quickly brought to bear. Several M79s dispersed through a moving unit would greatly improve that unit's chance of surviving an ambush.

6-47. Another consideration would be the adoption of shotguns as standard weapons for mounted troops conducting operations in dense terrain. Their unequaled killing ability at close range and less severe accuracy requirement would make them a good choice as a weapon for mounted troops. The M249 SAW would be the best choice for a general fire support weapon because of its size. The box magazine of the M249 is recommended because a belt of ammunition is too unwieldy around animals. The main problem with any of the weapons described is how their size relates to how they can be carried effectively and still be brought into action when needed. Larger weapon systems 50 pounds or less, such as the M60, M240, and M249 MG, should be laid across the top of the rucksacks that are attached to the animals by using a packer's knot to secure, using 550 cord, or by using straps with quick release for easy access to weapon systems. As discussed before, the selection of carbine-style or folding-stock weapons goes a long way in helping with this problem. However, further mention must be made about how these weapons should be carried. As stated before, a rider can use a scabbard but only when enemy contact is highly unlikely, such as traveling in a secure area. A cross-chest carry with a top-mounted sling is the best choice. Great care must be made that weapons **do not** endanger the rider or his mount by becoming entangled in reins and lead lines or by hitting the animal.

ADDITIONAL WEAPON CONSIDERATIONS

6-48. The nature of modern battle dictates that mounted units carry more types of weaponry than the cavalry of old. Mortars, antiarmor weapons, air defense weapons, and sniper weapons are just a few that must be considered. Again, the METT-TC factors determine what weapons will be carried and in what manner. This manual discusses only a few typical weapons and generic considerations of each.

Antiarmor Weapons

6-49. U.S. antiarmor weaponry of any effect is generally too cumbersome to be carried on horseback. The possible exception is the M72 light antitank weapon (LAW). The rider can use the LAW in many different roles, but it is sufficient against main armor vehicles in only selected manners. He can conveniently attach one or two LAWs to the rear of a saddle, behind the seat, and rig them to be quickly released for action. Backblast must be considered if LAWs are fired around animals. The larger antiarmor weapons (M47 Dragon and tube-launched, optically tracked, wire-guided missile [TOW]) are, in all respects, too heavy and large to be mounted with a rider, but can be mounted on a pack animal. The rider must keep in mind, though, that these weapons cannot be brought quickly to bear if needed.

Air Defense Weapons

6-50. Air defense weapons suitable for mounted operations are the man-portable generation of weapons (for example, the Stinger or SA-7 GRAIL). These are too unwieldy to be carried for any distance on a ridden animal but can be packed easily on a pack animal with consideration given to speedy access. They should be placed within the pack animal strings where the qualified users are as well.

Sniper Weapons

6-51. Sniper weapons are not fired from a mounted position and generally not from a hasty position. They usually will not have to be brought quickly to bear. The sensitivity of weapon sighting mechanisms demands that they be protected when packed on animals.

PERSONAL EQUIPMENT

6-52. Standard U.S. personal equipment will serve a mounted Soldier well when certain considerations are given. In most cases, an assault vest is preferable to the web-gear style because it fits closer to the body. The Soldier can carry all items higher and out of the way of lines and reins. A standard all-purpose, lightweight, individual carrying equipment (ALICE) pack is too large and heavy for the mounted Soldier to carry. However, it adapts easily to being packed on an animal. The Soldier can place the ALICE pack on packsaddles just like panniers. He should carry all essential and sensitive items in his LCE. Using saddlebags and a small day-pack style rucksack can greatly enhance his ability to survive if his ALICE pack gets lost.

6-53. The Soldier will need to tailor his mission and personal gear to meet the weight limitations while using pack animals as a transport. A mounted Soldier carries the essential items with him. These include, but are not limited to, the following:

- Knife.
- Water.
- Rope.
- Necessary bag.
- Personal hygiene kit.
- Required first-aid supplies.
- Compass.
- Chemlights, all colors, to include infrared.

ADDITIONAL EQUIPMENT

6-54. Modern combat operations depend on communications. If a Soldier is designated to carry unit radio equipment, it must be carried with him. For this reason, commanders should make every effort to provide a mounted unit with the smallest and lightest communications equipment.

NOTE

Soldiers must never carry sensitive or classified communications items on a pack animal.

CHAPTER 7

Techniques and Procedures

It is easier to demonstrate how to pack an animal than it is to try to explain how to do it. The only way to learn this skill is by attending a school on packing or spending time with a knowledgeable person who can demonstrate how it is done.

TYING AND USING KNOTS

7-1. There are a variety of knots useful in packing; this section introduces a few and is by no means inclusive. There are several knots most frequently used and the Soldier may perhaps know, or learn, of others equally useful. As horses and packing become more familiar, the Soldier may even come up with some of his own inventions. There is no one perfect way to throw a hitch or tie a sling; the Soldier should use what feels comfortable and works best with the horse equipment and the load that has to be packed.

7-2. A Soldier cannot learn to tie a knot just by reading about it. As with packing and horse handling, the only way to learn this skill is by doing it. Figure 7-1 explains and illustrates several commonly used knots. The recommended method of learning is for the Soldier to get a length of rope and practice tying the various knots until he becomes proficient.

WRAPPING CARGO WITH A MANTEE

7-3. A mantee is a tarp that is either lashed over the top of the load secured on a packsaddle or used to wrap up cargo that is to be placed or slung on a packsaddle. Mantee loads are more versatile than pannier loads. The size and shape of a load can be adjusted to the items packed, and weights can be adjusted daily to each animal's capacity without wasting space. Mantees are easily loaded by one person and, although they must balance, their shape permits considerable adjustment on the animal without unloading or rearranging gear. Mantee equipment is simple. The packer needs only two sheets of canvas and two cargo ropes. Properly folded, a mantee holds a load together at least as well as a pannier and is often more weatherproof. Cargo could be duffel bags, kit bags, sacks of grain, or hay for the animals. Large duffel and sleeping bags that are to be slung on a pack load should be wrapped regardless of the type of material with which they are made. If the packer slings the bags next to a pack animal without wrapping them, they will pick up the sweat and oil off the animal. Besides soiling the articles, the bags will end up smelling like a sweaty packhorse.

MANTEE MATERIALS

7-4. Most packers use an 8- by 8-foot square of 12 to 18 ounces untreated canvas for their mantees. Lighter canvas tears and abrades too easily, and heavier canvas gets too stiff to fold when wet or frozen. The packer should not use tarps of synthetics. Plastics and nylon are too slippery to hold corners and tend to snag on brush. Mantee cargo ropes are made from waxed manila or soft-twisted, spun nylon rope with a 3/8-inch diameter. These ropes should be 36 feet long, back-spliced on one end and eye-spliced on the other end. The advantages to nylon are that it is stronger, lasts longer, is easier on the hands, and does not soak up water that can freeze. Rope stretch will not be a problem with the tension that is used. There will be more give in the load that is being packed than the rope. Also, spun nylon holds knots well, particularly after it has begun to fray.

MANTEE LIMITATIONS

7-5. If the packer does not properly tie a mantee, he can wind up trickling gear along the trail. However, tying the mantee can be easily learned and once mastered is easier and faster than loading panniers. Also, mantee gear is relatively inaccessible. To get something from a mantee, the packer must unload the horse or mule and take the mantee apart. Good planning can reduce this problem, but if the packer has a string of several horses or mules, it would be wise to pack one with panniers for ease of obtaining equipment used frequently.

Type of Knot		Knot Uses
Figure 4 Quick Release		Used to tie a horse to the tree, high line, and hauling system for crossing bodies of water. No matter how hard the horse pulls, this knot will stay secure and still be easy to untie.
Half Hitch		Has many uses but is mostly used during the lashing process around the mantee or to secure the end of the figure 4 knot.
Bowline		Used in various ways. One of the best knots for forming a single loop that will not tighten or slip under strain. This is the **only** knot that should ever be tied around an animal's neck. The bowline forms a loop that may be of any length desired. (When tying a horse to a tree or a picket pin, the Soldier should use the bowline since it will not tighten.) The loop remains loose and will not wind up if the animal walks in a circle around the tree or picket pin.
Clove Hitch		Used to fasten a rope to a pole, bucks or arches on packsaddles, posts, or similar objects. It can be tied at the end of a rope or at any point along the length of a rope.
Timber Hitch		Used for moving heavy timbers or poles. The more tension applied, the tighter the hitch becomes. It will not slip, but will loosen easily when released.
Sheepshank		Used to shorten a rope without cutting it. Also used to take the strain off a weak spot in a rope. It is a temporary knot unless the eyes are fastened to the standing part on each end of the knot.
Packers		Used to secure the cargo rope around the mantee, barrel hitch, and basket hitch. It is secured with a half hitch.

Figure 7-1. Commonly used knots

Type of Knot	Knot Uses
Butterfly	Used to form a fixed loop or loops in place along the length of a rope without using the ends of the rope. It can be used to attach the middleman on a climbing party, tighten installed ropes, and make tie points on a picket line to attach the lead line of the pack animals.
Cat's Paw	Used to form a loop along the length of a rope without using the ends of the rope. It can be used to tighten installed ropes and to make tie points on a picket line.
Dutchman and Double Dutchman	Used to take the place of a pulley. The Dutchman can be used to make tie points on a picket line or to secure the high line around a tree. It can also be used to secure the hauling system when crossing rivers.
Locking	Used to secure billets on the offside of packsaddles.
Square	Used only in simple applications such as to tie packages and for binding rolls. It is easy to tie, will not jam, and is always easy to untie.

Figure 7-1. Commonly used knots (*Continued*)

HOW TO LOAD A MANTEE

7-6. If a packer can wrap a present, he can use a mantee on any item he wants to put on a pack animal. He must remember that the side next to the animal has to be flat and smooth. As in wrapping a present, the packer should take pride in the appearance of the finished package. The packer should drop two mantees so that the load will be balanced. The loads should weigh within five pounds of each other. The packer matches each item on one mantee with an item of equal weight on the other. He shapes the load to the practical limits of the pack animal and the design of the packsaddle. The packer loads the heavy item at a "third and a third." This means that the center of the heavy item should be one-third of the way down from the top of the load and should be in the center third of the load coming out from the pack animal. In this position, the weight rides on the tree of the saddle and directly under the sling rope when the packer uses a basket hitch. By focusing the weight at "a third and a third," the packer ensures that two loads of equal weight actually balance. For example, even though the weight is the same, if a load with the heavy weight at the bottom is loaded on the left side and a load of equal weight but with the weight concentrated at the top is loaded on the right side, the saddle will sag to the left. The gear should be arranged along the diagonal of each mantee ensuring no items have sharp edging that could damage the mantee or injure the animal.

7-7. When packing, the packer lays two mantees flat on the ground side by side. One will be for his onside and one for the offside. Cargo rope should be placed at the top of the mantee. The packer determines what his load will be and separates items into two separate piles of the same weight. The two piles should be within 3 to 5 pounds of each other. This method will give him a balanced load on the animal. The packer places one pile of the cargo on the onside mantee. He organizes (centers) the cargo with the heaviest weight to the bottom diagonally on the mantee. Figures 7-2 through 7-6, pages 327 through 332, illustrate how the packer uses four folds to mantee the cargo and also how to secure the mantee with the cargo rope.

The packer stands near the bottom of the load. He folds the top corner of the mantee located closest to the bottom of the load, near the heaviest part of the load up to the center of the load.

He pulls the corner tight with tension toward the top of the load. He places his left knee on the top corner to hold tight.

Figure 7-2. First fold of a mantee

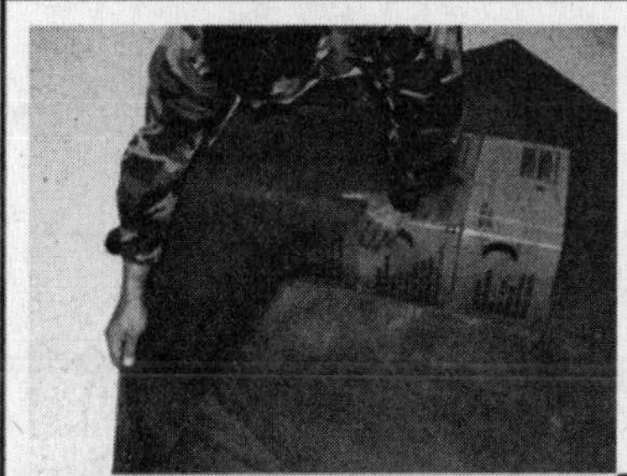

With his knee still on the mantee, the packer turns his body to the right side, reaches out and grabs the right corner.

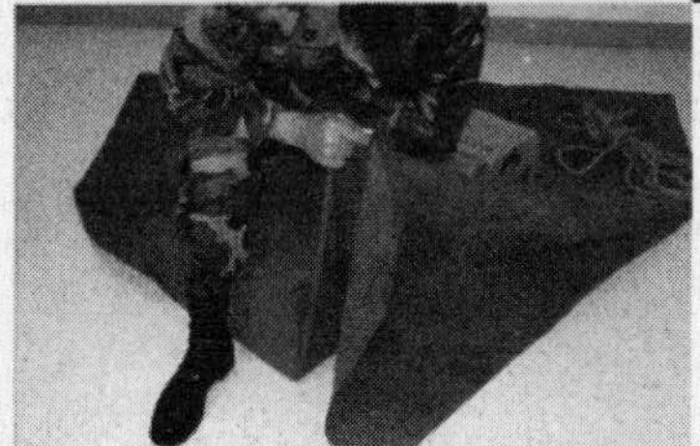

He pulls up and over the first fold, keeping tension on corner of mantee to ensure it is stretched tight. He ensures any mantee hanging out on the corner is dressed up and tucked in so the corner has a squared look.

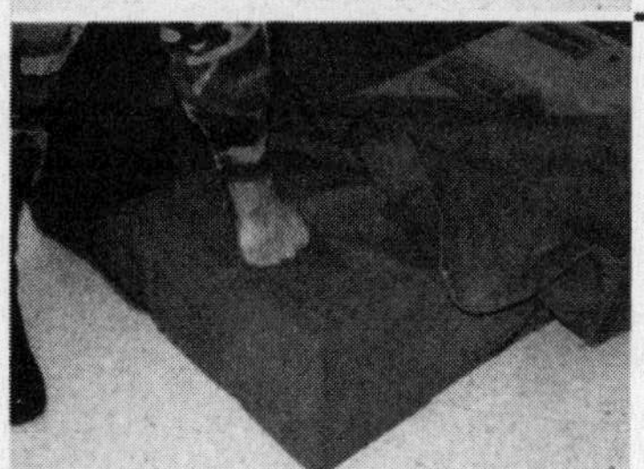

He brings the rest of the right side of the mantee up and over the cargo.

Figure 7-3. Second fold of a mantee

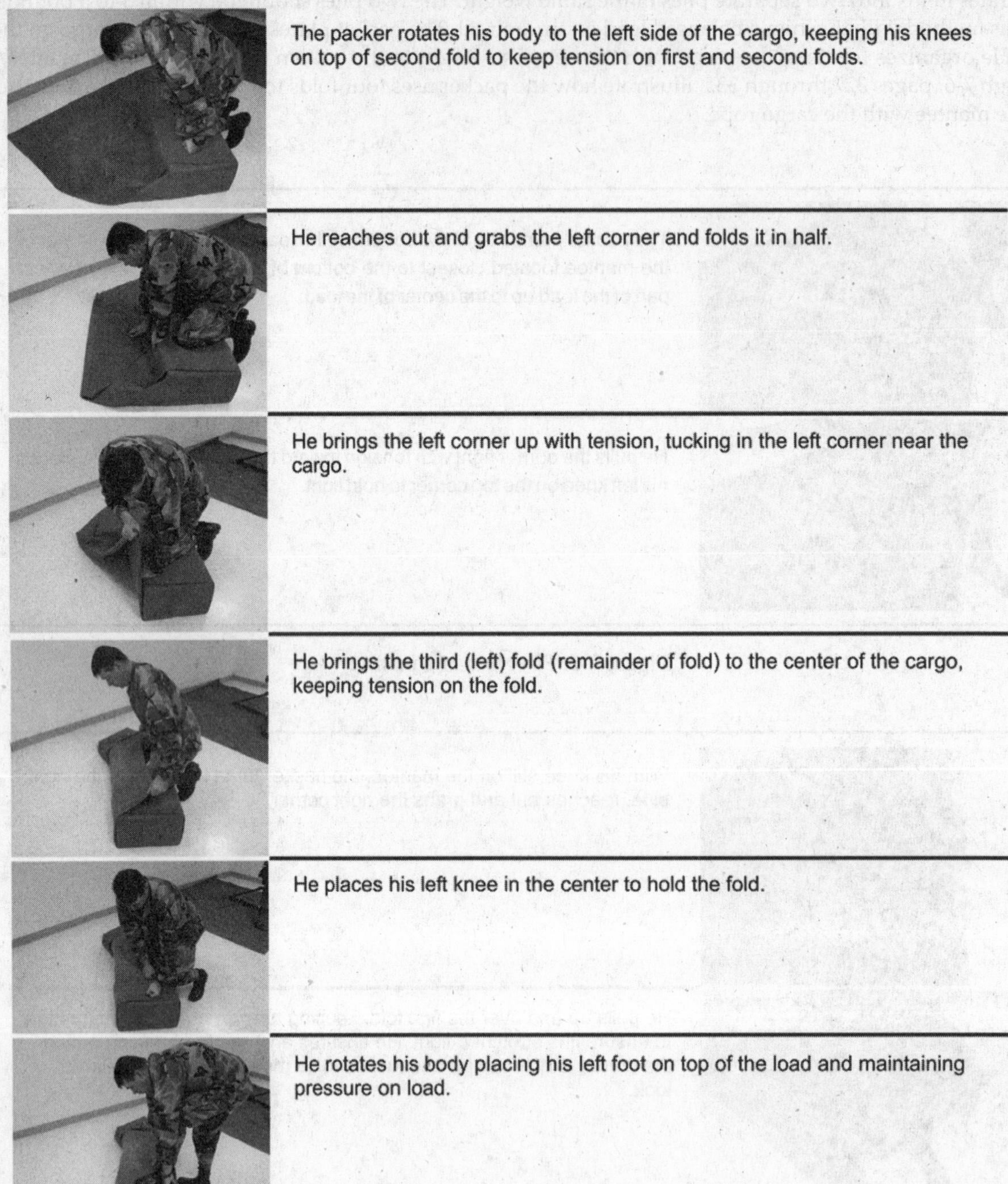

Figure 7-4. Third fold of a mantee

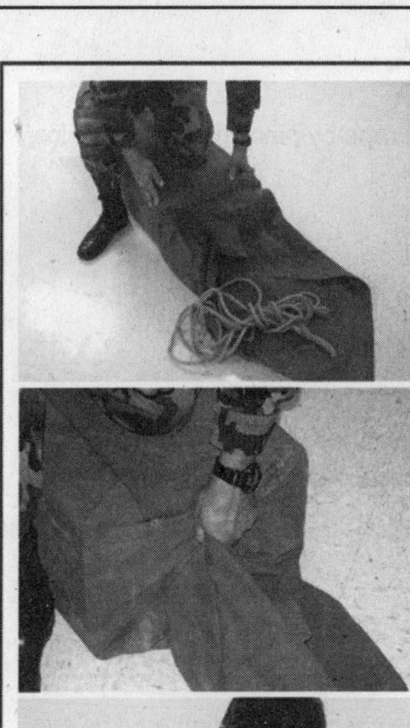

The packer continues to turn until he is facing the top of the load and places his left knee on the load to hold tension.

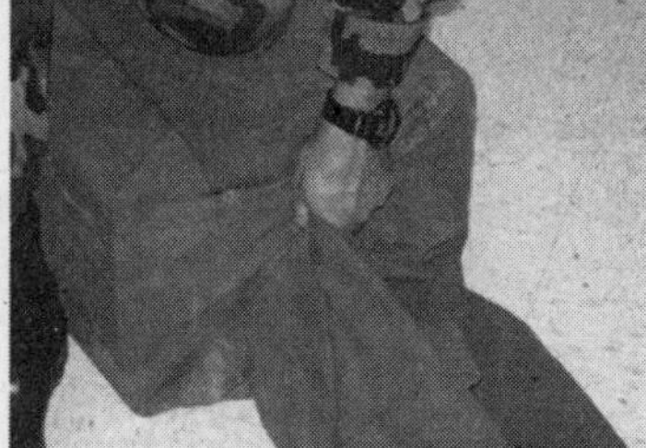

He reaches out and grabs the right and left corners, tucking and dressing the mantee.

He reaches out, grabs the bottom corner of the mantee and folds it toward him, ensuring the flap is as wide as the load to form a rain flap.

He tucks the bottom of the rain flap in so it ends up at half the distance down the cargo.

Figure 7-5. Fourth fold of a mantee

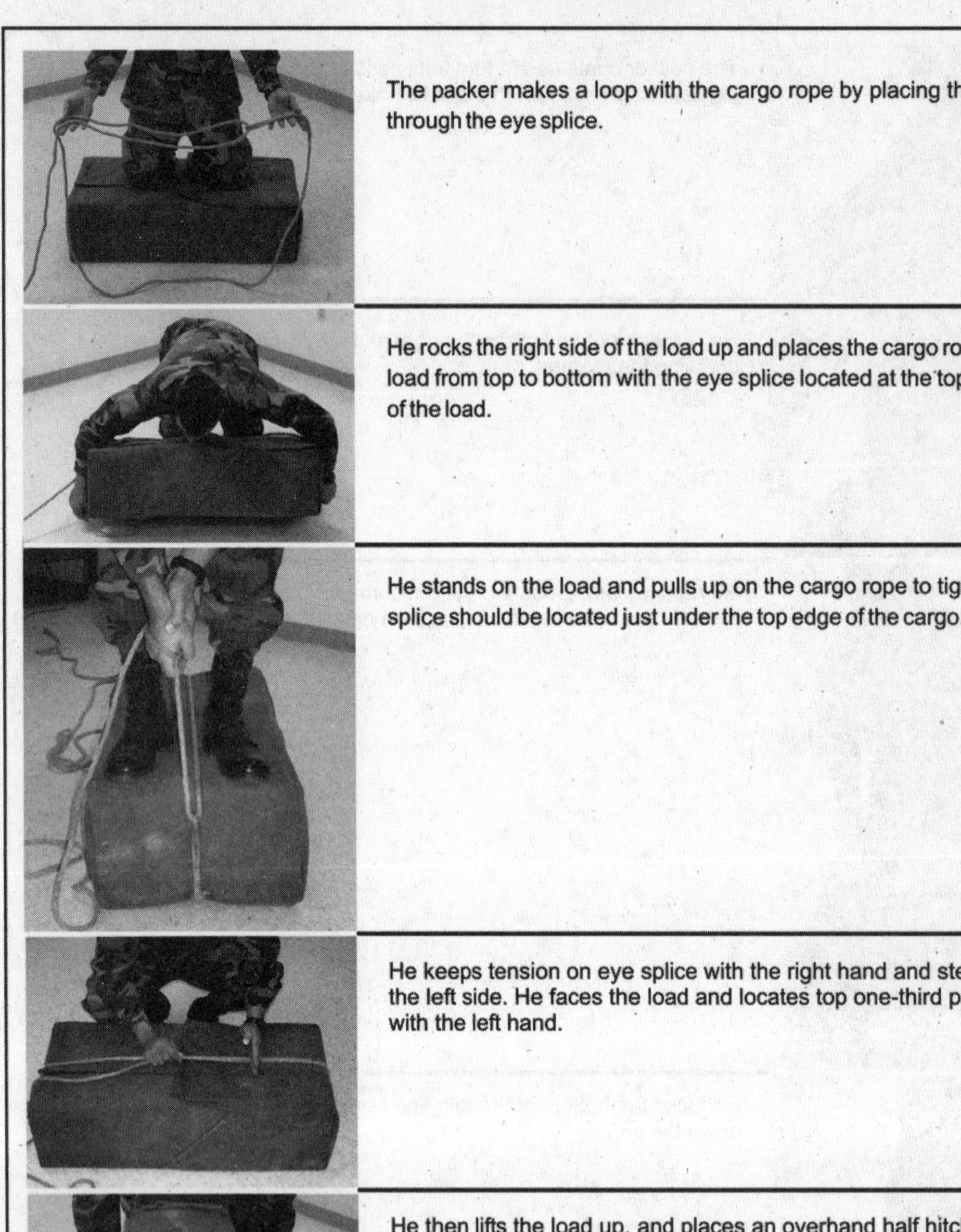

The packer makes a loop with the cargo rope by placing the back splice through the eye splice.

He rocks the right side of the load up and places the cargo rope around the load from top to bottom with the eye splice located at the top bottom edge of the load.

He stands on the load and pulls up on the cargo rope to tighten. The eye splice should be located just under the top edge of the cargo.

He keeps tension on eye splice with the right hand and steps off load to the left side. He faces the load and locates top one-third portion of load with the left hand.

He then lifts the load up, and places an overhand half hitch at the top one-third portion of the load.

Figure 7-6. How to secure a mantee to cargo with rope

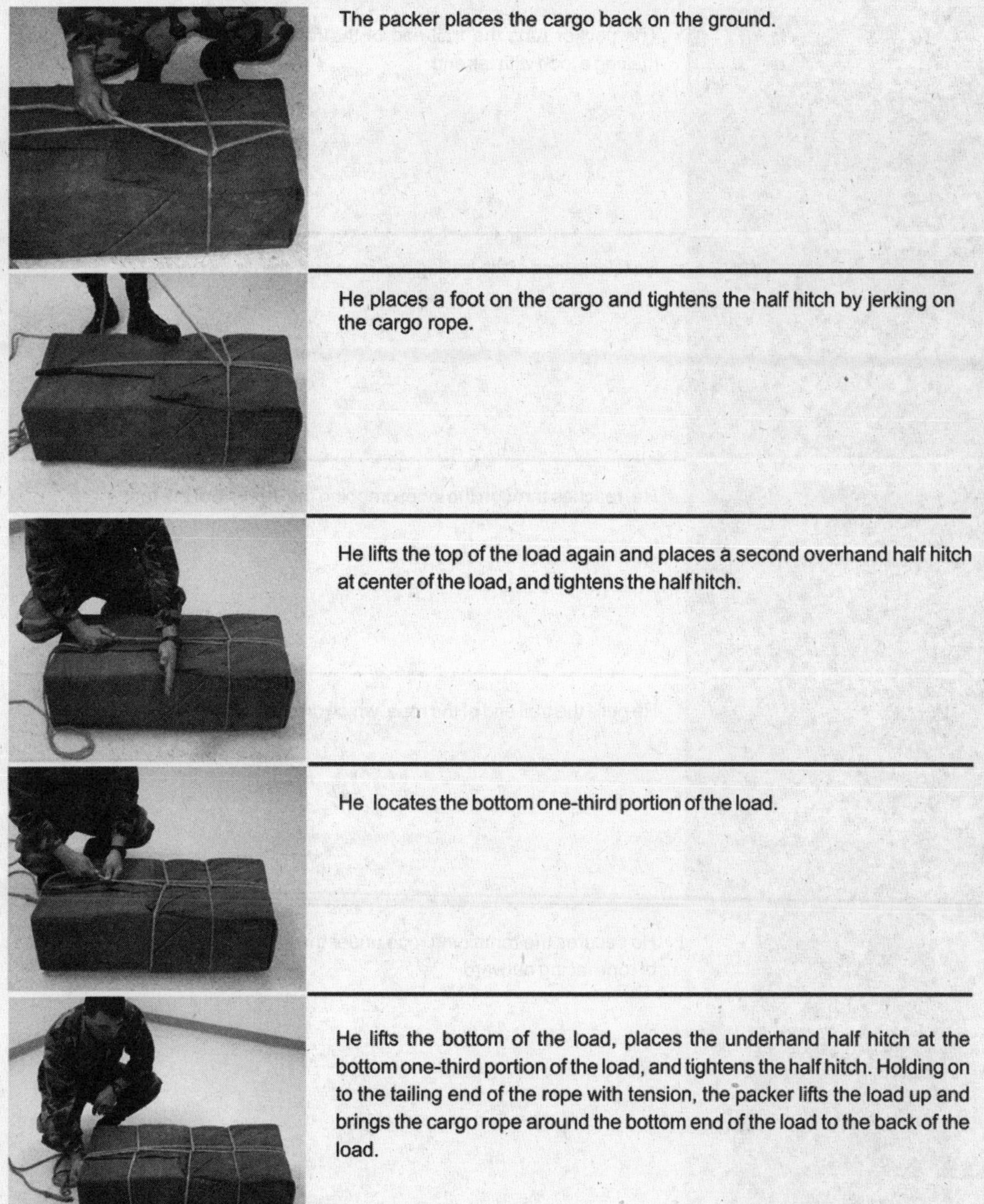

Figure 7-6. How to secure a mantee to cargo with rope (*Continued*)

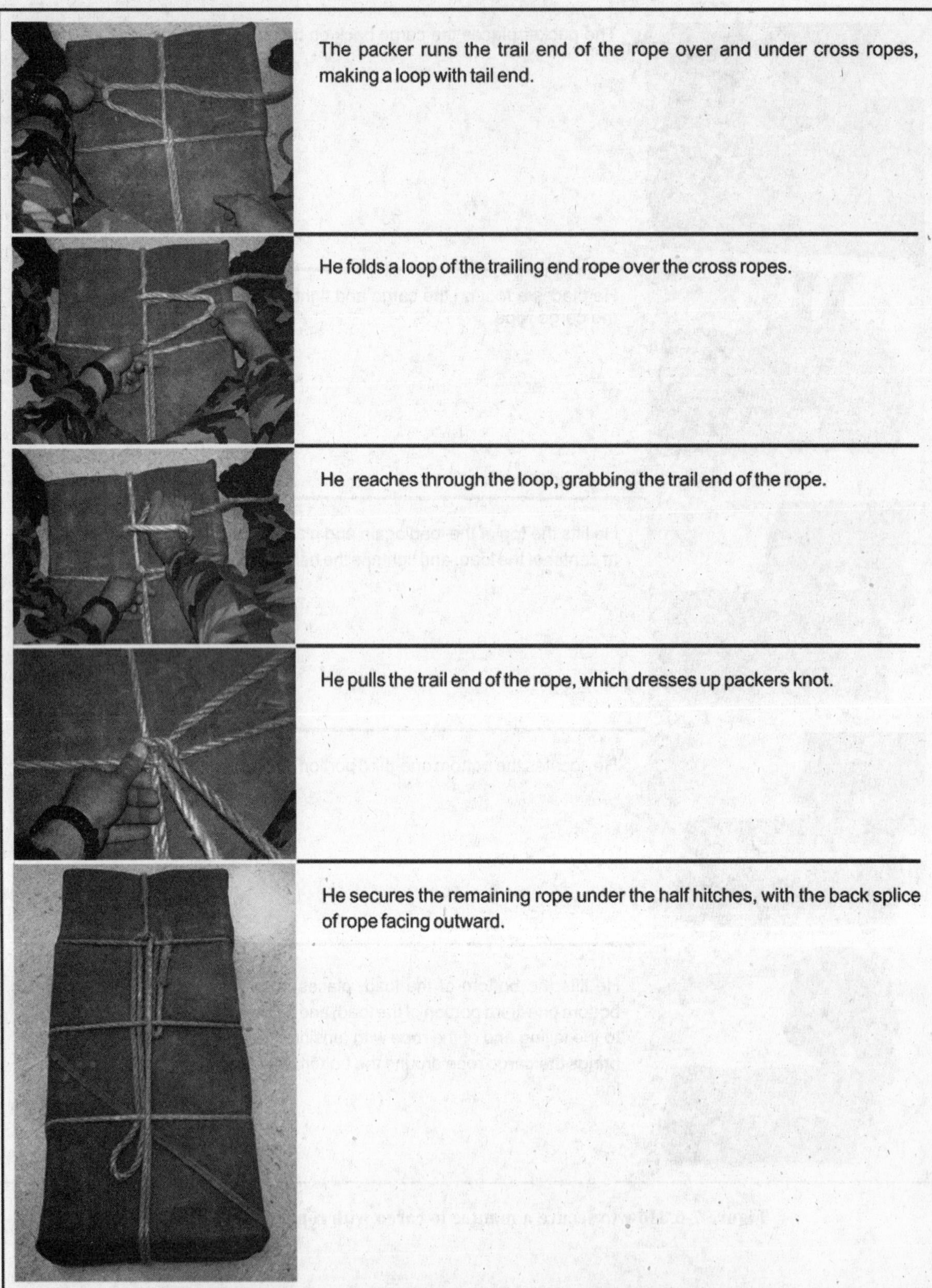

Figure 7-6. How to secure a mantee to cargo with rope (*Continued*)

NOTE

The packer then slings the load using a basket or barrel hitch. He can also use short ropes to loop the load to the bucks. He then ties off the load with a lash rope and box hitch.

BUILDING LOADS

7-8. Hard pack loads (Figure 7-7) are easier to mantee because of their shape. Hard pack loads consist of meal, ready to eat (MRE) boxes, ammunition boxes, water cans, and hard plastic cases, which all have a uniform shape.

Figure 7-7. Hard pack load

7-9. The packer mantees soft pack loads the same as hard pack loads. The soft pack load will be harder to organize and bulkier with no uniformity in shapes of different sizes. Soft pack items consist of kit bags, medical bags, rucksacks, demo bags, duffle bags, and a few hard items such as an MRE case or water can (Figure 7-8).

Figure 7-8. Soft pack load

SPECIAL WEAPONS LOADS

7-10. Weapons systems, such as the M2, MK-19, 60-millimeter (mm) and 81-mm mortar, can either be put in a mantee or into panniers designed for a heavy weapon system. If the packer uses a mantee, he must ensure all metal parts have padding to reduce the noise from movement. He ensures that the smooth side of the weapon is on the bottom of the mantee where it will be placed on the pack animal's back. He also equally divides the weapon system's weight when using the mantee. Table 7-1 shows one way to equally divide the weapon for the onside and offside of the animal. Ammunition may need to be loaded on different animals or broken down to equal the weight and packed with the weapon system to ensure loads are balanced on both sides of the animal. The packer also needs to throw five half hitches around the manteed weapon system for more security, instead of three as is done for the cargo loads.

Table 7-1. Onside and offside loads

Weapon	Onside of Load	Offside of Load
M2 Cal .50 Machine Gun	M2 Without Barrel, 61 pounds Cradle, 21 pounds T&E, 2.5 pounds Gloves, 1 pound Headspace and Timing Key, 2 ounces **Total Weight = 85.7 Pounds** **NOTE:** 1 each, case of cartridges, cal .50 Ball M33 linked, 77 pounds.	Tripod, 44 pounds Barrel, 24 pounds Barrel, 24 pounds **Total Weight = 92 Pounds**
MK-19 40-mm Grenade Machine Gun (MOD 3)	MK-19, 75.6 pounds T&E, 2.5 pounds **Total Weight = 78.1 Pounds** **NOTE:** 48 rounds of M548 in metal container, 62 pounds.	Tripod, 41.5 pounds Cradle, 21 pounds 1/3 Ammunition (Ammo) box, 16 rounds, 19 pounds **Total Weight = 81.5 Pounds**
M224/225, 60-mm Mortar	Mortar, 18 pounds M64A1 Sight, 2.5 pounds Bore Brush, 2.5 pounds M2/M2A2 Aiming Circle With Accessories, 12 pounds Without Batteries, 9 pounds **Total Weight = 32 Pounds** **NOTE:** High-explosive (HE) M888 ammo, 3.41 pounds per round. For hand-held mode, M8 base plate weighs 3.6 pounds.	Bipod, 15.2 pounds Base Plate, 14.4 pounds M14 Aiming Post With Case, 6 pounds **Total Weight = 35.6 Pounds**
M252, 81-mm Medium Extended Range Mortar	Mortar Barrel, 35 pounds Mortar Mount Assembly, 27 pounds **Total Weight = 62 Pounds** **NOTE:** HE M821 ammo, 9.5 pounds per round.	Base Plate, 29.5 pounds M64 Sight, 2.5 pounds Bore Brush, 3 pounds M22/M2A2 Aiming Circle With Accessories, 12 pounds Without Batteries, 9 pounds M14 Aiming Post With Case, 6 pounds **Total Weight = 50 Pounds**

NOTE

Ammunition or other equipment may be needed to adjust weight to the offside when packing.

7-11. Weapon systems like the AT-4s, LAWs, or Javelins (weights are shown in the special segment box below) can either be strapped together and left exposed or put in a mantee as in Figure 7-9. If the packer decides to mantee the weapon system, he must ensure all metal parts have padding to reduce the noise. He should also make sure the smooth side of the weapon is on the bottom of the mantee that will be placed on the pack animal's flanks. The packer makes sure to divide the weapon system's weight equally for the onside and offside. For more security, he should use five half hitches (three overhand and two underhand) around the mantee instead of the typical three.

Figure 7-9. Exposed javelins and AT-4s in a mantee

M98A1 Javelin, Surface Attack Guided Missile, 49 pounds
M72A2 Light Antitank Weapon (LAW), 5.1 pounds
M72A3 Light Antitank Weapon (LAW), 5.5 pounds
M136 Antiarmor Weapon (AT-4), 14.8 pounds

7-12. Top-loaded weapon systems are lighter in weight. The packer can secure the M249, M60, M240, and AT-4s across the top of two rucks or cargo packs that are in a mantee and hung on the onside and offside of the animal (Figure 7-10, page 335). These weapon systems will be secured with quick releases or straps to the mantee or rucksacks.

NOTE
No top-loaded weapon system should weigh over 50 pounds.

7-13. Rucksacks can easily be attached to the Decker or sawbuck saddle by using the single-point release system used for airborne operations. The packer attaches the single-point release system to the rucksack in the same configuration as if he were going to jump. He takes the two snap hooks and attaches to the saddle on the arches of the Decker saddle (Figure 7-11) or by running 550 cord around the saddle crosspieces on the sawbuck saddle.

Figure 7-10. Top-loading a weapon system

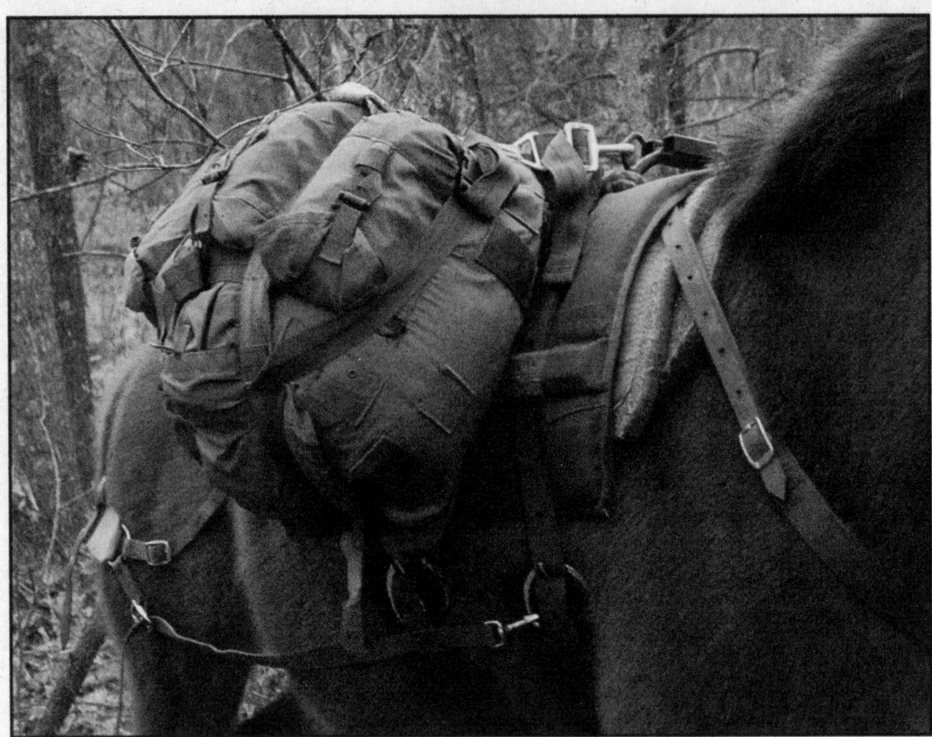

Figure 7-11. Rucksacks attached to decker saddle

7-14. Planning is the most important part of packing. Whether a person is packing one animal or twenty, it takes a plan of attack. In reality, a pack animal is packed in the packer's mind before the actual pack is ever loaded on the animal. A packer should decide which animal will carry which load best, which will be the lead pack, and which can be trusted to stand without trying to lie down or roll while the others are loaded.

7-15. A very good method to follow in planning the pack loads is to lay out several tarps or mantees on the ground to keep the items clean and dry. If the packer has several personnel whose gear is being loaded in the packs, he can have them put it all on the tarps. The packer should explain that once he starts to lay out the packs, they cannot take anything out or add to the pile of gear without asking him first. Any item taken out of a duffel bag that the packer has already hefted for weight will throw off the weight of the pack. This amount could be just enough weight variation to either cause sores on the pack animal or slip the pack on the trail.

7-16. When preparing to pack, the packer loads each individual's equipment onto one animal as neatly as possible, and if more than one animal is needed, he keeps them together in the string. This practice makes things simple at overnight halts and when the final destination is reached, so one individual does not have to go through the panniers of several different animals searching for his equipment.

7-17. One of the many secrets of packing—possibly the most important—is to keep the weight down at the bottom of the pack. This gives the packer a good solid foundation on which to build the rest of the load. A good load for most horses or mules (1,100- to 1,200-pound packhorses and 800- to 1,000- pound mules) is 160 to 170 pounds. However, if there are some small animals in the pack string, this amount could be too much for them. In extreme circumstances, the packer can load an animal with up to 250 pounds; however, this amount would limit his speed and endurance. The horse gear (shoes, nails, hobbles, bells, picket chains, ropes) usually will fit in one set of panniers (two panniers). The packer must remember this set of panniers well, as it will be the first item needed when he unpacks at the destination. He should try to keep all the camp tools (shovel, ax, saw, currycomb, brush) on this pack load; it will save a lot of time when he arrives at the camp for the night. The packer will know exactly where all his tools are located.

7-18. When loading the bottom of box panniers, the packer wants everything to fit as snugly as possible to keep from rattling. A pile of gunnysacks close at hand is good for chinking up any rattles. The packer can distribute the items through several sets of panniers, if necessary. Two layers of heavy items in a pannier are a big bottom load. If the packer has plenty of pack animals and box panniers, one layer of heavy items in several boxes will be better than trying to get it all on one pannier.

7-19. Canvas panniers come in all sizes, shapes, and forms. Their general use in packing is to load them with bulky items that will not fit the box panniers. The loading method as mentioned before is the same: the weight should stay down at the bottom. Just because a canvas pannier sometimes looks like a big sack, the packer should not make the serious mistake of loading it like a grocery bag. There is nothing between the load in the canvas pannier and the pack animal but a thin layer of canvas. The packer loads the canvas pannier so it is smooth and flat on the side next to the pack animal. If there are a lot of odd-shaped sleeping bags and duffel bags, here is a good place to put them. This method is also the best way to pack the grain for the animals. Having numbers on all the panniers is a great help in keeping them in sets of two. Whether there are numbers on the panniers or not, the packer should keep the sets together when he has finished loading.

7-20. When the packer has all the supplies, horse gear, grain, and other things packed in the panniers and any sling loads wrapped, he is ready to finish the pack loads with personal gear of the party. The packer selects two items of equal weight and puts one in each pannier, all the time keeping in mind what each pannier weighs. Next, he may need a top pack. He selects two duffel bags or sleeping bags of equal weight and places these in each pannier. Now is a good time to recheck the weight of his panniers to make sure they are still equal. The packer should have a scale that he can suspend from a tree limb to weigh the panniers; a difference of only a few pounds between them can make all the difference once the animal starts down the trail. If the packer feels that both panniers together weigh under 150 pounds, he should find a third sleeping bag or duffel bag for a center load. He then lays this third item across both panniers, showing it as the center load. He places a mantee and lash rope over the entire pile and allows no one to disturb it until he is ready to load it on a pack animal.

7-21. After the packer has gone through the pile of things to be packed, there will probably be several items that look like they will not fit any of the loads that have been laid out. If they are small and light enough to make another pack load, the packer can often find a place for them as he packs out the other loads. He will have to allow space for these items while loading the other panniers or he will end up with one or two things left out.

SADDLING

7-22. This section explains techniques and lessons learned that will keep a rider in good stead. (Chapter 5 provides saddling details.) There are quite a few different types of packsaddles, and each has to be rigged differently to get the pack on it. These saddles may have any number of different riggings and may or may not have quarter straps. Whatever the type, all saddles must properly fit the pack animal.

7-23. The padding between the pack animal and the saddle is a vital piece of pack gear. Pack pads as a rule are larger and thicker than regular riding pads. Once the animal is packed and the load rests on these pads, they will stay there until the animal is unpacked. Pack pads are made of many materials, the best being one that will stay soft and not pack down. The most commonly used pads have fiber, fleece, felt, or hair sewn to a light canvas.

7-24. Whatever type of pad is used, it should be checked thoroughly for any foreign objects before placing it on the animal. Sweat will build up but can be scratched off with the currycomb. Wet pads will gall or cause sores on a pack animal. The packer lays the saddle pads out where they can air out and dry when possible. He should always try to place the pack pads square on the packhorse, leaving at least 4 inches to the front of the packsaddle. Depending on the shape of the pack animal's back, the packer may need more than one pack pad. The best way to gauge is to set the packsaddle on the animal, then check the clearance between the saddle and the animal's withers; there should be enough space for two fingers.

7-25. The packer allows for the saddle settling down on the pads after the animal is loaded. If there is any chance of the saddle forks coming in contact with the top of the withers, he puts another pack pad or cheater pad under the saddle. He also makes sure not to put too much padding on the withers and cause the packsaddle to pinch from being too thick. Most good pack pads are thin down the center of the pads. The aim in a high-withered animal is to raise the packsaddle off the tops of the withers. Some packers use a cheater pad as explained in Chapter 5, page 297.

7-26. Now is the time to again check the pack animals to see if the saddles on them are rigged for the type load the animals will be carrying. If the packer has one or two sling loads, he knows to have that many sling ropes on the saddles and have them tied off ready to use in saddling the pack animal. He rechecks the pack pads to make sure they are loose over the withers of the animal and that the packsaddle sits in the middle of the pads.

7-27. During all the loading of the panniers and other gear, the packer should not lead the pack animal around to pick up parts of the load. It is a very serious mistake. He should have all the gear at hand that will be loaded onto the animal in one central location where he will be doing the loading. Once the packer begins loading an animal, he waits until the pack load is lashed down before he moves the animal, or he will be picking up parts of the load from the ground after they have slipped off.

7-28. If the packer is going to move the pack animal from where he was saddled to where the pack load is sitting, he pulls the cinches up snug before he leads him to the pack load, then finishes tightening the cinches just before loading. This technique is called "untracking" the animal. If pack animals that have been saddled and standing with a loose cinch have the cinches tightened and are then loaded without moving around first, they could experience some discomfort from being pinched or having a fold in their skin caught under the cinch. This pain will often cause them to throw the whole load off. When the packer pulls the cinch up on a pack animal, he untracks the animal before he puts the pack load on him. Moving around a bit allows the cinch to settle into place, and the animal will be more comfortable. This practice also applies when the packing is completed. The packer should continuously check the animals and monitor how the loads are riding. He should especially watch the animal as it takes the first few steps after being packed; if the load looks like it is shifting, he makes whatever adjustments are necessary.

7-29. Whenever possible, the packer should get help in loading the panniers onto the animals, because when packing alone, he will have to keep moving from side to side. While the packer is moving to the opposite side, the load on one side is pulling the packsaddle over and pinching the animal's withers. With a heavy load, this could cause the animal enough discomfort to buck off the load or at least turn the packsaddle.

7-30. Some panniers have ropes or straps that the packer can adjust to set the height at which the panniers will sit on the pack animal; others are slung with the sling rope. Regardless of the method used, the panniers must be even in height on the pack animal. A pannier low on one side pulls the saddle in that direction and either causes a sore on the animal or slips the entire pack. After loading the panniers on the animal, the packer steps to the rear and checks that they are evenly placed.

7-31. With any center load, such as a duffel bag, the packer must make sure the opening is to the front of the animal. The motion of the animal usually shifts things around. With the opening to the front, the packer can see if any items are working their way out of the bag while on the trail. Regardless of what is center-packed, the packer should make sure that after the load is lashed down it will not rub the animal.

7-32. The packer pulls the mantee down evenly on both sides of the boxes and tucks in the ends around the panniers. He keeps checking to make sure the pigtail on the packsaddle is clear and out where he can tie into it. A good solid pack will look sloppy if the packer does not take the time to use the mantee neatly and tie it up right.

SLINGS AND HITCHES

7-33. The packer uses the sling to initially attach the load (panniers, mantee, hay) to the saddle. Once attached, he throws a mantee across it and uses a hitch to secure the entire load to the animal. He then ties the sling to the saddle and the hitch to the animal.

7-34. The basic purpose of a hitch is to secure the entire load to the packsaddle and the animal as a balanced unit and still not have to use 100 feet of rope. The packer then throws these hitches so they can be taken off the load with little effort.

7-35. The different means of tying a load down on a pack animal are not as confusing as they might sound. Terms such as a one-man diamond, half diamond, full diamond, double diamond, squaw hitch, box hitch, and many other means of tying are frequently used during packing. The packer does not have to learn them all, but if he learns one or two of the most commonly used hitches, he can tie down almost any load encountered.

7-36. To throw a hitch means just that. The packer throws the loops and coils of his hitch on the pack in such a way that when he gives the hitch its last pull, all the ropes pull tight. When he releases the hitch to unpack the animal, the packer does not have to spend time unwinding or untying knots in the lash rope.

7-37. Most new lash ropes are approximately 36 feet long. They come in many diameters and are made of several materials. In most cases, lash ropes are approximately 1/2 inch in diameter and either of manila or nylon material. Polyester rope makes the best lash ropes because wet weather makes grass or hemp ropes very difficult to handle.

7-38. If a packer uses wet slings or lash ropes made of hemp to pack an animal, he may not go very far up the trail before the slings and hitches start to dry and stretch out. This stretching will make his pack loose or uneven and could cause a considerable delay in reaching his destination. In camp, or wherever the mission leads, the packer should keep all hemp lash and sling ropes dry if at all possible. The ropes should not be thrown on the wet ground while packing an animal. They should be hung on a tree limb or laid on a tarp or dry place until ready for use.

7-39. The lash cinch (on the end of the lash rope) needs checking often for signs of fatigue in the cinch materials. It has an eye splice in one end and a crown splice (back splice) in the other end to simplify the makings of a hitch. The lash cinch is really, in most hitches, the beginning and the end of a hitch. The packer throws the lash cinch across a loaded pack animal, and very often, the person on the offside forgets to duck or watch for it to come over. It does not take many knots on the head to learn respect for this piece of pack gear.

7-40. Whatever hitch the packer uses on the pack load must hold the ends, sides, and bottom of the panniers, besides holding the top pack. If the packer balances the pack on the animal properly, the lash rope can hold the pack down and together. He cannot balance a pack with the lash rope. After the packer puts everything inside so it will not rattle or break and the wrapping is on, he is ready to lash. He wants something that looks good yet holds the wrapping and box. Handling a lash rope while throwing a hitch can be dangerous if the packer becomes tangled in the rope and the animal gets spooked or starts bucking. The packer should always make sure there are no coils around his feet or arms, as they could cause him to get dragged or seriously injured. The safest way to handle this situation is to keep the tail, or excess, rope thrown out to the right while throwing the hitch.

7-41. The packer should always check the pigtail on the packsaddle to make sure it is still clear and ready for use. Again, he checks the entire load, front and rear, by conducting a press check to ensure packs and saddles are in line with the animal and are riding balanced on the animal. If it looks like the entire pack load has shifted to one side, the packer lifts up on the low sides and sees if it will rock back straight. If it does not, he completely repacks the entire load. This rechecking will save the packer time on the trail repacking where he may not have help or a place to tie up. It can also prevent sores from developing on the animal. He checks any loose rope or mantee ends sticking out and tucks them in the wrap.

7-42. The methods of securing cargo are slings, used to attach the load to the saddle, and hitches, used to secure the entire load to the horse. If the packer ties the sling on a sawbuck saddle, he can tie the same sling onto a Decker saddle by running the ropes through the loops (arches) at the top of the saddle rather than behind the bucks. With a little imagination and ingenuity, the packer can adapt any of the slings and hitches to whatever type saddle (to include riding saddles) and load he is packing.

LOAD BALANCING TIPS

7-43. The packer should make sure the animal is standing on level ground before he begins loading. He should beware of an animal resting a hind foot. The packer should quickly get the second mantee or pannier on the horse or mule. This can be accomplished with two packers better than one. The packers should balance each pair of loads after it is on the animal. This can be done by rocking the packs vigorously in place, releasing them, and seeing that the D-rings center perfectly on the animal's pack. If loads are not balanced, the packer should, whenever possible, lower the light side rather than raising the heavy side. He can snug the load up to within an inch of the D-rings, regardless of how high or low he positions a load.

BARREL HITCH

7-44. If the saddle does not already have a sling rope attached to it, the packer ties one onto the sawbuck saddle by using a clove hitch in the center of the cargo rope. He ties onto the Decker using the eye splice and back splice of the cargo rope attached to the front arch with one rope and to the rear arch with another cargo rope. He ensures the sling rope is around 36 feet long, though this may vary according to the size of the cargo.

7-45. Starting on the onside of the animal, the packer makes a large loop at the forward end of the saddle, passes the rope behind the bucks to the rear, then makes another large loop at the rear of the saddle. He then brings the rope back behind the rear buck and down to the sling ring (Figure 7-12A).

> **NOTE**
> The packer repeats this procedure on the offside of the animal.

7-46. The packer slips the cargo through the loops of the sling rope, then tightens up by running the end around the section of rope behind the bucks, pulls tight, and then ties off onto the sling ring (Figure 7-12B).

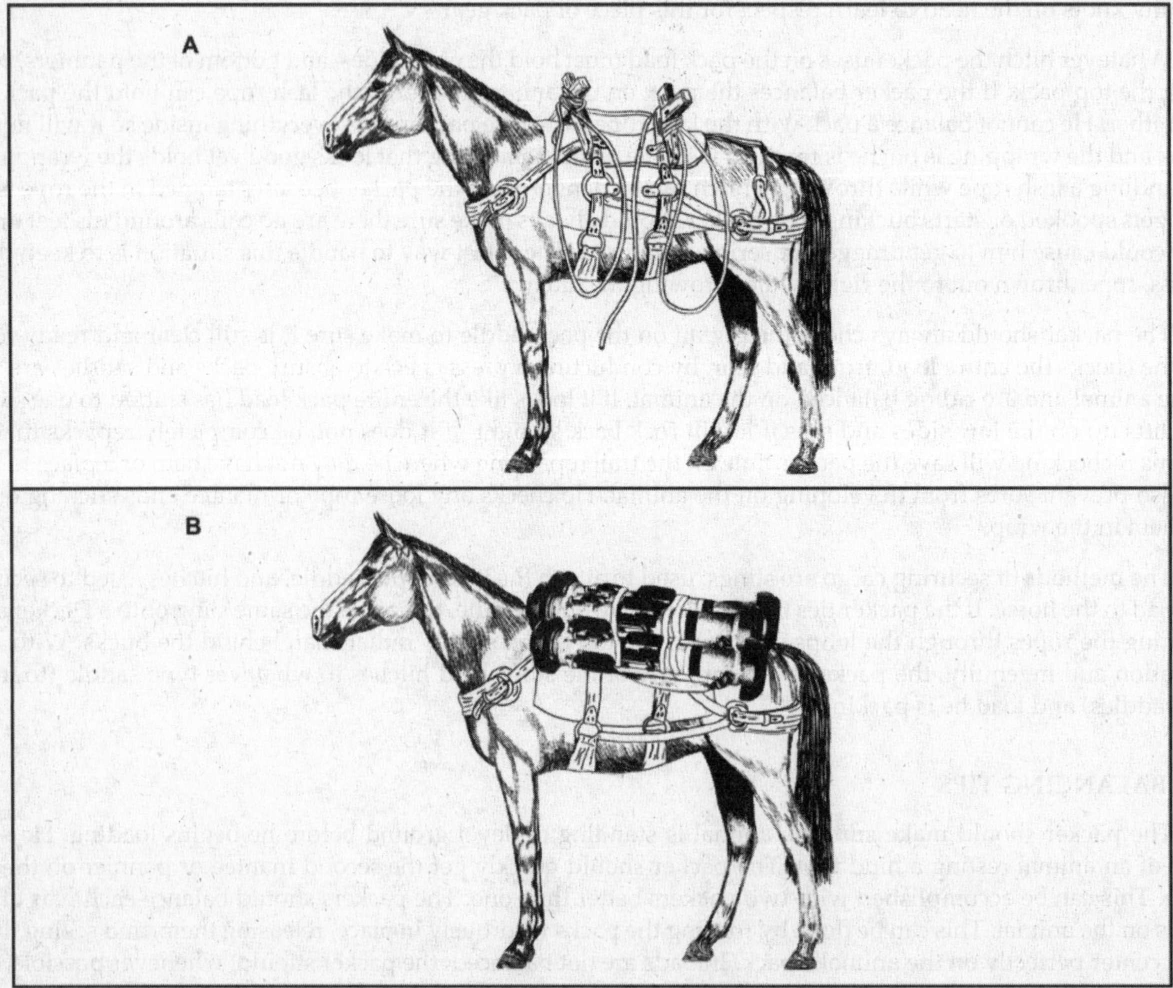

Figure 7-12. Barrel hitch

CAUTION

After running the ropes under the forks of a sawbuck saddle, the packer checks the clearance between the ropes and the withers to make sure the ropes will not rub the animal's back raw.

BASKET HITCH

7-47. As with the barrel hitch, the packer starts by tying a sling rope onto the saddle. He draws the rope around the cargo, through the back hoop, down between the cargo and the animal, then back out and up the center of the outside of the load.

7-48. The packer pulls one loop through the horizontal portion of the rope, then pulls another loop through that one. He pulls the first loop tight, then expands the second to fit around the bottom of the cargo. He allows enough slack so the bottom of the loop can pass through the cinch ring. He threads the end of the rope through this loop. The packer pulls the sling tight, then pulls another loop through the horizontal section and secures it with two half hitches (Figure 7-13).

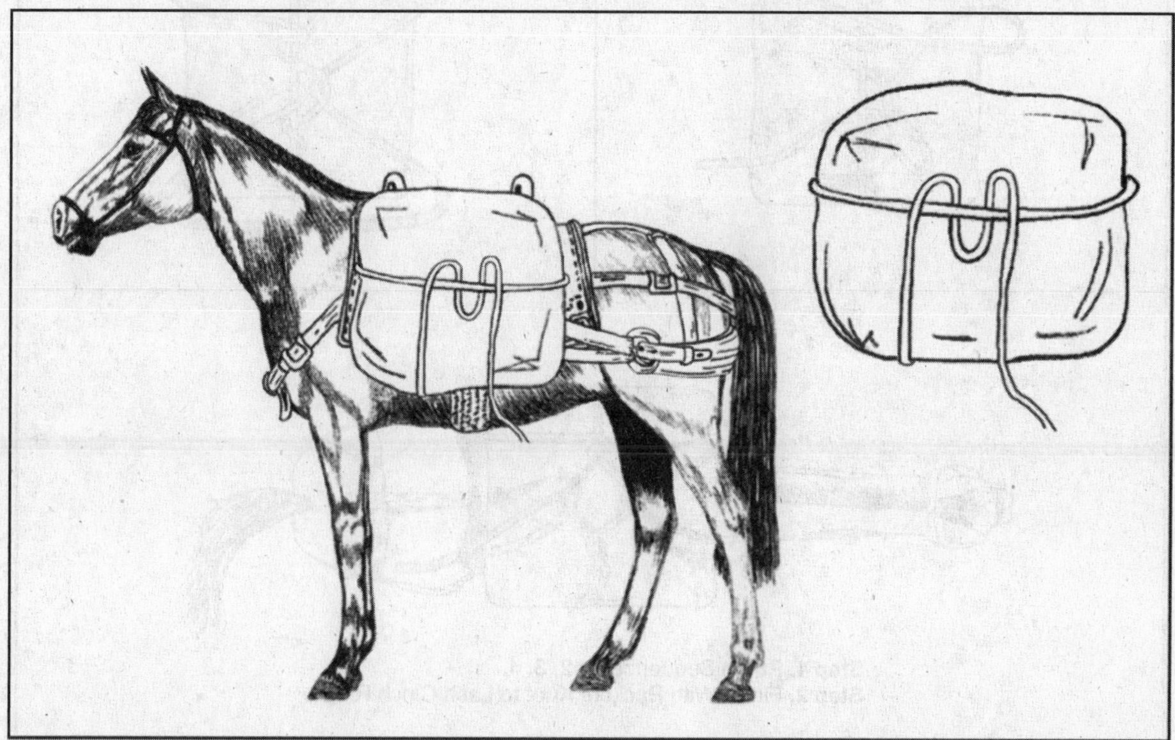

Figure 7-13. Basket hitch

DIAMOND HITCH

7-49. The diamond is useful for soft loads. The one-man diamond is easiest to tie (Figure 7-14). Again, this hitch does not tie off anywhere on the saddle.

7-50. This section is not meant to totally encompass slings and hitches—just enough of the basics to suffice for the most commonly encountered situations. As stated before, a person cannot learn this skill by reading about it; he must find someone knowledgeable on the subject and have him demonstrate how it is done.

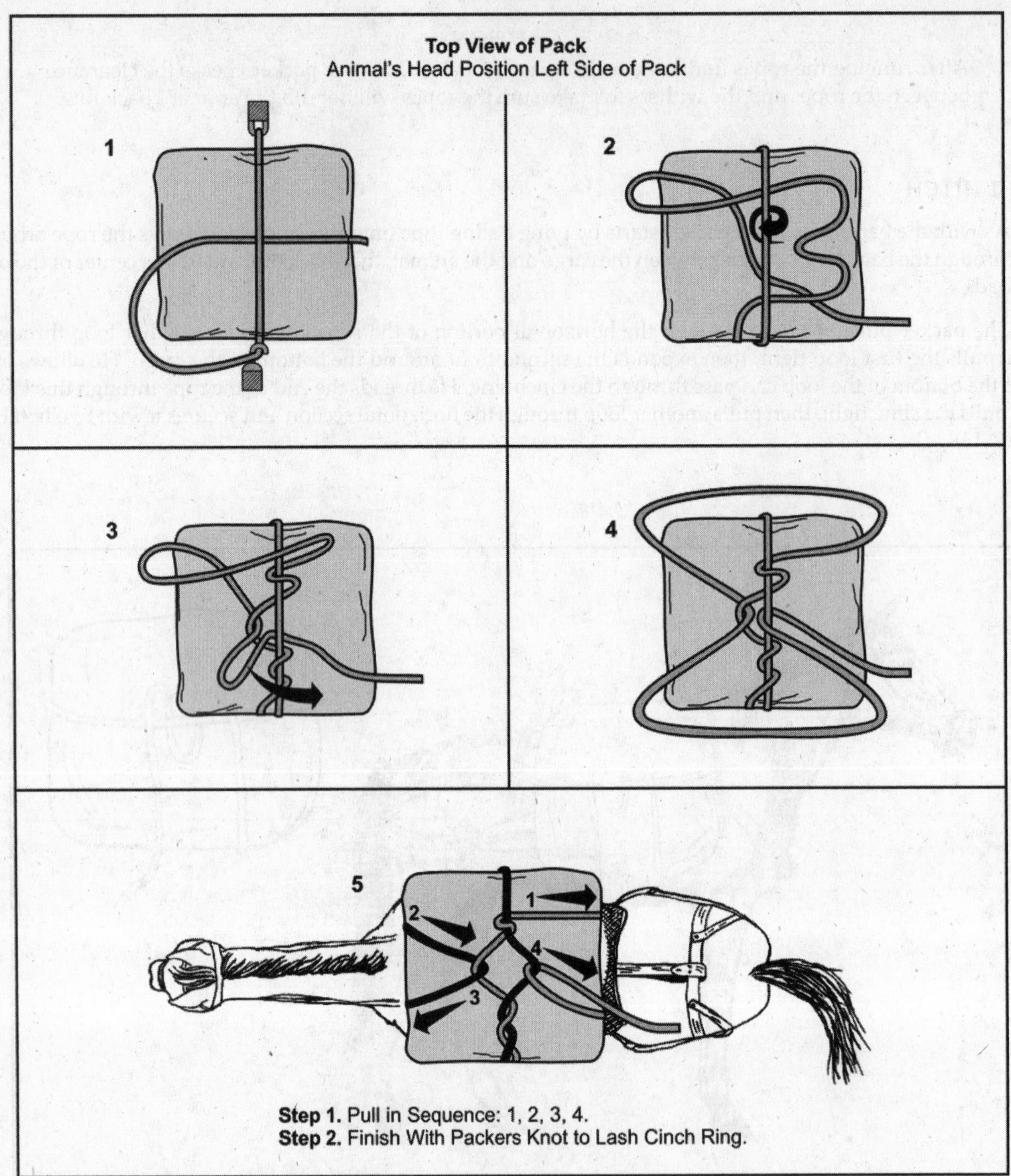

Figure 7-14. Diamond hitch

THE PACK STRING

7-51. Once the packer has first-class, well-balanced packs on the pack animals, he needs to make up the pack string. Being knowledgeable of how all his animals perform will help the packer greatly when he is selecting the lead animal. If the packer selects an animal that will not lead up on a slack rope, he will spend his time dragging this animal along all day. Many pack outfits using mules have a horse they call the Bell Mare. The outfit can put a bell on this particular horse and lead just the one animal and the rest will usually follow. Using horses as pack animals is another situation.

Horses and mules form habits, just as teams do, as to what position in the string they should be. If the packer knows this position when tying a string together, he will have a well-organized pack string going up the trail. Often, one of the pack animals will have a very fragile load that needs special attention on the trail. The packer may find that this is the animal he wants to lead and should focus on the pack items when loading out the packs.

7-52. Personnel should always stay in the clear whenever they are afoot around pack animals tied together. Many things can happen, even with the most gentle pack stock. Two animals with box panniers can definitely put the squeeze to a person caught between them. It does not have to be the pack animal that a person is working on that causes the trouble. It can be any one of the animals in the pack string. If one jumps or bucks, the whole string, being tied together, has to go along. If a person is in the middle of several loaded pack animals, he should try to keep them standing apart and in a line. A person should never get in the middle of the pack string when they are bunched up.

7-53. A person should never get off his saddle horse into a crowd of spooked and bucking pack animals. He should try to keep them circling or headed straight out until they settle down. He does not stand a chance afoot until he has them where he can get a hold on the head of whichever animal is causing the problem. A person may feel helpless sitting on his saddle horse, watching all that gear being thrown off and trampled, but he must remember that he could very easily be the one that is getting trampled or kicked.

7-54. Tying the pack string together takes just a little horse sense. The packer wants to give the animals all the room possible between them and yet not have so much lead rope that they can get a leg over the rope when their heads are down. A good gauge for the length of rope is to use the hoof of the pack animal that the packer is tying off to. If the animal being tied off is standing roughly nose-to-rump to the other animal, and the lead rope is down about to the hoof on the lead pack animal, this length is about right.

7-55. The packer can tie the pigtail on a packsaddle in several ways. One opinion is to run it through the rear forks of the packsaddle and down to the front rigging rings. Installing a pigtail this way pulls only on the cinch and not on the packsaddle. A nylon or polyester piece of 3/8-inch rope braided at the rings makes a very substantial pigtail.

7-56. Oftentimes, it is a good idea to have a "breakaway" in the end of the pigtail where the packer will be tying the lead ropes of the pack string. The packer can make the breakaway with light baling twine (40 to 60 pounds) or 1/4-inch 80-pound cotton webbing used for airborne operations. Should there be an emergency where the pack animal needs to break loose, it can usually break this light twine.

7-57. When leading a string of pack animals, the packer should be all eyes. The first mile on the trail is the most important. This short distance helps the packer find out if the packs are tight and well-balanced and if he missed some rattles in the panniers. He will want to look back over the pack string about as much as he looks ahead. When the packer comes to a turn in the trail, he should get a side view of the packs. Often, he can see something coming loose that can easily be fixed, but if left unattended could cause a pack to slip or something to be lost on the trail.

7-58. One of the most common mistakes a green packer makes is not giving the pack string time. When the packer crosses a ditch, rock, or downed trees in the trail, his saddle horse most likely will just step over or around it and keep right on going. Possibly, the next pack animal (the lead) will keep up easily enough, but the second pack animal will have to really hurry to get across the obstacle. When it comes to the third animal, it will either have to jump or pull back and so on down the line. When the packer crosses or goes around any obstacle on the trail, he should slow up until all his pack animals have gotten around or over it.

7-59. If the pack string has steep country to climb, the lead rider should give the animals a lot of time to stop and get their breath. He should pick a good spot where all the animals are standing square on the trail. The rider cannot use his saddle horse as a gauge for when to stop to breathe the pack string. The saddle horse may be carrying a 200-pound load, but that load is in balance with him while he is climbing. The pack animal has dead weight and needs more air to pack his load up the hill.

7-60. On long trips and especially when climbing, periodic rest stops will be necessary, but the packer should not overdo them. Stopping for long periods on the trail can cause more packs to needlessly slip. If a stop for lunch or whatever is necessary, the pack string should be taken apart and each animal tied to a tree. If at all possible, the pack string should be kept in motion. The pack load is continuous on the animals and the quicker it can be taken off, the better for the animals.

7-61. When crossing a stream or any fresh water, the animals should be allowed to drink. The lead horse should not just ride in and stop, the rider should, if possible, make sure there is room for all the animals to drink at once. When the animals are done drinking, the lead rider should make sure none of them has a foot over the lead ropes as he starts out. Whenever the lead rider stops on the trail for even a short time, he should always be sure the pack animals are ready to go before moving out. Often, one animal will be spread out relieving himself and is in no position to step out.

7-62. One of the most irritating things in leading a pack string is to have a pack animal that is always going around a tree the opposite way the rest of the string is going. Sometimes, shortening the lead rope will correct this problem. If that does not work, the rider may have to lead him. This behavior is usually a sign of a green pack animal and quite often disappears as the animal learns what is expected of it. Others just do not ever seem to learn. If the pack string has one of these problem learners, the packer should consider leaving it behind on the next mission.

7-63. As the packer becomes more proficient in packing and leading the string, he will learn specific techniques that worked well and will apply lessons learned through past mistakes. The more common tips to remember when positioning animals in a string are as follows:

- Make sure the lead animal is one who has a proven ability to lead easily and will not kick at the animal behind him.
- Do not put the fastest horse or mule at the head of the string. Put a steady, slower animal in this position—one with a walking pace that the entire string will find comfortable, and who will not be running up on the lead saddle horse or trying to pass him.
- Place the more quicker, more agile animals toward the end of the string to take advantage of their ability to negotiate obstacles and keep the string closed up.
- Put progressively taller animals toward the end of the string to make it easier to see how rear loads are riding.
- Put a problem animal, like a puller who knows how to break pigtails or a round-back mule whose saddle slips, in the number two position, so the packer will not have to squeeze past the whole string to adjust it.
- Keep the strings short. Leading two or three animals is not difficult. Leading six to ten can be a real headache. Short strings of five or less move faster than long strings.
- In difficult terrain, spend more time looking back at the string and between each animal's ears to see if the D-rings of the cross bucks of the packsaddles are centered on every animal's back.
- Resolve little problems, like unbalanced loads, quickly with the pack animal in place in the string. For major adjustments, remove the animal from the string to fix the load.

CAMPSITES

7-64. If there are several animals in the outfit, and the handler does not picket all of them, he might find it almost impossible to keep the loose animals in the area if there is insufficient grass. Unless he spends the entire night watching them, the animals might wander off in search of good pasture and be gone in the morning. Grass and water go together. An animal without water will act much the same as one with insufficient grass. For this reason, every handler should sleep with his weapon and bridle. A spring of good, cold water is by far the best, but these springs should run water far enough below the camp for the stock. Another problem in most all pack or saddle stock is the tendency to want to return to the last camp, or worse yet, go home. This urge is more evident in them if the string should be heading toward home after a few days out on a mission.

SETTING UP CAMP

7-65. If the packer remembers which items are in which pack, he will know which load goes where in the camp area. It will save a lot of time and labor to be able to lead each pack animal to wherever its load goes. As soon as the pack is off the animal, the handler should loosen the cinches on the packsaddle.

7-66. Keeping the saddles and pads off the ground even in dry weather is a sign of good organization. It only takes a minute to lash a pole between two trees to put the saddles and pads on. A tree limb makes a good hanger for lash ropes and halters. When unsaddling an animal, the pad and saddle should stay together. If the saddle is marked for which horse it fits, the handler will not have to refit the pad the next time he saddles up. If the weather is clear, the handler should let the pads air out and dry before covering them with the mantees off the pack loads that evening. While unsaddling the animals, the handler should ruffle the hair on the backs of the animals and check for any tenderness or sores. If a sore-backed animal is noted, it should be taken care of before being turned out.

7-67. When setting up for the night, many pack gear items will serve a dual purpose. Box panniers turn into tables and stools, lash ropes turn into high lines and corrals, and mantees turn into ground tarps and covers.

THE HIGH LINE

7-68. The high line is a section of rope strung between two or more trees, with tie points for the horses (Figure 7-15, page 345). The knot used for these tie points (sometimes called the high-line knot) can be the pulley knot used for a single or double dutchman, a butterfly knot, or a cat's paw. Another more permanent and faster way than tying knots is to insert snap links woven into the high line before the mission at 8- to 10-foot intervals used as the tie points for the animals.

7-69. The high line can often be temporarily put up when first arriving in camp. It will serve as an ideal place to tie up the pack string while laying out the camp area. Lariats will also serve for the first high line until the handler can get a lash rope off the packs. Tying up to a line upon arriving at camp can often prevent damaging equipment and gear on a pack. Tying keeps the pack animal from getting under low limbs or trying to rub the pack off against the tree he is tied to. A very frequent mistake is tying an animal to a small dead tree. Quite often just a light pull on the dead tree in the right direction will cause it to fall, possibly injuring the animal or spooking him and others into running off. The high-line area should be a level spot and have some shelter for the animals. Shade during the daytime will usually offer some shelter in a rainstorm.

7-70. In desert environments where no trees are available, the same high line can also be used at ground level. The high line can be anchored with wooden stakes or a screw-in-type ground anchor at each end and one in the center.

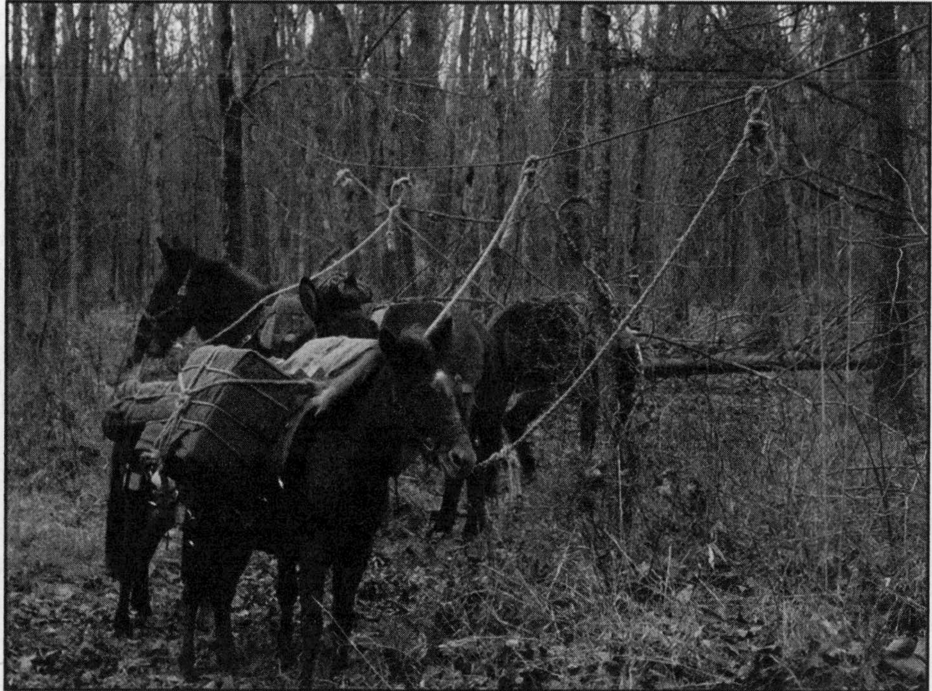

Figure 7-15. High line

The animals will need to be checked on more frequently if this system is used to ensure the animals do not get entangled in their lead line.

7-71. The handler puts up the high line by starting with the lash cinch and going around an average-sized tree approximately 8 feet off the ground. He hooks the lash cinch into the rope and, if possible, runs the line so another tree is approximately in the center of the line. He ties a high-line knot approximately every 8 to 10 feet until he comes to the first tree. The handler goes around this tree and ties high-line knots until he gets approximately 2 feet from the tree that he intends to tie off. He uses the last knot to set up a dutchman, then goes around the tree and pulls the whole line as tight as possible. The high line can be reached by throwing the lead line over the top of the high line and pulling the high line down to secure the animal's lead line to the high line. Other factors to consider are as follows:

- When tying to a high line, stagger the animals tied to it—one on one side and then one on the other side.
- The high line can also make a good line to dry saddle pads when they are not being used for the animals.

PICKETING

7-72. Picketing is tying an animal up by a line attached to either a stake or a heavy log. It allows the animal a certain freedom of movement to walk around, get to grass, and perhaps drink water but does not give him the chance to wander off.

7-73. The handler can picket an animal in several ways. He normally uses either a halter and picket line or a hobble and picket line off one front leg. Depending on the animal's experience with the picket line, picketing by a leg is the safest. An animal picketed with a halter will sometimes hook a shoe in the halter while scratching his ear with a hind leg. If the picketed animal hooks the shoe of his hind leg in the picket halter, he usually falls down. If not found soon after falling, he may just die in this position.

7-74. The anchor end of the picket line can be either a good dry stake driven into solid ground or a drag log. Picket stakes should be stout and not brittle. When placing the stakes, the handler makes sure there is plenty of room between the stakes so two picket lines cannot cross. The drag log, when used, should be heavy enough so the animal picketed to it cannot move it, yet light enough so, if need be, it can be pulled to another picket area using a saddle animal and a line off the saddle horn.

7-75. A small bowline knot should be used in tying off a picket line to the stake. It should be down at ground level on the stake. This level will let the line turn around the stake and still not turn the stake and loosen it in the ground. An animal that pulls a stake and runs loose with the line is a danger to himself and the mission. Should the animal get into the timber and hang up the stake and line, it could cause a day's delay. Should the animal not be found, it most likely will die a slow death of thirst and starvation.

7-76. The handler should consider several things when picketing by any method. He should determine how much feed is in the picket area and if there is any obstacle in the ring that the picket line can foul on, thus shortening the ring area. The best area is usually on a good, grassy creek bank where the animal can get both feed and water off the same picket line.

7-77. When selecting which animals will go on the picket line, the handler should pick out animals new to the outfit and those he knows to be leaders. He should also consider any renegades or loners who hole up by themselves when running loose. If there is a mare with a weaner colt at home, she needs to go on a picket or on the high line. Otherwise, after she has had time to fill up on grass, she just might decide to go home.

THE NIGHT HORSE

7-78. If some of the stock is running loose during the night, a night horse is a must. The night horse is one that is kept picketed near where its handler sleeps. The handler uses him for emergencies during the night and for running down loose stock in the morning.

7-79. The night horse does not come in any particular color, size, or shape. It could easily be the most inefficient looking animal in the outfit. What counts is what is between its ears. Many an animal used as a pack animal when on the trail, though not considered a riding horse, might make a good night horse. The only way to come up with a top night horse is to try them all at different times. A good night horse should have several good points. He should—

- Be trusted to graze and fill up during the night and not just run in circles and whinny at the other loose animals all night.
- Handle well while running loose animals. One of the best reining animals in the whole outfit may develop a lot of bad habits, such as trying to buck its rider off when with loose animals. Worse yet, after the loose animals are running, it may just stampede out of control with the rider, which is a very dangerous situation.
- Be easy to approach after dark and able to be ridden bareback. Quite often, should the loose animals start to leave during the night, it is possible to turn them very easily if the night horse is right there at the time. If the animal cannot be ridden bareback, the time it takes to saddle up might make it too late to easily turn the loose animals.

7-80. Many night horses develop the habit of watching where the loose animals go at night. Their hearing is far superior to humans. Often, while wrangling with a good night horse, it will want to head in a direction that the rider believes is wrong. The rider should trust the horse to help lead him to the loose animals. Quite often a night horse will want rein so he can smell the ground. Here again, its sense of smell is far better than the rider's and is being used to help locate the other animals. However, the horse is not totally in control; the rider most certainly will want to be reading tracks along with using the night horse's senses. Between the horse and the rider, loose animals are usually located quickly.

7-81. The night horse is often required to do quite a bit of running in bringing in the loose stock. This is bound to heat up the animal. Under such conditions, it must be cooled out. The most common mistake is for the rider to tie up the hot and lathered animal and head for the cook fire. In civilian pack outfits, many a supposedly experienced rider has been discharged for this one grave mistake. The best way to cool out a hot and lathered animal is to first unsaddle the animal. Using a currycomb and brush, the rider ruffles the hair over the back area. If he has some gunnysacks available, he should rub down the horse. Above all, the animal should not be fed grain or allowed any water until he is dry and cooled out. It could very possibly kill the animal or at the least cause a bellyache or colic. Walking the animal will also keep him from stiffening up. If the animal was good enough to keep on the night horse picket, he deserves the best of care when his job is done.

7-82. A night horse should be kept on the best grass and water and as close as possible to the sleeping area. A faint nicker from where the night horse is picketed may be the first sign that the other animals are moving out. The old mountain man may have slept with his rifle, but the handler should sleep with his bridle if he is the night horse rider.

TRANSPORTING SICK AND WOUNDED PERSONNEL

7-83. When confronted with an emergency, every situation varies according to what equipment is available. The unit leader should look over the horses to determine what can be used in a critical situation. There are many parts of saddles and gear strapped on them that can be pressed into service in ways other than those for which they were intended. This section is not meant to be an all-inclusive review of emergency procedures in the field. It is merely a brief look at things to consider and how they can be used expediently.

7-84. Using imagination and common sense and being observant of what is available to work with can help a person devise almost any type splint, bandage, sling, stretcher, or rig slings for transportation with equipment not necessarily intended for that purpose but which is at hand. However, using any part of the equipment may hinder the ability to ride out for help or transport the patient. Most of the items of equipment mentioned can be unbuckled or unsnapped rather than cut. If a strap needs to be cut, it should be cut close to a ring, buckle, or snap, so as to possibly save hours of needless repair later.

MOVEMENT

7-85. If the patient is subject to fainting or severe pain when moving, he should not be allowed to sit up in the saddle. If the person passes out and falls from the animal, the drop can be a meter or more. The fall will likely harm the patient and will upset the pack animal.

7-86. In most cases of back, neck, or spinal injury, it is best not to transfer the patient a great distance using horses. There is a lot to take into consideration, such as whether the patient is on an emergency backboard and how far it is to medical assistance. In most cases, where the patient will need to be transported only a short distance, a hand-held stretcher or travois pulled by a member of the team will be faster than rigging a horse for transportation. This way largely depends on how much help is available. There are several things that must not be done when transporting a victim with horses:

- Do not drape a wounded man head-down across a saddle.
- If the victim is inclined to pass out or is unsteady, do not let him ride by himself. Find out if the horse will ride double by sliding behind the saddle, without the victim. If the horse will ride double, ride behind the victim and hold him in the saddle.
- With a seriously sick or wounded patient, do not, in haste to get to help, trot or run the horse the victim is on. A slow, easy walk will get the patient to assistance in better condition.
- Do not at any time leave a horse unattended with a victim strapped or tied to the saddle. Maintain control of the horse's head at all times.

TRAVOIS OR PULKA LITTER

7-87. The difference between these two types of litters is in how the poles coming from the litter are attached to the pack animal. In the travois, the poles form an X over the back of the packsaddle. In the Pulka, the poles lie parallel along the sides of the animal's body. In most cases, the patient is below the level of the handler. This method makes most caregiving tasks easier since it is possible to reach over the patient without changing sides. The ends of the poles drag along the ground leaving ruts behind. This system does not work well if the ground is muddy or waterlogged. The patient will be soaked in only a few minutes. The handler must pick up the end of the litter and lift it over rocks, logs, or other obstructions. Crossing water obstacles requires the handler to hold up the litter and wade through the stream. Adrape stretching from the animal's rump to the poles of the litter will prevent gas or manure released from the animal to distress the patient (Figure 7-16).

7-88. One of the simplest and fastest means of transporting a patient who cannot ride is a travois drawn behind one horse. This method requires getting a gentle horse used to pulling the travois before putting the patient on one for

Figure 7-16. Travois litter

transportation. Personnel can construct a stretcher with two 15- to 20-foot strong poles that will support 200 pounds by running the poles through barrel hitches on the onside and offside of the animal. Again, it takes the horse a little while to get used to this rigging. If the emergency involves only two team members and the patient is conscious, the buddy should place the patient's head toward the horse and have him hold the reins. If this is not possible, he should tie the bridle reins to the poles, one on each side. This type of emergency stretcher is good for rough country or long-distance transportation. Most horses will tolerate the stretcher between them when they have a little time to become accustomed to the stretcher.

SUSPENDED LITTER

7-89. The suspended litter rides between two animals. It is long and requires a wide turning radius on any trail. The patient is about waist-high to the handler. It is easy to reach over and conduct any necessary task. The patient is kept high enough up to allow safe transport over rough ground, mud, low water, and other obstacles (Figure 7-17).

7-90. The primary problem with the suspended litter is that it requires two animals. If both are used to working together, only one handler is needed. If they march in stride, then the litter will rock from side to side. If they alternate legs, the litter may twitch. Both animals must keep the same speed and be very surefooted. The patient should be loaded with his head in the direction of travel. This way often helps prevent motion sickness.

Figure 7-17. Suspended litter

7-91. The handler can also stretch a large tarp or tent between two saddle horses that are side by side if he has a wide trail to travel. To rig the horses for this type of stretcher, it is wise to tie the horses' tails together to keep them from turning apart at the rear. A small pole tied between the bridle bits will keep them together at the head end. The tarp or tent should be pulled completely over the saddle and tied to the outside of the saddle. Two small poles, either run through or laced to the tarp, will make a stretcher in a very short time. In most cases, it is best to have the patient's head to the rear. Surprising as it may seem, this type of stretcher rides very comfortably.

STRETCHERS

7-92. The handler can use gunnysacks, canvas panniers, raincoats or saddle slickers, pannier tarps, saddle pads, mortuary adult shroud sheets (body bags), and blankets to make a stretcher. In most pack outfits, there are some gunnysacks used either to chink up a pannier or possibly to carry grain. By cutting two holes in the bottom corners of the sack and inserting two good poles, the handler has a first-class wilderness stretcher. Largely depending on what packhorses are present at the time, there is usually a set of deep canvas panniers. These canvas panniers have several emergency uses. The handler can make a stretcher with them, as with the gunnysacks. Another very important use is for lowering or raising an unconscious patient over such obstacles as a cliff or deep cut. The handler can cut two holes the size of the patient's legs in the bottom corners, slip his legs through these two holes, and pull the fabric up around his chest. The handler should test the knots used in tying a rope to the pannier with his own weight before trusting them on the patient. Raincoats, heavier coats, jackets, and saddle slickers also make a short distance stretcher by buttoning them up the front. Zippers are the best and most reliable. Two poles run through the inside of the garment and out the armholes make an emergency stretcher. Pannier tarps and large double saddle pads can make an emergency stretcher.

SPLINTS

7-93. The handler can use stirrup straps and fenders, pack pads, pannier tarps, pieces of wood, box panniers, and the bars out of packsaddles to make splints. There are many items of equipment, and often items loaded on a packhorse, that make an emergency splint. A backboard can be made by taking wood box panniers apart and either lashing or using the old nails in the box to nail or lash the flat boards to two small dry poles. The bars out of a packsaddle (using the flat surface) can also make a serviceable splint in a situation where other natural materials are not available. The stirrup straps and fenders out of a riding saddle are by far the best and simplest to obtain. The handler can unlace or unbuckle them and pull them out of the saddle without damaging the equipment. The stirrup straps and fenders from a riding saddle are already formed to the legs; therefore, using both straps and fenders can completely immobilize the legs of a victim. These work well also for the arms by using just one stirrup strap. Several small poles lashed flat and then padded with pack pads can make a backboard. An open rifle scabbard either down the seam or laid flat can make a splint.

STRAPS FOR LASHING TO BACKBOARDS

7-94. Latigos, lash cinches, saddle cinches, breast collars, brichens, and bridle reins can all be pressed into service. There are many large, heavy straps and cinches on a pack outfit or riding saddle. The handler can take off almost all of these very simply and make them serviceable for the bindings of splints or backboards. As mentioned before, he can also take off most all of these items without cutting them and thus damaging the equipment unnecessarily.

SMALL STRAPS TO BIND BANDAGES AND SPLINTS

7-95. Bridle reins, halter ropes, sling and lash ropes, saddle stirrups, and many of the straps on a packsaddle are useful as ties to hold things in place. There are many such straps on packsaddles and riding saddles. Bridle reins, for example, make a good long strap, and if needed for a long length of time, a person can still get by with one bridle rein. Almost all of the ropes, such as halter ropes and lash and sling ropes, can be unwound and one strand taken out while still leaving the rope serviceable. If small, tight bindings are required, the handler can use tail and mane hair from the horses. The handler should never use his or the patient's clothing to bind wounds and leave their bodies unprotected when there are so many other items available on the equipment. If the handler decides to leave the patient and ride for help, he can lay his saddle pads on the ground under the patient to help keep him warm and dry. Often there are two pads on a horse and, in an emergency, a rider could possibly get by with just one.

DIRECT PRESSURE IN SEVERE BLEEDING

7-96. Severe bleeding is always an emergency. If this situation arises and dressings are not readily available, the handler uses the sheepskin lining on the underside of the saddle to stop the blood flow. A small pad of this sheepskin with a clean dressing between it and the wound will in most instances pass for many layers of other dressings. A cool-back saddle pad also makes a good emergency compress for severe bleeding.

CHAPTER 8

Organization and Movement

Certain combinations of adverse weather, thick vegetation, and harsh terrain deny the use of wheeled or tracked vehicles in either a combat or logistics role. Mountainous terrain often restricts operations to those conducted by foot infantry. Heavily wooded areas, especially when associated with steep grades, have the same effect. Swamps, jungle-like vegetation, and certain types of cultivation may restrict the use of vehicles in lowlands. Weather, in combination with unfavorable terrain, may also deny or greatly restrict the use of aircraft in a combat or logistics role. In such situations, the commander who can move his troops, weapons, supplies, and equipment with the greatest speed and facility has a distinct advantage. Properly organizing, training, and equipping a combat pack animal detachment can give a commander this advantage.

ORGANIZATION

8-1. The pack animal detachment is usually the smallest fighting element. It can be a section, squad, or team of 10 to 20 individuals. The number of animals required to support these elements depends upon both the TOE and mission requirements.

8-2. The commander may task-organize the detachment squads or sections according to needs and requirements. For example, an 81-mm mortar section would not need as many individuals and animals to transport it as would a 107-mm mortar section. The mission will also have an impact on the size of the section; a raid with an 81-mm section will use fewer animals than sustained operations using the same weapons system. The squad or section requirements may vary from as few as five animals to as many as a dozen.

8-3. Other factors bearing on the organization of a pack detachment are load weight and the size of the items to be carried. The greater the total weight of the load, the more animals needed to carry it. If the items are large, even though lightweight, it will still take more animals.

DUTIES AND RESPONSIBILITIES

8-4. A pack animal detachment has unique duties and responsibilities. Most of these are leadership-related, and some are skills common to all.

8-5. The **train commander** is the commissioned officer or senior noncommissioned officer in charge of the pack train. He oversees the training, operation, and administration of the unit.

8-6. The **pack master** should be the platoon or team sergeant and the most knowledgeable about packing. He provides for the presence, care, and maintenance of all pack equipment and the animals in the unit. He rides the entire column to check all loads and to observe the condition of the individuals and animals. The pack master also—

- Trains personnel in the proper methods of packing, to include saddling, adjusting equipment, balancing loads, and tying of standard hitches.
- Trains personnel in the proper care of animals and maintenance of pack equipment.
- Ensures maximum unit effectiveness through daily inspection of pack animals for injury.
- Supervises packing, conducts the march, maintains the animals and equipment, and disciplines the soldiers.
- Inspects loads, makes sure the animals on the march are not injured by shifting loads or saddles, and ensures prompt correction of deficiencies.
- Inspects and directs prompt repair of pack saddlery.

8-7. The **cargadores**, usually squad or section leaders, assist the pack master in all his duties and are qualified to perform the duties of the pack master in his absence. In addition, cargadores must be able to make all repairs normally made by the unit saddler. The cargadores also—

- Assign a load to each pack animal, ensuring the loads are balanced.
- Assign pack equipment, loads, and animals to the packers.
- Maintain order and discipline among the packers and ensure quiet and gentle treatment of the animals.
- Select areas for cargo piles and rig line in bivouac.
- Ensure proper care of pack equipment.
- Keep a memorandum of all cargo and equipment under their care, marking and tagging it if necessary.

8-8. The packers must train and care for both pack and riding animals. In the field, their duties include the maintenance, adjustment, and use of pack and riding saddlery and associated equipment. In addition, they prepare the cargo for packing and sling and lash loads using a variety of hitches. All detachment personnel should be packer-qualified.

MOVEMENT PROCEDURES

8-9. The pack detachment begins movement soon after the pack animals are loaded. Packers mount their riding animals. Two detailed riders move ahead of the train to contain any animals that are out of control. The detachment moves out in the march order directed by the commander in pack strings of no more than five animals. One rider leads each string and another follows it. The rider should always lead the strings from the onside of the pack animals (the string will be on the rider's offside). Normally, the detachment moves in file with the riders keeping the pack strings closed up to ensure communication between strings and to maintain column integrity. However, terrain and the probability of enemy contact from ground or air dictates the distance between strings or squads. When moving during hours of limited visibility, the rider should keep the column close to facilitate control. Troops riding on the flanks and rear of the strings make frequent counts of the animals to ensure against strays. Halts should be made as necessary to inspect and adjust loads and saddles. The commander, pack master, and cargadores make frequent inspections of the detachment en route, whether moving during daylight or at night.

8-10. Operating the pack animal detachment with individually led animals is considered uneconomical in terms of personnel. However, there are certain circumstances under which other factors are more important. Members of the weapons crews lead the animals that are assigned to combat units for the transport of heavy weapons and accompanying ammunition. Animals used in proximity to known hostile action areas are usually led individually to take advantage of all available cover and concealment. Evacuating casualties to aid stations by animal transport also requires this method of operation to ensure the easiest ride for the casualty, as well as to take maximum advantage of existing cover and concealment. Although training time for the operation may be reduced, the following tasks need to be followed:

- Train personnel to pack both lashed and hanger loads. Although the animal will normally proceed at a walk, with the rate of march seldom exceeding 3 1/2 miles per hour, make sure the loads are balanced and securely tied.
- Ensure the pack driver (person leading the animal) only exerts sufficient control over the lead animal to maintain its position on the trail or in the column. He should not interfere with the animal's freedom of movement or balance. A clumsy driver can cause a loaded animal to fall.
- Train the driver to lead the animals from the onside. He should guide the animal with his right hand grasping the lead rope, with the remainder of the lead rope in the left hand. He should give the animal enough slack so there is room enough for the animal to walk without stepping on him. If there is noise, danger, or confusion on the offside, the driver may reverse his position to offer some protection to the animal and quiet it.
- Train personnel to regulate the speed of the animal by the gentle, but effective, use of the lead rope. In column, always maintain the prescribed interval to prevent accordion action and undue fatigue in the rear elements.
- Teach the driver to counter the tendency of the animal to trot down slopes or jump over obstacles so he can maintain the normal rate of march and prevent displacement of the load.

- When leading an animal up steep slopes or over very rugged terrain, make sure the driver precedes the animal with about 3 feet of loose lead rope so that the animal may pick his footing. If the terrain is very rough or steep and he falls behind, it may be best to drop the lead rope and let the animal go. He can then catch the animal after the obstacle is passed.

CAUTION

Under no circumstances will personnel hold the saddle breeching or the animal's tail to assist them in climbing.

STREAM CROSSING AT FORDS

8-11. Pack units will frequently come across streams or bodies of water where no bridges exist. These challenges, particularly in the spring or after a heavy rainfall, can be treacherous and demand special skills. Even small streams can cause problems when the water is rolling and muddy. All crossings should be checked carefully. If there is any doubt about a string's ability to cross easily, a single rider on a surefooted horse should be sent to check depth, bottom characteristics, and current strength. There is a huge difference in footing between a sandy or gravelly bottom and a bottom of large, mossy boulders. Similarly, fast water, deeper than a horse's belly, exerts its force against a much wider surface than water swirling around a horse's thin legs (Figure 8-1).

Figure 8-1. Stream crossing

8-12. Although horses and mules can ford fairly deep water and are generally good swimmers, the crossing of even fordable water requires care and good judgment. Unit training must include accepted methods and techniques of stream crossing. Units should conduct ford reconnaissance before attempting to cross with a loaded pack unit. The load makes the animal somewhat top-heavy. The unit should try to cross streams with the animals moving against the current (upstream). The loads in combination with swift current, water deep enough to bear against the animal's body, and poor footing may cause the animal to lose its balance, fall, and drown. Under such circumstances, the unit should unload the animals and either lead or herd them across the body of water. The unit can also ferry loads across in the same manner as described in the following paragraphs. Table 8-1 provides a water-crossing training schedule.

Table 8-1. Water-crossing training schedule

Day 1	Time	Subject
	0730–0930	Instruction in swimming, general rules and adjustment of equipment. Risk assessment reviewed and read to all involved with training.
	0930–1130	Entering the water. Wading and practice in adjusting the equipment.
	1130–1200	Care of animals and equipment.
	1200–1300	Feeding animals and lunch.
	1300–1430	Turning animals out to graze. Waterproof packing of equipment.
	1430–1500	Coffee break.
	1500–1700	Repeat of wading practice.
	1700–1800	Care of animals and equipment.
	1800	Dinner.
Day 2	0730–0930	Wading and equipment adjustment.
	0930–1000	Care of animals and equipment.
	1000–1030	Coffee break.
	1030–1200	Construction of bridges or rafts. Animals grazing.
	1200–1300	Feeding animals and lunch.
	1300–1400	Construction of bridges and rafts. Animals grazing.
	1400–1500	Towing animals across water.
	1500–1600	Care of animals and equipment.
	1600–1630	Coffee break.
	1630–1730	Water obstacle reconnaissance and analysis.
	1730	Dinner.
Day 3	0730–0930	Towing animals across water.
	0930–1030	Care of animals and equipment.
	1030–1100	Coffee break.
	1100–1200	Construction of bridges and rafts. Animals grazing.
	1200–1300	Feeding animals and lunch.
	1300–1400	Construction of bridges and rafts. Animals grazing.
	1400–1530	Swimming bareback.
	1530–1630	Care of animals and equipment.
	1630–1700	Coffee break.
	1700–1800	Water obstacle analysis.
	1800	Dinner.
Day 4	0730–0930	Swimming bareback.
	0930–1000	Care of animals and equipment.
	1000–1030	Coffee break.
	1030–1130	Care of animals in the field.
	1130–1230	Feeding animals and lunch.
	1230–1400	Construction of bridges and rafts. Animals grazing.

Table 8-1. Water-crossing training schedule (*Continued*)

Day 4 (Continued)	Time	Subject
	1400–1600	Swimming bareback.
	1600–1630	Care of animals and equipment.
	1630–1700	Coffee break.
	1700–1800	Correction of deficiencies.
	1800	Dinner.
Day 5	0730–0930	Instruction in swimming with saddles.
	0930–1000	Care of animals and equipment
	1000–1030	Coffee break.
	1030–1200	Construction of bridges and rafts. Animals grazing.
	1200–1300	Feeding animals and lunch.
	1300–1430	Medical treatment of swimming injuries.
	1430–1600	Swimming with saddles.
	1600–1630	Care of animals and equipment.
	1630–1700	Coffee break.
	1700–1800	Medical treatment of injuries.
	1800	Dinner.
Day 6	0730–0830	Instruction in swimming with full pack.
	0830–1030	Swimming with full packs.
	1030–1100	Care of animals and equipment.
	1100–1130	Coffee break.
	1130–1230	Medical treatment of injuries.
	1230–1330	Feeding animals and lunch.
	1330–1430	Terrain analysis and exercise.
	1430–1600	Swimming with full packs.
	1600–1630	Care of animals and equipment.
	1630–1800	Correction of deficiencies.
	1800	Dinner.
Day 7	0730–0930	Swimming with full packs.
	0930–1030	Care of animals and equipment.
	1030–1100	Coffee break.
	1100–1130	Care of animals and equipment.
	1130–1230	Feeding animals and lunch.
	1230–1400	Rescue procedures.
	1400–1600	Swimming with full packs.
	1600–1630	Care of animals and equipment.
	1630–1700	Coffee break.
	1700–1800	Rescue procedures.
	1800	Dinner.

Table 8-1. Water-crossing training schedule (*Continued*)

Day 8	Time	Subject
	0730–0930	Instruction in herd swimming.
	0930–1000	Care of animals and equipment.
	1000–1030	Coffee break.
	1030–1130	Terrain problems and terrain ride.
	1130–1230	Feeding animals and lunch.
	1230–1400	Team training.
	1400–1600	Herd swimming.
	1600–1630	Care of animals and equipment.
	1630–1700	Coffee break.
	1700–1800	Terrain problems and terrain ride.
	1800	Dinner.
Day 9	0730–0930	Herd swimming.
	0930–1000	Correction of deficiencies.
	1000–1030	Coffee break.
	1030–1100	Care of animals and equipment.
	1100–1200	Feeding animals and lunch.
	1200–1400	Instruction in special water-crossing problems, such as night and cold water.
	1400–1600	Swimming with full packs.
	1600–1630	Coffee break.
	1630–1730	Correction of deficiencies.
	1730–1800	Care of animals and equipment.
	1800	Dinner.
Day 10	0730–1000	Water-crossing problem.
	1000–1030	Coffee break.
	1030–1130	Correction of deficiencies.
	1130–1200	Care of animals and equipment.
	1200–1300	Feeding animals and lunch.
	1300–1400	Special problems in water crossing.
	1400–1600	Water-crossing exercise.
	1600–1630	Care of animals and equipment.
	1630–1700	Coffee break.
	1700–1800	Correction of deficiencies.
	1800	Dinner.
Day 11	0800–1600	Reserved for correction of deficiencies.

CROSSING UNFORDABLE WATER

8-13. Though an animal might be physically capable of swimming under a load, it upsets the animal's natural balance. When the pack unit must cross unfordable water, selected personnel swimming their riding animals should cross first to secure the farside, select the landing site on the far bank, and secure the hauling system for the pack animals. The nearside personnel should have animals ready to enter the body of water, ensure the hauling system is secure, and the pack animals' lead line is securely attached to the hauling system. The farside personnel should pull the pack animals and equipment to the far shore, disconnect lead lines from the hauling system, and secure the pack animals on the far bank. If the crossing is too wide for a hauling system, the unit can build poncho rafts to ferry the equipment and swim the animals freely across the body of water (Figure 8-2).

> **NOTE**
>
> Horses, mules, and dogs may cease to be effective when full-body immersion occurs (Figure 8-3) at water temperatures of 40 degrees F or below. Hypothermia will probably be noticeable within a half hour and life expectancy will be in jeopardy in an hour and a half. It will reach 50 percent loss in two hours and all but an overly fat animal will be dead or otherwise useless in three hours. At 32 degrees F, hypothermia will be obvious in 15 minutes, with 50 percent loss in one hour and total loss in an hour and a half. All of this is somewhat subjective and depends on body fat, physical condition, amount of food in the last 24 hours, general overall condition, and how well the animals are treated. All of this information is based on full-body immersion.

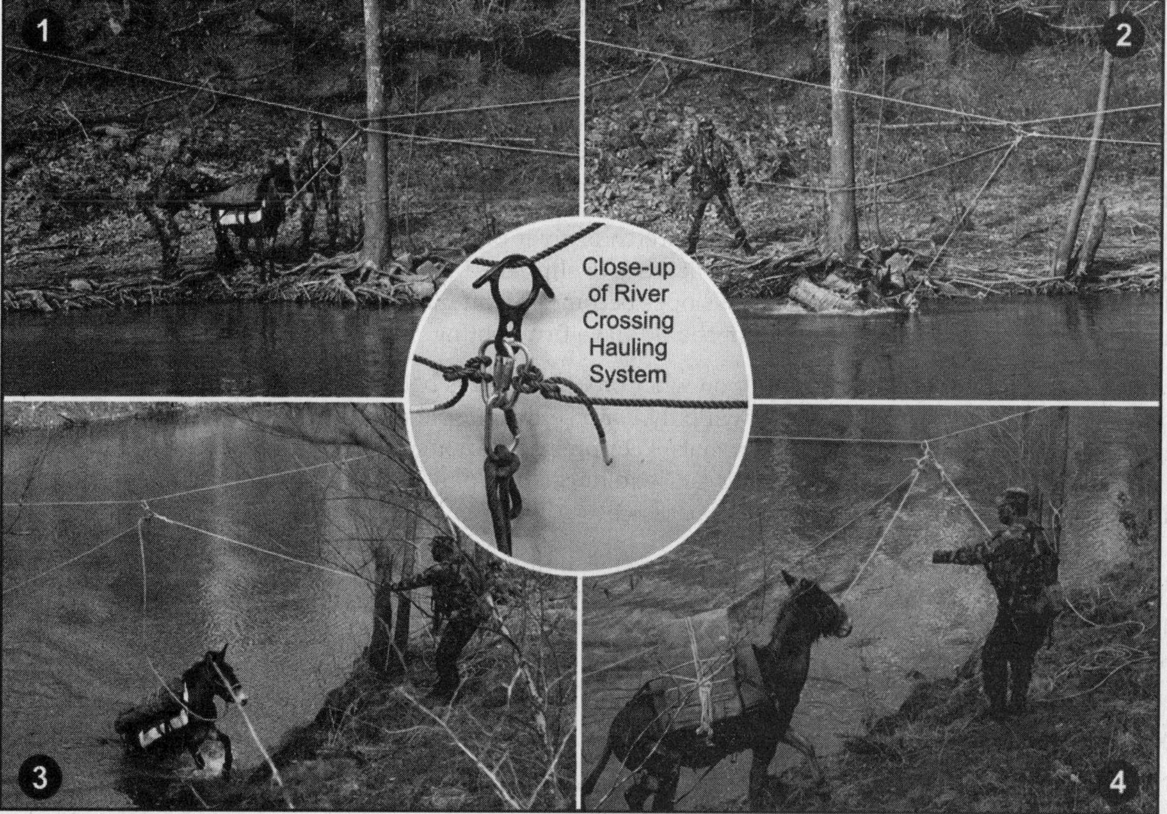

Figure 8-2. Crossing unfordable water

WATER TRAINING

8-14. Training animals to cross bodies of water is one of the most important activities if water obstacles are expected during an operation. The following procedures are recommended. All species can profit by this training, but it was originally developed for equines and may have to be modified for other animals.

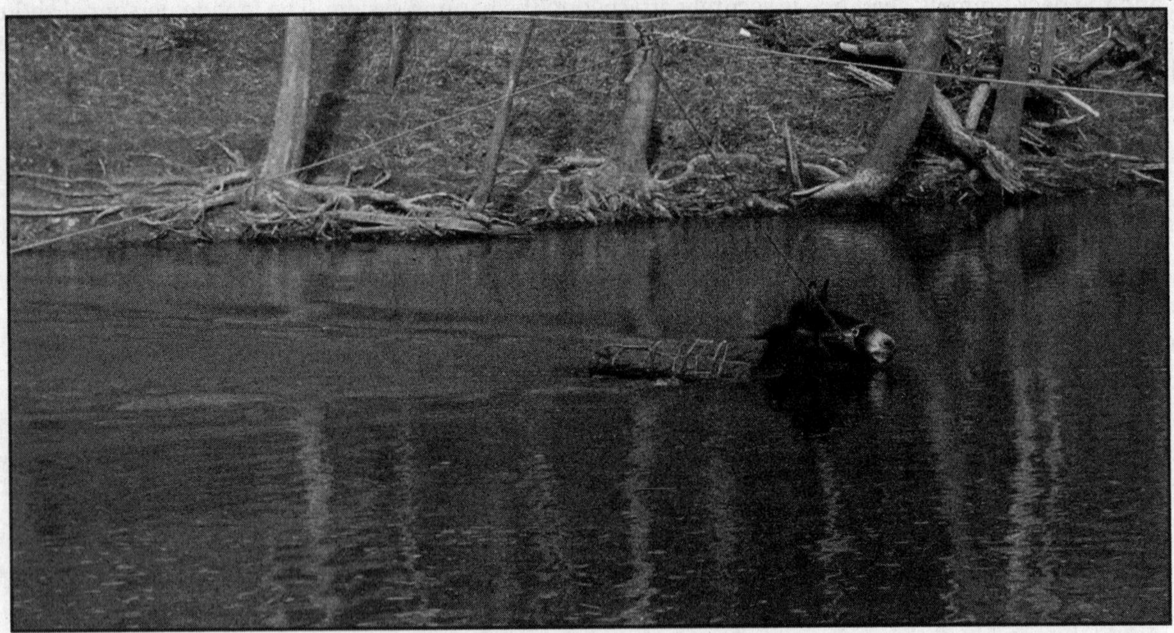

Figure 8-3. Full-body immersion

8-15. For safety, everyone involved should be questioned to see if they can swim and how well. The people who claim to be strong swimmers should be tested, and the best of them used as lifeguards. Good swimmers can also be used for mentoring beginners. Everyone must master survival floating.

8-16. The site of the training should be a quiet stretch of river or a small lake. Personnel should always check for quicksand or bad footing. The banks should not be steep or slippery. Many types of clay deposits are dangerous when wetted by splashing or tracked in water. Most slopes become soft after heavy traffic. The shore should be wide with a gradual shelving into the water. The bottom should have firm footing.

8-17. Each stage of training should be built on what precedes it. It is better to take longer than the times indicated here than to rush through training. Haste will only confuse the people and frighten the animals. Training should occur in groups of compatible people and animals. Peer pressure among the people and the herd instinct in the animals will help with instruction. Water training can be followed by a play period to further encourage both people and animals to look upon the water as a pleasant experience.

8-18. The unit should always use lifeguards and rescue equipment to prevent accidents. Unnecessary injuries will discourage students. Dangers should never be emphasized, but personnel should always be aware of the safety situation. Both animals and people lose body heat quickly even in warm water on a hot day. Personnel should watch for signs of chilling, such as shivering, and treat immediately.

TRAINING PROCEDURES

8-19. A 7/16-cm-thick rope should be stretched across the swimming area on the downstream side. Brightly colored floats should be attached at regular intervals. If possible, two motorboats or rowboats should be stationed at each side of the swimming area.

8-20. Poor or weak swimmers should wear life jackets during training. Voice amplification equipment should be available but used only in an emergency. Yelling only confuses the people and animals in the water.

8-21. A tent with cots, blankets, and a medic should be set up to care for anyone needing medical attention. Radio equipment should be operating at all times if an emergency occurs. Lifeguards should be posted at the entry and exit points. All lifeguards must be qualified in cardiopulmonary resuscitation (CPR). Two people should be assigned to catch any animals that break away from their riders.

ENTERING THE WATER

8-22. This phase is the most important part of training. Bad experiences at this stage can traumatize both humans and animals, resulting in problems for years to come. Patience on the part of the instructor can repay itself by reliable performance on the trail. The unit should use the madrina and mentors as examples.

8-23. Both humans and animals should be praised as each team moves deeper into the water. The animals can be rewarded with treats, which will produce a positive association with swimming and make training easier.

8-24. Wading should progress into deeper and deeper water until the animal must swim several strokes. At the same time, the animal must be required to turn in both directions while swimming.

8-25. Swimming animals move their legs in the same manner as walking but with exaggerated action. Most propulsion is from the forelegs. The hind legs keep the hindquarters afloat but they also reach further up than normal, which can cause them to become snagged in any straps or ropes trailing along. They can also kick a long-legged rider.

8-26. As the animal enters the water, it continues to keep contact with the bottom with all four legs as long as possible. An animal will remain calm even if the forehand begins to float as long as the hind legs are still solid.

8-27. The position of the rider significantly affects the balance of the animal. If the rider is too far forward, the forehand will sink and the head can go completely under. If the weight is too far back, the haunches go down and the forehand comes up. This impedes forward progress.

8-28. To get the animal to begin to swim, he must be ridden boldly into the water. Hesitation can cause balking. The rider sits well back to allow the forehand to float as soon as possible. As soon as the animal begins to struggle to find footing, the rider should quickly pull well up and force the hindquarters up. At this point, the animal floats and must begin to swim. The rider should keep the animal on a straight course, or as close as possible to straight, by aiming for the landing point on the opposite bank.

8-29. At no time should the animal be allowed to turn back to shore on its own. This movement will allow the animal to develop the conviction that it can refuse to cross. The first display of this behavior must be corrected and the animal required to swim properly. After that the trainer should be alert for subsequent attempts and make sure they are dealt with properly.

TOWING

8-30. If the unit decides to tow, it will need three ropes long enough to cross the body of water. Using a hauling system will require snap links. The unit will need the pack animal with packsaddles and the load. Animals must be haltered with a lead line attached to the chin ring.

8-31. The unit constructs a high line across the river attaching one end of the rope to a nearside tree and the other end to a farside tree. The high line should be at a height that allows the animal's head to be in a natural position when the lead line is attached. The handler places a snap link over the high-line rope. He attaches the nearside and farside hauling ropes to the snap link. Both ends of the hauling system ropes should be held by the pullers on both banks. Nearside personnel will attach the animal's lead line to the snap link using the figure 4 knot and move the animal to the water's edge. When nearside personnel signal they are ready, the farside hauler will begin to pull the animal into the water. The farside hauler must keep up with the animal's swimming speed to keep the rope from getting entangled around the animal's legs and cause drowning. When the animal reaches the farside bank, the hauler will

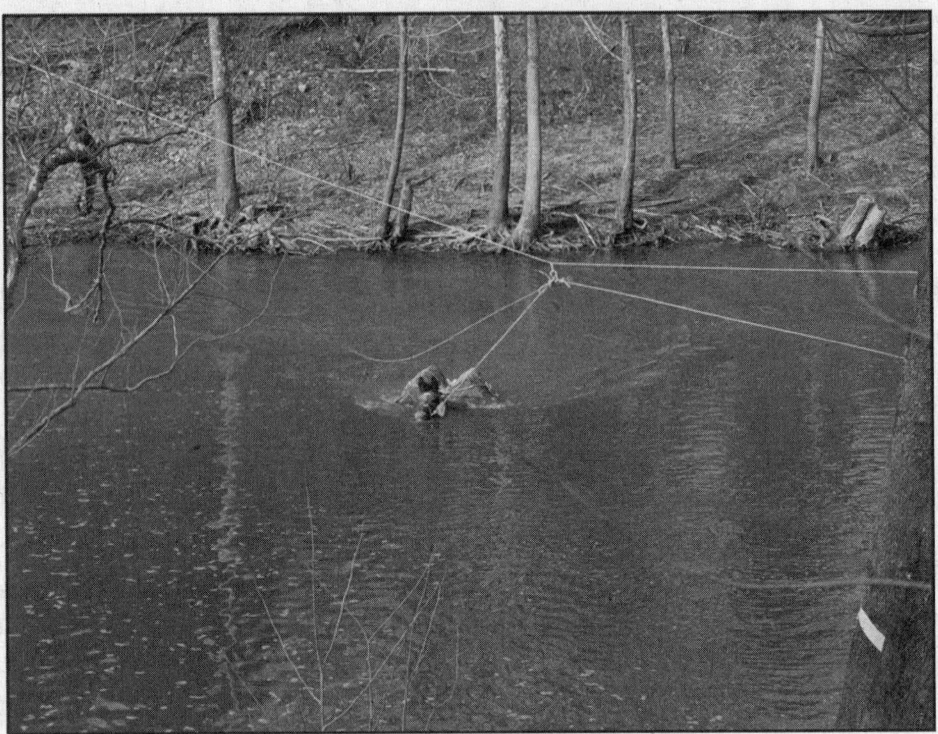

Figure 8-4. Hauling system

disconnect him from the snap link, and secure him on the farside bank. The nearside hauler will pull the hauling system back across the body of water and attach the next animal for crossing (Figure 8-4).

8-32. If more than one animal is to be hauled across the body of water, the hauler attaches only the lead animal's lead line to the snap link. All other animals will be tied into the lead animal using the pigtails on the packsaddles. To avoid having animals lingering in the water at the far bank, the hauler moves the lead animal far enough up the bank so the other animals can follow.

> **NOTE**
> The unit should haul only as many animals as it can handle on the farside bank.

8-33. The rider or pack animals should be allowed to swim at the animal's own pace and not be pulled across. Personnel on the opposite bank should take up the slack as the team approaches. A person should never put a foot in loose coils of rope since any sudden movement outward can drag him into and under the water.

SWIMMING BAREBACK

8-34. When swimming bareback, equines should have bridles with snaffle bits and no other gear. Neck ropes and breast straps should be avoided since animals will fight them in the water. A halter should be used for other species.

8-35. Each animal should be ridden straight into the water bareback and required to keep a straight course. The rider slips off on the upstream side and swims alongside the animal. If the person is a weak swimmer, he can hold onto the pommel or crosspiece of the packsaddle. He should never pull so hard that the saddle is displaced.

8-36. The rider should not hang onto the reins since they may be needed to steer the animal. He must never hang onto the tail since it can be dislocated, broken, or even torn at the roots. The mane can be used in an emergency. The rider should also be careful not to get stepped on or kicked when the animal enters shallow water on the opposite bank. The rider should stay at least two meters apart from the nearest animal or a kick can result.

8-37. The rider should never attempt to change an animal's direction abruptly. He should never swim an animal in a circle if it gets ahead of its group. At the first sign of trouble or the animal's head begins to go under water, the rider must let go and get clear. The animal may thrash or roll over and a serious kick can result.

NOTE
For minor adjustments, the following procedures can be used:

- If the animal attempts to turn downstream or away from the rider, the rider should gently pull the upstream rein and force the animal to turn its head toward him.
- If the animal turns toward the rider and splashes water in his face, the rider should *gently* pull the downstream rein and turn the animal's head away. A sudden pull back on the reins can cause the animal to tumble over backward.

SWIMMING A HERD

8-38. The unit can swim animals either individually or in groups. Herd crossing is especially useful with strong currents. A mixed horses and mules group will cross more readily than when separated. Strong swimmers should take the natural leaders and start off immediately. If a madrina is used, she should cross first with the bell on. When she reaches the bank, the bell should be rung to let the others know where she is. It has also been noted that the animals can be called from the opposite bank by people imitating the appropriate call.

8-39. The unit should cut a ramp into the bank that will allow no more than two animals abreast to pass. Animals are held in a two-abreast line with handlers on the left side, and everyone facing the water. When the crossing is about to begin, personnel hold bamboo or thin limbs to form a rail corral with an opening at the chute.

8-40. Once the leaders begin to cross, the rest will follow them into the water. The rails can be closed in behind to encourage them to move but they must not be crowded. Fighting and kicking of other animals can result. Handlers catch the animals as they exit on the opposite shore and bring them back to a picket line.

SWIMMING ANIMALS WITH STRIPPED PACK OR RIDING SADDLES

8-41. Personnel should use girth straps that are one or more holes looser than normal. A person should be able to get two hands, laid flat (palm to palm), between the girth and the belly. The blanket will swell as it soaks. Equines should wear a snaffle bit with the reins unfastened. Other species should wear a halter.

8-42. The animals should be ridden into the water on a short rein. Pack animals wear a set of blankets tied with a surcingle. The riders slip off on the upstream side and cross as previously trained.

SWIMMING SADDLE AND PACK ANIMALS TOGETHER

8-43. Pack animals should have increased loads placed on the saddle as training progresses. If problems develop, excessive loads should be reduced during the training period. Complete saddles, bridles, and halters should be worn, but neck, breast, and chest straps should be removed. These straps seem to panic many species and cause them to drown.

8-44. Riders lead the assigned pack animals into the water. At first, pack loads should consist of soft, lightweight materials that do not soak up water too quickly. As time goes on, the loads should reflect the cargo that will be carried.

BIVOUAC

8-45. The pack animal unit should select its camps based on the results of both map and ground reconnaissance, if feasible. The selection depends on the requirements for the safety, health, and comfort of individuals and animals and the operational plans of the unit. The night camp should be reached just before twilight. Guards around the camp and grazing stock aid in preventing surprise attacks. If the camp is found, it can be vacated before a major assault can be launched. The bivouac should have little or no tentage unless conditions (freezing rain, below freezing temperatures) require it. As little area disturbance as possible should be made. Trees should not be cut down or holes dug except for pit latrines and garbage disposal. In hostile environments, concealment from air or ground observation and as much cover as possible are essential. The first consideration is always security, but unless the unit is carrying all the feed the pack and saddle animals will need, the next concern should be grass and water for the stock. It is a grave mistake to sacrifice grass, water, wood, and shelter for anything but security considerations. In selecting the grass, it should allow the stock to feed all night. Just because a meadow looks green does not mean it has plenty of grass in it. Often in high, alpine meadows, most of the vegetation consists of flowers and weeds that a horse will not eat. If the unit is unfortunate enough to camp in such a meadow, the stock will be weakened from lack of grass the next day on the trail. It is very irritating to ride or be leading an animal that insists on trying to graze as it is going down the trail. After security, the next concern should always be the care of the animals. Reconnaissance personnel should next look for the best footing for animals available in the area. Picket lines, high lines or, in more secure and extended situations, temporary corrals should offer level standing and good drainage with little possibility of flooding in sudden rains. The selected area should be large enough to provide adequate dispersion and be free from briers, debris, and poisonous plants. An area convenient to the route of march offers additional operational advantages.

8-46. The detachment or train commander, accompanied by selected personnel, precedes the train into camp and selects areas for the rigging line, high line, and the cargo so that the animals and equipment will be arranged systematically and readily available night or day. Upon arrival in camp, the pack train conducts the following procedures:

- Select personnel designate the cooking and sleeping areas, keeping in mind that they will always be located upstream from the animals.
- Upon arrival of the train, all personnel (except for the wranglers) dismount, secure their riding animals, unload the cargo, and slack off the cinches. Personnel unpack all animals before the first is unsaddled, and coil the lash and sling ropes. The wranglers remain mounted and ready to stop any animals that try to bolt from the camp.
- Personnel secure the animals as they are unloaded.
- When all loads are removed, the train commander gives the command to unsaddle.
- If conditions are favorable, handlers turn the animals out to graze or picket so they may roll and relax. If not, the animals stay on the high line while personnel clean the equipment and improve the site.
- Handlers feed the animals 45 minutes after arrival and water them 1 hour after arrival. Personnel then prepare their equipment for the next day's movement.

CHAPTER 9

Tactical Considerations

A pack animal detachment during movement, regardless of its combat mission once it reaches its destination, is a logistic transportation element. This fact alone severely limits the detachment's tactical capabilities. Even though the detachment may be considered a highly mobile unit, the presence of pack animals precludes the capability of maneuver.

The mission of the detachment while moving is the safeguarding and delivery of the cargo to its destination, not to stand and fight. This point is not to say that all is lost tactically while moving; it just means that compensation has to be made for the lack of maneuver and concentrated fires.

SECURITY

9-1. The pack detachment configured for movement forms into pack strings and usually in column formation. This alignment presents a long, linear target for the enemy. The troops are dispersed, making it difficult to bring concentrated, effective fire to bear upon enemy contact. The diligent use of scouts and outriders for flank security, along with extreme caution, are needed to a greater extent than for dismounted troops to make up for maneuver limitations.

9-2. Two factors affect not using overwatch formations. The first is terrain. The primary reason for using pack animals is difficult terrain. This fact necessitates using column formations. Second, the act of bounding requires one element to remain static. Animals that are loaded, strung together, and not moving are an accident waiting to happen. The following paragraphs explain how the detachment should cross specific types of areas, and Appendix C illustrates the various formations that may be used.

9-3. When the scouts reach a linear danger area (roads, trails, streams), they conduct a thorough reconnaissance for the best possible crossing point and attempt to reach the farside. Once they establish farside security, the scout leader returns to the column to lead it to the crossing point. Once the column arrives at the crossing point, lead personnel take up farside security and free the scouts to continue.

9-4. Commanders should consider crossing open or large areas as dangerous. Their use must be negotiated accordingly. The scouts should provide as much information as possible about the area to the commander. With this information, the commander decides how best to negotiate the obstacle. Bypassing the area is by far the best method but is not always practical. However, in arriving at a decision about movement, the leader must also consider METT-TC.

9-5. Whether during long or short halts, lead personnel establish and maintain security using the same procedures as a dismounted combat unit. The difference is the terrain to be defended and whether the animals will be in or out of the perimeter. The following principles apply:

- Animals kept on a high line within the perimeter may offer a reduction to security personnel, but unique problems can arise if the position is attacked. Casualties may arise from animals becoming frightened and breaking loose or stampeding.
- Animals kept on picket lines outside of the perimeter require listening posts or observation posts placed at a greater distance. During an attack on the detachment, these animals are susceptible to both enemy and friendly fire. The chances are good that a large percentage of the animals will either flee or be wounded.

COVER AND CONCEALMENT

9-6. The pack detachment must continuously consider concealment options during movement. Admittedly, it is next to impossible to conceal the evidence (animal waste, disturbed vegetation, and tracks) that a pack unit has moved through an area. However, personnel can take the following precautions to avoid being observed while on the move:

- Avoid skylining.
- Stay well within the tree line (if any).
- Contour the terrain.
- Camouflage the loads.
- Avoid open areas, if possible, or cross them quickly.

9-7. During extended halts (when loads are unsaddled), personnel should use the proper camouflage. Cover for the animals, while desirable, may not be possible or practical. Personnel should be alert to animal noise, both vocal and from movement, and address the odors associated with animals. There are no clear-cut solutions to the problems of concealment. Personnel should use a common-sense approach and practice the following tips:

- Use as much natural cover and foliage as possible.
- Use camouflage nets.
- Apply proper field sanitation techniques, to include keeping animal waste policed.
- Control animal noise as much as possible. If the animals' vocal cords have not been cut, keep the animals quiet by maintaining a relaxed atmosphere.

ACTIONS ON CONTACT

9-8. As previously mentioned, a pack detachment organized for movement is not a maneuver unit. Therefore, it must act accordingly when contact is made.

9-9. When ambushed, those elements caught in the kill zone should quickly escape in any feasible direction. Forward elements, not in the kill zone, move in the direction of march as fast as possible. Those in the rear should move in the direction away from the kill zone, quickly but cautiously. All elements should make every effort to link up at a preplanned rally point. Elements not under direct fire should attempt to control and safeguard the animals.

9-10. Actions under indirect fire are handled in much the same way as an ambush. It may not be necessary to move to a rally point. The unit may stay out of harm's way until the barrage has been lifted and then continue in the direction of march. The commander states the actions for these events and incorporates them in the unit's SOP before movement.

9-11. The key to surviving an air attack is dispersion and continuous movement. The pack detachment always accounts for personnel, weapons, and equipment after it moves to the designated rally point, establishes security, and reestablishes the chain of command.

NOTE

Common sense, preparation, and good planning are the keys to surviving as a pack detachment in a hostile environment.

URBAN ENVIRONMENTS

9-12. Use of any kind of animals in an urban environment requires detailed planning and preparation. Even a clean, secure urban setting wears down an animal and its shoes rapidly. A damaged city with extensive rubble provides more danger in the form of sharp rock, broken glass, and other debris that can permanently damage animals. The best choice when planning to use pack animals to support an urban operation is to halt them at a secure location outside of any built-up areas and move the supplies in by foot. However, if the detachment must move the animals through a built-up area, it should try to avoid rubble, broken glass, nails, and other debris that will injure the animal.

9-13. A well-equipped farrier has special shoes for pack animals if the detachment is expected to stay in an urban environment for any period of time. Thick rubber horseshoes work well on pavement and concrete, but do not provide any traction on grass or any kind of dirt. Police departments sometimes use a complex shoe with a plastic plate to protect the inner hoof, a steel shoe over that, and carbide bits welded to the shoe. The carbide bits provide traction on asphalt and concrete, the shoe itself provides traction off-road, and the plastic protects the horse's inner hoof from nails, glass, and other debris.

9-14. Normally, the pack animal detachment will not have access to any special equipment to protect the animals. As mentioned earlier in this manual, shoes wear out much quicker on rocky or rough terrain. This is even more apparent when operating in any kind of urban environment. The detachment must check the animals' feet for any damage constantly throughout the day and must pay close attention to the animals during movement to watch for any injuries as soon as they occur. Routes must be selected and checked ahead of time to reduce the danger to the animals as they move. Special care must be taken to avoid any rubble, concrete, or asphalt along the route.

PART II

Observe, Assassinate, and Destroy

Special Forces Sniper Training and Employment

Preface

This field manual (FM) provides doctrinal guidance on the mission, personnel, organization, equipment, training, skills, and employment of the Special Forces (SF) sniper. It describes those segments of sniping that are unique to SF soldiers and those portions of conventional sniping that are necessary to train indigenous forces. It is intended for use by commanders, staffs, instructors, and soldiers at training posts, United States (U.S.) Army schools, and units.

This field manual addresses three distinct audiences:

- *Commanders.* It provides specific guidance on the nature, role, candidate selection, organization, and employment of sniper personnel.
- *Trainers.* It provides a reference for developing training programs.
- *Snipers.* It contains detailed information on the fundamental knowledge, skills, and employment methods of snipers throughout the entire operational continuum.

The most common measurements that the sniper uses are expressed throughout the text and in many cases are U.S. standard terms rather than metric.

CHAPTER 1

The Special Forces Sniper

The SF sniper is a selected volunteer specially trained in advanced marksmanship and fieldcraft skills. He can support special operations (SO) missions and is able to engage selected targets from concealed positions at ranges and under conditions that are not possible for the normal rifleman.

MISSION

1-1. Specially organized, trained, and equipped military and paramilitary forces conduct SF missions. Their goal is to achieve military, political, economic, or psychological objectives by unconventional means in hostile, denied, or politically sensitive areas. SF conduct missions in peacetime operations and war, independently or in coordination with operations of conventional forces. Politico-military considerations frequently shape SF operations, requiring clandestine, covert or low-visibility techniques, and oversight at the national level. SF operations usually differ from conventional operations in their degree of risk, operational techniques, mode of employment, independence from friendly support, and dependence upon operational intelligence and indigenous assets. Figure 1-1, lists the SF principal missions and collateral activities and the support that a sniper provides. Appendix B contains the sniper mission-essential task list.

SELECTION OF PERSONNEL

1-2. Commanders and assessors must carefully screen all candidates for sniper training. The rigorous training program and the great personal risk in combat require high motivation and the ability to learn a variety of skills. The proper mental conditioning cannot always be taught or instilled by training.

1-3. It is important for the commander to monitor evaluation and selection procedures, since each unit may have a different mission. There are no absolutes for selecting SF snipers. However, there are diagnostic tests, organizational indicators, and trends that help the commander identify potential snipers.

1-4. There are also several concrete prerequisites that should be met by the candidates before being accepted into the sniper program. Figure 1-2, lists the administrative prerequisites that the sniper candidate must meet.

1-5. The commander can determine personal qualities through background checks, interviews, records review, and counseling sessions. Recommended personal qualities should include, but are not limited to, those shown in Figure 1-3.

> **NOTE**
>
> Most of the prerequisites listed in Figure 1-2 are required to enter the Special Operations Target Interdiction Course (SOTIC) conducted at the USAJFKSWCS, Fort Bragg, North Carolina.

1-6. The first three personal qualities are particularly important when it comes to sustaining sniper skills, because the sniper with these characteristics will have a greater desire to practice these tasks as they are part of his avocation.

1-7. Commanders may implement diagnostic and aptitude testing. Certain testing procedures may be lengthy and tedious and are therefore subject to limitations of time, equipment, and facilities. It is recommended that the psychological evaluation of a candidate be at least partially determined through the use of the MMPI-2. This test, if properly

Principal Missions	**Collateral Activities**
Unconventional Warfare (UW)	Coalition Support
Foreign Internal Defense (FID)	Combat Search and Rescue (CSAR)
Information Operations (IO)	Counterdrug (CD) Activities
Direct Action (DA)	Humanitarian Demining (HD) Activities
Special Reconnaissance (SR)	Countermine (CM) Activities
Combatting Terrorism (CBT)	Foreign Humanitarian Assistance
Counterproliferation (CP)	Security Assistance
	Special Activities

The SF sniper supports the above functions by—

- Engaging long-range targets with precision fire.
- Obtaining and reporting enemy intelligence information.
- Providing training.

Figure 1-1. Special forces functions and how the sniper supports them

- Be a member of a special operations forces (SOF) unit having a validated sniper mission.
- Meet service physical fitness requirements (height and weight should be IAW AR 600-9).
- Have scored expert with the M4/M16A2 rifles in accordance with (IAW) FM 23-9. (Preferably, the candidate repeatedly scores expert during his biannual qualification.)
- Have no record of drug or alcohol abuse.
- Have no record of punishment under the Uniform Code of Military Justice during the current enlistment.
- Have a GT score of 110 or above and a CO score of 110 or above, or an SC score of 110 or above.
- Be in the pay grade of E4 or above and have a SECRET clearance.
- Have 20/20 vision or be correctable IAW AR 40-501. (Glasses are a liability unless the individual is otherwise highly qualified.)
- Have a psychological evaluation conducted under the direction of, and approved by, a qualified medical expert. (This examination includes, as a minimum, the Minnesota Multi-Phasic Personality Inventory [MMPI]-2 and a psychiatric history mental status examination.)
- Have at least 12 months of service remaining on active duty after completion of the course.
- Must not have been convicted of a domestic violence crime that would preclude him being issued a weapon IAW the Lautenberg Amendment.

Figure 1-2. Administrative prerequisites

administered, gives the commander a personality profile of the candidate. It helps him decide whether the candidate can function in confined spaces, work independently, and has the potential to be a sniper.

1-8. The tests are more than simple mental analyses. Psychological screening establishes a profile of characteristics that indicate if an individual would be a successful sniper. Testing eliminates candidates who would not perform well in combat. Psychological screening can identify individuals who have problems.

- Experience as a hunter or woodsman.
- Experience as a competitive marksman.
- Interest in weapons.
- Ability to make rapid, accurate assessments and mental calculations.
- Ability to maintain an emotionally stable personal life.
- Ability to function effectively under stress.
- Possession of character traits of patience, attention to detail, perseverance, and physical endurance.
- Ability to focus completely.
- Ability to endure solitude.
- Objectivity to the extent that one can stand outside oneself to evaluate a situation.
- Ability to work closely with another individual in confined spaces and under stress.
- Freedom from certain detrimental personal habits such as the use of tobacco products and alcohol. (Use of these is a liability unless the candidate is otherwise highly qualified. These traits, however, should not be the sole disqualifier.)
- First-class APFT scores with a high degree of stamina and, preferably, solid athletic skills and abilities.

Figure 1-3. Personal qualities

1-9. To select the best candidate, the commander talks to a qualified psychologist and explains what characteristics he is looking for. That way, once a candidate is tested, the psychologist can sit down with the commander and give him the best recommendation based on the candidate's psychological profile.

1-10. After the commander selects the sniper candidate, he must assess the individual's potential as a sniper. He may assess the candidate by conducting a thorough review of the candidate's records, objective tests, and subjective evaluations. The length of time a commander may devote to a candidate's assessment will vary with his resources and the mission. Normally, 2 or 3 days will suffice to complete an accurate assessment.

1-11. Assessment should include both written and practical tests. Practical examinations will actively measure the candidate's physical ability to perform the necessary tasks and subtasks involved in sniping. Written examinations will evaluate the candidate's comprehension of specific details.

1-12. Assessment testing must objectively and subjectively determine an individual's potential as a sniper. Objectivity measures the capacity to learn and perform in a sterile environment. Subjectivity assesses actual individual performance.

1-13. Objective assessment tests are presented as a battery grouped by subject matter and may be presented either as practical or written examinations. Some examples of objective testing are—

- Shooting battery tests that evaluate the theoretical and practical applications of rifle marksmanship.
- Observation and memory battery tests that measure the candidate's potential for observation and recall of specific facts.
- Intelligence battery tests that consist of standard military tests and previously mentioned specialized tests.
- Critical decision battery tests that evaluate the candidate's ability to think quickly and use sound judgment.
- Motor skills battery tests that assess hand-eye coordination.

1-14. Subjective assessment tests allow the assessor to gain insight into the candidate's personality. Although he is constantly observed in the selection and assessment process, specific tests may be designed to identify desirable and undesirable character traits. A trained psychologist (well versed in sniper selection) should conduct or monitor all subjective testing. Examples of possible subjective tests include, but are not limited to, the following:

- The interview—can identify the candidate's motivation for becoming a sniper and examine his expectations concerning the training.
- The suitability inventory—basically compares the candidate to a "predetermined profile" containing the characteristics, skills, motivations, and experience a sniper should possess.

1-15. A committee of assessors conducts the candidate selections at the end of the assessment program. While the commander should monitor all candidate selections, it is important for the committee to make the decision to preserve consistency and to rule out individual bias. The procedure for selection should be accomplished by a quorum during which the candidates are rated on a progressive scale. The committee should choose candidates based on their standing, in conjunction with the needs of the unit. At this time, the best-qualified soldiers should be selected; alternate and future candidates may also be identified. The committee should also adhere to the following guidelines:

- Do not apprise the candidates of their status during selection.
- Do not consider nonvolunteers.
- Select the best-qualified candidates first.
- Do not allow soldiers who do not meet set prerequisites into the program.
- Continue selection after SOTIC for "best qualified" determination and mission selection.

QUALIFICATIONS OF SOTIC GRADUATES

1-16. Upon completion of the SOTIC, the sniper has obtained a minimum of 700 course points and passed the "must pass" events to graduate. He must be able to—

- Detect, determine distances to, and engage multiple targets at distances between 150 to 800 meters.
- Stalk and reach a concealed position located no further than 220 meters from an observer as an individual or 330 meters as a team.
- Engage opportunity targets at 800 meters.
- Precisely engage snap targets at 200 and 400 meters with a 3-second exposure, and at 300 meters with a 6-second exposure.
- Engage moving targets at 200 and 300 meters.
- Understand camouflage and concealment, observation, techniques, reporting techniques, hide site selection, and hide construction.
- Make first-round hit on man-sized targets out to 600 meters 90 percent of the time, and out to 800 meters 50 percent of the time.

1-17. The only way the sniper can improve is through a comprehensive sniper sustainment training program. This program is not just to sustain the sniper at his present level, but it must challenge him to improve his skills. The program is mandatory IAW U.S. Army Special Operations Command (USASOC) Regulation 350-1, *Training*. It should be used as frequently as possible, at a minimum of 2 weeks every 6 months. Sniping skills are extremely perishable and without this program the sniper will rapidly lose his skills and become ineffective. Participating also aids in sniper selection after training.

THE SNIPER TEAM

1-18. Snipers conduct missions in pairs to enhance the team's effectiveness, provide mutual security, and maintain constant support for each other. Due to lowered stress, sniper pairs can engage targets more rapidly and stay in the field for longer periods of time than a single sniper due to lowered stress.

1-19. The more experienced of the pair will act as the observer during the shot. This method is especially important on a high priority target. The more experienced sniper is better able to read winds and give the shooter a compensated aim point to ensure a first-round hit. Also, a high-priority target may warrant that both snipers engage the target at the same time. The two-man concept allows this flexibility.

1-20. Past experience has shown that deploying as a sniper/observer team significantly increases the success rate of the missions. With few exceptions, snipers who are deployed singly have shown a marked decrease in their effectiveness and performance almost immediately after the start of the mission. This decrease is due to the sniper becoming overwhelmed with concern for his security, the tasks to be accomplished, and his own emotions (fear, loneliness).

SNIPER TEAM ORGANIZATION

1-21. Either member of the sniper team can perform the function of the sniper (with the M24 or a specially selected weapon); the other member performs the function of the observer. The two-man team is the smallest organization recommended. It offers mobility, concealment, and flexibility. The sniper team can maintain continuous observation of an area while alternating security, sleeping, eating, and relieving the stress inherent in a single-man operation. The sniper/observer relationship of the sniper pair is invaluable in target acquisition, estimation of range to targets, observation of bullet trace and impact, and in offering corrections to targets engaged. Also, the mutual support of two snipers working together is a significant morale factor in combat environments or extended missions.

1-22. Under certain circumstances the team may be augmented with a squad- to platoon-sized element. This element may be used for security, hide construction, or as a cover for a stay-behind operation. If the augmentation is for security purposes, the security element must be located far enough away from the team to prevent its compromise. A starting guideline is 800 to 1,000 meters that must be modified according to the situation and the terrain. It is critical to mission success that the sniper team and the augmentation unit be thoroughly familiar with each other and have well-developed standing operating procedures (SOPs).

1-23. Units may task-organize snipers for specific missions as opposed to sniper teams working independently. Regardless of any provisional or temporary sniper grouping, sniper teams should not be split. They are most effectively employed in the pairs in which they have been trained.

1-24. Sniper teams may also be augmented with additional observers or snipers. The additional personnel spread out the interval of observation periods and allow for longer rest cycles, which is important during extended missions with 24-hour observation. The primary team will act as the sniper/observer pair if a shot is required. The augmentees act only as observers during an observation cycle.

SNIPER TRAINING

1-25. Sniper training is conducted through two separate environments. The formal schoolhouse environment (SOTIC) is conducted by the USAJFKSWCS at Fort Bragg, North Carolina. This course produces Level I snipers for the SO community. The graduates receive a W3 identifier.

1-26. The second environment is the Unit Training Special Operations Target Interdiction Course. This course enables the unit commander to fill his needs within his mission parameters. A graduate of this course becomes a Level II sniper and is fully capable of filling an assigned team slot as a sniper. He also meets the requirements established by USASFC 350-1 for two snipers, either Level I or II, to be assigned to each Special Forces operational detachment A (SFODA). Once a sniper (Level I or II) is assigned to an SFODA, he is then a Category (CAT) I sniper for requesting training ammunition, equipment, and ranges.

1-27. Twice a year USAJFKSWCS conducts a 1-week Challenge Course. Level II snipers who successfully complete the Challenge Course will be awarded a SOTIC diploma and the Level I designator.

1-28. The primary differences in Levels I and II snipers are that Level I snipers are required to fire within close proximity of non-combatants and friendly forces in a Close Combat Situation. Level I snipers are required to run the SF Group Sustainment Program, which is usually conducted in conjunction with a Level II train up. Level I are required to train U.S. forces in Level II courses. Level II snipers may not train other U.S. forces to a Level II status. The Level II sniper may conduct sniper training for host nation courses.

1-29. The Level I sniper is tested to the maximum effective range of the M24 Sniper Weapon System 800 meters, while the Level II sniper furthest required range is 600 yards. However, the unit commander may designate his Level II snipers to be trained to a higher degree of efficiency and accuracy. The unit commander may have his Level II course mirror the Level I course or add greater emphasis in areas he feels are necessary to complete his assigned mission parameters. While the Level I course is a program-of-instruction-driven, 6-week course, the unit course may be 2 weeks or longer depending on the requirements of the command.

1-30. The Level I designation is to identify those snipers that have met a specific standard of training. These snipers have been trained by a cadre of instructors that have gone through the Instructor Training Course conducted by the SOTIC designators. The instructor's sole function is to train sniper students; he does not have to participate in the line unit's operations tempo.

1-31. The unit's Level II courses may train to a higher or lower standard depending upon the commander's needs and assessments. The instructors for the unit Level II course need to be identified as soon as possible, usually 6 to 8 weeks out, and permitted to prepare for the coming course. This lead time may not be possible due to the unit's operations tempo and red-cycle requirements. The longer the lead time, the better the course preparation and instruction.

1-32. Once a sniper is trained, whether Level I or II, he must maintain proficiency. His maintenance training must include the school "learning environment" and the unit "training environment." The school must teach a skill and thus remove variables so that the student may learn. Once the sniper has graduated, he must "train" in these skills with the variables added. Only imagination and desire on the sniper's part can limit the training scenarios.

CHAPTER 2

Equipment

Snipers, by the nature of their mission, must learn to exploit the maximum potential from all their equipment. The organizational level of employment and the mission will determine the type and amount of equipment needed. Snipers will carry only the equipment necessary for successfully completing their mission. Appendix A describes the M82A1 caliber .50 sniper weapon system (SWS). Appendix B describes the types of SWSs in other countries.

SNIPER WEAPON SYSTEM

2-1. The current SWS is the M24 sniper rifle with the Leopold & Stevens (L&S) ultra 10x M3A rifle scope. The M24 is based on the Remington Model 700 long action with an adjustable trigger. The barrel is a heavy, 5 groove, 11.2-inch twist, stainless steel target barrel. The stock is made of fiberglass, graphite, and Kevlar with an adjustable butt plate. The weapon is constructed to be accurate within 1/2 minute of angle (MOA) or 1/2-inch groups at 100 yards. The M24 is currently chambered for the 7.62-millimeter (mm) North Atlantic Treaty Organization (NATO) cartridge. Two M24s are issued per operational detachment. The parts of the M24 rifle include the bolt assembly, trigger assembly, adjustable stock, barreled action (H 700), and telescopic and iron sights. Because this weapon is the sniper's best friend, he must be proficient in inspecting and loading it. However, during the inspection, the extent of the sniper's repairs is limited. Figure 2-1 lists the M24 SWS components.

- Bolt-action rifle
- Fixed 10x telescope, L&S M3A
- System case
- Scope case
- Detachable iron sights (front and rear)
- Deployment case and kit
- Optional bipod
- Cleaning kit
- Soft rifle case
- Operator's manual

Figure 2-1. Components of the M24 SWS

SAFETY

2-2. The safety is located on the right rear side of the receiver and, when properly engaged, provides protection against accidental discharge under normal usage. The sniper should follow the rules below:

- To engage the safety, place it in the "S" position (Figure 2-2).
- Always place the safety in the "S" position before handling, loading, or unloading the weapon.
- When the weapon is ready to be fired, place the safety in the "F" position (Figure 2-2).

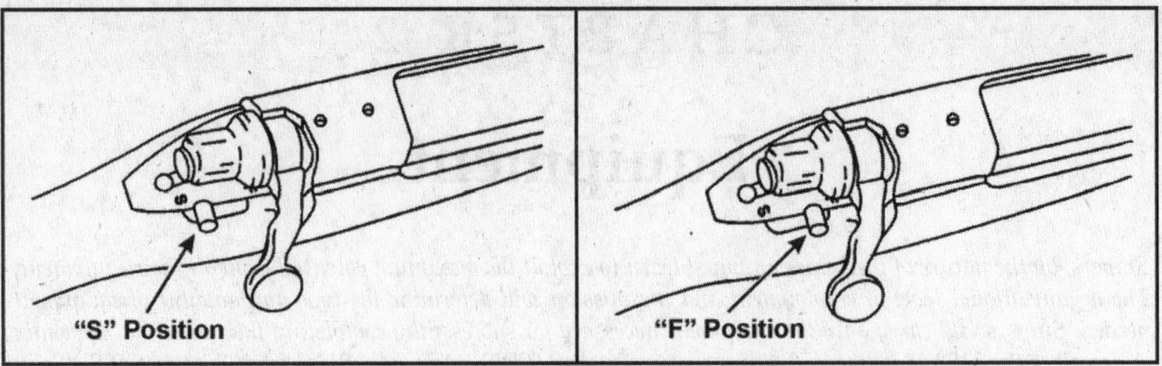

Figure 2-2. The M24 sniper weapon system in the SAFE and FIRE modes

BOLT ASSEMBLY

2-3. The bolt assembly locks the round into the chamber as well as extracts it. The sniper should follow the rules below:

- To remove the bolt from the receiver, place the safety in the "S" position, raise the bolt handle, and pull it back until it stops. Push the bolt stop release up (Figure 2-3) and pull the bolt from the receiver.
- To replace the bolt, ensure the safety is in the "S" position, align the lugs on the bolt assembly with the receiver (Figure 2-4), slide the bolt all the way into the receiver, and then push the bolt handle down.

TRIGGER ASSEMBLY

2-4. Pulling the trigger fires the rifle when the safety is in the "F" position. The sniper may adjust the trigger pull force from a minimum of 2.5 pounds to a maximum of 8 pounds. He can make this adjustment using the 1/16-inch Allen wrench provided in the deployment kit. Turning the trigger adjustment screw (Figure 2-5) clockwise will increase the force needed to pull the trigger. Turning it counterclockwise will decrease the force needed. This change is the only trigger adjustment the sniper will make. The trigger cannot be adjusted less than 2.5 pounds. The screw compresses an independent spring that increases the required pressure to make the sear disengage.

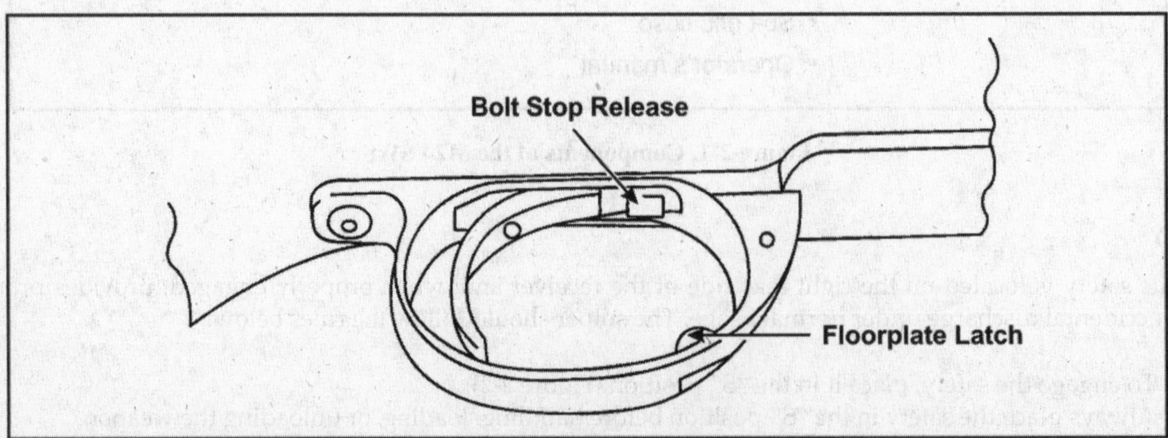

Figure 2-3. Bolt stop release

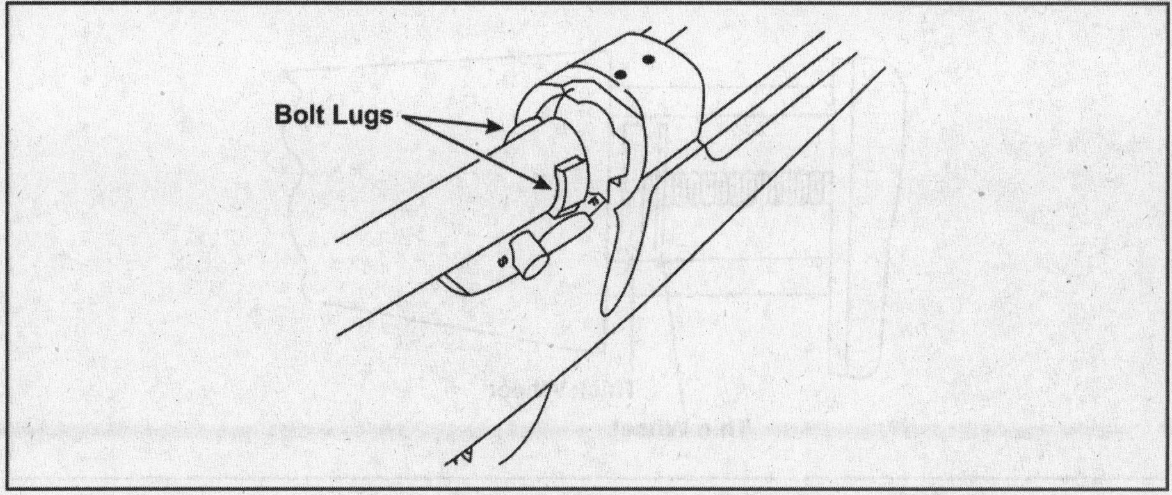

Figure 2-4. Bolt lugs aligned with the receiver

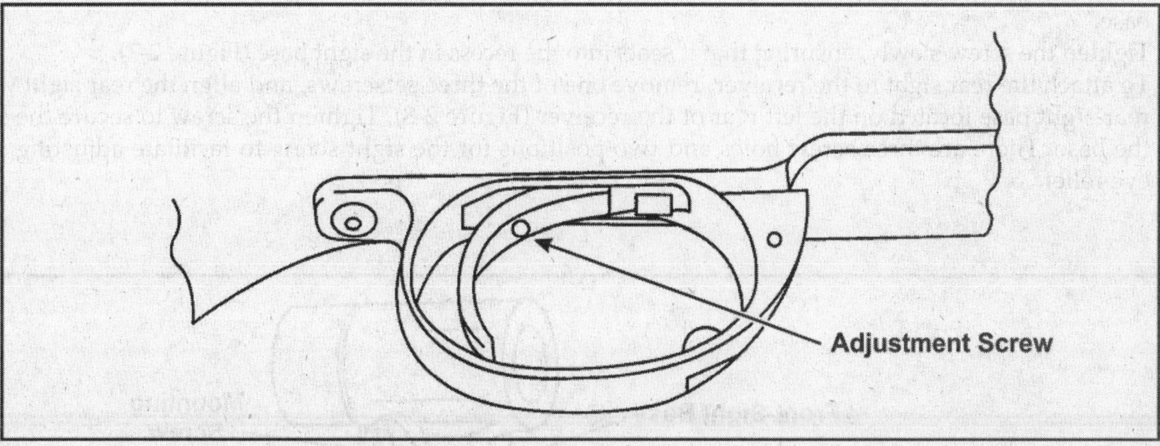

Figure 2-5. Location of the trigger adjustment screw

STOCK ADJUSTMENT

2-5. The M24 has a mechanism for making minor adjustments in the stock's length of pull. The thick wheel provides this adjustment. The thin wheel is for locking this adjustment (Figure 2-6). The sniper should turn the thick wheel clockwise to lengthen the stock or counterclockwise to shorten the stock. To lock the position of the shoulder stock, he should turn the thin wheel clockwise against the thick wheel. To unlock the position of the shoulder stock, he should turn the thin wheel counterclockwise away from the thick wheel. The sniper can adjust the length of pull so that the stock may be extended, but no more than three finger widths. Beyond this, the butt plate becomes unstable.

IRON SIGHTS

2-6. The M24 has a backup sighting system consisting of detachable front and rear iron sights. To install the iron sights, the sniper must first remove the telescope. The sniper should—

- Align the front sight and the front-sight base dovetail and slide the sight over the base to attach the front sight to the barrel.

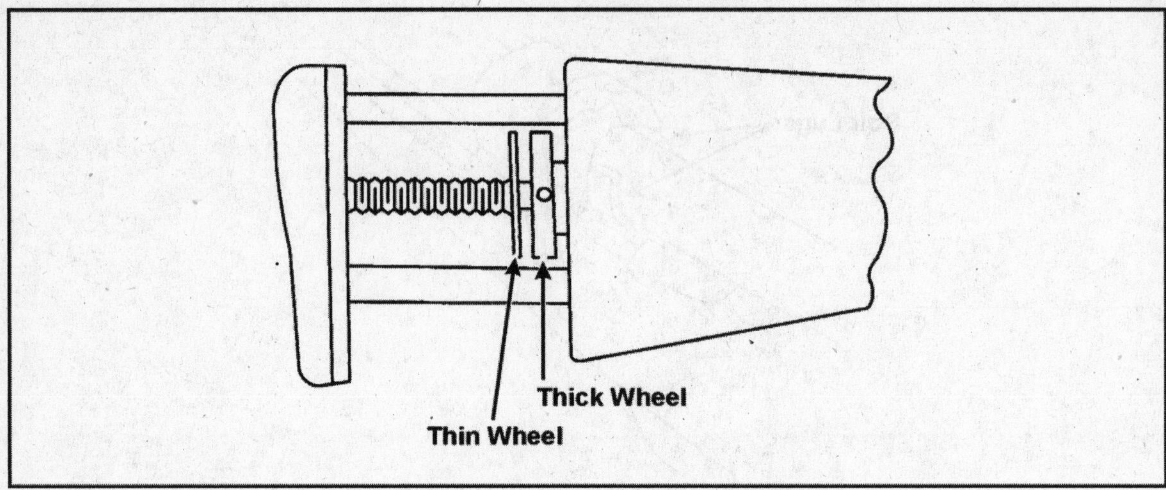

Figure 2-6. Stock length adjustment mechanism

- Ensure the fingernail projection of the front sight fits securely into the fingernail groove on the front-sight base.
- Tighten the screw slowly, ensuring that it seats into the recess in the sight base (Figure 2-7).
- To attach the rear sight to the receiver, remove one of the three setscrews, and align the rear sight with the rear-sight base located on the left rear of the receiver (Figure 2-8). Tighten the screw to secure the sight to the base. There are three screw holes and two positions for the sight screw to facilitate adjusting shooter eye relief.

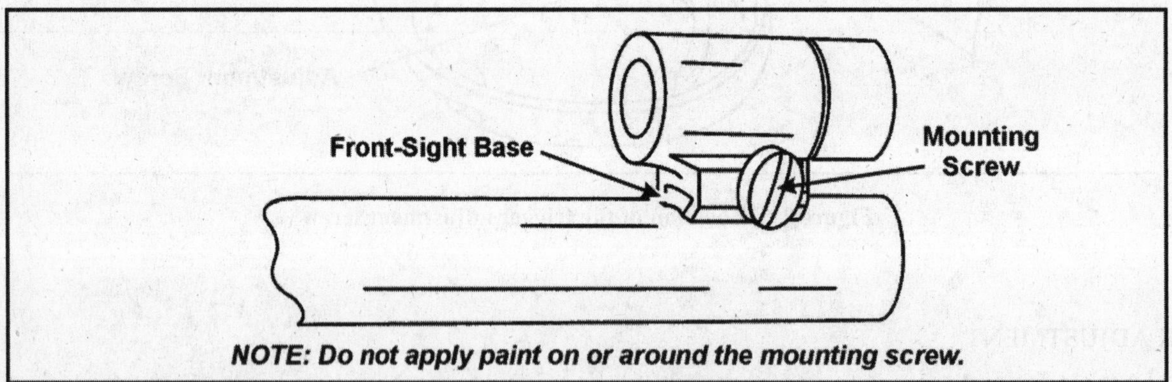

Figure 2-7. Front-sight mounting screw

2-7. The sniper should also make sure the other setscrews are below the level of the face of the rear sight base. If not, he should remove and store them.

INSPECTION

2-8. The M24's design enables the sniper to make some repairs. Deficiencies that the sniper is unable to repair will require manufacturer warranty work. When inspecting the M24, the sniper should check the—

- Appearance and completeness of all parts.
- Bolt to ensure it has the same serial number as the receiver and that it locks, unlocks, and moves smoothly.

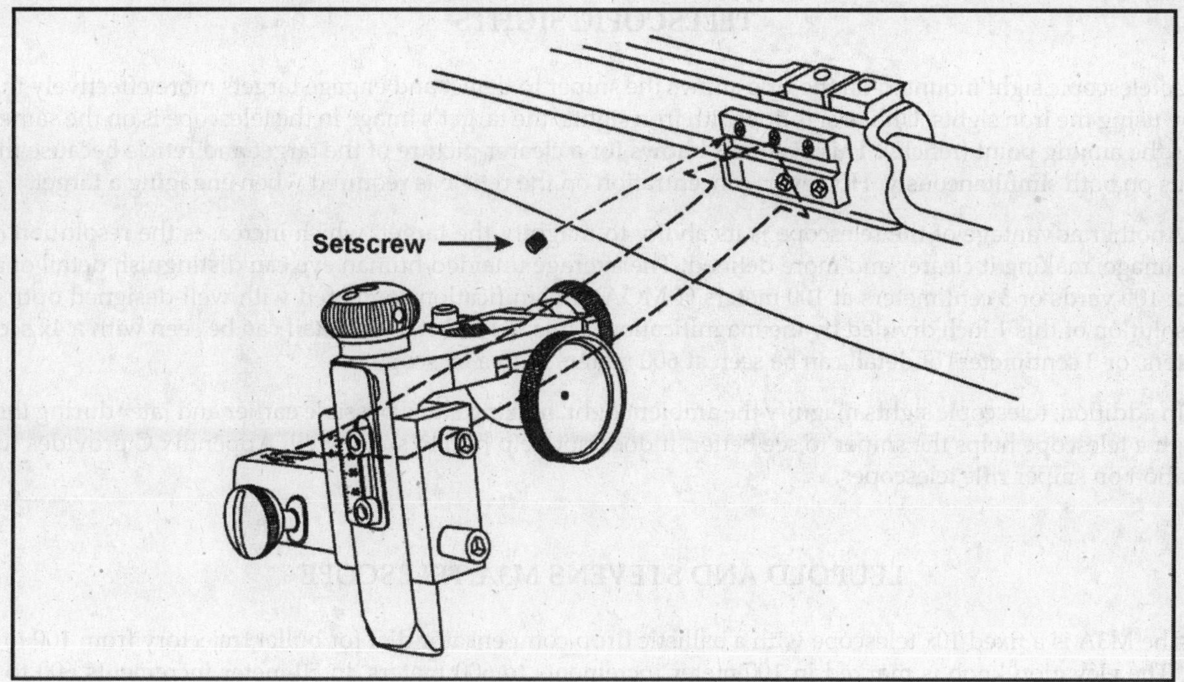

Figure 2-8. Attaching the rear sight assembly

- Safety to ensure it can be positively placed into the "S" and "F" positions without being too difficult or too easy to move.
- Trigger to ensure the weapon will not fire when the safety is in the "S" position and that it has a smooth, crisp trigger pull.
- Action screws (front of the internal magazine and rear of the trigger guard) for proper torque (65 inch-pounds).
- Telescope mounting ring nuts for proper torque (65 inch-pounds).
- Stock for any cracks, splits, or any contact it may have with the barrel.
- Telescope for obstructions such as dirt, dust, moisture, and loose or damaged lenses.

LOADING

2-9. The M24 has an internal, five-round capacity magazine. To load the rifle, the sniper should—

- Point the weapon in a safe direction.
- Ensure the safety is in the "S" position.
- Raise the bolt handle and pull it back until it stops.
- Push five rounds of 7.62-mm ammunition one at a time through the ejection port into the magazine. Ensure that the bullet end of the rounds is aligned toward the chamber.
- Push the rounds fully rearward in the magazine.
- Once the five rounds are in the magazine, push the rounds downward while slowly pushing the bolt forward over the top of the first round.
- Push the bolt handle down. The magazine is now loaded.
- To chamber a round, raise the bolt and pull it back to fully seat the round. Stopping the bolt early will cause an override situation.
- Push the bolt forward. The bolt strips a round from the magazine and pushes it into the chamber.
- Push the bolt handle down until it is fully seated. Failure will cause a light strike on the primer and a misfire.

2-10. To fire the rifle, place the safety in the "F" position and squeeze the trigger.

TELESCOPIC SIGHTS

2-11. A telescopic sight mounted on the rifle allows the sniper to detect and engage targets more effectively than he could by using the iron sights. Unlike sighting with iron sights, the target's image in the telescope is on the same focal plane as the aiming point (reticle). This evenness allows for a clearer picture of the target and reticle because the eye can focus on both simultaneously. However, concentration on the reticle is required when engaging a target.

2-12. Another advantage of the telescope is its ability to magnify the target, which increases the resolution of the target's image, making it clearer and more defined. The average unaided human eye can distinguish detail of about 1 inch at 100 yards or 3 centimeters at 100 meters (1 MOA). Magnification combined with well-designed optics permits resolution of this 1 inch divided by the magnification. Thus, a 1/4 MOA of detail can be seen with a 4x scope at 100 meters, or 3 centimeters of detail can be seen at 600 meters with a 6x scope.

2-13. In addition, telescopic sights magnify the ambient light, making shots possible earlier and later during the day. Although a telescope helps the sniper to see better, it does not help him to shoot well. Appendix C provides further information on sniper rifle telescopes.

LEUPOLD AND STEVENS M3A TELESCOPE

2-14. The M3A is a fixed 10x telescope with a ballistic drop compensator dial for bullet trajectory from 100 to 1,000 meters. The elevation knob is marked in 100-meter increments to 600 meters, in 50-meter increments 600 to 1,000 meters, and has 1 MOA elevation adjustment. The windage 1/2-MOA increments and a third knob provides for focus and parallax adjustment. The reticle is a duplex crosshair with 3/4-MOA mil dots (Figure 2-9). The mil dots are 1 mil apart, center to center, with a possible 10 mils vertical and 10 mils horizontal. The sniper uses mil dots for range estimation, holdover, windage holds, mover leads, and reference point holds.

2-15. The M3A consists of the telescope, a fixed mount, a detachable sunshade for the objective lens, and dust covers for the objective and ocular (eyepiece) lens. The telescope has a fixed 10x magnification that gives the sniper better resolution than with the adjustable ranging telescope (ART) series. There are three knobs located midway on the tube—the focus/parallax, elevation, and windage knobs (Figure 2-10).

ADJUSTMENTS

2-16. The sniper should always focus the reticle to his eye first. He should turn the ocular eyepiece to adjust the reticle until it is sharp, but should not force-focus his eye. He can adjust the eyepiece by turning it in or out of the tube until the reticle appears crisp and clear. The sniper should focus the eyepiece after mounting the telescope on the rifle. He should grasp the eyepiece and back it away from the lock ring. He should not attempt to loosen the lock ring first; it will automatically loosen when the eyepiece is backed away (no tools are needed). The sniper should rotate the eyepiece several turns to move it at least 1/8 inch. He will need this much change to achieve any measurable effect on the reticle clarity. The sniper then looks through the scope at the sky or a blank wall and checks to see if the reticle appears sharp and crisp. He must do this before adjusting the focus and parallax.

2-17. The focus/parallax knob sits on the left side of the tube. The sniper uses it to focus the target's image onto the same focal plane as the reticle, thereby reducing parallax to a minimum. Parallax is the apparent movement of the sight picture on the reticle when the eye is moved from side to side or up and down. The parallax adjustment knob has two extreme positions indicated by the infinity mark and the largest of four dots. Adjustments between these positions focus images from less than 50 meters to infinity. These markings are for reference only, after the sniper has initially adjusted his scope for parallax. He then slips the scale to match his requirements (for example, big ball references 100 or 200 meters). The sniper then writes each item and its distance in his log for reference whenever he engages targets at that range. Any change in reticle focus requires the sniper to readjust the focus/parallax setting.

2-18. The elevation knob sits on top of the tube. This knob has calibrated index markings from 1 to 10. These markings represent the elevation setting adjustments needed at varying distances; for example, 1 = 100 meters,

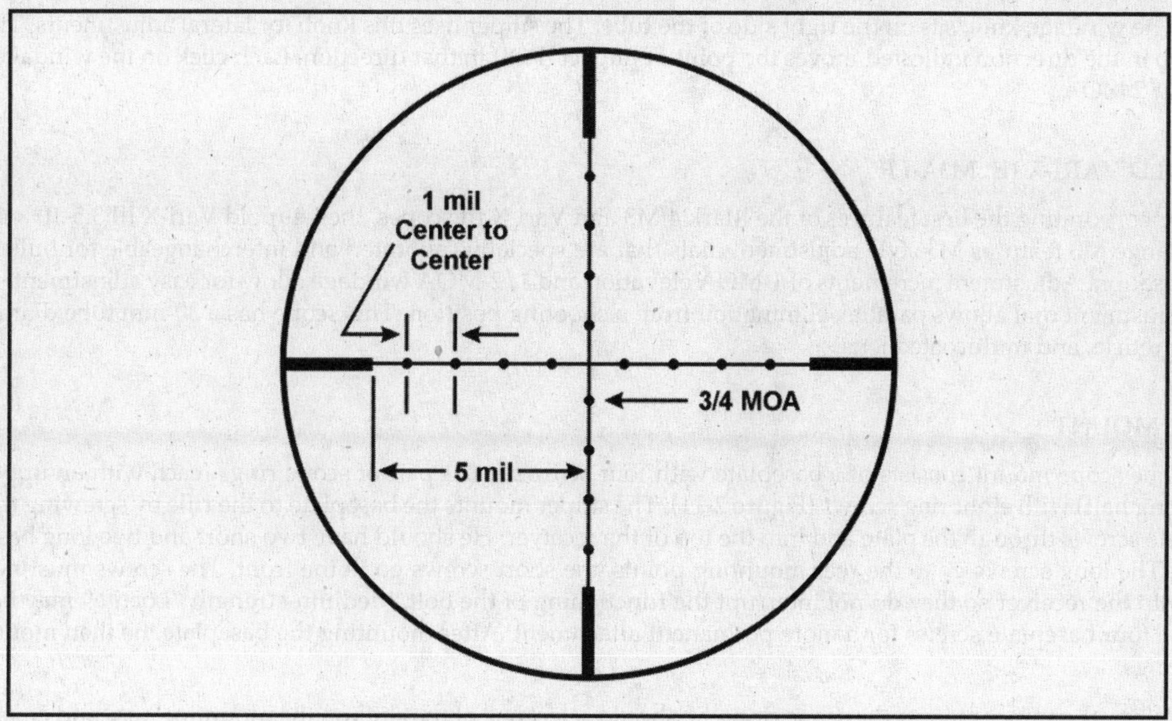

Figure 2-9. The M24 optical day sight reticle

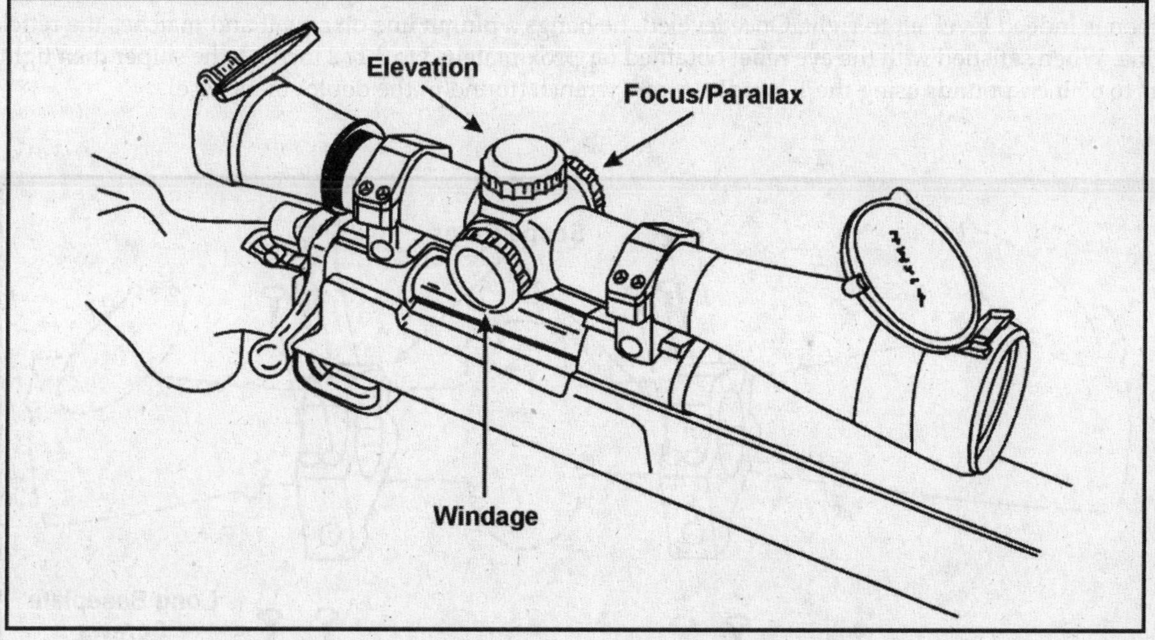

Figure 2-10. Focus/parallax, elevation, and windage knobs

10 = 1,000 meters. There are small hash marks between the 100-meter increments after 600 meters; these represent 50-meter increments. Each click of the elevation knob equals 1 MOA.

2-19. The windage knob sits on the right side of the tube. The sniper uses this knob for lateral adjustments. Turning the knob in the direction indicated moves the point of impact (POI) in that direction. Each click on the windage knob equals 1/2 MOA.

LEUPOLD VARI-X III, M3A-LR

2-20. Incorporating the best features of the Mark 4 M3 and Vari-X III scopes, the Leupold Vari-X III 3.5-10 × 40-mm Long-Range M3 features M3-style adjustment dials that are specially calibrated and interchangeable for bullet drop compensation. Adjustment increments of 1-MOA elevation and 1/2-MOA windage allow for easy adjustment. A parallax adjustment dial allows parallax elimination from a shooting position. This scope has a 30-mm tube diameter, a mil-dot reticle, and multicoated lens.

SCOPE MOUNT

2-21. The scope mount consists of a baseplate with four screws and a pair of scope rings (each with an upper and lower ring half) with eight ring screws (Figure 2-11). The sniper mounts the baseplate to the rifle by screwing the four baseplate screws through the plate and into the top of the receiver. He should have two short and two long baseplate screws. The long screws go to the rear mounting points, the short screws go to the front. The screws must not protrude into the receiver so they do not interrupt the functioning of the bolt. Medium-strength "Loctite" may be used on these four baseplate screws for a more permanent attachment. After mounting the baseplate, he then mounts the scope rings.

2-22. When the sniper mounts the scope rings, he should select one of the slots on the mounting base and engage the ringbolt spline with the selected slot. He should push the ring forward to get spline-to-base contact as the mount ring nut is tightened. He checks the eye relief. If the telescope needs to be adjusted, the sniper loosens the ring nuts and aligns the ringbolts with the other set of slots on the base; he then repeats the process. He makes sure that the crosshairs are perfectly aligned (vertically and horizontally) with the rifle. Any cant will cause misses at longer ranges. To ensure that the reticle is not canted in the rings, the sniper will need a level and plumb line. He uses the level to ensure the weapon is indeed level left to right. Once leveled, he hangs a plumb line on a wall and matches the reticle to the plumb line. When satisfied with the eye relief obtained (approximately 3 to 3 1/2 inches), the sniper then tightens the ring nuts to 65 inch-pounds using the T-handle torque wrench (found in the deployment case).

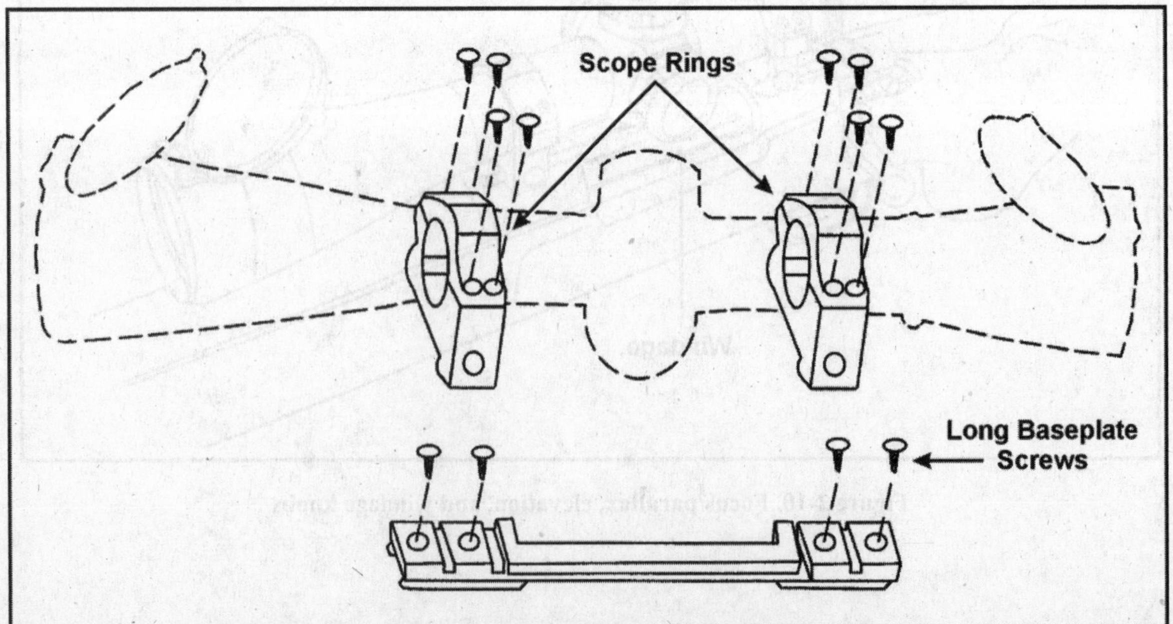

Figure 2-11. The M3A leupold and stevens scope mount

OPERATION

2-23. When using the telescope, the sniper simply places the reticle on the target, determines the distance to the target by using the mil dots on the reticle, sets parallax, and then adjusts the elevation knob for the estimated range. He then places the crosshair on the desired POI or quarters the target. The sniper then gives the observer a "READY" and awaits the wind call.

AMMUNITION

2-24. Snipers should always attempt to use match-grade ammunition when available because of its greater accuracy and lower sensitivity to environmental effects. However, if match-grade ammunition is not available, or if the situation requires, he may use a different grade of ammunition. Standard-grade ammunition may not provide the same level of accuracy or POI as match-grade ammunition. In the absence of match-grade ammunition, the sniper should conduct firing tests to determine the most accurate lot of ammunition available. Once he identifies a lot of ammunition as meeting the requirements, he should use this lot as long as it is available.

TYPES AND CHARACTERISTICS

2-25. The sniper should use 7.62- × 51-mm (.308 Winchester) NATO M118 Special Ball (SB), M852 National Match, or M118 Long Range (LR) ammunition with the SWS. He must rezero the SWS every time the type or lot of ammunition changes. The ammunition lot number appears on the cardboard box, metal can, and wooden crate that it is packaged in. The sniper should maintain this information in the weapon's data book.

M118 Special Ball

2-26. The M118SB bullet consists of a metal jacket and a lead antimony slug. It is a boat-tailed bullet (the rear of the bullet is tapered to reduce drag) and has a nominal weight of 173 grains. The tip of the bullet is not colored. The base of the cartridge is stamped with the NATO standardization mark (circle and crosshairs), manufacturer's code, and year of manufacture. Its primary use is against personnel. Its accuracy standard requires a 10-shot group to have an extreme spread of not more than 12 inches at 600 yards or 33 centimeters at 550 meters (2 MOAs) when fired from an accuracy barrel in a test cradle. The stated velocity of 2,550 feet per second (fps) is measured at 78 feet from the muzzle. The actual muzzle velocity of this ammunition is 2,600 fps. M118SB is the primary choice for the M24 SWS because the telescopic sights are ballistically matched to this ammunition out to 1,000 meters. This ammunition is being replaced by M118LR.

M852 National Match (Open Tip)

2-27. As of October 1990, the Department of State, Army General Counsel, and the Office of the Judge Advocate General concluded that the use of open-tip ammunition does not violate the law-of-war obligation of the United States. The U.S. Army, Navy, and Marine Corps may use this ammunition in peacetime or wartime missions.

2-28. The M852 bullet (Sierra Match King) is boat-tailed, 168 grains in weight, and has an open tip. The open tip is a small aperture (about the diameter of the wire in a standard-sized straight pin or paper clip) in the nose of the bullet. Describing this bullet as a hollow point is misleading in law-of-war terms. A hollow-point bullet is typically thought of in terms of its ability to expand upon impact with soft tissue. Physical examination of the M852 open-tip bullet reveals that its opening is small in comparison to the aperture of hollow-point hunting bullets. Its purpose is to improve the ballistic coefficient of the projectile. The swaging of the bullet from the base by the copper gilding leaves a small opening in the nose; it does not aid in expansion. The lead core of the M852 bullet is entirely covered by the copper bullet jacket.

2-29. Accuracy standard for the M852 ammunition is 9.5 inches average extreme spread (or slightly over 1.5 MOAs) at 600 yards. Other than its superior long-range accuracy capabilities, the M852 was examined with regard to its performance upon impact with the human body or in artificial material that approximates soft human tissue. In some cases, the bullet would break up or fragment after entry into soft tissue. Fragmentation depends on many factors, including the range to the target, velocity at the time of impact, degree of yaw of the bullet at the POI, or the distance traveled point-first within the body before yaw is induced. The M852 was not designed to yaw intentionally or break up upon impact. There was little discernible difference in bullet fragmentation between the M852 and other military small-arms bullets. Some military ball ammunition of foreign manufacture tends to fragment sooner in human tissue or to a greater degree, resulting in wounds that would be more severe than those caused by the M852 bullet.

NOTE

M852 is the best substitute for M118 taking the following limitations into consideration:

- The M852's trajectory is not identical to the M118's; therefore, it is not matched ballistically with the M3A telescope. The difference to 600 meters is minimal, predictable 700 becomes 725, and 800 requires 850. These are start-point ranges only.
- The M852 is not suited for target engagement beyond 700 meters because the 168-grain bullet is not ballistically suitable. This bullet will drop below the sound barrier just beyond this distance. The turbulence that it encounters as it becomes subsonic affects its accuracy at distances beyond 700 meters.

M118 Long-Range (Open Tip)

2-30. The M118LR bullet (Sierra Match King) is boat-tailed, 175 grains in weight, and has an open tip. The open tip is the same as the M852.

2-31. Accuracy standard for the M118LR ammunition is an average extreme horizontal spread of 10.3 inches and an average extreme vertical spread of 14.0 inches at 1,000 yards or slightly over 1 MOA horizontal and 1.4 MOAs vertical extreme spread. This data is stated in the Detail Specifications dated 3 March 1998. The trajectory of the M118LR will closely match the M118SB. Complete information is not available at this time. This is new ammunition being developed through the Navy and Marine Corps. It is scheduled to replace all lots of the M118SB and M852.

M82 Blank

2-32. Snipers use the M82 blank ammunition during field training. It provides the muzzle blast and flash that trainers can detect during the exercises that evaluate the sniper's ability to conceal himself while firing his weapon and activates the multiple integrated laser engagement system (MILES) training devices. MILES devices are an excellent tool for training the commander on the use of a sniper. However, these devices can cause problems in the sniper's training, because he does not have to lead targets or compensate for wind or range.

ALTERNATIVES

2-33. If match-grade ammunition is not available, snipers can use the standard 7.62- × 51-mm NATO ball ammunition. However, the M3A bullet drop compensator (BDC) is designed for M118SB, so there would be a significant change in zero. Snipers should always test-fire standard ammunition and record the ballistic data in the data book. They should use standard ball ammunition in an emergency situation only. Snipers should test-fire all ammunition for accuracy. Even match-grade ammunition can have a bad lot.

M80/M80E1 Ball

2-34. The M80 and M80E1 ball cartridge bullet consists of a metal jacket with a lead antimony slug. It is boat-tailed and weighs 147 grains. The tip of the bullet is not colored. This bullet is primarily used against personnel. Its accuracy standard requires a 10-shot group to have an extreme spread of not more than 4 MOAs or 24 inches at 600 yards (66 centimeters at 550 meters) when fired from an accuracy barrel in a test cradle. The muzzle velocity of this ammunition is 2,800 fps. The base of the cartridge is stamped with the NATO standardization mark, manufacturer's initials, and the date of manufacture. The sniper should test-fire several lots before using them due to the reduced accuracy and fluctuation in lots. The most accurate lot that is available in the largest quantity (to minimize test repetition) should be selected for use.

M62 Tracer

2-35. The M62 tracer bullet consists of a metal-clad steel jacket, a lead antimony slug, a tracer subigniter, and igniter composition. It has a closure cap and weighs 141 grains. The bullet tip is painted orange (NATO identification for tracer ammunition). It is used for observation of fire, incendiary, and signaling purposes. Tracer ammunition is manufactured to have an accuracy standard that requires 10-shot groups to have an extreme spread of not more than 6 MOAs or 36 inches at 600 yards (99 centimeters at 550 meters). The base of the cartridge is stamped with the NATO standardization mark, manufacturer's initials, and date of manufacture. The amount of tracer ammunition fired through the SWS should be minimized because of its harmful effect on the precision-made barrel.

ROUND COUNT BOOK

2-36. The sniper maintains a running count of the number and type of rounds fired through the SWS. It is imperative to accurately maintain the round count book. The SWS has shown to have a barrel life of about 8,000 to 10,000 rounds. The sniper should inspect the barrel at this time, or sooner if a loss of accuracy has been noted. He inspects the barrel for throat erosion and wear, and if excessive, schedules the SWS to be rebarreled. This inspection should be accomplished IAW the deployment schedule of the unit and the required break in time needed for the new barrel.

OBSERVATION DEVICES

2-37. Aside from the rifle and telescopic sight, the sniper's most important tools are optical devices. The categories of optical equipment that snipers normally use are binoculars, telescopes, night vision devices (NVDs), and range finders. The following paragraphs discuss selected optical equipment for special purposes.

BINOCULARS

2-38. Every sniper should be issued binoculars; they are the sniper's primary tool for observation. Binoculars provide an optical advantage not found with telescopes or other monocular optical devices. The binoculars' typically larger objective lens, lower magnification, and optical characteristics add depth and field of view to an observed area. Many types of binoculars are available. Snipers/observers should take the following into account when selecting binoculars:

- *Durability.* The binoculars must be able to withstand rough use under field conditions. They must be weatherproofed and sealed against moisture that would render them useless due to internal fogging. Binoculars with individually focused eyepieces can more easily be made waterproof than centrally focused binoculars. Most waterproof binoculars offered have individually focused eyepieces.
- *Size.* A sniper's binoculars should be relatively compact for ease of handling and concealment.
- *Moderate magnification.* Binoculars of 6 to 8 power are best suited for sniper work. Higher magnifications tend to limit the field of view for any given size of objective lens. Also, higher magnifications tend to intensify hand movements during observation and compress depth perception.
- *Lens diameter.* Binoculars with an objective lens diameter of 35 to 50 mm should be considered the best choice. Larger lenses permit more light to enter; therefore, the 50-mm lens would be more effective in low-light conditions.
- *Mil scale.* The binoculars should have a mil scale incorporated into the field of view for range estimation.

2-39. The M22 binoculars are the newest in the inventory and are general issue. These binoculars have the same features as the M19, plus fold-down eyepiece cups for personnel who wear glasses, to reduce the distance between the eyes and the eyepieces. They also has protective covers for the objective and eyepiece lenses. The binoculars have laser-protective filters on the inside of the objective lenses. Direct sunlight reflects off these lenses! The reticle pattern (Figure 2-12) is different from the M19's reticle. Laser filter also lowers the M22's light transmittance, which lowers its ability to gather light at dusk and dawn. Characteristics of the M19 and M22 are as follows:

- M19 Optical Characteristics:
  - Objective lens: 50 mm.
  - Magnification: 7x.
  - Field of view: 130 mils—130 meters at 1,000 meters.
- M19 Physical Characteristics:
  - Width (open position): 190.5 mm/7.5 inches.
  - Length: 152.4 mm/6 inches.
  - Weight: 966 kg/2.125 pounds.
  - Thickness: 63.5 mm/2.5 inches.
- M22 Optical Characteristics:
  - Objective lens: 50 mm.
  - Magnification: 7x.
  - Field of view: 130 mils—130 meters at 1,000 meters.
  - Depth of field: 12.5 meters to infinity.
- M22 Physical Characteristics:
  - Width (open position): 205 mm/8.1 inches.
  - Length: 180 mm/7.1 inches.
  - Weight: 1.2 kg/2.7 pounds.

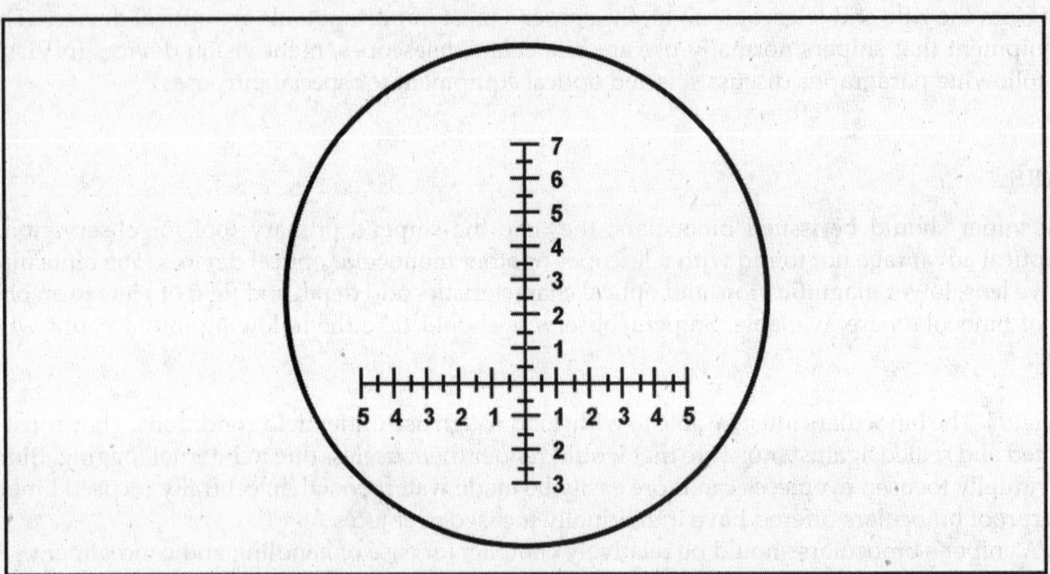

Figure 2-12. The reticle pattern in the M22 binoculars

Method of Holding Binoculars

2-40. Binoculars should be held lightly, resting on and supported by the heels of the hands. The thumbs are positioned to block out light that would enter between the eyes and the eyepieces. The eyepieces are held lightly to the eyes to avoid transmitting body movement. Whenever possible, a stationary rest should support the elbows. An alternate method for holding the binoculars is to move the hands forward, cupping them around the sides of the objective lenses. This method keeps light from reflecting off the lenses, which would reveal the sniper's position. The sniper should **always** be aware of reflecting light. He should operate from within shadows or cover the lens with an extension or thin veil, such as a nylon stocking.

Adjustments

2-41. Interpupillary distance is the space between the eyes. Interpupillary adjustment is moving the monocles to fit this distance. The monocles are hinged together for ease of adjustment. The hinge is adjusted until the field of vision ceases to be two overlapping circles and appears as a single, sharply defined circle. The setting on the hinge scale should be recorded for future use.

2-42. Each eye of every individual requires a different focus setting. The sniper should adjust the focus for each eye as follows:

- With **both** eyes open, look at a distant object, then through the binoculars at this same object.
- Place one hand over the objective lens of the right monocle and turn the focusing ring of the left monocle until the object is sharply defined.
- Uncover the right monocle and cover the left one. Rotate the focusing ring of the right monocle until the object is sharply defined.
- Uncover the left monocle. The object should be clear to both eyes.

The sniper should glance frequently at the distant object during this procedure to ensure that his eyes are not compensating for an out-of-focus condition. He then reads the diopter scale on each focusing ring and records the reading for future reference. Correctly focused binoculars will prevent eyestrain when observing for extended periods.

Eye Fatigue

2-43. Prolonged use of the binoculars or telescope will cause eye fatigue, reducing the effectiveness of observation. Periods of observation with optical devices should be limited to 30 minutes followed by a minimum of 15 minutes rest. A sniper can minimize eyestrain during observation by glancing away at green grass or any other subdued color.

M48/M49 OBSERVATION TELESCOPES AND TRIPOD

2-44. The M48/M49 observation telescopes are prismatic optical instruments of 20x magnification. Both scopes are essentially identical and this manual will refer mainly to the M49 from this point on. The lenses are coated with magnesium fluoride for improved light-transmitting capability. The sniper team carries the M49 when needed for the mission. The designated observer uses the telescope to assist in observation and selection of targets while the sniper is in the fire position. Properly used, the M49 telescope can significantly enhance the success of the team's mission by allowing it to conduct a superior target analysis, read the current environmental conditions, and make spot corrections by observing bullet trace and impact. The high magnification of the telescope makes observation, target detection, and target identification possible where conditions such as range would otherwise prevent identification. Camouflaged targets and those in deep shadows are more readily detected. Characteristics of the M48/M49 are as follows:

- M48 Observation Telescope:
  - Tripod: M14.
  - Carrying case (scope): M26.
  - Carrying case (tripod): M31.
  - Magnification: 19.6x.
  - Field of view: 37.2 mils.
  - Exit pupil: 0.100 inches.
  - Effective focal length (EFL) of objectives: 13.004 inches.
  - EFL of eyepiece: 0.662 inches.
  - Length: 13.5 inches.
- M49 Observation Telescope:
  - Tripod: M15.
  - Carrying case (scope): M27.
  - Carrying case (tripod): M42.
  - Magnification: 20x.

- Field of view: 38.37 mils.
- Exit pupil: 0.108 inches.
- EFL of objectives: 14.211 inches.
- EFL of eyepiece: 0.716 inches.
- Length: 14.5 inches.

Operating the M49

2-45. An eyepiece cover cap and objective lens cover protect the optics when the telescope is not in use. Snipers must take care to prevent cross-threading of the fine threads. They should turn the eyepiece focusing-sleeve clockwise or counterclockwise until the image is clearly seen.

Operating the M15 Tripod

2-46. The sniper uses the height adjusting collar to maintain a desired height for the telescope. The sniper keeps the collar in position by tightening the clamping screw. He uses the shaft rotation locking thumbscrew to clamp the tripod shaft at any desired azimuth. The elevating thumbscrew enables the sniper to adjust the cradle of the tripod and to increase or decrease the angle of elevation of the telescope. He can then tighten the screw nut at the upper end of each leg to hold the tripod legs in an adjusted position.

Setting Up the M49 and Tripod

2-47. The sniper spreads the tripod legs and places it in a level position on the ground so the cradle is level with the target area. He places the telescope through the strip loop of the tripod and tightens the strap to keep the telescope steady and in place. If the tripod is not carried, he uses an expedient rest for the scope. The sniper should always make sure the scope is in a steady position to maximize its capabilities and minimize eyestrain.

M144 OBSERVATION TELESCOPE

2-48. The M144 observation telescope is the new U.S. Army observation telescope and has a variable power eyepiece. The sniper/observer can adjust the eyepiece from 15x to 45x. This range permits the observer to adjust for a wider field of view or for magnification for clearer target identification. The observer should ensure that while reading winds or spotting trace, the scope should not be placed at a higher magnification than 20x. He can use the M144 in the same manner as the M49 scope that it replaces. Characteristics of the M144 are as follows:

- Objective lens: 60 mm.
- Magnification: 15x to 45x.
- Field of view: 125 ft at 15x and 62 ft at 45x at 100 meters.
- Focus range: 30 ft to infinity.
- Exit pupil: 4 mm at 15x and 1.4 mm at 45x.
- Eye relief: 20.5 mm at 15x and 13.5 mm at 45x.

2-49. The Army will soon replace the M144 observation telescope with a newer scope that is waterproof and more durable. The next scope will be a variable and possess better optics.

NIGHT VISION DEVICES

2-50. Snipers use NVDs to accomplish their mission during limited visibility operations. They can use NVDs as observation aids, weapons sights, or both. First- and second-generation NVDs amplify the ambient light to provide an image of the observed area or target. These NVDs require target illumination (with the exception of the NADS 750); they will not function in total darkness because they do not project their own light source. NVDs work best on bright, moonlit nights. When there is no light or the ambient light level is low (as in heavy vegetation), the use of artificial or infrared (IR) light improves the NVD's performance.

2-51. Fog, smoke, dust, hail, or rain limit the range and decrease the resolution of NVDs. NVDs do not allow the sniper to see through objects in the field of view. The sniper will experience the same range restrictions when viewing dense wood lines as he would when using other optical sights.

2-52. Initially, a sniper may experience eye fatigue when viewing for prolonged periods. He should limit initial exposure to 10 minutes, followed by a 15-minute rest period. After several periods of viewing, he can safely extend the observation time limit. To help maintain continuous observation and to reduce eye fatigue, the sniper should often alternate his viewing eyes.

Night Vision Sight, AN/PVS-2

2-53. The AN/PVS-2 is a first-generation NVD (Figure 2-13). It can resolve images in low, ambient light conditions better than second-generation NVDs. However, first-generation NVDs are larger and heavier. Characteristics of an AN/PVS-2 include the following:

- Length: 18.5 inches.
- Width: 3.34 inches.
- Weight: 5 pounds.
- Magnification: 4x.
- Range: varies depending on ambient light conditions.
- Field of view: 171 mils.
- Focus range: 4 meters to infinity.

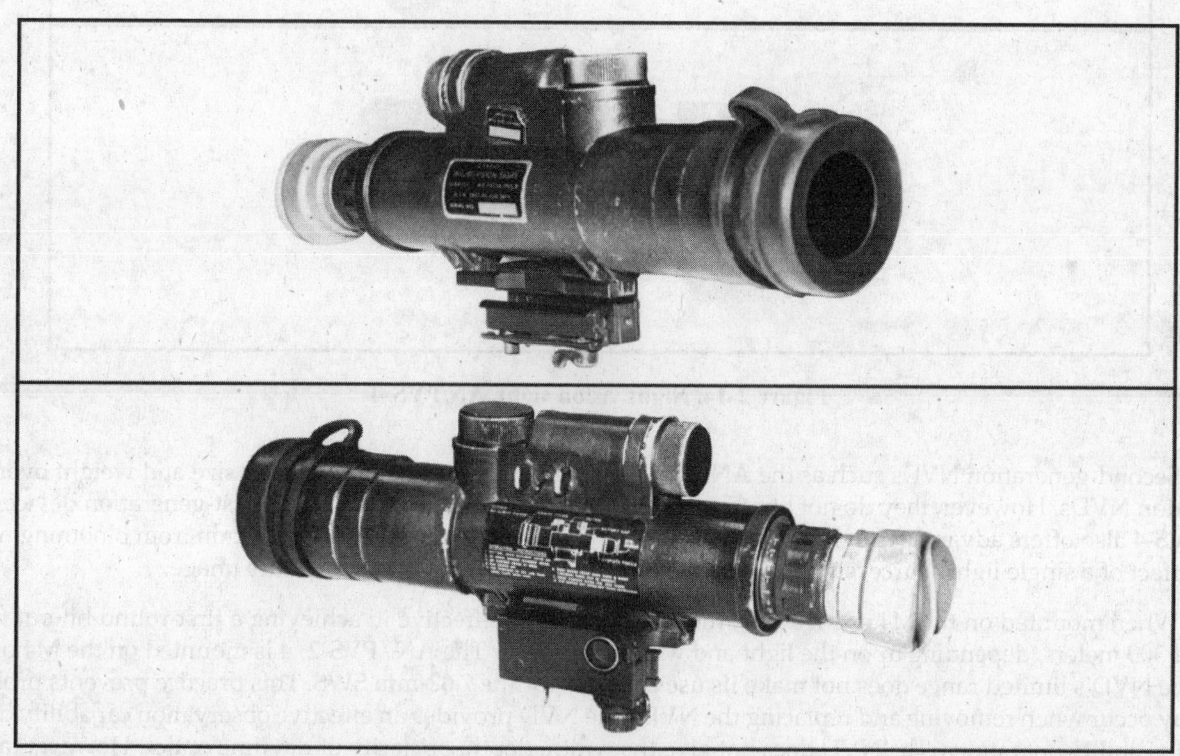

Figure 2-13. Night vision sight, AN/PVS-2

Night Vision Sight, AN/PVS-4

2-54. The AN/PVS-4 is a portable, battery-operated, electro-optical instrument that can be used for visual observation or weapon-mounted for precision fire at night (Figure 2-14). The sniper can detect and determine distant targets through the unique capability of the sight to amplify reflected ambient light (moon, stars, or sky glow). The sight is passive; thus, it is free from enemy detection by visual or electronic means. With the correct adapter bracket, the sniper can mount this sight on the M4, M16, M21, or M24. Characteristics of the AN/PVS-4 are as follows:

- Length: 12 inches.
- Width: 3.75 inches.
- Weight: 3.5 pounds.
- Magnification: 3.6x.
- Range: 400 meters/starlight, 600 meters/moonlight, for a man-sized target.
- Field of view: 258 mils.
- Focus range: 20 feet to infinity.

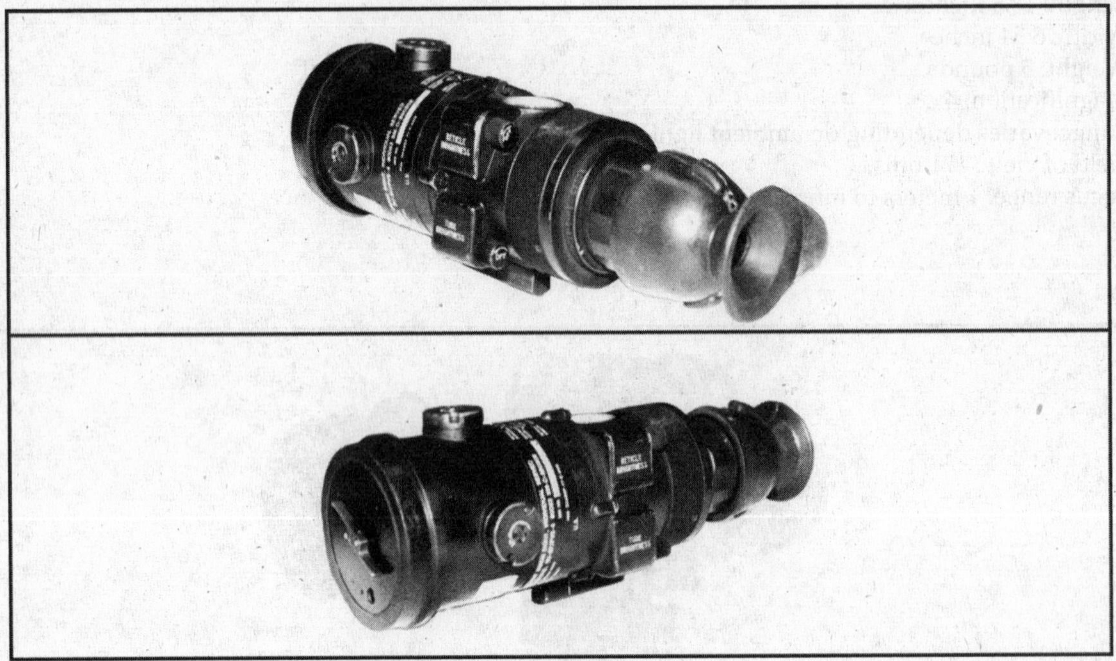

Figure 2-14. Night vision sight, AN/PVS-4

2-55. Second-generation NVDs such as the AN/PVS-4 possess the advantage of smaller size and weight over first-generation NVDs. However, they do not possess the extreme low-light capability of the first-generation devices. The AN/PVS-4 also offers advantages of internal adjustments, changeable reticles, and protection from blooming, which is the effect of a single light source, such as a flare or streetlight, overwhelming the entire image.

2-56. When mounted on the M4 or M16 rifle, the AN/PVS-2/4 is effective in achieving a first-round hit out to and beyond 300 meters, depending upon the light and wind conditions. The AN/PVS-2/4 is mounted on the M4 or M16 since the NVD's limited range does not make its use practical for the 7.62-mm SWS. This practice prevents problems that may occur when removing and replacing the NVD. The NVD provides an effective observation capability during limited visibility operations. The NVD does not give the width, depth, or clarity of daytime optics. However, a well-trained sniper can see enough to analyze the tactical situation, detect enemy targets, and engage targets effectively. The sniper team uses the AN/PVS-2/4 to—

- Enhance night observation capability.
- Locate and suppress hostile fire at night.
- Deny enemy movement at night.
- Demoralize the enemy with effective first-round hits at night.

2-57. When given a choice between AN/PVS-2 and AN/PVS-4, snipers should weigh their advantages and disadvantages. The proper training and knowledge with NVDs cannot be overemphasized. The results obtained with NVDs will be directly attributable to the sniper's skill and experience in their use. Generally the PVS-2 is better for very low-light observation while the PVS-4 is better for built-up areas.

KN200(PVS-9)/KN250(PVS-9A) Image Intensifier (SIMRAD)

2-58. The KN200/250 image intensifier (Figure 2-15) increases the use of the existing M3A telescope. It is mounted as an add-on unit and enables the sniper to aim through the eyepiece of the day sight both during day and night—an advantage not achieved with traditional types of NVDs. Sudden illumination of the scene does not affect sighting abilities. Depending on date of manufacture, these image intensifiers can be either second- or third-generation image intensifier tubes. Due to their unique design, the exact position of the image intensifier relative to the day sight is not critical. The mounting procedures take only a few seconds; however, boresighting will be required. The KN200/250 technical specifications include—

- Weight (excluding bracket): 1.4 kg/0.7 kg
- Magnification: 1x, +/− 1 percent.
- Field of view: 177/212 mils.
- Focus range: Fixed and adjustable.
- Objective lens: 100 mm/80 mm.
- Mounting tolerance: +/− 1 degree.
- Battery life: 40 hours at 25 degrees centigrade (C) with two AA alkaline cells.
- Operating temperature: −30 to +50 degrees C.

Figure 2-15. KN200(PVS-9)/KN250(PVS-9A) image intensifier (SIMRAD)

NADS 750, 850, 1000 Night Vision Imaging System

2-59. This system (Figures 2-16 and 2-17) is similar to the PVS-9 SIMRAD system as far as mounting and use. Its characteristics are as follows:

- Size (approximately): 4.5 × 7.1; 4.7 × 7.76; 5.8 × 12.1 inches.
- Weight: 2.6; 5.0; 6 lbs.

- Magnification: 1x.
- Field of view: 238, 210, and 120 mils.
- Immersion: 66 feet/2 hours.
- Tube type: Generation (Gen) III.
- Battery life: 24 hours at 73 degrees centigrade (C) with two AA alkaline cells.
- Illuminator: 750 only.

Figure 2-16. NADS 750, 850, and 1000

Figure 2-17. NADS 750 with AN/PEQ 2 IR pointer/illuminator mounted on SR-25

AN/PVS-10 Integrated Sniper Day/Night

2-60. This system (Figure 2-18) requires the sniper to remove his standard day scope and replace it with this system. The system splits the available light and directs part of the light to the daytime scope and part of the light to the night portion of the scope. Then the scope's daytime and nighttime portions do not receive the full available light and thus are not as efficient as stand-alone systems. Characteristics include the following:

- Weight: 4.9 pounds (lbs)/5.5 lbs.
- Magnification: 8.5/12.2x.
- Field of view: 35/26 mils.
- Tube types: Gen II, III, and III+.
- Batteries: 2 AA alkaline cells.

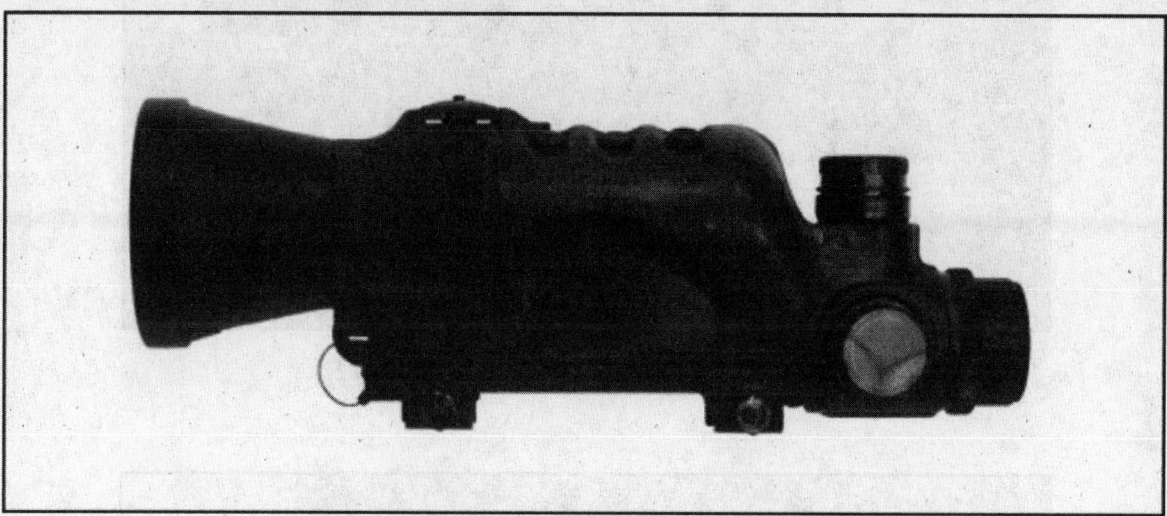

Figure 2-18. AN/PVS-10 sniper day/night scope

Model 007 "Universal Clip-On" Augmenting Weapon Night Sight

2-61. This clip-on sight (Figures 2-19 and 2-20) is similar to the SIMRAD and NADS. The sight clips onto the front of the day scope through a mounting system attached to the front scope-ring mount. The major difference is the size and weight of the system. Characteristics include the following:

- Magnification: 1x.
- Weight: 1.5 lbs.
- Length (approximately): 6 inches.
- Tube type: Gen III.
- Batteries: 2 AA alkaline cells.
- Boresight deviation upon mounting: < 1 MOA.

AN/PVS-17 Mini Night Vision Sight

2-62. This system (Figure 2-21) is designed for the M4 SOPMOD 2 Project and is easily adapted to the M24 for close-in urban work. The sniper must remove the day scope to mount and use this sight. Characteristics include the following:

- Magnification: 2.25x, 4.5x.
- Reticule: internal dot (presently).
- Tube types: Gen III and IV.
- Battery: 1 AA alkaline cell.
- Mount system: single-point, quick-release; two-point.

AN/PAS-13 Thermal Weapons Sight

2-63. The sniper can use this passive thermal imager (Figure 2-22) to detect targets in day or night conditions. It is also effective during periods of fog, rain, dust, or other conditions that will hinder the light amplification type of

Figure 2-19. Universal clip-on with AN/PEQ 2

Figure 2-20. Universal clip-on mounted on SR-25

Figure 2-21. AN/PVS-17 mini night vision sight

NVDs. The tube type is a Gen II forward-looking infrared (FLIR) and the reticle pattern is the same as the M3A day scope when the sniper uses the PAS-13 Heavy.

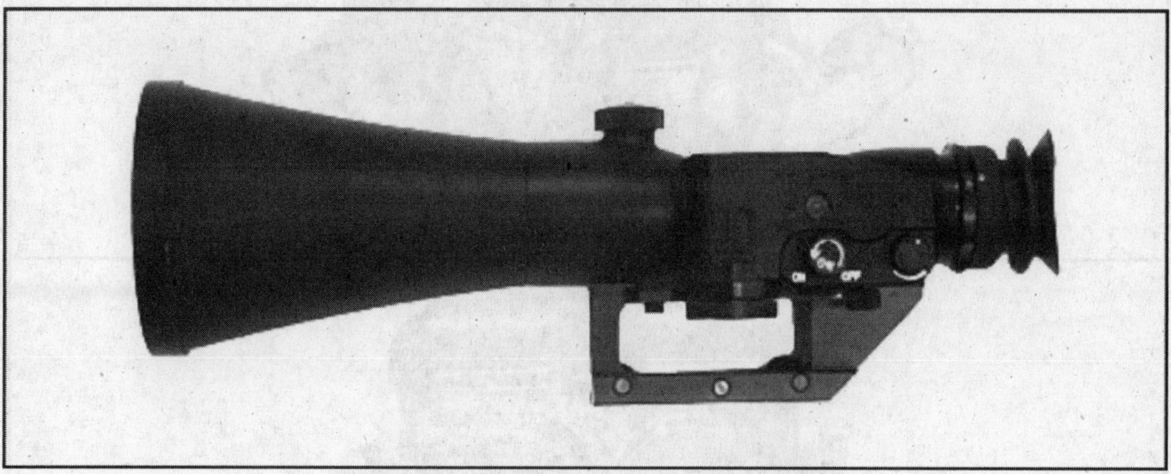

Figure 2-22. AN/PAS-13 thermal sight

Night Vision Goggles, AN/PVS-5

2-64. The AN/PVS-5 (Figure 2-23) is a lightweight, passive night vision system that gives the sniper team another means of observing an area during limited visibility. The sniper normally carries the goggles because the observer has the M16 mounted with the NVD. The design of the goggles makes viewing easier. However, the same limitations that apply to the night sight also apply to the goggles.

2-65. The sniper can use the AN/PVS-7 (Figure 2-24) instead of the AN/PVS-5 goggles. These goggles provide better resolution and viewing ability than the AN/PVS-5. The AN/PVS-7 series come with a head-mount assembly that allows them to be mounted in front of the face to free both hands. The sniper can also use the goggles without the mount assembly for handheld viewing. TM 11-5855-262-10-1, *Operator's Manual for Night Vision Goggles*, provides additional technical information.

AN/PVS-14 Monocular Night Vision Device

2-66. The AN/PVS-14 (Figure 2-25) is the replacement monocular for the PVS-7. The sniper can use either the 1x as a movement device or the 3x to 5x with an adapter as an observation device. The sniper can wear this NVD with a Kevlar helmet or a head harness for soft headgear. The NVD can also be handheld. It has a Gen III tube with a 40-degree field of view, and uses 2 AA batteries for power.

RANGE FINDERS

2-67. The sniper must use special equipment to reduce the possibility of detection. When necessary, he uses the following equipment to better determine the range to the target and provide greater accuracy upon engagement.

Laser Observation Set, AN/GVS-5

2-68. Depending on the mission, snipers can use the AN/GVS-5 to determine increased distances more accurately. The AN/GVS-5 is an individually operated, handheld, distance-measuring device designed for distances from 200 to 9,990 meters (with an error of +/– 10 meters). A sniper can use it to measure distances by firing an IR beam at a target and measuring the time the reflected beam takes to return to him. The AN/GVS-5 then displays the target distance, in meters, inside the viewer. The reticle pattern in the viewer is graduated in 10-mil increments and has display lights to indicate low battery and multiple target hits. If the beam hits more than one target, the display gives a reading of

Figure 2-23. Night vision goggles, AN/PVS-5

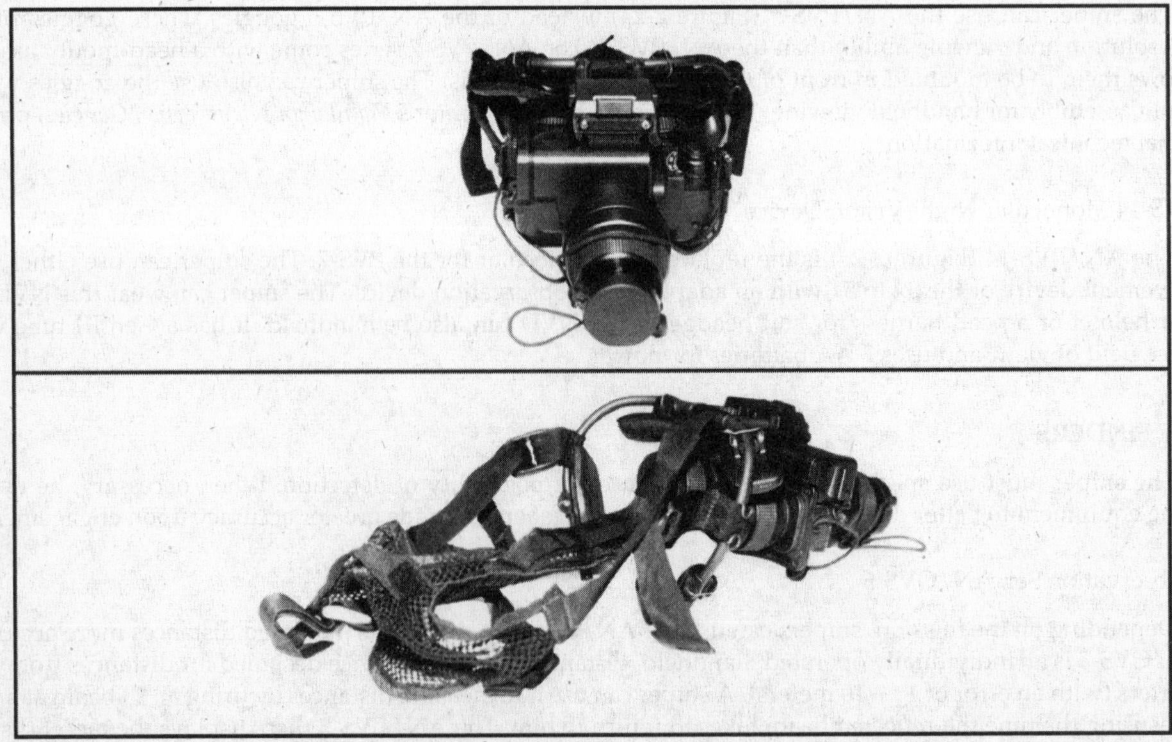

Figure 2-24. Night vision goggles, AN/PVS-7 series

Figure 2-25. AN/PVS-14 Mounted with helmet clip

Figure 2-26. Mini-eyesafe laser infrared observation set, AN/PVS-6

the closest target hit. The beam that is fired from the set poses a safety hazard; therefore, snipers that plan to use this equipment should be thoroughly trained in its safe operation. The AN/GVS-5 has two filters (red and yellow) that shorten the range of the range finder. The yellow filter is considered safe when viewed through other filtered optics. The red is considered eye safe. The sniper should use the yellow filter when operating near friendly forces.

Mini-Eyesafe Laser Infrared Observation Set, AN/PVS-6

2-69. The AN/PVS-6 (Figure 2-26) contains a mini-eyesafe laser range finder, nonrechargeable BA-6516/U batteries, lithium thionyl chloride, carrying case, shipping case, tripod, lens cleaning compound and tissues, and an operator's manual. The laser range finder is the major component of the AN/PVS-6. It is lightweight, individually operated, and handheld or tripod-mounted. It can accurately determine ranges from 50 to 9,995 meters in 5-meter increments and display the range in the eyepiece. The ranger finder can also be mounted with and boresighted to the AN/TAS-6 or other comparable long-range night observation device.

SNIPER TEAM EQUIPMENT

2-70. The sniper team carries only the equipment and supplies needed to complete the mission within an estimated time. In some instances, it may have to rely on mission support sites or caches to replenish supplies and equipment for either its operational role or survival. The following paragraphs explain the standard, additional, and special equipment that a sniper team may require.

STANDARD

2-71. The sniper team conducts a mission, enemy, terrain and weather, troops and support available, time available, and civil considerations (METT-TC) analysis to determine the type and quantity of equipment to carry. Due to unique mission requirements, each team should be equipped with the following:

- M24 SWS (with 100 rounds M118 or M852 ammunition).
- Sniper's data book, mission logbook, range cards, wind tables, and range adjustments for slope.
- Service rifle (w/NVD as appropriate) (with 200 to 210 rounds ammunition).
- M144 or M49 20x spotting scope with M15 tripod (or equivalent 15 to 20x fixed power scope or 15 to 45x zoomed spotting scope).
- Binoculars (preferably 7 power, 50 mm objective lens with mil scale).
- M9/service pistols (with 45 rounds 9-mm ball ammunition).
- NVDs (as needed).
- Radios.
- Camouflaged clothing (constructed by the sniper).
- Compass (the M2 is preferable).
- Watches (waterproof with sweep-second hand and luminous dial).
- Maps and sector sketch material.
- Special mission equipment.

ADDITIONAL

2-72. There is no limit to the diversity of equipment that the sniper may use for normal or special missions. After careful mission analysis, the sniper should select only what is necessary. Too much equipment can seriously hamper the sniper's mobility, endurance, and stealth. The next few paragraphs explain the recommended additional equipment for the team.

Sling

2-73. The sniper, to aid in firing the rifle if a solid rest is not available, uses the standard issue web sling or leather sling. However, the leather sling should be the primary sling used. A modified M14 web sling is superior to the leather sling in durability and easy use. The sniper must modify the sling for use but it is an easy modification. The M16 web sling is not suitable for sling-supported positions.

Ghillie Suit

2-74. The ghillie suit is a camouflage uniform that is covered with irregular strips of colored burlap or similar material. These strips are folded in half and sewn mainly to the back, legs, arms, and shoulders of the suit. The strips are then frayed or cut to break up the outline of the sniper and aid in blending him in with the surrounding vegetation or terrain. A close-net veil can be sewn to the back of the neck and shoulders of the suit and draped over the head when needed. The veil will help break the outline of the head, conceal the lens of the telescope, and contain the ejected brass cases.

NOTE

When deploying with regular troops, snipers should wear the uniform of those personnel. Wearing the ghillie suit in these situations will spotlight the snipers and make them a prime target to the enemy, especially enemy snipers.

Maintenance Equipment

2-75. During long and short missions, snipers never leave maintenance equipment in the rear area. Maintenance equipment can include weapon and optical cleaning equipment for short missions, or it can include tools and replacement parts for missions in protracted environments such as FID or UW operations. The amount and type of maintenance equipment for a mission will also be governed by support maintenance available in any given operations area.

Calculator

2-76. The sniper team needs a pocket-sized calculator to compute distances when using the mil-relation formula. Solar-powered calculators usually work fine, but under limited visibility conditions, battery power may be preferred. If the sniper must use a battery-powered calculator in low-light conditions, he should make sure it has a lighted display. However, he should never rely solely on a calculator.

Other Items

2-77. Knives, bayonets, entrenching tools, wire cutters, pruning shears, and rucksacks will be used as the mission and common sense dictate. The sniper team best determines which particular items will be carried for each given mission.

SPECIAL

2-78. Snipers use special equipment to meet a specific purpose or to complete unique mission requirements. Because sniper missions can vary, the special equipment that snipers use should have three basic characteristics: durability, simplicity, and accuracy. Special equipment can include weapons, suppressors, or surveillance devices.

Weapons

2-79. The weapons must be durable enough to withstand the conditions encountered in combat, simple enough to minimize failure, yet accurate enough for sniping. The weapons should be capable of grouping consistently into 2 MOAs out to 600 meters (approximately a 33-centimeter group). Various modifications to the weapons themselves or selection of certain types of ammunition may improve the accuracy of the following special weapons:

- Bolt-action target rifles.
- Foreign sniper weapons (procured out of need, compatibility, or to provide a foreign "signature").
- Large-bore, long-range sniper rifles.
- Telescope-mounted handguns (for example, XP100 or the Thompson Center Contender) for easy concealment or used as light multimission SWSs.
- Suppressed weapons.

Suppressors

2-80. The suppressor is a device that snipers can use to deceive observers (forward of the sniper) as to the exact location of the weapon and the sniper. This deception disguises the signature in two ways. First, it reduces the muzzle blast to such an extent that it becomes inaudible a short distance from the weapon. This reduction makes the exact sound location extremely difficult, if not impossible, to locate. Secondly, it suppresses the muzzle flash at night, making visual location equally difficult. Using the suppressor is critical during night operations.

2-81. When the sniper fires a rifle or any high-muzzle velocity weapon, the resulting noise is produced by two separate sources. These sounds are the muzzle blast and the ballistic crack (sonic boom) produced by the bullet:

- The muzzle blast appears when the blast wave (created by the high velocity gases) escapes into the atmosphere behind the bullet. This noise is relatively easy to locate as it emanates from a single, fixed point.
- Ballistic crack results from the supersonic speed of the bullet that compresses the air ahead of it exactly in the same fashion as a supersonic jet creates a sonic boom. The only difference is that the smaller bullet produces a sharp crack rather than a large overpressure wave with its resulting louder shock wave.

Depending on distance and direction from the weapon, the two noises may sound as one or as two different sounds. The further from the weapon the observer is, the more separate the sounds; for example, 600 meters—1 second elapses between the two.

2-82. Unlike the muzzle noise that emanates from a fixed point, the ballistic crack radiates backwards in a conical shape, similar to a bow wave from a boat, from a point slightly ahead of the moving bullet. Thus, the sonic boom created by the supersonic bullet moves at the velocity of the bullet away from the muzzle noise and in the direction of the target. Location and identification of the initial source of the shock wave is extremely difficult because the moving wave strikes the ear at nearly 90 degrees to the point of origin. Attention is thus drawn to the direction from which the wave is coming rather than toward the firing position (Figure 2-27).

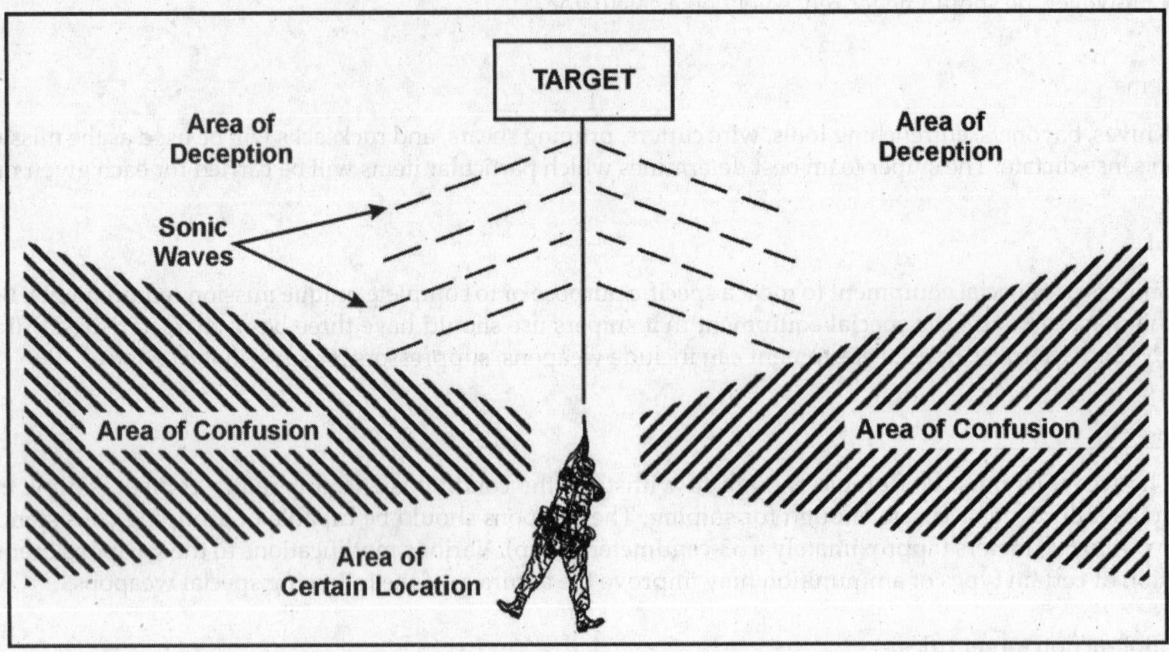

Figure 2-27. Deception caused by the sonic waves of the bullet breaking the speed of sound

Surveillance Devices

2-83. In some circumstances, a sniper may use special surveillance devices that will normally involve adding weight and bulk, which can limit his mobility. The sniper should consider using these devices mostly for fixed peacekeeping or Perimeter Force Protection roles. The following paragraphs explain a few of these devices.

2-84. **Single-Lens-Reflector (SLR), Digital, and Video Cameras**. Snipers spend more time observing than shooting. Collecting and reporting intelligence are critical tasks. SLR and digital cameras are important tools that significantly enhance the sniper's ability to meet intelligence collection requirements. Video surveillance kits are being fielded to the SF groups to support operations in urban and rural AOs. These kits are integrated with the sniper's communications package so that sniper teams can provide commanders with "near-real-time" video and still images of EEI. This ability to pass images significantly enhances a sniper team's utility and lethality.

2-85. **100-mm Team Spotting Scope.** This device is a standard team scope for most marksmanship units and should be used for sniper training purposes. The scope's increased field of view will greatly enhance the team's observation capability in static positions. While the Unertl is considered standard, the newer 100-mm Optolyth is clearer and more compact, as well as durable.

2-86. **Crew-Served NVDs**. Snipers commonly use these devices in conjunction with crew-served weapons (typified by the AN/TVS-5) or night observation (typified by the AN/TVS-4). These NVDs offer a significant advantage over their smaller counterparts in surveillance, target acquisition, and night observation (STANO). However, their weight and bulk normally limit their use to static operations.

2-87. **Thermal Imagery**. This relatively new tool is now available to the sniper team. Equipment such as the AN/PAS-7 offers a thermal imagery device in a portable package. Thermal imagery can enhance STANO operations when used with more conventional equipment, or it can provide continuous surveillance when ambient light conditions (such as starlight and moonlight) do not exist for light-intensification devices. Thermal devices offer an option when there is an abundance of light that would cause white out conditions with NVDs.

2-88. **Radars and Sensors.** Just as the sniper's surveillance operations should be integrated into the overall surveillance plan, the sniper should strive to make maximum use of any surveillance radars and sensors in the area of operation. Snipers will normally not use these items themselves, but through coordination with using or supporting units. The snipers may be able to use the target data that the radars and sensors can acquire. However, they must keep in mind that these devices are subject to human error, interpretation, and enemy countermeasures. Total reliance on the intelligence data obtained by using these devices could prove detrimental or misleading.

CARE AND CLEANING OF THE SNIPER WEAPON SYSTEM

2-89. Maintenance is any measure taken to keep the system in top operating condition. It includes inspection, repair, cleaning, and lubrication. Inspection reveals the need for the other measures. The sniper couples his cleaning with a program of detailed inspections for damage or defects. He uses the following maintenance items:

- One-piece plastic-coated caliber .30 cleaning rod with jags (36 inches).
- Field cleaning kit such as Kit and caboodle cleaning cable-with Muzzle Guard-Field.
- Bronze-bristled bore brushes (calibers .30 and .45).
- Muzzle guide.
- Cleaning patches (small and large sizes).
- Shooter's Choice Bore Solvent (SCBS) carbon cleaner.
- Sweets 7.62 Copper Remover (copper cleaner). (Shooter's Choice Copper Remover is the second choice.)
- Shooter's Choice Rust Prevent.
- Cleaner, lubricant, preservative (CLP). (Note: Do not use lubricating oil, weapons semifluid, Breakfree, or WD40 in the bore.)
- Rifle grease.
- Bore guide (long action).
- Q-tips or swabs.
- Pipe cleaners.
- Medicine dropper.
- Shaving brush.
- Toothbrush.
- Pistol cleaning rod.
- Rags.
- Camel-hair brush.
- Lens paper.
- Lens cleaning fluid or denatured alcohol.

NOTE
Never place cleaning fluid directly on lens surface. Use lens paper or cleaning pencil and place cleaning fluids on the tissue or pen.

WHEN TO CLEAN

2-90. Snipers must regularly inspect any weapon sheltered in garrison and infrequently used to detect dirt, moisture, and signs of corrosion and must clean it accordingly. However, a weapon in use and subject to the elements requires no inspection for cleanliness. The fact that it's used and exposed is sufficient evidence that it requires repeated cleaning and lubrication.

Before Firing

2-91. The sniper must always clean the rifle before firing. Firing a weapon with a dirty bore or chamber will multiply and speed up any corrosive action. Oil in the bore and chamber of even a clean rifle will cause pressures to vary and first-round accuracy will suffer. Hydrostatic pressure will also cause cases to blow or jam in the chamber. The sniper should clean and dry the bore and chamber before departing on a mission and use extreme care to keep the rifle clean and dry en route to the objective area. Before the sniper fires the weapon, he should ensure that the bore and chamber are still clean, dry, and no strings are left from the cleaning patches. Firing a rifle with oil or moisture in the bore will cause a puff of smoke that can disclose the firing position. It can also cause damage to the weapon system.

After Firing

2-92. The sniper must clean the rifle after it has been fired, because firing produces deposits of primer fouling, powder ashes, carbon, and metal fouling. Although modern ammunition has a noncorrosive primer that makes cleaning easier, the primer residue can still cause rust if not removed. Firing leaves two major types of fouling that requires different solvents to remove: **carbon** fouling and **copper jacket** fouling. The sniper must clean the rifle within a reasonable interval—a matter of hours—after a cessation of firing. Common sense should preclude the question as to the need for cleaning between rounds. Repeated firing will not damage the weapon if it is properly cleaned before the first round.

2-93. The M24 SWS will be disassembled only when absolutely necessary, not for daily cleaning. An example would be to remove an obstruction that is stuck between the stock and the barrel. When disassembly is required, the recommended procedure is to—

- Place the weapon so that it is pointing in a safe direction.
- Ensure the safety is in the "S" position.
- Remove the bolt assembly.
- Loosen the two mounting ring nuts (Figure 2-28) on the telescope and remove the telescope. (Not necessary when only cleaning the weapon.)
- Remove the two trigger action screws (Figure 2-29).
- Lift the stock from the barrel assembly.

> **NOTE**
> Always reassemble the weapon in the same sequence as the last time it was reassembled. This will keep the weapon zeroed to within .5 MOA. For further disassembly, refer to TM 9-1005-306-10.

HOW TO CLEAN

2-94. The sniper cleans the rifle by laying it on a cleaning table or other flat surface with the muzzle away from the body and the sling down. He makes sure not to strike the muzzle or telescopic sight on the table. The cleaning cradle is ideal for holding the rifle, or the sniper can use the bipod to support the weapon.

2-95. The sniper should always clean the bore from the chamber toward the muzzle, attempting to keep the muzzle lower than the chamber to prevent bore cleaner from running into the receiver or firing mechanism. When in garrison, he should always use the chamber guide to move the one-piece steel rod from chamber to muzzle. When in the field, he should use the muzzle guide and insert the one-piece cable down the bore to the chamber and pull the patches through to the muzzle. The sniper must be careful not to get solvents between the receiver and the stock. Solvents soften the bedding compound. When the rifle is fired, the action shifts in the soft bedding, which decreases accuracy and increases wear and tear on the bedding material. Solvents contribute to the accumulation of debris between the action and the stock interfering with barrel harmonics.

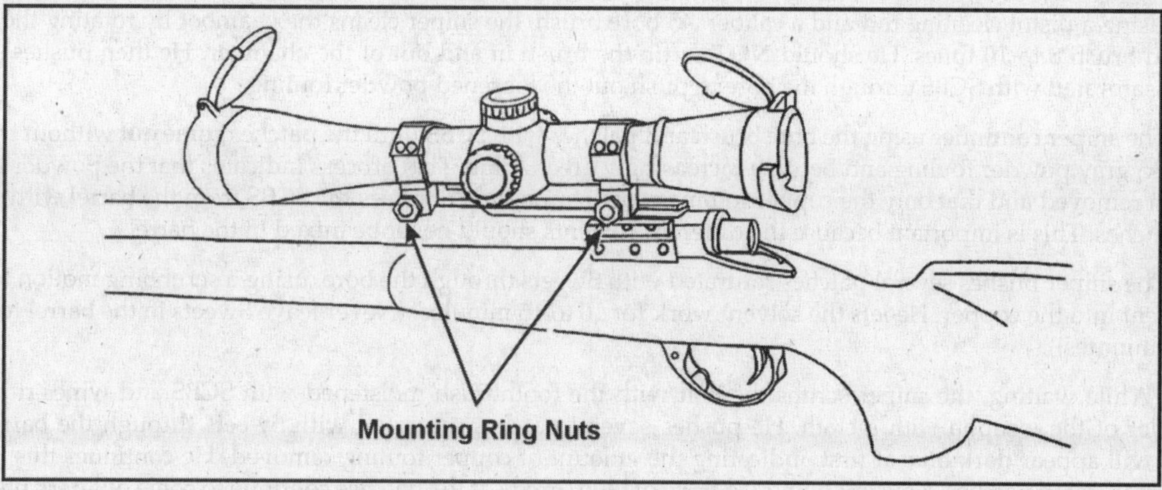

Figure 2-28. Location of the mounting ring nuts on the M24 SWS

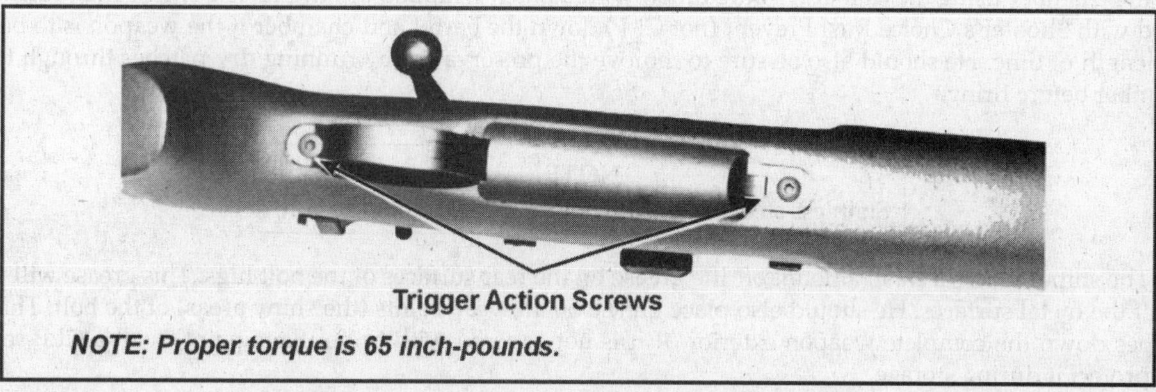

Figure 2-29. Location of the trigger action screws

> **NOTE**
>
> The sniper should always use a bore guide to keep the cleaning rod centered in the bore during the cleaning process.

2-96. The sniper first pushes several patches saturated with SCBS through the barrel to loosen the powder fouling and begin the solvent action on the copper jacket fouling. He then saturates the bronze-bristled brush (**Never use stainless steel bore brushes—they will scratch the barrel!**) with SCBS (shake bottle regularly to keep the ingredients mixed) using the medicine dropper to prevent contamination of the SCBS. He runs the bore brush through the barrel approximately 20 times. He makes sure that the bore brush passes completely through the barrel before reversing its direction; otherwise the bristles can break off.

> **NOTE**
>
> The sniper should never stick the bore brush into the bottle of SCBS. This will contaminate the fluid.

2-97. Using a pistol cleaning rod and a caliber .45 bore brush, the sniper cleans the chamber by rotating the patch-wrapped brush 8 to 10 times. He should **NOT** scrub the brush in and out of the chamber. He then pushes several patches saturated with SCBS through the bore to push out the loosened powder fouling.

2-98. The sniper continues using the bore brush and patches with SCBS until the patches come out without traces of the black/gray powder fouling and become increasingly green/blue. This process indicates that the powder fouling has been removed and that only the copper fouling remains. He then removes the SCBS from the barrel with several clean patches. This is important because the different solvents should never be mixed in the barrel.

2-99. The sniper pushes several patches saturated with Sweets through the bore, using a scrubbing motion to work the solvent into the copper. He lets the solvent work for 10 to 15 minutes. (Never leave Sweets in the barrel for more than 30 minutes!)

2-100. While waiting, the sniper scrubs the bolt with the toothbrush moistened with SCBS and wipes down the remainder of the weapon with a cloth. He pushes several patches saturated with Sweets through the barrel. The patches will appear dark blue at first, indicating the amount of copper fouling removed. He continues this process until the saturated patches come out without a trace of blue/green. If the patches continue to come out dark blue after several treatments with Sweets, he should run patches with SCBS through the bore deactivating the sweets and start the cleaning process over again.

2-101. When the barrel is completely clean, the sniper then dries it with several tight fitting patches. He should also dry out the chamber using the caliber .45 bore brush with a patch wrapped around it. The sniper then runs a patch saturated with Shooter's Choice Rust Prevent (not CLP) down the barrel and chamber if the weapon is to be stored for any length of time. He should also be sure to remove the preservative by running dry patches through the bore and chamber before firing.

NOTE

Stainless steel barrels are not immune from corrosion.

2-102. The sniper places a small amount of rifle grease on the rear surfaces of the bolt lugs. This grease will prevent galling of the metal surfaces. He should also place grease on all wear points (the shiny areas) of the bolt. The sniper then wipes down the complete weapon exterior (if it is not covered with camouflage paint) with a CLP-saturated cloth to protect it during storage.

Barrel Break-in Procedure

2-103. To maximize barrel life and accuracy and to minimize the cleaning requirement, the sniper must use the following barrel break-in procedure. This procedure is best done when the SWS is new or newly rebarreled. The break-in period "laps-in" the barrel by polishing the barrel surface under heat and pressure. The sniper must first completely clean the barrel of all fouling, both powder and copper. He dries the barrel and fires one round. He then completely cleans the barrel using Shooter's Choice Solvent, followed by Sweets 7.62 copper remover. Again, the barrel must be completely cleaned and another round fired. This procedure of firing one shot, then cleaning, must be done for a total of 10 rounds. After the 10th round, the sniper tests the SWS for groups by firing three-round shot groups, with a complete barrel cleaning between shot groups for a total of five shot groups (15 rounds total). The barrel comes from the factory with 60 test-fire rounds already through it. The barrel is now broken-in and will provide superior accuracy and a longer usable barrel life. It also will be easier to clean because the surface is smoother. Although the full accuracy potential may not be noticed until after 100 rounds or more have been fired, again, the sniper should clean the barrel at least every 100 rounds to maximize barrel life.

Storage

2-104. The M24 SWS should be properly stored to ensure it is protected and maintained at a specific level. The sniper should—

- Clear the SWS, close the bolt, and squeeze the trigger.
- Place all other items in the system case (M24).

- Transport the weapon in the system case during nontactical situations.
- Protect the weapon at all times during tactical movement.

OPTICAL EQUIPMENT MAINTENANCE

2-105. Dirt, rough handling, or abuse of optical equipment will result in inaccuracy and malfunction. When not in use during field conditions, the sniper should case the rifle and scope and cap the lenses.

Cleaning the Lenses

2-106. The sniper should coat the lenses with a special magnesium fluoride reflection-reducing material. The coat should be very thin and the sniper must take great care to prevent damaging the lenses. To remove dust, lint, or other foreign matter from the lens, he brushes it lightly with a clean camelhair brush.

2-107. The sniper must also remove oil or grease from all the optical surfaces. He applies a drop of lens cleaning fluid or denatured alcohol to a lens tissue and carefully wipes off the lens surface in circular motions, from the center to the outside edge. He dries off the lens with a clean lens tissue. In the field, if the proper supplies are not available, the sniper can breathe heavily on the glass and wipe with a soft, clean cloth.

Handling Telescopes

2-108. Telescopes are delicate instruments and the sniper must handle them with great care. The following precautions will prevent damage. The sniper should—

- Check the torque on all mounting screws periodically and always before any operation. He should also be careful not to change coarse windage adjustment.
- Keep lenses free from oil and grease and never touch them with the fingers. Body grease and perspiration can also injure them. Keep lenses capped.
- Not force elevation and windage screws or knobs.
- Not allow the telescope to remain in direct sunlight and avoid letting the sun's rays shine through the lens. Lenses magnify and concentrate sunlight into a pinpoint of intense heat, which is focused on the mil-scale reticle. This exposure may damage the telescope internally. Keep the lenses covered and the entire telescope covered when not firing or preparing to fire. Never use the rifle scope for observation purposes only.
- Avoid dropping the telescope or striking it with another object. This blow could damage it severely and permanently, as well as change the zero. When placing the weapon in the carrying case, he should place the scope away from the hinges. This will help protect the scope from vibration and dropping.
- Not allow just anyone to handle the equipment. The sniper or armorer should really be the only personnel that handle the telescope or any other sniper equipment.
- Once the scope is zeroed, note the reticle position on a bore scope grid for future reference.

WEAPON MAINTENANCE AND CARE

2-109. Maintenance is any measure that the sniper takes to keep the SWS in top operating condition. A sniper may have to operate in many different environments and every type requires him to care for his weapon in a specific manner. The following paragraphs explain each of these environments.

Cold Climates

2-110. In temperatures below freezing, the sniper must maintain and treat the rifle a specific way. He should—

- Always keep the rifle free of moisture and heavy oil (both will freeze) to prevent working parts from freezing or operating sluggishly.
- Store the rifle in a room with the temperature equal to the outside temperature.

- If the rifle is taken into a warm area, be sure to remove the condensation and thoroughly clean and dry the rifle before taking it into the cold. Otherwise, the condensation will cause icing on exposed metal parts and optics.
- Disassemble the firing pin, clean it thoroughly with a degreasing agent, and then lubricate it with CLP. Rifle grease will harden and cause the firing pin to fall sluggishly.

2-111. In extreme cold, the sniper must take the following care to avoid condensation and the congealing of oil on the weapon. He should—

- If not excessive, remove condensation by placing the instrument in a warm place. Not apply concentrated heat because it will cause expansion and damage.
- Blot moisture from the optics with a lens tissue or a soft, dry cloth.
- In cold temperatures, ensure the oil does not thicken and cause sluggish operation or failure. Remember that focusing parts are particularly sensitive to freezing oils.
- Remember that breathing will form frost, so he must clean the optical surfaces with lens tissue, preferably dampened lightly with lens cleaning fluid or denatured alcohol. Never apply the fluid directly to the glass.

Saltwater Exposure

2-112. Salt water and a saltwater atmosphere have extreme and very rapid corrosive effects on metal. During this type of exposure, the sniper must ensure the rifle is—

- Checked frequently and cleaned as often as possible, even if it means only lubricating the weapon.
- Always well lubricated, including the bore, except when actually firing.
- Thoroughly cleaned by running a dry patch through the bore before firing, if possible. To keep the patches dry, store them in a waterproof container.

Jungle Operations (High Humidity)

2-113. There is no standard jungle. The tropical area may be rain forests, secondary jungles, savannas, or saltwater swamps. When operating in any jungle environment, high temperatures, heavy rainfall, and oppressive humidity become a sniper's concern in maintaining his weapon. He should—

- Use more lubricant.
- Keep the rifle cased when not in use.
- Protect his rifle from rain and moisture whenever possible.
- Keep ammunition clean and dry.
- Clean the rifle, bore, and chamber daily.
- Keep the telescope caps on when not in use. If moisture or fungus develops inside the telescope, he should get a replacement.
- Keep cotton balls between lens caps and lens.
- Clean and dry the stock daily.
- Dry the carrying case and rifle in the sun whenever possible.
- Take an 8- or 9-inch strip of cloth and tie a knot in each end to protect the free-floating barrel of the weapon. Before going on a mission, he should slide the cloth between the barrel and stock all the way to the receiver and leave it there. When in position, he slides the cloth out, taking all restrictive debris and sand with it. (**This procedure should be done in all environments**.)

Desert Operations

2-114. Hot, dry climates are usually dusty and sandy areas. They are hot during daytime hours and cool during the nighttime. Dust and sand will get into the rifle and will cause malfunctions and excessive wear on component working surfaces through abrasive action during the firing operations. When operating in this type of environment, the sniper should—

- Keep the weapon completely dry and free of CLP and grease except on the rear of the bolt lugs.
- Keep the rifle free of sand by using a carrying sleeve or case when not in use.
- Protect the weapon by using a wrap. He should slide the wrap between the stock and barrel then cross over on top of the scope, cross under the weapon (over magazine), and secure. He can still place the weapon into immediate operation but all critical parts are covered. The sealed hard case is preferred in the desert if the situation permits.
- Keep the telescope protected from the direct rays of the sun.
- Keep ammunition clean and protected from the direct rays of the sun.
- Use a toothbrush to remove sand from the bolt and receiver.
- Clean the bore and chamber daily.
- Protect the muzzle and receiver from blowing sand by covering them with a clean cloth.
- Take an 8- or 9-inch strip of cloth and tie a knot in each end to protect the free-floating barrel of the weapon. Before going on a mission, he should slide the cloth between the barrel and stock all the way to the receiver and leave it there. When in position, he can slide the cloth out, taking all restrictive debris and sand with it. (**This procedure should be done in all environments**.)

Hot Climates and Saltwater Exposure

2-115. A hot climate and saltwater atmosphere may cause waves and wind. To keep these environmental hazards from affecting the optical equipment, a sniper must take precautionary measures. He should—

- Protect optics from hot, humid climates and saltwater atmosphere.
- **NOT** expose optical equipment to direct sunlight in a hot climate.
- In humidity and salt air, inspect and clean the optical instruments frequently to avoid rust and corrosion. A light film of oil is beneficial.
- Thoroughly dry and lightly oil optical instruments because perspiration from the hands is a contributing factor to rusting.

TROUBLESHOOTING THE SNIPER WEAPON SYSTEM

2-116. Table 2-1 lists some possible SWS malfunctions, causes, and corrective actions. If a malfunction is not correctable, the complete system must be sent to the proper maintenance / supply channel for return to the contractor. (TM 9-1005-306-10 provides further shipment information.)

Table 2-1. M24 SWS Malfunctions and corrective actions

Malfunctions	Causes	Corrections
Fail to Fire	Safety in "S" position.	Move safety to "F" position.
	Defective ammunition.	Eject round.
	Firing pin damaged.	Change firing pin assembly.
	Firing pin binds.	Change firing pin assembly.
	Firing pin protrudes.	Change firing pin assembly.
	Firing control out of adjustment.	Turn complete system in to the maintenance/supply channel for return to contractor.
	Trigger out of adjustment.	Turn in as above.
	Trigger binds on trigger guard.	Turn in as above.
	Trigger does not retract.	Turn in as above.
	Firing pin does not remain in cocked position with bolt closed.	Turn in as above.

Table 2-1. M24 SWS Malfunctions and Corrective Actions (*Continued*)

Malfunctions	Causes	Corrections
Bolt Binds	Action screw protrudes into bolt track.	Turn in as above.
	Scope base screw protrudes into bolt track.	Turn in as above.
Fail to Feed	Bolt override of cartridge.	Ensure bolt is pulled fully toward the rear.
	Cartridge stems chamber.	Pull bolt fully rearward; remove stemmed cartridge from ejection port area; reposition cartridge fully in the magazine.
	Magazine follower in backward.	Remove magazine spring and reinstall with long-leg follower.
	Weak or broken magazine spring.	Replace spring.
Fail to Eject	Broken ejector.	Turn complete weapon system in to the maintenance/ supply channel for return to contractor.
	Fouled ejector plunger.	Inspect and clean bolt face; if malfunction continues, turn in as above.
Fail to Extract	Broken extractor.	Turn in as above.
Bolt Release Fails	Bolt release mechanism fouled.	Disassemble rifle. Remove and clean bolt release mechanism. Lubricate with graphite lube.

CHAPTER 3

Marksmanship Training

The role of the SF sniper is to engage targets with precision rifle fire. A sniper's skill with a rifle is the most vital skill in the art of sniping. This skill is extremely perishable. Sniper marksmanship differs from basic rifle marksmanship only in the degree of expertise. The sniper, using basic and advanced marksmanship as building blocks, must adapt the conventional methods of firing to meet his unique requirements. The sniper must make first-round hits in a field environment under less than ideal conditions and become an expert in marksmanship. The fundamentals are developed into fixed and correct firing habits that become instinctive. This reaction is known as the "conditioning of the nervous system."

Snipers should maintain their proficiency at the following minimum standards:

- *90 percent first-round hits on stationary targets at ranges of 600 meters.*
- *50 percent first-round hits on stationary targets at ranges from 600 to 900 meters.*
- *70 percent first-round hits on moving targets at ranges to 300 meters.*
- *70 percent first-round hits on snap targets at ranges to 400 meters.*

FIRING POSITIONS

3-1. A sniper's firing position must be solid, stable, and durable. Solid—not influenced by outside factors; stable—for minimized movement of the weapon; and durable—able to hold the weapon and position for an extended period of time to accomplish the mission. Unlike the target shooter who must fire from different positions of varying stability to satisfy marksmanship rules, the sniper searches for the most stable position possible. He is not trying to see if he can hit the target; he must know he can hit the target. A miss could mean a failed mission or his life. A good position enables the sniper to relax and concentrate when preparing to fire.

3-2. Whether prone, kneeling, or standing, the sniper's position should be supported by firing rests or other means. Properly employed, the sling, in all but the standing position, provides a stable, supported position. Firing from a rest helps to minimize human factors such as heartbeat, muscular tension, and fatigue. A rest can support both the front and the rear of the rifle, as in the case of benchrest firing.

3-3. Regardless of the rest selected (tree, dirt, sandbag), the sniper will prevent any objects from contacting the barrel. During the firing process, the barrel vibrates like a tuning fork and any disturbance to this harmonic motion will result in an erratic shot. Also, a hard support will normally cause the rifle to change its POI. The sniper can help eliminate this problem by firing from objects of similar hardness. The sniper's hat, glove, or sock filled with sand or dirt can be placed between the rifle forestock and firing support to add consistency from range to combat. A support or rest greatly helps the sniper and he must use one whenever possible. Accuracy with a rifle is a product of consistency, and a rest aids consistency to firing positions.

3-4. On the battlefield, the sniper must assume a steady firing position with maximum use of cover and concealment. Considering the variables of terrain, vegetation, and the tactical situation, the sniper can use many variations of the basic positions. When assuming a firing position, he should adhere to the following basic rules:

- Use the prone position or its variations whenever possible because it is the most stable.
- Use any solid support available, when the bipod is not available or too short.
- Do not touch the support with the weapon's barrel since it interferes with the barrel harmonics and creates shot displacement.
- Use a cushion between the weapon and the support when not using the bipod.

- Do not allow the side of the weapon to rest against the support. This position will have an effect on the weapon during recoil and may affect the POI.
- Never cant the weapon while firing or aiming. The sniper should tilt his head to the weapon, not the weapon to his head.

ELEMENTS OF A GOOD POSITION

3-5. Three elements of a good position are bone support, muscular relaxation, and a natural point of aim (POA) on the aiming point. The following paragraphs explain each element.

Bone Support

3-6. Proper bone support is a learned process; only through practice (dry fire, live fire) will the sniper gain proficiency in this skill. Positions provide foundations for the rifle, and good foundations for the rifle are important to the sniper. When a sniper establishes a weak foundation (position) for the rifle, the position will not withstand the repeated recoil of the rifle in a string of rapid-fire shots or deliver the support necessary for precise firing. Therefore, the sniper will not be able to apply the marksmanship fundamentals properly.

Muscular Relaxation

3-7. The sniper must learn to relax as much as possible in the various firing positions. Undue muscle strain or tension causes trembling, which is transmitted to the rifle. However, in all positions, a certain amount of controlled muscular tension is needed. For example, in a rapid-fire position there should be pressure on the stock weld. Only through practice and achieving a natural POA will the sniper learn muscular relaxation.

Natural Point of Aim on the Aiming Point

3-8. In aiming, the rifle becomes an extension of the body. Therefore, the sniper must adjust the body position until the rifle points naturally at the target. To avoid using muscles to aim at a target, the sniper must shift his entire firing position to move his natural POA to the desired POI. The sniper reaches this point by—

- Assuming a good steady position.
- Closing both eyes and relaxing as if preparing to fire.
- Opening both eyes to see where the weapon is pointing.
- Leaving the nonfiring elbow in place and shifting the legs, torso, and firing elbow left or right.
- Repeating the process until the weapon points naturally at the desired POI.

If the sniper must push or pull the weapon onto target, he is not on his natural POA regardless of how small a movement is involved. Thus, muscle relaxation is not achieved, either.

3-9. The sniper can change the elevation of a natural POA by leaving the elbows in place and sliding the body forward or rearward. This movement causes the muzzle of the weapon to drop or rise, respectively. Minor adjustments to the natural POA can be made by the right leg (right-handed sniper). The sniper moves the lower leg in the opposite direction that he wants the sight to go. Another consideration is to maintain a natural POA after the weapon has been fired; therefore, proper bolt operation becomes critical. The sniper must practice reloading while in the prone position without removing the butt of the weapon from the firing shoulder.

COMMON FACTORS TO ALL POSITIONS

3-10. Establishing a mental checklist of steady position elements greatly enhances the sniper's ability to achieve a first-round hit. This checklist includes the factors discussed below that are inherent to a good firing position.

Nonfiring Hand

3-11. The sniper should use the nonfiring hand as a support. The nonfiring hand should either support the forestock or the butt of the weapon. The sniper should never grasp the forestock with the nonfiring hand. He should let the weapon rest in the nonfiring hand. If he grasps the weapon, the recoil and muscle tremor will cause erratic shots. If the sniper uses the nonfiring hand to support the butt, he should place the hand next to the chest and rest the tip of the butt on it. He then balls his hand into a fist to raise the butt or loosen the fist to lower the weapon's butt. The sniper can also use a firing sock in place of the fist. He must take care not to squeeze his fist as the trigger is squeezed. The muzzle will drop due to the rising of the stock causing a low shot. The sniper must not rest the nonfiring hand or fingers on the shooting side shoulder. Doing so will increase the transmission of the heartbeat to the weapon and destabilize the position.

Placement of the Rifle Butt

3-12. The sniper should place the rifle butt firmly in the pocket of the shoulder. Proper placement of the butt helps to steady the rifle and lessen recoil. The key to the correct rifle-butt method is consistent rearward pressure by the firing hand and correct placement in the shoulder. A hard hold versus a very light hold may change bullet impact. Again, consistency is important. A firm hold is necessary and using a shooting sock may cause a light hold and erratic groups.

Firing Hand

3-13. The sniper should grasp the small of the stock firmly but not rigidly with the firing hand. He then exerts pressure rearward, mainly with the middle and ring fingers of the firing hand. He should not "choke" the small of the stock. A choking-type grip can cause a twisting action during recoil. The sniper must not steer the rifle with the hand or shoulder. He should make large windage adjustments by altering the natural POA, not by leaning or steering the rifle, which will cause the rifle to steer in that direction during recoil. He can wrap his thumb over the top of the small of the stock and use it to grasp, or he can lay it alongside or on top of the stock in a relaxed manner. He places the index finger on the bottom or the trigger, ensuring that it does not touch the stock of the weapon and does not disturb the lay of the rifle when the trigger is pulled. The sniper must maintain steady rearward pressure on the weapon when firing. This tension will help steady the weapon.

Elbows

3-14. Each sniper must find a comfortable position that provides the greatest support. How a sniper uses his elbows will vary with each individual.

Stock Weld

3-15. The stock weld is the point of firm contact between the sniper's cheek and the stock. The sniper places his cheek on the stock in a position that gives proper eye relief. The stock weld will differ from position to position. However, due to the position of the telescope on the sniper rifle and the necessity to have eye relief, the sniper may not get a normal stock weld. An important factor is to get firm contact so that the head and weapon recoil as one unit, thereby facilitating rapid recovery. The point on the weapon should be a natural point where the sniper can maintain eye relief. The sniper should put his cheek in the same place on the stock with each shot. A change in stock weld tends to cause misalignment with the sights, thus creating misplaced shots. This change is more of a problem when using iron sights than with the telescopic sight that is properly adjusted.

3-16. Once the sniper obtains a spot or stock weld, he should use this same positioning for each shot. He must stay with the weapon, not lift his head from the stock during recoil, and maintain the spot or cheek weld. During the initial period of firing, the cheek may become tender and sore. To prevent this discomfort and to prevent flinching, the sniper should press the face firmly against the stock. Moving the head will only give the weapon a chance to build up speed before it impacts with the sniper's cheek.

TYPES OF POSITIONS

3-17. Due to the importance of delivering precision fire, the sniper makes maximum use of artificial support and eliminates any variable that may prevent adhering to the basic rules. He uses the following types of positions when engaging the target.

Prone Supported Position

3-18. The sniper first selects his firing position. He picks a position that gives the best observation, fields of fire, and concealment. He then assumes a comfortable prone position and prepares a firing platform for his rifle (Figure 3-1). The sniper should use the bipod whenever possible. The rifle platform should be as low to the ground as possible. The rifle should rest on the platform in a balanced position to the rear of the upper sling swivel and forward of the floor plate. The sniper must take care to ensure that the operating parts, the magazine, and the barrel do not touch the support, as contact will cause erratic shots. He then forms a wide, low bipod with his elbows. He grips the small of the stock with his firing hand, thumb over or alongside the small of the stock and the forefinger (just in front of the first joint) on the trigger, and pulls the butt of the rifle into his firing shoulder. He then places the nonfiring hand under the toe of the stock, palm down, and places the lower sling swivel into the web of the thumb and forefinger. The sniper can then adjust his fingers and thumb of the nonfiring hand by curling the fingers and thumb into a fist or relaxing the fingers and thumb and laying them flat. In this manner the sniper can raise or lower the barrel onto the target. He then relaxes into a comfortable supported position, removing his nonfiring hand from the stock when necessary to manipulate the scope. He can reload single rounds into the M24 with the firing hand while supporting the rifle at the toe of the stock with the nonfiring hand. When firing from this position, the sniper must have a clear field of fire because the shot may become erratic if the bullet strikes a leaf, grass, or a twig. For extended periods in the prone position, the sniper should cock the firing side leg up to relieve pressure off of the abdomen and reduce heartbeat pulse.

Figure 3-1. Prone supported position

Hawkins Position

3-19. The sniper uses this position when he needs a low silhouette. It is very useful when firing from a small depression, a slight rise in the ground, or from a roof (Figure 3-2). However, the sniper should make sure there are no obstructions above the boreline but below line of sight by removing the bolt and observing the target through the bore. This position is the steadiest of all firing positions. Concealment is also greatly aided by using the Hawkins position because the sniper is lying flat on the ground. The sniper will not use this position on level ground because he cannot raise the muzzle high enough to aim at the target.

3-20. The Hawkins position is similar to the prone supported position, except that the support of the weapon is provided by the nonfiring hand. The sniper grasps the front sling swivel with the nonfiring hand, forming a fist to support the front of the weapon. He makes sure the wrist and elbow are locked straight, and the recoil is taken up entirely by the nonfiring arm. Otherwise, his face will absorb the weapon's recoil. The sniper lies flat on the ground, either directly behind the rifle (Canadian version) or angled off to one side (British version). It will appear as though he is lying on the rifle. He can make minor adjustments in muzzle elevation by tightening or relaxing the fist of the nonfiring hand. If more elevation is required, he can place a support under the nonfiring fist.

3-21. If using the Canadian version, the sniper places the butt of the rifle in the shoulder. If using the British version, he tucks the butt under the armpit. The sniper should always use what is most comfortable.

Figure 3-2. Hawkins position

Sling-Supported Prone Position

3-22. The sniper faces the target squarely with the sling attached to the nonfiring arm above the bicep and lies down facing the target, legs straight to the rear (Figure 3-3). He extends the nonfiring elbow so it is in line with the body and the target and as far under the rifle as comfortable. With the firing hand, he pushes forward on the butt of the stock and fits it into the pocket of the shoulder. The sniper then places the firing side elbow down wherever it feels natural and grasps the grip of the stock, pulling it firmly into the shoulder. He lets his cheek rest naturally on the stock where he can see through the sights and acquire the target. He draws his firing side knee up to a comfortable position so as to take the weight off of the diaphragm. He can obtain a natural POA by adjusting the elevation. This can be done by sliding his body forward or rearward and adjusting his breathing.

Figure 3-3. Sling-supported prone position

Prone Backward Firing Position (Creedmore Firing Position)

3-23. The terrain or situation dictates when to use this firing position. It provides a higher angle of fire as required when firing uphill and other positions are inadequate. Also, the sniper can use this position when he must engage a target to his rear but cannot turn around because of the enemy situation or hide constrictions. The sniper assumes a comfortable position on his side with both legs bent for support and stability. He places the butt of the SWS into the pocket of his shoulder where it meets the armpit. He attempts to support his head for better stability and comfort. The small exit pupil of the telescope requires the sniper to maintain a solid hold and center the exit pupil in the field of the telescope to minimize the errors in sight alignment. This is an extreme firing position and not recommended under most circumstances.

Sitting Supported Position

3-24. To assume this position, the sniper prepares a firing platform for the rifle or rests the rifle on the raised portion of the position. If a platform is not available, then the sniper can use the observer to improvise this position (Figure 3-4). The sniper must ensure the barrel or operating parts do not touch the support. The sniper assumes a comfortable sitting position to the rear of the rifle, grasps the small of the stock with the firing hand, and places the butt of the rifle into the shoulder pocket. He places the nonfiring hand on the small of the stock to assist in getting a stock weld and the proper eye relief.

Figure 3-4. Sitting supported position

3-25. The sniper rests the elbows on the inside of the knees in a manner similar to the standard crossed-leg position. He changes position by varying the position of the elbows on the inside of the knees or by varying the body position. This position may be tiring; therefore, the firing mission should be alternated frequently between the sniper team members.

Sling-Supported Sitting Position

3-26. The sniper faces his body 30 degrees away from the target in the direction of the firing hand. He sits down and crosses his ankles so that the nonfiring side ankle is across the firing side ankle (Figure 3-5). He then adjusts the sling for the sitting position. The sniper uses the firing hand palm to place the butt of the stock into the shoulder while allowing the weapon to rest on the nonfiring hand. He uses his firing hand to pull the stock firmly into his shoulder. He rests his elbows inside the knees and leans his body forward. The sniper must not have direct contact between the points of the elbows and the knees. Avoiding direct contact ensures that the sniper uses bone support. He holds the stock high enough in the shoulder to require only a slight tilt of the head to acquire the sights, without canting the weapon. He lowers and raises the muzzle by moving the nonfiring hand forward and backward on the forestock. The sniper holds his breath when the sights are on the target.

3-27. The sniper assumes the crossed-leg position in the same way as the sitting position, but he faces 45 to 60 degrees away from the target and crosses his legs instead of his ankles.

Figure 3-5. Sling-supported sitting position

Supported Kneeling Position

3-28. The sniper uses the supported kneeling position when it is necessary to quickly assume a position and there is insufficient time to assume the prone position (Figure 3-6). This position can also be used on level ground or on ground that slopes upward where fields of fire or observation preclude using the prone position.

3-29. The sniper assumes this position in much the same way as the standard kneeling position, except he uses a tree or some other immovable object for support, cover, or concealment. He gains support by contact with the calf and knee of the leading leg, the upper forearm, or the shoulder. He might also rest the rifle on the hand lightly against the support. As with other supported positions, the sniper ensures that the operating parts and the barrel do not touch the support. Since the sniper's area of support is greatly reduced, he must maximize bone support.

3-30. This position differs between right- and left-handed snipers. Righthanded snipers use the following techniques and left-handed snipers do the opposite. The sniper faces 45 degrees to the right of the direction of the target. He kneels down and places the right knee on the ground, keeping the left leg as vertical as possible. He sits back on the right heel, placing it as directly under the spinal column as possible. A variation is to turn the toe inward and sit squarely on the right foot. The sniper grasps the small of the stock with the firing hand, and cradles the fore-end of the weapon in a crook formed with the left arm. He places the butt of the weapon in the pocket of the shoulder, then places the meaty underside of the left elbow on top of the left knee. Reaching under the weapon with the left hand, the sniper lightly grasps the firing arm. He relaxes forward and into the support, using the left shoulder as a contact

Figure 3-6. Supported kneeling position

point. This movement reduces transmission of the pulse beat into the sight picture. The sniper can use a tree, building, or vehicle for support.

Sling-Supported Kneeling Position

3-31. If vegetation height presents a problem, the sniper can raise his kneeling position by using the rifle sling (Figure 3-7). He takes this position by performing the first three steps for a kneeling supported position. With the

Figure 3-7. Sling-supported kneeling position

leather sling mounted to the weapon, the sniper turns the sling one-quarter turn to the left. The lower part of the sling then forms a loop. He places his left arm through the loop, pulls the sling up the arm, and places it on the upper arm above the bicep. He can tighten the sling on the arm by manipulating the upper and lower parts of the sling, if time permits. The sniper then rotates his arm in a clockwise motion around the sling and under the rifle with the sling secured to the upper arm. He places the fore-end of the stock in the "V" formed by the thumb and forefinger of the left hand. He can relax the left arm and let the sling support the weight of the weapon. Then he places the flat part of the rifle behind the point of the left elbow on top of the left knee. To add stability, the sniper can use his left hand to pull back along the fore-end of the rifle toward the trigger guard.

Squatting Position

3-32. The sniper uses the squatting position during hasty engagements or when other stable positions would be unacceptable due to inadequate height or concealment. He assumes this position by facing 45 degrees away from his direction of fire, putting his feet shoulder-width apart, and simply squatting. He can either rest his elbows on his knees or wrap them over his body. The sniper prefers this position when making engagements from rotary-winged aircraft as it reduces the amount of body contact with the inherent vibrations of the aircraft. Body configuration will determine the most comfortable and stable technique to use. The sniper can also use solid supports to lean up against or to lean back into.

Supported Standing Position

3-33. The sniper uses this position under the same circumstances as the supported kneeling position, where time, field of fire, or observation preclude the use of more stable positions. It is the least steady of the supported positions; the sniper should use it only as a last resort.

3-34. The sniper assumes this position in much the same manner as the standard standing position, except he uses a tree or some other immovable object for support. He gains support by contact with the leg, body, or arm. He might also rest the rifle lightly against the support. The sniper ensures the support makes no contact with operating parts or the barrel of the rifle.

3-35. This position also allows the sniper to use horizontal support, such as a wall or ledge. The sniper locates a solid object for support. He avoids branches because they tend to sway when the wind is present. He places the fore-end of the weapon on top of the support and the butt of the weapon into the pocket of the shoulder. The sniper forms a "V" with the thumb and forefinger of the nonfiring hand. He places the nonfiring hand, palm facing away, against the support with the fore-end of the weapon resting in the "V" of the hand. This hold steadies the weapon and allows quick recovery from recoil.

3-36. The sniper can also use a vertical support such as a tree, telephone pole, corner of building, or vehicle (Figure 3-8). He locates the stable support, faces 45 degrees to the right of the target, and places the palm of the nonfiring hand at arm's length against the support. He then locks the arm straight, lets the lead leg buckle, and places body weight against the nonfiring hand. He should keep the trail leg straight. The sniper places the fore-end of the weapon in the "V" formed by extending the thumb of the nonfiring hand. He should exert more pressure to the rear with the firing hand.

Standing Unsupported or Off-Hand Position

3-37. This position is the least desirable because it is least stable and most exposed of all the positions (Figure 3-9). The situation could dictate that the sniper use this position. The sniper faces perpendicular to the target, facing in the direction of his firing hand, with his legs spread about shoulder-width apart. He grasps the pistol grip of the stock with his firing hand and supports the fore-end with the nonfiring hand. He raises the stock of the weapon so the toe of the stock fits into the pocket of the shoulder and the weapon is lying on its side away from the body. The sniper rotates the weapon until it is vertical and the firing elbow is parallel with the ground. He pulls the nonfiring elbow into the side to support the weapon with the arm and rib cage. He then tilts his head slightly toward the weapon to obtain a natural spot or cheek weld and to align his eye with the sights. If his eye is not aligned with the sights, he adjusts his head position until the front sight and the target can be seen through the rear sight. Once in position, the sniper looks through his sights and moves his entire body to get the sights on target. He does not muscle the weapon onto the target. The sniper rests the rifle on a support to relax his arm muscles after firing the shot and following through.

Figure 3-8. Vertically supported standing position

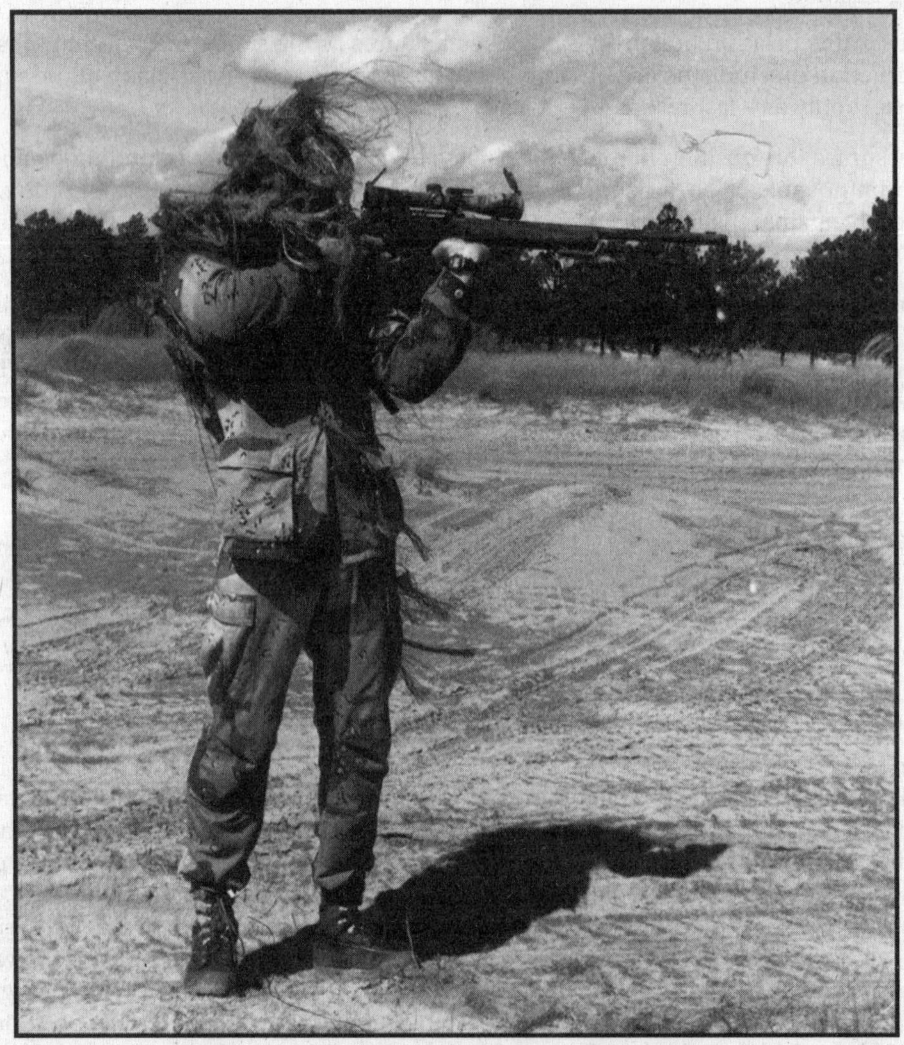

Figure 3-9. Standing unsupported or off-hand position

Other Supported Positions

3-38. During fundamental training, positions are taught in a step-by-step process. The sniper follows a series of precise movements until he obtains the correct position. Repetitive training ensures that he knows and correctly applies all the factors that can assist him in holding the rifle steady. As the sniper perfects the standard and supported positions, he can then use his ingenuity to devise other supported positions. Through practice he will gradually become accustomed to the feel of these positions and will know instinctively when his position is correct. This response is particularly important in combat because the sniper must be able to assume positions rapidly and stabilize the position by adapting it to any available artificial support. Figure 3-10 lists some significant nonstandard supported positions. The sniper must remember to adapt the position to his body so the position is solid, stable, and durable.

Foxhole-Supported Position	Used primarily in prepared defense areas where there is time for preparation. In this position, the sling, sandbags, or other material may be used to provide a stable firing platform.
Tree-Supported Position	Used when observation and firing into an area cannot be accomplished from the ground. When using this position, it is important to select a tree that is inconspicuous, is strong enough to support the sniper's weight, and affords concealment. **Remember: Avenues of escape are limited when in a tree.**
Bench Rest Position	Used when firing from a building, a cave, or a deeply shaded area. Sniper can use a built-up platform or table with a sitting aid and a rifle platform for stability. This position is very stable and will not tire the sniper. In this position, the sniper should stay deep in the shadows to prevent detection by the enemy.

Figure 3-10. Nonstandard supported positions

FIELD-EXPEDIENT WEAPON SUPPORT

3-39. Support of the weapon is critical to the sniper's success in engaging targets. Unlike a well-equipped firing range with sandbags for weapon support, the sniper will encounter situations where weapon support relies on common sense and imagination. The sniper should practice using the following supports at every opportunity and select the one that best suits his needs. He must train as if in combat to avoid confusion and self-doubt. While he should use the Harris Bipod when possible, the following items are commonly used as field-expedient weapon supports:

Sand Sock

3-40. The sniper may use the sand sock when delivering precision fire at long ranges. He uses a standard-issue, wool sock filled one-half to three-quarters full of sand or rice and knotted off. He places it under the rear-sling swivel when in the prone supported position for added stability. By limiting minor movements and reducing pulse beat, the sniper can concentrate on trigger control and aiming. He uses the nonfiring hand to grip the sand sock, rather than the rear sling swivel. The sniper makes minor changes in muzzle elevation by squeezing or relaxing his grip on the sock. He also uses the sand sock as padding between the weapon and a rigid support. The sniper must remember not to use a loose hold while firing the weapon.

> **NOTE**
> When using the sand sock, the sniper must be sure to grip the weapon firmly and hold it against his shoulder.

Rucksack

3-41. If the sniper is in terrain bare of any natural support, he may use his rucksack. He must consider the height and presence of rigid objects within the rucksack. The rucksack must conform to weapon contours to add stability.

Buttpack

3-42. The sniper can use a buttpack if the rucksack would give too high of a profile. He must also remember to consider the contents of the buttpack if he decides to change.

Sandbag

3-43. A sandbag is the simplest field-expedient support. The sniper can fill and empty a sandbag on site.

Tripod

3-44. The sniper can build a field-expedient tripod by tying together three 12-inch-long sticks with 550 cord or the equivalent (Figure 3-11). When tying the sticks, he wraps the cord at the center point and leaves enough slack to fold the legs out into a triangular base. Then he places the fore-end of the weapon between the three uprights. The juncture should be padded with a sand sock. A small camera table tripod padded with a sock full of sand or dirt can also be used.

Cross Sticks

3-45. The sniper can build a field-expedient bipod by tying together two 12-inch-long sticks, thick enough to support the weight of the weapon (Figure 3-11). Using 550 cord or the equivalent, he ties the sticks at the center point, leaving enough slack to fold them out in a scissorlike manner. He then places the weapon between the two uprights. The bipod is not as stable as other field-expedient items, and it should be used only in the absence of other techniques. The sniper should use a sling and grip the crossed stick juncture for stability.

Forked Stake

3-46. The tactical situation determines the use of the forked stake (Figure 3-11). Unless the sniper can drive a forked stake into the ground, this is the least desirable of the techniques; that is, he must use his nonfiring hand to hold the stake in an upright position. Delivering long-range precision fire is a near-impossibility due to the unsteadiness of the position.

SLINGS

3-47. The M1907 National Match leather sling is superior to the standard M16 web sling when used as a firing aid. Snipers who use a sling when firing should be aware of the possibility of a zero change. If the weapon is zeroed using a sling support, the POI may change when or if the sling is removed. This change is most noticeable in rifles with stocks that contact the barrel, such as the M21. The sling must be adjusted for each position. Each position will have a different point in which the sling is at the correct tightness. The sniper counts the number of holes in the sling and writes these down so that he can properly adjust the sling from position to position. An acceptable alternative is the cotton web M14 sling with a metal slide adjuster. The sniper must modify the sling for use.

TEAM FIRING TECHNIQUES

3-48. A successful sniper team consists of two intelligent and highly versatile members—the sniper and the observer. Each must be able to move and survive in a combat environment. The sniper's special mission is to deliver precision fire on targets that may not easily be engaged by conventional-fighting forces. The team must also—

- Calculate the range to the target.
- Determine the effects of the environment on ballistics.

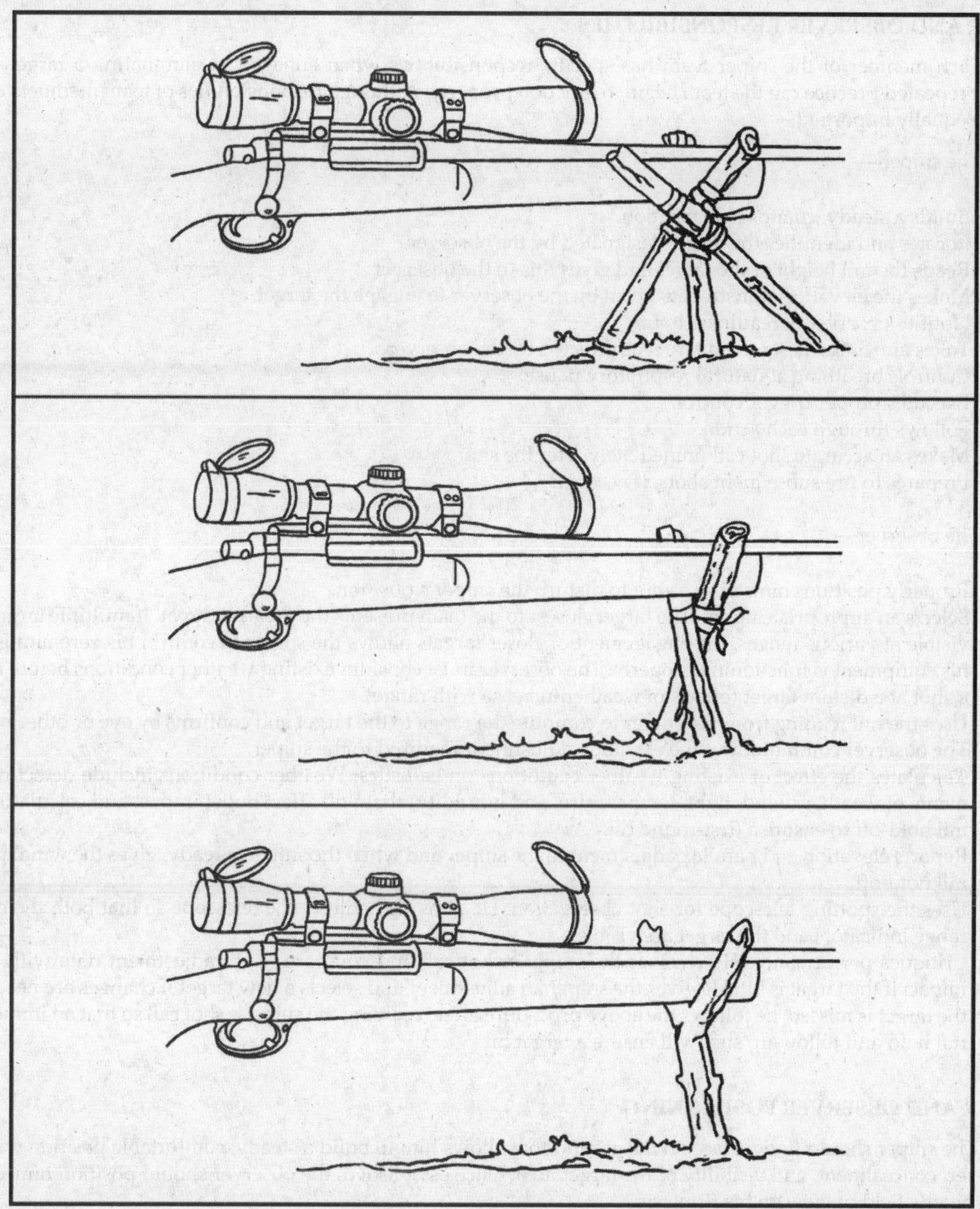

Figure 3-11. Tripod, cross sticks, and forked field-expedient weapon support

- Make necessary sight changes.
- Observe bullet impact.
- Quickly critique performance before any subsequent shots.

3-49. These tasks call for a coordinated, efficient team effort. Mission success occurs only if the sniper and observer thoroughly understand and react in a timely manner to one another.

SNIPER AND OBSERVER RESPONSIBILITIES

3-50. Each member of the sniper team has specific responsibilities when engaged in eliminating a target. Only through repeated practice can the team begin to function properly. Although responsibilities of team members differ, they are equally important.

3-51. The sniper—

- Builds a steady, comfortable position.
- Locates and identifies the target designated by the observer.
- Reads the mil height of the target and gives this to the observer.
- Makes the elevation adjustments given by the observer to engage the target.
- Notifies observer of readiness to fire.
- Takes aim at the designated target as directed by the observer.
- Controls breathing at natural respiratory pause.
- Executes proper trigger control.
- Follows through each action.
- Makes an accurate shot call immediately after the shot.
- Prepares to fire subsequent shots, if necessary.

3-52. The observer—

- Properly positions himself so as not to disturb the sniper's position.
- Selects an appropriate target. The target closest to the team presents the greatest threat. If multiple targets are visible at various ranges, the engagement of closer targets allows the sniper to confirm his zero and ensure his equipment is functioning properly. The observer must consider existing weather conditions before trying a shot at a distant target (effects of weather increase with range).
- Uses the mil reading from the sniper to compute the range to the target and confirms by eye or other means. The observer communicates the elevation adjustment required to the sniper.
- Calculates the effect of existing weather conditions on ballistics. Weather conditions include detecting elements of weather (wind, light, temperature, and humidity) that will affect bullet impact and calculating the mil hold-off to ensure a first-round hit.
- Reports elevation and parallax adjustment to the sniper and when the sniper is ready, gives the windage in a mil hold-off.
- Uses the spotting telescope for shot observation. He aims and adjusts the telescope so that both the downrange indicators and the target are visible.
- Critiques performance. He receives the sniper's shot call and compares sight adjustment data with bullet impact if the target is hit. He gives the sniper an adjustment and selects a new target if changes are needed. If the target is missed, he follows the above procedure after receiving the sniper's shot call so that an immediate mil hold and follow-up shot will ensure a target hit.

SNIPER AND OBSERVER POSITIONING

3-53. The sniper should find a place on the ground that allows him to build a steady, comfortable position with the best cover, concealment, and visibility of the target area. Once established, the observer should position himself out of the sniper's field of view on his firing side.

3-54. The closer the observer gets his spotting telescope to the sniper's gun target line, the easier it is to follow the trace (path) of the bullet and observe impact. A 4 to 5 o'clock position (7 to 8 o'clock for left-handed snipers) off the firing shoulder and close to (but not touching) the sniper is best (Figure 3-12).

SIGHTING AND AIMING

3-55. The sniper's use of iron sights serves mainly as a back-up system to his optical sight. However, iron sights are an excellent means of training for the sniper. The sniper is expected to be proficient in the use of iron sights before

Figure 3-12. Positioning of the observer's spotting telescope to the sniper

he obtains formal sniper training and he must remain proficient. By using iron sights during training, the sniper is forced to maintain his concentration on the fundamentals of firing. For a review of basic rifle marksmanship, see FM 23-9, *M16A1 and M16A2 Rifle Marksmanship*. While this manual is good for a basic review, some modifications in firing techniques must be made.

3-56. The sniper begins the aiming process by assuming a firing position and aligning the rifle with the target. He should point the rifle naturally at the desired POA. If his muscles are used to adjust the weapon onto the POA, they will automatically relax as the rifle fires, and the rifle will begin to move toward its natural POA. Because this movement begins just before the weapon discharges, the rifle is moving as the bullet leaves the muzzle. This movement causes displaced shots with no apparent cause (recoil disguises the movement). By adjusting the weapon and body as a single unit, rechecking, and readjusting as needed, the sniper achieves a true natural POA. Once the position is established, the sniper then aims the weapon at the exact point on the target. Aiming involves three factors: eye relief, sight alignment, and sight picture.

EYE RELIEF

3-57. Eye relief is the distance from the sniper's firing eye to the rear sight or the rear of the telescope tube (Figure 3-13). When using iron sights, the sniper ensures that this distance remains constant from shot to shot to preclude changing what he views through the rear sight. However, relief will vary from firing position to firing position and from sniper to sniper according to—

- The sniper's neck length.
- His angle of head approach to the stock.
- The depth of his shoulder pocket.
- The position of the butt of the stock in the shoulder.
- His firing position.

3-58. This distance is more rigidly controlled with telescopic sights than with iron sights. The sniper must take care to prevent eye injury caused by the rear sight or the telescope tube striking his eyebrow during recoil. Regardless of the sighting system he uses, he must place his head as upright as possible with his firing eye located directly behind the rear portion of the sighting system. This head placement also allows the muscles surrounding his eye to relax. Incorrect head placement causes the sniper to look out of the top or corner of his eye, which can result in blurred vision or eyestrain. The sniper can avoid eyestrain by not staring through the iron or telescopic sights for extended periods. The best aid to consistent eye relief is maintaining the same stock weld from shot to shot; because as the eye relief changes, a change in sight alignment will occur. Maintaining eye relief is a function of the position and stock weld use. Normal eye relief from the rear sight or scope on the M24 is 2 to 3 inches. Once the sniper is ready to fire, it is imperative that he concentrates on the front sight or reticle and not the target.

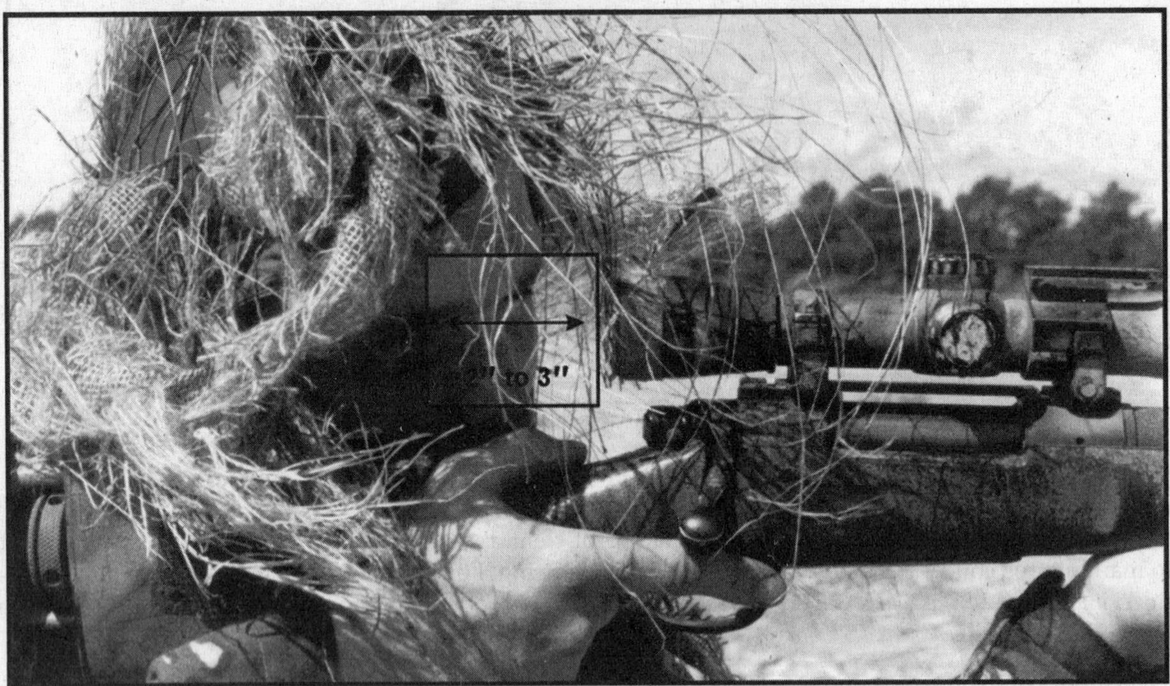

Figure 3-13. Eye relief

SIGHT ALIGNMENT

3-59. Sight alignment is the most critical factor in aiming. An error in sight alignment increases proportionately with range and will result in increased misses. The M24 has a hooded front sight that simplifies sight alignment. The front sight hood is centered in the rear sight aperture.

3-60. With iron sights, sight alignment is the relation between the front and rear sights as seen by the sniper (Figure 3-14). The sniper centers the front sight post horizontally and vertically within the rear aperture. (Centering the two circles is the easiest way for the eye to align the front and rear sights. This method allows the sniper to be consistent in

Figure 3-14. Proper sight alignment with the M24 sniper weapon iron sight system

blade location within the rear sight.) With telescopic sights, sight alignment is the relationship between the crosshairs and a full field of view as seen by the sniper. The sniper must place his head so that a full field of view fills the tube, with no dark shadows or crescents to cause misplaced shots. He centers the reticle in a full field of view, ensuring the vertical crosshair is straight up and down so that the rifle is not canted. Again, the center is easiest for the sniper to locate and allows for consistent reticle placement.

SIGHT PICTURE

3-61. With iron sights, the sight picture is the correlation between the front sight blade, the rear aperture, and the target as seen by the sniper (Figure 3-15). The sniper aligns his sights and places the top edge of the blade in the center (center hold) of the largest visible mass of the target (disregard the head and use the center of the torso). With telescopic sights, sight picture is the correlation between the reticle, full field of view, and the target as seen by the sniper (Figure 3-16). The sniper centers the reticle in a full field of view. He then places the reticle center on the largest visible

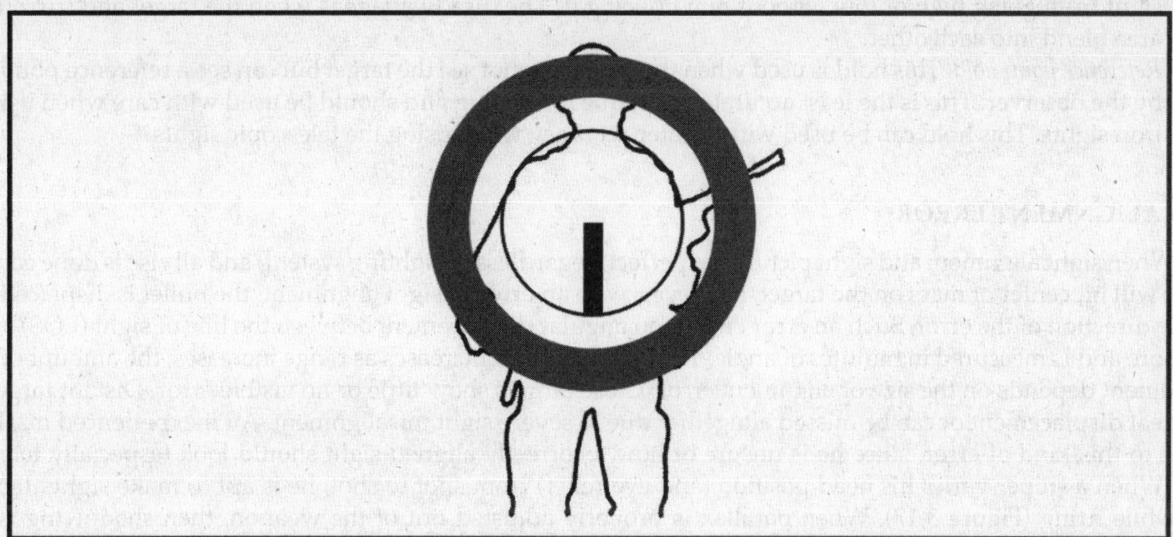

Figure 3-15. Correlation of sight picture using iron sights

Figure 3-16. Correlation of sight picture using telescopic sights

mass of the target (as in iron sights). The center of mass of the target is easiest for the sniper to locate, and it surrounds the intended POI with a maximum amount of target area. When aiming, the sniper concentrates on the front sight, or reticle, not the target. A clear front sight or focusing on the crosshairs is critical to detecting errors in sight alignment and is more important than the sight picture.

3-62. When aiming, the sniper has the following choices of where to hold the front sight:

- *Center hold.* This hold places the front sight on the desired POI. The problem with this hold is that the front sight blocks part of the target. **This hold is probably the best sight picture for combat** use because it is the most "natural" for U.S. Army-trained soldiers. Variation is the pimple hold.
- *6 o'clock hold.* This hold places the target on top of the front sight. The main problem is that it is easy for the front sight to "push up" into the target, causing the round to go high. Variation is the flat tire hold.
- *Line-of-white hold.* This hold allows a strip of contrasting color to show between the target and the front sight. The advantage of using this hold is that it permits the sniper to see the entire target and prevents the front sight from going high or low without him noticing it. The disadvantage is when the target and surrounding area blend into each other.
- *Reference point hold.* This hold is used when the sniper cannot see the target but can see a reference point given by the observer. This is the least accurate technique for aiming and should be used with care when using the iron sights. This hold can be used with greater accuracy when using the telescopic sights.

SIGHT ALIGNMENT ERROR

3-63. When sight alignment and sight picture are perfect (regardless of sighting system) and all else is done correctly, the shot will hit center of mass on the target. However, with an error in sight alignment, the bullet is displaced in the opposite direction of the error. Such an error creates an angular displacement between the line of sight (LOS) and the line of bore and is measured in minutes of angle. This displacement increases as range increases; the amount of bullet displacement depends on the size of alignment error. Close targets show little or no visible error. Distant targets can show great displacement or can be missed altogether due to severe sight misalignment. An inexperienced marksman is prone to this kind of error, since he is unsure of how a correctly aligned sight should look (especially telescopic sights). When a sniper varies his head position (and eye relief) from shot to shot, he is apt to make sight alignment errors while firing (Figure 3-17). When parallax is properly adjusted out of the weapon, then shadowing is not a problem.

SIGHT PICTURE ERROR

3-64. A sight picture error is an error in the placement of the aiming point. This mistake causes no displacement between the LOS and the line of bore. The weapon is simply pointed at the wrong spot on the target. Because no displacement exists as range increases, close and far targets are hit or missed depending on where the front sight or the reticle is when the rifle fires (Figure 3-18). All snipers face this kind of error every time they fire. Regardless of firing position stability, the weapon will always be moving. A supported rifle moves much less than an unsupported one, but both still move in what is known as a wobble area. The sniper must adjust his firing position so that his wobble area is as small as possible and centered on the target. With proper adjustments, the sniper should be able to fire the shot while the front sight blade or reticle is on the target at, or very near, the desired aiming point. How far the blade or reticle is from this point when the weapon fires is the amount of sight picture error all snipers face. Also, the sniper should not attempt to aim for more than 5 or 6 seconds without blinking. Doing so places an additional strain on the eye and "burns" the sight alignment and sight picture into the retina. The result could cause minor changes in sight alignment and sight picture to go unnoticed.

DOMINANT EYE

3-65. Some individuals may have difficulty aiming because of interferences from their dominant eye if it is not the eye used in the aiming process. This feature may require the sniper to fire from the other side of the weapon (right-handed sniper will fire left-handed). To determine which eye is dominant, hold an index finger 6 to 8 inches in front of your eyes. Close one eye at a time while looking past the finger at an object; one eye will make the finger

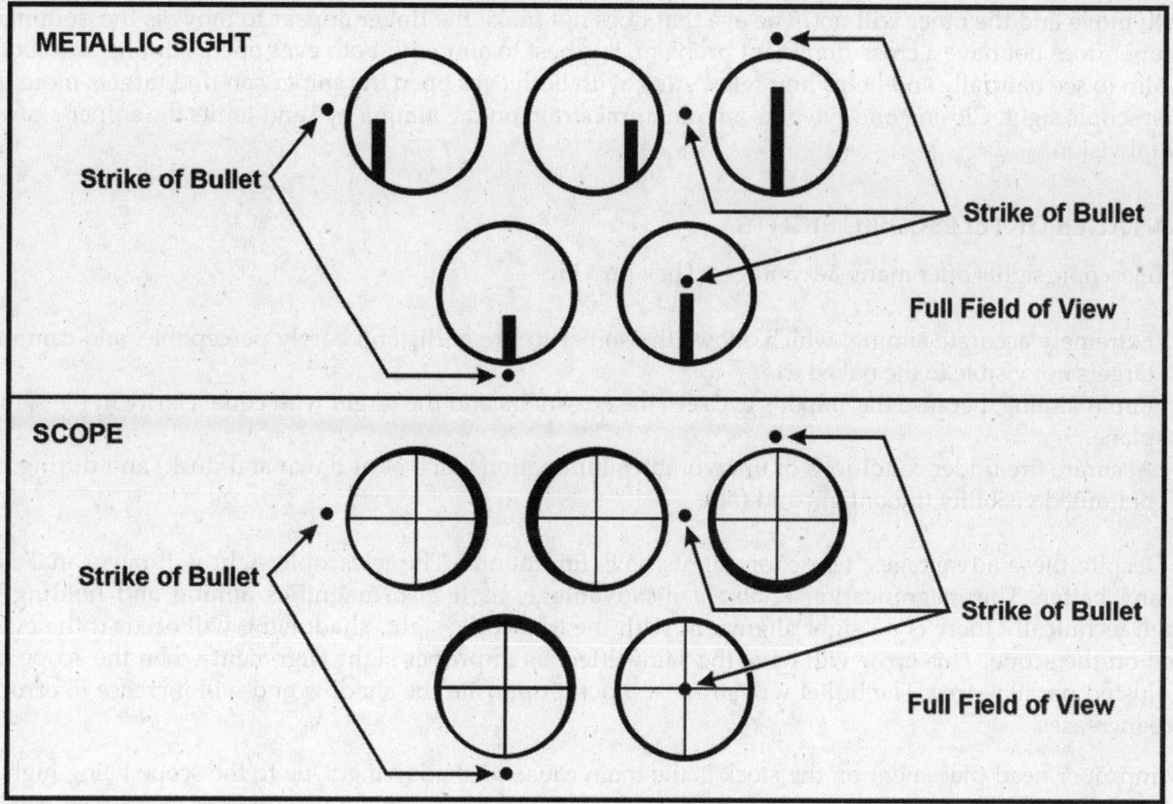

Figure 3-17. Possible sight alignment error

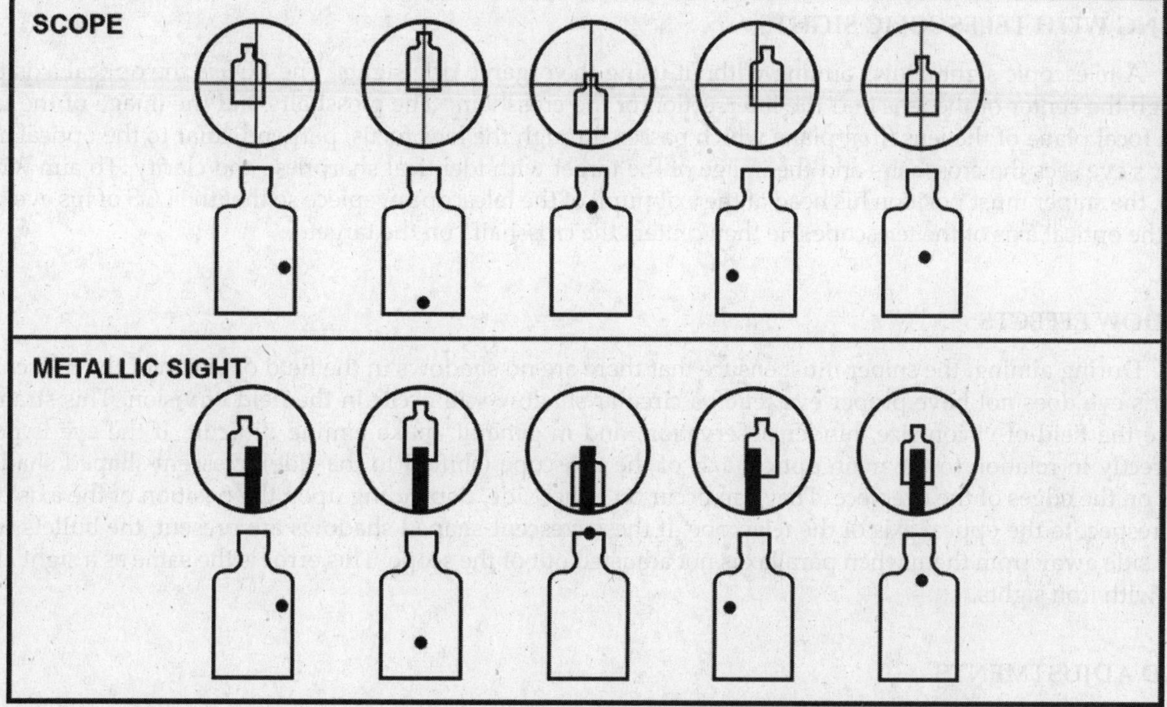

Figure 3-18. Possible sight picture error

appear to move and the other will not. The eye that does not make the finger appear to move is the dominant eye. If the sniper does not have a cross-dominant problem, it is best to aim with both eyes open. Aiming with both eyes allows him to see naturally and helps him relax. Also, with both eyes open the sniper can find targets more quickly in his telescopic sight. Closing one eye puts an unnatural strain on the aiming eye and limits the sniper's protective peripheral vision.

ADVANTAGES OF TELESCOPIC SIGHTS

3-66. Telescopic sights offer many advantages. They provide—

- Extremely accurate aiming, which allows the sniper to fire at distant, barely perceptible, and camouflaged targets not visible to the naked eye.
- Rapid aiming, because the sniper's eye sees the crosshairs and the target with equal clarity in the same focal plane.
- Accurate fire under conditions of unfavorable illumination (such as at dawn and dusk) and during periods of limited visibility (moonlight and fog).

3-67. Despite these advantages, telescopic sights have limitations. The telescopic sight will never make a poor sniper any better. The magnification is also a disadvantage, as it also magnifies aiming and holding errors. Although technically there is no sight alignment with the telescopic sight, shadowing will occur if the eye is not centered on the scope. This error will have the same effect as improper sight alignment when the scope has not been adjusted parallax-free. The bullet will strike at a point opposite the shadow and will increase in error as the distance increases.

3-68. Improper head placement on the stock is the main cause of shadowing. Due to the scope being higher than the iron sights, it is difficult to obtain a good solid stock weld. If this is a problem, temporary cheek rests can be constructed using T-shirts or any material that can be removed and replaced. The rest will assist the sniper in obtaining a good stock weld and will help keep his head held straight for sighting. It is recommended that the sniper learn to establish a solid position without these aids.

AIMING WITH TELESCOPIC SIGHTS

3-69. A telescopic sight allows aiming without using the organic rifle sights. The LOS is the optical axis that runs through the center of the lens and the intersection of the crosshairs. The crosshairs and the image of the target are in the focal plane of the lens (that plane which passes through the lens focus, perpendicular to the optical axis). The sniper's eye sees the crosshairs and the image of the target with identical sharpness and clarity. To aim with a telescope, the sniper must position his head at the exit pupil of the telescope eyepiece so that the LOS of his eye coincides with the optical axis of the telescope. He then centers the crosshairs on the target.

SHADOW EFFECTS

3-70. During aiming, the sniper must ensure that there are no shadows in the field of vision of the telescope. If the sniper's eye does not have proper eye relief, a circular shadow will occur in the field of vision. This straining will reduce the field-of-vision size, hinder observation, and in general, make aiming difficult. If the eye is positioned incorrectly in relation to the main optical axis of the telescope (shifted to the side), crescent-shaped shadows will occur on the edges of the eyepiece. They can occur on either side, depending upon the position of the axis of the eye with respect to the optical axis of the telescope. If these crescent-shaped shadows are present, the bullets will strike to the side away from them when parallax is not adjusted out of the scope. This error is the same as a sight alignment error with iron sights.

HEAD ADJUSTMENTS

3-71. If the sniper notices shadow on the edges of the field of vision during aiming, he must find a head position in which the eye will clearly see the entire field of vision of the telescope. Consequently, to ensure accurate aiming with a telescope, the sniper must direct his attention to keeping his eye on the optical axis of the telescope. He must also have the intersection of the crosshairs coincide exactly with the aiming point. However, his concentration must be on the crosshairs and not the target. It is important not to stare at the crosshairs while aiming.

CANTING

3-72. Canting is the act of tipping the rifle to either side of the vertical crosshair, causing misplaced and erratic shot grouping.

POINT OF AIM

3-73. The POA is mission- and range-dependent and should not be the center of mass unless required by the situation. The best POA between 300 and 600 meters is anywhere within the triangle formed by the base of the neck and the two nipples (Figure 3-19). This point will maximize the probability of hitting major organs and vessels and rendering a clean one-shot kill. The optional POA, at this range if the upper chest hold is not available, is the centerline below the belt. The pelvic girdle is rich in major blood vessels and nerves. A hit here will cause a mechanical collapse or mechanical dysfunction. A strike here is also an advantage if the target is wearing body armor, which usually covers only the upper chest. An alternate POA for closer than 300 meters is the head hold (Figure 3-20). This point is very difficult to achieve because of its size and constant motion. The advantage of the head hold is incapacitation well under 1 second if the correct placement is achieved. This hold is well suited for hostage situations where closer ranges are the norm and instant incapacitation is required. One hold is along the plane formed by the nose and the two ear canals. The target is the brain stem, thus severing the spinal cord from the medulla oblongata. Note that the POA is neither the forehead nor between the eyes, which would result in hits that would be too high. The sniper is best served by imagining a golf ball-sized shape inside the middle of the head. He is to hit that inner ball by aiming through the middle of the head regardless of position horizontally or vertically.

3-74. What the sniper is trying to sever or pulverize is the target's brain stem, the location where the spinal cord connects to the brain. Nerves that control motor function are channeled through here, and the lower third of the stem (the medulla) controls breathing and heartbeat. Hit here, the target will not experience even reflexive motor action. His entire body will instantly experience what is called "flaccid paralysis." The target's muscles will suddenly relax and he will become incapable of any motion of any kind thereafter. The sniper can tell how successful his headshot is by watching how his target falls. If the target goes straight down, limp,

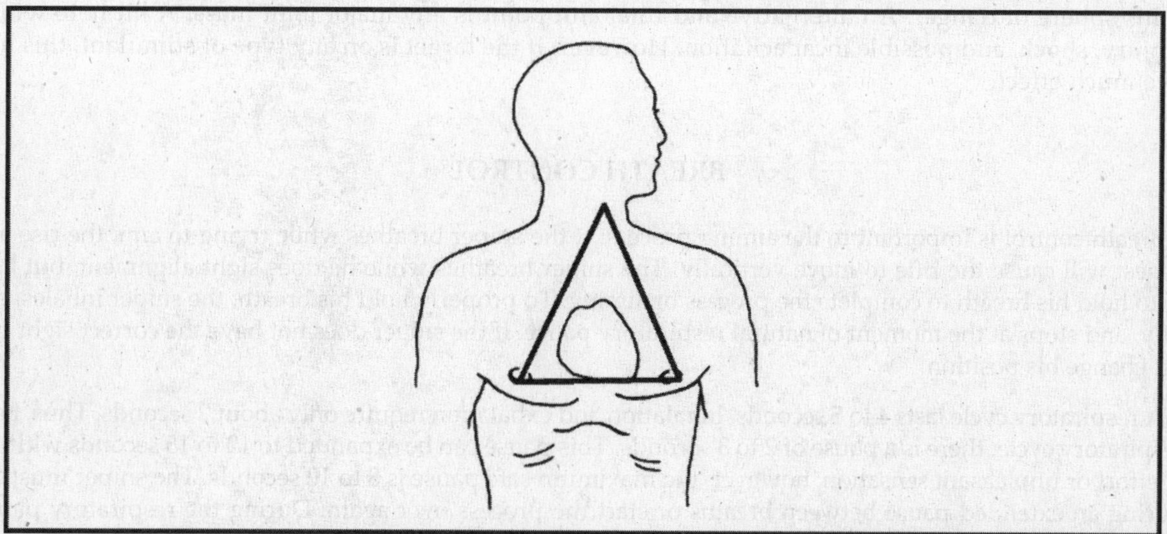

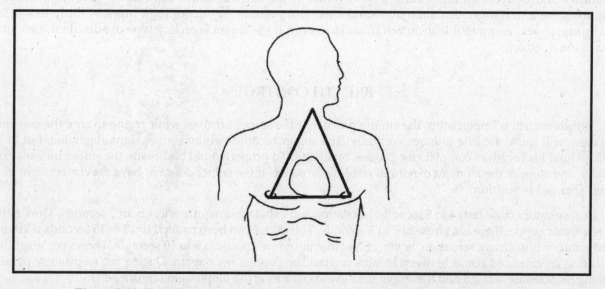

Figure 3-19. Triangular point of aim formed by the nipples and the base of the chin

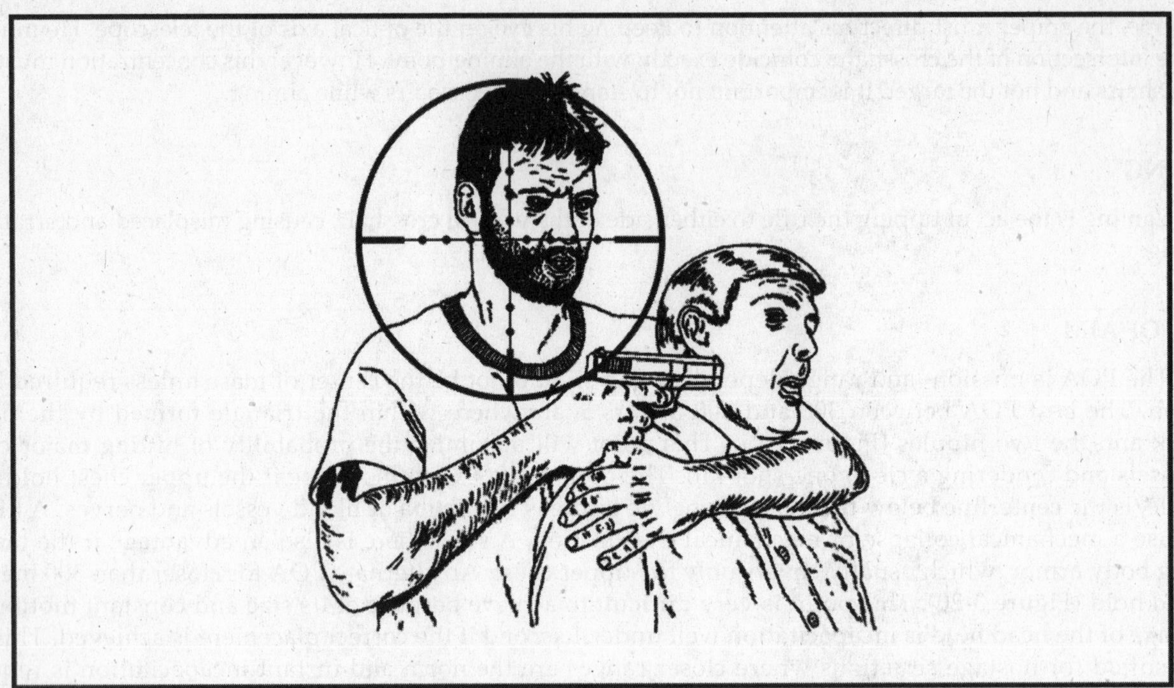

Figure 3-20. View of the final point of aim—head hold

there is a high assurance of fatality. If the target falls to the side or is "knocked" down, the target has only been partially incapacitated.

3-75. For a chest shot that is ideally placed (mid-sternum), the bullet will strike the largest and hardest of the bones overlying the vital organs. When the bullet strikes and severs the target's spine, his legs will buckle under flaccid paralysis. However, his arms may not be incapacitated instantly. With a chest shot, even though the suspect may technically be "dead" from the devastation of the round, there may be a brief and dangerous delay before he acts dead. His brain may not die for one to two minutes after his heart has ceased to function. During this time, his brain may command his arms to commit a simple, final act. The sniper anticipates these possibilities and delivers an immediate second round if the suspect is not fully down and out or anyone is within his sphere of danger. An alternative and final aim point is any major joint mass. A hit here will cause grave injury, shock, and possible incapacitation. However, if the target is on any type of stimulant, this hit may not have much effect.

BREATH CONTROL

3-76. Breath control is important to the aiming process. If the sniper breathes while trying to aim, the rise and fall of his chest will cause the rifle to move vertically. The sniper breathes while he does sight alignment, but he must be able to hold his breath to complete the process of aiming. To properly hold his breath, the sniper inhales, exhales normally, and stops at the moment of natural respiratory pause. If the sniper does not have the correct sight picture, he must change his position.

3-77. A respiratory cycle lasts 4 to 5 seconds. Inhalation and exhalation require only about 2 seconds. Thus, between each respiratory cycle, there is a pause of 2 to 3 seconds. This pause can be expanded to 12 to 15 seconds without any special effort or unpleasant sensation; however, the maximum safe pause is 8 to 10 seconds. The sniper must fire the shot during an extended pause between breaths or start the process over again. During the respiratory pause, the breathing muscles are relaxed and the sniper thus avoids straining the diaphragm (Figure 3-21).

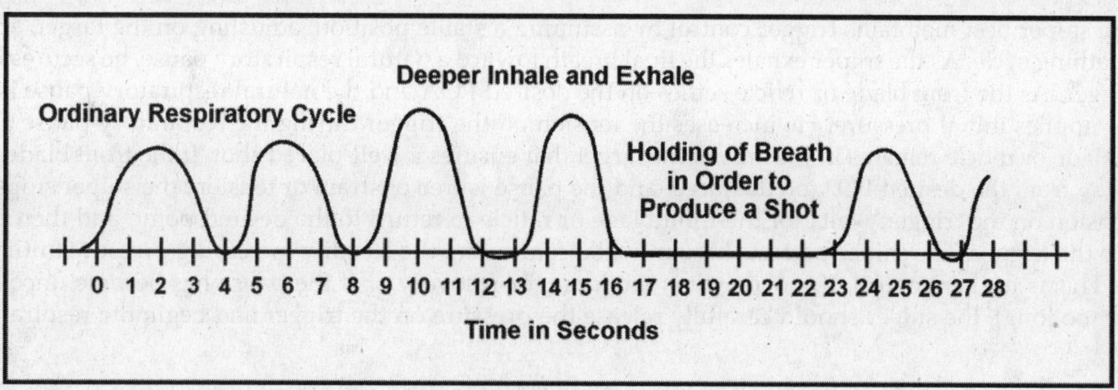

Figure 3-21. A sniper's respiratory pause before firing at the target

3-78. A sniper should assume his position and breathe naturally until his hold begins to settle. Many snipers then take a slightly deeper breath, exhale and pause, expecting to fire the shot during the pause. If the hold does not settle sufficiently to allow the shot to be fired, the sniper resumes normal breathing and repeats the process.

3-79. The respiratory pause should never feel unnatural. If the pause is extended for too long, the body suffers from oxygen deficiency and sends out signals to resume breathing. These signals produce slight involuntary movements in the diaphragm and interfere with the sniper's ability to concentrate. The heart rate also increases and there is a decrease of oxygen to the eyes. This lack of oxygen causes the eyes to have difficulty focusing and results in eyestrain. During multiple, rapid-fire engagements, the breathing cycle should be forced through a rapid, shallow cycle between shots instead of trying to hold the breath or breathing. Firing should be accomplished at the forced respiratory pause.

3-80. The natural tendency of the weapon to rise and fall during breathing allows the sniper to fine-tune his aim by holding his breath at the point in which the sights rest on the aiming point.

TRIGGER CONTROL

3-81. Trigger control is an important component of sniper marksmanship fundamentals. It is defined as causing the rifle to fire when the sight picture is at its best, without causing the rifle to move. Trigger squeeze, on the other hand, is defined as the independent action of the forefinger on the trigger, with a uniformly increasing pressure straight to the rear until the rifle fires. Trigger control is the last task to be accomplished before the weapon fires. This task is more difficult to apply when using a telescope or when a firing position becomes less stable. Misses are usually caused by the aim being disturbed as the bullet leaves the barrel or just before it leaves the barrel. This kind of miss results when a sniper jerks the trigger or flinches. The trigger need not be jerked violently to spoil the aim; even a slight, sudden pressure of the trigger finger is enough to cause the barrel to waver and spoil the sight alignment. Flinching is an involuntary movement of the body—tensing of the muscles of the arm, the neck, or the shoulder in anticipation of the shock of recoil or the sound of the rifle firing. A sniper can correct these errors by understanding and applying proper trigger control.

3-82. Proper trigger control occurs when the sniper places his firing finger as low on the trigger as possible and still clears the trigger guard, thereby achieving maximum mechanical advantage. The sniper engages the trigger with that part of his firing finger that allows him to pull the trigger straight to the rear. A firm grip on the rifle stock is essential for trigger control. If the sniper begins his trigger pull from a loose grip, he tends to squeeze the stock as well as the trigger and thus loses trigger control. To avoid transferring movement of the finger to the entire rifle, the sniper should see daylight between the trigger finger and the stock as he squeezes the trigger, straight to the rear. To ensure a well-placed shot, he fires the weapon when the front blade or reticle is on the desired POA.

3-83. The sniper best maintains trigger control by assuming a stable position, adjusting on the target, and beginning a breathing cycle. As the sniper exhales the final breath toward a natural respiratory pause, he secures his finger on the trigger. As the front blade or reticle settles on the desired POA and the natural respiratory pause is entered, the sniper applies initial pressure. He increases the tension on the trigger during the respiratory pause as long as the front blade or reticle remains in the area of the target that ensures a well-placed shot. If the front blade or reticle moves away from the desired POA on the target and the pause is free of strain or tension, the sniper stops increasing the tension on the trigger, waits for the front blade or reticle to return to the desired point, and then continues to squeeze the trigger. The sniper perfects his aim while continuing the steadily increasing pressure until the hammer falls. This is trigger control. If movement is too large for recovery or if the pause has become uncomfortable (extended too long), the sniper should carefully release the pressure on the trigger and begin the respiratory cycle again.

3-84. Most successful snipers agree that the trigger slack should be taken up with a heavy initial pressure. Concentration should be focused on the perfection of the sight picture as trigger control is automatically applied. Concentration, especially on the front sight or reticle, is the greatest aid to prevent flinching and jerking.

3-85. The methods of trigger control involve a mental process, while pulling the trigger is a mechanical process. The sniper uses two methods of trigger control to pull the trigger. They are as follows:

- *Smooth motion/constant pressure trigger pull.* The sniper takes up the slack with a heavy initial pressure and, when the sight picture settles, pulls the trigger with a single, smooth action. This method is used when there is a stationary target and the position is steady. This type of trigger control will help prevent flinching, jerking, and bucking the weapon.
- *Interrupted trigger pull.* The sniper applies pressure to the trigger when the sight picture begins to settle and as long as the sight picture looks good or continues to improve. If the sight picture deteriorates briefly, the sniper maintains the pressure at a constant level and increases it when the picture again begins to improve. He then continues the pressure or repeats this technique until he fires the rifle. The sniper does not jerk the trigger when the sights are aligned and the "perfect" sight picture occurs. This technique is used in the standing position to correct the wavering of the sights around, through, or in the target or aiming point due to the instability of the position.

3-86. Trigger control is not only the most important fundamental of marksmanship but also the most difficult to master. The majority of firing errors stems directly or indirectly from the improper application of trigger control. Failure to hit the target frequently results from the sniper jerking the trigger or applying pressure on both the trigger and the side of the rifle. Either of these actions can produce a miss. Therefore, instructors should always check for indications of improper trigger control, since an error in this technique can start a chain reaction of other errors.

3-87. Trigger control can be developed into a reflex action. The sniper can develop his trigger control to the point that pulling the trigger requires no conscious effort. The sniper will be aware of the pull, but he will not be consciously directing it. Everyone exhibits this type of reflex action in daily living. The individual who walks or drives a car while carrying on a conversation is an example. He is aware of his muscular activity but is not planning it. He is thinking about the conversation.

3-88. Trigger control is taught in conjunction with positions. When positions and trigger control are being taught, an effective training aid for demonstrating the technique of trigger control with reference to the interrupted or controlled pressure is the wobble sight and target simulator. The wobble sight may be used with a fixed target simulator to demonstrate wobble area, adjustment of natural POA, breathing, and trigger control.

3-89. In all positions, dry firing is one of the best methods of developing proper trigger control. In dry firing, not only is the coach able to detect errors, but the individual sniper is able to detect his own errors, since there is no recoil to conceal the rifle's undesirable movements. Where possible, trigger control practice should be integrated into all phases of marksmanship training. The mastery of trigger control takes patience, hard work, concentration, and a great deal of self-discipline.

THE INTEGRATED ACT OF FIRING ONE ROUND

3-90. Once the sniper has been taught the fundamentals of marksmanship, his primary concern is to apply this knowledge in the performance of his mission. An effective method of applying fundamentals is through the use of the integrated act of firing one round. The integrated act is a logical, step-by-step development of the fundamentals whereby the sniper develops habits to fire each shot exactly the same. Thus he achieves the marksmanship goal that a sniper must strive for: one shot—one kill. The integrated act of firing can be divided into the following four phases.

PREPARATION PHASE

3-91. Before departing the preparation area, the sniper ensures that—

- The team is mentally conditioned and knows what mission to accomplish.
- A systematic check is made of equipment for completeness and serviceability including, but not limited to—
  - Properly cleaned and lubricated rifles.
  - Properly mounted and torqued scopes.
  - Zero-sighted systems and recorded data in the sniper data book.
  - The study of weather conditions to determine the effects on the team's performance of the mission.

BEFORE-FIRING PHASE

3-92. On arrival at the mission site, the team exercises care in selecting positions. The sniper ensures that the selected positions complement the mission's goal. During this phase, the sniper—

- Maintains strict adherence to the fundamentals of position. He ensures that the firing position is as relaxed as possible, making the most of available external support. He also makes sure the support is stable, conforms to the position, and allows a correct, natural POA for each designated area or target.
- Once in position, removes the scope covers and checks the field of fire, making any needed corrections to ensure clear, unobstructed firing lanes.
- Checks the boreline for any obstructions.
- Makes dry-firing and natural POA checks.
- Double-checks ammunition for serviceability and completes final magazine loading.
- Notifies the observer he is ready to engage targets. The observer must constantly be aware of weather conditions that may affect the accuracy of the shots. He must also stay ahead of the tactical situation.

FIRING PHASE

3-93. Upon detection, or if directed to a suitable target, the sniper makes appropriate sight changes and aims, and tells the observer he is ready to fire. The observer then gives the needed windage and observes the target. To fire the rifle, the sniper should remember the key word, **BRASS.** Each letter is explained as follows:

- *Breathe.* The sniper inhales and exhales to the natural respiratory pause. He checks for consistent head placement and stock weld. He ensures eye relief is correct (full field of view through the scope, no shadows present). At the same time, he begins aligning the crosshairs or front blade with the target at the desired POA.
- *Relax.* As the sniper exhales, he relaxes as many muscles as possible while maintaining control of the weapon and position.
- *Aim.* If the sniper has a good, natural POA, the rifle points at the desired target during the respiratory pause. If the aim is off, the sniper should make a slight adjustment to acquire the desired POA. He avoids "muscling" the weapon toward the aiming point.

- *Slack.* (Does not apply to the M24 as issued.) The first stage of the two-stage trigger must be taken up with heavy initial pressure. Most experienced snipers actually take up the slack and get initial pressure as they reach the respiratory pause. In this way, the limited duration of the pause is not used up by manipulating the slack in the trigger.
- *Squeeze.* As long as the sight alignment and sight picture is satisfactory, the sniper should squeeze the trigger. The pressure applied to the trigger must be straight to the rear without disturbing the lay of the rifle or the desired POA.

3-94. After the shot, the sniper must remember to follow through with the recoil and recover back on target. He should make sure to call his shot so the observer can record any adjustment made.

AFTER-FIRING PHASE

3-95. The sniper's after-firing actions include observing the target area to certify the hit, observing the enemy reaction, acquiring another target, and avoiding compromise of his position. The sniper must analyze his performance. If the shot impacted at the desired spot (a target hit), it may be assumed that the integrated act of firing one round was correctly followed. However, if the shot was off call, the sniper and observer must check for the following possible errors:

- Failure to follow the key word BRASS (partial field of view, breath held incorrectly, trigger jerked, rifle muscled into position).
- Target improperly ranged with scope (causing high or low shots).
- Incorrectly compensated-for wind (causing right or left shots).
- Possible weapon or ammunition malfunction (used only as a last resort when no other errors are detected).

3-96. Once the probable reasons for an off-call shot are determined, the sniper must make note of the errors. He should pay close attention to the problem areas to increase the accuracy of future shots.

FOLLOW-THROUGH

3-97. Applying the fundamentals increases the odds of a well-aimed shot being fired. When mastered, the first-round kill becomes a certainty.

3-98. Follow-through is a continued mental and physical application of the fundamentals after each round is fired. It is the act of continuing to apply all of the sniper marksmanship fundamentals as the weapon fires and immediately after it fires. Follow-through consists of—

- Keeping the head in firm contact with the stock (stock weld).
- Keeping the finger on the trigger all the way to the rear.
- Continuing to look through the rear aperture or scope tube.
- Concentrating on the front sight or crosshairs.
- Keeping muscles relaxed.
- Avoiding reaction to recoil and noise.
- Releasing the trigger only after the recoil has stopped.

3-99. Good follow-through ensures that the weapon is allowed to fire and recoil naturally. The sniper and rifle combination reacts as a single unit to such actions. From a training viewpoint, follow-through may allow the observer to observe the strike of the bullet in relation to the sniper's point of aim and to help him rapidly correct and adjust his sights for a second shot. Also, a good follow-through will indicate to the sniper the quality of his natural POA. The weapon should settle back on target. If it does not, then muscles were used to get the weapon on target.

CALLING THE SHOT

3-100. Calling the shot is being able to tell where the round should impact on the target. Because live targets invariably move when hit, the sniper will find it almost impossible to use his telescope to locate the target after the round is fired. Using iron sights, the sniper will find that searching for a downrange hit is beyond his capabilities. He must be able to accurately call his shots. Proper follow-through will aid in calling the shot. However, the dominant factor in shot calling is where the reticle or post is located when the weapon discharges. The sniper refers to this location as his final focus point.

3-101. With iron sights, the final focus point should be on the top edge of the front sight blade. The blade is the only part of the sight picture that is moving (in the wobble area). Focusing on the blade aids in calling the shot and detecting any errors in sight alignment or sight picture. Of course, lining up the sights and the target initially requires the sniper to shift his focus from the target to the blade and back until he is satisfied that he is properly aligned with the target. This shifting exposes two more facts about eye focus. The eye can instantly shift focus from near objects (the blade) to far objects (the target). The eye cannot, however, be focused so that two objects at greatly different ranges (again the blade and target) are both in sharp focus. After years of experience, many snipers find that they no longer hold final focus on the front sight blade. Their focus is somewhere between the blade and the target. This act has been related to many things, from personal preference to failing eyesight. Regardless, inexperienced snipers are still advised to use the blade as a final focus point. With iron sights the final check before shooting will be sight alignment, as misalignment will cause a miss.

3-102. The sniper can easily place the final focus point with telescopic sights because of the sight's optical qualities. Properly focused, a scope should present both the field of view and the reticle in sharp detail. Final focus should then be on the reticle. While focusing on the reticle, the sniper moves his head slightly from side to side. The reticle may seem to move across the target face, even though the rifle and scope are motionless. Parallax is present when the target image is not correctly focused onto the reticule's focal plane. Therefore, the target image and the reticle appear to be in two separate positions inside the scope, causing the effect of reticle movement across the target. A certain amount of parallax is unavoidable throughout the range of the ART series of scopes. The M3A on the M24 has a focus/parallax adjustment that eliminates parallax. The sniper should adjust this knob until the target's image is on the same focal plane as the reticle. To determine if the target's image appears at the ideal location, the sniper should move his head slightly left and right to see if the reticle appears to move. If it does not move, the focus is properly adjusted and no parallax is present. The sniper will focus and concentrate on the reticle for the final shot, not the target.

3-103. In calling the shot, the sniper predicts where the shot will hit the target. The sniper calls the shot while dry firing and actual firing by noting the position of the sights in relation to the aiming point the instant the round is fired. If his shot is not on call, the sniper must review the fundamentals to isolate his problem or make a sight change as indicated to move his shot to his POA. Unless he can accurately call his shots, the sniper will not be able to effectively zero his rifle.

DETECTION AND CORRECTION OF ERRORS

3-104. During the process of teaching or using the fundamentals of marksmanship, it will become evident that errors may plague any sniper. When an error is detected, it must be corrected. Sometimes errors are not obvious to the sniper. Therefore, a coach or instructor will be invaluable. The procedure for correcting errors is to pinpoint or isolate the error, prove to the sniper that he is making this error, and convince him that through his own efforts and concentration he can correct his error. Knowing what to look for through analyzing the shot groups, observing the sniper, questioning the sniper, and reviewing the fundamentals of training exercises will assist the coach in this process. Even during sustainment a trained sniper will use detection and correction to ensure bad habits have not been developed.

TARGET ANALYSIS

3-105. Target or shot-group analysis is an important step in processing the detection and correction of errors. When analyzing a target, the coach should correlate errors in performance to loose groups, the shape of groups, and the size of groups. With some snipers, especially the experienced, this analysis cannot be done readily. However, the coach must be able to discuss the probable error. A bad shot group is seldom caused by only one error. Remember, in the initial analysis of groups, the coach must take into consideration the capabilities of the sniper, the weapon, and the ammunition.

OBSERVATION

3-106. When the coach or instructor has an indication that the sniper is committing one or more errors, it will usually be necessary for him to observe the sniper while he is in the act of firing to pinpoint his errors. If the instructor has no indication of the sniper's probable errors, the initial emphasis should be on his firing position and breath control. Next, the instructor should look for the most common errors—anticipation of the shot and improper trigger control. If observing the sniper fails to pinpoint his errors, the instructor must then question him.

QUESTIONING

3-107. The coach or instructor should ask the sniper if he could detect his errors. He should have the sniper explain the firing procedure, to include position, aiming, breath control, trigger control, and follow-through. If questioning does not reveal all of the errors, the instructor should talk the sniper through the procedures listed in Figure 3-22.

1. Set the sights. 2. Build the position. 3. Align the sight. 4. Check the natural POA. 5. Adjust the natural POA. 6. Control the breath.	7. Obtain a sight picture. 8. Focus on the front sight. 9. Control the trigger. 10. Follow through. 11. Call the shot.

Figure 3-22. Fundamental procedures for firing one round

NOTE

If errors still occur, there are several training exercises that can help to pinpoint them.

TRAINING EXERCISES

3-108. The instructor can use the following training exercises or devices at any time to supplement the detection procedure:

- Trigger exercise.
- Metal disk exercise.
- Ball and dummy exercise.
- Blank target-firing exercise.
- M2 aiming device.
- Air rifles.

3-109. When the sniper leaves the firing line, he compares weather conditions to the information needed to hit the POA or POI. Since he fires in all types of weather conditions, he must be aware of temperature, light, mirage, and wind. Other major tasks that the sniper must complete are as follows:

- Compare sight settings with previous firing sessions. If the sniper always has to fine-tune for windage or elevation, there is a chance he needs a sight change (slip a scale).
- Compare ammunition by lot number for the best rifle and ammunition combination.
- Compare all groups fired under each condition. Check the low and high shots and those to the left and right of the main group—the less dispersion, the better. If groups are tight, they are easily moved to the center of the target; if loose, there is a problem. Check the telescope focus and make sure the rifle is cleaned correctly. Remarks in the data book will also help.

- Make corrections. Record corrections in the data book, such as position and sight adjustment information, to ensure retention.
- Analyze a group on a target. These results are important for marksmanship training. The sniper may not notice errors during firing, but errors become apparent when analyzing a group. This study can only be done if the data book has been used correctly.

3-110. As the stability of a firing position decreases, the wobble area increases. The larger the wobble area, the harder it is to fire the shot without reacting to it. This reaction occurs when the sniper—

- Anticipates recoil.
- Jerks the trigger.
- Flinches.
- Avoids recoil.

APPLICATION OF FIRE

3-111. Following the Austrian-Prussian War of 1866, the Prussian Army began a systematic study of the effectiveness and control of small-arms fire. The result of this study, conducted over a 6-year period, was the introduction of the science of musketry, a misnomer as all major armies were by then equipped with rifles. Musketry is the science of small-arms fire under field conditions, as opposed to range conditions, and is concerned entirely with firing at unknown distances; thus the importance of musketry to the sniper. The material presented is merely an overview of the fundamentals of musketry. At the peak of the study of musketry as a martial science, musketry schools often extended their courses to six weeks. Only the introduction of machine guns and automatic small arms precipitated the doctrine of its study, although various aspects of musketry were retained as separate subjects, such as judging distances and issuing fire control orders. This study ties together the scattered remnants of the study of musketry as it pertains to sniping.

MINUTE OF ANGLE

3-112. Most weapon sights are constructed with a means of adjustment. Although the technicalities of adjustment may vary with weapon type or means of sighting, generally the weapon sight will be correctable for windage and elevation. The specific method by which adjustment is accomplished is angular displacement of the sight in relation to the bore of the rifle. This angular displacement is measured in MOAs, and establishes the angle of departure in relationship to LOS.

3-113. An MOA is the unit of angular measure that equals 1/60 of 1 degree of arc. With few exceptions the universal method of weapon sight adjustment is in fractions or multiples of MOAs. An MOA equals a distance of 1.0472 inches at 100 yards and 2.9 centimeters at 100 meters. Since an MOA is an angular unit of measure, the arc established by an MOA increases proportionately with distance (Figure 3-23).

3-114. Fractions are difficult to work with when making mental calculations. For this reason, snipers should assume that 1 MOA is the equivalent of 1 inch at 100 yards or 3 centimeters at 100 meters. By rounding off the angular displacement of the MOA in this manner, only 1/2 inch of accuracy at 1,000 yards and 1 centimeter at 1,000 meters are lost. This manual presents data in both the English and the metric system (Table 3-1), allowing the sniper to use whichever one he is most comfortable with.

SIGHT CORRECTIONS

3-115. With the knowledge of how much the displacement of 1 MOA at a given distance is, snipers can calculate sight corrections. All that the sniper needs to know is how many MOAs, or fractions of an MOA, each sight graduation (known as a "click") equals. This amount depends on the type of sight used.

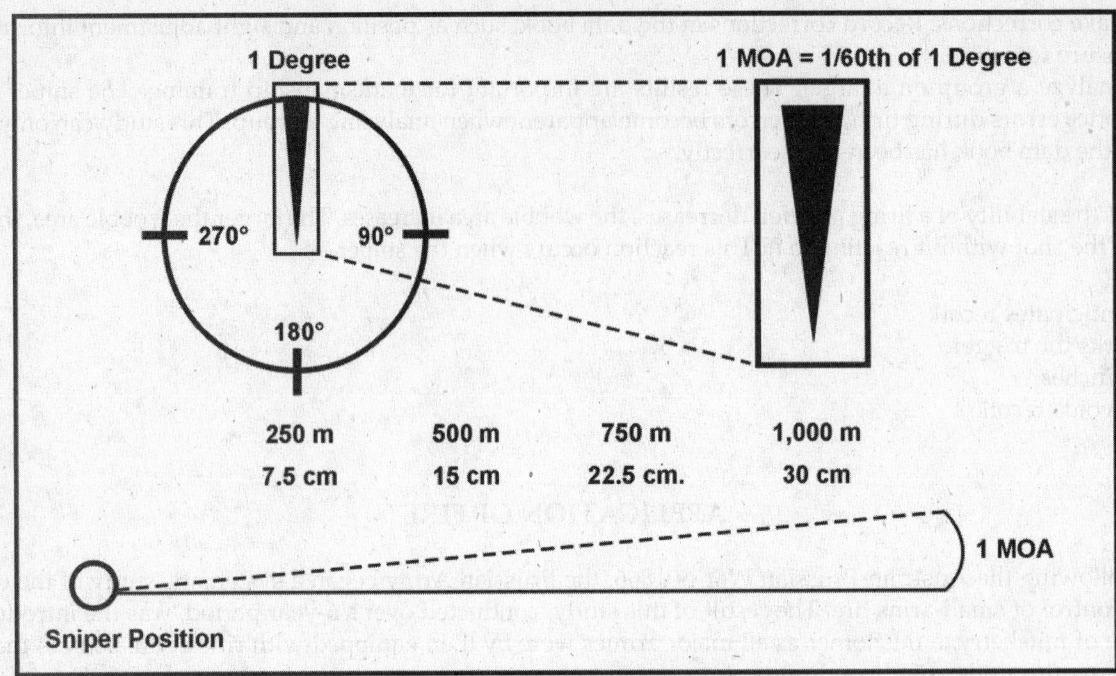

Figure 3-23. An MOA measurement

Table 3-1. Metric and English equivalents used to measure MOAs

Metric 1 MOA(cm)	Yards	Meters ←	Yards →	Meters	English 1 MOA (inches)
3	*109*	*100*		*91*	*1*
4.5	*164*	*150*		*137*	*1.5*
6	*219*	*200*		*183*	*2*
7.5	*273*	*250*		*228*	*2.5*
9	*328*	*300*		*274*	*3*
10.5	*383*	*350*		*320*	*3.5*
12	*437*	*400*		*365*	*4*
13.5	*492*	*450*		*411*	*4.5*
15	*546*	*500*		*457*	*5*
16.5	*602*	*550*		*503*	*5.5*
18	*656*	*600*		*548*	*6*
19.5	*711*	*650*		*594*	*6.5*
21	*766*	*700*		*640*	*7*
22.5	*820*	*750*		*686*	*7.5*
24	*875*	*800*		*731*	*8*
25.5	*929*	*850*		*777*	*8.5*
27	*984*	*900*		*823*	*9*
28.5	*1,039*	*950*		*869*	*9.5*
30	*1,094*	*1,000*		*914*	*10*
31.5	*1,148*	*1,050*		*960*	*10.5*
33	*1,203*	*1,100*		*1,005*	*11*

3-116. To determine the amount of correction required in MOAs for the English system, the error in inches is divided by the range expressed in whole numbers. The correction formula follows:

$$\text{Minutes} = \frac{\text{Error (inches)}}{\text{Range (expressed in whole numbers)}}$$

3-117. To determine the amount of correction required in MOAs using the metric system, the error in centimeters is divided by the range expressed in whole numbers, then the result is divided by 3. The correction formula follows:

$$\text{Minutes} = \frac{\text{Error (centimeters)}}{\text{Range (expressed in whole numbers)} \div 3}$$

3-118. There will be times when the impact of a shot is observed, but there is no accurate indication of how much the error is in inches or centimeters. Such occasions may occur when there is a great distance between the aiming point and the impact point or when there is a lack of an accurate reference. It is possible to determine the distance of the impact point from the POA in mils, then to convert the mils to MOAs. The conversion factor follows:

1 mil = 3.439 MOA (This is rounded to 3.5 for field use.)

EXAMPLE

When a round is fired, the observer sees the impact of the round to be several feet to the right of the target. He notes the impact point and determines it to be 2 mils to the right of the aiming point: 3.5 × 2 = 7 Minutes.

3-119. Table 3-2 gives the inch equivalents of mils at the given ranges of 91 meters to 1,000 meters and 100 yards to 1,000 yards. This data will aid the sniper in computing his sight change in mils for a given distance to the target with a given miss in estimated inches. For example, a miss of 28 inches left at 400 yards would be a 2-mil hold to the right.

Table 3-2. Inch equivalents of mils

Range (Meters/Yards)	Inches	Range (Meters/Yards)	Inches
91/100	*3.6*	*549/600*	*22.0*
100 m	*4.0*	*600 m*	*24.0*
183/200	*7.0*	*640/740*	*25.0*
200 m	*8.0*	*700 m*	*27.5*
274/300	*11.0*	*731/800*	*29.0*
300 m	*12.0*	*800 m*	*31.5*
365/400	*14.0*	*823/900*	*32.5*
400 m	*15.75*	*900 m*	*35.5*
457/500	*18.0*	*914/1,000*	*36.0*
500 m	*20.0*	*1,000 m*	*39.0*

BALLISTICS

3-120. As applied to sniper marksmanship, ballistics may be defined as the study of the firing, flight, and effect of ammunition. To fully understand ballistics, the sniper should be familiar with the terms listed in Table 3-3. Proper execution of marksmanship fundamentals and a thorough knowledge of ballistics ensure the successful completion of the mission. Tables and formulas in this section should be used only as guidelines since every rifle performs differently. Maintaining extensive ballistics data eventually results in a well-kept data book and provides the sniper with actual knowledge gained through experience. Appendix H provides additional ballistics data.

Table 3-3. Ballistics terminology

Muzzle Velocity	***The speed of a bullet as it leaves the rifle barrel, measured in fps. It varies according to various factors, such as ammunition type and lot number, temperature, and humidity.***
Line of Sight	***A straight line from the eye through the aiming devices to the POA.***
Line of Departure	***The line defined by the bore of the rifle or the path the bullet would take without gravity.***
Trajectory	***The path of the bullet as it flies to the target.***
Midrange Trajectory	***The high point the bullet reaches half way to the target. This point must be known to engage a target that requires firing underneath an overhead obstacle, such as a bridge or a tree. Inattention to midrange trajectory may cause the sniper to hit the obstacle instead of the target.***
Maximum Ordinate	***The highest point of elevation that a bullet reaches during its time of flight for a given distance.***
Bullet Drop	***How far the bullet drops from the line of departure to the POI.***
Time of Flight	***The amount of time it takes for the bullet to exit the rifle and reach the target.***
Retained Velocity	***The speed of the bullet when it reaches the target. Due to drag, the velocity will be reduced.***

APPLIED BALLISTICS

3-121. Ballistics can be broken down into three major areas. Interior or internal ballistics deals with the bullet in the rifle from primer detonation until it leaves the muzzle of the weapon. Exterior and external ballistics picks up after the bullet leaves the muzzle of the weapon and extends through the trajectory until the bullet impacts on the target or POA. Terminal ballistics is the study of what the bullet does upon impact with the target. The effectiveness of the terminal ballistics depends upon—

- Terminal velocity.
- Location of the hit.
- Bullet design and construction.

TARGET MATERIAL OR CONSTRUCTION

3-122. When it is fired, a bullet travels a straight path in the bore of the rifle as long as the bullet is confined in the barrel. As soon as the bullet is free of this constraint (exits the barrel), it immediately begins to fall due to the effects of gravity, and its motion is retarded due to air resistance. The path of the bullet through the air is called the bullet's trajectory.

3-123. If the barrel is horizontal, the forward motion imparted to the bullet by the detonation of the cartridge will cause it to travel in the direction of point A, but air resistance and the pull of gravity will cause it to strike point B (Figure 3-24). As soon as the bullet is free from the constraint of the barrel, it begins to pull from the horizontal.

3-124. For point A to be struck, the barrel of the rifle must be elevated to some predetermined angle (Figure 3-25). The bullet's initial impulse will be in the direction of point C. However, because of the initial angle, the bullet will fall to point A, due again to air resistance and gravity. This initial angle is known as the angle of departure.

3-125. The angle of departure is set by the sights and establishes the shape of the trajectory. The trajectory varies with the range to the target. For any given range, the angle of departure varies with the determining factors of the trajectory. The form of the trajectory is influenced by—

- The initial velocity (muzzle velocity).
- The angle of departure.

- Gravity.
- Air resistance.
- The rotation of the projectile (bullet) about its axis.

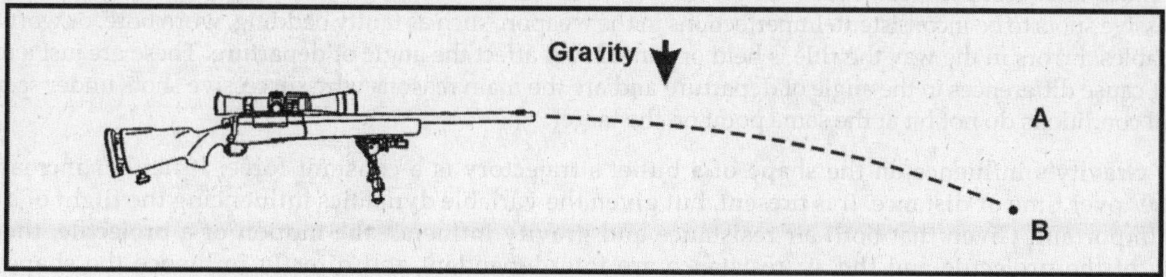

Figure 3-24. Bullet's trajectory when the sniper fires the rifle horizontally

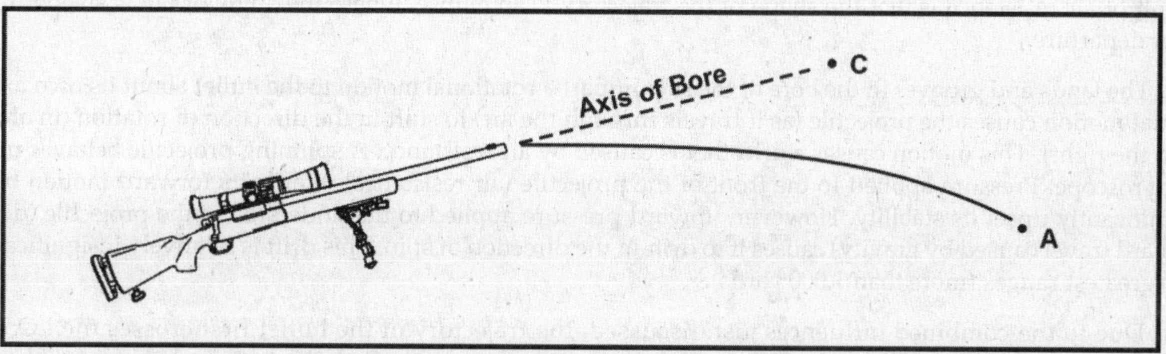

Figure 3-25. Bullet's trajectory when the sniper fires the rifle at an elevated angle

3-126. The relationship between initial velocity and air resistance is that the greater the amount of air resistance the bullet must overcome, the faster the bullet slows down as it travels through the air. A bullet with a lower initial velocity will be retarded less by air resistance and will retain a greater proportion of its initial velocity over a given distance. This relationship is important in that a light projectile with a higher initial (or short range) velocity will have a "flatter" initial trajectory but will have less initial and retained energy with which to incorporate the target, will be deflected more by wind, and will have a steeper trajectory at longer ranges. A comparatively heavy projectile will have a lower initial velocity and a steeper initial trajectory, will retain its energy over a great distance (retained energy is proportional to the mass of the projectile), will be deflected less by wind, and will have a "flatter" long-range trajectory.

3-127. Angle of departure is the angle to which the muzzle of the rifle must be elevated above the horizontal line in order for the bullet to strike a distant point. When the bullet departs the muzzle of the rifle, it immediately begins to fall to earth in relation to the angle of departure, due to the constant pull of gravity. The angle of departure increases the height the bullet must fall before it reaches the ground. If a rifle barrel were set horizontally in a vacuum, a bullet fired from the barrel would reach the ground at a distant point at the same moment that a bullet merely dropped from the same height as the barrel would reach the ground. Despite the horizontal motion of the bullet, its velocity in the vertical plane is constant (due to the constant effect of gravity). However, angle of departure in the air is directly related to the time of flight of the projectile in that medium. The greater the angle at which the projectile departs the muzzle, the longer it will remain in the air and the further it will travel before it strikes the ground. However, the effect of gravity causes the bullet to begin to lose distance at the 33-degree point.

3-128. The angle of departure is not constant. Although the angle of departure may remain fixed, a number of variables will influence the angle of departure in a series of shots fixed at the same given distance. The differences in the internal ballistics of a given lot of ammunition will have an effect. A muzzle velocity, within a proven lot, will often vary as much as 60 feet per second between shots. Imperfections in the human eye will cause the angles of departure of successive shots to be inconsistent. Imperfections in the weapon, such as faulty bedding, worn bore, or worn sights, are variables. Errors in the way the rifle is held or canted will affect the angle of departure. These are just a few factors that cause differences in the angle of departure and are the main reasons why successive shots under seemingly identical conditions do not hit at the same point on the target.

3-129. Gravity's influence on the shape of a bullet's trajectory is a constant force. It neither increases nor decreases over time or distance. It is present, but given the variable dynamics influencing the flight of a bullet, it is unimportant. Given that both air resistance and gravity influence the motion of a projectile, the initial velocity of the projectile and the air resistance are interdependent and directly influence the shape of the trajectory.

3-130. The single most important variable affecting the flight of a bullet is air resistance. It is not gravity that determines the shape of a bullet's trajectory. If gravity alone were the determining factor, the trajectory would have the shape of a parabola, where the angle of fall would be the same (or very nearly so) as the angle of departure. However, the result of air resistance is that the shape of the trajectory is an ellipse, where the angle of fall is steeper than the angle of departure.

3-131. The lands and grooves in the bore of the rifle impart a rotational motion to the bullet about its own axis. This rotational motion causes the projectile (as it travels through the air) to shift in the direction of rotation (in almost all cases to the right). This motion causes a drift that is caused by air resistance. A spinning projectile behaves precisely like a gyroscope. Pressure applied to the front of the projectile (air resistance) retards its forward motion but does not significantly upset its stability. However, upward pressure applied to the underside of the projectile (due to its downward travel caused by gravity) causes it to drift in the direction of spin. This drift is relatively insignificant at all but the greatest ranges (more than 1,000 yards).

3-132. Due to the combined influences just discussed, the trajectory of the bullet first crosses the LOS with a scarcely perceptible curve. The trajectory continues to rise to a point a little more than halfway to the target, called the maximum ordinate, beyond which it curves downward with a constantly increasing curve (possibly recrossing the LOS) until it hits the target (or ground). The point where the LOS meets the target is the POA. The point where the bullet (trajectory) strikes the target is the POI. Theoretically, the POA and the POI should coincide. In practical terms, because of one or more of the influences discussed, they rarely do. The greater the skill of the sniper and the more perfect the rifle and ammunition, the more often these two points will coincide (Figure 3-26).

3-133. The part of the trajectory between the muzzle and the maximum ordinate is called the rising branch of the trajectory; the part beyond the maximum ordinate is called the falling branch of the trajectory. Snipers are most concerned with the falling branch because this part of the trajectory contains the target and the ground in its vicinity. In computing the height of the trajectory, assuming the LOS is horizontal and at regular intervals (usually 100 yards), the sniper measures and records the height of the trajectory as the ordinate. The distance from the muzzle to the ordinate is known as the abscissa. The distance in front of the muzzle, within which the bullet does not rise higher than the target, is called the danger space of the rising branch of the trajectory. The falling branch of the trajectory also has a danger space. The danger space of the falling branch is the point where the bullet falls into the height of the target and continues to the ground.

3-134. Assuming that the POA is taken at the center of the target, the extent of the danger space depends on the following:

- Height of the sniper—whether he is standing, kneeling, or prone.
- Height of the target—whether he is standing, kneeling, or prone.

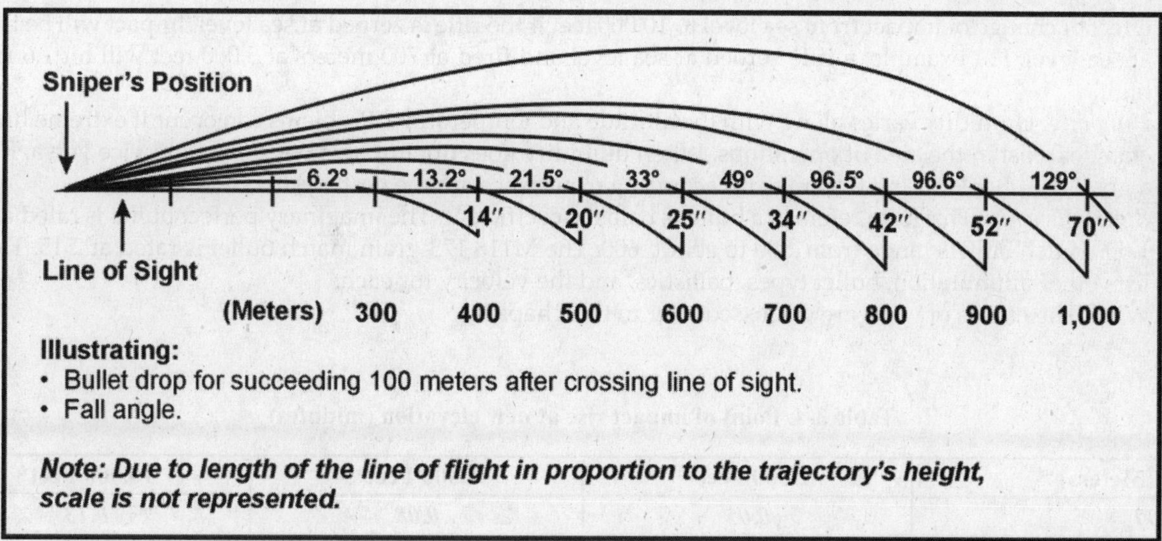

Figure 3-26. Sniper's line of sight with fall angles at various distances

- "Flatness" of the trajectory—the ballistic properties of the cartridge used.
- Angle of the LOS—above or below the horizontal.
- Slope of the ground—where the target resides.

3-135. The POA also has a significant influence on the extent of the danger space. If the sniper takes the POA at the top of the target, the total danger space will lie entirely behind the target. If he takes the POA at the foot of the target, the total danger space will lie entirely in front of the target. Thus, the extent of the total danger space, including the target, will be determined by where the POA is taken on the target. Only when the POA is at the center of the target will the total danger space (in relative terms) extend an equal distance in front of and behind the target.

EFFECTS ON TRAJECTORY

3-136. Mastery of marksmanship fundamentals and field skills are not the only requirements for being a sniper. Some of the factors that have an influence on the trajectory include the following:

- *Gravity.* The sniper would not have a maximum range without gravity; a fired bullet would continue to move much the same as items floating in space. As soon as the bullet exits the muzzle of the weapon, gravity begins to pull it down, requiring the sniper to use his elevation adjustment. At extended ranges, the sniper actually aims the muzzle of his rifle above his LOS and lets gravity pull the bullet down into the target. Gravity is always present, so the sniper must compensate for it through elevation adjustments or holdover techniques.
- *Drag.* It is the slowing effect the atmosphere has on the bullet. This effect either increases or decreases according to the air—that is, the less dense the air, the less drag and vice versa. Factors affecting drag and air density are—
- *Temperature.* The higher the temperature, the less dense the air. If the sniper zeroes at 60 degrees F and he fires at 80 degrees F, the air is less dense, thereby causing an increase in muzzle velocity and a higher impact. A 20-degree change equals a 1-minute elevation change on the rifle. This generally applies for a 7.62-mm weapon.
- *Altitude/barometric pressure.* Since the air pressure is less at higher altitudes, the air is less dense and there is less drag. Therefore, the bullet is more efficient and impacts higher. Table 3-4, page 448, shows the appropriate

effect of change of impact from sea level to 10,000 feet if the rifle is zeroed at sea level. Impact will be the POA at sea level. For example, a rifle zeroed at sea level and fired at 700 meters at 5,000 feet will hit 1.6 minutes high.

- *Humidity.* Humidity varies along with the altitude and temperature. Problems can occur if extreme humidity changes exist in the area of operations. When humidity goes up, impact goes down and vice versa. Keeping a good data book during training and acquiring experience are the best teachers.
- *Bullet efficiency.* This term refers to a bullet's ballistic coefficient. The imaginary perfect bullet is rated as being 1.00. Match bullets range from .500 to about .600. The M118 173-grain match bullet is rated at .515. Table 3-5 lists other ammunition, bullet types, ballistics, and the velocity for each.
- *Wind.* The effects of wind are discussed later in this chapter.

Table 3-4. Point of impact rise at new elevation (minutes)

Range (Meters)	2,500 Feet*	5,000 Feet*	10,000 Feet*
100	*0.05*	*0.08*	*0.13*
200	*0.1*	*0.2*	*0.34*
300	*0.2*	*0.4*	*0.6*
400	*0.4*	*0.5*	*0.9*
500	*0.5*	*0.9*	*1.4*
600	*0.6*	*1.0*	*1.8*
700	*1.0*	*1.6*	*2.4*
800	*1.3*	*1.9*	*3.3*
900	*1.6*	*2.8*	*4.8*
1,000	*1.8*	*3.7*	*6.0*

Above Sea Level

Table 3-5. Selected ballistics information

Ammunition	Bullet Type	Ballistic Coefficient	Muzzle Velocity
M193	*55 FMJBT*	*.260*	*3,200 fps*
M180	*147 FMJBT*	*.400*	*2,808 fps*
M118	*173 FMJBT*	*.515*	*2,610 fps*
M852	*168 HPBT*	*.475*	*2,675 fps*
M72	*173 FMJBT*	*.515*	*2,640 fps*

SHOT GROUPS

3-137. If a rifle is fired many times under uniform conditions, the bullets striking the target will group themselves about a central point called the center of impact and will form a circular or elliptical group. The dimensions and shape of this shot group will vary depending on the distance of the target from the sniper. The circle or ellipse formed by these shots constantly increases in size with the range. The line connecting the centers of impact of all shots at all ranges measured is called the mean trajectory, and the core containing the circumferences of all the circles would mark the limits of the sheaf. The mean trajectory is the average trajectory. All ordinates are compared to it, and angles of departure and fall refer only to it.

3-138. The pattern on the target made by all of the bullets is called the shot group. If the shot group is received on a vertical target, it is called a vertical shot group and is circular. If the group is received on a horizontal target, it is called a horizontal shot group and is elliptical. A large number of shots will form a shot group having the general shape of an ellipse, with its major axis vertical. The shots will be symmetrically grouped about the center of impact, not necessarily about the POA. They will be grouped more densely near the center of impact than at the edges, and half of all the shots will be found in a strip approximately 1/4 the size of the whole group. The width of this strip is called the mean vertical (or the 50 percent dispersion) if measured vertically or the mean lateral if measured laterally.

3-139. When considering the horizontal shot group, the mean lateral dispersion retains its same significance, but what is called the mean vertical dispersion on a vertical target is known as the mean longitudinal dispersion on a horizontal target. There is a significant relationship between the size or dimensions of a shot group and the size or dimensions of the target fired at. With a shot group of fixed dimensions, when the target is made sufficiently large, all shots fired will strike the target. Conversely, with a very small target, only a portion of the shots fired will strike the target. The rest of the shots will pass over, under, or to the sides of the target.

3-140. It is evident that the practical application of exterior ballistics—hitting a target of variable dimensions at unknown distances—is one probability of a shot group of fixed dimensions (the sniper's grouping ability) conforming to the dimensions of a given target. Added to this probability is the ability of the sniper to compensate for environmental conditions and maintain an accurate zero.

3-141. One of the greatest paradoxes of sniping is that an average marksman has a slightly higher chance of hitting targets at unknown distances than a good marksman, if their respective abilities to judge distances, determine effects of environmental conditions, and maintain an accurate zero are equal. (The classification of **good marksman** and **average marksman** refers only to the sniper's grouping ability.) A good marksman who has miscalculated wind or who is not accurately zeroed would expect to miss the target entirely. An average marksman, under identical conditions, would expect to obtain at least a few hits on the target; or if only one shot was fired, would have a slight chance of obtaining a first-round hit. The above statement does not mean that average marksmen make better snipers. It does mean that the better the individual shoots, the more precise his ability to judge distance, calculate wind, and maintain his zero must be.

3-142. Practical exterior ballistics is the state of applying a shot group or a sheaf of shots over an estimated distance against a target of unknown or estimated dimensions. It also includes estimating the probability of obtaining a hit with a single shot contained within the sheaf of shots previously determined through shot-group practices.

INFLUENCE OF GROUND ON THE SHOT GROUP (SHEAF OF SHOTS)

3-143. When firing at targets of unknown distances under field conditions, the sniper must take into consideration the lay of the ground and how it will affect his probable chances of hitting the target. Generally, the ground a sniper fires over will—

- Be level.
- Slope upward.
- Slope downward.

3-144. The extent of the danger space depends on the—

- Relationship between the trajectory and the LOS, angle of fall, and the range curvature of the trajectory.
- Height of the target.
- Point of aim.
- Point of impact.

> **NOTE**
>
> The longer the range, the shorter the danger space, due to the increasing curvature of the trajectory.

3-145. The displacing of the center of impact from the center of the target is a factor that the sniper must also consider. It will often be the controlling factor. The danger space at ranges under 700 yards is affected by the position of the sniper (height of the muzzle above the ground). The danger space increases as the height of the muzzle decreases. At longer ranges, no material effect is felt from different positions of the sniper.

3-146. The influence of the ground on computing hit probability on a target at unknown distances results in the necessity of distinguishing between danger space and swept space (which are functions of the mean trajectory), and between these (danger space and swept space) and the dangerous zone (which is a function of the whole or a part of the cone of fire). For a given height of target and POA, the danger space is of fixed dimensions. The swept space varies in relation with the slope of the ground. Swept space is shorter on rising ground and longer on falling ground than the danger space. All the functions of the danger zone, such as the density of the group at a given distance from the center of impact, are correspondingly modified.

SNIPER DATA BOOK

3-147. The sniper data book contains a collection of data cards. The sniper uses these cards to record firing results and all elements that have an effect on firing the weapon. This information could include weather conditions or even the sniper's attitude on a particular day. The sniper can refer to this information later to understand his weapon, the weather effects, and his firing ability on a given day. One of the most important items of information he will record is the cold barrel zero of his weapon. A cold barrel zero refers to the first round fired from the weapon. It is critical that the sniper know this by firing the first round at 200 meters. When the barrel warms up, later shots may begin to group 1 or 2 minutes higher or lower, depending on rifle specifics. Figure 3-27 shows a sample sniper data card.

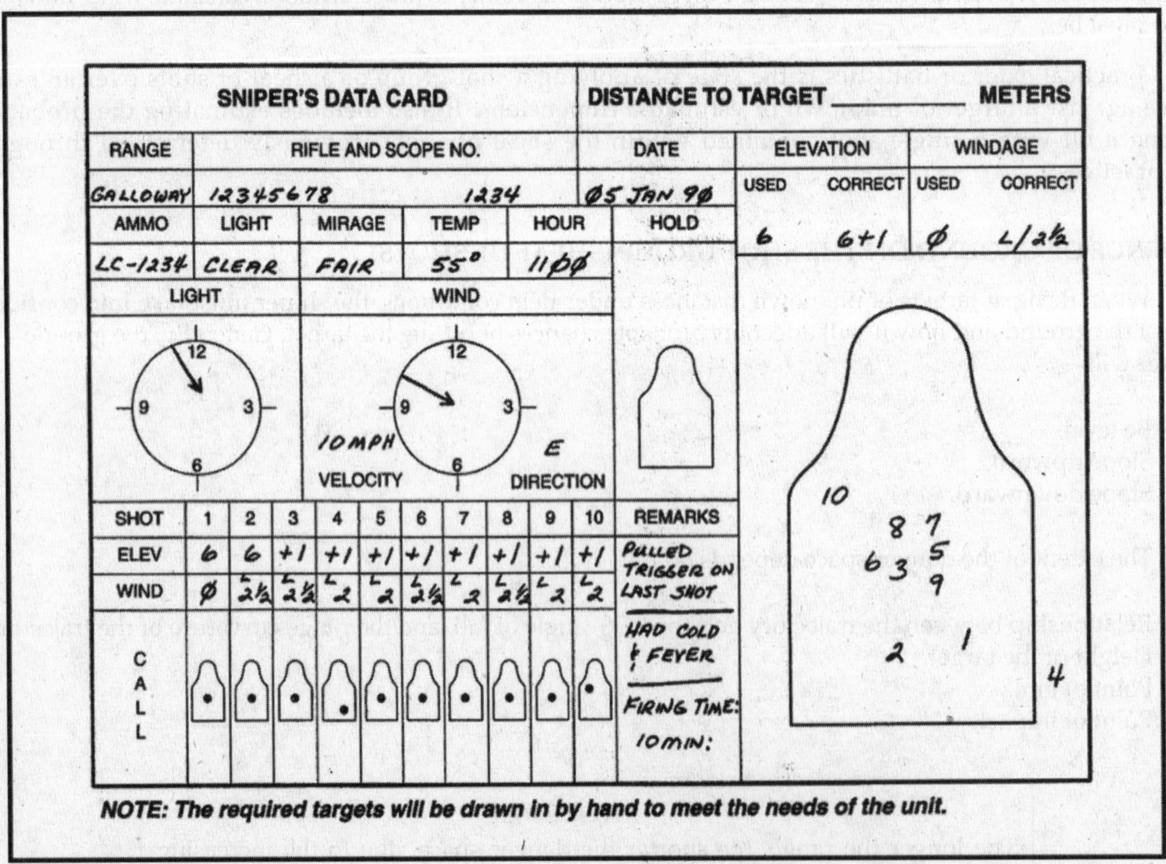

SNIPER'S DATA CARD — DISTANCE TO TARGET ______ METERS

RANGE	RIFLE AND SCOPE NO.	DATE	ELEVATION USED	ELEVATION CORRECT	WINDAGE USED	WINDAGE CORRECT
GALLOWAY	12345678 1234	Ø5 JAN 9Ø	6	6+1	Ø	L/2½

AMMO	LIGHT	MIRAGE	TEMP	HOUR	HOLD
LC-1234	CLEAR	FAIR	55°	11ØØ	

LIGHT: 12, 3, 6, 9

WIND: 12, 3, 6, 9 — 10MPH VELOCITY — E DIRECTION

SHOT	1	2	3	4	5	6	7	8	9	10	REMARKS
ELEV	6	6	+1	+1	+1	+1	+1	+1	+1	+1	PULLED TRIGGER ON LAST SHOT
WIND	Ø	L 2½	L 2½	L 2	L 2	L 2½	L 2	L 2½	L 2	L 2	HAD COLD & FEVER
CALL											FIRING TIME: 10MIN:

NOTE: The required targets will be drawn in by hand to meet the needs of the unit.

Figure 3-27. Sample of a sniper's data card

3-148. When used properly, the data card will provide the necessary information for initial sight settings at each distance or range. It also provides a basis for analyzing the performance of the sniper and his rifle and is a valuable aid in making bold and accurate sight changes. The most competent sniper would not be able to consistently hit the center of the target if he were unable to analyze his performance or if he had no record of his performance or conditions affecting his firing.

ENTRIES

3-149. The three phases in writing information on the data card are *before firing, during firing,* and *after firing*. Each phase requires specific data and provides an excellent learning tool for future training. Each sniper should complete the following information for each phase and analyze his performance to stay proficient at all times.

Phase I-Before Firing

3-150. Before the sniper fires, he should record the following data:

- *Range.* The distance to the target.
- *Rifle and telescope number.* The serial numbers of the rifle and telescope.
- *Date.* Date of firing.
- *Ammunition.* Type and lot number of ammunition.
- *Light.* Amount of light (overcast, clear).
- *Mirage.* Whether a mirage can be seen or not (bad, fair, good).
- *Temperature.* Temperature on the range.
- *Hour.* Time of firing.
- *Light (diagram).* He draws an arrow in the direction the light is shining.
- *Wind.* He draws an arrow in the direction that the wind is blowing and records its average velocity and cardinal direction (N, NE, S, SW).

Phase II-During Firing

3-151. The sniper should also record specific data during firing. This information includes the following:

- *Elevation.* Elevation setting used and any correction needed. (For example: The target distance is 600 meters; the sniper sets the elevation dial to 6. The sniper fires and the round hits the target 6 inches low of center. He then adds 1 minute [one click] of elevation.)
- *Windage.* Windage setting used and any correction needed. (For example: The sniper fires at a 600 meter target with a windage setting on 0; the round impacts 15 inches right of center. He will then add 2 1/2 minutes left to the windage dial [L/2 1/2].)
- *Shot.* The column of information about a particular shot. (For example: Column 1 is for the first round; column 10 is for the tenth round.)
- *Wind.* Windage used. (For example: L/2, 1/2, O, R/1/2.) This is for iron sights or compensation for spin drift. Mil holds are used for the scope.
- *Call.* Where the aiming point was when the weapon fired.
- *Large silhouette or target representation.* Used to record the exact impact of the round on the target. This is recorded by writing the shot's number on the large silhouette that is in the same place it hit the target.

Phase III-After Firing

3-152. The sniper also records data after firing that will enable him to better understand his results and to improve his performance. This data includes:

- Comments about the weapon, firing conditions (time allowed for fire), or his condition (nervous, felt bad, felt good).

- Corrected no-wind zero. Show the elevation and windage in minutes and clicks that was correct for this position and distance under no-wind conditions.
- Remarks. Note any equipment, performance, weather conditions, or range conditions that had a good or bad effect on the firing results.

ANALYSIS

3-153. When the sniper leaves the firing line, he compares weather conditions to the information needed to hit the POA or POI. Since he fires in all types of weather conditions, he must be aware of temperature, light, mirage, and wind. He must also consider the following possibilities:

- Compare sight settings with previous firing sessions. If the sniper always has to fine-tune for windage or elevation, there is a chance he needs a sight change (slip a scale).
- Compare the ammunition by lot number for the best rifle and ammunition combination.
- Compare all groups fired under each condition. Check the low and high shots as well as those to the left and the right of the main group. Of course, less dispersion is desired. If groups are tight, they are easily moved to the center of the target; if scattered, there is a problem. Check the telescope focus and ensure that the rifle is cleaned correctly. Remarks in the data book will also help.
- Make corrections. Record corrections in the data book, such as position and sight adjustment information, to ensure retention. The sniper should compare hits to calls. If they agree, the result is an indication that the zero is correct and that any compensation for the effects of the weather is correct. If the calls and hits are consistently out of the target, sight adjustment or more position and trigger control work is necessary.

3-154. The sniper should compare the weather conditions and location of the groups on the latest data sheet to previous data sheets to determine how much and in which direction the sights should be moved to compensate for the weather conditions. If better results are obtained with a different sight picture under an unusual light condition, he should use this sight picture whenever firing under that particular light condition. A different sight picture may necessitate adjusting the sights. After establishing how much to compensate for the effects of weather or which sight picture works best under various light conditions, the sniper should commit this information to memory.

3-155. The sniper should keep the training and zeroing data sheets for future reference. Rather than carry the firing data sheets during sniper training exercises or combat, he can carry or tape on his weapon stock a list of the elevation and windage zeros at various ranges.

ZEROING THE RIFLE

3-156. A zero is the alignment of the sights with the bore of the rifle so that the bullet will impact on the target at the desired POA. However, the aiming point, the sight, and the bore will coincide at two points. These points are called the zero.

3-157. Depending upon the situation, a sniper may have to deliver an effective shot at ranges up to 1,000 meters or more. This need requires the sniper to zero his rifle (with telescopic and iron sights) at most of the ranges that he may be expected to fire. When using telescopic sights, he needs only zero for elevation at 300 meters (100 meters for windage) and confirms at the more distant ranges. His success depends on a "one round, one hit" philosophy. He may not get a second shot. Therefore, he must accurately zero his rifle so that when applying the fundamentals he can be assured of an accurate hit.

CHARACTERISTICS OF THE SNIPER RIFLE IRON SIGHTS

3-158. The iron sights of the M24 are adjustable for both windage and elevation. While these sights are a backup to the telescope and used only under extraordinary circumstances, it is in the sniper's best interest to be fully capable with them. Iron sights are excellent for developing marksmanship skills. They force the sniper to concentrate on sight alignment, sight picture, and follow-through.

3-159. The M24 has a hooded front sight that has interchangeable inserts. These various-sized inserts range from circular discs to posts. The sniper should use the post front sight to develop the sight picture that is consistent with the majority of U.S. systems. The rear sight is the Palma match sight and has elevation and windage adjustments in 1/4 MOA. The elevation knob is on the top of the sight and the windage knob is on the right side of the sight. Turning the elevation knob in the direction marked "UP" raises the POI, and turning the windage knob in the direction marked "R" moves the POI to the right.

ADJUSTMENT OF THE REAR SIGHT

3-160. The sniper determines mechanical windage zero by aligning the sight base index line with the centerline of the windage gauge. The location of the movable index line indicates the windage used or the windage zero of the rifle. For example, if the index line is to the left of the centerline of the gauge, this point is a left reading. The sniper determines windage zero by simply counting the number of clicks back to the mechanical zero. He determines the elevation of any range by counting the number of clicks down to mechanical elevation zero.

3-161. Sight adjustment or manipulation is a very important aspect of training that must be thoroughly learned by the sniper. He can accomplish this goal best through explanation and practical work in manipulating the sights.

3-162. The sniper must move the rear sight in the direction that the shot or shot group is to be moved. To move the rear sight or a shot group to the right, he turns the windage knob clockwise. The rule to remember is *push left—pull right.* To raise the elevation or a shot group, he turns the elevation knob clockwise. To lower it, he turns counterclockwise.

ZEROING THE SNIPER RIFLE USING THE IRON SIGHTS

3-163. The most precise method of zeroing a sniper rifle with the iron sights is to fire the rifle and adjust the sights to hit a given point at a specific range. The rifle is zeroed in 100-meter increments from 100 to 900 meters. The targets are placed at each range, then the sniper fires one or more five-round shot groups at each aiming point. He must adjust the rear sight until the center of the shot group and the aiming point coincide at each range. The initial zeroing for each range should be accomplished from the prone supported position. The sniper can then zero from those positions and ranges that are most practical. There is no need to zero from the least steady positions at longer ranges.

3-164. The sniper should use the following zeroing procedure for M24 iron sights:

- *Elevation knob adjustments.* Turning the elevation knob located on the top of the rear sight in the UP direction raises the POI; turning the knob downward lowers the POI. Each click of adjustment equals 0.25 MOA.
- *Windage knob adjustments.* Turning the windage knob located on the right side of the rear sight in the R direction moves the impact of the round to the right; turning the knob in the opposite direction moves the POI to the left. Each click of adjustment equals 0.25 MOA. Windage should be zeroed at 100 meters to negate the effects of wind.
- *Calibrating rear sight.* After zeroing the sights to the rifle, the sniper loosens the elevation and windage indicator plate screws with the wrench provided. He should align the "0" on the plate with the "0" on the sight body, then retightens the plate screws. Next, he loosens the setscrews in each knob and aligns the "0" of the knob with the reference line on the sight. He presses the sight and tightens the setscrews. The sniper then sharpens or softens the click to preference by loosening or tightening the spring screws equally on the knob. He must now count down the number of clicks to the bottom of the sight. He then records this number and uses it as a reference whenever he believes there has been a problem with his rear sight. He only needs to bottom out the sight and count up the number of clicks required to the desired zero. Windage and elevation corrections can now be made, and the sniper can return quickly to the zero standard. Elevation should be zeroed at 200 meters to increase the accuracy of the zero.
- *Graduations.* There are 12 divisions or 3 MOA adjustments in each knob revolution. Total elevation adjustment is 60 MOAs and total windage adjustment is 36 MOAs. Adjustment scales are of the "vernier" type. Each graduation on the scale plate equals 3 MOAs. Each graduation on the sight base scale equals 1 MOA.

3-165. To use the scales, the sniper—

- Notes the point at which graduations on both scales are aligned (Figure 3-28).
- Counts the number of full 3 MOA graduations from "0" on the scale plate to "0" on the sight base scale.
- Adds this figure to the number of MOAs from "0" on the bottom scale to the point where the two graduations are aligned.

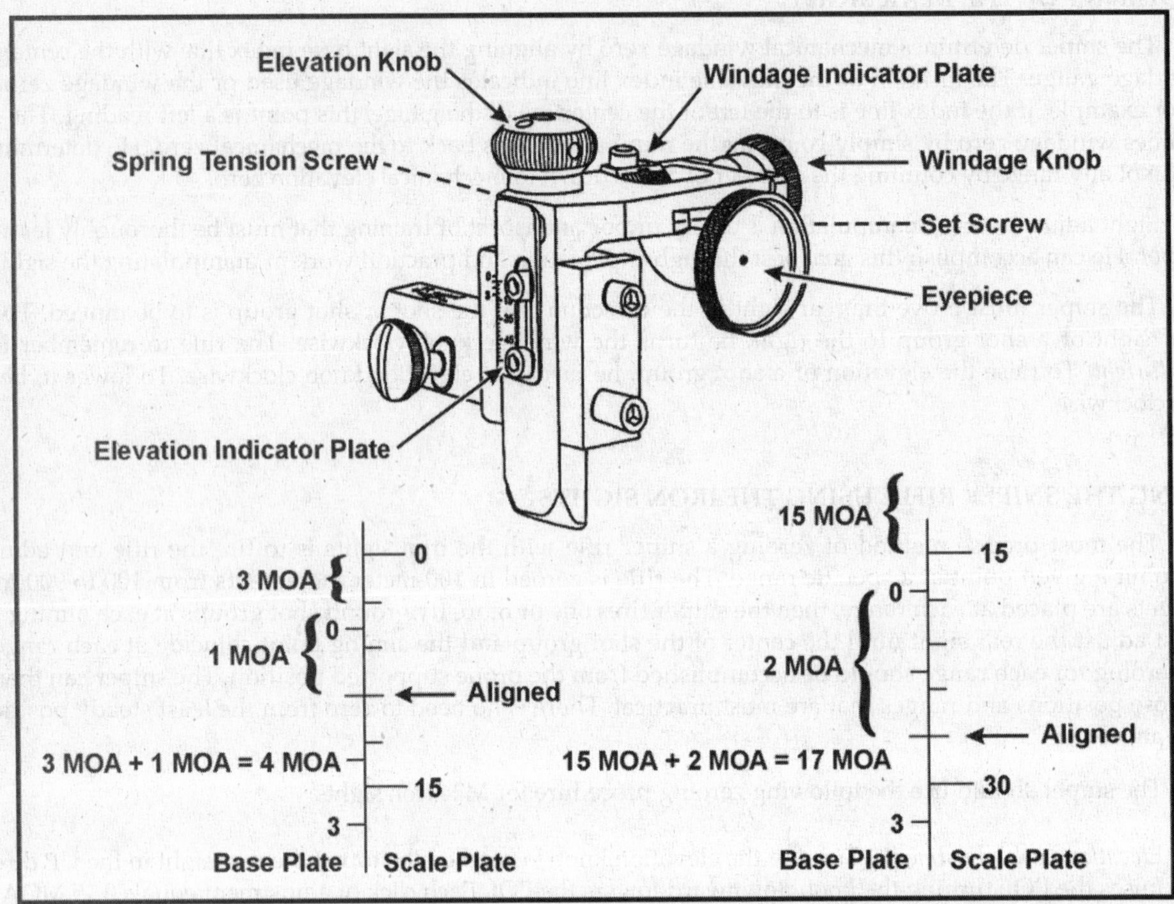

Figure 3-28. Adjusting the elevation and windage on the rear sight assembly

> **NOTE**
>
> The Redfield Palma sight is the issued sight of the SWS and no longer available commercially.

CHARACTERISTICS OF THE SNIPER RIFLE TELESCOPIC SIGHT

3-166. Sniper telescopic sights have turret assemblies for the adjustment of elevation and windage. The upper assembly is the elevation and the assembly on the right is for windage. These assemblies have knobs that are marked for corrections of a given value in the direction indicated by the arrow. The M3A and the ART series use a similar system for zeroing. The sniper moves the knobs in the direction that he wants the shot group to move on the target.

3-167. The M3A is graduated to provide 1 MOA of adjustment for each click of its elevation knob and 1/2 MOA of adjustment for each click of its windage knob. This sight is designed to provide audible and tactile clicks. The elevation turret knob is marked in 100-meter increments from 100 to 500, and 50-meter increments from 500 to 1,000.

ZEROING THE SNIPER WEAPON SYSTEM WITH THE TELESCOPIC SIGHT

3-168. The most precise method of zeroing the sniper rifle for elevation using the scope sight is to fire and adjust the sight to hit a given point at 200 meters. For windage, the scope should be zeroed at 100 meters. This point rules out as much wind effect as possible. After zeroing at 100 meters, the sniper should confirm his zero out to 900 meters in 100-meter increments. The bull's-eye-type target (200-yard targets, NSN SR1-6920-00-900-8204) can be used for zeroing. Another choice is a blank paper with black pastees forming a 1-MOA aim point.

3-169. The sniper should use the following zeroing procedures for a telescopic sight. He should—

- Properly mount the scope to the rifle.
- Select or prepare a distinct target (aiming cross) at 200 meters for elevation or 100 meters for windage. If 200 meters is used for windage, then impact must be compensated for a no-wind effect.
- Assume the prone supported position.
- Focus the reticle to his eye.
- Set parallax for target range.
- Boresight scope to ensure round on paper, considering that the M3A is a fixed 10x scope.
- Fire a single shot and determine its location and distance from the aiming cross.
- Using the elevation and windage rule, determine the number of clicks necessary to move the center of the group to the center of the aiming cross.
- Remove the elevation and windage turret caps and make the necessary sight adjustments. Then replace the turret caps. In making sight adjustments, the sniper must turn the adjusting screws in the direction that he wants to move the strike of the bullet or group.
- Fire 5-round groups as necessary to ensure that the center of the shot group coincides with the POA at 200 meters for elevation and compensated for wind.
- Zero the elevation and windage scales and replace the turret caps.

3-170. The rifle is now zeroed for 200 meters with a no-wind zero.

3-171. To engage targets at other ranges, set the range on the elevation turret. To engage targets at undetermined ranges, use the mil dots in the scope, determine the range to the target, and then manually set the elevation turret.

NOTE
Elevation and windage turrets should not be forced past the natural stops as damage may occur.

AN/PVS-2 Night Vision Device

3-172. The AN/PVS-2 may be zeroed during daylight hours or during hours of darkness. However, the operator may experience some difficulty in attempting to zero just before darkness (dusk). The light level is too low at dusk to permit the operator to resolve his zero target with the lens cap cover in place, but the light level at dusk is still intense enough to cause the sight to automatically cut off unless the lens cap cover is in position over the objective lens. The sniper will normally zero the sight for the maximum practical range that he can be expected to observe and fire, depending on the level of illumination.

3-173. The sniper should zero the sight in the following manner. He should—

- Place or select a distinct target at the desired zeroing range. A steel target provides the easiest target to spot because bullet splash is indicated by a spark as the bullet strikes the steel. He should assume the prone supported position, supporting the weapon and night vision sight combination with sandbags or other available equipment that will afford maximum stability.

- Boresight the sight to the rifle. The sniper places the iron sight windage and elevation zero on the rifle for the zeroing range and adjusts the weapon position until the correct sight picture is obtained on the aiming point at the zeroing range. He moves the eye to the night vision sight and observes the location of the reticle pattern in relation to the reference aiming point. If the reference aiming point on the target and the reference POA of the reticle pattern do not coincide, move the elevation and azimuth adjustment knobs until these aiming points coincide.
- Place the reference POA of the reticle pattern (Figure 3-29) on the center of mass of the target or on a distinct aiming point on the target. Then fire enough rounds to obtain a good shot group. Check the target to determine the center of the shot group in relation to the reticle POA.
- Adjust the night vision sight to move the reticle aiming reference point to the center of the shot group. When making adjustments for errors in elevation or azimuth, move the sight in the direction of the error. For example, if the shot group is high and to the left of the reticle POA, compensate for the error by moving the sight to the left and up.

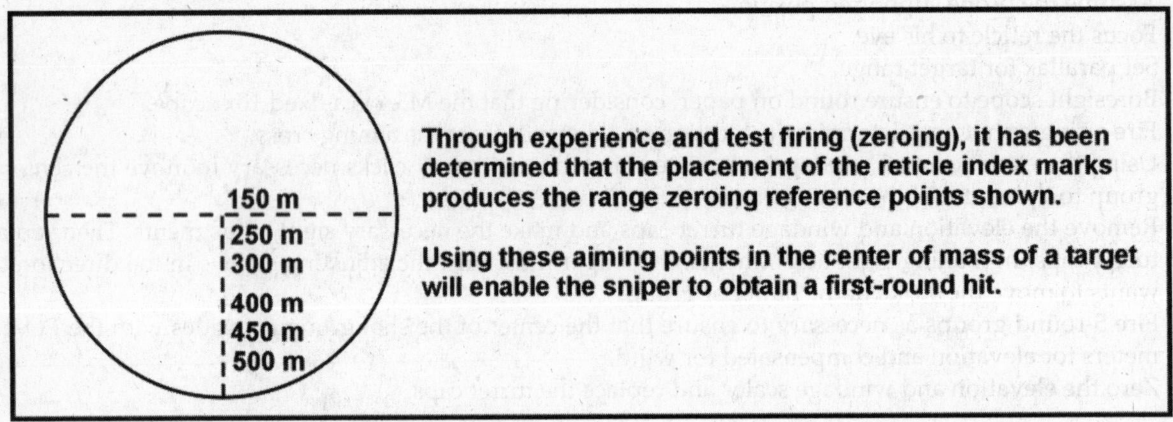

Figure 3-29. The range references and POAs for the AN/PVS-2 black line reticle pattern

> **NOTE**
> Each click of the azimuth or elevation knob will move the strike of the round 2 inches for each 100 meters of range.

3-174. To engage targets at ranges other than the zero range, apply hold-off to compensate for the rise and fall in the trajectory of the round.

AN/PVS-4 Night Vision Device

3-175. Zeroing the AN/PVS-4 is similar to zeroing with standard optical sights because (unlike the AN/PVS-2) the AN/PVS-4 mounts over the bore of the weapons system and has internal windage and elevation adjustments (Figure 3-30).

Periodic Checking

3-176. A sniper cannot expect his zero to remain absolutely constant. Periodic checking of the zero is required after disassembly of the sniper rifle for maintenance and cleaning, for changes in ammunition lots, as a result of severe weather changes, and to ensure first-shot hits. The rifle must be zeroed by the individual who will use it. Individual

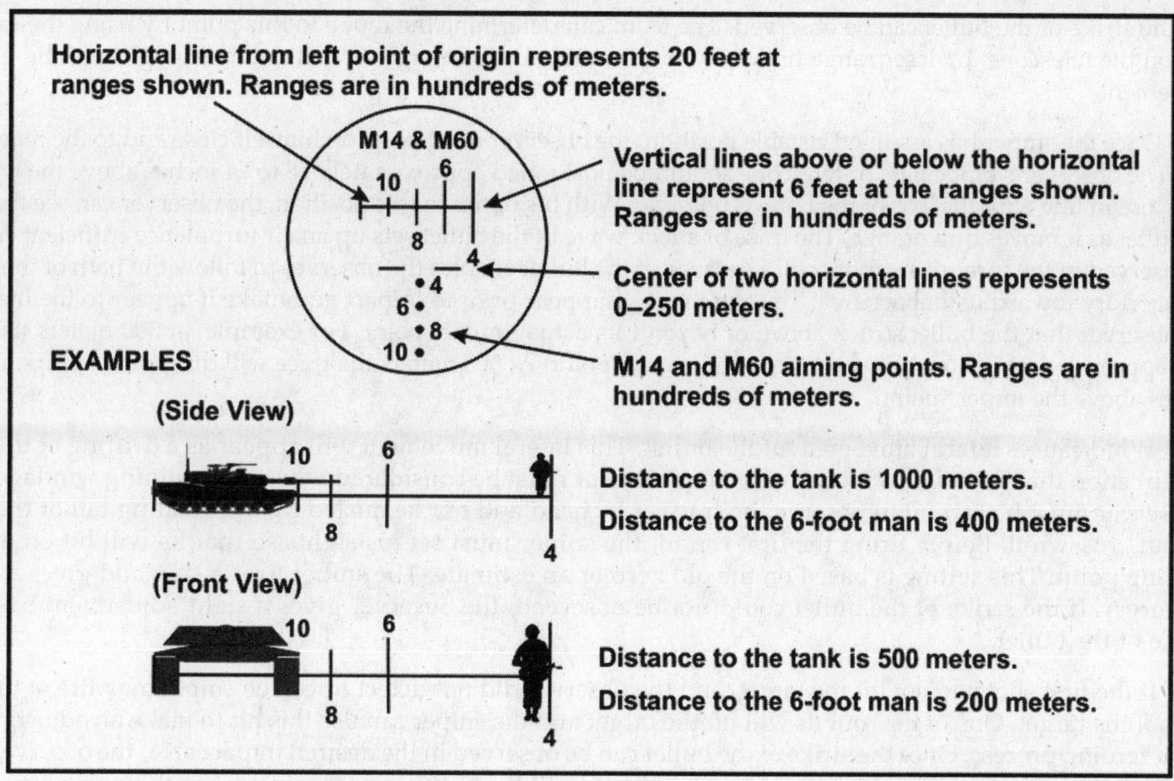

Figure 3-30. Using the M14 and M60 reticle of the AN/PVS-4 for range estimation and POA

differences in stock weld, eye relief, position, and trigger control usually result in each sniper having a different zero with the same rifle or a change in zero after moving from one position to another.

Confirming Zero

3-177. After a rifle has been zeroed and it becomes necessary to confirm this zero for any reason, the rifle can be zeroed again by firing at a known distance with the sight set on the old zero. If a sight adjustment is necessary to hit the aiming point, this zero change will remain constant at all ranges. For example, if a sniper is firing at a distance of 500 meters with the old zero and it becomes necessary to raise the elevation three clicks to hit the aiming point, he should raise the elevation zero three clicks at all ranges.

Changing Zero

3-178. Before changing the zero, windage, or elevation, the sniper must consider the effects of weather. Extreme changes of humidity or temperature can warp the stock or affect the ammunition. Wear, abuse, or repairs can also cause a sniper rifle's zero set to change.

Field-Expedient Zeroing

3-179. The sniper should use the boresight to confirm zero retention in a denied area. The sniper may need to confirm his zero in a field environment. Dropping a weapon or taking it through excessive climatic changes (by deploying worldwide) are good reasons for confirming the SWS's zero. The sniper may also use this method when the time or situation does not permit the use of a known distance range. This technique works best when confirming old zeros.

3-180. The sniper will need an observer equipped with binoculars or a spotting telescope to assist him. The sniper and observer pick out an aiming point in the center of an area; for example, a hillside, brick house, or any surface where the strike of the bullet can be observed. The team can determine the range to this point by using the ranging device on the telescope, by laser range finder, by map survey, by the range card of another weapon, or by ground measurement.

3-181. Once the sniper has assumed a stable position, the observer must position himself close and to the rear of the sniper. The observer's binoculars or telescope should be positioned approximately 18 to 24 inches above the weapon and as close in line with the axis of the bore as possible. With his optics in this position, the observer can see the trace of the bullet as it moves downrange. The trace or shock wave of the bullet sets up an air turbulence sufficient enough to be observed in the form of a vapor trail. The trace of the bullet enables the observer to follow the path of the bullet in its trajectory toward its impact area. The trace will disappear prior to impact and make it appear to the inexperienced observer that the bullet struck above or beyond its actual impact point. For example, at 300 meters the trace will disappear approximately 5 inches above the impact point. At 500 meters the trace will disappear approximately 25 inches above the impact point.

3-182. Wind causes lateral movement of the bullet. This lateral movement will appear as a drifting of the trace in the direction that the wind is blowing. This movement must be considered when determining windage zero. The observer must be careful to observe the trace at its head and not be misled by the bending tail of the trace in a stout crosswind. Before firing the first round, the sniper must set his sights so that he will hit on or near his aiming point. This setting is based on the old zero or an estimate. The sniper fires a shot and gives a call to the observer. If the strike of the bullet could not be observed, the observer gives a sight adjustment based on the trace of the bullet.

3-183. If the first shots do not hit the target, and the observer did not detect trace, the sniper may fire at the four corners of the target. One of the rounds will hit the target and the sniper can use this hit to make an adjustment to start the zeroing process. Once the strike of the bullet can be observed in the desired impact area, the observer compares the strike with the call and gives sight adjustments until the bullet impact coincides with the aiming point.

Firing at Targets With No Definite Zero Established

3-184. The sniper should use the 100-meter zero when firing on targets at a range of 100 meters or less. The difference between the impact of the bullet and the aiming point increases as the range increases if the sights are not moved. If the sniper's zero is 9 + 2 at 900 meters and 8 + 1 at 800 meters, and he establishes the range of the target at 850 meters, he should use a sight setting of 850+1 rather than using his 800- or 900-meter zero or the hold-off method. At any range, moving the sights is preferred over the hold-off method.

Firing the 25-Meter Range

3-185. The sniper should dial the telescope to 300 meters for elevation and to zero for windage. He then aims and fires at a target that is 25 yards away. He adjusts the telescope until rounds are impacting 1 inch above the POA. For the sniper to confirm, he fires the SWS on a known distance range out to its maximum effective range.

3-186. For iron sights, the sniper may fire on a 25-meter range to obtain a battle-sight zero. He then subtracts 1 minute (four clicks) of elevation from the battle-sight zero to get a 200-meter zero. The sniper may then use the following measures to determine the necessary increases in elevation to engage targets out to 600 meters:

- 200 to 300 meters—2 minutes.
- 300 to 400 meters—3 minutes.
- 400 to 500 meters—4 minutes.
- 500 to 600 meters—5 minutes.

NOTE

These measures are based on the average change of several sniper rifles. While the changes may not result in an "exact" POA or POI zero, the sniper should not miss his target.

ENVIRONMENTAL EFFECTS

3-187. For the highly trained sniper, the effects of weather are the main cause of error in the strike of the bullet. Wind, mirage, light, temperature, and humidity all have some effect on the bullet and the sniper. Some effects are insignificant, depending on average conditions of sniper employment.

3-188. It must be noted that all of the "rules of thumb" given here are for the 7.62-mm bullet (168 to 175 grains) at 2600 feet per second (fps). If the sniper is using a caliber 5.56, 300 Win Mag, .338 Lapua Mag, or any other round then these rules do not apply. It is incumbent on the sniper to find the specific wind constants and other "effects" for the round he will be using.

WIND

3-189. The condition that constantly presents the greatest problem to the sniper is the wind. The wind has a considerable effect on the bullet, and the effect increases with the range. This result is due mainly to the slowing of the bullet's velocity combined with a longer flight time. This slowing allows the wind to have a greater effect on the bullet as distances increase. The result is a loss of stability. Wind also has a considerable effect on the sniper. The stronger the wind, the more difficult it is for the sniper to hold the rifle steady. The effect on the sniper can be partially offset with good training, conditioning, and the use of supported positions.

Classification

3-190. Since the sniper must know how much effect the wind will have on the bullet, he must be able to classify the wind. The best method to use is the clock system (Figure 3-31, page 460). With the sniper at the center of the clock and the target at 12 o'clock, the wind is assigned the following three values:

- *Full value* means that the force of the wind will have a full effect on the flight of the bullet. These winds come from 3 and 9 o'clock.
- *Half value* means that a wind at the same speed, but from 1, 2, 4, 5, 7, 8, 10, and 11 o'clock will move the bullet only half as much as a full-value wind. While this half-value definition is generally accepted, it is not accurate. Applying basic math will illustrate that the actual half-value winds are from 1, 5, 7, and 11 on the clock. Winds from 2, 4, 8, and 10 have values of 86 percent.

> **NOTE**
>
> To determine the exact effect of the wind on the bullet when the wind is between full and no-value positions, multiply the wind speed by the following constants: 90-degree, full; 75 degree, 0.96; 60 degree, 0.86; 45 degree, 0.70; 30 degree, 0.50; 15 degree, 0.25.

- *No value* means that a wind from 6 or 12 o'clock will have little or no effect on the flight of the bullet at close ranges. The no-value wind has a definite effect on the bullet at long ranges (beyond 600 meters) if it is not blowing directly from 6 or 12 o'clock. This wind is the most difficult to fire in due to its switching or fishtail effect, which requires frequent sight changes. Depending on the velocity of this type of wind, it will have an effect on the vertical displacement of the bullet.

Velocity

3-191. Before adjusting the sight to compensate for wind, the sniper must determine wind direction and velocity. He may use certain indicators to make this determination. These indicators include range flags, smoke, trees, grass, rain, and the sense of feel. In most cases, wind direction can be determined simply by observing the indicators. However, the preferred method of determining wind direction and velocity is reading mirage.

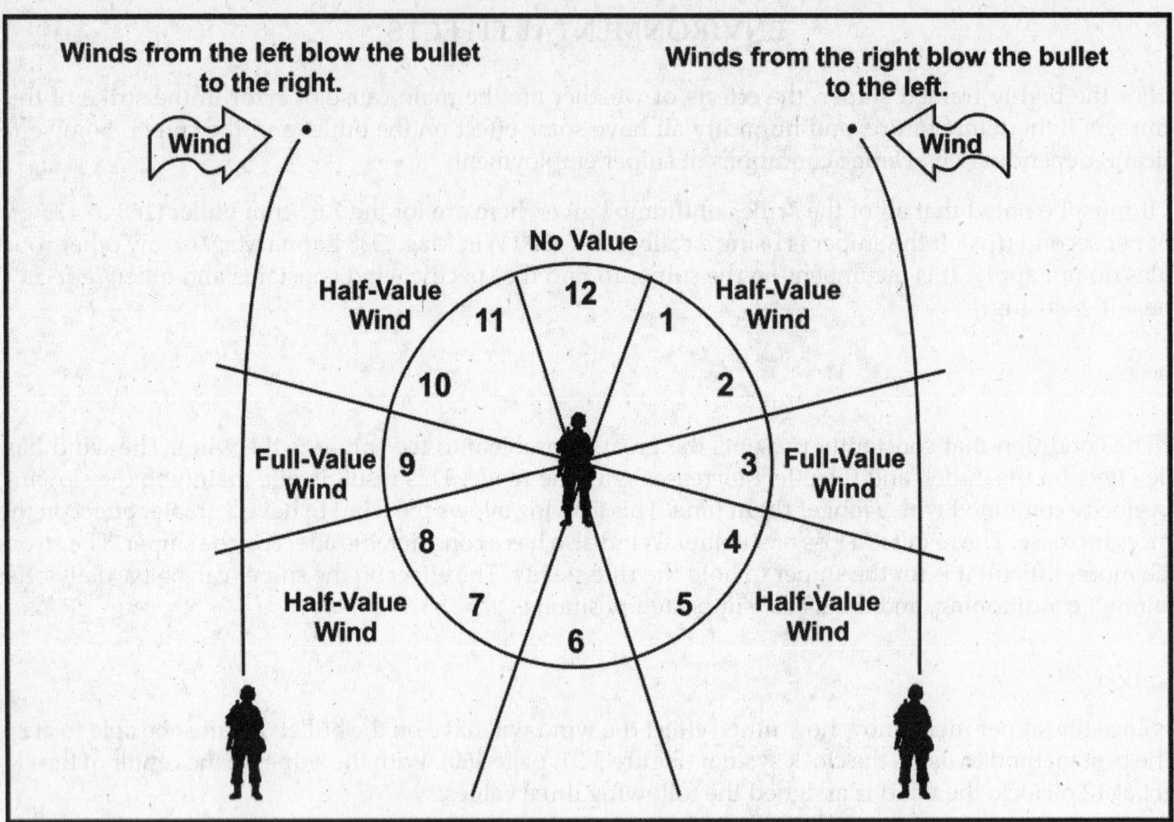

Figure 3-31. Using the clock system method to classify the wind

3-192. A method of estimating the velocity of the wind during training is to watch the range flag (Figure 3-32). The sniper determines the angle in degrees between the flag and pole, then divides by the constant number 4. The result gives the approximate velocity in miles per hour (mph). This amount is based on the use of the heavier cotton range flags, not nylon flags, which are now used on most ranges.

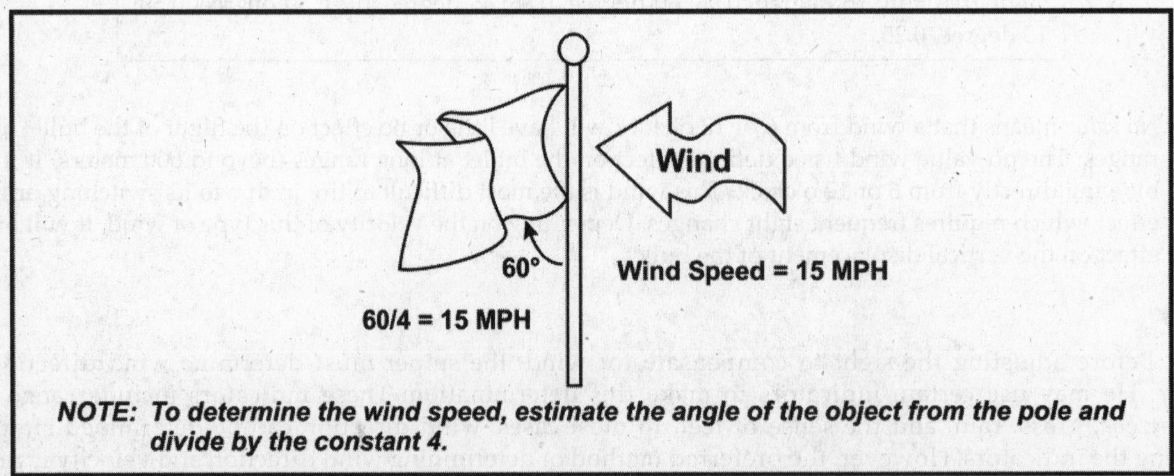

Figure 3-32. Estimating wind velocity using the range flag

> **NOTE**
> Nylon flags are not a reliable indicator for determining wind speed because of their susceptibility to minor wind speed variations.

3-193. If no flag is visible, the sniper holds a piece of paper, grass, cotton, or some other light material at shoulder level, then drops it. He then points directly at the spot where it lands and divides the angle between his body and arm by the constant number 4. This number gives him the approximate wind velocity in mph (Figure 3-33).

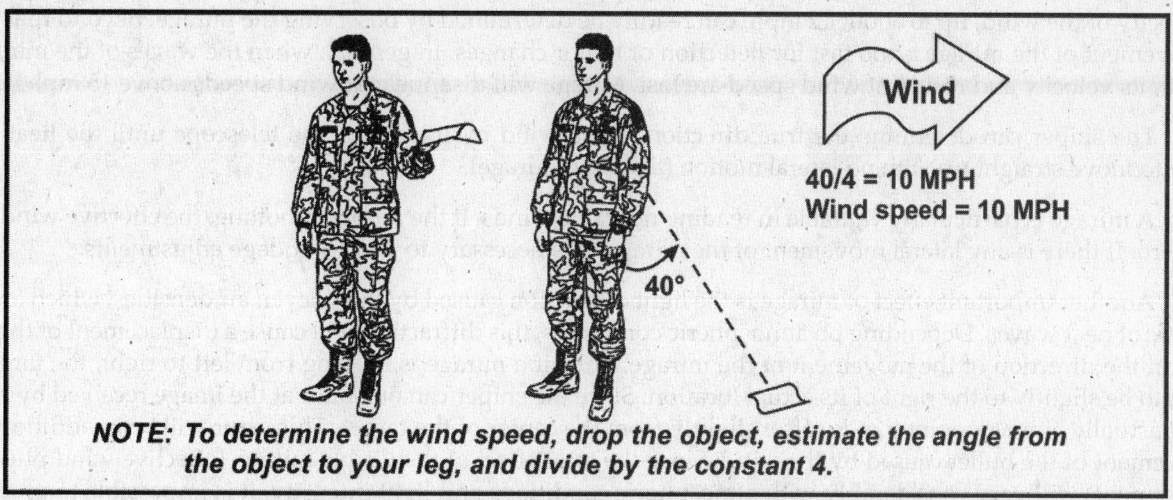

Figure 3-33. Estimating wind velocity by dropping a piece of paper

3-194. If the sniper is unable to use these methods, he can apply the information in Table 3-6 to determine velocity.

Table 3-6. Determining velocity

Wind Velocity (mph)	Effect
0–3	*The wind can barely be felt but may be seen by mirage or smoke drifts.*
3–5	*The wind can be felt on the face. Grass begins to move.*
5–8	*The leaves in the trees and long grass are in constant motion.*
8–12	*The wind raises dust and loose paper and moves small branches in trees.*
12–15	*The wind causes trees to sway.*

MIRAGE

3-195. A mirage is a reflection of the heat through layers of air at different temperatures and densities as seen on a warm, bright day. With the telescope, the sniper can see a mirage as long as there is a difference in ground and air temperatures. Proper reading of the mirage enables the sniper to estimate wind direction with a high degree of accuracy. The sniper uses the spotting scope to read the mirage. Since the wind nearest to midrange has the greatest effect on the bullet, he should try to determine velocity at that point. He can determine the amount in one of two ways:

- Focus on an object at midrange, then place the telescope back on to the target without readjusting the focus.

- Focus on the target, then back off the focus one-quarter turn counterclockwise. This movement makes the target appear fuzzy, but the mirage will be clear.

3-196. As observed through the telescope, the mirage appears to move with the same velocity as the wind, except when blowing straight into or away from the telescope. Then the mirage gives the appearance of moving straight upward with no lateral movement. It is then called a boiling mirage. A boiling mirage may also be seen when the wind is constantly changing direction; for example, a full-value wind blowing from 9 to 3 o'clock suddenly changes direction. The mirage will appear to stop moving from left to right and will present a boiling appearance. When this image occurs, the inexperienced observer may direct the sniper to fire with the "0" wind. As the sniper fires, the wind begins blowing from 3 to 9 o'clock and causes the bullet to miss the target. Therefore, firing in a "boil" can hamper shot placement. Unless there is a no-value wind, the sniper must wait until the boil disappears. In general, changes in the velocity of the wind, up to about 12 mph, can readily be determined by observing the mirage. Beyond that speed, the movement of the mirage is too fast for detection of minor changes. In general, when the waves of the mirage are shallow, its velocity and resultant wind speed are fast. Mirage will disappear at wind speeds above 15 mph.

3-197. The sniper can determine the true direction of the wind by traversing the telescope until the heat waves appear to move straight up with no lateral motion (a boiling mirage).

3-198. A mirage is particularly valuable in reading no-value winds. If the mirage is boiling, the effective wind velocity is zero. If there is any lateral movement of the mirage, it is necessary to make windage adjustments.

3-199. Another important effect of mirage is the light diffraction caused by the uneven air densities, which are characteristic of heat waves. Depending on atmospheric conditions, this diffraction will cause a displacement of the target image in the direction of the movement of the mirage. Thus if a mirage is moving from left to right, the target will appear to be slightly to the right of its actual location. Since the sniper can only aim at the image received by his eye, he will actually aim at a point that is offset slightly from the center of the target. This error will be in addition to the displacement of the bullet caused by the wind. Since the total effect of the visible mirage (effective wind plus target displacement) will vary considerably with atmospheric conditions and light intensity, it is impossible to predict the amount of error produced at any given place and time. It is only through considerable experience in reading mirage that the sniper will develop proficiency as a "wind doper."

3-200. Before firing, the sniper should check the mirage and make the necessary sight adjustments or hold-off to compensate for any wind. Immediately after firing, but before plotting the call in the scorebook, he again checks the mirage. If any changes are noted, they must be considered in relating the strike of the bullet to the call. The above procedure should be used for each shot.

CONVERSION OF WIND VELOCITY TO MINUTES OF ANGLE

3-201. All telescopic sights have windage adjustments that are graduated in MOAs or fractions thereof. An MOA is 1/60th of a degree. This number equals about 1 inch (1. 0472 inches) for every 100 yards and 3 centimeters (2.97 centimeters) for every meter.

EXAMPLE
1 MOA = 2 inches at 200 yards
1 MOA = 15 centimeters at 500 meters

3-202. Snipers use MOAs to determine and adjust the elevation and windage needed on the telescope. After finding the wind direction and velocity in mph, the sniper must then convert it into MOAs using the wind formula as a rule of thumb only. The wind formula is as follows:

$$\frac{\text{Range (hundreds)} \times \text{Velocity (mph)}}{\text{Given Variable}} = \text{Minutes Full-Value Wind}$$

3-203. The given variable (GV) for M80 ball depends on the target's range (R) and is due to bullet velocity loss:

- 100 to 500 GV = 15
- 600 GV = 14
- 700 to 800 V = 13
- 900 GV = 12
- 1,000 GV = 11

3-204. The variable for M118, M118LR, and M852 is 10 at all ranges.

3-205. If the target is 700 meters away and the wind velocity is 10 mph, the formula is as follows:

$$\frac{7 \times 10}{10} = 7 \text{ MOA}$$

NOTE

This formula determines the number of minutes for a full-value wind. For a half-value (1/2V) wind, the 7 MOA would be divided in half, resulting in 3.5 MOA.

3-206. The observer makes his own adjustment estimations and then compares them to the wind conversion table, which can be a valuable training tool. He must not rely on this table. If it is lost, his ability to perform the mission could be severely hampered. Until the observer gains skill in estimating wind speed (WS) and computing sight changes, he may refer to the wind conversion table (Table 3-7). The observer will give the sniper a sight adjustment for iron sights or a mil hold off for the scope.

Table 3-7. Wind conversion table in mils

WS / R(m)	2	4	6	8	10	12	14	16	18	20
100	*0.00*	*0.00*	*0.25*	*0.25*	*0.25*	*0.25*	*0.50*	*0.50*	*0.50*	*0.50*
1/2V	*0.00*	*0.00*	*0.00*	*0.00*	*0.00*	*0.00*	*0.25*	*0.25*	*0.25*	*0.25*
200	*0.00*	*0.25*	*0.25*	*0.50*	*0.50*	*0.75*	*0.75*	*1.00*	*1.00*	*1.25*
1/2V	*0.00*	*0.00*	*0.00*	*0.25*	*0.25*	*0.50*	*0.50*	*0.50*	*0.50*	*0.75*
300	*0.25*	*0.25*	*0.50*	*0.75*	*1.00*	*1.00*	*1.25*	*1.50*	*1.50*	*1.75*
1/2V	*0.00*	*0.00*	*0.25*	*0.50*	*0.50*	*0.50*	*0.75*	*0.75*	*0.75*	*1.00*
400	*0.25*	*0.50*	*0.75*	*1.00*	*1.25*	*1.50*	*1.50*	*2.00*	*2.25*	*2.25*
1/2V	*0.00*	*0.25*	*0.50*	*0.50*	*0.75*	*0.75*	*0.75*	*1.00*	*1.25*	*1.25*
500	*0.25*	*0.50*	*1.00*	*1.25*	*1.50*	*1.75*	*2.00*	*2.25*	*2.50*	*3.00*
1/2V	*0.00*	*0.25*	*0.50*	*0.75*	*0.75*	*1.00*	*1.00*	*1.25*	*1.25*	*1.50*
600	*0.25*	*0.75*	*1.00*	*1.50*	*1.75*	*2.25*	*2.50*	*2.75*	*3.25*	*3.50*
1/2V	*0.00*	*0.50*	*0.50*	*0.75*	*1.00*	*1.00*	*1.25*	*1.25*	*1.50*	*1.75*
700	*0.50*	*0.75*	*1.25*	*1.50*	*2.00*	*2.50*	*3.00*	*3.25*	*3.75*	*4.25*
1/2V	*0.25*	*0.50*	*0.75*	*0.75*	*1.00*	*1.25*	*1.50*	*1.75*	*2.00*	*2.25*
800	*0.50*	*1.00*	*1.50*	*2.00*	*2.25*	*2.75*	*3.25*	*3.75*	*4.25*	*4.75*
1/2V	*0.25*	*0.50*	*0.75*	*1.00*	*1.25*	*1.50*	*1.75*	*1.75*	*2.25*	*2.50*
900	*5.00*	*1.00*	*1.50*	*2.00*	*2.50*	*3.25*	*3.75*	*4.25*	*4.75*	*5.25*
1/2V	*2.50*	*0.50*	*0.75*	*1.00*	*1.25*	*1.50*	*1.75*	*2.25*	*2.50*	*2.50*
1,000	*5.00*	*1.25*	*1.75*	*2.50*	*3.00*	*3.50*	*4.25*	*4.75*	*5.25*	*6.00*
1/2V	*2.50*	*0.63*	*0.75*	*1.25*	*1.50*	*1.75*	*2.25*	*2.50*	*2.50*	*3.00*

LIGHT

3-207. Light does not affect the trajectory of the bullet. However, it may affect the way the sniper sees the target through the telescope. Light affects different people in different ways. The sniper generally fires high on a dull, cloudy day and low on a bright, clear day. Extreme light conditions from the left or the right may have an effect on the horizontal impact of a shot group.

3-208. This effect can be compared to the refraction (bending) of light through a medium, such as a prism or a fish bowl. The same effect can be observed on a day with high humidity and with sunlight from high angles. To solve the problem of light and its effects, the sniper must accurately record the light conditions under which he is firing. Through experience and study, he will eventually determine the effect of light on his zero. Light may also affect firing of unknown distance ranges since it affects range determination capabilities, by elongating the target.

TEMPERATURE

3-209. Temperature has a definite effect on the elevation setting required to hit the center of the target. This effect is caused by the fact that an increase in temperature of 20 degrees Fahrenheit (F) will increase the muzzle velocity by approximately 50 fps. When ammunition sits in direct sunlight, the burn rate of powder is increased. The greatest effect of temperature is on the density of the air. As the temperature rises, the air density is lowered. Since there is less resistance, velocity decreases at a slower rate and the impact rises. This increase is in relation to the temperature in which the rifle was zeroed. If the sniper zeroes at 50 degrees and he is now firing at 90 degrees, the impact rises considerably. How high it rises is best determined by past firing recorded in the data book. The general rule is that a 20-degree increase from zero temperature will raise the impact by 1 minute; conversely, a 20-degree decrease will drop impact by 1 minute from 100 to 500 meters, 15 degrees will affect the strike by 1 MOA from 600 to 900 meters, and 10 degrees over 900 meters will affect the strike by 1 MOA.

ELEVATION

3-210. Elevation above sea level can have an important effect on bullet trajectory. At higher elevations, air density, temperature, and air drag on the bullet decrease. The basic rule of thumb is that the bullet strike will vary by 1 MOA for every 5,000 feet of elevation. This amount will roughly correspond to the same barometric rule for changes in round strike.

BAROMETRIC PRESSURE

3-211. The effects of barometric pressure are that the higher the pressure, the denser the air. Thus the higher the pressure the lower the bullet will strike. As the pressure goes up, the sights go up. The basic rule is that from 100 to 500 meters, 1 inch in barometric pressure will affect the strike by 0.25 MOA; from 600 to 800 meters, a 1-inch change will affect the strike by 0.75 MOA, and from 900 to 1000 meters, a 1-inch change will effect the strike by 1.5 MOA.

HUMIDITY

3-212. Humidity varies along with the altitude and temperature. The sniper can encounter problems if drastic humidity changes occur in his area of operation. If humidity goes up, impact goes up; if humidity goes down, impact goes down. As a rule of thumb, a 20-percent change will equal about 1 minute affecting the impact. The sniper should keep a good data book during training and refer to his own record.

3-213. To understand the effects of humidity on the strike of the bullet, the sniper must realize that the higher the humidity, the thinner the air; thus there is less resistance to the flight of the bullet. This will tend to slow the bullet at a slower rate, and, as a result, the sniper must lower his elevation to compensate for these factors. The effect of humidity at short ranges is not as noticeable as at longer ranges. The sniper's experience and his analysis of hits and groups under varied conditions will determine the effect of humidity on his zero.

3-214. Some snipers fail to note all of the factors of weather. Certain combinations of weather will have different effects on the bullet. For this reason, a sniper may fire two successive days in the same location and under what appears to be the same conditions and yet use two different sight settings. For example, a 30-percent rise in humidity cannot always be determined readily. This rise in humidity makes the air less dense. If this thinner air is present with a 10-mile-per-hour wind, less elevation will be required to hit the same location than on a day when the humidity is 30 percent lower.

3-215. By not considering all the effects of weather, some snipers may overemphasize certain effects and therefore make bad shots from time to time. Snipers normally fire for a certain period of time under average conditions. As a result, they zero their rifles and (with the exception of minor displacements of shots and groups) have little difficulty except for the wind. However, a sniper can travel to a different location and fire again and find a change in his zero. Proper recording and study based on experience are all important in determining the effects of weather. Probably one of the most difficult things to impress upon a sniper is the evidence of a probable change in his zero. If a change is indicated, it should be applied to all ranges.

SLOPE FIRING

3-216. The sniper team conducts most firing practices by using the military range facilities, which are relatively flat. However, snipers may deploy to other regions of the world and have to operate in a mountainous or urban environment. This type of mission would require target engagements at higher and lower elevations. Unless the sniper takes corrective action, bullet impact will be above the POA. How high the bullet hits is determined by the range and angle to the target (Table 3-8). The amount of elevation change applied to the telescope of the rifle for angle firing is known as slope dope.

Table 3-8. Bullet rise at given angle and range in minutes

Range (Meters)	Slant Degrees											
	5	10	15	20	25	30	35	40	45	50	55	60
100	*0.01*	*0.04*	*0.09*	*0.16*	*0.25*	*0.36*	*0.49*	*0.63*	*0.79*	*0.97*	*1.2*	*1.4*
200	*0.03*	*0.09*	*0.2*	*0.34*	*0.53*	*0.76*	*1.0*	*1.3*	*1.7*	*2.0*	*2.4*	*2.9*
300	*0.03*	*0.1*	*0.3*	*0.5*	*0.9*	*1.2*	*1.6*	*2.1*	*2.7*	*3.2*	*3.9*	*4.5*
400	*0.05*	*0.19*	*0.43*	*0.76*	*1.2*	*1.7*	*2.3*	*2.9*	*3.7*	*4.5*	*5.4*	*6.3*
500	*0.06*	*0.26*	*0.57*	*1.0*	*1.6*	*2.3*	*3.0*	*3.9*	*4.9*	*6.0*	*7.2*	*8.4*
600	*0.08*	*0.31*	*0.73*	*1.3*	*2.0*	*2.9*	*3.9*	*5.0*	*6.3*	*7.7*	*9.2*	*10.7*
700	*0.1*	*0.4*	*0.9*	*1.6*	*2.5*	*3.6*	*4.9*	*6.3*	*7.9*	*9.6*	*11.5*	*13.4*
800	*0.13*	*0.5*	*1.0*	*2.0*	*3.0*	*4.4*	*5.9*	*7.7*	*9.6*	*11.7*	*14.0*	*16.4*
900	*0.15*	*0.6*	*1.3*	*2.4*	*3.7*	*5.3*	*7.2*	*9.3*	*11.6*	*14.1*	*16.9*	*19.8*
1,000	*0.2*	*0.7*	*1.6*	*2.8*	*4.5*	*6.4*	*8.6*	*11.0*	*13.9*	*16.9*	*20.2*	*23.7*

NOTE: Range given is slant range (meters), not map distance.

3-217. The following is a list of compensation factors to use in setting the sights of the SWS when firing from any of the following angles. To use Table 3-9, the sniper finds the angle at which he must fire and then multiplies the estimated range by the decimal figure shown to the right. For example, if the estimated range is 500 meters and the angle of fire is 35 degrees, the zero of the weapon should be set for 410 meters.

EXAMPLE

500 × .82 = 410 meters

Table 3-9. Compensation factors used when firing from a given angle

A	
Percent of Slope Angle Up or Down (Degrees)	**Multiply Range By**
5	*.99*
10	*.98*
15	*.96*
20	*.94*
25	*.91*
30	*.87*
35	*.82*
40	*.77*
45	*.70*
50	*.64*
55	*.57*
60	*.50*
65	*.42*
70	*.34*
75	*.26*
80	*.17*
85	*.09*
90	*.00*

NOTE: ***This chart can also be used to compensate for apparent size of a target when miling for distance; for example, a 5-meter target at 30 degrees to the viewer is .87 x 5 = 4.35, which is the apparent size of a 5-meter target.***

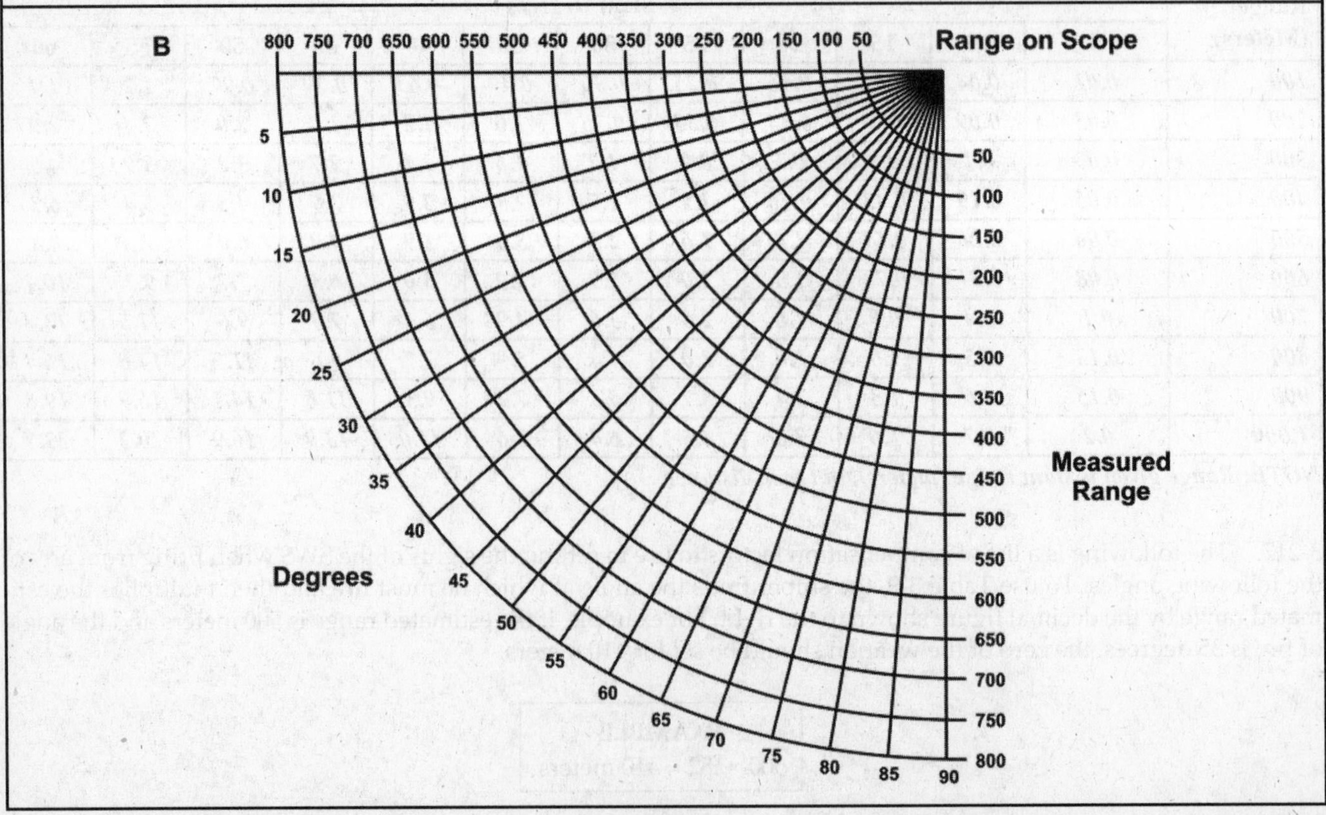

Table 3-9. Compensation factors used when firing from a given angle (*Continued*)

C																		
	Angular Degree																	
Range (m)	**5**	**10**	**15**	**20**	**25**	**30**	**35**	**40**	**45**	**50**	**55**	**60**	**65**	**70**	**75**	**80**	**85**	**90**
50	*49.5*	*49*	*48*	*47*	*45.5*	*43.5*	*41*	*38.5*	*35*	*32*	*28.5*	*25*	*21*	*17*	*13*	*8.5*	*4.5*	*0*
100	*99*	*98*	*96*	*94*	*91*	*87*	*82*	*77*	*70*	*64*	*57*	*50*	*42*	*34*	*26*	*17*	*9*	*0*
150	*149*	*147*	*144*	*141*	*137*	*131*	*123*	*116*	*105*	*96*	*85.5*	*75*	*63*	*51*	*39*	*25.5*	*13.5*	*0*
200	*198*	*196*	*192*	*188*	*182*	*174*	*164*	*154*	*140*	*128*	*114*	*100*	*84*	*68*	*52*	*34*	*18*	*0*
250	*248*	*245*	*240*	*235*	*228*	*218*	*205*	*193*	*175*	*160*	*143*	*125*	*105*	*85*	*65*	*42.5*	*22.5*	*0*
300	*297*	*294*	*288*	*282*	*273*	*261*	*246*	*231*	*210*	*192*	*171*	*150*	*126*	*102*	*78*	*51*	*27*	*0*
350	*347*	*343*	*336*	*329*	*319*	*305*	*287*	*270*	*245*	*224*	*200*	*175*	*147*	*119*	*91*	*59.5*	*31.5*	*0*
400	*396*	*392*	*384*	*376*	*364*	*348*	*328*	*308*	*280*	*256*	*228*	*200*	*168*	*136*	*104*	*68*	*36*	*0*
450	*446*	*441*	*432*	*423*	*410*	*392*	*369*	*347*	*315*	*288*	*257*	*225*	*189*	*153*	*117*	*76.5*	*40.5*	*0*
500	*595*	*490*	*480*	*470*	*455*	*435*	*410*	*385*	*350*	*320*	*285*	*250*	*210*	*170*	*130*	*85*	*45*	*0*
550	*545*	*539*	*528*	*517*	*501*	*479*	*451*	*424*	*385*	*352*	*314*	*275*	*231*	*187*	*143*	*93.5*	*49.5*	*0*
600	*594*	*588*	*576*	*564*	*546*	*522*	*492*	*462*	*420*	*384*	*342*	*300*	*252*	*204*	*156*	*102*	*54*	*0*
650	*644*	*637*	*624*	*611*	*592*	*566*	*533*	*501*	*455*	*416*	*371*	*325*	*273*	*221*	*169*	*111*	*58.5*	*0*
700	*693*	*686*	*672*	*658*	*637*	*609*	*574*	*539*	*490*	*448*	*399*	*350*	*294*	*238*	*182*	*119*	*63*	*0*
750	*743*	*735*	*720*	*705*	*683*	*653*	*615*	*578*	*525*	*480*	*428*	*375*	*315*	*255*	*195*	*128*	*67.5*	*0*
800	*792*	*784*	*768*	*752*	*728*	*696*	*656*	*616*	*560*	*512*	*456*	*400*	*336*	*272*	*208*	*136*	*72*	*0*
850	*842*	*833*	*816*	*799*	*774*	*740*	*697*	*655*	*595*	*544*	*485*	*425*	*357*	*289*	*221*	*145*	*76.5*	*0*
900	*891*	*882*	*864*	*846*	*819*	*783*	*738*	*693*	*630*	*576*	*513*	*450*	*378*	*306*	*234*	*153*	*81*	*0*
950	*941*	*931*	*912*	*893*	*865*	*827*	*779*	*732*	*665*	*608*	*542*	*475*	*399*	*323*	*247*	*162*	*85.5*	*0*
1,000	*990*	*980*	*960*	*940*	*910*	*870*	*820*	*770*	*700*	*640*	*570*	*500*	*420*	*340*	*260*	*170*	*90*	*0*

3-218. As can be seen, the steeper the angle, the shorter the range will be set on the scope or sights for a first-round hit. Also, the steeper the angle, the more precise the sniper must be in estimating or measuring the angle. Interpolation is necessary for angles between tens and fives.

EXAMPLE

Find the compensation factor for 72 degrees.
70 degrees = 0.34; 75 degrees = 0.26;
72 is 40 percent between 70 and 75 degrees.
0.34 - 0.26 = 0.08; 0.08 × 40 percent
(0.40) - 0.03; 0.34 - 0.03 - 0.31

NOTE

Table 3-9B and C, pages 466 and 467, are additional means of determining where to set the sights on the SWS to fire from a given angle. These tables are excellent references to reproduce and make into small cards for quick and easy access when conducting a mission. The data is for ranging only; the actual distance is used when determining the effects of the environment.

HOLD-OFF

3-219. Hold-off is shifting the POA to achieve a desired POI. Certain situations such as multiple targets at varying ranges do not allow proper elevation adjustments. Therefore, familiarization and practice of elevation hold-off techniques prepare the sniper to meet these situations. Windage is almost always held off by the sniper and will be practiced each range session.

ELEVATION

3-220. The sniper uses this technique only when he does not have time to change his sight setting. He rarely achieves pinpoint accuracy when holding off because a minor error in range determination or a lack of a precise aiming point might cause the bullet to miss the desired point. The sniper uses hold-off with the telescope only if several targets appear at various ranges and time does not permit adjusting the scope for each target.

3-221. The sniper uses hold-off to hit a target at ranges other than the range for which the rifle is presently adjusted. When he aims directly at a target at ranges greater than the set range, his bullet will hit below the POA. At closer distances, his bullet will hit higher than the POA. If the sniper understands this point and the effect of trajectory and bullet drop, he will be able to hit the target at ranges other than that for which the rifle was adjusted. For example, the sniper adjusts the rifle for a target located 500 meters downrange but another target appears at a range of 600 meters. The hold-off would be 25 inches; that is, the sniper should hold off 25 inches above the center of visible mass to hit the center of mass of that particular target (Figure 3-34). If another target were to appear at 400 meters, the sniper would aim 15 inches below the center of visible mass to hit the center of mass.

3-222. The vertical mil dots on the M3A's reticle can be used as aiming points when using elevation hold-offs (Figure 3-35). For example, if the sniper has to engage a target at 500 meters and the scope is set at 400 meters, he would place the first mil dot 5 inches below the vertical line on the target's center mass. This setting gives the sniper a 15-inch hold-off at 500 meters.

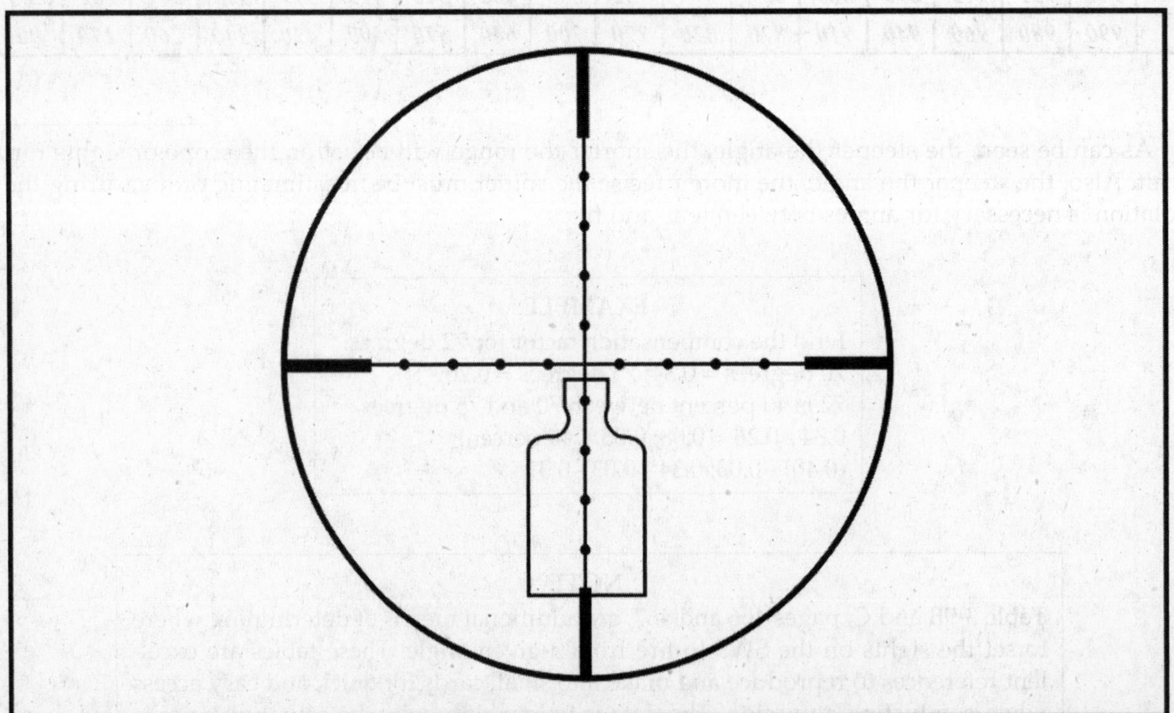

Figure 3-34. Elevation

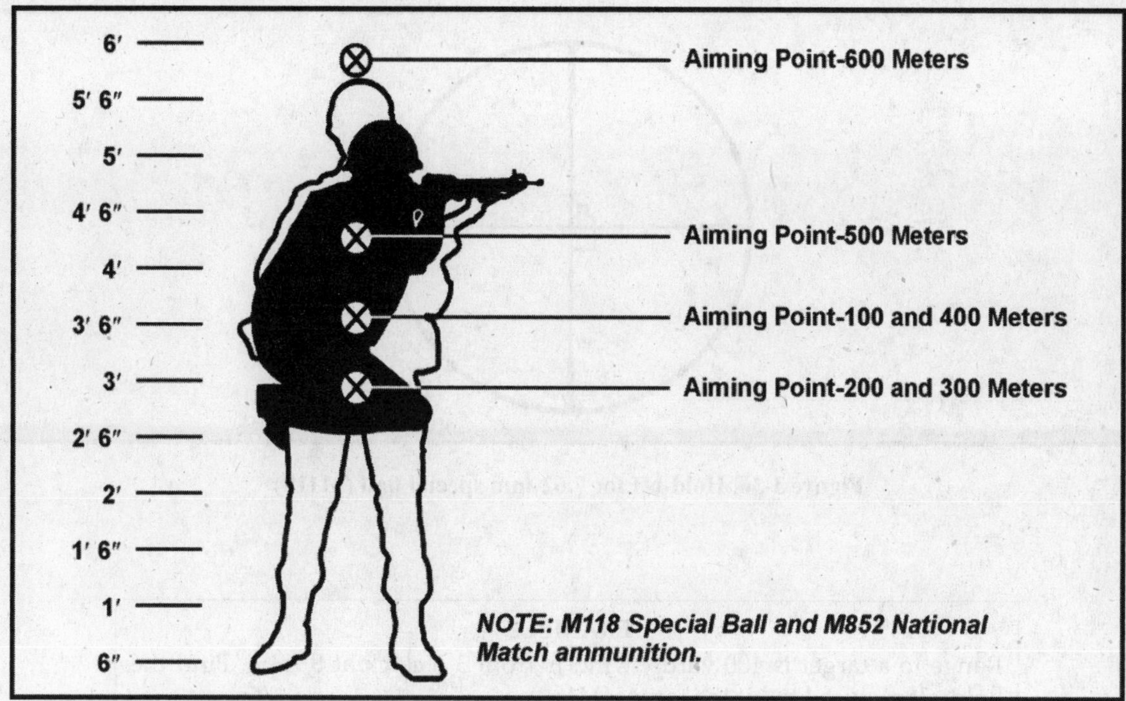

Figure 3-35. Correct holds for various ranges with sights set for 500 meters

3-223. For a 500-meter zero, the following measures apply:

- 100 and 400 meters, the waist or beltline.
- 200 and 300 meters, the groin.
- 500 meters, the chest.
- 600 meters, the top of the head.

WINDAGE

3-224. The sniper can use a hold-off to compensate for the effects of wind. When using the M3A scope, the sniper uses the horizontal mil dots on the reticle to hold off for wind. The space between each mil dot equals 3.375 MOAs, and a very accurate hold can be determined with the mil dots. For example, if the sniper has a target at 500 meters that requires a 10-inch hold-off, he would place the target's center mass halfway between the crosshairs and the first mil dot (1/2 mil) (Figure 3-36).

3-225. When holding off, the sniper aims into the wind. If the wind is moving from the right to left, his POA is to the right. If it is moving from left to right, his POA is to the left. Constant practice in wind estimation can bring about proficiency in making sight adjustments or learning to apply hold-off correctly. If the sniper misses the target and the impact of the round is observed, he notes the lateral distance of his error and refires, holding off that distance in the opposite direction. The formula used to find the hold-off distance is as follows:

$$\frac{\text{MOA (from wind formula)}}{3.5} = \text{Hold-off in mils}$$

> **NOTE**
> The wind formula must be computed first to find the MOA.

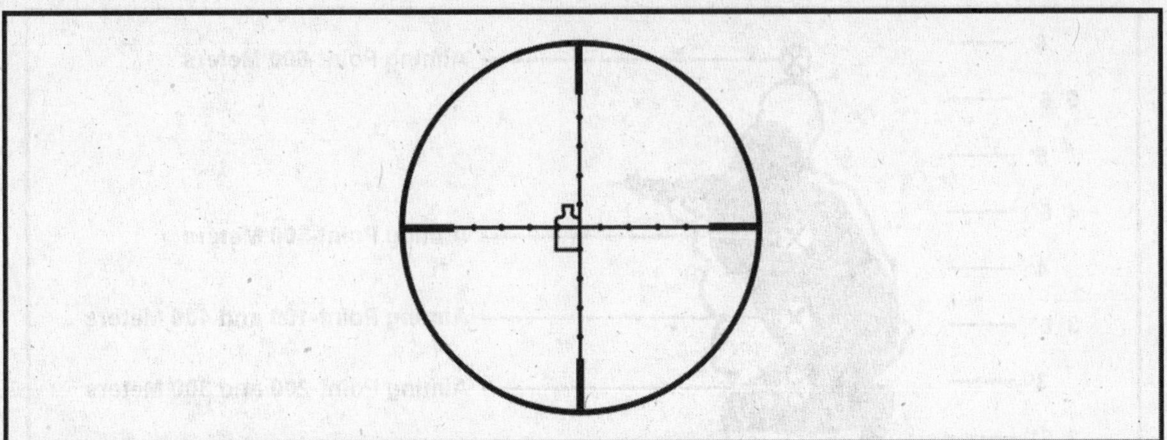

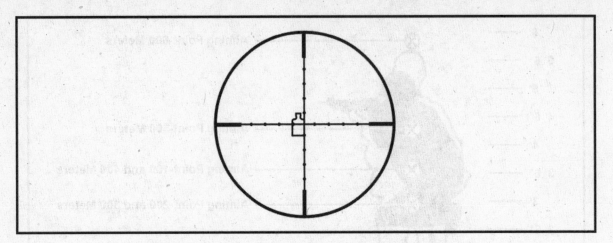

Figure 3-36. Hold-off for 7.62-mm special ball (M118)

EXAMPLE

Range to a target is 400 yards; wind is from 3 o'clock at 8 mph. Find the hold-off required to hit the target (M118).

$R \times V = MOA \qquad \frac{4 \times 8}{10} = \frac{32}{10} = 3.2 \text{ MOA}$

$\frac{MOA}{3.5} = \text{Hold-off in mils} \qquad \frac{3.2}{3.5} = .91 = \text{right 1 mil}$

For a half-value wind, divide mils by 2 for the hold-off.

ENGAGEMENT OF MOVING TARGETS

3-226. Moving targets are generally classified as walking or running and are the most difficult to hit. When engaging a target that is moving laterally across the LOS, the sniper must concentrate on moving his weapon with the target while aiming at a point some distance ahead. He must hold the lead, fire, and follow through after the shot. To engage moving targets, the sniper uses one of the techniques discussed below.

LEADING

3-227. A quarterback throwing a pass to his receiver can demonstrate the best example of a lead. He has to throw the ball at some point downfield in front of the receiver; the receiver will then run to that point. The same principle applies to firing at moving targets. Engaging moving targets requires the sniper to place the crosshairs ahead of the target's movement. The distance the crosshairs are placed in front of the target's movement is called a lead. The sniper uses the following four factors in determining leads.

Speed of the Target

3-228. Target speed will be a significant factor in determining the lead of the target. Running targets will require a greater lead than walking targets. Once target speed is determined, the sniper estimates the proper lead for the target at that specific range. Simultaneously, he applies the angle value to his lead estimation for the target (full-lead, half-lead).

3-229. For example, a target walking at a 45-degree angle toward the sniper at an average of 300 meters would require a 6-inch lead. This amount is determined by using the full-value lead of a walking target 300 meters away (a 12-inch lead) and dividing it in half for a half-value lead (as the target is moving at a 45-degree angle toward the sniper). Wind must also be considered, as it will affect the lead used. For a target moving with the wind, the sniper subtracts the wind value from the lead. For a target moving against the wind, he adds to the lead.

3-230. Double leads are sometimes necessary for a sniper who uses the swing-through method on a target that is moving toward his firing side. The double lead is necessary because of the difficulty that a person has in swinging his weapon smoothly toward his firing side. Practice on a known-distance range and meticulous record keeping are required to hone a sniper's moving target engagement skill.

Angle of Target Movement

3-231. A target moving perpendicular to the bullet's flight path moves a greater lateral distance during its flight time than a target moving at an angle away from or toward the bullet's path. A method of estimating the angle of movement of a target moving across the sniper's front follows (Figure 3-37):

- *Full-value lead target.* When only one arm and one side of the target are visible, the target is moving at or near a 90-degree angle and requires a full-value lead.
- *Half-value lead target.* When one arm and two-thirds of the front or back of the target are visible, the target is moving at approximately a 45-degree angle and requires a one-half value lead.
- *No-lead target.* When both arms and the entire front or back are visible, the target is moving directly toward or away from the sniper and requires no lead.

Range to the Target

3-232. The farther away a target is, the longer it takes for the bullet to reach it. Therefore, the lead must be increased as the distance to the target increases.

Wind Effects

3-233. The sniper must consider how the wind will affect the trajectory of the round. A wind blowing opposite to the target's direction requires more of a lead than a wind blowing in the same direction as the target's movement.

Figure 3-37. Leads for moving targets

When the target is moving against the wind, the wind effect is added to the lead. When he is moving with the wind, the wind effect is subtracted from the lead. Thus, "against add, with subtract."

3-234. Once the required lead has been determined (Table 3-9), the sniper should use the mil scale in the telescope for precise hold-off. The mil scale can be mentally sectioned into 1/4-mil increments for leads. The chosen point on the mil scale becomes the sniper's point of concentration, just as the crosshairs are for stationary targets. The sniper concentrates on the lead point and fires the weapon when the target is at this point.

Lead Values

3-235. Tables 3-10 through 3-12 list the recommended leads for movers at various ranges and speeds. Snipers should usually not engage movers beyond 400 yards due to the excessive lead required and low probability of a hit. If a mover is engaged at distances beyond 400 yards, an immediate follow-up shot must be ready.

3-236. The classification of a walker, fast walker, and a runner is based on a walker moving at 2 mph, a fast walker at 3 1/2 mph, and a runner at 5 mph.

3-237. These are starting point leads and are only guides. Each individual will have his own leads based on how he perceives movement and his reaction time to it.

Table 3-10. Recommended leads in mils for movers

Range (Meters)	Walkers	Fast Walkers	Runners
100	***Leading Edge***	*7/8*	*1 3/4*
200	*7/8*	*1 1/4*	*1 3/4*
300	*1 1/8*	*1 3/4*	*2 1/4*
400	*1 1/4*	*1 3/4*	*2 1/2*
500	*1 1/2*	*1 3/4*	*2 1/2*
600	*1 1/2*	*2 1/4*	*3*
700	*1 1/2*	*2 1/4*	*3*
800	*1 1/2*	*2 1/2*	*3*
900	*1 3/4*	*2 1/2*	*3 1/2*
1,000	*1 3/4*	*2 1/2*	*3 1/2*

Table 3-11. Recommended leads in minutes of angle for movers

Range (Meters)	Walkers	Fast Walkers	Runners
100	***Leading Edge***	*3*	*6*
200	*3*	*4.5*	*6*
300	*4*	*6*	*8*
400	*4.5*	*6*	*9*
500	*4.5*	*6*	*9*
600	*5*	*7.5*	*10*
700	*5*	*7.5*	*10*
800	*5.5*	*8*	*11*
900	*5.5*	*8*	*11*
1,000	*5.5*	*8*	*11*

Table 3-12. Recommended leads in feet for movers

Range (Meters)	Walkers	Fast Walkers	Runners
100	*Leading Edge*	*0.25*	*0.5*
200	*0.5*	*0.75*	*1*
300	*1*	*1.5*	*2*
400	*1.5*	*2.25*	*3*
500	*2*	*3*	*4*
600	*2.5*	*3.75*	*5*
700	*3*	*4.5*	*6*
800	*3.5*	*5.25*	*7*
900	*4*	*6*	*8*
1,000	*4.5*	*7.25*	*9*

TRACKING

3-238. Tracking requires the sniper to establish an aiming point ahead of the target's movement and to maintain it as the weapon is fired. This technique requires the weapon and body position to be moved while following the target and firing. This method is preferred and needs to be perfected after the basics are mastered.

TRAPPING OR AMBUSHING

3-239. Trapping or ambushing is the sniper's alternate method of engaging moving targets. The sniper must establish an aiming point ahead of the target that is the correct lead for speed and distance. As the target reaches this point, the sniper fires his weapon. This method allows the sniper's weapon and body position to remain motionless. With practice, a sniper can determine exact leads and aiming points using the horizontal stadia lines in the ART scopes or the mil dots in the M3A. The sniper must remember to concentrate on the crosshairs and not on the target. He must also not jerk the trigger. However, he must make the weapon go off the lead. The sniper can use a combination of tracking and ambushing to aid in determining target speed and direction. This technique is best suited for sentries who walk a set pattern.

TRACKING AND HOLDING

3-240. The sniper uses this technique to engage an erratically moving target. While the target is moving, the sniper keeps his crosshairs centered as much as possible and adjusts his position with the target. When the target stops, the sniper quickly perfects his hold and fires. This technique requires concentration and discipline to keep from firing before the target comes to a complete halt.

FIRING A SNAPSHOT

3-241. A sniper may often attempt to engage a target that only presents itself briefly, then resumes cover. Once he establishes a pattern, he can aim in the vicinity of the target's expected appearance and fire a snapshot at the moment of exposure.

COMMON ERRORS WITH MOVING TARGETS

3-242. When engaging moving targets, the sniper makes common errors because he is under greater stress than with a stationary target. There are more considerations, such as retaining a steady position and the correct aiming point, how fast the target is moving, and how far away it is. The more practice a sniper has firing at moving targets the better he will become. Some common mistakes that a sniper makes are when he—

- Watches his target instead of his aiming point. He must force himself to watch his lead point.
- Jerks or flinches at the moment his weapon fires because he thinks he must fire **NOW**. This reflex can be overcome through practice on a live-fire range.
- Hurries and thus forgets to adjust for wind speed and direction as needed. Windage must be calculated for moving targets just as for stationary targets. Failing to estimate when acquiring a lead will result in a miss.

3-243. Engaging moving targets requires the sniper to determine target distance and wind effects on the round, the lateral speed of the target, the round's time of flight, and the placement of a proper lead to compensate for both. These added variables increase the chance of a miss. Therefore, the sniper should engage moving targets when it is the only option.

ENGAGEMENT OF SNAP TARGETS

3-244. Many times the sniper will see a target that shows itself for only a brief moment, especially in urban and countersniper environments. Under these circumstances it is very important to concentrate on trigger control. Trigger control is modified to a very rapid pull of the finger directly to the rear without disturbing the lay of the weapon, similar to the moving target trigger control.

3-245. Another valuable skill for the sniper to learn is the quick-kill firing technique. He is most vulnerable during movement. Not only is he compromised because of the heavier equipment requirement, but also because of his large, optically sighted sniper rifle. Using the quick-kill technique, the sniper or observer can engage a target very rapidly at close range. This method is very useful for chance encounters with the enemy and when security is threatened. The sniper carries the rifle pointed toward the front, with the muzzle always pointing where he is looking and not at port arms. When the rifle is raised to fire, the eye is looking at the target. As the sniper looks at his target, the weapon lines on the target and he fires in the same movement. This technique must be practiced to obtain proficiency. It is not "wild firing," but a learned technique. A close analogy could be made to a skeet shooter who points his shotgun as opposed to sighting it.

FIRING THROUGH OBSTACLES AND BARRIERS

3-246. Another variable the sniper may encounter is the effect that glass penetration has on exterior and terminal ballistics. Firing through glass is unpredictable, and unless the target is close to the glass, more than one shot may be required. The sniper should never shoot through glass if it is close to his position. He is better off opening the window or having someone else break the window for him. The U.S. Army conducted a penetration test by firing through a glass plate from a distance of 1 yard at a silhouette target 100 yards away. Of the 14 test shots through various types of glass, only 2 shots hit the target.

GLASS PENETRATION

3-247. The United States Marine Corps (USMC) conducted a test by firing at an 8- by 9-inch pane of safety glass at 90- and 45-degree angles with the following results:

- Regardless of the angle, the path of the test bullet core was not greatly affected up to 5 feet beyond the point of initial impact; further from the glass, the apparent deflection became more pronounced.
- At an angle, glass fragments were always blown perpendicular to the glass plate.
- The Ml 18 173 grain bullet's copper jacket fragments upon impact. All of the bullet fragments followed an erratic path both in height and width. Each of the main cores (lead) began to tumble about 2 feet from the initial impact point.

- Due to the lamination of safety glass with a sheet plastic, large fragments of plastic were embedded in the target 1 foot from the POI. These fragments were large enough to cause severe wounds.
- Glass fragments did not penetrate targets farther than 1 foot from the POI.
- It can be concluded that anyone near the glass would be injured.

3-248. Therefore, as indicated by both the USMC and U.S. Army tests, snipers should try to avoid engaging targets requiring glass penetration.

PENETRATION PERFORMANCE OF M118 SPECIAL BALL

3-249. To support the M24 SWS program, two tests were conducted with the M118 Special Ball ammunition at a range of 800 meters. The first test used a test sample of ballistic Kevlar, and the second test used a 10-gauge, mild steel plate. Testing personnel positioned a witness plate behind each of these targets. Witness plates consist of a 0.5-mm sheet of 2024T3 aluminum to measure residual velocity or energy. To pass the test, the bullet had to penetrate both the target and witness plate. Results of these tests follow:

- *M118 versus ballistic Kevlar.* When 10 rounds were fired at 13 layers of ballistic Kevlar (equivalent to the U.S. personal armor system ground troop vest), full penetration was achieved of both the test sample and the aluminum witness plate.
- *M118 versus mild steel plate.* When 20 rounds were fired at a 3.42-mm thick (10-gauge) SAE 1010 or 1020 steel plate (Rockwell hardness of B55 to B70), 16 achieved full penetration of both the test sample and aluminum witness plate. The 4 failing rounds penetrated the steel plate but only dented the witness plate. These 4 rounds were considered to have insufficient terminal energy to be effective.

COLD BORE FIRST-SHOT HIT

3-250. On a mission, a sniper will rarely get a second shot at the intended target. Therefore, he must be 98 percent sure that he will hit his target with the first shot. This requirement places a great deal of importance on the maintenance of a sniper's logbook. Whenever the sniper conducts a live-fire exercise, he should develop a database on his SWS and its cold bore zero. The sniper uses the integrated act of firing one round to hone his sniping skills. By maintaining a detailed logbook, he develops confidence in his system's ability to provide the "one shot-one kill" goal of every sniper. The sniper must pay close attention to the maintenance and cleanliness of his rifle. He must also maintain proficiency in the marksmanship fundamentals. He should attempt to obtain his cold bore data at all ranges and climatic conditions. The bore and chamber must be completely dry and free of all lubricants. The exact POI of the bullet should be annotated in the logbook. Also keeping a file of the actual paper targets used is even better. This data will help detect trends that can be used to improve the sniper's performance. This exercise also develops the teamwork required for the sniper pair to accomplish the mission. A sniper going on a mission will foul his bore with 5 shots to preclude problems with the so-called cold bore shot.

LIMITED VISIBILITY FIRING

3-251. The U.S. Army currently fields the AN/PVS 10 as the night vision sight for its SWS. If unavailable, then the sniper can compromise by using issued equipment to mount a PVS-4 onto an M4 or M16. This NVD should be kept permanently mounted to avoid zeroing problems. This system is adequate because the rifle's effective range matches that of the NVD's ability to distinguish target details. The M24 can be used during limited visibility operations if the conditions are favorable. Moonlight, artificial illumination, and terrain will determine the potential effectiveness. The sniper will find that the reticle will fade out during limited visibility. Rather than trying to strain his eyes to make out the reticle, he should use the entire field of view of the telescope as the aiming device. Live-fire exercises will help the sniper determine his own maximum effective range. The sniper needs to use off-center vision in the rifle scope to see the heavy crosshair post and target.

3-252. The PVS-10 and the Universal Night Sight (UNS) are now standard issue. The NAD 750 and KN 200/250 (mentioned in Chapter 2), as well as the other NVDs, are not yet a standard-issue item. These sights are available for contingency operations and are in contingency stocks. Every effort should be made to acquire these sights for training. It is the best sight currently available for precision firing during limited visibility. It has a longer effective range for discriminating targets and does not need to be mounted and dismounted from the rifle.

3-253. Another consideration during limited visibility firing is that of muzzle flash. Both the M4 and the M16 are equipped with an excellent flash suppressor. The enemy would have to be very close or using NVDs to pinpoint a couple of muzzle flashes. The M24 has a flash suppressor that attaches to the front sight block and is locked in place by a ring. To minimize the compromising effects of muzzle flash, the sniper should carefully select hide sites and ammunition lots. However, at a range of greater than 100 meters, the muzzle flash is not noticeable, and even with NVDs the flash is barely noticeable. Snipers should not use flash hiders because they increase the muzzle blast signature of the weapon and increase the likelihood of detection. They also change the barrel harmonics and are detrimental to the weapon's accuracy.

NUCLEAR, BIOLOGICAL, AND CHEMICAL FIRING

3-254. Performance of long-range precision fire is difficult at best during nuclear, biological, and chemical (NBC) conditions. Enemy NBC warfare creates new problems for the sniper. Not only must the sniper properly execute the fundamentals of marksmanship and contend with the forces of nature, he must overcome obstacles presented by protective equipment.

3-255. Firing in mission-oriented protective posture (MOPP) has a significant effect on the ability to deliver precision fire. The following problems and solutions have been identified:

- *Eye relief.* Special emphasis must be made in maintaining proper eye relief and the absence of scope shadow. It is a must to maintain consistent stock weld. However, care must be taken not to break the mask's seal.
- *Trigger control.* Problems encountered with trigger control consist of the following:
  - *Sense of touch.* When gloves are worn, the sniper cannot determine the amount of pressure he is applying to the trigger. This point is particularly important if the sniper has his trigger adjusted for a light pull. Training with a glove will be beneficial; however, the trigger should be adjusted to allow the sniper to feel the trigger without accidental discharge.
  - *Stock drag.* While training, the sniper should have his observer watch his trigger finger to ensure that the finger and glove are not touching any part of the rifle but the trigger. The glove or finger resting on the trigger guard moves the rifle as the trigger is pulled to the rear. The sniper must wear a well-fitted glove.
- *Vertical sight picture.* The sniper naturally cants the rifle into the cheek of the face while firing with a protective mask. Using the crosshair of the reticle as a reference mark, he keeps the weapon in a vertical position. Failure to stay upright will cause shots to hit low and in the direction of the cant. Also, windage and elevation corrections will not be true.
- *Sniper/observer communications.* The absence of a voice-emitter on the M25-series protective mask creates an obstacle in relaying information. The team either speaks louder or uses written messages. A system of foot taps, finger taps, or hand signals may be devised. Communication is a must; training should include the development and practice of communications at different MOPP levels.

3-256. The easiest solution to NBC firing with the M24 SWS is to use the Harris bipod. The bipod helps stabilize the rifle and allows the sniper to maintain a solid position behind the rifle as he cants his head to achieve a proper sight picture. The sniper can also try tilting his head down so he is looking up through the telescope. NBC firing must be incorporated into live-fire ranges so that the most comfortable and effective position can be developed. Also, a detailed logbook should be developed that addresses the effects of NBC firing.

CHAPTER 4

Field Skills

The sniper's primary mission is to interdict selected enemy targets with long-range precision fire. How well he accomplishes his mission depends on the knowledge, understanding, and application of various field techniques and skills that allow him to move, hide, observe, and detect targets. This chapter discusses those techniques and skills that the sniper must learn before employment in support of combat operations. The sniper's application of these skills will affect his survival on the battlefield.

CAMOUFLAGE

4-1. Camouflage is one of the basic weapons of war. To the sniper team, it can mean the difference between life and death. Camouflage measures are important since the team cannot afford to be detected at any time while moving alone, as part of another element, or while operating from a firing position. Marksmanship training teaches the sniper to hit a target. Knowing how and when to camouflage can enable the sniper to escape becoming a target. He must be camouflage-conscious from the time he departs on a mission until he returns. Paying attention to camouflage fundamentals is a mark of a well-trained sniper.

FUNDAMENTALS

4-2. The sniper must pay careful attention when using camouflage clothing and equipment (artificial and natural). He should apply the following fundamental rules when determining his camouflage needs:

- Take advantage of all available natural concealment such as trees, bushes, grass, earth, man-made structures, and shadows.
- Alter the form, shadow, texture, and color of objects.
- Camouflage against ground and air observation.
- Camouflage a sniper post as it is prepared.
  - Study the terrain and vegetation in the area. Arrange grass, leaves, brush, and other natural camouflage to conform to the area.
  - Use only as much material as is needed. Excessive use of material (natural or artificial) can reveal a sniper's position.
  - Obtain natural material over a wide area. Do not strip an area, as this may attract the enemy's attention.
  - Dispose of excess soil by covering it with leaves and grass or by dumping it under bushes, into streams, or into ravines. Piles of fresh dirt indicate that an area is occupied and reduce the effectiveness of camouflage.

4-3. The sniper and his equipment must blend with the natural background. Remember that vegetation changes color many times in an area.

VARIOUS GEOGRAPHICAL AREAS

4-4. A sniper cannot use one type of camouflage in all types of terrain and geographic areas. Before operations in an area, a sniper should study the terrain, the vegetation, and the lay of the land to determine the best possible type of personal camouflage.

4-5. In areas with heavy snow or in wooded areas with snow-covered brush, the sniper should use a full, white camouflage suit with gray shading. With snow on the ground and the brush not covered, he should wear white trousers and green-brown tops. A hood or veil in snow areas is very effective, and equipment should be striped or totally covered in white. In snow regions, visibility during a bright night is nearly as good as during the day. This advantage gives the sniper full-time capabilities, but he must move along carefully concealed routes.

4-6. In sandy and desert areas that have minimal vegetation, textured camouflage is normally not necessary. Still, proper coloring of a suit that breaks up the sniper's human outline is needed. Blending tan and brown colors is most effective. A bulky-type smock of light material with a hood works well. The sniper must be sure his hands, face, and all equipment blend into a solid pattern that corresponds with the terrain. The sniper must make full use of the terrain by using properly selected and concealed routes of movement.

4-7. When deployed with regular troops in an urban area, the sniper should be dressed like the troops in the area. When the sniper is in position, he should be camouflaged to match his area of operations. He can use a bulky, shapeless, gray camouflage suit that has been colored to match rubble and debris. He should make sure some type of hood breaks up the outline of the head. Movement during daylight hours should be extremely slow and careful, if at all, because of the unlimited amount of possible enemy sniper positions.

4-8. In jungle areas, the sniper can use foliage, artificial camouflage, and camouflage paint in a contrasting pattern that will blend with the texture of the terrain. In a very hot and humid area, he should wear only a light camouflage suit. A heavy suit will cause a loss of too much body fluid. The vegetation is usually very thick in jungle areas, so the sniper can rely more on the natural foliage for concealment.

DISCIPLINE

4-9. The sniper must always practice camouflage discipline. The sniper will change his camouflage to match the terrain patterns and foliage as he moves and as it dries or wilts. He ensures his camouflage presents a natural appearance at all times.

CONFIGURATION

4-10. The sniper must constantly observe the terrain and vegetation changes to pick the most concealed routes of advance and be certain he is camouflaged properly. He should use shadows caused by vegetation, terrain features, and man-made features to remain undetected. He must master the techniques of hiding, blending, and deceiving.

Hiding

4-11. This technique enables the sniper to completely conceal his body from observation by lying in thick vegetation, lying under leaves, or even by digging a shallow trench and covering up in it. Hiding may be used if the sniper stumbles upon an enemy patrol and immediate concealment is needed or if he wishes to stay out of sight during daylight hours to await darkness. However, the sniper should not use the hiding technique in the final firing position (FFP), as he would be unable to see his target.

Blending

4-12. A sniper should use this technique since it is not possible to completely camouflage in such a way as to be indistinguishable from the surrounding area. Camouflage needs to be so nearly perfect that the sniper cannot be recognized through optical gear or with the human eye. He must be able to be looked at directly and not be seen. This trait takes much practice and experience. The ghillie suit is a form of blending.

NOTE

A sniper should not attempt to use disguising as a camouflage technique. This requires him to change his appearance to look like another object.

Deceiving

4-13. In this method, the sniper tricks the enemy into a false conclusion regarding his location, intentions, or movement. By planting objects such as ammunition cans, food cartons, or something intriguing, the sniper decoys the enemy into the open where he can be brought under fire. Cutting enemy communications wire and waiting for the repair personnel is another technique. After a unit has left a bivouac area, a sniper can stay behind to watch for enemy scouts that may search the area. The unit can also use mannequins to lure the enemy sniper into firing, thereby revealing his position.

TARGET INDICATORS

4-14. A target indicator is anything a sniper does or fails to do that will reveal his position to an enemy. A sniper must know these indicators if he is to locate the enemy and prevent the enemy from locating him. There are four general areas: olfactory, tactile, auditory, and visual.

Olfactory

4-15. The enemy can smell these target indicators. Cooking food, fires, cigarettes, aftershave lotion, soap, and insect repellents are examples. Most of these indicators are caused by the sniper's bodily functions. The sniper usually can eliminate this target indicator by washing the body, burying body wastes, and eliminating the cause. The indicator only gives a sign that the sniper is in the area.

Tactile

4-16. The sniper can touch these indicators; for example, trip wire, phone wire, and hide positions. He uses them mainly at night. Tactile indicators are defeated through the proper construction of sniper hides, and awareness of the altered vegetation he has left behind while constructing his hide.

Auditory

4-17. This indicator is a sound that the sniper might make by moving, rattling equipment, or talking, and is most noticeable during hours of darkness. The enemy may dismiss small noises as natural, but when they hear someone speak, they know for certain that others are near. The sniper should silence all equipment before a mission so that he will make no sound while running or walking. He can defeat auditory indicators through noise discipline and proper equipment preparation.

Visual

4-18. This factor is the most important target indicator. The main reason a sniper is detected is because the enemy sees him. Being familiar with subcategories of visual target indicators can help the sniper locate the enemy and prevent him from being detected. The sniper can overcome the following visual indicators by properly using the principles of concealment.

4-19. **Why Things are Seen.** The proper understanding and application of the principles of concealment used with the proper camouflage techniques can protect the sniper from enemy observation. The following principles explain why things are seen:

- *Siting.* This detection involves anything that is out of place or in a location that it does not belong. It includes wrong foliage or items in an area that the sniper is occupying. Siting is dependent upon—
  - Mission.
  - Dispersion (more than one sniper team per objective).
  - Terrain patterns (rural, urban, wooded, barren).
- *Shape.* Military equipment and personnel have familiar outlines and specific shapes that are easily recognizable. A sniper must alter or disguise these revealing shapes and outlines. Geometric shapes are manmade.
- *Shadows.* If used correctly, shadows can be very effective in hiding a sniper's position. They can be found under most conditions of day and night. However, the sniper can cast a shadow that can give him away.
- *Silhouettes.* They can easily be seen in the daytime as well as at night. A sniper must break up the outline of his body and his equipment so it blends with the background to reduce the chance of his silhouette being recognized.
- *Surface.* Reflections of light on shiny surfaces can instantly attract attention and can be seen for great distances. The sniper must camouflage all objects that have a distinguishable surface, such as hats, gloves, and shirtsleeves. He must also consider the texture of the surface he is camouflaging.

- *Spacing.* This factor is normally more important when two or more sniper teams are deployed together. Teams should coordinate their locations so that one does not compromise another. Teams should also coordinate their movements so that only one team is moving near the objective at one time. Spacing is also a factor when dealing with one sniper team. A sniper team must consider the distance between team members when moving to, and when at, the objective or firing position. Team members may need to move forward into the firing position individually so as not to compromise the firing position. This movement will normally depend on the terrain and the enemy situation.
- *Color.* Changing seasons cause vegetation to change. A sniper must be aware of the color of vegetation so that he does not contrast with it. The sniper must never use points of color, as the eye will notice any movement in the color.
- *Movement.* The main reason a sniper's position is revealed to the enemy is due to movement. Even if all other indicators are absent, movement can give a sniper's position away. Rapid or jerky movement is very noticeable; while slow movement may be seen, it is not as noticeable nor will it attract the eye as readily. The sniper must also remember that animal and foliage movements can give him away.

4-20. **Effects of Terrain Patterns and Weather Conditions.** The sniper must consider the weather conditions throughout the mission because they can constantly change. He must also consider terrain patterns because the patterns at the objective may be quite different from the ones en route to and from the objective.

TYPES OF CAMOUFLAGE

4-21. The two types of camouflage that the sniper team can use to camouflage itself and its equipment are natural and artificial. Each type has specific effects that can help the sniper remain undetected.

4-22. Natural camouflage is vegetation or materials that are native to the given area. The sniper team should always augment its appearance by using some natural camouflage. Natural foliage, properly applied, is preferred to artificial material, but the sniper must be aware of wilting.

4-23. Artificial camouflage is any manmade material or substance that the sniper uses for coloring or covering something to conceal it. He can use camouflage sticks or face paints to cover all exposed areas of skin such as face, hands, and the back of the neck. He should darken the parts of the face that form shadows. The sniper team uses the following types of camouflage patterns:

- *Striping.* Used when in heavily wooded areas, and leafy vegetation is scarce.
- *Blotching.* Used when an area is thick with leafy vegetation.
- *Combination.* Used when moving through changing terrain. It is normally the best all-round pattern.

MATERIALS

4-24. There are many types of camouflage materials. The sniper can use any of the following items to cover exposed skin:

- Artificial materials (or manufactured materials).
- Army-issued camouflage paint sticks:
  - Loam and light green—used for light-skinned personnel in all but snow regions.
  - Sand and light green—used for dark-skinned personnel in all but snow regions.
  - Loam and white—used for all personnel in snow-covered terrain.

> **NOTE**
> The use of camouflage in a cold weather environment will make detecting cold weather injuries more difficult.

- Commercial hunter's paint. There are many different colors.

- Stage makeup.
- Bear grease.
- Natural materials (or self-made materials):
  - Burnt cork.
  - Charcoal.
  - Lampblack (carbide).
  - Mud.

CAUTION

Dyes or paints should not be used, as they do not come off. Mud may contain dangerous parasites.

CLOTHING

4-25. The sniper can wear many types of clothing to conceal himself from the enemy. Battle dress uniforms (BDUs) have a camouflage pattern but often require additional camouflaging, especially in operations that occur very close to the enemy. The sniper can wear any of the following:

- U.S. Army uniforms:
  - Camouflage fatigues.
  - BDUs.
  - Desert BDUs.
  - Overwhites.
  - Desert night camouflage uniforms.
- Nonstandard uniforms with other camouflage patterns may help blend into the surrounding population.
- Gloves or mittens.
- Head masks:
  - Balaclavas.
  - Veils.
  - Head covers.
  - Kaffiyehs.
  - Ghillie or sniper hats.

GHILLIE SUIT

4-26. The term "ghillie suit" originated in Scotland during the 1800s. ("Ghillie" is a Scottish and Irish term for a fishing and hunting guide.) Scottish game wardens made special camouflage suits to catch poachers. Today the ghillie suit is a specially made camouflage uniform that is covered with irregular patterns of garnish or netting (Figure 4-1, page 482).

4-27. The sniper can make a ghillie suit from BDUs or one-piece aviator-type uniforms. Turning the uniform inside out places the pockets inside the suit and protects items in the pockets from damage caused by crawling on the ground. The sniper should cover the front of the ghillie suit with canvas or some type of heavy cloth to reinforce it. He should cover the knees and elbows with two layers of canvas, and reinforce the seam of the crotch with heavy nylon thread since these areas are prone to wear out more often. Shoo-goo is excellent for attaching the canvas to the uniform.

4-28. The next step is to make a garnish or net cover. The sniper should make sure the garnish or netting covers the shoulders and reaches down to the elbows on the sleeves. The garnish applied to the back of the suit should be long enough to cover the sides of the sniper when he is in the prone position. A bush hat is also covered with garnish or netting. The garnish should be long enough to break up the outline of the sniper's neck, but should not be so long in front to obscure his vision or hinder movement. A cut-up hammock makes an excellent foundation for the garnish.

Figure 4-1. Construction of the ghillie suit

4-29. A veil can be made from a net or pieces of cloth covered with garnish or netting. It covers the weapon and the sniper's head when he is in a firing position. The sniper can sew the veil into the ghillie suit or a boonie hat, or he can carry it separately. He must remember that a ghillie suit does not make him invisible but is only a camouflage base. The sniper can add natural vegetation to help blend with the surroundings, at a rate of 60 to 70 percent natural to 30 to 40 percent man-made.

> **NOTE**
>
> The ghillie suit is made to meet the sniper's need. However, he must take great care to ensure that he does not place an excessive amount of material on the netting. Doing so may form a new outline that can be seen by the enemy, or create a suit that will overheat him.

> **NOTE**
>
> It may be to the advantage of the sniper to use only a veil, as a full ghillie suit will be very bulky and difficult to pack and transport.

CAUTION

If using camouflage netting as a base, remove the radar scattering rings. Also remember the plastic camouflage shines when wet and the netting may catch on foliage when the sniper is crawling.

CAMOUFLAGE FOR EQUIPMENT

4-30. The sniper must camouflage all the equipment that he will use. However, he must ensure that the camouflage does not interfere with or hinder the operation of the equipment. Equipment that the sniper should camouflage is as follows:

- *Rifles.* The SWS and the M4/M16/M203 should also be camouflaged to break up their outlines. The SWS can be carried in a "drag bag" (Figure 4-2), which is a rifle case made of canvas and covered with garnish similar to the ghillie suit. However, the rifle will not be combat ready while it is in the drag bag. The drag bag can become a liability in many circumstances.

NOTE

The sniper should use drag bags carefully because they grab and snag on foliage during movement, but are beneficial when climbing buildings.

- *Optics.* The sniper must also camouflage optics to break up the outline and to reduce the possibility of light reflecting off the lenses. He can cover the lenses with mesh-type webbing or nylon hose material. He can also use a cover cutout that changes the circular appearance of the optic's objective lens.

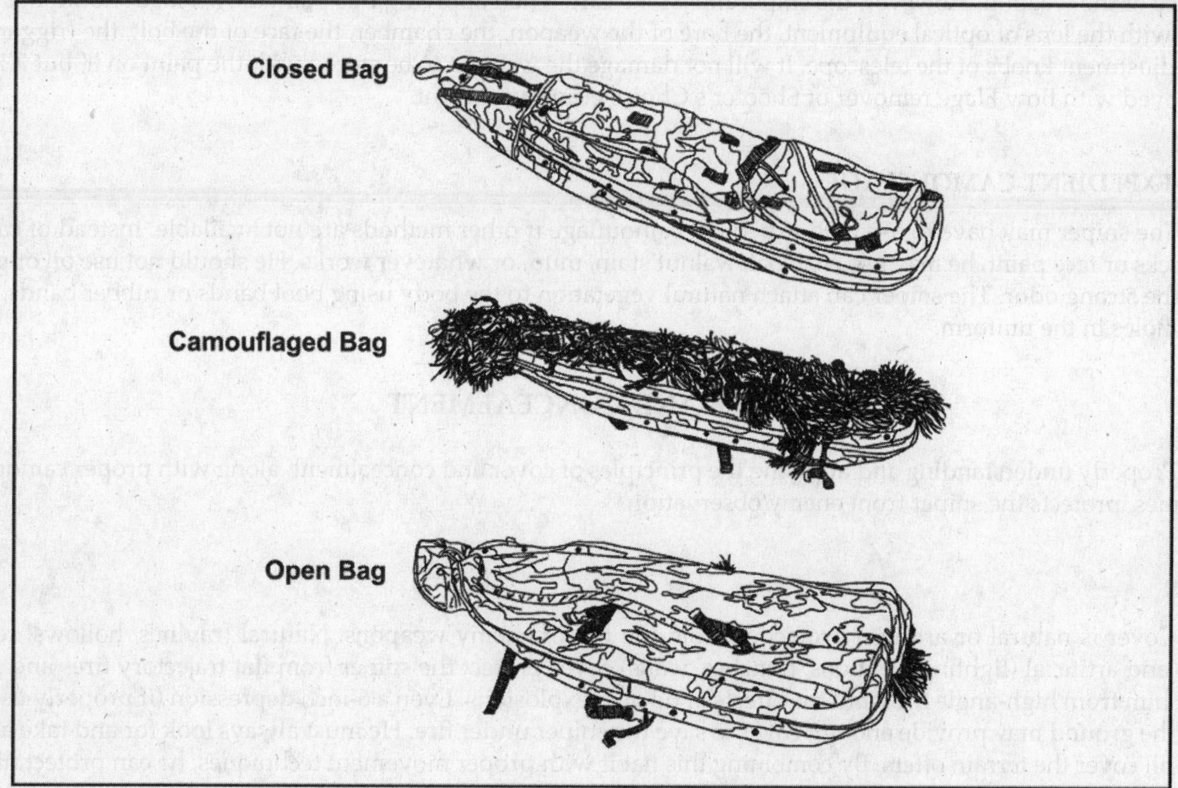

Figure 4-2. Construction of an equipment "drag bag"

- *ALICE Packs.* If the sniper uses the ALICE pack while wearing the ghillie suit, he must camouflage the pack the same as the suit. He can use paints, dyes, netting, and garnish. However, the sniper should avoid wearing the ALICE pack with the ghillie suit.

FACIAL CAMOUFLAGE PATTERNS

4-31. Facial patterns can vary from irregular stripes across the face to bold splotching. The best pattern, perhaps, is a combination of both strips and blotches. The sniper should avoid wild types of designs and colors that stand out from the background. He should cover all exposed skin, to include the—

- Hands and forearms.
- Neck, front and back.
- Ears, as well as behind the ears.
- Face:
  - Forehead-darkened.
  - Cheekbones-darkened.
  - Nose-darkened.
  - Chin—darkened.
  - Under eyes-lightened.
  - Under nose-lightened.
  - Under chin-lightened.

USING REMOVABLE CAMOUFLAGE SPRAY PAINT ON THE SWS AND EQUIPMENT

4-32. The sniper should paint his weapon with a removable paint (such as Bow Flage) so that he can change the colors to suit different vegetation and changing seasons. Bow Flage spray paint will not affect the accuracy or performance of the weapon. However, the sniper must take care when applying this paint. Bow Flage should not make contact with the lens of optical equipment, the bore of the weapon, the chamber, the face of the bolt, the trigger area, or the adjustment knobs of the telescope. It will not damage the weapon to be stored with the paint on it, but it is easily removed with Bow Flage remover or Shooter's Choice cleaning solvent.

FIELD-EXPEDIENT CAMOUFLAGE

4-33. The sniper may have to use field-expedient camouflage if other methods are not available. Instead of camouflage sticks or face paint, he may use charcoal, walnut stain, mud, or whatever works. He should not use oil or grease due to the strong odor. The sniper can attach natural vegetation to the body using boot bands or rubber bands, or by cutting holes in the uniform.

COVER AND CONCEALMENT

4-34. Properly understanding and applying the principles of cover and concealment, along with proper camouflage techniques, protects the sniper from enemy observation.

COVER

4-35. Cover is natural or artificial protection from the fire of enemy weapons. Natural (ravines, hollows, reverse slopes) and artificial (fighting positions, trenches, walls) cover protect the sniper from flat trajectory fires and partly protect him from high-angle fires and the effects of nuclear explosions. Even a 6-inch depression (if properly used) or fold in the ground may provide enough cover to save the sniper under fire. He must always look for and take advantage of all cover the terrain offers. By combining this habit with proper movement techniques, he can protect himself from enemy fire. To get protection from enemy fire when moving, the sniper should use routes that put cover between himself and the places where the enemy is known or thought to be. He should use natural and artificial cover to keep the enemy from seeing him and firing at him.

CONCEALMENT

4-36. Concealment is natural or artificial protection from enemy observation. The surroundings may provide natural concealment that needs no change before use (bushes, grass, and shadows). The sniper can create artificial concealment from materials such as burlap and camouflage nets, or he can move natural materials (bushes, leaves, and grass) from their original location. He must consider the effects of the change of seasons on the concealment provided by both natural and artificial materials.

4-37. The principles of concealment include the following:

- *Avoid Unnecessary Movement.* Remain still; movement attracts attention. The sniper's position may be concealed when he remains still, yet easily detected if he moves. This movement against a stationary background will make the sniper stand out. When he must change positions, he should move carefully over a concealed route to the new position, preferably during limited visibility. He should move inches at a time, slowly and cautiously, always scanning ahead for the next position.
- *Use All Available Concealment.* Background is important; the sniper must blend in to avoid detection. The trees, bushes, grass, earth, and man-made structures that form the background vary in color and appearance. This feature makes it possible for the sniper to blend in with them. The sniper should select trees or bushes to blend with the uniform and to absorb the figure outline. He must always assume that his area is under observation. The sniper in the open stands out clearly, but the sniper in the shadows is difficult to see. Shadows exist under most conditions, day and night. A sniper should never fire from the edge of a woodline; he should fire from a position inside the woodline (in the shade or shadows provided by the treetops).
- *Stay Low to Observe.* A low silhouette makes it difficult for the enemy to see a sniper. Therefore, he should observe from a crouch, a squat, or a prone position.
- *Expose Nothing That Shines.* Reflection of light on a shiny surface instantly attracts attention and can be seen from great distances. The sniper should uncover his rifle scope only when indexing and reducing a target. He should then use optics cautiously in bright sunshine because of the reflections they cause.
- *Avoid Skylining.* Figures on the skyline can be seen from a great distance, even at night, because a dark outline stands out against the lighter sky. The silhouette formed by the body makes a good target.
- *Alter Familiar Outlines.* Military equipment and the human body are familiar outlines to the enemy. The sniper should alter or disguise these revealing shapes by using a ghillie suit or outer smock that is covered with irregular patterns of garnish. He must alter his outline from his head to the soles of his boots.
- *Keep Quiet.* Noise, such as talking, can be picked up by enemy patrols or observation posts. The sniper should silence gear before a mission so that it makes no sound when he walks or runs.

INDIVIDUAL AND TEAM MOVEMENT

4-38. In many cases the success of a sniper's mission will depend upon his being able to close the range to his target, engage or observe the target, and withdraw without being detected. To succeed, he must be able to move silently through different types of terrain.

PREPARATION FOR MOVEMENT

4-39. As with any mission, the sniper must make preparations before moving. He must make a detailed study of large-scale maps and aerial photographs of the area, interview inhabitants and people who have been through the areas before, and review any other intelligence available about the area. He may construct sand tables of the area of operations (AO) to assist in forming and rehearsing the plan. The sniper must select camouflage to suit the area. He must also allow enough time for the selection of the proper camouflage, which should match the type of terrain the team will be moving through. Before moving, personnel should make sure that all shiny equipment is toned down and all gear is silenced. The sniper must ensure that only mission-essential gear is taken along.

Route Selection

4-40. A sniper should try to avoid known enemy positions and obstacles, open areas, and areas believed to be under enemy observation. He should select routes that make maximum use of cover and concealment and should never use trails. A sniper should try to take advantage of the more difficult terrain such as swamps or dense woods.

Movement

4-41. The sniper team cannot afford to be seen at any time by anyone. Therefore, its movement will be slow and deliberate. The movement over any given distance will be considerably slower than infantry units. Stealth is a sniper's security.

Rules of Movement

4-42. When moving, the sniper should always remember the following rules:

- Always assume that the area is under enemy observation.
- Move slowly; progress by feet and inches.
- Do not cause the overhead movement of trees, bushes, or tall grasses by rubbing against them.
- Plan every movement and traverse the route in segments.
- Stop, look, and listen often.
- Move during disturbances such as gunfire, explosions, aircraft noise, wind, or anything that will distract the enemy's attention or conceal the team's movement.

TYPES OF MOVEMENT

4-43. The sniper team will always move with caution. It will use various methods of walking and crawling based upon the enemy threat and the speed of movement required.

Walking

4-44. Walking is the fastest, easiest, and most useful way to move when extreme silence is desired. It is used when threat is low and speed is important. The sniper walks in a crouch to maintain a low profile with shadows and bushes so as not to be silhouetted. To ensure solid footing, he keeps his weight on one foot as he raises the other, being sure to clear all brush. He then gently sets the moving foot down, toes first, and then the heel. He takes short steps to maintain balance and carries the weapon in-line with the body by grasping the forward sling swivel (muzzle pointed down). At night, he holds the weapon close to his body to free his other hand to feel for obstacles. The sniper should use this walking technique when near the enemy; otherwise, he would use the standard patrol walk.

Hands and Knees Crawl

4-45. The sniper uses this self-explanatory crawl when cover is adequate or silence is necessary (Figure 4-3). The sniper holds the rifle in one hand close to the chest and in-line with the body, or places it on the ground alongside the body. The weight of the upper body is supported by the opposite arm. While supporting the rifle in one hand, the sniper picks a

Figure 4-3. Hands and knees crawl

point ahead to position the opposite hand and slowly and quietly moves the hand into position. When moving the hand into position, the sniper can support the weight of his upper body on the opposite elbow. The sniper then alternately moves his hands forward, being careful not to make any noise. Leaves, twigs, and pebbles can be moved out of the way with the hand if absolute silence is required.

High Crawl

4-46. When cover is more prevalent or when speed is required, the sniper uses this movement (Figure 4-4). The body is kept free of the ground and the weight rests on the forearms and the lower legs (shins). The rifle can either be carried, as in the low crawl, or cradled in the arms. Movement is made by alternately pulling with each arm and pushing with one leg. The sniper can alternate legs for pushing when cover is adequate. An alternate method is to pull with both arms and push with one leg. The sniper should always keep in mind that the head and buttocks cannot be raised too high and the legs must not be allowed to make excessive noise when being dragged over brush and debris. Both heels must remain in contact with the ground. This is the standard Army high crawl.

Medium Crawl

4-47. The medium crawl allows the sniper to move in fairly low cover because it is faster and less tiring to the body (Figure 4-5). This movement is similar to the low crawl, except that one leg is cocked forward to push with. One leg is used until tired, then the other leg is used. However, the sniper must not alternate legs, as this causes the lower portion of the body to rise into the air. This is the standard Army low crawl and is conducted in the same manner.

Low Crawl

4-48. The sniper uses the low crawl when an enemy is near, when vegetation is sparse, or when moving in or out of position to fire or to observe (Figure 4-6). To low crawl, he lies face down on the ground, legs together, feet flat on the ground, and arms to the front and flat on the ground. To carry the rifle, he grasps the upper portion of the sling and lays the stock on the back of his hand or wrist, with the rifle lying on the inside of his body under one arm. He can push the rifle forward as he moves. However, care must be taken to ensure that the muzzle does not protrude into the air or stick into the ground. To move forward, the sniper extends his arms and pulls with his arms while pushing with his toes, being careful not to raise his heels or head. This movement is extremely slow and requires practice to keep from using quick or jerky movements. The head is maintained down one side of the face.

Turning While Crawling

4-49. It may be necessary to change direction or turn completely around while crawling. To execute a right turn, the sniper moves his upper body as far to the right as possible and then moves his left leg to the left as far as possible. He

Figure 4-4. High crawl

Figure 4-5. Medium crawl

Figure 4-6. Low crawl

then closes the right leg to the left leg. This turn will create a pivot-type movement (Figure 4-7). Left turns are done in the opposite fashion.

Backward Movement

4-50. The sniper moves backward by reversing the crawling movement.

Assuming the Prone Position

4-51. The sniper assumes the prone position from a walk by stopping, tucking his rifle under his arm, and crouching slowly. Simultaneously, he feels the ground with the free hand for a clear spot. He then lowers his knees, one at a time,

Figure 4-7. Turning while crawling

to the ground. He shifts his weight to one knee and lifts and extends the free leg to the rear. The sniper uses his toes to feel for a clear spot. Rolling onto that side, he then lowers the rest of his body into position.

Night Movement

4-52. Movement at night is basically the same as during the day except it is slower and more deliberate because of the limited visibility. The sniper has to rely on the senses of touch and hearing to a greater extent. If at all possible, the sniper should move under the cover of darkness, fog, haze, rain, or high winds to conceal his movement. This is a safety factor; however, it makes the enemy harder to spot and specific positions or landmarks harder to locate.

STALKING

4-53. Stalking is the sniper's art of moving unseen into a firing position within a range that will ensure a first-round kill and then withdrawing undetected. Stalking incorporates all aspects of fieldcraft and can only be effectively learned by repeated practice over various types of ground.

Reconnaissance

4-54. The sniper should conduct a complete reconnaissance before his mission. Seldom will he have an opportunity to view the ground. He must rely on maps and aerial photographs for his information. The sniper should address the following before stalking:

- Location, position, or target to be stalked.
- Cover and concealment.
- Best possible firing position to engage targets.
- Best line of advance to stalk.
- Obstacles, whether natural or artificial.
- Observation points along the route.
- Known or suspected enemy locations.
- Method of movement throughout the mission.
- Withdrawal route (to include method of movement).

Conduct of the Stalk

4-55. A sniper may lose his sense of direction while stalking, particularly if he has to crawl a great distance. Losing direction can be reduced if the sniper—

- Uses a compass, map, and aerial photograph, and thoroughly and accurately plans the route, direction, and distance to various checkpoints.
- Memorizes a distinct landmark or two, or even a series.
- Notes the direction of the wind and sun. However, he must bear in mind that over a long period of time the wind direction can change and the sun will change position.
- Has the ability to use terrain association.

4-56. The sniper must be alert at all times. Any relaxation on a stalk can lead to carelessness, resulting in an unsuccessful mission and even death. He should also conduct an observation at periodic intervals. If the sniper is surprised or exposed during the stalk, immediate reaction is necessary. The sniper must decide whether to freeze or move quickly to the nearest cover and hide.

4-57. Disturbed animals or birds can draw attention to the area of approach. If animals are alarmed, the sniper should stop, wait, and listen. Their flight may indicate someone's approach or call attention to his position. However, advantage should be taken of any local disturbances or distractions that could enable him to move more quickly than would otherwise be possible. It should be emphasized that such movement includes a degree of risk, and when the enemy is close, risks should be avoided.

4-58. While halted, the sniper identifies his next position and the position after that position. If he is moving through tall grass, he should occasionally make a slight change of direction to keep the grass from waving in an unnatural motion. If crossing roads or trails, he should look for a low spot or cross on the leading edge of a curve and always avoid cleared areas, steep slopes, and loose rocks. The sniper should never skyline himself. He should also be aware of any changes in local cover, since such changes will usually require an alteration to his personal camouflage.

4-59. During route selection, the sniper must always plan one or two points ahead of his next point. Doing so prevents the sniper from crawling into a dead-end position.

Night Stalking

4-60. A sniper is less adapted to stalking at night than during the day. He must use slower, more deliberate movement to occupy an observation post or a firing position. The principal differences between day and night stalking are that at night—

- There is a degree of protection offered by the darkness against aimed enemy fire. However, a false sense of security may compromise the sniper.
- The sniper should use NVDs to aid in movement.

- While observation is still important, much more use is made of hearing, making silence vital.
- Cover is less important than background. The sniper should particularly avoid crests and skylines against which he may be silhouetted. He should use lunar shadows to hide in to help defeat NVDs.
- Maintaining direction is much more difficult to achieve, which places greater emphasis on a thorough reconnaissance. A compass or knowledge of the stars may help.

Silent Movement Techniques

4-61. Stealthful movement is critical to a sniper. Survival and mission success require the sniper to learn the skills of memorizing the ground and the surrounding terrain, applying silent and stealth movement, moving over different terrain, and using various noise obstacles. The sniper must memorize the terrain, select a route, move, communicate using touch signals, and avoid or negotiate obstacles using stealth techniques. The sniper can accomplish his mission by—

- Using binoculars to observe the terrain to the front, simultaneously selecting a route of advance and memorizing the terrain.
- Specifying signals with his team partner for different obstacles. Considerations include—
  - Finding the obstacles.
  - Identifying the obstacles (barbed wire, explosives, mines).
  - Negotiating the obstacles (Should the team go around, over, or under the obstacles?).
  - Clearing the obstacles (or getting caught in the obstacle).
  - Signaling partner (a signal must be relayed to the sniper's partner).
- Using stealth and silent movement techniques. They include—
  - Cautious and deliberate movement.
  - Frequent halts to listen and observe.
  - No unnecessary movement.
  - Silent movement. All equipment is taped and padded.
  - Looking where the next move is going to be made.
  - Clearing foliage or debris from the next position.
  - Constant awareness of the natural habitat of birds and animals in your area.
- Obtaining a safe passage of obstacles. Factors include—
  - Avoiding or bypassing noise obstacles.
  - If noise obstacles must be moved through, checking the debris and clearing loose noise obstacles from the path.
  - Memorizing locations of obstacles for night movement.
- Using the basic elements of walking stealthily. They are—
  - Maintaining balance.
  - Shifting weight gradually from the rear foot to the front foot.
  - Moving the rear foot to the front, taking care to clear brush. The moving foot may be placed either heel first, toe first, edge of foot first, or flat on the ground.
- Knowing how to move through rubble and debris. The sniper must—
  - Test the debris with his hand.
  - Remove debris that will break.
  - Put his feet down flat-footed. This way will reduce noise.
- Avoiding movement through mud and muck. If it cannot be avoided, the boots should be wrapped with burlap rags or socks.
- Crossing in the sand. Movement is noiseless and can be fairly fast.
- Keeping a low silhouette when moving over an obstacle. Trying not to brush or scrape against the obstacle, he should lower himself silently on the other side and move away at a medium-slow pace.
- Always maintaining positive control of his weapon.
- Never pulling or tugging at snagged equipment to free it; he should untangle or cut it free.

Detection Devices

4-62. The sniper must be constantly vigilant in his movements and acts to defeat enemy detection. He should be able to use the following devices:

- *Passive and Active Light Intensification Devices.* The sniper must be aware of enemy detection devices and remember that he could unknowingly be under observation. Where there is the possibility that NVDs are being used, the sniper can combat them by moving very slowly and staying very low to the ground. This way his dark silhouette will be broken up by vegetation. Preferably, he will move in dark shadows or tree lines that will obscure the enemy's vision. Also, moving in defilade through ground haze, fog, or rain will greatly benefit the sniper by helping him to remain undetected. Using the new IR reflecting material (used in equipment netting) as a base for the ghillie suit will limit the enemy's IR viewing capabilities. This should be used with caution, and the sniper must experiment with the correct balance.
- *Sensors.* Sensors are remote monitoring devices with seismic sensors, magnetic sensors, motion sensors, IR sensors, or thermal sensors planted in the ground along likely avenues of advance or perimeters. These devices normally vary in sensitivity. They are triggered by vibration of the ground, metal, movement, breaking a beam of light, or heat within their area of influence. The sniper can move past these devices undetected only by using the slowest, most careful, and errorless movement. He can help combat the effects of seismic devices by moving when other actions that will activate the devices, such as artillery fire, low-flying aircraft, rain, snow, or even a heavy wind, are in progress or, in some instances, moving without rhythm. The sniper can defeat most other sensors if he knows their limitations and capabilities.
- *Ground Surveillance Radars.* Ground surveillance radars can detect troop or vehicle movement at an extended range, but only along its line of sight and only if the object is moving at a given speed or faster. It takes a well-trained individual to properly monitor the device. A sniper can combat the use of ground surveillance radars by moving in defilade, out of the direct line of sight of the equipment, or slower than the radar can detect. He should move extremely slow and low to the ground, using natural objects and vegetation to mask the movement. The more laterally to the radar the sniper moves, the easier it is for the radar to detect the sniper's movement.
- *Thermal Imagers.* Thermal imagers are infrared heat detectors that locate body heat. The difference between heat sources is what is registered. These devices could locate even a motionless and camouflaged sniper. One possible way to confuse such a detector would be to attach a space blanket (Mylar) to the inside of the camouflage suit. The blanket would reflect the body heat inward and could possibly keep the sniper from being distinguished from the heat pattern of the surrounding terrain. This method would work best when the temperature is warm and the greatest amount of radiant heat is rising from the ground. Active infrared spotlights and metascopes may be used against the sniper. The sniper must always avoid the IR light or he will be detected.

CAUTION

By trapping the body heat and not allowing it to dissipate, the sniper increases the chance of becoming a heat casualty.

Selecting Lines of Advance

4-63. Part of the sniper's mission will be to analyze the terrain, select a good route to the target, use obstacles (man-made and natural) and terrain to their best advantage, and determine the best method of movement to arrive at his target. Once at the target site, he must be able to select firing positions and plan a stalk.

4-64. On the ground, the sniper looks for a route that will provide the best cover and concealment. He should fully use low ground, dead space, and shadows and avoid open areas. He looks for a route that will provide easy movement, yet will allow quiet movement at night. The sniper selects the route, then chooses the movement techniques that will allow undetected movement over that specific terrain.

4-65. Position selection is also critical to mission success. The sniper should not select a position that looks obvious and ideal; it will appear that way to the enemy. He should select a position away from prominent terrain features of contrasting background. When possible, he selects an area that has an obstacle (natural or man-made) between him and the target.

4-66. Stalk planning involves map and ground reconnaissance, selection of a route to the objective, selection of the type of movement, notation of known or suspected enemy locations, and selection of a route of withdrawal.

Sniper teams must not be detected or even suspected by the enemy. To maintain efficiency, each sniper must master *individual* movement techniques and ensure team effort is kept at the highest possible level.

Sniper Team Movement and Navigation

4-67. Normally, the sniper carries the SWS, the observer carries an M4/M16/M203, and both have sidearms. Due to the number of personnel and firepower, the sniper team cannot afford to be detected by the enemy nor can it successfully meet the enemy in sustained engagements. Another technique is for the sniper to carry the M24 bagged and on his back, while carrying an M4 at the ready. This gives the team greater firepower.

4-68. When possible, the sniper team should have a security element (squad/platoon) attached. The security element allows the team to reach its area of operations quicker and safer. Plus, it provides the team a reaction force should the team be detected.

4-69. Snipers use the following guidelines when attaching a security element:

- The security element leader is in charge of the team while it is attached.
- Sniper teams always appear as an integral part of the element.
- Sniper teams wear the same uniform as the element members.
- Sniper teams maintain proper intervals and positions in all formations.
- The SWS is carried in-line and close to the body, hiding its outline and barrel length, or it is bagged and the shooter carries an M4.
- All equipment that is unique to sniper teams is concealed from view (optics, ghillie suits).
- Once in the area of operations, the sniper team separates from the security element and operates alone.

4-70. Two examples of sniper teams separating from security elements follow:

- The security element provides security while the team prepares for its operation. The team—
  - Dons the ghillie suits and camouflages itself and its equipment (if mission requires).
  - Ensures that all equipment is secure and caches any nonessential equipment (if mission requires).
  - Once it is prepared, assumes a concealed position, and the security element departs the area.
  - Once the security element has departed, waits in position long enough to ensure neither it nor the security element have been compromised. The team then moves to its tentative position.
- The security element conducts a short security halt at the separation point. The snipers halt, ensuring they have good available concealment and know each other's location. The security element then proceeds, leaving the sniper team in place. The sniper team remains in position until the security element is clear of the area. The team then organizes itself as required by the mission and moves on to its tentative position. This type of separation also works well in military operations in urban terrain (MOUT) situations.

4-71. When selecting routes, the sniper team must remember its strengths and weaknesses. The following guidelines should be used when selecting routes:

- Avoid known enemy positions and obstacles.
- Seek terrain that offers the best cover and concealment.
- Take advantage of difficult terrain (swamps, dense woods).
- Avoid natural lines of drift.
- Do not use trails, roads, or footpaths.
- Avoid built-up or populated areas.
- Avoid areas of heavy enemy guerrilla activity.
- Avoid areas between opposing forces in contact with each other.

4-72. When the sniper team moves, it must always assume its area is under enemy observation. Because of this threat and the small amount of firepower that the team has, it can use only one type of formation—the sniper movement formation. Characteristics are as follows:

- The observer is the point man; the sniper follows.
- The observer's sector of security is 9 o'clock to 3 o'clock; the sniper's sector of security is 3 o'clock to 9 o'clock (overlapping each other).
- Team members maintain visual contact, even when lying on the ground.
- Team members maintain an interval of no more than 2 meters.
- The sniper reacts to the point man's actions.
- Team leader designates the movement techniques and routes used.
- Team leader designates rally points.
- During the stalk, team moves by using individual bounding techniques. It can move by successive bounds or alternating bounds.
- Team crosses linear danger areas by moving together across the danger area after a security or listing halt.

Sniper Team Immediate Action Drills

4-73. A sniper team must never become decisively engaged with the enemy. It must rehearse immediate action drills so they become a natural and immediate reaction should it make unexpected contact with the enemy. Examples of such actions are as follows:

- *Visual Contact.* If the sniper team sees the enemy and the enemy does not see the team, it freezes. If the team has time, it will do the following:
  - Assume the best covered and concealed position.
  - Remain in position until the enemy has passed.

NOTE
The team will not initiate contact.

- *Ambush.* The sniper team's objective is to break contact immediately during an ambush. One example of this technique involves performing the following:
  - The observer delivers rapid fire on the enemy and the team immediately moves out of the area.
  - The team moves to a location where the enemy cannot observe or place direct fire on it.
  - If contact cannot be broken, the sniper calls for indirect fire or security element (if attached).
  - If team members get separated, they should either link up at the objective rally point (ORP) or move to the next designated rally point. This move will depend upon the team SOP.
- *Indirect Fire.* Indirect fire can cause the team to move out of the area as quickly as possible and may result in its exact location and direction being pinpointed. Therefore, the team must not only react to indirect fire but also take the following actions to conceal its movement once it is out of the impact area:
  - The team leader moves the team out of the impact area using the quickest route by giving the direction and distance (clock method).
- Both members move out of the impact area the designated distance and direction.
  - The team leader then moves the team farther away from the impact area by using the most direct concealed route. They continue the mission using an alternate route.
- If the team members get separated, they should either link up at the ORP or move next designated rally point.
- *Air Attack.* If the sniper team finds itself caught in an air attack or its position is about to be destroyed, it should react as follows:
  - Assume the best available covered and concealed positions.
  - Between passes of aircraft, move to a position that offers better cover and concealment.
  - Do not engage the aircraft.
  - Remain in position until the attacking aircraft departs.
- Link up at the ORP or move to the next designated rally point if the members get separated.

Navigational Aids

4-74. To aid the sniper team in navigation, it should memorize the route by studying maps, aerial photos, or sketches. The team notes distinctive features (hills, streams, and roads) and its location in relation to the route. It plans an alternate route in case the primary route cannot be used. It plans an offset to circumvent known obstacles to movement. The team uses terrain countdown, which involves memorizing terrain features from the start to the objective, to maintain the route. During the mission, the sniper team mentally counts each terrain feature, thus ensuring it maintains the proper route. The team designates all en route rally points along the routes.

4-75. The sniper team maintains orientation at all times. As it moves, it observes the terrain carefully and mentally checks off the distinctive features noted in the planning and study of the route. The team must be aware of the map terrain interval to prevent counting low terrain features not represented on a map.

4-76. The following aids are available to ensure orientation:

- Global positioning system (GPS).
- The location and direction of flow of principal streams.
- Hills, valleys, roads, and other peculiar terrain features.
- Railroad tracks, power lines, and other man-made objects.

TRACKING AND COUNTERTRACKING

4-77. Tracking is the art of being able to follow a person or an animal by the signs that they leave during their movement. It is nearly impossible to move cross-country and not leave signs of one's passage. These signs, no matter how small, can be detected by a trained and experienced tracker. However, a person who is trained in tracking techniques can use deception drills that can minimize telltale signs and throw off or confuse trackers who are not well trained or who do not have the experience to spot the signs of a deception.

4-78. As a tracker follows a trail, he builds a picture of the enemy in his mind by asking himself these questions: How many persons am I following? What is their state of training? How are they equipped? Are they healthy? What is their state of morale? Do they know they are being followed? To answer these questions, the tracker uses available indicators—that is, signs that tell an action occurred at a specific time and place (Figure 4-8). By comparing indicators, the tracker obtains answers to his questions.

NOTE

Throughout this section, the terms tracker and sniper are used interchangeably.

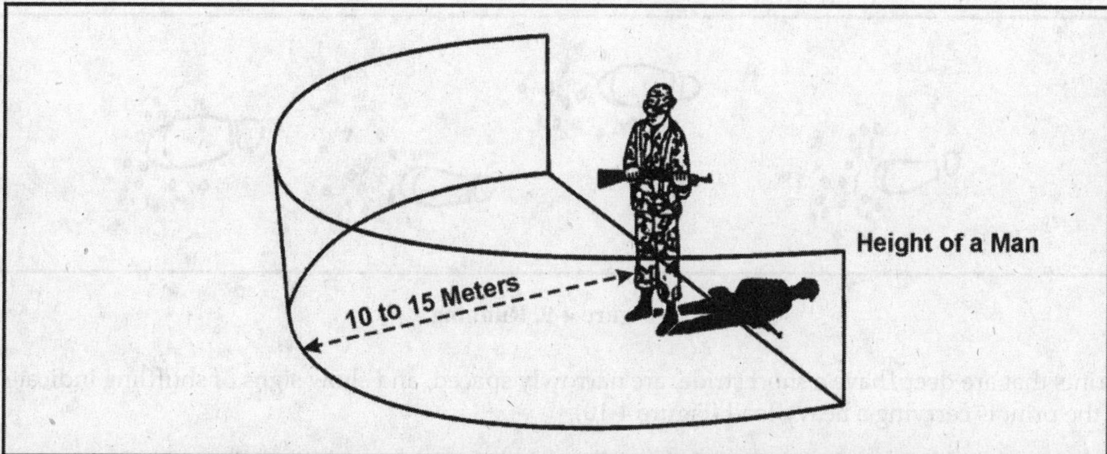

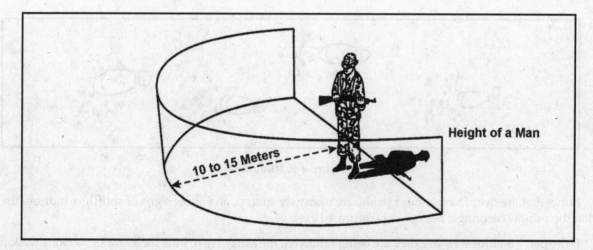

Figure 4-8. The area a tracker surveys to find tracking indicators

TRACKING SIGNS

4-79. Signs are visible marks left by individuals or animals as they pass through an area. The sniper must know the following categories of signs:

- *Ground Signs.* These are signs left below the knees. All ground signs are further divided as follows:
  - *Large signs* are caused by the movement of ten or more individuals through the area.
  - *Small signs are* caused by the movement of one to nine individuals through the area.
- *High Signs (also known as top signs).* These are signs left above the knees. They are also divided into large and small top signs.
- *Temporary Signs.* These signs will eventually fade with time (for example, a footprint).
- *Permanent Signs.* These signs require weeks to fade or will leave a mark forever (for example, broken branches or chipped bark).

TRACKING INDICATORS

4-80. Any sign the tracker discovers can be defined by one of six tracking indicators. They include displacement, stains, weathering, litter, camouflage, and immediate-use intelligence.

Displacement

4-81. Displacement takes place when anything is moved from its original position. A well-defined footprint in soft, moist ground is a good example of displacement. The footgear or bare feet of the person who left the print displaced the soil by compression, leaving an indentation in the ground. The tracker can study this sign and determine several important facts. For example, a print left by worn footgear or by bare feet may indicate lack of proper equipment. Displacement can also result from clearing a trail by breaking or cutting through heavy vegetation with a machete; these trails are obvious to the most inexperienced tracker. Individuals may unconsciously break more branches as they move behind someone who is cutting the path. Displacement indicators can also be made by persons carrying heavy loads who stop to rest; prints made by box edges can help to identify the load. When loads are set down at a rest halt or campsite, they usually crush grass and twigs. A reclining man can also flatten the vegetation.

4-82. **Analyzing Footprints.** Footprints can indicate direction, rate of movement, number, sex, and whether the individual knows he is being tracked. Figures 4-9 through 4-12 show different appearances of tracks made during various activities and countertracking techniques. The footprint can be the whole print but is usually only the "heel dig" and "toe push" footprint. They may also be found on the underside of large leaves that have not dried out and are lying on the ground.

4-83. If footprints are deep and the pace is long, rapid movement is apparent. Extremely long strides and deep prints with toe prints deeper than heel prints indicate running (Figure 4-9).

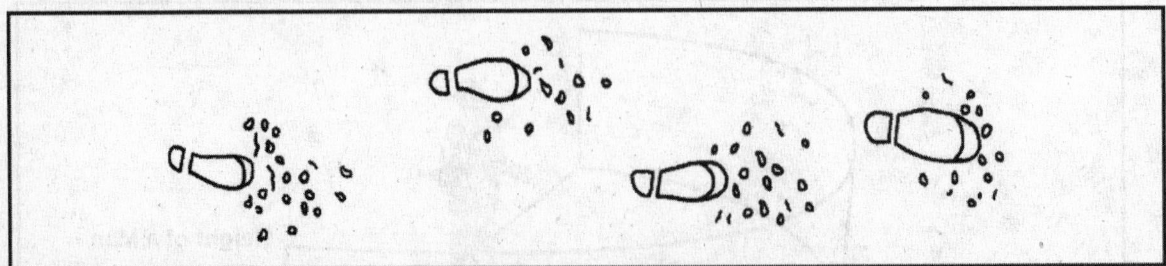

Figure 4-9. Running

4-84. Prints that are deep, have a short stride, are narrowly spaced, and show signs of shuffling indicate the person who left the print is carrying a heavy load (Figure 4-10).

4-85. If the party members realize they are being followed, they may try to hide their tracks. Persons walking backward have a short, irregular stride (Figure 4-11). The prints have an unnaturally deep toe, and soil is displaced in

Figure 4-10. Carrying a heavy load

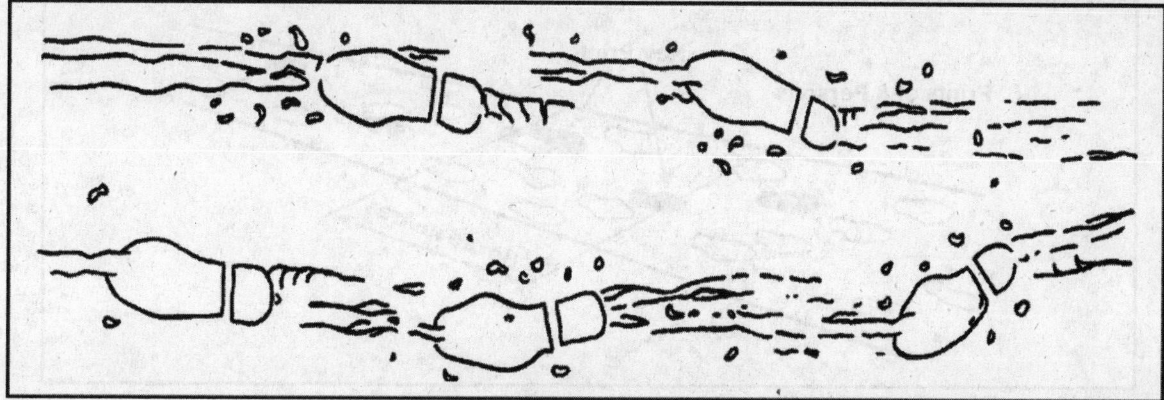

Figure 4-11. Walking backward

the direction of movement. These types of prints are characterized by "toe digs" and "heel push" as opposed to the normal footprint.

4-86. To determine the sex of a member of the party being followed, the tracker should study the size and position of the footprints (Figure 4-12). Women tend to be pigeon-toed; men walk with their feet straight ahead or pointed slightly to the outside. Prints left by women are usually smaller and the stride is usually shorter than that taken by men.

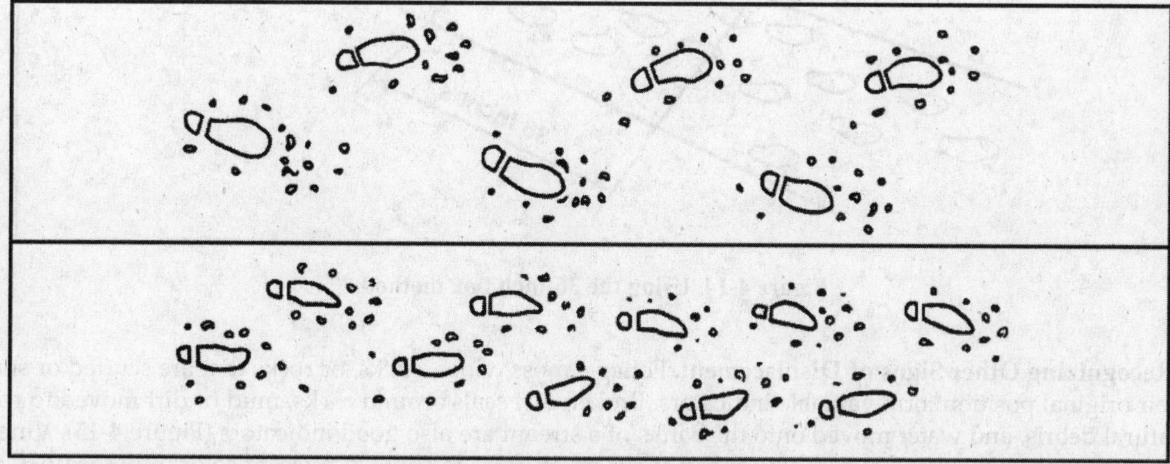

Figure 4-12. Man versus woman

4-87. **Determining Key Prints.** Normally, the last man in the file leaves the clearest footprints; these should be the key prints. The tracker cuts a stick to match the length of the prints and notches it to show the length and widest part of the sole. He can then study the angle of the key prints in relation to the direction of march. He looks for an identifying mark or feature, such as worn or frayed footgear, to identify the key prints. If the trail becomes vague, erased, or merges with another, the tracker can employ his stick-measuring device and identify the key prints with close study. This method helps him to stay on the trail. By using the box method, he can count up to 18 persons. The tracker can—

- Use the stride as a unit of measure when determining key prints (Figure 4-13). He uses these prints and the edges of the road or trail to box in an area to analyze.
- Also use the 36-inch box method if key prints are not evident (Figure 4-14). To use this method, the tracker uses the edges of the road or trail as the sides of the box. He measures a cross section of the area 36 inches long, counting each indentation in the box and dividing by two. This method gives a close estimate of the number of individuals who made the prints; however, this system is not as accurate as the stride measurement.

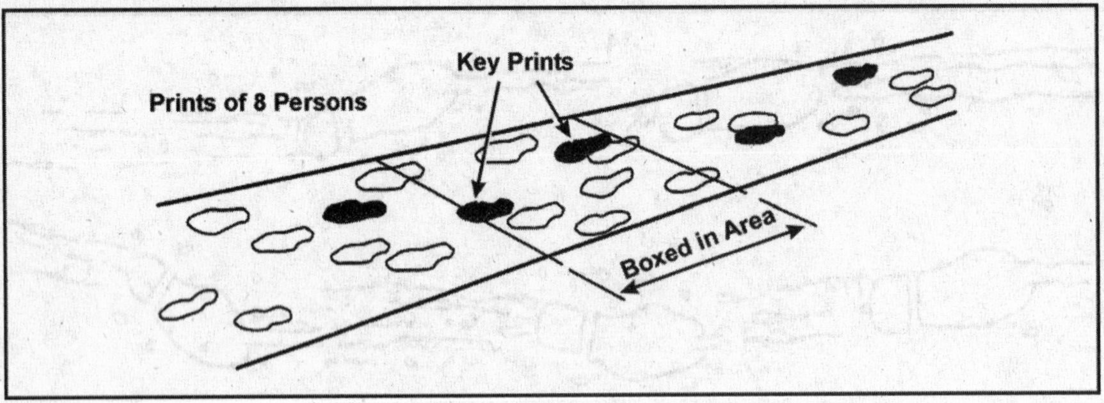

Figure 4-13. Using the stride as a unit of measure

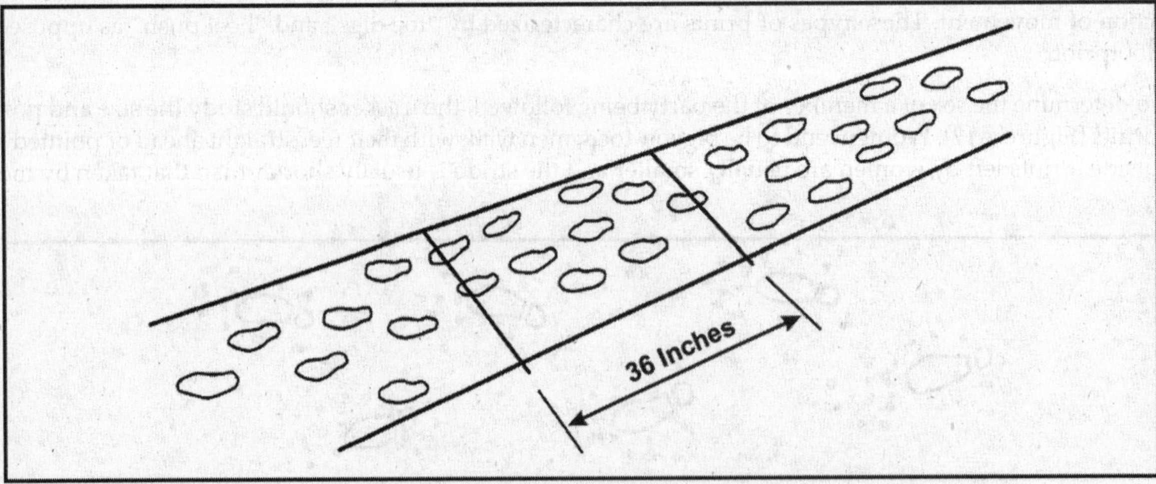

Figure 4-14. Using the 36-inch box method

4-88. **Recognizing Other Signs of Displacement.** Foliage, moss, vines, sticks, or rocks that are scuffed or snapped from their original position form valuable indicators. Broken dirt seals around rocks, mud or dirt moved to rocks or other natural debris, and water moved onto the banks of a stream are also good indicators (Figure 4-15). Vines may be dragged, dew droplets displaced, or stones and sticks overturned to show a different color underneath. Grass or other vegetation may be bent or broken in the direction of movement (Figure 4-16).

Figure 4-15. Turned over rocks and sticks

Figure 4-16. Crushed or disturbed vegetation

4-89. The tracker inspects all areas for bits of clothing, threads, or dirt from torn footgear or can fall and be left on thorns, snags, or the ground.

4-90. Flushed from their natural habitat, wild animals and birds are another example of displacement. Cries of birds excited by unnatural movement are an indicator; moving tops of tall grass or brush on a windless day indicate that something is moving the vegetation.

4-91. Changes in the normal life of insects and spiders may indicate that someone has recently passed. Valuable clues are disturbed bees, ant holes covered by someone moving over them, or torn spider webs. Spiders often spin webs across open areas, trails, or roads to trap flying insects. If the tracked person does not avoid these webs, he leaves an indicator to an observant tracker.

4-92. If the person being followed tries to use a stream to cover his trail, the tracker can still follow successfully. Algae and other water plants can be displaced by lost footing or by careless walking. Rocks can be displaced from their original position or overturned to indicate a lighter or darker color on the opposite side. The person entering or exiting a stream creates slide marks or footprints, or scuffs the bark on roots or sticks (Figure 4-17). Normally, a

Figure 4-17. Slip marks and waterfilled footprints on stream banks

person or animal seeks the path of least resistance; therefore, when searching the stream for an indication of departures, trackers will find signs in open areas along the banks.

Stains

4-93. A stain occurs when any substance from one organism or article is smeared or deposited on something else. The best example of staining is blood from a profusely bleeding wound. Bloodstains often appear as spatters or drops and are not always on the ground; they also appear smeared on leaves or twigs of trees and bushes. The tracker can determine the seriousness of the wound and how far the wounded person can move unassisted. This process may lead the tracker to enemy bodies or indicate where they have been carried.

4-94. By studying bloodstains, the tracker can determine the wound's location as follows:

- If the blood seems to be dripping steadily, it probably came from a wound on the trunk.
- If the blood appears to be slung toward the front, rear, or sides, the wound is probably in the extremity.
- Arterial wounds appear to pour blood at regular intervals as if poured from a pitcher. If the wound is veinous, the blood pours steadily.
- A lung wound deposits pink, bubbly, and frothy bloodstains.
- A bloodstain from a head wound appears heavy, wet, and slimy.
- Abdominal wounds often mix blood with digestive juices so the deposit has an odor and is light in color.

4-95. Any body fluids such as urine or feces deposited on the ground, trees, bushes, or rocks will leave a stain.

4-96. On a calm, clear day, leaves of bushes and small trees are generally turned so that the dark top side shows. However, when a man passes through an area and disturbs the leaves, he will generally cause the lighter side of the leaf to show. This movement is also true with some varieties of grass. Moving causes an unnatural discoloration of the area, which is called "shine." Grass or leaves that have been stepped on will have a bruise on the lighter side.

4-97. Staining can also occur when muddy footgear is dragged over grass, stones, and shrubs. Thus, staining and displacement combine to indicate movement and direction. Crushed leaves may stain rocky ground that is too hard to show footprints. Roots, stones, and vines may be stained where leaves or berries are crushed by moving feet.

4-98. The tracker may have difficulty determining the difference between staining and displacement since both terms can be applied to some indicators. For example, muddied water may indicate recent movement; displaced mud also stains the water. Muddy footgear can stain stones in streams, and algae can be displaced from stones in streams and can stain other stones or the bank. Muddy water collects in new footprints in swampy ground; however, the mud settles and the water clears with time. The tracker can use this information to indicate time. Normally, the mud clears in about one hour, although time varies with the terrain. Since muddied water travels with the current, it is usually best to move downstream.

Weathering

4-99. Weathering either aids or hinders the tracker. It also affects indicators in certain ways so that the tracker can determine their relative ages. However, wind, snow, rain, or sunlight can erase indicators entirely and hinder the tracker. The tracker should know how weathering affects soil, vegetation, and other indicators in his area. He cannot properly determine the age of indicators until he understands the effects that weathering has on trail signs.

4-100. For example, when bloodstains are fresh, they are bright red. Air and sunlight first change blood to a deep ruby-red color, then to a dark brown crust when the moisture evaporates. Scuff marks on trees or bushes darken with time. Sap oozes on trees and then hardens when it makes contact with the air.

4-101. Weather greatly affects footprints (Figure 4-18). By carefully studying this weathering process, the tracker can estimate the age of the print. If particles of soil are just beginning to fall into the print, this is a sign that the print is very recent. At this point, the tracker should then focus on becoming a stalker. If the edges of the print are dried and crusty, the prints are probably about 1 hour old. This process varies with terrain and is only a guide.

4-102. A light rain may round the edges of the print. By remembering when the last rain occurred, the tracker can place the print into a time frame. A heavy rain may erase all signs.

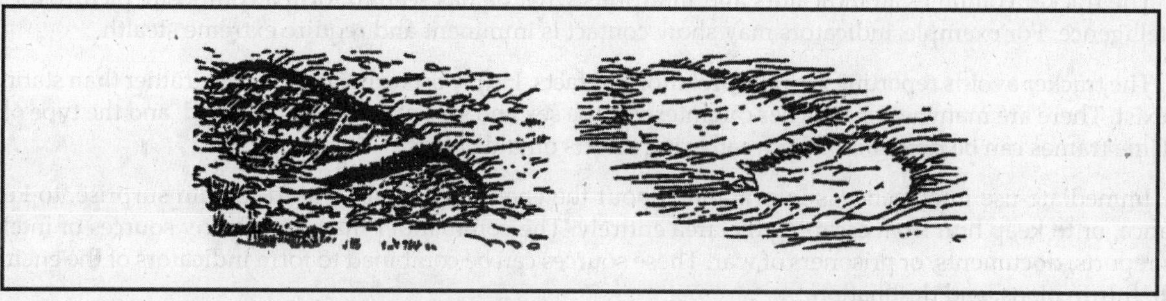

Figure 4-18. Effects of weather on the clarity of footprints

4-103. Trails exiting streams may appear weathered by rain due to water running from clothing or equipment into the tracks. This trait is especially true if the party exits the stream single file. Then, each person deposits water into the tracks. The existence of a wet, weathered trail slowly fading into a dry trail indicates the trail is fresh.

4-104. Wind dries out tracks and blows litter, sticks, or leaves into prints. By recalling wind activity, the tracker may estimate the age of the tracks. For example, the tracker may reason "the wind is calm at the present but blew hard about an hour ago. These tracks have litter blown into them, so they must be over an hour old." However, he must be sure that the litter was blown into the prints and not crushed into them when the prints were made.

4-105. Wind affects sound and odors. If the wind is blowing down the trail (toward the tracker), sounds and odors may be carried to him; conversely, if the wind is blowing up the trail (away from the tracker), he must be extremely cautious since wind also carries sounds toward the enemy. The tracker can determine wind direction by dropping a handful of dust or dried grass from shoulder height. By pointing in the same direction the wind is blowing, the tracker can localize sounds by cupping his hands behind his ears and turning slowly. When sounds are loudest, the tracker is facing the origin.

4-106. In calm weather (no wind), air currents that may be too light to detect can carry sounds to the tracker. Air cools in the evening and moves downhill toward the valleys. If the tracker is moving uphill late in the day or night, air currents will probably be moving toward him if no other wind is blowing. As the morning sun warms the air in the valleys, it moves uphill. The tracker considers these factors when plotting patrol routes or other operations. If he keeps the wind in his face, sounds and odors will be carried to him from his objective or from the party being tracked.

4-107. The tracker should also consider the sun. It is difficult to fire directly into the sun, but if the tracker has the sun at his back and the wind in his face, he has a slight advantage.

Litter

4-108. Litter consists of anything not indigenous to the area that is left on the ground. A poorly trained or poorly disciplined unit moving over terrain is apt to leave a trail of litter. Unmistakable signs of recent movement are gum or candy wrappers, ration cans, cigarette butts, remains of fires, urine, and bloody bandages. Rain flattens or washes litter away and turns paper into pulp. Exposure to weather can cause ration cans to rust at the opened edge; then, the rust moves toward the center. The tracker must consider weather conditions when estimating the age of litter. He can use the last rain or strong wind as the basis for a time frame.

4-109. The sniper should also know the wildlife in the area. Even sumps, regardless of how well camouflaged, are a potential source of litter. The best policy you can follow is to take out with you everything you bring in.

Camouflage

4-110. Camouflage applies to tracking when the followed party uses techniques to baffle or slow the tracker—that is, walking backward to leave confusing prints, brushing out trails, and moving over rocky ground or through streams. Camouflaged movement indicates a trained adversary.

Immediate-Use Intelligence

4-111. The tracker combines all indicators and interprets what he has seen to form a composite picture for on-the-spot intelligence. For example, indicators may show contact is imminent and require extreme stealth.

4-112. The tracker avoids reporting his interpretations as facts. He reports what he has seen, rather than stating these things exist. There are many ways a tracker can interpret the sex and size of the party, the load, and the type of equipment. Time frames can be determined by weathering effects on indicators.

4-113. Immediate-use intelligence is information about the enemy that can be used to gain surprise, to keep him off balance, or to keep him from escaping the area entirely. The commander may have many sources of intelligence such as reports, documents, or prisoners of war. These sources can be combined to form indicators of the enemy's last location, future plans, and destination.

4-114. However, tracking gives the commander definite information on which to act immediately. For example, a unit may report there are no men of military age in a village. This information is of value only if it is combined with other information to make a composite enemy picture in the area. Therefore, a tracker who interprets trail signs and reports that he is 30 minutes behind a known enemy unit, moving north, and located at a specific location, gives the commander information on which he can act.

DOG-TRACKER TEAMS

4-115. The three types of tracker dogs are as follows:

- *Visual dogs* rely upon their acute vision. They usually are the final part of tracking before shifting over to the attack mode.
- *Search dogs* are allowed to run free and search using airborne scents.
- *Tracker dogs* run on leashes and use ground scents.

4-116. Many myths surround the abilities and limitations of canine trackers. The first and perhaps greatest myth is that tracking involves only the dog's sense of smell. Canine tracking involves a team—a merging of man and dog. Dogs use both their eyes and ears; the tracker uses his eyes and knowledge of the quarry. Together, they create an effective team that maximizes their strengths and minimizes their weaknesses. The sniper team is not only trying to evade and outwit "just" a dog but also the dog's handler. The most common breed of dog used is the German shepherd. These dogs are trained to respond independently to a variety of situations and threats. Good tracking dogs are a rare and difficult-to-replace asset.

4-117. A visual tracker assists the dog handlers in finding a track if the dog loses the trail. He can radio ahead to another tracker and give him an oral account of the track picture. A visual tracker is slower than dogs because he must always use his powers of observation, which creates fatigue. His effectiveness is limited at night.

4-118. Tracker dogs smell microbes in the earth that are released from disturbed soil. The trail has no innate smell of a specific quarry, although trails do vary depending on the size and number of the quarry. For example, a scent is like the wake a ship leaves in the ocean, but no part of the ship is left in the wake. It is the white, foamy, disturbed water that is the trail. The result is entirely different from a point smell of the quarry such as sweat, urine, or cigarette smoke. The same training that makes tracking dogs adept at tracking a scent trail applies to finding a point smell.

4-119. Smelling is a highly complex process and many variables affect it. The most important element in tracking is the actual ground such as earth and grass. It contains living microbes that are always disturbed by the quarry's passage. Artificial surfaces (concrete and macadam) and mainly inorganic surfaces (stone) provide little or no living microbes to form a scent track.

4-120. A search or a scent-discrimination dog builds a scent picture of the person that he is tracking. Scent may be short-lived and its life span is dependent upon the weather and the area that the person last passed through. The sun and the wind, as well as time, destroy the scent. There are both airborne and ground scents. Airborne scents can be blown away within minutes or a few hours. Ground scents can last longer than 48 hours under ideal conditions. Bloodhounds have been known to successfully track a scent that was left behind 7 days before.

4-121. Wind and moisture are other major variables that affect tracking. Foggy and drizzly weather that keeps the ground moist is best. Too much rain can wash a trail away; depending on the strength of the trail, it takes persistent, hard rain to erase a scent trail. Usually, the scent is not washed away but only sealed beneath a layer of ground water. A short, violent rainfall could deposit enough water to seal the scent track, but after the rain stops and the water layer evaporates, the microbe trail would again be detectable by dogs. Hard, dry ground releases the fewest microbes and is the most difficult terrain for dogs to track on. A dog may also have difficulty following a trail on a beach or dusty path, but his human tracker could easily follow the footprints visually. Snipers must always remember they are being tracked by a man and a dog team. Tracker dogs track on the tail of the sniper while search dogs track downwind of the trail.

4-122. Wind strength and direction are important factors in tracking. Basically, strong wind inhibits tracking a scent trail but makes it easier for a dog to find a point scent source—like a hide. A general rule is that a dog can smell a man-size source downwind out to 50 meters and a group-size source—a hide—out to 200 meters under ideal conditions. Upwind, a source 1 meter away could be missed.

	Wind Direction→		
Wind Speed:		Still	Windy
	D—X	D	D
Distance:	1 Meter	30 to 50 Meters	Maximum 150 to 200 Meters

D = Dog Team
X = Sniper/Sniper Team

4-123. A strong wind disperses microbes that arise from the ground, hindering a dog's ability to follow a trail. However, a strong wind increases the size of a point scent, helping a dog to find the target in an area search.

4-124. An inflexible rule for the life of a scent trail cannot be provided. In Germany, trackers rate their chance of following a trail that is more than 3 days old as negligible. Terrain, weather, and the sensitivity of the tracking dog are some of the many variables that affect the scent trail. A point smell will last as long as the target emits odors.

4-125. While dogs are mainly scent hunters, they also have good short-range vision. Dogs are colorblind and do not have good distance vision (camouflage works extremely well against dogs). However, they can detect slight movements. Dogs also have a phenomenal sense of hearing, extending far beyond human norms in both the frequency range and in sensitivity. Dogs use smell to approximate a target, and then rely on sound and movement to pinpoint that target.

4-126. Although dogs have tremendous detection abilities, they also have limitations. Following a scent trail is the most difficult task a tracking dog can perform. The level of effort is so intense that most dogs cannot work longer than

20 to 30 minutes at a time, followed by a 10- to 20-minute rest. Dogs can perform this cycle no more than five or six times in a 24-hour period before reaching complete exhaustion. The efficiency of the search also decreases as the dog tires. In wartime, the situation will force the maximum from men and equipment, but times should remain constant for dogs because they always give 100 percent. If the snipers keep moving and stay out of the detection range of the human handlers, then they could outlast the dog-scent trackers.

4-127. When looking for sniper teams, trackers mainly use wood line sweeps and area searches. A wood line sweep consists of walking the dog **upwind** of a suspected wood line or brush line—the key is upwind. If the wind is blowing through the woods and out of the wood line, trackers move 50 to 100 meters inside a wooded area to sweep the woods' edge. Since wood line sweeps tend to be less specific, trackers perform them faster. Trackers perform an area search when a team's location is specific, such as a small wooded area or block of houses. The search area is cordoned off, if possible and the dog-tracker teams are brought on-line about 25 to 150 meters apart, depending on terrain and visibility. The handlers then advance, each moving their dogs through a specific corridor. The handler controls the dog entirely with voice commands and gestures. He remains undercover, directing the dog in a search pattern or to a likely target area. The search line moves forward with each dog dashing back and forth in assigned sectors.

TECHNIQUES TO DEFEAT DOG-TRACKER TEAMS

4-128. Although dog and handler tracking teams are a potent threat, there are counters available to the sniper team. As always, the best defenses are basic infantry techniques: good camouflage and light, noise, and trash discipline. Dogs find a team either by detecting a trail or by a point source such as human waste odors at the hide site. It is critical to try to obscure or limit trails around the hide, especially along the wood line or area closest to the team's target area. Surveillance targets are usually major axes of advance. "Trolling the Wood lines" along likely-looking roads or intersections is a favorite tactic of dog-tracker teams. When moving into a target area, the sniper team should take the following countermeasures:

- Remain as far away from the target area as the situation allows.
- Never establish a position at the edge of cover and concealment nearest the target area.
- Minimize the track. Try to approach the position area on hard, dry ground or along a stream or river.
- Urinate in a hole and cover it up. Never urinate more than once in exactly the same spot.
- Deeply bury fecal matter. If the duration of the mission permits, use meals, ready to eat (MRE) bags sealed with tape and take it with you.
- Never smoke.
- Carry all trash until it can be buried elsewhere.

4-129. When dogs are being used against a sniper team, they use other odors left behind or around the team to find it. Sweat from exertion or fear is one of these. Wet clothing or material from damp environments holds in the scent. Soap or deodorant used before infiltration helps the dogs to find the team. Foreign odors such as oils, preservatives, polish, and petroleum products also aid the dogs. Time permitting, the sniper should try to change his diet to that of the local inhabitants before infiltration.

4-130. When the sniper team first arrives in its AO, it is best to move initially in a direction that is from 90 to 170 degrees away from the objective. Objects or items of clothing not belonging to any of the team members should be carried into the AO in a plastic bag. When the team first starts moving, it should drop an item of clothing or piece of cloth out of the bag and leave it on a back trail. This step can confuse a dog long enough to give the team more of a head start. Also, if dogs are brought in late, the team's scent will be very faint while this scent will still be strong.

4-131. While traveling, the team should try to avoid heavily foliaged areas, as these areas hold the scent longer. Periodically, when the situation permits, move across an open area that the sun shines on during the day and that has the potential of being windswept. The wind moves the scent and will eventually blow it away; the sun destroys scent very rapidly.

4-132. When the situation permits, make changes in direction at the open points of terrain to force the dog to cast for a scent. If dogs are very close behind, moving through water does not confuse them, as scent will be hanging in the air above the water. Moving through water will only slow the team down. Throwing CS gas to the rear or using blood, spice mixtures, or any other concoctions will prevent a dog from smelling the team's scent, but it will not be effective on a trained tracker dog.

4-133. While a dog will not be confused by water if he is close, running water, such as a rapidly moving stream, will confuse a dog if he is several hours behind. However, areas with foliage, stagnant air, and little sunlight will hold the scent longer. Therefore, the team should try to avoid any swampy areas.

4-134. The sniper team should move through areas that have been frequently traveled by other people, as this will confuse the scent picture to the dog. Team members should split up from time to time to confuse the dogs. The best place for this is in areas frequently traveled by indigenous personnel.

4-135. If a dog-tracker is on the sniper team's trail, it should not run because the scent will become stronger. The team may attempt to wear out the dog handler and confuse the dog but should always be on the lookout for a good ambush site that it can fishhook into. If it becomes necessary to ambush the tracking party, fishhook into the ambush site and kill or wound the handler, not the dog. A tracker dog is trained with his handler and will protect him should he become wounded. This practice will allow the team to move off and away from the area while the rest of the tracking party tries to give assistance to the handler. Also, that dog will not work well with anyone other than his handler.

4-136. If a dog search team moves into the area, the sniper team should first check wind direction and strength. If the team is downwind of the estimated search area, the chances are minimal that the team's point smells will be detected. If upwind of the search area, the team should attempt to move downwind. Terrain and visibility dictate whether the team can move without being detected visually by the handlers. Remember, sweeps are not always conducted just outside of a wood line. Wind direction determines whether the sweep will be parallel to the outside or 50 to 100 meters inside the wood line.

4-137. The team has options if caught inside the search area of a line search. The handlers rely on radio communications and often do not have visual contact with each other. If the team has been generally localized through enemy radio detection-finding equipment, the search net will still be loose during the initial sweep. A sniper team has a small chance of hiding and escaping detection in deep brush or in woodpiles. Larger groups will almost certainly be found. Yet, the team may have the chance to eliminate the handler and to escape the search net.

4-138. The handler hides behind cover with the dog. He searches for movement and then sends the dog out in a straight line toward the front. Usually, when the dog has moved about 50 to 75 meters, the handler calls the dog back. The handler then moves slowly forward and always from covered position to covered position. Commands are by voice and gesture with a backup whistle to signal the dog to return. If a handler is killed or badly injured after he has released the dog, but before he has recalled it, the dog continues to randomly search out and away from the handler. The dog usually returns to another handler or to his former handler's last position within several minutes. This time lapse creates a gap from 25 to 150 meters wide in the search pattern. Response times by the other searchers tend to be fast. Given the high degree of radio "chatter," the injured handler will probably be quickly missed from the radio net. Killing the dog before the handler will probably delay discovery only by moments. Dogs are so reliable that if the dog does not return immediately, the handler knows something is wrong.

4-139. If the sniper does not have a firearm, human versus dog combat is a hazard. One dog can be dealt with relatively easily if a knife or large club is available. The sniper must keep low and strike upward using the wrist, never overhand. Dogs are quick and will try to strike the groin or legs. Most attack dogs are trained to go for the groin or throat. If alone and faced with two or more dogs, the sniper should flee the situation.

4-140. Dog-tracker teams are a potent threat to the sniper team. Although small and lightly armed, they can greatly increase the area that a rear area security unit can search. Due to the dog-tracker team's effectiveness and its lack of firepower, a sniper team may be tempted to destroy such an "easy" target. Whether a team should fight or run depends on the situation and the team leader. Eliminating or injuring the dog-tracker team only confirms to threat security forces that there is a hostile team operating in the area. The techniques for attacking a dog-tracker team should be used only in extreme situations or as a last measure.

COUNTERTRACKING

4-141. There are two types of human trackers—combat trackers and professional trackers. Combat trackers look ahead for signs and do not necessarily look for each individual sign. Professional trackers go from sign to sign. If they cannot find any sign, they will stop and search till they find one. The only way to lose a trained professional tracker is to fishhook into an area and then ambush him.

4-142. If an enemy tracker finds tracks of two men, it tells him that a highly trained specialty team may be operating in his area. However, a knowledge of countertracking enables the sniper team to survive by remaining undetected.

4-143. As with the dogs, to confuse the combat tracker and throw him off the track, the sniper always starts his movement away from his objective. He travels in a straight line for about an hour and then changes direction. Changing will cause the tracker to cast in different directions to find the track.

Evasion

4-144. Evasion of the tracker or pursuit team is a difficult task that requires the use of immediate-action drills mostly designed to counter the threat. A team skilled in tracking techniques can successfully use deception drills to minimize signs that the enemy can use against them. However, it is very difficult for a person, especially a group, to move across any area without leaving signs noticeable to the trained eye.

Camouflage

4-145. The followed party may use two types of routes to cover its movement. It must also remember that travel time reduces when trying to camouflage the trail. Two types of routes include:

- *Most-Used Routes.* Movement on lightly-traveled sandy or soft trails is easily tracked. However, a person may try to confuse the tracker by moving on hard-surfaced, often-traveled roads or by merging with civilians. These routes should be carefully examined. If a well-defined approach leads to the enemy, it will probably be mined, ambushed, or covered by snipers.
- *Least-Used Routes.* These routes avoid all man-made trails or roads and confuse the tracker. They are normally magnetic azimuths between two points. However, the tracker can use the proper concepts to follow the party if he is experienced and persistent.

Reduction of Trail Signs

4-146. A sniper who tries to hide his trail moves at reduced speed; therefore, the experienced tracker gains time. A sniper should use the following methods to reduce trail signs:

- Wrap footgear with rags or wear soft-soled sneakers that make footprints rounded and less distinctive.
- Change into footgear with a different tread immediately following a deceptive maneuver.
- Walk on hard or rocky ground.

Deception Techniques

4-147. Evading a skilled and persistent enemy tracker requires skillfully executed maneuvers to deceive the tracker and cause him to lose the trail. An enemy tracker cannot be outrun by a sniper team that is carrying equipment, because he travels light and is escorted by enemy forces designed for pursuit. The size of the pursuing force dictates the sniper team's chances of success in using ambush-type maneuvers. Sniper teams use some of the following techniques in immediate-action drills and deception drills.

4-148. **Backward Walking**. One of the most basic techniques is walking backward (Figure 4-19) in tracks already made, and then stepping off the trail onto terrain or objects that leave little to no signs. Skillful use of this maneuver causes the tracker to look in the wrong direction once he has lost the trail. This must be used in conjunction with another deception technique. This technique will probably fail if a professional tracker is on your trail.

4-149. **Big Tree.** A good deception tactic is to change directions at large trees (Figure 4-20). To change, the sniper moves in any given direction and walks past large tree (12 inches wide or larger) from 5 to 10 paces. He carefully walks backward to the forward side of the tree and makes a 90-degree change in the direction of travel, passing the tree on its forward side. This technique uses the tree as a screen to hide the new trail from the pursuing tracker. A variation used near a clear area would be for the sniper to pass by the side of the tree that he wishes to change direction to on his next leg. He walks past the tree into a clear area for 75 to 100 meters and then walks backwards to the tree. At this time he moves 90 degrees and passes on the side away from the tracker. This method could cause the tracker to follow his sign into the open area where, when he loses the track, he might cast in the wrong direction for the track. This technique works only on combat trackers and not professional trackers.

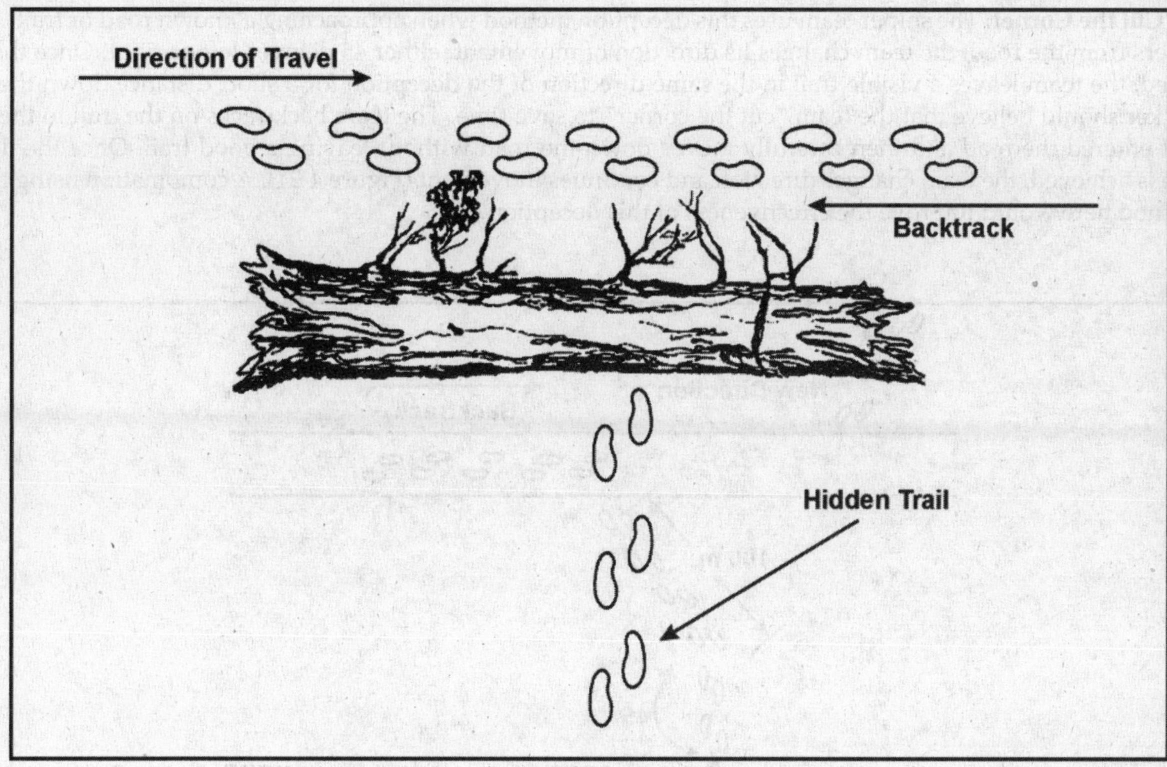

Figure 4-19. Backward-walking deception technique

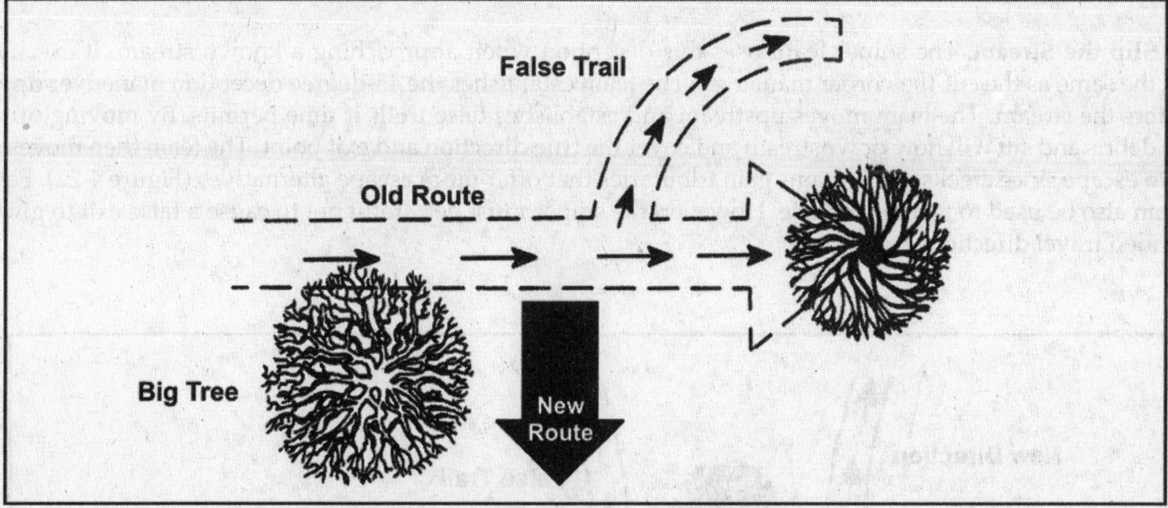

Figure 4-20. Big tree deception technique

NOTE

By studying signs, an observant tracker can determine if an attempt is being made to confuse him. If the sniper team tries to lose the tracker by walking backward, footprints will be deepened at the toe and soil will be scuffed or dragged in the direction of movement. By following carefully, the tracker can normally find a turnaround point.

4-150. **Cut the Corner.** The sniper team uses this deception method when approaching a known road or trail. About 100 meters from the road, the team changes its direction of movement, either 45 degrees left or right. Once the road is reached, the team leaves a visible trail in the same direction of the deception for a short distance down the road. The tracker should believe that the team "cut the corner" to save time. The team backtracks on the trail to the point where it entered the road and then carefully moves down the road without leaving a good trail. Once the desired distance is achieved, the team changes direction and continues movement (Figure 4-21). A combination using the big tree method here would improve the effectiveness of this deception.

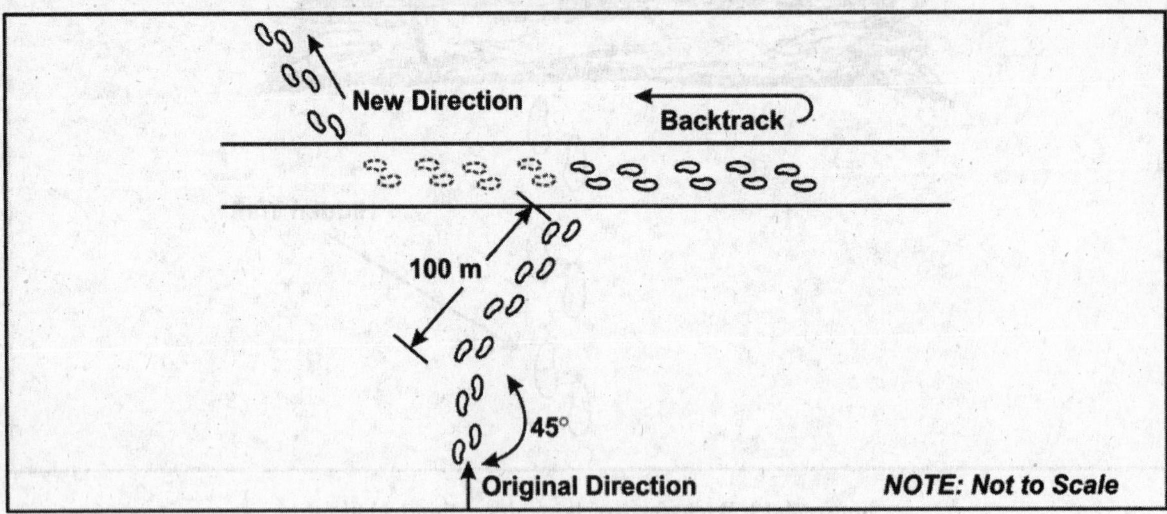

Figure 4-21. Cut-the-corner deception technique

4-151. **Slip the Stream.** The sniper team uses this deception when approaching a known stream. It executes this method the same as the cut-the-corner maneuver. The team establishes the 45-degree deception maneuver upstream, then enters the stream. The team moves upstream and establishes false trails if time permits. By moving upstream, floating debris and silt will flow downstream and cover the true direction and exit point. The team then moves downstream to escape since creeks and streams gain tributaries that offer more escape alternatives (Figure 4-22). False exit points can also be used to further confuse. However, the sniper must be careful not to cause a false exit to give away his intended travel direction.

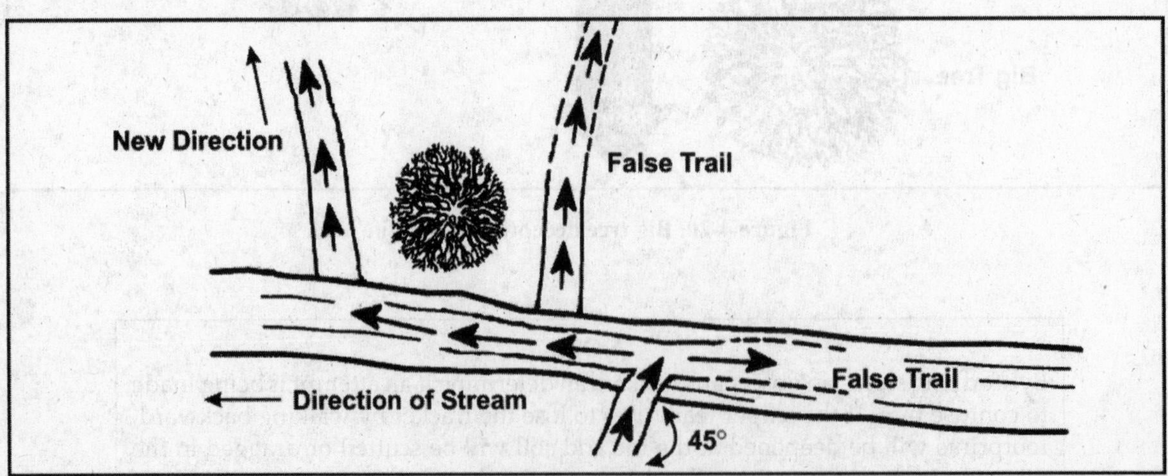

Figure 4-22. Slip-the-stream deception technique

4-152. **Arctic Circle**. The team uses this deception in snow-covered terrain to escape pursuers or to hide a patrol base. It establishes a trail in a circle as large as possible (Figure 4-23). The trail that starts on a road and returns to the same start point is effective. At some point along the circular trail, the team removes snowshoes (if used) and carefully steps off the trail, leaving one set of tracks. The large tree maneuver can be used to screen the trail. From the hide position, the team returns over the same steps and carefully fills them with snow one at a time. This technique is especially effective if it is snowing.

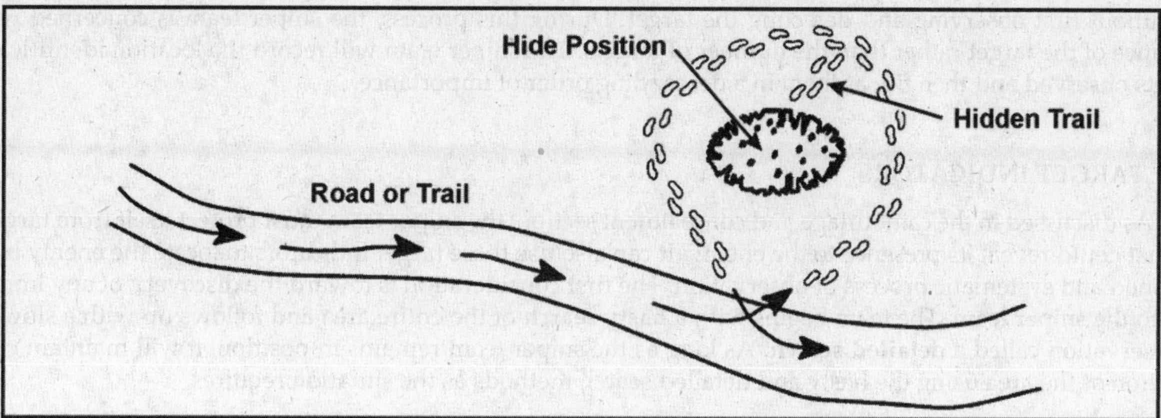

Figure 4-23. Arctic circle deception technique

4-153. **Fishhook.** The team uses this technique to double back on its own trail in an overwatch position (Figure 4-24). It can observe the back trail for trackers or ambush pursuers. If the pursuing force is too large to be destroyed, the team strives to eliminate the tracker. It uses hit-and-run tactics, then moves to another ambush position. The terrain must be used to advantage.

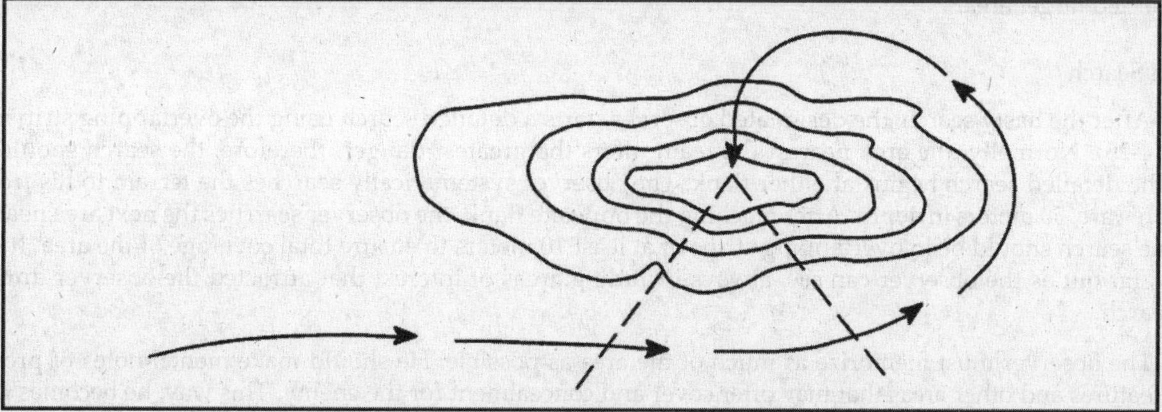

Figure 4-24. The fishhook deception technique

4-154. Dog and visual trackers are not infallible; they can be confused with simple techniques and clear thinking. The sniper should not panic and try to outrun a dog or visual tracker. It only makes it easier for the tracking party. The successful sniper keeps his head and always plans two steps ahead. Even if trackers are not in the area, it is best to always use countertracking techniques.

> **NOTE**
> Snipers must always **remember** that there is no way to hide a trail from a professional tracker!

OBSERVATION AND TARGET DETECTION

4-155. The sniper's mission requires that he deliver precision fire to selected targets. He cannot meet this requirement without first observing and detecting the target. During this process, the sniper team is concerned with the significance of the target rather than the number of targets. The sniper team will record the location identification of all targets observed and then fire at them in a descending order of importance.

USE OF TARGET INDICATORS

4-156. As discussed in the camouflage and concealment section, the sniper team must protect itself from target indicators that could reveal its presence to the enemy. It can also use these target indicators to locate the enemy by using the planned and systematic process of observation. The first consideration is toward the discovery of any immediate danger to the sniper team. The team begins with a **hasty search** of the entire area and follows up with a slow, deliberate observation called a **detailed search**. As long as the sniper team remains in position, it will maintain constant observation of the area using the hasty and detailed search methods as the situation requires.

Hasty Search

4-157. This process is the first phase of observing a target area. The observer conducts a hasty search (about 10 seconds) for any enemy activity immediately after the team occupies the firing position. The search is carried out by making quick glances at specific points, terrain features, or other areas that could conceal the enemy. The sniper should not sweep his eyes across the terrain in one continuous movement; it will prevent him from detecting motion. The observer views the area closest to the team's position first since it could pose the most immediate threat. The observer then searches farther out until the entire target area has been searched. The hasty search is effective because the eyes are sensitive to the slightest movement occurring within a wide arc of the object. This spot is called "side vision" or "seeing out of the corner of the eye." The eye must be focused on a specific point to have this sensitivity. When the observer sees or suspects a target, he uses the binoculars or the observation telescope for a detailed view of the suspected target area.

Detailed Search

4-158. After the hasty search, the designated observer starts a detailed search using the overlapping strip method (Figure 4-25). Normally, the area nearest the team offers the greatest danger, therefore, the search should begin there. The detailed search begins at either flank. The observer systematically searches the terrain to his front in a 180-degree arc, 50 meters in depth. After reaching the opposite flank, the observer searches the next area nearest his post. The search should be in overlapping strips of at least 10 meters to ensure total coverage of the area. It should cover as far out as the observer can see, always including areas of interest that attracted the observer during the hasty search.

4-159. The observer must memorize as much of the area as possible. He should make mental notes of prominent terrain features and other areas that may offer cover and concealment for the enemy. This way, he becomes familiar with the terrain as he searches. These become his key points of interest for his hasty searches.

4-160. This cycle of a hasty search followed by a detailed search should be repeated every 15 to 20 minutes depending upon the terrain and area of responsibility. Repetition allows the sniper team to become accustomed to the area and to look closer at various points with each consecutive pass over the area. After the initial searches, the observer should view the area using a combination of both hasty and detailed searches. While the observer conducts the initial searches of the area, the sniper should record prominent features, reference points, and distances on a range card.

Figure 4-25. Overlapping strip method

MAINTAINING OBSERVATION

4-161. The team members should alternate the task of observing the area about every 30 minutes. When maintaining observation, the observer keeps movement of his head and body to a minimum. He should not expose his head any higher than is necessary to see the area being observed. After completing his detailed search, the observer maintains observation of the area by using a method similar to the hasty search. He glances quickly at various points throughout the entire area and focuses his eyes on specific features that he had designated during his detailed search.

4-162. While maintaining observation, the observer should devise a set sequence for searching to ensure coverage of all terrain. Since it is entirely possible that his hasty search may fail to detect the enemy, he should periodically repeat a detailed search.

WHY OBJECTS ARE SEEN

4-163. The relative ease or difficulty in seeing objects depends upon several factors. The observer may determine objects by—

- *Shape.* Some objects can be recognized instantly by their shape, particularly if it contrasts with the background. Experience teaches people to associate an object with its shape or outline. At a distance, the outline of objects can be seen well before the details can be determined. The human body and the equipment that a soldier carries are easily identified unless the outline has been altered. Areas of importance when considering shape during observation are—
  - The clear-cut outline of a soldier or his equipment, either partially or fully exposed.
  - Man-made objects, which have geometric shapes.
  - Geometric shapes, which do not occur in nature on a large scale.
- *Shadow.* In sunlight, an object or a man will cast a shadow that can give away his presence. Shadows may be more revealing than the object itself. Care must be taken to detect alterations of the natural shape of a shadow. Where light is excessively bright, shadows will look especially black. Contrast will be extreme, and in this exaggerated contrast the observer's eye cannot adjust to both areas simultaneously. This requires the observer to "isolate" the shadowed area from the bright sunlight so that his eye can adapt to the shadow.

- *Silhouette.* Any object silhouetted against a contrasting background is conspicuous. Any smooth, flat background, such as water, a field, or best of all, the sky, will cause an object to become well delineated. However, special care must be taken when searching areas with an uneven background, as it is more difficult to detect the silhouette of an object.
- *Surface.* If an object has a surface that contrasts with its surroundings, it becomes conspicuous. An object with a smooth surface reflects light and becomes more obvious than an object with a rough surface that casts shadows on itself. An extremely smooth object becomes shiny. The reflections from a belt buckle, watch, or optical device can be seen over a mile away from the source. Any shine will attract the observer's attention.
- *Spacing.* Nature never places objects in a regular, equally spaced pattern. Only man uses rows and equal spacing.
- *Siting.* Anything that does not belong in the immediate surroundings are obvious and become readily detectable. This evidence should arouse the observer's curiosity and cause him to investigate the area more thoroughly.
- *Color.* The greater the contrasting color, the more visible the object becomes. This point is especially true when the color is not natural for that area. Color alone will usually not identify the object but is often an aid in locating it.
- *Movement.* This final reason why things are seen will seldom reveal the identity of an object, but it is the most common reason an enemy's position is revealed. Even when all other indicators are absent, movement will give a position away. A stationary object may be impossible to see and a slow-moving object difficult to detect, but a quick or jerky movement will be seen.

ELEMENTS OF OBSERVATION

4-164. Four elements in the process of observation include awareness, understanding, recording, and response. Each of these elements may be construed as a separate process or as occurring at the same time.

Awareness

4-165. Awareness is being consciously attuned to a specific fact. A sniper team must always be aware of the surroundings and take nothing for granted. The team should consider the following points because they may influence and distort awareness:

- An object's size and shape can be misinterpreted if viewed incompletely or inaccurately.
- Distractions can occur during observation.
- Active participation or degree of interest can diminish toward the event.
- Physical abilities (five senses) can be limited.
- Environmental changes can affect or occur at the time of observation.
- Imagination or perception can cause possible exaggerations or inaccuracies when reporting or recalling facts.

Understanding

4-166. Understanding is derived from education, training, practice, and experience. It enhances the sniper team's knowledge about what should be observed, broadens its ability to view and consider all factors, and aids in its evaluation of the information.

Recording

4-167. Recording is the ability to save and recall what was observed. Usually, the sniper team has mechanical aids such as writing utensils, logbooks, sketch kits, tape recordings, and cameras to support the recording of events. However, the most accessible method is memory. The ability to record, retain, and recall depends on the team's mental capacity (and alertness) and ability to recognize what is essential to record. Added factors that affect recording include:

- The amount of training and practice in observation.
- Skill through experience.
- Similarity of previous incidents.
- Time interval between observing and recording.
- The ability to understand or convey messages through oral or other communication.
- Preconceived perception of the event as to what or how it occurred and who was involved.

Response

4-168. Response is the sniper team's action toward information. It may be as simple as recording events in a logbook, making a communications call, or firing a well-aimed shot.

TARGET INDICATION AT UNKNOWN DISTANCES

4-169. Snipers usually deploy in pairs and can recognize and direct each other to targets quickly and efficiently. To recognize targets quickly, the sniper uses standard methods of indication, with slight variations to meet his individual needs.

4-170. The three methods of indicating targets are the direct method, the reference-point method, and the clock-ray method. It is easier to recognize a target if the area of ground in which it is likely to appear is known. Such an area of ground is called an "arc of fire." An arc of fire is indicated in the following sequence:

- The axis (the middle of the arc).
- The left and right limits of the arc.
- Reference points (prominent objects). These should be as permanent as possible (woods, mounds), a reasonable distance apart, and easy to identify. A specific point of the object is nominated and given a name and range (mound–bottom left corner; to be known as mound–range 400) the same as on your range card.

Direct Method

4-171. The sniper uses this method to indicate obvious targets. The range, where to look, and a description of the target are given. Terms used for where to look include the following:

- Axis of arc—for targets on or very near the axis.
- Left or right—for targets 90 degrees from the axis.
- Slightly, quarter, half, or three-quarters and left or right—for targets between the axis and the left or right limits.

Reference-Point Method

4-172. To indicate less obvious targets, the sniper may use a reference point together with the direct method, and perhaps the words above and below as well. For example:

- 300-mound (reference point—slightly right—small bush [target]).
- 200-mound (reference point—slightly right and below—gate [target]).

Clock-Ray Method

4-173. To indicate less-obvious targets, a reference-point target with a clock ray may be used. To use this method, it is imagined that there is a clock face standing up on the landscape with its center on the reference point. To indicate a target, the range, the reference point and whether the target is to the left or to the right of it, and the approximate hour on the clock face are given. For example: 300-mound—right—4 o'clock—small bush.

4-174. When indicating targets, the following points must be considered:

- *Range.* Its main purpose is to give an indication of how far to look but it should also be as accurate as possible. The sniper sets the range given to him by his observer as indicated by his shooter's data book.
- *Detailed Indication.* This value may require more detail than a normal indication; nevertheless, it should still be as brief and as clear as possible.

4-175. The sniper can use mil measurements along with the methods of indication to specify the distance between an object and the reference point used (for example, mound—reference point; go left 50 mils, lone tree, base of tree—target). The mil scale in binoculars can assist in accurate indication, although occasionally the use of hand angles will have to suffice. It is important that each sniper is conversant with the angles subtended by the various parts of his hand when the arm is outstretched.

4-176. Sniper teams must always be aware of the difficulties that can be caused when the observer and the sniper are observing through instruments with different magnifications and fields of view (telescope, binoculars). If time and concealment allow it, the observer and the sniper should use the same viewing instrument, particularly if the mil scale in the binoculars is being used to give accurate measurements from a reference point.

4-177. It is necessary that both the observer and the sniper know exactly what the other is doing and what he is saying when locating the target. Any method that is understandable to both and is fast to use is acceptable. They must use short and concise words to locate the target. Each must always be aware of what the other is doing so that the sniper does not shoot before the observer is ready. An example of this dialogue would be:

- Observer: "60—HALF RIGHT, BARN, RIGHT 50 MILS, 2 O'CLOCK, LARGE ROCK, BOTTOM LEFT CORNER, TARGET."
- Sniper: "TARGET IDENTIFIED, READY" (or describe back to observer the target).
- Sniper: "TARGET IS 2 MILS TALL; 1 MIL WIDE."
- Observer: "SET ELEVATION AT 5+1, WINDAGE 0, PARALLAX 2D BALL."
- Sniper: (repeats directions upon setting scope) "READY."
- Observer: "HOLD OF RIGHT" (wind correction). The sniper should have a round downrange within 1 to 2 seconds after the wind call.

4-178. It is extremely important that the sniper fires as soon as possible after the wind call to preclude any wind change that could affect the impact of his bullet. If the wind does change, then the observer stops the firing sequence and gives new wind readings to the sniper. The sniper and the observer must not be afraid to talk to each other, but they should keep everything said as short and concise as possible.

INDEXING TARGETS

4-179. The sniper must have some system for remembering or indexing target locations. He may want to fire at the highest priority target first. He must be selective, patient, and not fire at a target just to have a kill. Indiscriminate firing may alert more valuable and closer targets. Engagement of a distant target may result in disclosure of the sniper post to a closer enemy.

4-180. Since several targets may be sighted at the same time, the observer needs some system to remember all of the locations. To remember, he uses aiming points and reference points and records this information on the sector sketch or range card and observer's log.

4-181. To index targets, the sniper team uses the prepared range card for a reference since it can greatly reduce the engagement time. When indexing a target to the sniper, the observer locates a prominent terrain feature near the target. He indicates this feature and any other information to the sniper to assist in finding the target. Information between team members varies with the situation. The observer may sound like a forward observer (FO) giving a call for fire to a fire direction center (FDC), depending on the condition of the battlefield and the total number of possible targets from which to choose.

4-182. The sniper team must also consider the following factors:

- *Exposure Time.* Moving targets may expose themselves for only a short time. The sniper team must be alert to note the points of disappearance of as many targets as possible before engaging any one of them. By doing so, the sniper team may be able to take several targets under fire in rapid succession.
- *Number of Targets.* When the sniper team is unable to remember and plot all target locations, it should concentrate only on the most important target. By concentrating only on the most important targets, the team will effectively locate and engage high-priority targets or those targets that represent the greatest threat.
- *Spacing.* The greater the space interval between targets, the more difficult it is to note their movements. In such cases, the sniper team should accurately locate and engage the nearest target.
- *Aiming Points.* Targets that disappear behind good aiming points are easily recorded and remembered. Targets with poor aiming points are easily lost. If two such targets are of equal value and a threat to the team, the poor aiming point target should be engaged first, until the target with a good aiming point becomes a greater threat.

TARGET SELECTION

4-183. Snipers select targets according to their value. Certain enemy personnel and equipment can be listed as key targets, but their real worth must be decided by the sniper team in relation to the circumstances in which they are located.

4-184. As stated in the discussion of recording targets, the sniper team may have no choice of targets. It may lose a rapidly moving target if it waits to identify target details. It must also consider any enemy threatening its position as an "extremely high-value" target. When forced to choose a target, the sniper team will consider the following factors:

- *Certainty of Target's Identity.* The sniper team must be reasonably certain that the target it is considering is the key target.
- *Target Effect on the Enemy.* The sniper team must consider what effect the elimination of the target will have on the enemy's fighting ability. It must determine that the target is the one available target that will cause the greatest harm to the enemy.
- *Enemy Reaction to Sniper Fire.* The sniper team must consider what the enemy will do once the shot has been fired. The team must be prepared for such actions as immediate suppression by indirect fires and enemy sweeps of the area.
- *Effect on the Overall Mission.* The sniper team must consider how the engagement will affect the overall mission. The mission may be one of intelligence-gathering for a certain period. Firing will not only alert the enemy to a team's presence, but it may also terminate the mission if the team has to move from its position as a result of the engagement.
- *Probability of First-Round Hit.* The sniper team must determine the chances of hitting the target with the first shot by considering the following:
  - Distance to the target.
  - Direction and velocity of the wind.
  - Visibility of the target area.
  - Amount of the target that is exposed.
  - Length of time the target is exposed.
  - Speed and direction of target movement.
  - Nature of the terrain and vegetation surrounding the target.
- *Distance.* Although the sniper may be capable of hitting a human target at a range of 800 meters, he should not risk such a distant shot without a special reason. The sniper has been trained to stalk to within 200 meters of a trained observer and plan his retrograde. He must make use of this ability and ensure his first shot hits the target. A clean, one-shot kill is far more demoralizing to the enemy than a near-miss from 600 meters.
- *Multiple Targets.* The sniper should carefully weigh the possible consequences of firing at one of a number of targets, especially when the target cannot be identified in detail. The sniper may trade his life for an unimportant target by putting himself in a position where he must fire repeatedly in self-defense.
- *Equipment as Targets.* A well-placed shot can disable crew-served weapons, radios, vehicles, or other equipment. Such equipment may serve as "bait" and allow the sniper to make repeated engagements of crew members or radio operators while keeping the equipment idle, to be disabled at the sniper's convenience. Retaliation by indirect fire must be considered in these circumstances.
- *Intelligence Collection.* Intelligence is an important collateral function of the sniper team. When in a location near to the enemy, the sniper team must be very judicious in its decision to fire. The sniper may interrupt a pattern of activity that, if observed longer, would allow the pair to report facts that would far outweigh the value of a kill. The well-trained sniper team will carefully evaluate such situations.
- *Key Target Selection.* A sniper selects targets according to their value. A target's real worth is determined by the sniper and the nature of his mission. Key personnel targets can be identified by actions, mannerisms, positions within formations, rank or insignias, and equipment being worn or carried. Key personnel targets are as follows:
  - *Snipers.* Snipers are the number one target of a sniper team. The fleeting nature of a sniper is reason enough to engage him because he may never be seen again.
  - *Dog-Tracking Teams.* Dog-tracking teams pose a great threat to sniper teams and other special teams that may be working in the area. It is hard to fool a trained dog; therefore, the dog-tracking team must be stopped. When engaging a dog-tracking team, the sniper should engage the dog's handler first, unless it is known that the dogs are trained to attack on gunshot.

- *Scouts.* Scouts are keen observers, provide valuable information about friendly units, and control indirect fires, which make them dangerous on the battlefield.
- *Officers (Military and Political).* These individuals are also targets because in some forces losing key officers is a major disruption and causes coordination loss for hours.
- *Noncommissioned Officers (NCOs).* Losing NCOs not only affects the operation of a unit but also affects the morale of lower-ranking personnel.
- *Vehicle Commanders and Drivers.* Many vehicles are rendered useless or the capabilities are greatly degraded without a commander or driver.
- *Communications Personnel.* Eliminating these personnel can seriously cripple the enemy's communication network, because in some forces only highly trained personnel can operate various radios.
- *Weapons Crews.* Eliminating these personnel reduces the amount and accuracy of enemy fire on friendly troops.
- *Optics on Vehicles.* Personnel who are in closed vehicles are limited to viewing through optics. The sniper can blind a vehicle by damaging these optic systems.
- *Communications and Radar Equipment.* The right shot in the right place can completely ruin a tactically valuable radar or communications system. Also, only highly trained personnel may attempt to repair these systems in place. Eliminating these personnel may impair the enemy's ability to perform field repair.
- *Weapons Systems.* Many high-technology weapons, especially computer-guided systems, can be rendered useless by one well-placed round in the guidance controller of the system.

PRINCIPLES OF VISION

4-185. To fully understand and accomplish the principles of training the eye, the sniper must know its capabilities and limitations. The parts of the eye correspond to the parts of the camera and react in much the same way (Figure 4-26). The eye has a lens like a camera; however, the lens of the eye focuses automatically and more rapidly than the camera lens. The eye also has a diaphragm, called the iris, that regulates the amount of light into the eye. It permits the individual to see in bright light or in dark shadows. Just as with the camera, the eye cannot accomplish both at the same time. The eye's film is the photoreceptor cells located on the back wall, or retina, of the eye. There are two types of cells:

- *Cone Cells.* They are located in the central portion of the retina, used for day vision, and enable one to distinguish color, shape, and sharp contrast. The eye needs a lot of light to activate the cone cells, so these cells are blind during periods of low light.
- *Rod Cells.* They are located peripheral to the cone cells and are used for night vision. They see mostly in black and white and are excellent at seeing movement. These are the cells that give the observer peripheral and night vision.

OBSERVATION TECHNIQUES

4-186. Training the eye requires training the mind as well. The sniper's proficiency as an observer will come from a good mental attitude and a trained eye. As an observer, just as with a hunter, the eye must be trained to notice little

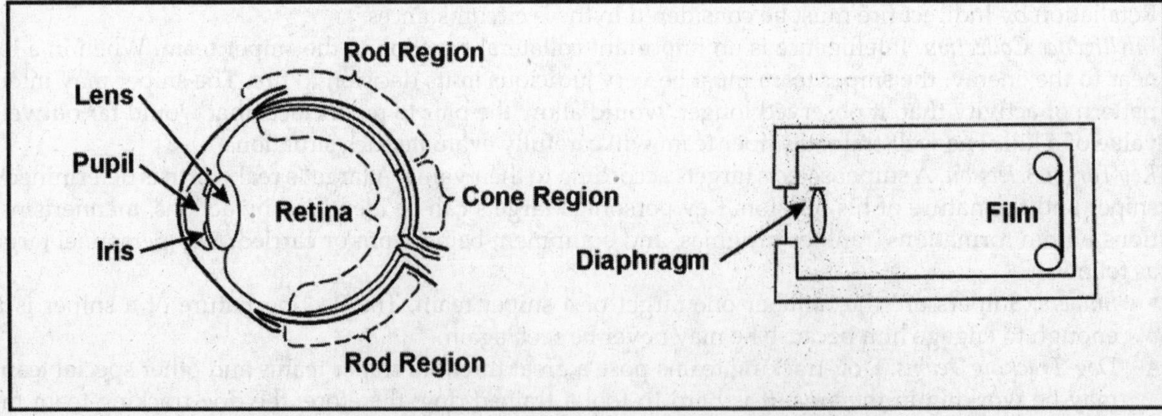

Figure 4-26. Functional similarities between the eye and a camera

things, such as the bending of grass when there is no wind, the unnatural shape of a shadow, or the wisp of vapor in cold air. Even when the enemy cannot be seen, his location can be given away by little things, such as a window that is now open when it was closed before, a puff of smoke, signs of fresh soil, or disturbed undergrowth.

4-187. Observers should learn the habits of the animals in the area or watch the domestic animals. A chicken suddenly darting from behind a building; sheep, goats, or cows suddenly moving or just becoming more alert in a field; wild birds flying or becoming quiet; insects becoming quiet at night; or animals startled from their positions should alert the observer of possible enemy activity in his area.

4-188. The observer should study and memorize the AO. Any change will alert the prepared mind to the possibility of the enemy. The observer should inspect all changes to determine the cause. He should also remember some key rules while observing. He must learn to—

- Look for the reasons why things are seen.
- Look for objects that seem out of place. Almost every object in the wild is vertical; only man-made objects such as a gun barrel are horizontal.
- See things in the proper perspective at distances. Learn to see movement, color, shape, and contrast in miniature.
- Look through vegetation, not at it. The observer should not be satisfied until he has seen as far as possible into the vegetation.

4-189. Due to constantly changing clouds and the sun's positions, light is a changing factor in observation. The sniper should always be ready to watch the changing contrast and shadows. An area that the sniper first thought held no enemy may prove different when the light changes. When the sun is to the sniper's back, light will reflect from the enemy's optical devices. But when the light changes and is to the front, the enemy will be able to see the light reflected from the sniper's optical devices.

4-190. It is also more tiring for the sniper to observe when the light shines in his eyes. He should arrange for a relief observer more frequently at this time if possible. If not, the use of some type of shading will help to cut down on the amount of light coming into the eyes.

LIMITED VISIBILITY TECHNIQUES

4-191. Twilight is another time of light changes. The eye begins to produce visual purple and the cone cells begin shutting down. Also, the iris opens more to let more light in. This reaction causes the eye to constantly change focus, and consequently, tires the eye quicker. However, during twilight the enemy will usually become more careless, allowing an alert observer to spot that last change in position or that last cigarette before dark. The sniper should also remember this is not a time for him to become relaxed.

4-192. Limited visibility runs the gamut from bright moonlight to utter darkness. But no matter how bright the night is, the eye cannot function with daylight precision. For maximum effectiveness, an observer must apply the following principles of night vision when training the eye:

- *Night Adaptation.* Allow approximately 30 minutes for the eye to adjust.
- *Off-Center Vision.* Never look directly at an object at night. This look will cause the object to disappear. When it reappears, it could appear to change shape or move.
- *Scanning.* It is important that the eye stops movement for a few seconds during the scan to be able to see an object. When scanning around an object, the temptation to look directly at the object "just to make sure" should be resisted.

4-193. The sniper should remember that the following factors can affect night vision:

- Lack of Vitamin A.
- Colds, headaches, fatigue, narcotics, alcohol, and heavy smoking.
- Exposure to bright light. It will destroy night vision for about 10 to 30 minutes, depending on the brightness and duration of the light.

4-194. Darkness blots out detail, so the eye must be trained to recognize objects by outline alone. While some people can see better than others at night, everyone can use the following techniques to improve their vision at night:

- Train the eye to actually see all the detail possible at nighttime. When the sniper sees a tree, he actually sees the tree, not a faint outline that he thinks may be a tree.
- Open the iris. While the iris of the eye is basically automatic, the eye can be trained to open up the iris even more to gather more light, which allows more detail to be seen.
- Practice roofing, which is silhouetting objects against a light background.
- Maneuver to catch the light. At night, noticeable light will only be in patches where it filters through the trees. The sniper must maneuver to place an object between his eyes and that patch of light.
- Lower the body. By lowering the body or even lying down, the sniper will be able to pick up more light and therefore see things that might otherwise go unnoticed.

OBSERVATION BY SOUND

4-195. Many times sound will warn the sniper long before the enemy is actually seen. Also, the sounds or lack of sounds from birds or animals may alert one to the possible presence of the enemy. It is therefore important to train the ears along with the eyes.

4-196. The ear nearest the origin of the sound will pick up the sound first and will hear it slightly louder than the other ear. The difference is what enables the sniper to detect the direction of the sound. When the sound hits both ears equally then the sound is to his front or rear. The brain will determine front or rear. However, if the sound reaches both ears at the same time and with the same intensity, as in fog or extremely humid weather, then the direction that the sound came from will not be discernible or will be confusing.

4-197. Sound also loses its intensity with distance traveled. The ears must be trained to become familiar with the different sounds at different distances so that the distance to the sound can be estimated. This estimate would then give the sniper a general location of the sound.

4-198. The sniper must learn to actually hear all sounds. Most people rely on sight for most of their information. A trained sniper must learn to use his ears as well as his eyes. The observer must make a conscious effort to hear all of the sounds, so that when a sound changes or a new one occurs, he will be alerted to it. He should close his eyes and listen to the sounds around him. He must categorize the sounds and remember them. Detailed observation includes a recheck of the surrounding sounds.

4-199. By cupping his hand behind one ear, the sniper can increase his ability to hear and pinpoint the direction of a sound.

TARGET LOCATION BY THE "CRACK-THUMP" METHOD

4-200. A trained ear enables the sniper to determine the approximate location of a shot being fired by using the "crack-thump" method. When the sniper is being fired at, he will hear two distinct sounds. One sound is the crack of the bullet as it breaks the sound barrier as it passes by his position. The other sound is the thump created by the muzzle blast of the weapon being fired. The crack-thump relationship is the time that passes between the two sounds. This time interval can be used to estimate the distance to the weapon being fired.

4-201. When the sniper hears the crack, he does not look into the direction of the crack. The sound will give him a false location because the sonic waves of the bullet strike objects perpendicular to the bullet's path (Figure 2-27). The sniper would mistakenly look 90 degrees from the enemy's true position. The crack should instead alert the sniper to start counting seconds.

4-202. The second sound heard is the thump of the weapon being fired. This point is the enemy's location. The time passed in seconds is the distance to the enemy. Sound travels at 340 meters per second at 30 degrees F. The speed of the bullet is twice that, which means it arrives before the sound of the muzzle blast. Therefore, half a second is approximately 300 meters, and a full second 600 meters. It becomes easier to distinguish between the two sounds as the distance increases. By listening for the thump and then looking in the direction of the thump, it is possible to determine the approximate location of the weapon being fired.

4-203. Flash-bang may be used to determine the distance to a weapon fired or and explosion seen. Since the light is instantaneous, the count will equal approximately 350 meters every second or 1,000 meters every 3 seconds or 1 mile every 5 seconds.

4-204. The speed of light is far greater than the speed of sound or of bullets. Remember that the crack-thump and flash-bang relationships are a double-edged sword that may be used against the sniper.

4-205. The speed, size, and shape of the bullet will produce different sounds. Initially, they will sound alike, but with practice the sniper will be able to distinguish between different types of weapons. A 7.62 × 39-mm bullet is just going subsonic at 600 meters. Since the crack-thump sounds differ from weapon to weapon, with practice the experienced sniper will be able to distinguish enemy fire from friendly fire.

4-206. The crack-thump method has the following limitations:

- Isolating the crack and thump is difficult when many shots are being fired.
- Mountainous areas and tall buildings cause echoes and make this method ineffective.

4-207. To overcome these limitations, the innovative sniper team can use—

- *Dummy Targets.* The sniper team can use polystyrene plastic heads or mannequins dressed to resemble a soldier to lure enemy snipers into firing. The head is placed on a stick and slowly raised into the enemy's view while another team observes the area for muzzle blast or flash.
- *The Shot-Hole Analysis.* Locating two or more shot holes in trees, walls, or dummy heads may make it possible to determine the direction of the shots. The team can use the dummy-head method and triangulate on the enemy sniper's position. However, this method only works if all shots come from the same position.

OBSERVATION DEVICE USE AND SELECTION

4-208. The sniper team's success depends upon its powers of observation. In addition to the rifle telescope, which is not used for observation, the team has an observation telescope, binoculars, night vision sight, and night vision goggles to enhance its ability to observe and engage targets. Team members must relieve each other often when using this equipment since prolonged use can cause eye fatigue, which greatly reduces the effectiveness of observation. Periods of observation during daylight should be limited to 30 minutes followed by at least 15 minutes of rest. When using NVDs, the observer should limit his initial period of viewing to 10 minutes followed by a 15-minute rest period. After several periods of viewing, he can extend the viewing period to 15 and then 20 minutes.

4-209. The M19 or M22 binoculars are the fastest and easiest aid to use when greater magnification is not needed. The binoculars also have a mil scale that can aid the sniper in judging sizes and distances. The M19 and M22 binoculars can also be used to observe at twilight by gathering more light than the naked eye. Using this reticle pattern aids the sniper in determining range and adjusting indirect fires. The sniper uses the binoculars to—

- Observe target areas.
- Observe enemy movement and positions.
- Identify aircraft.
- Improve low-light-level viewing.
- Estimate range.
- Call for and adjust indirect fires.

4-210. The M22 binoculars are the latest in the inventory but have several flaws. The M22's flaws are directly attributable to its antilaser protective coating. This coating reflects light like a mirror and is an excellent target indicator. Also, this coating reduces the amount of light that is transmitted through the lens system and greatly reduces the observation capability of the sniper during dawn and dusk.

4-211. The M49 is a fixed 20x observation-spotting telescope and can be used to discern much more detail at a greater distance than the binoculars or the sniper telescope. With good moonlight, the observer can see a target up to 800 meters away. However, the high magnification of the observation scope decreases its field of view. Moreover, the terrain will not be in focus unless it is near the object being inspected. The sniper should use the observation scope for the inspection and identification of a specific point only, not for observation of an area. The M144 is a variable power (15x to 45x) observation scope and a replacement for the M49. More modern and higher-quality spotting scopes are available in limited quantities. The sniper team should research the availability of these improved observation devices.

RANGE ESTIMATION

4-212. Range estimation is the process of determining the distance between two points. The ability to accurately determine range is the key skill needed by the sniper to accomplish his mission.

FACTORS AFFECTING ESTIMATION

4-213. Range can be determined by measuring or by estimating. Below are three main factors that affect the appearance of objects when determining range by eye.

Nature of the Target

4-214. Objects of regular outline, such as a house, will appear closer than one of irregular outline, such as a clump of trees. A target that contrasts with its background will appear to be closer than it actually is. A partially exposed target will appear more distant than it actually is.

Nature of the Terrain

4-215. Observing over smooth terrain, such as sand, water, or snow, causes the observer to underestimate distance targets. Objects will appear nearer than they really are when the viewer is looking across a depression, most of which is hidden from view. They will also appear nearer when the viewer is looking downward from high ground or when the viewer is looking down on a straight, open road or along railroad tracks.

4-216. As the observer's eye follows the contour of the terrain, he tends to overestimate the distance to targets. Objects will appear more distant than they really are when the viewer is looking across a depression, all of which is visible. They also appear more distant than they really are when the viewer is looking from low ground toward nigh ground and when the field of vision is narrowly confined, such as in twisted streets or on forest trails.

Light Conditions

4-217. The more clearly a target can be seen, the closer it will appear. A target viewed in full sunlight appears to be closer than the same target viewed at dusk or dawn or through smoke, fog, or rain. The position of the sun in relation to the target also affects the apparent range. When the sun is behind the viewer, the target appears closer. When the sun appears behind the target, the target is more difficult to see and appears farther away.

MILING THE TARGET FOR RANGE

4-218. When ranging on a human target, the sniper may use two different methods. The first method is to range on the target using the vertical crosshairs and mil dots. The second method is to use the horizontal crosshairs and mil dots.

Vertical Method

4-219. The sniper most often uses this method of range finding when using the M3A. He must become very good at estimating the height of the target in either meters or feet and inches. The sniper has the option of using a 1-meter (head to crotch) target frame or using the entire target (head to toe) as the target frame. To use the vertical method, the sniper places the crosshairs at either the feet or crotch, and measures to the top of the head of the target. The mil value is then read for that target. The sniper must determine the height of the target if he is not using the 1-meter target frame. Since the telescope is graduated in meters, the height of the target must be converted into meters. The sniper then calculates the range using the mil-relation formula. The estimation of the height of the target may be the most important factor in this formula. An error of 3 inches on a 5-foot 9-inch target that is actually 5 feet 6 inches results in a 19-meter error at a reading of 4 mils.

Normal height of the human = 69 inches

$$\frac{\text{69 inches} \times 25.4}{\text{Size of target in mils (4)}} = \text{Range to target in meters (438.5 or 440 meters)}$$

NOTE

This example may prove to be of specific use when facing an enemy entrenched in bunkers or in dense vegetation.

Horizontal Method

4-220. The horizontal method is based upon a target width of 19 inches at the shoulders. This technique can be very accurate out to ranges of 350 meters, and is very effective in an urban environment. Beyond this range it is no longer effective. The sniper should use this method to double-check ranges derived from groin to head. For example, a range estimate derived from a groin to head (1 meter) measurement of 2 mils would be equal to a 1 mil shoulder to shoulder measurement (horizontal = 1/2 vertical). A good rule of thumb is that if the target is smaller than 1 1/2 mils (322 meters), it is more accurate to use the vertical method in combination with the horizontal method.

4-221. The mil dots in the M3A are 3/4 MOA in diameter. Therefore, it is important to note where on the dots the bottom or the top of the target falls within the mil dot. The mil dots are spaced 1 mil from center to center, or cross to center of first dot.

4-222. Objects viewed from an oblique angle may cause the sniper to overestimate the range to that object. Snipers should be aware of this effect and compensate accordingly.

DETERMINING RANGE TECHNIQUES

4-223. A sniper team must accurately determine distance, properly adjust elevation on the SWS, and prepare topographic sketches or range cards. To meet these needs, team members have to be skilled in various range estimation techniques. The team can use any of the following methods to determine distance between its position and the target.

Sniper Telescope

4-224. The M3A has a mil dot reticle and the mil-relation formula is used for range determination. Using the telescope for range estimation is especially helpful when establishing known ranges for a range card or a reference mark. The sniper rifle's inherent stability helps to improve the accuracy of the measurements. The sniper can determine range by using the range feature of the sniping telescope and the following:

- *Personnel.* The distance from the individual's head to his waist is normally 30 inches; from the top of his head to his groin is 1 meter (39.4 inches). The head to groin is the most common measuring point for the human body. The 1-meter measurement will not vary but an inch or two from the 6-foot-6-inch man to the 5-foot-6-inch man.
- *Tanks.* The distance from the ground line to the deck or from the deck to the turret top of a Soviet-style tank is approximately 30 inches.
- *Vehicles.* The distance from the ground line to the fender above the wheel is approximately 30 inches. The distance to the roofline is 3 1/2 to 4 feet.
- *Trees.* The width of the trees in the vicinity of the sniper will be a good indication of the width of the trees in the target area.
- *Window Frames.* The vertical length of a standard frame is approximately 60 inches. This distance is 1.5 meters by 2.0 meters in Europe.

NOTE

Through the process of interpolation, the sniper can range on any object of known size. For example, the head of any individual will measure approximately 12 inches. The M3A has a mil-dot reticle. On this telescope a mil dot equals 3/4 of an MOA, and the space between mil dots equals 1 mil or 3.44 MOA (round to 3.5 in the field). The figure 3.44 is the true number of MOA in a mil as one radian is equal to 57.295 degrees. This makes 6.283 radians in a circle or 6283 mils in a circle. With 21,600 MOA in a circle, the result is 3.44 MOA in a mil.

Mil-Relation Formula

4-225. The sniper can also use the mil-relation formula to determine ranges. The M3A rifle telescope has 10 mils vertical and horizontal measurement between the heavy duplex reticle lines; the space between each dot represents 1 mil. Military binoculars also have a mil scale in the left ocular eyepiece. By using the known measured sizes of objects, the sniper can use the mil-relation formula to determine the range.

NOTE

The size of objects in meters yields ranges in meters; the size of objects in yards yields ranges in yards. Other relationships must also be understood: 1 mil equals 3.44 MOA or 3.6 inches at 100 yards; 1 meter at 1,000 meters or approximately 1 yard at 1,000 yards.

4-226. The sniper uses the following formula to determine the range to the target:

$$\text{Range to target} = \frac{\text{Size of object in meters and yards} \times 1{,}000}{\text{Size of object in mils}}$$

EXAMPLE 1

Object = 2 meters, Mils = 4 mils (as measured in the M3A scope)

$$\frac{2 \times 1{,}000}{4} = \frac{2{,}000}{4} = 500 \text{ meters} = \text{Range to target}$$

EXAMPLE 2

Object = 2 yards, Mils = 5 mils (as measured in the M3A scope)

$$\frac{2 \times 1{,}000}{5} = \frac{2{,}000}{5} = 400 \text{ yards} = \text{Range to target}$$

EXAMPLE 3

Object = 69 inches, Mils = 4 mils (To convert inches to meters, multiply by 25.4.)

$$\frac{69 \times 25.4}{4} = \frac{1752.6}{4} = 438 \text{ meters}$$

NOTE

The distance to the target in yards must be converted to meters to correctly set the M3A's ballistic cam.

4-227. Once the sniper understands the formula, he must become proficient at estimating the actual height of the target in his scope. At longer ranges the measurements must be accurate to within 1/10 mil. Otherwise, the data will be more than the allowable ballistic error. The ability of the sniper team to accurately estimate the height of the target is the single most important factor in using this formula.

Mil Relation (Worm Formula)

Sample Problems:

No. 1: As a member of a sniper team, you and your partner are in your hide site and are preparing a range card. To your front you see a Soviet-type truck that you determine to be 4 meters long. Your team is equipped with an M24 system. Through your binoculars the truck is 5 mils in length. Determine the range to this reference for your system.

Solution: STEP 1. No conversion needed.
STEP 2. Determine the range.

$$\text{Width} = \frac{4 \text{ meters} \times 1{,}000}{5 \text{ mils}} = 800 \text{ meters}$$

No. 2: You are a member of a sniper team assigned to cover a certain area of ground. You are making a range card and determining ranges to reference points in that area. You see a tank located to your front. Through your binoculars you find the width of the tank to be 8 mils. You determine the length of the tank to be 5 meters. Determine the correct range for your system.

Solution: STEP 1. No conversion needed.
STEP 2. Determine the range.

$$\text{Width} = \frac{5 \text{ meters} \times 1{,}000}{8 \text{ mils}} = 625 \text{ meters}$$

Military Binoculars

4-228. The sniper can calculate the range to a target by using the M3, M19, and M22 binoculars, or any other optical device that has vertical and horizontal mil reticles.

4-229. M3 Binoculars. The graduations between the numbers on the horizontal reference line are in 10-mil graduations. The height of the vertical lines along the horizontal reference line is 2 1/2 mils. The graduation of the horizontal reference lines on the left of the reticle is 5 mils (vertical) between the reference lines. These lines are also 5 mils long (horizontal). The small horizontal lines located above the horizontal reference line in the center of the reticle are 5 mils apart (vertical) and are also 5 mils long (horizontal). The vertical scale on the reticle is not to be used for range finding purposes.

4-230. **M19 Binoculars**. The graduation between the number lines on the horizontal and the vertical lines on the reticle is 10 mils (Figure 4-27). The total height of the vertical lines on the horizontal reference lines is 5 mils. These lines are further graduated 2 1/2 mils above the horizontal line and 2 1/2 mils below the line. The total width of the horizontal lines on the vertical reference line is 5 mils. These lines are further graduated into 2 1/2 mils on the left side of the line and 2 1/2 mils on the right side of the vertical reference line.

4-231. **M22 Binoculars**. The graduation between the numbered lines on the horizontal and vertical reference lines is 10 mils. There are 5 mils between a numbered graduation and the 2 1/2-mil tall line that falls between the numbered graduations. The value of the longer lines that intersect the horizontal and vertical lines on the reticle is 5 mils. The value of the shorter lines that intersect the horizontal and vertical reference lines on the reticle is 2 1/2 mils. These are the lines that fall between the 5-mil lines.

Estimation

4-232. There will be times when the sniper must estimate the range to the target. This method requires no equipment and can be accomplished without exposing the observer's position. There are two methods of estimation that meet these requirements: the 100-meter unit-of-measure method and the appearance-of-objects method.

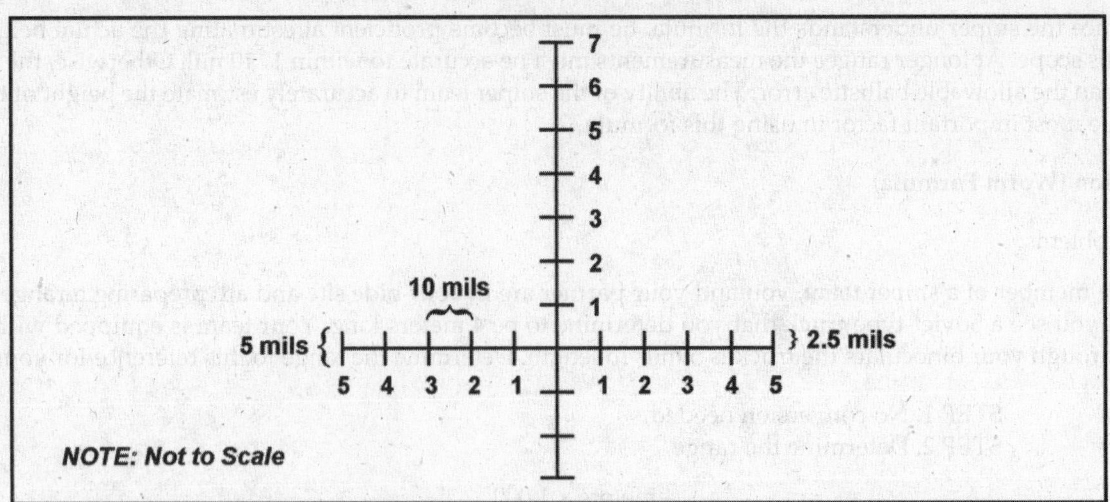

Figure 4-27. The M19 binocular reticle showing the mil measurements of the stadia lines

4-233. **The 100-Meter Unit-of-Measure Method.** The sniper must be able to visualize a distance of 100 meters on the ground. For ranges up to 500 meters, he determines the number of 100-meter increments between the two points that he wishes to measure. Beyond 500 meters, the sniper must select a point halfway to the target, determine the number of 100-meter increments of the halfway point, and then double this number to find the range to the target (Figure 4-28).

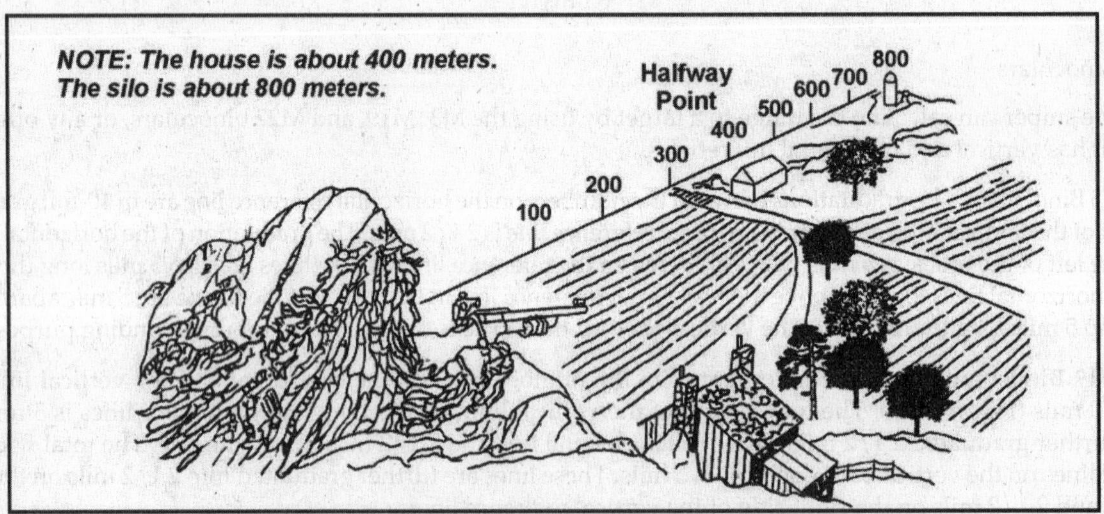

Figure 4-28. The "Halfway Point" distance estimation process

4-234. During training exercises, the sniper must become familiar with the effect that sloping ground has on the appearance of a 100-meter increment. Ground that slopes upward gives the illusion of a shorter distance, and the observer's tendency is to overestimate a 100-meter increment. Conversely, ground that slopes downward gives the illusion of a longer distance. In this case, the sniper's tendency is to underestimate.

4-235. Proficiency in the 100-meter unit-of-measure method requires constant practice. Throughout the training in this technique, comparisons should continuously be made between the range as determined by the sniper and the actual range as determined by pacing or other more accurate means of measurement. The best training technique is to require the sniper to pace the range after he has visually determined it. In this way he discovers the actual range for himself, which makes a greater impression than if he were simply told the correct range.

4-236. The greatest limitation of the 100-meter unit of measure is that its accuracy is directly related to how much of the terrain is visible at the greater ranges. This point is particularly true at a range of 500 meters or more when the sniper can only see a portion of the ground between himself and the target. It becomes very difficult to use the 100-meter unit-of-measure method of range determination with any degree of accuracy.

4-237. **The Appearance-of-Objects Method**. The appearance-of-objects method is the means of determining range by the size and other characteristic details of the object in question. It is a common method of determining distances and used by most people in their everyday living. For example, a motorist attempting to pass another car must judge the distance of oncoming vehicles based on his knowledge of how vehicles appear at various distances. Of course, in this example, the motorist is not interested in precise distances, but only that he has sufficient road space to safely pass the car in front of him. This same technique can be used by the sniper to determine ranges on the battlefield. If he knows the characteristic size and detail of personnel and equipment at known ranges, then he can compare these characteristics to similar objects at unknown ranges. When the characteristics match, so does the range.

4-238. To use this method with any degree of accuracy, the sniper must be familiar with the characteristic details of objects as they appear at various ranges. For example, the sniper should study the appearance of a man when he is standing at a range of 100 meters. He fixes the man's appearance firmly in his mind, carefully noting details of size and characteristics of uniform and equipment. Next, he studies the same man in a kneeling position and then in a prone position. By comparing the appearance of these positions at known ranges from 100 to 500 meters, the sniper can establish a series of mental images that will help him determine range on unfamiliar terrain. Training should also be conducted in the appearance of other familiar objects such as weapons or vehicles. Because the successful use of this method depends upon visibility, anything that limits the visibility (such as weather, smoke, or darkness) will also limit the effectiveness of this method.

Combination of Methods

4-239. Under proper conditions, either the 100-meter unit-of-measure method or the appearance-of-objects method is an effective way of determining range. However, proper conditions do not always exist on the battlefield and the sniper will need to use a combination of methods. The terrain might limit using the 100-meter unit-of-measure method and the visibility could limit using the appearance-of-objects method. For example, an observer may not be able to see all of the terrain out to the target; however, he may see enough to get a general idea of the distance within 100 meters. A slight haze may obscure many of the target details, but the observer should still be able to judge its size. Thus, by carefully considering the approximate ranges as determined by both methods, an experienced observer should arrive at a figure close to the true range.

Measuring

4-240. The sniper can measure distance on a map or pace the distance between two points. The following paragraphs discuss each method.

4-241. **Map (Paper-Strip Method)**. The paper-strip method is useful when determining longer distances (1,000 meters plus). When using this method, the sniper places the edge of a strip of paper on the map and ensures it is long enough to reach between the two points. Then he pencils in a tick mark on the paper at the team position and another at the distant location. He places the paper on the map's bar scale, located at the bottom center of the map, and aligns the left tick mark with the 0 on the scale. Then he reads to the right to the second mark and notes the corresponding distance represented between the two marks.

4-242. **Actual Measurement**. The sniper uses this method by pacing the distance between two points, provided the enemy is not in the vicinity. This method obviously has limited applications and can be very hazardous to the sniper team. It is one of the least desirable methods.

Bracketing Method

4-243. The bracketing method is used when the sniper assumes that the target is no less than "X" meters away, but no more than "Y" meters away. The sniper then uses the average of the two distances as the estimated range. Snipers can increase their accuracy of eye-range estimation by using an average of both team members' estimate.

Halving Method

4-244. The sniper uses this method for distances beyond 500 meters. He selects a point midway to the target, determines the number of 100-meter increments to the halfway point, and then doubles the estimate. Again, it is best to average the results of both team members.

Range Card

4-245. This method is a very accurate means of estimating range. The fact that the sniper has established a range card means he has been in the area long enough to know the target area. He has already determined ranges to indicated reference points. The observer will give his targets to the sniper by giving deflections and distances from known reference points in the target field of view. The sniper can adjust his telescope for a good median distance in the target area and simply adjust fire from that point. **There are multiple key distances that should be calculated and noted with references on the range card.** The first is the point blank zero of the weapon. With a 300-meter zero, the point-blank zero of the M118 ammunition is 375 meters. Targets under this range do not need to be corrected for. The other key distances are merely a point of reference against which further distance determinations can be judged. These are marked as target reference points (TRP) and are also used as reference points for directing the sniper onto a target.

Speed of Sound

4-246. The sniper can estimate the approximate distance from the observer to a sound source (bursting shell, weapon firing) by timing the sound. The speed of sound in still air at 50 degrees F is about 340 meters per second. However, wind and variations in temperature alter this speed somewhat. For practical use, the sniper may assume the speed of sound is 350 meters per second under all conditions. He can time the sound either with a watch or by counting from the time the flash appears until the sound is heard by the observer. The sniper counts "one-1,000, two-1,000," and so on, to determine the approximate time in seconds. He then multiplies the time in seconds by 350 to get the approximate distance in meters to the source of the fire.

MEASUREMENT BY BULLET IMPACT

4-247. Another undesirable but potentially useful method is to actually fire a round at the point in question. This practice is possible if you know your target is coming into the area at a later time and you plan to ambush the target. However, this method is not tactically sound and is also very hazardous to the sniper team.

LASER RANGE FINDERS

4-248. These can also be used to determine range to a very high degree of accuracy. When aiming the laser at a specific target, the sniper should support it much the same way as his weapon to ensure accuracy. If the target is too small, aiming the laser at a larger object near the target will suffice—that is, a building, vehicle, tree, or terrain feature. The range finder must be used with yellow filters to keep the laser eye-safe for the sniper and observer when observing through optics, as the AN/GVS 5 is not eye safe. This cover limits the range; however, the limitations are well within the range of the sniper. Rain, fog, or smoke will severely limit the use of laser range finders. Laser detectors and NVDs that are set to the correct wavelength may also intercept laser range finders.

CAUTION

Viewing an "eye-safe" laser through magnifying optics increases the laser's intensity to unsafe levels.

Sniper Cheat Book

4-249. The sniper team should keep a "cheat book" complete with measurements. The team fills in the cheat book during its area analysis, mission planning, isolation, and once in the AO. A tape measure will prove invaluable. Each cheat book should include the following:

- Average height of human targets in AO.
- Vehicles:
  - Height of road wheels.
  - Vehicle dimensions.
  - Length of main gun tubes on tanks.
  - Lengths and sizes of different weapon systems.
- Urban environment:
  - Average size of doorways.
  - Average size of windows.
  - Average width of streets and lanes (average width of a paved road in the United States is 10 feet).

4-250. As the sniper team develops its cheat book, all measurements are converted into constants and computed with different mil readings. These measurements should also be incorporated into the sniper's logbook. The team should use the "worm formula" (paragraph 4-227) when preparing the cheat book.

SELECTION AND PREPARATION OF HIDES

4-251. To effectively accomplish its mission or to support combat operations, the sniper team must select a position called a sniper hide or post. Once constructed, it will provide the sniper team with a well-concealed post from which to observe and fire without fear of enemy detection. Selecting the location of a position is one of the most important tasks a sniper team must accomplish during the mission planning phase of an operation. After selecting the location, the team must also determine how it will move into the area and locate and occupy the final position.

HIDE SELECTION

4-252. Upon receiving a mission, the sniper team locates the target area and then determines the best location for a tentative position by using one or more of the following sources of information:

- Topographic maps.
- Aerial photographs.
- Visual reconnaissance before the mission.
- Information gained from units operating in the area.

4-253. In selecting a sniper hide, maximum consideration is given to the fundamentals and principles of camouflage, cover, and concealment. Once on the ground, the sniper team ensures the position provides an optimum balance between the following considerations:

- Maximum fields of fire and observation of the target area.
- Maximum concealment from enemy observation.
- Covered routes into and out of the position.
- Located no closer than 300 meters from the target area whenever possible.
- A natural or man-made obstacle between the position and the target area.

4-254. A sniper team must remember that if a position appears ideal, it may also appear that way to the enemy. Therefore, the team should avoid choosing locations that are—

- On a point or crest of prominent terrain features.
- Close to isolated objects.
- At bends or ends of roads, trails, or streams.
- In populated areas, unless mission-essential.

4-255. The sniper team must use its imagination and ingenuity in choosing a good location for the given mission. The team must choose a location that not only allows the team to be effective but also must appear to the enemy to be the least likely place for a team position. Examples of such positions are—

- Under logs in a deadfall area.
- Tunnels bored from one side of a knoll to the other.
- Swamps.
- Deep shadows.
- Inside rubble piles.

HIDE SITE LOCATION

4-256. The sniper team should determine the site location by the following factors of area effectiveness:

- Mission.
- Dispersion.
- Terrain patterns.

4-257. Various factors can affect the team's site location. The sniper team should select tentative sites and routes to the objective area by using—

- Aerial photographs.
- Maps.
- Reconnaissance and after-action reports.
- Interrogations of indigenous personnel, prisoners of war, and other sources.
- Weather reports.
- Area studies.

4-258. When the team is selecting a site, it should look for—

- Terrain patterns (urban, rural, wooded, barren).
- Soil type (to determine tools).
- Population density.
- Weather conditions (snow, rain).
- Drainage.
- Types of vegetation.
- Drinking water.

4-259. The sniper team must also consider some additional requirements when selecting the hide site. It should conduct a reconnaissance of the area to determine—

- Fields of fire.
- Cover and concealment.
- Avenues of approach.
- Isolated and conspicuous patterns.
- Terrain features lying between your position and the objectives.

SNIPER HIDE CHECKLIST

4-260. There are many factors to consider in the selection, construction, and use of a sniper hide. The sniper team must remain alert to the danger of compromise and consider its mission as an overriding factor. Figure 4-29 lists the guidelines that the sniper team should use when selecting a site and constructing the sniper hide.

HIDE SITE OCCUPATION

4-261. During the mission planning phase, the sniper also selects an ORP. From this point, the sniper team reconnoiters the tentative position to determine the exact location of its final position. The location of the ORP should provide cover and concealment from enemy fire and observation, be located as close to the selected area as possible, and have good routes into and out of the selected area.

- ❑ Select and construct a sniper hide from which to observe and fire. Because the slightest movement is the only requirement for detection, construction is usually accomplished at night. Caution must still be exercised, as the enemy may employ NVDs, and sound travels greater distances at night.
- ❑ Do not place the sniper hide against a contrasting background or near a prominent terrain feature. These features are usually under observation or used as registration points.
- ❑ Consider those areas that are least likely to be occupied by the enemy.
- ❑ Ensure that the position is located within effective range of the expected targets and that it affords a clear field of fire.
- ❑ Construct or empty alternate hides where necessary to effectively cover an area.
- ❑ Assume that the sniper hide is under enemy observation.
- ❑ Avoid making sounds.
- ❑ Avoid unnecessary movement.
- ❑ Avoid observing over a skyline or the top of cover or concealment that has an even outline or contrasting background.
- ❑ Avoid using the binoculars or telescope where light may reflect from lenses.
- ❑ Observe around a tree from a position near the ground. The snipers should stay in the shadows when observing from a sniper hide.
- ❑ Give careful consideration to the route into or out of the hide. A worn path can easily be detected. The route should be concealed and covered, if possible.
- ❑ Use resourcefulness and ingenuity to determine the type of hide to be constructed.
- ❑ When possible, choose a position that has a terrain obstacle (for example, a river, thick brush) between it and the target and/or known or suspected enemy location.

Figure 4-29. Checklist for selecting and constructing a hide

4-262. From the ORP, the team moves forward to a location that allows the team to view the tentative position area. Once a suitable location has been found, the team member moves to the position. While conducting the reconnaissance or moving to the position, the team—

- Moves slowly and deliberately, using the sniper low crawl.
- Avoids unnecessary movement of trees, bushes, and grass.
- Avoids making any noises.
- Stays in the shadows, if there are any.
- Stops, looks, and listens every few feet.
- Looks for locations to hide spoil if a hide is to be dug into the terrain.

4-263. When the sniper team arrives at the firing position, it—

- Conducts a hasty and detailed search of the target area.
- Starts construction of the firing position, if required.
- Organizes equipment so that it is easily accessible.
- Establishes a system of observing, eating, resting, and using the latrine.

HASTY SNIPER HIDE OR FINAL FIRING POSITION

4-264. The sniper team uses a hasty position when it will be in position for a short time, cannot construct a position due to the proximity of the enemy, or must immediately assume a position. Due to the limited nature of sniper missions and the requirement to stalk, the sniper team will most often use a hasty position.

4-265. This position (fast find) provides protection from enemy fire or observation. Natural cover (ravines, hollows, reverse slopes) and artificial cover (foxholes, trenches, walls) protect the sniper from flat trajectory fires and enemy observation. Snipers must form the habit of looking for and taking advantage of every bit of cover and concealment the terrain offers. They must combine this habit with proper use of movement techniques to provide adequate protection from enemy fire and observation.

4-266. Cover and concealment in a hasty position provide protection from enemy fire and observation. The cover and concealment may be artificial or natural. Concealment may not provide protection from enemy fire. A sniper team should not make the mistake of believing they are protected from enemy fire merely because they are concealed from enemy eyes.

4-267. There should be no limitation on ingenuity of the sniper team in selecting a hasty sniper hide. Under certain circumstances it may be necessary to fire from trees, rooftops, steeples, logs, tunnels, deep shadows, buildings, swamps, woods, and an unlimited variety of open areas. The sniper team's success depends to a large degree on its knowledge, understanding, and application of the various field techniques or skills that allow them to move, hide, observe, and detect the enemy (Table 4-1).

Table 4-1. Hasty sniper hide advantages and disadvantages

Advantages	Disadvantages
• ***Requires no construction. The sniper team uses what is available for cover and concealment.*** • ***Can be occupied in a short time. As soon as a suitable position is found, the team need only prepare loopholes by moving small amounts of vegetation or by simply backing several meters away from the vegetation that is already there to conceal the weapon's muzzle blast.*** **Note:** ***Loopholes may be various objects or constructed by the team, but must provide an adequate view for firing.***	• ***Affords no freedom of movement. Any movement that is not slow and deliberate may result in the team being compromised.*** • ***Restricts observation of large areas. This type of position is normally used to observe a specific target area (intersection, passage, or crossing).*** • ***Offers no protection from direct or indirect fires. The team has only available cover for protection from direct fires.*** • ***Relies heavily on personal camouflage. The team's only protection against detection is personal camouflage and the ability to use the available terrain.***

Occupation Time: ***The team should not remain in this type of position longer than 8 hours; it will only result in loss of effectiveness. This is due to muscle strain or cramps, which is a result of lack of freedom of movement combined with eye fatigue.***

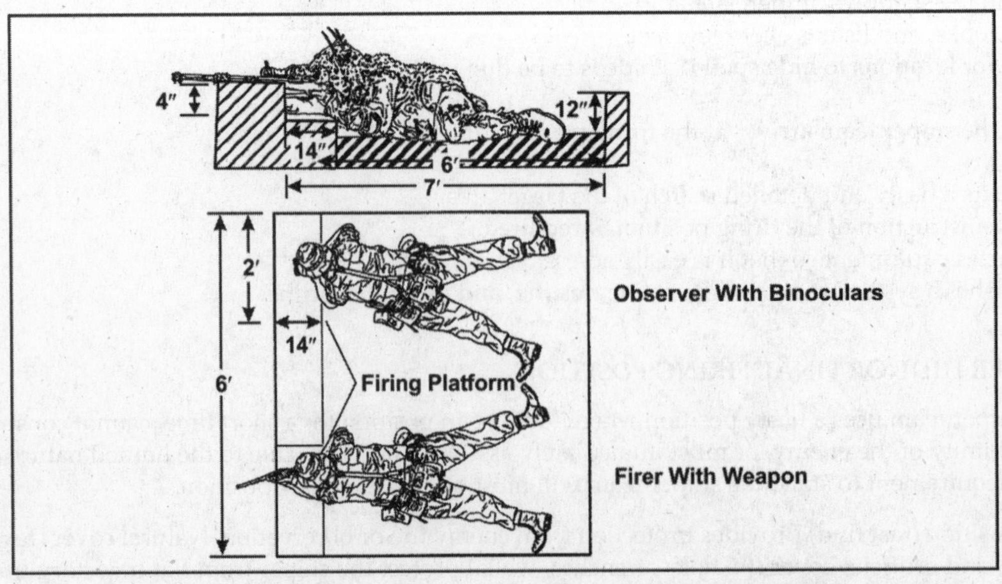

Figure 4-30. Overhead and side view of the expedient sniper hide site

EXPEDIENT SNIPER HIDE

Table 4-2. Expedient sniper hide advantages and disadvantages

Advantages	Disadvantages
• ***Requires little construction. This position is constructed by digging a hole in the ground just large enough for the team and its equipment. Soil dug from this position can be placed in sandbags and used for building firing platforms.*** • ***Conceals most of the body and equipment. The optics, rifles, and heads of the sniper team are the only items that are above ground level in this position.*** • ***Provides some protection from direct fires due to its lower silhouette.***	• ***Affords little freedom of movement. The team has more freedom of movement in this position than in the hasty position. However, teams must remember that stretching or reaching for a canteen causes the exposed head to move unless controlled. Team members can lower the head below ground level, but this movement should be done slowly to ensure a target indicator is not produced.*** • ***Allows little protection from indirect fires. This position does not protect the team from shrapnel and debris falling into the position.*** • ***Exposes the head, weapons, and optics. The team must rely heavily on the camouflaging of these exposed items.***

Construction Time: ***1 to 3 hours (depending on the situation).***
Occupation Time: ***6 to 12 hours.***

4-268. When a sniper team has to remain in position for a longer time than the hasty position can provide, it should construct an expedient position (Figure 4-30). The expedient position lowers the sniper's silhouette as low to the ground as possible, but it still allows him to fire and observe effectively. Table 4-2 lists characteristics of an expedient sniper hide.

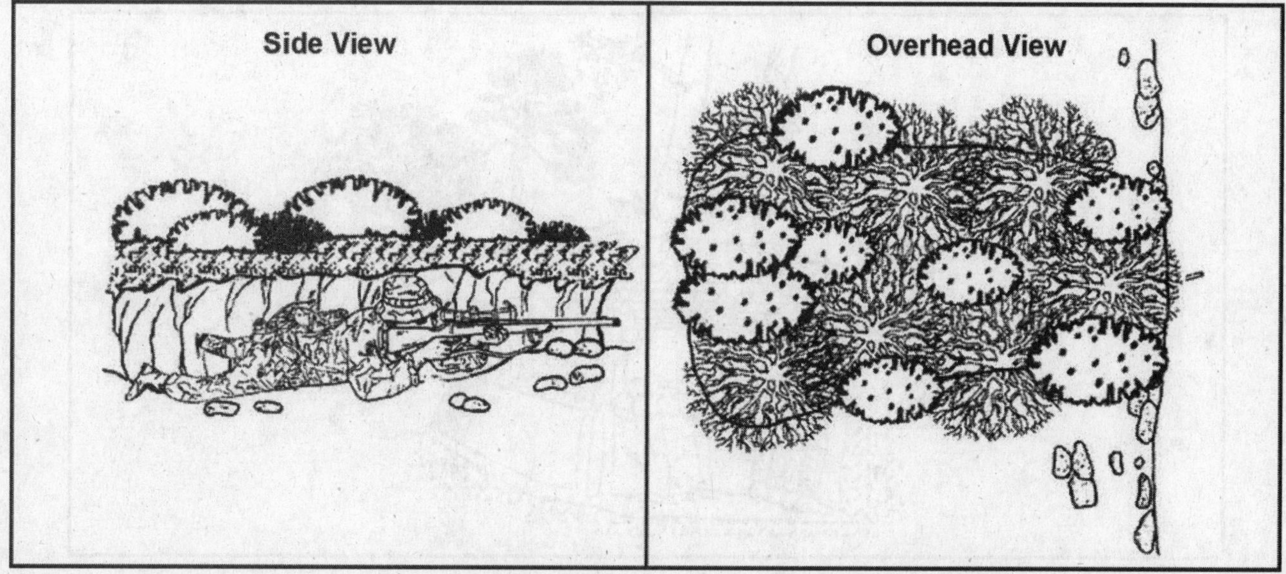

Figure 4-31. Overhead and side view of the expedient belly hide site

BELLY HIDE

4-269. The belly hide (Figure 4-31) is similar to the expedient position, but it has overhead cover that not only protects the team from the effects of indirect fires but also allows more freedom of movement. A belly hide is most useful in mobile situations or when the sniper does not intend to be in the position for extended periods of time. This position can be dug out under a tree, a rock, or any available object that will provide overhead protection and a concealed entrance and exit. Table 4-3 lists the belly hide characteristics.

Table 4-3. Belly hide advantages, disadvantages, and construction

Advantages	Disadvantages
• ***Allows some freedom of movement. The darkened area inside this position allows the team to move freely. The team should cover the entrance/exit hole with a poncho or piece of canvas so outside light does not silhouette the team inside the position.*** • ***Conceals all but the rifle barrel. All equipment is inside the position except the rifle barrels, but the barrels could be inside, depending on the room available to construct the position.*** • ***Provides protection from direct and indirect fires. The team should try to choose a position that has an object that will provide good overhead protection (rock, tracked vehicle, rubble pile, and so forth), or prepare it in the same manner as overhead cover for other infantry positions.*** • ***Is simple and can be quickly built. This hide can be used when the sniper is mobile, because many can be built.***	• ***Is uncomfortable.*** • ***Cannot be occupied for long periods of time.*** • ***The sniper is exposed while firing.*** • ***Provides limited protection from the weather or fire.*** • ***Requires extra construction time.*** • ***Requires extra materials and tools. Construction of overhead cover will require saws or axes, waterproof material, and so forth.*** • ***Has limited space. The sniper team will have to lie in the belly hide without a lot of variation in body position due to limited space and design of the position.***
Construction	

Figure 4-32. The semipermanent sniper hide

• *Dig a pit (shallow) for the prone position.* • *Build an overhead cover using:* ▪ *Dirt and sod.* ▪ *A drop cloth.* ▪ *Woven saplings.* ▪ *Corrugated metal, shell boxes, scrap metal, doors, chicken wire, or scrap lumber.*

Construction Time: ***4 to 6 hours.***
Occupation Time: ***12 to 48 hours.***

SEMIPERMANENT SNIPER HIDE

4-270. The sniper uses the semipermanent hide mostly in a defensive or outpost situation (Figure 4-32). Construction of this position requires additional equipment and personnel. However, it will allow sniper teams to remain there for extended periods or be relieved in place by other sniper teams. Like the belly hide, the sniper can construct this position by tunneling through a knoll or under natural objects already in place. This prepared sniper hide should provide sufficient room for movement without fear of detection, some protection from weather and overhead or direct fire, and a covered route to and from the hide.

Table 4-4. Semipermanent sniper hide advantages and disadvantages

Advantages	Disadvantages
• ***Offers total freedom of movement inside the position. The team members can move about freely. They can stand, sit, or even lie down.*** • ***Protects against direct and indirect fires. The sniper team should look for the same items as mentioned in the belly hide.*** • ***Is completely concealed. Loopholes are the only part of the position that can be detected. They allow for the smallest exposure possible; yet, they still allow the sniper and observer to view the target area. The entrance and exit to the position must be covered to prevent light from entering and highlighting the loopholes. Loopholes that are not in use should be covered from the inside with a piece of canvas or suitable material.*** • ***Is easily maintained for extended periods. This position allows the team to operate effectively for a longer period.***	• ***Requires extra personnel and tools to construct. This position requires extensive work and more tools. Very seldom can a position like this be constructed near the enemy, but it should be constructed during darkness and be completed before dawn.*** • ***Increases risk of detection. Using a position for several days or having teams relieve each other in a position always increases the risk of the position being detected. Snipers should never continue to fire from the same position.***

Construction Time: ***4 to 6 hours (4 personnel).***
Occupation Time: ***48 hours plus (relieved by other teams).***

4-271. A semipermanent hide can be an enlargement of the standard one- or two-man fighting position with overhead cover. The sniper constructs this type of hide when in a defensive posture, since construction requires considerable time. It would be suitable when integrated into the perimeter defense of a base camp, during static warfare, or during a stay-behind infiltration. It can be constructed as a standing or lying type of hide.

4-272. The construction of loopholes requires care and practice to ensure that they afford an adequate view of the required fields of fire. The sniper should construct the loopholes so that they are wide at the back where he is and

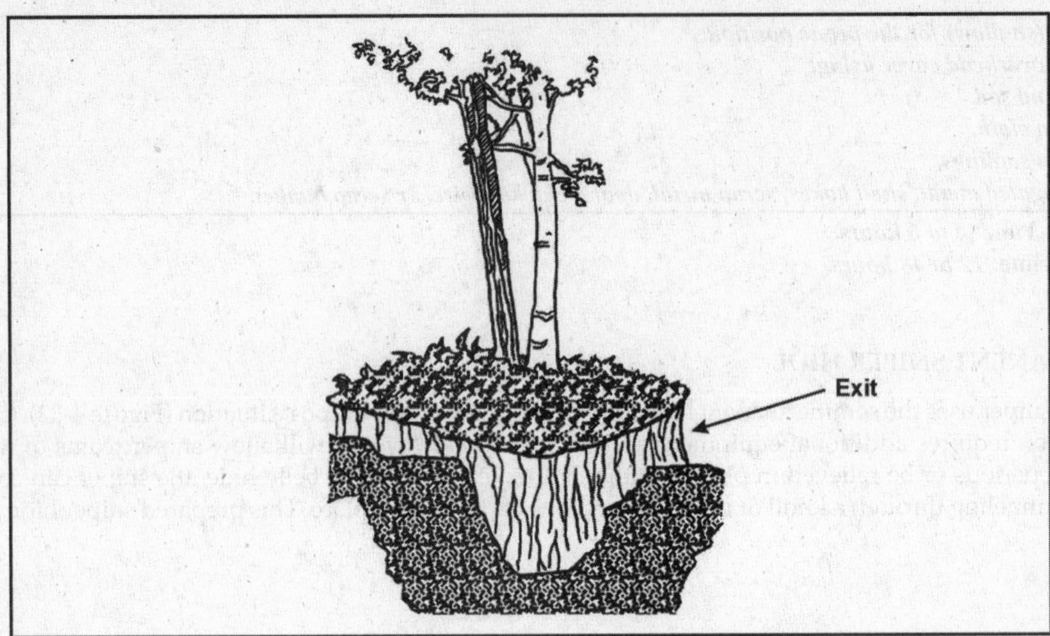

Figure 4-33. Tree or stump sniper hide

Table 4-5. Tree or stump hide advantages, disadvantages, and construction

Advantages	Disadvantages
• ***Can be rapidly occupied.*** • ***The sniper team is protected from fire and shrapnel.*** • ***The sniper team has freedom of movement.*** • ***Provides comfort.***	• ***Takes time to construct.*** • ***The sniper team requires pioneer equipment for construction of the hide (picks, shovels, axes).***
Construction	
• ***Use trees that have a good, deep root such as oak, chestnut, or hickory. During heavy winds these trees tend to remain steady better than a pine tree, which has surface roots and sways a bit in a breeze.*** • ***Use a large tree that is set back from the woodline. This location may limit the view but will provide better cover and concealment.***	

narrow in the front, but not so narrow that observation is restricted. Loopholes may be made of old coffee cans, old boots, or any other rubbish, provided that it is natural to the surroundings or that it can be properly and cleverly concealed.

4-273. Loopholes may be holes in windows, shutters, roofs, walls, or fences, or they may be constructed by the sniper team. Loopholes must blend in with the surrounding area. Table 4-4 lists the semipermanent sniper hide characteristics.

TREE OR STUMP HIDES

4-274. Nature can provide these types of hides but they also require the sniper to do some heavy construction (Figure 4-33). Table 4-5 lists the tree or stump hide characteristics.

TYPES OF HASTY SNIPER HIDES

4-275. The sniper can also use different types of deliberate hides to increase his chances for mission success and maintain the sniper training objectives. The various positions are explained below.

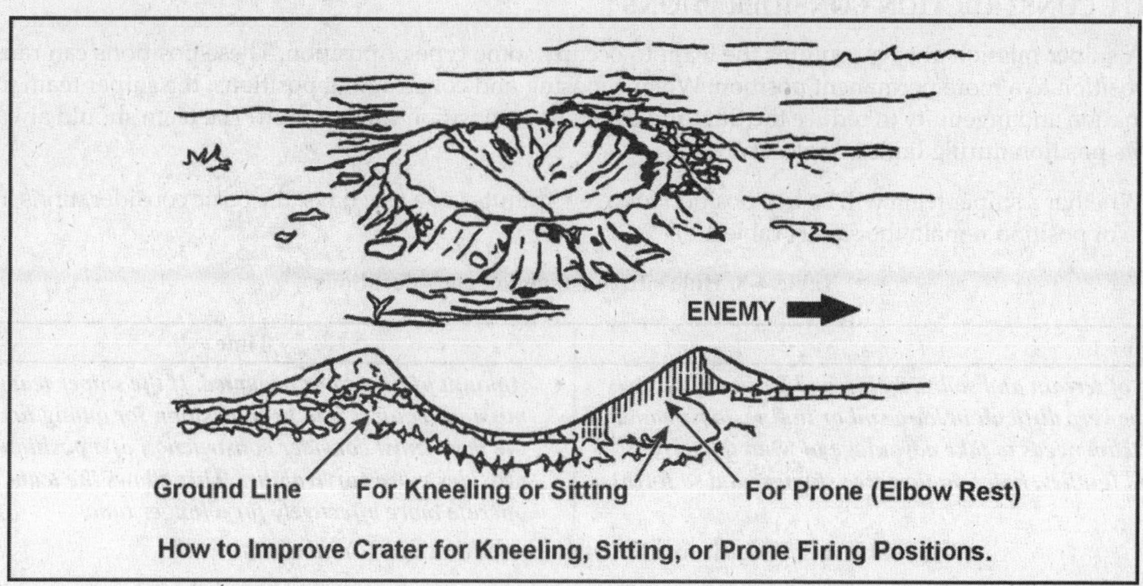

Figure 4-34. The shell-hole sniper hide

Enlarged Fire Trench Hides

4-276. This hide is actually an enlarged fighting position. Table 4-6 lists the enlarged fire trench hide characteristics.

Table 4-6. Enlarged fire trench hide advantages, disadvantages, and construction

Advantages	Disadvantages
• *The sniper team is able to maintain a low silhouette.* • *Simple to construct.* • *Can be occupied for a moderate period of time with some degree of comfort.*	• *Is not easily entered into or exited from.* • *The sniper team has no overhead cover when in firing position.* • *The sniper team is exposed while firing or observing.*
Construction	
• *Enlarge and repair the sides and the parapet.* • *Camouflage the hide with a drop cloth.*	

Shell-Hole Hides

4-277. This sniper hide is a crater improved for kneeling, sitting, or prone firing positions (Figure 4-34). Table 4-7 lists the shell-hole hide characteristics.

Table 4-7.Shell-hole hide advantages, disadvantages, and construction

Advantages	Disadvantages
• *Requires little digging.*	• *Requires material to secure the sides.* • *Affords no drainage.*
Construction	

- ***Dig platforms for either the prone, the kneeling, or the sitting positions.***
- ***Reinforce the sides of the craters.***

HIDE SITE CONSTRUCTION CONSIDERATIONS

4-278. A sniper mission always requires the team to occupy some type of position. These positions can range from a hasty position to a more permanent position. When choosing and constructing positions, the sniper team must use its imagination and ingenuity to reduce the time and difficulty of position construction. The team should always plan to build its position during limited visibility.

4-279. Whether a sniper team will be in a position for a few minutes or a few days, the basic considerations in choosing a type of position remain the same (Table 4-8).

Table 4-8. Hide site construction considerations

Location	Time
• ***Type of terrain and soil. Digging and boring of tunnels can be very difficult in hard soil or in fine, loose sand. The team needs to take advantage of what the terrain offers (gullies, holes, hollow tree stumps, and so forth).***	• ***Amount of time to be occupied. If the sniper team's mission requires it to be in position for a long time, the team must consider construction of a position that provides more survivability. This allows the team to operate more effectively for a longer time.***

Table 4-8. Hide site construction considerations (*Continued*)

Location	Time
• ***Enemy location and capabilities. Enemy patrols in the area may be close enough to the position to hear any noises that may accidentally be made during any construction. The team also needs to consider the enemy's night vision and detection capabilities.***	• ***Time needed for construction. The time needed to build a position must be a consideration, especially during the mission planning phase.***
Personnel and Equipment	
• ***Equipment needed for construction. The team must plan the use of any extra equipment needed for construction (bow saws, picks, axes).*** • ***Personnel needed for construction. Coordination must take place if the position requires more personnel to build it or a security element to secure the area during construction.***	

STEPS USED IN THE CONSTRUCTION OF A SNIPER HIDE

4-280. When the sniper team is en route to the objective area, it should mark all material that can be used for constructing a hide. The team should establish an ORP, reconnoiter the objective area, select a site, and mark the fields of fire and observation. After collecting additional material, the team returns to the sniper hide site under the cover of darkness and begins constructing the hide. Team personnel—

- Post security.
- Remove the topsoil (observe construction discipline).
- Dig a pit. Dispose of soil properly and reinforce the sides. Ensure the pit has—
  - Loopholes.
  - A bench rest.
  - A bed.
  - A drainage sump (if appropriate).
- Construct an overhead cover.
- Construct an entrance and exit by escape routes selected.
- Camouflage the hide.
- Inspect the hide for improper concealment (continuous).

HIDE SITE CONSTRUCTION TECHNIQUES

4-281. The sniper can construct belly and semipermanent hide sites of stone, brick, wood, or turf. Regardless of material, he should ensure the following measures are taken to prevent enemy observation, provide adequate protection, and allow for sufficient fields of fire:

- *Frontal Protection.* Regardless of material, every effort is made to bulletproof the front of the hide position. The most readily available material for frontal protection is the soil taken from the hide site excavation. It can be packed or bagged. While many exotic materials can be used, including Kevlar vests and armor plate, weight is always a consideration. Several dozen empty sandbags can be carried for the same weight as a Kevlar vest or a small piece of armor plate.
- *Pit.* Hide construction begins with the pit since it protects the sniper team. All excavated dirt is removed (placed in sandbags, taken away on a poncho, and so forth) and hidden (plowed fields, under a log, or away from the hide site).
- *Overhead Cover.* In a semipermanent hide position, logs should be used as the base of the roof. The sniper team places a dust cover over the base (such as a poncho, layers of empty sandbags, or canvas), a layer of dirt. The team spreads another layer of dirt, and then adds camouflage. Due to the various materials, the roof is difficult to conceal if not countersunk.
- *Entrance.* To prevent detection, the sniper team should construct an entrance door sturdy enough to bear a man's weight. The entrance must be closed while the loopholes are open.

- Entrenching tools.
- Bayonets.
- GP nets.
- Ponchos.
- Waterproof bags.
- Rucksacks.
- Shovels.
- Axes and hatchets.
- Hammers.
- Machetes.
- Chisels.
- Saws (Hacksaws).
- Screwdrivers, pliers, garden tools.
- Garbage bags.
- Wood glue.
- Nails.
- Chicken wire, newspapers, flour, water.

Figure 4-35. Items used to construct the sniper hide

- *Loopholes.* The construction of loopholes requires care and practice to ensure that they afford adequate fields of fire. These loopholes should have a large diameter (10 to 14 inches) in the interior of the position and taper down to a smaller diameter (4 to 8 inches) on the outside of the position. A position may have more than two sets of loopholes if needed to cover large areas. Foliage or other material that blends with or is natural to the surroundings must camouflage loopholes. The loopholes must be capable of being closed when the door is open.
- *Approaches.* It is vital that the natural appearance of the ground remains unaltered and camouflage blends with the surroundings. Remember, construction time is wasted if the enemy observes a team entering the hide; therefore, approaches must be concealed whenever possible. Teams should try to enter the hide during darkness, keeping movement around it to a minimum and adhering to trail discipline. In built-up areas, a secure and quiet approach is needed. Teams should avoid drawing attention to the mission and carefully plan movement. A possible ploy is to use a house search with sniper gear hidden among other gear. Sewers may be used for movement, also.

WARNING

When moving through sewers, teams must be alert for booby traps and poisonous gases.

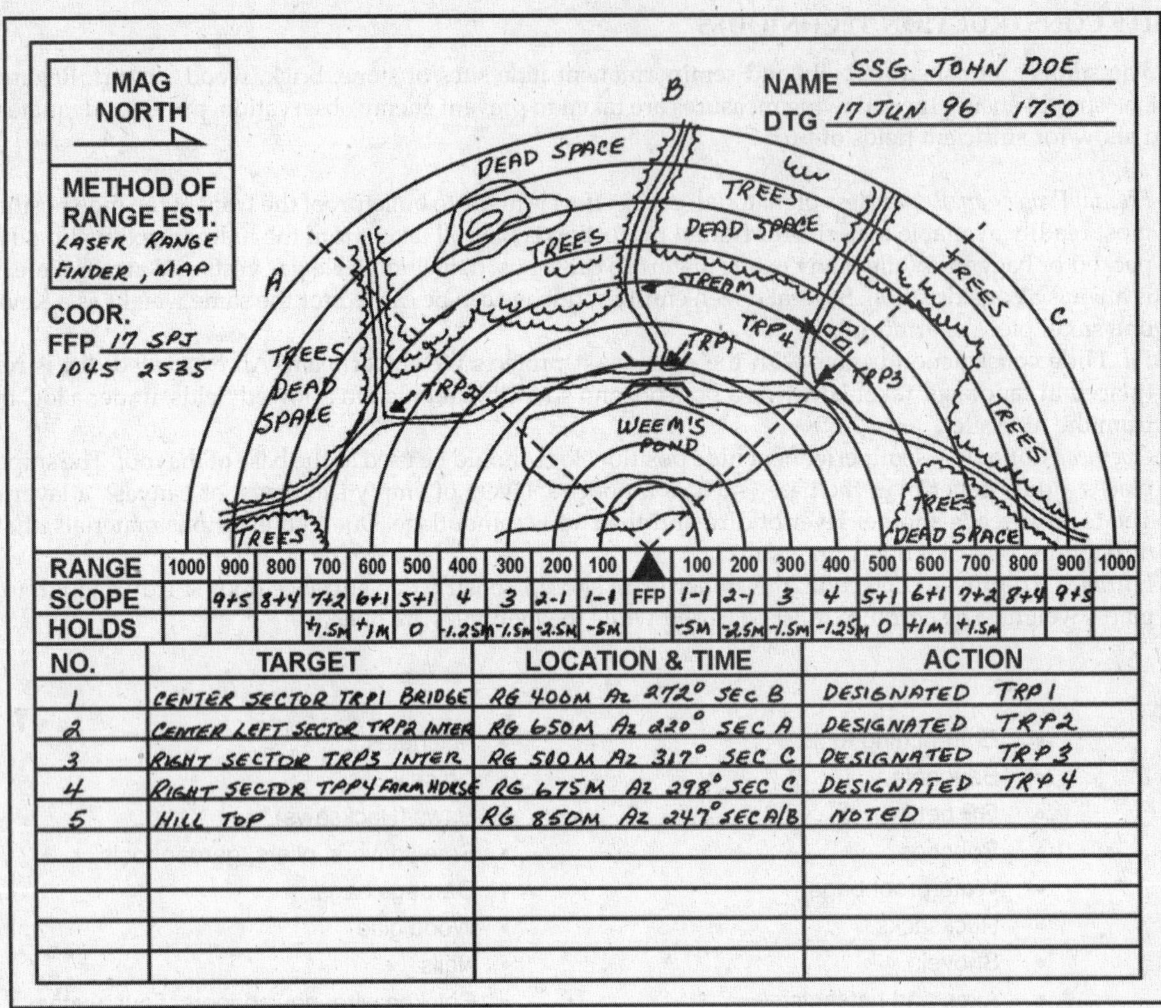

RANGE	1000	900	800	700	600	500	400	300	200	100	▲	100	200	300	400	500	600	700	800	900	1000
SCOPE		9+5	8+4	7+2	6+1	5+1	4	3	2-1	1-1	FFP	1-1	2-1	3	4	5+1	6+1	7+2	8+4	9+5	
HOLDS				+1.5M	+1M	0	-1.25M	-1.5M	-2.5M	-5M		-5M	-2.5M	-1.5M	-1.25M	0	+1M	+1.5M			

NO.	TARGET	LOCATION & TIME	ACTION
1	CENTER SECTOR TRP1 BRIDGE	RG 400M Az 272° SEC B	DESIGNATED TRP1
2	CENTER LEFT SECTOR TRP2 INTER	RG 650M Az 220° SEC A	DESIGNATED TRP2
3	RIGHT SECTOR TRP3 INTER	RG 500M Az 317° SEC C	DESIGNATED TRP3
4	RIGHT SECTOR TPP4 FARMHOUSE	RG 675M Az 298° SEC C	DESIGNATED TRP4
5	HILL TOP	RG 850M Az 247° SEC A/B	NOTED

Figure 4-36. Sample range card

TOOLS AND MATERIALS NEEDED TO CONSTRUCT A SNIPER HIDE

4-282. The tools and materials needed to build a sniper hide depend on the soil, the terrain, and the type of hide to be built. Figure 4-35 lists various items that the sniper team should consider during construction.

HIDE SITE ROUTINES

4-283. Although the construction of positions may differ, the routines while in position are the same. The sniper should have a stable firing platform for his weapon and the observer needs a steady platform for the optics. When rotating observation duties, the sniper weapon should remain in place, and the optics are handed from one member to the other. Data books, observation logs, range cards, and the radio should be placed within the site where both members have easy access to them. The team must arrange a system of resting, eating, and making latrine calls. All latrine calls should be done during darkness, if possible. A hole should be dug to conceal any traces of latrine calls.

SNIPER RANGE CARD, OBSERVATION LOG, AND MILITARY SKETCH

4-284. The sniper team uses range cards, observation logs, and military sketches to enable it to rapidly engage targets. These items also enable the sniper to maintain a record of his employment during an operation.

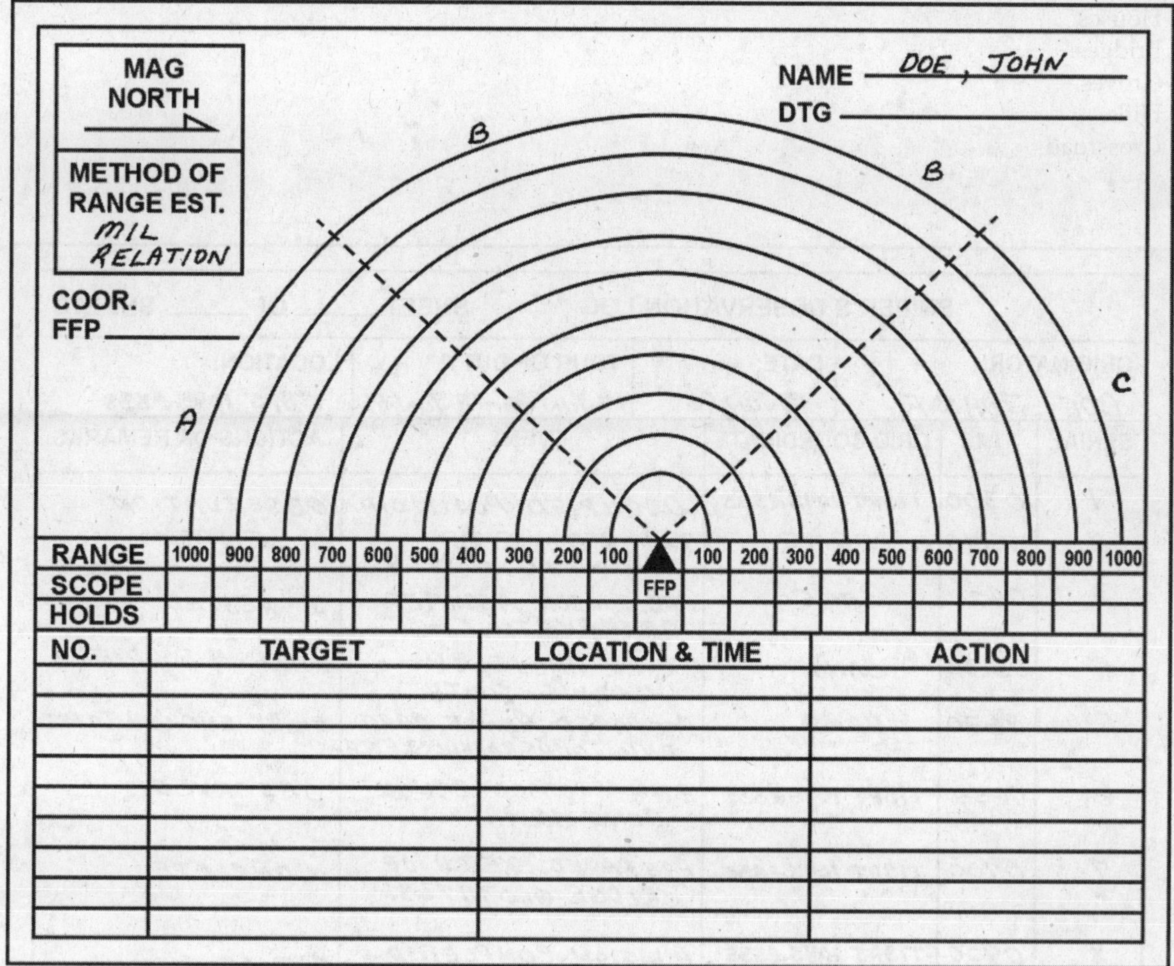

Figure 4-37. Range card divided into sectors

RANGE CARD

4-285. The range card (Figure 4-36) represents the target area as seen from above with annotations indicating distances throughout the target area. It provides the sniper team with a quick-range reference and a means to record target locations since it has preprinted range rings on it. These cards can be divided into sectors by using dashed lines (Figure 4-37, page 539). This break provides the team members with a quick reference when locating targets. A field-expedient range card can be prepared on any paper the team has available. The sniper team position and distances to prominent objects and terrain features are drawn on the card. There is not a set maximum range on either range card, because the team may also label any indirect fire targets on its range card. Information contained on both range cards includes the—

- Sniper's name and method of obtaining range.
- Left and right limits of engageable area.
- Major terrain features, roads, and structures.
- Ranges, elevation, and windage needed at various distances.
- Distances throughout the area.
- Temperature and wind. (Cross out previous entry whenever temperature, wind direction, or wind velocity changes.)
- Target reference points (azimuth, distance, and description).

4-286. Relative locations of dominant objects and terrain features should be included. Examples include—

- Houses.
- Bridges.
- Groves.
- Hills.
- Crossroads.

SNIPER'S OBSERVATION LOG SHEET ____ OF ____ SHEETS

ORIGINATOR:	DATE:	TOUR OF DUTY:	LOCATION:
DOE, JOHN R.	17 JUN 96	17 JUN 96–18 JUN 96	17SPJ 10452535

SERIAL	TIME	GRID COORDINATE	EVENT	ACTIONS OR REMARKS
1	0300	17SPJ 10452535	OCCUPIED POSITION	OBSERVATION
2	0340	SAME	TRUCK DROVE BY HEADING NORTH	EMPTY
3	0420	SAME	PFC JUDSON ASSUMED OBSERVATION	I RESTED
4	0530	SAME	TRUCK DROVE BY HEADING SOUTH	WITH 4 SOLDIERS
5	0630	SAME	PREPARED RANGE CARD AND TOPOGRAPHIC SKETCH	LIGHT ENOUGH TO SEE
6	0655	17SPJ 10452535	BRM CROSSED BRIDGE GONE SOUTH	OBSERVED
7	0700	17SPJ 10452535	PREPARED SKETCH OF BRIDGE GL03117631	COMPLETE
8	0900	17SPJ 10452535	MISSION COMPLETED–RETURN TO CP	END OF MISSION

Figure 4-38. Sample observation log

4-287. The sniper team will indicate the range to each object by estimating or measuring. All drawings on the range card are from the perspective of the sniper looking straight down on the observation area.

4-288. The range card is a record of the sniper's area of responsibility. Its proper preparation and use provides a quick reference to key terrain features and targets. It also allows the sniper team to quickly acquire new targets that come into their area of observation. The sniper always uses the range card and the observation log in conjunction with each other.

OBSERVATION LOG

4-289. The observation log (Figure 4-38) is a written, chronological record of all activities and events that take place in a sniper team's area. The log starts immediately upon infiltration. It is used with military sketches and range cards; this combination not only gives commanders and intelligence personnel information about the appearance of the area, but it also provides an accurate record of the activity in the area. Information in the observation log includes the—

- Grid coordinates of the sniper team's position.

- Observer's name.
- Date and time of observation and visibility.
- Sheet number and number of total sheets.
- Series number, time, and grid coordinates of each event.
- Events that have taken place.
- Action taken.

4-290. The sniper log will always be used in conjunction with a military sketch. The sketch helps to serve as a pictorial reference to the written log. If the sniper team is relieved in place, a new sniper team can easily locate earlier sightings using these two documents as references. The observer's log is a ready means of recording enemy activity, and if properly maintained, it enables the sniper team to report all information required.

4-291. Sniper observation logs will be filled out using the key word SALUTE for enemy activity and OAKOC for terrain. When using these key words to fill out the logs, the sniper should not use generalities; he should be very specific (for example, give the exact number of troops, the exact location, the dispersion location).

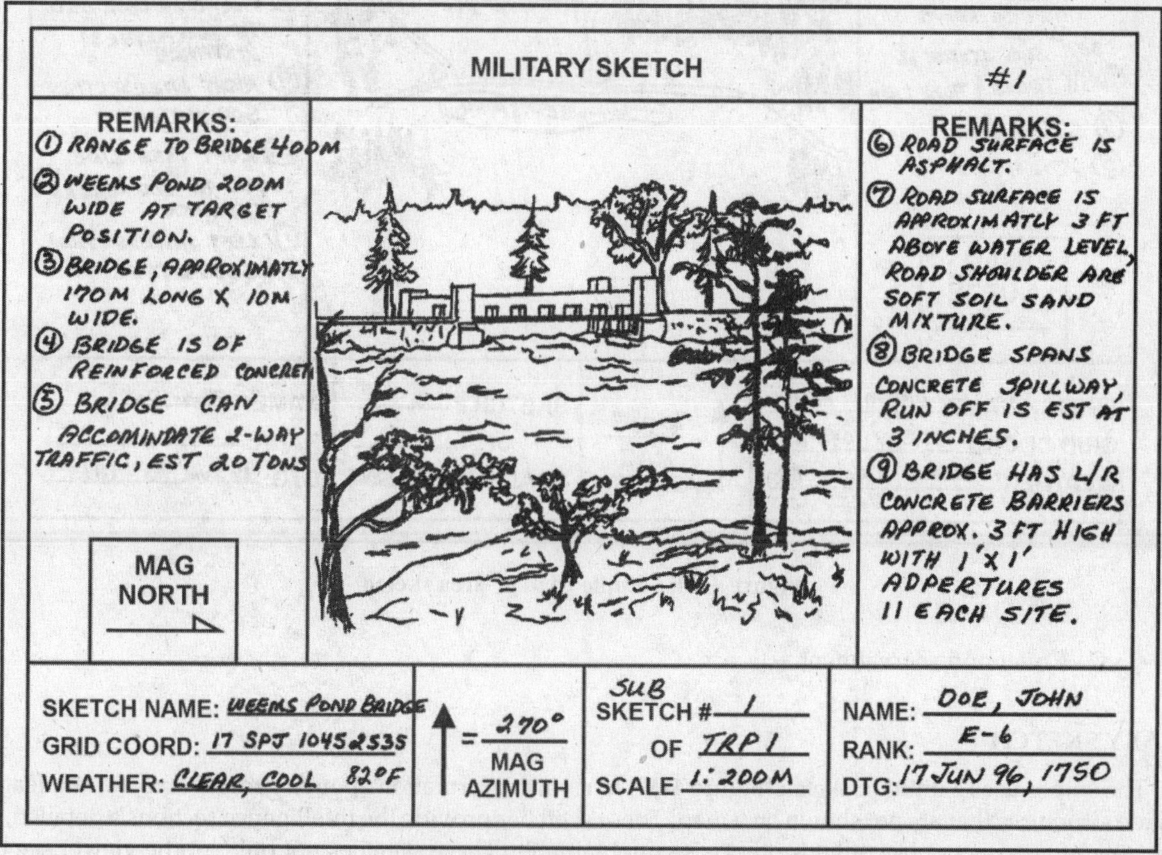

Figure 4-39. Sample military sketch

- The key word SALUTE:
  - S - Size.
  - A - Activity.
  - L - Location.
  - U - Unit/Uniform.
  - T - Time.
  - E - Equipment.

- The key word OAKOC:
  - O - Observation and fields of fire.
  - A - Avenues of approach.
  - K - Key terrain.
  - O - Obstacles.

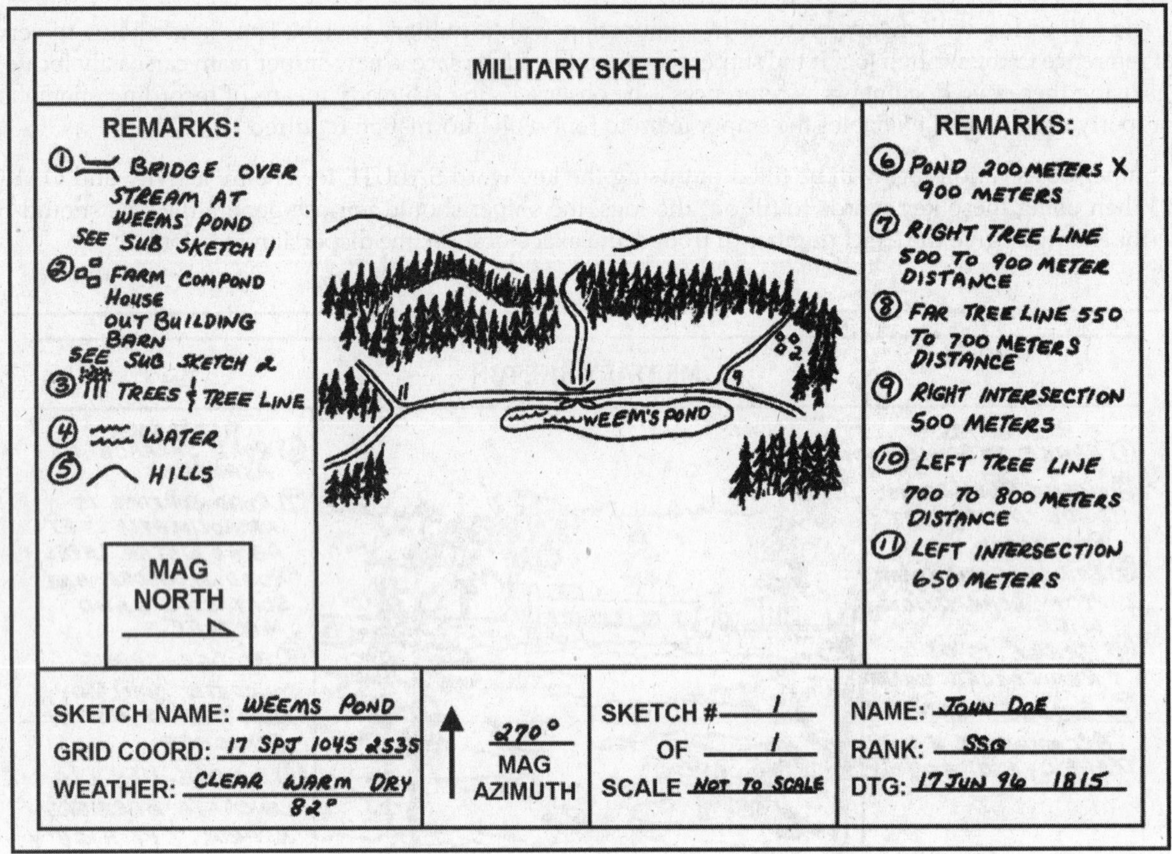

Figure 4-40. Sample road or area sketch

  - C - Cover and concealment.

MILITARY SKETCH

4-292. The sniper uses a military sketch (Figure 4-39) to record information about a general area, terrain features, or man-made structures that are not shown on a map. These sketches provide the intelligence sections a detailed, on-the-ground view of an area or object that is otherwise unobtainable. These sketches not only let the viewer see the area in different perspectives but also provide detail such as type of fences, number of telephone wires, present depth of streams, and other pertinent data. There are two types of military sketches: road or area sketches and field sketches. The sniper should not include people in either of these sketches.

Road or Area Sketch

4-293. This sketch is a panoramic representation of an area or object drawn to scale as seen from the sniper team's perspective. It shows details about a specific area or a man-made structure (Figure 4-40). Information considered in a road or area sketch includes—

- Grid coordinates of sniper team's position.

- Magnetic azimuth through the center of sketch.
- Sketch name and number.
- Scale of sketch.

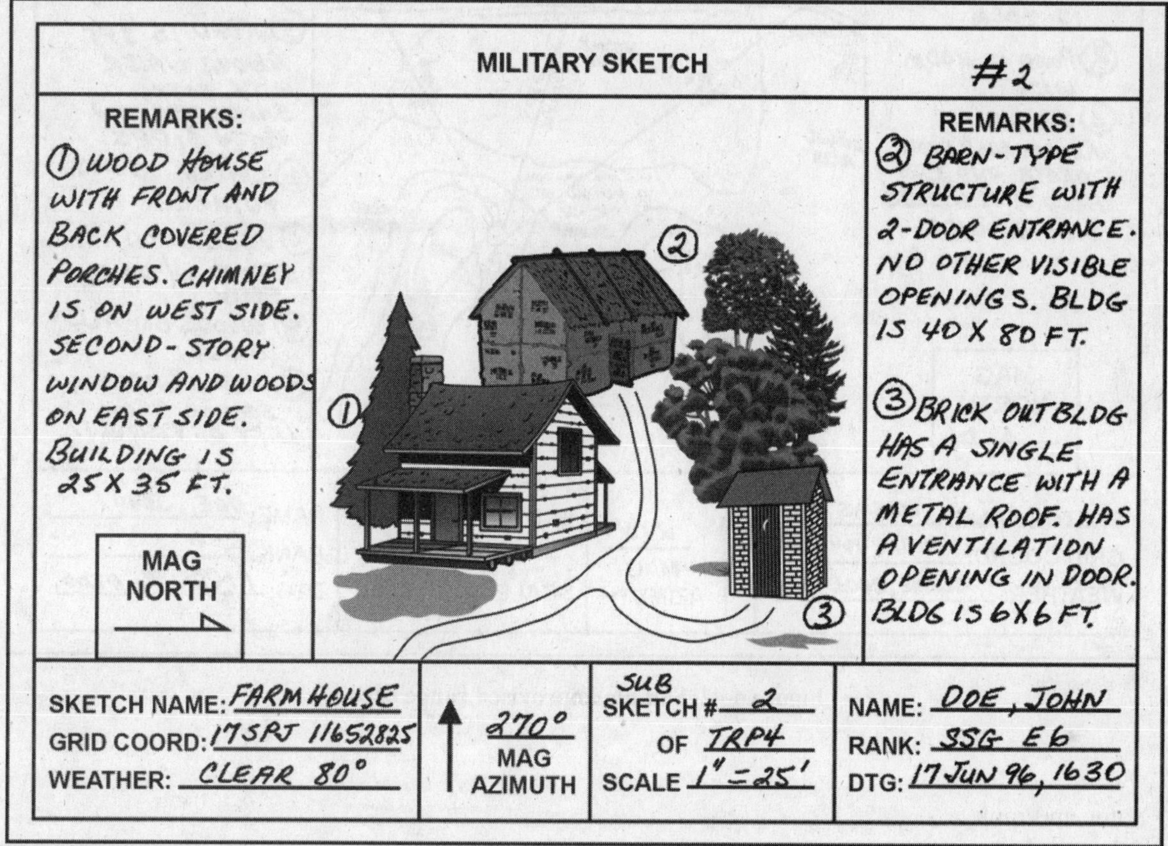

Figure 4-41. Subsketch of buildings in figure 4-40

- Remarks section.
- Name and rank.
- Date and time.
- Weather.

Field Sketches

4-294. A field sketch is a topographic representation of an area drawn to scale as seen from above. It provides the sniper team with a method for describing large areas while showing reliable distance and azimuths between major features. This type of sketch is useful in describing road systems, flow of streams and rivers, or locations of natural and man-made obstacles. The field sketch can also be used as an overlay on the range card. Information contained in a field sketch includes—

- Grid coordinates of the sniper team's position.
- Left and right limits with azimuths.
- Rear reference with azimuth and distance.
- Target reference points.
- Sketch name and number.

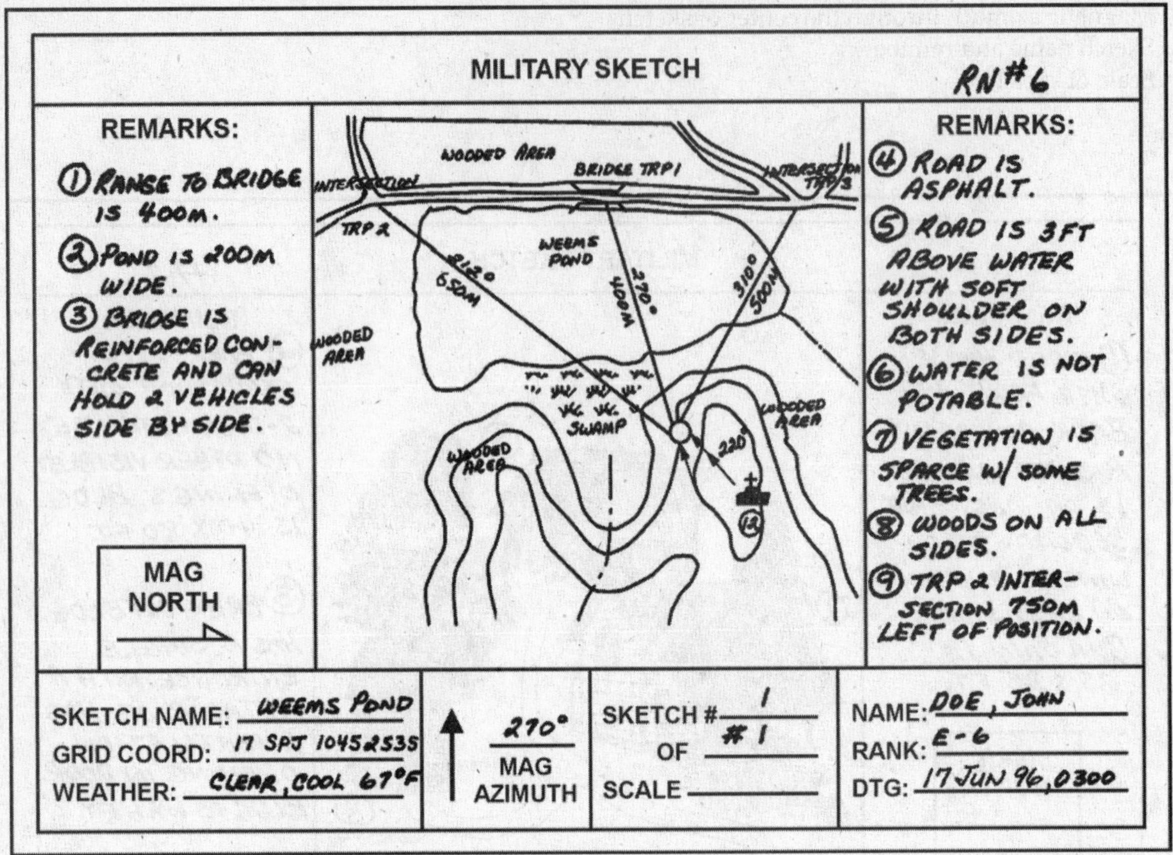

Figure 4-42. Sample improvised range card

- Name and rank.
- Date and time.
- Weather and visibility.

4-295. The field sketch serves to reinforce the observation log. A military sketch is either panoramic or topographic.

PANORAMIC SKETCH

4-296. The panoramic sketch is a picture of the terrain in elevation and perspective as seen from one point of observation (Figure 4-41).

TOPOGRAPHIC SKETCH

4-297. The topographic sketch is similar to a map or pictorial representation from an overhead perspective. It is generally less desirable than the panoramic sketch because it is difficult to relate this type of sketch to the observer's log. It is drawn in a fashion similar to the range card. Figure 4-42 represents a topographic sketch or an improvised range card.

GUIDELINES FOR DRAWING SKETCHES

4-298. As with all drawings, artistic skill is an asset, but satisfactory sketches can be drawn by anyone with practice. The sniper should use the following guidelines when drawing sketches:

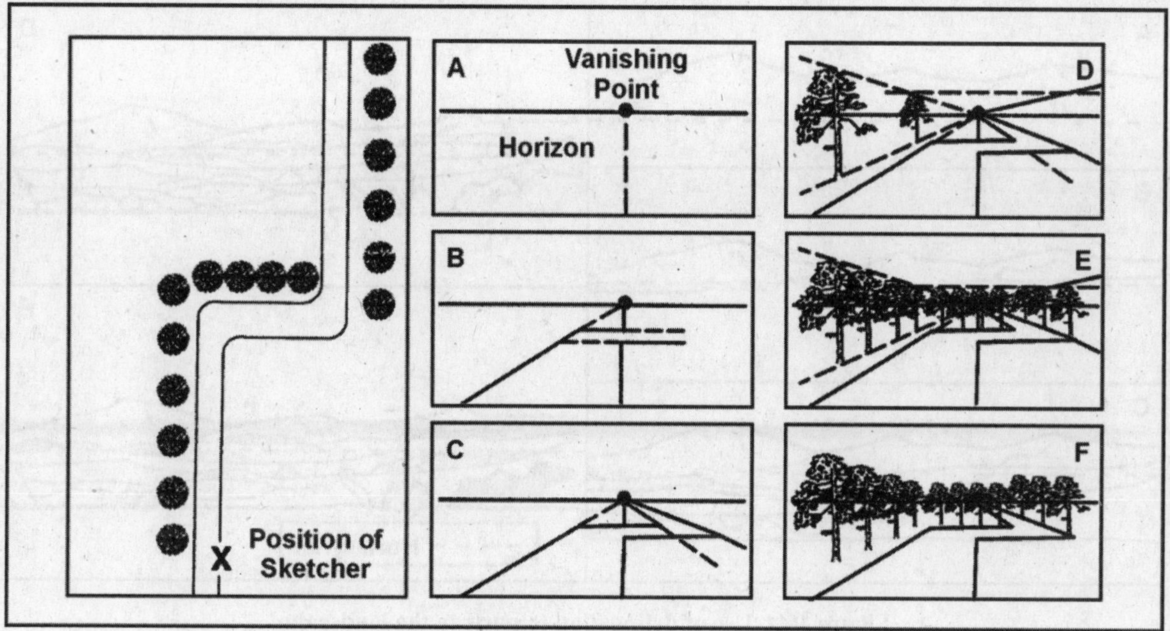

Figure 4-43. Sample sketch using vanishing points

- *Work from the whole to the part.* First determine the boundaries of the sketch. Then sketch the larger objects such as hills, mountains, or outlines of large buildings. After drawing the large objects in the sketch, start drawing the smaller details.
- *Use common shapes to show common objects.* Do not sketch each individual tree, hedgerow, or wood line exactly. Use common shapes to show these types of objects. Do not concentrate on the fine details unless they are of tactical importance.
- *Draw in perspective; use vanishing points.* Try to draw sketches in perspective. To do this, recognize the vanishing points of the area to be sketched. Parallel lines on the ground that are horizontal vanish at a point on the horizon. Parallel lines on the ground that slope downward away from the observer vanish at a point below the horizon. Parallel lines on the ground that slope upward, away from the observer, vanish at a point above the horizon. Parallel lines that recede to the right vanish on the right and those that recede to the left vanish on the left (Figure 4-43).

4-299. For the sniper team to thoroughly and effectively observe its area of responsibility, it must be aware of the slightest change in the area. These otherwise insignificant changes could be an indicator of targets or enemy activity that needs to be reported. By constructing a panoramic sketch, the team has a basis for comparing small changes in the surrounding terrain. Updating data permits the team to better report intelligence and complete its mission.

GENERAL PRINCIPLES OF SKETCHING

4-300. The sniper initiates the panoramic sketch only after the observer's log and range card have been initiated and after the sniper team has settled into the AO.

4-301. The sniper studies the terrain with the naked eye first to get an overall impression of the area. After he obtains his overall impression, he uses binoculars to further study those areas that attracted his attention before the first mark is made on a sketch pad.

4-302. Too much detail is not desirable unless it is of tactical importance. If additional detail is required on a specific area, the sniper can make subdrawings to supplement the main drawing.

Principles of Perspective and Proportionality

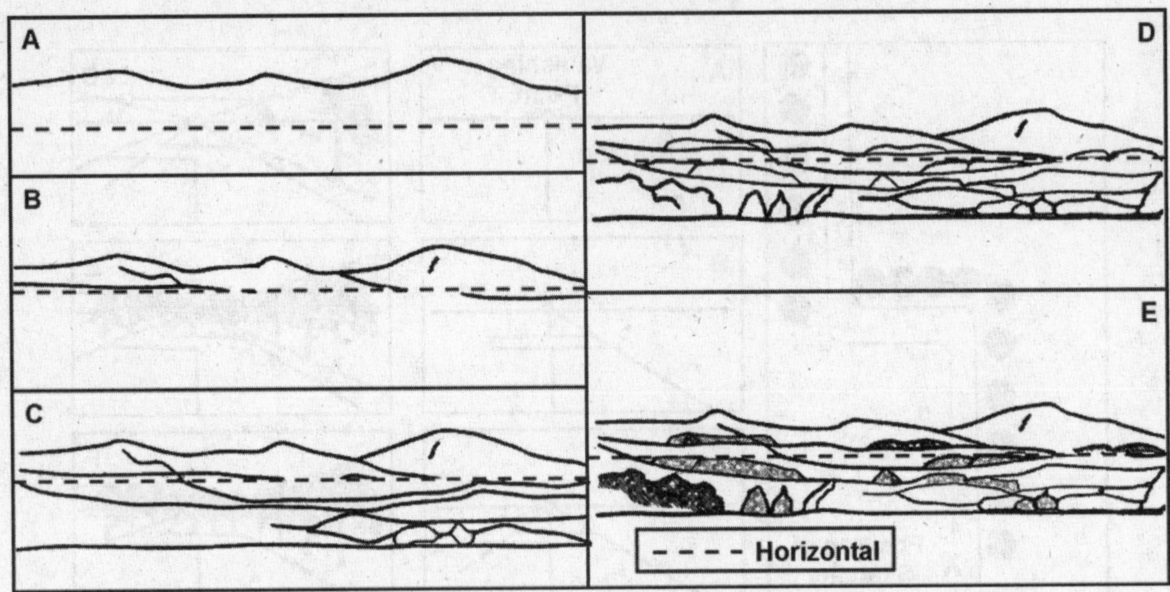

Figure 4-44. Use of delineation to portray the landscape

4-303. Sketches are drawn to perspective whenever possible. To be in perspective, the sketcher must remember that the farther away an object is, the smaller it will appear in the drawing. Vertical lines will remain vertical throughout the drawing; however, a series of vertical lines (such as telephone poles or a picket fence) will diminish in height as they approach the horizon. Proportionality is representing a larger object as larger than a smaller object. This gives depth along with perspective.

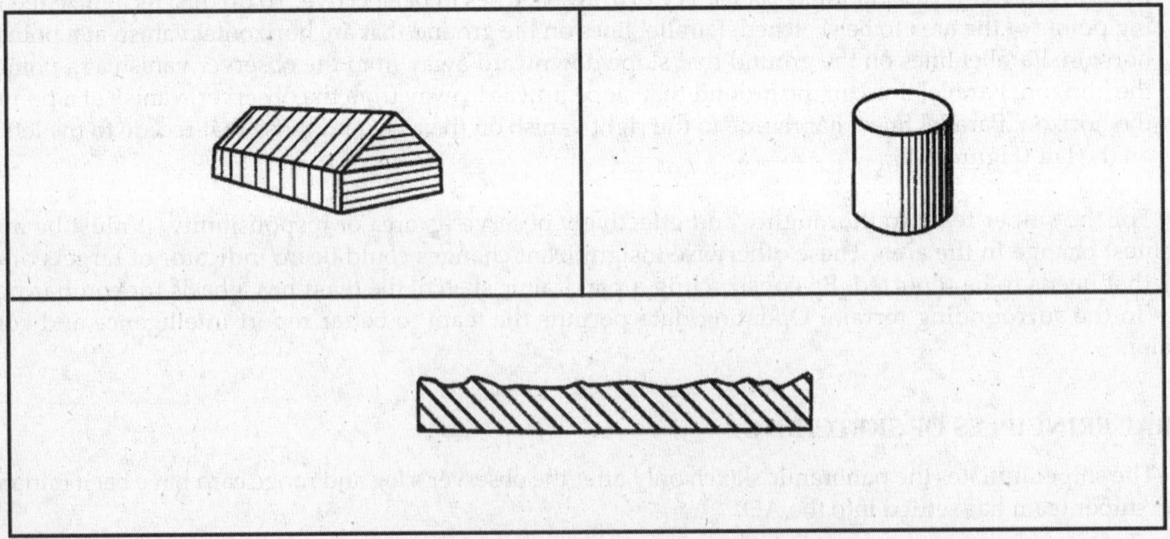

Figure 4-45. Hatchings that can add depth to objects

Using Delineation to Portray Objects or Features of the Landscape

4-304. The sketcher forms a horizontal line with the horizontal plane at the height of his eye. This is known as the eye-level line and the initial control line. The skyline or the horizon and crests, roads, and rivers form other "control lines" of the sketch. These areas are drawn first to form the framework within which the details can be placed. The sketcher should represent features with a few, rather than many, lines. He should create the effect of distance by making lines in the foreground heavy and making distance lines lighter as the distance increases. He can use a light "hatching" to distinguish wooded areas, but the hatching should follow the natural lines of the object (Figure 4-44).

Using Conventional Methods to Portray Objects

4-305. If possible, the sketcher should show the actual shape of all prominent features that may be readily selected as reference points. These features may be marked with an arrow and with a line to a description; for example, a prominent tree with a withered branch. The sketcher should also show—

- Rivers and roads as two lines that diminish in width to the vanishing point as they recede.
- Railroads in the foreground as a double line with small crosslines (which represent ties). The crosslines will distinguish them from roads. To portray railroads in the distance, a single line with vertical ticks to represent the telegraph poles is drawn. When rivers, roads, and railroads are all present in the same sketch, they may have to be labeled to show what they are.
- Trees in outline only, unless a particular tree is to be used as a reference point. If a particular tree is to be used as a reference point, the tree must be drawn in more detail to show why it was picked.
- Woods in the distance by outline only. If the woods are in the foreground, the tops of individual trees can be drawn.
- Churches in outline only, but it should be noted whether they have a tower or a spire.
- Towns and villages as definite rectangular shapes to denote houses, he also shows the locations of towers, factory chimneys, and prominent buildings in the sketch. Again, detail can be added in subdrawings or hatchings (Figure 4-45).
- Cuts, fills, depressions, swamps, and marshes are shown by using the usual topographic symbols.

Using a Legend to Label the Sketch

4-306. The legend includes the title of the sketch, the date-time group, and the sketcher's signature. It also includes an explanation of the topographic symbols used in the sketch.

KIM GAMES

4-307. The name of the game comes from the book *Kim* by Rudyard Kipling. The story is about a young Indian boy who was trained to remember intelligence information during the British occupation of India. To assist some in remembering the name of the game, it has been misnamed—Keep in Mind (KIM). Sniper operations encompass a much larger scope than hiding in the woods, spotting targets of opportunity, and engaging them. The sniper must observe vast areas and accurately record any and all information. Because many situations occur suddenly and do not offer prolonged observation, snipers must learn to observe for short periods of time and extract the maximum amount of information from any situation.

4-308. KIM games are a series of exercises that can help increase the sniper's abilities to both perceive reality and retain information. They can be conducted anywhere, in very little time, with a large return for the trainer's investment of effort and imagination. Although the various time limits of viewing, waiting, and recording the objects are often not reflected in tactical reality, KIM games are designed to exercise the mind through overload (much the same as weight training overloads the muscles).

4-309. Advancement in KIM games is measured by shortening the viewing and recording times and lengthening the waiting time. Greater results can be realized by gradually adding additional elements to increase confusion and uncertainty. In the sniper's trade, the perception of reality often means penetrating the enemy's deception measures. These measures may include, but are not limited to—

- Misdirection.
- Disguise.
- Exchange.

4-310. There is a marked similarity between the above list and the principles of stage magic. Just as knowing how a magician performs a trick takes the "magic" from it, knowing how one is being deceived negates the deception.

THE BASIC GAME

4-311. The instructor will require a table, a cover, and an assortment of objects. He selects ten objects and randomly places them on the table. He should not place the objects in orderly rows, since studies have shown that objects placed in rows make memorization easier. He then covers the objects. The instructor briefs the students on the following rules before each iteration:

- No talking is allowed.
- Objects may not be touched.
- Students will not write until told to do so.

4-312. The students gather around the table. The instructor removes the cover, and the time for viewing begins. When the time is up, he replaces the cover, and students return to their seats. After a designated interval, the students begin to write their observations within a designated time limit. To aid in retaining and recording their observations, the following standardized categories are used throughout:

- Size.
- Shape
- Color.
- Condition.
- What the object appears to be.

4-313. It must be stressed that the above categories are not intended for use in a tactical setting.

THE SAVELLI SHUFFLE

4-314. A variation of the KIM game that trains the eyes to "look faster" and coordinates hand-to-eye movement is the Savelli Shuffle. Two individuals face each other approximately 5 meters apart. The first man has a bag containing a number of yellow rubber balls and a smaller number of red rubber balls. The second man has an empty bag. The first man reaches into his bag and picks out a ball, concealing it from the second man. The first man tosses the ball to the second man. Speed will depend on level of experience.

4-315. The second man has a quick decision to make—catch yellow balls with the left hand and red balls with the right hand. The second man then places the caught balls into his bag.

4-316. This process is repeated until the first man's bag is emptied. Positions of the first man and the second man are exchanged. Advancement in this exercise is measured by the speed at which the balls are thrown and the distance between men.

INTEREST AND ATTENTION

4-317. When learning to observe, team members must make a distinction between interest and attention. Interest is a sense of being involved in some process, actual or potential. Attention is a simple response to a stimulus, such as a loud noise. Attention without interest cannot be maintained for very long. During long periods of uneventful observation, attention must be maintained through interest. Deception at the individual level can be thought of as manipulation of interest.

CHAPTER 5

Employment

SF sniper employment is complex. When employed intelligently, skillfully, and with originality, the SF sniper will provide a payoff far greater than would be expected from the assets used. For this to happen, the planner must have more than a basic knowledge of the SWS. He must understand the capabilities and limitations of the sniper. However, sniping is an individual talent and skill that varies with each sniper. This trait compounds the planner's challenge, but he can minimize these variables with careful planning. The SF sniper, when properly trained and employed, can be one of the SO forces' most versatile weapons systems. See Appendix D for some specific tricks of the trade that a sniper must master to maintain employment proficiency.

METHODS

5-1. The sniper planner must apply methods of interdiction in relation to the necessary target and the desired effects against it. The employment of SF snipers generally falls into the following four categories.

SURVEILLANCE AND RECONNAISSANCE

5-2. Sniping, by nature of its execution (stealthful movement, infiltration, use of long-range optics, and limited-visibility operations), is closely related to reconnaissance and surveillance. The techniques a sniper uses to hunt a target are similar to those the scout uses to conduct surveillance—only the end results are different. Also, human intelligence (HUMINT) collection is a secondary function to sniping. Operational planners should refrain from employing snipers in solely HUMINT roles but should take advantage of the HUMINT function when possible. Combining both functions would be analogous to using a long-range guard—the sniper provides needed information and can intercede if necessary.

POINT INTERDICTION

5-3. The sniper's goal is to interdict targets for the purpose of impeding, destroying, or preventing enemy influence in a particular area. A point interdiction is essentially hunting a specific target. The SF sniper can interdict both personnel and material point targets in support of SO missions. Such missions tend to be complex and may require difficult infiltration, precise navigation to the target, evasion of enemy forces, the broaching of sophisticated security systems, and external mission support systems (safe houses, special intelligence). Normally, the more complex the target or the more protected it is, the greater the degree of sophistication required to defeat it. For instance, a protected personnel target may require detailed intelligence and a highly skilled sniper for successful interdiction. Point interdiction also includes firing situations like those encountered in counterterrorist situations.

LONG-RANGE HARASSMENT

5-4. Long-range harassment is not intended to be decisive; creating psychological fear in the enemy and restricting his freedom of action are the sniper's primary goals. The sniper has the greatest latitude of employment in harassment missions. He can often engage opportunity targets at his discretion but always within the constraints of the mission. This method may include harassing specific kinds of targets to disrupt key functions such as command and control (C2) procedures. In some situations, the sniper can afford to engage targets at extreme ranges and risk nonfatal or missed shots, which maximizes harassment by interdicting more targets. Snipers normally conduct harassment at extended ranges to take advantage of their ability to engage targets at distances beyond the enemy's small-arms fire. This practice normally means they will not engage targets closer than 400 meters—100 meters beyond the common effective-fire range of conventional small arms. The average range for harassing fire is 600 meters.

SECURITY OPERATIONS

5-5. Snipers can provide long-range security to deny an enemy freedom of action in a particular area. The sniper security mission can take the form of a series of mutually supporting sniper outposts or cordons. An example of security operations where snipers proved invaluable was during the USMC operations in Beirut, Lebanon. The Marine snipers were interwoven with traditional defenses and proved to be effective in long-range protection of local U.S. facilities and interests. Security and cordon missions normally entail static, defenselike operations. However, with the austere firepower of sniper teams and their inability to maneuver in defensive warfare, they are vulnerable to becoming decisively engaged. Therefore, security operations are best integrated into conventional security and reaction forces to help snipers increase their defensive capability. Without such support, snipers can easily be suppressed and maneuvered upon with fire and maneuver tactics.

PLANNING

5-6. When employing snipers, the operational planner must consider many factors. Tactical planning considerations of the sniper include hide selection, deception plans, and movement techniques. However, the planner must consider sniper employment from an even higher level of operational perspective. He must realize that snipers are a unique weapon system and possess entirely different attributes from conventional forces, among which (the one most frequently misunderstood) is the sniper's firepower. Unlike conventional small-arms fire that emphasizes volume, the sniper's firepower emphasizes precision. Sniper fire is most effective when combined with a mind that can exploit long-range precision. A two-man sniper team can deliver only limited volumes of fire, and no matter how accurate, the volume seldom equals that of even the most austere military units. If employed incorrectly, the sniper easily becomes another soldier on the battlefield—except that he is handicapped with a slow-firing weapon. The sniper's unique employment considerations should be guided by the following factors.

STANDOFF

5-7. The planner should base employment around the sniper's ability to engage targets at extended ranges. The maximum effective range will vary with each sniper. However, planners can establish nominal engagement ranges based on the sniper's ability to group his shots into a specified area or shot group. This measurement can, in turn, be applied to specific targets. The sniper should be able to keep his fire within 2 MOA shot groups under simulated combat conditions.

5-8. The application of group size is important for determining maximum standoff in relation to target size. For planning, SF snipers should be expected to provide instant incapacitation (nonreflexive impact) first-round shots on personnel to 200 meters; personnel interdiction with 90-percent probability to 600 meters on stationary targets; and 50-percent probability to 800 meters. Engagement of more complicated targets, such as those moving or in adverse environmental conditions, depends on the individual sniper's skill and his weapon's capability. The sniper should be able to hit 100 percent of assigned moving targets at 200 meters and 90 percent at 300 meters. The sniper should also be able to hit 100 percent of short, 3-second, exposure targets at 200 meters and 90 percent at 300 meters. Sniper employment planning should also consider the probability of error against the risks incurred if the shot misses. Such analysis will help determine the minimum standoff range for a reliable chance of a hit on the target.

DECEPTION

5-9. The sniper's most critical tools are his deceptive talents. To planners, deception is also important for operational needs. The SF sniper may use a weapon from another country to duplicate using that weapon's characteristic signature (ballistic characteristics, cartridge case, bullets) for cover. He must consider both operational and tactical deception methods when conducting each mission.

Operational

5-10. Planners may center operational deception on infiltrating the target area using a clandestine (concealed) sniper weapon. Operational deception may also require plausible deniability of the operation and lead the enemy to believe the target damage was the result of normal failure, accident, or some other form of sabotage. With such interdiction requirements, the sniper can use special weapons and munitions and aim for vulnerable points to purposely obtain such results. (Such targets include those that tend to burn, detonate, or self-destruct when shot.) However, this kind of deception is not possible with many targets and is especially difficult to conceal in personnel interdiction. Deception also means a sniper can seldom fire more than twice from any location as the sound of shots (even suppressed) is increasingly easier to locate with repetition. (This concept differs greatly from many media and war stories, where the sniper engages his enemy on a protracted basis from the same location—firing shot after shot with apparent impunity.) In reality, snipers locked in a decisive dual with enemy forces and firing defensively will normally lose as sniping seldom succeeds in such situations. Planners should refrain from employing snipers in missions that will not allow deception or concealment after firing.

Tactical

5-11. The sniper's use of tactical deception is often his only real security. Employment planners must consider security from operational aspects of the mission when using snipers. These include infiltration means, communications procedures, and methods of C2. These procedures are important because the sniper must remain covert before interdiction to ensure success. Normally, once the sniper fires, he is no longer covert and must rely on other plans to facilitate escape. Many environments may permit sniper employment, but few allow plausible denial for the sponsor or operation after interdiction. In other words, such covert operations may be easy to perform, but the risk of compromise, no matter how small, may overshadow the mission. Missions to collect information concerning another country's hostile intentions may themselves provoke serious repercussions if discovered. Moreover, using snipers will assuredly indicate an alternative motive to actually interdicting a target—which could compromise the mission even more.

TIME

5-12. The sniper's mission normally requires more time than conventional operations. Because the sniper normally moves on foot with stealth, his only defense is that of remaining unseen. If the sniper does not have enough time to execute the mission, he may hurry and unnecessarily compromise the mission or fail to reach the target.

TEAM EMPLOYMENT

5-13. Teams provide limited security for self-protection and allow near-continuous operations, yet are small enough to allow concealment for execution. In practice, one sniper fires while the other observes. The sniper-observer identifies and selects targets, adjusts the sniper-firer to environmental factors, provides security, and helps correct missed shots. However, the greatest advantage is the sniper-observer's detachment from the firing process, leaving the sniper-firer to concentrate on the act of firing. In other words, firing does not complicate the sniper-observer's decision process—a task requiring total concentration. Mission needs may also require snipers to be part of a larger force or in multiple sniper teams to engage the same target. Both techniques of employment can enhance the sniper's effect; however, the basic sniper team should always be retained. Snipers will never be employed in elements smaller than a two-man team, larger elements of three or four men may be required depending upon mission, duration, visibility expected in the target area, and size of target area.

TERRAIN

5-14. Terrain features are extremely important to the sniper's mission. Some areas, such as those that are densely wooded, tightly compartmented, or heavily vegetated, are not suitable for sniper employment because they reduce the sniper's ability to employ the full standoff capability of his weapons system. The threat can quickly suppress snipers that engage targets inside their minimum standoff envelope (usually 400 meters). Moreover, restrictive terrain offers the threat cover and concealment that can mask his attack against the sniper. The sniper must always consider both maximum and minimum engagement ranges; he must never get so close to the target as to compromise the mission.

INNOVATION

5-15. A sniper's most important attribute is his ability to improvise. The operational planner must also be innovative in the planning process. The sniper is a weapon of opportunity, not one to be used as a matter of course. Planners must actively seek missions and opportunities to apply the sniper's unique attributes of long-range precision rifle fire and concealment. Often the sniper's greatest handicap is the planner's inability to fully use his potential because of the planner's lack of familiarity with the sniper's true role and capability. Planners should include the sniper team in the planning process. Multiple sniper teams can often suggest a better solution when planning from the bottom up. Staff officers with little practical sniper experience or lacking innovative thought will never be able to fully take advantage of the sniper's capabilities.

ORGANIZATION

5-16. Organizational grouping of snipers above the sniper-team level normally occurs through expedient pooling of sniper pairs into larger organizations. Such centralized grouping of sniper assets can prove beneficial to their employment for specific missions. In all cases, the sniper specialist within the unit should manage control of the snipers. Regardless of any provisional or temporary sniper grouping, sniper teams should not be split. They function best in the pairs in which they have trained, with all members being fully qualified snipers.

5-17. The level at which sniping is organized and managed directly influences the ability of sniping to provide direct or indirect support to friendly operations. Centralized organization and management of sniping provides a great degree of flexibility regarding deployment. This flexibility permits snipers to be deployed to areas or locations where they will have the greatest influence on the enemy and provide the maximum support to friendly operations.

5-18. The organization of sniper teams will magnify their effectiveness against the enemy. Sniping, like any other supporting arm, is an individual specialty that requires independent action to achieve its greatest potential effect on the enemy. Requiring special organization, snipers may be organized into teams, squads, sections, and platoons.

SNIPER TEAM

5-19. The base element of any sniper unit is that the team consists of two equally trained snipers and is assigned to the company. The company is the lowest level at which sniping can be centralized and still maintain operational effectiveness. Sniper teams should not be attached to the tactical subunits of the company. However, a subunit, squad or platoon, may be attached to the sniper team as security or cover for a stay-behind type mission. When organized into a team, snipers are able to—

- Provide mutual security.
- Diminish stress.
- Lengthen their duration of employment.
- Aid in the engagement of targets more rapidly.

SNIPER SQUAD

5-20. A sniper squad is composed of three to four sniper teams and is located at battalion level. The organization of the sniper squad is as follows:

- Squad leader.
- Assistant squad leader.
- Three senior snipers.
- Three junior snipers.
- The sniper pairs include a senior sniper and a junior sniper.

5-21. The mission of the sniper squad is to support the operations of the battalion. The squad may be broken and the separate teams attached to any company in the battalion.

SNIPER SECTION

5-22. The sniper section's mission is to directly or indirectly support the combat operations of brigade or regiment subordinate units. In direct support, sniper teams are attached to company or battalion headquarters elements as needed, and employment considerations are identical to those of company sniper teams. Indirect support gives the sniper teams assigned sectors of responsibility as part of the battalion fire plan. The sniper section is attached to the brigade regiment headquarters S-2 or S-3, and the section commander acts as the brigade sniper coordinator. The sniper section consists of a **command element** (section commander, assistant section leader), a **support element** (armorer, radio operator), and **8 to 10 operational two-man sniper teams** (per team-senior sniper, junior sniper).

SNIPER PLATOON

5-23. The mission of a sniper platoon is to support division combat and intelligence operations independently or by attachment to division subunits. When attached, sniper squads should remain intact and should be attached no lower than battalion level. The sniper platoon is composed of a platoon leader, a platoon sergeant, a radiotelephone operator or driver, an armorer, and three sniper squads consisting of a squad leader and five two-man sniper teams. The sniper platoon falls under direct operational control of the division intelligence officer or indirect control through liaison with the sniper platoon leader. Sniper platoon operations may include deep penetration of the enemy rear areas, stay-behind operations, and rear-area protection.

COMMAND AND CONTROL

5-24. C2 of snipers is accomplished using indirect and direct control procedures. These procedures complement the sniper's self-discipline in executing his assigned mission. The sniper team will often operate in situations where direct control methods will not be possible. Therefore, the sniper must execute his mission (within the parameters of the commander's intent) on personal initiative and determination. This reaction is a major reason (in the sniper-selection process) why personnel with motivation and self-determination are required as snipers. Without these personal traits, the sniper's decentralized execution allows total disregard for the mission and its completion. In other words, he can go out to perform a mission and merely stay out of sight until time to return.

INDIRECT CONTROL OF SNIPERS

5-25. Commanders can accomplish indirect control of snipers through a variety of methods, the simplest being rules of engagement (ROE) and fire control measures. Even with strict direct control (voice radio, wire) of sniper teams, commanders should establish ROE and fire control to maximize flexibility and prevent unnecessary engagements. The ROE will normally designate combatant forces and situations that will allow the sniper to engage the enemy.

5-26. One significant problem with contemporary ROE is the restrictive measures used in peacetime operations. Often, such ROE will specify enemy personnel as only those presenting a direct threat to friendly forces or requiring verbal warning before engagement. The paradox is that a sniper's modus operandi is to engage targets that are not a direct threat to him (outside small-arms effective fire range) at the moment, but which later may be. It is extremely difficult for the sniper to stay within ROE because once the enemy gets within his minimum standoff, the conflict can become one of close-quarters battle and a 12-pound, scope-sighted sniper rifle is no match for an AK47 or M16 at close quarters—despite the fact that it may be a semiautomatic rifle. Therefore, ROE for the sniper must provide for his safety by adding security forces or by removing him from the operation.

5-27. Fire control measures are just as important for the sniper as they are for indirect-fire weapons and aircraft. As with any long-range weapons system, positive target identification is difficult at extended ranges—even with the advanced optics the sniper will carry. Establishment of no-fire zones or times, fire coordination lines, and free-fire zones or times will help in sniper C2 by establishing guidelines for when and where he can fire. If positive target identification is required, then appropriate security measures are required to prevent decisive engagement to the sniper.

DIRECT CONTROL OF SNIPERS

5-28. Commanders can maintain direct control of SF snipers by using technical and nontechnical systems, including radio and wire communications. In some circumstances, direct control means may include commercial telephones or other nontraditional tactical forms of communications. The mission and the operational environment will determine the exact methods of control.

5-29. Nontechnical control of snipers involves using prearranged methods including rendezvous, message pick-ups and drops, and other clandestine methods of secure communications. In denied areas, or those with electronic interception capabilities, these methods may be the only secure techniques for communicating with the sniper teams. These systems, although often quite secure, tend to be slow, and execution is complex.

5-30. Snipers can also use many forms of technical communications systems such as radio and wire. Both radio and wire offer near-instant message traffic and facilitate C2 with two-way communications. Snipers most often use radios as their method of communications because they are responsive and provide real-time control and reporting capabilities. Also, radio (voice, data burst, or satellites) provides the mobility that snipers require for their mobile-employment methodology. The major advantage to radio is its ability to transmit mission changes, updates, and intelligence in a timely manner. However, when properly arrayed, enemy direction-finding assets can determine the location of even the most focused and directional transmissions. To avoid detection, SO must use specialized communications techniques and procedures. Even then, the deployed teams will still have the problem of transmitting from their location to confirm messages or send data.

5-31. The major drawback to radio communications is the transmitter's electronic signature. In the sniper's operational area, enemy detection of any electronic signature can be just as damaging as reception of a message. Once the enemy is aware of the sniper's presence (through spurious transmissions), it becomes an academic problem to hunt him down. Even with successful evasion from threats (for example, scent- and visual-tracking dogs), the sniper team will be preoccupied with evasion and escape (E&E) instead of the target. Of course, this act can also be an objective—to divert enemy internal security forces to a rear-area sniper threat.

5-32. Under all conditions, the sniper team must have a method for immediate recall. This method allows for immediate reaction forces to be available for the sniper. This factor is imperative in an unstable battlefield.

5-33. Wire communications can provide protection from enemy deception, jamming, and interception. Static security operations, defensive positions, and extended surveillance posts are suitable for the use of wire communications. However, the sniper team must also calculate the disadvantages of wire, such as time to emplace, lack of mobility, and relative ease of compromise if found by the enemy. When possible, the team should back up wire communications by more flexible forms of control, such as radio.

5-34. Certain environments (FID or CBT missions) may allow for more flexible communications techniques. For example, the use of commercial telephones may be more appropriate than traditional military communications. Also, many environments possess a low threat from actual message interception or direction-finding assets, which allows the sniper team more liberal use of the radio. However, planners would be wise to remember the time-tested proverb: Never underestimate your enemy.

COORDINATION

5-35. There must be meticulous coordination with both supported and unsupported units that fall within the sniper team's AO. This coordination is the sniper coordinator's main focus; however, the sniper team must ensure that the coordination has been accomplished. Coordination with supported and unsupported units includes the following:

- Nature, duration, and extent of local and extended patrols.
- Friendly, direct, and indirect fire plans.
- Local security measures.
- Location and extent of obstacles and barrier plan.
- Rendezvous and linkup points.
- Passage and reentry of friendly lines.
- Unit mission and area of responsibility.
- Routes and limits of advance.
- Location and description of friendly units.
- Communication plan.

5-36. Although it is important that the sniper team receives as much information as possible for mission success, the sniper coordinator must not tell the team so much that, if captured, the entire sector would be compromised. This objective demands that everyone involved—the sniper teams, the sniper coordinator, supported and unsupported units in the area of operations—communicate and remain "coordinated." The sniper coordinator will establish control measures to assist in the deployment of the teams. This will keep the teams and units from committing fratricide, while not compromising the units if the teams are captured.

5-37. Once coordination begins, the team must establish control measures to protect the sniper and the supported and unsupported friendly units. Also, if the situation changes, there will be a recall capability to prevent the sniper team from unnecessary danger. The sniper team must also receive warning that friendly operations are in the area and it could be subjected to friendly fire. The team must have enough latitude to avoid engagement with the enemy by remaining mobile, elusive, and unpredictable. However, the team must understand that operational areas with lines of advance, exclusion areas, and no-fire zones are designed to protect him and friendlies and are not to be violated.

SUPPORT RELATIONSHIPS

5-38. Sniping is a combat support activity. Snipers should augment only those units that have a specific need for it. Sniping provides either indirect or direct support. Deployed as human intelligence (HUMINT) assets, snipers indirectly support friendly units and operations. There are two types of direct support.

Operational Control

5-39. Snipers are under the operational control (OPCON) of the supported unit only for the duration of a specific operation. At the end of the mission, they return to the control of the parent unit. This practice is the optimal method of supporting operations, as it is flexible and efficient toward the unit to which the snipers are attached.

Attachment

5-40. For extended operations or distances, snipers may support a specific unit. This unit responds to all the sniper team's requirements for the duration of attachment. The sniping specialist or coordinator should also be attached to advise the unit on assignment of proper employment methods. If it is not possible to attach the sniper coordinator, then the senior and most experienced sniper on the attachment orders must assume the job as sniper coordinator for the period of attachment. The receiving unit must also understand the status of the sniper coordinator and the importance of his position. Normally, attachment for extended periods will include supply and logistics support to the sniper element from the unit of attachment.

5-41. The support given to the unit and support received from the unit can also determine the planning, coordination, and control requirements. The four types of support given to a unit are as follows:

- Offensive operational.
- Defensive operational.
- Retrograde operational.
- Special operations.

TARGET ANALYSIS

5-42. There are two general classes of sniper targets—personnel and material. The sniper coordinator can further categorize these targets as having either tactical or strategic value. Tactical targets have local, short-term value to the current battle or situation. Tactical personnel targets are normally of enough significance to warrant the risk of detection when firing. Such targets include enemy snipers, key leaders, scouts, and crew-served weapons personnel. Tactical material targets are of particular importance to the current operation.

5-43. Strategic personnel targets are not as well-defined as tactical personnel targets because of problems with the concept and definition of assassination. The definition of assassination versus the elimination of a military target is based on the end result. If the end result is military, then the target is classified as military ambush. However, if the end result is political in nature, then the target is classified as assassination and possibly illegal. This is a simplified definition of a complex issue and further discussion is beyond the scope of this manual.

5-44. Strategic material targets consist of all types of objects of a military nature, including components or systems within a target (such as a turbine in an aircraft). The sniper must always consider criticality, accessibility, recuperability, vulnerability, effect, recognizability (CARVER) in evaluating the target.

TARGET SYSTEMS AND CRITICAL NODES

5-45. SF snipers should be directed at the enemy's C2 facilities and the critical nodes supporting them. Snipers can frequently regard targets as being in an interrelated system; that is, any one component may be essential to the target's entire operation. These interrelated and essential components are known as critical nodes. Critical C2 nodes are components, functions, or systems that support a military force's C2. These will differ for each target, but they will generally consist of the following:

- *Procedures.* Snipers can easily interdict the procedures, routines, and habits the enemy uses to conduct operations. Of most significance, snipers can create fear in the enemy that will cause him to take extreme measures in security or to modify procedures to keep from being shot. The enemy may curtail certain functions, divert assets for security, or restrict movement in his own rear areas to prevent interdiction.
- *Persônnel.* Personnel targets are critical, depending on their importance or function. The target does not necessarily need to be a high-ranking officer but may be a lower-ranking person or a select group of people, such as a skill or occupational group, who are vital to the enemy's warfighting apparatus.
- *Equipment.* Equipment is critical when the loss of it will impact the enemy's conduct of operations. Seldom will singular equipment targets be so critical as to impact the enemy in any significant fashion. However, targets or components that are not singularly critical may, collectively, be vital to the enemy. Common targets include objects common to all other similar targets or systems vulnerable to interdiction, such as a particular component (a radar antenna) which is common to many other radars. Interdicting only one antenna would have limited effect; it would merely be replaced. However, interdicting other radar components would significantly impair the enemy's logistics.
- *Facilities.* These activities and complexes support the enemy's operations or C2 functions. In the larger context, snipers are not suited for such interdiction. However, where possible, the sniper can focus on critical elements, such as C2 nodes or logistics capabilities of the larger facility (power generation systems or transportation equipment).
- *Communications.* Communications nodes often are the most fragile components of C2 systems. Snipers can usually interdict these nodes because they are easy to recognize and frequently quite vulnerable. Attacking other targets, not critical in some fashion, serves no purpose in using SF snipers and only wastes resources without a definable objective. Target analysis helps determine which critical nodes to interdict and predict how effective the sniper will be.

CARVER PROCESS

5-46. Target analysis includes selecting the appropriate method to use against a target, such as an aircraft, a strike force, or snipers. In doing so, the planner can match the sniper's capabilities to the potential target. Sniper capabilities include using special weapons and performing covert operations.

5-47. Attacking targets by sniper fire requires detailed planning and coordination; the sniper should not attack these targets indiscriminately. Interdiction must occur within the parameters of the assigned mission from higher headquarters to the stated results, maximizing the target's vulnerabilities and the priority of interdiction (on multiple targets or components).

5-48. The target analysis system that snipers use is based on the acronym CARVER. The CARVER analysis process is a generic model for SO interdiction missions. It is also suitable for sniper interdiction, particularly during material interdiction planning, which is similar to interdiction with special munitions or demolitions. The sniper can apply sniper fire within the framework of the CARVER model to better determine if sniping would be the appropriate interdiction method and precisely how and where to apply it. Mission planners apply the CARVER analysis to sniper interdiction based on the following criteria:

- *Criticality.* A target is critical in relation to the impact its destruction would have on the enemy. The mission order will largely determine critical targets. However, within a target system there may be components that may be critical for the operation of the entire target. For example, a turbine is a critical component of a jet aircraft. The concept of attacking a critical component (using accurate fire) allows the sniper to engage a much greater variety of targets than commonly accepted.
- *Accessibility.* This factor is based on how readily the target can be attacked. For the sniper, target accessibility includes getting through the target's security systems (security police or intrusion detectors) and knowing

what the reaction will be to the sniper's stand-off interdiction. Accessibility for sniper interdiction is unique, because the sniper can frequently engage targets without violating security systems, and in turn, reduce the enemy's ability to detect the sniper before the interdiction. Again, the sniper must base accessibility on both maximum and minimum ranges. He must also be able to get off the target after he shoots.

- *Recuperability.* The sniper measures recuperability of a target based on the time it takes the target to be repaired, replaced, bypassed, or substituted. Frequently, planners think only in terms of total destruction as opposed to a lesser degree of destruction. However, the same effect can be achieved by simply shutting down the target or destroying one vulnerable component. The advantage of interdiction short of total destruction is in the application of force; complete destruction normally requires a more elaborate force and more units. Also, the ability to control target destruction with precision fire can prevent unnecessary damage. It can limit adverse effects to systems that the local populace may depend on for electrical power, food, or water. However, the planners must take into consideration repair time. If the target can be repaired in less time than the target window allows, the another destruction technique must be considered.
- *Vulnerability.* A target (or component) is vulnerable to the sniper if he has the weapons and skill required to interdict the critical points that the target analysis has identified. The key to target vulnerability is identifying the weakest critical link in the target system and destroying it. The sniper must match the weapon to the target.
- *Effect.* A wide range of interdiction effects are possible. Target effect is the desired result of attacking the target, including all possible implications—political, economic, and social effects of the interdiction. Occasionally, the planner must decide what is the desired effect. It may be the removal of key personnel, the psychological impact of the interdiction, or the threat of interdiction. Planners must always consider the balance of effect on the overall mission and the effect on the populace. When an adverse effect on the populace outweighs the effect on the mission, the sniper must reconsider the mission.
- *Recognizability.* A target is recognizable if it can be effectively acquired by the sniper. A target may be well within the sniper's standoff range but cannot be effectively engaged because the target is masked or concealed. For example, the sniper's recognition of targets using night-vision equipment might be restricted because of the technological limitations of the device. Positive identification of targets, as well as small target components, is difficult given the characteristics of the phosphor screen in NVDs. Other factors complicating recognizability include the time of day, light conditions, terrain masking, environmental factors, and similar nontargets in the area.

5-49. The fear of interdiction is evident in the German attempts to kill Winston Churchill in World War II, which forced him to remain hidden for some time. Conversely, John M. Collins' book, *Green Berets, SEALs, and SPETSNAZ,* details the political implications of a DA mission to kill a figure such as Emperor Hirohito of Japan, the "emperor-god," during World War II. Such action, Collins states, "would have had an adverse impact by rallying the Japanese people." A similar reaction was seen when the U.S. bombed Libya in 1986. During the raid, U.S. bombs seriously injured one of Colonel Mu ammar Gadhafi's children and resulted in negative media and international backlash. (Despite Gadhafi's unscrupulous acts, endangering his family was unacceptable to the international public.)

5-50. Material target interdiction by sniper fire is much more limited than it is with personnel targets. The SF sniper's abilities could increase by his choice of special weapons to interdict material targets, but he might still be limited by the relative vulnerability of the target. The greatest obstacle for successful interdiction of material targets rests primarily with the identification of the vulnerable nodes. The goal of the snipers fire on these nodes is to be as effective as more powerful weapons—using precision fire at key points instead of brute force in the general area.

MISSION PLANNING

5-51. Successful accomplishment of a sniper mission relates directly to the planning and preparation that takes place. Each mission requires the expertise of different people at each planning level.

LEVELS OF PLANNING

5-52. The two levels of mission planning are above-team level and team level. At above-team level the sniper employment officer (SEO) or sniper leader plans and coordinates the actions of more than one sniper team. The intent of this directive is to have several teams carry out coordinated or independent missions toward the same objective.

1. **SITUATION**
   a. Enemy forces.
      (1) Weather. Light data, precipitation, temperature, effect on the enemy and the sniper team.
      (2) Terrain. Terrain pattern, profile, soil type, vegetation, and fauna, effect on the enemy and the sniper team.
      (3) Enemy. Type unit(s), identification, training, and presence of countersnipers, significant activities, and effect on the sniper team.
   b. Friendly forces. Adjacent units, left, right, front, and rear. Since sniper teams are vulnerable to capture, they should not receive this information. Rather, they should receive information such as the location of free-fire and no-fire zones.
2. **MISSION**
   Who, what, where, when.
3. **EXECUTION**
   a. Commander's intent. This paragraph relates specifically what is to be accomplished, in a short, precise statement. It should include the commander's measure of success.
   b. Concept of the operation. This paragraph relates step-by-step how the mission will proceed. Breaking the mission down into phases works best. Specific tasks will be carried out in each phase, usually starting from preinfiltration to exfiltration and debriefing.
   c. Fire support. Normally, in a deep operation, fire support will not be available. However, in other situations, the assets may exist.
   d. Follow-on missions. This paragraph will outline any follow-on missions that may be needed. Once the primary mission is accomplished, the sniper team may be tasked to carry out another mission in the AO before exfiltration. This duty may consist of another sniper mission or a linkup with another team, unit, or indigenous persons as a means of exfiltration.
   e. Coordinating instructions. Consist of the following:
      (1) Actions at the objective. This paragraph contains specifically the duties of each member of the team and their rotation to include—
         (a) Security.
         (b) Selection and construction of the hide.
         (c) Removal of spoils.
         (d) Camouflage and fields of fire.
         (e) Observer's log, range card, and military sketch.
         (f) Placement of equipment in the hide.
         (g) Maintenance of weapons and equipment.
         (h) Observation rotation.
      (2) Movement techniques. This paragraph will cover the movement techniques, security at halts, and responsibilities during movement to and from the ORP and the hide and during the return trip.

Figure 5-1. Sniper operation order

(3) Route. This paragraph covers the primary and alternate routes to and from the objective area. It may also include the fire support plan if it is not included in the fire support annex.

(4) Departure and reentry of friendly positions. This information is normally used in the support of conventional forces, but it could be used when dealing with indigenous persons, for example, during a linkup.

(5) Rally points and actions at rally points. In some instances, these points can be used, but for a two-man element a rendezvous is much more advisable. For example, several rendezvous points en route should be preplanned with a specific time or period for linkup. These designations are set so that movement is constantly toward the objective, preventing the lead man from backtracking and wasting time. It is not advisable for a two-man team to attempt to use en route rally points.

(6) Actions on enemy contact. This paragraph stresses minimal contact with the enemy. The team should avoid contact and not engage in a firefight. It is best to avoid contact, even in an ambush; evade as best as possible. The team should not attempt to throw smoke or lay down a base of fire. This action calls attention to the team's position and will cause the enemy to pursue with a much larger element. If an air attack occurs, hide. It is not possible for a two-man team to successfully engage an enemy aircraft.

(7) Actions at danger areas. Avoid danger areas by moving around them, unless this is not possible or time is critical. When moving across large open areas, stalk across; do not move in an upright posture. Linear danger areas are best crossed by having both team members move across the area at the same time after an extended listening halt. This will avoid splitting the team in case of enemy contact and lower the risk of compromise while traversing the danger area.

(8) Actions at halts. Security is critical even when taking a break and nobody is expected in the area. Stay alert.

(9) Rehearsals. If time is not available, at the minimum, always practice actions at the objective. During rehearsals, practice immediate action drills (IADs) and discuss actions at rally and rendezvous points. The team must know these points and the routes on the map. It is also important that the team rehearses any previously untrained actions.

(10) Inspections. Team members should inspect their equipment. Use a checklist for equipment and ensure that everything works. The team should have the proper equipment and camouflage for the terrain and the environment that it will encounter. Inspections should be conducted prior to infiltration, after infiltration, and finally in the ORP before occupying the FFP.

(11) Debriefing. This paragraph covers who will attend the debriefing, where it will occur, and when it will take place. The observer's log and military sketches become useful information-gathering tools during the debriefing (Appendix M).

(12) Priority intelligence requirements (PIR)/information requirements (IRs). These requirements are given to the sniper team as information that should be gathered when the team is employed.

(13) Annexes. This section contains specific maps and sketches showing items such as routes, the fire support plan, the tentative ORPs, and the hide sites. It will also include the evasion and recovery (E&R) plan, sunrise sunset overlay, and terrain profiles.

Figure 5-1. Sniper operation order (*Continued*)

4. **SERVICE SUPPORT**

This paragraph covers, but is not limited to, administrative items such as—

a. Rations.
b. Arms and ammunition that each team member will carry.
c. Uniform and equipment that each team member will carry.
d. Method of handling the dead and wounded.
e. Prisoners and captured equipment. This paragraph is not likely to be used, unless the equipment can be carried, photographed, or sketched.
f. Caches and mission support sites (MSSs).

5. **COMMAND AND SIGNAL**

a. Frequencies and call signs. It is not necessary to list all the frequencies and call signs. You need only to refer to the current signal operating instructions (SOI).
b. Pyrotechnics and signals, to include hand and arm signals. It is best to have a team SOP to which you can refer. Otherwise, you must list all the pyrotechnics and hand and arm signals.
c. Challenge and password. The challenge and password will be necessary when linking up at rendezvous points and passing through friendly lines.
d. Code words and reports. This refers to any contact made with higher headquarters or possibly a linkup with indigenous persons.
e. Chain of command.

Figure 5-1. Sniper operation order (*Continued*)

At team level, the members of the sniper team will carry out the planning, preparation, and coordination for the mission. Therefore, warning orders are not necessary at this level, and the following sniper operation order (Figure 5-1, pages 558 through 560) itself is a mission planning tool.

TERRAIN PROFILE

5-53. A terrain profile is an exaggerated side view of a portion of the earth's surface between two points. The profile will determine if LOS is available. The sniper leader can use line of sight to determine—

- Defilade positions.
- Dead space.
- Potential direct-fire weapon positions.

5-54. The sniper leader can construct a profile from any contoured map. Its construction requires the following steps:

- Draw a line from where the profile begins to where it ends.
- Find the highest and lowest value of the contour lines that cross or touch the profile line. Add one contour value above the highest and one below the lowest to take care of hills and valleys.
- Select a piece of notebook paper with as many lines as contours on the profile line. The standard Army green pocket notebook or any paper with quarter-inch lines is ideal. If lined paper is not available, draw equally spaced lines on a blank sheet.
- Number the top line with the highest value and the rest of the lines in sequence with the contour interval down to the lowest value.

- Place the paper on the map with the lines parallel to the profile line.
- From every point on the profile line where a contour line, a stream, an intermittent stream, or a body of water crosses or touches, drop a perpendicular line to the line having the same value. Where trees are present, add the height of the trees to the contour.
- After all perpendicular lines are drawn and tick marks placed on the corresponding elevation line, draw a smooth line connecting the marks to form a horizontal view or profile of the terrain. (The profile drawn may be exaggerated. The space of lines on the notebook paper will determine the amount of exaggeration.)
- Draw a straight line from the start point to the finish point on the profile. If the straight line intersects the curved profile, line of sight is not available.

SUNRISE/SUNSET OVERLAY

5-55. A sunrise/sunset overlay (SSO) is a graphic representation of the angle to the rising and setting sun and the objective. An SSO enables a team to plan a line of advance or tentative hide sites to take best advantage of the light. An SSO requires a table showing the true azimuth of the rising sun and the relative bearing of the setting sun for all months of the year. An SSO is constructed in the following manner:

- Using the projected date of the mission and the latitude of the target, determine the true azimuth of the sunrise from Table 5-1, pages 562 and 564.
- Using a protractor and a straightedge, draw a line from the objective along the true azimuth.
- Subtract the true azimuth from 360 to find the sunset azimuth.
- Using a protractor and a straightedge, draw another line from the objective along the sunset azimuth.
- Convert each azimuth to a back azimuth and write it on the appropriate line.
- Label the appropriate lines sunrise and sunset.
- Write down the latitude and the date that was used to construct the overlay.

SNIPER SUPPORT IN SPECIAL OPERATIONS MISSIONS AND COLLATERAL ACTIVITIES

5-56. Special operations (SO) forces plan, conduct, and support activities in all operational environments. The following paragraphs explain how the SF sniper supports each mission and activity.

CIVIL AFFAIRS AND PSYCHOLOGICAL OPERATIONS

5-57. The misuse of sniper interdiction can adversely affect Civil Affairs (CA) and civic action programs sponsored by friendly organizations. The sniper is a very efficient killer and given a target will go to extreme efforts to interdict it. Therefore, planners must temper the use of force with common sense and the future goals of the operation. It may be easier to eliminate threats than to negotiate, but in the long run, negotiations may open the door for settlement where sniping may close it or may set the stage for undesirable reactions.

5-58. Planners must also consider the psychological operations (PSYOP) aspects of the mission, including both positive and negative impacts. The sniper can project not only accurate weapons fire but also tremendous psychological destruction. Such impact was given as rationale for the Vietnam My Lai massacre. There, in defense of their actions, some soldiers claimed that enemy sniper fire (and friendly casualties) over prolonged time drove them to commit the war crimes. On the other end of the spectrum, U.S. use of snipers can also cause adverse reaction on enemy forces. As at My Lai, the enemy may focus on innocent noncombatants and commit inappropriate reprisals in response to intense sniper pressure. This practice is especially true in UW and FID environments where U.S. SO forces may use local populations as guerrillas and security forces.

5-59. The psychological impact of sniping has received little attention in the overall scheme of war. Historians often focus on the large weapons systems and overlook the stress and fear that sniping adds to the battlefield. Yet, this psychological impact can ruin the fiber and morale of an entire army; for example, in World War I, the sniper's bullet was often feared far more than many other ways of dying.

5-60. The U.S. military has only recently recognized the psychological impact of sustained combat, although the sniper has always contributed as much to fear as he has to fighting. Operational planners may consider this PSYOP capability when planning sniper missions, especially when using PSYOP in UW where it plays a vital role.

Table 5-1. Finding direction from the rising or setting sun

Date		Angle to North From the Rising or Setting Sun (level terrain) Latitude												
		0°	5°	10°	15°	20°	25°	30°	35°	40°	45°	50°	55°	60°
January	1	113	113	113	114	115	116	117	118	121	124	127	155	141
	6	112	113	113	113	114	115	116	118	120	123	127	132	140
	11	112	112	112	113	113	114	115	117	119	122	125	130	138
	16	111	111	111	112	112	113	114	116	118	120	124	129	136
	21	110	110	110	111	111	112	113	115	117	119	122	127	133
	26	109	109	109	109	110	111	112	113	115	117	120	124	130
February	1	107	107	108	108	108	109	110	111	113	115	117	121	126
	6	106	106	106	106	107	107	108	109	111	113	115	118	123
	11	104	104	105	105	105	106	107	108	100	110	112	116	120
	16	103	103	103	103	103	104	105	106	107	108	110	112	116
	21	101	101	101	101	101	102	102	103	104	105	107	109	112
	26	99	99	99	99	100	100	100	101	102	103	104	106	108
March	1	98	98	98	98	99	99	99	100	100	101	102	104	106
	6	96	96	96	96	96	97	97	97	98	98	99	100	102
	11	94	94	94	94	94	94	95	95	95	96	96	97	98
	16	92	92	92	92	92	92	92	92	93	93	93	93	94
	21	90	90	90	90	90	90	90	90	90	90	90	90	90
	26	88	88	88	88	88	88	88	88	87	87	87	87	96
April	1	86	86	86	86	85	85	85	85	84	84	83	82	81
	6	84	84	84	83	83	83	83	82	82	81	80	79	77
	11	82	82	82	82	81	81	81	80	80	79	77	76	74
	16	80	80	80	80	79	70	78	78	77	76	74	72	70
	21	78	78	78	78	78	77	76	76	75	73	72	69	66
	26	77	77	76	76	76	75	75	74	72	71	69	66	63
May	1	75	75	75	74	74	73	73	72	70	69	66	63	59
	6	74	74	73	73	73	72	71	70	68	67	64	61	56
	11	72	72	72	72	71	70	69	68	67	64	62	58	52
	16	71	71	71	70	70	69	68	67	65	63	60	55	49
	21	70	70	70	69	69	68	67	65	63	61	58	53	47
	26	69	69	69	68	68	67	66	64	62	60	56	51	44

Table 5-1. Finding direction from the rising or setting sun (*Continued*)

Date		Angle to North From the Rising or Setting Sun (level terrain) Latitude												
		0°	**5°**	**10°**	**15°**	**20°**	**25°**	**30°**	**35°**	**40°**	**45°**	**50°**	**55°**	**60°**
June	1	68	68	68	67	66	66	64	63	61	58	54	49	40
	6	67	67	67	67	66	65	64	62	60	59	53	48	40
	11	67	67	67	66	66	64	63	62	59	56	53	47	39
	16	67	67	67	66	65	64	63	62	59	56	53	47	39
	21	67	67	67	66	66	64	63	62	59	56	53	47	39
	26	67	67	67	66	65	64	63	62	59	56	53	47	39
July	1	67	67	67	66	65	64	63	62	59	56	53	47	39
	6	67	67	67	66	66	65	64	62	60	57	53	48	40
	11	68	68	68	67	66	65	64	63	61	58	54	49	41
	16	69	68	68	68	67	66	65	64	62	59	55	50	43
	21	69	69	69	69	68	67	66	65	63	60	57	52	45
	26	70	70	70	70	69	68	67	66	64	62	59	54	48
August	1	72	72	72	71	71	70	69	68	66	64	61	57	51
	6	73	73	73	73	72	71	71	69	68	68	63	60	55
	11	75	75	74	74	74	73	72	71	70	68	66	63	58
	16	76	76	76	76	75	75	74	73	72	70	68	65	61
	21	78	78	77	77	77	76	76	75	74	72	71	68	65
	26	79	79	79	79	79	78	78	77	76	75	73	71	68
September	1	82	82	82	81	81	81	80	80	79	78	77	75	73
	6	83	83	83	83	83	83	82	82	81	81	80	78	77
	11	85	85	85	85	85	85	85	84	84	83	83	82	81
	16	87	87	87	87	87	87	87	86	86	86	85	85	84
	21	89	89	89	89	89	89	89	89	89	89	88	88	88
	26	91	91	91	91	91	91	91	91	91	91	92	92	92
October	1	93	93	93	93	93	93	93	94	94	94	95	95	96
	6	95	95	95	95	95	96	96	96	97	97	98	98	100
	11	97	97	97	97	97	98	98	99	99	100	101	102	104
	16	99	99	99	99	99	100	100	101	101	102	104	105	108
	21	101	101	101	101	101	102	102	103	104	105	107	109	112
	26	102	102	193	103	103	104	104	105	106	108	109	112	115
November	1	104	104	105	105	105	106	107	108	109	110	113	116	120
	6	106	106	106	107	107	108	109	110	111	113	115	119	123
	11	107	107	108	108	108	109	110	111	113	115	117	121	126
	16	109	109	109	109	110	111	112	113	115	117	120	124	130
	21	110	110	110	111	111	112	113	114	116	119	122	126	133
	26	111	111	111	112	112	113	114	116	118	120	124	128	135

Table 5-1. Finding direction from the rising or setting sun (*Continued*)

Date		Angle to North From the Rising or Setting Sun (level terrain) Latitude												
		0°	5°	10°	15°	20°	25°	30°	35°	40°	45°	50°	55°	60°
December	1	112	112	112	113	113	114	115	117	119	122	125	130	138
	6	112	112	113	113	114	115	116	118	120	123	126	132	140
	11	113	113	113	114	115	116	117	118	121	124	127	133	141
	16	113	113	113	114	115	116	117	118	121	124	127	133	141
	21	113	113	113	114	115	116	117	118	121	124	127	133	141
	26	113	113	113	114	115	116	117	118	121	124	127	133	141

NOTES 1. When the sun is rising, the angle is reckoned from east to north. When the sun is setting, the angle is reckoned from the west to north.
2. This chart is for the Northern Hemisphere.

UNCONVENTIONAL WARFARE OPERATIONS

5-61. In a UW environment, the SF sniper provides an additional capability to the resistance force. The primary mission of the resistance force is to support conventional forces during times of war. Therefore, the SF sniper must know conventional sniper tactics as well as unconventional techniques to effectively train a U.S.-sponsored resistance force. During peacetime, mobile training teams (MTTs) can train foreign military or paramilitary forces. In times of war, the training takes place during the organization and training phase of the resistance force after linkup.

5-62. The importance of a sniper in UW cannot be measured only by the number of casualties he inflicts upon the enemy. Realization of the sniper's presence instills fear in enemy troops and influences their decisions and actions. Selective and discriminate target interdiction not only instills fear in the enemy, but can lead to general confusion and relocation of significant enemy strengths to counter such activity.

5-63. In UW, the SF sniper can perform as a fighter and a trainer. Not only can he teach sniper skills to the force he is training; he can act as a direct action asset when needed. The sniper's ancillary skills in camouflage, stalking, surveillance, and deception are also useful in the UW environments. The impact of these talents is magnified when the sniper acts as a trainer. By training others he is, in effect, performing interdiction much more efficiently than he could alone.

5-64. UW or guerrilla warfare (GW) consists of three major phases: buildup, consolidation, and linkup. Snipers will play an important role in all three phases.

Buildup

5-65. During initial contact and buildup, SF snipers will mainly train the indigenous force snipers and then act as sniper coordinators.

5-66. During the buildup, snipers are extremely effective when used in the harassing and sniper ambush role. By using the snipers' ability to deliver long-range precision rifle fire, the UW force can accomplish the following objectives all at once:

- Be able to strike at the enemy forces while minimizing their own exposure.
- Deny the comfort of a secure area to the enemy.
- Build UW force morale with successes while minimizing the amount of UW force exposure.
- Since the fires are discriminatory, maintain a positive effect on the civilian population, as civilian casualties are minimized. This also reinforces in the civilians' minds the inability of government forces to control that part of the countryside.

5-67. However, it is very important that the snipers go after targets with a military objective only. The line between sniper ambush and assassination at this point can be unclear. The sniper must remember that an ambush is for military gain, while an assassination is for political gain. Assassination, under any guise, is illegal due to Executive Order 12333, Part n, paragraph 2-11, dated 4 December 1981.

5-68. During the end of the buildup and before the consolidation phase, the UW snipers will be used the same as strike operations snipers; that is, in support of small raids and ambushes. As the size of the UW force grows, so will the size of the missions that are similar to strike missions.

Consolidation

5-69. During consolidation, as the UW force becomes larger, the role of the sniper reverts to that of the conventional sniper. The same missions, tactics, and employment principles apply.

Linkup

5-70. During and after linkup, the snipers will mainly act as part of the security force and rear area protection (RAP) force. The UW force snipers will be particularly suited for this role. They have spent their time in that area and should know most, if not all, of the main areas that could support the enemy during infiltration and rear area attacks.

5-71. During the initial contact phase of a resistance movement, sniper employment will normally be limited to supporting small-unit operations and will include such actions as—

- *Harassment of Enemy Personnel.* When performed at ranges greater than 500 meters, harassment serves to lower the enemy's morale and inhibit his freedom of movement.
- *Infiltration.* Before an attack, snipers may infiltrate enemy units' positions and establish themselves in the enemy's rear area. During the attack, the infiltrated snipers engage specific targets of opportunity to divert the enemy's attention from the attacking units and to disrupt his freedom of movement in his rear areas.
- *Interdiction.* The snipers will delay or interdict reinforcing elements to a target and deny the enemy use of an area or routes by any means.
- *Multiple Team, Area Sniper Ambush.* This type of ambush involves multiple sniper teams operating together to engage targets by timed or simultaneous fire. Each sniper will fire a fixed number of rounds, and the ambush will end when either the targets have been successfully engaged or the predetermined number of shots have been fired. Planning considerations must include how the ambush is to be initiated, how the snipers will communicate with each other, and what methods the snipers will use to engage the targets.
- *Security and Surveillance.* Snipers are employed to gather information or to confirm existing intelligence by long-term surveillance of a target site. They may also be used to provide early warning of impending counterattacks. Snipers will normally establish a hide position to conduct their surveillance.
- *Offensive Operations.* During the advanced stages of the combat phase of a resistance movement, snipers may be used to detect and engage long-range targets that could impede the progress of the offensive element. The teams must be ready to assume the defensive role immediately after the offensive operation.
- *Defensive Operations.* Snipers are best used in defensive operations outside the forward line of troops (FLOT) to provide early warning of enemy approach, disorganize his attack, and cause him to deploy early. Snipers may also be used to delay the enemy's advance by interdicting enemy movements using a series of interlocking delay positions, thus allowing the friendly forces to withdraw.

FOREIGN INTERNAL DEFENSE OPERATIONS

5-72. The primary role of SF snipers in FID is that of a teacher. During the passive FID role, SF snipers will be in-country for training and advising only and will not have an active role. During active FID, the SF snipers could find themselves in both a trainer's role and an active role. In either case, passive or active, the primary tactics will be that of conventional warfare—offense, defense, and withdrawal.

5-73. During active FID, the SF sniper will conduct counterguerrilla operations, sniper cordons and periphery observation posts (OPs), sniper ambushes, urban surveillance, and civil disorders.

5-74. Sniper participation in RAP is the main line of attack in accomplishing counterguerrilla operations. Snipers can enhance the protective measures surrounding sensitive facilities or installations by setting up observation posts along routes of access, acting as part of a reaction force when the rear area has been penetrated or patrolling the area (as members of established security patrols). They can then operate in a stay-behind role once the security patrol has moved on. In RAP operations, the sniper—

- Protects critical installations and sites.
- Covers gaps between units to avoid infiltration.
- Prevents removal of obstacles.
- Tracks enemy patrols known to have penetrated into the rear area.

5-75. The sniper's ancillary skills in camouflage, stalking, surveillance, and deception are also useful in the FID environment. The impact of these talents is magnified when the sniper acts as a trainer. By training others he is, in effect, performing interdiction much more efficiently than he could alone. Appendix N provides a sample sniper range complex (SRC) for the trainer's use.

SNIPER ELEMENT ORGANIZATION IN UW AND FID

5-76. In a UW or FID role, the sniper elements organize above-team-level size with elements under the control of the commander and the S-2. Depending upon the availability of trained personnel, the sniper elements should organize as a squad at battalion level (10 men or 5 teams) and as a section at regimental or brigade level. A sniper coordinator is required at regimental level and desirable at battalion level. He should be assigned to the S-2/G-2 staff for intelligence purposes. However, he must work closely with the S-3/G-3 staff for planning purposes. The sniper coordinator should be a sniper-qualified senior NCO, warrant officer, or officer who is well versed in mission planning. He must also be strong enough to ensure that the sniper teams are not improperly deployed. All other members of the squads, the platoon, and the platoon headquarters element must be sniper-qualified.

DIRECT ACTION OPERATIONS

5-77. DA operations are short-duration strikes and other small-scale offensive actions conducted by SOF to seize, destroy, or inflict damage on a specified target. When employed in DA missions, snipers will perform one or more of the following four functions.

Harassment

5-78. Snipers use deliberate harassment to impede, destroy, or prevent movement of enemy units. The degree of harassment depends on the amount of time and planning put into the operation. Harassment is best suited for protracted or unconventional operations. During such operations sniper casualties will be high, and provisions for their replacement must be included in the harassment plan.

Multiple Team, Area Sniper Ambush

5-79. The "sniper ambush" is when multiple sniper teams operate together to engage targets by timed or simultaneous fire. Each sniper fires a fixed number of rounds; the ambush ends either after target engagement or after all shots are fired. The planners for each ambush should always consider how the ambush will start, how the snipers will communicate with each other, and how they will engage the targets in the kill zone.

Sniper Cordon

5-80. A sniper cordon is a series of outposts surrounding a specific area. A sniper cordon can prevent the enemy from entering or leaving a target location. Snipers may operate in cordon operations by being integrated into the overall fire plan as a supporting force or in cordon areas as independent elements. Snipers should be used during cordon operations to maximize their precision long-range fire capabilities. Due to the snipers' limited volume of fire and reliance on stealth, they possess little capability to become decisively engaged during such operations. Once the snipers have been located, they may be suppressed by fire and maneuver or indirect fire. Therefore, the snipers' ability to hold or cordon an area will be directly commensurate to the enemy force encountered and the support from friendly units.

Interdiction

5-81. Interdiction is preventing or hindering enemy use of an area or route by any means. When deployed for interdiction, the snipers can restrain dismounted avenues of approach. Their ability to interdict vehicular traffic is limited to harassment unless armed with large-caliber SWSs. Snipers can deploy with vehicular interdiction elements to harass the enemy when it is forced to dismount. They can also cause armor vehicles to "button up," making them more vulnerable to antitank weapons.

THE STRIKE FORCE OF DA OPERATIONS

5-82. The size of the strike force depends on the mission, location of the target, and enemy situation. Planners tailor the strike force in size and capability to perform a specific mission. It can be a small team to interdict a personnel target or a larger force to destroy a large facility or plant. Regardless of size, most strike operations consist of command, security, support, and assault elements. Snipers can provide support to any of these elements depending on the objectives and needs of the commander. The requirements for the SF sniper in strike operations may include the elements discussed below.

Command Element

5-83. This element forms the primary command post and normally consists of the strike force commander and, as a minimum, his S-2/S-3 and fire support element controllers. The sniper coordinator also works with the command element. The snipers assigned to the command element are formed by the expedient pooling of strike force snipers. They are under the control of the sniping specialist. Regardless of their origin, pooled snipers stay in their original teams. Under the command element, snipers will be able to conduct reconnaissance and DA missions supporting the entire strike force or multiple missions supporting one or more strike force elements throughout the operation. Examples of these missions may include—

- Reconnoitering the ORPs, routes, or exfiltration sites.
- Reconnoitering and observing the objective (once action is initiated, covert OP snipers may perform a DA function in support of the strike force).
- Establishing a reserve to intervene or reinforce elements with precision rifle fire.
- Screening danger areas and vulnerable flanks or sealing off the enemy rear.

Security Element

5-84. Snipers may operate in conjunction with a larger security force or independently in support of the security mission. When sniper teams work with a larger security force, they should not collocate with crew-served weapons. This step will ensure that sniper fire is not suppressed by enemy fire directed at the crew-served weapons. The element will determine sniper employment by the scope of the operation and personnel constraints. The security element's missions include—

- Securing rallying points.
- Providing early warning of enemy approach.
- Blocking avenues of approach into the objective area.
- Preventing enemy escape.
- Acting as left, right, and rear security elements for the strike force.

5-85. In smaller operations, the security element could consists entirely of snipers. This would reduce personnel requirements. In larger operations, a larger, more flexible (antiarmor, demolitions) security force would be necessary, and snipers would serve to complement this security element's capabilities. For example, armored threats require augmentation by appropriate antiarmor weapons. Snipers can provide accurate long-range suppressive fire to separate infantry from their armored units and to force tanks to button up, which will hinder their ability to detect the launch of wire-guided missiles. The sniper team can employ large-bore sniper weapons to help delay and interdict light material targets.

5-86. Snipers performing security missions in DA operations are well suited to perform successive or simultaneous missions. They also provide early warning of delaying and harassing reaction forces. Reaction forces located some distance from the objective will approach using vehicles or aircraft. The mobility assets of the reaction force can be dedicated to that mission and can subsequently present an actual threat to the strike force. Snipers may operate as part of the security force to interdict or harass reaction force avenues of approach or landing zones (if known or obvious). In addition to the main role of security, the snipers may also—

- Report information before an assault.
- Support the assault force by fire (caution must be used here).
- Assist in sealing the objective during the assault.
- Maintain contact after the assault.
- Act as a rear guard during the withdrawal of the assault force.

Support Element

5-87. This element of the strike force must be capable of placing accurate supporting fire on the objective. It must deliver a sufficient volume of fire to suppress the objective and provide cover to the assault element. It also provides fire support to cover the withdrawal of the assault element from the objective.

5-88. Snipers in the support element provide discriminate fire in support of the assault force. The sniper's optics facilitate positive target identification and acquisition, which allows him to fire in close proximity to friendly forces with reduced risk of fratricide. This practice is opposed to more traditional automatic or indirect supporting fire that must terminate or shift as friendly forces approach the target area (referred to as "lift and shift"). At night, friendly troops can wear distinctive markings such as reflective tapes or infrared devices (visible to the sniper's night-vision equipment) to aid identification.

5-89. When assigned to the support element, snipers should organize into four-man sniper teams (two pairs working together). There are several reasons for this type of organization. First, the sniper team leader can better control the snipers' rate and control of supporting fire. Second, sniper elements centrally located can better redeploy to critical locations to delay pursuing forces. Third, limited vantage points from which to deliver precision rifle fire may exist. Concentrating snipers at these vantage points may be the only effective way to maximize their capabilities of long-range precision rifle fire. Again, as in the support role, snipers should not be collocated with crew-served weapon systems.

5-90. When snipers are assigned to the support element, their mission should be specific. The effectiveness of sniper fire is not in the volume, but the precision with which it is delivered. Sniper missions include—

- Disrupting C2 by engaging officers or NCOs directing the defense.
- Suppressing guards and enemy security forces.
- Providing precision covering force to the assault element.
- Precision reduction of hard points.
- Delaying pursuing forces after withdrawal.
- Maintaining contact with displaced enemy forces after the attack.
- Observing for enemy counterattacks or continued harassment of the enemy to disorganize any counterattack efforts.

5-91. One advantage of snipers in the support element is that they do not have to lift and shift as crew-served weapons do once the assault element is on the objective. The snipers can continue to support through precision rifle fire.

Assault Element

5-92. Snipers seldom operate with the assault element, mainly because of the need for rapid movement combined with suppressive fire. This type of maneuver seldom allows for the snipers' deliberate (sedentary) firing process.

In addition, the assault element often participates in close-quarter battle—nullifying the snipers' standoff capability. However, snipers can support the element when C2 would be better effected or in circumstances where they can enhance the element's mission. They may provide cover fire when the assault element must pass through an area that is dead space from other supporting elements. However, the snipers would then support the assault element's movement to the objective and not be an actual part of it. They may also provide support by using aerial platforms (Appendix O).

ENEMY CONSIDERATIONS DURING DIRECT ACTION OPERATIONS

5-93. The type and number of enemy security forces likely to be manning the target or available for reaction must be considered in the plan. These forces may be static, foot-mobile, vehicle-mounted, or airmobile.

Enemy Security Forces

5-94. Mission planners will generally position armored vehicles on the perimeter; light vehicles will normally remain in a vehicle park. Armored vehicles are likely to become centers of resistance, around which defenders will concentrate during the action. This position will present the snipers with a high density of targets, particularly officers and NCOs who will tend to use static-armored vehicles as rally points. The lack of vehicular mobility on the part of the strike force renders them vulnerable to a mobile threat. In such circumstances, snipers should be delegated the task of interdicting routes of access to vehicle parks. Drivers of light vehicles are the primary targets; track or tank commanders are the prime armored-vehicle targets.

On-Site Defensive Positions

5-95. DA targets deep within enemy lines will generally have less protection and a lower defensive posture than those located close to the main battle area. Target site defenses can be either hasty or permanent.

5-96. Hasty defensive positions provide less protection to defending personnel than prepared ones. Strike force snipers are able to engage such positions at a greater distance with more effectiveness due to the limited protection to the targets. Snipers should consider any object or location at the target site that affords protection to the enemy (for example, behind light vehicles or in buildings) as a hasty defensive position.

5-97. Permanent defensive positions consist of bunkers, sandbagged fighting positions, or prepared buildings. Such targets present unique circumstances to the snipers. These well-protected targets, which often have narrow firing ports and are mutually supportive, make engagement difficult and require the snipers to move closer to the targets than normal. As the range to the targets decreases, the probability of detection and engagement from the enemy forces increases.

Enemy Reaction Force

5-98. Strike force snipers functioning in a support capacity, or as part of the strike force security element, will primarily target the enemy reaction force.

SPECIAL RECONNAISSANCE OPERATIONS

5-99. The SF sniper offers some advantages to SR missions. He is well trained in surveillance and his ability to interdict material targets at extended range is often complementary to follow-on SR missions. If interdiction of C2 systems is the goal of the follow-on mission, then snipers can carry significant potential destruction in the form of large-bore sniper rifles.

5-100. Snipers make extensive use of fixed and roving surveillance to acquire targets or assess their vulnerabilities. They will normally establish a hide position to conduct their surveillance. Once hidden, they will continue noting detailed information in their observation log. The log will serve as a record of events and assist in mission debriefing. The snipers will report all PIR and IRs as required.

5-101. Because of their mission-essential equipment, snipers are ideally suited to perform reconnaissance in conjunction with their primary DA mission. They can obtain information about the activity and resources of an enemy or potential enemy and secure data concerning the meteorological, hydrographic, or geographic characteristics of a particular area.

5-102. Snipers may need to reconnoiter enemy positions that are of specific interest to supported units. Information gathered by snipers includes, but is not limited to the locations of—

- FDCs.
- Crew-served weapons.
- Tactical operations centers (TOCs).
- Gaps in enemy wire.
- Listening posts (LPs) and OPs.
- Gaps between enemy units and positions.
- Infiltration routes.

5-103. Snipers may also infiltrate through enemy positions in support of offensive operations or to harass enemy rear areas. Once sniper teams have infiltrated enemy positions, their tasks may be to report information on—

- Troop strength and movements.
- Concentrations and reserve locations.
- OPs and weapons locations.
- Command, control, and communications facilities.

COUNTERTERRORISM OPERATIONS

5-104. The primary mission of SOF in counterterrorism (CT) is to apply specialized capabilities to preclude, preempt, and resolve terrorist incidents abroad. Snipers provide three primary functions in CT operations. They—

- Deliver discriminate fire to interdict hostile targets.
- Cover the entry teams into the objective area with rifle fire.
- Provide the CT force commander with his most accurate target intelligence.

5-105. In the last case, the commander will normally position the sniper in an ideal position to observe the enemy. Most frequently, this position will be the commander's only view of the target.

5-106. Counterterrorism operations require extensive training and coordination. Most important, the sniper teams must know the plans and actions of the entry teams to avoid possible injury to friendly personnel, and they must fire when told to do so. Failure to engage and neutralize a target can have devastating consequences, similar to what occurred in the 1972 Olympic games in Munich, Federal Republic of Germany. Snipers did not neutralize their terrorist targets on command. The result was that the terrorists were free to execute the hostages. To compound the problem, the snipers were so confused that they shot and killed several of their own men. Of course, overzealous snipers can create results similar to what occurred in Los Angeles, California. Police snipers shot and killed a bank president who was indicating a gunman by pointing his finger. The overanxious police sniper thought the man was pointing a gun and shot him. Obviously, the line between shoot and do not shoot is thin and can be stretched thinner by haste or indecisiveness.

5-107. Part of the solution to these problems lies in the selection and training process. During the selection process, an individual's mind is the one variable that a psychologist cannot effectively measure. In fact, oftentimes psychologists cannot agree on what traits to look for in a sniper. How does one pick a man to deliberately kill another man who presents no immediate threat to him personally? Unfortunately, the real test of a sniper comes only when it is time to pull the trigger. Only then will the sniper's reliability definitely be known.

5-108. Another problem that seems to manifest itself in CT scenarios is the Stockholm Syndrome. This type of reaction occurs when the sniper is unable to shoot a person who has become familiar to him. The syndrome manifests itself when the sniper has conducted constant surveillance of his target and becomes so familiar with the target's actions, habits, and mannerisms that the target becomes more human, almost well acquainted—too familiar to shoot. On the other hand, some reports have indicated the opposite to be true; some snipers hope to have the opportunity to shoot someone from some twisted, personal motivation. Perhaps this happened in Los Angeles. Nevertheless, these psychological extremes—eager or reluctant firers—are inappropriate to the sniper's function; the sniper must be somewhere in between.

COMBAT SEARCH AND RESCUE

5-109. In CSAR operations, the sniper's role is extremely limited because the mission is to rescue and not to interdict. However, the sniper can provide traditional long-range security and early warning to rescue forces. His ability to operate in denied areas can greatly assist the rescue forces by providing accurate information regarding the rescue. The sniper can infiltrate before the rescue and conduct surveillance of the rescue area unnoticed. The U.S. Air Force is considering using snipers with their pararescue units (in place of machine guns) to provide long-range security during rescue operations. This method would give them the benefit of selectively interdicting threat targets while not endangering innocent bystanders.

COUNTERSNIPER

5-110. A sniper team is the best asset available to a commander for a countersniper operation. The team plans and coordinates the operation to eliminate the enemy sniper threat. A countersniper operation occurs between two highly trained elements—the sniper team and the enemy sniper—each knowing the capabilities and limits of the other.

5-111. A sniper team's first task is to determine if there is a sniper threat. If so, it then identifies information that may be gained from the unit in the operations area, such as—

- Enemy soldiers in special camouflage uniforms.
- Enemy soldiers with weapons in cases or drag bags, which includes:
  - Rifles of unusual configuration
  - Long-barrel rifles.
  - Mounted telescopes.
  - Bolt-action rifles.
- Single-shot fire at key personnel (commanders, platoon leaders, senior NCOs, or weapons crews).
- Lack or reduction of enemy patrols during single-shot fires.
- Light reflecting from optical lenses.
- Reconnaissance patrols reporting of small groups of enemy (one to three men) by visual sighting or tracking.
- Discovery of single, expending casings (usually of rifle calibers 7.62x54R, 7.26NM, 300WM, 338 Lapua)

5-112. The sniper team next determines the best method to eliminate the enemy sniper. It—

- Gathers information, which includes:
  - Times of day precision fire occurs.
  - Locations where enemy sniper fire was encountered.
  - Locations of enemy sniper sightings.
  - Material evidence of enemy snipers such as empty brass casings or equipment.
- Determines patterns.

5-113. The sniper team evaluates the information to detect the enemy's established patterns or routines. It conducts a map reconnaissance, studies aerial photos, or carries out a ground reconnaissance to determine travel patterns. The sniper must picture himself in the enemy's position and ask, "How would I accomplish this mission?"

5-114. Once a pattern or routine is detected, the sniper team determines the best location and time to engage the enemy sniper. It also requests—

- Coordinating routes and preplanned fires (direct and indirect).
- Additional preplotted targets (fire support).
- Infantry support to canalize or ambush the sniper.
- Additional sniper teams for mutual supporting fire.
- Baiting of likely engagement areas to deceive the enemy sniper into commitment by firing.
- All elements be in place 12 hours before the expected engagement time.

5-115. During a countersniper operation, the team must ignore battle activity and concentrate on one objective—the enemy sniper. When an enemy sniper is operating in a unit's area, the sniper team ensures that the unit uses the following passive countermeasures to defend against enemy sniper fire:

- Do not establish routines—for example, consistent meal times, ammunition resupply, assembly area procedures, or day-to-day activities that have developed into a routine.
- Conduct all meetings, briefings, or gatherings of personnel under cover or during limited visibility.
- Cover or conceal equipment.
- Remove rank from helmets and collars. Do not salute officers. Leaders should not use authoritative mannerisms.
- Increase OPs and use other methods to increase the unit's observation capabilities. All information should be consolidated at the S-2 for analysis and logged-in regardless of insignificance.
- Brief patrols on what to look for, such as single, expended rounds or different camouflage materials.
- Do not display awareness of the enemy's presence at any time.
- Be aware that some of the enemy snipers may be women. Patrols and OPs must not be misled when sighting a woman with a mounted telescope on her rifle. She is a deadly opponent.
- Be aware of resupply operations by women and children into suspected or possible sniper locations. Watch for movement and scheduled patterns.

CONVENTIONAL OFFENSIVE OPERATIONS

5-116. Snipers can add deception to the battlefield and provide economy-of-force to allow the conventional force commander to focus combat power elsewhere. Commanders must also think of sniper operations in unilateral terms. The effect of snipers on a scale of ones and twos is small. However, when employed in coordinated actions on a broad front, their effect can be substantial, not only throughout the battlefield but also before, during, and after the battle. They can provide support to conventional units in the following critical phases of offensive operations:

PREOFFENSIVE MISSIONS

5-117. Any missions before offensive operations will primarily be in the deep battle area to gather information on the enemy's disposition. Snipers can help collect this information and interdict selected targets, if necessary. If the objective is to divert enemy assets from the main effort, then snipers can imitate the actions that the Russian partisans conducted against the Germans in World War II. The result of such actions can impair logistics operations and demoralize enemy soldiers in their own rear areas. The preoffensive missions are generally HUMINT-oriented. However, the sniper can perform the following DA functions as a natural consequence of his proximity to the enemy as a HUMINT asset.

Reconnoitering

5-118. The sniper's tasks can vary with each reconnoitering mission. Some of his functions are to—

- Gather (real-time) information on enemy dispositions, terrain, and weather.
- Penetrate enemy security zones in an effort to determine the extent and nature of enemy deception efforts.
- Confirm or deny existing intelligence as requested by the commander or S-2.
- Locate securable routes or axes of advance.

- Locate enemy reserve forces and the possible routes they could use to reinforce the objective.
- Establish or modify preplanned fires of indirect weapons to more effectively reduce TOCs, FDCs, crew-served weapons, hard points, avenues of approach, and retreat.
- Locate enemy security measures, such as mines, obstacles, or barriers.

Harassment

5-119. This function serves to lower the enemy's morale and inhibit his freedom of movement within his own lines. It takes the feeling of a secure area away from the enemy and inhibits his ability to rest his troops. The sniper generally performs this type of harassment at ranges greater than 500 meters.

Infiltration

5-120. Before an attack, snipers infiltrate the gaps between enemy units and positions and establish themselves in the enemy's rear area. During the attack the infiltrated snipers will engage specific targets and targets of opportunity both on the main line of resistance and in the rear area. This method diverts the enemy's attention from the attacking units and disrupts the freedom of movement in its own rear areas. Specific targets engaged by infiltrating snipers include—

- Enemy snipers.
- Command, control, and communications facilities and personnel.
- Crew-served weapons personnel.
- Artillery and forward air controllers.
- Dismounted reserve forces.
- Military policemen.
- Wire repair and resupply parties.

MISSIONS DURING THE OFFENSE

5-121. Sniping during the offensive is DA-oriented. Snipers are attached to friendly units to provide immediate direct support by means of precision rifle fire. The main function of attached snipers will be the suppression of enemy crew-served weapons, enemy snipers, and C2 personnel. Snipers can also support the offensive by interdicting follow-on or reserve forces (such as second-echelon combat forces or logistics). Conventional snipers, assigned to their parent units, can also interdict key targets in the main battle area. Also, attached snipers can be used to screen the flanks of advancing units, cover dead space from supporting crew-served weapons, and engage specific selected targets of the defending enemy units. Snipers maintain pressure on the retreating forces to prevent assembly and reconsolidation. The sniper will pursue retreating forces until he reaches his limit of advance. Then he will prepare for postoffensive operations.

POSTOFFENSIVE MISSIONS

5-122. Snipers' postoffensive role begins during the consolidation of the objective. Snipers are deployed forward of the consolidating unit's OP or LP line. The snipers will observe for enemy assembly for counterattack and either harass with direct fire or call for indirect fire. Once the enemy begins movement to the line of departure, the sniper will interdict the advance of dismounted counterattacking forces or button up advancing armor. This interdiction will give the antitank weapons a better chance of success and survival. When sufficient numbers of snipers are available, hasty sniper ambushes are established to interdict patrols, probing elements, and enemy sniper teams that normally precede a counterattack. Snipers can also use these ambushes to harass the displaced enemy to prevent him from establishing a base to counterattack. One of the primary jobs of the sniper is to get the enemy to deploy early in the attack formation. This will cost the enemy positive control of his attack formation.

Interdiction

5-123. In the interdiction mission, snipers push out beyond the range of friendly support in an effort to preinfiltrate reestablished first-echelon defenses, infiltrate second-echelon defenses, or engage counterattacking forces from the rear.

They will interdict lines of communication in the enemy's rear areas and force him to commit more troops to the rear areas and weaken his forward lines. This can also cause the enemy to reinforce the wrong areas before the next attack.

Security

5-124. Because of their ability to remain undetected in close proximity to the enemy, snipers can maintain contact with displaced enemy forces. During consolidation, snipers range ahead of the main LP or OP line, determine the enemy's whereabouts, and continue to harass until the attack is resumed. Forward deployment also permits snipers to provide early warning of impending counterattacks.

Countersniping

5-125. Displaced enemy forces will often result in individuals or small groups getting cut off from their parent units. Oftentimes snipers will stay behind to disrupt the attacker's consolidation efforts. As these threats are small, snipers can track down and eliminate stay-behinds and isolated pockets of resistance. At the very least, snipers can suppress them until suitable forces can be spared to deal with them.

RESERVE MISSIONS

5-126. In a reserve role, snipers can give support where needed. They can reinforce success or react to enemy incursions. They can also provide stopgap measures until the commander can rally forces that are more appropriate. Snipers can maintain security in their own rear areas by using stealth and unconventional skills to seek out enemy forces. Their main support roles are as follows:

- Reinforcement involves attaching themselves directly to the unit engaged and adding their fires to those of the unit.
- Intervention enables the sniper to outflank the local resistance and suppress it with precision rifle fire.

5-127. Snipers may also conduct a dismounted movement to contact by deploying before the movement. Once deployed, they will move along the route to reconnoiter the route and select sniper hide positions to secure the route for the moving element. Depending on the number of snipers available, it is possible to secure a corridor over 1,500 meters at the widest (depending on the terrain) and as deep as permitted by the number of sniper teams and terrain. During reconnaissance and combat patrols, snipers may function as part of the security or support elements.

CONVENTIONAL DEFENSIVE OPERATIONS

5-128. The SF sniper's support to conventional defensive operations is similar to offensive operations. He can lend support anywhere on the battlefield including deep, rear, and main battle areas. However, conventional snipers normally operate in the main battle area in concert with their parent units—making SF sniper support seldom necessary in this area. The SF sniper's most important role is in the deep battle area. The rear battle area is also an area of employment, providing a rear-area threat exists.

5-129. Sniper operations in the deep battle area can be used to keep enemy efforts off-balance and directed toward rear area protection. The more enemy assets the sniper eliminates from the deep battle area, the fewer forces the enemy will have to execute attacks against the main effort. The sniper can also provide information on enemy strengths, location of reserves, and intentions.

SNIPER INTERDICTION

5-130. Just as in offensive operations, SOF units using snipers should deploy on a broad front to disrupt the enemy's order of battle. The main goal is to disrupt follow-on forces in the deep battle area. Snipers can assist in interdicting the enemy's soft underbelly—his unarmored logistics columns, fragile C2 nodes, and critical military weapons such as missiles and fire control equipment.

5-131. Defensive operations that could involve the sniper are—

- Area defense.
- Perimeter defense.
- Security forces.
- Reverse slope defense.
- Defense of built-up or fortified positions.
- River line defense.
- Mobile defense.
- Economy-of-force.
- Withdrawal operations.

5-132. Threat doctrine calls for simultaneous attacks at critical nodes located in U.S. rear areas. The sniper is ideally suited to locate and interdict the threat of enemy SO units that conduct such operations. The sniper uses the following methods to achieve these objectives:

Harassment

5-133. Snipers operate best in defensive operations beyond the FLOT to provide early warning of the approaching enemy, disorganize his attack, and cause him to deploy early. If armored vehicles are being used, it will cause the vehicle commanders to button up early. Snipers should closely integrate in the security force while performing this mission.

5-134. Snipers can also work directly into the FLOT defensive positions or assume their positions after withdrawal of the security fire. Snipers in defense of the FLOT should operate similarly to the crew-served weapons. Snipers can obtain optimum results by maximizing their standoff range to the targets, positioning on lucrative avenues of approach, and engaging targets of opportunity. Sniper positions should not be emplaced near obvious indirect fire targets. No matter how well concealed a hide is, if it is in the bursting radius of an indirect fire weapon, it can be compromised and destroyed.

5-135. The use of skilled marksmen will enhance the overall combat effectiveness of the defensive positions. Skilled marksmen are not necessarily snipers. They are simply skilled rifle shots who, for whatever reason, have neither the inclination nor the background skill to be successful snipers. However, they do possess the ability to engage targets at long ranges. When equipped with special weapons, such as caliber .50 or high-powered target rifles, they are particularly useful for conducting long-range harassment.

Delay

5-136. When friendly forces need to withdraw from contact with the enemy, snipers can delay and impede the enemy's advance. They deploy throughout the withdrawing unit's sector. By using a series of interlocking delay positions, a handful of snipers can interdict dismounted avenues of approach and severely impede advancing enemy forces. They can use successive delay positions to permit the withdrawing forces to reassemble and establish new defensive positions. Sniper elements must remain mobile to avoid decisive engagement with the attacking enemy. They can operate during the withdrawal to cover obstacles with precision rifle fire and thus increase the effectiveness of the obstacles. They can also be the stay-behind element and attack the enemy forces' rear area and supply columns.

Rear Area Protection

5-137. In this mission, snipers can enhance the protective measures surrounding sensitive facilities or installations. They can strengthen these measures by either establishing OPs along routes of access, acting as a reaction force to rear area penetrations, or by patrolling. Snipers will not normally patrol by themselves but as members of established security patrols.

5-138. The role of sniping in security operations is that of extending the depth and scope of the security effort. Specific roles include—

- Protecting critical installations, sites, or projects from infiltration.
- Dominating the gaps between units to prevent infiltration by enemy combat elements or patrols.
- Preventing the removal or breaching of obstacles.
- Tracking enemy patrols known to have penetrated into the rear area.

SNIPER SUPPORT TO DEFENSIVE HUMINT COLLECTION

5-139. Using snipers in defensive operations provides a variety of means to maintain constant offensive pressure on the enemy. Sniping in the defense is dependent on the collection and use of information. When the snipers collect information for their personal use, it is known as targeting. Information collected for organizational use is but an element of the total HUMINT collection effort of the snipers' unit. OPs are the snipers' primary means of collecting information in the defense. In the role of the observers, the snipers establish a series of OPs that dominate their sector. These OPs are of two types—overt and covert.

Overt Observation Post

5-140. This OP is not overt in that its location or function is known to the enemy, but that the snipers may engage high-priority targets from it. While firing from the OP may not necessarily reveal its exact location, it will certainly reveal the snipers' presence and the fact that such a location exists.

Covert Observation Post

5-141. The sniper uses this OP because it offers a commanding view of enemy positions. These posts should remain unknown to the enemy and should never be fired from, regardless of the temptation to do so. The information that the sniper collects from a well-sited covert OP is far more valuable than any targets that may appear.

CIVIL DISTURBANCE ASSISTANCE

5-142. The U.S. Army provides military assistance to civil authorities in civil disturbances when it is requested or directed IAW prevailing laws. When such assistance is requested, the military forces assist local authorities in the restoration and maintenance of law and order.

5-143. Military assistance is considered as a last resort. When committed, involvement is to the degree justified by the circumstances to restore law and order with a minimum loss of life and property. When using force, the guiding principle should be minimum force consistent with mission accomplishment.

5-144. The sniper team's precision fire and observation abilities give authorities a way to detect and eliminate criminal threats with low risk to innocent personnel. The use of sniper teams in civil disorders must be planned and controlled. They may be an important factor in the control and elimination of weapons fire directed against riot control authorities. Snipers functioning in this role must operate under strict ROE. However the team must never allow itself to be overrun. The team should always plan its multiple covert positions.

CHARACTERISTICS OF URBAN VIOLENCE

5-145. Crowd behavior during a civil disturbance is essentially emotional and without reason. The feelings and the momentum generated have a tendency to make the whole group act like its worst members. Skillful agitators or subversive elements exploit these psychological factors during these disorders. Regardless of the reason for violence, the results may consist of indiscriminate looting and burning or open and violent attacks on officials, buildings, and innocent passersby. Rioters may set fire to buildings and vehicles to—

- Block the advance of troops.
- Create confusion and diversion.
- Achieve goals of property destruction, looting, and sniping.

5-146. In addition, organized rioters or agitators may use sniper fire to cause government forces to overreact.

SNIPER SUPPORT DURING CIVIL DISTURBANCES

5-147. The sniper team uses planning factors to estimate the amount of time, coordination, and effort that it will take to support local authorities, when faced with an enemy sniper threat or any type of civil disturbance such as a riot. For the team's mission to run smoothly and be a success, all participants should consider the following factors.

Briefings

5-148. Sniper teams must receive a detailed briefing on the areas and routes within the riot area. Representatives of local authorities should be assigned to the sniper teams for protection and communications with local indigenous personnel.

Adequate Personnel

5-149. The civil authorities should have sufficient sniper teams to provide maximum versatility to the riot control personnel. Sniper teams should also have at least one reaction team assigned to them. This capability will permit the team to direct a reaction team to a troublemaker for apprehension without the requirement to fire a weapon. These teams should consist of both military and local authority personnel.

Observation Areas and Fields of Fire

5-150. Observation areas and fields of fire are clearly defined by streets and highways. However, surveillance and detection are complicated by the numerous rooftops, windows, and doorways from which hostile fire may be directed. Sniper teams take maximum advantage of dominant buildings or rooftops to maintain continuous observation of a riot scene. Mutually supporting teams cover blind spots or dead space within the area. Sniper teams must place themselves at various heights to give them view into the different multistoried buildings.

Cover and Concealment

5-151. Built-up areas offer excellent cover and concealment for both the rioters and the sniper teams.

Avenues of Approach

5-152. The best avenues of approach to a riot scene, or to points of observation and firing positions, are through building interiors. Movement through streets may be difficult and easily detected by rioters. Sniper teams should also consider underground passages such as cableways.

Operations

5-153. Sniper teams should operate in each established area. The teams remain at a sufficient distance from control troops to keep from getting involved in direct riot actions.

Firing Positions

5-154. The firing position should provide the maximum stability, because precision fire is used to wound and not to kill. A stray shot that wounds or kills a woman, child, or unarmed rioter may only inflame an already riotous situation. When firing from a window, the sniper team should fire, if possible, from a supported position in the back of the room. The distance will muffle the muzzle blast and keep the muzzle flash from being noticed. If the sniper shows his rifle or part of his body, it may invite fire from weapons-equipped rioting personnel. When possible, he should use a silencer on his sniper rifle.

Camouflage

5-155. Sniper teams should dress in drab or blending clothing to prevent identification or observation. However, snipers must wear an identifying mark so as not to be engaged by friendly forces.

Civil Authorities

5-156. Since civil authorities are in charge, snipers maintain a direct line of communications (LOC) with the civilian who permits or directs snipers to engage. Civil authorities also determine the caliber of weapon as well as the type of ammunition. However, usually anything within 300 meters is engaged with 5.56-mm ammunition unless special penetration capability is required.

Sniper Team Control

5-157. A key to effective sniper team use is control. When directed to engage in countersniping activities, the sniper team's actions must be swift and precise. The sniper leader must maintain positive control over the teams at all times.

Rules of Engagement

5-158. When countersniping is required, the sniper team should direct its precision fire to wound rather than to kill, if possible, unless in direct defense of human life.

5-159. Snipers employed to counteract sniper fire from a street disorder require quick and decisive action. When directed to support the control forces during a street disorder, the sniper team—

- Deploys to rooftops or vantage points providing observation and fields of fire into the riot area.
- Institutes communications with the commander.
- Begins observation immediately and continues it.
- Relays information continuously to the commander.
- Conducts countersniping actions as directed.

5-160. During civil disorders, rioters may seize control of buildings for the purpose of using the vantage points of rooftops or windows from which to direct hostile sniper fire on riot control forces. The sniper team may have to provide covering fire to allow the searching or clearing team to approach and clear the building. On the other hand, the sniper may have to use precision fire to engage the hostile sniper if the hostile sniping is directed at control authorities in mob control actions.

5-161. Upon identifying or locating a riotous sniper who is directing fire at fire-fighting personnel, the sniper immediately reacts to reduce the hostile sniper fire. He directs this countersniper fire with accuracy to kill.

5-162. Civil authorities must try to quickly control looting because it may also lead to more serious acts of murder and arson, often against innocent nonparticipants. The sniper team's employment to assist in looting control is mainly for observation, communication, and to act as a covering force should the looters fire upon the control forces. When control forces are fired upon, the sniper team immediately engages the riotous sniper to facilitate apprehension by the control forces.

5-163. The sniper team's role in support of riot control forces is equally important during the hours of darkness. Optical equipment, to include NVDs, allows the sniper team to provide prolonged night observation. Therefore, the team can sufficiently accompany patrol forces, man observation posts and roadblocks, or cover control troops during mob control activities.

5-164. Use of snipers during civil disturbances can become a source of greater agitation among the rioters. Civil authorities should publicly remove compromised snipers while leaving the other snipers in place. In many instances this removal will embolden the agitators and permit rapid identification for quick apprehension by control personnel. In the same vein, firers may become more relaxed and show themselves for easier identification by the posted countersnipers.

CHAPTER 6

Sniper Operations in Urban Terrain

Snipers are extremely effective in urban terrain. Their long-range precision fire can engage targets at a distance; their advanced optics can discriminate individual point targets to save innocent bystanders or protect property; and their observation skills can offer superior intelligence-collection capabilities. In an urban environment, the sniper is both a casualty producer and an intimidating psychological weapon.

URBAN TERRAIN

6-1. Urban terrain consists mainly of man-made structures. Buildings are the main components of urban terrain. They provide cover and concealment, limit fields of fire and observation, and impair movement. Thick-walled buildings provide excellent protection from hostile fire.

6-2. Urban streets are generally avenues of approach. However, forces moving along streets are often channalized by buildings and terrain that offer minimal off-road maneuver space. Obstacles on streets prove difficult to bypass, due to these restrictive avenues of approach.

6-3. Underground systems found in some urban areas are easily overlooked but can be important to the outcome of operations. They include subways, sewers, cellars, and utility systems.

6-4. Civilians will be present in urban operations, often in great numbers. Concern for the safety of noncombatants may restrict fire and limit maneuver options available to the commander.

CATEGORIES OF URBAN TERRAIN

6-5. The world is largely urban in terms of population concentration. Commanders categorize urban terrain as large cities, towns and small cities, villages, and strip areas.

Large Cities (population greater than 100,000)

6-6. In Europe, other than the former Soviet Union, there are approximately 410 cities with a population of more than 100,000. Large cities frequently form the core of a larger, densely populated urban complex consisting of the city, its suburban areas, and small towns. Such complexes have the appearance of a single large and continuous city containing millions of people and occupying vast areas of land.

Towns and Small Cities (population of 3,000 to 100,000)

6-7. These areas are mostly located along major lines of communications and situated in river valleys. Similar to larger cities, these areas are continuing to expand and will eventually form new concentrations or merge with existing ones.

Villages (population of less than 3,000)

6-8. In most cases, villages are agriculturally oriented and usually exist among the more open cultivated areas.

Strip Areas

6-9. These built-up areas generally form connecting links between villages and towns. These areas also exist among LOCs leading to larger complexes.

DESCRIPTIONS OF URBAN TERRAIN

6-10. Within the city, urban terrain differs based on size, location, and history. The areas within the city are generally categorized as follows:

- *Industrial Areas and Residential Sprawl.* Residential areas consist of some houses or small dwellings with yards, gardens, trees, and fences. Street patterns are normally rectangular or curving. Industrial areas consist of one- to three-story buildings of low, flat-roofed factories or warehouses, generally located on or along major rail and highway routes. In both regions, there are many open areas.
- *Core Periphery.* The core periphery consists of narrow streets (12 to 20 meters wide) with continuous fronts of brick and heavy-walled concrete buildings. The height of the buildings is generally uniform, two to three stories in small towns and five to ten stories in large cities.
- *City Cores and Outlying High-Rise Areas.* Typical city cores of today are made of high-rise buildings that vary greatly in height and allow for more open space between buildings. Outlying high-rise areas are dominated by this open-construction style to a greater degree than city cores. Generally, streets form a rectangular pattern.
- *Commercial Ribbons.* These are rows of stores, shops, or boutiques built along either side of major streets through the built-up areas. Generally, these streets are 25 meters wide or wider. The buildings are uniformly two to three stories tall.

NATURE OF URBAN COMBAT

6-11. Urban combat usually occurs when a city is between two natural obstacles and it cannot be bypassed, the seizure of the city contributes to the attainment of an overall objective, or political or humanitarian concerns require the seizure or retention of the city.

6-12. In the city, the ranges of observation and fields of fire are reduced by the structures as well as the smoke and dust of combat. Targets will generally be seen briefly at ranges of 200 meters or less.

6-13. Units fighting in urban areas often become isolated by an enemy. Therefore, snipers must have the skill, initiative, and courage to operate effectively while isolated from their unit. Combat in more up-to-date nations can no longer avoid urban areas; therefore, snipers must train and be psychologically prepared for the demands of urban combat.

6-14. The defender will generally have the advantage over the attacker in urban combat. The defender occupies strong positions, whereas the attacker must expose himself to advance. Also, the greatly reduced LOS ranges, built-in obstacles, and compartmented terrain require the commitment of more troops for a given frontage. Troop density may be three to five times greater for both attacker and defender in urban combat than in natural environments.

6-15. Density of structures degrades radio communications. This factor, combined with limited observation, makes control of forces difficult. The well-established defender will probably use wire communications to enhance control, thus adding to his advantage.

6-16. Soldiers may encounter a greater degree of stress during urban combat. Continual close combat, intense pressure, high casualties, the fleeting nature of targets, and fire from an unseen enemy may produce increased psychological strain and physical fatigue.

6-17. Commanders may have to restrict their use of weapons and tactics to minimize collateral damage. This restriction may be necessary to preserve a nation's cultural heritage and gain the support of the population. In such cases, snipers are ideally suited to deliver discriminatory fire against selected targets.

6-18. Attacks will generally limit artillery fires to the direct fire mode. Units use this method to avoid reducing the city to rubble. Direct fire causes few casualties and tends to enhance the defender's fortifications and concealment. It also restricts the attacker's avenues of approach.

6-19. Forces engaged in urban fighting use large quantities of munitions. Units committed to urban combat must also have special equipment, such as grappling hooks, ropes, snaplinks, construction materials, axes, sandbags, and ladders.

6-20. Urban combat historically has presented chances for looting. Looting can break down discipline, reduce alertness, increase vulnerability, and delay the progress of the unit. It also alienates the civilian population.

EVALUATING URBAN TERRAIN

6-21. When the sniper evaluates urban terrain, he should consider the following factors:

- *Observation and Fields of Fire.* Buildings on the edge of a city provide better fields of fire than buildings in the interior. In the city, tall buildings with numerous windows often provide the best fields of fire, especially if the buildings have spaces between them. However, the sniper should never choose the outermost buildings as they are usually subjected to the greater amount of fire and preparatory bombardment.
- *Avenues of Approach.* The best way to gain entry into a building is from the top. Therefore, the most important avenue of approach to look for is one that quickly leads to the top (fire escapes, drainpipes, or adjacent buildings). Personnel must protect these when the sniper is in the defense and allow him use when required.
- *Key Control Points.* The key points in a building are entrances, hallways, and stairs; troops that control these areas control the building.
- *Obstacles.* Doors and fire barriers are common in commercial buildings. They become obstacles if they are shut and secured. Furniture and appliances can also be obstacles in a building. Snipers can also use barbed wire effectively inside a building because it further restricts movement.
- *Cover and Concealment.* Buildings with brick walls and few, narrow windows provide the best balance between cover and concealment and fields of fire. Roofs provide little protection; snipers usually have better protection in the lower stories than directly under the roof. (An exception to this rule is the parking garage.) Floor layouts with many small rooms provide more protection than floor layouts with larger rooms.
- *Intra-City Distribution of Building Types.* The sniper can generally determine the layout of a city by the distribution of the buildings within the city. Types and layout are as follows:
  - Mass construction buildings (older apartments and hotels) are the most common structures in old city cores and older built-up areas (two-thirds of the total area). They are usually constructed of bricks or cement block.
  - Frame and heavy clad, steel and concrete-framed, as well light clad, glass, multistory buildings are found in the core area—a city's most valuable land—where, as centers of economic and political power they have potentially high military significance.
  - Open spaces (for example, parks, athletic fields, and golf courses) account for about 15 percent of an average city's area. Most of this area is suitable for airmobile operations.
  - Frame and light clad, wood, and cosmetic brick structures dominate residential sprawl areas.
- *Environmental Considerations.* Environmental factors will influence the effectiveness of the sniper. He should closely evaluate these factors during the selection and preparation of the urban sniper hide site.

6-22. Population density will affect the ease of movement to and from the hide as well as the ability of the team to remain undetected. The sniper must also consider the safety of the local civilian population. Dependent upon the type of operation, eliminating civilian collateral damage may be an overriding factor for measuring success. In urban areas, the sniper team must be prepared to deal with pet animals. If these pets pose a threat to the sniper team (detection or actual attack), it may be necessary to eliminate or silence the pets. Snipers should be aware of the possible consequences if these animals should suddenly disappear.

6-23. The media, in the form of international news television and radio commentators, will probably be present in some strength in all future conflicts. Their presence may compromise or negate the effectiveness of the snipers' mission and must be a consideration.

6-24. Glass or windows can cause problems for the sniper. Depending on the mission, the sniper may be able to remove the glass during hide construction. If not, he must devise a method of emergency glass removal.

6-25. Natural and artificial lighting will impact on the effectiveness of standoff optics and NVDs. All lights in the hide should be off and secured or deactivated to avoid inadvertent activation.

6-26. Ambient noise levels may aid in the occupation and construction of the hide. It could also provide a desirable time window for the snipers to engage targets. In urban areas, most noise levels will go in cycles from high levels during the day to low levels at night.

LINE OF-SIGHT FACTORS

6-27. Streets serving areas composed mostly of one type of building normally have a common pattern. Street widths are grouped into three major classes:

- Narrow (7 to 15 meters)—such places as medieval sections of European cities.
- Medium (15 to 25 meters)—newer, planned sections of most cities.
- Wide (25 to 50 meters)—areas where buildings are located along broad boulevards or set far apart on large parcels of land.

6-28. When a street is narrow, observing or firing into windows of a building across the street can be difficult because an observer must look along the building rather than into the windows. When the street is wide, the observer has a better chance to look and fire into and out of the window openings.

6-29. The same limitation on LOS occurs when looking up or down tall buildings.

SOURCES OF INFORMATION IN URBAN TERRAIN

6-30. Operations in urban terrain require detailed intelligence. Snipers should have the following materials for planning operations:

- *Maps and Aerial Photos.* Although tactical maps do not show man-made objects in enough detail for tactical operations in urban terrain, they do show the details of terrain adjacent to urban areas. The sniper should supplement tactical maps with both vertical and oblique aerial photos. From the aerial photos, the sniper should construct plan view sketches to locate the best LOS positions.
- *Civil Government and Local Military Information.* The sniper can obtain considerable current information on practically all details of a city from civil governments and local military forces. Items include:
  - Large-scale city maps.
  - Diagrams of underground sewer, utility, transport, and miscellaneous systems.
  - Key public buildings and rosters of key personnel.
  - Size and density of the population.
  - Police and security capabilities.
  - Civil defense, air raid shelters, and firefighting capabilities.
  - Utility systems, medical facilities, and mass communications facilities.

CAMOUFLAGE TECHNIQUES FOR URBAN TERRAIN

6-31. To survive in urban combat, the sniper must supplement cover and concealment with camouflage. He must study the surroundings in the area to properly camouflage himself. He must make the firing positions look like the surrounding terrain. For instance, if there is no damage to buildings, he will not make loopholes for firing and will use only the materials needed. Any excess material can reveal his position. For example, if defending the city park, the sniper will use the entire park for resources; he will not denude a small area near the position for camouflage material.

6-32. Buildings provide numerous concealed positions. Thick masonry, stone, or brick walls offer excellent protection from direct fire and provide concealed routes. If the tactical situation permits, the sniper will inspect positions from the enemy's viewpoint. He will conduct routine checks to see if the camouflage remains material-looking and actually conceals the position. He should not remove his shirt because exposed skin reflects light and could attract the enemy's attention.

6-33. When using urban camouflage techniques, the sniper must consider the following:

- *Use of Shadows.* Buildings in urban areas throw sharp shadows. The sniper can use the shadow to aid in concealment during movement. He will avoid lighted areas around windows and loopholes. A lace curtain or a piece of cheesecloth provides additional concealment to snipers in interiors of rooms, if curtains are common in the area.

- *Color and Texture.* The need to break up the silhouette of helmets and individual equipment exists in urban areas as elsewhere. However, burlap or canvas strips are a more effective camouflage garnish than foliage. Predominant colors are normally browns, tans, and sometimes grays, rather than greens; but the sniper should evaluate each camouflage location separately.
- *Dust.* In weapons emplacements, the sniper should use a wet blanket, canvas, or type of cloth to keep dust from rising when the weapons are fired.
- *Background.* Snipers must pay attention to the background to ensure that they are not silhouetted or skylined, but rather blend into their surroundings. Use of a neutral drop cloth to his rear will help the sniper blend with his background.
- *Common Camouflage Errors.* To defeat enemy urban camouflage, the sniper should look for errors such as tracks or other evidence of activity, shine or shadows, unnatural or peculiar colors or textures, muzzle flash smoke or dust, unnatural sounds and smells, and finally, movements. Things to remember when camouflaging include—
  - Use dummy positions to distract the enemy and make him reveal his position by firing.
  - Use the terrain and alter camouflage habits to suit the surroundings.
  - Do not forget deceptive camouflage of buildings.
  - Continue to improve positions. Reinforce fighting positions with sandbags or other shrapnel and blast absorbing material.
  - Do not upset the natural look of the area.
  - Do not make positions obvious by clearing away too much debris for fields of fire.
  - Choose firing ports in inconspicuous spots when available.

INFILTRATION AND EXFILTRATION IN URBAN TERRAIN

6-34. A sniper can more easily infiltrate into the outskirts of a town because the outskirts are usually not strongly defended. Its defenders may only have a series of antitank positions, security elements on the principal approach, or positions blocking the approaches to key features in the town. The strong points and reserves are deeper in the city.

6-35. As part of a larger force, the sniper moves by stealth on secondary streets using cover and concealment of back alleys and buildings. These moves enable him to assist in seizing key terrain features and isolating enemy positions, thus aiding following units' entry into the urban area. Sniper teams may also infiltrate into the city after the initial force has seized a foothold and move into their respective sniper positions.

6-36. Snipers may use mortar and artillery fire to attract the enemy's attention and cover the sound of infiltrating troops. They should infiltrate when visibility is poor; chances of success are greater if there are no civilians in the area. Snipers may also infiltrate into a city (as part of a larger force) during an airborne or airmobile operation.

6-37. During exfiltration, snipers must be extremely careful to avoid detection. As in infiltration, snipers must use stealth and all available cover and concealment when leaving their positions. Snipers should always try to exfiltrate during darkness.

MOVEMENT TECHNIQUES IN URBAN TERRAIN

6-38. Movement in urban areas is one of the first fundamental skills that a sniper must master. He must practice movement techniques until they become second nature. To minimize exposure to enemy fire, the urban sniper must move so that he—

- Does not silhouette himself, but keeps low at all times.
- Avoids open areas (streets, alleys, parks).
- Selects the next covered position before moving.
- Conceals movement by using buildings, rubble, foliage, smoke, or limited visibility.
- Advances rapidly from one position to another, but not so rapidly that he creates dust clouds or noise that will help the enemy locate him.
- Does not mask his covering fire.
- Remains alert, ready for the unexpected.

6-39. Specific movement techniques used frequently in urban operations must be learned by all snipers. They are—

- *Crossing a Wall.* After the sniper has reconnoitered the other side, he quickly rolls over the wall, keeping a low silhouette. The speed and the low silhouette will deny the enemy a good target.
- *Moving Around a Corner.* Corners are dangerous. The sniper must observe the area around the corner before he moves beyond the corner. The most common mistake that a sniper makes at a corner is allowing his weapon to extend beyond the corner, exposing his position (flagging). Also, a sniper should not show his head at the height that an enemy soldier would expect to see it. When using the correct technique for looking around a corner, the sniper lies flat on the ground and does not extend his weapon beyond the corner of the building. He exposes his head or a hand-held mirror (at ground level) only enough to permit observation around the corner.
- *Moving Past Windows.* When using the correct technique for passing a window, the sniper stays below the window level, taking care not to silhouette himself in the window. He hugs the side of the building. An enemy gunner inside the building would have to expose himself to fire from another position if he wished to engage the sniper.
- *Moving Past Basement Windows.* When using the correct procedure of negotiating a basement window, the sniper stays close to the wall of the building and steps or jumps over the window without exposing his legs.
- *Using Doorways.* The sniper should not use doorways as entrances or exits. If he must use a doorway as an exit, he should move quickly through it to his next covered position, staying as low as possible to avoid silhouetting himself.
- *Moving Parallel to a Building.* At times, it may not be possible to use interiors of buildings for a route of advance. To correctly move along the outside of a building, the sniper moves along the side of the building, staying in the shadows, presenting a low silhouette, and moves deliberately to his next position. He must plan one position ahead of his next position. This will prevent getting into a dead-end position with nowhere to go.
- *Crossing Open Areas.* Snipers should avoid open areas such as streets, alleys, and parks whenever possible. However, they can be crossed safely if the sniper applies certain fundamentals. Even using the correct method for crossing, the sniper may employ a distraction or limited visibility to conceal his movement. He crosses the open area at the shortest distance between two points.

6-40. Before moving from one position to another, a sniper should make a visual reconnaissance and select the position that will give him the best cover and concealment. At the same time, he should select the route that he will take to that position.

> **NOTE**
> The sniper team should not move together when crossing from one building to another or across an open area.

BUILDING ENTRY TECHNIQUES

6-41. When entering a building, a sniper may be required to enter by means other than through doorways or reach top levels of buildings by means other than stairs.

6-42. The sniper team can use various means, such as ladders, drainpipes, vines, helicopters, or the roofs and windows of adjoining buildings, to reach the top floor or roof of a building. Additional aids and methods to reach higher levels include—

- The two-man lift, supported and unsupported; the two-man lift with heels raised; the one-man lift; the two-man pull; and individual climbing techniques. These techniques are more commonly used to gain entry into areas at lower levels.
- Ladders or grappling hooks with knotted ropes. By attaching a grappling hook to the end of a scaling rope, a sniper can scale a wall, swing from one building to another, or gain entry to an upstairs window.
- Rappelling. The sniper can use this combat technique to descend from the roof of a tall building to other levels or to a window.

SNIPER SUPPORT IN URBAN OPERATIONS

6-43. A sniper should be given general areas (buildings or a group of buildings) in which to position himself, but he selects the best positions for engagements. Sniper positions should cover obstacles, roofs, gaps in the final protective fires, and dead space. The sniper also selects numerous secondary and supplementary positions to cover his areas of responsibility. He should think three-dimensionally.

6-44. The sniper determines his engagement priorities by the relative importance of the targets to the effective operations of the enemy. The following are normally sniper targets:

- Enemy snipers.
- Key leaders.
- Tank commanders.
- Direct fire-support weapons crewmen.
- Crew-served weapons personnel.
- Forward observers.
- Radiotelephone operators.
- Protected equipment.

6-45. The characteristics of built-up areas and the nature of urban warfare impact on both the effectiveness of the SWS and how the sniper can use it. The sniper must consider the following basic factors during urban operations:

- *Relative Location of the Shooter and the Target.* Both the target and the shooter may be inside or outside of buildings, or either one may be inside a building while the other is outside.
- *Structural Configuration of Buildings.* The basic classes of structures encountered in a built-up area can generally be classified as concrete, masonry, or wooden. However, any one building may include a combination of these materials. All buildings offer concealment, although the degree of protection varies with the material used.
- *Firing Ranges and Angles.* Engagement ranges may vary from distances of less than 100 meters up to the maximum effective range of a sniper system. Depression and elevation limits may create dead space. Target engagement from oblique angles, either vertical or horizontal, demands increased marksmanship skills. Urban areas often limit snipers to firing down or across streets, but open spaces of urban areas permit engagements at long ranges.
- *Visibility Limitations.* Added to the weather conditions that limit visibility are the urban factors of target masking and increased dead space caused by buildings and rubble. Observation through smoke, dust, and concealment offered by shaded areas, rubble, and man-made structures influence visibility.

DURING AN ATTACK IN URBAN TERRAIN

6-46. Snipers employed during the attack of a built-up area are usually divided into three phases:

- Phase I should allow snipers to isolate the battle area by seizing terrain features that dominate the avenues of approach. Snipers deliver long-range precision fire at targets of opportunity.
- Phase II consists of the advance to the built-up area and seizure of a foothold on its edge. It is during this period that snipers displace forward and assume their initial position from which to support continuation of the attack.
- Phase III consists of the advance through the built-up area IAW the plan of attack. Sniper teams should operate in each zone of action, moving with and supporting the infantry units. They should operate at a sufficient distance from the riflemen to keep from getting involved in firefights but close enough to kill more distant targets that threaten the advance. Some sniper teams can operate independently of the infantry on missions of search for targets of opportunity, particularly the search for enemy snipers.

6-47. Snipers that are in a defensive posture should place themselves in buildings that offer the best long-range fields of fire and all-around observation. They are assigned various missions, such as—

- Providing countersniper fire.
- Firing at targets of opportunity.

- Denying the enemy access to certain areas or avenues of approach.
- Providing fire support over barricades and obstacles.
- Observing the flank and rear areas.
- Supporting counterattacks.
- Preventing enemy observation.

INTERNAL SECURITY OPERATIONS

6-48. Commanders can use snipers in internal security operations during urban guerrilla warfare and hostage situations. The following paragraphs explain each situation.

Urban Guerrilla Warfare

6-49. In this type of environment, the sniper dominates the AO by delivery of selective, aimed fire against specific targets as authorized by local commanders. Usually this authorization comes when targets are about to employ firearms or other lethal weapons against the peacekeeping force or innocent civilians. The sniper's other role, almost equally as important as his primary role, is the gathering and reporting of intelligence. Within the above roles, some specific tasks that may be assigned include—

- When authorized by local commanders, engaging dissidents or urban guerrillas who are involved in hijacking, kidnapping, or holding hostages.
- Engaging urban guerrilla snipers as opportunity targets or as part of a deliberate clearance operation.
- Covertly occupying concealed positions to observe selected areas.
- Recording and reporting all suspicious activities in the area of observations.
- Assisting in coordinating the activities of other elements by taking advantage of hidden observation posts.
- Providing protection for other elements of the peacekeeping force, including firemen and repair crews.

6-50. In urban guerrilla operations, there are several limiting factors that snipers would not encounter in unconventional warfare. Some of these limitations follow:

- There is no forward edge of the battle area (FEBA) and therefore no "no man's land" in which to operate. Snipers can therefore expect to operate in entirely hostile surroundings in most circumstances.
- The enemy is hidden from or perfectly camouflaged among the everyday populace that surrounds the sniper. The guerrilla force usually uses an identifying clothing code each day to distinguish themselves from civilians. This code is a PIR each day. The sooner the sniper can begin to distinguish this code, the easier his job will be.
- In areas where confrontation between peacekeeping forces and the urban guerrillas takes place, the guerrilla dominates the ground entirely from the point of view of continued presence and observation. He knows every yard of ground; it is ground of his own choosing. Anything approximating a conventional stalk to and occupation of a hide is doomed to failure.
- Although the sniper is not subject to the same difficult conditions as he is in conventional war, he is subject to other pressures. These include not only legal and political restraints but also requirements to kill or wound without the motivational stimulus normally associated with the battlefield.
- In conventional war, the sniper normally needs no clearance to fire his shot. In urban guerrilla warfare, the sniper must make every effort possible to determine the need to open fire, and that doing so constitutes reasonable or minimum force under the circumstances.

Hostage Situations

6-51. Snipers and commanding officers must appreciate that even a well-placed shot may not always result in the instantaneous incapacitation of a terrorist. Even the best sniper, armed with the best weapon and bullet combination, cannot guarantee the desired results. Even an instantly fatal shot may not prevent the death of a hostage when muscle spasms in the terrorist's body trigger his weapon. As a rule then, the commander should use a sniper only when all other means of solving a hostage situation have been exhausted.

6-52. **Accuracy Requirements.** The sniper must consider the size of the target in a hostage situation. The head is the only place on the human body where a bullet strike can cause instantaneous death. (Generally, the normal human being will live 8 to 10 seconds after being shot directly in the heart.) The entire head of a man is a relatively large target, measuring approximately 7 inches wide and 10 inches high. But the area where a bullet strike can cause instantaneous death is a much smaller target. The portion of the brain that controls all motor reflex actions is the medulla. When viewed at eye level, it is located directly behind the eyes, runs generally from ear lobe to ear lobe, and is roughly 2 inches wide. In reality then, the size of the sniper's target is 2 inches, not 7 inches. The easiest way for the sniper to view this area under all circumstances is to visualize a 2-inch ball (the medulla) directly in the middle of the 7-inch ball (the head).

6-53. Application of the windage and elevation rule makes it clear that the average sniper cannot and should not attempt to deliver an instantly killing head shot beyond 200 meters. To ask him to do so requires him to do something that the rifle and ammunition combination available to him will not do.

6-54. **Position Selection.** Generally, the selection of a firing position for a hostage situation is not much different from selecting a firing position for any other form of combat. The same guidelines and rules apply. The terrain and situation will dictate the choice of firing positions.

6-55. Although the commander should use the sniper only as a last resort, he should place the sniper into position as early as possible. Early positioning will enable him to precisely estimate his ranges, positively identify both the hostages and the terrorists, and select alternate firing positions for use if the situation should change. He is also the main HUMINT asset to the command element.

Command and Control

6-56. Once the commander decides to use the sniper, all C2 of his actions should pass to the sniper team leader. At no time should the sniper receive the command to fire from someone not in command. When he receives clearance to fire, then he and the sniper team leader alone will decide exactly when.

6-57. If the commander uses more than one sniper team to engage one or more targets, it is imperative that the same ROE apply to all teams. However, it will be necessary for snipers to communicate with each other. The most reliable method is to establish a "land line" or TA-312 telephone loop much like a gun loop used in artillery battery firing positions. This loop enables all teams to communicate with all the others without confusion about frequencies or radio procedures.

SNIPER AMBUSH IN URBAN TERRAIN

6-58. In cases where intelligence is forthcoming that a target will be in a specific place at a specific time, a sniper ambush is frequently a better alternative than a more cumbersome cordon operation.

6-59. Close reconnaissance is easier than in normal operations. The sniper can carry it out as part of a normal patrol without raising any undue suspicion. The principal difficulty is getting the ambush party to its hide undetected. To place snipers in positions that are undetected will require some form of deception plan. The team leader often forms a routine search operation in at least platoon strength. During the course of the search, the snipers position themselves in their hide. They remain in position when the remainder of the force withdraws. This tactic is especially effective when carried out at night.

6-60. Once in position, the snipers must be able to remain for lengthy periods in the closest proximity to the enemy and their sympathizers. Their security is tenuous at best. Most urban OPs have "dead spots." This trait, combined with the fact that special ambush positions are frequently out of direct observation by other friendly forces, makes them highly susceptible to attack, especially from guerrillas armed with explosives. The uncertainty about being observed on entry is a constant worry to the snipers. This feeling can and does have a most disquieting effect on the sniper and underlines the need for highly trained men of stable character.

6-61. If the ambush position cannot be directly supported from a permanent position, the commander must place a "backup" force on immediate notice to extract the snipers after the ambush or in case of compromise. Commanders normally assume that during the ambush the snipers cannot make their exit without assistance. They will be surrounded by large, extremely hostile crowds. Consequently, backup forces must not only be nearby but also be sufficient in size to handle the extraction of the snipers.

URBAN HIDES

6-62. A sniper team's success or failure greatly depends on each sniper's ability to place accurate fire on the enemy with the least possible exposure to enemy fire. Consequently, the sniper must constantly seek firing positions and use them properly when he finds them. Positions in urban terrain are quite different from positions in the field. The sniper team can normally choose from inside attics to street-level positions in basements. This type of terrain is ideal for a sniper and can provide the team a means of stopping an enemy's advance through its area of responsibility. However, one important fact for the team to remember is that in this type of terrain the enemy will use every asset it has to detect and eliminate them. The following paragraphs explain the two categories of urban hide positions.

HASTY HIDE

6-63. The sniper normally occupies a hasty hide in the attack or the early stages of the defense. This position allows the sniper to place fire upon the enemy while using available cover to gain protection from enemy fire. There are some common hasty firing positions in a built-up area and techniques for occupying them are as follows:

- *Firing From Corners of Buildings.* The corner of a building, used properly, provides cover for a hasty firing position. A sniper must be capable of firing his weapon from either shoulder to minimize body exposure to the enemy. A common mistake when firing around corners is firing from the standing position. The sniper exposes himself at the height the enemy would expect a target to appear and risks exposing the entire length of his body as a target.
- *Firing From Behind Walls.* When firing from behind a wall, the sniper should attempt to fire around cover rather than over it.
- *Firing From Windows.* In a built-up area windows provide readily accessible firing ports. However, the sniper must not allow his weapon to protrude beyond the window. It is an obvious sign of the firer's position, especially at night when the muzzle flash can easily be seen. A sniper should position himself as far into the room as possible to prevent the muzzle flash from being seen. He should fire from a supported position (table and sandbag) low enough to avoid silhouetting himself. He should use room shadow during darkness and leave blinds or shades drawn to a maximum to avoid being seen. The sniper must be careful when firing to prevent the drapes or curtains from moving due to the muzzle blast. He can do this by tacking them down or using sufficient standoff. He should also use drop cloths behind himself to cut down on silhouetting.
- *Firing From an Unprepared Loophole.* The sniper may fire through a hole torn in the wall, thus avoiding the windows. He should stay as far from the loophole as possible so the muzzle does not protrude beyond the wall, thus concealing the muzzle flash. If the hole is natural damage, he should ensure that it is not the only hole in the building. If the sniper constructs it, then the hole must blend with the building or he should construct multiple holes. There are several openings in a building that naturally occur and the sniper can enlarge or use them.
- *Firing From the Peak of a Roof.* This position provides a vantage point for snipers that increases their field of vision and the ranges at which they can engage targets. A chimney, a smokestack, or any other object protruding from the roof of a building can reduce the size of the target exposed, and the sniper should use it. However, his head and weapon breaks the clean line of a rooftop and this position is a "last choice" position.
- *Firing When No Cover Is Available.* When no cover is available, target exposure can be reduced by firing from the prone position, firing from shadows, presenting no silhouette against buildings or skyline, and using tall grass, weeds, or shrubbery for concealment if available.

PREPARED HIDE

6-64. A prepared hide is one built or improved to allow the sniper to engage a particular area, avenue of approach, or enemy position while reducing his exposure to return fire. Common sense and imagination are the sniper team's only limitation in the construction of urban hides. The sniper must follow several principles in urban and field environments. In urban environments, the sniper must still avoid silhouetting, consider reflections and light refraction, and be sure to minimize muzzle blast effects on dust, curtains, and other surroundings. The team constructs and occupies one of the following positions or a variation thereof:

- *Chimney Hide.* The sniper can use a chimney or any other structure that protrudes through the roof as a base to build his sniper position. Part of the roofing material is removed to allow the sniper to fire around the chimney while standing inside the building on beams or a platform with only his head and shoulders above the roof (behind the chimney). He should use sandbags on the sides of the position to protect his flanks.

- *Roof Hide.* When preparing a sniper position on a roof that has no protruding structure to provide protection, the sniper should prepare his position underneath on the enemy side of the roof (Figure 6-1, page 589). He should remove a small piece of roofing material to allow him to engage targets in his sector. He then reinforces the position with sandbags and prepares it so that the only sign that a position exists is the missing piece of roofing material. The sniper should also remove other pieces of roofing to deceive the enemy as to the true sniper position. The sniper should not be visible from outside the building. Care must be taken to hide the muzzle flash from outside the building.

Figure 6-1. Roof hide

- *Room Hide.* In a room hide, the sniper team uses an existing room and fires through a window or loophole (Figure 6-2). It can use existing furniture, such as desks or tables to establish weapon support. When selecting a position, teams must notice both front and back window positions. To avoid silhouetting, they may need to use a backdrop, such as a dark-colored blanket, canvas, carpet, and a screen. Screens (common screening material) are important since they allow the sniper teams maximum observation and deny observation by the enemy. They must not remove curtains; however, they can open windows or remove single panes of glass. Remember, teams can randomly remove panes in other windows so the position is not obvious.

Figure 6-2. Internal view of a room hide

- *Crawl Space Hide.* The sniper team builds this position into the space between floors in multistory buildings (Figure 6-3). Loopholes are difficult to construct, but a damaged building helps considerably. Escape routes can be holes knocked into the floor or ceiling. Carpet or furniture placed over escape holes or replaced ceiling tiles will conceal them until needed.

Figure 6-3. Crawl space hide

PRINCIPLES FOR SELECTING AND OCCUPYING SNIPER FIRING POSITIONS

6-65. Upon receiving a mission, the sniper team locates the target area and then determines the best location for a tentative position by using various sources of information. The team ensures the position provides optimum balance between the following principles:

- Avoid obvious sniper positions.
- Make maximum use of available cover and concealment.
- Carefully select a new firing position before leaving an old one.
- Avoid setting a pattern. The sniper should fire from both barricaded and unbarricaded windows.
- Never subject the sniper position to traffic of other personnel, regardless of how well the sniper is hidden. Traffic invites observation and the sniper may be detected by optical devices. He should also be aware of backlighting that might silhouette him to the enemy.
- Abandon a position from which two or three misses have been fired; detection is almost certain.
- Operate from separate positions. In built-up areas, it is desirable that sniper teams operate from separate positions. Detection of two teams in close proximity is very probable, considering the number of positions from which the enemy may be observing. The snipers should position themselves where they can provide mutual support.
- Select alternate positions as well as supplementary positions to engage targets in any direction.
- Always plan the escape route ahead of time.
- Minimize the combustibility of selected positions (fireproofing).
- Select a secure and quiet approach route. This route should, if possible, be free of garbage cans, crumbling walls, barking dogs, and other impediments.

- Select a secure entry and exit point. The more obvious and easily accessible entry and exit points are not necessarily the best, as their constant use during subsequent relief of sniper teams may more readily lead to compromise.
- Pick good arcs of observation. Restricted arcs are inevitable, but the greater the arc, the better.
- Ensure the least impedance of communications equipment.
- Consider all aspects of security.
- Try to pick positions of comfort. This rule is important but should be the lowest priority. Uncomfortable observation and firing positions can be maintained only for short periods. If there is no adequate relief from observation, hides can rarely remain effective for more than a few hours.
- Never return to a sniper position that the sniper has fired from, no matter how good it is.

CHARACTERISTICS OF URBAN HIDES

6-66. The overriding requirement of a hide is that it must dominate its area of responsibility and provide maximum observation of the target area.

6-67. When selecting a suitable location, there is always a tendency to go for height. In an urban operation, this can be a mistake. The greater the height attained, the more the sniper has to look out over an area and away from his immediate surroundings. For example, if a hide were established on the tenth floor of an apartment building to see a road beneath, the sniper would have to lean out of the window, which does little for security. The sniper should get only close enough to provide observation and fire without compromise. The sniper should stay at the second and third floor levels unless his area of interest is on a higher floor in another building. He would then want to be slightly above that floor if possible.

6-68. The locations of incidents that the sniper might have to deal with are largely unpredictable, but the ranges are usually relatively short. Consequently, a hide must cover its immediate surroundings, as well as middle and far distances. In residential areas, this goal is rarely possible, as hides are forced off ground floor levels by passing pedestrians. However, it is not advisable to go above the second floor because to go higher greatly increases the dead space in front of the hide. This practice is not a cardinal rule, however. Local conditions, such as being on a bus route, may force the sniper to go higher to avoid direct observation by passengers.

6-69. In view of this weakness in local defense of urban hides, the principle of mutual support between hides assumes even greater importance and is one reason why coordination and planning must take place at battalion level.

CONSTRUCTING AN URBAN POSITION

6-70. Positions in urban terrain are quite different from in the field. When the sniper team must construct an urban position, it should consider the following factors:

- Use a backdrop to minimize detection from the outside of the structure.
- Position the weapon to ensure adequate observation and engagement of the target area and mark the vertical and horizontal limits of observation.
- If adequate time and materials are available, hang drop cloths to limit the possibility of observation from the outside of the structure. Cut loopholes in the drop cloth fabric to allow observation of the target area.
- Always be aware of the outside appearance of the structure. Firing through loopholes in barricaded windows is preferred, but the team must also barricade all other windows.
- Build loopholes in other windows to provide more than one firing position. When building loopholes, the team should make them different shapes (not perfect squares or circles). Dummy loopholes also confuse the enemy.
- Establish positions in attics. The team removes the shingles and cuts out loopholes in the roof; however, they must make sure there are other shingles missing from the roof so that the firing position loophole is not obvious.
- Do not locate the position against contrasting background or in prominent buildings that automatically draw attention. The team must stay in the shadows while moving, observing, and engaging targets. **AVOID** obvious locations.

- Never fire close to a loophole. The team must always back away from the hole as far as possible to hide the muzzle flash and to muffle the sound of the weapon when it fires.
- Locate positions in a different room than the one the loophole is in by making a hole through a wall to connect the two and fire from inside the far room. Thus, the sniper is forming a "double baffle" with his loopholes by constructing two loopholes in succession. This method will further reduce his muzzle flash and blast and improve his concealment from enemy observation.
- Do not fire continually from one position.

> **NOTE**
> These factors are why the sniper should construct more than one position if time and the situation permit. When constructing other positions, the team should make sure it can observe the target area. Sniper team positions should never be used by any personnel other than a sniper team.

POSSIBLE HIDE AND OBSERVATION POST LOCATIONS

6-71. Common sense and imagination are the sniper team's only limitation in determining urban hide or OP locations. Below are just a few options that the team can use to maximize cover and meet mission requirements:

- *Old Derelict Buildings.* The team should pay special attention to the possibility of encountering booby traps. One proven method of detecting guerrilla booby traps is to notice if the locals (especially children) move in and about the building freely.
- *Occupied Houses.* After carefully observing the inhabitants' daily routine, snipers can move into occupied homes and establish hides or OPs in basements and attics. This method was used very successfully by the British in Northern Ireland. However, these locations cannot be occupied for extended periods due to the strict noise discipline required.
- *Shops.*
- *Schools and Churches.* When using these buildings, the snipers risk possible damage to what might already be strained public relations. They should not use these positions if they are still active buildings in the community.
- *Factories, Sheds, and Garages.*
- *Basements and Between Floors in Buildings.* It is possible for the sniper team to locate itself in these positions, although there may be no window or readily usable firing port available. These locations require the sniper to remove bricks or stones without leaving any noticeable evidence outside the building. The sniper should try to locate those crawl spaces that already vent to the outside.
- *Rural Areas From Which Urban Areas Can Be Observed.*

MANNING THE SNIPER HIDES AND OBSERVATION POSTS

6-72. Before moving into the hide or OP, the snipers must have the following information:

- The exact nature of the mission (observe, fire).
- The length of stay.
- The local situation.
- Procedure and timing for entry.
- Emergency recall code and procedures.
- Emergency evacuation procedures.
- Radio procedures.
- Movement of any friendly troops.
- Procedure and timing for exit.
- Any special equipment needed.

6-73. The well-tried and understood principle of remaining back from windows and other apertures when in buildings has a marked effect on the manning of hides or OPs. The field of view from the back of a room through a window is limited. To enable a worthwhile area to be covered, two or even three men may have to observe at one time from different parts of the room.

SNIPER TECHNIQUES IN URBAN HIDES

6-74. Although the construction of hide positions may differ, the techniques or routines while in position are the same. Sniper teams use the technique best suited for the urban position. These may include any of the following:

- The second floor of a building is usually the best location for the position. It presents minimal dead space but provides the team more protection since passersby cannot easily spot it.
- Normally, a window is the best viewing aperture or loophole.
  - If the window is dirty, do not clean it for better viewing.
  - If curtains are prevalent in the area, do not remove those in the position. Lace or net-type curtains can be seen through from the inside, but they are difficult to see through from the outside.
  - If strong winds blow the curtains open, staple, tack, or weigh them down. However, do the same with all other curtains in open windows or the nonmovement of the curtains will attract attention.
  - Firing a round through a curtain has little effect on accuracy; however, ensure the muzzle is far enough away to avoid muzzle blast.
  - When area routine indicates open curtains, follow suit. Set up well away from the viewing aperture; however, ensure effective coverage of the assigned target area, or place a secondary drop cloth behind the open curtain where it would not be noticeable. With the sniper sandwiched between the two drop cloths, his movement and activities will be more difficult to observe with open curtains.
- Firing through glass should be avoided since more than one shot may be required. The copper jacket of the M118 round is usually stripped as the round passes through the glass. However, the mass of the core will continue and should stay on target for approximately 5 feet after penetrating standard house pane glass. The sniper should consider the following variables when shooting through glass:
  - Type and thickness of glass (tempered or safety glass reacts much differently from pane glass).
  - Distance of weapon to glass.
  - Type of weapon and ammunition.
  - Distance of glass to target.
  - Angle of bullet path to glass; if possible, he should fire at a 90-degree angle to the glass.
- If firing through glass, the team should also consider the following options:
  - Break or open several windows throughout the position before occupation. This can be done during the reconnaissance phase of the operation; however, avoid drawing attention to the area.
  - Remove or replace panes of glass with plastic sheeting of the heat-shrink type. The sheeting will not disrupt the bullet but will deceive the enemy into believing that the glass is still in place.
- Other loopholes or viewing apertures are nearly unlimited, such as—
  - Battle damage.
  - Drilled holes (hand drill).
  - Brick removal.
  - Loose boards or derelict houses.
- Positions can also be set up in attics or between the ceiling and roof:
  - Gable ends close to the eaves (shadow adding to concealment).
  - Battle damage to gables or roof.
  - Loose or removed tiles, shingles, or slates.
  - Skylights.
- The sniper makes sure the bullet clears the loophole. The muzzle must be far enough from the loophole and the rifle boresighted to ensure the bullet's path is not in line with the bottom of the loophole. The observer and sniper must clear the muzzle before firing.
- Front drops, usually netting, may have to be changed (if the situation permits) from dark to light colors at beginning morning nautical twilight or ending evening nautical twilight due to sunlight or lack of sunlight into the position.
- If the site is not multiroomed, partitions can be made by hanging blankets or nets to separate the operating area from the rest and administrative areas.
- If sandbags are required, the team can fill and carry them inside of rucksacks, or fill them in the basement, depending on the situation or location of the position site.

- There should always be a planned escape route that leads to the ORP. When forced to vacate the position, the team meets the reaction force at the ORP. Normally, the team will not be able to leave from the same point at which it gained access; therefore, a separate escape point may be required in emergencies. The team must consider windows (other than the viewing apertures), anchored ropes to climb down the building, or a small, preset explosive charge situation on a wall or floor for access into adjoining rooms, buildings, or the outside.
- The type of uniform or camouflage that the team will wear is dictated by the tactical situation, the rules of engagement, the team's mission, and the AO. The following applies:
  - Most often, the normal BDU and required equipment are worn.
  - Urban-camouflaged uniforms can be made or purchased. Urban areas vary greatly in color (mostly gray [cinder block]; red [brick]; white [marble]; dark gray [granite]; or stucco, clay, or wood). Regardless of area color, uniforms should include angular-lined patterns.
  - When necessary, most woodland-patterned BDUs can be worn inside out, as they are a green-gray color underneath.
  - Soft-soled shoes or boots are the preferred footwear in the urban environment.
  - The team can reduce its visual profile during movement by using nonstandard uniforms or a mixture of civilian clothes as part of a deliberate deception plan. With theater approval, civilian clothing can be worn (native or host country populace).
  - Tradesmen's or construction workers' uniforms and accessories can aid in the deception plan.

WEAPONS CHARACTERISTICS IN URBAN TERRAIN

6-75. The characteristics of built-up areas and the nature of urban warfare influence the effectiveness of sniper systems and how they may be employed. The sniper must consider the following basic factors during all urban operations:

STRUCTURAL CONFIGURATION OF BUILDINGS

6-76. The basic classes of structures encountered in a built-up area can generally be classified as concrete, masonry, or wooden. However, any one building may include a combination of these materials. All buildings offer concealment, although the degree of protection varies with the material used. The 7.62- × 51-mm NATO ball cartridge will penetrate at 200 meters—

- Fifty inches of pinewood boards.
- Ten inches of loose sand.
- Three inches of concrete.

GLASS PENETRATION

6-77. If the situation should require firing through glass, the sniper should know—

- When the M118 ammunition penetrates glass, in most cases, the copper jacket is stripped of its lead core and the core fragments. These fragments will injure or kill should they hit either the hostage or the terrorist. The fragments show no standard pattern, but randomly fly in a cone-shaped pattern, much like shot from a shotgun. Even when the glass is angled to as much as 45 degrees, the lead core will not show minimum signs of deflection up to approximately 5 feet past the point of impact with standard house pane glass.
- When the bullet impacts with the glass, the glass will shatter and explode back into the room. The angle of the bullet impact with the glass has no bearing on the direction of the shattered glass. The shattered glass will always fly perpendicular to the pane of the glass.

6-78. The U.S. Secret Service tested the efficiency of Federal 168 grain Sierra hollow-point boattail ammunition on several types of glass and found that—

- Targets placed up to 20 feet behind the glass were neutralized when the weapon was fired from 100 meters away, from a 0- to 45-degree angle of deflection.

NOTE

These results do not fit with the tests run by the Marine Corps, U.S. Army, or the FBI. Their tests showed a deviation that was acceptable to 5 or 7 feet.

- Glass fragmentation formed a cone-shaped hazard area 10 feet deep and 6 feet in diameter; the axis of which is perpendicular to the line and angle of fire.
- The jacket separated from the round but both jacket and round maintained an integrated trajectory.

ENGAGEMENT TECHNIQUES

6-79. Engaging targets not only requires the sniper to determine specific variables, but also to be trained and proficient in the methods below.

SIMULTANEOUS SHOOTING

6-80. Shooting simultaneously by command fire with another sniper is a very important skill to develop and requires much practice. The senior man in the command post (CP) will usually give this command. He may delegate the actual firing decision to the assault element team leader, so that the sniper fire may be better coordinated with the rescue effort. The actual command "standby, (pause) ready, ready, fire" must be given clearly, without emotion, or tonal change. Procedure is as follows:

- Team leader requests, "SNIPER STATUS."
- Snipers respond by numbers on availability of targets, "ONE ON," "TWO ON," "THREE OFF," "FOUR ON."
- Team leader will respond with "STANDBY," or "HOLD," depending on availability of targets.
- If assault is a GO, the command "READY, READY FIRE" is given. All snipers with targets will shoot simultaneously. (This action should sound as one shot.)
- Or the team leader may indicate specific snipers to fire.
- Alert commands should be repeated twice, "READY, READY, FIRE."
- After shooting the sniper will acknowledge, "SHOT OUT." He will then confirm results.

6-81. Reactive targets give a positive visual indication of simultaneous impact and should be used whenever possible for this exercise.

COUNTDOWN SYSTEM

6-82. During a multiple action engagement or a sniper-initiated assault, a countdown technique will be used. The CP or team leader gives a verbal countdown as follows:

STANDBY
(PAUSE)
5-
4-
3-
2- SNIPERS FIRE.
1- BLAST FROM GRENADES OR BREACHING CHARGE.

6-83. If glass must be shattered to provide the primary sniper a clear shot at his target, it is best if the support sniper also aims his "window breaking" bullet at the target. This way, the sniper team has two projectiles aimed at the target, increasing the likelihood of a hit.

APPENDIX A

M82A1 Caliber .50 Sniper Weapon System

Changes in modern warfare required an expansion of the sniper's role. On the fluid, modern battlefield, the sniper must be prepared to engage a wide range of targets at even greater distances. After years of research and development, the military adopted the M82A1 caliber .50 SWS. However, even after having been deployed to operational units, no comprehensive training plan has been developed to train snipers on this new role. The basic approach to the large-bore sniper rifle has been that it is nothing more than a big M24 (7.62-mm sniper rifle). This logic has its obvious flaws. Many of the techniques learned by the sniper need to be modified to compensate for this new weapon system. Some of these changes include movement techniques, maintenance requirements, sniper team size and configuration, support requirements, and the marksmanship skills necessary to engage targets at ranges in excess of 1,800 meters. To keep up with the battles fought in-depth, as well as smaller-scale conflicts, the need for a sniper trained and equipped with a large-bore rifle is apparent.

ROLE OF THE M82A1 CALIBER .50 SWS

A-1. The military can use the M82A1 in several different roles—as the long-range rifle, the infantry support rifle, and the explosive ordnance disposal tool. Personnel use the M82A1 as—

- A long-range rifle to disable valuable targets that are located outside the range or the capabilities of conventional weapons, many times doing so in situations that may preclude the use of more sophisticated weapons.
- An infantry support rifle to engage lightly armored vehicles and to penetrate light fortifications that the 5.56 mm and the 7.62 mm cannot defeat.
- An explosive ordnance disposal tool to engage and disrupt several types of munitions at ranges from 100 to 500 meters. In most cases, the munitions are destroyed or disrupted with a single hit and without a high-order detonation.

A-2. When used in any of its roles, the caliber .50 SWS and personnel trained to use it are vital assets to the commander. In light of this, a training program is necessary to maximize their potential.

M82A1 CALIBER .50 SWS CHARACTERISTICS

A-3. The Barrett Caliber .50 Model 82A1 is a short recoil-operated, magazine-fed, air-cooled, semiautomatic rifle (Figure A-1). Its specifications are as follows:

- Caliber: .50 Browning machine gun cartridge (12.7 × 99 mm).
- Weight: 30 lbs (13.6 kg).
- Overall Length: 57 inches (144.78 cm).
- Barrel Length: 29 inches (73.67 cm).
- Muzzle Velocity: 2,850 fps (M33 ball).
- Maximum Range M2 Ball: 6,800 meters (7,450 yds).
- Maximum Effective Range: 1,830 meters on an area target and 1200 to 1400 on a point target, depending on target size.
- Magazine Capacity: 10 rounds.

Figure A-1. The barrett caliber .50 Model 82A1

THE SWAROVSKI RANGING RETICLE RIFLE SCOPE

A-4. A qualified sniper has already been taught the fundamentals of scoped rifle fire. However, the scope that the M82A1 is equipped with differs from most of the scopes. Figure A-2, lists the specifications for the Swarovski rifle scope.

USING THE M82A1 CALIBER .50 SWS

A-5. A qualified sniper has also already been taught the considerations necessary for proper employment of a sniper team. With the caliber .50 SWS, many of these have changed. The effective range, signature, weight, support requirements, and terminal performance of the round are all increased over the 7.62 SWS. As a result, the sniper must do the following to ensure proper use of this system:

- Maximize the range of the M82A1. Always engage targets at the maximum range that the weapon, target, and terrain will permit. Make sure to—
  - Select the appropriate ammunition (by effective range and terminal performance).
  - Use range finder whenever possible.
  - When in doubt of range estimation, aim low and adjust using the sight-to-burst method. Second shots are frowned upon with a 7.62 SWS because of two things—the target getting into a prone position (which most people do when shot at) and the sniper revealing his position. Neither of these principles apply to the caliber .50 SWS when it is used against armored or fortified targets. Armored personnel carriers (APCs) cannot "duck," nor is an enemy buttoned into a bunker or an APC as observant as he could be. The sniper needs to have carefully observed his area before assuming the above to be always true.
- Conduct movement into or occupy an FFP with the M82A1 SWS. Sniper should—
  - Modify his movement techniques to accommodate for the following:
    - Increased weight of the system, ammunition, and team equipment.
    - Better route selection (amount of crawling is reduced).
    - Better selection of withdrawal routes (after the shot, the sniper becomes a higher-priority target and must select route for quick egress).

Design Characteristics
• 30-mm main tube is compatible with existing SWS mounting rings. • Made of aluminum alloy. • NOVA ocular system filled with dry nitrogen after pressure-testing to prevent fogging. • Available add-on battery-operated reticle illuminator for low-light conditions. • Recoiling eyepiece offers added protection from scope "bite." • Sloped scope rail enables use of **only** the Swarovski reticle-equipped scope, rail is between 0.030 and 0.035 inches higher at rear. The sloped rail also aids in the M3A to zero at the longer ranges due to the additional slope in the rail. **NOTE:** Under no circumstances will the scope rail be removed.
Technical Data
• Magnification: 10x. • Objective Lens Diameter: 42 mm. • Field of View: 12 feet at 100 yards/4 meters at 100 meters. • Parallax-Free Distance of the Reticle: 500 meters (tolerance 250 meters to infinity). • Windage and Elevation Adjustments: 1 click: 1/5 inch at 100 yards, (1/5 MOA) maximum: 80 inches at 100 yards (80 MOA). • Operating Temperature: 131 degrees Fahrenheit/ –4 degrees Fahrenheit. • Weight: approximately 13.5 ounces.
Reticle
• Offers "ranging" capabilities from 500 to 1,800 meters. • No range estimation abilities (500 meters to 600 meters stadia lines approximately 1 mil apart, 3.5 MOA). • 5 and 10 mph wind hold-offs, also usable for moving targets. • Lack of mil dots require different hold-offs for wind and drift.

Figure A-2. Scope specifications

- Occupy an FFP and adjust for the following:
  - Much larger signature to front, clear area and dampen soil.
  - Signature also at 65 degrees, fan to right and left of sniper.
  - Size requirement for a 3-man sniper team in a permanent hide may make it unfeasible for many applications.
  - FFP should prevent long-range "skylined" targets.
- Understand additional support requirements for the M82A1. Sniper should—
  - Maintain an M82A1 SWS as follows:
    - Clean after 10 rounds for better accuracy.
    - Be aware that a chamber pressure of 55,000 copper units of pressure (CUP) could cause fatal maintenance failures.
  - Modify existing training and sustainment programs as follows:
    - Cannot fire the M82A1 on existing small-arms sniper ranges.
    - Requires special considerations for the use of ammunition other than the standard ball and tracer (for example, multipurpose ammunition, armor-piercing incendiary [API]).

- Understand the following additional transportation requirements:
  - Additional weight of system makes vehicular movement desirable.
  - As there is no existing approved method for parachute or underwater infiltration with the M82A1, the sniper must plan for alternate methods of getting the SWS to the battlefield.

A-6. A sniper's ability to deploy to the battlefield with an M82A1 depends on whether he can adapt what he has learned in the past. The rules of sniper employment haven't changed, but many of the finer points have.

MAINTENANCE

A-7. Maintenance of the M82A1 SWS involves assembly and disassembly, inspection, cleaning and lubrication, and replacement of parts.

A-8. The sniper normally stores and transports the M82A1 SWS in the carrying case. The following procedure covers the initial assembly of the rifle as it would come from the case.

A-9. The sniper first removes the lower receiver from the carrying case. He extends the bipod legs by pulling them back and swinging them down to the front where they will lock into place. He places the lower receiver on the ground.

A-10. The sniper removes the rear lock pin from its stored position in the lower receiver, found just forward of the recoil pad.

A-11. He frees the bolt carrier. The bolt carrier is held in place under tension in the lower receiver by the midlock pin. He grasps the charging handle of the bolt carrier with the right hand and pulls back against the tension of the main spring. The sniper then removes the midlock pin and allows the bolt carrier to come forward slowly until there is no more spring tension.

CAUTION

Do not pull the midlock pin without hands-on control of the bolt carrier; it can be launched from the lower receiver.

A-12. The sniper removes the upper receiver from the case. He maintains control of the barrel that is retracted in the upper receiver to prevent it from sliding and injuring his fingers. The barrel may have rotated in shipping and he will need to index it so that the feed ramp is to the bottom. The sniper then fully extends the barrel from the upper receiver.

A-13. The impact bumper that surrounds the barrel must be placed into proper position by the barrel lug. The sniper grasps the barrel key (not the springs) with the thumb and middle of the index finger. He pulls the key into place on the key slot of the barrel. This is a difficult operation, at first, because the tension of the barrel spring is approximately 70 pounds.

A-14. The sniper positions the upper receiver, rear-end up, muzzle down; over the lower receiver. He engages the front hook of the lower receiver.

NOTE

The sniper should make sure of the proper mating of the hook and bar to avoid receiver damage during the final assembly motion.

A-15. He grasps the charging handle on the bolt carrier and pulls back against the tension of the main spring until the bolt clears the barrel when the upper receiver is lowered.

A-16. The sniper lowers and closes the upper receiver onto the lower receiver. He releases the charging handle. Then he places the mid and rear lock pins into the lock pin holes in the receiver.

A-17. He places thumb safety in the "on safe" position (horizontal).

DISASSEMBLY AND ASSEMBLY

A-18. The two types of disassembly and assembly are general and detailed. General disassembly and assembly involves removing and replacing the three major weapon groups. Detailed disassembly and assembly involves removing and replacing the component parts of the major groups.

General Disassembly

> **NOTE**
> Only SOTIC personnel are authorized to perform complete disassembly.

A-19. The three major weapon groups are the upper receiver, bolt carrier, and lower receiver. As the sniper disassembles the weapon, he should note each part position, configuration, and part name. He—

- Begins by clearing the weapon and supporting the rifle on the bipod, with the magazine removed.
- Removes the mid and rear lock pins.
- Grasps the charging handle and pulls back until the bolt withdraws from and clears the barrel.
- Lifts the upper receiver at its rear. When the receiver has raised enough to clear the bolt, he slowly releases the pull on the charging handle so that the bolt carrier comes to rest.
- Continues to raise the upper receiver until the front hinge is disengaged and then lifts it from the lower receiver.
- Withdraws the barrel by resting the upper receiver group on the muzzle brake by placing it on any surface that will not damage the end of the brake.
- Withdraws the barrel key from the slot in the barrel by slowly working it out and grasping it between his thumb and the middle of the index finger (he should be prepared to assume the tension of the barrel springs upon the release of the barrel key from the slot—tension is approximately 70 pounds). Slowly lowers the key until the tension of the springs are at rest.

> **NOTE**
> The sniper should never pull on the barrel springs to remove the barrel key.

- Lowers the receiver down around the barrel.
- Grasps the charging handle and lifts the bolt carrier group from the lower receiver.
- Decocks the firing mechanism by depressing the sear with the rear lock pin.
- With the bolt in the left hand, uses the mid lock to depress the bolt latch against the palm. He uses the rear lock pin to lift the cam pin and frees the bolt with the right hand. The bolt will rise under the power of the bolt spring. He should never lift the cam pin more than needed to release the bolt.
- Removes the bolt and bolt spring.
- If it is necessary to remove the extractor, inserts a pin punch or paper clip through the extractor hole and slides the extractor out either side of the slot. He should be prepared to capture or contain the plunger and the plunger spring. He reverses the procedure for replacement.

Assembly

A-20. The sniper reverses the procedure for reassembly of the bolt. He—

- Replaces the bolt carrier. With the lower receiver group standing on its bipod, places the bolt carrier into the lower receiver.
- Replaces the upper receiver by—
  - Positioning the upper receiver (rear up and muzzle down) over the lower receiver so the hook of the front hinge can fully engage the hinge bar on the lower receiver.
  - **NOTE**: If not properly seated, the hinge bar can be pried off due to leverage the operator can apply when closing the receiver.

- While positioned directly behind the rifle, preparing to close the upper receiver with the left hand.
- Grasping the charging handle of the bolt carrier and pulling the bolt carrier back into the main spring, so the bolt clears the barrel while lowering the upper receiver.
- Lowering and closing the upper receiver and releasing the charging handle.
- Replacing mid and rear lock pins.

INSPECTION

A-21. Inspection begins with the weapon disassembled into its three major groups. Figure A-3 describes each group and the steps that the sniper must perform to inspect for proper functioning.

CLEANING AND LUBRICATION

A-22. The rifle's size makes it relatively easy to clean. The sniper should clean it at the completion of each day's firing or during the day if fouling is causing the weapon to malfunction. He—

- Cleans the bore with rifle bore cleaner (RBC) or a suitable substitute. Each cleaning should include at least six passes back and forth with the bronze-bristle brush, followed by cloth patches until the patches come out

Upper Receiver Group
• Makes sure barrel springs are not overstretched and each coil is tight with no space between the coils.
• Checks to see if impact bumper is in good condition.
• Ensures the muzzle brake is tight.
• Inspects the upper receiver for signs of being cracked, bent, or burred.
• Makes sure scope mounting rings are tight.
Bolt Carrier Group
• Checks the ejector and extractor to see that they are under spring pressure and not chipped or worn.
• Decocks firing mechanism, depresses the bolt latch, and manually works the bolt in and out, feeling for any roughness.
• Holding the bolt down, inspects firing pin protrusion and for any erosion of the firing pin hole.
• Inspects bolt latch for deformation and free movement.
• Swings cocking lever forward. The sear should capture the firing pin extension before the cocking lever is fully depressed.
Lower Receiver Group
• With the bolt carrier in place, pulls it rearwards and checks to see that the mainspring moves freely.
• Holds bolt carrier under mainspring housing approximately 10 mm and checks for excessive lift that would prevent the trigger from firing.
• Ensures the lower receiver is not cracked, bent, or burred.
• Checks the bipod assembly to ensure it functions properly.

Figure A-3. Steps in sniper's inspection of major weapon groups

clean. Immediately after using bore cleaner, he dries the bore and any parts of the rifle exposed to the bore cleaner and applies a thin coat of oil. He should always clean the bore from the chamber end.

- Cleans the rest of the weapon with a weapons cleaning toothbrush, rags, and cleaning solvent. When using cleaning solvent, he should not expose plastic or rubber parts to it. He dries and lubricates all metal surfaces when clean.

A-23. The sniper should lightly lubricate all exposed metal. These parts are as follows:

- Bolt (locking lugs and cam slot).
- Bolt carrier (receiver bearing surfaces).
- Barrel bolt locking surfaces (receiver bearing surfaces).
- Receiver (bearing surfaces for recoiling parts).

NOTE
The sniper lubricates according to the conditions in the AO.

A-24. The sniper should dust off the scope and keep it free of dirt. He should dust the lenses with a lens cleaning brush and only clean them with lens cleaning solvent and lens tissue.

NOTE
The Barrett is easy to maintain, but because of the size of its components the sniper must pay attention to what he is doing, or he may damage the weapon, injure himself, or hurt others around him if not careful.

APPENDIX B

Sniper Rifle Telescopes

A scope mounted on the rifle allows the sniper to detect and engage targets more effectively. Another advantage of the scope is its ability to magnify the target. As previously stated, a scope does not make a soldier a better sniper, it only helps him see better. This appendix explains the characteristics and types of scopes.

CHARACTERISTICS OF RIFLE TELESCOPES

B-1. The telescope is an optical instrument that the sniper uses to improve his ability to see his target clearly in most situations. It also helps him to quickly identify or recognize the target and enables him to engage with a higher rate of success. The following characteristics apply to most types of scopes.

TELESCOPE MAGNIFICATION

B-2. The average unaided human eye can distinguish 1-inch detail at 100 meters. Magnification, combined with quality lens manufacture and design, permits resolution of this 1 inch divided by the optical magnification. The general rule is 1x magnification per 100 meters. The magnification (power) of a telescope should correspond to the maximum effective range of the weapon system being used. This amount of power will enable the operator to identify precise corrections. For example, a 5x telescope is adequate out to 500 meters; a 10x is good out to 1,000 meters. The best all-around magnification determined for field-type sniping is the 10x because it permits the operator to identify precise corrections out to 1,000 meters. The field of view of a 10x at close range, while small, is still enough to see large and small targets. Higher-powered telescopes have very limited fields of view, making close range and snap target engagements difficult. Substandard high-powered telescopes may be hard to focus and have parallax problems. Some marksmen still prefer lower-powered telescopes. Recent advances in the construction of variable-powered rifle telescopes have negated the problems that once plagued them. Advantages of the variable power scopes in both urban and clip-on style night vision devices make them very desirable in the long run. A number of scope manufacturers now make reliable variable powers in the 2.5 to 10 or 14 range. This allows the sniper to power down so as not to overpower the phosphorus matrix of the NVD or to gain a wider field of view in close in sniping.

PARALLAX

B-3. Parallax results when the target is not focused on the same focal plane as the reticle. When parallax is present, the target will move in relation to the reticle when the sniper moves his head (changes his spot weld) while looking through the telescope. It is more apparent in high-powered telescopes. With parallax, the error will affect the strike of the bullet by the amount seen in the scope. If the crosshairs move from one side of the target to the other, then the potential error is from one side of the target to the other. Therefore, the sniper should zero his system, for elevation, at the greatest distance possible. For a 1,000-meter system, the sniper should confirm his zero at 500 meters for elevation. The initial zero of the weapon system for elevation and windage should be at 100 or 200 meters. This will keep the shooter on paper. The 100-meter range will negate most wind effect; however, the shooter is capable of computing the wind effect and zero with the bullet strike at that point on the target. The M1A and M3A Ultra/Mark IV by Leupold and Stevens have a focus/parallax knob on the left side of the telescope. With the M1A and M3A, it is imperative that the sniper adjusts his focus/parallax when he zeros his system for each range and that he records this data in his shooter's log. If there is a zero-shift while adjusting parallax from range to range, then the scope is defective and requires replacement. The reticle must be focused for the eye prior to focusing on the target. If the reticle is perfectly focused, then the target will be in focus and the scope will be parallax-free. If the target is focused and the scope is not parallax-free, then the shooter may wish to refocus the reticle and recheck parallax. Once both reticle and target are focused on the same plane, the scope will be parallax-free at that range only. The snipers will be required to then focus the target for each range to obtain a parallax-free scope. This information is then recorded in the shooter's log for use when firing over unknown distances and will become part of the sniper and observer dialogue. As an example, "Range 650+1, windage left 1 click spin drift, parallax second ball."

ADJUSTABLE OBJECTIVE LENS

B-4. Adjustable objective lenses for focusing at different magnifications and ranges are becoming quite common. Some target telescopes (such as the M1A and M3A) have a third turret knob on the side of the telescope that will focus the objective lens. Doing so will focus the target and reticle on the same plane, eliminating parallax. Unfortunately, many telescopes have neither and must be dealt with on an individual basis. The best way to deal with the problem is to eliminate shadow. Once shadow is eliminated, the sniper must ensure that the reticle moves the same distance left and right on the target as well as up and down. Doing so will assist in attaining the same aim point even with parallax. If shadow is present, with parallax error, then the strike of the bullet will be opposite of the shadow. The shadow indicates that the sniper is looking down that side of the scope's exit pupil and the crosshairs will appear to have moved to that side as well. The sniper will then compensate by moving the weapon right to get the crosshair back on target, causing the strike of the bullet to be opposite of the shadow.

VARIABLE-POWERED TELESCOPES

B-5. Older variable-powered telescopes often shifted the POI if the magnification was changed from its original setting when sighting the system. Modern, high-quality, variable-powered telescopes do not have this problem. This type of movement has been tested on a number of quality variable-powered telescopes. After zeroing, the scopes showed no variation in the POA versus the POI at any range or any power. Of course, it is prudent to test the system during live-fire exercises to establish the optic's reliability.

TELESCOPE ADJUSTMENTS

B-6. One telescope will not automatically work in the same manner for every sniper. Each sniper's vision is different and requires different adjustments. The following factors vary with each use.

FOCUSING

B-7. Focusing the telescope to the sniper assigned the weapon is important. He can adjust the ocular lens of most telescopes to obtain a crisp, clear picture of the reticle. To do this, the sniper should look at a distant object for several seconds without using the telescope. Then he should shift his vision quickly, looking through the telescope at a plain background. The reticle pattern should be sharp and clear before his eye refocuses. If he needs to make an adjustment to match his eyes, he should hold the eyepiece lock ring and loosen the eyepiece by turning it two turns clockwise to compensate for nearsightedness and counterclockwise to compensate for farsightedness. Then, with a quick glance he should recheck the image. If the focus is worse, he then turns it four revolutions in the opposite direction. It will normally take two full revolutions to see a noticeable difference in the focus. Once the reticle appears focused, the sniper leaves the sights alone and allows the eye to rest for 5 to 10 minutes and then rechecks the reticle. If he force-focuses the reticle, his eye will tire and he will see two reticles after shooting for a period of time. After determining the precise focus for his eye, the sniper should make sure to retighten the lock ring securely against the eyepiece to hold it in position.

CAUTION

Never look at the sun through the telescope. Concentration of strong solar rays can cause serious eye damage.

EYE RELIEF

B-8. Proper eye relief is established very simply. First, the sniper loosens the scope rings' Allen screws so that the telescope is free to move. He gets into the shooting position that will be used most frequently and slides the scope forward or back until a full, crisp picture is obtained. There should be no shading in the view. This view will be anywhere from 2 to 4 inches from his eye depending on the telescope. He rotates the telescope until the reticle crosshairs are perfectly vertical and horizontal, then he tightens the rings' screws.

B-9. The M24 has a one-piece telescope base that has two sets of machined grooves that allow the telescope to be mounted either forward or back to adjust for personal comfort. If that range of adjustment is not sufficient, the telescope can be adjusted after the mounting ring lock screws are loosened.

UNITED STATES TELESCOPES

B-10. The sniper team carries the telescope on all missions. The observer uses the telescope to determine wind speed and direction. The sniper uses this information to make quick and accurate adjustments for wind conditions. The team also uses the telescope for quicker and easier target identification during troop movement. The following discussion applies to the U.S. rifle telescopes currently in use.

M84 TELESCOPIC SIGHT

B-11. The M84 telescopic sight has a magnification of 2.2x. It has a field of view of 27 feet at 100 yards. The maximum field of view is obtained with an eye relief of 3 1/2 to 5 inches. The reticle consists of a vertical post and a horizontal crosshair. The post is 3 MOA in width. The sight is sealed with rubber seals and may be submerged without damage (not recommended due to age). The windage knob has 60 MOA of adjustment, 30 MOA from center left or right. However, there are a total of 100 MOA adjustments available to zero the telescope for misalignment. To adjust the strike of the bullet vertically, the sniper turns the knob to the higher numbers to raise the POI, and to lower numbers to lower the POI. A complete turn of the elevation knob provides 40 MOA of adjustment. One click of the elevation or windage knob equals 1 MOA. The elevation scale starts at 0 yards and goes up to 900 yards with graduations every 50 yards. There is a numbered graduation every 100 yards.

B-12. To zero the scope, the sniper shoots at a target at 100 or 200 yards. He adjusts the elevation and windage until the POA and POI are the same. He turns out the setscrews on both the elevation and windage knobs to "zero" them. The sniper then lifts and rotates the windage dial until the windage (deflection) is on the zero marking for the no-wind zero. He lifts and rotates the range (elevation) knob to the distance used for the zeroing procedure. He can mount this telescope on both the M1C and M2D, the M1 Marine sniper, and the 1903A4 Springfield using a Redfield scope mount.

ADJUSTABLE RANGING TELESCOPE I (ART I)

B-13. The ART I automatically compensates for trajectory when a target of the proper size is adjusted between the stadia lines. It is a 3–9x variable that compensates for targets from 300 to 900 meters. It has a one-piece ballistic cam/ power ring. The ballistic cam is set for the ballistic trajectory of the M118 Match or Special Ball ammunition (173 grain FMJBT @ 2610 fps). Each click or tick mark on the adjustment screws is worth 1/2 MOA in value. The ART I is zeroed at 300 meters. The sniper sets the power ring to 3 (3x/300m) and removes the adjustment turret caps. He fires the rifle and adjusts the elevation and windage adjustment screws until the POI is the same as the POA. Then he screws the turret caps back on to maximize the waterproofing of the telescope.

B-14. The reticle has four stadia lines on it (Figure B-1). The two horizontal stadia lines are on the vertical crosshair, are 30 inches apart at the designated distance, and are used for ranging. The vertical crosshair and horizontal stadia lines are used to range targets from the beltline to the top of the head. The sniper adjusts the power/cam until the stadia lines are bracketing the target's beltline and top of head. The numeral on the power ring is the target distance. For example, if the power ring reads 5, the target is at 500 m, and the scope is at 5x magnification. The ballistic cam has automatically adjusted the telescope for the trajectory of the round by changing the telescope's POA. The sniper aims center mass on the target to obtain a hit in a no-wind situation. The two vertical stadia lines are on the horizontal

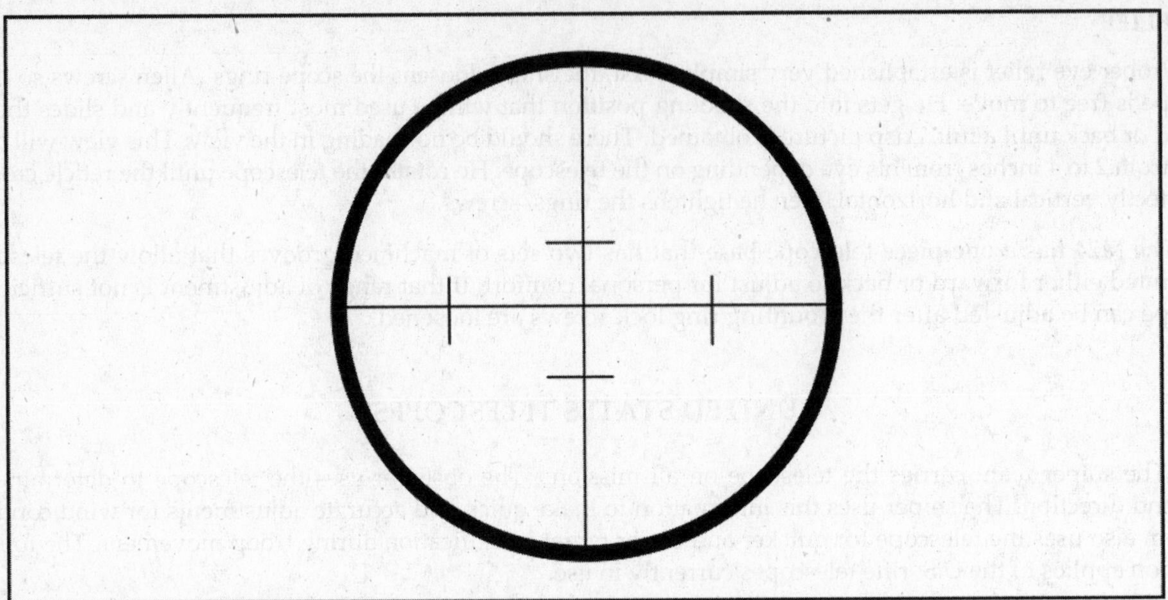

Figure B-1. ART I telescope reticle

crosshair, are 60 inches apart at the designated distance, and are used for wind hold-offs and leads. If necessary, he holds off for environmental effects or target movement.

> **NOTE**
>
> It is imperative to keep the scope base clean. The cam slides along the mount and pushes the telescope off from the bearing surface. Debris can interfere with the precise camming and ranging functions.

ADJUSTABLE RANGING TELESCOPE II (ART II)

B-15. The ART II is similar in operation and design to the ART I, with two major modifications. The ballistic cam and the power ring are now separate and can be moved independently of each other. This modification was made so that after ranging a target, the ballistic cam can be locked to permit the sniper to increase the magnification for greater definition. The problem with this system is that it seldom works correctly. The two rings are locked together in poker-chip-tooth fashion, and even when locked together, they can move independently. When unlocked, it is very difficult to move one without the other moving, creating a change in the camming action, and ultimately, causing misses. It is best to lock them together and keep them together. The mount is similar to the ART I mount, and the bearing surface must be kept clean. The ART II mount has two mounting screws, one of which is threaded into a modified clip guide. The reticle is the second major modification. The reticle pattern is a standard crosshair, with thick outer bars on the left, right, and bottom crosshairs (Figure B-2). The horizontal crosshair has two dots, one on each side of the crosshair intersection. Each dot is 30 inches from the center and a total of 60 inches apart. The heavy bars are 1 meter in height or thickness at the range indicated. To determine the range to a target, the sniper adjusts the power ring and cam together until the target is of equal height to the bar. The correct placement of the bar is from the crotch to the top of head (1 meter). He aims center mass for a no-wind hit. He can read the cam to determine the range.

LEUPOLD AND STEVENS M1A AND M3A ULTRA/MARK 4 10X OR 16X

B-16. The M1A comes in either 10x or 16x. It has three large, oversized target knobs. The left knob (as seen from the sniper) is for focus/parallax adjustment. The top knob is for elevation adjustment. The right knob is for windage adjustment. Table B-1 explains the scope adjustments. The M3A is only available in l0x. It has the same knob arrangement as the M1A, but the knobs are smaller, and they have different click values. All Leupold and Stevens sniper telescopes use the mil-dot reticle (Figure B-3).

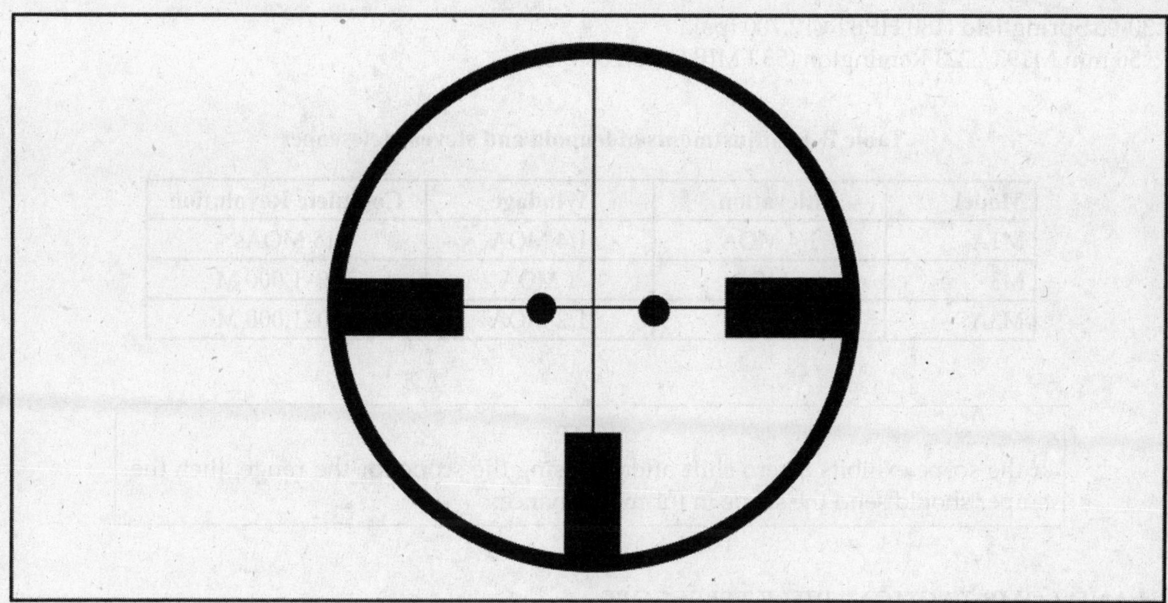

Figure B-2. ART II telescope reticle

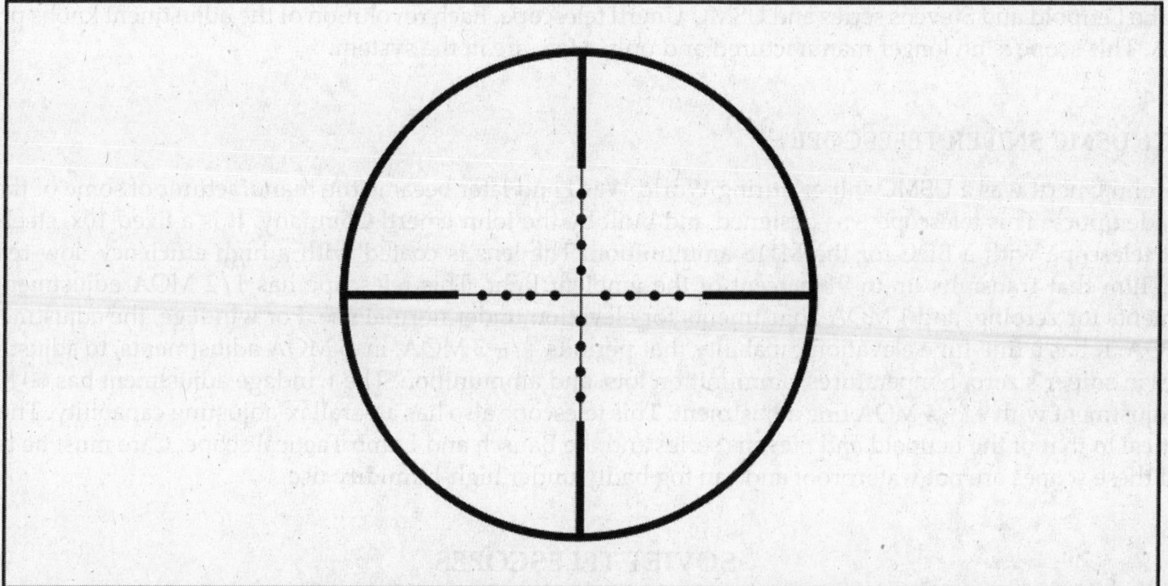

Figure B-3. Leupold and stevens telescope with a mil-dot reticle

B-17. The M3A has a ballistic collar to compensate for the trajectory of the specified cartridge. The collar is calibrated for bullet drop compensation from 100 meters to 1,000 meters. The following are available:

- 7.62 mm NATO M118 (173 FMJBT @ 2,610 fps).
- .300 Winchester Magnum (190 HPBT @ 2900 fps).

NOTE

This collar is erroneously marked as 220 grain.

- .30-06 Springfield (180 HPBT @ 2,700 fps).
- 5.56 mm M193/.223 Remington (55 FMJBT @ 3,200 fps).

Table B-1. Adjustments of leupold and stevens telescopes

Model	Elevation	Windage	Complete Revolution
M1A	1/4 MOA	1/4 MOA	15 MOAs
M3	1 MOA	1 MOA	100–1,000 M
M3A	1 MOA	1/2 MOA	100–1,000 M

NOTE
If the scope exhibits a zero shift after focusing the scope for the range, then the sniper should send the scope in for maintenance.

BAUSCH AND LOMB TACTICAL RIFLE TELESCOPE

B-18. The Bausch and Lomb is a 10- × 40-mm fixed-magnification telescope with 1/4 MOA adjustments. It has two large, target-type knobs. The upper knob is for elevation, and the knob on the right is for windage. The eyepiece houses the range-focus adjustment ring that is calibrated from 50 yards to infinity. It has the same mil-dot reticle pattern as the Leupold and Stevens series and USMC Unertl telescope. Each revolution of the adjustment knobs provides 12 MOA. This scope is no longer manufactured and only a few are in the system.

UNERTL USMC SNIPER TELESCOPE

B-19. John Unertl was a USMC sniper during World War I and later became the manufacturer of some of the finest U.S.-made optics. This telescope was designed and built by the John Unertl Company. It is a fixed 10x, steel-tubed, mil-dot telescope with a BDC for the M118 ammunition. The lens is coated with a high-efficiency, low-reflection (HELR) film that transmits up to 91 percent of the ambient light. This telescope has 1/2 MOA adjustments, fine adjustments for zeroing, and 1 MOA adjustments for elevation under normal use. For windage, the adjustments are in .5 MOA. It has a fine-tune elevation capability that permits +/− 3 MOA, in .5 MOA adjustments, to adjust for differences in sniper's zero, temperatures, ammunition lots, and ammunition. The windage adjustment has 60 MOA of main adjustment with +/− 4 MOA fine adjustment. This telescope also has a parallax-adjusting capability. The reticle is identical to that of the Leupold and Stevens series and the Bausch and Lomb Tactical scope. Care must be taken as most of these scopes are not waterproof and can fog badly under high-humidity use.

SOVIET TELESCOPES

B-20. The Soviet telescopes are made on machinery purchased from Carl Zeiss of Germany during the 1930s. Their optical quality is therefore good to excellent. Their operation is rather simple. Only the PE series has the capability of individually focusing to the user. The top turret is for elevation adjustment and has a ballistic cam that is calibrated for the 7.62- × 54-mm Rimmed L ball ammunition (150 gn FMJ flat base @ 2,800 fps). The turret on the left is for windage adjustments. Table B-2 lists various models and their characteristics.

B-21. The zeroing procedures are identical for all Soviet telescopes. The sniper should zero at 100 meters. To do so, he loosens the small screws on the turrets that hold the top plate to the cam that is engraved with the tick marks and numerals. Several turns are all that is necessary. He should not remove these screws completely; they are not captive and are easily lost. Using a small screwdriver, he gently pries the top plate and cam apart so that the top plate can move independently of the cam. Firing three-shot groups, he adjusts the elevation and windage knobs until the POA and the POI are the same. When making adjustments, the sniper should move **the reticle to the shot group**. This adjustment is the major difference from zeroing these telescopes when compared to zeroing modern, U.S.-style telescopes where the shot group is moved to the reticle (POA). When the rifle and telescope system is zeroed, the sniper should "zero out" the cams. He should turn the elevation cam until the "1," which represents 100 meters, is aligned with the reference tick mark. He makes sure the top plate does not rotate when the cam is moved. The windage cam is also centered on its "0" marking. The sniper then pushes down on the top plates until they mate with the cams. He carefully tightens the small metal screws. The telescope is now zeroed.

Table B-2. M1891/30 sniper telescopes

Model	Magnification	BDC (out to)	Tube Diameter
PE	4x	1,400 m	1 inch
PU	3.5x	1,300 m	300mm
PV	3.5x	1,300 m	30 mm

SOVIET MANUAL DESCRIPTION

B-22. Telescopes can be any of various tubular optical instruments. Soviet technical manuals describe the telescope in two parts: a telescope tube and a mount.

Telescope Tube

B-23. On the top of the tube is an elevation range knob, consisting of a screw and a drum, marked with numbers from 1 to 14 on the PE scope and from 1 to 13 on the PU scope. Each graduation is equivalent to 100 meters in distance.

B-24. At the left rear side of the scope is a windage knob. The components of the windage knob are the same as that of the elevation-range knob. The sniper uses the windage knob to compensate for the effects of wind on the trajectory of the bullet. The windage knob has 10 graduations; the middle one is marked with the number 0.

B-25. To move the strike of the bullet to the right, the sniper turns the windage knob to the direction of the mark "+," and conversely, turns the knob to the direction of the mark "–" to move the strike of the bullet to the left. Each click of windage corresponds to 1 mil.

B-26. The telescope tube contains a system of optical glasses including convex lenses, prisms, and an eyepiece. The reticle is a cross-wire type. When aiming the rifle at the objective, the sniper places the vertical line of the reticle right on the objective. He uses the horizontal line to adjust the aim. The two knobs provide horizontal and vertical movement of the reticle.

B-27. The telescope tube PE has adjusting devices. When taking aim, the sniper adjusts the knobs on the tube to fit with the observer's eye.

B-28. The telescope tube PU has no adjusting (focusing) devices. Therefore, when aiming, the observer looks through the telescope and moves his head until the sighted object is in focus.

B-29. When using a telescope to aim at the objective, the sniper places the eye at the center of the eyepiece, thus forming a sight alignment toward the objective. If aiming inaccurately, the sniper will see a small, black, crescent-shaped spot in the telescope.

Mount

B-30. The mount for PE consists of a base and a body. The sniper fixes the base to the receiver of the rifle with six screws. He uses the body of the mount, after it is fastened to the base, to fix the telescope to the rifle.

B-31. The mount for PU also includes a base and a body. The sniper connects the base, after it is screwed to the receiver of the rifle, with the body of the mount by guide lugs and screws. The body of the mount may be moved up and down on the base using the two screws on the upper side and the rear lower side of the base. The sniper uses the body to fix the telescope to the rifle.

B-32. The sniper then loosens three screws to rotate the sighting telescope, but only loosens the screws when firing for adjustment at the repair station of the regiment.

PSO-1

B-33. The PSO-l scope will be found mounted on the Soviet SVD and the Romanian FPK. The PSO-1 is 4x, and has an illuminated reticle powered by a small battery. The battery housing is located at the bottom rear of the telescopic sight mount. To change batteries, the sniper presses in and rotates the battery housing counterclockwise. He removes the old battery and replaces it with the same type. He can replace the reticle lamp by unscrewing its housing and removing the bulb (the RPG-7 sight uses the same bulb). The reticle light is turned on or off by its switch. The lens cap should always be in place except when the telescope is in use. Two covers are issued with each rifle: one is for the telescopic sight alone and the other covers the sight and breech when the PSO-1 is mounted. A belt pouch is provided for carrying the telescope when dismounted from the rifle, four magazines, a cleaning kit, and an extra battery and lamp.

B-34. If the sniper needs to use open sights, he sets the rear sight by pressing in the locks on the rear sight slide, then moves the slide along the rear sight leaf. He then aligns the front edge of the slide with the numeral that corresponds in hundreds of meters. He can use the same sight picture as for firing a pistol.

B-35. If the sniper uses the PSO-1, he rotates the elevation knob until the index aligns with the figure that corresponds to the range in hundreds of meters. He can closely determine the range by using the range finder located in the lower left of the telescopic reticle. This range finder is graduated to the height of a man (5 feet 7 inches) from 200 to 1,000 meters. The sniper looks through the telescope and places the horizontal line at the bottom of the target. He moves the telescope until the upper (curved) line just touches the top of the target's head. The number indicates the range in hundreds of meters. If the target falls between numbers, he must estimate the remaining distance. When the range is determined and set into the elevation knob, he uses the point of the top chevron on the reticle as an aiming point. He uses the three lower chevrons for firing at 1,100, 1,200, and 1,300 meters with the elevation knob set at 10.

B-36. The sniper uses the horizontal scale extending out from the sides of the top chevron for hasty wind and lead corrections; each tick mark is worth 1 Soviet mil (6,000 Soviet mils per 360 degrees). The horizontal scale is numbered every 5 and 10 mils. Rotating the windage knob makes deliberate changes. The windage knob is graduated every 1/2 Soviet mil. The windage knob scale has two clicks per graduation, each click representing 1/2 mil (.5 mil), each graduation one mil. At 1,000 meters, each click moves the impact of the round .5 meters (20 inches), each graduation moves the impact 1 meter (40 inches). The numbers on the windage knob are colored. Right windage corrections are black and are obtained when the knob is rotated clockwise. Left windage corrections are red and are obtained when the knob is rotated counterclockwise.

B-37. When the sniper must fire in dim light, he illuminates the reticle by turning on the switch in the telescopic sight mount. If active infrared light sources are believed to be used by the enemy, he sets the range drum at four and switches the infrared detector into place. He then scans the area to the front; if any active infrared light sources are in use, they will appear as orange-red blobs in the telescope. He aligns the point of the reticle on the light and fires. The sniper should turn off the reticle when not in use to conserve the battery and swing the infrared detector out of the way so that it will be activated by light during the day. Several hours of direct sunlight are required to activate the infrared detector.

B-38. If the sniper is unable to obtain the correct dry cell batteries, he can easily assemble a suitable expedient. The Soviet dry cell is 5.0 volts. The following are required:

- Two 1.25 volt/625 camera batteries (lithium).
- One 3.0 volt/DL2025 camera battery (lithium).
- One plastic bushing Outside Diameter–0.85," Inside Diameter–0.60," Length–0.73."

B-39. The sniper should place the batteries' positive "+" side into the battery compartment first. He places the large, flat DL2025 in first, then the bushing, then the two 625 batteries, and replaces the battery compartment cap.

Improvised Munitions Handbook

Introduction

PURPOSE AND SCOPE

In Unconventional Warfare operations it may be impossible or unwise to use conventional military munitions as tools in the conduct of certain missions. It may be necessary instead to fabricate the required munitions from locally available or unassuming materials. The purpose of this manual is to increase the potential of Special Forces and guerrilla troops by describing in detail the manufacture of munitions from seemingly innocuous locally available materials.

Manufactured, precision devices almost always will be more effective, more reliable, and easier to use than improvised ones, but shelf items will just not be available for certain operations for security or logistical reasons. Therefore the operator will have to rely on materials he can buy in a drug or paint store, find in a junk pile, or scrounge from military stocks. Also, many of the ingredients and materials used in fabricating homemade items are so commonplace or innocuous they can be carried without arousing suspicion. The completed item itself often is more easily concealed or camouflaged. In addition, the field expedient item can be tailored for the intended target, thereby providing an advantage over the standard item in flexibility and versatility.

The manual contains simple explanations and illustrations to permit construction of the items by personnel not normally familiar with making and handling munitions. These items were conceived in-house or, obtained from other publications or personnel engaged in munitions or special warfare work. This manual includes methods for fabricating explosives, detonators, propellants, shaped charges, small arms, mortars, incendiaries, delays, switches, and similar items from indigenous materials.

SAFETY AND RELIABILITY

Each item was evaluated both theoretically and experimentally to assure safety and reliability. A large number of items were discarded because of inherent hazards or unreliable performance. Safety warnings are prominently inserted in the procedures where they apply but it is emphasized that safety is a matter of attitude. It is a proven fact that men who are alert, who think out a situation, and who take correct precautions have fewer accidents than the careless and indifferent. It is important that work be planned and that instructions be followed to the letter; all work should be done in a neat and orderly manner. In the manufacture of explosives, detonators, propellants and incendiaries, equipment must be kept clean and such energy concentrations as sparks, friction, impact, hot objects, flame, chemical reactions, and excessive pressure should be avoided.

These items were found to be effective in most environments; however, samples should be made and tested remotely prior to actual use to assure proper performance. Chemical items should be used as soon as possible after preparation and kept free of moisture, dirt, and the above energy concentrations. Special care should be taken in any attempt at substitution or use of items for purposes other than that specified or intended.

SECTION 1

Explosives and Propellants (Including Igniters)

1.1 PLASTIC EXPLOSIVE FILLER

A plastic explosive filler can be made from potassium chlorate and petroleum jelly. This explosive can be detonated with commercial #8 or any military blasting cap.

Materials Required	How Used
Potassium chlorate	Medicine Manufacture of matches
Petroleum jelly (Vaseline)	Medicine Lubricant
Piece of round stick	
Wide bowl or other container for mixing ingredients	

Procedure

1. Spread potassium chlorate crystals thinly on a hard surface. Roll the round stick over crystals to crush into a very fine powder until it looks like face powder or wheat flour.

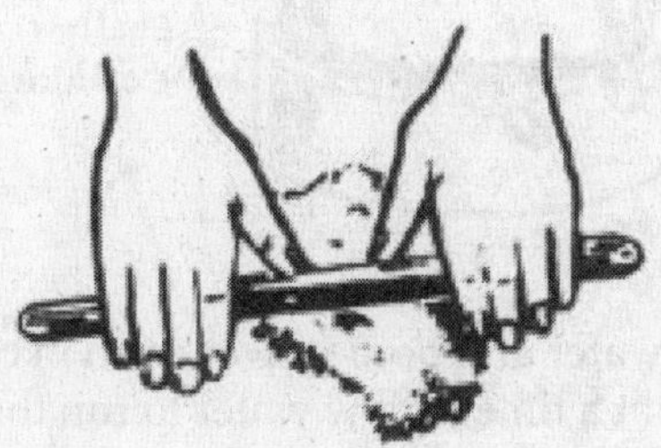

2. Place 9 parts powdered potassium chlorate and 1 part petroleum jelly in a wide bowl or similar container. Mix ingredients with hands (knead) until a uniform paste is obtained.

NOTE
Store explosive in a waterproof container until ready to use.

1.2 POTASSIUM NITRATE

Potassium nitrate (saltpeter) can be extracted from many natural sources and can be used to make nitric acid, black powder and many pyrotechnics. The yield ranges from 0.1 to 10% by weight, depending on the fertility of the soil.

Materials	Source
Nitrate bearing earth or other material, about 3-1/2 gallons (13-1/2 liters)	Soil containing old decayed vegetable or animal matter Old cellars and/or farm dirt floors Earth from old burial grounds Decayed stone or mortar building foundations
Fine wood ashes, about 1/2 cup (1/8 liter)	Totally burned whitish wood ash powder Totally burned paper (black)

Bucket or similar container, about 5 gallons (19 liters) in volume (plastic, metal, or wood)	
2 pieces of finely woven cloth, each slightly larger than bottom of bucket	
Shallow pan or dish, at least as large as bottom of bucket	
Shallow heat resistant container (ceramic, metal, etc.)	
Water – 1-3/4 gallons (6-3/4 liters)	
Awl, knife, screwdriver, or other hole producing instrument	
Alcohol about 1 gallon (4 liters) (whiskey, rubbing alcohol, etc.)	
Heat source (fire, electric heater, etc.)	
Paper	
Tape	

NOTE

Only the ratios of the amounts of ingredients are important. Thus, for twice as much potassium nitrate, double quantities used.

Procedure

1. Punch holes in bottom of bucket. Spread one piece of cloth over holes inside of bucket.

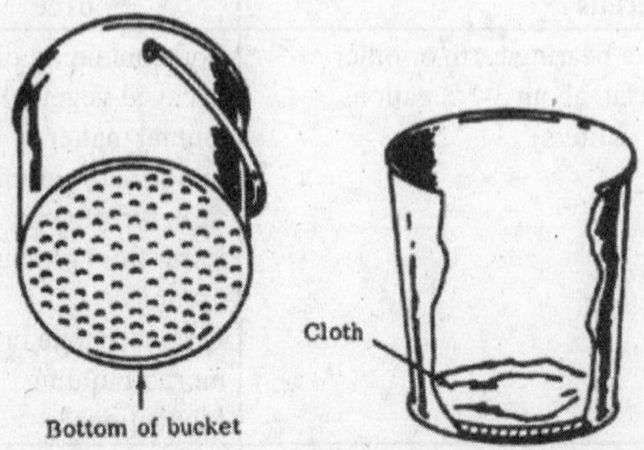

2. Place wood ashes on cloth and spread to make a layer about the thickness of the cloth. Place second piece of cloth on top of ashes.

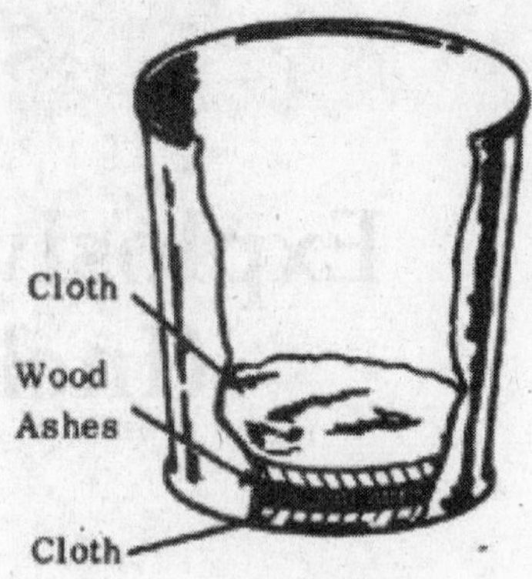

3. Place dirt in bucket.

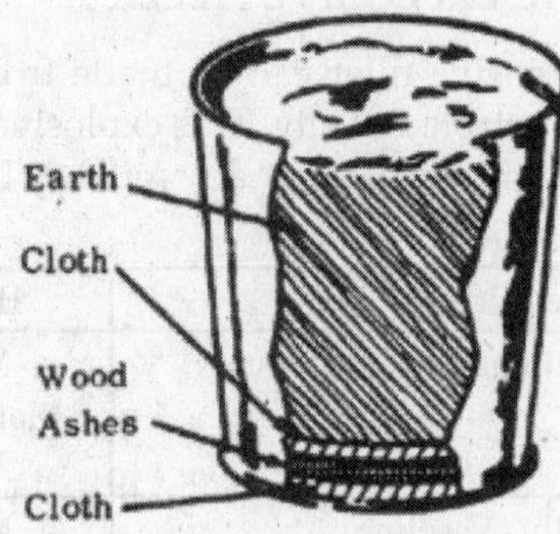

4. Place bucket over shallow container. Bucket may be a ported on sticks if necessary.

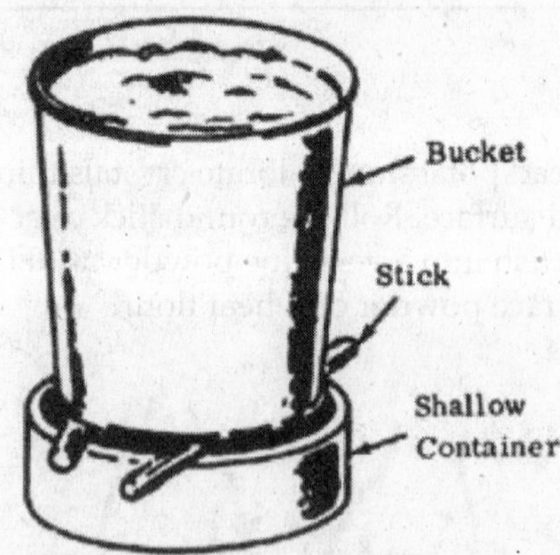

5. Boil water and pour it over earth in bucket a little at a time. Allow water to run through holes in bucket into shallow container. Be sure water goes through *all* of the earth. Allow drained liquid to cool and settle for 1 to 2 hours.

NOTE

Do not pour all of the water at once, since this may cause stoppage.

6. Carefully drain off liquid into heat resistant container. Discard any sludge remaining in bottom of the shallow container.

7. Boil mixture over hot fire for at least 2 hours. Small grains of salt will begin to appear in the solution. Scoop these out as they form, using any type of improvised strainer (paper, etc.).

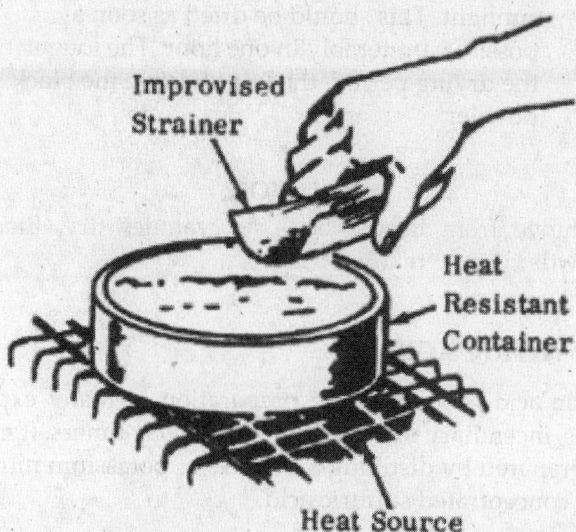

8. When liquid has boiled down to approximately half its original volume, remove from fire and let sit. After half an hour add an equal volume of alcohol. When mixture is poured through paper, small white crystals will collect on top of it.

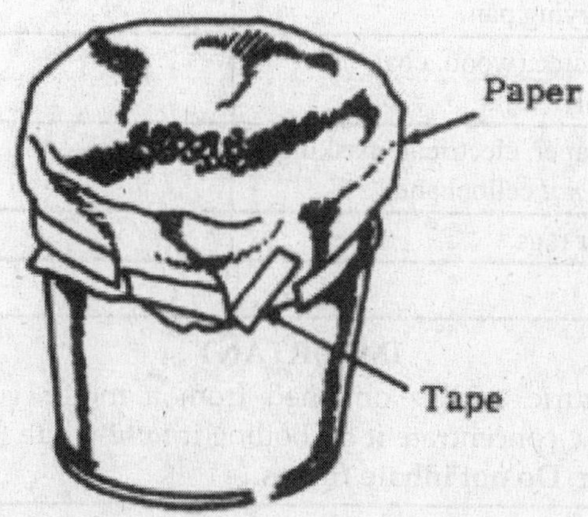

9. To purify the potassium nitrate, redissolve the dry crystals in the smallest possible amount of boiled water. Remove any salt crystals that appear (step 7); pour through an improvised filter made of several pieces of paper and evaporate or gently heat the concentrated solution to dryness.

10. Spread crystals on flat surface and allow to dry. The potassium nitrate crystals are now ready for use.

1.3 IMPROVISED BLACK POWDER

Black powder can be prepared in a simple, safe manner. It may be used as blasting or gun powder.

Materials Required
Potassium nitrate, granulated, 3 cups (3/4 liter) (section 1.2)
Wood charcoal, powdered, 2 cups (1/2 liter)
Sulfur, powdered, 1/2 cup (1/8 liter)
Alcohol, 5 pints (2-1/2 liters) (whiskey, rubbing alcohol, etc.)
Water, 3 cups (3/4 liter)
Heat source
2 Buckets – each 2 gallon (7-1/2 liters) capacity, at least one of which is heat resistant (metal, ceramic, etc.)
Flat window screening, at least 1 foot (30 cm) square
Large wooden stick
Cloth, at least 2 feet (60 cm) square

Note: The above amounts will yield two pounds (900 grams) of black powder. However, only the ratios of the amounts of ingredients are important. Thus, for twice as much black powder, double all quantities used.

Procedure

1. Place alcohol in one of the buckets.

2. Place potassium nitrate, charcoal, and sulfur in the heat resistant bucket. Add 1 cup water and mix thoroughly with wooden stick until all ingredients are dissolved.

3. Add remaining water (2 cups) to mixture. Place bucket on heat source and stir until small bubbles begin to form.

CAUTION

Do not boil mixture. Be sure *all* mixture stays wet. If any is dry, as on sides of pan, it may ignite.

4. Remove bucket from heat and pour mixture into alcohol while stirring vigorously.

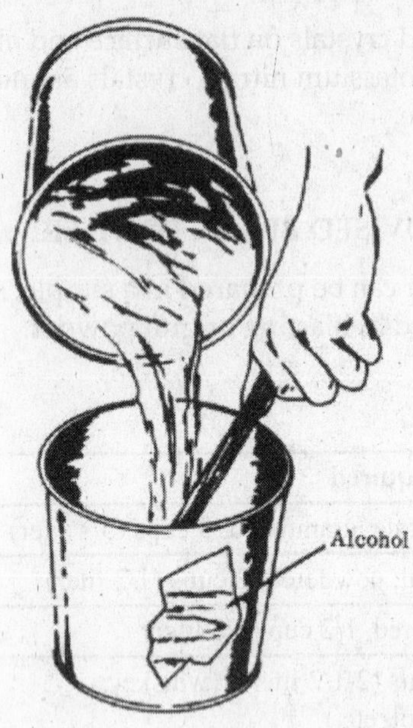

5. Let alcohol mixture stand about 5 minutes. Strain mixture through cloth to obtain black powder. Discard liquid. Wrap cloth around black powder and squeeze to remove all excess liquid.

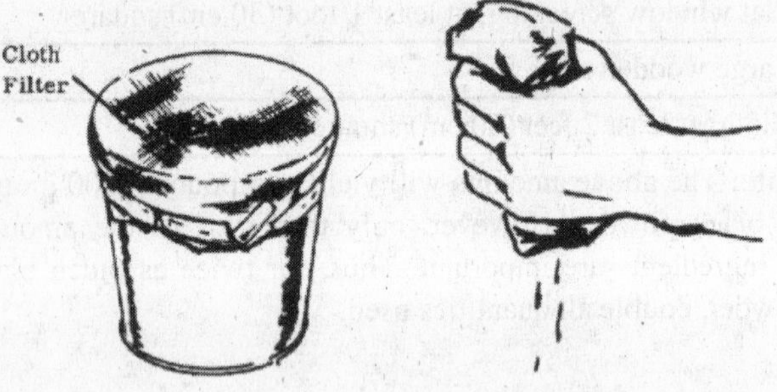

6. Place screening over dry bucket. Place workable amount of damp powder on screen and granulate by rubbing solid through screen.

NOTE

If granulated particles appear to stick together and change shape, recombine entire batch of powder and repeat steps 5 and 6.

7. Spread granulated black powder on flat dry surface so that layer about 1/2 inch (1-1/4 cm) is formed. Allow to dry. Use radiator, or direct sunlight. This should be dried as soon as possible, preferably in one hour. The longer the drying period, the less effective the black powder.

CAUTION

Remove from heat *as soon as* granules dry. Black powder is now ready for use.

1.4 NITRIC ACID

Nitric acid is used in the preparation of many explosives, incendiary mixtures, and acid delay timers. It may be prepared by distilling a mixture of potassium nitrate and concentrated sulfuric acid.

Materials Required	**Source**
Potassium nitrate (2 parts by volume)	Drug Store Improvised (section 1.2)
Concentrated sulfuric acid (1 part by volume)	Motor vehicle batteries Industrial plants
2 bottles or ceramic jugs (narrow necks are preferable)	
Pot or frying pan	
Heat source (wood, coal, or charcoal)	
Tape (paper, electrical, masking, etc. but *not* cellophane)	
Paper or rags	

IMPORTANT

If sulfuric acid is obtained from a motor vehicle battery, concentrate it by boiling it *until* white fumes appear. **Do not inhale fumes.**

NOTE

The amount of nitric acid produced is the same as the amount of potassium nitrate. Thus, for 2 tablespoonfuls of nitric acid, use 2 tablespoonfuls of potassium nitrate and 1 tablespoonful of concentrated sulfuric acid.

Procedure

1. Place dry potassium nitrate in bottle or jug. Add sulfuric acid. Do not fill bottle more than 1/4 full. Mix until paste is formed.

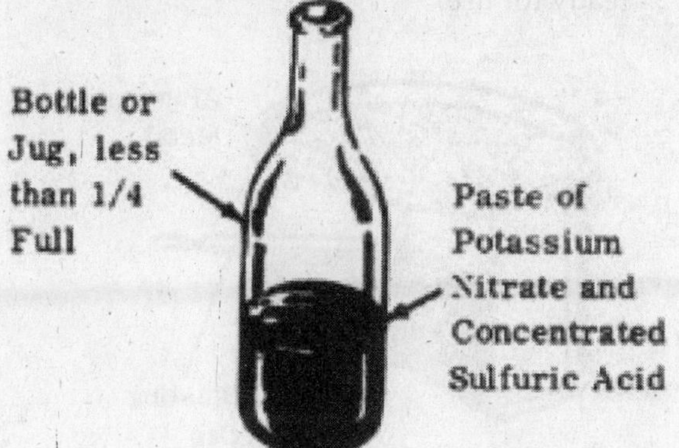

CAUTION

Sulfuric acid will burn skin and destroy clothing. If any is spilled, wash it away with a large quantity of water. Fumes are also dangerous and should not be inhaled.

2. Wrap paper or rags around necks of 2 bottles. Securely tape necks of bottles together. Be sure bottles are flush against each other and that there are no air spaces.

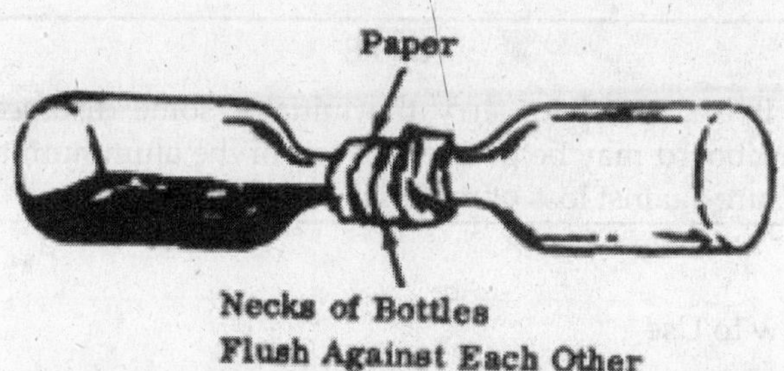

3. Support bottles on rocks or cans so that empty bottle is *slightly* lower than bottle containing paste so that nitric acid that is formed in receiving bottle will not run into other bottle.

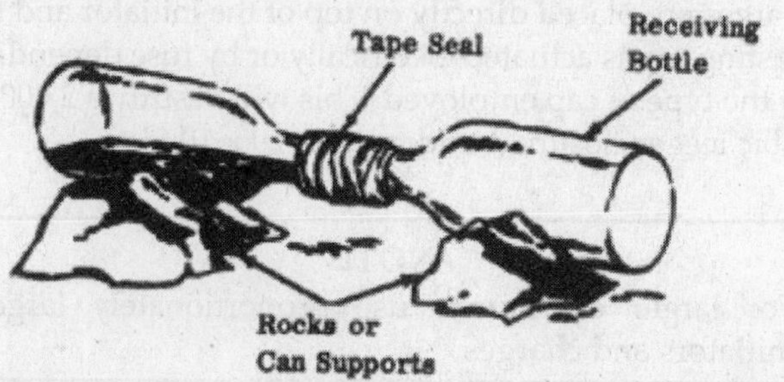

4. Build fire in pot or frying pan.

5. Gently heat bottle containing mixture by moving fire in and out. As red fumes begin to appear periodically pour cool water over empty receiving bottle. Nitric acid will begin to form in the receiving bottle.

CAUTION

Do not overheat or wet bottle containing mixture or it may shatter. As an added precaution, place bottle to be heated in heat resistant container filled with sand or gravel. Heat this outer container to produce nitric acid.

6. Continue the above process until no more red fumes are formed. If the nitric acid formed in the receiving bottle is not clear (cloudy) pour it into cleaned bottle and repeat steps 2–6.

CAUTION

Nitric acid will burn skin and destroy clothing. If any is spilled, wash it away with a large quantity of water. Fumes are also dangerous and should not be inhaled. Nitric acid should be kept away from all combustibles and should be kept in a *sealed ceramic or glass* container.

1.5 INITIATOR FOR DUST EXPLOSIONS

An initiator which will initiate common material to produce dust explosions can be rapidly and easily constructed. This type of charge is ideal for the destruction of enclosed areas such as rooms or buildings.

Materials Required
A flat can, 3 inches (8 cm) diameter and 1-1/2 inch (3-3/4 cm) high. A 6-1/2 ounce (185 g) tuna can serves the purpose quite well.
Blasting cap
Explosive
Aluminum (may be wire, cut sheet, flattened can or powder
Large nail, 4 inches (10 cm) long
Wooden rod – 1/4 inch (6 mm) diameter
Flour, gasoline and powder or chipped aluminum

NOTE

Plastic explosives (Composition C4, etc.) produce better explosions than cast explosives (Composition B, etc.).

Procedure

1. Using the nail, press a hole through the side of the tuna can 3/8 to 1/2 inch (1 to 1-1/2 cm) from the bottom. Using a rotating and lever action, enlarge the hole until it will accommodate the blasting cap.

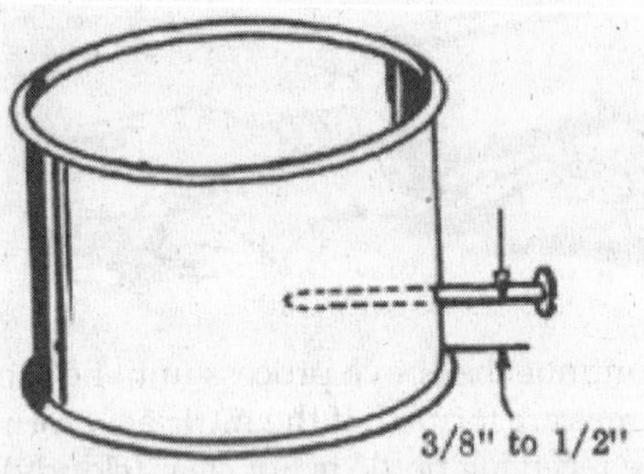

2. Place the wooden rod in the hole and position the end of the rod at the center of the can.

3. Press explosive into the can, being sure to surround the rod, until it is 3/4 inch (2 cm) from top of the can. Carefully remove the wooden rod.

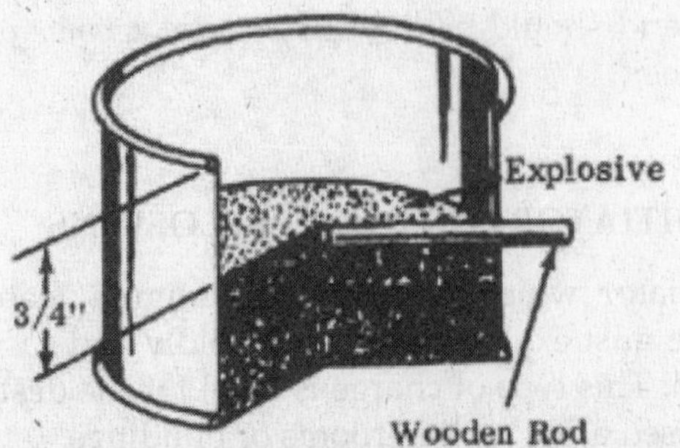

4. Place the aluminum metal on top of the explosive.

5. Just before use, insert the blasting cap into the cavity made by the rod. The initiator is now ready for use.

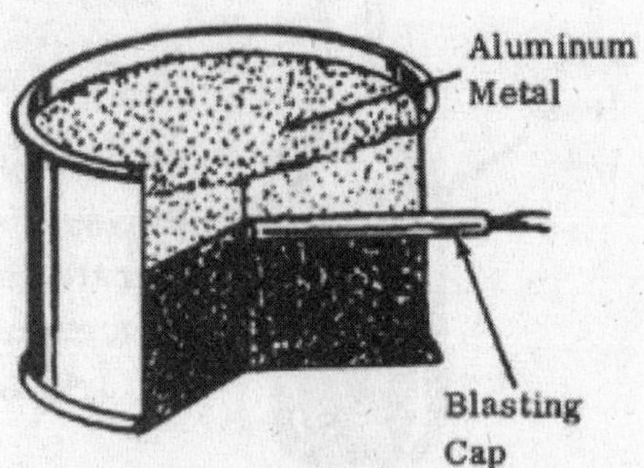

NOTE

If it is desired to carry the initiator some distance, cardboard may be pressed on top of the aluminum to insure against loss of material.

How to Use

This particular unit works quite well to initiate charges of five pounds of flour, 1/2 gallon (1-2/3 liters) of gasoline or two pounds of flake painters aluminum. The solid materials may merely be contained in sacks or cardboard cartons. The gasoline may be placed in plastic coated paper milk cartons, plastic or glass bottles. The charges are placed directly on top of the initiator and the blasting cap is actuated electrically or by fuse depending on the type of cap employed. This will destroy a 2,000 cubic feet enclosure (building 10 × 20 × 10 feet).

NOTE

For larger enclosures, use proportionately larger initiators and charges.

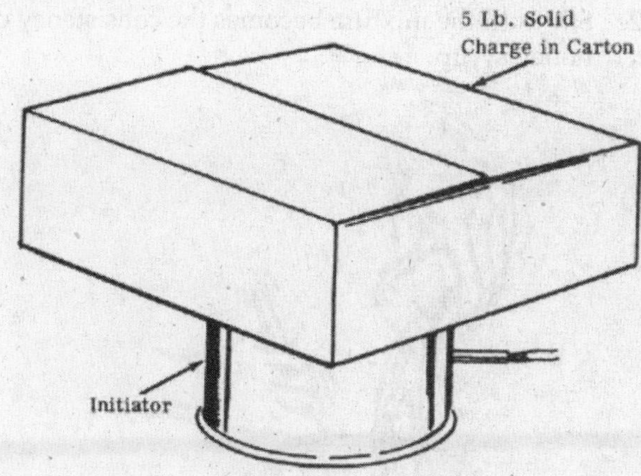

1.6 FERTILIZER EXPLOSIVE

An explosive munition can be made from fertilizer grade ammonium nitrate and either fuel oil or a mixture of equal parts of motor oil and gasoline. When properly prepared, this explosive munition can be detonated with a blasting cap.

Materials Required
Ammonium nitrate (not less than 32% nitrogen)
Fuel oil or gasoline and motor oil 1:1 ratio)
Two flat boards. (At least one of these should be comfortably held in the hand, i.e. 2 × 4 and 36 × 36.)
Bucket or other container for mixing ingredients
Iron or steel pipe or bottle, tin can or heavy-walled cardboard tube
Blasting cap
Wooden rod – 1/4 inch diameter
Spoon or similar measuring container

Procedure

1. Spread a handful of the ammonium nitrate on the large flat board and rub vigorously with the other board until the large particles are crushed into a very fine powder that looks like flour (approximately 10 minutes).

NOTE
Proceed with step 2 as soon as possible since the powder may take moisture from the air and become spoiled.

2. Mix one measure (cup, tablespoon, etc.) of fuel oil with 16 measures of the finely ground ammonium nitrate in a dry bucket or other suitable container and stir with the wooden rod. If fuel oil is not available, use one half measure of gasoline and one half measure of motor oil. Store in a waterproof container until ready to use.

3. Spoon this mixture into an iron or steel pipe which has an end cap threaded on one end. If a pipe is not available, you may use a dry tin can, a glass jar or a heavy-walled cardboard tube.

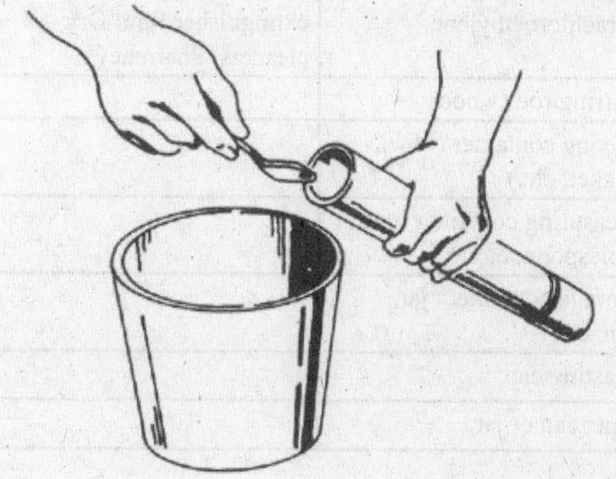

NOTE
Take care not to tamp or shake the mixture in the pipe. If mixture becomes tightly packed, one cap will not be sufficient to initiate the explosive.

4. Insert blasting cap just beneath the surface of the explosive mix.

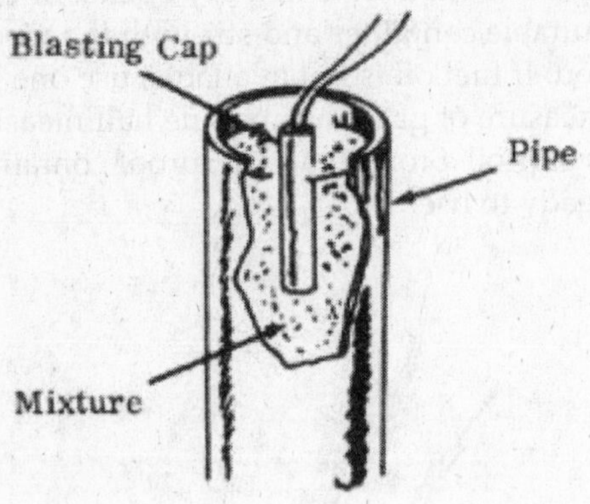

> **NOTE**
>
> Confining the open end of the container will add to the effectiveness of the explosive.

1.7 CARBON TET–EXPLOSIVE

A moist explosive mixture can be made from fine aluminum powder combined with carbon tetrachloride or tetrachloroethylene. This explosive can be detonated with a blasting cap.

Materials Required	Source
Fine aluminum bronzing powder	Paint Store
Carbon tetrachloride, or tetrachloroethylene	Pharmacy, or fire extinguisher fluid Dry cleaners, Pharmacy
Stirring rod (wood)	
Mixing container (bowl, bucket, etc.)	
Measuring container (cup, tablespoon, etc.)	
Storage container (jar, can, etc.)	
Blasting cap	
Pipe, can or jar	

Procedure

1. Measure out two parts aluminum powder to one part carbon tetrachloride or tetrachloroethylene liquid into mixing container, adding liquid to powder while stirring with the wooden rod.
2. Stir until the mixture becomes the consistency of honey syrup.

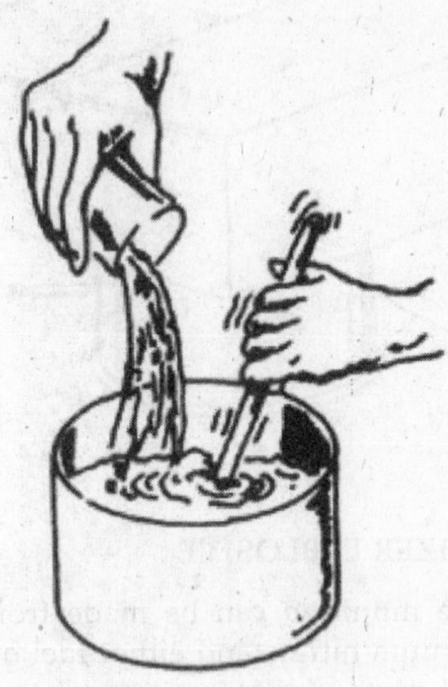

> **CAUTION**
>
> Fumes from the liquid are dangerous and should not be inhaled.

3. Store explosive in a jar or similar water proof container until ready to use. The liquid in the mixture evaporates quickly when not confined.

> **NOTE**
>
> Mixture will detonate in this manner for a period of 72 hours.

How to Use

1. Pour this mixture into an iron or steel pipe which has an end cap threaded on one end. If a pipe is not available, you may use a dry tin can or a glass jar.

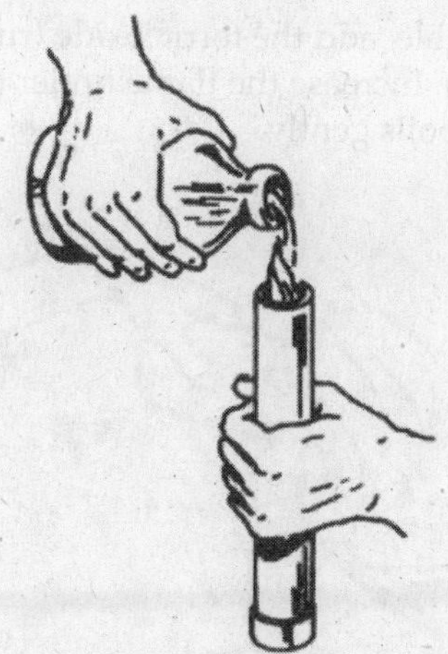

2. Insert blasting cap just beneath the surface of the explosive mix.

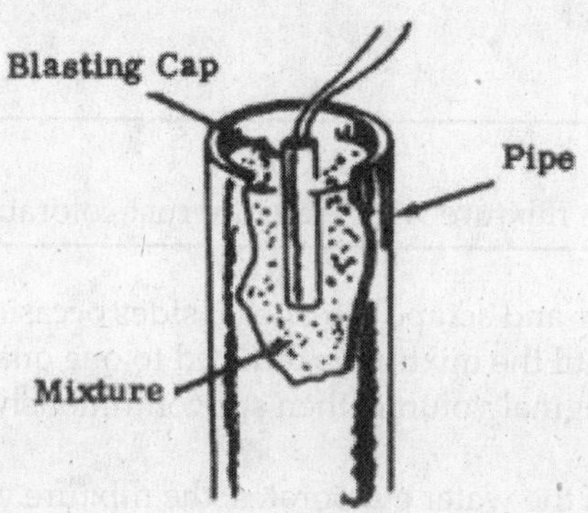

NOTE
Confining the open end of the container will add to the effectiveness of the explosive.

1.8 FERTILIZER AN-AI EXPLOSIVE

A dry explosive mixture can be made from ammonium nitrate fertilizer combined with fine aluminum powder. This explosive can be detonated with a blasting cap.

Materials Required	Source
Ammonium nitrate fertilizer (not less than 32% nitrogen)	Farm or Feed Store
Fine aluminum bronzing powder	Paint Store
Measuring container (cup, tablespoon, etc.)	
Mixing container (wide bowl, can, etc.)	
Two flat boards (one should be comfortably held in hand and one very large, i.e. 2 × 4 and 36 × 36 inches)	
Storage container (jar, can, etc.)	
Blasting cap	
Wooden rod – 1/4 inch diameter	
Pipe, can or jar	

Procedure

1. *Method I – To Obtain a Low Velocity Explosive*
   a. Use measuring container to measure four parts fertilizer to one part aluminum powder and pour into the mixing container. (Example: 4 cups of fertilizer to 1 cup aluminum powder.)
   b. Mix ingredients well with the wooden rod.

2. *Method II – To Obtain a Much Higher Velocity Explosive*
   a. Spread a handful at a time of the fertilizer on the large flat board and rub vigorously with the other board until the large particles are crushed into a very fine powder that looks like flour (approximately 10 minutes per handful).

NOTE
Proceed with step b below as soon as possible since the powder may take moisture from the air and become spoiled.

   b. Follow steps a and b of Method I.

3. Store the explosive mixture in a waterproof container, such as glass jar, steel pipe, etc., until ready to use.

How to Use

Follow steps 1 and 2 of How to Use in section 1.7.

1.9 "RED OR WHITE POWDER" PROPELLANT

"Red or White Powder" Propellant may be prepared in a simple, safe manner. The formulation described below will result in approximately 2-1/2 pounds of powder. This is a small arms propellant and should only be used in weapons with 1/2 inch inside diameter or less, such as the Match Gun or the 7.62 Carbine, but not pistols.

Materials Required
Heat source (kitchen stove or open fire)
2 gallon metal bucket
Measuring cup (8 ounces or 240 milliliters)
Wooden spoon or rubber spatula
Metal sheet or aluminum foil (at least 18 inches square)
Flat window screen (at least 1 foot square)
Potassium nitrate (granulated) 2-1/3 cups (560 milliliters)
White sugar (granulated) 2 cups (480 milliliters)
Powdered ferric oxide (rust) 1/8 cup (30 milliliters) (if available)
Clear water, 3-1/2 cups (840 milliliters)

Procedure

1. Place the sugar, potassium nitrate, and water in the bucket. Heat with a low flame, stirring occasionally until the sugar and potassium nitrate dissolve.

2. If available, add the ferric oxide (rust) to the solution. Increase the flame under the mixture until it boils gently.

NOTE
The mixture will retain the rust coloration.

3. Stir and scrape the bucket sides occasionally until the mixture is reduced to one quarter of its original volume, then stir continuously.

4. As the water evaporates, the mixture will become thicker until it reaches the consistency of cooked breakfast cereal or homemade fudge. At this stage of thickness, remove the bucket from the heat source, and spread the mass on the metal sheet.

5. While the material cools, score it with the spoon or spatula in crisscrossed furrows about 1 inch apart.

6. Allow the material to air dry, preferably in the sun. As it dries, rescore it occasionally (about every 20 minutes) to aid drying.

7. When the material has dried to a point where it is moist and soft but not sticky to the touch, place a small spoonful on the screen. Rub the material back and forth against the screen mesh with spoon or other flat object until the material is granulated into small worm-like particles.

8. After granulation, return me material to me sun to dry completely.

1.10 NITRIC ACID/NITROBENZENE ("HELLHOFFITE") EXPLOSIVE

An explosive munition can be made from mononitrobenzene and nitric acid. It is a simple explosive to prepare. Just pour the mononitrobenzene into the acid and stir.

Materials Required	Source
Nitric acid	Field grade or 90% concentrated (specific gravity of 1.48)
Mononitrobenzene (also known as nitrobenzene)	Drug store (oil of mirbane) Chemical supply house Industries (used as solvent)
Acid resistant measuring containers	Glass, clay, etc.
Acid resistant mixing rod	
Blasting cap	
Wax	
Steel pipe, end cap and tape	
Bottle or jar	

NOTE
Prepare mixture just before use.

Procedure

1. Add 1 volume (cup, quart, etc.) mononitrobenzene to 2 volumes nitric acid in bottle or jar.

2. Mix ingredients well by stirring with acid resistant rod.

CAUTION
Nitric acid will burn skin and destroy clothing. If any is spilled, wash off immediately with large amount of water. Nitrobenzene is toxic; do not inhale fumes.

How to Use

1. Wax blasting cap, pipe and end cap.
2. Thread end cap onto pipe.
3. Pour mixture into pipe.

4. Insert and tape blasting cap just beneath surface of mixture.

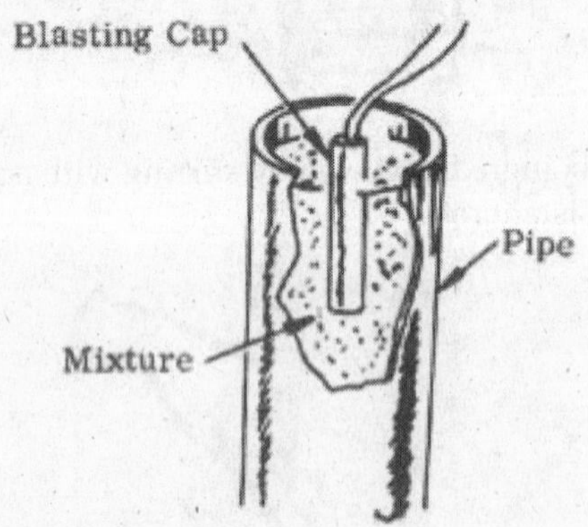

> **NOTE**
> Combining the open end of the pipe will add to the effectiveness of the explosive.

1.11 OPTIMIZED PROCESS FOR CELLULOSE/ ACID EXPLOSIVES

An acid type explosive can be made from nitric acid and white paper or cotton cloth. This explosive can be detonated with a commercial #8 or any military blasting cap.

Materials Required	Source
Nitric Acid	Industrial metal processors, 90% concentrated (specific gravity of 1.48) Field grade (section 1,4)
White unprinted, unsized paper	Paper towels, napkins
Clean white cotton cloth	Clothing, sheets, etc.
Acid resistant container	Wax coated pipe or can, ceramic pipe, glass jar, etc. Heavy-walled glass containers
Aluminum foil or acid resistant material	Food stores
Protective gloves	
Blasting cap	
Wax	

Procedure

1. Put on gloves.
2. Spread out a layer of paper or cloth on aluminum foil and sprinkle with nitric acid until thoroughly soaked. If aluminum foil is unavailable, use an acid resistant material (glass, ceramic or wood).

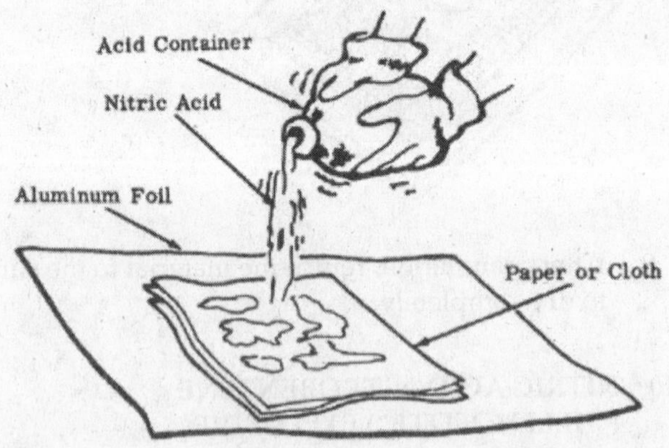

> **CAUTION**
> Acid will burn skin and destroy clothing. If any is spilled, wash it away with a large quantity of water. Do not inhale fumes.

3. Place another layer of paper or cloth on top of the acid-soaked sheet and repeat step 2 above. Repeat as often as necessary.

4. Roll up the aluminum foil containing the acid-soaked sheets and insert the roll into the acid resistant container.

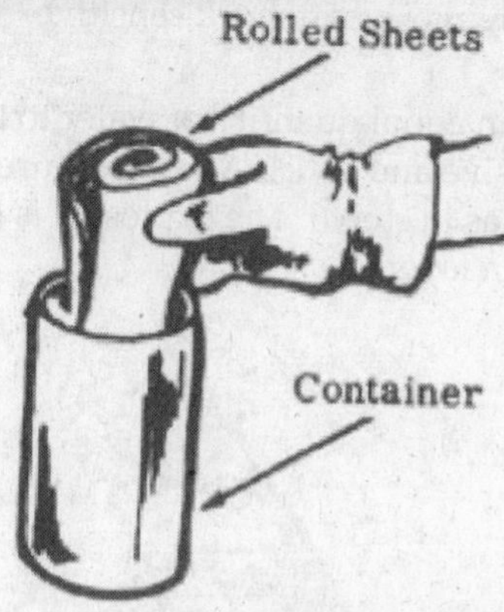

NOTE
If glass, ceramic or wooden tray is used, pick up sheets with two wooden sticks and load into container.

5. Wax blasting cap.

6. Insert the blasting cap in the center of the rolled sheets. Allow 5 minutes before detonating the explosive.

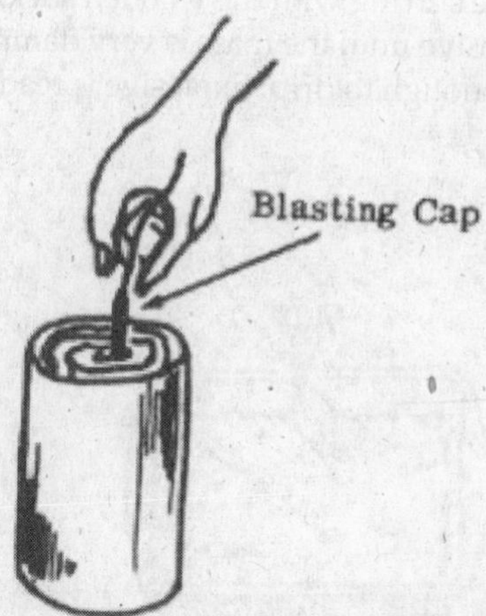

1.12 METHYL NITRATE DYNAMITE

A moist explosive mixture can be made from sulfuric acid, nitric acid and methyl alcohol. This explosive can be detonated with a blasting cap.

Materials Required	Source
Sulfuric acid	Clear battery acid boiled until white fumes appear
Nitric acid	Field grade nitric acid (section 1.4) or 90% concentration (1.48 specific gravity)
Methyl alcohol	Methanol Wood alcohol (not denatured alcohol) Antifreeze (nonpermanent)
Eyedropper or syringe with glass tube	
Large diameter glass (2 quart) jar	
Narrow glass jars (1 quart)	
Absorbent (fine sawdust, shredded paper, shredded cloth)	
Cup	
Pan (3 to 5 gallon)	
Teaspoon	
Wooden stick	
Steel pipe with end cap	
Blasting cap	
Water	
Tray	

Procedure

1. Add 24 teaspoons of sulfuric acid to 16-1/2 teaspoons of nitric acid in the 2 quart jar.

CAUTION

Acid will burn skin and destroy clothing. If any is spilled, wash it away with a large quantity of water. Do not inhale fumes.

2. Place the jar in the pan (3 to 5 gallon) filled with cold water or a stream and allow acid to cool.

3. Rapidly swirl the jar to create a whirlpool in the liquid (without splashing) while keeping the bottom portion of the jar in the water.

4. While continually swirling, add to mixture, 1/2 teaspoon at a time, 13-1/2 teaspoons of methyl alcohol, allowing mixture to cool at least one minute between additions.

CAUTION

If there is a sudden increase in the amount of fumes produced or if the solution suddenly turns much darker or begins to froth, dump solution in the water *within 10 seconds*. This will halt the reaction and prevent an accident.

5. After the final addition of methyl alcohol, swirl for another 30 to 45 seconds.

6. Carefully pour the solution into one of the narrow glass jars. Allow jar to stand in water for xapproximately 5 minutes until two layers separate.

7. With an eyedropper or syringe, remove top layer and *carefully* put into another narrow glass jar. This liquid is the explosive.

CAUTION

Explosive is shock sensitive.

8. Add an equal quantity of water to the explosive and swirl. Allow mixture to separate again as in step 6. The explosive is now the bottom layer.

9. Carefully remove the top layer with the eyedropper or syringe and discard.

10. Place one firmly packed cup of absorbent in the tray.

11. While stirring with the wooden stick, slowly add explosive until the mass is very damp but not wet enough to drip. Explosive is ready to use.

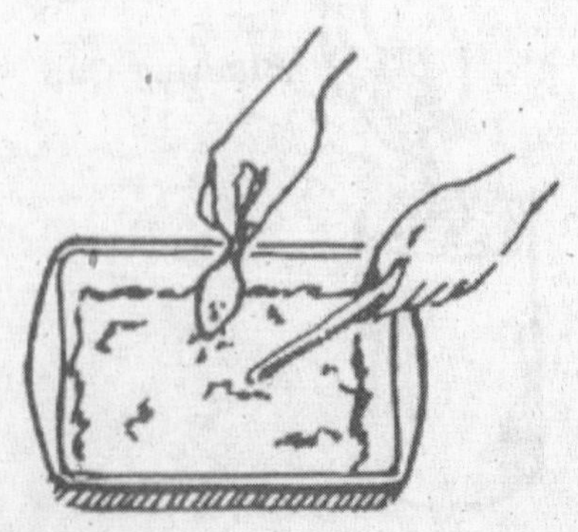

NOTE

If mixture becomes too wet, add more absorbent.

If storage of explosive is required, store in a sealed container to prevent evaporation.

CAUTION

Do not handle liquid explosive or allow to contact skin. If this happens, flush away immediately with large quantity of water. Keep grit, sand or dirt out of mixture.

How to Use

1. Spoon this mixture into an iron or steel pipe which has an end cap threaded on one end. If a pipe is not available, you may use a dry tin can or a glass jar.

2. Insert blasting cap just beneath the surface of the explosive mix.

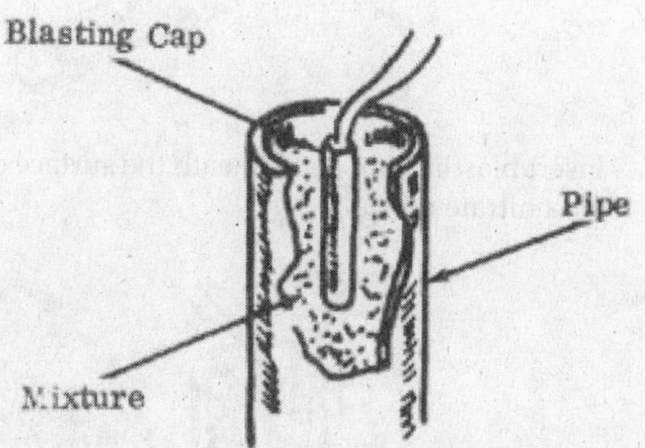

NOTE

Confining the open end of the container will add to the effectiveness of the explosive.

1.13 UREA NITRATE EXPLOSIVE

Urea nitrate can be used as an explosive munition. It is easy to prepare from nitric acid and urine. It can be detonated with a blasting cap.

Materials Required	Source
Nitric acid, 90% concentration (1.48 specific gravity)	Field grade (section 1.4) or industrial metal processors
Urine	Animals (including humans)
2 one gallon heat and acid-resistant containers (glass, clay, etc.)	
Filtering material	Paper towel or finely textured cotton cloth (shirt, sheet, etc.)
Aluminum powder (optional or if available)	Paint stores
Heat source	
Measuring containers (cup and spoon)	
Water	
Tape	
Blasting cap	
Steel pipe and end cap(s)	

NOTE

Prepare mixture just before use.

Procedure

1. Boil a large quantity of urine (10 cups) to approximately 1/10 its volume (1 cup) in one of the containers over the heat source.

2. Filter the urine into the other container through the filtering material to remove impurities.

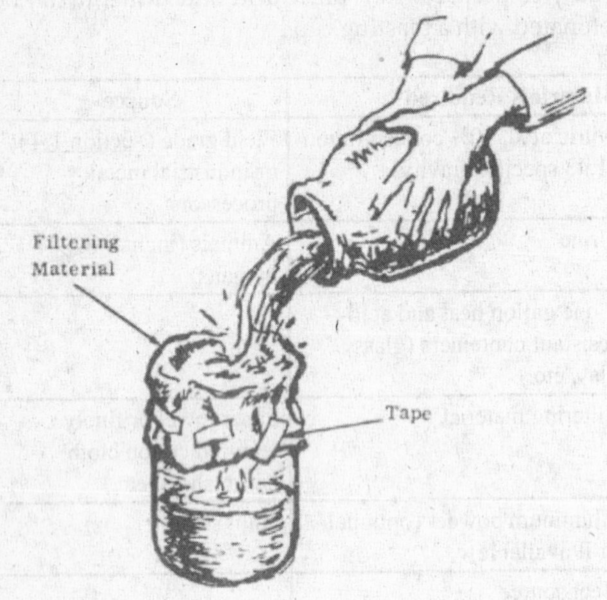

3. Slowly add 1/3 cup of nitric acid to the filtered urine, and let mixture stand for 1 hour.

CAUTION

Acid will burn skin and destroy clothing. If any is spilled, wash it away with a large quantity of water. Do not inhale fumes.

4. Filter mixture as in step 2. Urea nitrate crystals will collect on the paper.

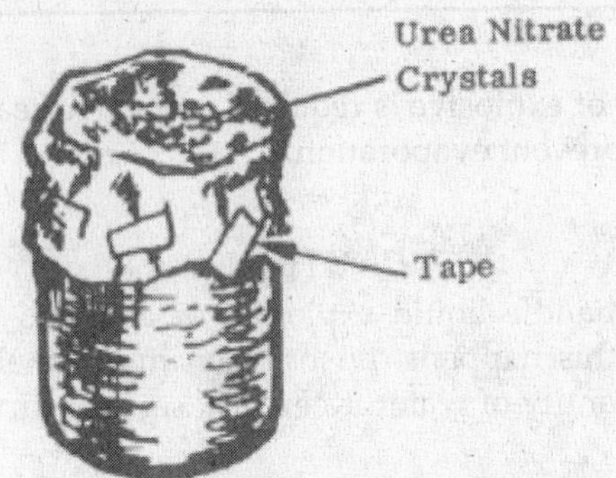

5. Wash the urea nitrate by pouring water over it.
6. Remove urea nitrate crystals from the filtering material and allow to dry thoroughly (approximately 16 hours).

NOTE

The drying time can be reduced to two hours if a hot (not boiling) water bath is used. See step 5 of section 1.15.

How to Use

1. Spoon the urea nitrate crystals into an iron or steel pipe which has an end cap threaded on one end.

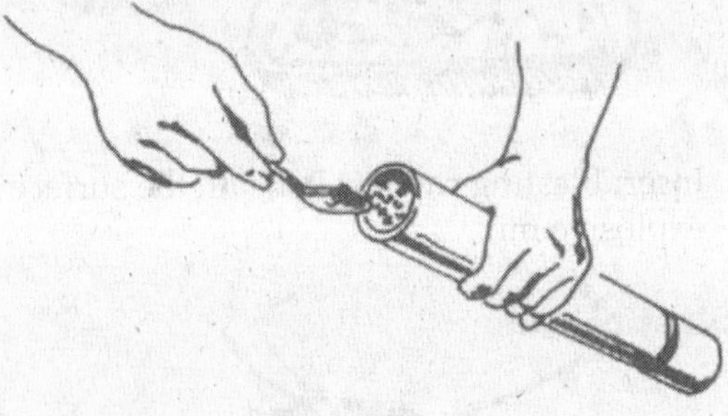

2. Insert blasting cap just beneath the surface of the urea nitrate crystals.

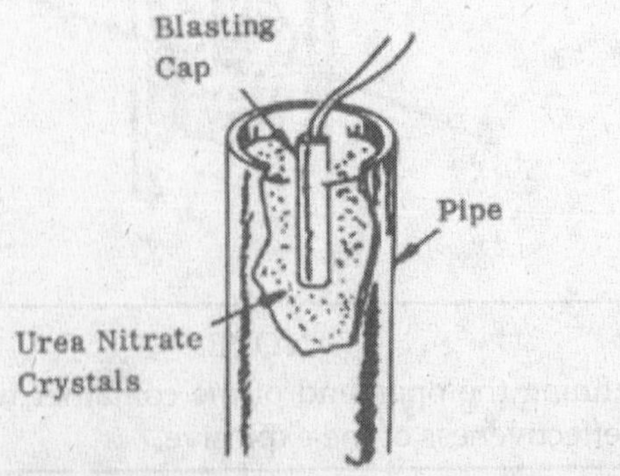

NOTES

This explosive can be made more effective by mixing with aluminum powder (can be obtained in paint stores) in the ratio of 4 to 1. For example, mix 1 cup of aluminum powder with 4 cups of urea nitrate.

Confining the open end of the container will add to the effectiveness of the explosive.

1.14 PREPARATION OF COPPER SULFATE (PENTAHYDRATE)

Copper sulfate is a required material for the preparation of TACC (section 1.16).

Materials Required
Pieces of copper or copper wire
Dilute sulfuric acid (battery acid)
Potassium nitrate (section 1.2) or nitric acid, 90% concentration (1.48 specific gravity) (section 1.4)
Alcohol
Water
Two 1 pint jars or glasses, heat resistant
Paper towels
Pan
Wooden rod or stick
Improvised scale (section 7.8)
Cup
Container
Heat source
Teaspoon

Procedure

1. Place 10 grams of copper pieces into one of the pint jars. Add 1 cup (240 milliliters) of dilute sulfuric acid to the copper.

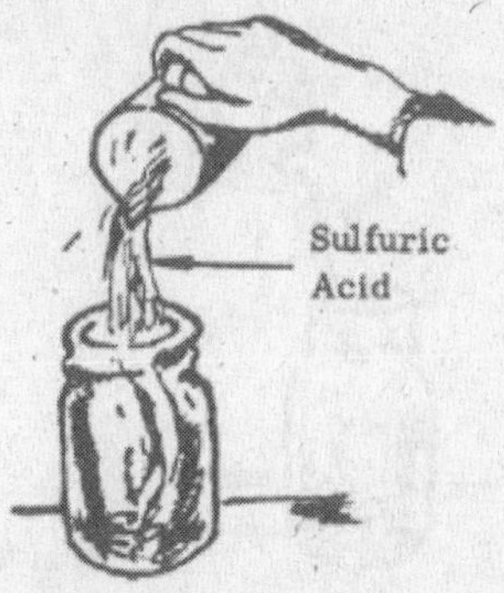

2. Add 12 grams of potassium nitrate or 1-1/2 teaspoons of nitric acid to the mixture.

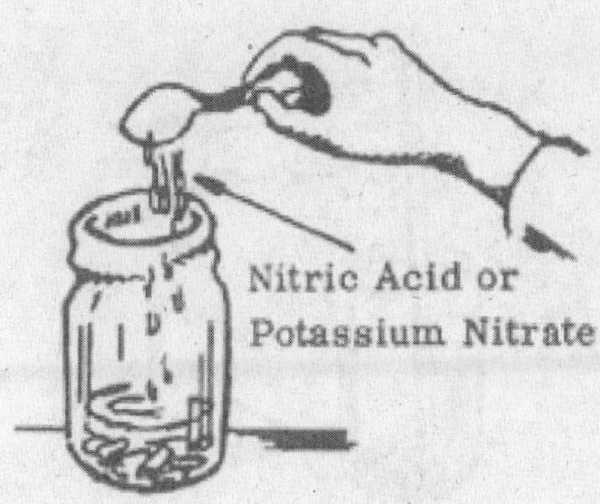

NOTE

Nitric acid gives a product of greater purity.

3. Heat the mixture in a pan of simmering hot water bath until the bubbling has ceased (approximately 2 hours). The mixture will turn to a blue color.

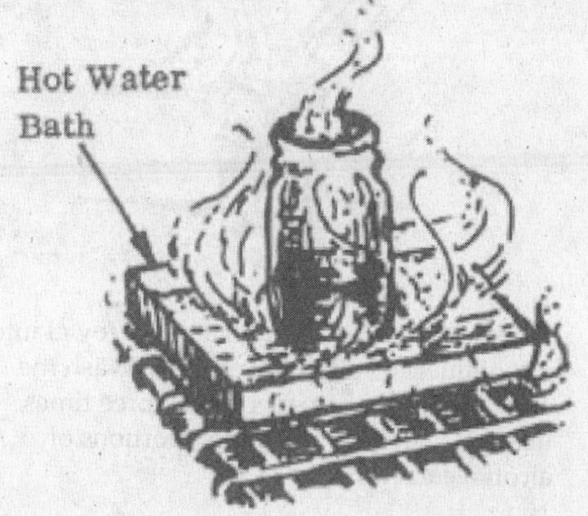

CAUTION

The above procedure will cause strong toxic fumes. Perform step 3 in an open, well ventilated area.

4. Pour the hot blue solution, but not the copper, into the other pint jar. Allow solution to cool at room temperature. Crystals will form at the bottom of the jar. Discard the unreacted copper pieces in the first jar.

5. Carefully pour away the liquid from the crystals. Crush crystals into a powder with wooden rod or stick.

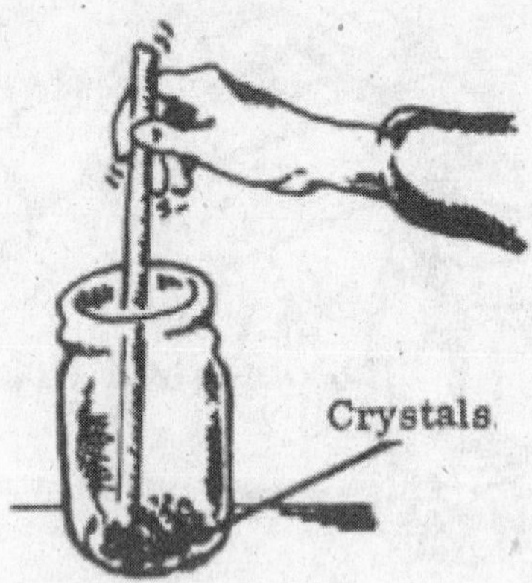

6. Add 1/2 cup (120 milliliters) of alcohol to the powder while stirring.

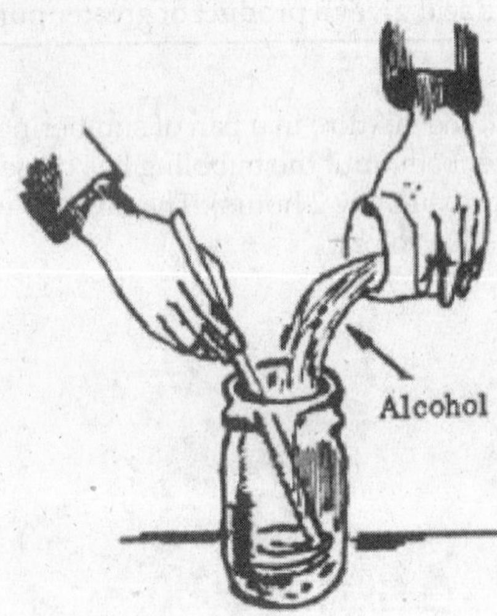

7. Filter the solution through a paper towel into a container to collect the crystals. Wash the crystals left on the paper towel three times, using 1/2 cup (120 milliliters) portions of alcohol each time.

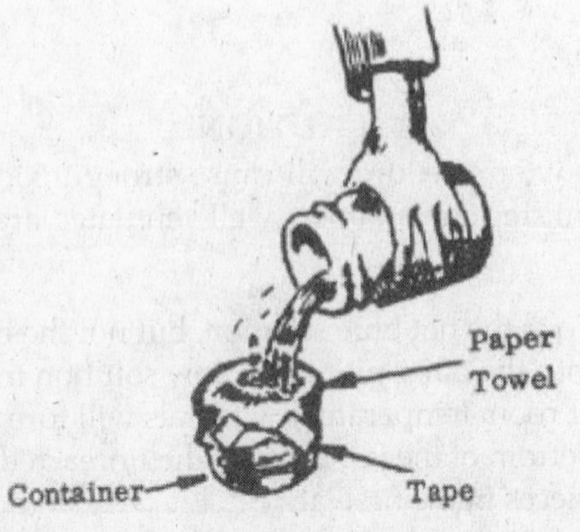

8. Air dry the copper sulfate crystals for 2 hours.

NOTE

Drying time can be reduced to 1/2 hour by use of hot, not boiling, water bath (see step 3).

1.15 RECLAMATION OF RDX FROM C4

RDX can be obtained from C4 explosive with the use of gasoline. It can be used as a booster explosive for detonators (section 6.13) or as a high explosive charge.

Materials Required	
Gasoline	
C4 explosive	
2 pint glass jars, wide mouth	
Paper towels	
Stirring rod (glass or wood)	
Water	Optional (RDX can be air dried instead)
Ceramic or glass dish	
Pan	
Heat Source	
Teaspoon	
Cup	
Tape	

Procedure

1. Place 1-1/2 teaspoons (15 grams) of C4 explosive in one of the pint jars. Add 1 cup (240 milliliters) of gasoline.

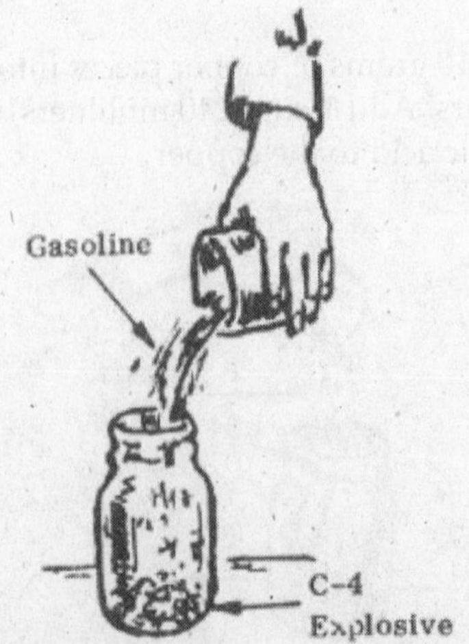

> **NOTE**
> These quantities can be in creased to obtain more RDX. For example, use 2 gallons of gasoline per 1 cup of C4.

2. Knead and stir the C4 with the rod until the C4 has broken down into small particles. Allow mixture to stand for 1/2 hour.

3. Stir the mixture again until a fine white powder remains on the bottom of the jar.

4. Filter the mixture through a paper towel into the other glass jar. Wash the particles collected on the paper towel with 1/2 cup (120 milliliters) of gasoline. Discard the waste liquid.

5. Place the RDX particles in a glass or ceramic dish. Set the dish in a pan of hot water, not boiling, and dry for a period of 1 hour.

> **NOTE**
> The RDX particles may be air dried for a period of 2 to 3 hours.

1.16 TACC (TETRAMMINECOPPER (II) CHLORATE)

Tetramminecopper (II) chlorate is a primary explosive that can be made from sodium chlorate, copper sulfate and ammonia. This explosive is to be used with a booster explosive such as picric acid (section 1.21) or RDX (section 1.15) in the fabrication of detonators (section 6.13).

Materials Required	Source
Sodium chlorate	Section 1,23 Medicine Weed killer, hardware store
Copper sulfate	Section 1.14 Insecticide, hardware store Water purifying agent
Ammonia hydroxide	Household ammonia Smelling salts
Alcohol, 95% pure	
Wax, clay, pitch, etc.	
Water	
Bottle, narrow mouth (wine or Coke)	
Bottles, wide month (mason jars)	
Tubing (rubber, copper, steel) to fit narrow mouth bottle	
Teaspoon	
Improvised scale	Section 7.8
Heat source	
Paper towel	
Pan	
Tape	
Cup	

Procedure

1. Measure 1/3 teaspoon (2-1/2 grams) of sodium chlorate into a wide mouth bottle. Add 10 teaspoons of alcohol.

2. Place the wide mouth bottle in a pan of hot water. Add 1 teaspoon (4 grams) of copper sulfate to the mixture. Heat for a period of 30 minutes just under the boiling point and stir occasionally.

CAUTION
Keep solution away from flame.

NOTE
Keep volume of solution constant by adding additional alcohol approximately every 10 minutes.

3. Remove solution from pan and allow to cool. Color of solution will change from blue to light green. Filter solution through a paper towel into another wide mouth bottle. Store solution until ready for step 6.

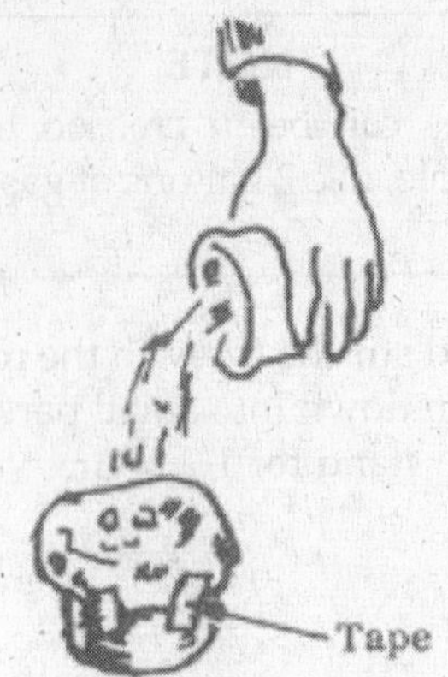

4. Add 1 cup (250 milliliters) of ammonia to the narrow mouth bottle.

5. Place tubing into the neck of bottle so that it extends about 1-1/2 inches (4 cm) inside bottle. Seal tubing to bottle with wax, clay, pitch, etc.

6. Place free end of tubing into the chlorate-alcohol-sulfate solution (step 3). Heat bottle containing ammonia in a pan of hot water, but not boiling, for approximately 10 minutes.

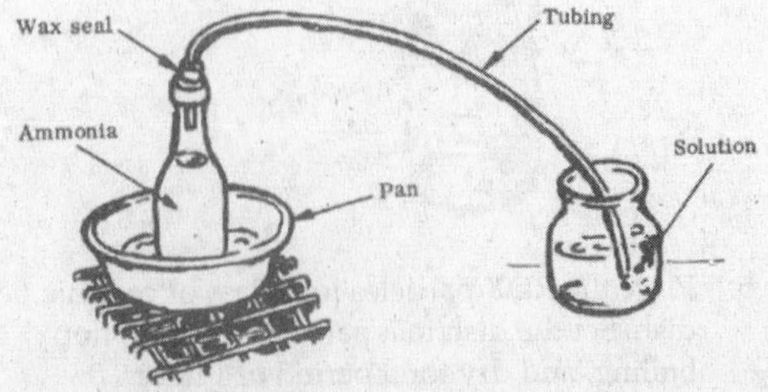

7. Bubble ammonia gas through the chlorate-alcohol-sulfate solution, approximately 10 minutes, until the color changes from light green to dark blue. Continue bubbling for another 10 minutes.

CAUTION
At this point the solution is a primary explosive. Keep away from flame.

8. Remove the solution from the pan and reduce the volume to about 1/3 of its original volume by evaporating in the open air or in a stream of air.

NOTE
Pour solution into a flat container for faster evaporation.

9. Filter the solution through a paper towel into a wide mouth bottle to collect crystals. Wash crystals with 1 teaspoon of alcohol. Tape and set aside to dry (approximately 16 hours).

CAUTION
Explosive is shock and flame sensitive. Store in a capped container.

NOTE
The drying time can be reduced to 2 hours if a hot (not boiling) water bath is used.

1.17 HMTD:

HMTD is a primary explosive that can be made from hexamethylenetetramine, hydrogen peroxide and citric acid. This explosive is to be used with a booster explosive such as picric acid (section 1.21) or RDX (section 1.15) in the fabrication of detonators (section 6.13).

Materials Required	Source
Hexamethylene-tetramine	Drugstores under names of urotropine, hexamin, methenamine, etc. Army heat tablets
Hydrogen peroxide	6% hair bleach (or stronger if possible)
Citric acid	Drug stores or food stores ("Sour Salt")
Containers, bottles or glasses	
Paper towels	
Teaspoon	
Pan	
Water	
Tape	

Procedure

1. Measure 9 teaspoons of hydrogen peroxide into a container.

2. In 3 portions, dissolve 2-1/2 teaspoons of crushed hexamethylenetetramine in the peroxide.

3. Keep the solution cool for 30 minutes by placing container in a pan of cold water.

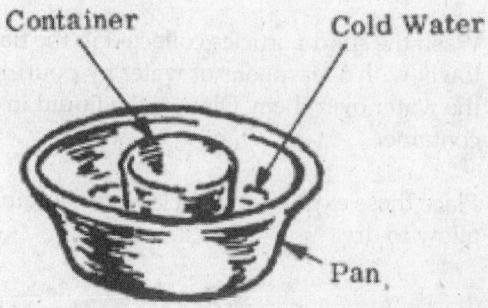

4. In 5 portions, dissolve 4-1/2 teaspoons of crushed citric acid in the hexamethylenetetramine-peroxide solution.

5. Permit solution to stand at room temperature until solid particles form at the bottom of container.

NOTE
Complete precipitation will take place in 8 to 24 hours.

CAUTION
At this point the mixture is a primary explosive. Keep away from flame.

6. Filter the mixture through a paper towel into a container to collect the solid particles.

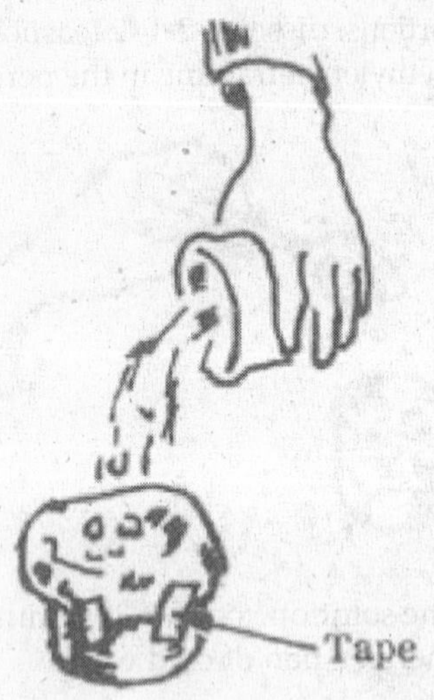

7. Wash the solid particles collected in the paper towel with 6 teaspoons of water by pouring the water over them. Discard the liquid in the container.

8. Place these explosive particles in a container and allow to dry.

CAUTION
Handle dry explosive with great care. Do not scrape or handle it roughly. Keep away from sparks or open flames. Store in cool, dry place.

1.18 POTASSIUM OR SODIUM NITRATE AND LITHARGE (LEAD MONOXIDE)

Potassium or sodium nitrite is needed to prepare DDNP (section 1.19), and litharge is required for the preparation of lead picrate (section 1.20).

Materials Required	Source
Lead metal (small pieces or chips)	Plumbing supply store
Potassium (or sodium) nitrate	Field grade (section 1.2) or Drug Store
Methyl (wood) alcohol	
Iron pipe with end cap	
Iron rod or screwdriver	
Paper towels	
2 glass jars, wide mouth	
Metal pan	
Heat source (hot coals or blow torch)	
Improvised scale (section 7.8)	
Cup	
Water	
Pan	

Procedure

1. Mix 12 grams of lead and 4 grams of potassium or sodium nitrate in a jar. Place the mixture in the iron pipe.

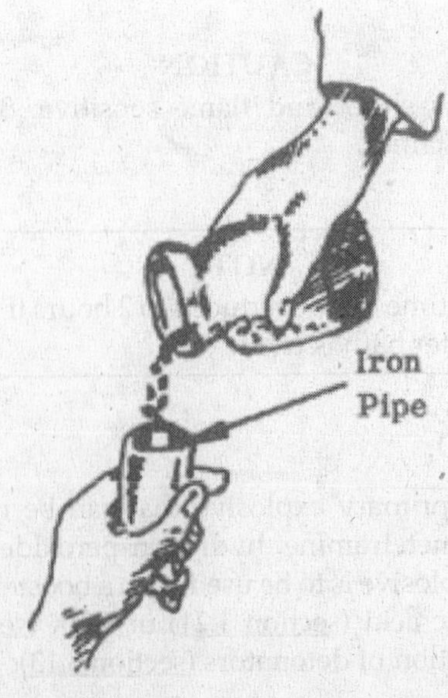

2. Heat iron pipe in a bed of hot coals or with blow torch for 30 minutes to 1 hour. (Mixture will change to a yellow color.)

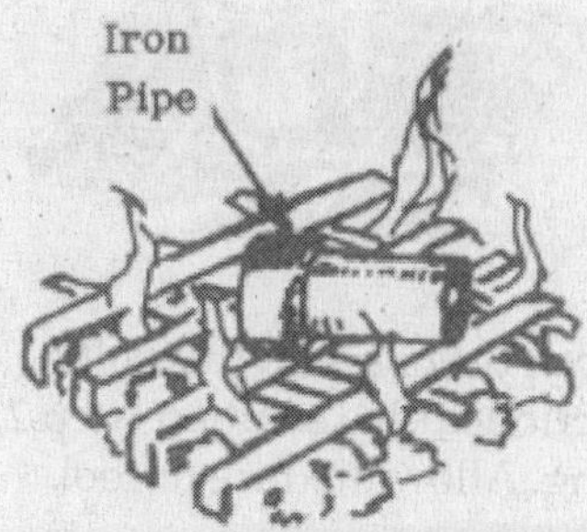

3. Remove the iron pipe from the heat source and allow to cool. Chip out the yellow material formed in the iron pipe and place the chips in the glass jar.

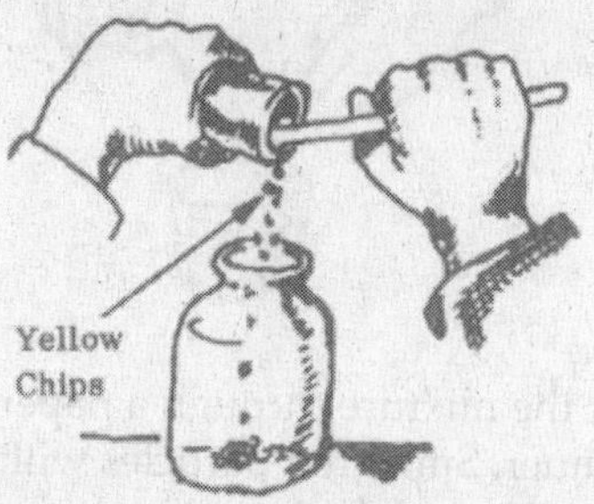

4. Add 1/2 cup (120 milliliters) of methyl alcohol to the chips.

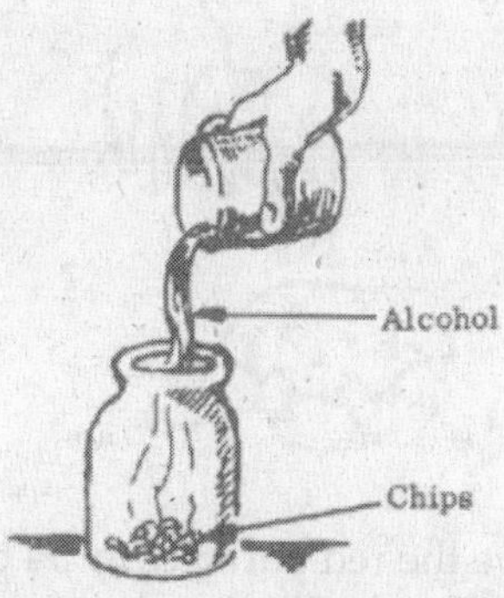

5. Heat the glass jar containing the mixture in a hot water bath for approximately 2 minutes (heat until there is a noticeable reaction between chips and alcohol; solution will turn darker).

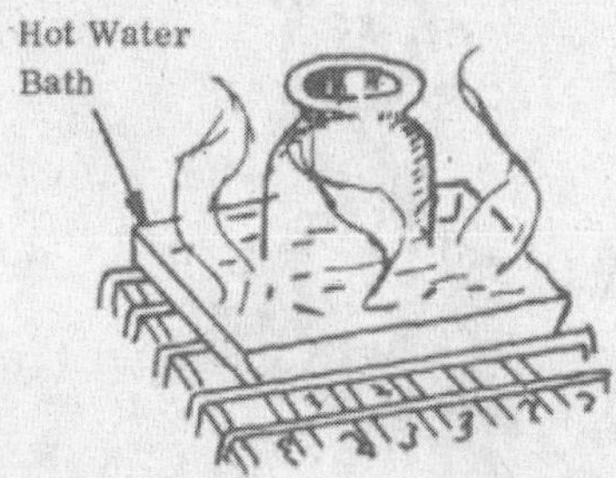

6. Filter the mixture through a paper towel into the other glass jar. The material left on the paper towel is lead monoxide.

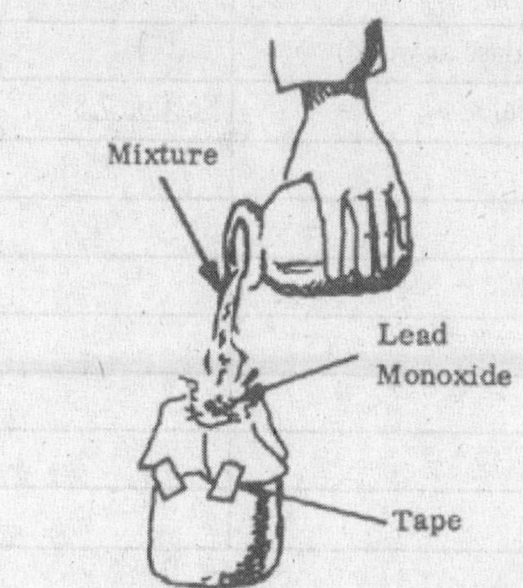

7. Remove the lead monoxide and wash it twice through a paper towel using 1/2 cup (120 millimeters) of hot water each time. Air dry before using.

8. Place the jar with the liquid (from step 6) in a hot water bath (as in step 5) and heat until the alcohol has evaporated. The powder remaining in the jar after evaporation is potassium or sodium nitrite.

> **NOTE**
>
> Nitrite has a strong tendency to absorb water from the atmosphere and should be stored in a closed container.

1.19 DDNP

DDNP is a primary explosive used in the fabrication of detonators (section 6.13). It is to be used with a booster explosive such as picric acid (section. 1.21.) or RDX (section 1.15).

Materials Required	Source
Picric acid	Section 1.21
Flowers of sulfur	
Lye (sodium hydroxide)	
Sulfuric acid, diluted	Motor vehicle batteries
Potassium or sodium nitrite	Section 1.18
Water	

Materials Required	**Source**
2 glass cups, heat resistant, (Pyrex)	
Stirring rod (glass or wood)	
Improvised scale	Section 7.8
Paper towels	
Teaspoon	
Tablespoon	
Eyedropper	
Heat source	
Containers	
Tape	

Procedure

1. In one of the glass cups, mix 1/2 gram of lye with 2 tablespoons (30 milliliters) of warm water.

2. Dissolve 1 teaspoon (3 grams) of picric acid in the water-lye solution. Store until ready for step 5.

3. Place 1/4 teaspoon (1 milliliter) of water in the other glass cup. Add 1/2 teaspoon (2-1/2 grams) of sulfur and 1/3 teaspoon (2-1/2 grams) of lye to the water.

4. Boil solution over heat source until color turns dark red. Remove and allow solution to cool.

5. In three portions, add this sulfur-lye solution to the picric acid-lye solution (step 2); stir while pouring. Allow mixture to cool.

6. Filter the mixture through a paper towel into a container. Small red particles will collect on the paper. Discard the liquid in the container.

7. Dissolve the red particles in 1/4 cup (60 milliliters) of boiling water.

8. Remove and filter the mixture through a paper towel as in step 6. Discard the particles left on the paper.
9. Using an eyedropper, slowly add the sulfuric acid to the filtered solution until it turns orange-brown.

10. Add 1/2 teaspoon (2-1/2 grams) more of sulfuric acid to the solution. Allow the solution to cool to room temperature.
11. In a separate container, dissolve 1/4 teaspoon (1.8 grams) of potassium or sodium nitrite in 1/3 cup (80 milliliters) of water.
12. Add this solution in one portion, while stirring, to the orange-solution. Allow the mixture to stand for 10 minutes. The mixture will turn light brown.

CAUTION

At this point the mixture is a primary explosive. Keep away from flame.

13. Filter the mixture through a paper towel. Wash the particles left on the paper with 4 teaspoons (20 milliliters) of water.

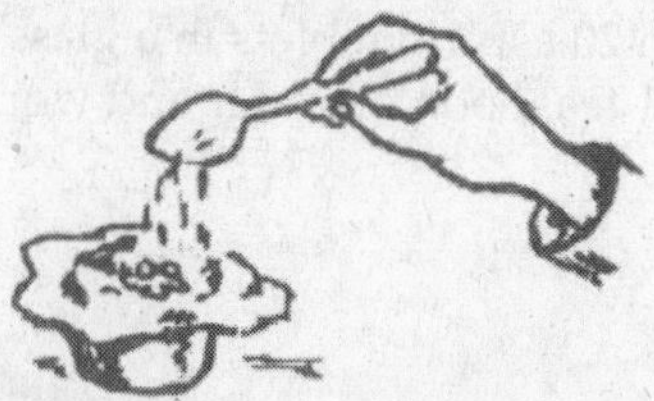

14. Allow the particles to dry (approximately 16 hours).

CAUTION

Explosive is shock and flame sensitive. Store explosive in a capped container.

NOTE

The drying time can be reduced to 2 hours if a hot (not boiling) water bath is used. See section 1.16.

1.20 PREPARATION OF LEAD PICRATE

Lead picrate is used as a primary explosive in the fabrication of detonators (section 6.13). It is to be used with a booster explosive such as picric acid (section 1.21) or RDX (section 1.15).

Materials Required	Source
Litharge (lead monoxide)	Section 1.18 or plumbing supplies
Picric Acid	Section 1.21
Wood alcohol (methanol)	Paint removers; some antifreezes
Wooden or plastic rod	
Dish or saucer (china or glass)	
Teaspoon	
Improvised Scale	Section 7.8
Containers	
Flat pan	
Heat source (optional)	
Water (optional)	

Procedure

1. Weigh 2 grams each of picric acid and lead monoxide. Place each in a separate container.
2. Place 2 teaspoons (10 milliliters) of the alcohol in a dish. Add the picric acid to the alcohol and stir with the wooden or plastic rod.

3. Add the lead monoxide to the mixture while stirring.

CAUTION

At this point the solution is a primary explosive. Keep away from flame.

4. Continue stirring the mixture until the alcohol has evaporated. The mixture will suddenly thicken.

5. Stir mixture occasionally (to stop lumps from forming) until a powder is formed. A few lumps will remain.

CAUTION

Be very careful of dry material forming on the inside of the container.

6. Spread this powdered mixture, the lead picrate, in a flat pan to air dry.

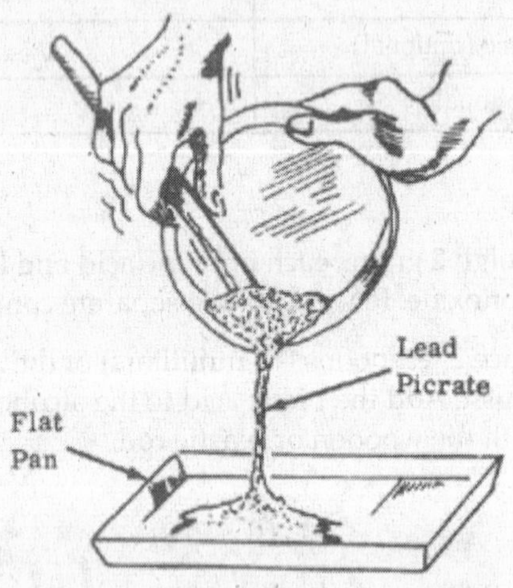

NOTE

If possible, dry the mixture in a hot, not boiling, water bath for a period of 2 hours.

1.21 PREPARATION OF PICRIC ACID FROM ASPIRIN

Picric acid can be used as a booster explosive in detonators (section 6.13), a high explosive charge, or as an intermediate to preparing lead picrate (section 1.20) or DDNP (section 1.19).

Materials Required
Aspirin tablets (5 grains or 325 mg per tablet)
Alcohol, 95% pure
Sulfuric acid, concentrated, (battery acid – boil until white fumes appear)
Potassium nitrate (section 1.2)
Water
Paper towels
Canning jar, 1 pint
Rod (glass or wood)
Glass containers
Ceramic or glass dish
Cup
Teaspoon
Tablespoon
Pan
Heat Source
Tape

Procedure

1. Crush 20 aspirin tablets in a glass container. Add 1 teaspoon of water and work into a paste.

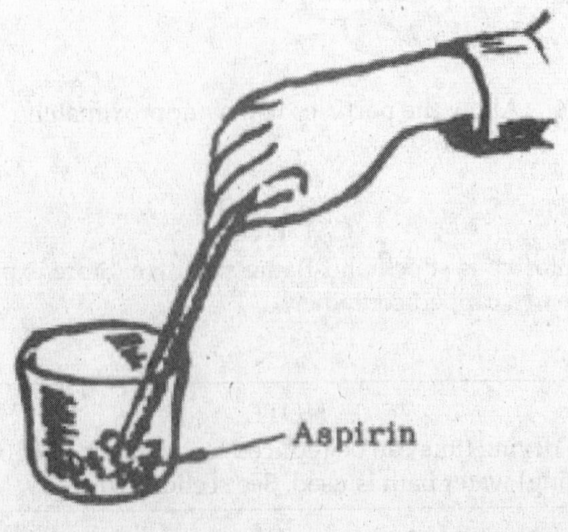

2. Add approximately 1/3 to 1/2 cup of alcohol (100 milliliters) to the aspirin paste; stir while pouring.

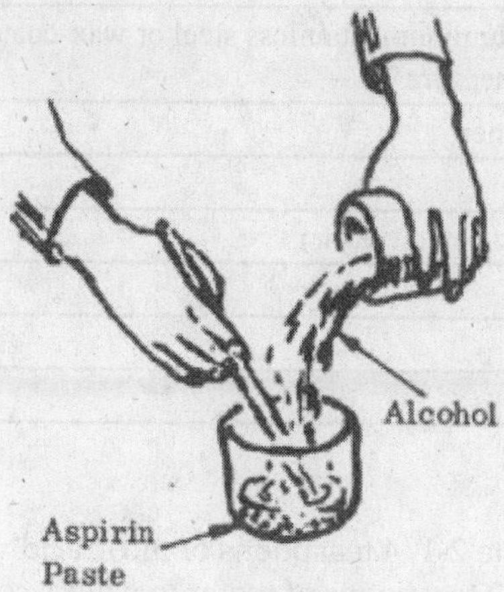

3. Filter the alcohol-aspirin solution through a paper towel into another glass container. Discard the solid left on the paper towel.

4. Pour the filtered solution into a ceramic or glass dish.

5. Evaporate the alcohol and water from the solution by placing the dish into a pan of hot water. White powder will remain in the dish after evaporation.

NOTE

Water in pan should be at hot bath temperature, not boiling, approximately 160° to 180°F. It should not burn the hands.

6. Pour 1/3 cup (80 milliliters) of concentrated sulfuric acid into a canning jar. Add the white powder to the sulfuric acid.

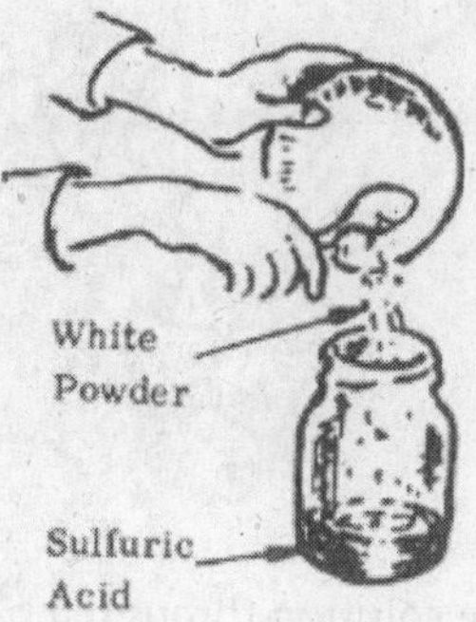

7. Heat canning jar of sulfuric acid in a pan of simmering hot water bath for 15 minutes; then remove jar from the bath. Solution will turn to a yellow-orange color.

8. Add 3 level teaspoons (15 grams) of potassium nitrate in three portions to the yellow-orange solution; stir vigorously during additions. Solution will turn red, and then back to a yellow-orange color.

9. Allow the solution to cool to ambient or room temperature while stirring occasionally.
10. Slowly pour the solution, while stirring, into 1-1/4 cup (300 milliliters) of cold water and allow to cool.

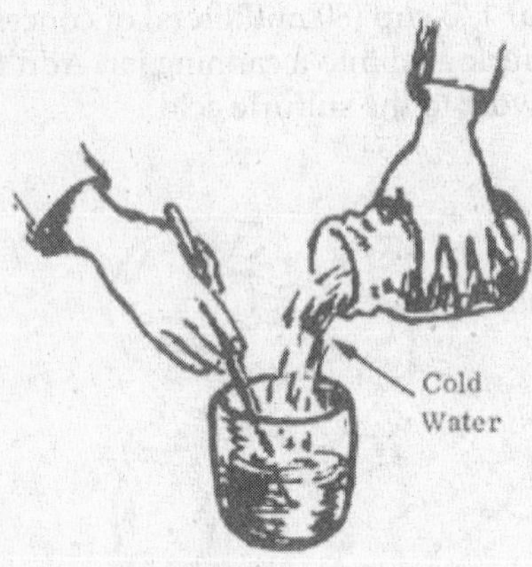

11. Filter the solution through a paper towel into a glass container. Light yellow particles will collect on the paper towel.
12. Wash the light yellow particles with 2 tablespoons (25 milliliters) of water. Discard the waste liquid in the container.

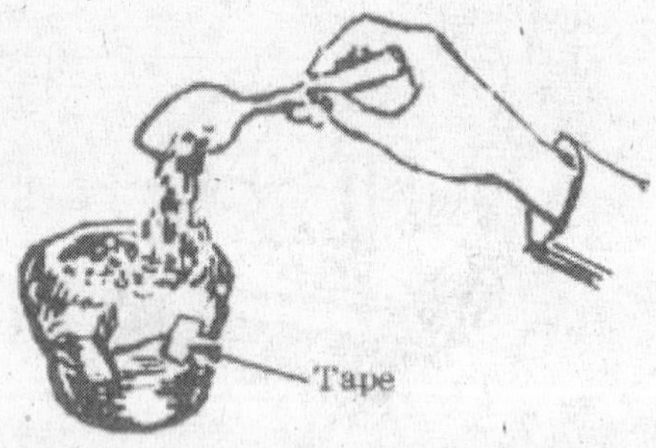

13. Place particles in ceramic dish and set in a hot water bath, as in step 5, for 2 hours.

1.22 DOUBLE SALTS

Double salts is used as a primary explosive in the fabrication of detonators (section 6.13). It can be made in the field from silver (coins), nitric acid, calcium carbide, and water.

Materials Required
Nitric acid (90% concentration) (section 1.4)
Silver metal (silver coin, about 5/8 inch diameter)
Calcium carbide (acetylene or calcium carbide lamps)
Rubber and glass tubing (approximately 1/4 inch inside diameter)
Paper towels
Heat-resistant bottles or ceramic jugs, 1 to 2 quart capacity, and one cork to fit. (Punch hole in cork to fit tubing.)
Teaspoon (aluminum, stainless steel or wax-coated) or equivalent measure
Glass container
Heat source
Long narrow jar (olive jar)
Tape
Water
Alcohol

Procedure

1. Dilute 2-1/4 teaspoons of nitric acid with 1-1/2 teaspoons of water in a glass container by adding the acid to the water.

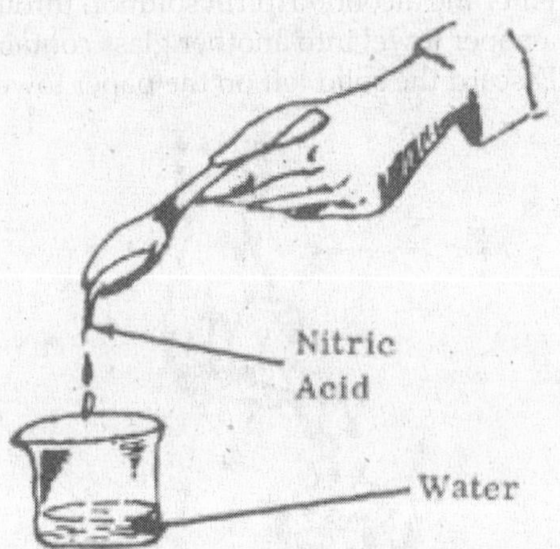

2. Dissolve a silver coin (a silver dime) in the diluted nitric acid. The solution will turn to a green color.

NOTE
It may be necessary to warm the container to completely dissolve the silver coin.

CAUTION
Acid will burn skin and destroy clothing. If any is spilled, wash it away with a large quantity of water. Do not inhale fumes.

3. Pour solution into a long narrow (olive) jar and place it in a bottle of hot water. Crystals will form in the solution; heat until crystals dissolve.

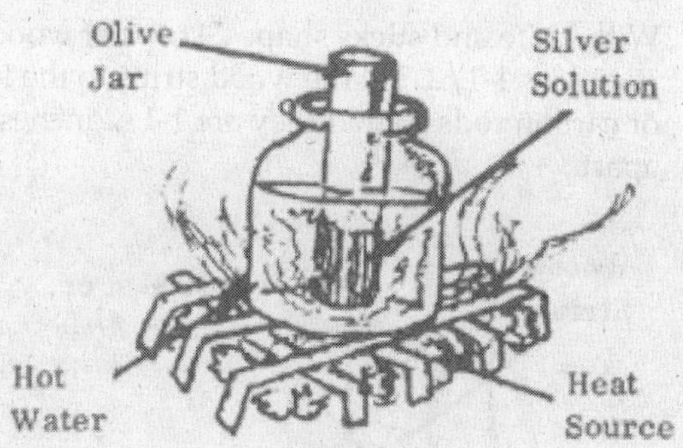

4. While still heating and after crystals have dissolved, place 10 teaspoons of calcium carbide in another glass bottle and add 1 teaspoon of water. After the reaction has started add another teaspoon of water. Then set up as shown.

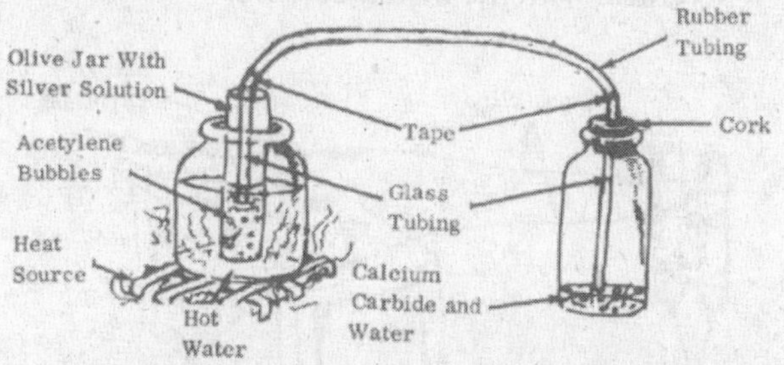

5. Bubble acetylene through the solution for 5 to 8 minutes. A brown vapor will be given off and white flakes will appear in the silver solution.
6. Remove the silver solution from the heat source and allow it to cool. Filter the solution through a paper towel into a glass container. Green crystals will collect on the paper.

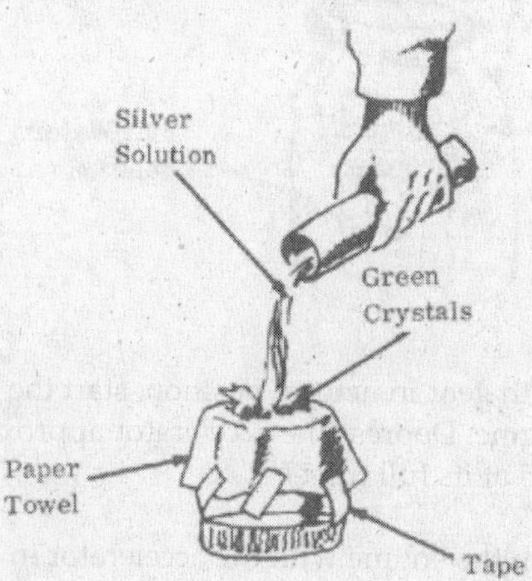

7. Wash the solids collected on the paper towel with 12 teaspoons of alcohol. The solid material will turn white while the solvent in the container will have a green color.

8. Place the white solid material on a clean paper towel to air dry.

CAUTION

Handle dry explosive with great care. Do not scrape or handle it roughly. Keep away from sparks or open flames. Store in cool, dry place.

1.23 SODIUM CHLORATE

Sodium chlorate is a strong oxidizer used in the manufacture of explosives. It can be used in place of potassium chlorate (section 1.1).

Materials Required	Source
2 carbon or lead rods (1 inch diameter × 5 inches long)	Dry cell batteries (2-1/2 inches diameter × 7 inches long) or plumbing supply store
Salt or, ocean water	Grocery store or ocean
Sulfuric acid, diluted	Motor vehicle batteries
Motor vehicle	
Water	
2 wires, 16 gauge (3/64 inch diameter approximately), 6 feet long, insulated	
Gasoline	
1 gallon glass jar, wide mouth (5 inches diameter × 6 inches high approximately)	
Sticks	
String	
Teaspoon	
Trays	
Cup	

Materials Required	Source
Heavy cloth	
Knife	
Large flat pan or tray	

Procedure

1. Mix 1/2 cup of salt into the one gallon glass jar with 3 liters (3 quarts) of water.

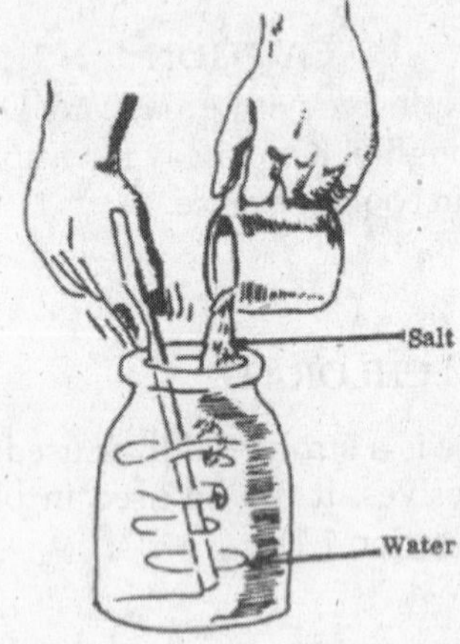

2. Add 2 teaspoons of battery acid to the solution and stir vigorously for 5 minutes.

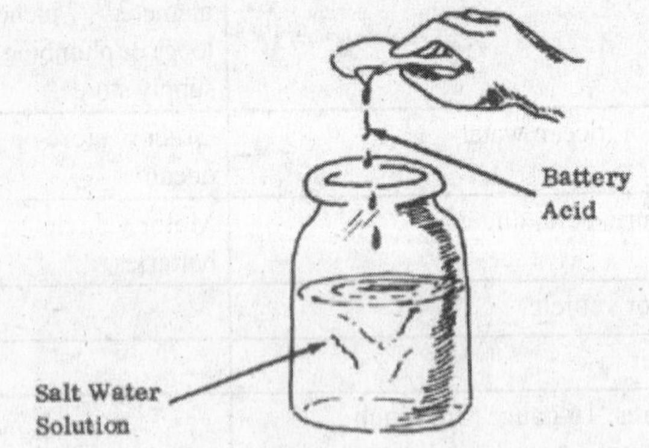

3. Strip about 4 inches of insulation from both ends of the 2 wires.

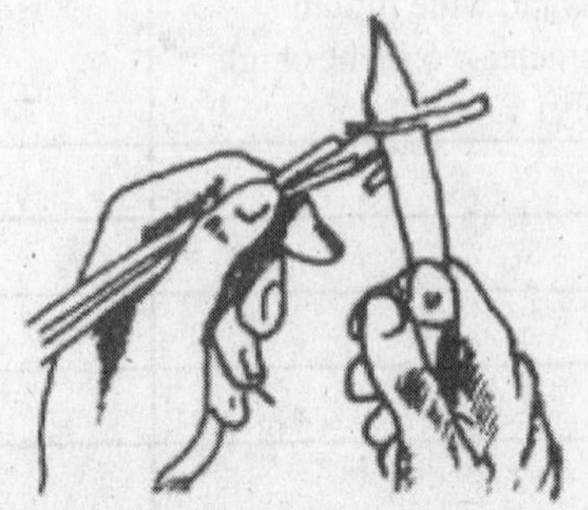

4. With knife and sticks shape 2 strips of wood 1 × 1/8 × 1-1/2. Tie the wood strips to the lead or carbon rods so that they are 1-1/2 inches apart.

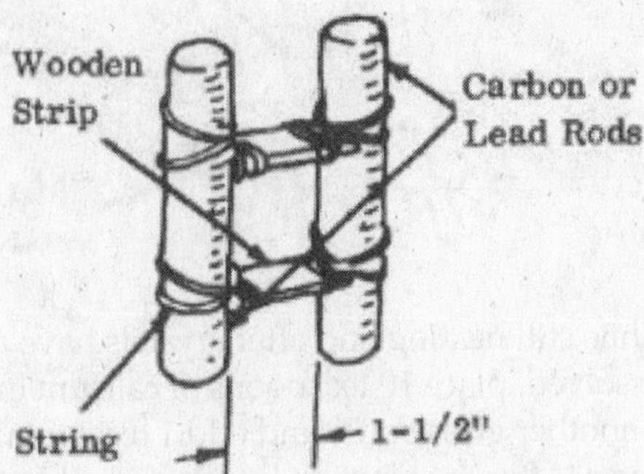

5. Connect the rods to the battery in a motor vehicle with the insulated wire.

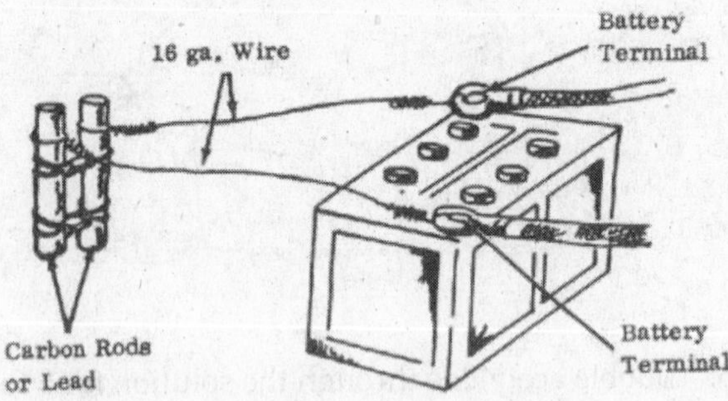

6. Submerge 4-1/2 inches of the rods into the salt water solution.

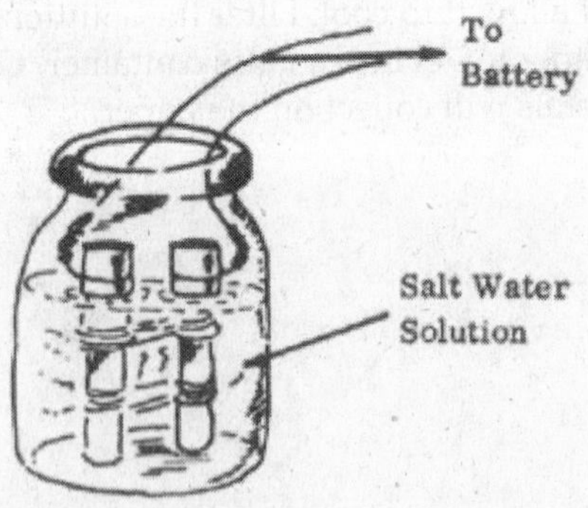

7. With gear in neutral position, start the vehicle engine. Depress the accelerator approximately 1/5 of its full travel.

8. Run the engine with the accelerator in this position for 2 hours; then, shut it down 2 hours.

9. Repeat this cycle for a total of 64 hours while maintaining the level of the acid-salt water solution in the glass jar.

CAUTION

This arrangement employs voltages which may be dangerous to personnel. Do not touch bare wire leads while engine is running.

10. Shut off the engine. Remove the rods from the glass jar and disconnect wire leads from the battery.

11. Filter the solution through the heavy cloth into a flat pan or tray, leaving the sediment at the bottom of the glass jar.

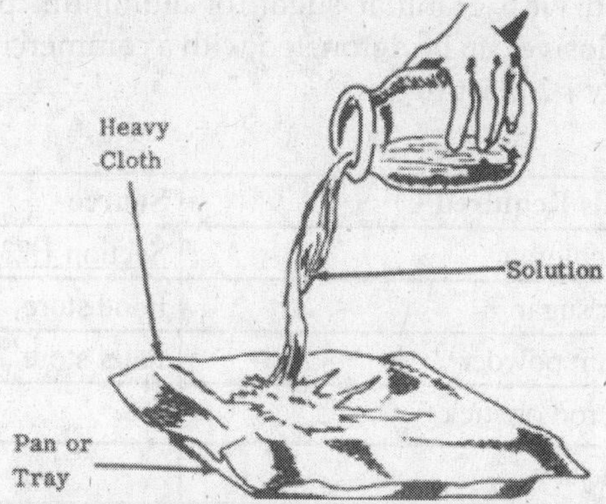

12. Allow the water in the filtered solution to evaporate at room temperature (approximately 16 hours). The residue is approximately 60% or more sodium chlorate which is pure enough to be used as an explosive ingredient.

1.24 MERCURY FULMINATE

Mercury fulminate is used as a primary explosive in the fabrication of detonators (section 6.13). It is to be used with a booster explosive such as picric acid (section 1.21) or RDX (section 1.15).

Materials Required	Source
Nitric Acid, 90% concentration (1.48 specific gravity)	Field grade (section 1.4) or industrial metal processors
Mercury	Thermometers, mercury switches, old radio tubes
Ethyl (grain) alcohol (90%)	
Filtering material	Paper towels
Teaspoon measure (1/4, 1/2, and 1 teaspoon capacity) – aluminum, stainless steel or wax-coated	
Heat source	
Clean wooden stick	
Clean water	
Glass containers	
Tape	
Syringe	

Procedure

1. Dilute 5 teaspoons of nitric acid with 2-1/2 teaspoons of clean water in a glass container by adding the acid to the water.

2. Dissolve 1/8 teaspoon of mercury in the diluted nitric acid. This will yield dark red fumes.

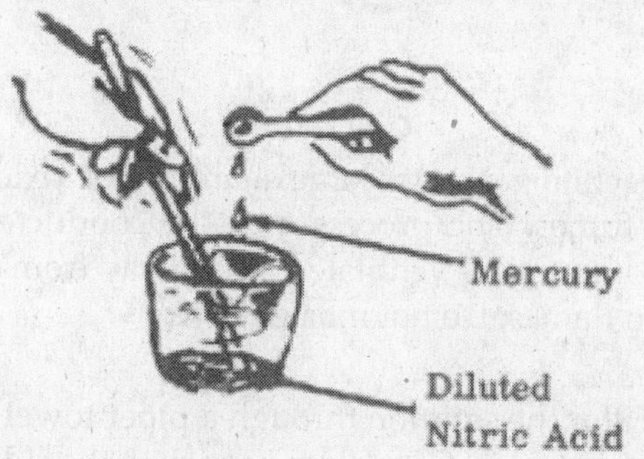

NOTE

It may be necessary to add water, one drop at a time, to the mercury-acid solution in order to start reaction.

CAUTION

Acid will burn skin and destroy clothing. If any is spilled, wash it away with a large quantity of water. Do not inhale fumes.

3. Warm 10 teaspoons of the alcohol in a container until the alcohol feels warm to the inside of the wrist.

4. Pour the metal-acid solution into the warm alcohol. Reaction should start in less than 5 minutes. Dense white fumes will be given off during reaction. As time lapses, the fumes will become less dense. Allow 10 to 15 minutes to complete reaction. Fulminate will settle to bottom.

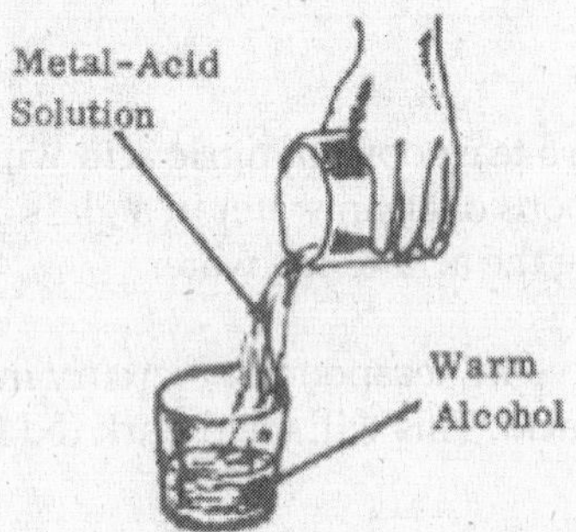

CAUTION

This reaction generates large quantities of toxic, flammable fumes. The process must be conducted outdoors or in a well ventilated area, away from sparks or open flames. Do not inhale fumes.

5. Filter the solution through a piper towel into a container. Crystals may stick to the side of the container. If so, tilt and squirt water down the sides of the container until all the material collects on the filter paper.

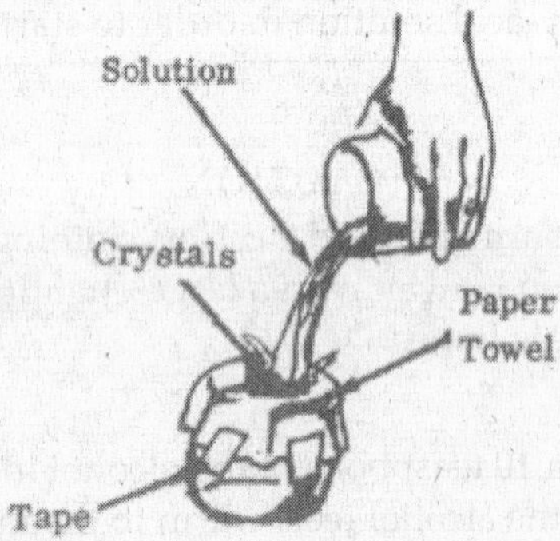

6. Wash the crystals with 6 teaspoons of ethyl alcohol.

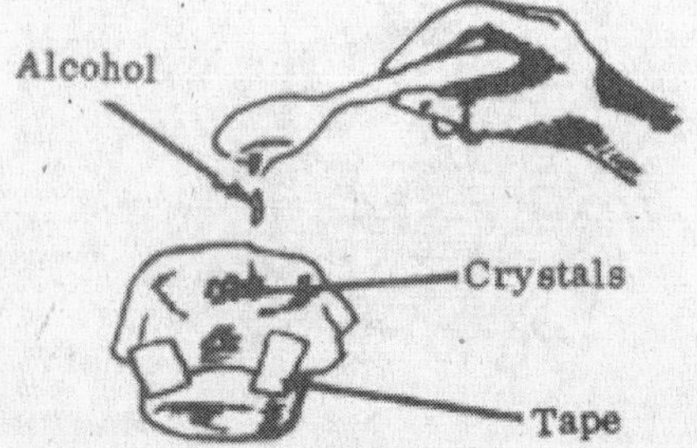

7. Allow these mercury fulminate crystals to air dry.

CAUTION

Handle dry explosive with great care. Do not scrape or handle it roughly. Keep away from sparks or open flames. Store in cool, dry place.

1.25 SODIUM CHLORATE AND SUGAR OR ALUMINUM EXPLOSIVE

An explosive munition can be made from sodium chlorate combined with granular sugar, or aluminum powder. This explosive can be detonated with a commercial #8 or a Military J-2 blasting cap.

Materials Required	Source
Sodium chlorate	Section 1.23
Granular sugar	Food store
Aluminum powder	Paint store
Wooden rod or stick	
Bottle or jar	
Blasting cap	
Steel pipe (threaded at one end), end cap and tape	
Wax	
Measuring container (cup, quart, etc.)	

Procedure

1. Add three volumes (cups, quarts, etc.) sodium chlorate to one volume aluminum, or two granular sugar, in bottle or jar.

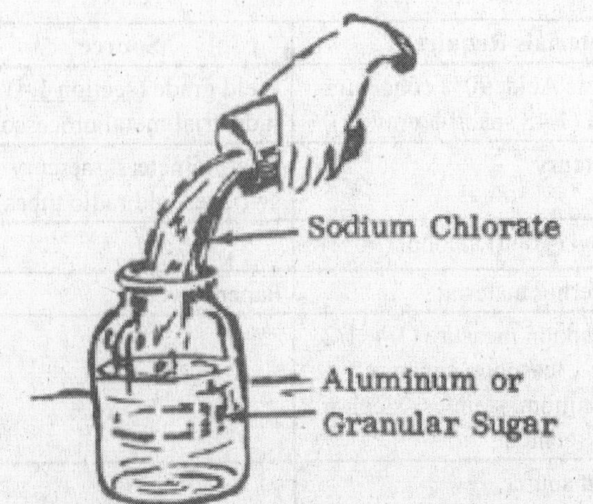

2. Mix ingredients well by stirring with the wooden rod or stick.

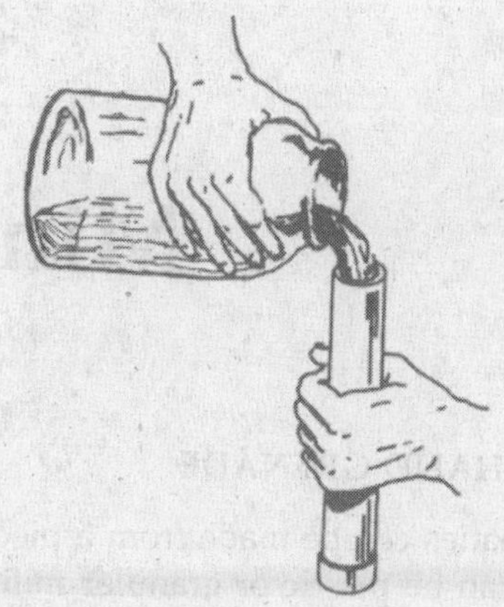

> **NOTE**
> Confining the open end of the pipe will add to the effectiveness of the explosive.

How to Use

1. Wax blasting cap, pipe and end cap.
2. Thread end cap onto pipe.
3. Pour mixture into pipe.
4. Insert and tape blasting cap just beneath surface of mixture.

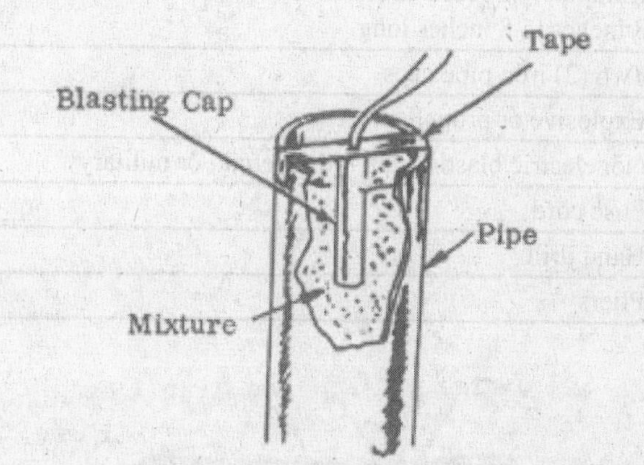

SECTION 2

Mines and Grenades

2.1 PIPE HAND GRENADE

Hand grenades can be made from a piece of iron pipe. The filler can be plastic or granular military explosive, improvised explosive, or propellant from shotgun or small arms ammunition.

Materials Required
Iron pipe, threaded ends, 1-1/2 inch to 3 inches diameter, 3 inches to 8 inches long
Two (2) iron pipe caps
Explosive or propellant
Nonelectric blasting cap (commercial or military)
Fuse cord
Hand drill
Pliers

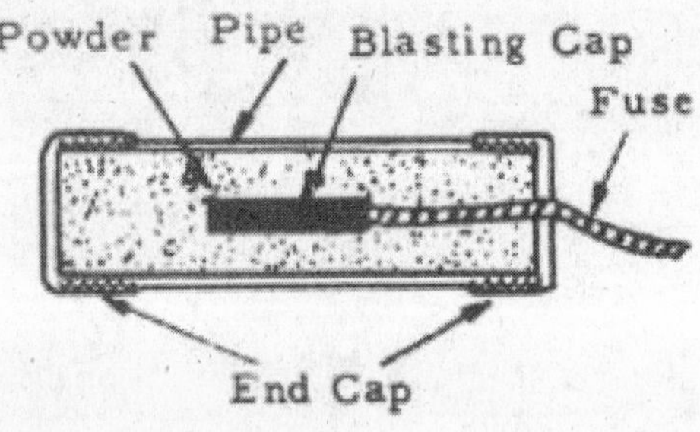

Procedure

1. Place sblasting cap on one end of fuse cord and crimp with pliers.

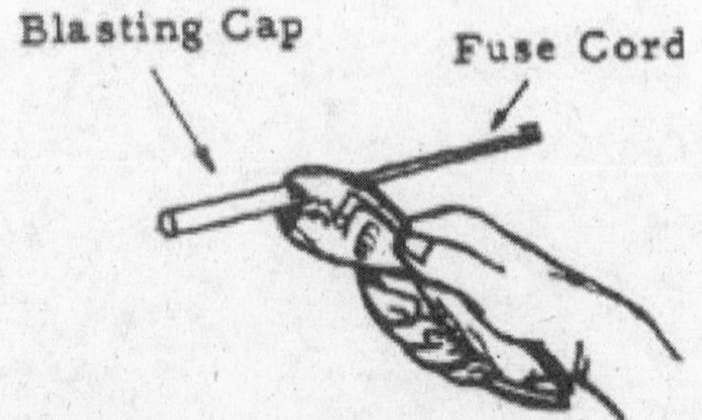

> **NOTE**
> To find out how long the fuse cord should be, check the time it takes a known length to burn. If 12 inches burns in 30 seconds, a 6-inch cord will ignite the grenade in 15 seconds.

2. Screw pipe cap to one and of pipe. Place fuse cord with blasting cap into the opposite end so that the blasting cap in near the center of the pipe.

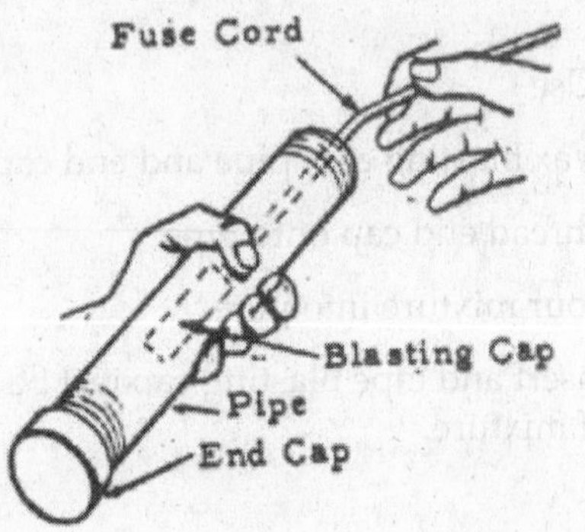

> **NOTE**
> If plastic explosive is to be used, fill pipe before inserting blasting cap. Push a round stick into the center of the explosive to make a hole and then insert the blasting cap.

3. Pour explosive or propellant into pipe a little bit at a time. Tap the base of the pipe frequently to settle filler.

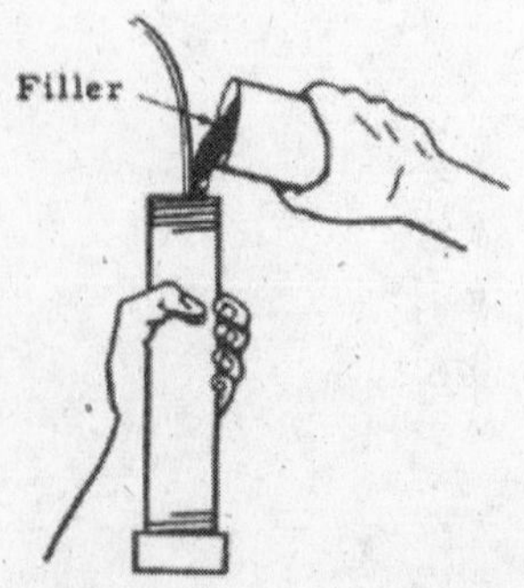

4. Drill a hole in the center of the unassembled pipe cap large enough for the fume cord to pass through.

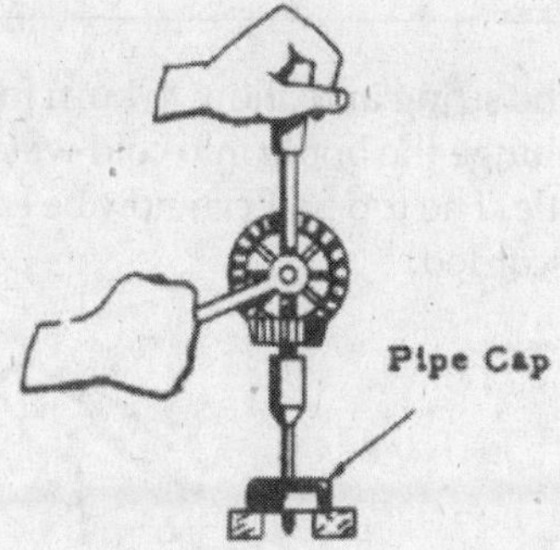

5. Wipe pipe threads to remove any filler material. Slide the drilled pipe cap over the fuse and screw hand tight onto the pipe.

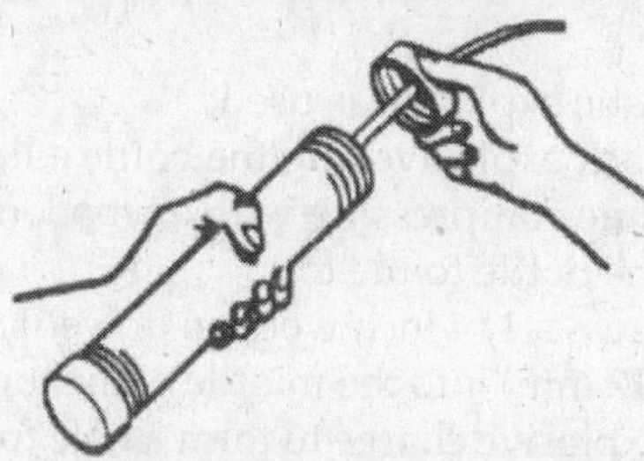

2.2 NAIL GRENADE

Effective fragmentation grenades can be made from a block of TNT or other blasting explosive and nails.

Materials Required
Block of TNT or other blasting explosive
Nails
Nonelectric military blasting cap
Fuse Cord
Tape, string, wire or glue

Procedure

1. If an explosive charge other than a standard TNT block is used, make a hole in the center of the charge for inserting the blasting cap. TNT can be drilled with relative safety. With plastic explosives, a hole can be made by pressing a round stick into the center of the charge. The hole should be deep enough that the blasting cap is totally within the explosive.

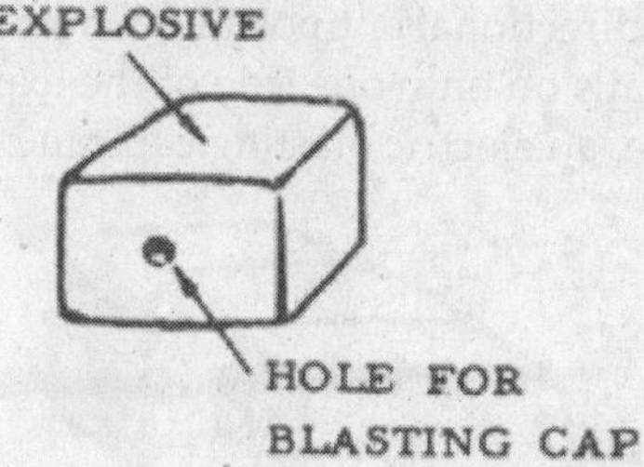

2. Tape, tie or glue one or two rows of closely packed nails to sides of explosive block. Nails should completely cover the four surfaces of the block.

3. Place blasting cap on one end of the fuse cord and crimp with pliers.

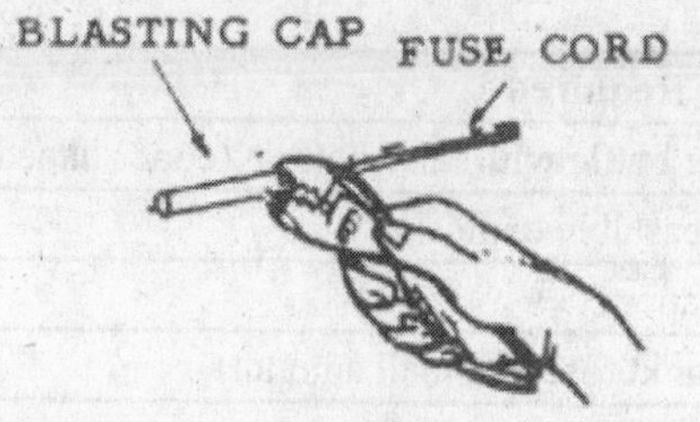

NOTE

To find out how long the fuse cord should be, check the time it takes a known length to burn. If 12 inches (30 cm) burns for 30 seconds, a 10 second delay will require a 4 inch (10 cm) fuse.

4.

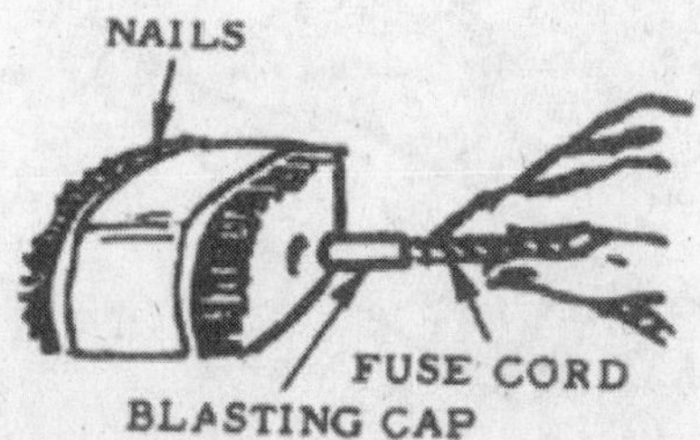

Insert the blasting cap in the hole in the block of explosive. Tape or tie fuse cord securely in place so that it will not fall out when the grenade is thrown.

Alternate Use

An effective directional antipersonnel mine can be made by placing nails on only one side of the explosive block. For this came, an electric blasting cap can be used.

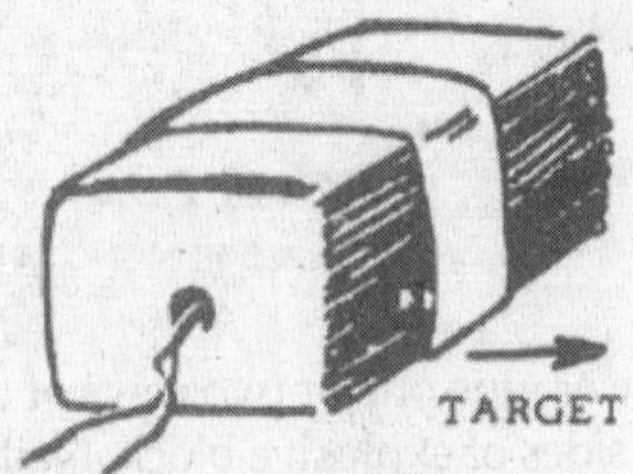

2.3 WINE BOTTLE CONE CHARGE

This cone charge will penetrate 3 to 4 inches of armor. Placed on an engine or engine compartment it will disable a tank or other vehicle.

Materials Required
Glass wine bottle with false bottom (cone shaped)
Plastic or castable explosive
Blasting cap
Gasoline or kerosene (small amount)
String
Adhesive tape

Procedure

1. Soak a piece of string in gasoline or kerosene. Double wrap this string around the wine bottle approximately 3 inches (7-1/2 cm) above the top of the cone.

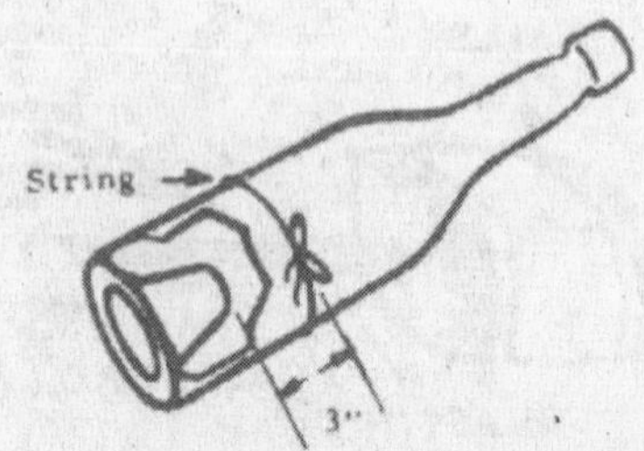

NOTE
A small amount of motor oil added to the gasoline or kerosene will improve results.

2. Ignite the string and allow to burn for 2 minutes. Then plunge the bottle into cold water to crack the bottle. The top half can now be easily removed and discarded.

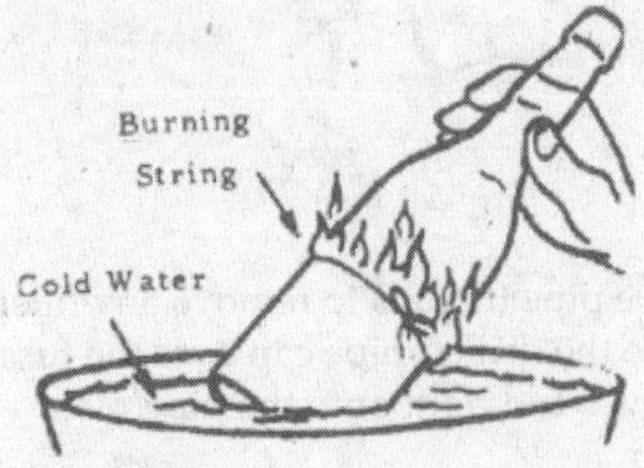

3. If plastic explosive is used:
   a. Pack explosive into the bottle a little at a time compressing with a wooden rod. Fill the bottle to the top.
   b. Press a 1/4 inch wooden dowel 1/2 inch (12 mm) into the middle of the top of the explosive charge to form a hole for the blasting cap.

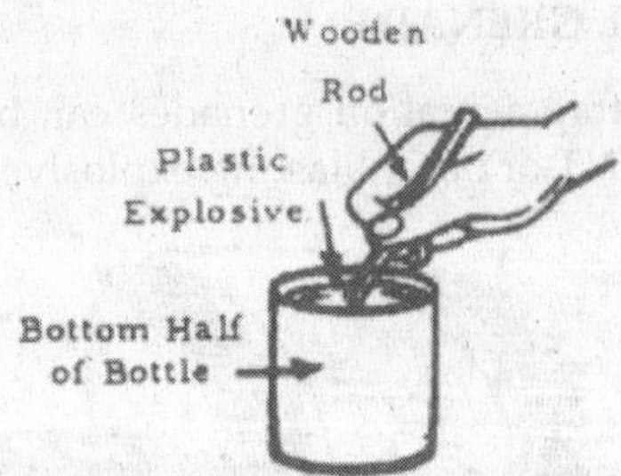

4. If TNT or other castable explosive is used:
   a. Break explosive into small pieces using a wooden mallet or nonsparking metal tools. Place pieces in a tin can.
   b. Suspend this can in a larger container which is partly filled with water. A stiff wire or stick pushed through the smaller can will accomplish this.

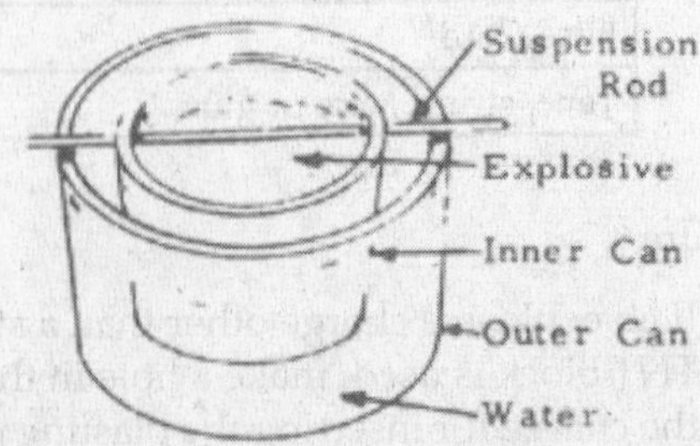

CAUTION

The inner can *must not* rest on the bottom of the outer container.

c. Heat the container on an electric hot plate or other heat source. Stir the explosive frequently with a wooden stick while it is melting.

CAUTION

Keep area well ventilated while melting explosive. Fumes may be poisonous.

d. When all the explosive has melted, remove the inner container and stir the molten explosive until it begins to thicken. During this time the bottom half of the wine bottle should be placed in the container of hot water. This will preheat the bottle so that it will not crack when the explosive is poured.

e. Remove the bottle from hot water and dry thoroughly. Pour molten explosive into the bottle and allow to cool. The crust which forms on top of the charge during cooling should be broken with a wooden stick and more explosive added. Do this as often as necessary until the bottle is filled to the top.

f. When explosive has completely hardened, bore a hole for the blasting cap in the middle of the top of the charge about 1/2 inch (12 mm) deep.

How to Use

1. Place blasting cap in the hole in the top of the charge. If nonelectric cap is used be sure cap is crimped around fuze and fuze is long enough to provide safe delay.

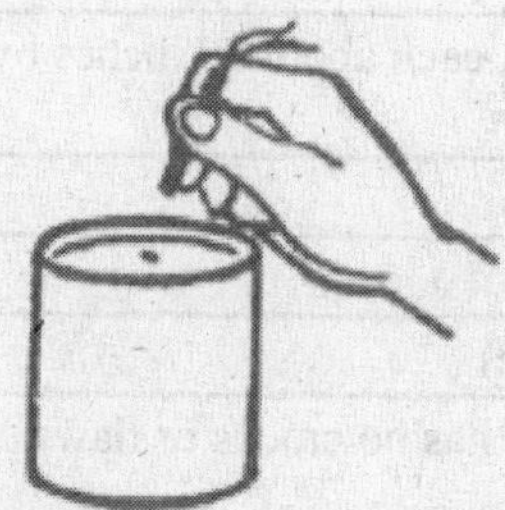

2. Place the charge so that the bottom is 3 to 4 inches (7-1/2 to 10 cm) from the target. This can be done by taping legs to the charge or any other convenient means as long as there is nothing between the base of the charge and the target.

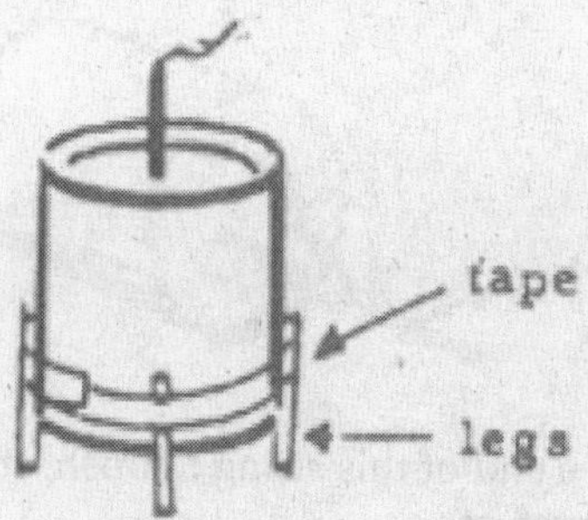

3. If electric cap is used, connect blasting cap wires to firing circuit.

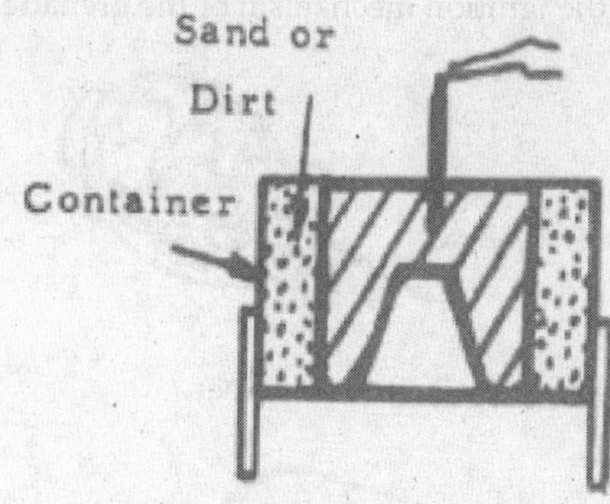

NOTE

The effectiveness of this charge can be increased by placing it inside a can, box, or similar container and packing sand or dirt between the charge and the container.

2.4 GRENADE-TIN CAN LAND MINE

This device cant be used as a land mine that will explode when the trip wire is pulled.

Materials Required
Hand grenade having side safety lever
Sturdy container, open at one end, that is just large enough to fit over grenade and its safety lever (tin can of proper size is suitable)
Strong string or wire

Note: The container must be of such a size that, when the grenade is placed in it and the safety pin removed, its sides will prevent the safety lever from springing open. One end must be completely open.

Procedure

1. Fasten one piece of string to the closed end of container, making a strong connection. This can be done by punching 2 holes in the can, looping the string through them, and tying a knot.

2. Tie free end of this string to bush, stake, fencepost, etc.

3. Fasten another length of string to the grenade such that it cannot interfere with the functioning of the ignition mechanism of the grenade.

4. Insert grenade into container.

5. Lay free length of string across path and fasten to stake, bush, etc. The string should remain taut.

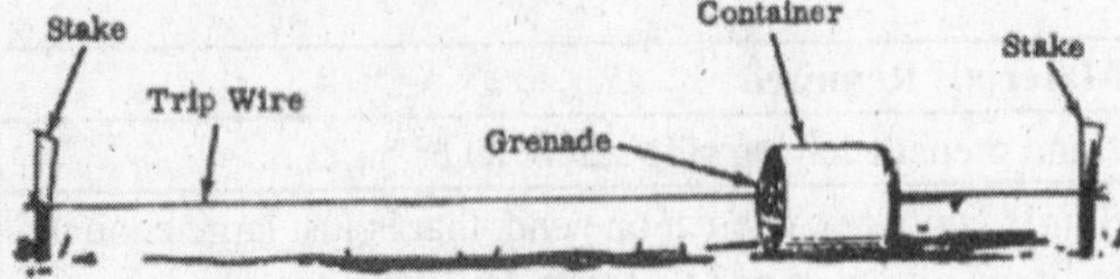

How to Use

1. Carefully withdraw safety pin by pulling on ring. Be sure safety lever is restrained during this operation. Grenade will function in normal manner when trip wire is pulled.

> **NOTE**
> In areas where concealment is possible, a greater effect may be obtained by suspending the grenade several feet above ground, as illustrated below.

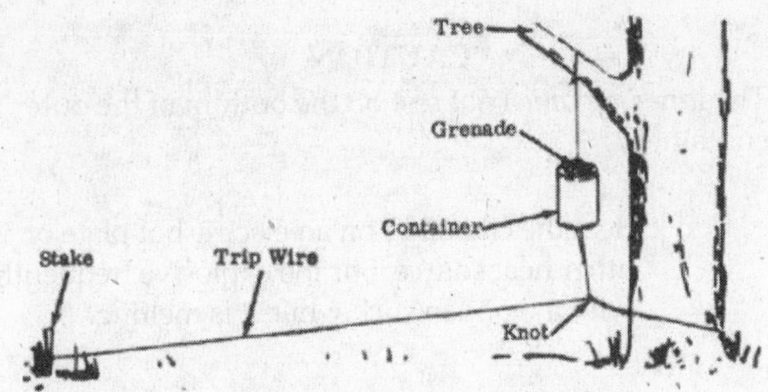

2.5 MORTAR SCRAP MINE

A directional shrapnel launcher that can be placed in the path of advancing troops.

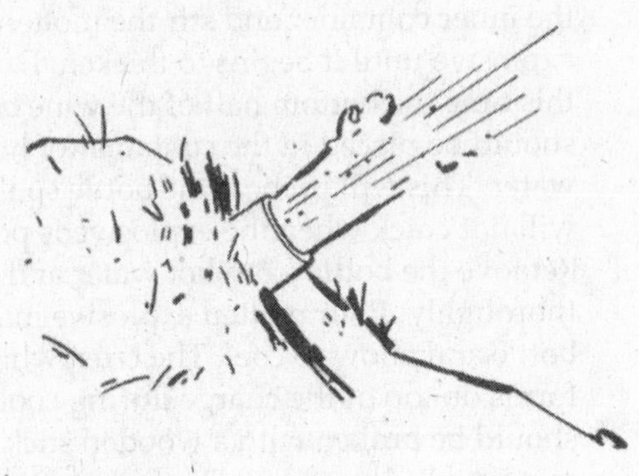

Materials Required
Iron pipe approximately 3 feet (1 meter) long and 2 inches to 4 inches (5 to 10 cm) in diameter and threaded on at least one end. Salvaged artillery cartridge case may also be used.
Threaded cap to fit pipe
Black powder or salvaged artillery propellant about 1/2 pound (200 grams) total
Electrical igniter (commercial squib or improvised igniter, section 6.1). Safety or improvised fuse may also be used.
Small stones about 1 inch (2-1/2 cm) in diameter or small size scrap; about 1 pound (400 grams) total
Rags for wadding, each about 20 inches by 20 inches (50 cm × 50 cm)
Paper or bag
Battery and wire
Stick (nonmetallic)

Note: Be sure pipe has no cracks or flaws.

Procedure

1. Screw threaded cap onto pipe.

2. Place propellant and igniter in paper or rag and tie package with string so contents will not fall out.

CAUTION
Be sure that base of bottle is flush against target and that there is nothing between the target and the base of the bottle.

3. Connect leads from blasting cap to firing circuit.

Method II – If Nonelectrical Blasting Cap is Used

1. Crimp cap around fuse.

CAUTION
Be sure fuse is long enough to provide a safe delay.

2. Follow steps 1, 2, and **cautions** of Method I.
3. Light fuse when ready to fire.

2.7 CYLINDRICAL CAVITY SHAPED CHARGE

A shaped charge can be made from common pipe. It will penetrate 1-1/2 inch (3-1/2 cm) of steel, producing a hole 1-1/2 inch (3-1/2 cm) in diameter.

Materials Required	
Iron or steel pipe, 2 to 2-1/2 inches (5 to 6-1/2 cm) in diameter and 3 to 4 inches (7-1/2 to 10 cm) long	
Metal pipe, 1/2 to 3/4 inch (1-1/2 to 2 cm) in diameter and 1-1/2 inch (3-1/2 cm) long, open at both ends. (The wall of the pipe should be as thin as possible.)	
Blasting cap	
Nonmetallic rod, 1/4 inch (6 mm) in diameter	
Plastic or castable explosive	
2 metal cans of different sizes	If castable explosive is used
Stick or wire	
Heat source	

Procedure

1. If plastic explosive is used:
   a. Place larger pipe on flat surface. *Hand* pack and tamp explosive into pipe. Leave approximately 1/4 inch (6 mm) space at top.

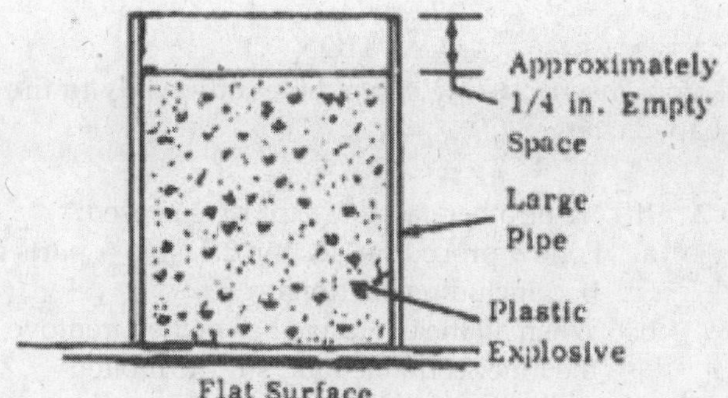

   b. Push rod into *center* of explosive. Enlarge hole in explosive to diameter and length of small pipe.
   c. Insert small pipe into hole.

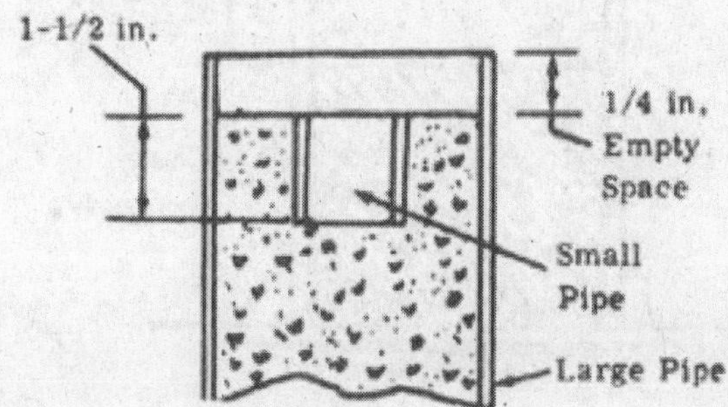

IMPORTANT
Be sure direct contact is made between explosive and small pipe. Tamp explosive around pipe *by hand* if necessary.

   d. Make sure that there is 1/4 inch (6 mm) empty space above small pipe. Remove explosive if necessary.
   e. Turn pipe upside down and push rod 1/2 inch (1-1/4 cm) into center of opposite end of explosive to form a hole for the blasting cap.

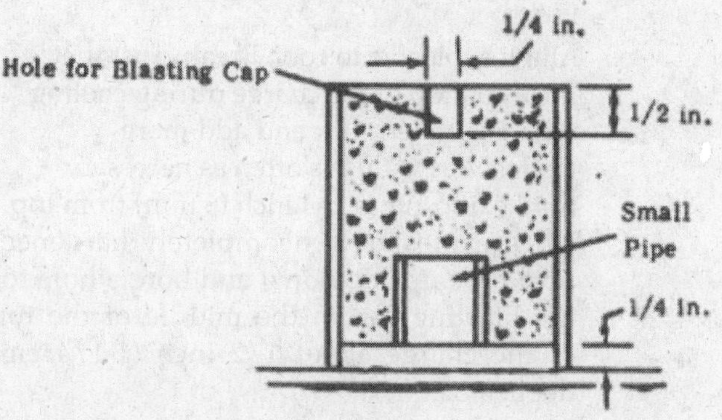

CAUTION

Do not insert blasting cap in hole until ready to fire shaped charge.

2. If TNT or other castable explosive is used:
   a. Follow procedure, section 2.3, step 4, parts a, b, c, including **cautions**.
   b. When all the explosive has melted, remove the inner container and stir the molten explosive until it begins to thicken.
   c. Place large pipe on flat surface. Pour explosive into pipe until it is 1-3/4 inch (4 cm) from the top.

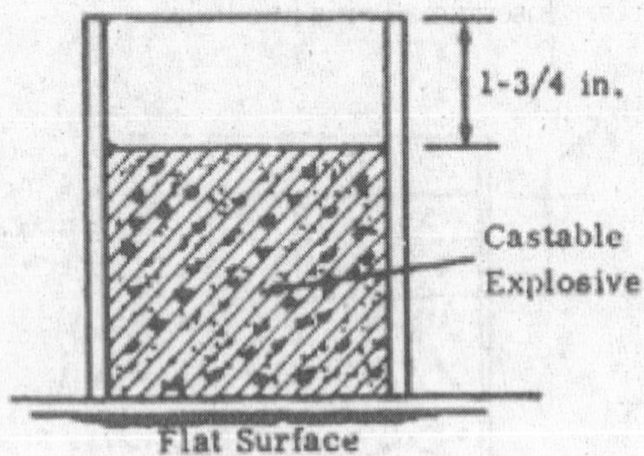

   d. Place small pipe in *center* of large pipe so that it rests on top of explosive. Holding small pipe in place, pour explosive around small pipe until explosive is 1/4 inch (6 mm) from top of large pipe.

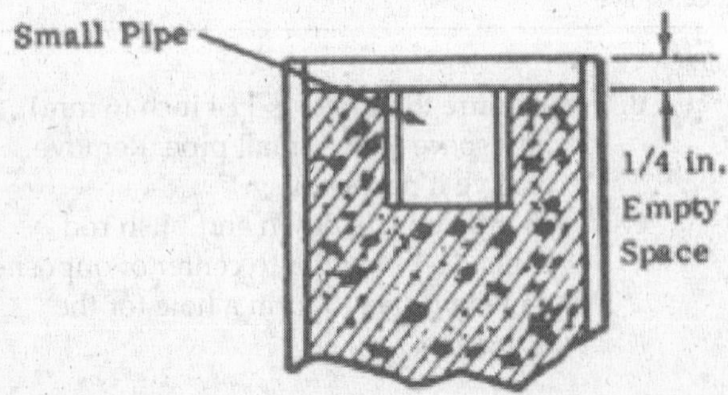

   e. Allow explosive to cool. Break crust that forms on top of the charge during cooling with a wooden stick and add more explosive. Do this as often as necessary until explosive is 1/4 inch (6 mm) from top.
   f. When explosive has completely hardened, turn pipe upside down and bore a hole for the blasting cap in the middle of the top of the charge about 1/2 inch (1-1/4 cm) deep.

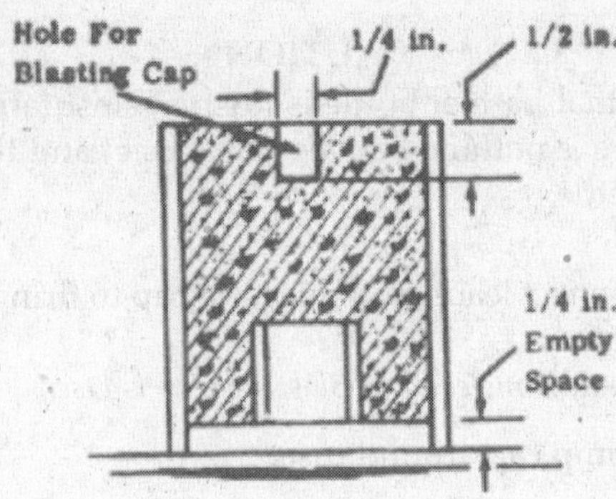

How to Use

Method I – If Electrical Blasting Cap is Used

1. Place blasting cap in hole made for it.

CAUTION

Do not insert blasting cap until charge is ready to fire.

2. Place other end of pipe flush against the target. Fasten pipe to target by any convenient means, such as by placing tape or string around target and top of pipe, if target is not flat and horizontal.

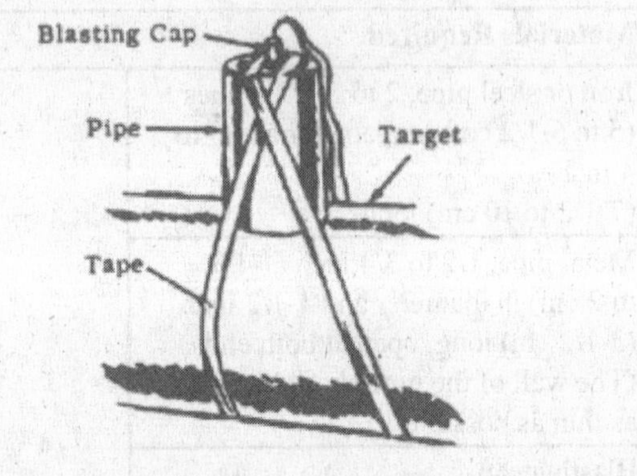

CAUTION

Be sure that base of pipe is flush against target and that there is nothing between the target and the base of the pipe.

3. Connect leads from blasting cap to firing circuit.

Method II – If Nonelectrical Blasting Cap is Used

1. Crimp cap around fuse.

CAUTION

Be sure fuse is long enough to provide a safe delay.

2. Follow steps 1, 2, and **caution** of Method I.
3. Light fuse when ready to fire.

2.8 NOT AVAILABLE

The original printed document from which this electronic edition was produced goes directly from section 2.7 to 2.9. There was no section 2.8.

2.9 FUNNEL SHAPED CHARGE

An effective shaped charge can be made using various types of commercial funnels. See table for penetration capabilities.

Materials Required
Container (soda or beer can, etc.), approximately 2-1/2 inches diameter × 5 inches long (6-1/4 cm × 12-1/2 cm)
Funnel(s) (glass, steel, or aluminum) 2-1/2 inches (6-1/2 cm) in diameter
Wooden rod or stick, 1/4 inch (6 mm) in diameter
Tape
Blasting cap (electrical or nonelectrical)
Sharp cutting edge
Explosive

Procedure

1. Remove the top and bottom from can and discard.

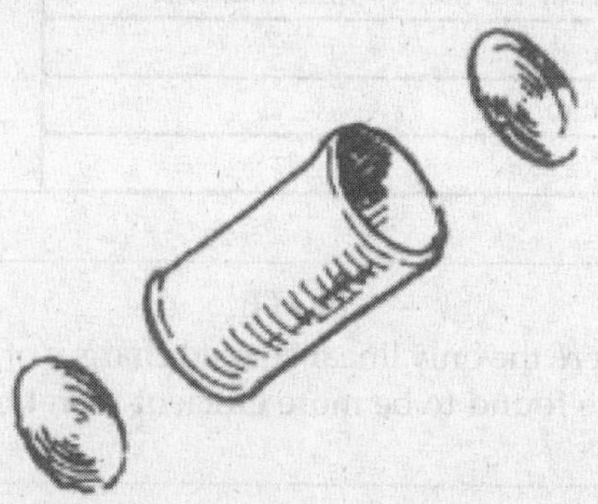

2. Cut off and throw away the spout of the funnel(s).

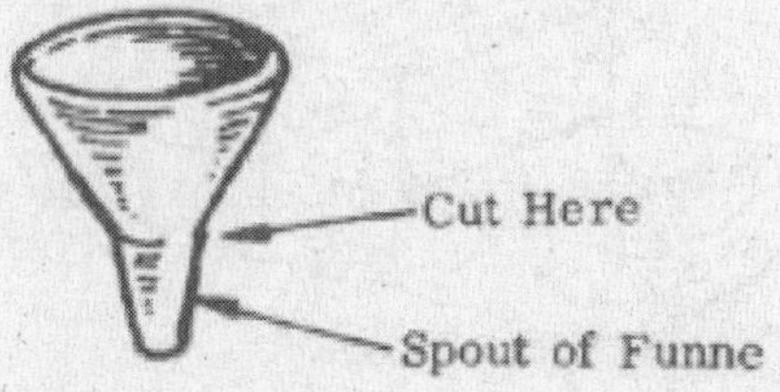

NOTE

When using 3 funnels (see table), place the modified funnels together as tight and as straight as possible. Tape the funnels together at the outer ridges.

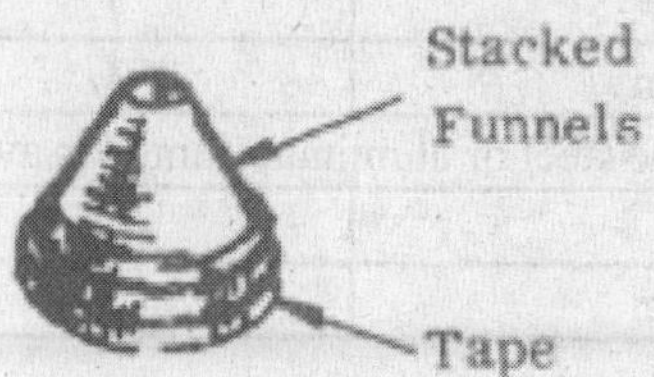

3. Place the funnel(s) in the modified can. Tape on outer ridges to hold funnel(s) to can.

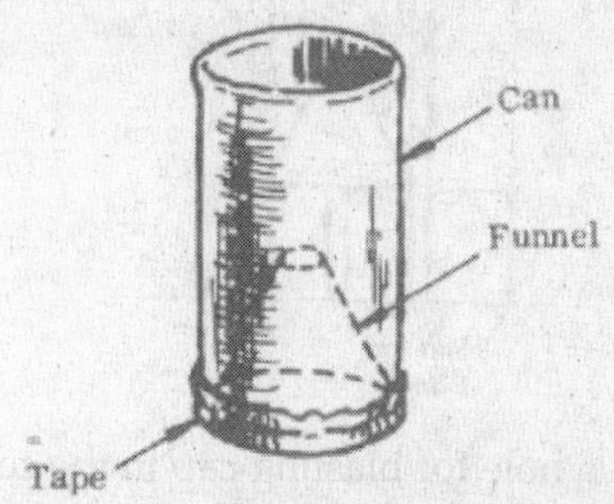

4. If plastic explosive is used, fill the can with the explosive using small quantities, and tamp with wooden rod or stick.

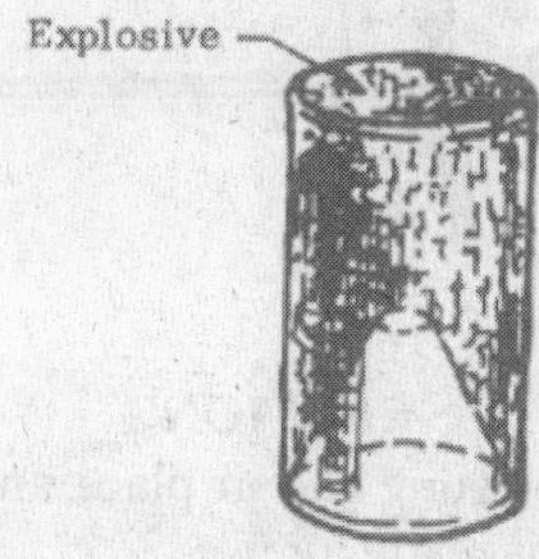

NOTE

If castable explosive is used, refer to <u>step 4</u> of section 2.3.

5. Cut wooden rod to lengths 3 inches longer than the standoff length. (See table.) Position three of these rods around the explosive filled can and hold in place with tape.

NOTE

The position of the rods on the container *must* conform to standoff dimensions to obtain the penetrations given in the table.

Table

Funnel Material	Number of Funnels	Standoff		Penetration	
		inches	metric	inches	metric
Glass	1	3-1/2	9 cm	4	10 cm
Steel	3	1	2-1/2 cm	2-1/2	6 cm
Aluminum	3	3-1/2	9 cm	2-1/2	6 cm
If only one steel or aluminum funnel is available:					
Steel	1	1	2-1/2 cm	1-1/2	4 cm
Aluminum	1	1	2-1/2 cm	1-1/2	4 cm

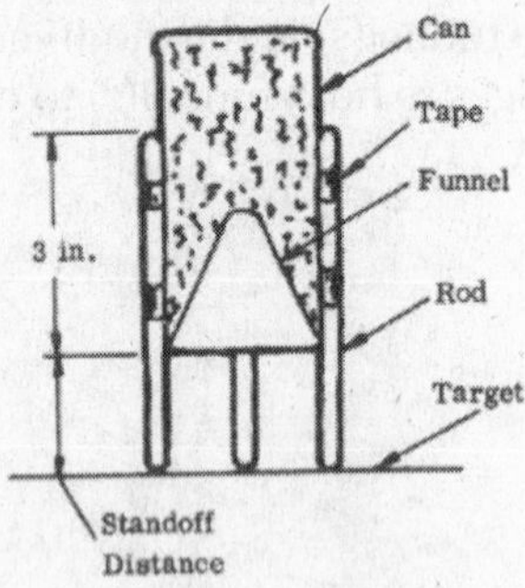

6. Make a hole for blasting cap in the center of the explosive with rod or stick.

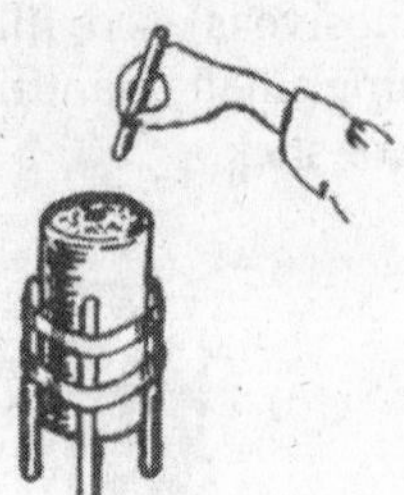

CAUTION

Do not place blasting cap in place until the funnel shaped charge is ready for use.

How to Use

1. Place blasting cap in the hole in top of the charge. If nonelectric cap is used, be sure cap is crimped around fuse and fuse is long enough to provide safe delay.

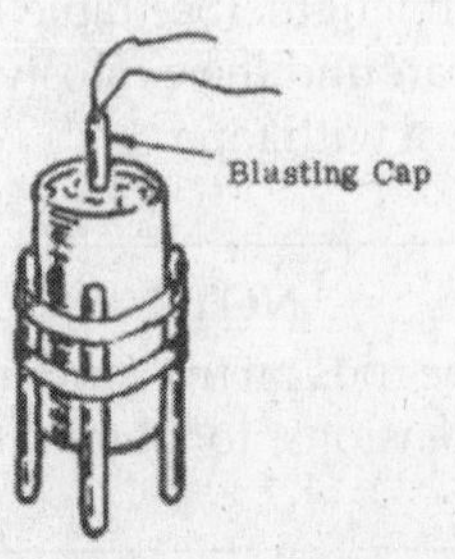

2. Place (tape if necessary) the funnel shaped charge on the target so that nothing is between the base of charge and target.
3. If electric cap is used, connect blasting cap wires to firing circuit.

2.10 LINEAR SHAPED CHARGE

This shaped charge made from construction materials will cut through up to nearly 3 inches of armor depending upon the liner used (see table).

Materials Required	
Standard structural angle or pipe (see table)	
Wood or cardboard container	
Hacksaw	If pipe is used
Vice	
Wooden rod, 1/4 inch (6 mm) diameter	
Explosive	
Blasting cap	
Tape	

NOTE

These were the only linear shaped charges of this type that were found to be more efficient than the Ribbon Charge.

Ribbon Charge: No standoff is required; just place on target.

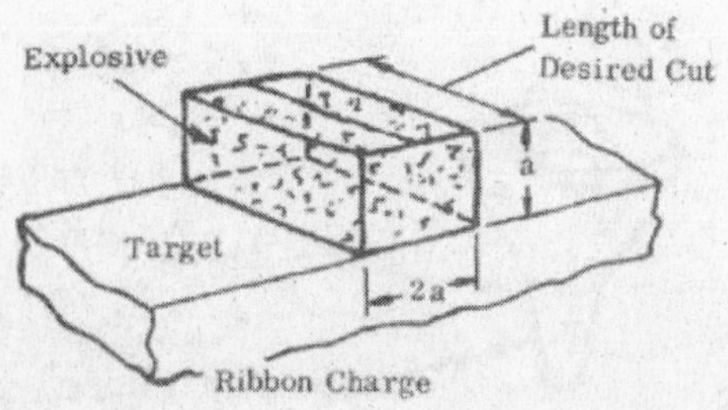

Table

Type	Material	Liner Size inches – nominal	Standoff		Penetration	
			inches	metric	inches	metric
angle	steel	3 × 3 legs × 1/4 web	2	5 cm	2-3/4	7 cm
angle	aluminum	2 × 2 legs × 3/16 web	5-1/2	14 cm	2-1/2	6 cm
pipe half section	aluminum	2 diameter	2	5 cm	2	5 cm
pipe half section	copper	2 diameter	1	2-1/2 cm	1-3/4	4 cm

Procedure

1. If pipe is used:
   a. Place the pipe in the vise and cut pipe in half lengthwise. Remove the pipe half sections from vise.
   b. Discard one of the pipe half sections, or save for another charge.

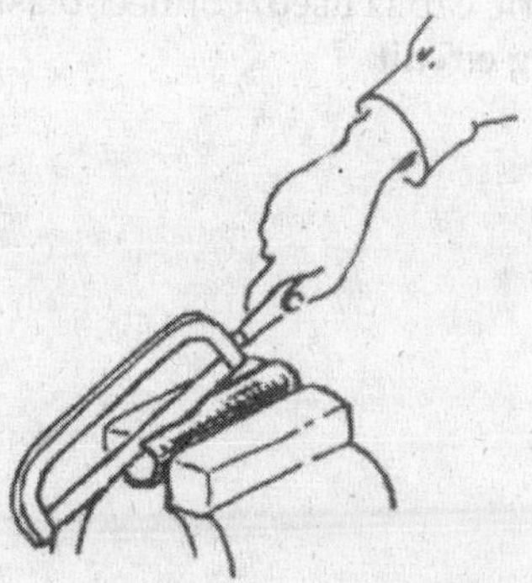

2. Place angle or pipe half section with open end face down on a flat surface.
3. Make container from any material available. The container must be as wide as the angle or pipe half section, twice as high, and as long as the desired cut to be made with the charge.
4. Place container over the liner (angle or pipe half section) and tape liner to container.

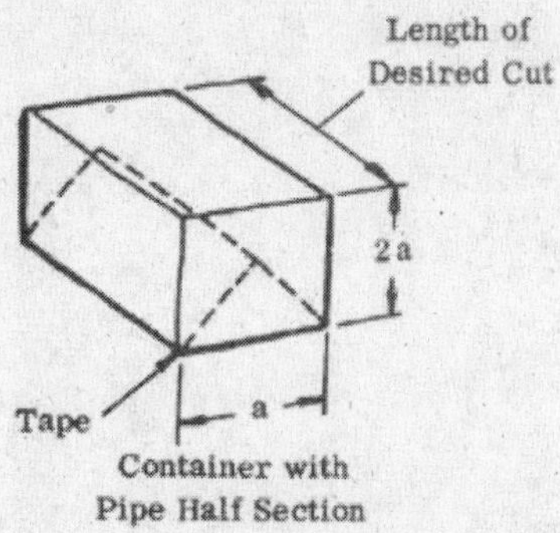

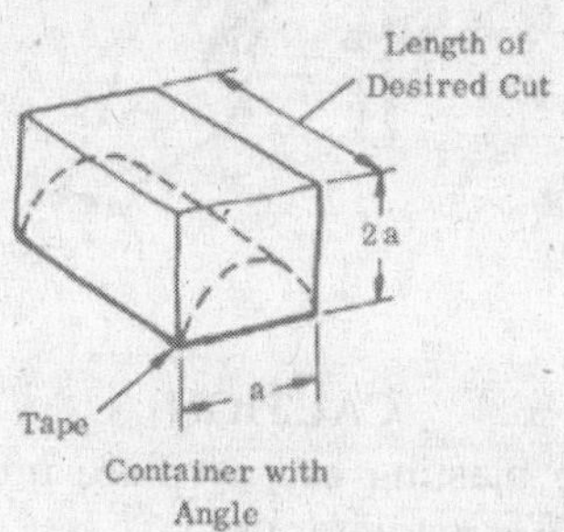

5. If plastic explosive is used, fill the container with the explosive using small quantities, and tamp explosive with wooden rod or stick.

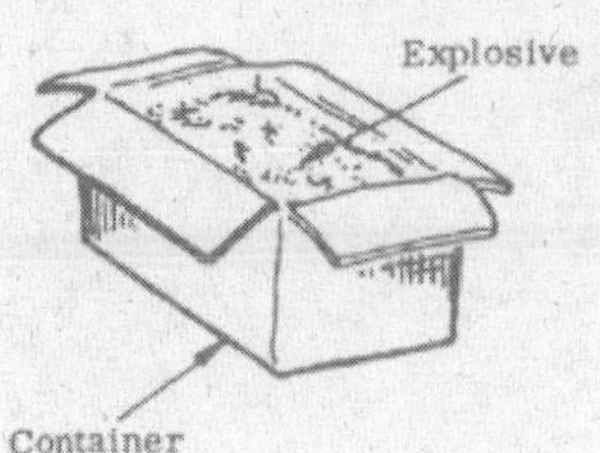

NOTE

If castable explosive is used, refer to step 4 of section 2.3.

6. Cut wooden rod to lengths 2 inches longer than the standoff length (see table). Position the rods at the corners of the explosive filled container and hold in place with tape.

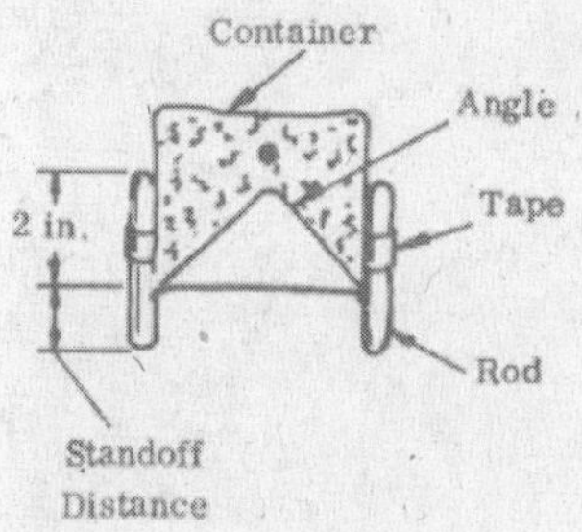

NOTE

The position of the rods on the container must conform to standoff and penetration dimensions given in the table.

7. Make a hole for blasting cap in the side of the container 1/2 inch above the liner and centered with the wooden rod.

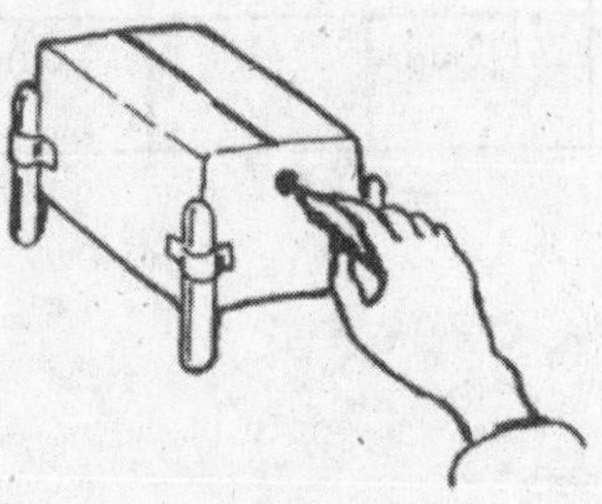

CAUTION

Do not place blasting cap in place until the linear shaped charge is ready for use.

How to Use

1. Place blasting cap into hole on the side of the container. If nonelectric cap is used, be sure cap is crimped around fuse and fuse is long enough to provide safe delay.

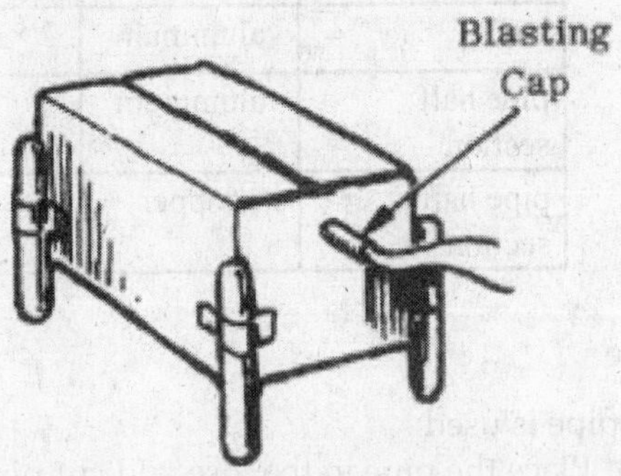

2. Place (tape if necessary) the linear shaped charge on the target so that nothing is between base of charge and target.

3. If electric cap is used, connect blasting cap wires to firing circuit.

SECTION 3

Small Arms Weapons and Ammunition

3.1 PIPE PISTOL FOR 9 MM AMMUNITION

A 9 mm pistol can be made from 1/4 inch steel gas or water pipe and fittings.

Materials Required
1/4 inch nominal size steel pipe4 to 6 inches long with threaded ends
1/4 inch solid pipe plug
Two (2) steel pipe couplings
Metal strap – roughly 1/8 inch × 1/4 inch × 5 inch
Two (2) elastic bands
Flat head nail – 6D or 8D (approximately 1/16 inch diameter)
Two (2) wood screws #8
Wood 8 inch × 5 inch × 1 inch
Drill
1/4 inch wood or metal rod, (approximately 8 inches long)

Procedure

1. Carefully inspect pipe and fittings.
   a. Make sure that there are **no** cracks or other flaws in the pipe or fittings.
   b. Check inside diameter of pipe using a 9 mm cartridge as a gauge. The bullet should closely fit into the pipe without forcing but the cartridge case **should not** fit into pipe.
   c. Outside diameter of pipe **must not be** less than 1-1/2 times bullet diameter (0.536 inches; 1.37 cm)
2. Drill a 9/16 inch (1.43 cm) diameter hole 3/8 inch (approximately 1 cm) into one coupling to remove the thread.

Drilled section should fit tightly over smooth section of pipe.

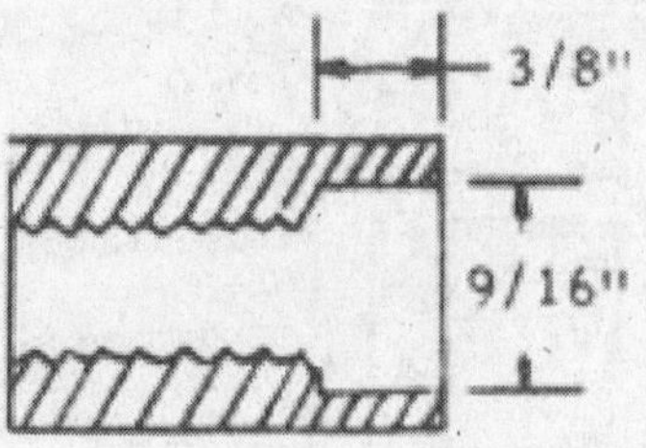

3. Drill a 25/64 inch (1 cm) diameter hole 3/4 inch (1.9 cm) into pipe. Use cartridge as a gauge; when a cartridge is inserted into the pipe, the base of the case should be even with the end of the pipe. Thread coupling tightly onto pipe, drilled end first.

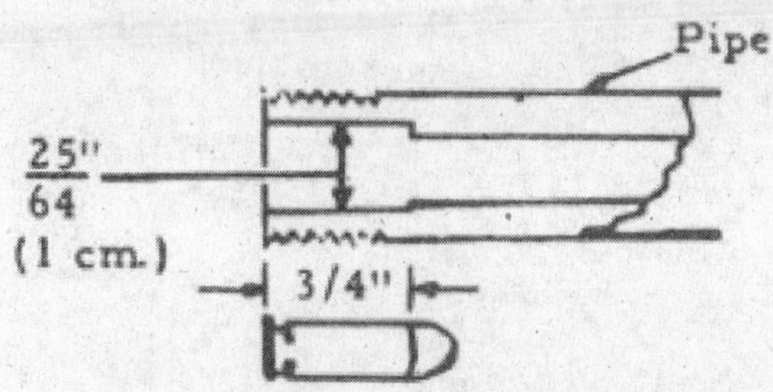

4. Drill a hole in the center of the pipe plug just large enough for the nail to fit through.

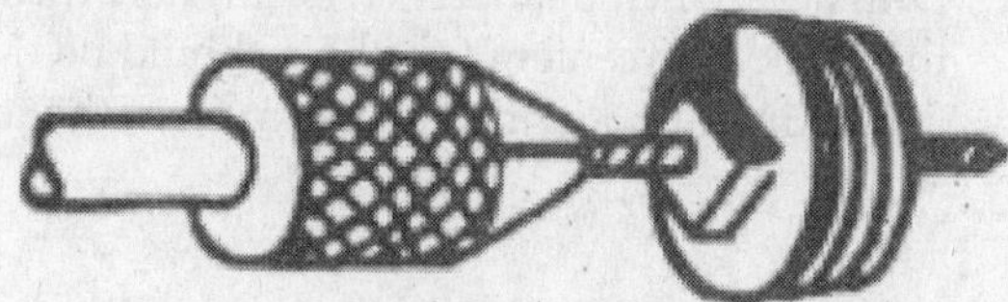

Hole must be centered in plug.

5. Push nail through plug until head of nail is flush with square end. Cut nail off at other end

1/16 inch (0.158 cm) away from plug. Round off end of nail with file.

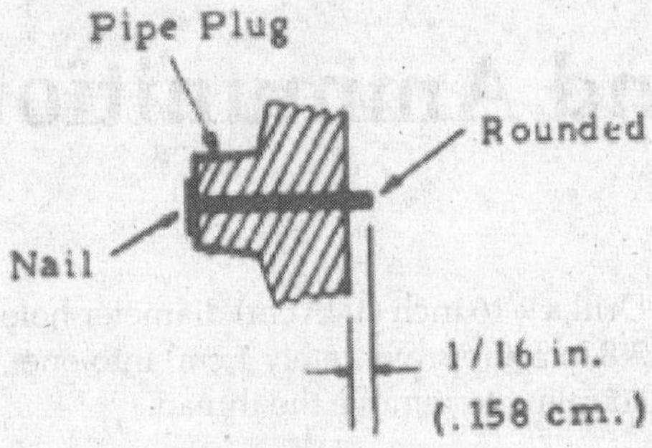

6. Bend metal strap to "U" shape and drill holes for wood screws. File two small notches at top.

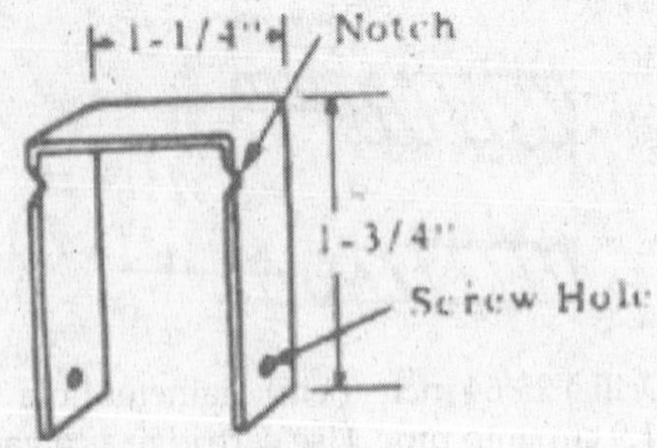

7. Saw or otherwise shape 1 inch (2.54 cm) thick hard wood into stock.

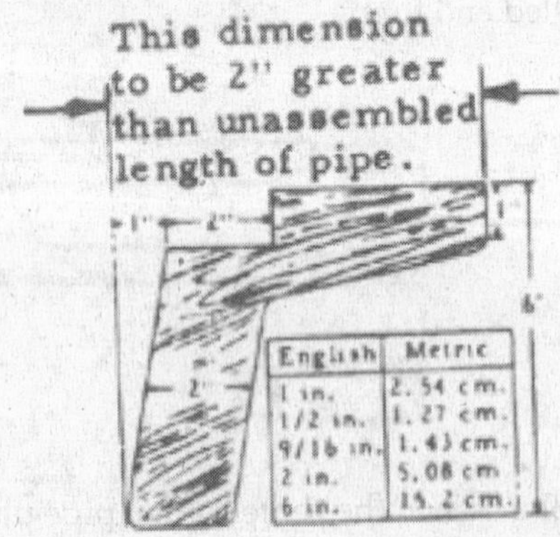

English	Metric
1 in.	2.54 cm.
1/2 in.	1.27 cm.
9/16 in.	1.43 cm.
2 in.	5.08 cm
6 in.	15.2 cm.

8. Drill a 9/16 inch diameter (1.43 cm) hole through the stock. The center of the hole should be approximately 1/2 inch (1.27 cm) from the top.

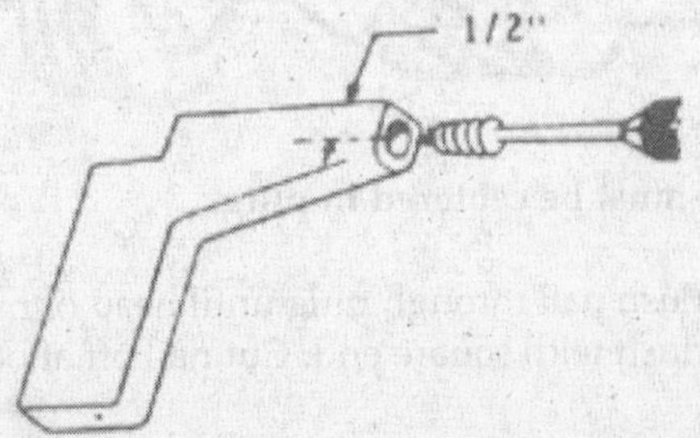

9. Slide the pipe through this hole and attach front coupling. Screw drilled plug into rear coupling.

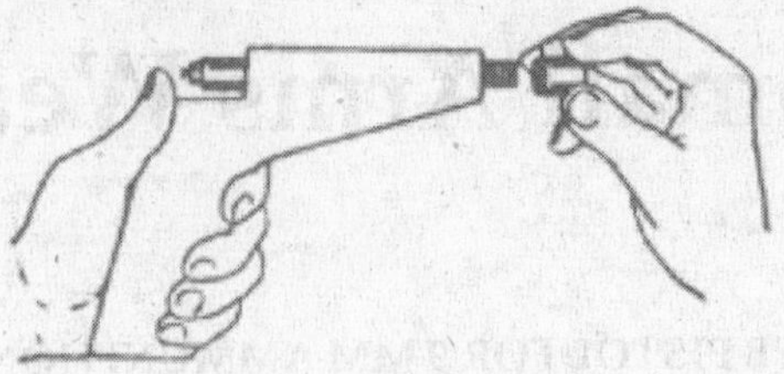

NOTE

If 9/16 inch drill is not available cut a "V" groove in the top of the stock and tape pipe securely in place.

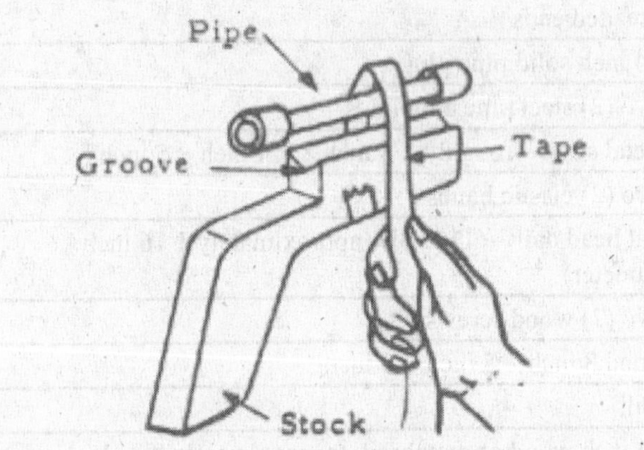

10. Position metal strap on stock so that top will hit the head of the nail. Attach to stock with wood screw on each side.

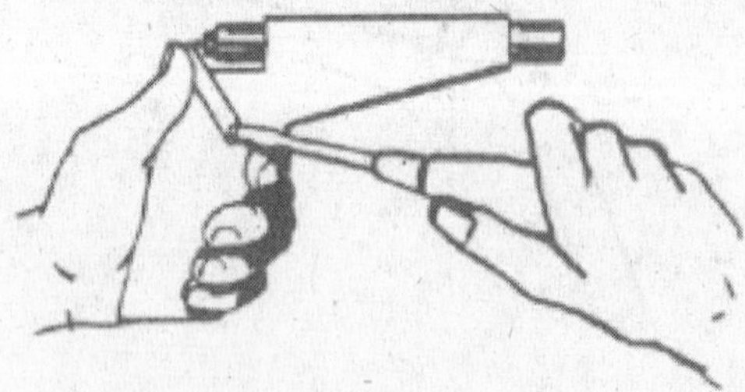

11. String elastic bands from front coupling to notch on each side of the strap.

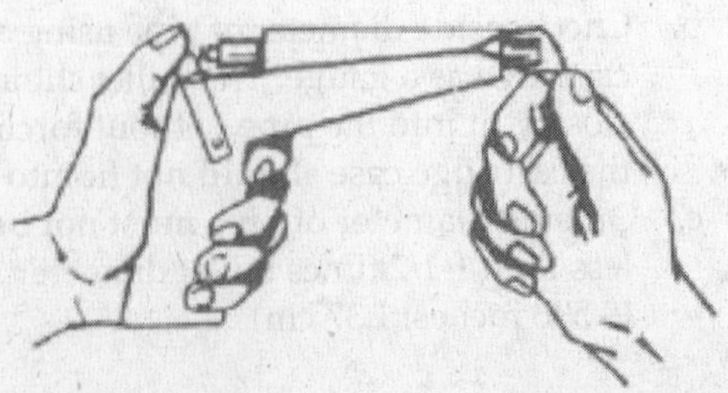

Safety Check – Test Fire Pistol Before Hand Firing

1. Locate a barrier such as a stone wall or large tree which you can stand behind in case the pistol ruptures when fired.

2. Mount pistol solidly to a table or other rigid support at least ten feet in front of the barrier.

3. Attach a cord to the firing strap on the pistol.

4. Holding the other end of the cord, go behind the barrier.

5. Pull the cord so that the firing strap is held back.

6. Release the cord to fire the pistol. (If pistol does not fire, shorten the elastic bands or increase their number.)

> **IMPORTANT**
> Fire at least five rounds from behind the barrier and then reinspect the pistol before you attempt to hand fire it.

How to Operate Pistol

1. *To Load:*
   a. Remove plug from rear coupling.

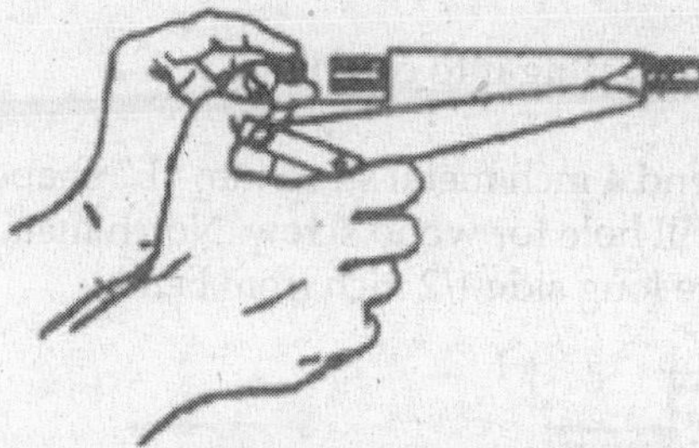

   b. Place cartridge into pipe.

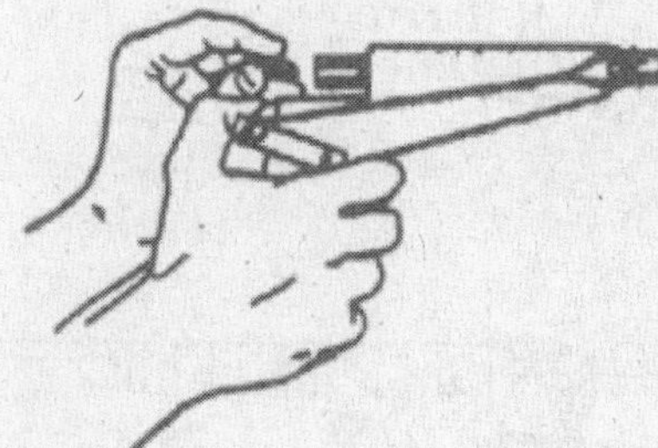

   c. Replace plug.

2. *To Fire:*
   a. Pull strap back and hold with thumb until ready.

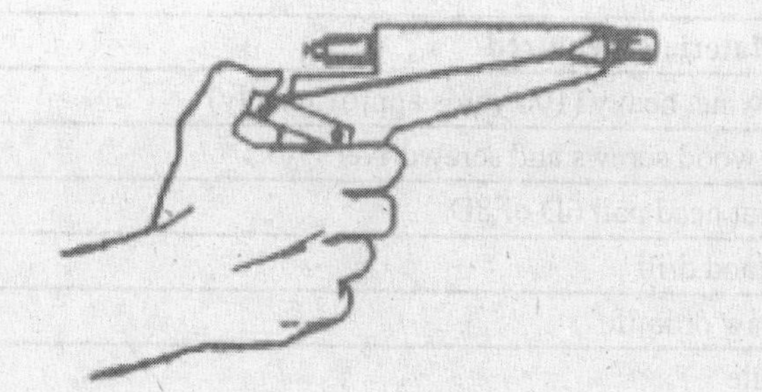

   b. Release strap.

3. *To Remove Shell Case:*
   a. Remove plug from rear coupling.
   b. Insert 1/4 inch diameter steel or wooden rod into front of pistol and push shell case out.

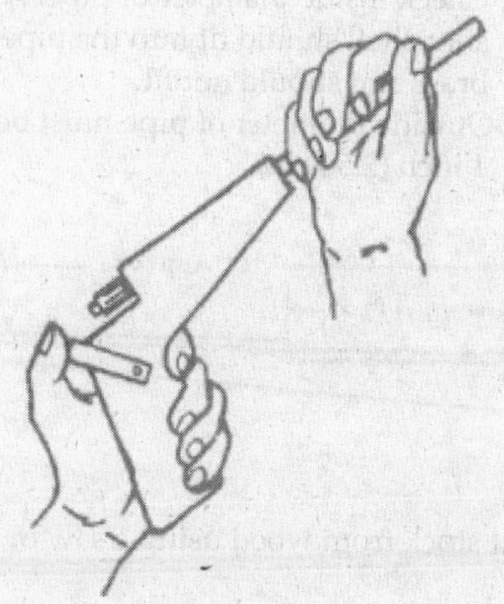

3.2 SHOTGUN (12 GAUGE)

A 12-gauge shotgun can be made from 3/4 inch water or gas pipe and fittings.

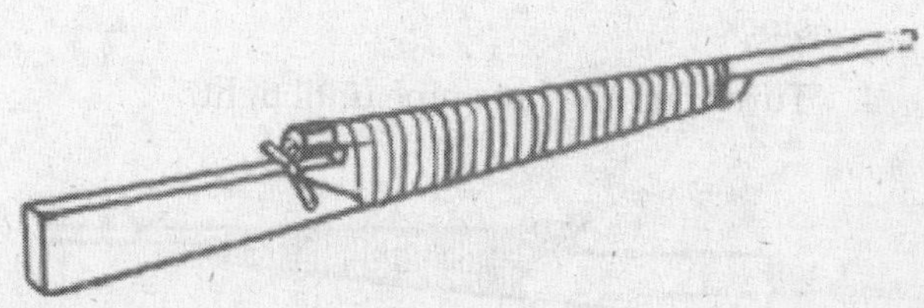

Materials Required
Wood 2 inches × 4 inches × 32 inches
3/4 inch nominal size water or gas pipe 20 inches to 30 inches long threaded on one end
3/4 inch steel coupling
Solid 3/4 inch pipe plug
Metal strap (1/4 inch × 1/16 inch × 4 inch)

Materials Required
Twine, heavy (100 yards approximately)
3 wood screws and screwdriver
Hat head nail 6D or 8D
Hand drill
Saw or knife
File
Shellac or lacquer
Elastic Bands

Procedure

1. Carefully inspect pipe and fittings.
   a. Make sure that there are no cracks or other flaws.
   b. Check inside diameter of pipe. A 12-gauge shot shell should fit into the pipe but the brass rim should not fit.
   c. Outside diameter of pipe must be at least 1 inch (2.54 cm).

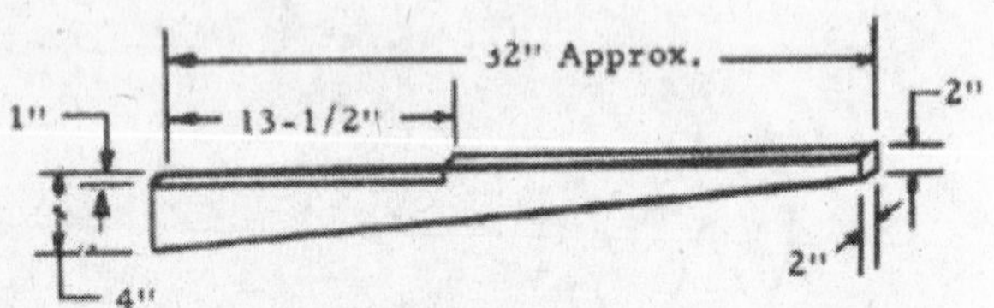

2. Cut stock from wood using a saw or knife.

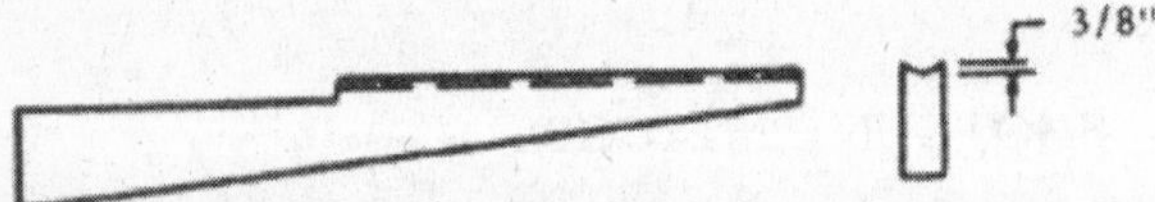

3. Cut a 3/8 inch deep "V" groove in top of the stock.
4. Turn coupling onto pipe until tight.

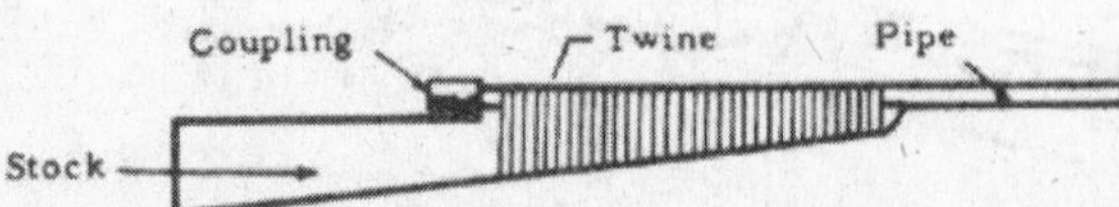

5. Coat pipe and "V" groove of stock with shellac or lacquer and, while still wet, place pipe in "V" groove and wrap pipe and stock together using two heavy layers of twine. Coat twine with shellac or lacquer after each layer.
6. Drill a hole through center of pipe plug large enough for nail to pass through.

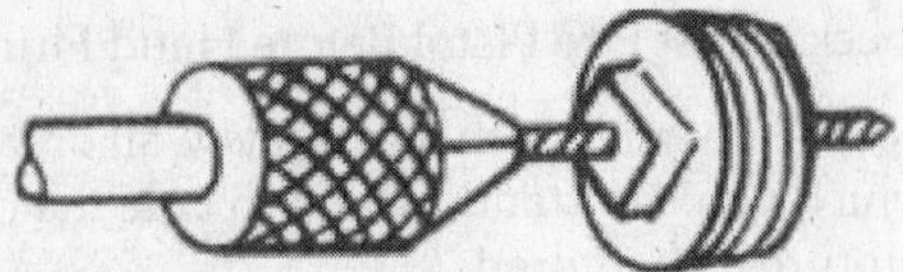

7. File threaded end of plug flat.

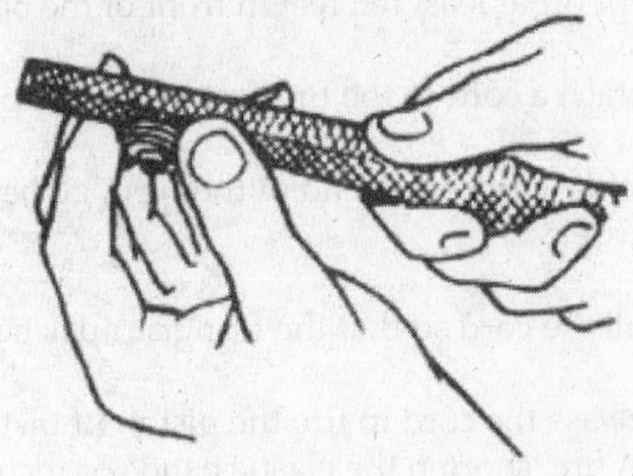

8. Push nail through plug and cut off flat 1/32 inch past the plug.

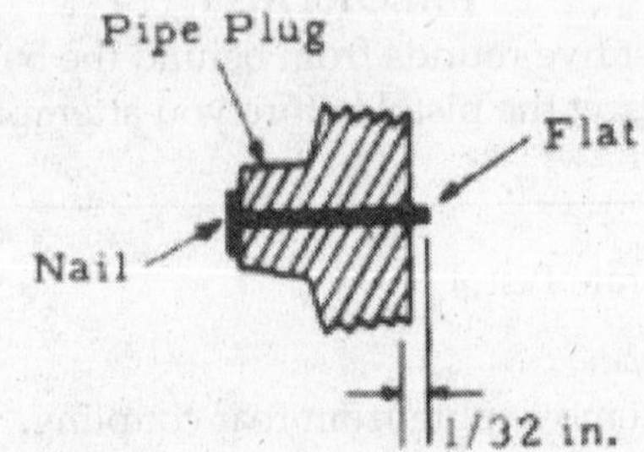

9. Screw plug into coupling.
10. Bend 4 inch metal strap into "L" shape and drill hole for wood screw. Notch metal strap on the long side 1/2 inch from bend.

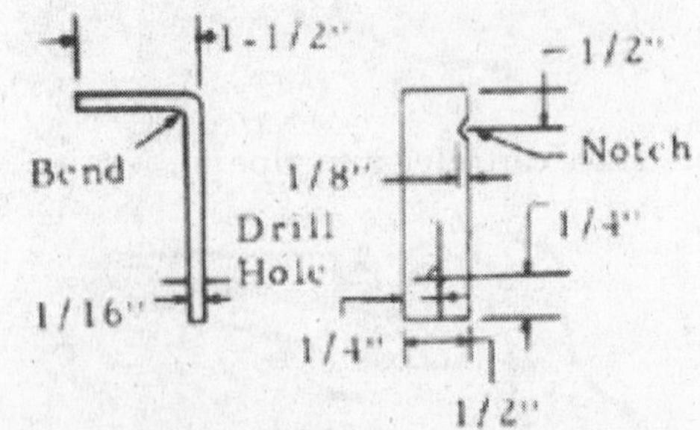

11. Position metal strap on stock so that top will hit the head of the nail. Attach to stock with wood screw.

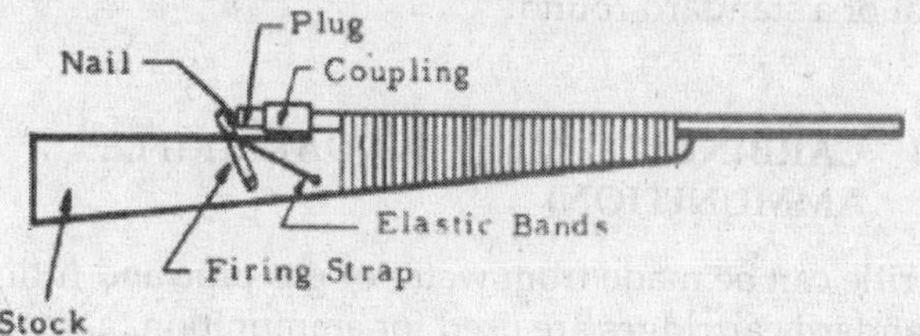

12. Place screw in each side of stock about 4 inch in front of metal strap. Pass elastic bands through notch in metal strap and attach to screw on each side of the stock.

Safety Check – Test Fire Shotgun Before Hand Firing

1. Locate a barrier such as a stone wall or large tree which you can stand behind in case the weapon explodes when fired.
2. Mount shotgun solidly to a table or other rigid support at least ten feet in front of the barrier.
3. Attach a long cord to the firing strap on the shotgun.
4. Holding the other end of the cord, go behind the barrier.
5. Pull the cord so that the firing strap is held back.
6. Release the cord to fire the shotgun. (If shotgun does not fire, shorten the elastic bands or increase their number.)

> **IMPORTANT**
> Fire at least five rounds from behind the barrier and then reinspect the shotgun before you attempt to shoulder fire it.

How to Operate Shotgun

1. *To Load:*

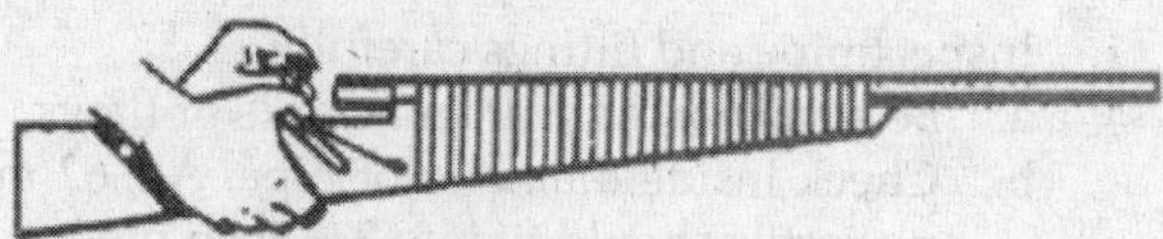

   a. Take plug out of coupling.

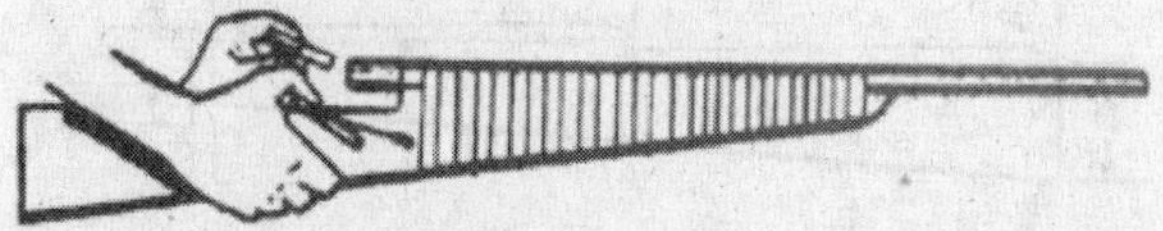

   b. Put shotgun shell into pipe.
   c. Screw plug hand tight into coupling.

2. *To Fire:*

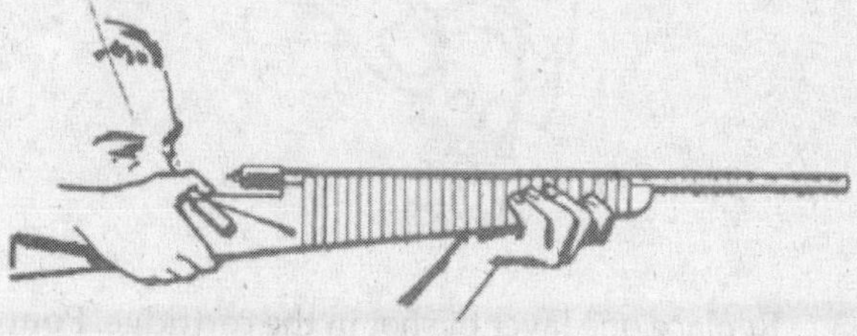

   a. Pull strap back and hold with thumb.
   b. Release strap.

3. *To Unload Gun:*
   a. Take plug out of coupling.
   b. Shake out used cartridge.

3.3 SHOTSHELL DISPERSION CONTROL

When desired, shotshell can be modified to reduce shot dispersion.

Materials Required
Shotshell
Screwdriver or knife
Any of the following filler materials: Crushed rice Rice flour Dry bread crumbs Fine dry sawdust

Procedure

1. Carefully remove crimp from shotshell using a screwdriver or knife.

> **NOTE**
> If cartridge is of roll-crimp type, remove top wad.

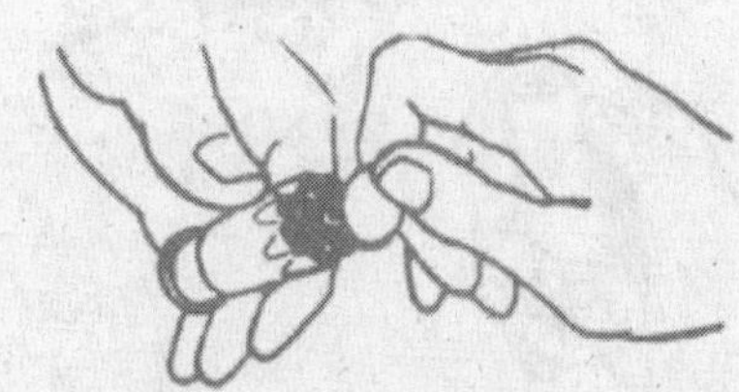

2. Pour shot from shell.

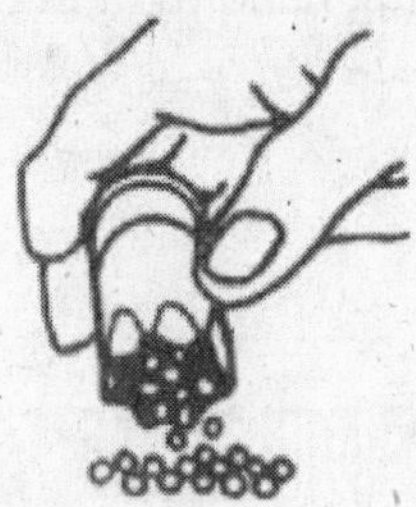

3. Replace one layer of shot in the cartridge. Pour in filler material to fill the spaces between the shot.

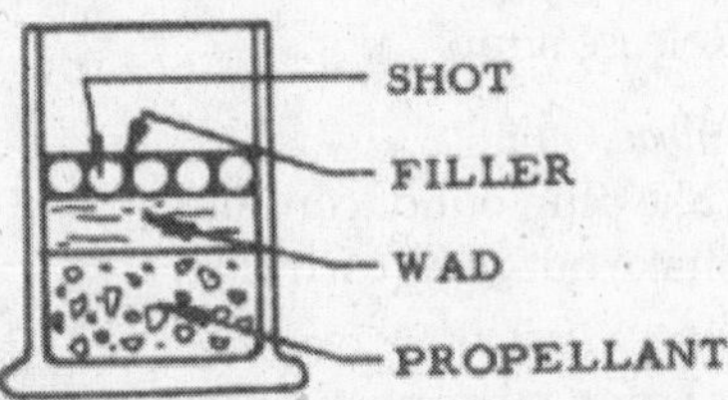

4. Repeat step 3 until all shot has been replaced.
5. Replace top wad (if applicable) and refold crimp.
6. Roll shell on flat surface to smooth out crimp and restore roundness.

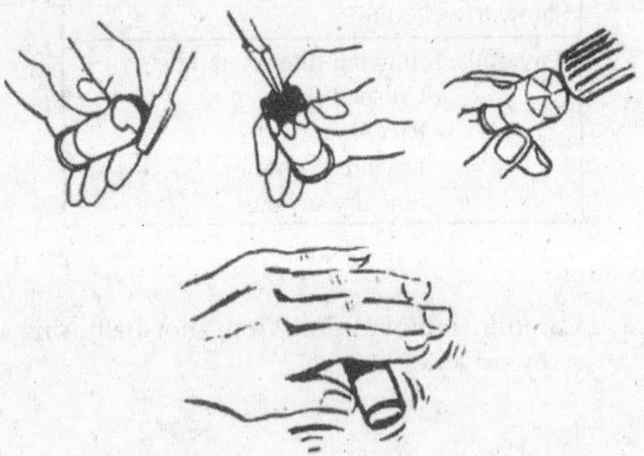

7. Seal end of case with wax.

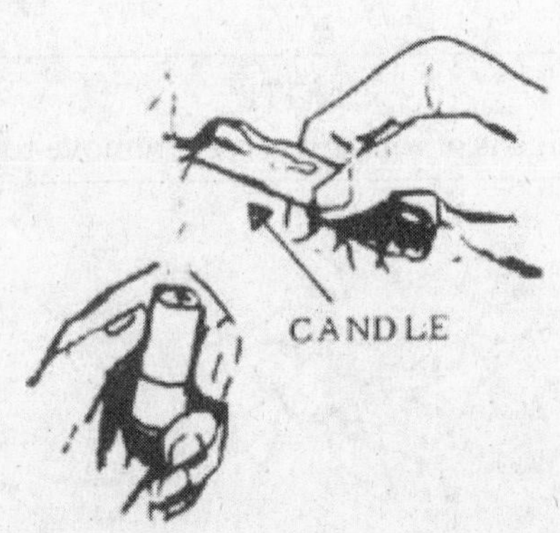

How to Use

This round is loaded and fired in the same manner as standard shotshell. The shot spread will be about 2/3 that of a standard round.

3.4 CARBINE (7.62 MM STANDARD RIFLE AMMUNITION)

A rifle can be made from water or gas pipe and fittings. Standard cartridges are used for ammunition.

Materials Required
Wood approximately 2 inches × 4inches × 30 inches
1/4 inch nominal size iron water or gas pipe 20 inches long threaded at one end
3/8 inch to 1/4 inch reducer
3/8 inch × 1-1/2 inch threaded pipe
3/8 inch pipe coupling
Metal strap approximately 1/2 inch × 1/16inch × 4inches
Twine, heavy (100 yards approximately)
3 wood screws and screwdriver
Flat head hail about 1 inch long
Hand drill
Saworknife
File
Pipe wrench
Shellac or lacquer
Elastic bands
Solid 3/8 inch pipe plug

Procedure

1. Inspect pipe and fittings carefully.
   a. Be sure that there are no cracks or flaws.
   b. Check inside diameter of pipe. A 7.62 mm projectile should fit into 3/8 inch pipe.

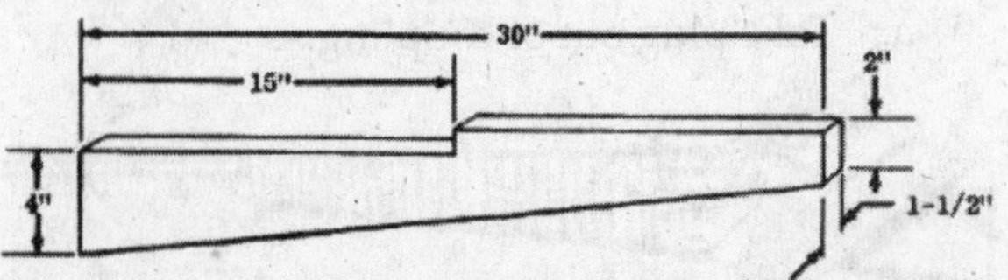

2. Cut stock from wood using saw or knife.

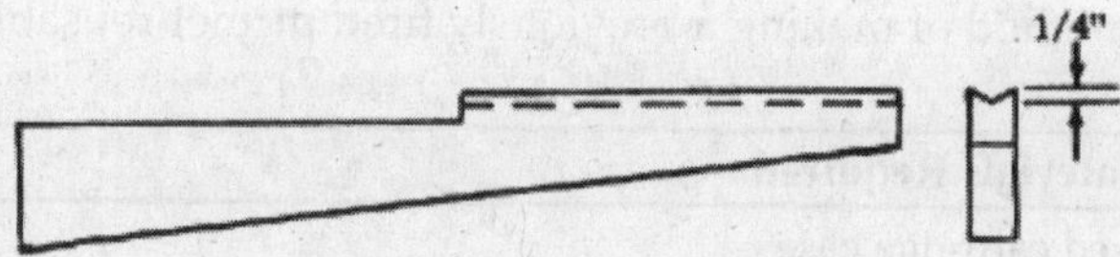

3. Cut a 1/4 inch deep "V" groove in top of the stock.
4. Fabricate rifle barrel from pipe.
   a. File or drill inside diameter of threaded end of 20 inch pipe for about 1/4 inch so neck of cartridge case will fit in.
   b. Screw reducer onto threaded pipe using pipe wrench.
   c. Screw short threaded pipe into reducer.
   d. Turn 3/8 pipe coupling onto threaded pipe using pipe wrench. *All* fittings *should* be as tight as possible. Do not split fittings.

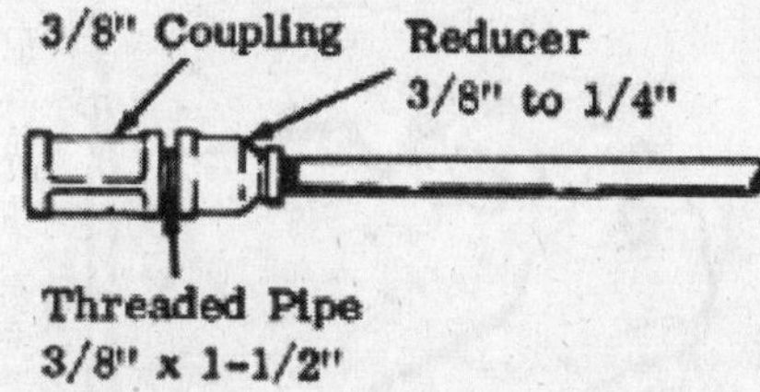

5. Coat pipe and "V" groove of stock with shellac or lacquer. While still wet, place pipe in "V" groove and wrap pipe and stock together using two layers of twine. Coat twine with shellac or lacquer after each layer.
6. Drill a hole through center of pipe plug large enough for nail to pass through.

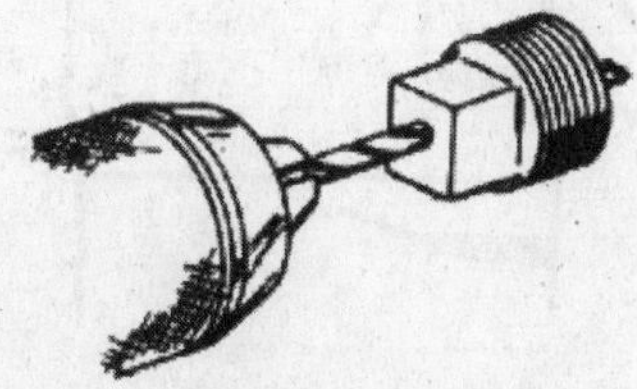

7. File threaded end of plug flat.

8. Push nail through plug and out off rounded 1/32 inch (2 mm) past the plug.

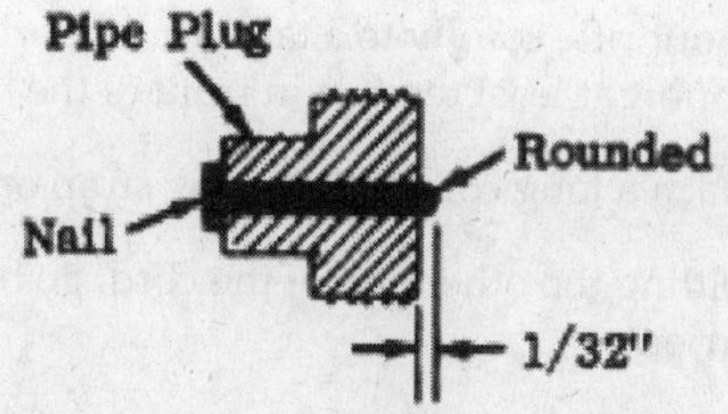

9. Screw plug into coupling.
10. Bend 4 inch metal strap into "L" shape and drill hole for wood screw. Notch metal strap on the long side 1/2 inch from bend.

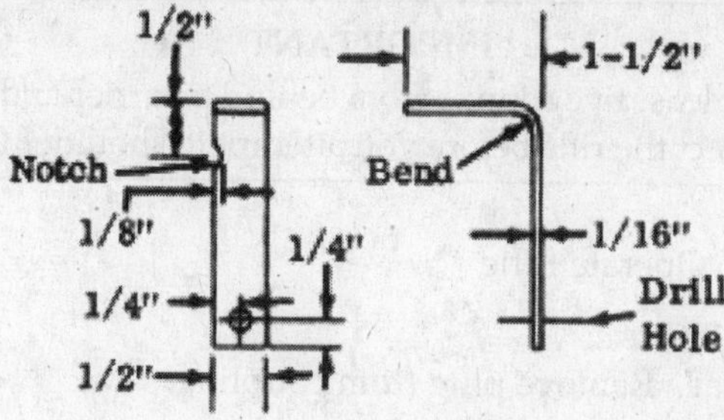

11. Position metal strap on stock so that top will hit the head of the nail. Attach to stock with wood screw.

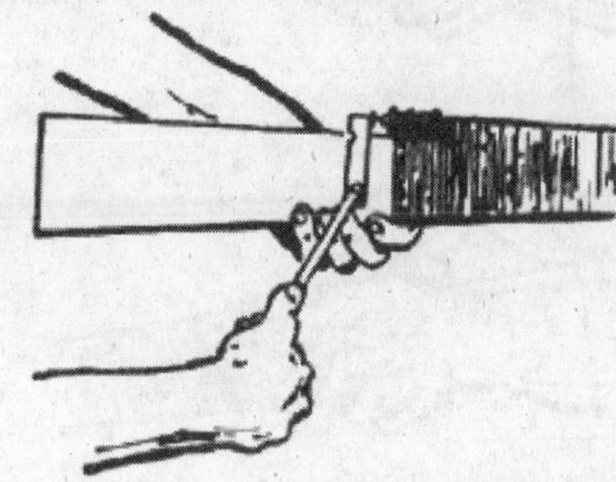

12. Place screw in each side of stock about 4 inches in front of metal strap. Pass elastic bands through notch in metal strap and attach to screw on each side of the stock.

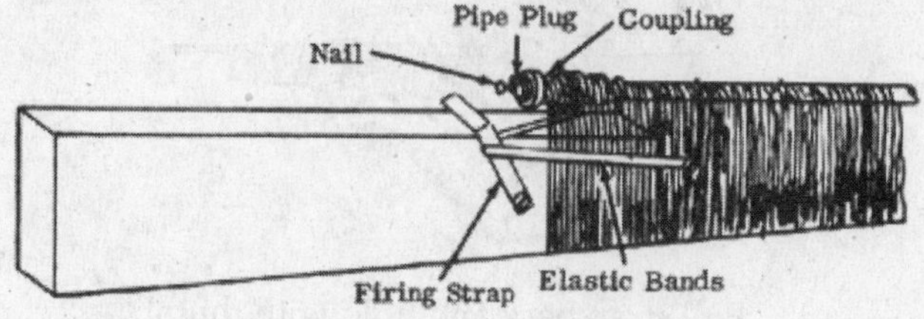

Safety Check – Test Fire Rifle Before Hand Firing

1. Locate a barrier such as a stone wall or large tree which you can stand behind to test fire weapon.

2. Mount rifle solidly to a table or other rigid support at least ten feet in front of the barrier.

3. Attach a long cord to the firing strap on the rifle.

4. Holding the other end of the cord, go behind the barrier.

5. Pull the cord so that the firing strap is held back.

6. Release the cord to fire the rifle. (If the rifle does not fire, shorten the elastic bands or increase their number.)

IMPORTANT

Fire at least five rounds from behind a barrier and then reinspect the rifle before you attempt to shoulder fire it.

How to Operate Rifle

1. *To Load:*
   a. Remove plug from coupling.

   b. Put cartridge into pipe.

   c. Screw plug hand tight into coupling.

2. *To Fire:*

   a. Pull strap back and hold with thumb.
   b. Release strap.

3. *To Unload Gun:*
   a. Take plug out of coupling.
   b. Drive out used case using stick or twig.

3.5 REUSABLE PRIMER

A method of making a previously fired primer reusable.

Materials Required
Used cartridge case
2 long nails having approximately the same diameter as the inside of the primer pocket
"Strike-anywhere" matches – 2 or 3 are needed for *each* primer
Vise
Hammer
Knife or other sharp edged instrument

Procedure

1. File one nail to a needle point so that it is small enough to fit through hole in primer pocket.

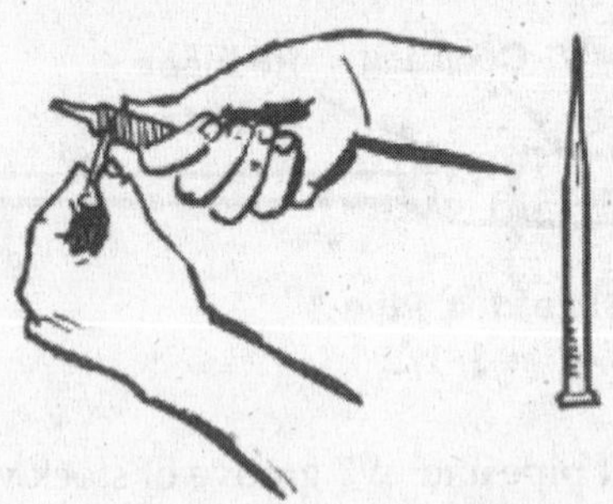

2. Place cartridge case and nail between jaws of vise. Force out fired primer with nail as shown:

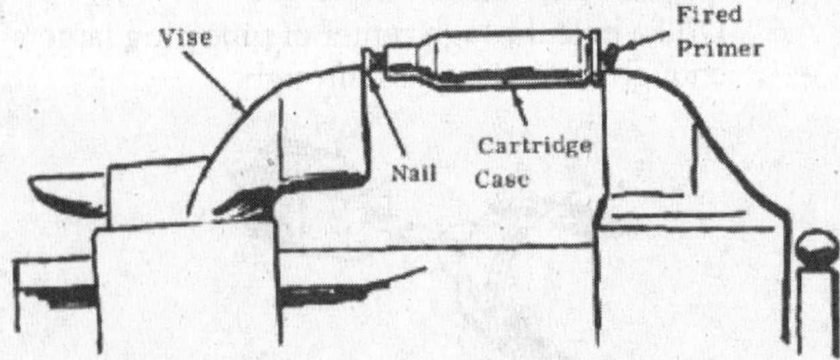

3. Remove anvil from primer cup.

4. File down point of second nail until tip is flat.

5. Remove indentations from face of primer cup with hammer and flattened nail.

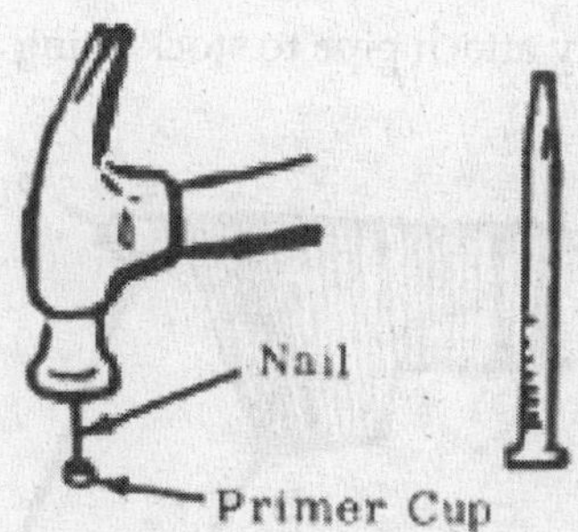

6. Cut off tips of the heads of "strike-anywhere" matches using knife. Carefully crush the match tips on dry surface with wooden match stick until the mixture is the consistency of sugar.

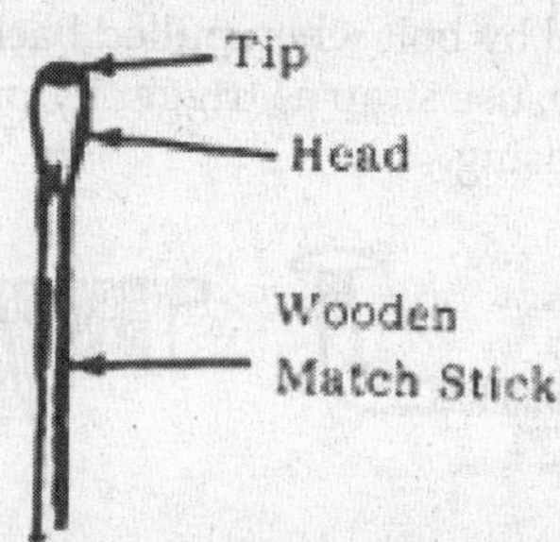

CAUTION

Do not crush more than 3 match tips at one time or the mixture may explode.

7. Pour mixture into primer cup. Compress mixture with wooden match stick until primer cup is fully packed.

8. Place anvil in primer pocket with legs down.

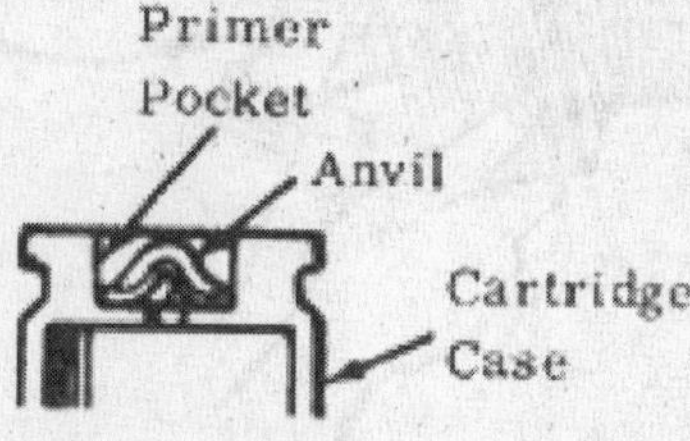

9. Place cup in pocket with mixture facing downward.

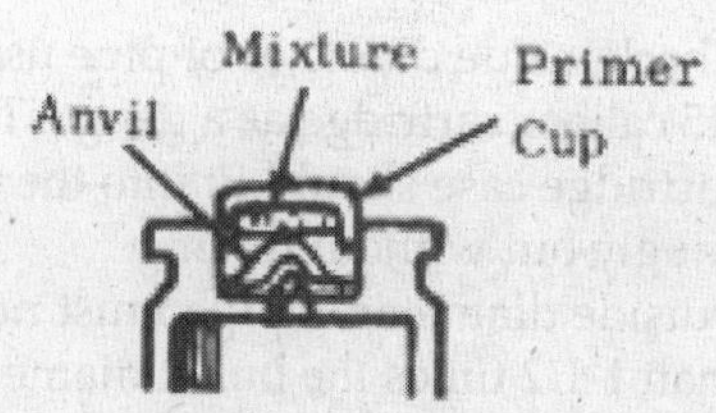

10. Place cartridge case and primer cup between vise jaws, and press slowly until primer is seated into bottom of pocket. The primer is now ready to use.

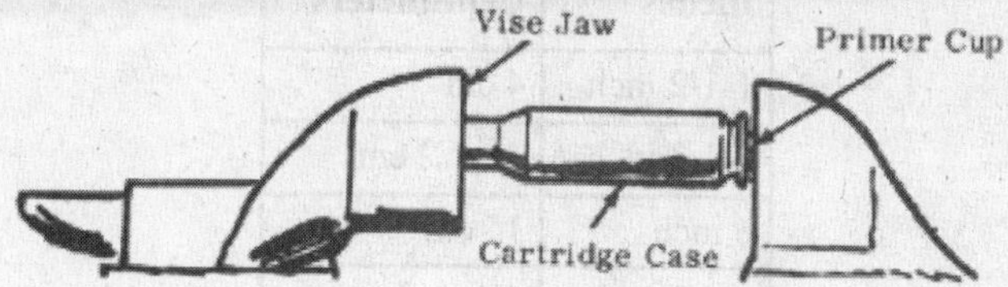

3.6 PIPE PISTOL FOR .45 CALIBER AMMUNITION

A .45 caliber pistol can be made from 3/8 inch nominal diameter steel gas or water pipe and fittings. Lethal range is about 15 yards (13-1/2 meters).

Materials Required
Steel pipe, 3/8 inch (1 cm) nominal diameter and 6 inches (15 cm) long with threaded ends
2 threaded couplings to fit pipe
Solid pipe plug to fit pipe coupling
Hard wood, 8-1/2 inches × 6-1/2 inches × 1 inch (21 cm × 16-1/2 cm × 2-1/2 cm)
Tape or string
Flat head nail, approximately 1/16 inch (1-1/2 mm) in diameter
2 wood screws, approximately 1/16 inch (1-172 mm) in diameter
Metal strap, 5 inches × 1/4 inch × 1/8 inch (12-1/2 cm × 6 mm × 1 mm)
Bolt, 4 inches (10 cm) long, with nut (optional)
Elastic bands
Drills, one 1/16 inch (1-1/2 mm) in diameter, and one having same diameter as bolt (optional)
Rod, 1/4 inch (6 mm) in diameter and 8 inches (20 cm) long
Saw or knife

Procedure

1. Carefully inspect pipe and fittings.
   a. Make sure that there are no cracks or other flaws in the pipe and fittings.

b. Check inside diameter of pipe using a .45 caliber cartridge as a gauge. The cartridge case should fit into the pipe snugly but without forcing.
c. Outside diameter of pipe **must not be** less than 1-1/2 times the bullet diameter.

2. Follow procedure of section 3.1, steps 4, 5, and 6.
3. Cut stock from wood using saw or knife.

Inches	Centimeters
1-1/2 inch	4 cm
8-1/2 inch	21-1/2 cm
6 inch	15 cm
1-1/2 inch	4 cm
5 inch	12-1/2 cm

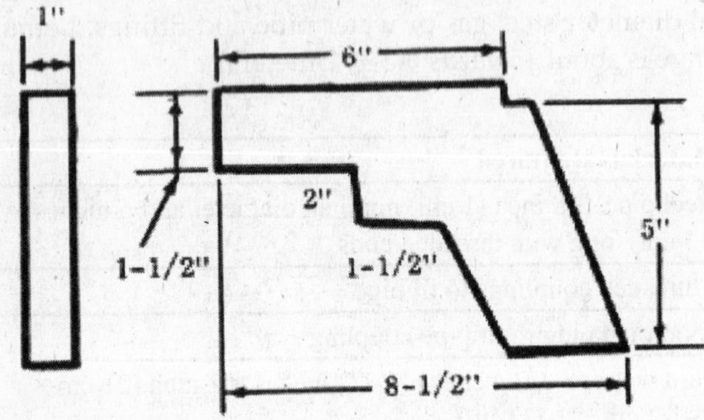

4. Cut a 3/8 inch (9-1/2 mm) deep groove in top of stock.

5. Screw couplings onto pipe. Screw plug into one coupling.

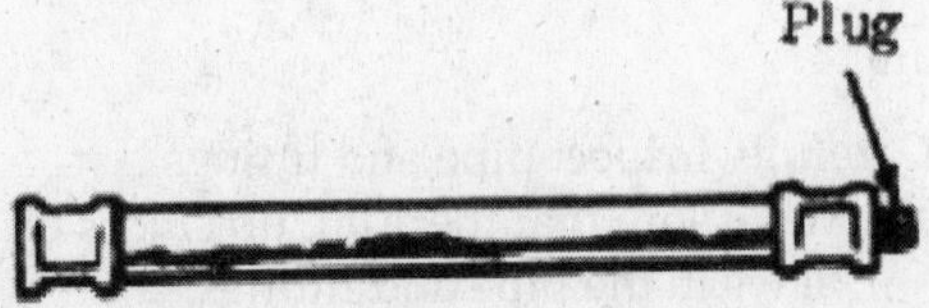

6. Securely attach pipe to stock using string or tape.

7. Follow procedures of section 3.1, steps 10 and 11.
8. (Optional) Bend bolt for trigger. Drill hole in stock and place bolt in hole so strap will be anchored by bolt when pulled back. If bolt is not available, use strap as trigger by pulling back and releasing.

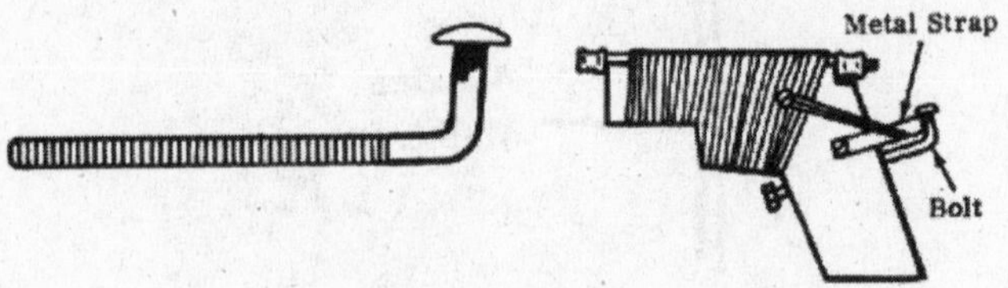

9. Follow Safety Check, section 3.1.

How to Use

1. *To Load:*
   a. Remove plug from rear coupling.
   b. Wrap string or elastic band around extractor groove so case will seat into barrel securely.

   c. Place cartridge in pipe.

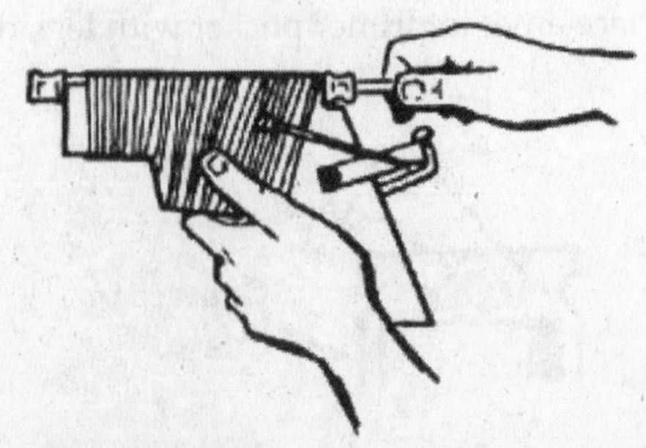

   d. Replace plug.

2. *To Fire:*
   a. Pull metal strap back and anchor in trigger.
   b. Pull trigger when ready to fire.

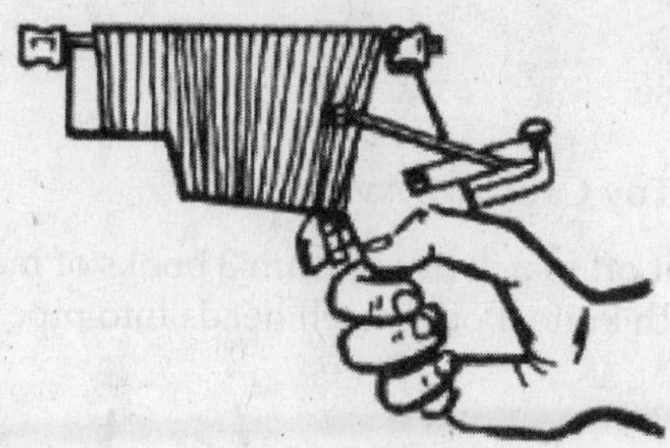

NOTE
If bolt is not used, pull strap back and release.

3. *To Remove Cartridge Case:*
   a. Remove plug from rear coupling.
   b. Insert rod into front of pistol and push cartridge case out.

3.7 MATCH GUN

An improvised weapon using safety match heads as the propellant and a metal object as the projectile. Lethal range is about 40 yards (36 meters).

Materials Required
Metal pipe 24 inches (61 cm) long and 3/8 inch (1 cm) in diameter (nominal size) or its equivalent, threaded on one end
End cap to tit pipe
Safety matches – 3books of 20 matches each
Wood – 28 inches × 4 inches × 1 inch (70 cm × 10 cm × 2.5cm)
Toy caps **or** safety fuse **or** "Strike-anywhere" matches (2)
Electrical tape or string
Metal strap, about 4 inches × 1/4 inch × 3/16 inch (10 cm × 6 mm × 4.5 mm)
2 rags, about 1 in × 12 inches and 1 inch × 3 inches (2-1/2 cm × 30 cm and 2-1/2 cm × 8 cm)
Wood screws
Elastic bands
Metal object (steel rod, bolt with head cut off, etc.), approximately 7/16 inch (11 mm) in diameter, and 7/16 inch (11 mm) long if iron or steel, 1-1/4 inch (31 mm) long if aluminum, 5/16 inch (8 mm) long if lead
Metal disk 1 inch (2-1/2 cm) in diameter and 1/16 inch (1-1/2 mm) thick
Bolt, 3/32 inch (2-1/2 nun) or smaller in diameter and nut to fit
Saw or knife

Procedure

1. Carefully inspect pipe and fittings. Be sure that there are no cracks or other flaws.

2. Drill small hole in center of end cap. If safety fuse is used, be sure it will pass through this hole.

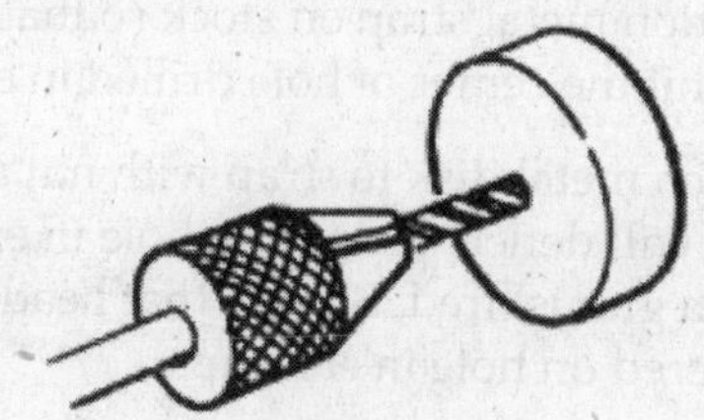

3. Cut stock from wood using saw or knife.

Metric	English
5 cm	2 inches
10 cm	4 inches
36 cm	14 inches
71 cm	28 inches

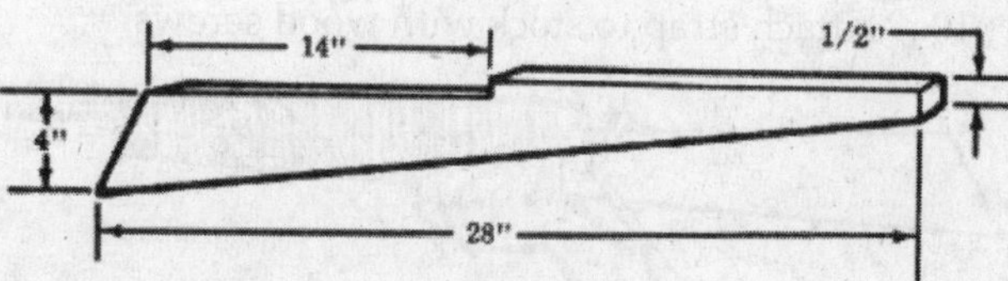

4. Cut 3/8 inch (9-1/2 mm) deep "V" groove in top of stock.

5. Screw end cap onto pipe until finger tight.

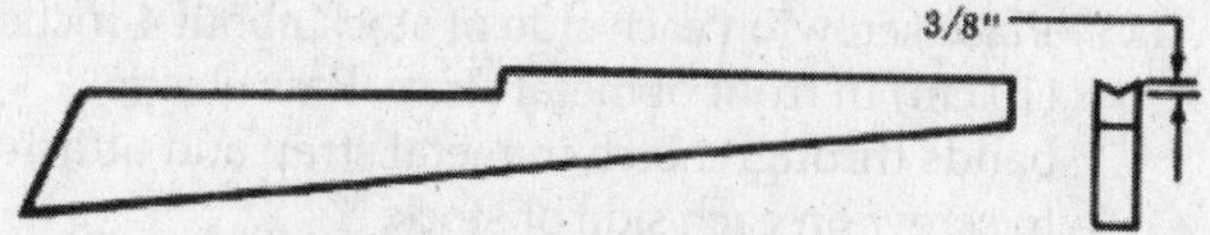

6. Attach pipe to stock with string or tape.

7. Bend metal strap into "L" shape and drill holes for wood screw. Notch metal strap on long side 1/2 inch (1 cm) from bend.

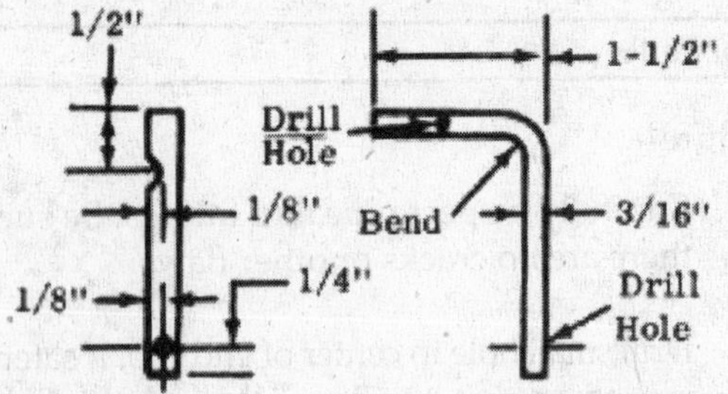

8. Position metal strap on stock so that the top will hit the center of hole drilled in end cap.
9. Attach metal disk to strap with nut and bolt. This will deflect blast from hole in end cap when gun is fired. Be sure that head of bolt is centered on hole in end cap.

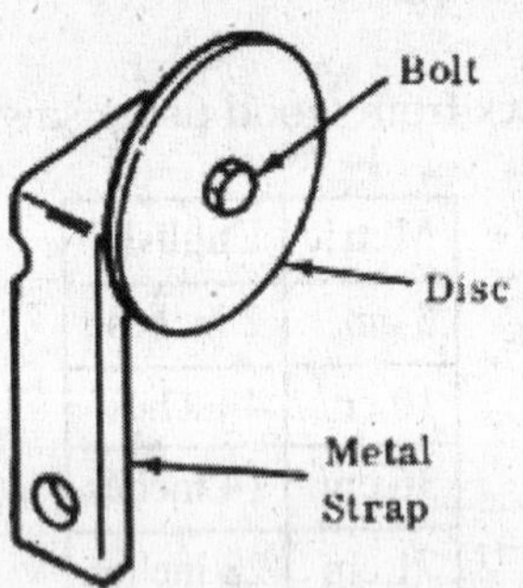

10. Attach strap to stock with wood screws.

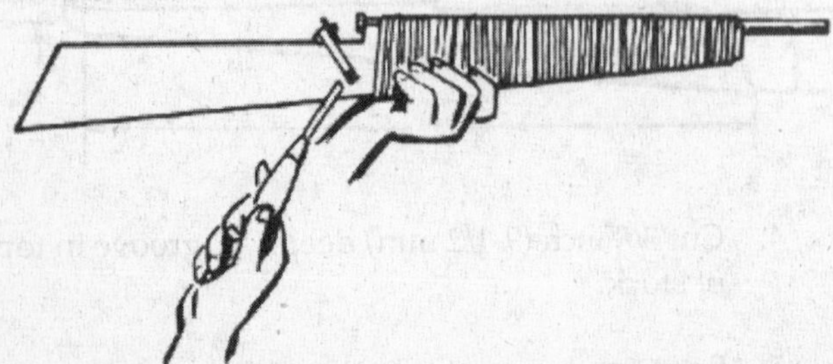

11. Place screw on each side of stock about 4 inches (10 cm) in front of metal strap. Pass elastic bands through notch in metal strap and attach to screw on each side of stock.

How to Use

A. When Toy Caps Are Available:

1. Cut off match heads from 3 books of matches with knife. Pour match heads into pipe.

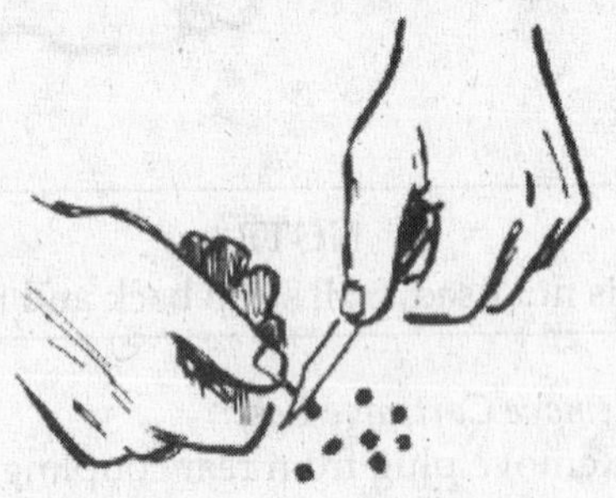

2. Fold one end of 1 inch × 12 inch rag 3 times so that it becomes a one inch square of 3 thicknesses. Place rag into pipe to cover match heads, folded end first. Tamp firmly **with caution.**

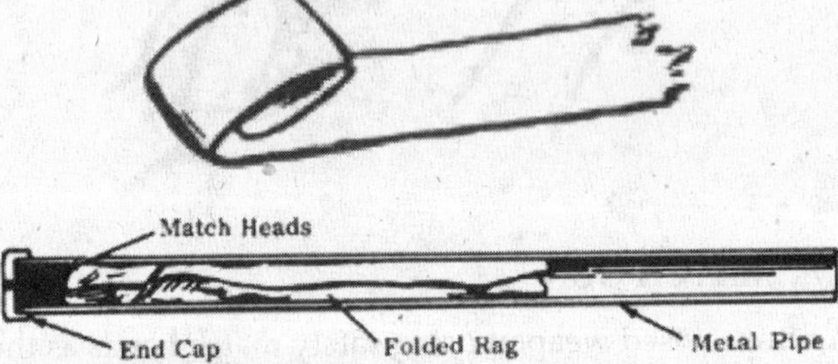

3. Place metal object into pipe. Place 1 inch × 3 inch rag into pipe to cover projectile. Tamp firmly **with caution.**
4. Place 2 toy caps over small hole in end cap. Be sure metal strap will hit caps when it is released.

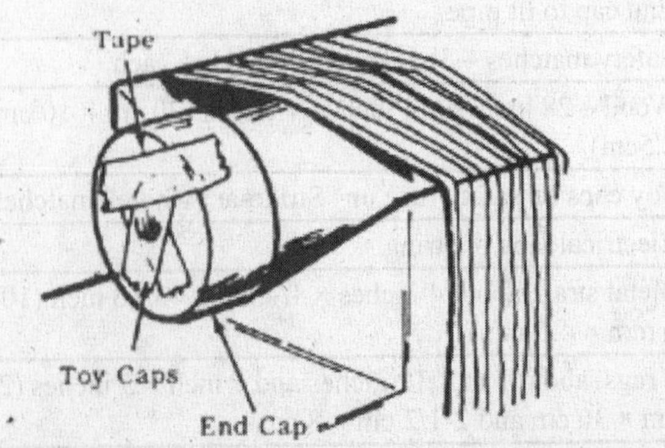

> **NOTE**
> It may be necessary to tape toy caps to end cap.

5. When ready to fire, pull metal strap back and release.

B. When "Strike-Anywhere" Matches Are Available:

1. Follow steps 1 through 3 in A.
2. Carefully cut off tips of heads of 2 "strike-anywhere" matches with knife.

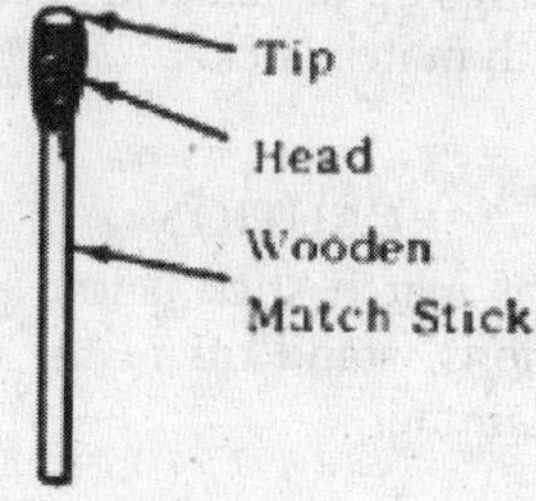

3. Place one tip in hole in end cap. Push in with wooden end of match stick.
4. Place second match tip on a piece of tape. Place tape so match tip is directly over hole in end cap.

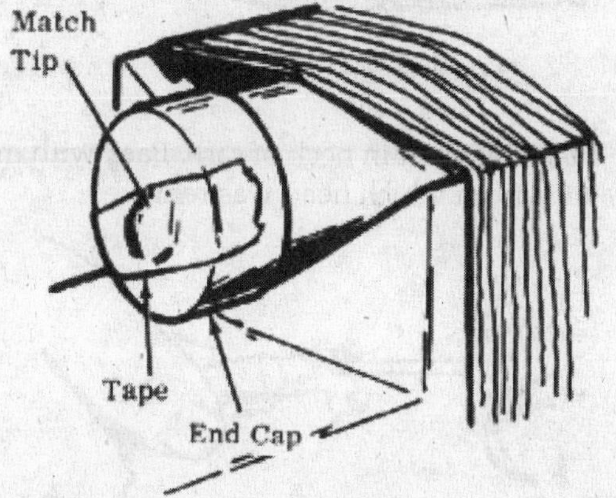

5. When ready to fire, pull metal strap back and release.

C. When Safety Fuse is Available: (Recommended for Booby Traps)

1. Remove end cap from pipe. Knot one end of safety fuse. Thread safety fuse through hole in end cap so that knot is on *inside* of end cap.
2. Follow steps 1 through 3 in A.
3. Tie several matches to safety fuse near outside of end cap.

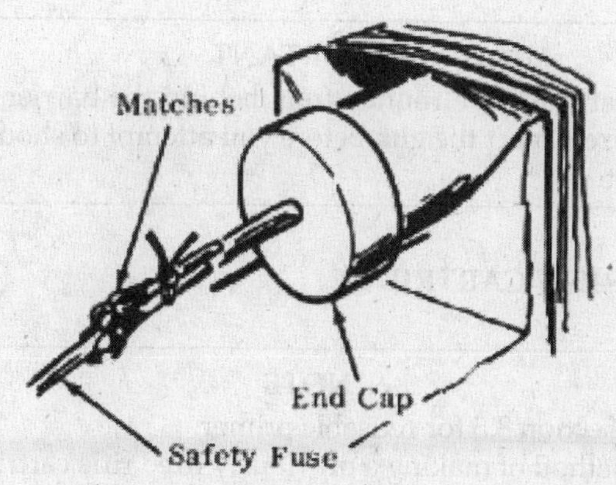

> **NOTE**
> Bare end of safety fuse should be inside match head cluster.

4. Wrap match covers around matches and tie. Striker should be in contact with match bands.

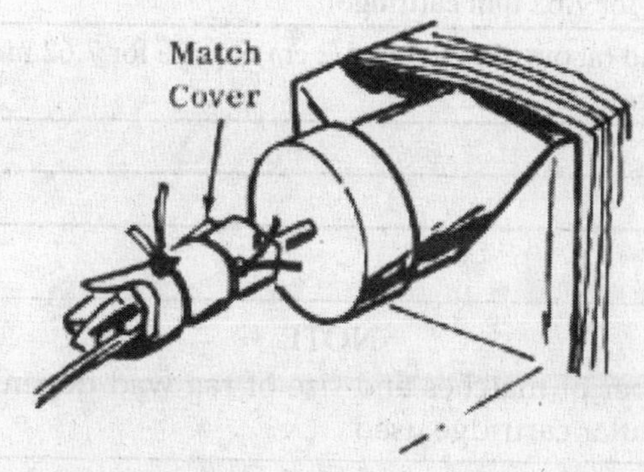

5. Replace end cap on pipe.
6. When ready to fire, pull match cover off with strong, firm, quick motion.

Safety Check – Test Fire Gun Before Hand Firing

1. Locate a barrier such as a stone wall or large tree which you can stand behind in case the weapon explodes when fired.
2. Mount gun solidly to a table or other rigid support at least ten feet in front of the barrier.
3. Attach a long cord to the firing strap on the gun.
4. Holding the other end of the cord, go behind the barrier.
5. Pull the cord so that the firing strap is held back.
6. Release the cord to fire the gun. (If gun does not fire, shorten the elastic bands or increase their number.)

IMPORTANT

Fire at least five rounds from behind the barrier and then reinspect the gun before you attempt to shoulder fire it.

3.8 RIFLE CARTRIDGE

NOTE

See section 3.5 for reusable primer.
A method of making a previously fired rifle cartridge reusable.

Materials Required
Empty rifle cartridge, be sure that it still fits inside gun
Threaded bolt that fits into neck of cartridge at least 1-1/4 inch (3 cm) long
Safety or "strike-anywhere" matches (about 58 matches are needed for 7.62 mm cartridge)
Rag wad (about 3/4 inch (1-1/2 cm) square for 7.62 mm cartridge)
Knife
Saw

NOTE

Number of matches and size of rag wad depend on particular cartridge used.

Procedure

1. Remove coating on heads of matches by scraping match sticks with sharp edge.

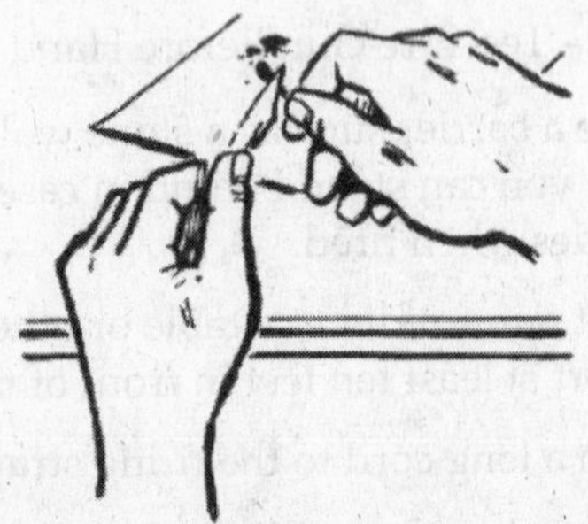

CAUTION

If wooden "strike-anywhere" matches are used, cut off tips *first*. Discard tips or use for Reusable Primer, section 3.5.

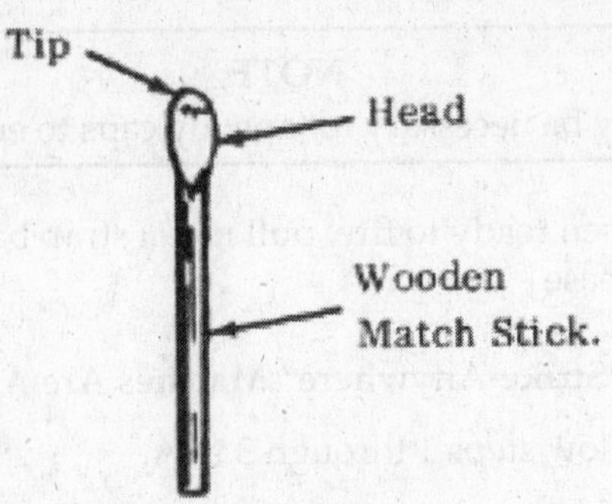

2. Fill previously primed cartridge case with match head coatings up to its neck. Pack evenly and tightly with match stick.

CAUTION

Remove head of match stick before packing. In all packing operations, stand off to the side and pack *gently*. Do not hammer.

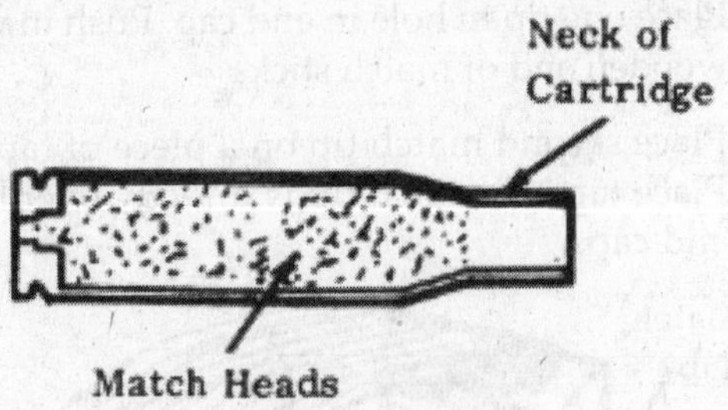

3. Place rag wad in neck of case. Pack with match stick from which head was removed.

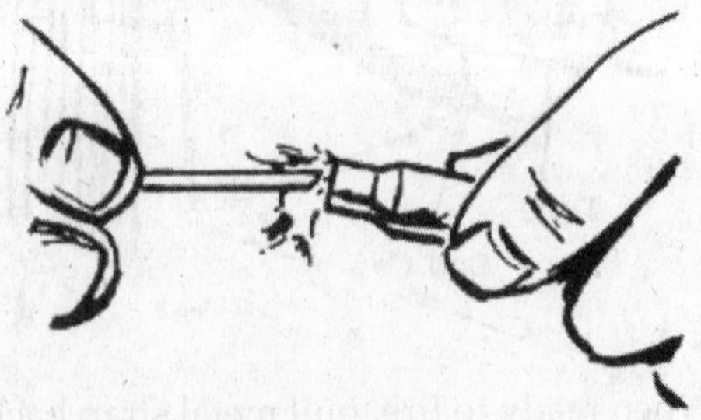

4. Saw off head end of bolt so remainder is approximately the length of the standard bullet.

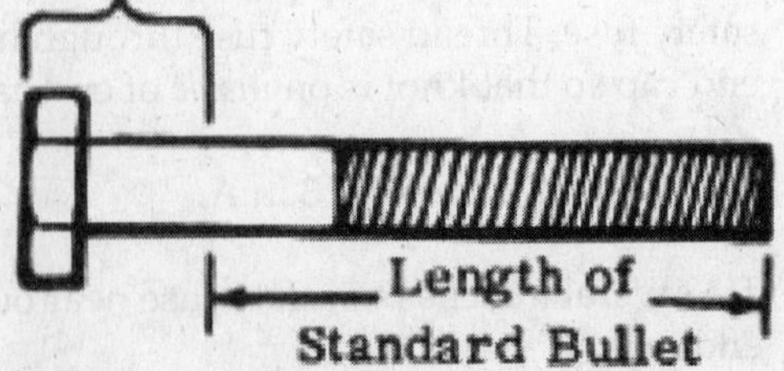

5. Place bolt in cartridge case so that it sticks out about the same length as the original bullet.

> **NOTE**
> If bolt does not fit snugly, force paper or match sticks between bolt and case, or wrap tape around bolt before inserting in case.

3.9 PIPE PISTOL FOR .38 CALIBER AMMUNITION

A .38 caliber pistol can be made from 1/4 inch nominal diameter steel gas or water pipe and fittings. Lethal range is approximately 33 yards (30 meters).

Materials Required
Steel pipe, 1 /4 inch (6 mm) nominal diameter and 6 inches (15 cm) long with threaded ends (nipple)
Solid pipe plug, 1/4 inch (6 mm) nominal diameter
2 steel pipe couplings, 1/4 inch (6 mm) nominal diameter
Metal strap, approximately 1/8 inch × 1/4 inch × 5 inches (3 mm × 6 mm × 125 mm or 12-1/2 cm)
Elastic bands
Flat head nail – 6D or 8D, approximately 1/16 inch diameter (1-1/2 mm)
2 wood screws, #8
Hard wood, 8 inches × 5 inches × 1 inch (20 cm × 12-1/2 cm × 2-1/2 cm)
Drill
Wood or metal rod, 1/4 inch (6 mm) diameter and 8 inches (20 cm) long
Saw or knife

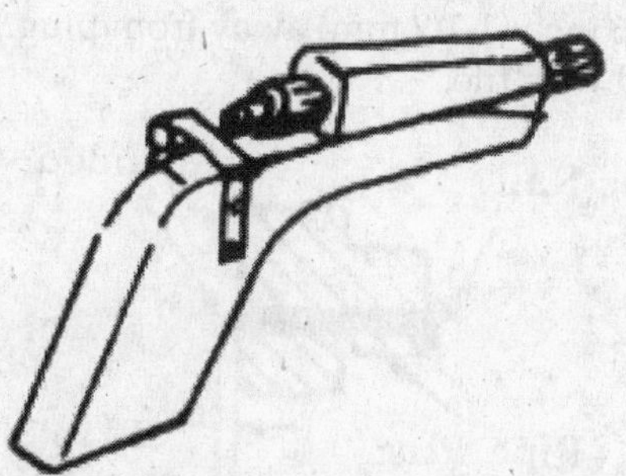

Procedure

1. Carefully inspect pipe and fittings.
   a. Make sure that there are no cracks or other flaws in the pipe or fittings.
   b. Check inside diameter of pipe using a .38 caliber cartridge as a gauge. The bullet should fit closely into the pipe without forcing, but the cartridge case should not fit into the pipe.
   c. Outside diameter of pipe must not be less than 1-1/2 times the bullet diameter.
2. Drill a 35/64 inch (14 mm) diameter hole 3/4 inch (2 cm) into one coupling to remove the thread. Drilled section should fit tightly over smooth section of pipe.

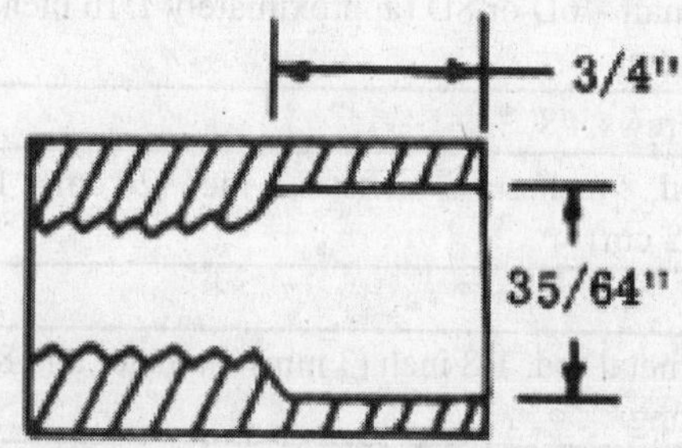

3. Drill a 25/64 inch (1 cm) diameter hole 1-1/8 inch (2.86 cm) into pipe. Use cartridge as a gauge; when a cartridge is inserted into the pipe, the shoulder of the case should butt against the end of the pipe. Thread coupling tightly onto pipe, drilled end first.

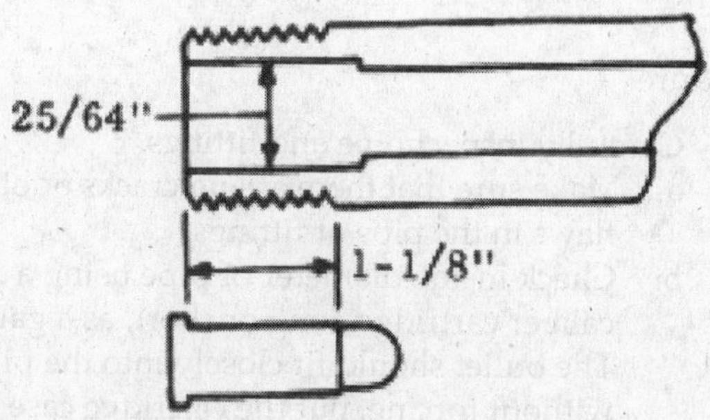

4. Follow procedures of section 3.1, steps 4 through 11.
5. Follow Safety Check, section 3.1.

How to Operate Pistol

Follow procedures of How to Operate Pistol, section 3.1, steps 1, 2, and 3.

3.10 PIPE PISTOL FOR .22 CALIBER AMMUNITION — LONG OR SHORT CARTRIDGE

A .22 caliber pistol can be made from 1/8 inch nominal diameter extra heavy, steel gas or water pipe and fittings. Lethal range is approximately 33 yards (30 meters).

Materials Required
Steel pipe, extra heavy, 1/8 inch (3 mm) nominal diameter and 6 inches (15 cm) long with threaded ends (nipple)
Solid pipe plug, 1/8 inch (3 mm) nominal diameter
2 steel pipe couplings, 1/8 inch (3 mm) nominal diameter
Metal strap, approximately 1/8 inch × 1/4 inch × 5 inches (3 mm × 6 mm × 125 mm or 12-1/2 cm)
Elastic bands
Flat head nail – 6D or 8D (approximately 1/16 inch (1-1/2 mm) diameter
2 wood screws, #8
Hard wood, 8 inches × 5 inches × 1 inch (20 cm × 12-1/2 cm × 2-1/2 cm)
Drill
Wood or metal rod, 1/8 inch (3 mm) diameter and 8 inches (20 cm) long
Saw or knife

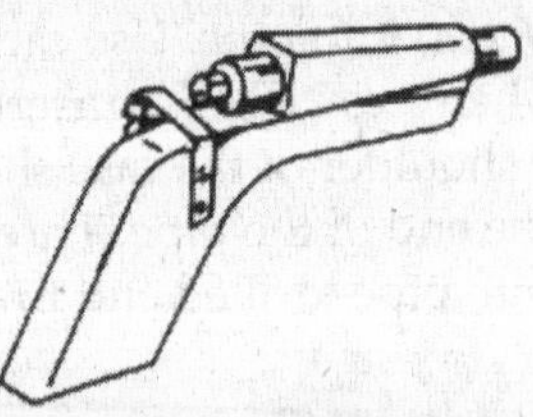

Procedure

1. Carefully inspect pipe and fittings.
   a. Make sure that there are **no** cracks or other flaws in the pipe or fittings.
   b. Check inside diameter of pipe using a .22 caliber cartridge, long or short, as a gauge. The bullet should fit closely into the pipe without forcing, but the cartridge case **should not fit** into the Pipe.
   c. Outside diameter of pipe **must not be** less than 1-1/2 times the bullet diameter.
2. Drill a 15/64 inch (1/2 cm) diameter hole 9/16 inch (1-1/2 cm) deep in pipe for long cartridge. (If a short cartridge is used, drill hole 3/8 inch (1 cm) deep.) When a cartridge is inserted into the pipe, the shoulder of the case should butt against the end of the pipe.

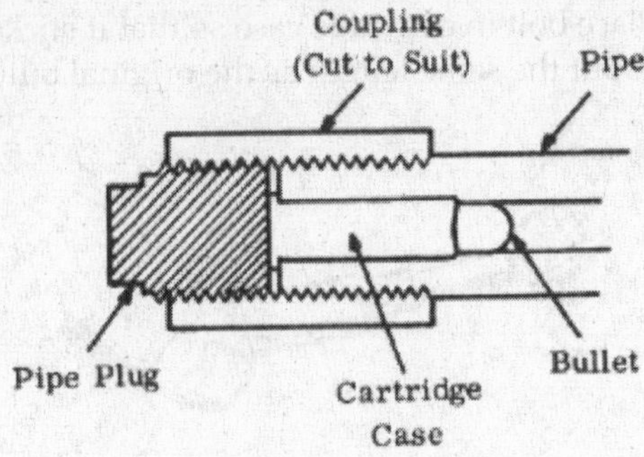

3. Screw the coupling onto the pipe. Cut coupling length to allow pipe plug to thread in pipe flush against the cartridge case.

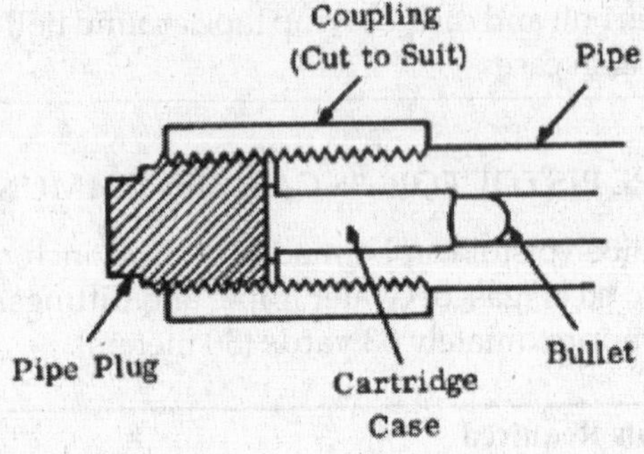

4. Drill a hole off center of the pipe plug just large enough for the nail to fit through.

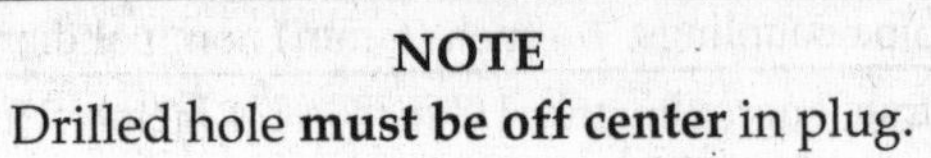
NOTE
Drilled hole **must be off center** in plug.

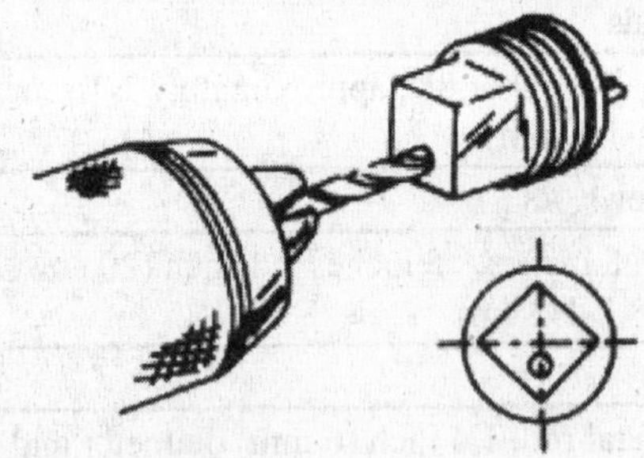

5. Push nail through pipe plug until head of nail is flush with square end. Cut nail off at other end 1/16 inch (1-1/2 mm) away from plug. Round off end with file.

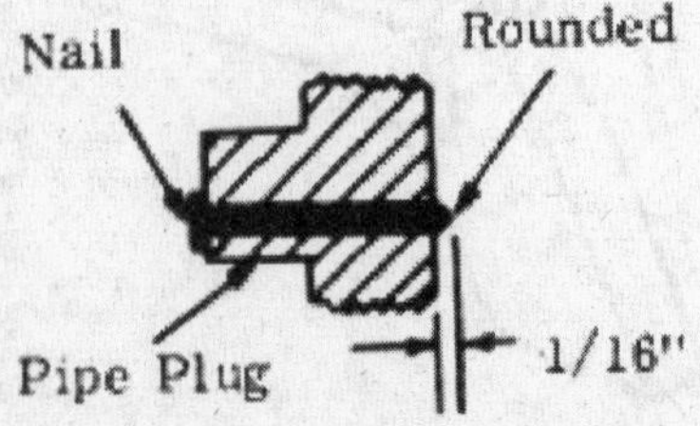

6. Follow procedures of section 3.1, steps 6 through 11.

7. Follow Safety Check, section 3.1.

How to Operate

Follow procedures of How to Operate Pistol, section 3.1, steps 1, 2, and 3.

3.11 LOW SIGNATURE SYSTEM

Low signature systems (silencers) for improvised small arms weapons (section 3) can be made from steel gas or water pipe and fittings.

Materials Required
Grenade container
Steel pipe nipple, 6 inches (15 cm) long – see Table I for diameter
2 steel pipe couplings – see Table II for dimensions
Cotton cloth – see Table II for dimensions
Drill
Absorbent cotton

Procedure

1. Drill hole in grenade container at both ends to fit outside diameter of pipe nipple. (See Table I.)

2. Drill four (4) rows of holes in pipe nipple. Use Table I for diameter and location of holes.

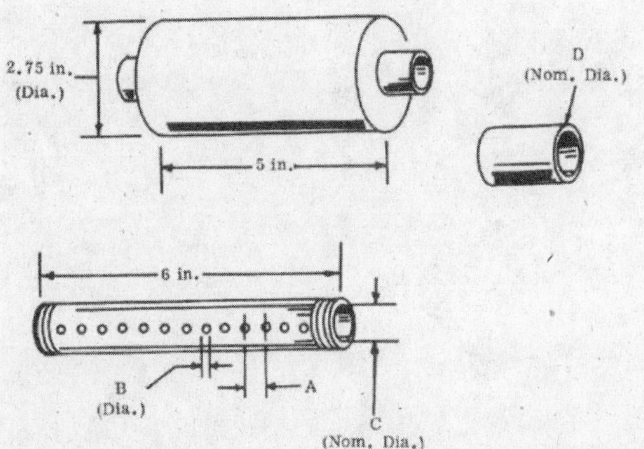

Table I. Low Signature System Dimensions

	A	B	C	(Coupling) D	Holes per Row	(4-Rows) Total
.45 caliber	3/8	1/4	3/8	3/8	12	48
.38 caliber	3/8	1/4	1/4	1/4	12	48
9 mm	3/8	1/4	1/4	1/4	12	48
7.62 mm	3/8	1/4	1/4	1/4	12	48
.22 caliber	1/4	5/32	1/8*	1/8	14	50

*Extra heavy pipe
All dimensions in inches

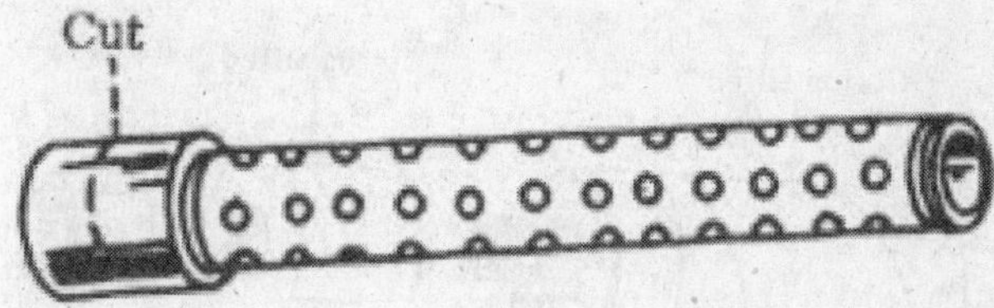

3. Thread one of the pipe couplings on the drilled pipe nipple.

4. Cut coupling length to allow barrel of weapon to thread fully into low signature system. Barrel should butt against end of the drilled pipe nipple.

5. Separate the top half of the grenade container from the bottom half.

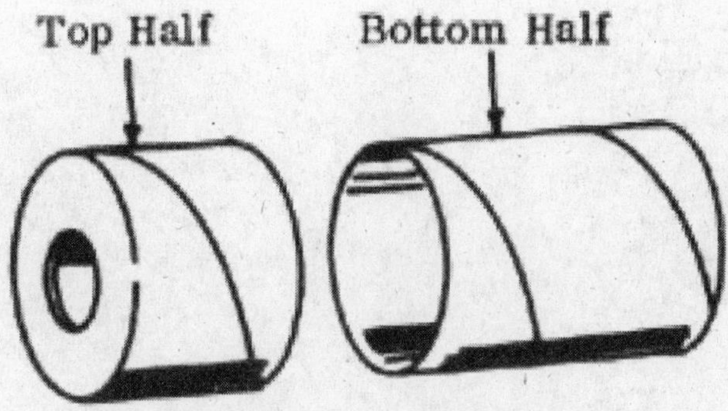

6. Insert the pipe nipple in the drilled hole at the base of the bottom half of container. Pack the absorbent cotton inside the container and around the pipe nipple.

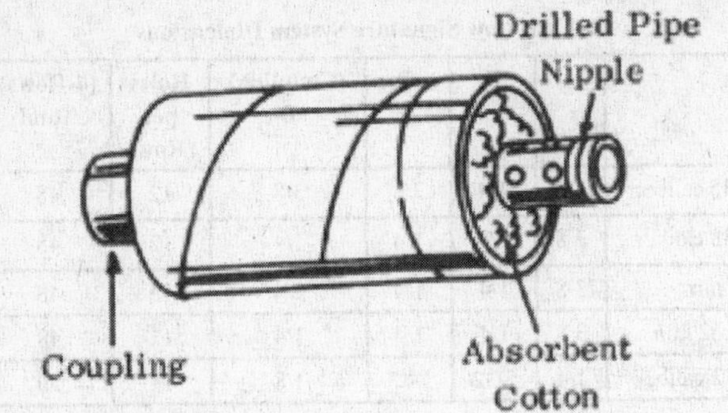

7. Pack the absorbent cotton in top half of grenade container leaving hole in center. Assemble container to the bottom half.

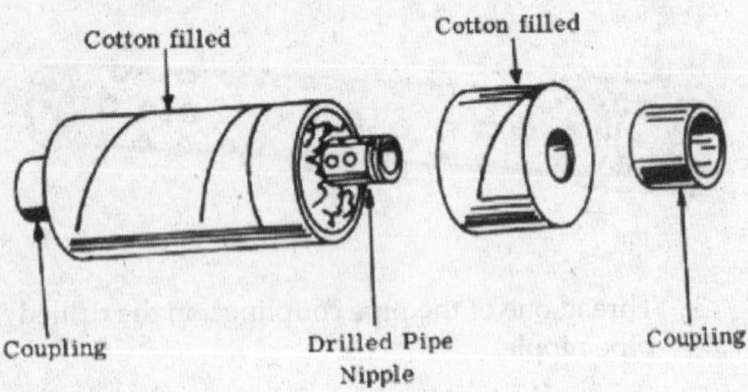

8. Thread the other coupling onto the pipe nipple.

NOTE

A longer container and pipe nipple, with same "A" and "B" dimensions as those given, will further reduce the signature of the system.

How to Use

1. Thread the low signature system on the selected weapon securely.

2. Place the proper cotton wad size into the muzzle end of the system.

Table II. Cotton Wadding – Sizes

Weapon	Cotton Wad Size
.45 caliber	1-1/2 × 6 inches
.38 caliber	1 × 4 inches
9 mm	1 × 4 inches
7.62 mm	1 × 4 inches
.22 caliber	Not needed

3. Load weapon.

4. Weapon is now ready for use.

SECTION 4

Mortars and Rockets

4.1 RECOILLESS LAUNCHER

A dual directional scrap fragment launcher which can be placed to cover the path of advancing troops.

Materials Required
Iron water pipe approximately 4 feet (1 meter) long and 2 to 4 inches (5 to 10 cm) in diameter
Black powder (commercial) or salvaged artillery propellant about 1/2 pound (200 grams)
Safety or improvised fuse (section 6.7) or improvised electrical igniter (section 6.2)
Stones and/or metal scrap chunks approximately 1/2 inch (1 cm) in diameter – about 1 pound (400 grams) total
4 rags for waddings, each about 20 inches by 20 inches (50 cm by 50 cm)
Wire
Paper or rag

NOTE

Be sure that the water pipe has no cracks or flaws.

Procedure

1. Place propellant and igniter in paper or rag and tie with string so contents cannot fall out.

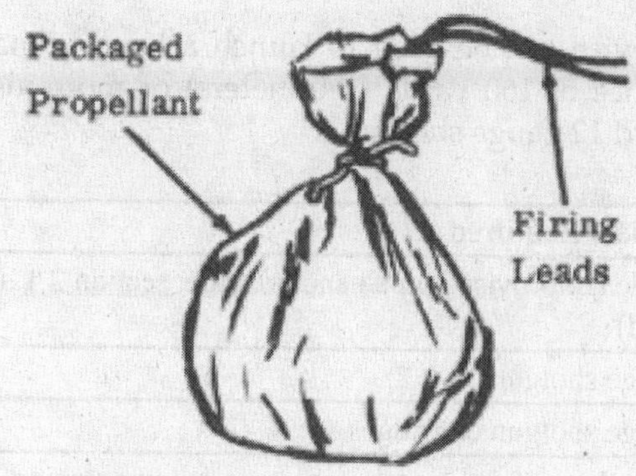

2. Insert packaged propellant and igniter in center of pipe. Pull firing leads out one end of pipe.
3. Stuff a rag wad into each end of pipe and lightly tamp using a flat end stick.
4. Insert stones and/or scrap metal into each end of pipe. Be sure the same weight of material is used in each side.

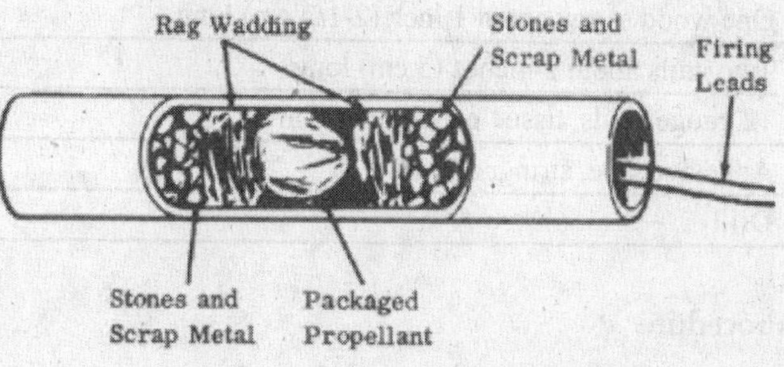

5. Insert a rag wad into each end of the pipe and pack tightly as before.

How to Use

1. Place scrap mine in a tree or pointed in the path of the enemy. Attach igniter lead to the firing circuit. The recoilless launcher is now ready to fire.
2. If safety or improvised fuse is used instead of the detonator, place the fuse into the packaged propellant through a hole drilled in the center

of the pipe. Light free end of fuse when ready to fire. Allow for normal delay time.

CAUTION
Scrap will be ejected from both ends of the launcher.

4.2 SHOTGUN GRENADE LAUNCHER

This device can be used to launch a hand grenade to a distance of 160 yards (150 meters) or more, using a standard 12 gauge shotgun.

Materials Required
Grenade (Improvised pipe hand grenade, section 2.1, may be used)
12 gauge shotgun
12 gauge shotgun cartridges
Two washers, (brass, steel, iron, etc.), having outside diameter of 5/8 inch (1-1/2 cm)
Rubber disk 3/4 inch (2 cm) in diameter and 1/4 inch (6 mm) thick (leather, neoprene, etc. can be used)
A 30 inch (75 cm) long piece of hard wood (maple, oak, etc.) approximately 5/8 inch (1-1/2 cm) in diameter. Be sure that wood will slide into barrel easily.
Tin can (grenade and its safety lever must fit into can)
Two wooden blocks about 2 inches (5 cm) square and 1-1/2 inch (4 cm) thick
One wood screw about 1 inch (2-1/2 cm) long
Two nails about 2 inches (5 cm) long
12 gauge wads, tissue paper, or cotton
Adhesive tape, string, or wire
Drill

Procedure

1. Punch hole in center of rubber disk large enough for screw to pass through.
2. Make pushrod as shown.

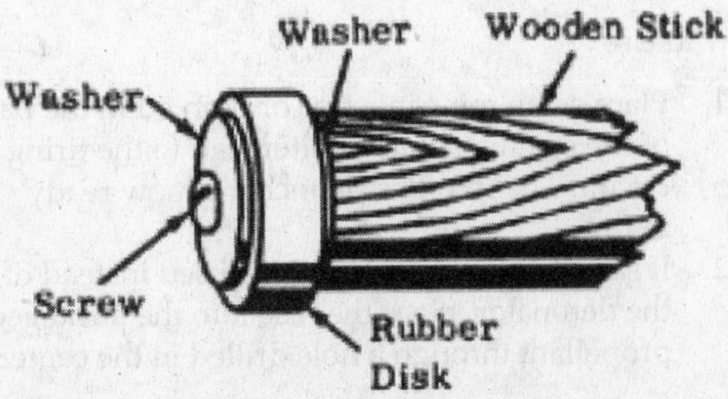

NOTE
Gun barrel is slightly less than 3/4 inch in diameter. If rubber disk does not fit in barrel, file or trim it very slightly. It should fit tightly.

3. Drill a hole through the center of one wooden block of such size that the pushrod will fit tightly. Whittle a depression around the hole on one side approximately 1/8 inch (3 mm) and large enough for the grenade to rest in.

4. Place the base of the grenade in the depression in the wooden block. Securely fasten grenade to block by wrapping tape (or wire) around entire grenade and block.

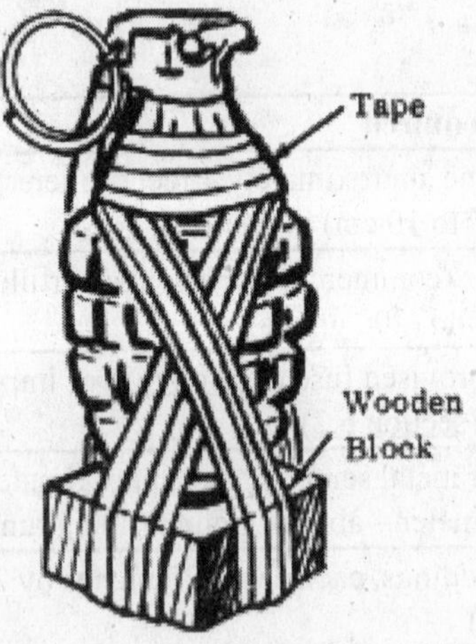

NOTE
Be sure that the tape (or wire) does not cover hole in block or interfere with the operation of the grenade safety lever.

5. Drill hole through the center of the second wooden block, so that it will just slide over the outside of the gun barrel.
6. Drill a hole in the center of the bottom of the tin can the same size as the hole in the block.

7. Attach can to block as shown.

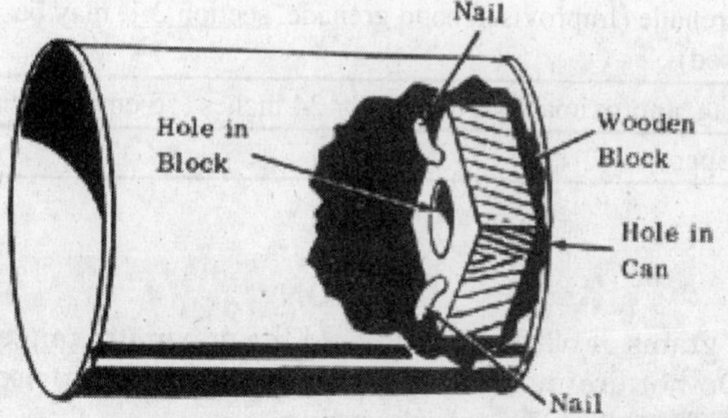

8. Slide the can and block onto the barrel until muzzle passes can open end. Wrap a small piece of tape around the barrel an inch or two from the end. Tightly wrapped string may be used instead of tape. Force the can and wooden block forward against the tape so that they are securely held in place. Wrap tape around the barrel behind the can.

CAUTION

Be sure that the can is securely fastened to the gun barrel. If the can should become loose and slip down the barrel after the launcher is assembled, the grenade will explode after the regular delay time.

9. Remove crimp from a 12 gauge shotgun cartridge with pen knife. Open cartridge. Pour shot from shell. Remove wads and plastic liner if present.

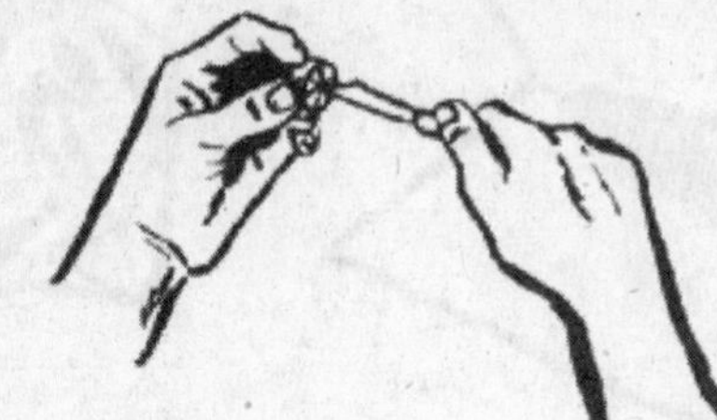

10. Empty the propellant onto a piece of paper. Using a knife, divide the propellant in half.

Replace half of the propellant into the cartridge case.

11. Replace the 12 gauge cardboard wads into cartridge case.

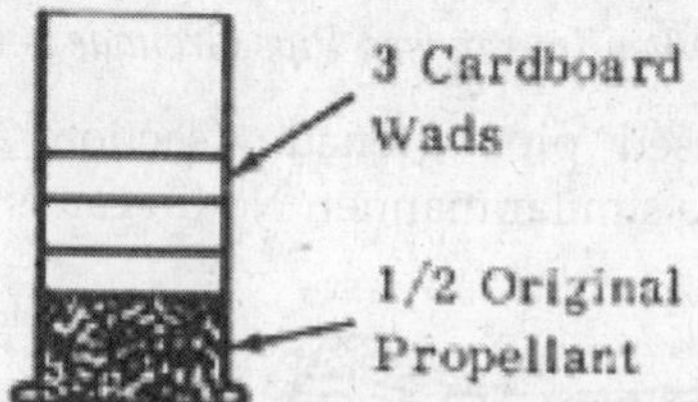

NOTE

If wads are not available, stuff tissue paper or cotton into the cartridge case. Pack tightly.

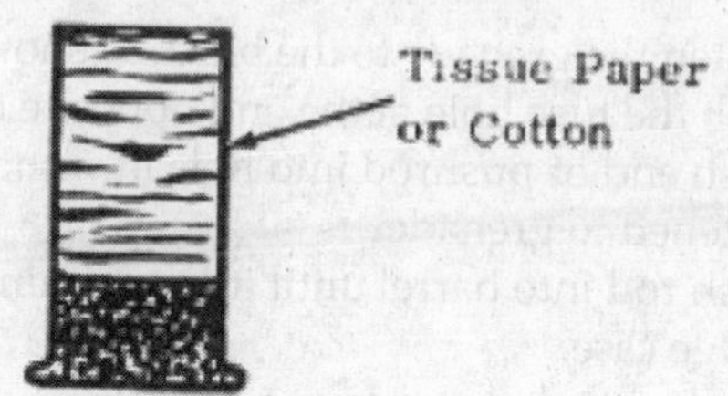

How to Use

Method I – When Ordinary Grenade is Used

1. Load cartridge in gun.
2. Push end of pushrod without the rubber disk into hole in wooden block fastened to grenade.
3. Slowly push rod into barrel until it rests against the cartridge case and grenade is in can. If the grenade is not in the can, remove rod and cut to proper size. Push rod back into barrel.

4. With can holding safety lever of grenade in place, carefully remove safety pin.

CAUTION

Be sure that the sides of the can restrain the grenade safety lever. If the safety lever should be released for any reason, grenade will explode after regular grenade delay time.

5. To fire grenade launcher, rest gun in ground at angle determined by range desired. A 45 degree angle should give about 150 meters (160 yards).

Method II – When Improvised Pipe Grenade is Used

An improvised pipe grenade (section 2.1) may be launched in a similar manner. No tin can is needed.

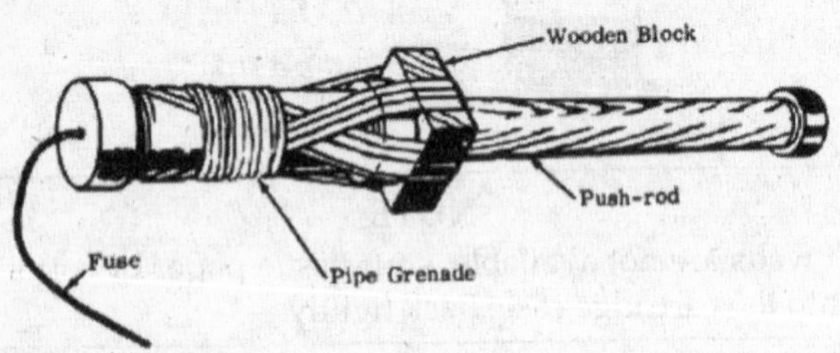

1. Fasten the grenade to the block as shown above with the fuse hole at the end opposite the block.
2. Push end of pushrod into hole in wooden block fastened to grenade.
3. Push rod into barrel until it rests against cartridge case.
4. Load cartridge in gun.
5. Follow step 5 of Method I.
6. Using a fuse with *at least* a 10 second delay, light the fuse before firing.
7. Fire when the fuse burns to 1/2 its original length.

4.3 GRENADE LAUNCHER (57 MM CARDBOARD CONTAINER)

An improvised method of launching a standard grenade 150 yards (135 meters) or an improvised grenade 90 yards (81 meters) using a discarded cardboard ammunition container.

Materials Required
Heavy cardboard container with inside diameter of 2-1/2 to 3 inches (5-1/2 to 8 cm) and at least 12 inches (30 cm) long (ammunition container is suitable)
Black powder – 8 grams (124 grains) or less
Safety or improvised fuse (section 6.7)
Grenade (Improvised hand grenade, section 2.1, may be used)
Rag, approximately 30 inches × 24 inches (75 cm × 60 cm)
Paper

CAUTION

8 grams of black powder yield the maximum ranges. Do not use more than this amount. See Improvised Scale, section 7.8. for measuring.

Procedure

Method I – If Standard Grenade is Used

1. Discard top of container. Make small hole in bottom.

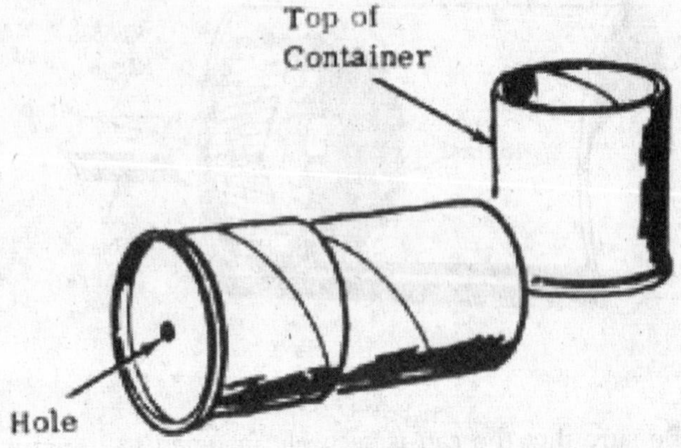

2. Place black powder in paper. Tie end with string so contents cannot fall out. Place package in container.

3. Insert rag wadding into container. Pack tightly with **caution**.

4. Measure off a length of fuse that will give the desired delay. Thread this through hole in bottom of container so that it penetrates into the black powder package.

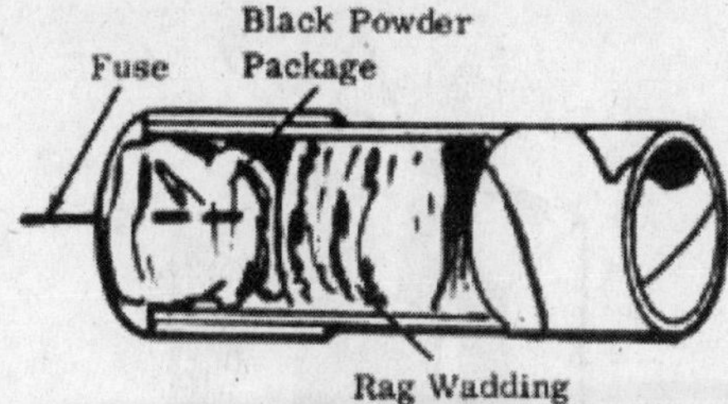

NOTE

If improvised fuse is used, be sure fuse fits loosely through hole in bottom of container.

5. Hold grenade safety lever and carefully withdraw safety pin from grenade. Insert grenade into container, lever end first.

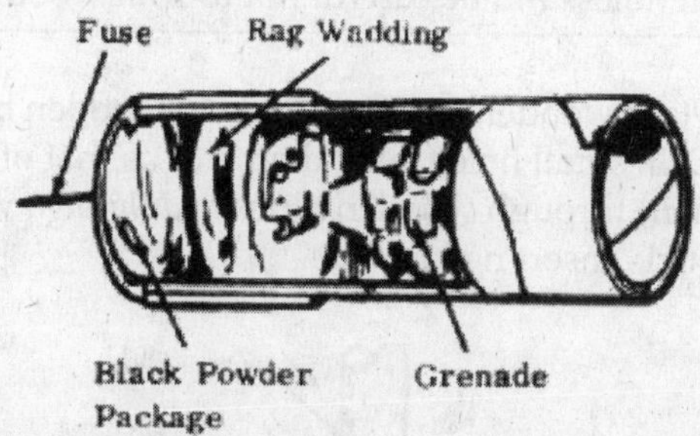

CAUTION

If grenade safety lever should be released for any reason, grenade will explode after normal delay time.

6. Bury container about 6 inches (15 cm) in the ground at 30° angle, bringing fuse up alongside container. Pack ground tightly around container.

CAUTION

The tightly packed dirt helps to hold the tube together during the firing. Do not fire unless at least the bottom half of the container is buried in solidly packed dirt.

Method II – If Improvised Pipe Hand Grenade is Used

1. Follow step 1 of above procedure.
2. Measure off a piece of fuse at least as long as the cardboard container. Tape one end of this to the fuse from the blasting cap in the improvised grenade. Be sure ends of fuse are in contact with *each* other.

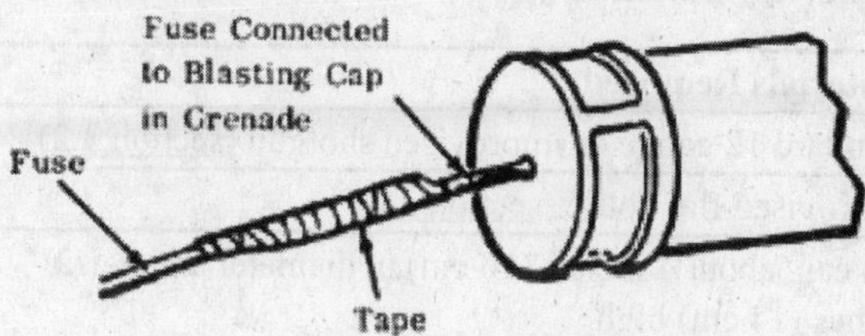

3. Place free end of fuse and black powder on piece of paper. Tie ends with string so contents will not fall out.

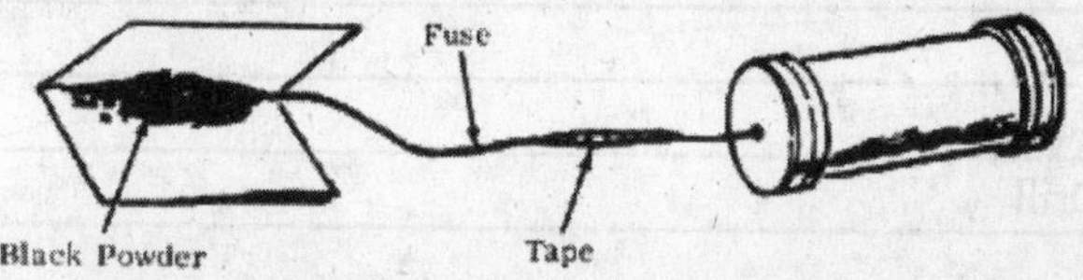

4. Place package in tube. Insert rag wadding. Pack so it fits snugly. Place pipe hand grenade into tube. Be sure it fits snugly.

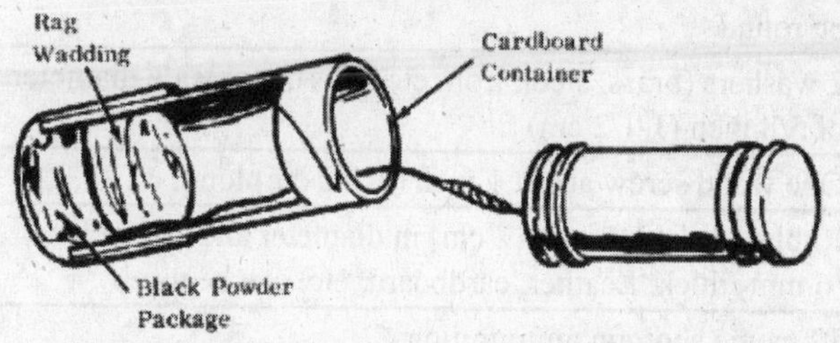

5. Insert fuse through hole in end of cardboard container. Be sure it goes into black powder package.

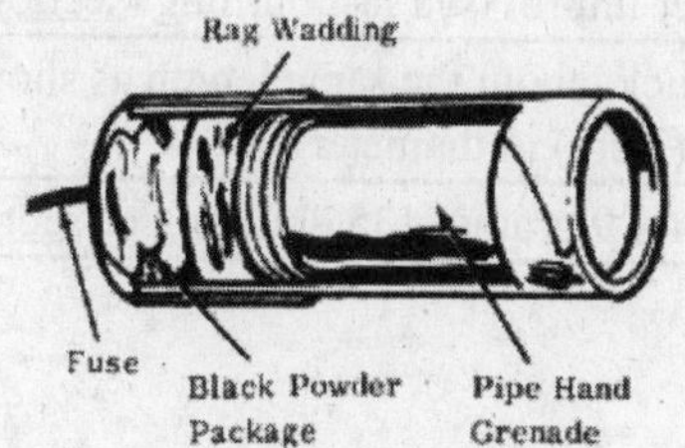

NOTE

Cardboard container may be used for only *one* firing.

6. Follow step 6 of Method I.

How to Use

Light fuse when ready to fire.

4.4 FIRE BOTTLE LAUNCHER

A device using 2 items (shotgun and chemical fire bottle) that can be used to start or place a fire 80 yards (72 meters) from launcher.

Materials Required
Standard 12 gauge or improvised shotgun (section 3.2)
Improvised fire bottle (section 5.1)
Tin can, about 4 inches (10 cm) in diameter and 5-1/2 inches (14 cm) high
Wood, about 3 inches × 3 inches × 2 inches (7-172 cm × 7-1/2 cm × 5 cm)
Nail, at least 3 inches (7-1/2 cm) long
Nuts and bolts or nails, at least 2-1/2 inches (6-1/2 cm) long
Rag
Paper
Drill

If Standard Shotgun is Used
Hard wood stick, about the same length as shotgun barrel and about 5/8 inch (1-1/2 cm) in diameter. Stick need not be round.
2 washers (brass, steel, iron, etc.) having outside diameter of 5/8 inch (1-1/2 cm)
One wood screw about 1 inch (2-1/2 cm) long
Rubber disk, 3/4 inch (2 cm) in diameter and 1/4 inch (6 mm) thick. Leather, cardboard, etc. can be used.
12 gauge shotgun ammunition

If Improvised Shotgun is Used
Fuse, safety or improvised fast burning (section 6.7)
Hard wood stick, about the same length as shotgun barrel and 3/4 inch (2 cm) in diameter
Black powder – 9 grams (135 grains). See section 7.8.

Procedure

Method I – If Improvised Shotgun is Used

1. Drill hole in center of wood block approximately 1 inch (2-1/2 cm) deep. Hole should have approximately the same diameter as the wooden stick.
2. Drill 2 small holes on opposite sides of the wooden block. Hole should be large enough for bolts to pass through.

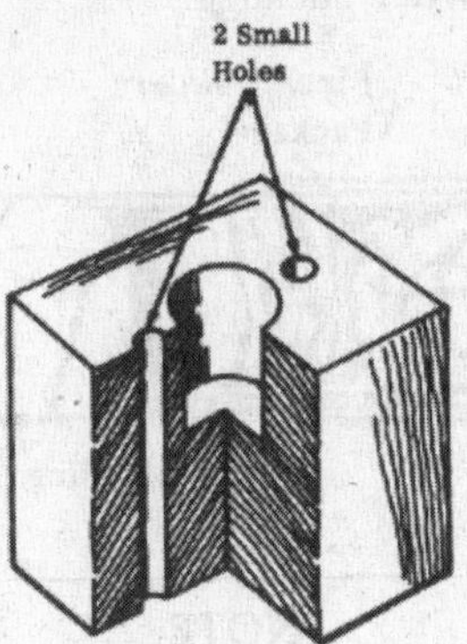

3. Fasten can to block with nuts and bolts.

> **NOTE**
> Can may also be securely fastened to block by hammering several nails through can and block. Do not drill holes, and be careful not to split wood.

4. Place wooden stick into hole in wooden block. Drill small hole (same diameter as that of 3 inch nail) through wooden block *and through* wooden stick. Insert nail in hole.

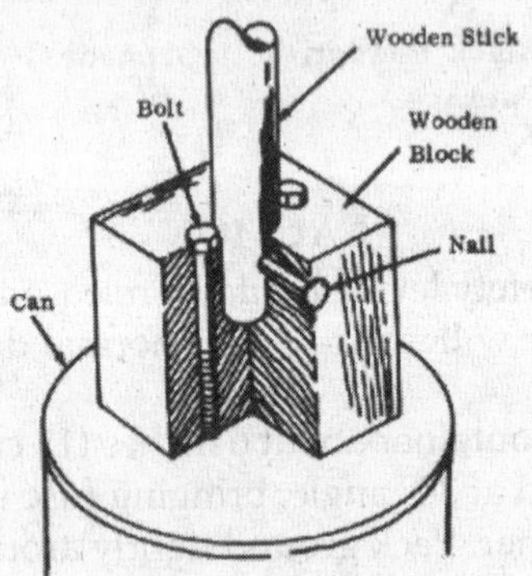

5. Crumple paper and place in bottom of can. Place another piece of paper around fire bottle and insert in can. Use enough paper so that bottle will fit snugly.

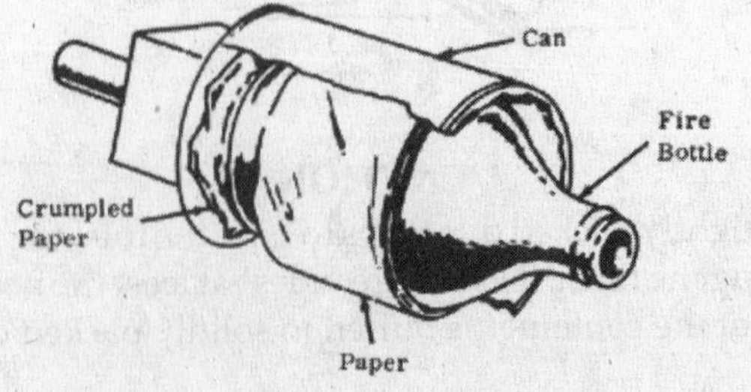

6. Place safety fuse and black powder on paper. Tie each end with string.

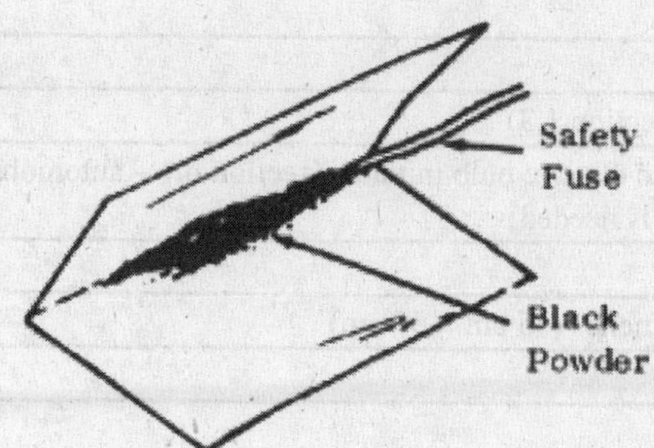

7. Thread fuse through hole in plug. Place powder package in rear of shotgun. Screw plug finger tight into coupling.

> **NOTE**
> Hole in plug may have to be enlarged for fuse.

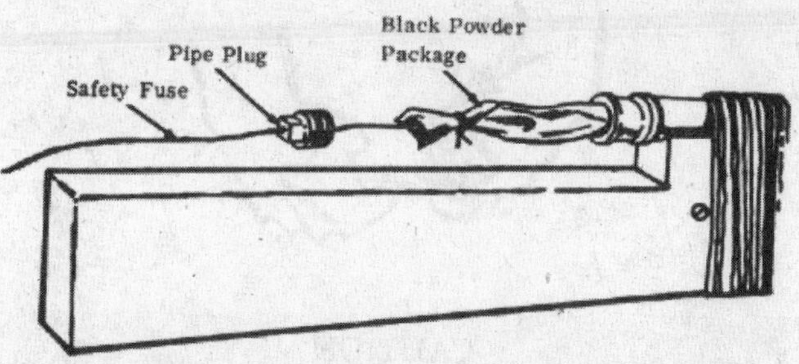

8. Insert rag into front of shotgun. Pick rag against powder package with stick. Use **caution**.

Method II – If Standard Shotgun is Used

1. Follow steps 1 and 2, Shotgun Grenade Launcher, section 4.2.
2. Follow procedure of Method I, steps 1–5.
3. Follow steps 9, 10, 11, Shotgun Grenade Launcher, section 4.2, using 1/3 of total propellant instead of 1/2.
4. Load cartridge in gun.

How to Use

1. Insert stick and holder containing chemical fire bottle.

> **CAUTION**
> Do not tilt muzzle downward.

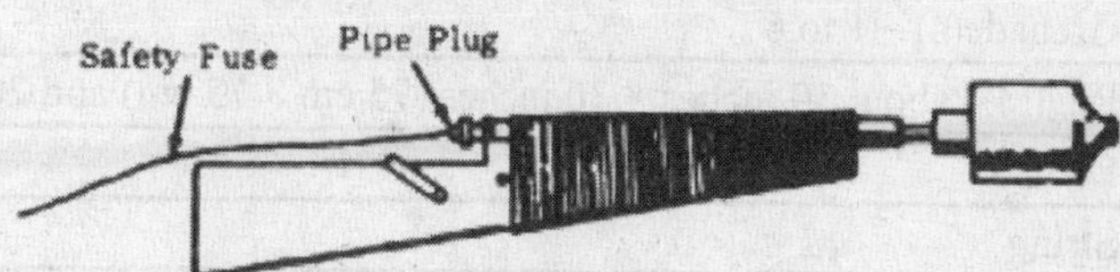

2. Hold gun against ground at 45° angle and light fuse.

> **NOTE**
> Steps 1 and 2, *How to Use*, same for both standard and improvised shotguns.

> **CAUTION**
> Severe burns may result if bottle shatters when fired. If possible, obtain a bottle identical to that being used as the fire bottle. Fill about 2/3 full of water and fire as above. If bottle shatters when fired instead of being launched intact, use a different type of bottle.

4.5 GRENADE LAUNCHERS

A variety of grenade launchers can be fabricated from metal pipes and fittings. Ranges up to 600 meters (660 yards) can be obtained depending on length of tube, charge, number of grenades, and angle of firing.

Materials Required		
Metal pipe, threaded on one end and approximately 2-1/2 inches (6-1/4 cm) in diameter and 14 inches to 4 feet (35 cm to 119 cm) long depending on range desired and number of grenades used		
End cap to fit pipe		
Black powder, 15 to 50 grams, approximately 1-1/4 to 4-1/4 tablespoons (section 1.3)		
Safety fuse, fast burning improvised fuse (section 6.7)	or	Improvised electric bulb initiator (**section 6.1** – automobile light bulb is needed)
Grenade(s) – 1 to 6		
Rag(s) – about 30 inches × 30 inches (75 cm × 75 cm) and 20 inches × 20 inches (55 cm × 55 cm)		
Drill		
String		

> **NOTE**
> Examine pipe carefully to be sure there are no cracks or other flaws.

Procedure

Method I – If Fuse is Used

1. Drill small hole through center of end cap.

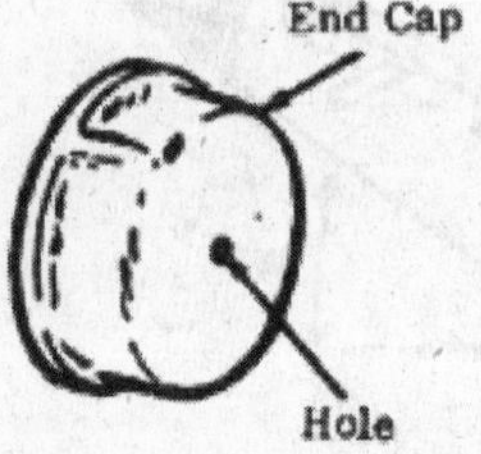

2. Make small knot near one end of fuse. Place black powder and knotted end of fuse in paper and tie with string.

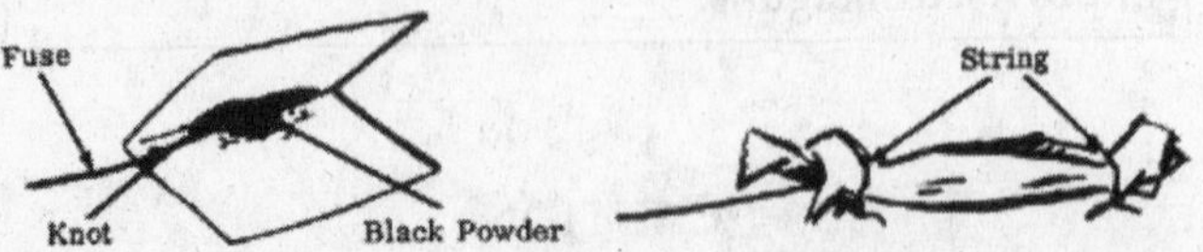

3. Thread fuse through hole in end cap and place package in end cap. Screw end cap onto pipe, being careful that black powder package is not caught between the threads.

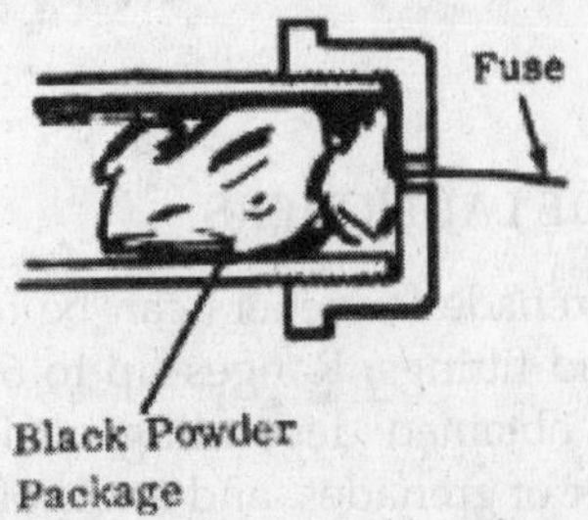

4. Roll rag wad so that it is about 6 inches (15 cm) long and has approximately the same diameter as the pipe. Push rolled rag into open-end of pipe until it rests against black powder package.

5. Hold grenade safety lever in place and carefully withdraw safety pin.

> **CAUTION**
> If grenade safety lever is released for any reason, grenade will explode after regular time (4–5 seconds).

6. Holding safety lever in place, carefully push grenade into pipe, lever end first, until it rests against rag wad.

7. The following table lists various types of grenade launchers and their performance characteristics.

Desired Range	Number of Grenades Launched	Black Powder Charge	Pipe Length	Firing Angle
250 m	1	15 grams	14 inches	30°
500 m	1	50 grams	48 inches	10°
600 m(a)	1	50 grams	48 inches	30°
200 m	6(b)	25 grams	48 inches	30°

(a) For this range, an additional delay is required. See section 6.11 and section 6.12.
(b) For multiple grenade launcher, load as shown.

> **NOTE**
> Since performance of different black powder varies, fire several test rounds to determine the exact amount of powder necessary to achieve the desired range.

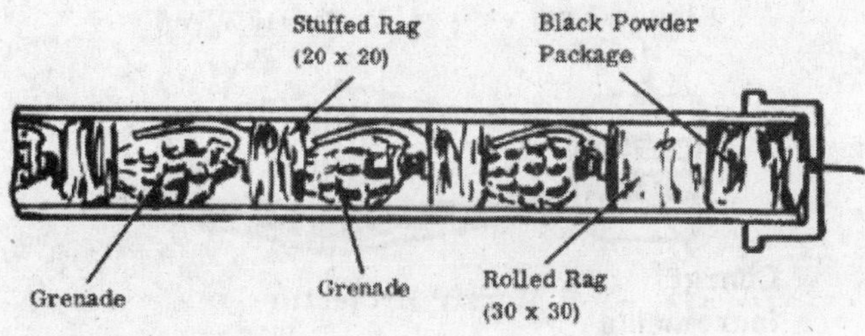

How to Use

1. Bury at least 1/2 of the launcher pipe in the ground at desired angle. Open end should face the expected path of the enemy. Muzzle may be covered with cardboard and a thin layer of dirt and/or leaves as camouflage. Be sure cardboard prevents dirt from entering pipe.

> **NOTE**
> The 14 inch launcher may be hand held against the ground instead of being buried.

2. Light fuse when ready to fire.

Method II – If Electrical Igniter is Used

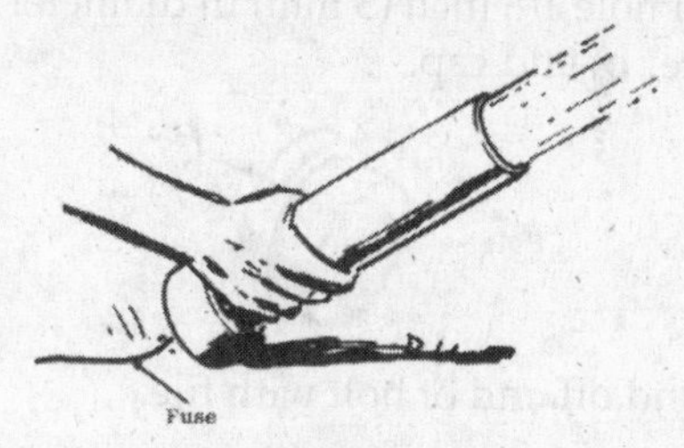

> **NOTE**
> Be sure that bulb is in good operating condition.

1. Prepare electric bulb initiator as described in section 6.1.
2. Place electric initiator and black powder charge in paper. Tie ends of paper with string.

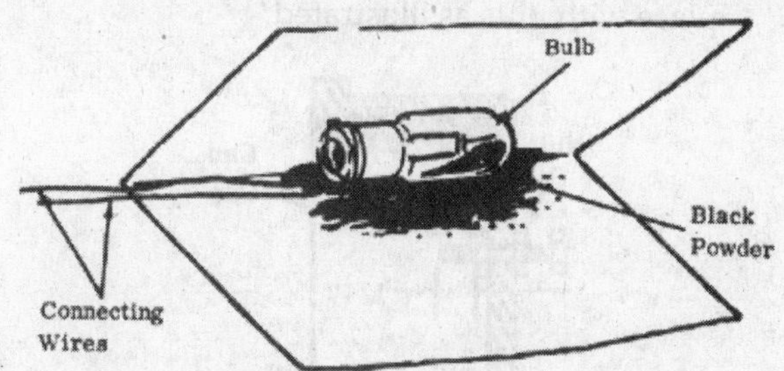

3. Follow above procedure, steps 3 to end.

How to Use

1. Follow above *How to Use*, step 1.
2. Connect leads to tiring circuit. Close circuit when ready to fire.

4.6 60 MM MORTAR PROJECTILE LAUNCHER

A device to launch 60 mm mortar rounds using a metal pipe 2-1/2 inches (6 cm) in diameter and 4 feet (120 cm) long as the launching tube.

Materials Required
Mortar, projectile (60 mm) and charge increments
Metal pipe 2-1/2 inches (6 cm) in diameter and 4 feet (120 cm) long, threaded on one end
Threaded end cap to fit pipe
Bolt, 1/8 inch (3 mm) in diameter and at least 1 inch (2-1/2 cm) long
Two (2) nuts to fit bolt
File
Drill

Procedure

1. Drill hole 1/8 inch (3 mm) in diameter through center of end cap.

2. Round off end of bolt with file.

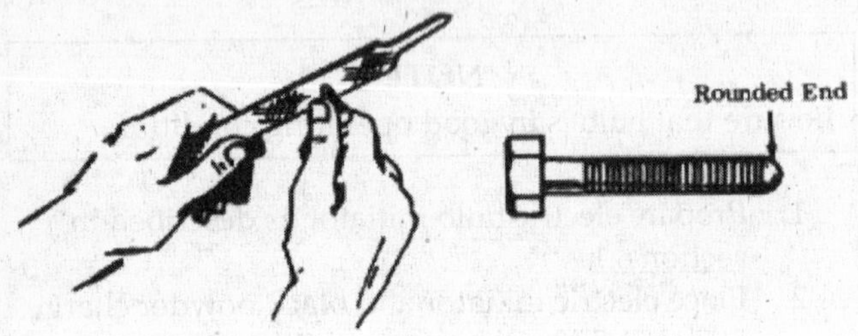

3. Place bolt through hole in end cap. Secure in place with nuts as illustrated.

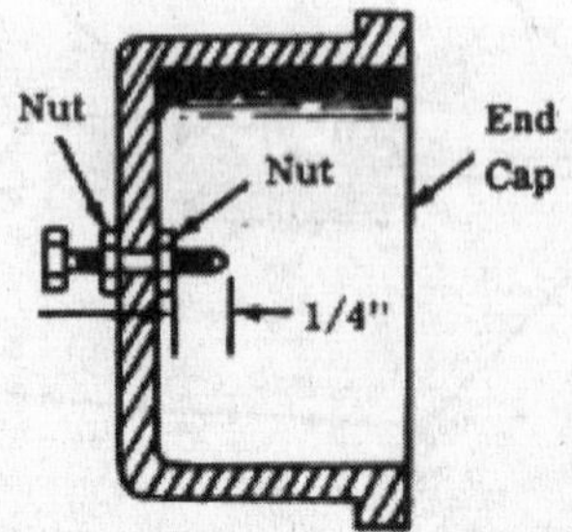

4. Screw end cap onto pipe tightly. Tube is now ready for use.

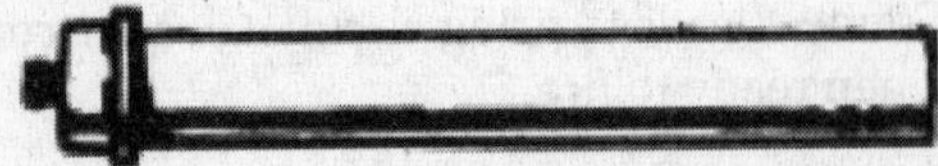

How to Use

1. Bury launching tube in ground at desired angle so that bottom of tube is at least 2 feet (60 cm) under ground. Adjust the number of increments in rear finned end of mortar projectile. See following table for launching angle and number of increments used.

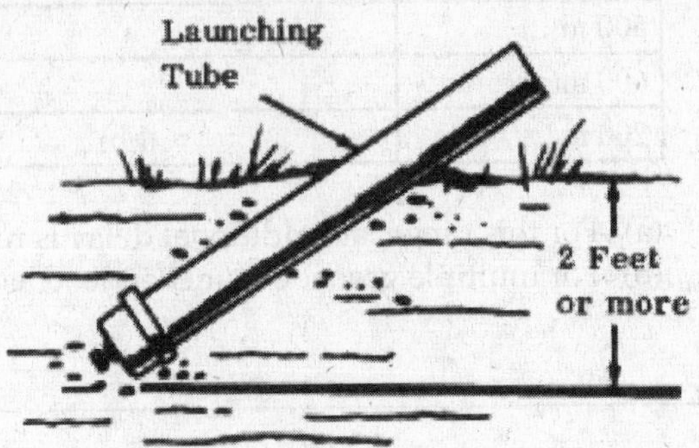

2. When ready to fire, withdraw safety wire from mortar projectile. Drop projectile into launching tube, finned end first.

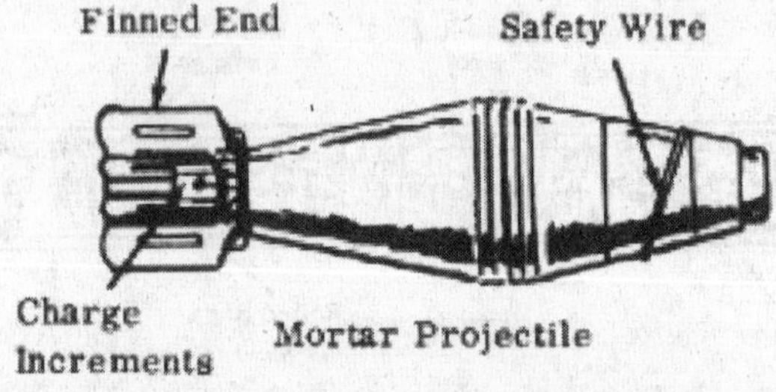

CAUTION

Be sure bore riding pin is in place in fuse when mortar projectile is dropped into tube. A live mortar round could explode in the tube if the fit is loose enough to permit the bore riding pin to come out partway.

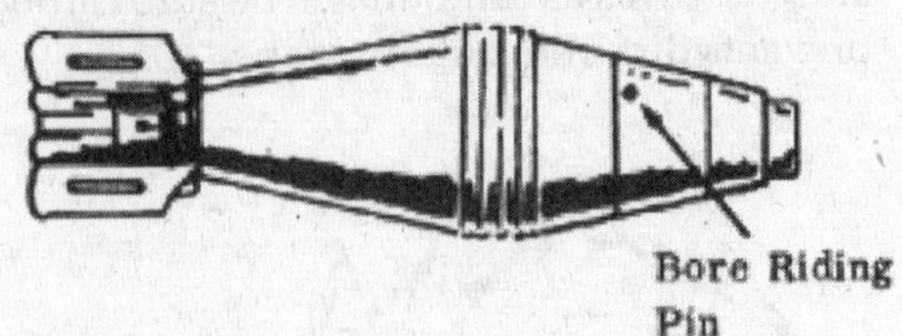

CAUTION
The round will fire as soon as the projectile is dropped into tube. Keep all parts of body behind the open end of the tube.

Desired Range (Yards)	Maximum Height Mortar Will Reach (Yards)	Required Angle of Elevation of Tube (Measured from Horizontal Degrees)	Charge – Number of Increments
150	25	40	0
300	50	40	1
700	150	40	2
1000	225	40	3
1500	300	40	4
125	75	60	0
300	125	60	1
550	250	60	2
1000	375	60	3
1440	600	60	4
Desired Range (Yards)	**Maximum Height Mortar Will Reach (Yards)**	**Required Angle of Elevation of Tube (Measured from Horizontal Degrees)**	**Charge – Number of Increments**
75	100	80	0
150	200	80	1
300	350	80	2
400	600	80	3
550	750	80	4

SECTION 5

Incendiary Devices

5.1 CHEMICAL FIRE BOTTLE

This incendiary bottle is self-igniting on target impact.

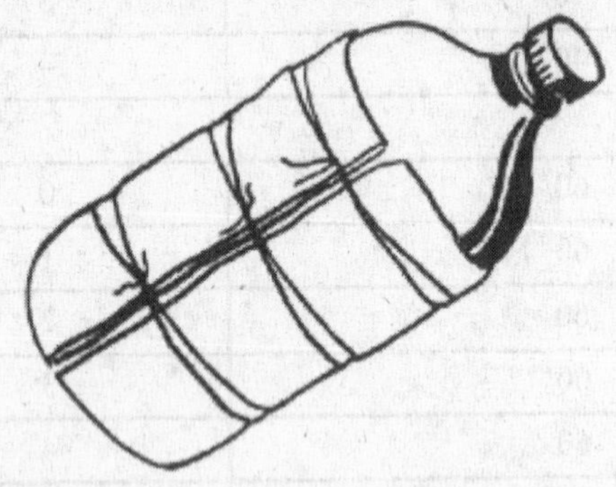

Materials Required	How Used	Source
Sulfuric acid	Storage batteries Material processing	Motor vehicles Industrial plants
Gasoline	Motor fuel	Gas station or motor vehicles
Potassium chlorate	Medicine	Drug store
Sugar	Sweetening foods	Food store
Glass bottle with stopper (roughly 1 quart size)		
Small bottle or jar with lid		
Rag or absorbent paper (paper towels, newspaper)		
String or rubber bands		

Procedure

1. *Sulfuric acid must be concentrated.* If battery acid or other dilute acid is used, concentrate it by boiling until dense white fumes are given off. Container used should be of enamelware or oven glass.

CAUTION

Sulfuric acid will burn skin and destroy clothing. If any is spilled, wash it away with a large quantity of water. Fumes are also dangerous and should not be inhaled.

2. Remove the acid from heat and allow to cool to room temperature.
3. Pour gasoline into the large (1 quart) bottle until it is approximately 1/3 full.
4. Add concentrated sulfuric acid to gasoline slowly until the bottle is filled to within 1 inch to 2 inches from top. Place the stopper on the bottle.
5. Wash the outside of the bottle thoroughly with clear water.

CAUTION

If this is *not* done, the fire bottle may be dangerous to handle during use.

6. Wrap a clean cloth or several sheets of absorbent paper around the outside of the bottle. Tie with string or fasten with rubber bands.

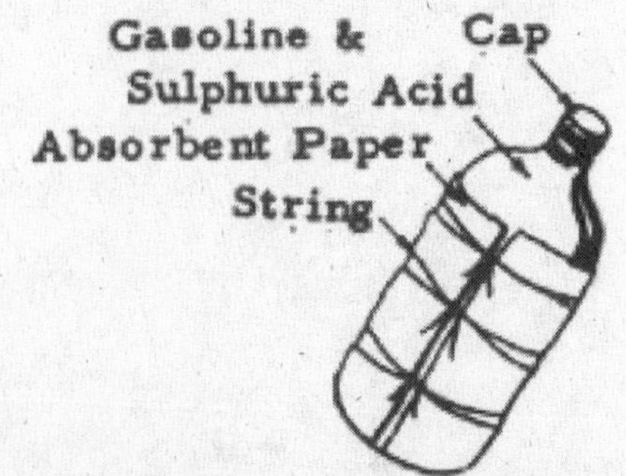

7. Dissolve 1/2 cup (100 grams) of potassium chlorate and 1/2 cup (100 grams) of sugar in one cup (250 milliliters) of boiling water.

8. Allow the solution to cool, pour into the small bottle and cap tightly. The cooled solution should be approximately 2/3 crystals and 2/3 liquid. If there is more liquid than this, pour off excess before using.

CAUTION

Store this bottle separately from the other bottle.

How to Use

1. Shake the small bottle to mix contents and pour onto the cloth or paper around the large bottle. Bottle can be used wet or after solution has dried. However, when dry, the sugar – potassium chlorate mixture in very sensitive to spark or flame and should be handled accordingly.

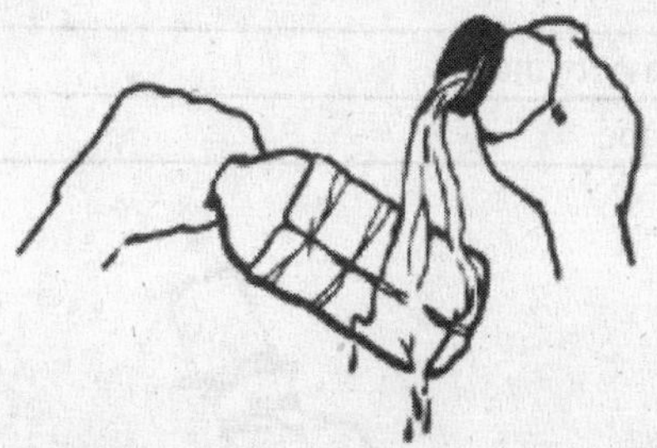

2. Throw or launch the bottle. When the bottle breaks against a hard surface (target) the fuel will ignite.

5.2 IGNITER FROM BOOK MATCHES

This is a hot igniter made from paper book matches for use with molotov cocktail and other incendiaries.

Materials Required
Paper book matches
Adhesive or friction tape

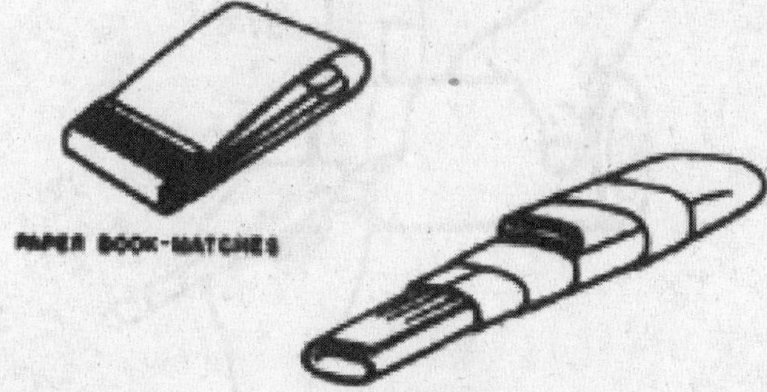

Procedure

1. Remove the staple(s) from match book and separate matches from cover.

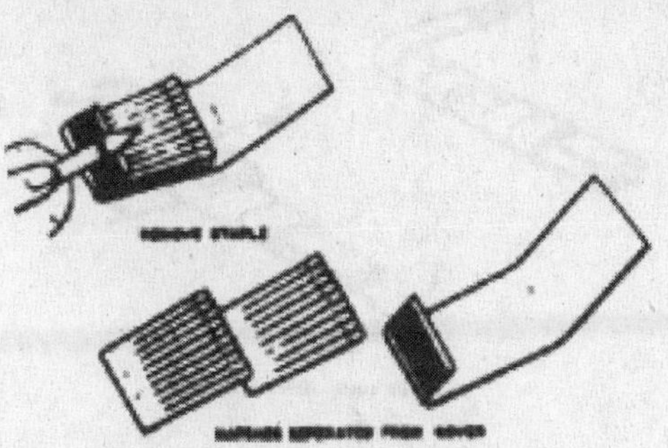

2. Fold and tape one row of matches.

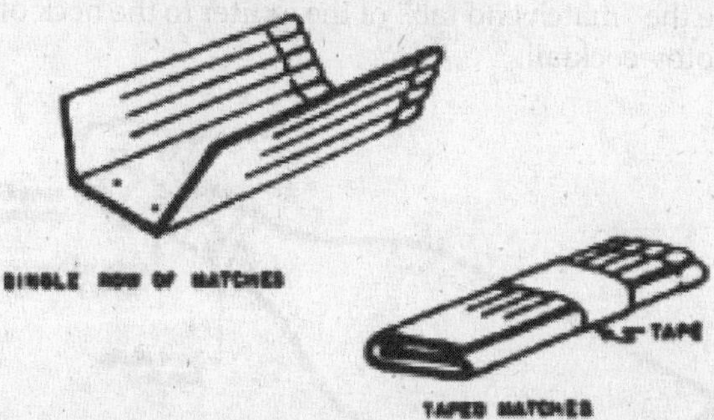

3. Shape the cover into a tube with striking surface on the inside and tape. Make sure the folded cover will fit tightly around the taped match heads. Leave cover open at opposite end for insertion of the matches.

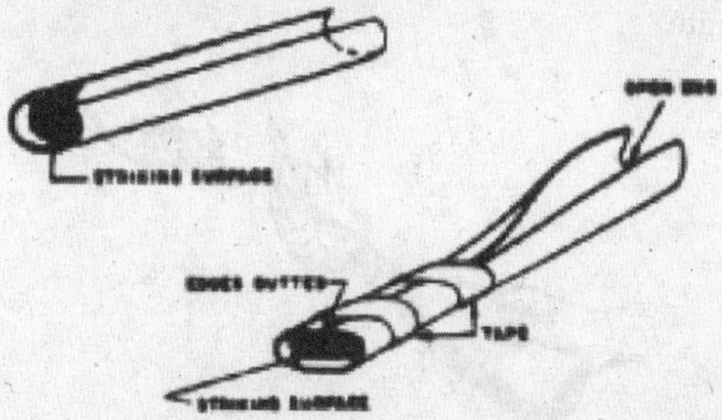

4. Push the taped matches into the tube until the bottom ends are exposed about 3/4 inch (2 cm).

5. Flatten and fold the open end of the tube so that it laps over about 1 inch (2-1/2 cm); tape in place.

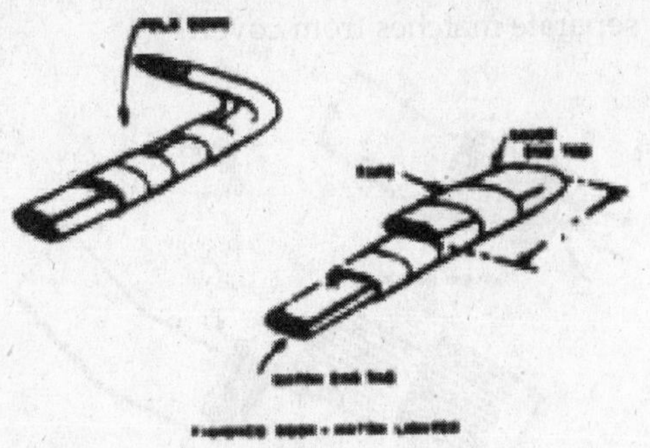

Use with Molotov Cocktail

Tape the "match end tab" of the igniter to the neck of the molotov cocktail.

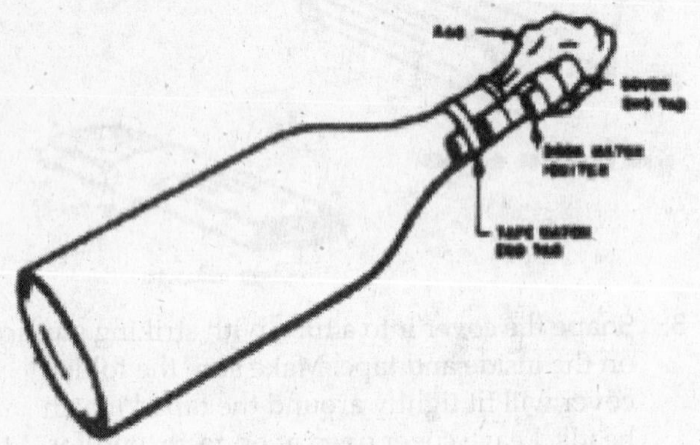

Grasp the "cover end tab" and pull sharply or quickly to ignite.

General Use

The book match igniter can be used by itself to ignite flammable liquids, fuse cords and similar items requiring hot ignition.

CAUTION

Store matches and completed igniter in moisture-proof containers such as rubber or plastic bags until ready for use. Damp or wet paper book matches will not ignite.

5.3 MECHANICALLY INITIATED FIRE BOTTLE

The mechanically initiated fire bottle is an incendiary device which ignites when thrown against a hard surface.

Materials Required
Glass jar or short neck bottle with a leakproof lid or stopper
"Tin" can or similar container just large enough to fit over the lid of the jar
Coil spring (compression) approximately 1/2 the diameter of the can and 1-1/2 times as long
Gasoline
Four (4) "blue tip" matches
Flat stick or piece of metal (roughly 1/2 inch × 1/16 inch × 4 inches)
Wire or heavy twine
Adhesive tape

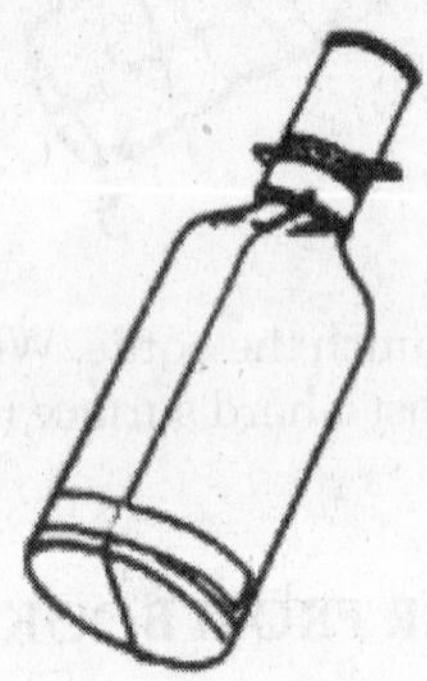

Procedure

1. Draw or scratch two lines around the can – one 3/4 inch (19 mm) and the other 1-1/4 inch (30 mm) from the open end.

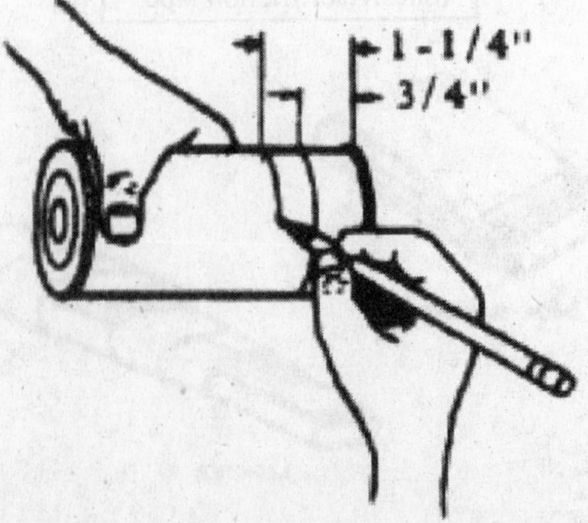

2. Cut 2 slots on opposite sides of the tin can at the line farthest from the open end. Make slots large enough for the flat stick or piece of metal to pass through.

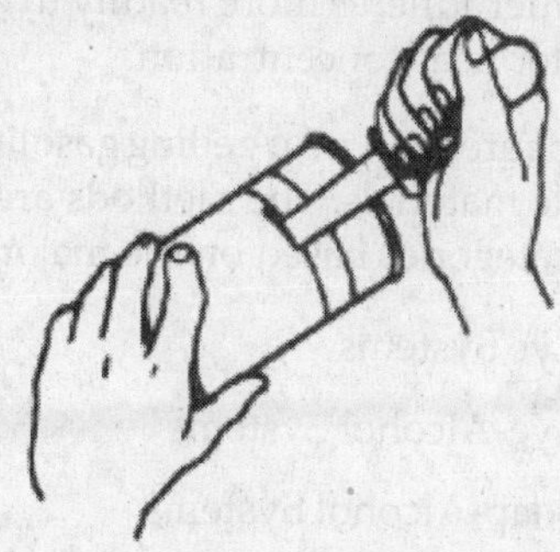

3. Punch 2 small holes just below the rim of the open end of the can.

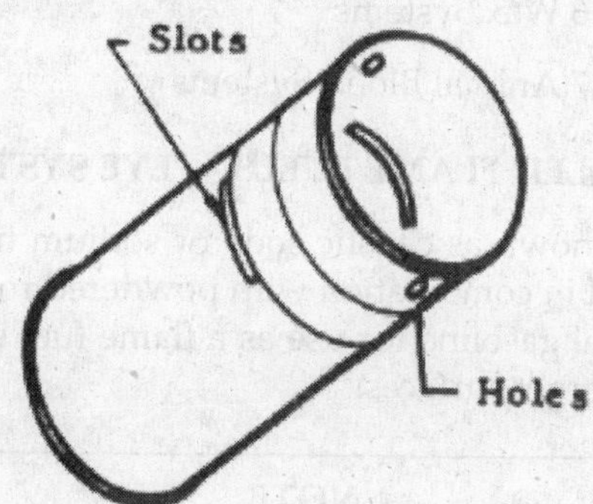

4. Tape blue tip matches together in pairs. The distance between the match heads should equal the inside diameter of the can. Two pairs are sufficient.

5. Attach paired matches to second and third coils of the spring, using thin wire.

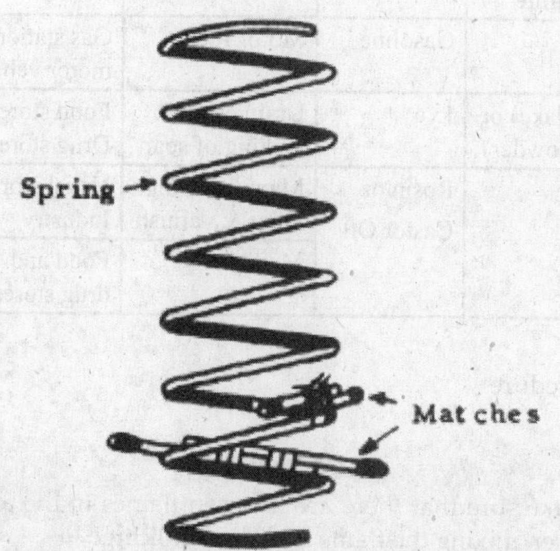

6. Insert the end of the spring opposite the matches into the tin can.

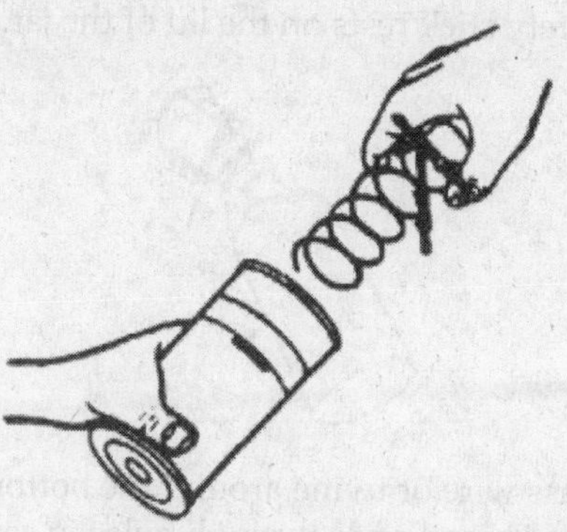

7. Compress the spring until the end with the matches passes the slot in the can. Pass the flat stick or piece of metal through slots in can to hold spring in place. This acts as a safety device.

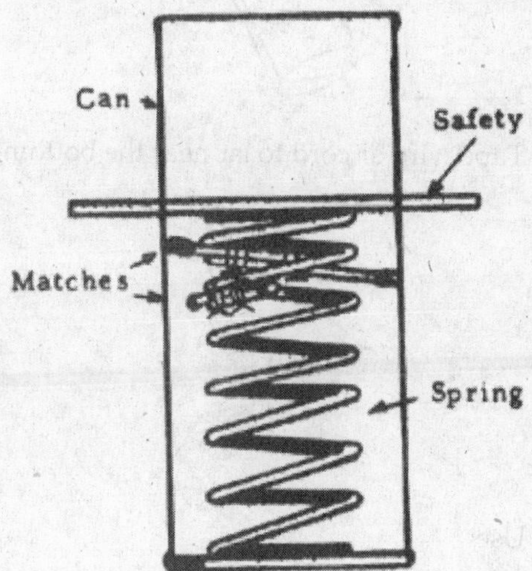

8. Punch many closely spaced small holes between the lines marked on the can to form a striking surface for the matches. Be careful not to seriously deform can.

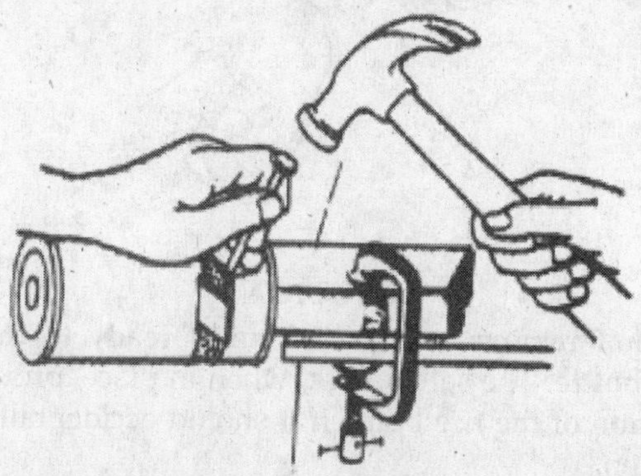

9. Fill the jar with gasoline and cap tightly.
10. Turn can over and place over the jar so that the safety stick rests on the lid of the jar.

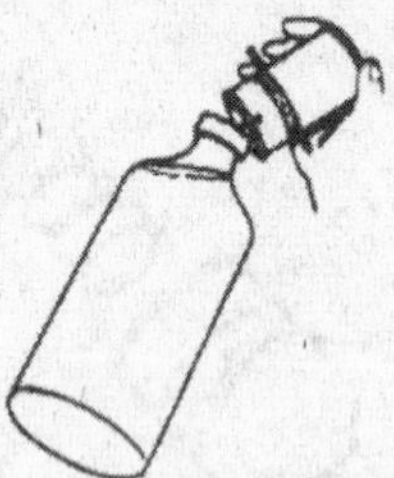

11. Pass wire or twine around the bottom of the jar. Thread ends through holes in can and bind tightly to jar.

12. Tape wire or cord to jar near the bottom.

How to Use

1. Carefully withdraw flat safety stick.
2. Throw jar at hard surface.

CAUTION

Do not remove safety stick until ready to throw fire bottle. The safety stick, when in place, prevents ignition of the fire bottle if it should accidentally be broken.

5.4 GELLED FLAME FUELS

Gelled or paste type fuels are often preferable to raw gasoline for use in incendiary devices such as fire bottles. This type fuel adheres more readily to the target and produces greater heat concentration.

Several methods are shown for gelling gasoline using commonly available materials. The methods are divided into the following categories based on the major ingredient:

5.4.1 Lye Systems

5.4.2 Lye-Alcohol Systems

5.4.3 Soap-Alcohol Systems

5.4.4 Egg White Systems

5.4.5 Latex Systems

5.4.6 Wax Systems

5.4.7 Animal Blood Systems

5.4.1 GELLED FLAME FUELS — LYE SYSTEMS

Lye (also known as caustic soda or sodium hydroxide) can be used in combination with powdered rosin or castor oil to gel gasoline for use as a flame fuel which will adhere to target surfaces.

NOTE

This fuel is not suitable for use in the chemical (sulfuric acid) type of fire bottle section 5.1. The acid will react with the lye and break down the gel.

Materials Required

Parts by Volume	Ingredient	How Used	Source
60	Gasoline	Motor fuel	Gas station or motor vehicle
2 (flake) or 1 (powder)	Lye	Drain cleaner, making of soap	Food store Drug store
15	Rosin or Castor Oil	Manufacturing Paint & varnish	Naval stores Industry
		Medicine	Food and drug stores

Procedure

CAUTION

Make sure that there are no open flames in the area when mixing the flame fuel. **No smoking!**

1. Pour gasoline into jar, bottle or other container. **(Do not use an aluminum container.)**
2. If rosin is in **cake** form, crush into small pieces.
3. Add rosin or castor oil to the gasoline and stir for about five (5) minutes to mix thoroughly.
4. In a second container **(not aluminum)** add lye to an equal volume of water slowly with stirring.

CAUTION

Lye solution can burn skin and destroy clothing. If any is spilled, wash away immediately with large quantities of water.

5. Add lye solution to the gasoline mix and stir until mixture thickens (about one minute).

NOTE

The sample will eventually thicken to a very firm paste. This can be thinned, if desired, by stirring in additional gasoline.

5.4.2 GELLED FLAME FUELS — LYE-ALCOHOL SYSTEMS

Lye (also known as caustic soda or sodium hydroxide) can be used in combination with alcohol and any of several fats to gel gasoline for use as a flame fuel.

NOTE

This fuel is not suitable for use in the chemical (sulfuric acid) type of fire bottle section 5.1. The acid will react with the lye and break down the gel.

Materials Required			
Parts by Volume	**Ingredient**	**How Used**	**Source**
60	Gasoline	Motor fuel	Gas station or motor vehicles
2 (flake) or 1 (powder)	Lye	Drain cleaner Making of soap	Food store Drug store
3	Ethyl alcohol*	Whiskey Medicine	Liquor store Drug store
14	Tallow	Food Making of soap	Fat rendered by cooking the meat or suet of animals

*Methyl (wood) alcohol or isopropyl (rubbing) alcohol can be substituted for ethyl alcohol, but their use produces softer gels.

NOTE

The following can be substituted for the tallow:

a. Wool grease (lanolin) (very good) – fat extracted from sheep wool
b. Castor oil (good)
c. Any vegetable oil (corn, cottonseed, peanut, linseed, etc.)
d. Any fish oil
e. Butter or oleomargarine

It is necessary when using substitutes (c) to (e) to double the given amount of fat and of lye for satisfactory bodying.

Procedure

CAUTION

Make sure that there are no open flames in the area when mixing flame fuels. **No smoking!**

1. Pour gasoline into bottle, jar or other container. **(Do not use an aluminum container.)**
2. Add tallow (or substitute) to the gasoline and stir for about 1/2 minute to dissolve fat.
3. Add alcohol to the gasoline mixture.
4. In a separate container **(not aluminum)** slowly add lye to an equal amount of water. Mixture should be stirred constantly while adding lye.

CAUTION

Lye solution can burn skin and destroy clothing. If any is spilled, wash away immediately with large quantities of water.

5. Add lye solution to the gasoline mixture and stir occasionally until thickened (about 1/2 hour).

NOTE

The mixture will eventually (1 to 2 days) thicken to a very firm paste. This can be thinned, if desired, by stirring in additional gasoline.

5.4.3 GELLED FLAME FUELS — SOAP-ALCOHOL SYSTEM

Common household soap can be used in combination with alcohol to gel gasoline for use as a flame fuel which will adhere to target surfaces.

Materials Required			
Parts by Volume	**Ingredient**	**How Used**	**Source**
36	Gasoline	Motor fuel	Gas station Motor vehicles
1	Ethyl alcohol*	Whiskey Medicine	Liquor store Drug store
20 (powdered) or 28 (flake)	Laundry soap	Washing clothes	Stores

*Methyl (wood) or isopropyl (rubbing) alcohols can be substituted for the whiskey.

NOTE

Unless the word "soap" actually appears somewhere on the container or wrapper, a washing compound is probably a detergent. **These can not be used.**

Procedure

CAUTION

Make sure that there are no open flames in the area when mixing flame fuels. **No smoking!**

1. If bar soap is used, carve into thin flakes using a knife.
2. Pour alcohol and gasoline into a jar, bottle or other container and mix thoroughly.
3. Add soap powder or flakes to gasoline-alcohol mix and stir occasionally until thickened (about 15 minutes).

5.4.4 GELLED FLAME FUELS — EGG WHITE SYSTEMS

The white of any bird egg can be used to gel gasoline for use as a flame fuel which will adhere to target surfaces.

Materials Required			
Parts by Volume	**Ingredient**	**How Used**	**Source**
85	Gasoline	Motor fuel Stove fuel Solvent	Gas station Motor vehicles
14	Egg whites	Food Industrial processes	Food store Farms
Any one of the following:			
1	Table salt	Food Industrial processes	Sea water Natural brine Food store
3	Ground coffee	Food	Coffee plant Food store
3	Dried tea leaves	Food	Tea plant Food store
3	Cocoa	Food	Cacao tree Food store
2	Sugar	Sweetening foods Industrial processes	Sugar cane Food store
1	Saltpeter (Niter) (Potassium nitrate)	Pyrotechnics Explosives Matches Medicine	Natural deposits Drug store
1	Epsom salts	Medicine Mineral water Industrial processes	Natural deposits Kieserite Drug store Food store

Materials Required			
Parts by Volume	**Ingredient**	**How Used**	**Source**
2	Washing soda (Sal soda)	Washing cleaner Medicine Photography	Food store Drug store Photo supply store
1-1/2	Baking Soda	Baking Manufacture of: Beverages, Mineral waters and Medicines	Food store Drug store
1-1/2	Aspirin	Medicine	Drug store Food store

Procedure

CAUTION

Make sure that there are no open flames in the area when mixing flame fuels. **No smoking!**

1. Separate egg white from yolk. This can be done by breaking the egg into a dish and carefully removing the yolk with a spoon.

NOTE

Do not get the yellow egg yolk mixed into the egg white. If egg yolk gets into the egg white, discard the egg.

2. Pour egg white into a jar, bottle, or other container and add gasoline.
3. Add the salt (or other additive) to the mixture and stir occasionally until gel forms (about 5 to 10 minutes).

NOTE

A thicker gelled flame fuel can be obtained by putting the capped jar in hot (65° C) water for about 1/2 hour and then letting them cool to room temperature. **(Do not heat the gelled fuel containing coffee.)**

5.4.5 GELLED FLAME FUELS — LATEX SYSTEMS

Any milky white plant fluid is a potential source of latex which can be used to gel gasoline.

Materials Required		
Ingredient	**How Used**	**Source**
Gasoline	Motor fuel Solvent	Gas station Motor vehicle
Latex, commercial or natural	Paints Adhesives	Natural from tree or plant Rubber cement
One of the following acids:		
Acetic acid (Vinegar)	Salad dressing Developing film	Food stores Fermented apple cider Photographic supply
Sulfuric acid (Oil of vitriol)	Storage batteries Material processing	Motor vehicles Industrial plants
Hydrochloric acid (Muriatic acid)	Petroleum wells Pickling and metal cleaning Industrial processes	Hardware store Industrial plants

NOTE

If acids are not available, use acid salt (alum, sulfates and chlorides other than sodium or potassium). The formic acid from crushed red ants can also be used.

Procedure

CAUTION

Make sure that there are no open flames in the area when mixing flame fuels. **No smoking!**

1. With commercial rubber latex:
   a. Place 7 parts by volume of latex and 92 parts by volume of gasoline in bottle. Cap bottle and shake to mix well.
   b. Add 1 part by volume vinegar (or other acid) and shake until gel forms.

CAUTION

Concentrated acids will burn skin and destroy clothing. If any is spilled, wash away immediately with large quantities of water.

2. With natural latex:
   a. Natural latex should form lumps as it comes from the plant. If lumps do not form, add a small amount of acid to the latex.
   b. Strain off the latex lumps and allow to dry in air.
   c. Place 20 parts by volume of latex in bottle and add 80 parts by volume of gasoline. Cover bottle and allow to stand until a swollen gel mass is obtained (2 to 3 days).

5.4.6 GELLED FLAME FUELS — WAX SYSTEMS

Any of several common waxes can be used to gel gasoline for use as a flame fuel which will adhere to target surfaces.

Materials Required			
Parts by Volume	**Ingredient**	**How Used**	**Source**
80	Gasoline	Motor fuel Solvent	Gas station Motor vehicles
Any one of the following:			
20	Ozocerite Mineral wax Fossil wax Ceresin wax	Leather polish Sealing wax Candles Crayons Waxed paper Textile sizing	Natural deposits General stores Department store
	Beeswax	Furniture and floor waxes Artificial fruit and flowers Lithographing Wax paper Textile finish Candles	Honeycomb of bee General store Department store
	Bayberry wax Myrtle wax	Candles Soaps Leather polish Medicine	Natural form Myrica berries General store Department store Drug store

Procedure

1. Obtaining wax from natural sources: Plants and berries are potential sources of natural waxes. Place the plants and/or berries in boiling water. The natural waxes will melt. Let the water cool. The natural waxes will form a solid layer on the water surface. Skim off the solid wax and let it dry. With natural waxes which have suspended matter when melted, screen the wax through a cloth.
2. Melt the wax and pour into jar or bottle which has been placed in a hot water bath.
3. Add gasoline to the bottle.
4. When wax has completely dissolved in the gasoline, allow the water bath to cool slowly to room temperature.

NOTE

If a gel does not form, add additional wax (up to 40% by volume) and repeat the above steps. If no gel forms with 40% wax, make a lye solution by dissolving a small amount of lye (sodium hydroxide) in an equal amount of water. Add this solution (1/2% forms by volume) to the gasoline wax mix and shake bottle until a gel forms.

5.4.7 GELLED FLAME FUELS — ANIMAL BLOOD SYSTEMS

Animal blood can be used to gel gasoline for use as a flame fuel which will adhere to target surfaces.

Materials Required			
Parts by Volume	**Ingredient**	**How Used**	**Source**
68	Gasoline	Motor fuel Solvent	Gas station Motor vehicles
30	Animal blood serum	Food Medicine	Slaughter House Natural habitat
Any one of the following:			
2	Salt	Food Industrial processes	Sea Water Natural brine Food store
	Ground Coffee	Food Caffeine source Beverage	Coffee plant Food store

Materials Required			
Parts by Volume	**Ingredient**	**How Used**	**Source**
	Dried tea leaves	Food Beverage	Tea plant Food store
	Sugar	Sweetening foods Industrial processes	Sugar cane Food store
	Lime	Mortar Plaster Medicine Ceramics Steel making Industrial processes	From calcium carbonate Hardware store Drug store Garden supply store
	Baking soda	Baking Beverages Medicine Industrial processes	Food store Drug store
	Epsom salts	Medicine Mineral water Industrial processes	Drug store Natural deposits Food store

Procedure

1. Preparation of animal blood serum:
   a. Slit animal's throat by jugular vein. Hang upside down to drain.
   b. Place coagulated (lumpy) blood in a cloth or on a screen and catch the red fluid (serum) which drains through.
   c. Store in cool place if possible.

CAUTION

Do not get aged animal blood or the serum into an open cut. This can cause infections.

2. Pour blood serum into jar, bottle, or other container and add gasoline.
3. Add the salt (or other additive) to the mixture and stir until a gel forms.

5.5 ACID DELAY INCENDIARY

This device will ignite automatically after a given time delay.

Materials Required
Small jar with cap
Cardboard
Adhesive tape
Potassium chlorate
Sugar
Sulfuric acid (battery acid)
Rubber sheeting (automotive inner tube)

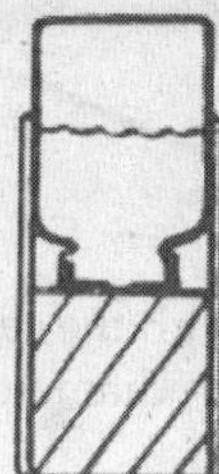

Procedure

1. *Sulfuric acid must be concentrated.* If battery acid or other dilute acid is used, concentrate it by boiling. Container used should be of enamelware or oven glass. When dense white fumes begin to appear, immediately remove the acid from heat and allow to cool to room temperature.

CAUTION

Sulfuric acid will burn skin and destroy clothing. If any is spilled, wash it away with a larger quantity of water. Fumes are also dangerous and should not be inhaled.

2. Dissolve one part by volume of potassium chlorate and one part by volume of sugar in two parts by volume of boiling water.
3. Allow the solution to cool. When crystals settle, pour off and discard the liquid.
4. Form a tube from cardboard just large enough to fit around the outside of the jar and 2 to 3 times the height of the jar. Tape one end of the tube closed.

5. Pour wet potassium chlorate-sugar crystals into the tube until it is about 2/3 full. Stand the tube aside to dry.

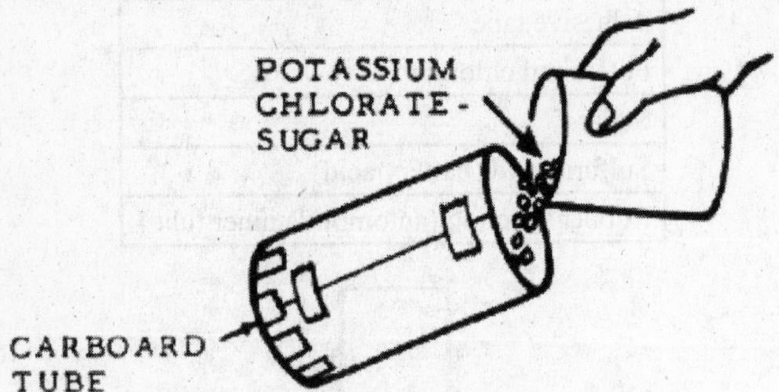

6. Drill a hole through the cap of the jar about 1/2 inch (1-1/4 cm) in diameter.

7. Cut a disc from rubber sheet so that it just fits snugly inside the lid of the jar.

8. Partly fill jar with water, cover with rubber disc and cap tightly with the drilled lid. Invert bottle and allow to stand for a few minutes to make sure that there are no leaks. **This is extremely important.**
9. Pour water from jar and fill about 1/3 full with concentrated sulfuric acid. Replace the rubber disc and cap tightly.

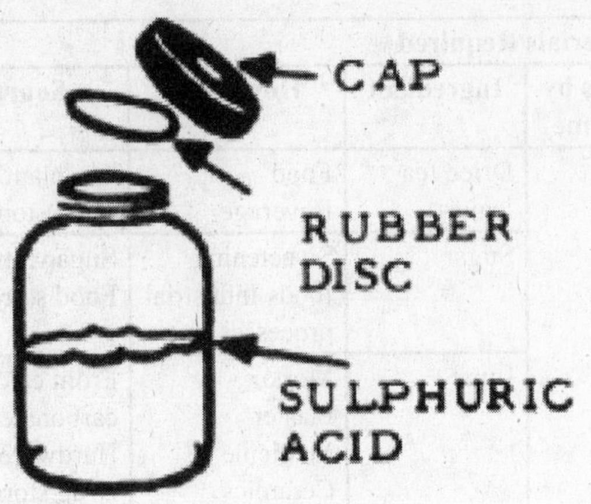

IMPORTANT

Wash outside of jar thoroughly with clear water. If this is not done, the jar may be dangerous to handle during use.

How to Use

1. Place the tube containing the sugar chlorate crystals on an incendiary or flammable material taped end down.
2. Turn the jar of sulfuric acid cap end down and slide it into the open end of the tube.

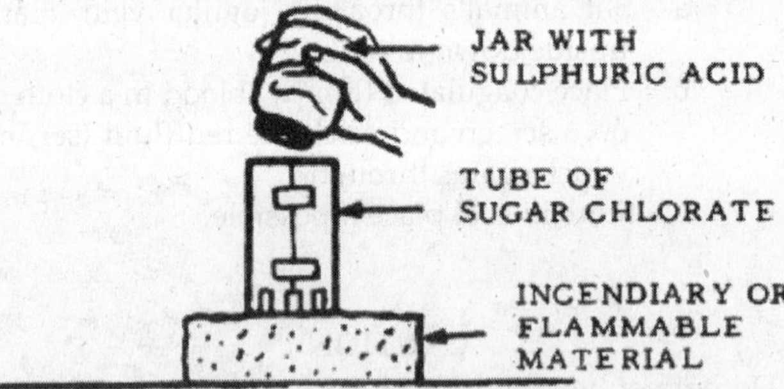

After a time delay, the acid will eat through the rubber disc and ignite the sugar chlorate mix. The delay time depends upon the thickness and type of rubber used for the disc. Before using this device, tests should be conducted to determine the delay time that can be expected.

NOTE

A piece of standard automobile inner tube (about 1/32 inch thick) will provide a delay time of approximately 45 minutes.

5.6 IMPROVISED WHITE FLARE

An improvised white flare can be made from potassium nitrate, aluminum powder and shellac. it has a time duration of approximately 2 minutes.

Materials Required	Source
Potassium nitrate	Field grade (section 1.2) Drug Store
Aluminum powder (bronzing)	Hardware or paint store
Shellac	Hardware or paint store
Quart jar with lid	
Fuse, 15 inches long	
Wooden rod, 1/4 inch diameter	
Tin can, 2-1/2 inch diameter × 5 inches long	
Flat window screen	
Wooden block	

NOTE
All of the above dimensions are approximate.

Procedure

1. Place the potassium nitrate crystals on the screen. Rub the material back and forth against the screen mesh with the wooden block until the nitrate is granulated into a powder.

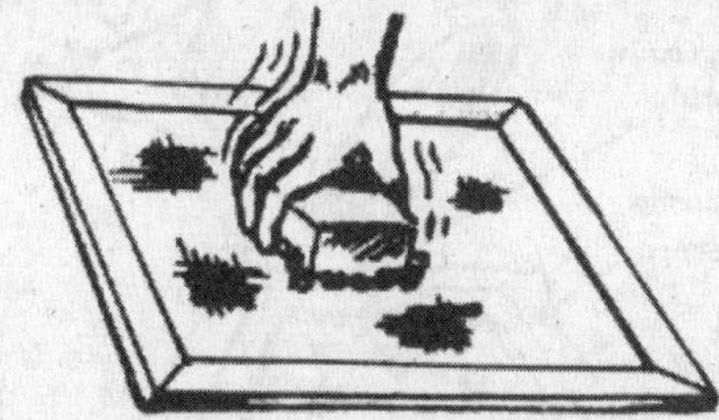

2. Measure 21 tablespoons of the powdered nitrate into a quart jar. Add 21 tablespoons of the aluminum powder to the nitrate.

3. Place lid on the jar and shake ingredients vigorously until well mixed.

4. Add 12 tablespoons of shellac to the mixture and stir with the wooden rod. Store mixture until ready for step 7.

5. Knot one end of the fuse.
6. Wrap the knotted end of the fuse once around the inside bottom of the can with the knot at the center. Then, run the rest of the fuse out the center top of the can.

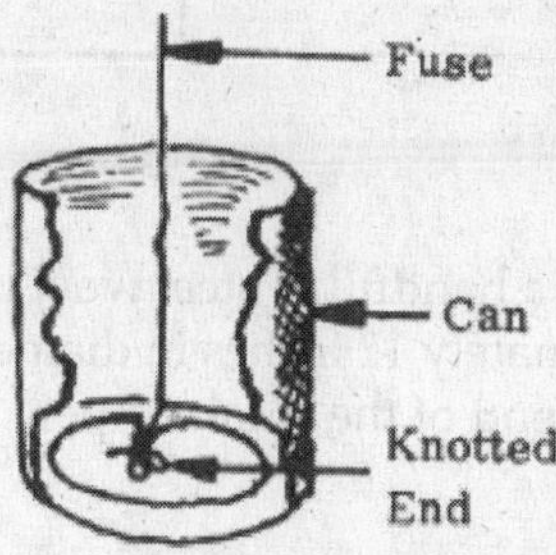

7. Pour the mixture in the can and around the fuse.

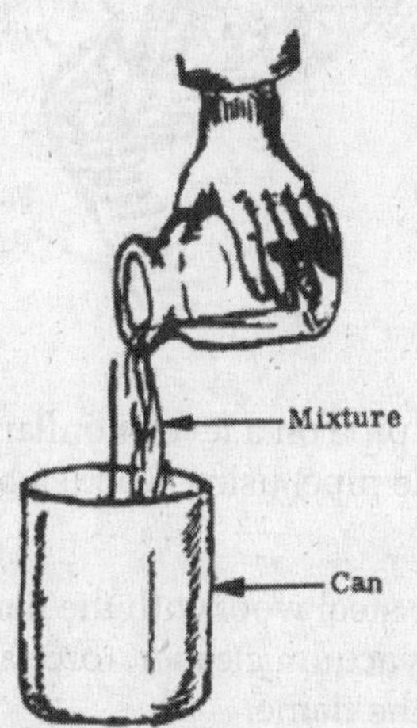

8. Store flare mixture away from heat and flame until ready for use, but no longer than 3 weeks.

5.7 IMPROVISED IRON OXIDE

Iron oxide can be made from steel wool. It is used in the preparation of Improvised Yellow Flare (section 5.8), Improvised White Smoke Munition (section 5.9) and Improvised Black Smoke Munition (section 5.10).

Materials Required	Source
Steel wool (without soap), approximately 16 large pads	Hardware or general store
Smoke pipe, approximately 4 feet long × 12 inches in diameter, 1/16 inch thick	Hardware store
Vacuum cleaner	Hardware store
Electrical source (110 V, A.C.)	Modern commercial and domestic buildings
Window screen	
Newspaper	
2 containers	
Wooden blocks, if necessary	
Flame source (matches, lighter, etc.)	

Procedure

1. Separate a handful of steel wool into a fluffy ball approximately 12 inches in diameter and place into one end of the smoke pipe.

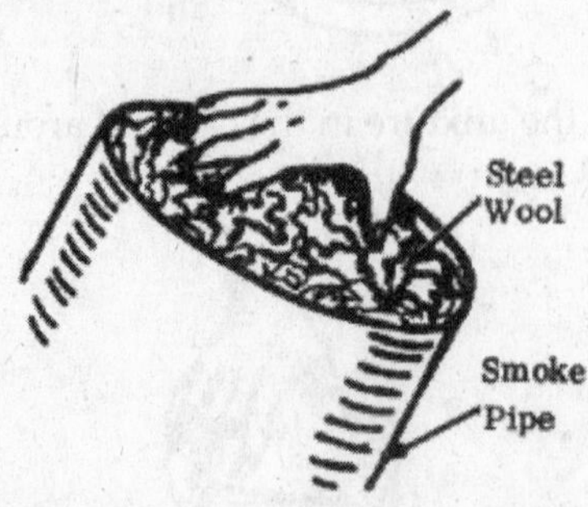

2. Place the pipe on a level, nonflammable surface. Steady the pipe, using wooden blocks if necessary.

3. Ignite the steel wool with the flame source and, with the vacuum cleaner, force a stream of air through the flame.

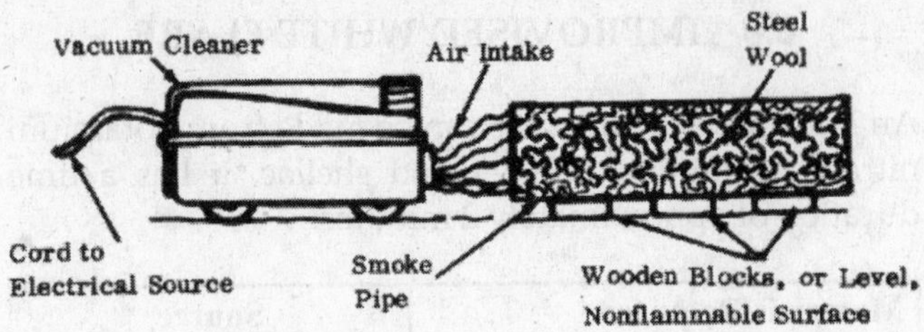

NOTE

The forced air provided by the vacuum cleaner aids in the burning of the steel wool. If the steel wool does not completely burn, more separation of the wool is needed.

4. When the steel wool has almost completely burned, add another handful of the fluffed steel wool (step 1).

5. Continue adding to the flame a single handful of fluffed wool at a time until a sufficient amount of iron oxide granules have accumulated in the stove pipe.

6. Place a window screen on a sheet of newspaper. Pour the burned steel wool granules onto the window screen and shake screen until all the fine particles have passed through.

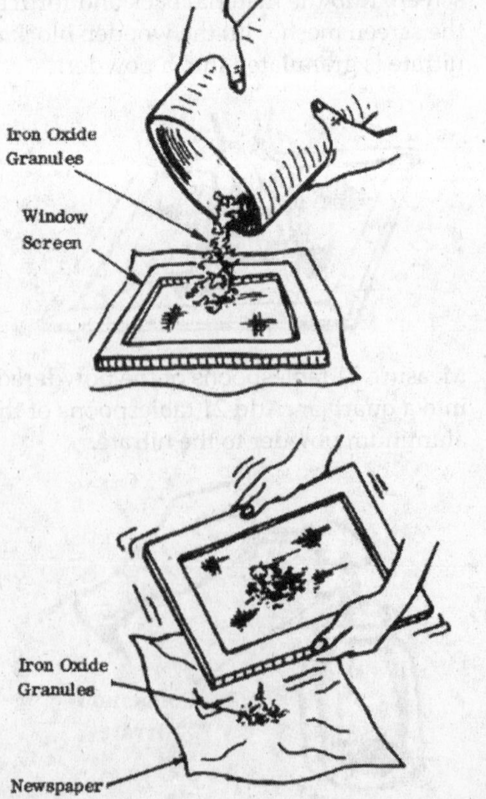

7. Discard those particles on the newspaper which are fibrous and unburned.

8. Save the particles which were too large to pass through the screen in one of the containers for future burning.

9. Store particles of iron oxide (left on newspaper) in another container until ready for use.

5.8 IMPROVISED YELLOW FLARE

A yellow flare can be made from shellac, sulfur, aluminum powder, iron oxide and baking soda. It can be used either for signaling or lighting up a dark area.

Materials Required	Source
Shellac	Hardware or paint store
Sulfur	Drug or agricultural supply store
Aluminum powder (bronzing)	Hardware or paint store
Black iron oxide	Section 5.7
Sodium bicarbonate (baking soda)	Food store
Improvised white flare mix	Section 5.6
Window Screen	
Wooden rod or stick	
Tablespoon	
Quart jar with lid	
Newspaper	
Wooden block	
Fuse, 15 inches long	
Tin can, 2-1/2 inches diameter × 5 inches long	
Aluminum foil	
Flame source (matches, lighter, etc.)	

Procedure

1. Measure 6 firm level tablespoons of sulfur into a quart jar.

2. Add 7 firm level tablespoons of sodium bicarbonate to the sulfur.

3. Add 2 heaping tablespoons of black iron oxide.

4. Place the lid on the quart jar and shake ingredients 10 times.

5. Place the mixed ingredients on the window screen.

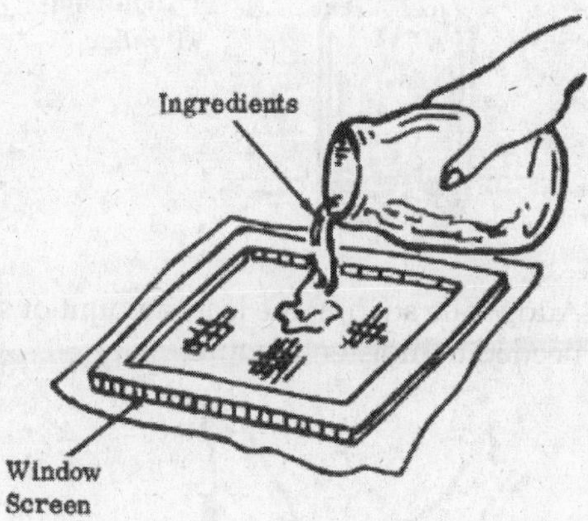

6. Mix ingredients thoroughly by forcing material through screen mesh onto the newspaper, using a wooden rod or stick. Repeat screening 2 times to insure thorough mixing.

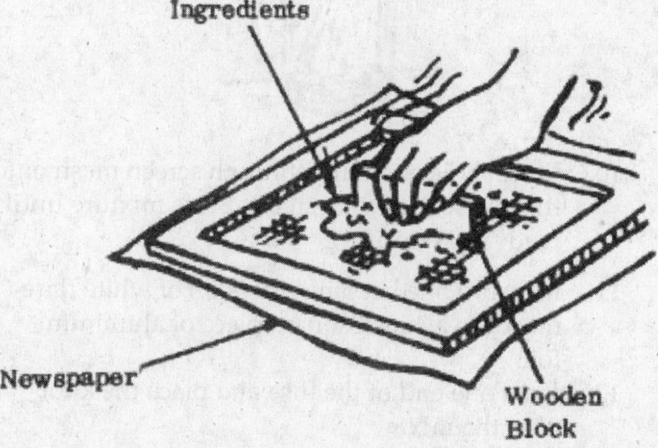

7. Pour mixed ingredients back into the jar.

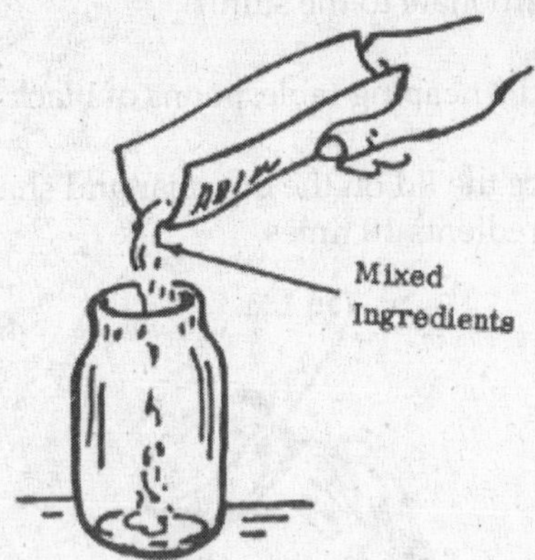

8. Add 20 heaping tablespoons of aluminum powder to the ingredients.

9. Add while stirring the least amount of shellac needed to moisten mixture.

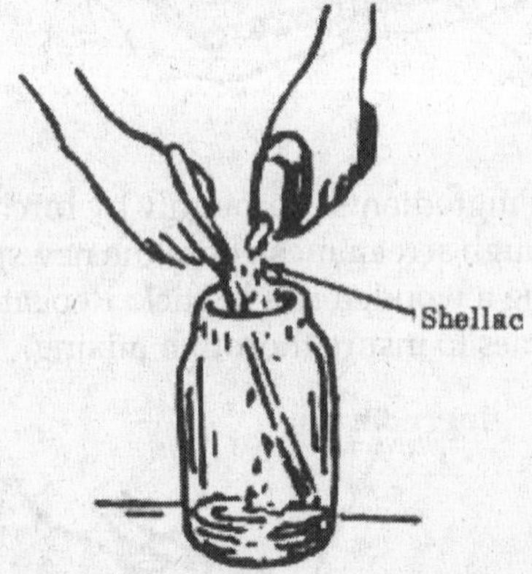

10. Force moistened mix through screen mesh onto the newspaper as in step 6. Store mixture until ready for step 14.

11. Measure one heaping teaspoon of white flare mix onto a 4 inch square piece of aluminum foil.

12. Knot one end of the fuse and place the knot onto the mix.

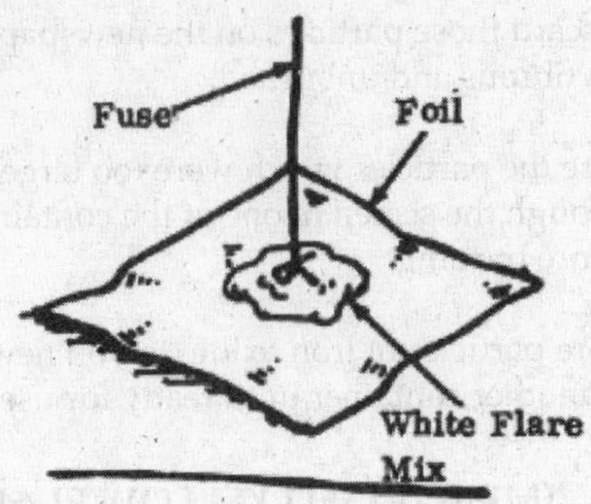

13. Fold the corners of the foil tightly around the fuse.

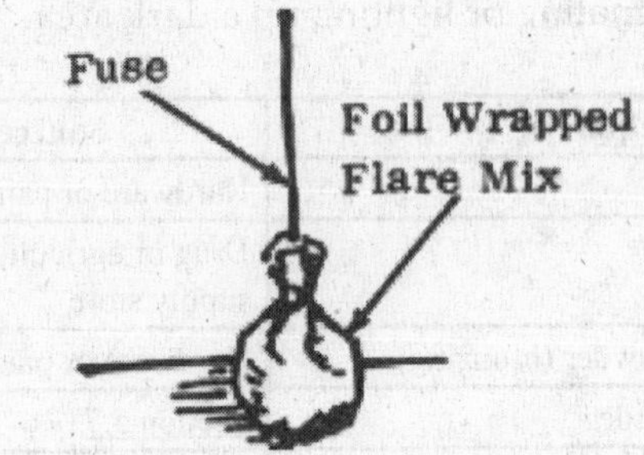

14. Now place the yellow flare mix into the can.

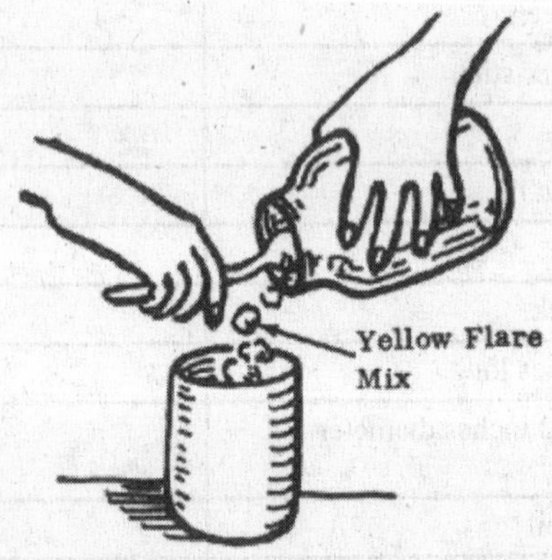

15. Place the fused white flare mix in the foil below the surface of the yellow flare mix in the can.

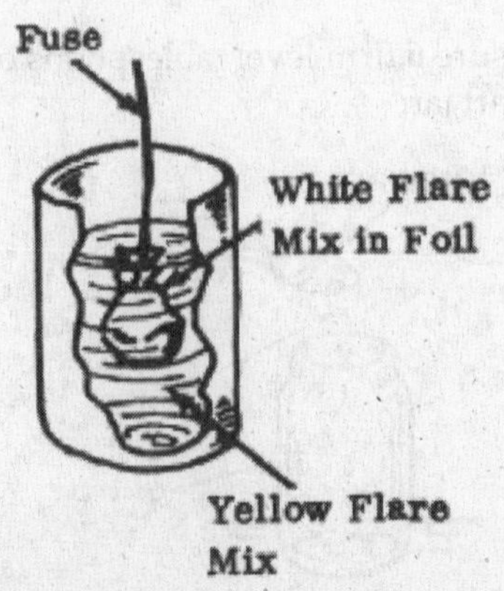

16. Light the fuse with the flame source when ready.

5.9 IMPROVISED WHITE SMOKE MUNITION

A white smoke munition can be made from sulfur, potassium nitrate, black powder, aluminum powder, iron oxide and carbon tetrachloride. It can be used either for signaling or screening.

Materials Required	Source
Sulfur	Drug or agricultural supply store
Potassium nitrate (saltpeter)	Drug store or section 1.2
Improvised black powder	Section 1.3
Aluminum powder (bronzing)	Hardware or paint store
Black iron oxide	Section 5.7
Carbon tetrachloride	Hardware or paint store
Improvised white flare mix	Section 5.6
Tablespoon	
Wooden rod or stick	
Newspaper	
Quart Jar with lid	
Window screen	
Fuse, 15 inches long	
Tin can, 2-1/2 inches diameter × 5 inches long	
Flame source (matches, lighter, etc.)	

Procedure

1. Measure 3 level tablespoons of powdered dry sulfur into the quart jar.

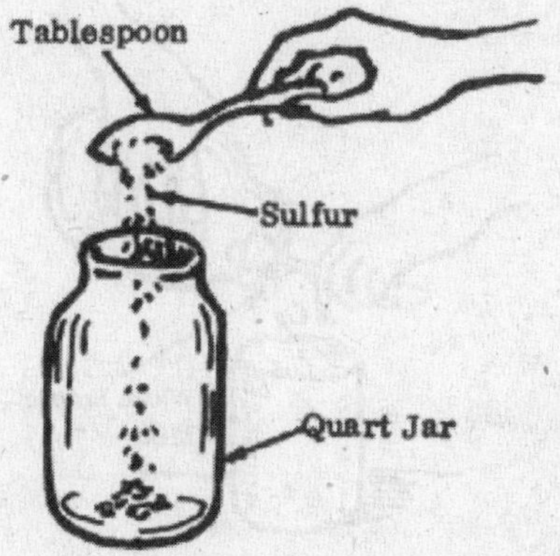

2. Add 4 level tablespoons of powdered dry potassium nitrate to the sulfur.

NOTE

It may be necessary to crush the potassium nitrate crystals and sulfur to obtain an accurate measure in tablespoon.

3. Add 2 heaping tablespoons of black iron oxide.

4. Place all ingredients on the window screen.

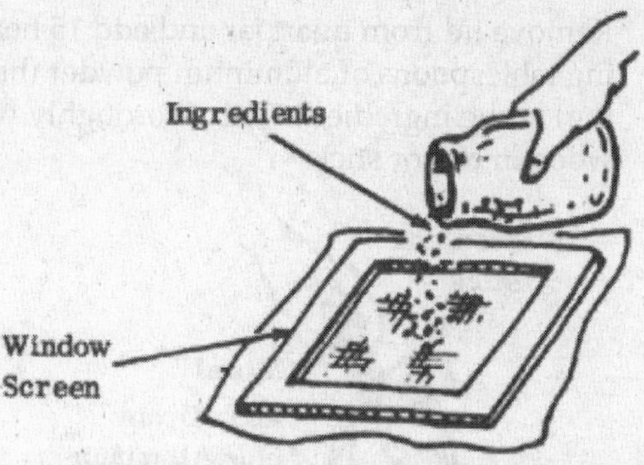

5. Mix ingredients thoroughly by sieving them onto the newspaper. Repeat screening 3 times to insure thorough mixing.

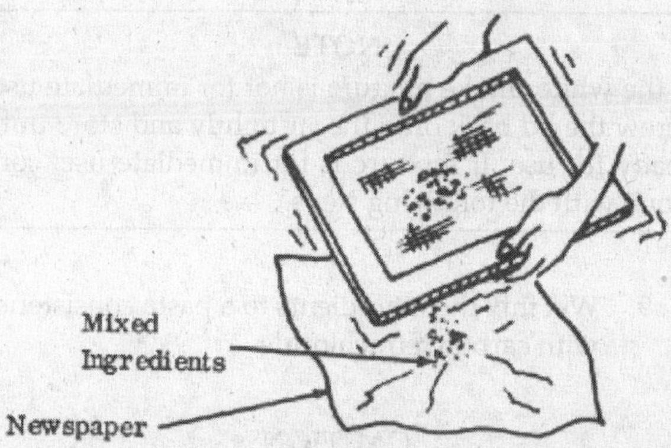

6. Pour mixed ingredients back into the jar.

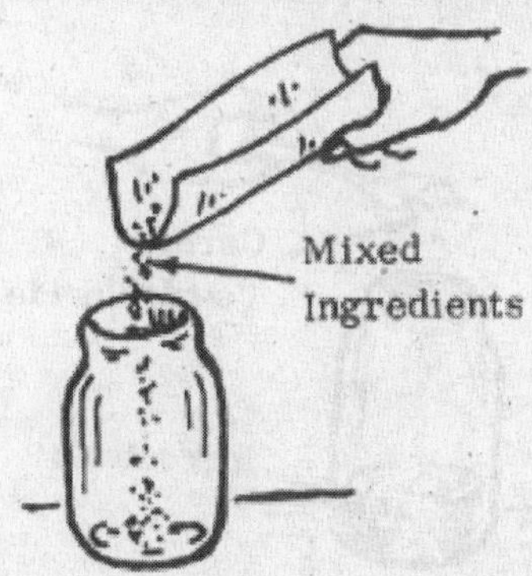

7. Screw lid onto the quart jar and shake vigorously until the ingredients are evenly mixed.

8. Remove lid from quart jar and add 15 heaping tablespoons of aluminum powder (bronzing) to the ingredients. Mix thoroughly with wooden rod or stick.

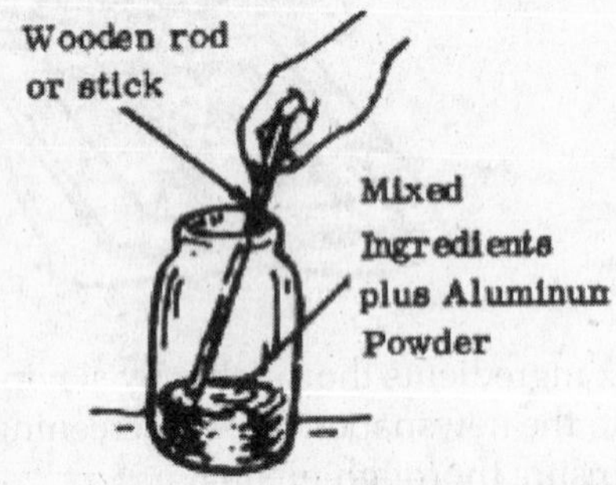

NOTE

If the white smoke mixture is not for immediate use, screw the lid back onto the jar tightly and store until ready for use. If mixture is for immediate use, continue with the following steps.

9. Wet mix the ingredients to a paste consistency with carbon tetrachloride.

CAUTION

Fumes of carbon tetrachloride are hazardous. Perform step 10 in a well ventilated area.

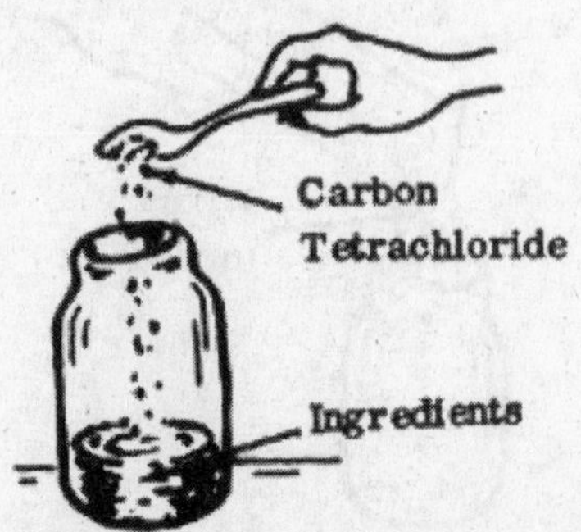

10. Add 1/2 cup of black powder to the ingredients and carefully mix with wooden rod or stick.

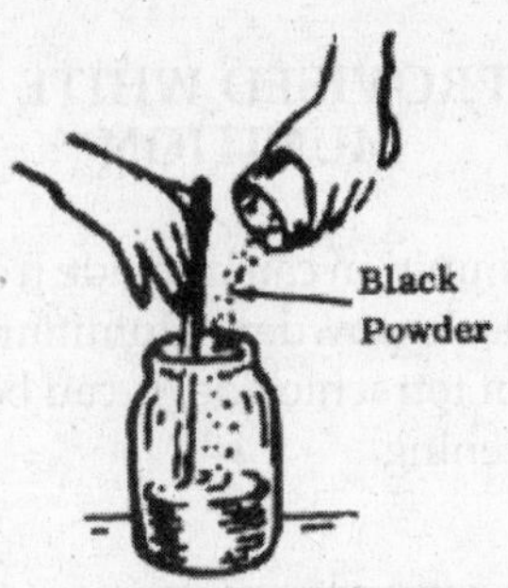

How to Use

1. Measure one heaping teaspoon of white flare mix onto a 4 inch square piece of aluminum foil.
2. Knot one end of the fuse and place the knot into the mix.

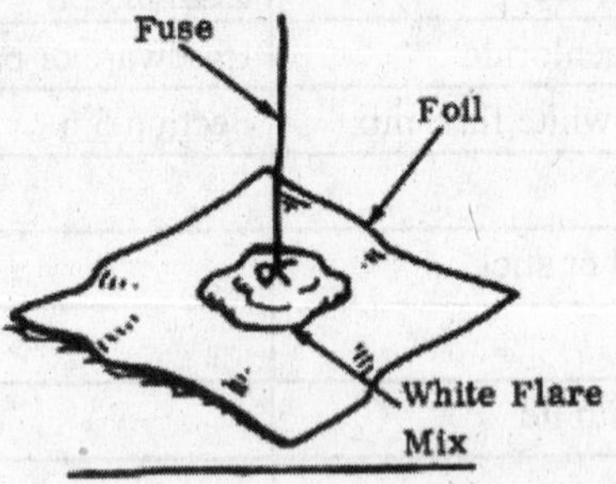

3. Fold the corners of the foil tightly around the fuse.

4. Now place the white smoke mix into the can.

5. Place the fused white flare mix in the foil below the surface of the white smoke mix in the can.

6. Light the fuse with the flame source when ready.

5.10 IMPROVISED BLACK SMOKE MUNITION

A black smoke munition can be made from sulfur, aluminum powder, iron oxide, moth crystals and carbon tetrachloride. It can be used either for signaling or screening.

Materials Required	Source
Sulfur	Drug store
Aluminum powder (bronzing)	Paint or hardware store
Improvised black iron oxide	Section 5.7
Moth crystals (paradichlorobenzene)	Hardware store
Carbon tetrachloride	Paint or hardware store
Improvised white flare mix	Section 5.6
Table salt	Food store
Teaspoon	
Tablespoon	
Quart jar or container	
Wooden rod or stick	
Wooden block	
Window screen	
Newspaper	
Fuse, 15 inches long	
Tin can, 2-1/2 inch diameter × 5 inches long	
Aluminum foil	
Flame source (matches, lighter, etc.)	

Procedure

1. Measure 3 level teaspoons of sulfur into a quart jar.

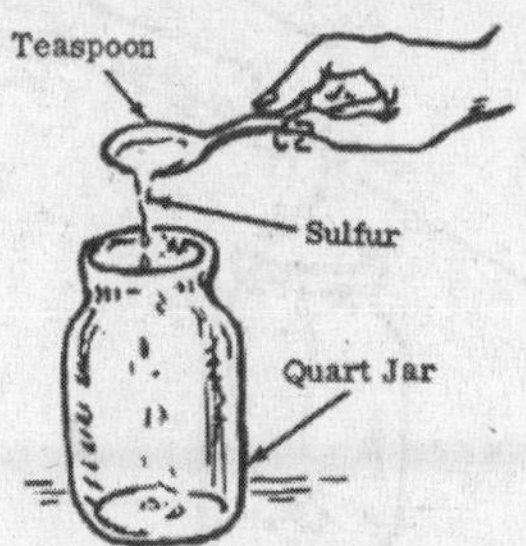

2. Add 1 heaping tablespoon of improvised iron oxide to the sulfur.
3. Add 2 level teaspoons of table salt.
4. Crush 5 heaping tablespoons of moth crystal into a fine powder using a wooden block.

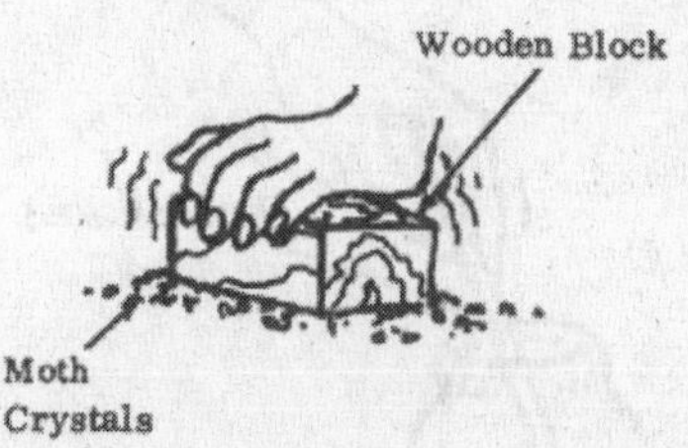

5. Add 4 heaping tablespoons of powdered moth crystals to the other ingredients in jar.
6. Place all ingredients on the window screen.

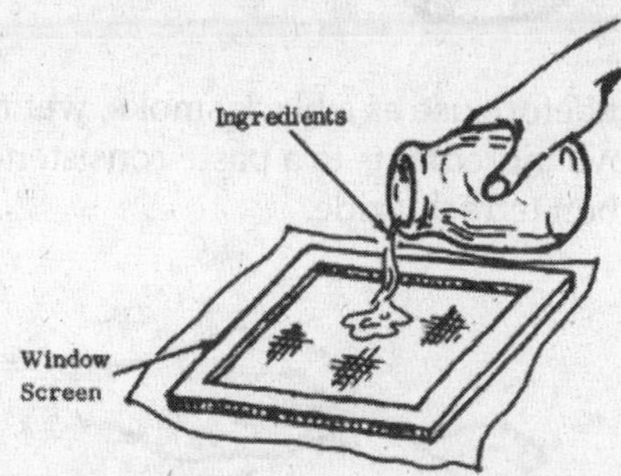

7. Mix ingredients thoroughly by sieving them onto the newspaper. Repeat screening 3 times to insure thorough mixing.

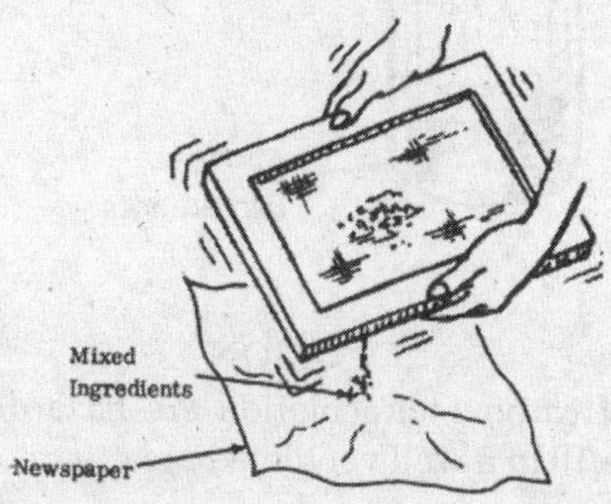

8. Pour mixed ingredients back into the jar.

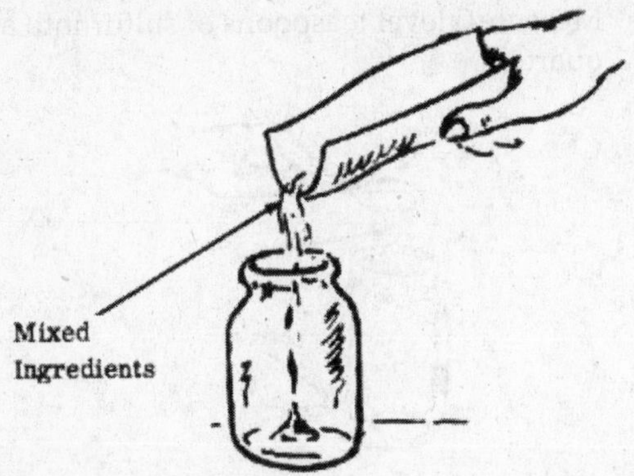

9. Add 12 heaping tablespoons of aluminum powder to the ingredients and mix by stirring with wooden rod or stick.

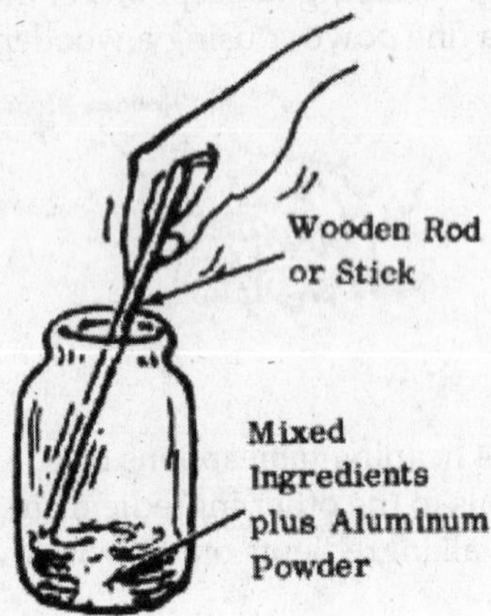

10. Just before use as a black smoke, wet mix the above ingredients to a paste consistency with carbon tetrachloride.

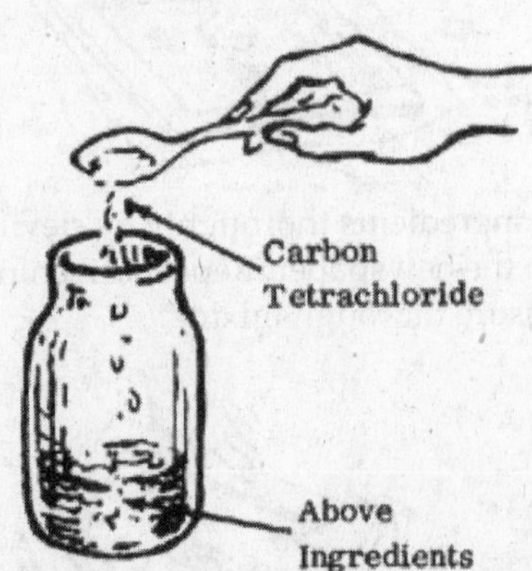

CAUTION

Fumes of carbon tetrachloride are hazardous. Perform step 10 in a well ventilated area.

How to Use

1. Measure one heaping teaspoon of white flare mix onto a 4 inch square piece of aluminum foil.
2. Knot one end of the fuse and place the knot into the mix.

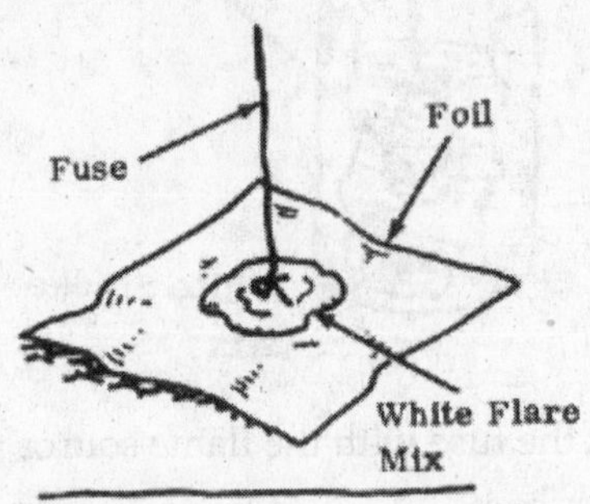

3. Fold the corners of the foil tightly around the fuse.

4. Now place the black smoke mix into the can.

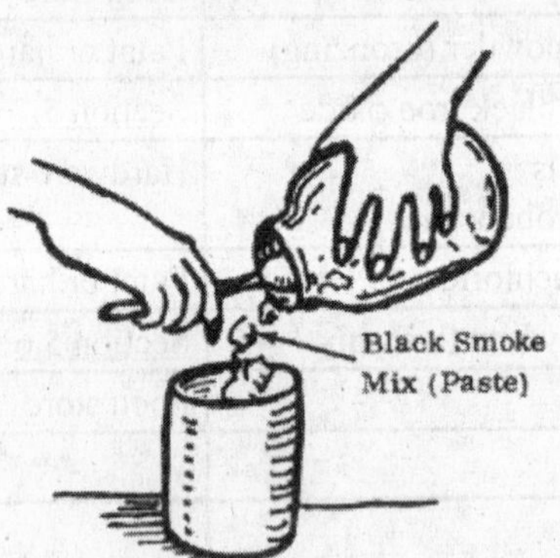

5. Place the fused white flare mix in the foil below the surface of the black smoke mix in the can.

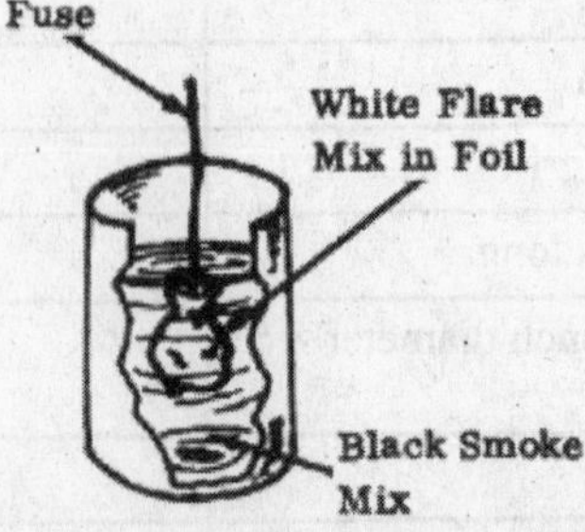

6. Light the fuse with the flame source when ready.

SECTION 6

Fuses, Detonators & Delay Mechanisms

6.1 ELECTRIC BULB INITIATOR

Mortars, mines and similar weapons often make use of electric initiators. An electric initiator can be made using a flash light or automobile electric light bulb.

Materials Required
Electric light bulb and mating socket
Cardboard or heavy paper
Black powder
Adhesive tape

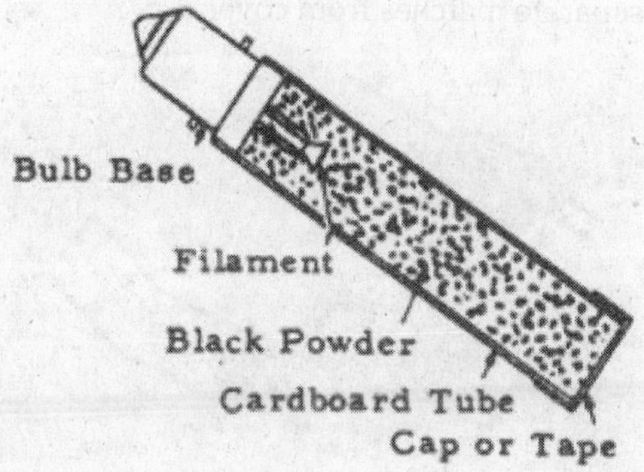

Procedure

Method I

1. Break the glass of the electric light bulb. Take care not to damage the filament. The initiator will not work if the filament is broken. Remove all glass above the base of the bulb.

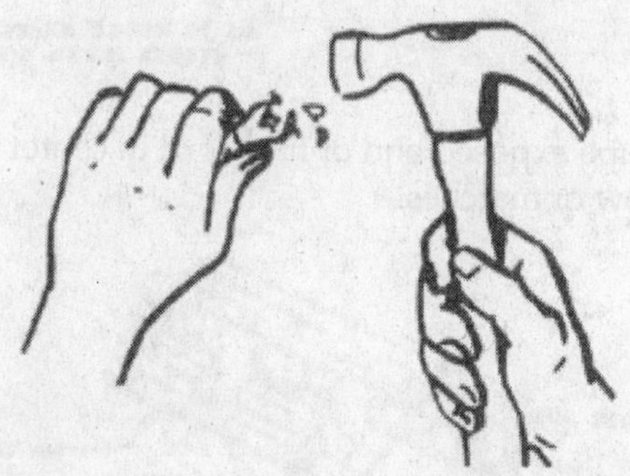

2. Form a tube 3 to 4 inches long from cardboard or heavy paper to fit around the base of the bulb. Join the tube with adhesive tape.

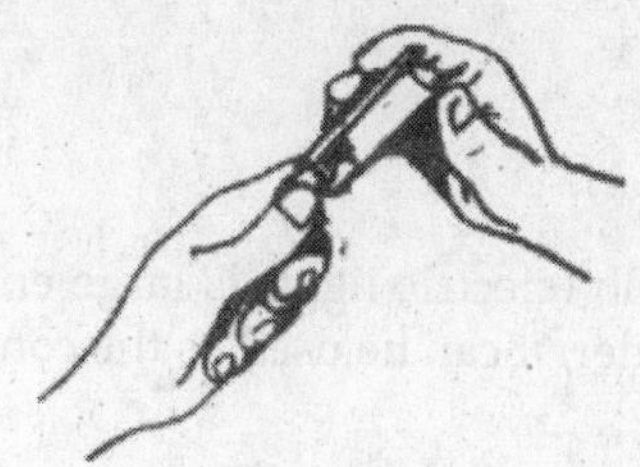

3. Fit the tube to the bulb base and tape in place. Make sure that the tube does not cover that portion of the bulb base that fits into the socket.

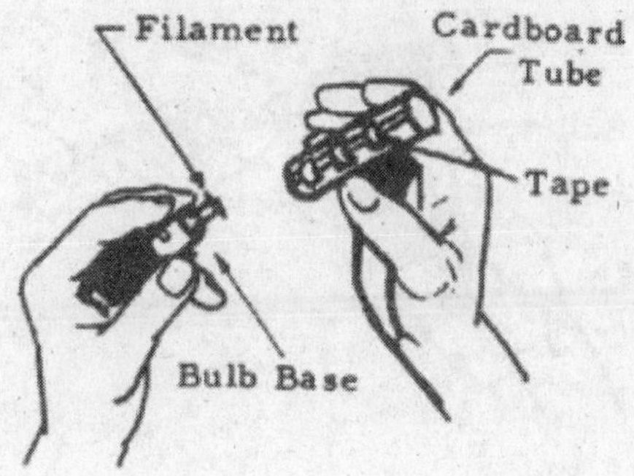

4. If no socket is available for connecting the initiator to the firing circuit, solder the connecting wires to the bulb base.

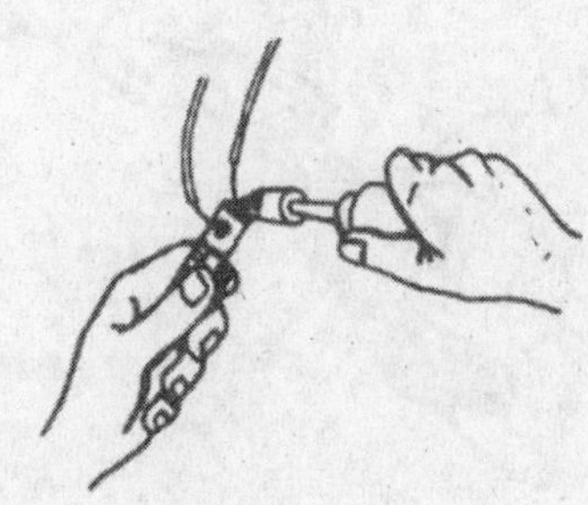

CAUTION

Do **not** use a hot soldering iron on the completed igniter since it may ignite the black powder.

5. Fill the tube with black powder and tape the open end of the tube closed.

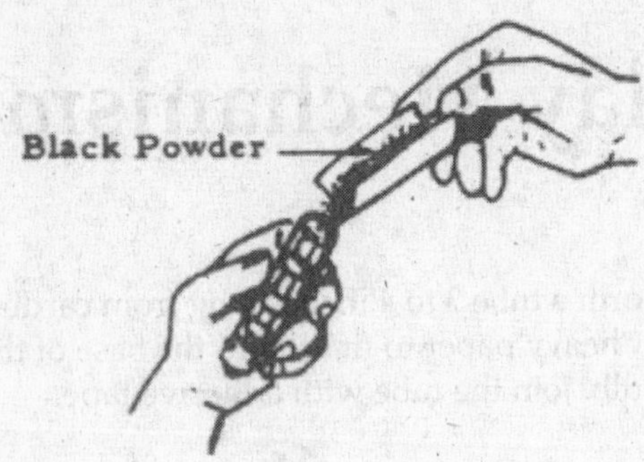

Method II

If the glass bulb (electric light) is large enough to hold the black powder, it can he used as the container.

Procedure

1. File a small hole in the top of the bulb.

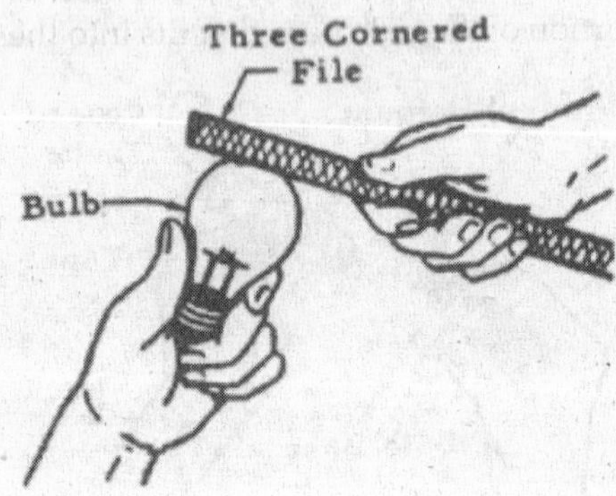

2. Fill the bulb with black powder and tape the hole closed.

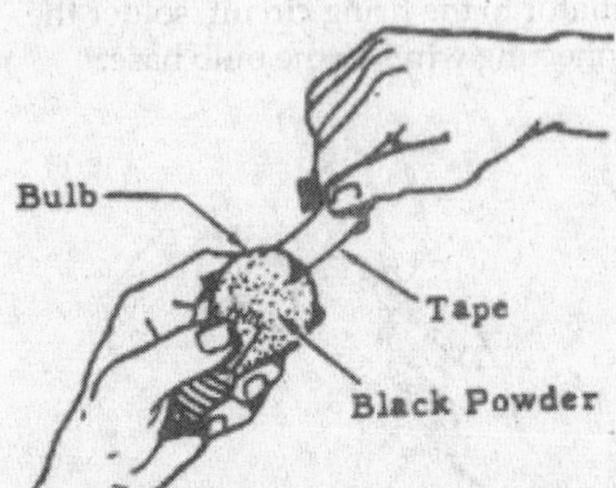

6.2 FUSE IGNITER FROM BOOK MATCHES

A simple, reliable fuse igniter can be made from paper book matches.

Materials Required
Paper book matches
Adhesive or friction tape
Fuse cord (improvised or commercial)
Pin or small nail

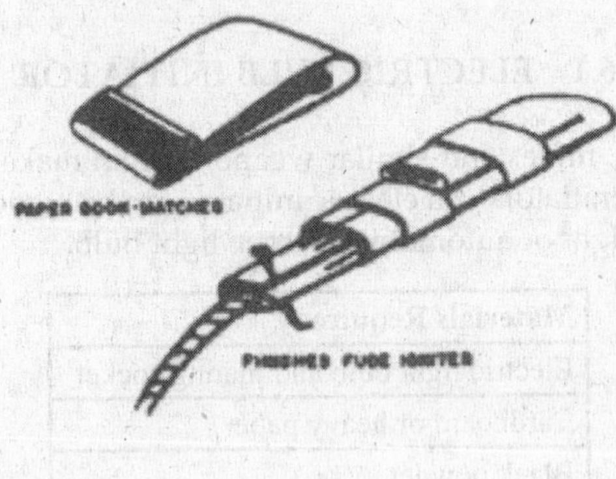

Procedure

1. Remove the staple(s) from match book and separate matches from cover.

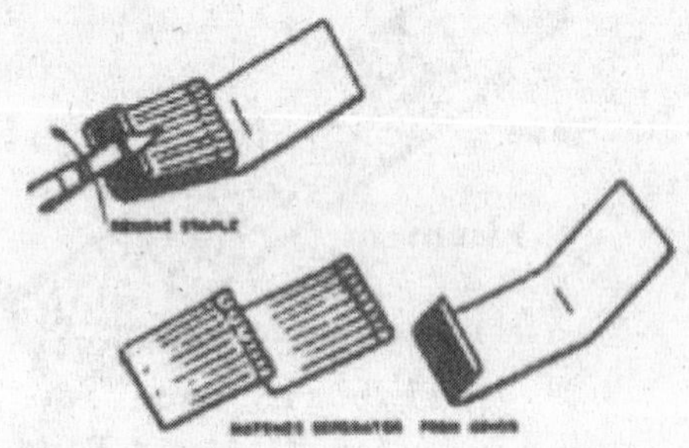

2. Cut fuse cord so that inner core is exposed.

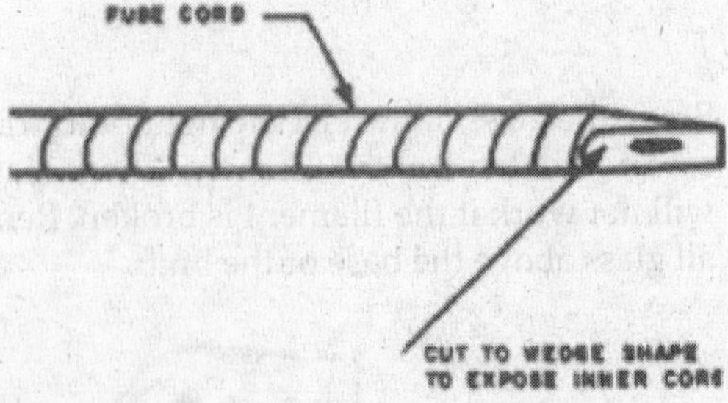

3. Tape exposed end of fuse cord in center of one row of matches.

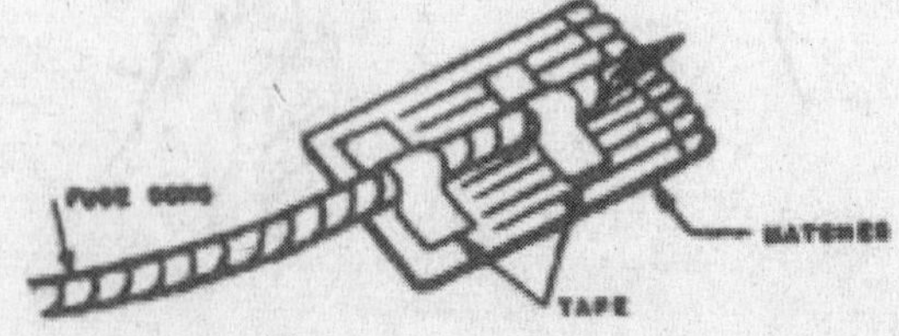

4. Fold matches over fuse and tape.

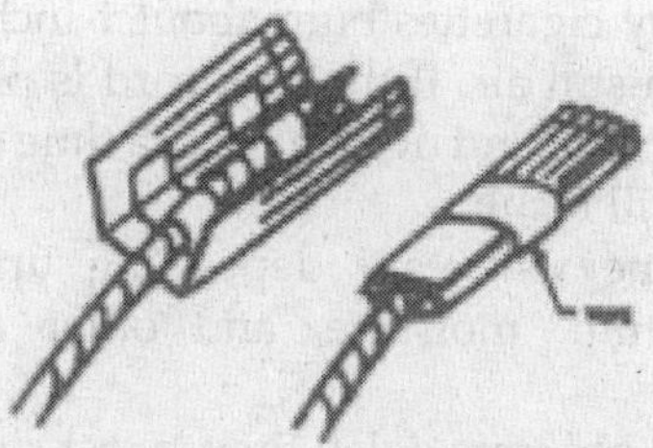

5. Shape the cover into a tube with the striking surface on the inside and tape. Make sure the edges of the cover at the striking end are butted. Leave cover open at opposite end for insertion of the matches.

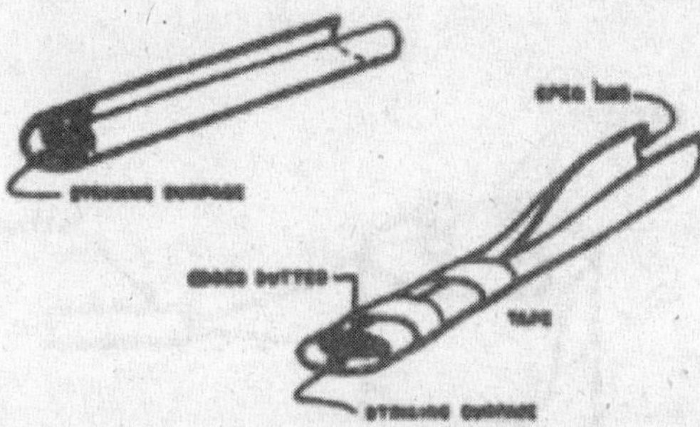

6. Push the taped matches with fuse cord into the tube until the bottom ends of the matches are exposed about 3/4 inch (2 cm).

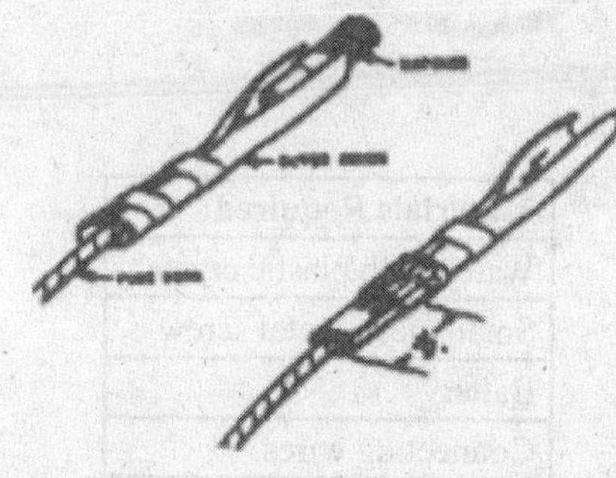

7. Flatten and fold the open end of the tube so that it laps over about 1 inch (2-1/2 cm); tape in place.

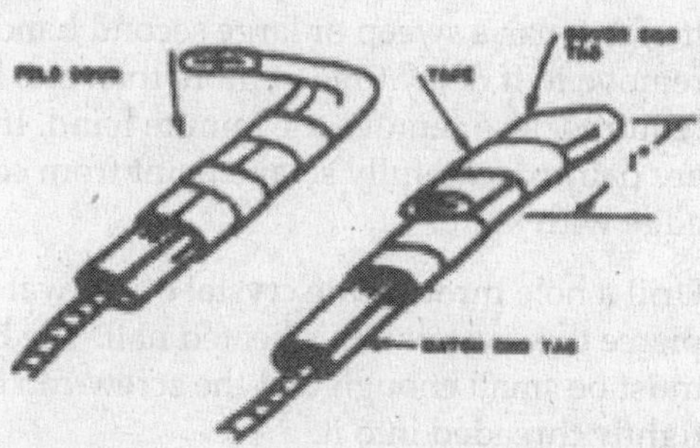

8. Push pin or small nail through matches and fuse cord. Bend end of pin or nail.

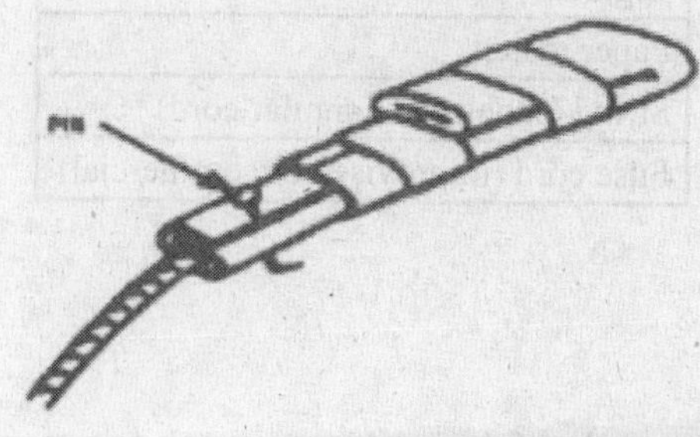

Method of Use

To light the fuse cord, the igniter is held by both hands and pulled sharply or quickly.

CAUTION

Store matches and completed fuse igniters in moistureproof containers such as plastic or rubber type bags until ready for use. Damp or wet paper book matches will not ignite. Fuse lengths should not exceed 12 inches (30 cm) for easy storage. These can be spliced to main fuses when needed.

6.3 DELAY IGNITER FROM CIGARETTE

A simple and economical time delay can be made with a common cigarette.

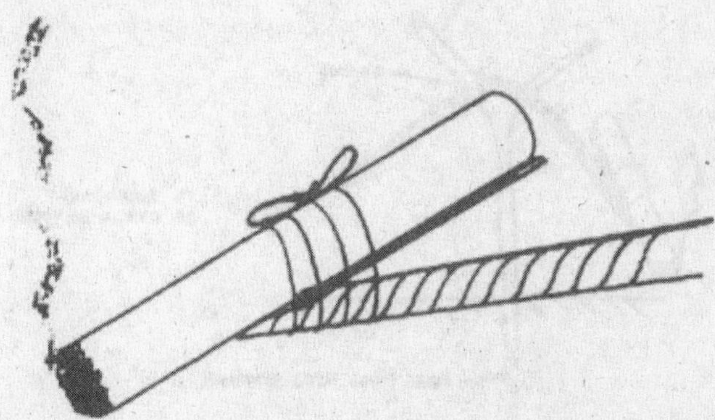

Materials Required
Cigarette
Paper match
String (shoelace or similar cord)
Fuse cord (improvised or commercial)

Procedure

1. Cut end of fuse cord to expose inner core.

2. Light cigarette in normal fashion. Place a paper match so that the head is over exposed end of fuse cord and tie both to the side of the burning cigarette with string.

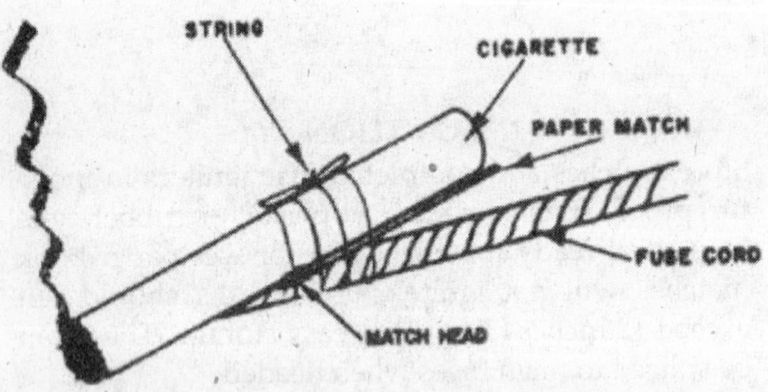

3. Position the burning cigarette with fuse so that it burns freely. A suggested method is to hang the delay on a twig.

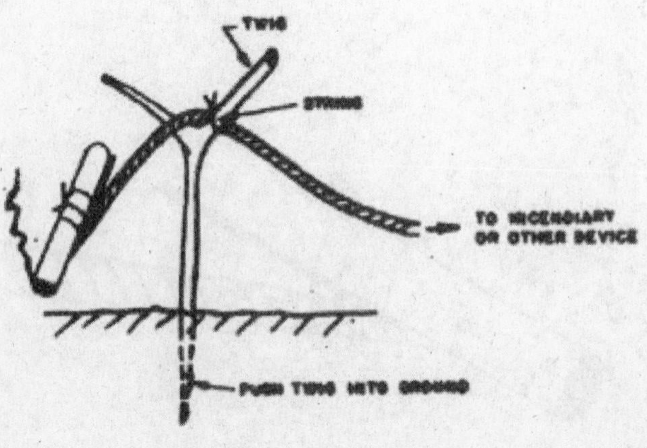

NOTE

Common dry cigarettes bum about 1 inch every 7 or 8 minutes in still air. If the fuse cord is placed 1 inch from the burning end of a cigarette a time delay of 7 or 8 minutes will result.

Delay time will vary depending upon type of cigarette, wind, moisture, and other atmospheric conditions.

To obtain accurate delay time, a test run should be made under "use" conditions.

6.4 WATCH DELAY TIMER

A time delay device for use with electrical firing circuits can be made by using a watch with a plastic crystal.

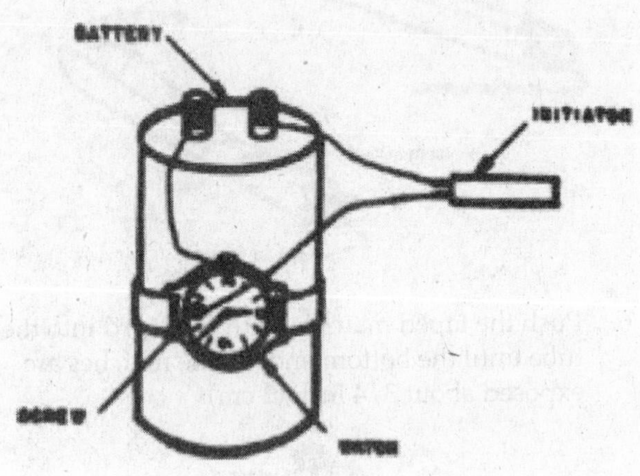

Materials Required
Watch with plastic crystal
Small clean metal screw
Battery
Connecting wires
Drill or nail

Procedure

1. If watch has a sweep or large second hand, remove it. If delay time of more than one hour is required, also remove the minute hand. If hands are painted, carefully scrape paint from contact edge with knife.
2. Drill a hole through the crystal of the watch or pierce the crystal with a heated nail. The hole must be small enough that the screw can be tightly threaded into it.

3. Place the screw in the hole and turn down as far as possible without making contact with the face of the watch. If screw has a pointed tip, it may be necessary to grind the tip flat.

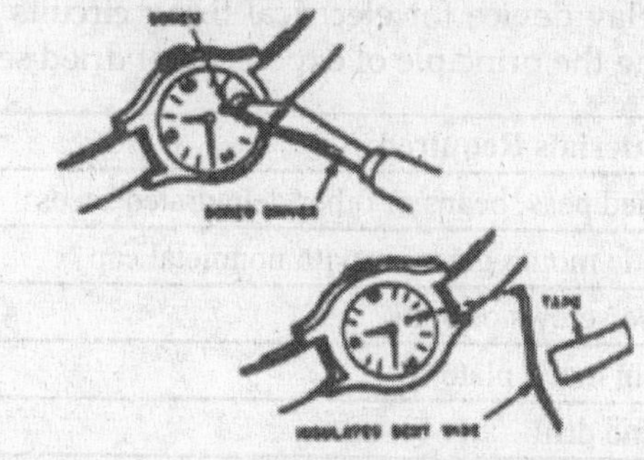

If no screw is available, pass bent stiff wire through the hole and tape to the crystal.

> **IMPORTANT**
> Check to make sure hand of watch cannot pass screw or wire without contacting it.

How to Use

1. Set the watch so that a hand will reach the screw or wire at the time you want the firing circuit completed.
2. Wind the watch.
3. Attach a wire from the case of the watch to one terminal of the battery.
4. Attach one wire from an electric initiator (blasting cap, squib, or alarm device) to the screw or wire on the face of the watch.
5. After thorough inspection is made to assure that the screw or the wire connected to it is not touching the face or case of the watch, attach the other wire from the initiator to the second terminal of the battery.

> **CAUTION**
> Follow step 5 carefully to prevent premature initiation.

6.5 NO-FLASH FUSE IGNITER

A simple no-flash fuse igniter can be made from common pipe fittings.

Materials Required
1/4 inch (6 mm) pipe cap
Solid 1/4 inch (6 mm) pipe plug
Flat head nail about 1/16 inch (1-1/2 mm) in diameter
Hand drill
Common "strike-anywhere" matches
Adhesive tape

Procedure

1. Screw the pipe plug tightly into the pipe cap.

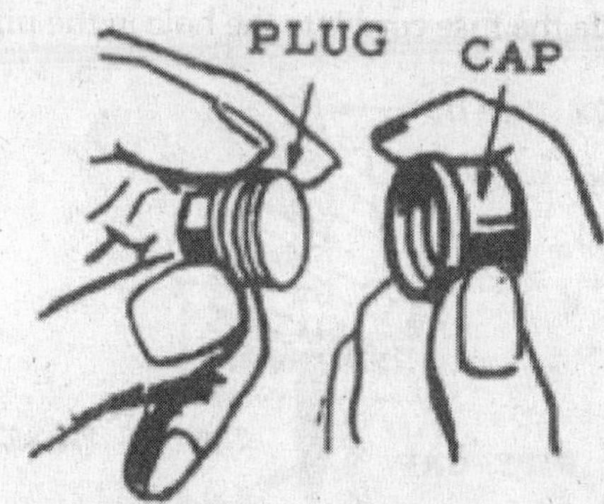

2. Drill hole completely through the center of the plug and cap large enough that the nail fits loosely.

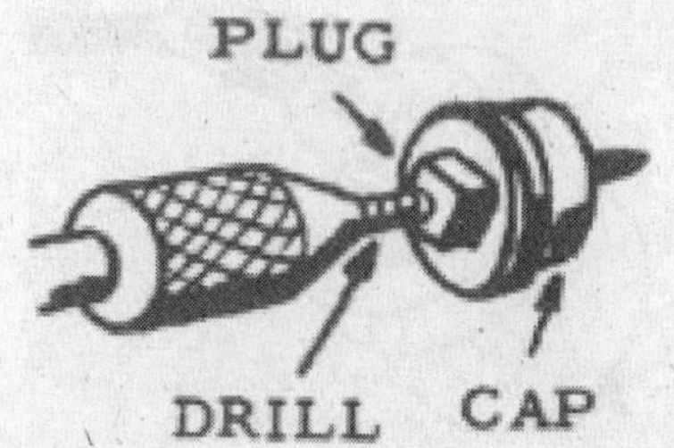

3. Enlarge the hole in the plug except for the last 1/8 inch (3 mm) so that the fuse cord will just fit.

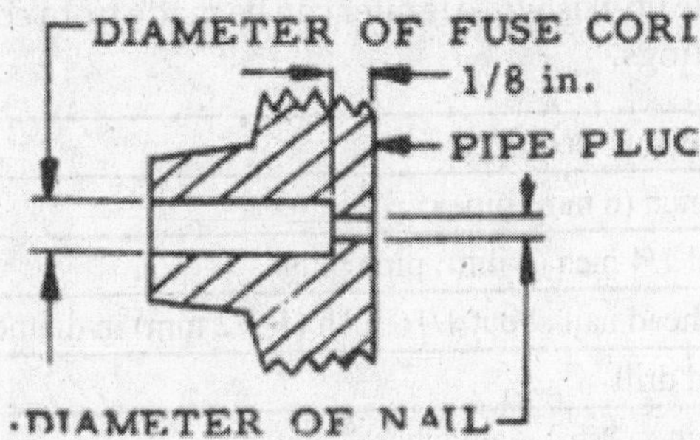

4. Remove the plug from the cap and push the flat head nail through the hole in the cap from the inside.

5. Cut the striking tips from approximately 10 "strike-anywhere" matches. Place match tips inside pipe cap and screw plug in finger tight.

How to Use

1. Slide the fuse cord into the hole in the pipe plug.

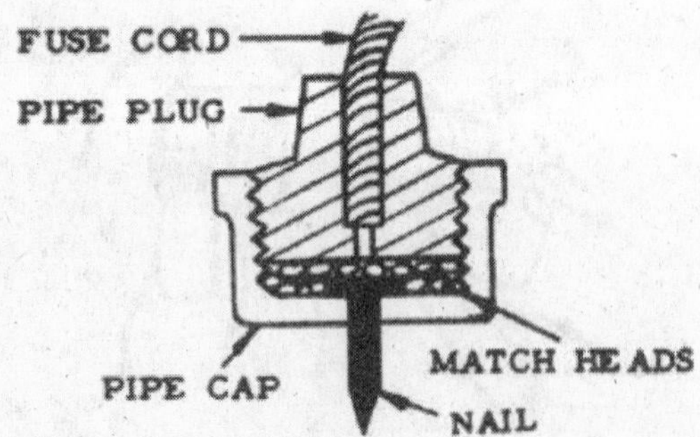

2. Tape igniter to fuse cord.

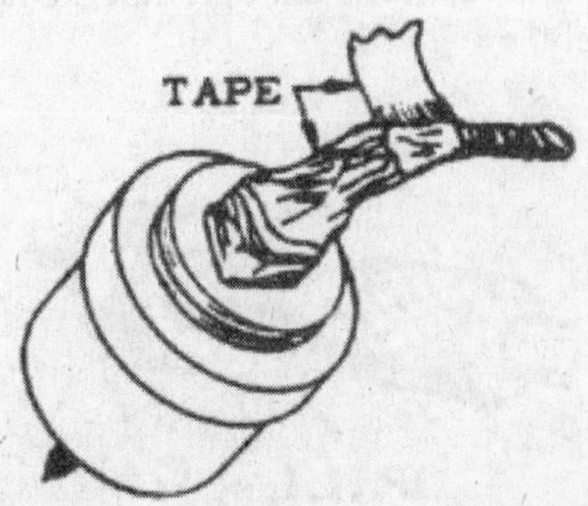

3. Tap point of nail on a hard surface to ignite the fuse.

6.6 DRIED SEED TIMER

A time delay device for electrical firing circuits can be made using the principle of expansion of dried seeds.

Materials Required
Dried peas, beans or other dehydrated seeds
Wide mouth glass jar with nonmetal cap
Two screws or bolts
Thin metal plate
Hand drill
Screwdriver

Procedure

1. Determine the rate of rise of the dried seeds selected. This is necessary to determine delay time of the timer.
   a. Place a sample of the dried seeds in the jar and cover with water.
   b. Measure the time it takes for the seeds to rise a given height. Most dried seeds increase 50% in one to two hours.
2. Cut a disc from thin metal plate. Disc should fit loosely inside the jar.

NOTE

If metal is painted, rusty or otherwise coated, it must be scraped or sanded to obtain a clean metal surface.

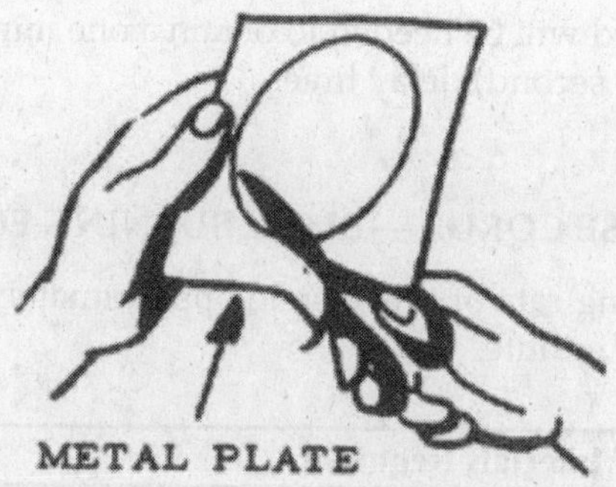

3. Drill two holes in the cap of the jar about 2 inches apart. Diameter of holes should be such that screws or bolts will thread tightly into them. If the jar has a metal cap or no cap, a piece of wood or plastic **(not metal)** can be used as a cover.

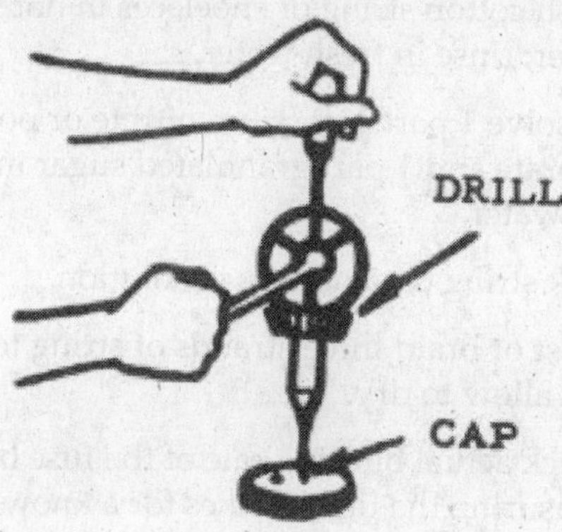

4. Turn the two screws or bolts through the holes in the cap. Bolts should extend about one inch (2-1/2 cm) into the jar.

IMPORTANT

Both bolts must extend the same distance below the container cover.

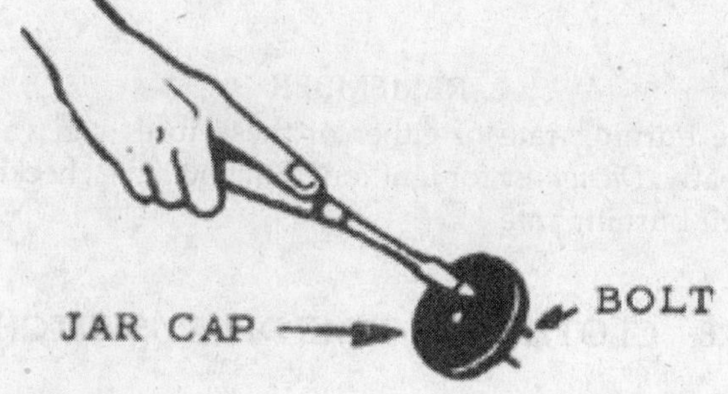

5. Pour dried seeds into the container. The level will depend upon the previously measured rise time and the desired delay.

6. Place the metal disc in the jar on top of the seeds.

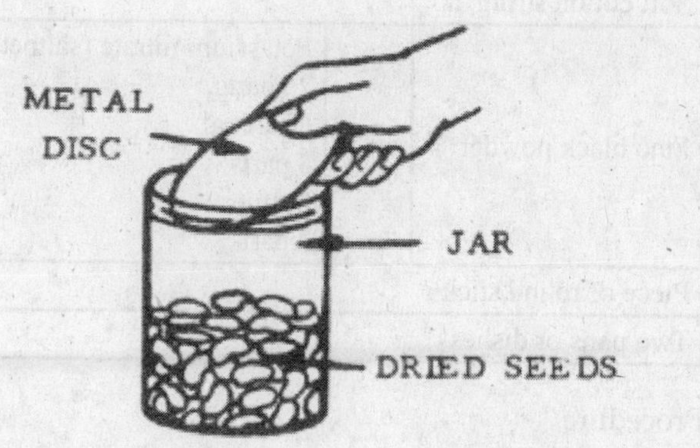

How to Use

1. Add just enough water to completely cover the seeds and place the cap on the jar.
2. Attach connecting wires from the firing circuit to the two screws on the cap.

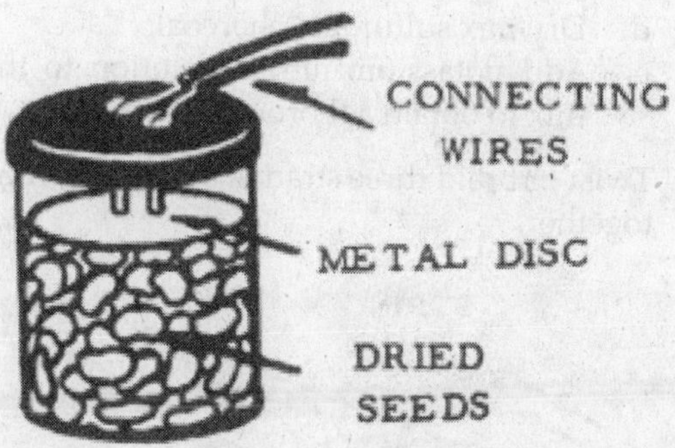

Expansion of the seeds will raise the metal disc until it contacts the screws and closes the circuit.

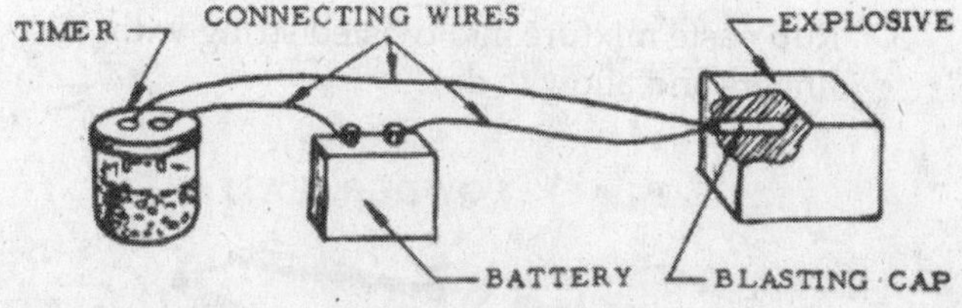

6.7 FUSE CORDS

These fuse cords are used for igniting propellants and incendiaries or, with a nonelectric blasting cap, to detonate explosives.

6.7.1 FUSE CORDS — FAST BURNING FUSE

The burning rate of this fuse is approximately 40 inches (100 cm) per minute.

Materials Required		
Soft cotton string		
Fine black powder	**or**	Potassium nitrate (saltpeter) 25 parts Charcoal 3 parts Sulfur 2 parts
Piece of round stick		
Two pans or dishes		

Procedure

1. Moisten fine black powder to form a paste or prepare a substitute as follows:
   a. Dissolve potassium nitrate in an equal amount of water.
   b. Pulverize charcoal by spreading thinly on a hard surface and rolling the round stick over it to crush to a fine powder.
   c. Pulverize sulfur in the same manner.
   d. Dry mix sulfur and charcoal.
   e. Add potassium nitrate solution to the dry mix to obtain a thoroughly wet paste.
2. Twist or braid three strands of cotton string together.

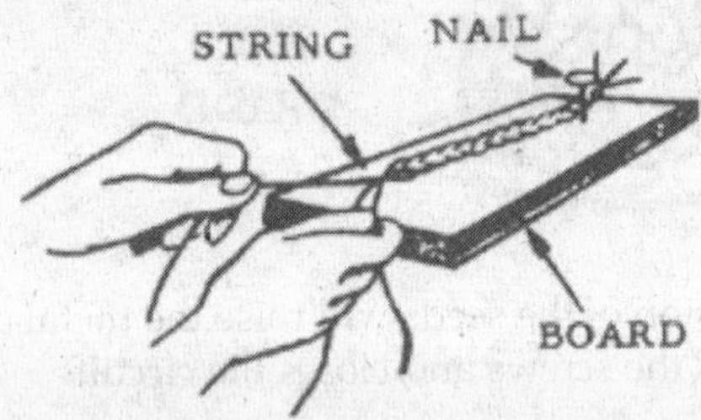

3. Rub paste mixture into twisted string with fingers and allow to dry.

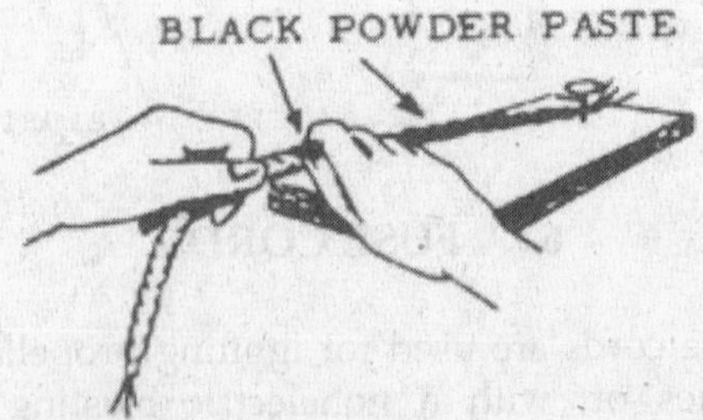

4. Check actual burning rate of fuse by measuring the time it takes for a known length to burn. This is used to determine the length needed for a desired delay time. If 5 inches (12-1/2 cm) burns for 6 seconds, 50 inches (125 cm) of fuse cord will be needed to obtain a one minute (60 second) delay time.

6.7.2 FUSE CORDS — SLOW BURNING FUSE

The burning rate of this fuse in approximately 2 inches (5 cm) per minute.

Materials Required
Cotton string or 3 shoelaces
Potassium nitrate or potassium chlorate
Granulated sugar

Procedure

1. Wash cotton string or shoelaces in hot soapy water; rinse in fresh water.
2. Dissolve 1 part potassium nitrate or potassium chlorate and 1 part granulated sugar in 2 parts hot water.
3. Soak string or shoelaces in solution.
4. Twist or braid three strands of string together and allow to dry.
5. Check actual burning rate of the fuse by measuring the time it takes for a known length to burn. This is used to determine the length needed for the desired delay time. If 2 inches (5 cm) burns for 1 minute, 10 inches (25 cm) will be needed to obtain a 5 minute delay.

NOTE

The last few inches of this cord (the end inserted in the material to be ignited) should be coated with the fast burning black powder paste if possible. This *must be done* when the fuse is used to ignite a blasting cap.

REMEMBER

The burning rate of either of these fuses can vary greatly. *Do not use* for ignition until you have checked their burning rate.

6.8 CLOTHESPIN TIME DELAY SWITCH

A 3 to 5 minute time delay switch can be made from the clothespin switch (section 7.1) and a cigarette. The system can be used for initiation of explosive charges, mines, and booby traps.

Materials Required
Spring type clothespin
Solid or stranded copper wire about 1/16 inch (2 mm) in diameter (field or bell wire is suitable)
Fine string, about 6 inches in length
Cigarette
Knife

NOTE

Delay time may be adjusted by varying the burning length of the cigarette. Burning rate in still air is approximately 7 minutes per inch (2.5 cm). Since this rate varies with environment and brand of cigarette, it should be tested in each case if accurate delay time is desired.

Procedure

1. Strip about 4 inches (10 cm) of insulation from the ends of 2 copper wires. Scrape copper wires with pocket knife until metal is shiny.

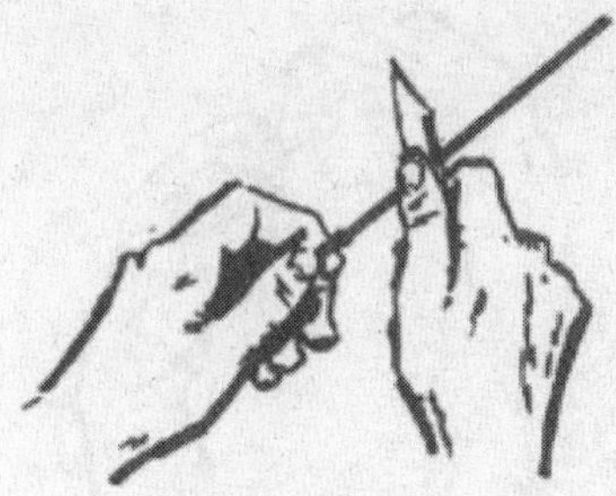

2. Wind one scraped wire tightly on one jaw of the clothespin, and the other wire on the other jaw so that the wires will be in contact with each other when the jaws are closed.

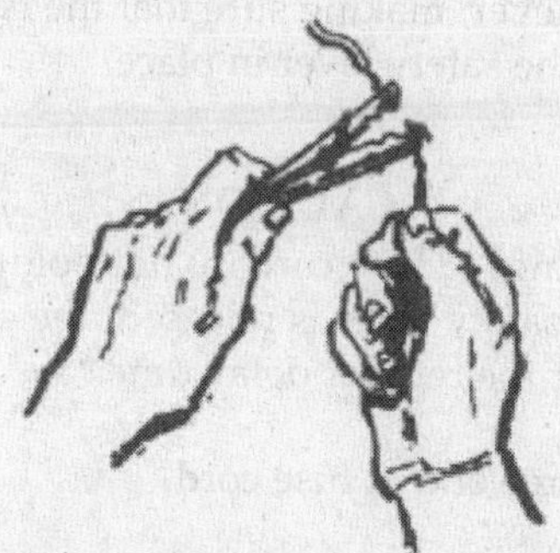

3. Measuring from tip of cigarette measure a length of cigarette that will correspond to the desired delay time. Make a hole in cigarette at this point, using wire or pin.

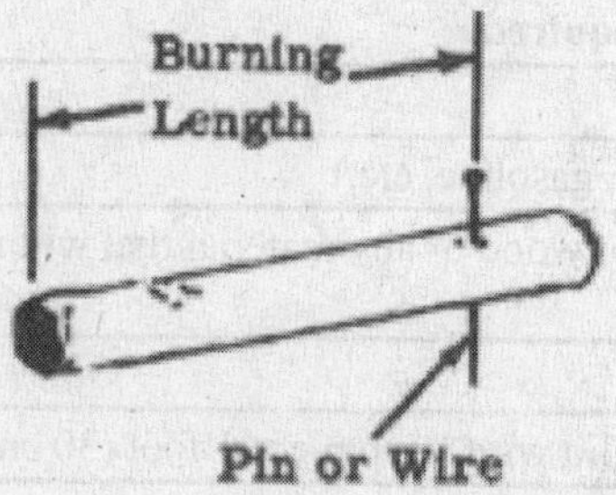

4. Thread string through hole in cigarette.

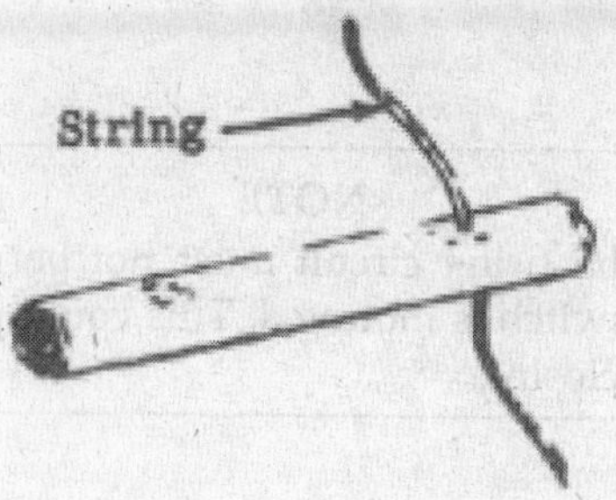

5. Tie string around rear of clothespin, 1/8 inch or less from end. The clothespin may be notched to hold the string in place.

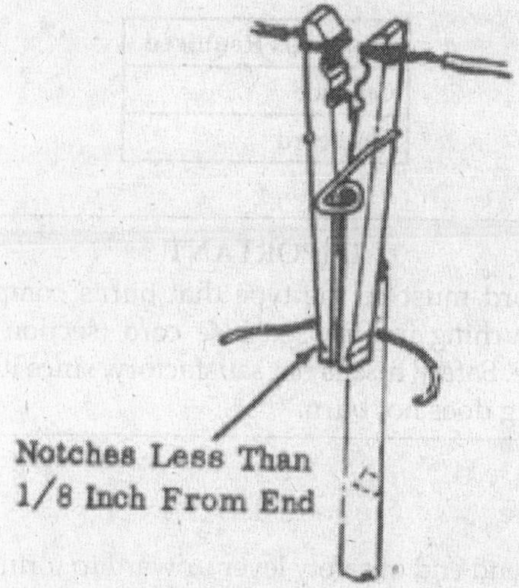

NOTE

The string must keep the rear end of the clothespin closed so that the jaws stay open and no contact is made between the wire.

How to Use

Suspend the entire system vertically with the cigarette tip down. Light tip of cigarette. Switch will close and initiation will occur when the cigarette burns up to and through the string.

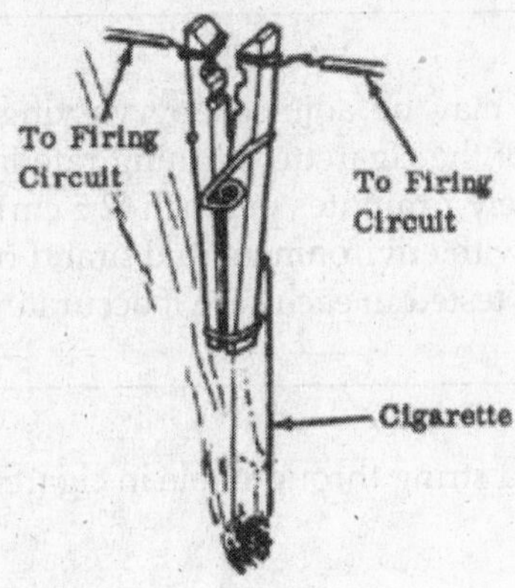

NOTE

Wires to the firing circuit must not be pulled taut when the switch is mounted. This could prevent the jaws from closing.

6.9 TIME DELAY GRENADE

This delay mechanism makes it possible to use an ordinary grenade as a time bomb.

Materials Required
Grenade
Fuse cord

IMPORTANT

Fuse cord must be the type that burns completely. Slow burning improvised fuse cord (section 6.7) is suitable. Safety fuse is not satisfactory, since its outer covering does not burn.

Procedure

1. Bend end of safety lever upward to form a hook. Make a single loop of fuse cord around the center of the grenade body and safety lever. Tie a knot of the nonslip variety at the safety lever.

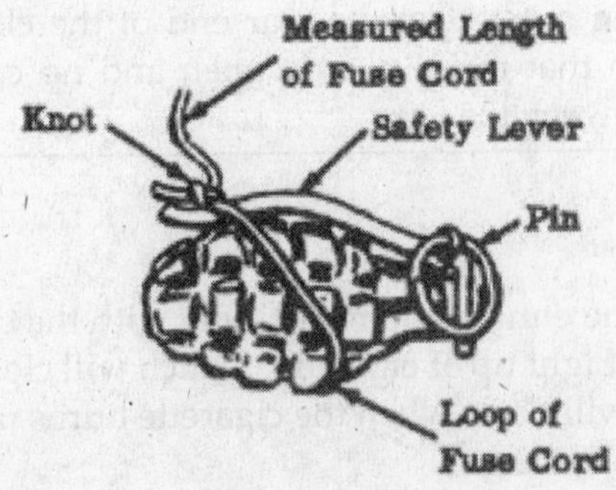

NOTE

The loop must be tight enough to hold the safety lever in position when the pin is removed.

2. Measuring from the knot along the free length of the fuse cord, measure off a length of fuse cord that will give the desired delay time. Cut off the excess fuse cord.

How to Use

1. Place hand around grenade and safety lever so safety lever is held in place. Carefully remove pin.

2. Emplace grenade in desired location while holding grenade and safety lever.
3. Very carefully remove hand from grenade and safety lever, making sure that the fuse cord holds the safety lever in place.

CAUTION

If loop and knot of fuse cord do not hold for any reason and the safety lever is released, the grenade will explode after the regular delay time.

4. Light free end of fuse cord.

6.10 CAN-LIQUID TIME DELAY

A time delay device for electrical firing circuits can be made using a can and liquid.

Materials Required
Can
Liquid (water, gasoline, etc.)
Small block of wood or any material that will float on the liquid used
Knife
2 pieces of solid wire, each piece 1 foot (30 cm) or longer

Procedure

1. Make 2 small holes at opposite sides of the can very close to the top.

2. Remove insulation from a long piece of wire for a distance a little greater than the diameter of the can.

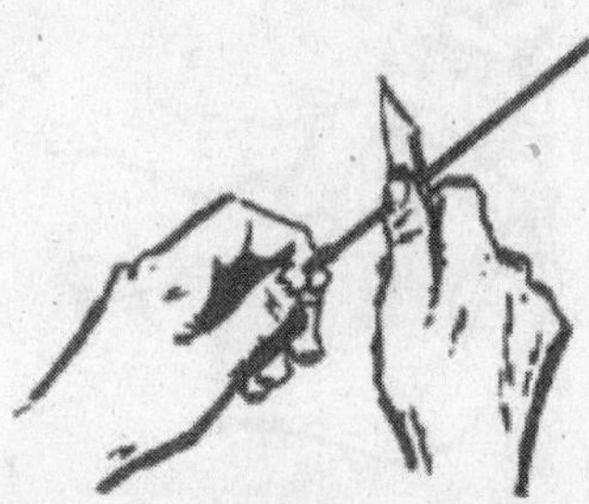

3. Secure the wire in place across the top of the can by threading it through the holes and twisting in place, leaving some slack. Make loop in center or wire. Be sure a long piece of wire extends from one end of the can.

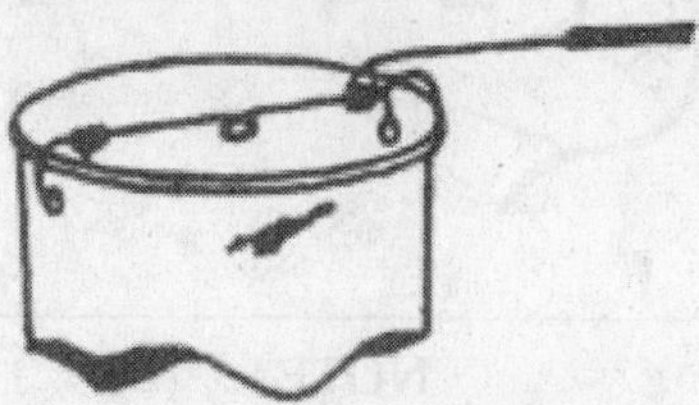

4. Wrap a piece of insulated wire around the block of wood. Scrape insulation from a small section of this wire and bend as shown so that wire contacts loop before wood touches bottom of container. Thread this wire through the loop of bare wire.

5. Make a very small hole (pinhole) in the side of the container. Fill container with a quantity of liquid corresponding to the desired delay time. Since the rate at which liquid leaves the can depends upon weather conditions, liquid used, size of hole, amount of liquid in the container, etc., determine the delay time for each individual case. Delays from a few minutes to many hours are possible. Vary time by adjusting liquid level, type of liquid (water, oil) and hole size.

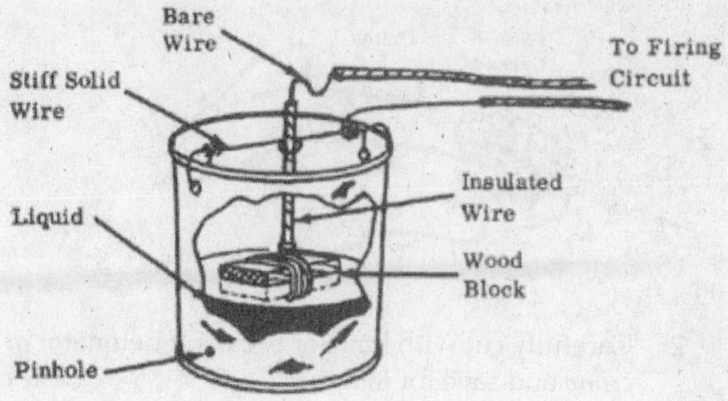

How to Use

1. Fill can with liquid to the same level as during experimental run (step 5 above). Be sure that wooden block floats on liquid and that wire is free to move down as liquid leaves container.

2. Connect wires to firing circuit.

> **NOTE**
>
> A long term delay can be obtained by placing a volatile liquid (gasoline, ether, etc.) in the can instead of water and relying on evaporation to lower the level. Be sure that the wood will float on the liquid used. **Do not make pinhole in side of can!**

6.11 SHORT TERM TIME DELAY FOR GRENADE

A simple modification can produce delays of approximately 12 seconds for grenades when fired from Grenade Launchers (section 4.5).

Materials Required	
Grenade	
Nail	
Knife	May not be needed
Pliers	
Safety fuse	

> **NOTE**
>
> Any safety or improvised fuse may be used. However, since different time delays will result, determine the burning rate of the fuse first.

Procedure

1. Unscrew fuse mechanism from body of grenade and remove. Pliers may have to be used.

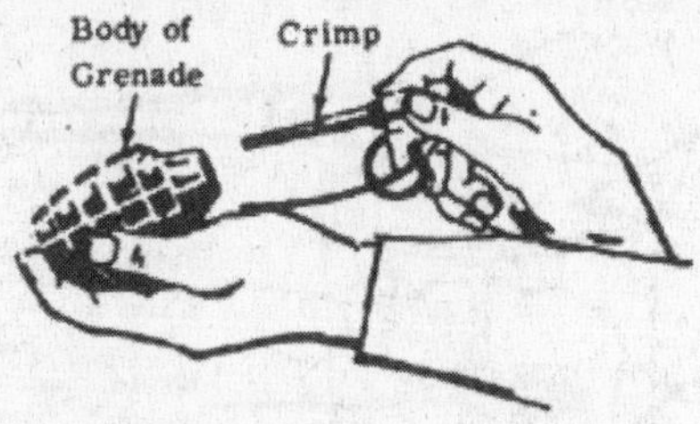

2. Carefully cut with knife or break off detonator *at crimp* and save for later use.

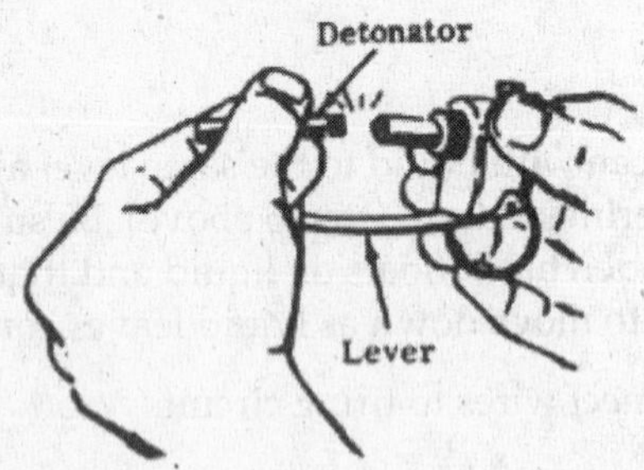

CAUTION

If detonator is cut or broken below the crimp, detonation may occur and severe injuries could result.

3. Remove safety pin pull ring and lever, letting striker hit the primer. Place fuse mechanism aside until delay fuse powder mix in mechanism is completely burned.

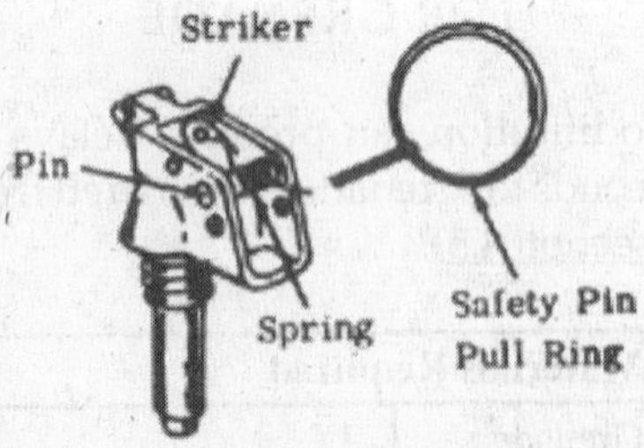

4. Remove pin, spring, and striker.

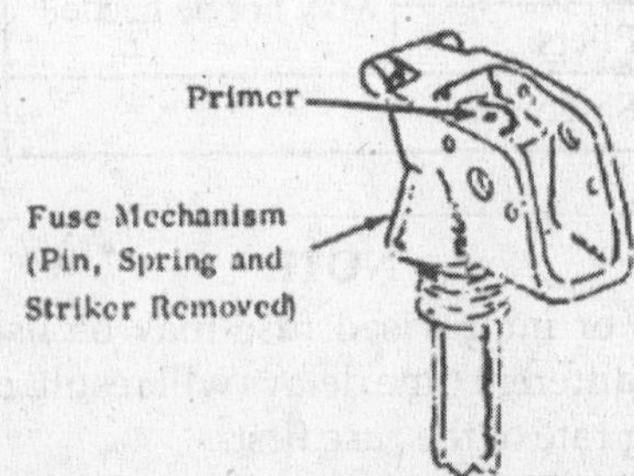

5. Remove primer from fuse mechanism by pushing nail through *bottom* end of primer hole and tapping with hammer.

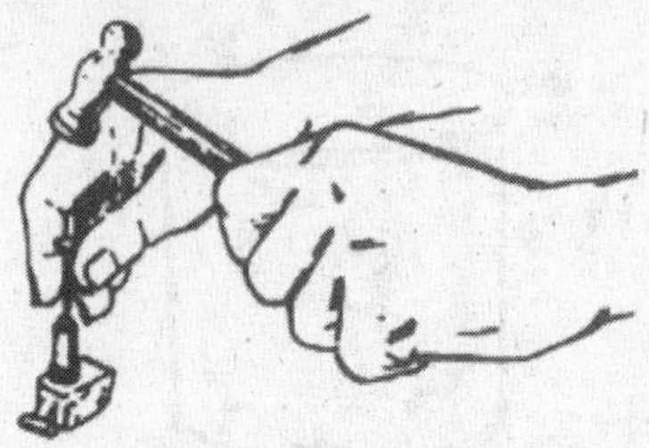

6. Insert safety fuse through top of primer hole. Enlarge hole if necessary. The fuse should go completely through the hole.

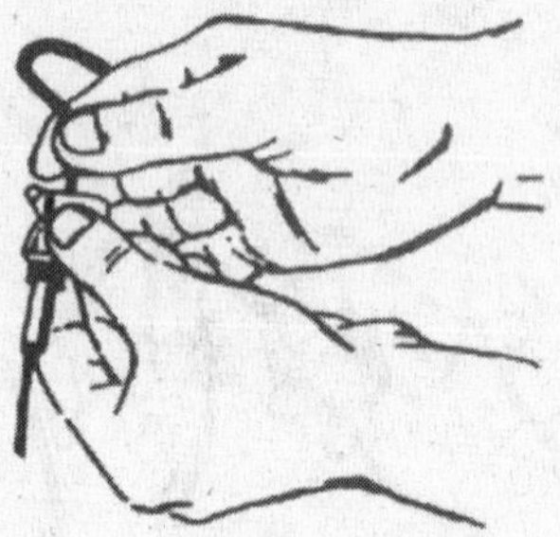

7. Insert fuse into detonator and tape it securely to modified fuse mechanism.

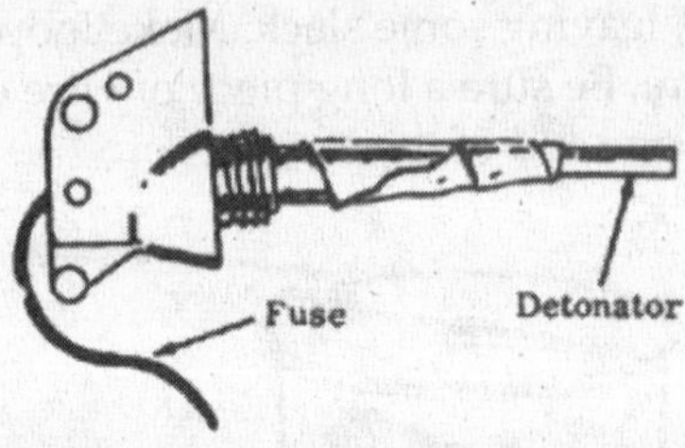

NOTE

Be sure that fuse rests firmly against detonator at all times.

8. Screw modified fuse mechanism back into grenade. Grenade is now ready for use.

NOTE

If time delay is used for Improvised Grenade Launchers (section 4.5):

1. Wrap tape around safety fuse.
2. Securely tape fuse to grenade.
3. Load grenade in launcher. Grenade will explode in approximately 12 seconds after safety fuse burns up to bottom of grenade.

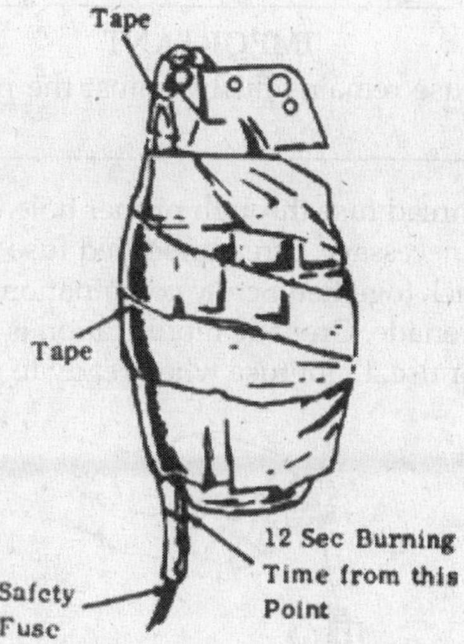

6.12 LONG TERM TIME DELAY FOR GRENADE

A simple modification can produce delays of approximately 20 seconds for grenades when fired from Grenade Launchers (section 4.5).

Materials Required
Grenade
Nail
"Strike-anywhere" matches, 6 to 8
Pliers (may not be needed)
Knife or sharp cutting edge
Piece of wood
Safety fuse

NOTE
Any safety or improvised fuse may be used. However, since different time delays will result, determine the burning rate of the fuse first.

Procedure

1. Unscrew fuse mechanism from body of grenade and remove. Pliers may have to be used.

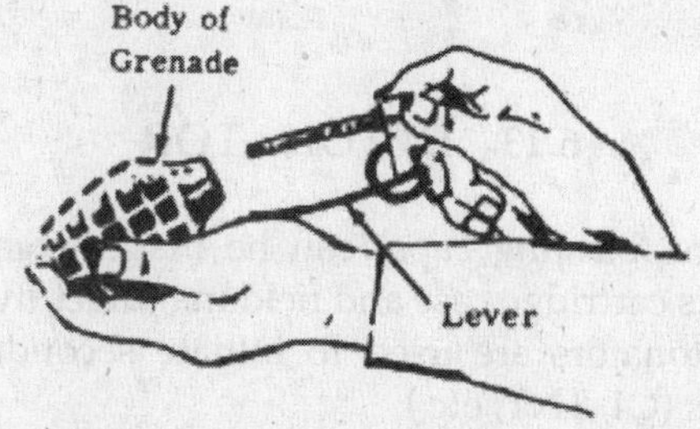

2. Insert nail completely through safety hole (hole over primer).
3. Carefully remove safety pin pull ring and lever, and allow striker to hit nail.

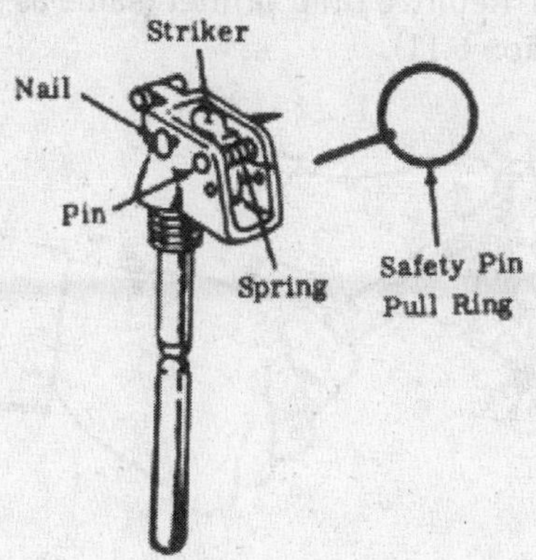

CAUTION
If for any reason, striker should hit primer instead of nail, detonator will explode after (4–5 second) delay time.

4. Push pin out and remove spring and striker. Remove nail.

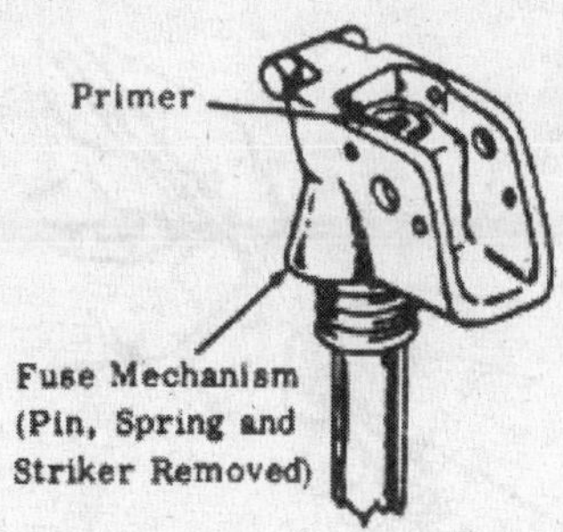

5. Carefully remove top section of fuse mechanism from bottom section by unscrewing. Pliers may have to be used.

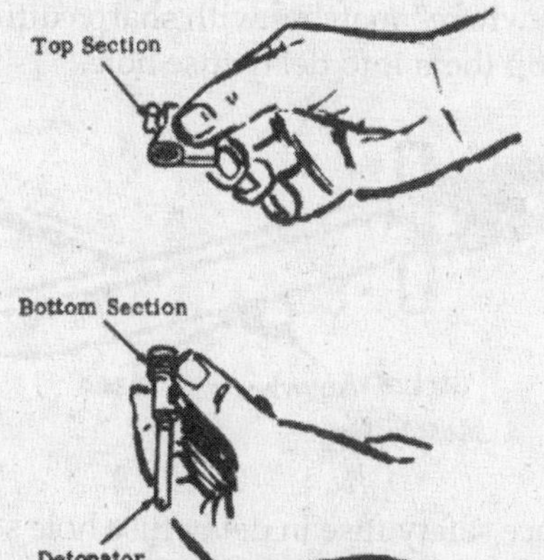

CAUTION

Use extreme care—sudden shock may set off detonator.

6. Fire primer by hitting nail placed against top of it. Remove fired primer (same as step 5 of section 6.11).

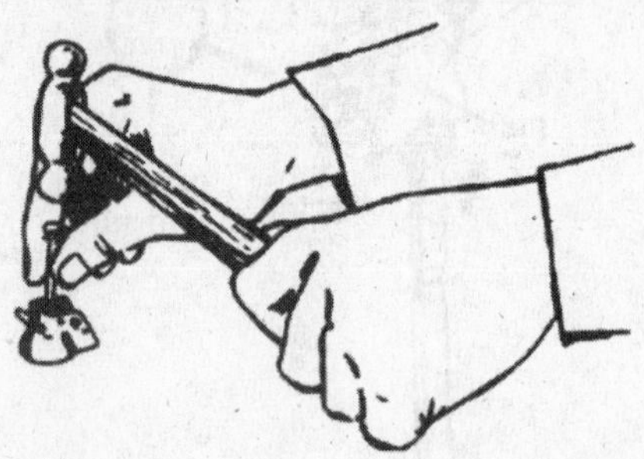

CAUTION

Do not hold assembly in your hand during above operation, as serious burns may result.

7. Scrape delay fuse powder with a sharpened stick. Loosen about 1/4 inch (6 mm) of powder in cavity.

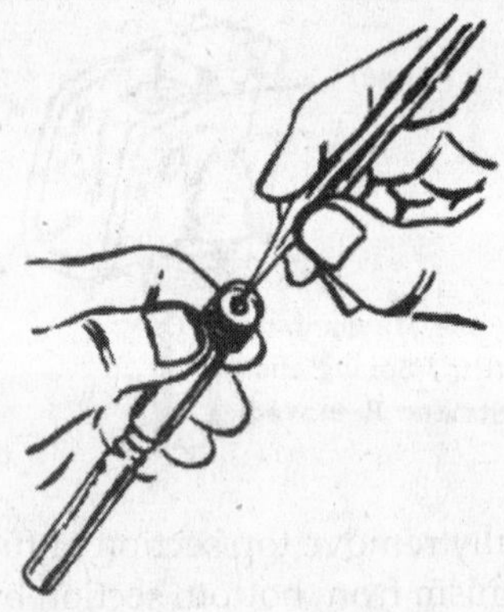

8. Cut off tips (not whole head) of 6 "strike-anywhere" matches with sharp cutting edge. Drop them into delay fuse hole.

9. Place safety fuse in delay fuse hole so that it is flush against the match tips.

IMPORTANT

Be sure fuse remains flush against the match tips at all times.

10. Thread fuse through primer hole. Enlarge hole if necessary. Screw modified fuse mechanism back together. Screw combination back into grenade. Grenade modification is now ready for use. Light fuse when ready to use.

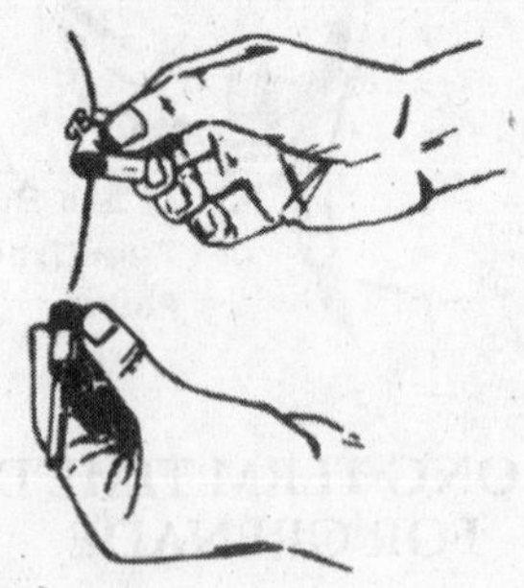

NOTE

If time delay is used for Improvised Grenade Launchers (section 4.5):

1. Wrap tape around safety fuse.
2. Securely tape fuse to grenade.
3. Load grenade in launcher. Grenade will explode in approximately 20 seconds after safety fuse burns up to bottom of grenade.

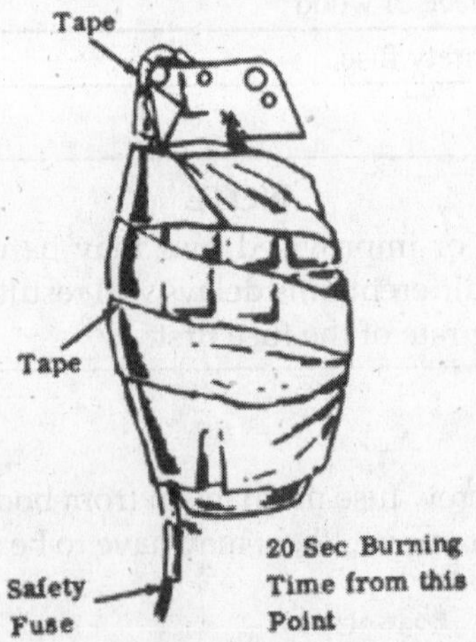

6.13 DETONATOR

Detonators (blasting caps) can be made from a used small arms cartridge case and field manufactured explosives. Detonators are used to initiate secondary high explosives (C4, TNT, etc.).

Materials Required	Source
Primary explosive	See table
Booster explosive	RDX (section 1.15) or picric acid (section 1.21)
Improvised scale	Section 7.8
Used cartridge case	.22 caliber or larger
Fuse, 12 inches long	
Round wooden stick (small enough just to fit in the neck of the cartridge case)	
Drill or knife	
Long nail with sharpened end	
Vise	
Improvised loading fixture	

Procedure

1. Remove fired primer from a used cartridge case using a sharpened nail. (See section 3.5.)
2. If necessary, open out flash hole in the primer pocket using a drill or knife. Make it large enough to receive fuse.

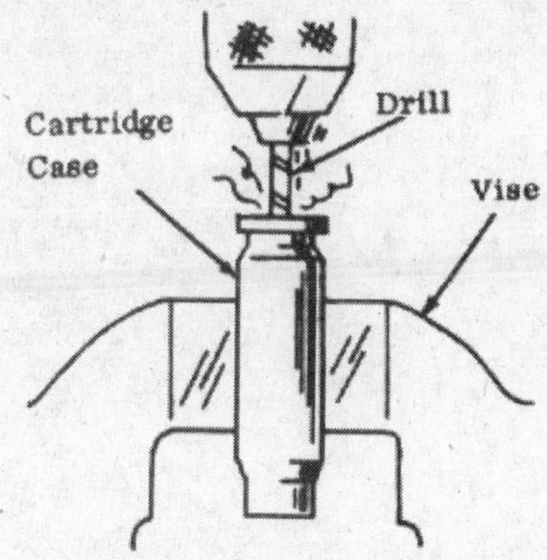

3. Place one end of fuse in the flash hole and extend it through the case until it becomes exposed at the open end. Knot this end and then pull fuse in cartridge case thus preventing fuse from falling out.

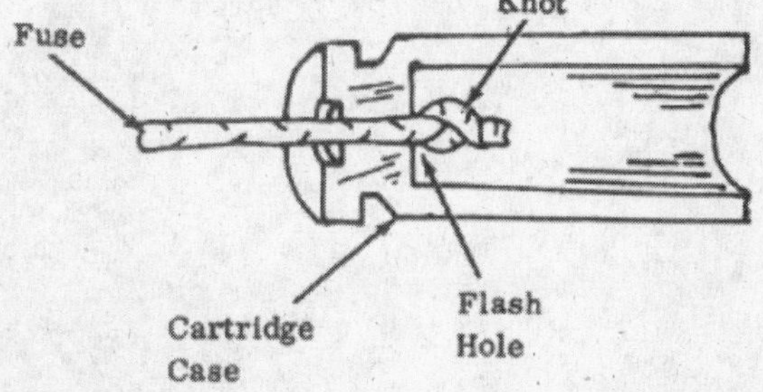

4. Load the primary explosive in the cartridge case, using the following table for the proper amount.

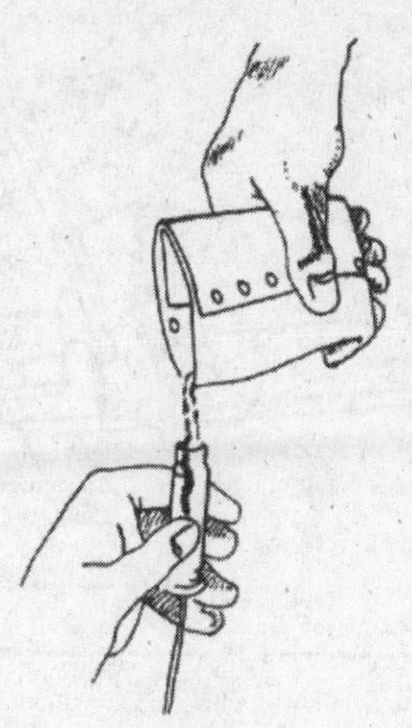

Primary Explosive	Primary Explosive Source	Minimum Weight*
Lead picrate**	Section 1.20	3 grams (3 handbook pages)
TACC (tetramminecopper chlorate)	Section 1.16	1 gram (1 handbook page)
DDNP (diazodinitrophenol)	Section 1.19	0.5 gram (1/2 handbook page)
Mercury fulminate	Section 1.24	0.75 gram (3/4 handbook page)
HMTD	Section 1.17	
Double salts	Section 1.22	

*See section 7.8 for details on improvised scale.
**.22 caliber cartridge case cannot be used with lead picrate as there is not enough volume to contain the explosive train.

5. Compress the primary explosive into the cartridge case with the wooden stick and the following improvised loading fixture.

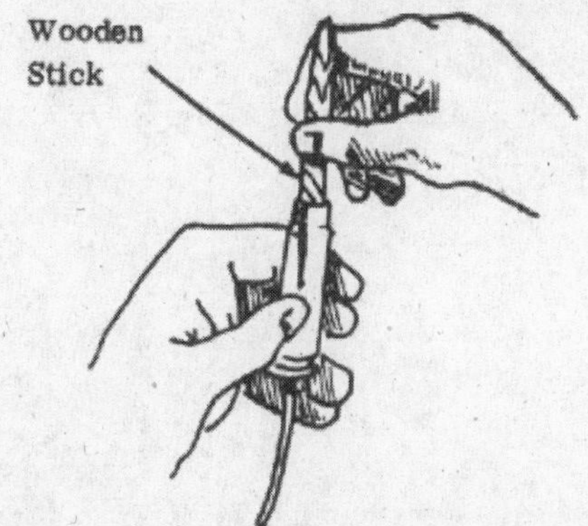

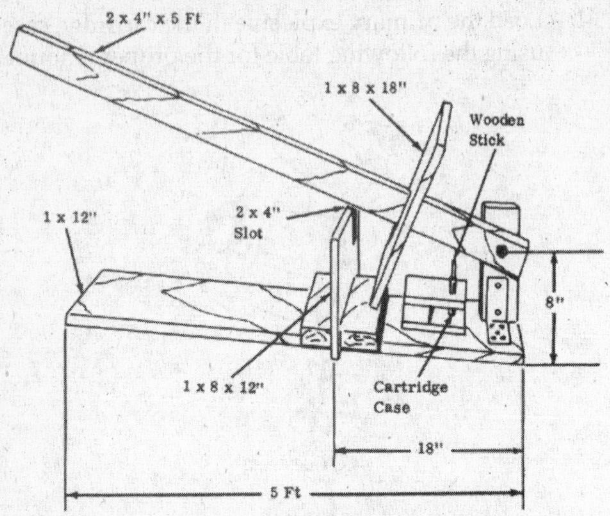

CAUTION
The primary explosive is shock and flame sensitive.

NOTE
Tamping is not needed when TACC is used.

6. Add one gram of booster explosive. The booster can be RDX (section 1.15), or picric acid (section 1.21).
7. Compress the booster explosive into the cartridge case with wooden stick and the loading fixture.
8. If the case is not full, fill the remainder with the secondary explosive to be detonated.

CAUTION
Detonator has considerably more power than a military blasting cap and should be handled carefully.

SECTION 7

Miscellaneous

7.1 CLOTHESPIN SWITCH

A spring type clothespin is used to make a circuit closing switch to actuate explosive charges, mines, booby traps and alarm systems.

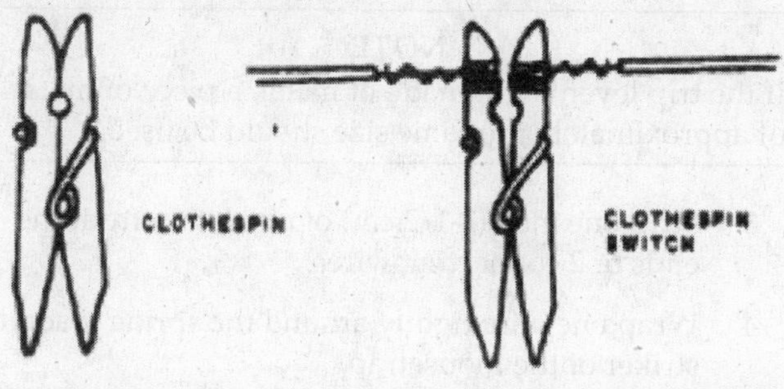

Materials Required
Spring type clothespin
Solid copper wire, 1/16 inch (2 mm) in diameter
Strong string on wire
Flat piece of wood (roughly 1/8 inch × 1 inch × 2 inches)
Knife

Procedure

1. Strip four inches (10 cm) of insulation from the ends of 2 solid copper wires. Scrape copper wires with pocket knife until metal is shiny.

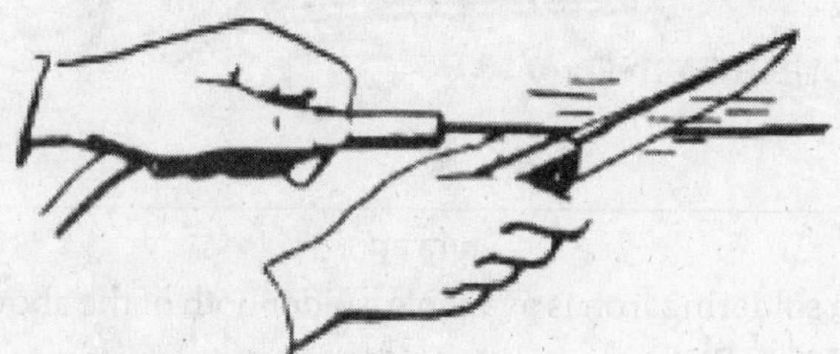

2. Wind one scraped wire tightly on one jaw of the clothespin, and the other wire on the other jaw.

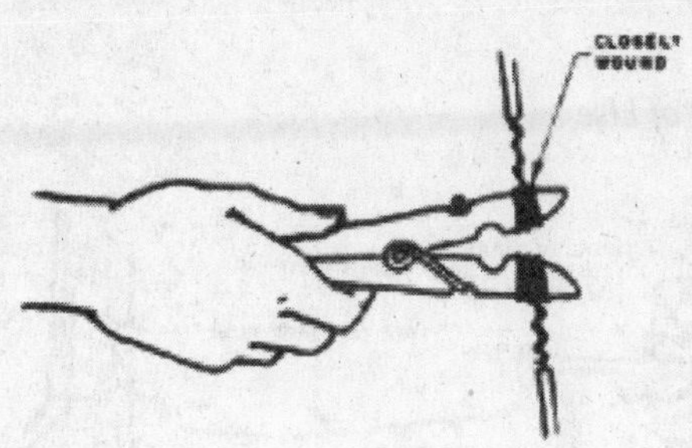

3. Make a hole in one end of the flat piece of wood using a knife, heated nail or drill. Tie strong string or wire through the hole.

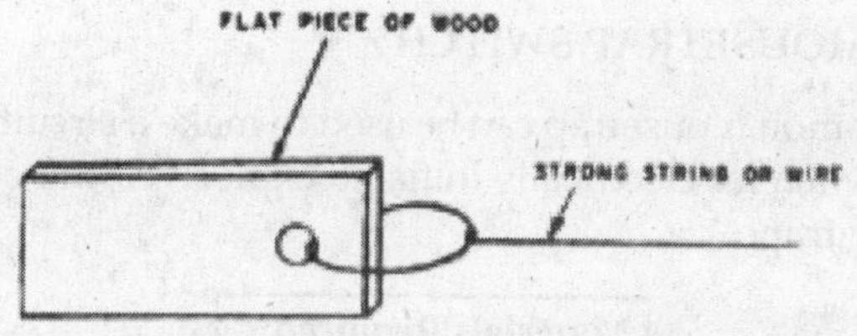

4. Place flat piece of wood between jaws of the clothespin switch.

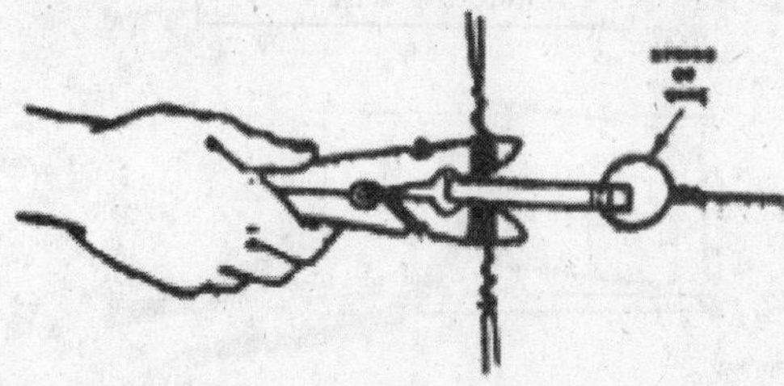

Basic Firing Circuit

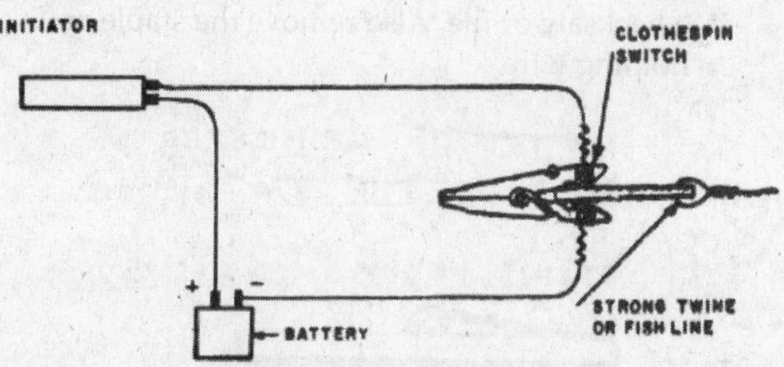

When the flat piece of wood is removed by pulling the string, the jaws of the clothespin will close completing the circuit.

> **CAUTION**
> Do not attach the battery until the switch and trip wire have been emplaced and examined. Be sure the flat piece of wood is separating the jaws of the switch.

A Method of Use

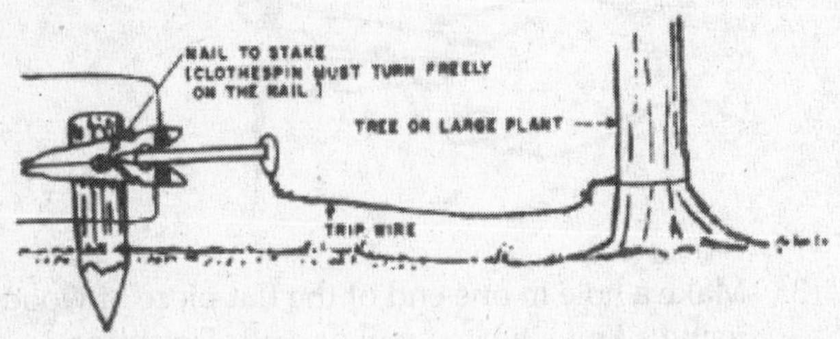

7.2 MOUSETRAP SWITCH

A common mousetrap can be used to make a circuit closing switch for electrically initiated explosives, mines and booby traps.

Materials Required
Mousetrap
Hacksaw or file
Connecting wires

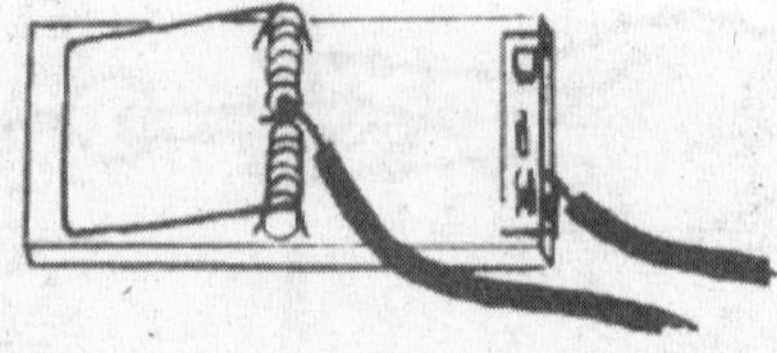

Procedure

1. Remove the trip lever from the mousetrap using a hacksaw or file. Also remove the staple and holding wire.

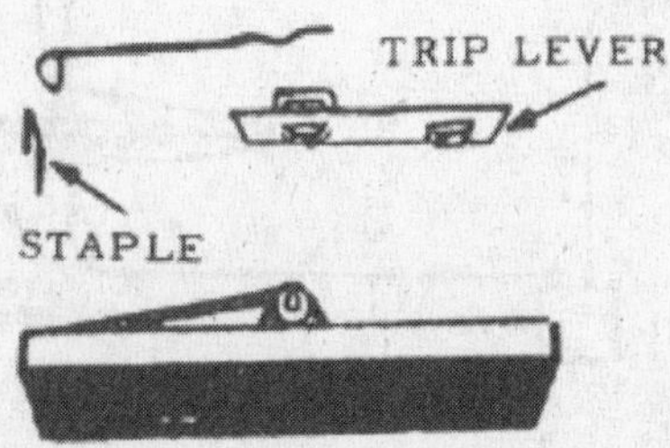

2. Retract the striker of the mousetrap and attach the trip lever across the end of the wood base using the staple with which the holding wire was attached.

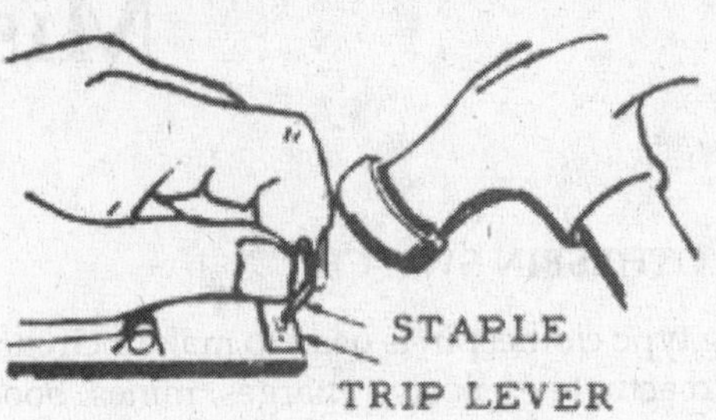

> **NOTE**
> If the trip lever is not made of metal, a piece of metal of approximately the same size should be used.

3. Strip one inch (2-1/2 cm) of insulation from the ends of 2 connecting wires.
4. Wrap one wire tightly around the spring loaded striker of the mousetrap.

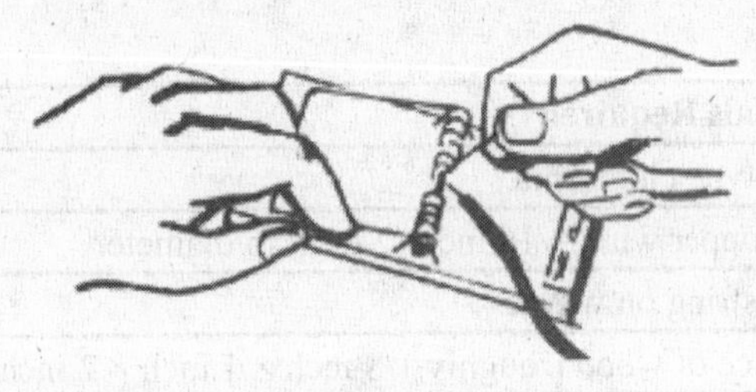

5. Wrap the second wire around some part of the trip lever or piece of metal.

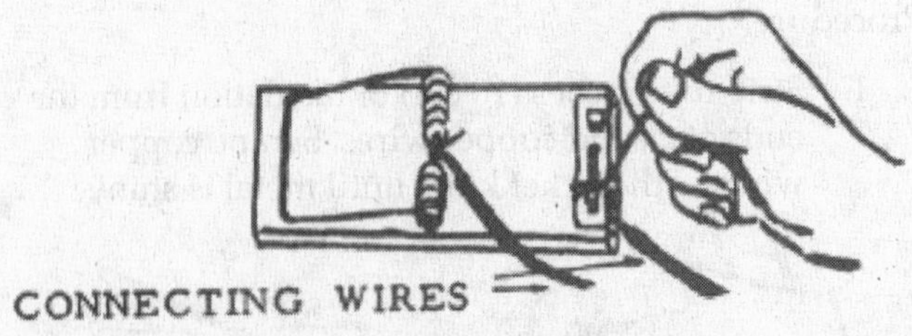

> **NOTE**
> If a soldering iron is available, solder both of the above wires in place.

How to Use

This switch can be used in a number of ways—one typical method is presented here.

The switch is placed inside a box which also contains the explosive and batteries. The spring loaded striker is held back by the lid of the box and when the box is opened the circuit is closed.

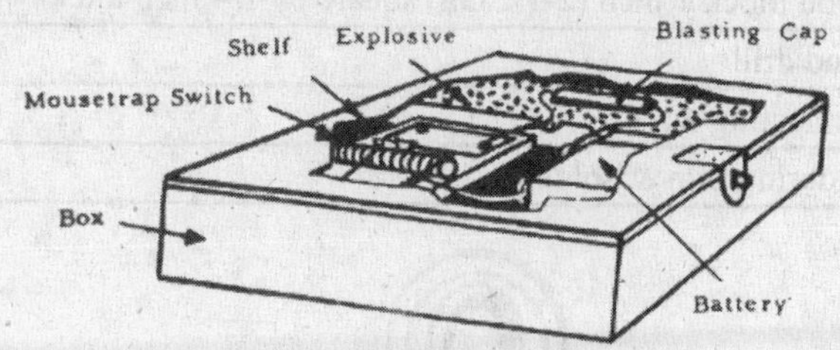

7.3 FLEXIBLE PLATE SWITCH

This pressure sensitive switch is used for initiating emplaced mines and explosives.

Materials Required
Two flexible metal sheets: one approximately 10 inches (25 cm) square one approximately 10 inches × 8 inches (20 cm)
Piece of wood 10 inches square by 1 inch thick
Four soft wood blocks 1 inch × 1 inch × 1/4 inch
Eight flat head nails, 1 inch long
Connecting wires
Adhesive tape

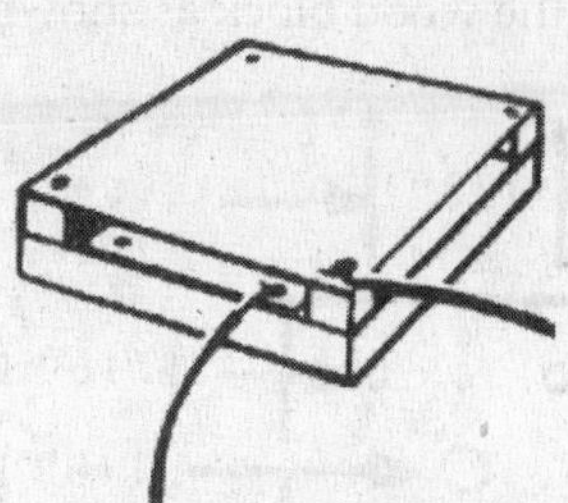

Procedure

1. Nail 10 inch × 8 inch metal sheet to 10 inches square piece of wood so that 1 inch of wood shows on each side of metal. Leave one of the nails sticking up about 1/4 inch.

2. Strip insulation from the end of one connecting wire. Wrap this end around the nail and drive the nail all the way in.

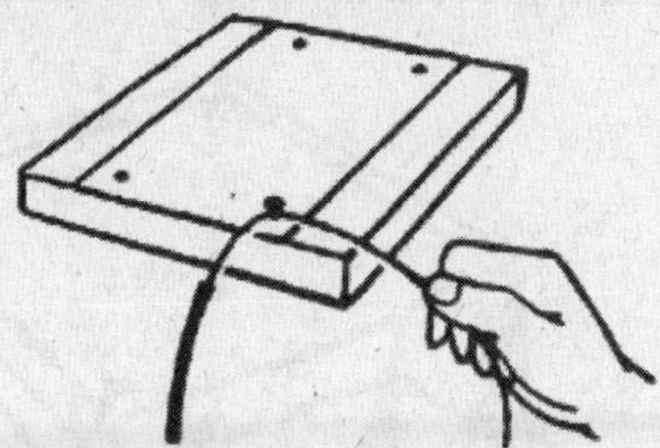

3. Place the four wood blocks on the corners of the wood base.

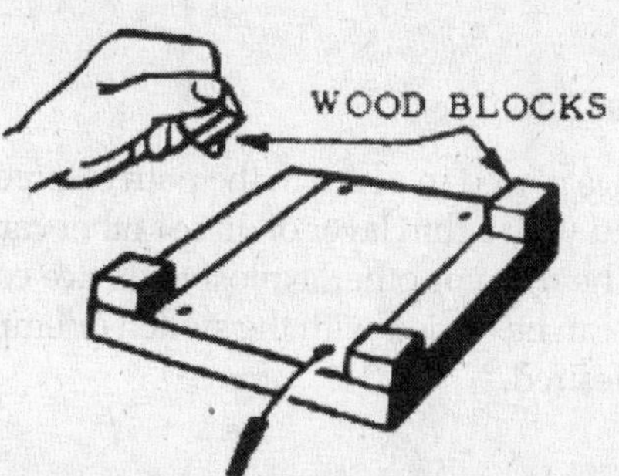

4. Place the 10 inch square flexible metal sheet so that it rests on the blocks in line with the wood base.

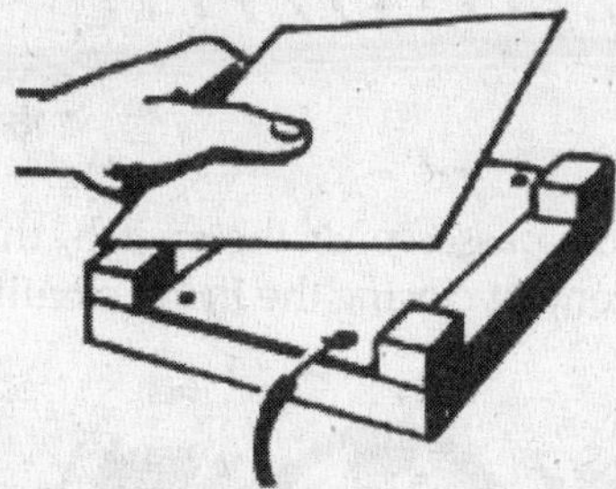

5. Drive four nails through the metal sheet and the blocks to fasten to the wood base. A second connecting wire is attached to one of the nails as in step 2.

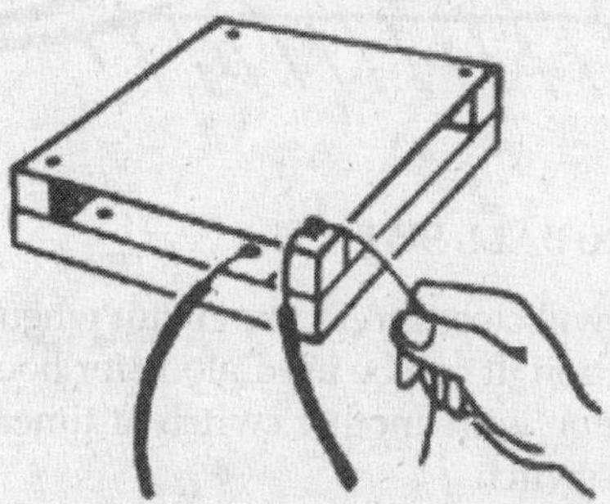

6. Wrap adhesive tape around the edges of the plate and wood base. This will assure that no dirt or other foreign matter will get between the plates and prevent the switch from operating.

How to Use

The switch is placed in a hole in the path of expected traffic and covered with a thin layer of dirt or other camouflaging material. The mine or other explosive device connected to the switch can be buried with the switch or emplaced elsewhere as desired.

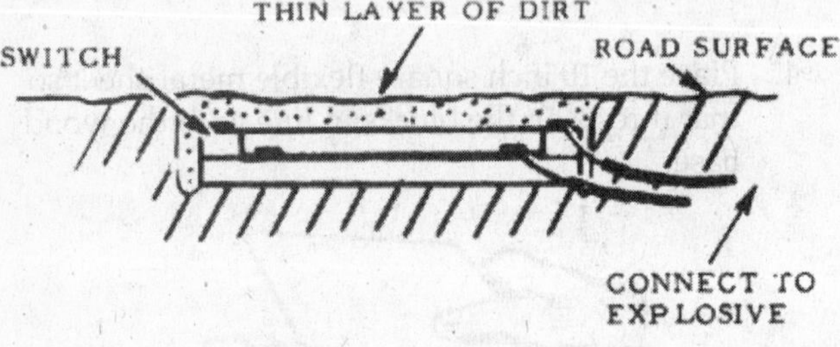

When a vehicle passes over the switch, the two metal plates make contact closing the firing circuit.

7.4 METAL BALL SWITCH

This switch will close an electric circuit when it is tipped in any direction. It can be used alone for booby traps or in combination with another switch or timer as an anti-disturbance switch.

Materials Required
Metal Ball 1/2 inch (1-1/4 cm) diameter (see note)
Solid copper wire 1/16 inch (1/4 cm) diameter
Wood block 1 inch (2-1/2 cm) square by 1/4 inch thick
Hand drill
Connecting wires
Soldering iron & solder

NOTE

If other than a 1/2 inch diameter ball is used, other dimension must be changed so that the ball will rest in the center hole of the block without touching either of the wires.

Procedure

1. Drill four 1/16 inch holes and one 1/8 inch hole through the wood block as shown.

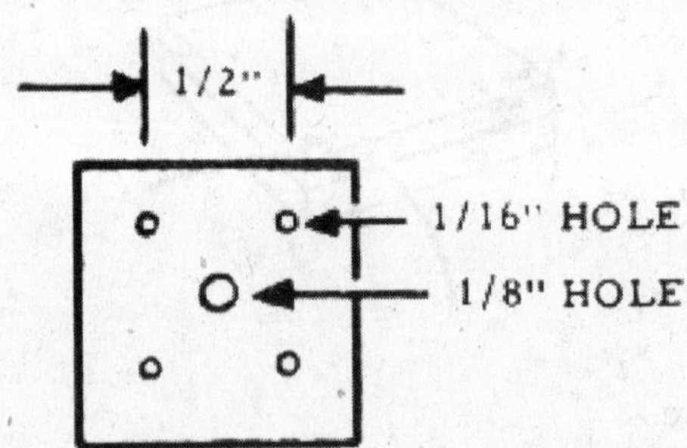

2. Form two "U" shaped pieces from 1/16 inch copper wire to the dimensions shown.

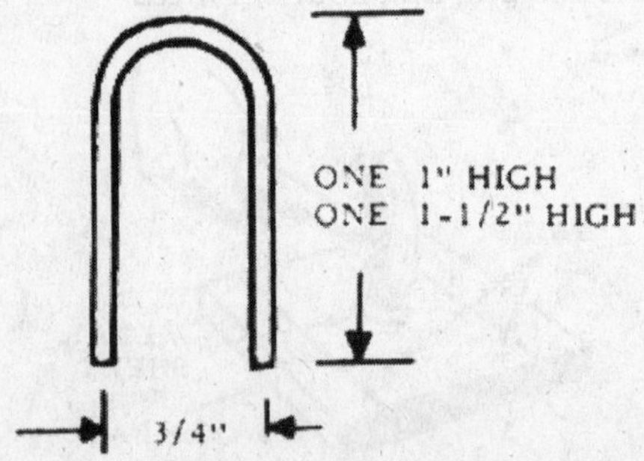

3. Wrap a connecting wire around one leg of each "U" at least 1/4 inch from the end and solder in place.

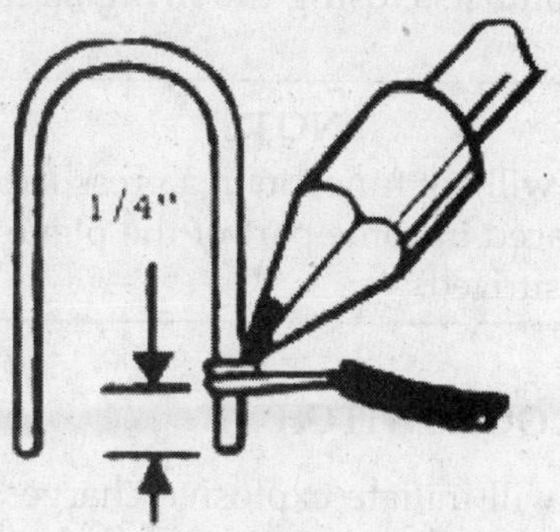

4. Place metal ball on block so that it rests in the center hole.

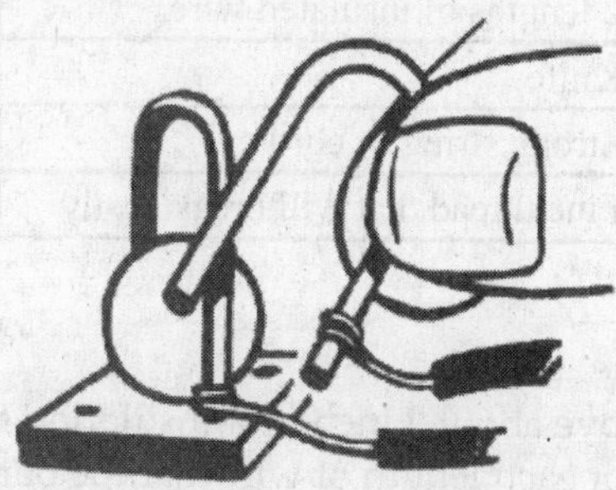

5. Insert the ends of the small "U" into two holes in thae block. Insert large "U" into the remaining two holes.

CAUTION
Make sure that the metal does not touch either "U" shaped wire when the switch is standing on its base. If the ball does touch, bend wires outward slightly.

How to Use

Mount switch vertically and connect in electrical firing circuit as with any other switch. When tipped in any direction it will close the circuit.

CAUTION
Switch must be mounted vertically and not disturbed while completing connections.

7.5 ALTIMETER SWITCH

This switch is designed for use with explosives placed on aircraft. It will close an electrical firing circuit when an altitude of approximately 5000 feet (1-1/2 km) is reached.

Materials Required
Jar or tin can
Thin sheet of flexible plastic or waxed paper
Thin metal sheet (cut from tin can)
Adhesive tape
Connecting wires

Procedure

1. Place sheet of plastic or waxed paper over the top of the can or jar and tape tightly to sides of container.

NOTE
Plastic sheet should not be stretched tight. A small depression should be left in the top.

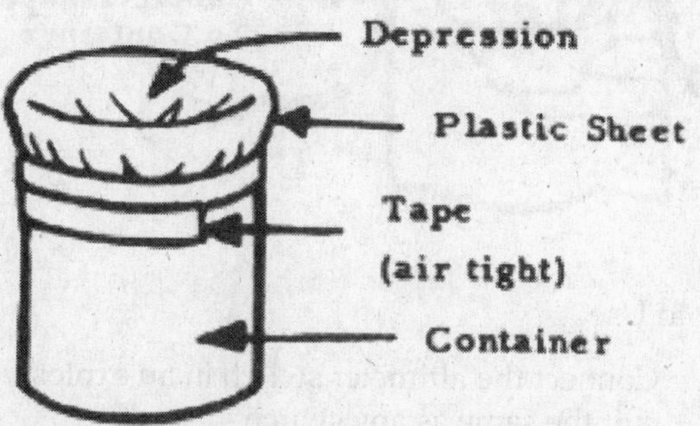

2. Cut two contact strips from thin metal and bend to the shapes shown.

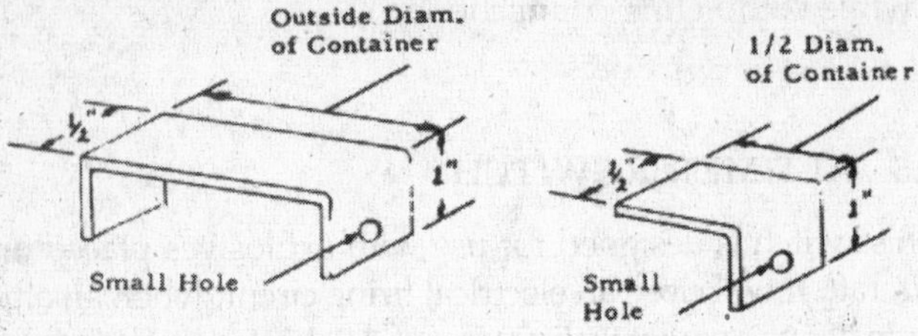

3. Strip insulation from the ends of two connecting wires. Attach one wire to each contact strip.

> **NOTE**
> If a soldering iron in available solder wires in place.

4. Place contact strips over container so that the larger contact is above the smaller with a very small clearance between the two.

5. Securely tape contact strips to sides of container.

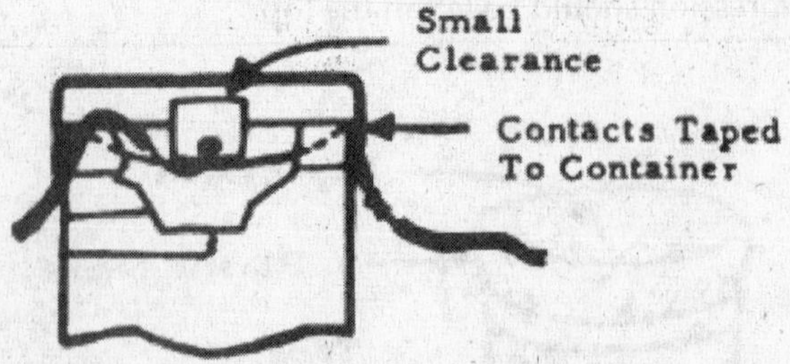

How to Use

1. Connect the altimeter switch in an explosive circuit the same as any switch.
2. Place the explosive package on airplane. As the plane rises the air inside the container will expand. This forces the plastic sheet against the contacts closing the firing circuit.

> **NOTE**
> The switch will not function in a pressurized cabin. It must be placed in some part of the plane which will not be pressurized.

7.6 PULL-LOOP SWITCH

This switch will initiate explosive charges, mines, and booby traps when the trip wire is pulled.

Materials Required
2 lengths of insulated wire
Knife
Strong string or cord
Fine thread that will break easily

Procedure

1. Remove about 2 inches of insulation from one end of each length of wire. Scrape bare wire with knife until metal is shiny.

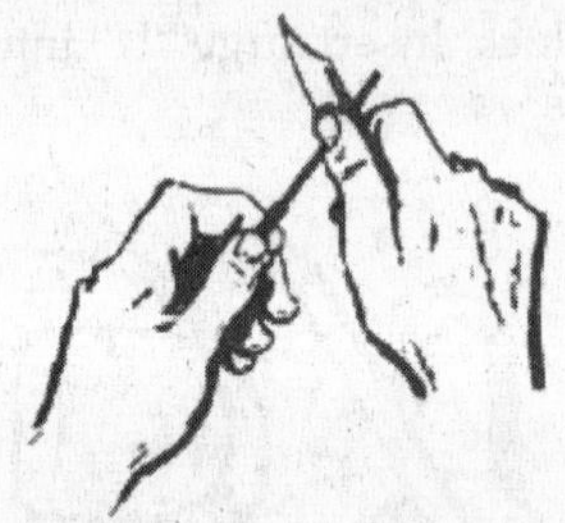

2. Make a loop out of each piece of bare wire.

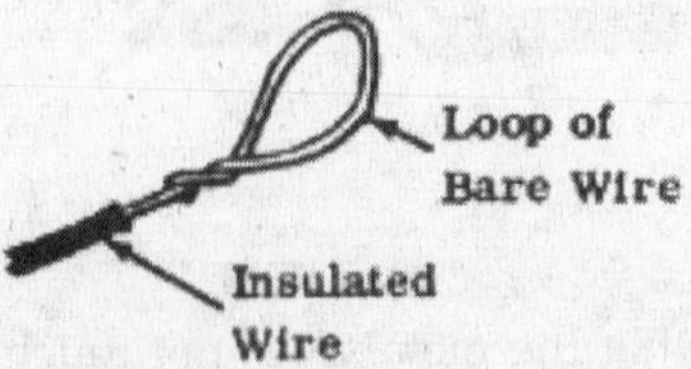

3. Thread each wire through the loop of the other wire so the wires can slide along each other.

NOTE
The loops should contact each other when the two wires are pulled taut.

How to Use

1. Separate loops by about 2 inches. Tie piece of fine thread around wires near each loop. Thread should be taut enough to support loops and wire, yet fine enough that it will break under a very slight pull.

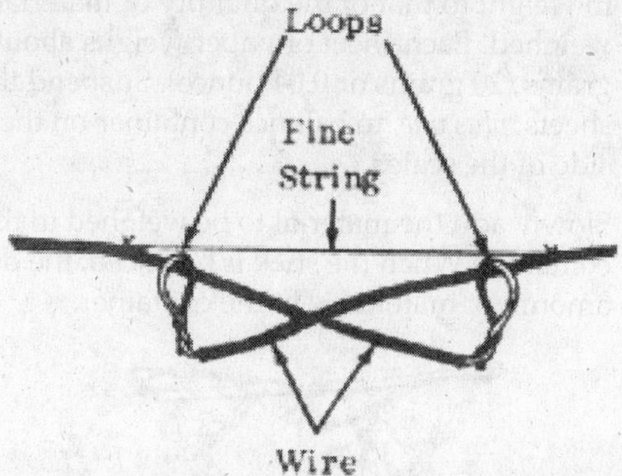

2. Fasten one wire to tree or stake and connect end to firing circuit.
3. Tie a piece of cord or string around the other piece of wire a few inches from the loop. Tie free end of cord around tree, bush, or stake. Connect the free end of the wire to the firing circuit. Initiation will occur when the tripcord is pulled.

CAUTION
Be sure that the loops do not contact each other when the wires are connected to the firing circuit.

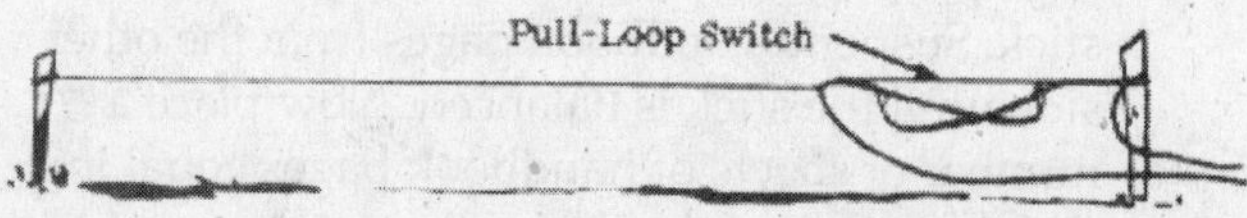

Other uses: The switch minus the fine thread may be used to activate a booby trap by such means as attaching it between the lid and a rigid portion of a box, between a door and a door jamb, and in similar manners.

7.7 KNIFE SWITCH

This device will close the firing circuit charges, mines, and booby traps when the trip wire is pulled or cut.

Materials Required
Knife or hack saw blade
6 nails
Strong string or light rope
Sturdy wooden board
Wire

Procedure

1. Place knife on board. Drive 2 nails into board on each side of knife handle so knife is held in place.
2. Drive one nail into board so that it touches blade of knife near the point.
3. Attach rope to knife. Place rope across path. Apply tension to rope, pulling knife blade away from nail slightly. Tie rope to tree, bush, or stake.
4. Drive another nail into board near the tip of the knife blade as shown below. Connect the two nails with a piece of conducting wire. Nail should be positioned so that it will contact the second nail when blade is pulled about 1 inch (2-1/2 cm) to the side.

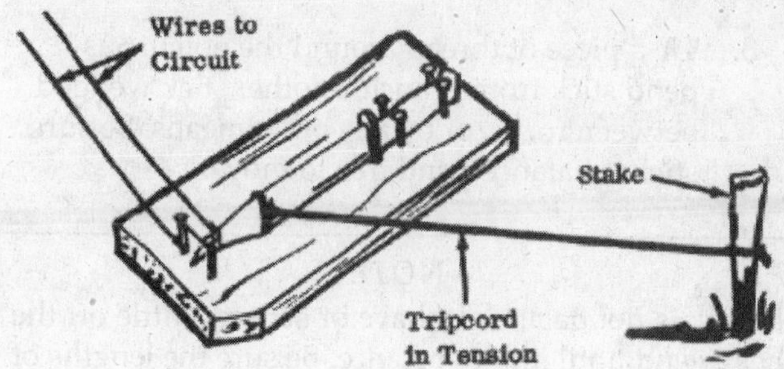

NOTE
Check position of nails to knife blade. The nails should be placed so that the knife blade will contact either one when the rope is pulled or released.

How to Use

Attach one wire from firing circuit to one of the nails and the other to the knife blade. The circuit will be completed when the tripcord is pulled or released.

7.8 IMPROVISED SCALE

This scale provides a means of weighing propellant and other items when conventional scales or balances are not available.

Materials Required
Pages from *Improvised Munitions Handbook*
Straight sticks about 1 foot (30 cm) long and 1/4 inch (5 mm) in diameter
Thread or fine string

Procedure

1. Make a notch about 1/2 inch (1 cm) from each end of stick. Be sure that the two notches are the same distance from the end of the stick.
2. Find the exact center of the stick by folding in half a piece of thread the same length as the stick and placing it alongside the stick as a ruler. Make a small notch at the center of the stick.

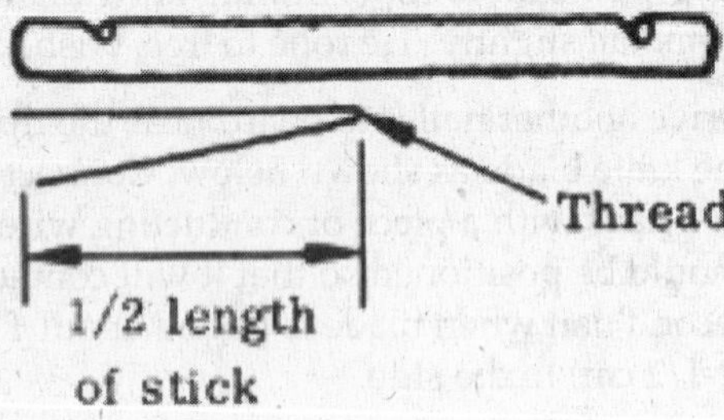

3. Tie a piece of thread around the notch. Suspend stick from branch, another stick wedged between rocks, or by any other means. Be sure stick is balanced and free to move.

NOTE
If stick is not balanced, shave or scrape a little off the heavy end until it does balance. Be sure the lengths of the arms are the same.

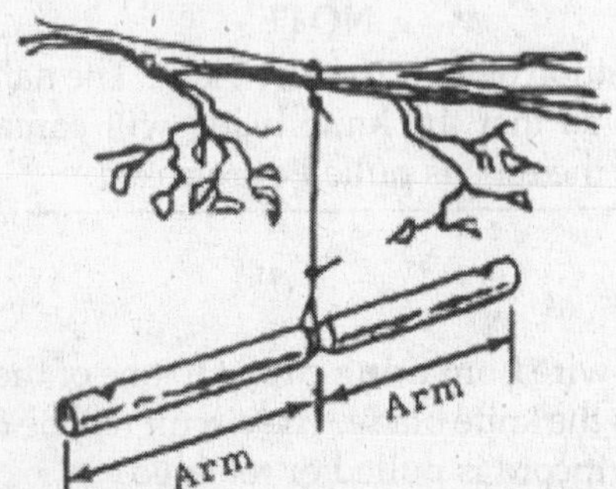

4. Make a container out of one piece of paper. This can be done by rolling the paper into a cylinder and folding up the bottom a few times.
5. Punch 2 holes at opposite sides of paper container. Suspend container from one side of stick.

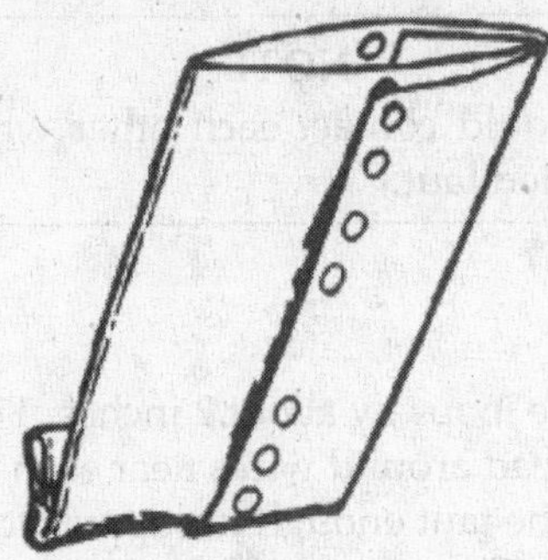

6. Count out the number of handbook pages equal in weight to that of the quantity of material to be weighed. Each sheet of paper weighs about 1.3 grams (20 grains or 0.04 ounce). Suspend these sheets, *plus one*, to balance container on the other side of the scale.
7. Slowly add the material to be weighed to the container. When the stick is balanced, the desired amount of material is in the container.

8. If it is desired to weigh a quantity of material larger than that which would fit in the above container, make a container out of a larger paper or paper bag, and suspend from one side of the stick. Suspend handbook pages from the other side until the stick is balanced. Now place a number of sheets of handbook pages equal in weight to that of the desired amount of material to be weighed on one side, and fill the container with the material until the stick is balanced.
9. A similar method may be used to measure parts or percentage by weight. The weight units are unimportant. Suspend equal weight containers from each side of the stick. Bags, tin cans, etc. can be used. Place one material in one of the containers. Fill the other container with the other material until they balance. Empty and

refill the number of times necessary to get the required parts by weight (e.g., 5 to 1 parts by weight would require 5 fillings of one can for one filling of the other).

7.9 ROPE GRENADE LAUNCHING TECHNIQUE

A method of increasing the distance a grenade may be thrown. Safety fuse is used to increase the delay time.

Materials Required
Hand grenade (improvised pipe hand grenade, section 2.3, may be used)
Safety fuse or fast burning improvised fuse (section 6.7)
Light rope, cord, or string

Procedure

1. Tie a 4 to 6 foot (a meter) length Rope of cord to the grenade. Be sure that the rope will not prevent the grenade handle from coming off.

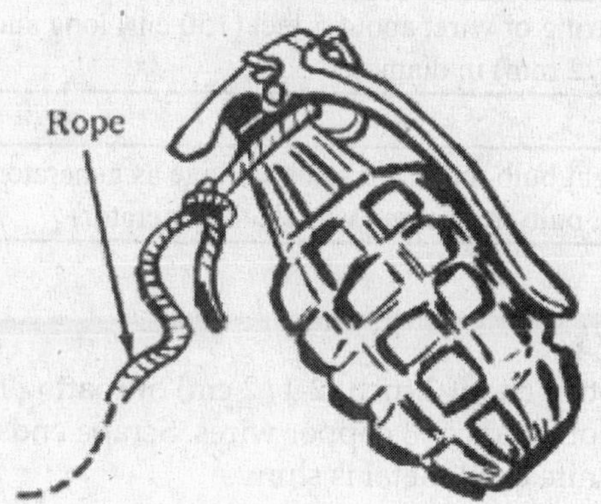

NOTE
If improvised grenade is used, tie cord around grenade near the end cap. Tape in place if necessary.

2. Tie a large knot in the other end of the cord for use as a handle.

3. Carefully remove safety pin from grenade, holding safety lever in place. Enlarge safety pin hole with point of knife, awl, or drill so that safety fuse will pass through hole.

4. Insert *safety fuse* in hole. Be sure that safety fuse is long enough to provide a 10 second or more time delay. Slowly release safety lever to make sure fuse holds safety lever in place.

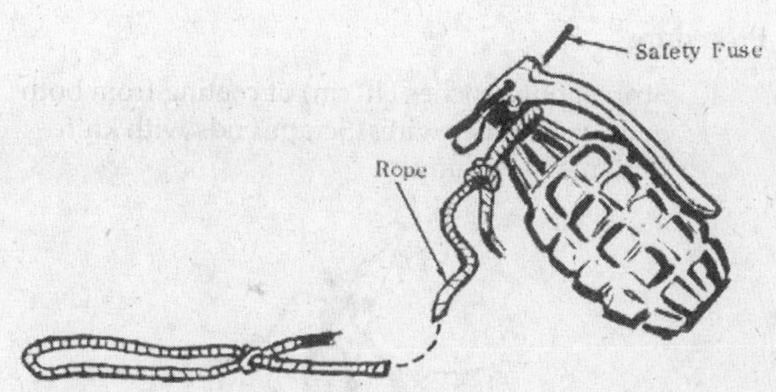

CAUTION
If safety lever should be released for any reason, grenade will explode after regular delay time (4–5 seconds).

NOTE
If diameter of safety fuse is too large to fit in hole (step 4), follow *Procedure* and *How to Use* of Time Delay Grenade, section 6.9, instead of steps 3 and 4 above.

How to Use

1. Light fuse.

2. Whirl grenade overhead, holding knot at end of rope, until grenade picks up speed (3 or 4 turns).

3. Release when sighted on target.

CAUTION
Be sure to release grenade 10 seconds after fuse is it.

NOTE
It is helpful to practice first with a dummy grenade or a rock to improve accuracy. With practice, accurate launching up to 100 meters (300 feet) can be obtained.

7.10 BICYCLE GENERATOR POWER SOURCE

A 6 volt, 3 watt bicycle generator will set off one or two blasting caps (connected in series) or an igniter.

Materials Required
Bicycle generator (6 volt, 3 watt)
Copper wire
Knife

Procedure

1. Strip about 4 inches (10 cm) of coating from both ends of 2 copper wires. Scrape ends with knife until metal is shiny.

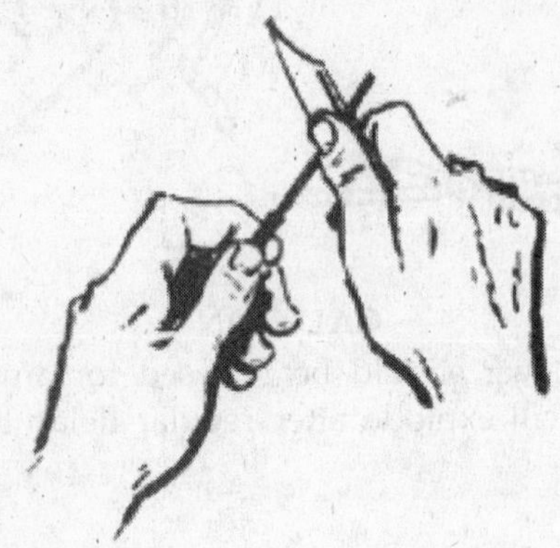

2. Connect the end of one wire to the generator terminal.
3. Attach the end of the second wire to generator case. This wire may be wrapped around a convenient projection, taped, or simply held against the case with the hand.

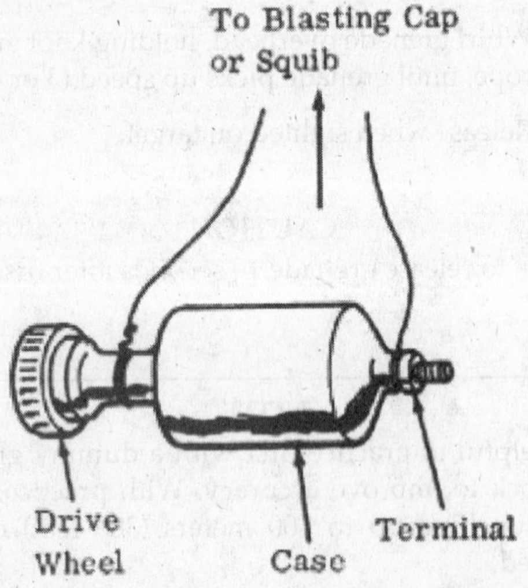

How to Use

1. Connect free ends of wires to blasting cap or squib leads.

CAUTION

If drive wheel is rotated, explosive may be set off.

2. Run the drive wheel firmly and rapidly across the palm of the hand to activate generator.

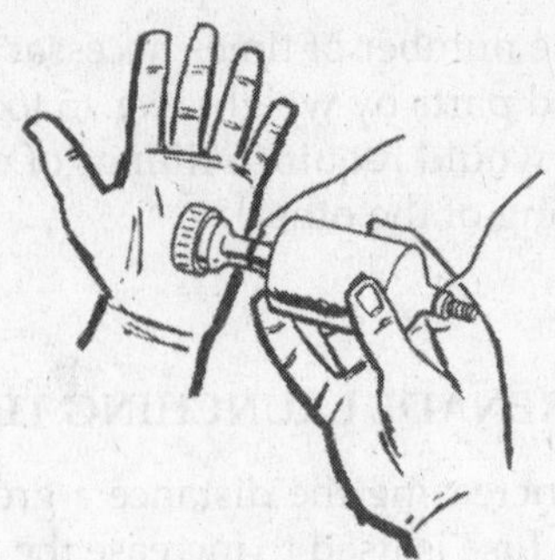

7.11 AUTOMOBILE GENERATOR POWER SOURCE

An automobile generator can be used as a means of firing one blasting cap or igniter. (Improvised Igniter, section 5.2, may be used.)

Materials Required
Automobile generator (6, 12, or 28 volt) (an alternator will *not* work.)
Copper wire
Strong string or wire, about 5 feet (150 cm) long and 1/16 inch (1-1/2 mm) in diameter
Knife
Small light bulb requiring same voltage as generator (for example, bulb from same vehicle as generator)

Procedure

1. Strip about 1 inch (2-1/2 cm) of coating from both ends of 3 copper wires. Scrape ends with knife until metal is shiny.

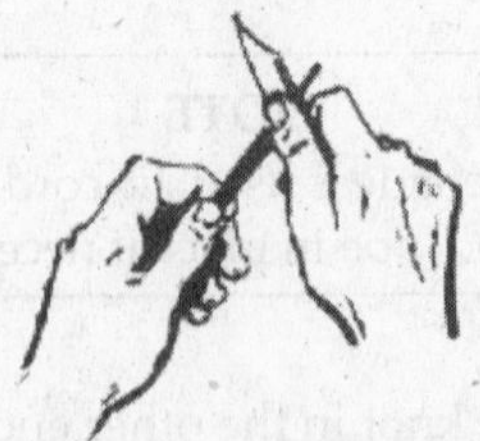

2. Connect the A and F terminals with one piece of wire.
3. Connect a wire to the A terminal. Connect another to the G terminal.

NOTE

The F and G or C terminals may not be labeled; in this case, connect wires as shown. The F terminal is *usually* smaller in size than the C or G terminal.

4. Wrap several turns of string or wire clockwise around the drive pulley.

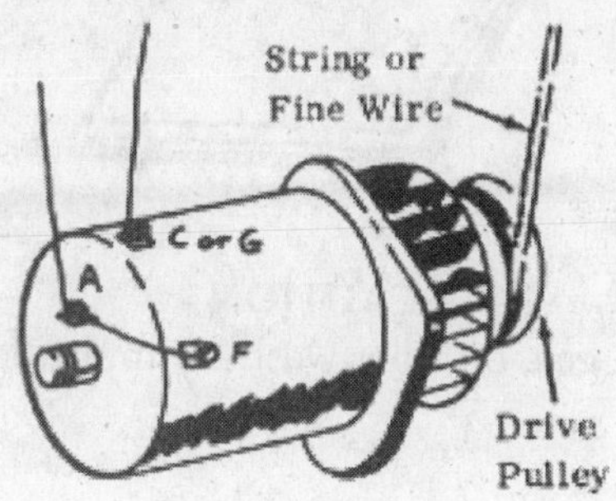

How to Use

1. Connect the free ends of the wires to the light bulb.

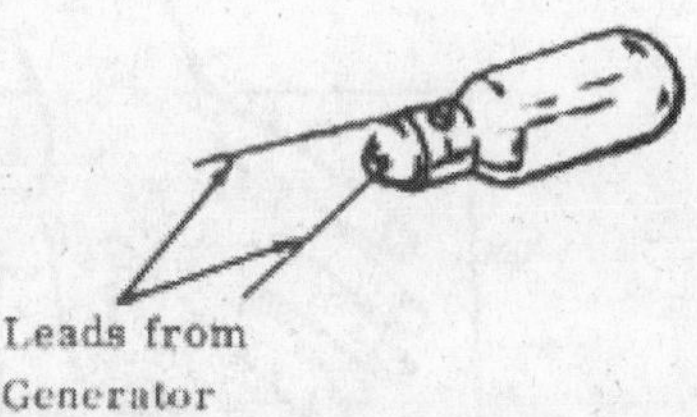

2. Place one foot on the generator to secure it in place. Give the string or wire a *very hard* pull to light the bulb.

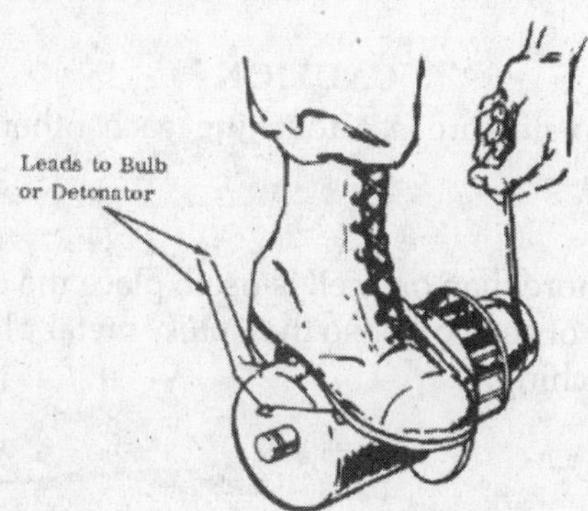

NOTE

If not successful at first, rewind string and try again several times. After repeating this operation and the bulb still does not light, follow step 4, *How to Use.*

3. If light bulb lights, follow steps 1 and 2 of above, *How to Use,* connecting free ends of wires to blasting cap or igniter instead of to light bulb.
4. If light bulb does not light after several pulls, switch leads connected to F and G terminals. Repeat above *How to Use,* steps 1 to 3.

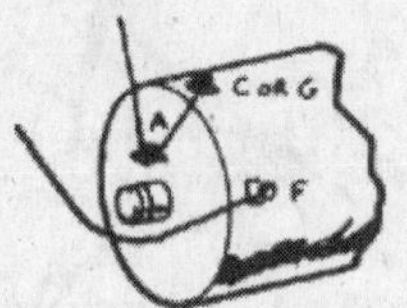

7.12 IMPROVISED BATTERY (SHORT LASTING)

This battery is powerful but must be used within 15 minutes after fabrication. One cell of this battery will detonate one blasting cap or one igniter. Two cells, connected in series, will detonate two of these devices and so on. Larger cells have a longer life as well as greater power.

Materials Required	Source
Water	
Sodium hydroxide (lye, solid or concentrated solution)	Soap manufacturing Disinfectants Sewer cleaner
Copper or brass plate about 4 inches (10 cm) square and 1/16 inch (2 mm) thick	
Aluminum plate or sheet, same size as copper plate	
Charcoal powder	
Container for mixing	
Knife	
One of the following:	
Potassium permanganate, solid	Disinfectants Deodorants
Calcium hypochlorite, solid	Disinfectants Water treating chemicals Chlorine bleaches
Manganese dioxide (pyrolucite)	Dead dry cell batteries

NOTE

Be sure sodium hydroxide solution is at least a 45% solution by weight. If not, boil off some of the water. If solid sodium hydroxide is available, dissolve some sodium hydroxide in about twice as much water (by volume).

Procedure

1. Scrape coating off both ends of wires with knife until metal is shiny.

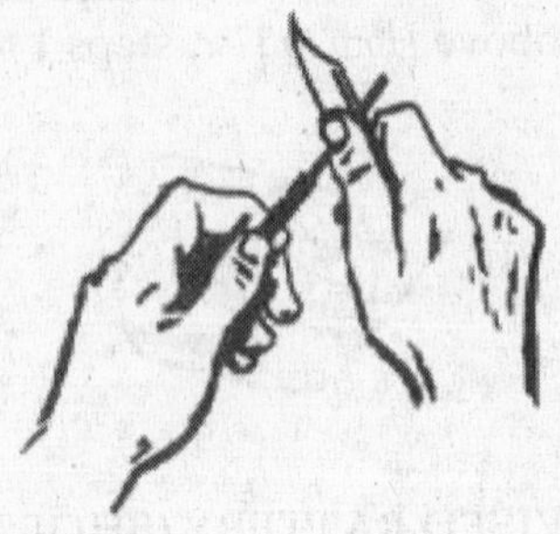

2. Mix thoroughly (do not grind) approximately equal volumes of powdered charcoal and *one* of the following: potassium permanganate, calcium hypochlorite, or manganese dioxide. Add water until a very thick paste is formed.

CAUTION

Avoid getting any of the ingredient on the skin or in the eyes.

3. Spread a layer of this mixture about 1/8 inch (2 mm) thick on the copper or brass plate. Be sure mixture is thick enough so that when mixture is sandwiched between two metal plates, the plates will not touch each other at any point.

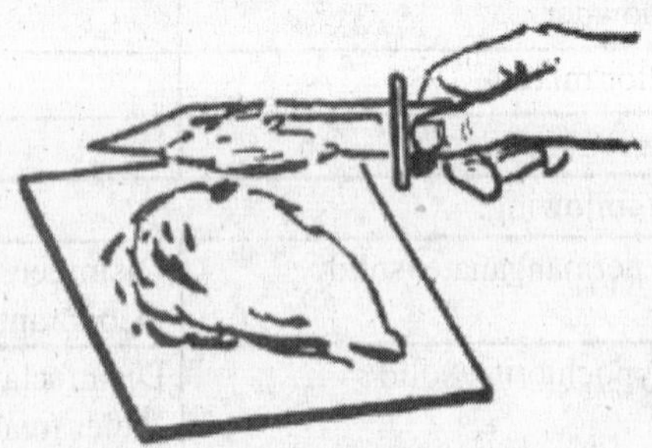

NOTE

If more power is required, prepare several plates as above.

How to Use

1. Just prior to use (no more than 15 minutes), carefully pour a small quantity of sodium hydroxide solution over the mixture on each plate used.

CAUTION

If solution gets on skin, wash off immediately with water.

2. Place an aluminum plate on top of the mixture on each copper plate. Press firmly. Remove any excess that oozes out between the plates.

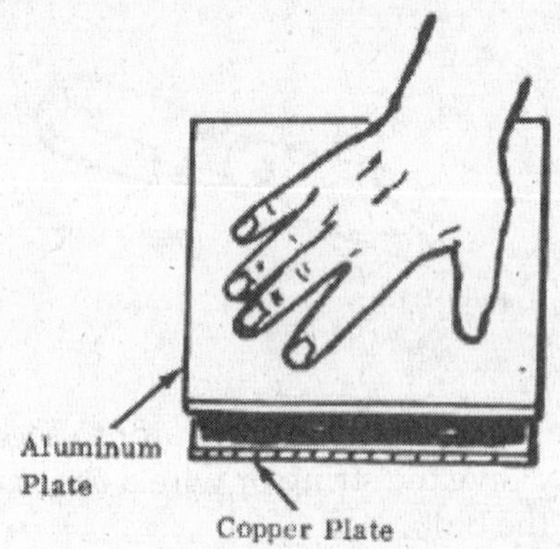

CAUTION

Be sure plates are not touching each other at any point.

3. If more than one cell is used, place the cells on top of each other so that *unlike* metal plates are touching.

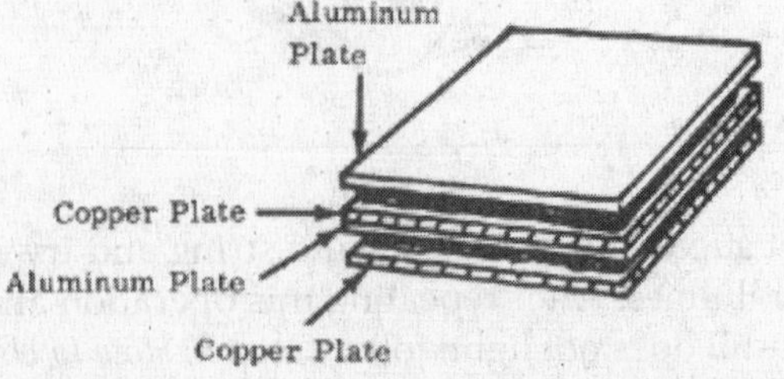

4. When ready to fire, clean plates with knife where connections are to be made. Connect one

wire to the outer aluminum plate. This may be done by holding the wires against the plates or by hooking them through holes punched through plates. If wires are hooked through plates, be sure they do not touch mixture between plates.

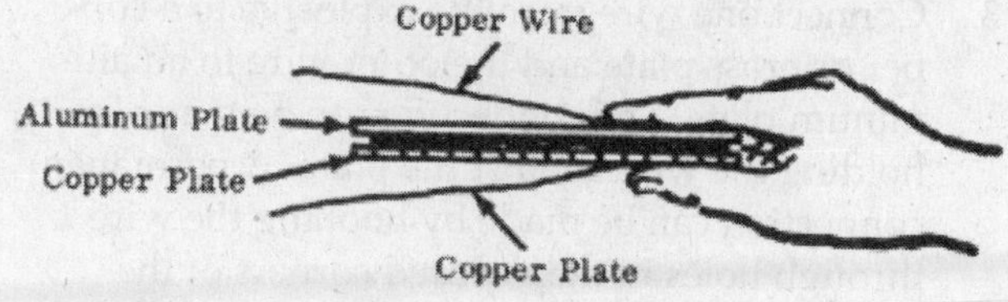

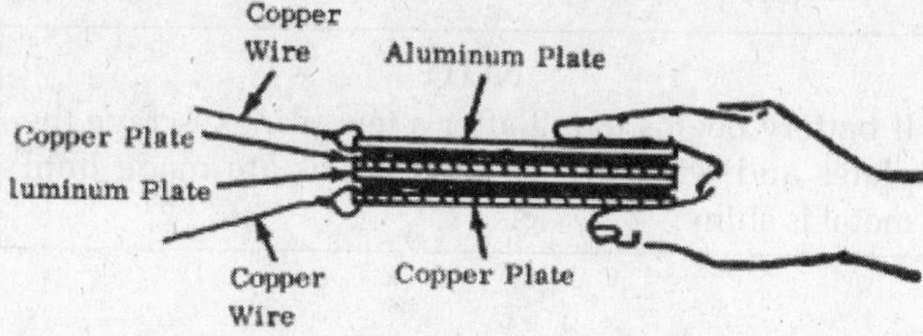

7.13 IMPROVISED BATTERY (2 HOUR DURATION)

This battery should be used within 2 hours and should be *securely wrapped.* Three cells will detonate one blasting cap or one igniter. Five cells, connected in series, will detonate two of these devices and so on. Larger cells have a longer life and will yield more power.

If depolarizing materials such as potassium permanganate or manganese dioxide cannot be obtained, ten cells without depolarizer, arranged as described below, (step 4) will detonate one blasting cap.

Materials Required	Source
Water	
Ammonium chloride (sal ammoniac) (solid or concentrated solution)	Medicines Soldering fluxes Fertilizers Ice melting chemicals for roads
Charcoal powder	
Copper or brass plate about 4 inches (10 cm) square and 1/16 inch (2 mm) thick	
Aluminum plate same size as copper or brass plate	
Wax and pajper (or waxed paper)	Candles
Wire, string or tape	
Container for mixing	
Knife	
One of the following:	
Potassium permanganate, solid	Disinfectants Deodorants
Manganese dioxide	Dead dry batteries

NOTE

If ammonium chloride solution is not concentrated (at least 45% by weight) boil off some of the water.

Procedure

1. Mix thoroughly (do not grind) approximately equal volumes of powdered charcoal, ammonium chloride and *one* of the following: potassium permanganate or manganese dioxide. Add water until a very thick paste is formed. If ammonium chloride is in solution form, it may not be necessary to add water.

2. Spread a layer of this mixture, about 1/8 inch (3 mm) thick on a clean copper or brass plate. The layer must be thick enough to prevent a second plate from touching the copper plate when it is pressed on top.

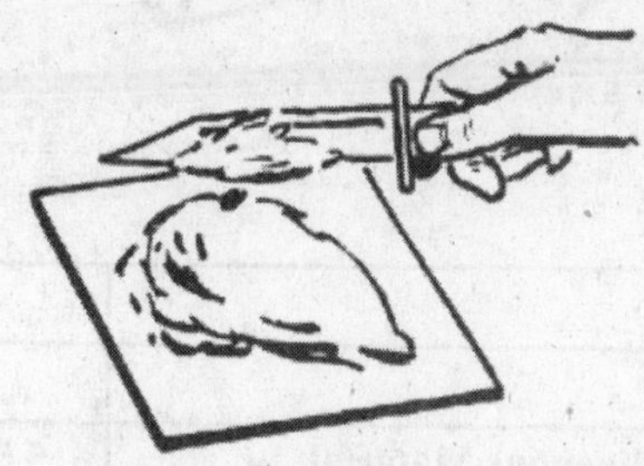

3. Press an aluminum plate very firmly upon the mixture on the copper plate. Remove completely any of the mixture that squeezes out between the plates. *The plates must not touch.*

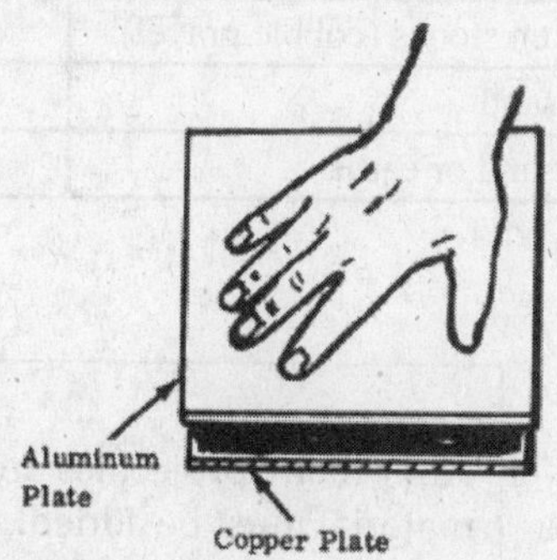

4. If more than one cell is desired:
   a. Place one cell on top of the other so that *unlike* metal plates are touching.

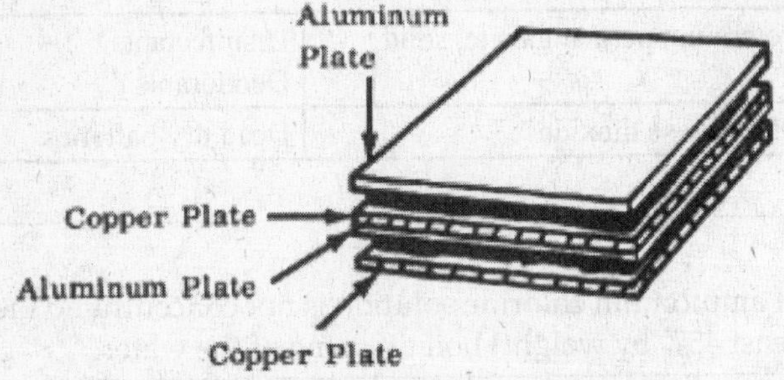

   b. Wrap the combined cells in heavy waxed paper. The waxed paper can be made by rubbing candle wax over one side of a piece of paper. Secure the paper around the battery with string, wire or tape. Expose the top and bottom metal plates at one corner.

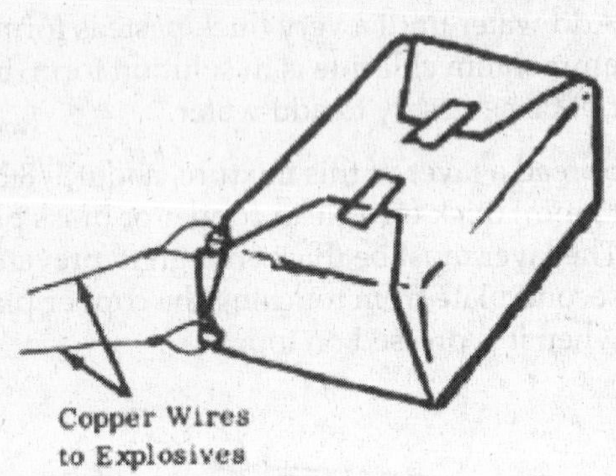

How to Use

1. Scrape a few inches off each end of two wires with knife till metal is shiny.
2. Clean plates with knife until metal is shiny where connections are to be made.
3. Connect one wire from the explosive to a copper or brass plate and the other wire to an aluminum plate. The connection can be made by holding the wire against the plate. A permanent connection can be made by hooking the wire through holes in the exposed corners of the plates. The battery is now ready for use.

NOTE

If battery begins to fail after a few firings, scrape the plates and wires where connections are made until metal is shiny.

7.14 ARMOR MATERIALS

The following table shows the amount of indigenous materials needed to stop ball type projectiles of the 5.56 mm, . 30 caliber, and .50 caliber ammunition fired from their respective weapons at a distance of 10 feet (3 m).

	Thickness of Materials					
	Inches			Centimeters		
Indigenous Material	**5.56 mm**	**.30 caliber 7.62 mm**	**.50 caliber 12.70 mm**	**5.56 mm**	**.30 caliber 7.62 mm**	**.50 caliber 12.70 mm**
Mild steel (structural)	1/2	1/2	3/4	1-1/4	1-1/4	2
Mid aluminum (structural)	1	1	2	2-1/2	2-1/2	5
Pine wood (soft)	14	22	32	36	56	82
Broken stones (cobble gravel)	3	4	11	8	11	28
Dry sand	4	5	14	11	13	36
Wet sand or earth	6	13	21	16	33	54

NOTE

After many projectiles are fired into the armor, the armor will break down. More material must be added.

APPENDIX 1

Primary High Explosives

A1.1 MERCURY FULMINATE

Description

Mercury fulminate is an initiating explosive, commonly appearing as white or gray crystals. It is extremely sensitive to initiation by heat, friction, spark or flame, and impact. It detonates when initiated by any of these means. It is pressed into containers, usually at 3000 pounds per square inch (20 mPa), for use in detonators and blasting caps. However, when compressed at greater and greater pressure (up to 30,000 pounds per square inch or 200 mPa), it becomes "dead pressed." In this condition, it can only be exploded by another initial detonating agent. Mercury fulminate gradually becomes inert when stored continuously above 100°F. A dark-colored product of deterioration gives evidence of this effect. Mercury fulminate is stored underwater except when there is danger of freezing. Then it is stored under a mixture of water and alcohol.

Comments

This material was tested. It is effective.

References

TM 9-1900, Ammunition, General, page 59.

TM 9-1910, Military Explosives, page 98.

A1.2 LEAD STYPHNATE

Description

Lead styphnate is an initiating explosive, commonly appearing in the form of orange or brown crystals. It is easily ignited by heat and static discharge but cannot be used to initiate secondary high explosives reliably. Lead styphnate is used as an igniting charge for lead azide and as an ingredient in priming mixtures for small arms ammunition. In these applications, it is usually mixed with other materials first and then pressed into a metallic container (detonators and primers). Lead styphnate is stored under water except when there is danger of freezing. Then it is stored under a mixture of water and alcohol.

Comments

This item was tested. It is effective.

References

TM 9-1900, Ammunition, General, page 59.

TM 9-1910, Military Explosives, page 107.

A1.3 LEAD AZIDE

Description

Lead azide is an initiating explosive and is produced as a white to buff crystalline substance. It is a more efficient detonating agent than mercury fulminate and it does not decompose on long continued storage at moderately elevated temperatures. It is sensitive to both flame and impact but requires a layer of lead styphnate priming mixture to produce reliable initiation when it is used in detonators that are initiated by a firing pin or electrical energy. It is generally loaded into aluminum detonator housings and must not be loaded into housing of copper or brass because extremely sensitive copper azide can be formed in the presence of moisture.

Comments

This material was tested. It is effective.

References

TM 9-1900, Ammunition, General, page 60.

TM 9-1910, Military Explosives, page 103.

A1.4 DDNP

Description

DDNP (diazodinitrophenol is a primary high explosive. It is extensively used in commercial blasting caps that are initiated by black powder safety fuse. It is superior to mercury fulminate in stability but is not as stable as lead azide. DDNP is desensitized by immersion in water.

Comments

This material was tested. It is effective.

References

TM 9-1900, Ammunition, General, page 60.

TM 9-1910, Military Explosives, page 103.

APPENDIX 2

Secondary High Explosives

A2.1 TNT

Description

TNT (Trinitrotoluene) is produced from toluene, sulfuric acid, and nitric acid. It is a powerful high explosive. It is well suited for steel cutting, concrete breaching, general demolition, and for under water demolition. It is a stable explosive and is relatively insensitive to shock. It may be detonated with a blasting cap or by primacord. TNT is issued in 1-pound and 1/2-pound containers and 50-pounds to a wooden box.

Comments

This material was tested. It is effective. TNT is toxic and its dust should not be inhaled or allowed to contact the skin.

References

TM 9-1900, Ammunition, General, page 263.

FM 5-25, Explosives and Demolitions, page 3.

A2.2 NITROSTARCH

Description

Nitrostarch is composed of starch nitrate, barium nitrate, and sodium nitrate. It is more sensitive to flame, friction, and impact than TNT but is less powerful. It is initiated by detonating cord. Nitrostarch is issued in 1-pound and 1-1/2-pound blocks. The 1-pound packages can be broken into 1/4-pound blocks. Fifty 1-pound packages and one hundred 1-1/2-pound packages are packed in boxes.

Comments

This material was tested. It is effective.

Reference

TM 9-1900, Ammunition, General, page 263.

A2.3 TETRYL

Description

Tetryl is a fine, yellow, crystalline material and exhibits a very high shattering power. It is commonly used as a booster in explosive trains. It is stable in storage. Tetryl is used in detonators. It is pressed into the bottom of the detonator housing and covered with a small priming charge of mercury fulminate or lead azide.

Comments

This material was tested. It is effective.

References

TM 9-1900, Ammunition, General, page 52.

TM 31-201-1, Unconventional Warfare Devices and Techniques, para 1509.

A2.4 RDX

Description

RDX (cyclonite) is a white crystalline solid that exhibits very high shattering power. It is commonly used as a booster in explosive trains or as a main bursting charge. It is stable in storage, and when combined with proper additives, may be cast or press loaded. It may be initiated by lead azide or mercury fulminate.

Comments

This material was tested. It is effective.

References

TM 9-1900, Ammunition, General, page 52.

TM 31-201-1, Unconventional Warfare Devices and Techniques, para 1501.

A2.5 NITROGLYCERIN

Description

Nitroglycerin is manufactured by treating glycerin with a nitrating mixture of nitric and sulfuric acid. It is a thick, clear to yellow-brownish liquid that is an extremely powerful and shock-sensitive high explosive. Nitroglycerin freezes at 56°F, in which state it is less sensitive to shock than in liquid form.

Comments

This material was tested. It is effective.

References

TM 9-1910, Military Explosives, page 123.

TM 31-201-1, Unconventional Warfare Devices and Techniques, para 1502.

A2.6 COMMERCIAL DYNAMITE

Description

There are three principal types of commercial dynamite: straight dynamite, ammonia dynamite, and gelatin dynamite. Each type is further subdivided into a series of grades. All dynamites contain nitroglycerin in varying amounts and the strength or force of the explosive is related to the nitroglycerin content. Dynamites range in velocity of detonation from about 4000 to 23,000 feet per second and are sensitive to shock. The types and grades of dynamite are each used for specific purposes such as rock blasting or underground explosives. Dynamite is initiated by electric or nonelectric blasting caps. Although dynamites are furnished in a wide variety of packages, the most common unit is the 1/2 pound cartridge. Fifty pounds is the maximum weight per case.

Comments

This material was tested. It is effective.

References

TM 9-1900, Ammunition, General, page 265.

FM 5-25, Explosives and Demolitions, page 8.

A2.7 MILITARY DYNAMITE

Description

Military (construction) dynamite, unlike commercial dynamite, does not absorb or retain moisture, contains no nitroglycerin, and is much safer to store, handle, and transport. It comes in standard sticks 1-1/4 inches in diameter by 8 inches long, weighing approximately 1/2 pound. It detonates at a velocity of about 20,000 feet per second and is very satisfactory for military construction, quarrying, and demolition work. It may be detonated with an electric or nonelectric military blasting cap or detonating cord.

Comments

This material was tested. It is effective.

References

FM 5-25, Explosives and Demolitions, page 7.

TM 9-1910, Military Explosives, page 204.

A2.8 AMATOL

Description

Amatol is a high explosive, white to buff in color. It is a mixture of ammonium nitrate and TNT, with a relative effectiveness slightly higher than that of TNT alone. Common compositions vary from 80% ammonium nitrate and 20% TNT to 40% ammonium nitrate and 60% TNT. Amatol is used as the main bursting charge in artillery shell and bombs. Amatol absorbs moisture and can form dangerous compounds with copper and brass. Therefore it should not be housed in containers of such metals.

Comments

This material was tested. It is effective.

References

FM 5-25, Explosives and Demolitions, page 7.

TM 9-1910, Military Explosives, page 182.

A2.9 PETN

Description

PETN (pentaerythrite tetranitrate), the high explosive used in detonating cord, is one of the most powerful of military explosives, almost equal in force to nitroglycerin and RDX. When used in detonating cord, it has a detonation velocity of 21,000 feet per second and is relatively insensitive to friction and shock from handling and transportation.

Comments

This material was tested. It is effective.

References

FM 5-25, Explosives and Demolitions, page 7.

TM 9-1910, Military Explosives, page 135.

TM 31-201-1, Unconventional Warfare Devices and Techniques, para 1508.

A2.10 BLASTING GELATIN

Description

Blasting gelatin is a translucent material of an elastic, jellylike texture and is manufactured in a number of different colors. It is considered to be the most powerful industrial explosive. Its characteristics are similar to those of gelatin dynamite except that blasting gelatin is more water resistant.

Comments

This material was tested. It is effective.

References

TM 9-1910, Military Explosives, page 204.

A2.11 COMPOSITION B

Description

Composition B is a high-explosive mixture with a relative effectiveness higher than that of TNT. It is also more sensitive than TNT. It is composed of RDX (59%), TNT (40%), and wax (1%). Because of its shattering power and high rate of detonation, Composition B is used as the main charge in certain models of bangalore torpedoes and shaped charges.

Comments

This material was tested. It is effective.

References

FM 5-25, Explosives and Demolitions, page 7.

TM 9-1900, Ammunition, General, page 57.

TM 9-1910, Military Explosives, page 193.

A2.12 COMPOSITION C4

Description

Composition C4 is a white plastic high explosive more powerful than TNT. It consists of 91% RDX and 9% plastic binder. It remains plastic over a wide range of temperatures (-70°F to 170°F), and is about as sensitive as TNT. It is eroded less than other plastic explosives when immersed under water for long periods. Because of its high detonation velocity and its plasticity, C4 is well suited for cutting steel and timber and for breaching concrete.

Comments

This material was tested. It is effective.

Reference

TM 9-1910, Military Explosives, page 204.

A2.13 AMMONIUM NITRATE

Description

Ammonium nitrate is a white crystalline substance that is extremely water absorbent and is therefore usually packed in a sealed metal container. It has a low velocity of detonation (3600 feet per second or 1100 meters per second) and is used primarily as an additive in other explosive compounds. When it is used alone, it must be initiated by a powerful booster or primer. It is only 55% as powerful as TNT, hence larger quantities are required to produce similar results.

Comments

This material was tested. It is effective.

CAUTION

Never use copper or brass containers because ammonium nitrate reacts with these metals.

References

TM 9-1900, Ammunition, General, page 264.

TM 9-1910, Military Explosives, page 119.

PART III

Fight Your Way Out, Ranger

CHAPTER 1

Leadership

Leadership, the most essential element of combat power, gives purpose, direction, and motivation in combat. The leader balances and maximizes maneuver, firepower, and protection against the enemy. This chapter discusses how he does this by exploring the principles of leadership (BE, KNOW, DO); the duties, responsibilities, and actions of an effective leader; and the leader's assumption of command.

1-1. PRINCIPLES

The principles of leadership are BE, KNOW, and DO.

BE

- Technically and tactically proficient.
- Able to accomplish to standard all tasks required for the wartime mission.
- Courageous, committed, and candid.
- A leader with integrity.

KNOW

- The four major factors of leadership and how they affect each other are–
  —Led
  —Leader
  —Situation
  —Communications
- Yourself, and the strengths and weaknesses in your character, knowledge, and skills. Seek continual self-improvement, that is, develop your strengths and work to overcome your weaknesses.
- Your Rangers, and look out for their well-being by training them for the rigors of combat, taking care of their physical and safety needs, and disciplining and rewarding them.

DO–

- Seek responsibility and take responsibility for your actions; exercise initiative; demonstrate resourcefulness; and take advantage of opportunities on the battlefield that will lead to you to victory; accept fair criticism, and take corrective actions for your mistakes.
- Assess situations rapidly, make sound and timely decisions, gather essential information, announce decisions in time for Rangers to react, and consider the short- and long-term effects of your decision.
- Set the example by serving as a role model for your Rangers. Set high but attainable standards; be willing do what you require of your Rangers; and share dangers and hardships with them.
- Keep your subordinates informed to help them make decisions and execute plans within your intent, encourage initiative, improve teamwork, and enhance morale.
- Develop a sense of responsibility in subordinates by teaching, challenging, and developing them. Delegate to show you trust them. This makes them want more responsibility.
- Ensure the Rangers understand the task; supervise them, and ensure they accomplish it. Rangers need to know what you expect: when and what you want them to do, and to what standard.
- Build the team by training and cross-training your Rangers until they are confident in their technical and tactical abilities. Develop a team spirit that motivates them to go willingly and confidently into combat.
- Know your unit's capabilities and limitations, and employ them accordingly.

1-2. DUTIES, RESPONSIBILITIES, AND ACTIONS

To complete all assigned tasks, every Ranger in the patrol must do his job. Each must accomplish his specific duties and responsibilities and be a part of the team.

PLATOON LEADER (PL)

- Is responsible for what the patrol does or fails to do. This includes tactical employment, training, administration, personnel management, and logistics. He does this by planning, making timely decisions, issuing orders, assigning tasks, and supervising patrol activities. He must know his Rangers and how to employ the patrol's weapons. He is responsible for positioning and employing all assigned or attached crew-served weapons and employment of supporting weapons.
- Establishes time schedule using backwards planning. Considers time for execution, movement to the objective, and the planning and preparation phase of the operation.
- Takes the initiative to accomplish the mission in the absence of orders. Keeps higher informed by using periodic situation reports (SITREP).
- Plans with the help of the platoon sergeant (PSG), squad leaders, and other key personnel (team leaders, FO, attachment leaders).
- Stays abreast of the situation through coordination with adjacent patrols and higher HQ; supervises, issues FRAGOs, and accomplishes the mission.
- If needed to perform the mission, requests more support for his patrol from higher headquarters.
- Directs and assists the platoon sergeant in planning and coordinating the patrol's sustainment effort and casualty evacuation (CASEVAC) plan.
- During planning, receives on-hand status reports from the platoon sergeant and squad leaders.
- Reviews patrol requirements based on the tactical plan.
- Ensures that all-round security is maintained at all times.
- Supervises and spot-checks all assigned tasks, and corrects unsatisfactory actions.
- During execution, positions himself where he can influence the most critical task for mission accomplishment; usually with the main effort, to ensure that his platoon achieves its decisive point.
- Is responsible for positioning and employing all assigned and attached crew-served weapons.
- Commands through his squad leaders IAW the intent of the two levels higher commanders.
- Conducts rehearsals.

PLATOON SERGEANT (PSG)

The PSG is the senior NCO in the patrol and second in succession of command. He helps and advises the patrol leader, and leads the patrol in the leader's absence. He supervises the patrol's administration, logistics, and maintenance, and he prepares and issues paragraph 4 of the patrol OPORD.

DUTIES

- Organizes and controls the patrol CP IAW the unit SOP, patrol leader's guidance, and METT-TC factors.
- Receives squad leader's requests for rations, water, and ammunition. Work with the company first sergeant or XO to request resupply. Directs the routing of supplies and mail.
- Supervises and directs the patrol medic and patrol aid-litter teams in moving casualties to the rear.
- Maintains patrol status of personnel, weapons, and equipment; consolidates and forwards the patrol's casualty reports (DA Forms 1155 and 1156); and receives and orients replacements.
- Monitors the morale, discipline, and health of patrol members.
- Supervises task-organized elements of patrol:
  - — Quartering parties.
  - — Security forces during withdrawals.
  - — Support elements during raids or attacks.
  - — Security patrols during night attacks.
- Coordinates and supervises patrol resupply operations.
- Ensures that supplies are distributed IAW the patrol leader's guidance and direction.

- Ensures that ammunition, supplies, and loads are properly and evenly distributed (a critical task during consolidation and reorganization).
- Ensures the casualty evacuation plan is complete and executed properly.
- Ensures that the patrol adheres to the platoon leader's time schedule.
- Assists the platoon leader in supervising and spot-checking all assigned tasks, and corrects unsatisfactory actions.

ACTIONS DURING MOVEMENT AND HALTS

- Takes actions necessary to facilitate movement.
- Supervises rear security during movement.
- Establishes, supervises, and maintains security during halts.
- Knows unit location.
- Performs additional tasks as required by the patrol leader and assists in every way possible. Focuses on security and control of patrol.

ACTIONS AT DANGER AREAS

- Directs positioning of near-side security (usually conducted by the trail squad or team).
- Maintains accountability of personnel.

ACTIONS ON THE OBJECTIVE AREA

- Assists with ORP occupation.
- Supervises, establishes, and maintains security at the ORP.
- Supervises the final preparation of men, weapons, and equipment in the ORP IAW the patrol leader's guidance.
- Assists the patrol leader in control and security.
- Supervises the consolidation and reorganization of ammunition and equipment.
- Establishes, marks, and supervises the planned CCP, and ensures that the personnel status (to include WIA/KIA) is accurately reported to higher.
- Performs additional tasks assigned by the patrol leader and reports status to platoon leader.

ACTIONS IN THE PATROL BASE

- Assists in patrol base occupation.
- Assist in establishing and adjusting perimeter.
- Enforces security in the patrol base.
- Keeps movement and noise to a minimum.
- Supervises and enforces camouflage.
- Assigns sectors of fire.
- Ensures designated personnel remain alert and equipment is maintained to a high state of readiness.
- Requisitions supplies, water, and ammunition, and supervises their distribution.
- Supervises the priority of work and ensures its accomplishment.
    - — Security plan.
        - Ensures crew-served weapons have interlocking sectors of fire.
        - Ensures Claymores are emplaced to cover dead space.
        - Ensures range cards and sector sketch are complete.
    - — Alert plan.
    - — Evacuation plan.
    - — Withdrawal plan.
    - — Alternate patrol base.
    - — Maintenance plan.
    - — Hygiene plan.
    - — Messing plan.
    - — Water plan.
    - — Rest plan.
- Performs additional tasks assigned by the patrol leader and assists him in every way possible.

SQUAD LEADER (SL)

Is responsible for what the squad does or fails to do. He is a tactical leader who leads by example.

DUTIES

- Completes casualty feeder reports and reviews the casualty reports completed by squad members.
- Directs the maintenance of the squad's weapons and equipment.
- Inspects the condition of Rangers' weapons, clothing, and equipment.
- Keeps the PL and PSG informed on status of squad.
- Submits ACE report to PSG.

ACTIONS THROUGHOUT THE MISSION

- Obtains status report from team leaders and submits reports to the PL and PSG.
- Makes a recommendation to the PL/PSG when problems are observed.
- Delegates priority task to team leaders, and supervises their accomplishment IAW squad leader's guidance.
- Uses initiative in the absence of orders.
- Follows the PL's plan and makes recommendations.

ACTIONS DURING MOVEMENT AND HALTS

- Ensures heavy equipment is rotated among members and difficult duties are shared.
- Notifies PL of the status of the squad.
- Maintains proper movement techniques while monitoring route, pace, and azimuth.
- Ensures the squad maintains security throughout the movement and at halts.
- Prevents breaks in contact.
- Ensures subordinate leaders are disseminating information, assigning sectors of fire, and checking personnel.

ACTION IN THE OBJECTIVE AREA

- Ensures special equipment has been prepared for actions at the objective.
- Maintains positive control of squad during the execution of the mission.
- Positions key weapons systems during and after assault on the objective.
- Obtains status reports from team leaders and ensures ammunition is redistributed and reports status to PL.

ACTIONS IN THE PATROL BASE

- Ensures patrol base is occupied according to the plan.
- Ensures that his sector of the patrol base is covered by interlocking fires; makes final adjustments, if necessary.
- Sends out LP or OPs in front of assigned sector. (METT-TC dependent).
- Ensures priorities of work are being accomplished, and reports accomplished priorities to the PL and PSG.
- Adheres to time schedule.
- Ensures personnel know the alert and evacuation plans, and the locations of key leaders, OPs, and the alternate patrol base.

WEAPONS SQUAD LEADER

Is responsible for all that the weapons squad does or fails to do. His duties are the same as those of the squad leader. Also, he controls the machine guns in support of the patrol's mission. He advises the PL on employment of his squad.

DUTIES

- Supervises machine gun teams to ensure they follow priorities of work.
- Inspects machine gun teams for correct range cards, fighting positions, and understanding of fire plan.

- Supervises maintenance of machine guns, that is, ensures that maintenance is performed correctly, that deficiencies are corrected and reported, and that the performance of maintenance does not violate the security plan.
- Assists PL in planning.
- Positions at halts and danger areas and according to the patrol SOP any machine guns not attached to squads.
- Rotates loads. Machine gunners normally get tired first.
- Submits ACE report to PSG.
- Designates sectors of fire, principal direction of fire (PDF), and secondary sectors of fire for all guns.
- Gives fire commands to achieve maximum effectiveness of firepower:
  — Shifts fires.
  — Corrects windage or elevation to increase accuracy.
  — Alternates firing guns.
  — Controls rates of fire and fire distribution.
- Knows locations of assault and security elements, and prevents fratricide.
- Reports to the PL.

TEAM LEADER (TL)

Controls the movement of his fire team and the rate and placement of fire. To do this, leads from the front and uses the proper commands and signals. Maintains accountability of his Rangers, weapons, and equipment. Ensures his Rangers maintain unit standards in all areas, and are knowledgeable of their tasks and the operation. The following checklist outlines specific duties and responsibilities of team leaders during mission planning and execution. The TL leads by example:

ACTIONS DURING PLANNING AND PREPARATION

- Warning Order.
  — Assists in control of the squad.
  — Monitors squad during issuance of the order.
- OPORD Preparation.
  — Posts changes to schedule.
  — Posts and updates team duties on warning order board.
  — Submits ammunition and supply requests.
  — Picks up ammunition and supplies.
  — Distributes ammunition and special equipment.
  — Performs all tasks given in the SL's special instructions paragraph.
- OPORD Issuance and Rehearsal.
  — Monitors squad during issuance of the order.
  — Assists SL during rehearsals.
- Takes actions necessary to facilitate movement.
- Enforces rear security.
- Establishes, supervises, and maintains security at all times.
- Performs additional tasks as required by the SL, and assists him in every way possible, particularly in control and security.

ACTION IN THE ORP

- Assists in the occupation of the ORP.
- Helps supervise, establish, and maintain security.
- Supervises the final preparation of Rangers, weapons, and equipment in the ORP IAW the SL's guidance.
- Assists in control of personnel departing and entering the ORP.
- Reorganizes perimeter after the reconnaissance party departs.
- Maintains communication with higher headquarters.
- Upon return of reconnaissance party, helps reorganize personnel and redistribute ammunition and equipment; ensures accountability of all personnel and equipment is maintained.

- Disseminates PIR to his team.
- Performs additional tasks assigned by the SL.

ACTIONS IN THE PATROL BASE

- Inspects the perimeter to ensure team has interlocking sectors of fire; prepares team sector sketch.
- Enforces the priority of work and ensures it is properly accomplished.
- Performs additional tasks assigned by the SL and assists him in every way possible.

MEDIC

Assists the PSG in directing aid and litter teams; monitors the health and hygiene of the platoon.

DUTIES

- Treats casualties, conducts triage, and assists in CASEVAC under the control of the PSG.
- Aids the PL or PSG in field hygiene matters. Personally checks the health and physical condition of platoon members.
- Requests Class VIII (medical) supplies through the PSG.
- Provides technical expertise to and supervision of combat lifesavers.
- Ensures casualty feeder reports are correct and attached to each evacuated casualty.
- Carries out other tasks assigned by the PL or PSG.

RADIO OPERATOR

Is responsible for establishing and maintaining communications with higher headquarters and within the patrol.

DUTIES DURING PLANNING

- Enters the net at the specified time.
- Ensures that all frequencies, COMSEC fills, and net IDs, are preset in squad/platoon radios.
- Informs SL and PL of changes to call signs, frequencies, challenge and password, and number combination based on the appropriate time in the ANCD.
- Ensures the proper function of all radios and troubleshoots and reports deficiencies to higher.
- Weatherproofs all communications equipment.

DUTIES DURING EXECUTION

- Serves as en route recorder during all phases of the mission.
- Records all enemy contact and reports it to higher in a SALUTE format.
- Reports all OPSKEDs to higher.
- Consolidates and records all PIR.

FORWARD OBSERVER (FO)

Works for the PL. Serves as the eyes of the FA and mortars. Is mainly responsible for locating targets, and for calling for and adjusting indirect fire support. Knows the terrain where the platoon is operating; knows the tactical situation. Knows the mission, the concept, and the unit's scheme of maneuver and priority of fires.

DUTIES DURING PLANNING

- Selects targets to support the platoon's mission based on the company OPORD, platoon leader's guidance, and analysis of METT-TC factors.
- Prepares and uses situation maps, overlays, and terrain sketches.

DUTIES DURING EXECUTION

- Informs the FIST headquarters of platoon activities and of the fire support situation.
- Selects new targets to support the platoon's mission based on the company OPORD, the platoon leader's guidance, and an analysis of METT-TC factors.
- Calls for and adjusts fire support.
- Operates as a team with the radio operator.
- Selects OPs.
- Maintains communications as prescribed by the FSO.
- Maintains the current 8-digit coordinate of his location at all times.

1-3. ASSUMPTION OF COMMAND

Any platoon/squad member might have to take command of his element in an emergency, so every Ranger must be prepared to do so. During an assumption of command, situation permitting, the Ranger assuming command accomplishes the following tasks (not necessarily in this order) based on METT-TC:

- *Informs* the unit's subordinate leaders of the command and notifies higher.
- *Checks* security.
- *Checks* crew-served weapons.
- *Pinpoints* location.
- *Coordinates* and *checks* equipment.
- *Checks* personnel status.
- *Issues* FRAGO (if required).
- *Reorganizes* as needed, maintaining unit integrity when possible.
- *Maintains* noise and light discipline.
- *Continues* patrol base activities, especially security, if assuming command in a patrol base.
- *Reconnoiters* or, at the least, conducts a map reconnaissance.
- *Finalizes* plan.
- *Executes* the mission.

CHAPTER 2

Movement

To survive on the battlefield, stealth, dispersion, and security must be enforced in all tactical movements. The leader must be skilled in all movement techniques.

2-1. FORMATIONS

Movement formations are comprised of elements and Soldiers in relation to each other. Fire teams, squads and platoons use several movement formations. Formations provide the leader control based on a METT-TC analysis. Leaders position themselves where they can best command and control formations. The formations below allow the fire team leader to lead by example, *"Follow me, and do as I do."* All Soldiers in the team must be able to see their leader. The formations in Figure 2-1 reflect fire team formations. Squad formations are very similar with more Soldiers. Squads can operate in lines and files similar to fire teams. When squads operate in wedges or in echelon, the fire teams use those formations and simply arrange themselves in column or one team behind the other. Squads may also use the vee, with one team forming the lines of the vee, and the SL at the apex for command and control. Platoons work on the same basic formations as the Squads. When operating as a platoon, the platoon leader must carefully select the location for his machine guns in the movement formation.

a. **Techniques**. A movement technique is the method a unit uses to traverse terrain. There are three movement techniques: traveling, traveling overwatch, and bounding overwatch. The selection of a movement technique is based on the likelihood of enemy contact and the need for speed. Factors to consider for each technique are control, dispersion, speed, and security. Movement techniques are not fixed formations. They refer to the distances between Soldiers, teams, and squads that vary based on METT-TC. Soldiers must be able to see their fire team leaders. The platoon leader should be able to see his lead squad leader. Leaders control movement with hand-and-arm signals and use radios only when needed.

b. **Standards**.
   (1) Unit moves on designated route or arrives at specified location IAW OPORD maintaining accountability of all assigned/attached personnel.
   (2) Unit uses movement formation and technique ordered by the leader based on METT-TC.
   (3) Leaders remain oriented (within 200 meters) and follow planned route unless METT-TC dictates otherwise.
   (4) Unit maintains 360 degree security and remains 100% alert during movement.

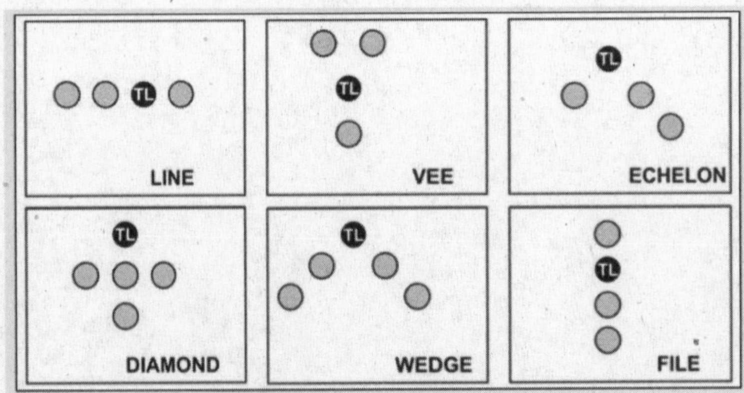

Figure 2-1. Formations

(5) Unit maintains 360 degree security and a minimum of 75% security during halts.
(6) If contact with the enemy is made, it is made with the smallest element possible.
(7) Control measures are used during movement such as head counts, rally points, or phase lines.

c. **Fundamentals.**

(1) ***Land Navigation.*** Mission accomplishment depends on successful land navigation. The patrol should use stealth and vigilance to avoid chance contact. Designate a primary and alternate compass and pace man per patrol.

> **NOTE**
> The point man will not be tasked to perform compass or pace duties. The point man's sole responsibility is forward security for the element.

(2) ***Avoidance of Detection.*** Patrols must use stealth, and use the cover and concealment of the terrain to its maximum advantage. Whenever possible, move during limited visibility in order to maximize technological advantages gained by night vision devices and to hinder the enemy's ability to detect the patrol. Exploit the enemy's weaknesses, and attempt to time movements to coincide with other operations that distract the enemy. The enemy threat and terrain determines which of the three movement techniques will be used:

(a) Fire teams maintain visual contact, but the distance between them is such that the entire patrol does not become engaged if contact is made. Fire teams can spread their formations as necessary to gain better observation to the flanks. Although widely spaced, men retain their relative position in their wedge and follow their team leader. Only in extreme situations should the file be used.

(b) The lead squad must secure the front along with assuming responsibility for navigation. For a long movement, the PL may rotate the lead squad responsibilities. The fire team/squad in the rear is charged with rear security.

(c) Vary movement techniques to meet the changing situation.

(d) With the exception of fire team leaders, leaders move inside their formations where they can maintain the best control.

(3) ***Security.*** The patrol must use both active and passive security measures constantly. Assign subunits responsibility for security at danger areas, patrol bases, and most importantly in the objective area.

(4) ***Fire Support.*** Plan fire support (mortars, artillery, tactical air, attack helicopter, naval gunfire).

(5) ***Three-Dimensional Battlefield.*** 360 Degree Security is achieved through high and low security. Within a fire team, squad, and so on, the leader must assign appropriate sectors of fire to their subordinate in order to ensure all aspects of the battlefield are covered. This includes trees, multiple storied structures, tunnels, sewers, ditches.

d. **Movement Techniques.**

(1) The traveling technique is used when enemy contact is not likely but speed is necessary.
(2) The traveling overwatch technique is used when enemy contact is possible.
(3) The bounding overwatch technique is used when enemy contact is likely, or when crossing a danger area.

e. **Traveling.** In the traveling technique, the distance between individuals is about 10 meters with 20 meters between squads. It has the following characteristics:

(1) More control than traveling overwatch but less than bounding overwatch.
(2) Minimum dispersion.
(3) Maximum speed.
(4) Minimum security.

f. **Traveling Overwatch.** The traveling overwatch technique is the basic movement technique. The distance between individuals is about 20 meters, between teams about 50 meters.

(1) In platoon traveling overwatch, the lead squad must be far enough ahead of the rest of the platoon to detect or engage any enemy before the enemy observes or fires on the main body. However, it must be close enough to be supported by the platoon's small arm's fires. This is normally between 50 to 100 meters, depending on terrain, vegetation, and light and weather conditions.

(2) In a column formation, only the lead squad should use the traveling overwatch; however, if greater dispersion is desired, all squads may use it.

(3) In other formations, all squads use traveling overwatch unless the platoon leader specifies otherwise.

(4) Traveling overwatch has the following characteristics:
- Good control.
- Good dispersion.
- Good speed.
- Good security forward.

g. **Bounding Overwatch**. In the bounding overwatch technique (Figure 2-2), the distance between men remains about 20 meters. The distance between teams and squads varies.

(1) The squad or platoon has a bounding element and an overwatch element. The bounding element moves while the overwatch element occupies an overwatch position that can cover the route of the bounding element by fire. Each bound is within supporting range of the overwatch element.

(2) There are two types of bounding, successive and alternating (Figure 2-2). Successive is nothing more than one squad moving to a position, then the overwatching squad moving to a position generally online with the first squad. Alternating bounding is when one squad moves into position, then the overwatching squad moves to a position in front of the first squad.

(3) The length of a bound depends on the terrain, visibility, and control.

(4) Before a bound, the leader gives the following instructions to his subordinates:
- Direction of the enemy if known
- Position of overwatch elements
- Next overwatch position
- Route of the bounding element
- What to do after the bounding element reaches the next position
- How the elements receive follow-on orders

(5) The characteristics of bounding overwatch are:
- Maximum control
- Maximum dispersion
- Minimum speed
- Maximum security

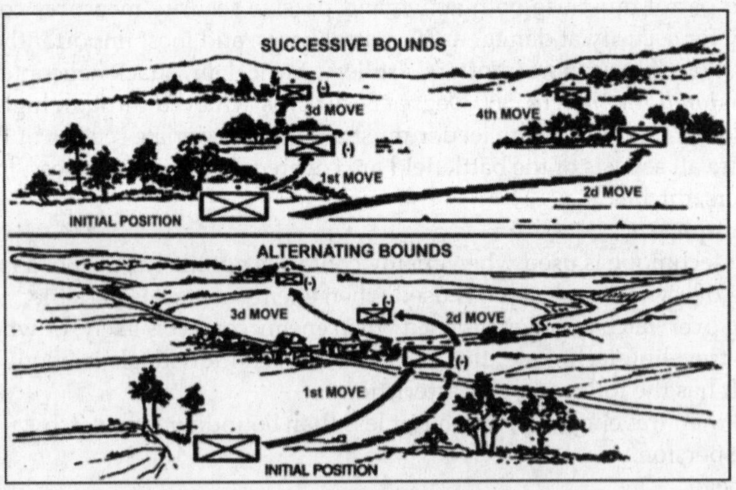

Figure 2-2. Squad bounding overwatch

h. **Platoon Bounding Overwatch** (Figure 2-3).

(1) ***Method One***. When platoons use bounding overwatch, one squad bounds and one squad overwatches; the third squad awaits orders. Forward observers stay with the overwatching squad to call for fire. Platoon leaders normally stay with the overwatching squad who use machine guns and attached weapons to support the bounding squad.

(2) ***Method Two***. Another way is to have one squad use bounding overwatch and have the other two squads use traveling or traveling overwatch technique.

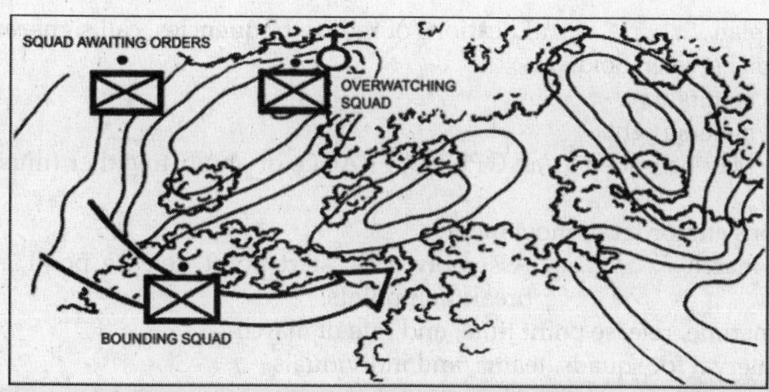

Figure 2-3. Platoon bounding overwatch

(3) ***Movement Considerations***. When deciding where to move the bounding element, consider–

- Where the enemy is likely to be.
- The mission.
- The routes to the next overwatch position.
- The weapons ranges of the overwatching unit.
- The responsiveness of the rest of the unit.
- The fields of fire at the next overwatch position.

2-2 TACTICAL MARCHES

Platoons conduct two types of marches with the company: foot marches and motor (road) marches.

a. **Purpose/General**. A successful foot march is when troops arrive at their destination at the prescribed time, physically able to execute their tactical mission.

b. **Standard**.

(1) The unit crosses the start point and release point at the time specified in the order.

(2) The unit follows the prescribed route, rate of march, and interval without deviation unless required otherwise by enemy action or higher headquarters action.

c. **Fundamentals**.

(1) Effective control.

(2) Detailed planning.

(3) Rehearsals.

d. **Considerations**.

(1) ***METT-TC***.

- Mission....................................Task and purpose.
- Enemy.......................................Intentions, capabilities, and course of action.
- Terrain and weather................Road condition/trafficability, and visibility.
- Troops/equipment...................Condition of Soldiers and their loads, numbers and types of weapons and radios.
- Time..Start time, release time, rate of march, time available.
- Civilians ....Movement through populated areas, refugees, OPSEC.

(2) ***Task Organization***:

- Security.....................................Advance and trail teams.
- Main body.................................Two remaining line squads and weapons squad.
- Headquarters............................Command and control.
- Control measures.

(3) ***Start Point and Release Point*** (given by higher):

(a) Checkpoints...........................At checkpoints report to higher and use checkpoint to remain oriented.

(b) Rally or rendezvous points..Used when elements become separated.

(c) Location of leaders ....Where they can best control their elements.

(d) Commo plan ....Locations of radios, frequencies, call signs, and OPSKEDs.
(e) Dispersion between Soldiers–
- 3 to 5 meters/day.
- 1 to 3 meters/night.

(4) *March Order*. May be issued as an OPORD, FRAGO, or annex to either (must use operational overlay or strip map):
(a) Formations and order of movement.
(b) Route of march ....Assembly area, start point, release point, rally points, checkpoints, break/halt points.
(c) Start point time, release point time, and rate of march.
(d) March interval for squads, teams, and individuals.
(e) Actions on enemy contact ....Air and ground.
(f) Actions at halts.
(g) Fires ....Detailed plan of fire support for the march.
(h) Water supply plan.
(i) MEDEVAC plan.

e. ***Duties and Responsibilities***.

(1) ***Platoon Leader***:
- Before......................................Issues warning order and FRAGO; inspects and supervises.
- During ....Ensures unit makes movement time; ensures interval is maintained and that unit remains oriented; maintains security; checks condition of men; and enforces water discipline and field sanitation.
- After...Ensures men are prepared to accomplish their mission, supervises SLs, and ensures medical coverage is provided to men as needed.

(2) ***Platoon Sergeant***:
- Before......................................Assists PL, makes recommendations, and enforces uniform and packing lists.
- During ....Controls stragglers, helps platoon leader maintain proper interval and security.
- At Halts ....Enforces security, ensures welfare of men, enforces field sanitation and litter discipline, and enforces use of preventive medicine.
- After...Coordinates for water, rations, and medical supplies. Recovers casualties.

(3) ***Squad Leaders***:
- Before......................................Provides detailed instruction to TLs, inspects boots and socks for serviceability and proper fit, inspects adjustment of equipment, inspects to ensure canteens are full, and ensures equal distribution of loads.
- During ....Controls squad, maintains proper interval between men and equipment, enforces security, remains oriented.
- At Halts ....Ensures security is maintained, provides men for water resupply as detailed. Physically checks the men in his squad, ensures they drink water, and that they change socks as necessary. Rotates heavy equipment. (Units should plan this in detail to avoid confusion before, during, and after halts.)
- After...Occupies squad sector of assembly area, conducts foot inspection, reports condition of men to PL, and prepares men to accomplish the mission.

(4) ***Security Squad***:
- Lead Team.
  - Serves as point element for platoon.
  - Recons route to SP.
  - Calls in checkpoints.
  - Provides early warning.
  - Maintains rate of march.
  - Moves 10 to 20 meters in front of main body.

- Trail Team.
  - Provides rear security.
  - Moves 10 to 20 meters behind main body.

(5) *Medic*:
- Assesses and treats march casualties.
- Advise chain of command on evacuation and transportation requirements of casualties.

(6) *Individual*:
- Maintains interval.
- Follows TL's examples.
- Relays hand and arm signals; remains alert during movement and at halts.
- Remains alert during movement and at halts.

2-3. MOVEMENT IN LIMITED VISIBILITY CONDITIONS

During hours of limited visibility, a platoon will use surveillance, target acquisition, and night observation (STANO) devices to enhance their effectiveness. Leaders must be able to control, navigate, maintain security, and move during limited visibility.

a. **Control**. When visibility is poor, the following methods aid in control.
(1) Use of night vision devices.
(2) Leaders move closer to the front.
(3) Platoon reduces speed.
(4) Use of luminescent tape on equipment.
(5) Reduce intervals between men and elements.
(6) Conducts headcount regularly.

b. **Navigation**. While navigating during limited visibility the same techniques are used as during the day; however, leaders exercise more care to keep the patrol oriented.

c. **Security**.
(1) Enforce strict noise and light discipline.
(2) Use radio-listening silence.
(3) Use camouflage.
(4) Use terrain to avoid detection by enemy surveillance or night vision devices.
(5) Make frequent listening halts; Conduct SLLS (Stop, Look, Listen, Smell).
(6) Mask the sounds of movement when possible. (Rain, wind, and flowing water will mask the sounds of movement).

d. **Rally Points**. Plan actions to be taken at rally points in detail. All elements must maintain communications at all time. There are two techniques for actions at rally points:
(1) ***Minimum Force***: Patrol members assemble at the rally point, and the senior leader assumes command. When the minimum force (designated in the OPORD) is assembled and organized the patrol will continue the mission.
(2) ***Time Available***: The senior leader determines if the patrol has enough time remaining to accomplish the mission.

e. **Actions at Halts**. During halts, post security and cover all approaches into the sector with key weapons.
(1) ***Short Halt***. Typically 1-2 minutes long. Soldiers seek immediate cover and concealment and take a knee. Leaders assign sectors of fire.
(2) ***Long Halt***. More than 2 minutes. Soldiers assume the prone position behind cover and concealment. (Ensure soldiers have clear fields of fire.) Leaders assign sectors of fire.

2-4. DANGER AREAS

A danger area is any place on a unit's route where the leader determines his unit may be exposed to enemy observation or fire. Some examples of danger areas are open areas, roads and trails, built-up areas, enemy positions, and natural and man-made obstacles. Bypass danger areas whenever possible.

a. **Standards.**
   (1) The unit prevents the enemy from surprising the main body.
   (2) The unit moves all personnel and equipment across the danger area.
   (3) The unit prevents decisive engagement by the enemy.
b. **Fundamentals.**
   (1) Designate near and far side rally points.
   (2) Secure near side, left and right flank, and rear security.
   (3) Recon and secure the far side.
   (4) Cross the danger area.
   (5) Plan for fires on all known danger areas.
c. **Technique for Crossing Danger Areas.**
   (1) *Linear Danger Area* (LDA, Figure 2-4) Actions for a Squad:

STEP 1: The alpha team leader (ATL) observes the linear danger area and sends the hand and arm signal to the SL who determines to bound across.

STEP 2: SL directs the ATL to move his team across the LDA far enough to fit the remainder of the squad on the far side of the LDA. Bravo team moves to the LDA to the right or left to provide an overwatch position prior to A team crossing.

STEP 3: SL receives the hand and arm signal that it is safe to move the rest of the squad across (B team is still providing overwatch).

STEP 4: SL moves himself, radio operator, and B team across the LDA. (A team provides overwatch for squad missions.)

STEP 5: A team assumes original azimuth at SL's command or hand and arm signal.

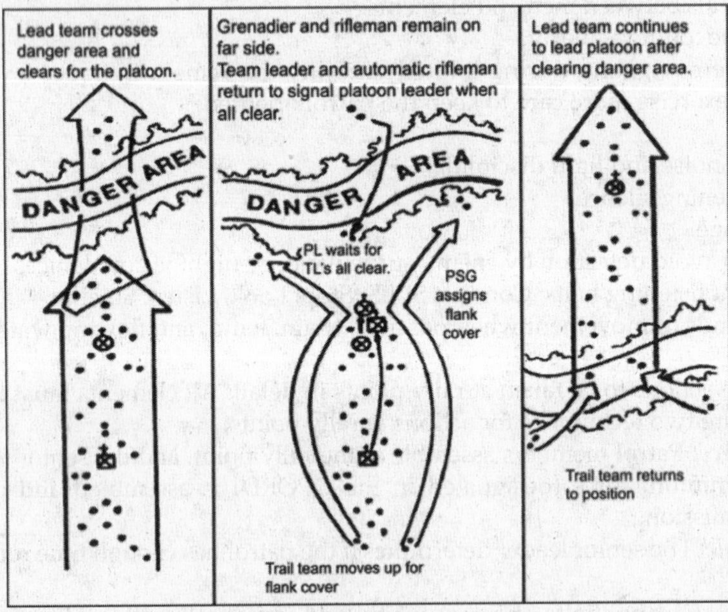

Figure 2-4. Linear danger area

(2) *LDA Crossing for a Platoon:*
   (a) The lead squad halts the platoon, and signals danger area.
   (b) The platoon leader moves forward to the lead squad to confirm the danger area and decides if current location is a suitable crossing site.
   (c) The platoon leader confirms danger area/crossing site and establishes near and far side rally points.
   (d) On the platoon leader's signal, the A team of the lead squad establishes an overwatch position to the left of the crossing site. Prior to crossing, the compassman with the lead two squads confirm azimuth and pace data.
   (e) B team of the lead squad establishes an overwatch position to the right of the crossing site.

(f) Once overwatch positions are established, the platoon leader gives the second squad in movement the signal to bound across by fire team.
(g) Once across, the squad is now lead in movement and continues on azimuth.
(h) Once Stop, Look, Listen, and Smell (SLLS) is conducted, squad leader signals platoon leader all clear.
- Day time—hand and arm signal such as thumbs up.
- Night time—Clandestine signal such as IR, red lens.

(i) Platoon leader receives all clear and crosses with radio operator, FO, WSL, and 2 gun teams.
(j) Once across, PL signals the 3rd squad in movement to cross.
(k) PSG with medic and one gun team crosses after 2nd squad is across (sterilizing central crossing site).
(l) PSG signals security squad to cross at their location.

> **NOTE**
> Platoon leader will plan for fires at all known LDA crossing sites. Nearside security in overwatch will sterilize signs of the patrol.

(3) ***Danger Area (Small/Open)***
(a) The lead squad halts the platoon and signals danger area.
(b) The PL moves forward to the lead squad to confirm the danger area.
(c) The platoon leader confirms danger area and establishes near and far side rally points.
(d) The PL designates lead squad to bypass danger area using the detour-bypass method.
(e) Paceman suspends current pace count and initiates an interim pace count. Alternate pace/compass man moves forward and offsets compass 90 degrees left or right as designated and moves in that direction until clear of danger area.
(f) After moving set distance (x-meters as instructed by PL). Lead squad assumes original azimuth, and primary pace man resumes original pace.
(g) After the open area, the alternate pace/compass man offsets his compass 90 degrees left or right and leads the platoon/squad the same distance (x-meters) back to the original azimuth.

(4) ***Danger Areas (Series):*** A series of danger areas is two or more danger areas within an area that can be either observed or covered by fire.
- Double linear danger area (use linear danger area technique and cross as one LDA).
- Linear/small open danger area (use by-pass/contour technique. Figure 2-5).
- Linear/large open danger area (use platoon wedge when crossing).

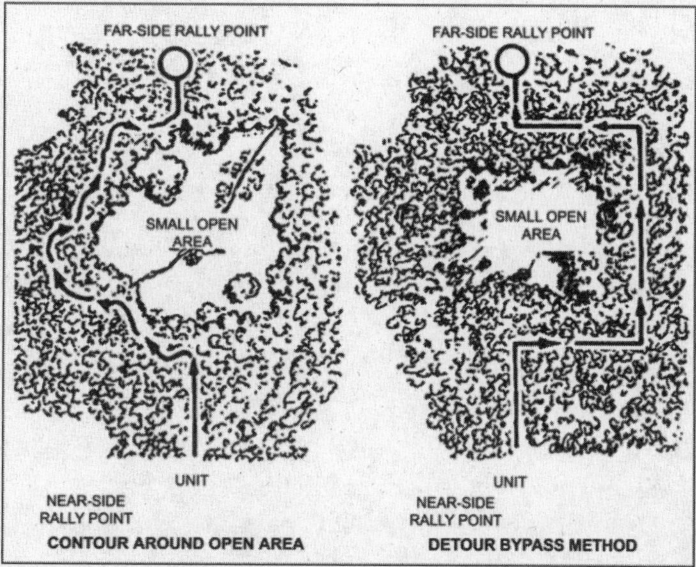

Figure 2-5. Small open area

NOTE

A series of danger areas is crossed using the technique which provides the most security.

(5) ***Danger Area (Large):***

(a) Lead squad halts the platoon, and signals danger area.
(b) The platoon leader moves forward with RTO and FO and confirms danger area.
(c) The platoon leader confirms danger area and establishes near and far side rally points.
(d) PL designates direction of movement.
(e) PL designates change of formation as necessary to ensure security.

NOTE

Before point man steps into danger area, PL and FO adjust targets to cover movement.

If far side of danger area is within 250 meters, PL establishes overwatch, and designates lead squad to clear wood line on far side.

CHAPTER 3

Patrols

Infantry platoons and squads primarily conduct two types of patrols: reconnaissance and combat. This chapter describes the principles of patrolling, planning considerations, types of patrols, supporting tasks, patrol base, and movement to contact. In this chapter, the terms *"element"* and *"team"* refer to the squads, fire teams, or buddy teams that perform the tasks as described.

3-1. PRINCIPLES

All patrols are governed by five principles:

a. **Planning**. Quickly make a simple plan and effectively communicate it to the lowest level. A great plan that takes forever to complete and is poorly disseminated isn't a great plan. Plan and prepare to a realistic standard and rehearse everything.

b. **Reconnaissance.** Your responsibility as a Ranger leader is to confirm what you think you know, and to team that which you do not already know.

c. **Security**. Preserve your force as a whole. Every Ranger and every rifle counts; anyone could be the difference between victory and defeat.

d. **Control**. Clear understanding of the concept of the operation and commander's intent, coupled with disciplined communications, to bring every man and weapon available to overwhelm the enemy at the decisive point.

e. **Common Sense**. Use all available information and good judgment to make sound, timely decisions.

3-2. PLANNING

This paragraph provides the planning considerations common to most patrols. It discusses task organization, initial planning and coordination, completion of the plan, and contingency planning.

a. **Task Organization**. A patrol is a mission, not an organization. To accomplish the patrolling mission, a platoon or squad must perform specific tasks, for example, secure itself, cross danger areas, recon the patrol objective, breach, support, or assault. As with other missions, the leader tasks elements of his unit in accordance with his estimate of the situation, identifying those tasks his unit must perform and designating which elements of his unit will perform which tasks. Where possible, in assigning tasks, the leader should maintain squad and fire team integrity. The chain of command continues to lead its elements during a patrol. Squads and fire teams may perform more than one task in an assigned sequence; others may perform only one task. The leader must plan carefully to ensure that he has identified and assigned all required tasks in the most efficient way. Elements and teams for platoons conducting patrols include—

(1) Elements common to all patrols:

(a) *Headquarters Element.* The headquarters consists of the platoon leader (PL), RTO, platoon sergeant (PSG), FO, RTO, and medic. It may include any attachments that the PL decides that he or the PSG must control directly.

(b) *Aid and Litter Team.* Aid and litter teams are responsible for buddy aid and evacuation of casualties.

(c) *Enemy Prisoner of War Team.* EPW teams control enemy prisoners using the five S's and the leader's guidance.

(d) *Surveillance Team.* The surveillance team keeps watch on the objective from the time that the leader's reconnaissance ends until the unit deploys for actions on the objective. They then rejoin their parent element.

(e) *En Route Recorder.* Part of the HQ element, maintains communications with higher and acts as the recorder for all CCIR collected during the mission.

(f) *Compass Man.* The compass man assists in navigation by ensuring the patrol remains on course at all times. Instructions to the compass man must include initial and subsequent azimuths. As a technique, the compass man should preset his compass on the initial azimuth before the unit moves out, especially if the move win be during limited visibility conditions. The platoon or squad leader should also designate an alternate compass man.

(g) *Point/Pace Man.* As required, the PL designates a primary and alternate point man and a pace man for the patrol. The pace man aids in navigation by keeping an accurate count of distance traveled. The point man selects the actual route through the terrain, guided by the compass man or team leader. In addition, the point man also provides frontal security.

(2) Elements common to all combat patrols:

(a) *Assault Element.* The assault element seizes and secures the objective and protects special teams as they complete their assigned actions on the objective.

(b) *Security Element.* The security element provides security at danger areas, secures the ORP, isolates the objective, and supports the withdrawal of the rest of the patrol once actions on the objective are complete. The security element may have separate security teams, each with an assigned task or sequence of tasks.

(c) *Support Element.* The support element provides direct and indirect fire support for the unit. Direct fires include machine guns, medium and light antiarmor weapons, small recoilless rifles. Indirect fires available may include mortars, artillery, CAS, and organic M203 weapon systems.

(d) *Demolition Team.* Demolition teams are responsible for preparing and detonating the charges to destroy designated equipment, vehicles, or facilities on the objective.

(e) *EPW and Search Teams.* The assault element may provide two-man (buddy teams) or four-man (fire team) search teams to search bunkers, buildings, or tunnels on the objective. These teams will search the objective or kill zone for any PIR that may give the PL an idea of the enemy concept for future operations. Primary and alternate teams may be assigned to ensure enough prepared personnel are available on the objective.

(f) *Breach Element.* The breach team conducts initial penetration of enemy obstacles to seize a foothold and allow the patrol to enter an objective. This is typically done IAW METT-TC and the steps outlined in the *"Conduct an Initial Breach of a Mined Wire Obstacle"* battle drill in Chapter 5 of this Handbook.

(3) Elements common to all reconnaissance patrols:

(a) *Reconnaissance Team.* Reconnaissance teams reconnoiter the objective area once the security teams are in position. Normally these are two-man teams (buddy teams) to reduce the possibility of detection.

(b) *Reconnaissance and Security Teams.* R&S teams are normally used in a zone reconnaissance, but may be useful in any situation when it is impractical to separate the responsibilities for reconnaissance and security.

(c) *Security Element.* When the responsibilities of reconnaissance and security are separate, the security element provides security at danger areas, secures the ORP, isolates the objective, and supports the withdrawal of the rest of the platoon once the recon is complete. The security element may have separate security teams, each with an assigned task or sequence of tasks.

b. **Initial Planning and Coordination.** Leaders plan and prepare for patrols using the troop-leading procedures and the estimate of the situation, as described in Chapter 2. Through an estimate of the situation, leaders identify required actions on the objective (mission analysis) and plan backward to departure from friendly lines and forward to reentry of friendly lines. Because patrolling units act independently, move beyond the direct-fire support of the parent unit, and operate forward of friendly units, coordination must be thorough and detailed. Coordination is continuous throughout planning and preparation. PLs use checklists to preclude omitting any items vital to the accomplishment of the mission.

(1) ***Coordination with Higher Headquarters.*** This coordination Includes intelligence, Operations, and Fire Support. This initial coordination is an integral part of Step 3 of Troop-Leading Procedures, *Make a Tentative Plan.*

(2) ***Coordination with Adjacent Units.*** The leader also coordinates his unit's patrol activities with the leaders of other units that will be patrolling in adjacent areas at the same time, IAW.

c. **Completion of Plan.** As the PL completes his plan, he considers–

(1) ***Specified and Implied Tasks.*** The PL ensures that he has assigned all specified tasks to be performed on the objective, at rally points, at danger areas, at security or surveillance locations, along the

route(s), and at passage lanes. These make up the maneuver and tasks to maneuver units subparagraphs of the Execution paragraph.

(2) ***Key travel and Execution Times.*** The leader estimates time requirements for movement to the objective, leader's reconnaissance of the objective, establishment of security and surveillance, completion of all assigned tasks on the objective, and passage through friendly lines. Some planning factors are–
- Movement: Average of 1 Kmph during daylight hours in Woodland Terrain; Average limited visibility ½ Kmph. Add additional time for restrictive, or severely restrictive terrain such as mountains, swamps, or thick vegetation.
- Leader's recon: NLT 1.5 hr.
- Establishment of security and surveillance: 0.5 hr.

(3) ***Primary and Alternate Routes.*** The leader selects primary and alternate routes to and from the objective. The return routes should differ from the routes to the objective. The PL may delegate route selection to a subordinate, but is ultimately responsible for the routes selected.

(4) ***Signals.*** The leader should consider the use of special signals. These include hand-and-arm signals, flares, voice, whistles, radios, and infrared equipment. Primary and alternate signals must be identified and rehearsed so that all Soldiers know their meaning.

(5) ***Challenge and Password Forward of Friendly Lines.*** The challenge and password from the unit's ANCD must not be used beyond the FLOT.

(a) *Odd-Number System.* The leader specifies an odd number. The challenge can be any number less than the specified number. The password will be the number that must be added to it to equal the specified number, for example, the number is 7, the challenge is 3, and the password is 4.

(b) *Running Password.* ANCDs may also designate a running password. This code word alerts a unit that friendly Soldiers are approaching in a less than organized manner and possibly under pressure. The number of Soldiers approaching follows the running password. For example, if the running password is *"Ranger,"* and five friendly Soldiers are approaching, they would say *"Ranger five."*

(6) ***Location of Leaders.*** The PL considers where he and the PSG and other key leaders are located during each phase of the mission. The PL positions himself where he can best control the actions of the patrol. The PSG is normally located with the assault element during a raid or attack to help the PL control the use of additional assaulting squads, and will assist with securing the OBJ. The PSG will locate himself at the CCP to facilitate casualty treatment and evacuation. During a reconnaissance mission, the PSG will stay behind in the ORP to facilitate the transfer of Intel to the higher headquarters, and control the recon elements movement into and out of the ORP.

(7) ***Actions on Enemy Contact.*** Unless required by the mission, the unit avoids enemy contact. The leader's plan must address actions on chance contact at each phase of the patrol mission. The unit's ability to continue will depend on how early contact is made, whether the platoon is able to break contact successfully (so that its subsequent direction of movement is undetected), and whether the unit receives any casualties because of the contact. The plan must address the handling of seriously wounded Soldiers and KIAs. The plan must also address the handling of prisoners who are captured because of chance contact and are not part of the planned mission.

(8) ***Contingency Plans.*** The leader leaves his unit for many reasons throughout the planning, coordination, preparation, and execution of his patrol mission. Each time the leader departs the patrol main body, he must issue a five-point contingency plan to the leader left in charge of the unit. The contingency plan is described by the acronym GOTWA, as follows. The patrol leader will additionally issue specific guidance stating what tasks are to be accomplished in the ORP in his absence:
- G: Where the leader is GOING.
- O: OTHERS he is taking with him.
- T: TIME he plans to be gone.
- W: WHAT to do if the leader does not return in time.
- A: The unit's and the leader's ACTIONS on chance contact while the leader is gone.

(9) ***Rally Points.*** The leader considers the use and location of rally points. A rally point is a place designated by the leader where the unit moves to reassemble and reorganize if it becomes dispersed. Soldiers must know which rally point to move to at each phase of the patrol mission should they become separated from the unit. They must also know what actions are required there and how long they are to wait at each rally point before moving to another.

(a) *Criteria.* Rally points must be—
- Easily identifiable in daylight and limited visibility.
- Show no signs of recent enemy activity.
- Covered and concealed.
- Away from natural lines of drift and high-speed avenues of approach.
- Defendable for short periods of time.

(b) *Types.* The most common types of rally points are initial, en route, objective, and near-and-far-side rally points.

(10) ***Objective Rally Point.*** The ORP is typically 200 to 400m from the objective, or at a minimum, one major terrain feature away. Actions at the ORP include—
- Conduct SLLS and pinpoint location.
- Leaders Recon of the Objective.
- Issuing a FRAGO, if needed.
- Making final preparations before continuing operations, for example, recamouflaging, preparing demolitions, lining up rucksacks for quick recovery. Preparing EPW bindings, first aid kits, litters, and inspecting weapons.
- Accounting for Soldiers and equipment after actions at the objective are complete.
- Reestablishing the chain of command after actions at the objective are complete.
- Disseminating information from reconnaissance, if contact was not made.

(11) ***Leader's reconnaissance of the objective.*** The plan must include a leader's reconnaissance of the objective once the platoon or squad establishes the ORP. Before departing, the leader must issue a 5-point contingency plan. During his reconnaissance, the leader pinpoints the objective, selects reconnaissance, security, support, and assault positions for his elements, and adjusts his plan based on his observation of the objective. Each type of patrol requires different tasks during the leader's reconnaissance. The platoon leader will bring different elements with him. (These are discussed separately under each type of patrol). The leader must plan time to return to the ORP, complete his plan, disseminate information, issue orders and instructions, and allow his squads to make any additional preparations. During the Leader's Reconnaissance tor a Raid or Ambush, the PL will leave surveillance on the OBJ.

(12) ***Actions on the objective.*** Each type of patrol requires different actions on the objective. Actions on the objective are discussed under each type of patrol.

3-3. RECONNAISSANCE PATROLS

Recon patrols are one of the two types of patrols, provide timely and accurate information on the enemy and terrain. They confirm the leader's plan before it is executed. Units on reconnaissance operations collect specific information (*priority intelligence requirements* [PIR] or general information (*information requirements* [IR]) based on the instructions from their higher commander. The two types of recon patrols discussed here are area and zone. This section discusses the fundamentals of reconnaissance, task standards for the two most common types of recon, and actions on the objective for those types of recon.

a. **Fundamentals of Reconnaissance.** In order to have a successful area reconnaissance, the platoon leader must apply the fundamentals of the reconnaissance to his plan during the conduct of the operation.

(1) ***Gain all required information.*** The parent unit tells the patrol leader (PL) what information is required. This is in the form of the IR and PIR. The platoon's mission is then tailored to what information is required. During the entire patrol, members must continuously gain and exchange at information gathered, but cannot consider the mission accomplished unless all PIR has been gathered.

(2) ***Avoid detection by the enemy.*** A patrol must not let the enemy know that it is in the objective area. If the enemy knows he is being observed, he may move, change his plans, or increase his security measures. Methods of avoiding detection are—

(a) Minimize movement in the objective area (area reconnaissance).
(b) Move no closer to the enemy than necessary.
(c) If possible, use long-range surveillance or night vision devices.
(d) Camouflage, stealth, noise, and light discipline.
(e) Minimize radio traffic.

(3) ***Employ security measures.*** A patrol must be able to break contact and return to the friendly unit with what information is gathered. If necessary, break contact and continue the mission. Security elements

are emplaced so that they can overwatch the reconnaissance elements and suppress the enemy so the reconnaissance element can break contact.

(4) ***Task organization.*** When the platoon leader receives the order, he analyzes his mission to ensure he understands what must be done. Then he task organizes his platoon to best accomplish the mission LAW METT-TC. Recons are typically squad-sized missions.

b. **Task Standards.**

(1) ***Area Reconnaissance.*** The area recon patrol collects all available information on PIR and other intelligence not specified in the order for the area. The patrol completes the recon and reports all information by the time specified in the order. The patrol is not compromised.

(2) ***Zone Reconnaissance.*** The zone recon patrol determines all PIR and other intelligence not specified in the order for its assigned zone. The patrol reconnoiters without detection by the enemy. The patrol completes the recon and reports all information by the time specified in the order.

c. **Actions on the Objective, Area Reconnaissance** (Figure 3-1).

(1) The element occupies the ORP as discussed in the section on occupation of the ORP. The RTO calls in spare for occupation of ORP. The leader confirms his location on map while subordinate leaders make necessary perimeter adjustments.

(2) The PL organizes the platoon in one of two ways: separate recon and security elements, or combined recon and security elements.

(3) The PL takes subordinates leaders and key personnel on a leader's recon to confirm the objective and plan.

(a) Issues a 5-point contingency plan before departure.

(b) Establishes a suitable release point that is beyond sight and sound of the objective if possible, but that is definitely out of sight. The RP should also have good rally point characteristics.

(c) Allow all personnel to become familiar with the release point and surrounding area.

(d) Identifies the objective and emplaces surveillance. Designates a surveillance team to keep the objective under surveillance. Issues a contingency plan to the senior man remaining with the surveillance team. The surveillance team is positioned with one man facing the objective, and one facing back in the direction of the release point.

(e) Takes subordinate leaders forward to pinpoint the objective, emplace surveillance, establish a limit of advance, and choose vantage points.

(f) Maintains commo with the platoon throughout the leader's recon.

(4) The PSG maintains security and supervises priorities of work in the ORP.

(a) Reestablishes security at the ORP.

(b) Disseminates the PLs contingency plan.

(c) Oversees preparation of recon personnel (personnel recamouflaged, NVDs and binos prepared, weapons on safe with a round in the chamber).

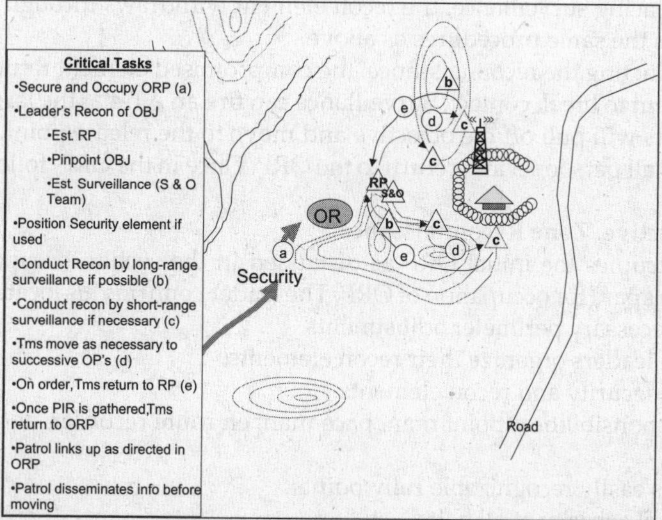

Figure 3-1. Actions on the objective, area reconnaissance

(5) The PL and his recon party return to the ORP.
   (a) Confirms the plan or issues a FRAGO.
   (b) Allows subordinate leaders time to disseminate the plan.
(6) The patrol conducts the recon by long-range observation and surveillance if possible.
   (a) R & S elements move to observation points that offer cover and concealment and that are outside of small-arms range.
   (b) Establishes a series of observation posts (OP) if information cannot be gathered from one location.
   (c) Gathers all PIR using the SALUTE format.
(7) If necessary, the patrol conducts its recon by short-range observation and surveillance.
   (a) Moves to an OP near the objective.
   (b) Passes close enough to the objective to gain information.
   (c) Gathers all PIR using the SALUTE format.
(8) R&S teams move using a technique such as the cloverleaf method to move to successive OP's. In this method, R&S teams avoid paralleling the objective site, maintain extreme stealth, do not cross the limit of advance, and maximize the use of available cover and concealment.
(9) During the conduct of the recon, each R&S team will return to the release point when any of the following occurs:
   - They have gathered all their PIR.
   - They have reached the limit of advance.
   - The allocated time to conduct the recon has elapsed.
   - Contact has been made.
(10) At the release point, the leader will analyze what information has been gathered and determine if he has met the PIR requirements.
(11) If the leader determines that he has not gathered sufficient information to meet the PIR requirements, or if the information he and the subordinate leader gathered differs drastically, he may have to send R&S teams back to the objective site. In this case, R&S teams will alternate areas of responsibilities. For example, if one team reconnoitered from the 6-3-12, then that team will now recon from the 6-9-12.
(12) The R&S element returns undetected to the ORP by the specified time.
   (a) Disseminates information to all patrol members through key leaders at the ORP, or moves to a position at least one terrain feature or one kilometer away to disseminate. To disseminate, the leader has the RTO prepare three sketches of the objective site based on the leader's sketch and provides the copies to the subordinate leaders to assist in dissemination.
   (b) Reports any information requirements and/or any information requiring immediate attention to higher headquarters, and departs for the designated area.
(13) If contact is made, move to the release point. The recon element tries to break contact and return to the ORP, secure rucksacks, and quickly move out of the area. Once they have moved a safe distance away, the leader will inform higher HQ of the situation and take further instructions from them.
   (a) While emplacing surveillance, the recon element withdraws through the release point to the ORP, and follows the same procedures as above.
   (b) While conducting the reconnaissance, the compromised element returns a sufficient volume of fire to allow them to break contact. Surveillance can fire an AT-4 at the largest weapon on the objective. All elements will pull off the objective and move to the release point. The senior man will quickly account for all personnel and return to the ORP. Once in the ORP, follow the procedures previously described.

d. **Actions on the Objective, Zone Reconnaissance.**
   (1) The element occupies the initial ORP as discussed in the section occupation on the ORP. The radio operator calls in spare for occupation of ORP. The leader confirms his location on map white subordinate leaders make necessary perimeter adjustments.
   (2) The recon team leaders organize their recon elements.
      (a) Designate security and recon elements.
      (b) Assign responsibilities (point man, pace man, en route recorder, and rear security), if not already assigned.
      (c) Designates easily recognizable rally points.
      (d) Ensure local security at all halts.

(3) The patrol recons the zone.
(a) Moves tactically to the ORPs.
(b) Occupies designated ORPs.
(c) Follows the method designated by the PL (fan, converging routes, or box method, Figure 3-2).

FAN METHOD	*CONVERGING ROUTES METHOD*	*BOX METHOD*
• Uses a series (fan) of ORPs. • Patrol establishes security at first ORP. • Each recon element moves from ORP along a different fan-shaped route. Route overlaps with that of other recon elements. This ensures recon of entire area. • Leader maintains reserve at ORP. • When all recon elements return to ORP, PL collects and disseminates all info before moving to next ORP.	• PL selects routes from ORP thru zone to a linkup point at the far side of the zone from the ORP. Each recon element moves and recons along a specified route. They converge (link up) at one time and place.	• PL sends recon elements from the first ORP along routes that form a box. He sends other elements along routes throughout the box. All teams link up at the far side of the box from the ORP.

Figure 3-2. Comparison of zone reconnaissance methods

(d) The recon teams reconnoiter.
- During movement, the squad will gather all PIR specified by the order.
- Recon team leaders will ensure sketches are drawn or digital photos are taken of all enemy hard sites, roads, and trails.
- Return to the ORP, or link up at the rendezvous point on time.
- When the squad arrives at new rendezvous point or ORP, the recon team leaders report to the PL with all information gathered.

(e) The PL continues to control the recon elements.
- PL moves with the recon element that establishes the linkup point.
- PL changes recon methods as required.
- PL designates times for the elements to return to the ORP or to linkup.
- PL collects all information and disseminates it to the entire patrol. PL will brief all key subordinate leaders on information gathered by other squads, establishing one consolidated sketch if possible, and allow team leaders time to brief their teams.
- PL and PSG account for all personnel.

(f) The patrol continues the recon until all designated areas have been reconned, and returns undetected to friendly lines.

3-4. COMBAT PATROLS

Combat patrols are the second type of patrol. Combat patrols are further divided into raids and ambushes Units conduct combat patrols to destroy or capture enemy Soldiers or equipment; destroy installations, facilities, or key points; or harass enemy forces. Combat patrols also provide security for larger units. This section describes overall combat patrol planning considerations, task considerations for each type of combat patrol, and finally actions on the objective for each type.

a. **Planning Considerations (General).** In planning a combat patrol, the PL considers the following:
(1) ***Tasks to Maneuver Units.*** Normally the platoon headquarters element controls the patrol on a combat patrol mission. The PL makes every try to maintain squad and fire team integrity as he assigns tasks to subordinates units.
(a) The PL must consider the requirements for assaulting the objective, supporting the assault by fire, and security of the entire unit throughout the mission.
- For the assault on the objective, the PL considers the required actions on the objective, the size of the objective, and the known or presumed strength and disposition of the enemy on and near the objective.
- The PL considers the weapons available, and the type and volume of fires required to provide fire support for the assault on the objective.
- The PL considers the requirement to secure the platoon at points along the route, at danger areas, at the ORP, along enemy avenues of approach into the objective, and elsewhere during the mission.
- The PL will also designate engagement/disengagement criteria.

(b) The PL assigns additional tasks to his squads for demolition, search of EPWs, guarding of EPWs, treatment and evacuation (litter teams) of friendly casualties, and other tasks required for successful completion of patrol mission (if not already in the SOP).

(c) The PL determines who will control any attachments of skilled personnel or special equipment.

(2) ***Leader's Reconnaissance of the Objective.*** In a combat patrol, the PL has additional considerations for the conduct of his reconnaissance of the objective from the ORP.

(a) *Composition of the leader's reconnaissance party.* The platoon leader will normally bring the following personnel.

- Squad leaders to include the weapons squad leader.
- Surveillance team.
- Forward observer.
- Security element (dependent on time available).

(b) Conduct of the leader's reconnaissance. In a combat patrol, the PL considers the following additional actions in the conduct of the leader's reconnaissance of the objective.

- The PL designates a release point approximately halfway between the ORP and this objective. The PL posts the surveillance team. Squads and fire teams separate at the release point and then they move to their assigned positions.
- The PL confirms the location of the objective or kill zone. He notes the terrain and identifies where he can emplace claymores to cover dead space. Any change to his plan is issued to the squad leaders (while overlooking the objective if possible).
- If the objective is the kill zone for an ambush, the leader's reconnaissance party should not cross the objective; to do so will leave tracks that may compromise the mission.
- The PL confirms the suitability of the assault and support positions and routes from them back to the ORP.
- The PL issues a five-point contingency plan before returning to the ORP.

b. **Ambush.**

(1) ***Planning Considerations.*** An ambush is a surprise attack form a concealed position on a moving or temporarily halted target. Ambushes are classified by category-hasty or deliberate; type-point or area; and formation-linear or L-shaped. The leader uses a combination of category, type, and formation in developing his ambush plan. The key planning considerations include—

(a) Coverage of entire kill zone by fire.

(b) METT-TC.

(c) Use of existing or reinforcing obstacles, including Claymores, to keep the enemy in the kill zone.

(d) Security teams (typically equipped with hand-held antitank weapons such as AT-4 or LAW; Claymores; and various means of communication.

(e) Protect the assault and support elements with claymores or explosives.

(f) Use security elements or teams to isolate the kill zone.

(g) Assault through the kill zone to the limit of advance (LOA). (The assault element must be able to move quickly through its own protective obstacles.)

(h) Time the actions of all elements of the platoon to preclude loss of surprise. In the event any member of the ambush is compromised, he may immediately initiate the ambush.

(i) When the ambush must be manned for a long time, use only one squad to conduct the entire ambush and determining movement time of rotating squads from the ORP to the ambush site.

(2) **Categories.**

(a) *Hasty Ambush.* A unit conducts a hasty ambush when it makes visual contact with an enemy force and has time to establish an ambush without being detected. The actions for a hasty ambush must be well rehearsed so that Soldiers know what to do on the leader's signal. They must also know what action to take if the unit is detected before it is ready to initiate the ambush.

(b) *Deliberate Ambush.* A deliberate ambush is conducted at a predetermined location against any enemy element that meets the commander's engagement criteria. The leader requires the following detailed information in planning a deliberate ambush: size and composition of the targeted enemy, and weapons and equipment available to the enemy.

(3) ***Types***
  (a) Point ambush. In a point ambush, Soldiers deploy to attack an enemy in a single kill zone.
  (b) Area ambush. In an area, Soldiers deploy in two or more related point ambushes.
(4) ***Formations.*** (Figure 3-3).
  (a) *Linear Ambush.* In an ambush using a linear formation, the assault and support elements deploy parallel to the enemy's route. This positions both elements on the long axis of the kill zone and subjects the enemy to flanking fire. This formation can be used in close terrain that restricts the enemy's ability to maneuver against the platoon, or in open terrain provided a means of keeping the enemy in the kill zone can be effected.
  (b) *L-Shaped Ambush.* In an L-shaped ambush, the assault element forms the long leg parallel to the enemy's direction of movement along the kill zone. The support element forms the short leg at one end of and at right angles to the assault element. This provides both flanking (long leg) and enfilading fires (short leg) against the enemy. The L-shaped ambush can be used at a sharp bend in a trail, road, or stream. It should not be used where the short leg would have to cross a straight road or trail.

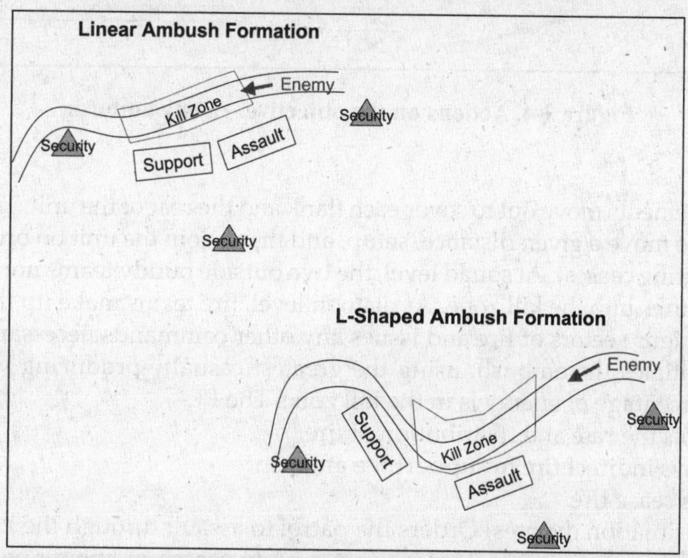

Figure 3-3. Ambush formations

c. **Hatty Ambush.**
(1) ***Task Standards.*** The platoon moves quickly to concealed positions. The ambush is not initiated until the majority of the enemy is in the kill zone. The unit does not become decisively engaged. The platoon surprises the enemy. The patrol captures, kills, or forces the withdrawal of all of the enemy within the kill zone. On order, the patrol withdraws all personnel and equipment in the kill zone from observation and direct fire. The unit does not become decisively engaged by follow-on elements. The platoon continues follow-on operations.
(2) ***Actions on the Objective (Hasty Ambush).*** See Figure 3-4.
  (a) Using visual signals, any Soldier alerts the unit that an enemy force is in sight. The Soldier continues to monitor the location and activities of the enemy force until his team or squad leader relieves him, and gives the enemy location and direction of movement.
  (b) The platoon or squad halts and remains motionless.
  - The PL gives the signal to conduct a hasty ambush, taking care not to alert the enemy of the patrol's presence.
  - The leader determines the best nearby location tor a hasty ambush. He uses arm-and-hand signals to direct the unit members to covered and concealed positions.
  (c) The leader designates the location and extent of the kill zone.
  (d) Teams and squads move silently to covered and concealed positions, ensuring positions are undetected and have good observation and fields of fire into the kill zone.

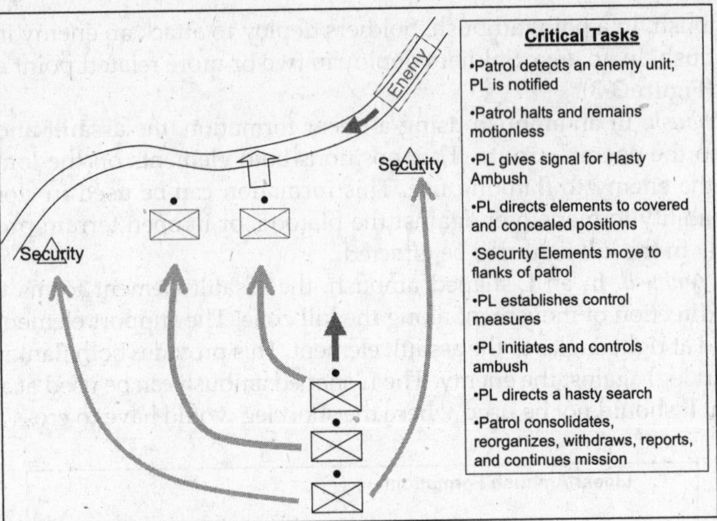

Figure 3-4. Actions on the objective – hasty ambush

(e) Security elements move out to cover each flank and the rear of the unit. The leader directs the security elements to move a given distance, setup, and then rejoin the unit on order or, after the ambush (the sound of firing ceases). At squad level, the two outside buddy teams normally provide flank security as well as fires into the kill zone. At platoon level, fire teams make up the security elements.

(f) The PL assigns sectors of fire and issues any other commands necessary such as control measures.

(g) The PL initiates the ambush, using the greatest casualty-producing weapon available, when the largest percentage of enemy is in the kill zone. The PL-

- Controls the rate and distribution of fire.
- Employs indirect fire to support the ambush.
- Orders cease fire.
- (If the situation dictates) Orders the patrol to assault through the kill zone.

(h) The PL designates personnel to conduct a hasty search of enemy personnel and process enemy prisoners and equipment.

(i) The PL orders the platoon to withdraw from the ambush site along a covered and concealed route.

(j) The PL gains accountability, reorganizes as necessary, disseminates information, reports the situation, and continues the mission as directed.

d. **Deliberate (Point/Area) Ambush.**

(1) ***Task Standards.*** The ambush is emplaced NLT the time specified in the order. The patrol surprises the enemy and engages the enemy main body. The patrol kills or captures all enemy in the kill zone and destroys equipment based on the commander's intent. The patrol withdraws all personnel and equipment from the objective, on order, within the time specified in the order. The patrol obtains all available PIR from the ambush and continues follow-on operations.

(2) ***Actions on the Objective (Deliberate Ambush).*** See Figure 3-5.

(a) The PL prepares the patrol for the ambush in the ORP.

(b) The PL prepares to conduct a leader's reconnaissance. He—

- Designates the members of the leader's recon party (typically includes squad leaders, surveillance team, FO, and possibly the security element.
- Issues a contingency plan to the PSG.

(c) The PL conducts his leader's reconnaissance. He–

- Ensures the leader's recon party moves undetected.
- Confirms the objective location and suitability for the ambush.
- Selects a kill zone.
- Posts the surveillance team at the site and issues a contingency plan.

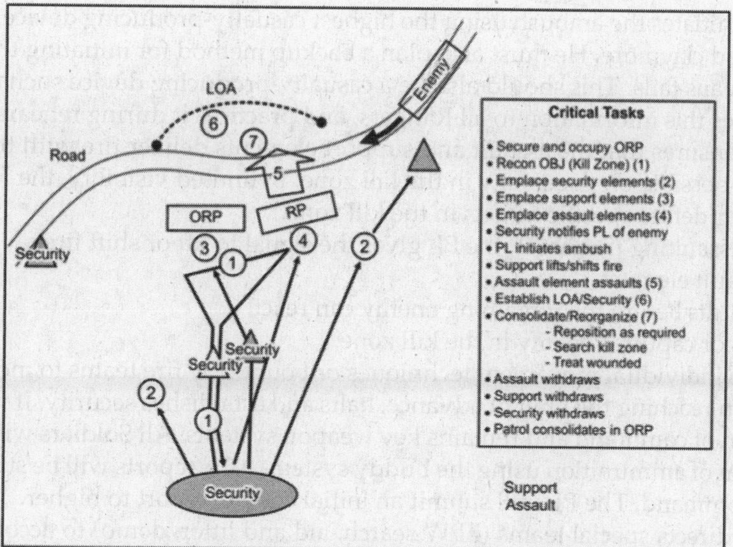

Figure 3-5. Actions on the objective - deliberate ambush

- Confirms suitability of assault and support positions, and routes from them to the ORP.
- Selects the position of each weapon system in the support-by-fire position, and then designates sectors of fire.
- Identifies all offensive control measures to be used. Identifies PLD, the assault position, LOA, any boundaries or other control measures. If available, the PL can use infrared aiming devices to identify these positions on the ground.

(d) The PL adjusts his plan based on info from the reconnaissance. He–
- Assigns positions.
- Designates withdrawal routes.

(e) The PL confirms the ambush formation.

(f) The security team(s) occupy first, securing the flanks of the ambush site, and providing early warning. The security element must be in position before the support and assault elements move forward of the release point. A security team remains in the ORP if the patrol plans to return to the ORP after actions on the objective. If the ORP is abandoned, a rear security team should be emplaced.

(g) Support element leader assigns sectors of fire. He–
- Emplaces claymores and obstacles as designated.
- Identifies sectors of fire and emplaces limiting stakes to prevent friendly fires from hitting other elements.
- Overwatches the movement of the assault element into position.

(h) Once the support element is in position, or on the PLs order, the assault element–
- Departs the ORP and moves into position.
- Upon reaching the PLD, the assault element transitions from the movement formation to the battle formation.
- Identifies individual sectors of fire as assigned by the PL. Emplaces aiming stakes or uses metal-to-metal contact with the machine gun tripods to prevent fratricide on the objective.
- Emplaces claymores to help destroy the enemy in the kill zone.
- Camouflages positions.

(i) The security element spots the enemy and notifies the PL, and reports the direction of movement, size of the target, and any special weapons or equipment carried. The security element also keeps the platoon leader informed if any enemy forces are following the lead force.

(j) The PL alerts other elements, and determines if the enemy force is too large, or if the ambush can engage the enemy successfully.

(k) The PL initiates the ambush using the highest casualty-producing device. He may use a command-detonated claymore. He must also plan a backup method for initiating the ambush, in case his primary means fails. This should also be a casualty-producing device such as his individual weapon. He passes this information to all Rangers, and practices it during rehearsals.

(l) The PL ensures that the assault and support elements deliver fire with the heaviest, most accurate volume possible on the enemy in the kill zone. In limited visibility, the PL may use infrared lasers to further define specific targets in the kill zone.

(m) Before assaulting the target, the PL gives the signal to lift or shift fires.

(n) The assault element–
- Assaults before the remaining enemy can react.
- Kills or captures enemy in the kill zone.
- Uses individual movement techniques or bounds by fire teams to move.
- Upon reaching the limit of advance, halts and establishes security. If needed, it reestablishes the chain of command and remains key weapon systems. All Soldiers will load a fresh magazine or drum of ammunition using the buddy system. ACE reports will be submitted through the chain of command. The PL will submit an initial contact report to higher.

(o) The PL directs special teams (EPW search, aid and litter, demo) to accomplish their assigned task once the assault element has established its LOA.
- Once the kill zone had been cleared, collect and secure all EPWs and move them out of the kill zone before searching bodies. Coordinate for an EPW exchange point to link up with higher to extract all EPWs and treat them IAW the five S's.
- Search from one side to the other and mark bodies that have been searched to ensure the area is thoroughly covered. Units should use the *"clear out, search in"* technique, clear from the center of the objective out ensuring the area is clear of all enemy combatants; then search all enemy personnel towards the center of the objective. Search all dead enemy personnel using two-man search techniques.
  - As the search team approaches a dead enemy Soldier, one-man guards while the other man searches. First, he kicks the enemy weapon away.
  - Second, he rolls the body over (if on the stomach) by lying on top and when given the go ahead by the guard (who is positioned at the enemy's head), the searcher rolls the body over on him. This is done for protection in case the enemy Soldier has a grenade with the pin pulled underneath him.
  - The searchers then conduct a systematic search of the dead Soldier from head to toe removing all papers and anything new (different type rank, shoulder boards, different unit patch, pistol, weapon, or NVD). They note if the enemy has a fresh or shabby haircut and the condition of his uniform and boots. They note the radio frequency, and then they secure the SOI, maps, documents, and overlays.
  - Once the body has been thoroughly searched, the search team will continue in this manner until all enemy personnel in and near the kill zone have been searched.
- Identify, collect, and prepare all equipment to be carried back or destroyed.
- Evacuate and treat friendly wounded first, then enemy wounded, time permitting.
- The demolition team prepares dual-primed explosives or incendiary grenades and awaits the signal to initiate. This is normally the last action performed before the unit departs the objective and may signal the security elements to return to the ORP.
- Actions on the objective with stationary assault line; all actions are the same with the exception of the search teams. To provide security within the teams to the far side of the kill zone during the search, they work in three-Ranger teams. Before the search begins, the Rangers move all KIAs to the near side of the kill zone.

(p) If enemy reinforcements try to penetrate the kill zone, the flank security will engage to prevent the assault element from being compromised.

(q) The platoon leader directs the unit's withdrawal from the ambush site:
- Elements normally withdraw in the reverse order that they established their positions.
- The elements may return to the RP or directly to the ORP, depending on the distance between elements.

- The security element of the ORP must be alert to assist the platoon's return to the ORP. It maintains security for the ORP while the rest of the platoon prepares to leave.
- If possible, all elements should return to the location at which they separated from the main body. This location should usually be the RP.

(r) The PL and PSG direct actions at the ORP, to include accountability of personnel and equipment and recovery of rucksacks and other equipment left at the ORP during the ambush.

(s) The platoon leader disseminates information, or moves the platoon to a safe location (no less than one kilometer or one terrain feature away from the objective) and disseminates information.

(t) As required, the PL and FO execute indirect fires to cover the platoon's withdrawal.

e. **Perform Raid.** The patrol initiates the raid NLT the time specified in the order, surprises the enemy, assaults the objective, and accomplishes its assigned mission within the commander's intent. The patrol does not become decisively engaged en route to the objective. The patrol obtains all available PIR from the raid objective and continues follow-on operations.

(1) ***Planning Considerations.*** A Raid is a form of attack, usually small scale, involving a swift entry into hostile territory to secure information, confuse the enemy, or destroy installations followed by a planned withdrawal. Squads do not conduct raids. The sequence of platoon actions for a raid is similar to those for an ambush. Additionally, the assault element of the platoon may have to conduct a breach of an obstacle. It may have additional tasks to perform on the objective such as demolition of fixed facilities. Fundamentals of the raid include—

- Surprise and speed. Infiltrate and surprise the enemy without being detected.
- Coordinated fires. Seal off the objective with well-synchronized direct and indirect fires.
- Violence of action. Overwhelm the enemy with fire and maneuver.
- Planned withdrawal. Withdraw from the objective in an organized manner, maintaining security.

(2) **Actions on the Objective (Raid).** See Figure 3-6.

(a) The patrol moves to and occupies the ORP IAW the patrol SOP. The patrol prepares for the leader's recon.

(b) The PL, squad leaders, and selected personnel conduct a leader's recon.

- PL leaves a five point contingency plan with the PSG.
- PL establishes the RP, pinpoints the objective, contacts the PSG to prep men, weapons, and equipment. Emplaces the surveillance team to observe the objective, and verifies and updates intelligence information.
- Leader's recon verifies location of and routes to security, support, and assault positions.
- Security teams are brought forward on the leader's reconnaissance and emplaced before the leader's recon leaves the RP
- Leaders conduct the recon without compromising the patrol.
- Leaders normally recon support by fire position first, then the assault position.

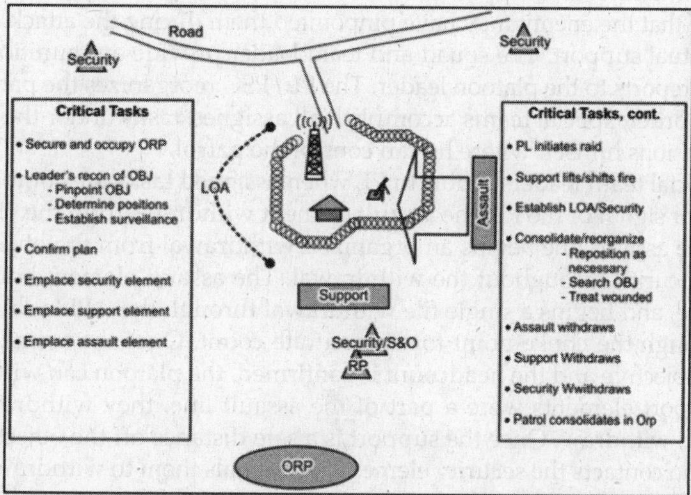

Figure 3-6. Actions on the objective – raid

(c) The PL confirms, denies, or modifies his plan and issues instructions to his squad leaders.
- Assigns positions and withdrawal routes to all elements.
- Designates control measures on the objective (element objectives, lanes, limits of advance, target reference points, and assault line).
- Allows SLs time to disseminate information, and confirm that their elements are ready.

(d) Security elements occupy designated positions, moving undetected into positions that provide early warning and can seal off the objective from outside support or reinforcement.

(e) The support element leader moves the support element to designated positions. The support element leader ensures his element can place well-aimed fire on the objective.

(f) The PL moves with the assault element into the assault position. The assault position is normally the last covered and concealed position before reaching the objective. As it passes through the assault position the platoon deploys into its assault formation; that is, its squads and fire teams deploy to place the bulk of their firepower to the front as they assault the objective.
- Makes contact with the surveillance team to confirm any enemy activity on the objective.
- Ensures that the assault position is close enough for immediate assault if the assault element is detected early.
- Moves into position undetected, and establish local security and fire control measures.

(g) Element leaders inform the PL when their elements are in position and ready.

(h) The PL directs the support element to fire.

(i) Upon gaining fire superiority, the PL directs the assault element to move towards the objective.
- Assault element holds fire until engaged, or until ready to penetrate the objective.
- PL signals the support element to lift or shift fires. The support element lifts or shifts fires as directed, shifting fire to the flanks of targets or areas as directed in the FRAGO.

(j) The assault element attacks and secures the objective. The assault element may be required to breech a wire obstacle. As the platoon, or its assault element moves onto the objective, it must increase the volume and accuracy of fires. Squad leaders assign specific targets or objectives for their fire teams. Only when these direct fires keep the enemy suppressed can the rest of the unit maneuver. As the assault element gets closer to the enemy, there is more emphasis on suppression and less on maneuver. Ultimately, all but one fire team may be suppressing to allow that one fire team to break into the enemy position. Throughout the assault, Soldiers use proper individual movement techniques, and fire teams retain their basic shallow wedge formation. The platoon does not get *"on-line"* to sweep across the objective.
- Assault element assaults through the objective to the designated LOA.
- Assault element leaders establish local security along the LOA, and consolidate and reorganize as necessary. They provide ACE reports to the PL and PSG. The platoon establishes security, operates key weapons, provides first aid, and prepares wounded Soldiers for MEDEVAC. They redistribute ammunition and supplies, and they relocate selected weapons to alternate positions if leaders believe that the enemy may have pinpointed them during the attack. They adjust other positions for mutual support. The squad and team leader provide ammunition, casualty, and equipment (ACE) reports to the platoon leader. The PL/PSG reorganizes the patrol based on the contact.
  - On order, special teams accomplish all assigned tasks under the supervision of the PL, who positions himself where he can control the patrol.
  - Special team leaders report to PL when assigned tasks are complete.

(k) On order or signal of the PL, the assault element withdraws from the objective. Using prearranged signals, the assault line begins an organized withdrawal from the objective site, maintaining control and security throughout the withdrawal. The assault element bounds back near the original assault line, and begins a single file withdrawal through the APL's choke point. All Rangers must move through the choke point for an accurate count. Once the assault element is a safe distance from the objective and the headcount is confirmed, the platoon can withdraw the support element. If the support elements were a part of the assault line, they withdraw together, and security is signaled to withdraw. Once the support is a safe distance off the objective, they notify the platoon leader, who contacts the security element and signals them to withdraw. All security teams link up at the release point and notify the platoon leader before moving to the ORP. Personnel returning to the ORP immediately secure their equipment and establish all-round security. Once the security element returns, the platoon moves out of the objective area as soon as possible, normally in two to three minutes.

- Before withdrawing, the demo team activates demo devices and charges.
- Support element or designated personnel in the assault element maintain local security during the withdrawal.
- Leaders report updated accountability and status (ACE report) to the PL and PSG.

(l) Squads withdraw from the objective in the order designated in the FRAGO to the ORP.

- Account for personnel and equipment.
- Disseminate information.
- Redistribute ammunition and equipment as required.

(m) The PL reports mission accomplishment to higher and continues the mission.

- Reports raid assessment to higher.
- Informs higher of any IR/PIR gathered.

3-5 SUPPORTING TASKS

This section covers Linkup, Patrol Debriefing, and Occupation of an ORP.

a. **Linkup.** A linkup is a meeting of friendly ground forces. Linkups depend on control, detailed planning, communications, and stealth.

(1) **Task Standard.** The units link up at the time and place specified in the order. The enemy does not surprise the main bodies. The linkup units establish a consolidated chain of command.

(2) *Linkup Site Selection.* The leader identifies a tentative linkup site by map reconnaissance, other imagery, or higher headquarters designates a linkup site. The linkup site should have the following characteristics:

- Ease of recognition.
- Cover and concealment.
- No tactical value to the enemy.
- Location away from natural lines of drift.
- Defendable for a short period of time.
- N=Mutiple access and escape routes.

(3) *Execution.* Linkup procedure begins as the unit moves to the linkup point. The steps of this procedure are:

(a) The stationary unit performs linkup actions.

- Occupies the linkup rally point (LRP) NLT the time specified in the order.
- Establishes all-around security, establishes commo, and prepares to accept the moving unit.
- The security team clears the immediate area around the linkup point. It then marks the linkup point with the coordinated recognition signal. The security team moves to a covered and concealed position and observes the linkup point and immediate area around it.

(b) The moving unit—

- Performs linkup actions.
- The unit reports its location using phase lines, checkpoints, or other control measures.
- Halts at a safe distance from the linkup point in a covered and concealed position (the linkup rally point).

(c) The PL and a contact team—

- Prepare to make physical contact with the stationary unit.
- Issue a contingency plan to the PSG.
- Maintain commo with the platoon; verify near and far recognition signals for linkup (good visibility and limited visibility).
- Exchange far and near recognition signals with the linkup unit; conduct final coordination with the linkup unit.

(d) The stationary unit—

- Guides the patrol from its linkup rally point to the stationary unit linkup rally point.
- Linkup is complete by the time specified in the order.
- The main body of the stationary unit is alerted before the moving unit is brought forward.

(e) The patrol continues its mission IAW the order.

(4) ***Coordination Checklist.*** The PL coordinates or obtains the following information from the unit that his patrol will link up with:
- Exchange frequencies, call signs, codes, and other communication information.
- Verify near and far recognition signals.
- Exchange fire coordination measures.
- Determine command relationship with the linkup unit; plan for consolidation of chain of command.
- Plan actions following linkup.
- Exchange control measures such as contact points, phase lines, contact points, as appropriate.

b. **Debrief.** Immediately after the platoon or squad returns, personnel from higher headquarters conduct a through debrief. This may include all members of the platoon or the leaders, RTOs, and any attached personnel. Normally the debriefing is oral. Sometimes a written report is required. Information on the written report should include—
- Size and composition of the unit conducing the patrol.
- Mission of the platoon such as type of patrol, location, and purpose.
- Departure and return times.
- Routes. Use checkpoints, grid coordinates for each leg or include an overlay.
- Detailed description of terrain and enemy positions that were identified.
- Results of any contact with the enemy.
- Unit status at the conclusion of the patrol mission, including the disposition of dead or wounded Soldiers.
- Conclusions or recommendations.

c. **Objective Rally Point.** The ORP is a point out of sight, sound, and small arms range of the objective area. It is normally located in the direction that the platoon plans to move after completion of actions on the objective. The ORP is tentative until the objective is pinpointed.

(1) ***Occupation of the ORP.*** See Figure 3-7.

(a) The patrol halts beyond sight and sound of the tentative ORP (200-400m in good visibility, 100–200m in limited visibility).

(b) The patrol establishes a security halt IAW the unit SOP.

(c) After issuing a five-point contingency plan to the PSG, the PL moves forward with a recon element to conduct a leader's recon of the ORP.

(d) For a squad-sized patrol, the PL moves forward with a compass man and one member of each fire team to confirm the ORP.
- After physically cleaning the ORP location, the PL leaves two Rangers at the 6 o'clock position facing in opposite directions.

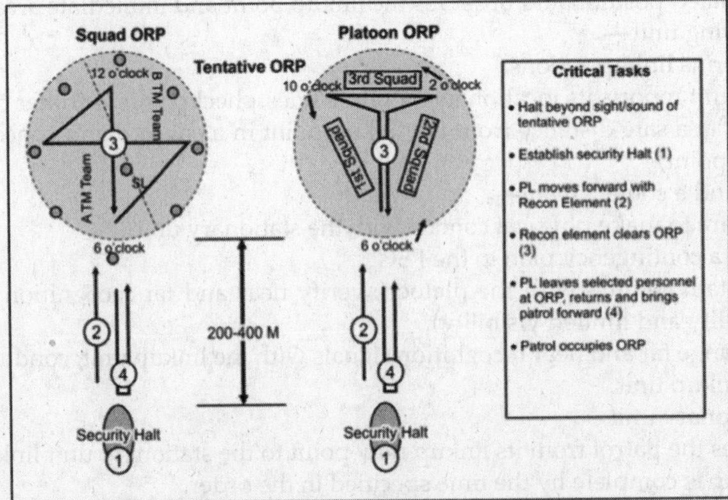

Figure 3-7. Occupation of the ORP

- The PL issues a contingency plan and returns with the compass man to guide the patrol forward.
- The PL guides the patrol forward into the ORP, with one team occupying from 3 o'clock through 12 o'clock to 9 o'clock, and the other occupying from 9 o'clock through 6 o'clock to 3 o'clock.

(e) For a platoon-size patrol, the PL, RTO, WSL, three ammo bearers, a team leader, a SAW gunner, and riflemen go on the leaders recon for the ORP and position themselves at 10, 2, and 6 o'clock.
- The first squad in the order of march is the base squad, occupying from 10 to 2 o'clock.
- The trail squads occupy from 2 to 6 o'clock and 6 to 10 o'clock, respectively.
- The patrol headquarters element occupies the center of the triangle.

(2) ***Actions in the ORP.*** The unit prepares for the mission in the ORP. Once the leader's recon pinpoints the objective, the PSG generally lines up rucks IAW unit SOP In the center of the ORP.

d. **Patrol Base.** A patrol base is a security perimeter that is set up when a squad or platoon conducting a patrol halts for an extended period. Patrol bases should not be occupied for more than a 24-hour period (except in emergency). A patrol never uses the same patrol base twice.

(1) ***Use.*** Patrol bases are typically used—
- To avoid detection by eliminating movement.
- To hide a unit during a long detailed reconnaissance.
- To perform maintenance on weapons, equipment, eat and rest.
- To plan and issue orders.
- To reorganize after infiltrating on an enemy area.
- To establish a base from which to execute several consecutive or concurrent operations.

(2) ***Site Selection.*** The leader selects the tentative site from a map or by aerial reconnaissance. The site's suitability must be confirmed and secured before the unit moves into it. Plans to establish a patrol base must include selecting an alternate patrol base site. The alternate site is used if the first site is unsuitable or if the patrol must unexpectedly evacuate the first patrol base.

(3) ***Planning Considerations.*** Leaders planning for a patrol base must consider the mission and passive and active security measures. A patrol base (PB) must be located so it allows the unit to accomplish its mission.
- Observation posts and communication with observation posts.
- Patrol or platoon fire plan.
- Alert plan.
- Withdrawal plan from the patrol base to include withdrawal routes and a rally point, rendezvous point, or alternate patrol base.
- A security system to make sure that specific Soldiers are awake at all times.
- Enforcement of camouflage, noise, and light discipline.
- The conduct of required activities with minimum movement and noise.
- Priorities of Work.

(4) ***Security Measures.***
- Select terrain the enemy would probably consider of little tactical value.
- Select terrain that is off main lines of drift.
- Select difficult terrain that would impede foot movement, such as an area of dense vegetation, preferably bushes and trees that spread dose to the ground.
- Select terrain near a source of water.
- Select terrain that can be defended for a short period and that offers good cover and concealment.
- Avoid known or suspected enemy positions.
- Avoid built-up areas.
- Avoid ridges and hilltops, except as needed for maintaining communications.
- Avoid small valleys.
- Avoid roads and trails.

(5) ***Occupation.*** See Figure 3-8.

(a) A PB is reconned and occupied in the same manner as an ORP, with the exception that the platoon will typically plan to enter at a 90 degree turn. The PL leaves a two-man OP at the turn, and the patrol covers any tracks from the turn to the PB.

(b) The platoon moves into the PB. Squad-sized patrols will generally occupy a cigar-shaped perimeter; platoon-sized patrols will generally occupy a triangle-shaped perimeter.

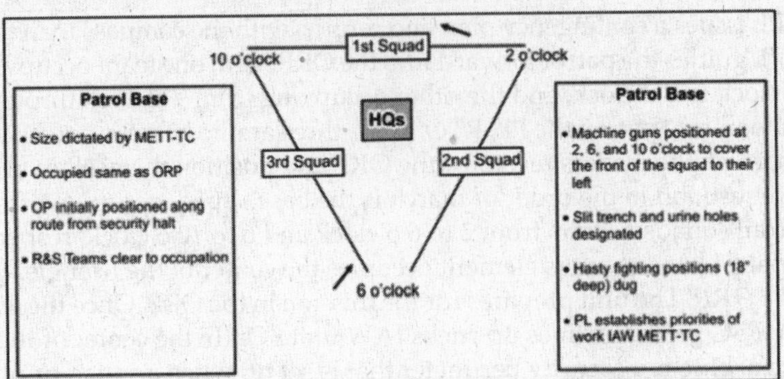

Figure 3-8. Patrol base

(c) The PL and another designated leader Inspect and adjust the entire perimeter as necessary.

(d) After the PL has checked each squad sector, each SL sends a two-man R&S team to the PL at the CP. The PL issues the three R&S teams a contingency plan, reconnaissance method, and detailed guidance on what to look for (enemy, water, built-up areas or human habitat, roads, trails, or possible rally points).

(e) Where each R&S team departs is based on the PLs guidance. The R&S team moves a prescribed distance and direction, and reenters where the PL dictates.

- Squad-sized patrols do not normally send out an R&S team at night.
- R&S teams will prepare a sketch of the area to the squad front if possible.
- The patrol remains at 100 % alert during this recon.
- If the PL feels the patrol was tracked or followed, he may elect to wait in silence at 100 % alert before sending out R&S teams.
- The R&S teams may use methods such as the "*I*," the "*Box*," or the "*T*." Regardless of the method chosen, the R&S team must be able to provide the PL with the same information.
- Upon completion of R&S, the PL confirms or denies the patrol base location, and either moves the patrol or begins priorities of work.

(6) ***Passive (Clandestine) Patrol Base (Squad).***

- The purpose of a passive patrol base is for the rest of a squad or smaller size element.
- Unit moves as a whole and occupies in force.
- Squad leader ensures that the unit moves in at a 90-degree angle to the order of movement.
- A claymore mine is emplaced on route entering patrol base.
- Alpha and Bravo teams sit back-to-back facing outward, ensuring that at least one individual per team is alert and providing security.

(7) ***Priorities of Work (Platoon and Squad).*** Once the PL is briefed by the R&S teams and determines the area is suitable for a patrol base, the leader establishes or modifies defensive work priorities in order to establish the defense for the patrol base. Priorities of work are not a laundry list of tasks to be completed; to be effective, priorities of work must consist of a task, a given time, and a measurable performance standard. For each priority of work, a clear standard must be issued to guide the element in the successful accomplishment of each task. It must also be designated whether the work will be controlled in a centralized or decentralized manner. Priorities of work are determined IAW METT-TC. Priorities of Work may include, but are not limited to the following tasks:

(a) *Security (Continuous).*

- Prepare to use all passive and active measures to cover all of the perimeter all of the time, regardless of the percentage of weapons used to cover that all of the terrain.
- Readjust after R&S teams return, or based on current priority of work {such as weapons maintenance).
- Employ all elements, weapons, and personnel to meet conditions of the terrain, enemy, or situation.
- Assign sectors of fire to all personnel and weapons. Develop squad sector sketches and platoon fire plan.

- Confirm location of fighting positions for cover, concealment, and observation and fields of fire. SLs supervise placement of aiming stakes and claymores.
- Only use one point of entry and exit, and count personnel in and out. Everyone is challenged IAW the unit SOP.
- Hasty fighting positions are prepared at least 18 inches deep (at the front), and sloping gently from front to rear, with a grenade sump if possible.

(b) *Withdrawal Plan.* The PL designates the signal for withdrawal, order of withdrawal, and the platoon rendezvous point and / or alternate patrol base.

(c) *Communication (Continuous).* Commo must be maintained with higher headquarters, OP's, and within the unit. May be rotated between the patrol's RTOs to allow accomplishment of continuous radio monitoring, radio maintenance, act as runners for PL, or conduct other priorities of work.

(d) *Mission Preparation and Planning.* The PL uses the patrol base to plan, issue orders, rehearse, inspect, and prepare for future missions.

(e) *Weapons and Equipment Maintenance.* The PL ensures that machine guns, weapon systems, commo equipment and night vision devices (as well as other equipment) are maintained. These items are not disassembled at the same time for maintenance (no more than 33 percent at a time), and weapons are not disassembled at night. If one machine gun is down, then security for all remaining systems is raised.

(f) *Water Resupply.* The PSG organizes watering parties as necessary. The watering party carries canteens in an empty rucksack or duffel bag, and must have commo and a contingency plan prior to departure.

(g) *Mess Plan.* At a minimum, security and weapons maintenance are performed prior to mess. Normally no more than half the platoon eats at one time. Rangers typically eat 1 to 3 meters behind their fighting positions.

- Rest / sleep plan management. The patrol conducts rest as necessary to prepare for future operations.
- Alert Plan and Stand-to. The PL states the alert posture and the stand-to time. He develops the plan to ensure all positions are checked periodically, OP's are relieved periodically, and at least one leader Is always alert. The patrol typically conducts stand-to at a time specified by unit SOP (such as 30 minutes before and after BMNT or EENT).
- Resupply. Distribute or cross-load ammunition, meals, equipment, etc.
- Sanitation and personal hygiene. The PSG and medic ensure a slit trench is prepared and marked. All Soldiers will brush teeth, wash face, shave, wash hands, armpits, groin, feet, and darken (brush shine) boots daily. The patrol will not leave trash behind.

3-6. MOVEMENT TO CONTACT

The MTC is one of the five types of offensive operations. An MTC gains or regains contact with the enemy. Once contact is made, the unit develops the situation. Normally a platoon conducts an MTC as part of a larger force.

a. **Techniques.** The two techniques of conducting a movement to contact are search and attach and approach march.

(1) ***Search and Attack (S&A).*** This technique is used when the enemy is dispersed, is expected to avoid contact, disengage or withdraw, or you have to deny his movement in an area. The search and attack technique involves the use of multiple platoons, squads, and fire teams coordinating their actions to make contact with the enemy. Platoons typically try to find the enemy and then fix and finish him. They combine patrolling techniques with the requirement to conduct hasty or deliberate attacks once the enemy has been found.

(a) *Planning Considerations.*

- The factors of METT-TC.
- The requirement for decentralized execution.
- The requirement for mutual support.
- The length of operations.
- Minimize Soldier's load to improve stealth and speed.

- Resupply and MEDEVAC.
- Positioning key leaders and equipment.
- Employment of key weapons.
- Requirement for patrol bases.
- Concept tor entering the zone of action.
- The concept for linkups while in contact.

(b) *Critical Performance Measures.*
- The platoon locates the enemy without being detected.
- Once engaged, fixes the enemy in position and maneuvers against the enemy.
- Maintains security throughout actions to avoid being flanked.

(2) ***Approach March.*** The concept of the approach march is to make contact with the smallest element, allowing the commander the flexibility of destroying or bypassing the enemy. A platoon uses the approach march method as part of a larger unit. It can be tasked as the advance guard, move as part of the main body, or provide flank or rear security for the company or battalion. They may also receive on-order missions as part of the main body.

(a) *Fundamentals.* These basics are common to all movements to contact.
- Make enemy contact with smallest element possible.
- Rapidly develop combat power upon enemy contact.
- Provide all-round security for the unit.
- Support higher unit's concept.
- Reports all information rapidly and accurately and strives to gain and maintain contact with the enemy.
- Requires decentralized execution.

(b) *Planning Considerations.* The following issues should be considered heavily for MTC operations:
- Factors of METT-TC.
- Reduced Soldier's load.

(c) Critical Performance Measures.
- PL selects the appropriate movement formation based on likelihood of enemy contact.
- Maintains contact, once contact is made, until ordered to do otherwise.

b. **Task Standards**. The platoon moves NLT the time specified in the order, the platoon makes contact with the smallest element possible, and the main body is not surprised by the enemy. Once the platoon makes contact, it maintains contact. The platoon destroys squad and smaller-sized elements, and fixes elements larger than a squad. The platoon maintains sufficient fighting force capable of conducting further combat operations. Reports of enemy locations and contact are forwarded. If not detected by the enemy, the PL initiates a hasty attack. The platoon sustains no casualties from friendly fire. The platoon is prepared to initiate further movement within 25 minutes of contact, and all personnel and equipment are accounted for.

CHAPTER 4

Battle Drills

Infantry battle drills describe how platoons and squads apply fire and maneuver to commonly encountered situations. They require leaders to make decisions rapidly and to issue brief oral orders quickly.

SECTION I. INTRODUCTION

This section defines and describes the format for battle drills.

4-1. DEFINITION

FM7-1 defines a battle drill as *"a collective action rapidly executed without applying a deliberate decision-making process."*

a. Characteristics of a battle drill are—
   - They require minimal leader orders to accomplish and are standard throughout the Army.
   - Sequential actions are vital to success in combat or critical to preserving life.
   - They apply to platoon or smaller units.
   - They are trained responses to enemy actions or leader's orders.
   - They represent mental steps followed for offensive and defensive actions in training and combat.

b. A unit's ability to accomplish its mission often depends on Soldiers and leaders to execute key actions quickly. All Soldiers and their leaders must know their immediate reaction to enemy contact, as well as follow-up actions. Drills are limited to situations requiring instantaneous response; therefore, Soldiers must execute drills instinctively. This results from continual practice. Drills provide small units with standard procedures essential for building strength and aggressiveness.
   (1) They identify key actions that leaders and Soldiers must perform quickly.
   (2) They provide for a smooth transition from one activity to another; for example, from movement to offensive action to defensive action.
   (3) They provide standardized actions that link Soldier and collective tasks at platoon level and below. (Soldiers perform individual tasks to CTT or SDT standard.)
   (4) They require the full understanding of each individual and leader, and continual practice.

4.2 FORMAT

Drills Include a ***title***, ***a situation*** to cue the unit or leader to start the drill, the ***required actions*** in sequence, and supporting illustrations. Where applicable, drills are cross-referenced with material in other chapters, or other drills, or both. Training standards for battle drills are in the mission training plan (MTP).

SECTION II. DRILLS

This section provides the battle drills for small units.

BATTLE DRILL 1
REACT TO CONTACT

SITUATION: A squad or platoon receives fires from enemy individual or crew-served weapons.

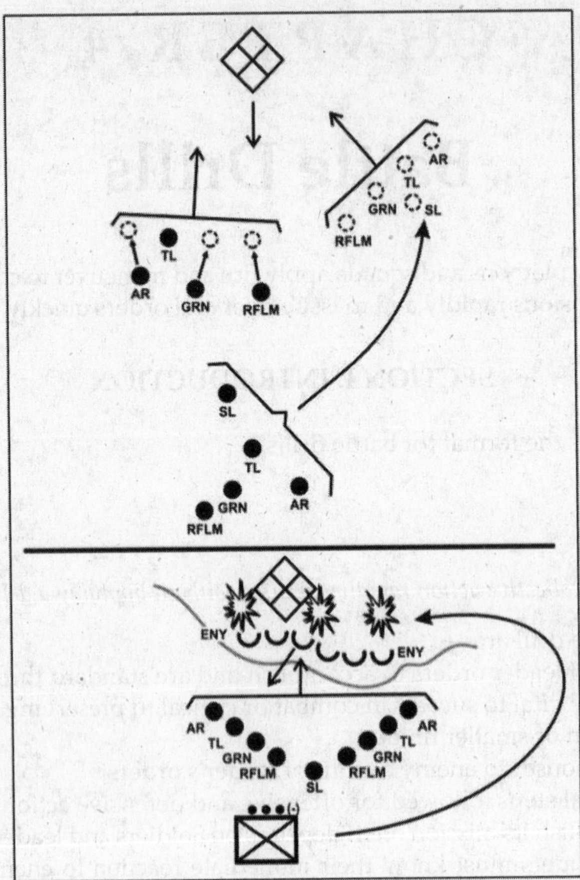

Figure 4-1. React to contact

REQUIRED ACTIONS: See Figure 4-1.

1. Solders immediately assume the nearest covered positions.
2. Soldiers return fire immediately on reaching the covered positions.
3. Squad/team leaders locate and engage known or suspected enemy positions with well-aimed fire, and they pass information to the platoon/squad leader.
4. Fire team leaders control the fire of their Soldiers by using standard fire commands (initial and supplemental) containing the following elements:
   - Alert
   - Direction
   - Description of target
   - Range
   - Method of fire (manipulation and rate of fire)
   - Command to commence firing
5. Soldiers maintain contact (visual or oral) with the Soldiers on their left and right.
6. Soldiers maintain contact with their team leaders and indicate the location of enemy positions.
7. The leaders (visual or oral) check the status of their personnel.
8. The squad/team leaders maintain visual contact with the platoon/squad leader.
9. The platoon/squad leader moves up to the squad/fire team in contact and links up with its leader.
   a. The platoon leader brings his RTO, platoon FO, the nearest squad's squad leader, and one machine gun team.
   b. The squad leader of the trail squad moves to the front of his lead fire team.
   c. The PSG also moves forward with the second machine gun team and links up with the platoon leader, ready to assume control of the base-of-fire element.

10. The platoon/squad leader determines whether or not his unit must move out of an EA.
11. The platoon/squad leader determines whether his unit can gain and maintain suppressive fires with the element already in contact (based on the volume and accuracy of enemy fires against the element in contact). The platoon/squad leader assesses the situation. He identifies—
    - The location of the enemy position and obstacles.
    - The size of the enemy force engaging the unit in contact. The number of enemy automatic weapons, the presence of any vehicles, and the employment of indirect fires are indicators of the enemy strength.
    - Vulnerable flanks.
    - Covered and concealed flanking routes to the enemy position.
12. The platoon/squad leader determines the next COA, such as fire and movement, assault, breach, knock out bunker, enter and clear a building or trench.
13. The platoon/squad leader reports the situation to the company commander/platoon leader and begins to maneuver his unit.
14. Platoon leader directs platoon FO to call for and adjust indirect fires (mortars or artillery). Squad leaders relay requests through the platoon leader. The platoon/squad leader in conjunction with the platoon FO maintains accurate battle tracking of all friendly elements to facilitate quick clearance of fires.
15. Leaders relay all commands and signals from the platoon chain of command.
16. The PSG positions the base of fire element to observe and to provide supporting fires.

NOTE

Once the platoon has executed the React to Contact drill, the platoon leader quickly assesses the situation, for example, enemy size and location. He picks a COA. The platoon leader reports the situation to the company commander.

BATTLE DRILL 2

BREAK CONTACT

SITUATION: The squad or platoon is under enemy fire and must break contact.

REQUIRED ACTIONS: See Figure 4-2.

1. The platoon/squad leader directs fire support for the disengagement. He accomplishes this by—
    - Directing one squad/fire team in contact to support the disengagement of the remainder of the unit.
    - Considering the use of indirect fires for breaking contact.
    - Clearing the location, task, purpose, and method of conducting the fire mission with the platoon FO.
2. The platoon/squad leader orders a distance and direction, a terrain feature, or last ORP for the movement of the first squad/fire team. In conjunction with the platoon FO, the leader maintains accurate battle tracking of all friendly elements to facilitate quick clearance of fires.
3. The base of fire squad/team continues to suppress the enemy. The platoon/squad leader directs the platoon FO to execute the fire mission, if needed.
4. The moving squad/team assumes the overwatch position. The squad/team should use M203 grenade launchers, throw fragmentation and concussion grenades, and use smoke grenades to mask movement. The platoon/squad leader directs the platoon FO to execute smoke mission to screen friendly elements movement, if needed.
5. The moving squad/team takes up the designated position and engages the enemy position.
6. The platoon leader directs the base-of-fire element to move to its next location. Based on the terrain and the volume and accuracy of the enemy's fire, the moving fire team or squad may need to use fire and movement techniques.
7. The platoon/squad continues to bound away from the enemy until—
    - It breaks contact. It must continue to suppress the enemy as it does this.
    - It passes through a higher-level SBF position.
    - Its squad/fire teams are In the assigned position to conduct the next mission.
8. The leader should consider changing his unit's direction of movement once contact is broken. This will reduce the ability of the enemy to place effective indirect fires on the unit.

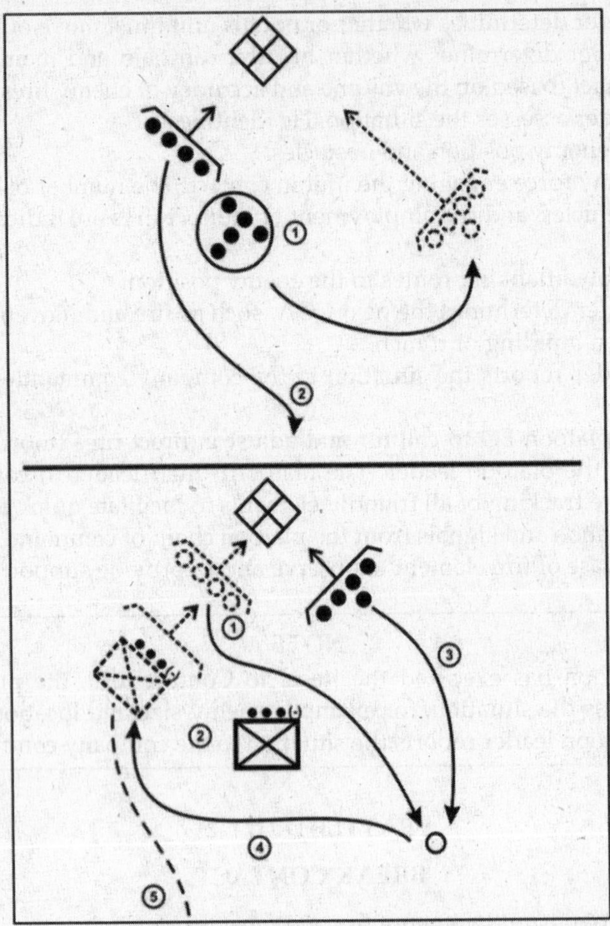

Figure 4-2. Break contact

9. If the platoon/squad becomes disrupted. Soldiers stay together and move to the last designated rally point.
10. The platoon/squad leaders account for Soldiers, report, reorganize as necessary, and continue the mission. With the platoon FO, the platoon/squad develops a quick fire plan to support the hasty defense or new route of march.

BATTLE DRILL 3

REACT TO AMBUSH

SITUATION: The squad or platoon enters a kill zone and the enemy initiates an ambush with a casualty-producing device and a high volume of fire.

REQUIRED ACTIONS: See Figure 4-3.

1. Near ambush (within hand-grenade range).
   a. Soldiers in the kill zone return fire immediately. How they go about this depends on the terrain. If—
      - Cover is not available. Soldiers immediately, without order or signal, assume prone position and throw concussion or fragmentation and smoke grenades.
      - Cover is available, without order or signal, Soldiers seek the nearest covered position, assume the prone position, and throw fragmentation or concussion and smoke grenades.
   b. Immediately after the explosion of the concussion or fragmentation grenades, Soldiers in the kill zone return fire and assault through the ambush position using fire and movement.

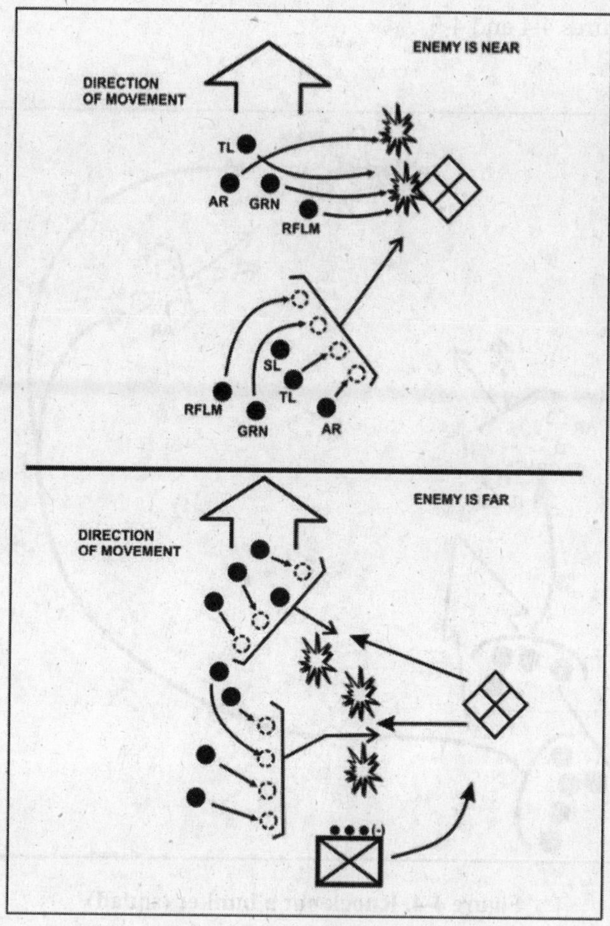

Figure 4-3. React to ambush

c. Soldiers not in the kill zone identify the enemy's position. Fire is shifted as the personnel in the kill zone begin to assault.

d. Soldiers in the kill zone continue the assault to eliminate the ambush or until contact is broken.

e. The platoon/squad conducts consolidation and reorganization.

2. Far ambush (out of hand-grenade range). Soldiers receiving fire immediately return fire, take up covered positions, and suppress the enemy by—
   - Destroying or suppressing enemy crew-served weapons.
   - Sustaining suppressive fires.
3. Soldiers (squad/teams) not receiving fires move by a covered and concealed route to a vulnerable flank of the enemy position and assault using fire and movement techniques.
4. Soldiers in the kill zone continue suppressive fires and shift fires as the assaulting squad/team fights through the enemy position.
5. The platoon FO calls for and adjusts indirect fires as directed by the platoon leader. On order, he shifts or ceases fires to isolate the enemy position or to attack them with indirect fires as they retreat.
6. The platoon/squad leader reports, reorganizes as necessary, and continues the mission.

BATTLE DRILL 4

KNOCK OUT BUNKERS

SITUATION: While moving as part of a larger force, the platoon identifies the enemy in bunkers.

REQUIRED ACTIONS: See Figures 4-4 and 4-5.

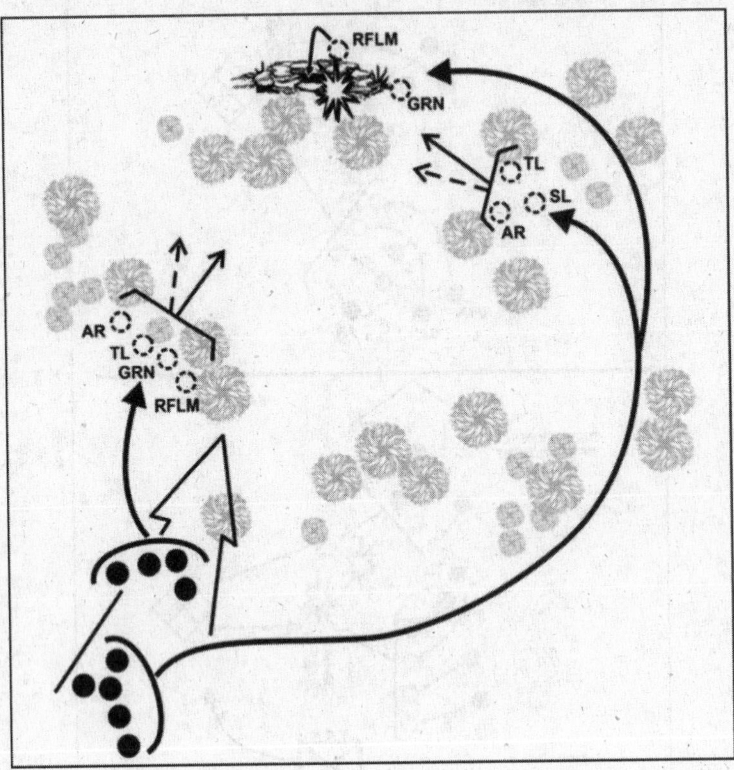

Figure 4-4. Knock out a bunker (squad)

1. The platoon initiates contact.
   a. The squad in contact establishes a base of fire.
   b. The platoon leader, his RTO, platoon FO, and one machine gun team move forward to link up with the squad leader of the squad in contact.
   c. The PSG moves forward with the second machine gun team and assumes control of the base-of-fire squad.
   d. The base-of-fire squad—
      - Destroys or suppresses enemy crew-served weapons first.
      - Obscures the enemy position with smoke (M203).
      - Sustains suppressive fires at the lowest possible level.
   e. The platoon leader directs platoon FO to call for and adjust indirect fires. The platoon leader in conjunction with the platoon FO maintains accurate battle tracking of all friendly elements to facilitate quick clearance of fires.
2. The platoon leader determines that he can maneuver by identifying—
   - Enemy bunkers, other supporting positions, and any obstacles.
   - Size of the enemy force engaging the platoon. The number of enemy automatic weapons, the presence of any vehicles, and the employment of indirect fires are indicators of enemy strength.
   - A vulnerable flank of at least one bunker.
   - A covered and concealed flanking route to the flank of the bunker.
3. The platoon leader determines which bunker is to be assaulted first and directs one squad (not in contact) to knock it out.
4. If necessary, the PSG repositions a squad, fire team, or machine gun team to isolate toe bunker as well as to continue suppressive fires.

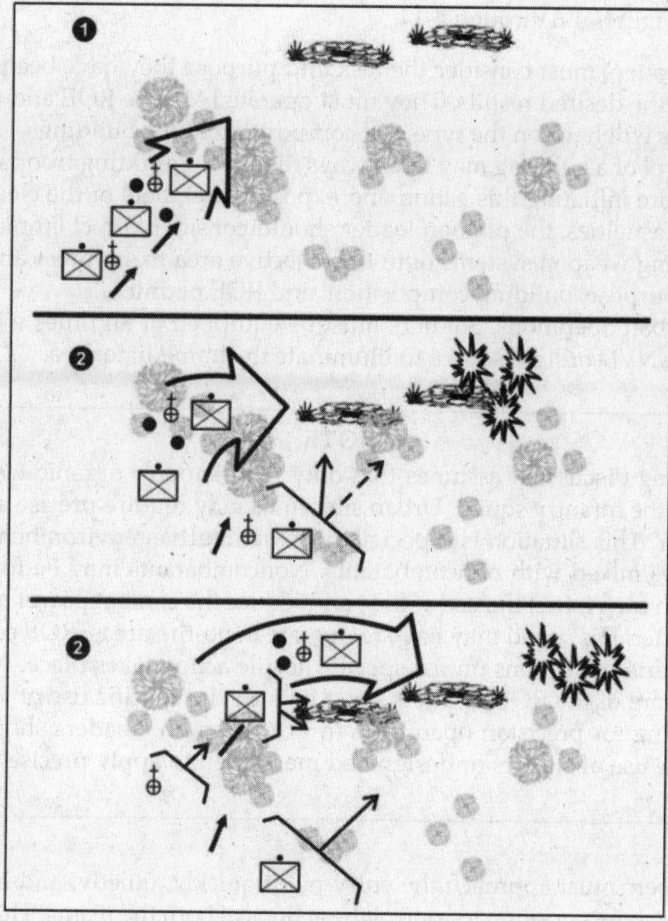

Figure 4-5. Knock out bunker (platoon)

5. The assaulting squad, with the platoon leader and his RTO, move along the covered and concealed route and take action to knock out the bunker. The following occurs.
   a. On the platoon leader's signal, the support squad ceases or shifts fires to the opposite side of the bunker from which the squad is assaulting.
   b. At the same time, the platoon FO shifts indirect fires to isolate enemy positions.
6. The assaulting squad leader reports to the platoon leader and reorganizes his squad.
7. The platoon leader—
   - Directs the supporting squad to move up and knock out the next bunker.
   - Directs the assaulting squad to continue and knock out the next bunker.
   - Rotates squads as necessary.
8. The platoon leader reports, reorganizes as necessary, and continues the mission. The company follows up the success of the platoon attack and continues to assault enemy positions.

BATTLE DRILL 5
ENTER BUILDING/CLEAR ROOM

SITUATION: Operating as part of a larger force (in daylight or darkness), the squad is tasked to participate in clearing a building. The platoon leader directs the squad to enter the building or to clear a room. An entry point or breach has already been identified or will be created before initiating the entry. For a detailed discussion of urban entry breaching techniques, see FM 3.06-11. Enemy forces and noncombatants may or may not be present in the room and or building to be cleared.

REQUIRED ACTIONS: See Figures 4-6 through 4-14.

1. Platoon and squad leaders must consider the task and purpose they have been given and the method they are to use to achieve the desired results. They must operate IAW the ROE and must be aware of the affects that platoon weapons will have on the type and composition of the buildings.
2. To seize or gain control of a building may not always require committing troops into the structure or closing with the enemy. Before initiating this action and exposing members of the clearing squad to direct enemy contact and risking casualties, the platoon leader should consider/direct employment of all organic, crew-served, and supporting weapon systems onto the objective area to suppress and neutralize the threat, providing the mission, purpose, building composition, and ROE permit.
3. When conducting urban operations, Soldiers must be equipped at all times with a properly-mounted and immediately-useable NVD or light source to illuminate the immediate area.

> **NOTE**
>
> The following discussion assumes that only the platoon's organic weapons are supporting the infantry squad. Urban situations may require precise application of firepower. This situation is especially true of an urban environment in which the enemy is mixed with noncombatants. Noncombatants may be found in the room, which can restrict the use of fires and reduce the combat power available to a squad leader. His squad may have to operate in no-fire areas. ROE can prohibit the use of certain weapons until a specific hostile action takes place. All Soldiers must be aware of the ROE. Leaders must include the specific use of weapons in their planning for precision operations in urban terrain. Leaders should always consider the use of snipers or designated marksmen to apply precise fires to the objective.

4. Clearing team members must approach the entry point quickly, quietly, and in standard order. The squad leader must ensure he is in a position to control the actions of both fire teams. This approach preserves the element of surprise and allows for quick entry and domination of the room. If a breach is required, the order may be slightly modified based on the breach technique (FM 3-06, 11). The members of the fire team are assigned numbers one through four. The rifleman is #1 and the grenadier is #3. If one member of the Clearing team is armed with the SAW rather than anM16 rifle or carbine, he should be designated #4. The team leader is normally the # 2 man, because he will have the most Immediate decision to make as he enters the room.
5. The entire team enters the room as quickly and smoothly as possible and clears the doorway immediately. If possible, the team moves from a covered or concealed position already in their entry order. Ideally, the team arrives and passes through the entry point without having to stop. If the team must stop to effectively *"stack"* outside the entry point, if must do so only momentarily, and it must provide cover.
6. The door is the focal point of anyone in the room. It is known as the "fatal funnel," because it focuses attention at the precise point where the Individual team members are the most vulnerable. Moving into the room quickly reduces the chance of anyone being hit by enemy fire directed at the doorway.
7. For this battle to be effectively employed, each member of the team must know his sector of fire and how his sector overlaps and links with the sectors of the other team members. Team members do not move to the points of domination and then engage their targets. Rather, they engage targets as they calmly and quickly move to their designated points. Engagements must not slow movement to their points of domination. Team members may shoot from as short a range as 1 to 2 inches. They engage the most immediate threat first and then the less immediate threats in sector. Immediate threats are personnel who—
   - Are armed and prepared to return fire immediately.
   - Block movement to the position of domination.
   - Are within arm's reach of a clearing team member.
   - Are within 3 to 5 feet of the breach point.
8. The squad leader designates the assault team and identifies the location of the entry point for them.
9. The squad leader positions the follow-on assault team to provide overwatch and supporting fires for the initial assault team.

10. Assault team members use available cover and concealment, and move as close to the entry point as possible.
    a. If an explosive breach or a ballistic breach is to be performed by a supporting element, the assault team remains in a covered position until the breach is made. They may provide overwatch and fire support for the breaching element it necessary.
    b. All team members must signal one another that they are ready before the team moves to the entry point.
    c. If stealth is a consideration, team members avoid the use of verbal signals, which may alert the enemy and remove the element of surprise.
    d. Assault team members must move quickly from the covered position to the entry point, minimizing the time they are exposed to enemy fire.
11. The assault team enters through the entry point or breach. Unless a grenade will be thrown prior to entry, the team should avoid stopping outside the point of entry.
    a. If required, the # 2 man throws a grenade of some type (fragmentary, concussion, stun) into the room before entry.
    b. The use of grenades should be consistent with the ROE and building structure. The grenade should be cooked off before being thrown, if applicable to the type of grenade used.
    c. If stealth is not a factor, the thrower should sound off with a verbal indication (*"Frag out"* "*Concussion out,*" "*Stun out*") that a grenade of some type is being thrown. If stealth is a factor, only visual signals are given as the grenade is thrown.

CAUTION

If walls and floors are thin, fragments from fragmentation grenades and debris created by concussion grenades can injure Soldiers outside the room. If the structure has been stressed by previous explosive engagements, the use of these grenades could cause it to collapse. Leaders must determine the effectiveness of these types of grenades compared to possibilities of harm to friendly troops.

12. On the signal to go, or after the grenade detonates, the assault team moves through the entry point (Figure 4-6 through Figure 4-9) and quickly takes up positions inside the room that allow it to completely dominate the room and eliminate the threat. Unless restricted or impeded, team members Stop movement only after they have cleared the door and reached their designated point of domination. In addition to dominating the room, an team members are responsible for identifying possible loopholes and mouseholes in the ceiling, walls, and floor.

NOTE

Where enemy forces may be concentrated and the presence of noncombatants is highly unlikely, the assault team can precede their entry by throwing a fragmentation or concussion grenade (structure dependent) into the room, followed by bursts of automatic small-arms fire by the # 1 man as he enters. Caref ully consider the ROE and building composition before employing this method.

13. The # 1 and # 2 men are initially concerned with the area directly to their front, then along the wall on either side of the door or entry point. This area is in their path of movement, and it is their primary sector of fire. Their alternate sector of fire is from the wall they are moving toward, back to the opposite far corner.
14. The # 3 and # 4 men start at the center of the wall opposite their point of entry and clear to the left if moving toward the left, or to the right if moving toward the right. They stop short of their respective team member (either the # 1 man or the # 2 man).
15. The team members move toward their points of domination, engaging all threat or hostile targets in sequence in their sector. Team members must exercise fire control and discriminate between hostile and noncombatant room occupants. (The most practical way to do this is to identify whether or not the target has a weapon in his or her hands.) Shooting is done without stopping, using reflexive shooting techniques. Because the Soldiers are

moving and shooting at the same time, they must move using the careful hurry. Figure 4-10, shows all four team members at their points of domination for a room with a center door and their overlapping sectors of fire.

16. The first man (rifleman) enters the room and eliminates the immediate threat. He has the option of going left or right, normally moving along the path of least resistance to one of two corners. When using a doorway as the point of entry, the team uses the path of least resistance, which they determine initially based on the way the door opens. If the door opens inward, the first man plans to move away from the hinges. If the door opens outward, he plans to move toward the hinged side. Upon entering, his direction is influenced by the size of the room, the enemy situation, and furniture or other obstacles that hinder or channel his movement.
17. The direction each man moves in should not be preplanned unless the exact room layout is known. Each man should go in a direction opposite the man in front of him (Figure 4-6), Every team member must know the sectors and duties of each position.

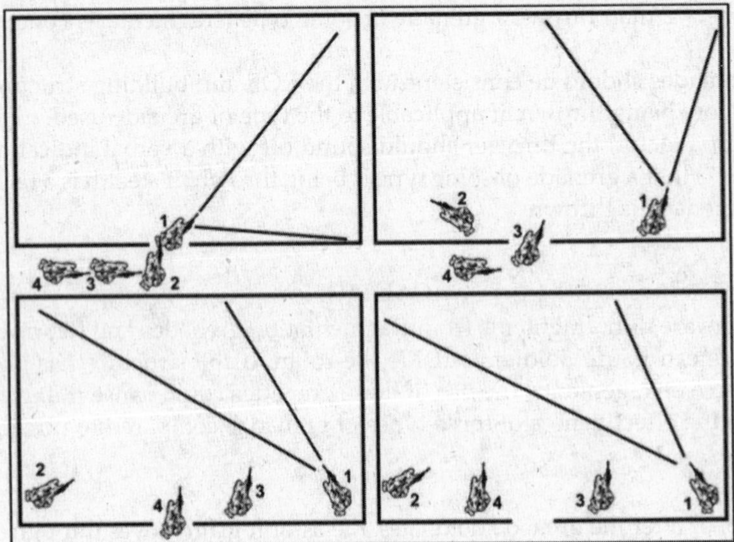

Figure 4-6. First man enters a room, followed by team leader

18. As the first man goes through the entry point, he can usually see into the far corner of the room. He eliminates any immediate threat and continues to move along the wall if possible and to the first corner, where he assumes a position of domination facing into the room.

NOTE

Team members must always stay within 1 meter of the wall. If a team member finds his progress blocked by some object that will force him more than 1 meter from the wall, ha must either step over it (if able) or stop where he is and clear the rest of his sector from where he is. If this action creates dead space in the room, the team leader directs which clearing actions to take once other members of the team have reached their points of domination.

19. The second man (normally the team leader), entering almost simultaneously with the first, moves in the opposite direction, following the wall (Figure 4-7). The second man must clear the entry point, clear the immediate threat area, clear his corner, and move to a dominating position on his side of the room. The second man must also immediately determine if he is entering a center door or corner door and act accordingly (Figure 4-7 and Figure 4-10).

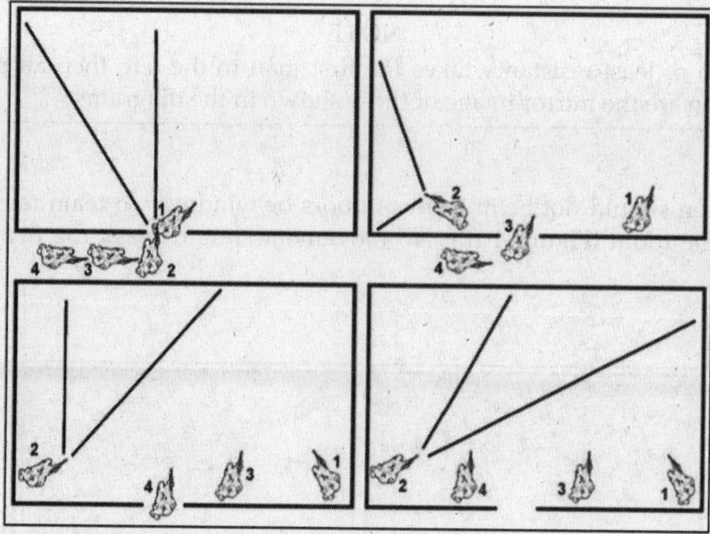

Figure 4-7. Second man (team leader) enters a room

20. The third man (normally the grenadier) simply goes opposite of the second man inside the room, moves at least 1 meter from the entry point, and takes a position that dominates his sector (Figure 4-8).

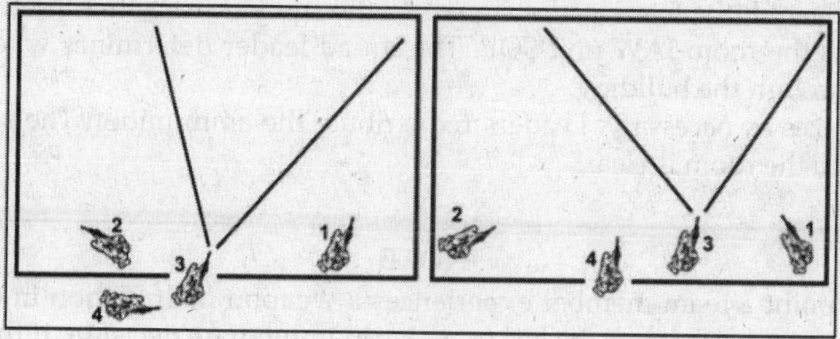

Figure 4-8. Third man enters a room

21. The fourth man (normally the SAW gunner) moves opposite of the third man, clears the doorway by at least 1 meter, and moves to a position that dominates his sector (Figure 4-9.)

Figure 4-9. Fourth man in a room

> **NOTE**
> If the path of least resistance takes the first man to the left, then all points of domination are the mirror image of those shown in the diagrams.

22. Points of domination should not be in front of doors or windows so team members are not silhouetted to the outside of the room (Figure 4-10). No movement should mask the fire of any of the other team members.

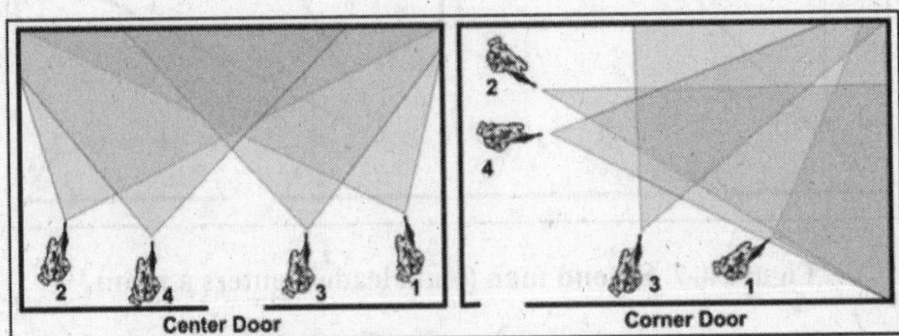

Figure 4-10. Points of domination and sectors of fire, center door versus corner door

23. On order, any member of the assault team may move deeper info the room overwatched by the other team members. The team leader must control this action.
24. Once the room is cleared, the team leader signals to the squad leader that the room has been cleared. The squad leader marks the room IAW unit SOP. The squad leader determines whether or not his squad can continue to clear through the building.
25. The squad reorganizes as necessary. Leaders redistribute the ammunition The squad leader reports to the platoon leader when the room is clear.

> **NOTE**
> If at any point a team member experiences a weapon malfunction in the presence of enemy combatants, he has to make an immediate decision. If the enemy is outside immediate danger distance from the Soldier, then the Soldier should drop to one knee, which indicates that he has experienced a weapon malfunction and prevents fratricide by ensuring that the next Soldier's fields of fire are clear. Once on a knee, the Soldier must remain there until the team leader directs him to stand up. If the kneeling Soldier corrects his weapon malfunction, he can continue to engage targets from his kneeling position. If, however, the enemy Soldier is so close that he presents an immediate threat, and if dropping to a knee would expose the US Soldier to immediate harm, then the US Soldier must try to subdue or disable the enemy Soldier. He can strike the enemy with the muzzle of his weapon or a bayonet to the face, throat, or chest. Or, he could grapple with the enemy soldier and lake him to the ground immediately to clear the other team members' fields of fire. Once they have cleared their sectors and eliminated any other threats m the room, the other members of the clearing team assist.

26. Although this battle drill is effective, leaders might have to modify if for the situation. Some reasons and methods for modifying the technique are shown in Table 4-1.

Table 4-1. Reasons for and methods of modifying entry techniques

Reason	Method
Objective rooms are consistently small	Clear in teams of 2 or 3
Shortage of personnel	Clear in teams of 2 or 3
Enemy poses no immediate threat	2 or 3 men search rooms to ensure no enemy or noncombatants are present
No immediate threat, speed is critical	1 to 3 men visually search each room

27. When full four-man teams are not available for room clearing, two- and three-man teams can be used. If the # 1 or # 2 man discovers that the room is very small, he can yell, *"Short room"* or *"Short,"* which tells the # 3 or # 4 man (whoever following the # 1 or # 2 man) to stay outside the room. Figures 4-11 and 4-12 show the points of domination and sectors of fire for a two-man clearing team. Figures 4-13 and 4-14 show the actions for a three-man team.

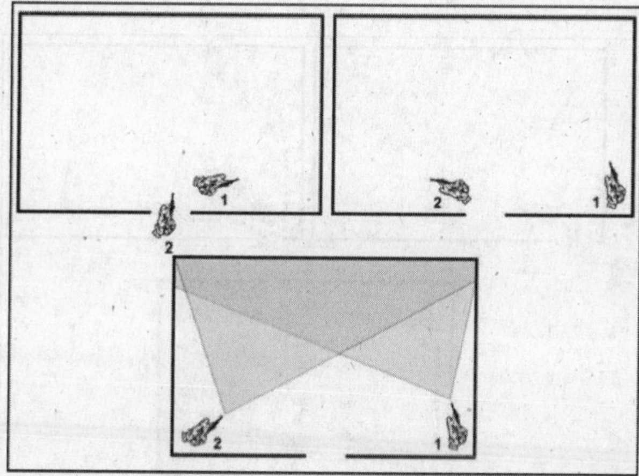

Figure 4-11. Points of domination and sectors of fire (two-man team, center door)

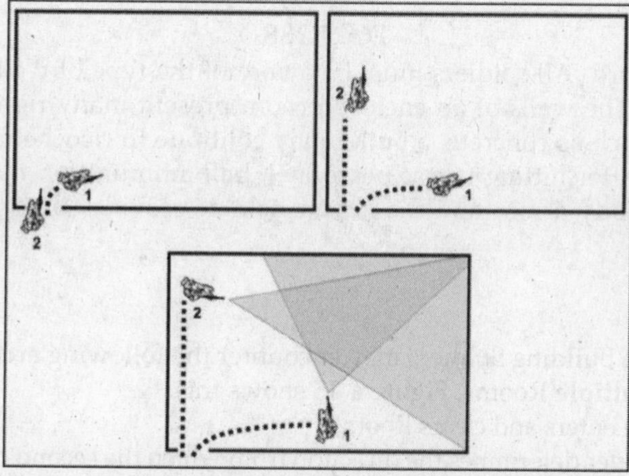

Figure 4-12. Points of domination and sectors of fire (two-man team, corner door)

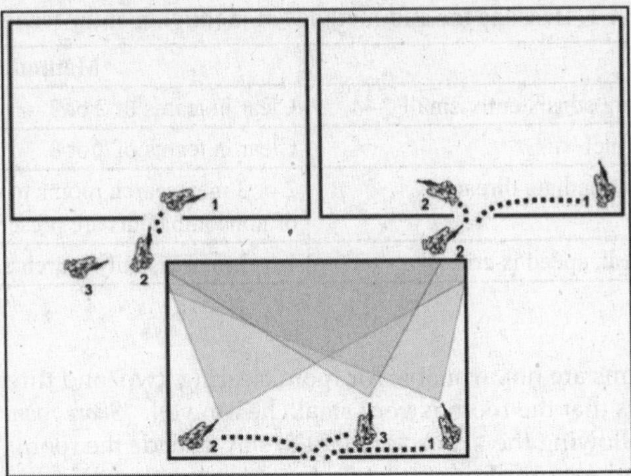

Figure 4-13. Points of domination and sectors of fire (three-man team, center door)

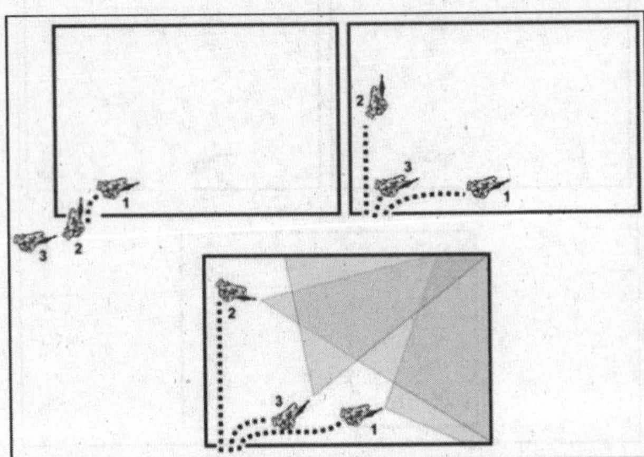

Figure 4-14. Points of domination and sectors of fire (three-man team, corner door)

> **DANGER**
>
> Ricochets pose a hazard. All soldiers must be aware of the type of wall construction of the room being cleared. The walls of an enclosed room present many right angles. Combined with hard surfaces such as concrete, a bullet may continue to ricochet around a room until its energy is spent. After hitting threat personnel, ball ammunition may pass through the body and ricochet. Body armor and the kevlar helmet provide some protection from this hazard.

28. White moving through a building Soldiers may encounter the following architectural building features.
    a. **Multiple Team/Multiple Rooms.** Figure 4-15 shows this.
    STEP 1: First team enters and clears Room 1.
    STEP 2: Squad leader determines the direction from which the second clearing team must enter Room 1, based on the location of the Room 2 entry point.
    STEP 3: First team collapses inward to allow the second team to move into the room.
    STEP 4: Second team 'stacks left' and prepares to enter Room 2.

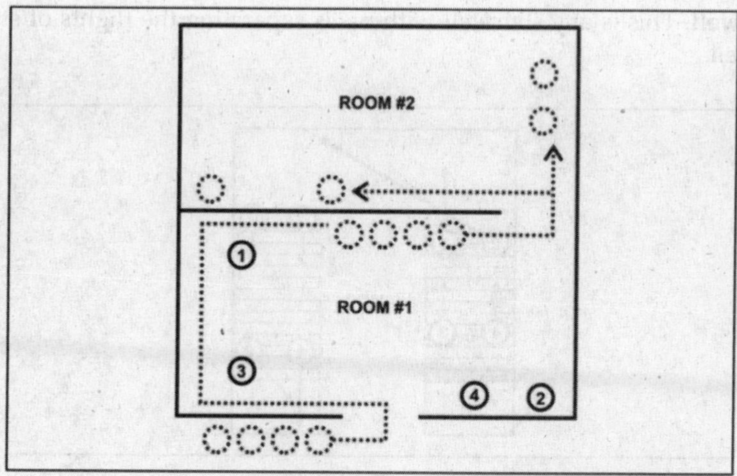

Figure 4-15. Multiple teams/multiple rooms

b. **Open Stairwell.** This is a gap between flights of stairs that allows a person to look up and down between the flights. Figure 4-16 shows an open stairwell.

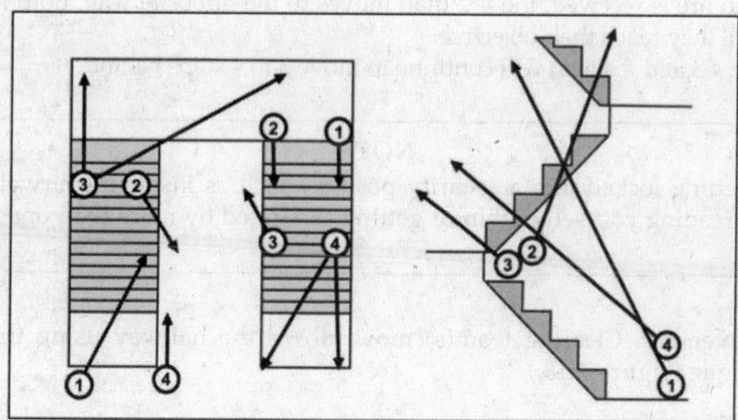

Figure 4-16. Open stairwell

STEP 1: The # 1 man pulls security on the highest point he can see/engage.
STEP 2: The # 2 man moves up the stairs on the inside with the # 3 man to a point that he can see/engage the next landing, where he turns around and continues to move up to the next landing.
STEP 3: The # 3 man moves up the stairs with the # 2 man on the outside and engages the threat on the immediate landing.
STEP 4: The # 4 man moves up the stairs with the # 1 man, on the squeeze, the # 2 man turns around to engage the next landing.
STEP 5: The flow continues with the # 2 man picking up the sector of the # 1 man had. The # 3 man picks up where the # 2 man was. The # 4 man picks up where the # 3 man was. The # 1 man picks up where the # 4 man was.

NOTE
Most stairwells require a second team.

c. **Closed Stairwell.** This is any stairwell with walls separating the flights of stairs. Figure 4-17 shows a closed stairwell.

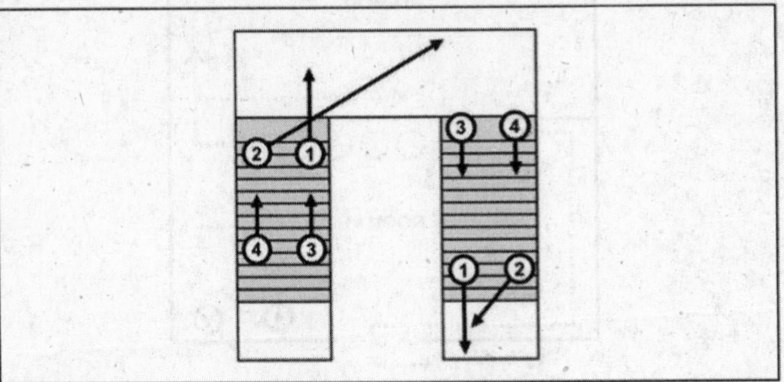

Figure 4-17. Closed stairwell

STEP 1: The # 1 man checks high to ensure there is no opening on the landing or between the stairs.
STEP 2: The # 2 man pulls long security to the next bend or landing.
STEP 3: The # 1 or # 3 man moves up the steps with the # 2 man. As they approach the corner, the # 2 man signals his presence by tapping the # 1 man on the shoulder.
STEP 4: Keying off the # 1 man's movement, the other men simultaneously break around the corner.
STEP 5: If no fire is received, the # 2 man moves to the opposite wall. Both men continue to move up until they reach their objective.
STEP 6: The # 3 and # 4 men will continue to move 3 to 4 steps behind.

NOTE

Avoid getting locked into a security position such as inside a stairwell. Also, avoid spreading yourselves thin or getting separated by more than one floor of stairs.

d. **Hallway Movement.** Clearing team(s) move down the hallway using the frontal security (cross cover) technique (Figure 4-18.)

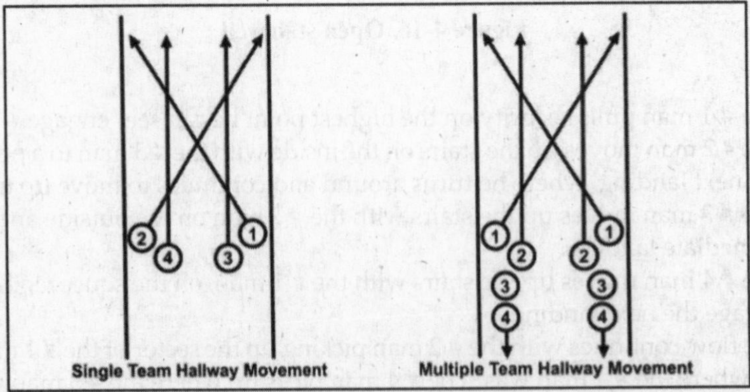

Figure 4-18. Hallway movement

e. **T-Shaped Intersection.** See Figure 4-19. This technique can incorporate the dynamic corner clear (Figure 4-20).

STEP 1: Each # 1 man goes to a knee covering his sector.
STEP 2: On a predetermined signal, each two-man team will break the corner, picking up their sectors of fire.

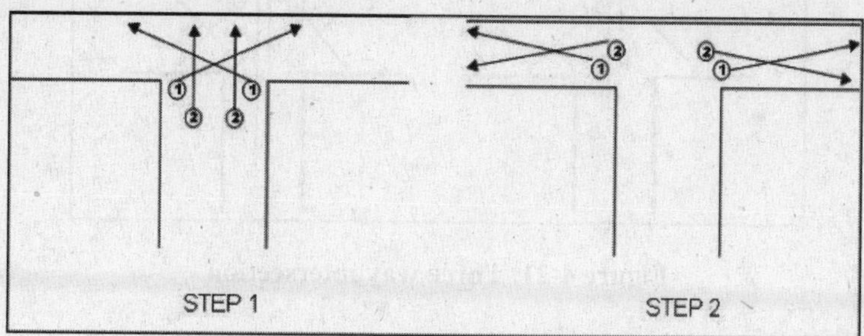

Figure 4-19. T-Shaped intersection

f. Dynamic Corner. (See Figure 4-20.)

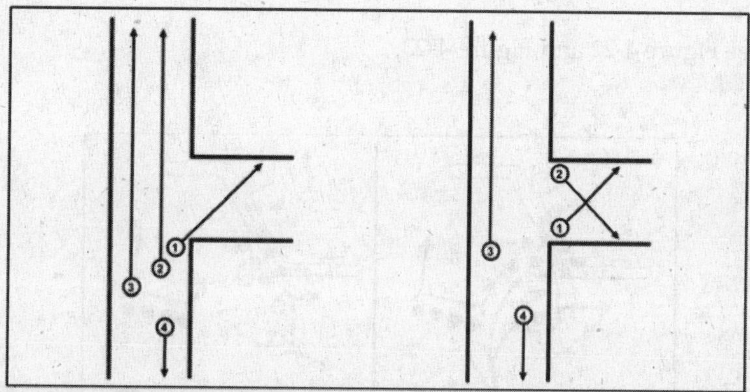

Figure 4-20. Dynamic corner

STEP 1: The #1 and #2 man, as they approach the corner, have to clear. Do not slow down.
STEP 2: The #2 man will tap the #1 man on the shoulder about 2–3 meters away from the corner letting the #1 man know the #2 man is with him.
STEP 3: Keying off of the #1 man's movement, they both break the comer simultaneously.
STEP 4: The #1 man goes tow to a knee, the #2 man stays high.
STEP 5: If the Rangers are not receiving fire the #2 man rabbits, or moves, to the far side.
STEP 6: The #1 and #2 man take up sectors of fire.
STEP 7: The #3 and #4 man take long security in the direction of movement.

g. Three-Way Intersection. (See Figure 4-21.)

STEP 1: The #1 through #4 man will use one of the corner clearing techniques to clear the intersection.
STEP 2: When the intersection is secure, the #5 and #6 man move through the intersection and enter either more hallway or a room. If they are entering more hallway, the #1 through #4 man provide cross coverage as the #5 and #6 man move through the intersection into more hallway. If they are moving into a room, the #5 and #6 man move to one side of the door and signal the #1 and #3 or #2 and #4 man to enter the stack depending on which side of the door they stack on. The remaining members of the team, not in the stack, will continue to provide security down the hallway.
STEP 3: If the #5 and #6 man move into more hallway the #1 through #4 man will enter the stack and proceed down the hallway with the #3 and #4 man providing rear security.

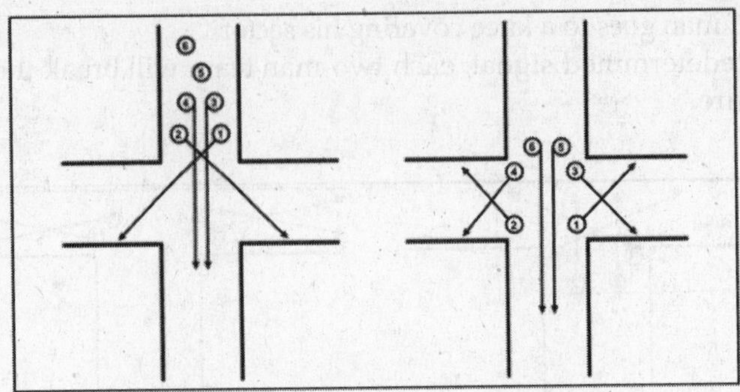

Figure 4-21. Three way intersection

BATTLE DRILL 6

ENTER/CLEAR A TRENCH

SITUATION: The platoon is attacking as part of a larger force and identifies the enemy in a trench line. The platoon deploys and establishes a base of fire. The platoon leader determines that he has sufficient combat power to maneuver and assault the trench line.

REQUIRED ACTIONS: See Figure 4-22 and Figure 4-23.

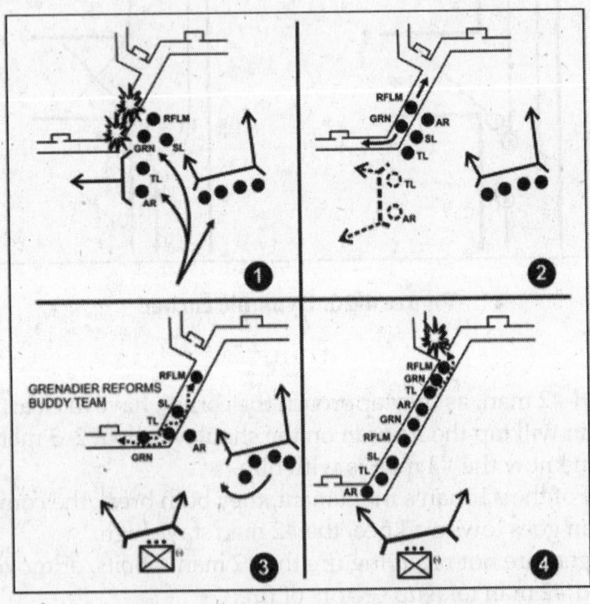

Figure 4-22. Enter a trench (squad)

1. The platoon leader directs one squad to enter the trench and secure a foothold.
2. The platoon leader designates the entry point of the trench line and the direction of movement once the platoon begins clearing.
3. The PSG positions Soldiers and machine guns to suppress the trench and isolate the entry point.
4. Platoon leader directs platoon FO to initiate fire mission, if necessary, in support of assault. They maintain accurate battle tracking of all friendly elements to facilitate quick clearance of fires. The platoon FO ceases or shifts fires to isolate the OBJ as assault team advances.
5. The assaulting squad executes actions to enter the trench and establish a foothold. The squad leader signals to the platoon leader that the foothold is secure, and the follow on elements can move into the trench. The

squad leader remains at the entry point and marks it. The platoon follows the success of the seizure of the foothold with the remainder of the platoon as part of the platoon actions to clear a trench line.

6. The platoon leader moves into the trench with the assaulting squad.
7. The platoon leader directs one of the base-of-fire squads to move into the trench and begin clearing it in the direction of movement from the foothold.
8. The base-of-fire element repositions as necessary to continue suppressive fires.
9. The assaulting squad passes the squad that has secured the foothold and executes actions to take the lead and clear the trench.
   a. The squad leader designates a lead fire team and a trail fire team.
   b. The lead fire team and the squad leader move to the forward most secure comer or intersection. The squad leader tells the team securing that corner or intersection that his squad is ready to continue clearing the trench. The trail fire team follows, maintaining visual contact with the last Soldier of the lead team.

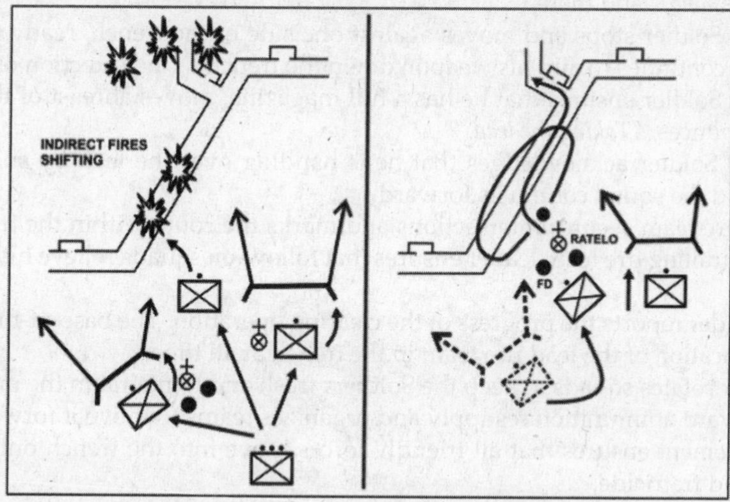

Figure 4-23. Clear a trench line (platoon)

NOTES

1. The fire support element must be able to identify the location of the lead fire team in the trench at all times.
2. Throughout this battle drill, the team leader positions himself at the rear of the fire team to have direct control (physically, if necessary) of his Soldiers. Other Soldiers in the fire team rotate the lead to change magazines and prepare grenades. Rotating the lead provides constant suppressive fires down the trench and maintains the momentum of the attack as the squad clears the trench.

   c. The lead fire team passes the element securing the foothold. The following then occurs.
      (1) The lead Soldier of the fire team moves abreast of the Soldier securing the corner or intersection, taps him, and announces. *"Taking the lead."*
      (2) The Soldier securing the comer or intersection acknowledges that he is handing over the lead by shouting, *"Okay!"* He allows the fire team to pass him.
   d. The lead fire team starts clearing in the direction of movement. They arrive at a corner or intersection. The following then occurs.
      (1) Allowing for cook-off (2 seconds maximum) and shouting, *"Frag out,"* the second Soldier prepares and throws a grenade around the corner.

(2) Upon detonation of the grenade, the lead Soldier moves around the corner firing three-round bursts and advancing as he fires. The entire fire team follows him to the next comer or intersection.

e. The squad leader—
- Follows behind the team.
- Ensures that the trailing fire team moves up and is ready to pass the lead at his direction.
- Rotates fire teams as necessary to keep his Soldiers fresh and to maintain the momentum of the attack.
- Requests indirect fires, if required, through the platoon leader. The squad leader also directs the employment of the M203 to provide immediate suppression against positions along the trench line.
- Ensures fire teams maintain sufficient interval to prevent them from being engaged by the same enemy fires.

f. At each corner or intersection, the lead fire team performs the same actions previously described.

g. If the lead Soldier finds that he is nearly out of ammunition before reaching a comer or intersection, he announces, *"Ammo,"* and then–

(1) The lead Soldier stops and moves against one side of the trench, ready to let the rest of the team pass. He continues to aim his weapon down the trench in the direction of movement.

(2) The next Soldier ensures that he has a full magazine, moves abreast of the lead Soldier, taps him, and announces, *"Taking the lead."*

(3) The lead Soldier acknowledges that he is handing over the lead by shouting, *"Okay."* Positions rotate and the squad continues forward.

h. The trailing fire team secures intersections and marks the route within the trench as the squad moves forward. The trailing fire team leader ensures that follow-on squads relieve his buddy teams to maintain security.

i. The squad leader reports the progress of the clearing operation. The base-of-fire element must be able to identify the location of the lead fire team in the trench at all times.

10. The platoon leader rotates squads to keep the Soldiers fresh and to maintain the momentum of the assault.
11. The PSG calls forward ammunition resupply and organizes teams to move it forward into the trench.
12. The base-of-fire element ensures that all friendly forces move into the trench only through the designated entry point to avoid fratricide.
13. The platoon leader reports to the company commander that the trench line is secured, or he is no longer able to continue clearing, if trench line is secured, then platoon leader directs platoon FO to develop a fire plan to support the defense of the platoon position.

DANGER

Fire teams: Maintain sufficient intervals to avoid engagement by the same enemy fires.

BATTLE DRILL 7

CONDUCT INITIAL BREACH OF A MINED WIRE OBSTACLE (PLATOON)

SITUATION: The platoon is operating as part of a larger force. The lead squad identifies a wire obstacle reinforced with mines that cannot be bypassed and enemy positions on the far side of the obstacle.

REQUIRED ACTIONS: See Figure 4-24 and Figure 4-25.

1. The squad in contact reacts to contact.
2 The platoon gains suppressive fires. The following then occurs.
   a. The squad in contact establishes a base-of-fire position.
   b. The platoon leader, his RTO, platoon FO, and the squad leader of the next squad with one machine gun team move forward to link up with the squad leader of the squad in contact.
3. The platoon leader determines that he can maneuver by identifying—
   - The obstacle and enemy positions.
   - The size of the enemy force engaging the squad, for example, the number of enemy automatic weapons, the presence of any vehicles, and the employment of indirect fires are indicators of enemy strength.

- A breach point.
- A covered and concealed route to the breach point.

4. The platoon leader directs the squad in contact to support the movement of another squad to the breach point. He indicates the base-of-fire position and the route to it, the enemy position to be suppressed, and the breach point and route the rest of the platoon will take to it. The platoon leader also clears the location, task, purpose, and method of conducting the fire mission with the platoon FO.
5. On the platoon leader's signal, the base-of-fire squad—
   - Destroys or suppresses enemy weapons that are firing effectively against the platoon.
   - Obscures the enemy position with smoke.
   - Continues suppressive fires at the lowest possible level.
6. The platoon leader designates one squad as the breach squad and the remaining squad as the assault squad once the breach has been made. The assault squad may add its fires to the base-of-fire squad. Normally, it follows the covered and concealed route of the breach squad and assaults through immediately after the breach is made.
7. The base-of-fire squad moves to the breach point and establishes a base of fire.
8. The PSG moves forward to the base-of-fire squad with the second machine gun and assumes control of the squad.
9. The platoon leader leads the breach and assault squads along the covered and concealed route.
10. The platoon FO calls for and adjusts indirect fires as directed by the platoon leader. The platoon leader in conjunction with the platoon FO maintains accurate battle tracking of all friendly elements to facilitate quick clearance of fires.
11. The breach squad executes actions to breach the obstacle.

a. The squad leader directs one fire team to support the movement of the other fire team to the breach point.
b. The squad leader identifies the breach point.

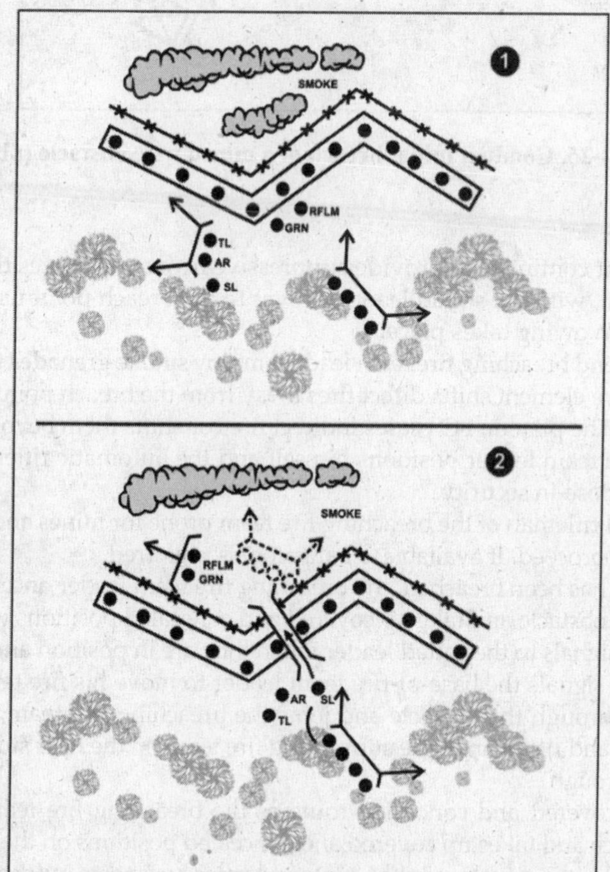

Figure 4-24. Conduct initial breach of a mined wire obstacle (squad)

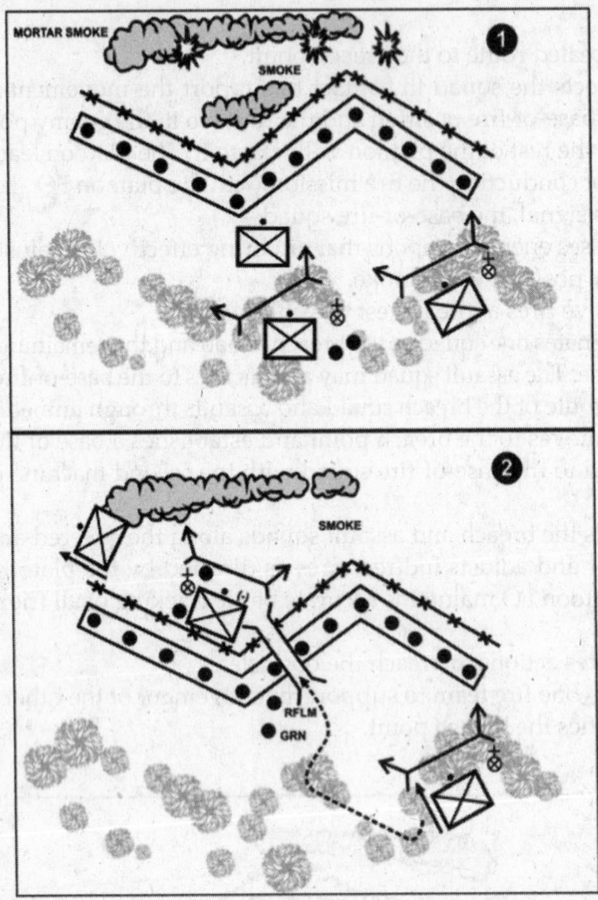

Figure 4-25. Conduct initial breach of a mined wire obstacle (platoon)

c. The base-of-fire element continues to provide suppressive fires and isolates the breach point.

d. The breaching fire team, with the squad leader, moves to the breach point using the covered and concealed route. From there, the Wowing takes place:

(1) The squad leader and breaching fire team leader employ smoke grenades to obscure the breach point. The platoon base-of-fire element shifts direct fires away from the breach point and continues to suppress key enemy positions. The platoon FO ceases indirect fires or shifts them beyond the obstacle.

(2) The breaching fire team leader positions himself and the automatic rifleman on one flank of the breach point to provide close-in security.

(3) The grenadier and rifleman of the breaching fire team probe for mines and cut the wire obstacle, marking their path as they proceed. If available, a bangalore is preferred.

(4) Once the obstacle has been breached, the breaching fire team leader and the automatic rifleman move to the far side of the obstacle and take up covered and concealed positions with the rifleman and grenadier. The team leader signals to the squad leader when they are in position and ready to support.

(5) The squad leader signals the base-of-fire team leader to move his fire team up and through the breach. He then moves through the obstacle and joins the breaching fire team, leaving the grenadier (or anti-armor specialist) and rifleman of the supporting fire team on the near side of the breach to guide the rest of the platoon through.

(6) Using the same covered and concealed route as the breaching fire team, the base-of-fire team moves through the breach and takes up covered and concealed positions on the far side.

12. The squad leader reports the situation to the platoon leader and posts guides at the breach point.

13. The platoon leader leads the assault squad through the breach in the obstacle and positions them beyond the breach to support the movement of the remainder of the platoon or assaults the enemy position covering the obstacle. Platoon leader directs the platoon FO to shift indirect fires off the enemy position.
14. The breaching squad continues to widen the breach to allow vehicles to pass through.
15. The platoon leader reports the situation to the company commander, and then he directs his base-of-fire squad to move up and through the obstacle. The platoon leader appoints Soldiers to guide the company through the breach point.
16. The PSG brings the remaining elements forward and through the breach on the platoon leader's command.
17. The company follows up the success of the platoon as it conducts the breach and continues the assault against the enemy positions.

BATTLE DRILL 8

REACT TO INDIRECT FIRE

SITUATION: A platoon or squad while moving or at the halt (not dug in) receives indirect fire.

REQUIRED ACTIONS: NA

Any Soldier announces, *"Incoming."* Then, if the platoon/squad is moving, the following takes place:

1. The platoon/squad leader gives direction and distance for the platoon/squad to move to a rally point by ordering direction and distance, for example, *"Four o'clock, three hundred meters."*
2. Platoon/squad members move rapidly along the direction and distance to the rally point.
3. At the rally point, the leader immediately accounts for personnel and equipment, and forms the platoon/squad for a move to an alternate position.
4. The senior leader submits a SITREP to higher headquarters.
5. If the platoon/squad is halted (not dug in) or is preparing to move because they hear incoming artillery, the following takes place:
   a. The platoon/squad leader gives direction and distance for the platoon/squad to move to a rally point by ordering direction and distance, for example, *"Four o'clock three hundred meters."*
   b. Platoon/squad members secure all mission-essential equipment and ammunition and move rapidly along the direction and distance to the rally point.
   c. At the rally point the leader immediately accounts for personnel and equipment, and forms the platoon/squad for a move to an alternate position.
   d. The senior leader submits a SITREP to higher headquarters.

NOTE

If platoon/squad members are in defensive (dug in) positions, then members will remain in those positions if appropriate. Senior leader submits SITREP.

CHAPTER 5

Military Mountaineering

In the mountains, commanders face the challenge of maintaining their units' combat effectiveness and efficiency. To meet this challenge, commanders conduct training that provides Rangers with the mountaineering skills necessary to apply combat power in a rugged mountain environment, and they develop leaders capable of applying doctrine to the distinct characteristics of mountain warfare.

5-1. TRAINING

Military mountaineering training provides tactical and fundamental mobility skills needed to move units safely and efficiently in mountainous terrain. Rangers should receive extensive training prior to executing combat operations in mountainous environments. Some of the areas to train are as follows:

- Characteristics of the mountain environment.
- Care and use of basic mountaineering equipment.
- Mountain bivouac techniques.
- Mountain communications.
- Mountain travel and walking techniques.
- Mountain navigation, hazard recognition and route selection.
- Rope management and knots.
- Natural and artificial anchors.
- Belay and rappel techniques.
- Installation construction and use such as rope bridges.
- Rock climbing fundamentals.
- Rope bridges and lowering systems.
- Individual movement on snow and ice.
- Mountain stream crossings (to include water survival techniques).

5-2. DISMOUNTED MOBILITY

Movement in more technical terrain demands specialized skills and equipment. Before Rangers can move in such terrain, a technical mountaineering team might have to secure the high ground.

5-3. MOUNTAINEERING EQUIPMENT

Mountaineering equipment is everything that allows the trained Ranger to accomplish many tasks in the mountains. The importance of this gear to the mountaineer is no less than that of the rifle to the infantry Soldier.

a. **Ropes and Cords**. Ropes and cords are the most important pieces of mountaineering equipment. They secure climbers and equipment during steep ascents and descents. They are also used to install other ropes and to haul equipment. From WWII until the 1980's, US armed forces mainly used 7/16 *nylon laid rope*, often referred to as green line for all mountaineering operations. Since kemmantle ropes were introduced, other, more specialized ropes have in many cases replaced the all-purpose green line. Kemmantle ropes are made much like parachute cord, with a smooth sheath around a braided or woven core. Laid ropes are still used, but should be avoided whenever rope failure could cause injury or loss of equipment.

(1) ***Types***. Kemmantle rope is classified as *dynamic* or static:

(a) *Dynamic Ropes.* Ropes used for climbing are classified as *dynamic ropes.* These rope stretch or elongate 8 to 12 percent once subjected to weight or impact. This stretching is critical in reducing the impact force on the climber, anchors, and belayer during a fall by softening the catch. An 11-mm by 150-meter rope is standard for military use. Other sizes are available.

(b) *Static Ropes.* Static ropes are used in situations where rope stretch is undesired, and when the rope is subjected to heavy static weight. Static ropes should never be used while climbing, since even a fall of a few feet could generate enough impact force to injure climber and belayer, and/or cause anchor failure. Static Ropes are usually used when constructing rope bridges, fixed rope installations, vertical haul lines, and so on.

(2) ***Sling Ropes and Cordelettes.*** A short section of static rope or static cord is referred to as a sling rope or cordelette. These are a critical piece of personal equipment during mountaineering operations. They are usually 7 to 8mm diameter and up to 21 feet long. The minimum Ranger standard is 8mm by 15 feet.

(3) ***Rope Care.*** Ropes used daily should be used no longer that one year. An occasionally used rope can be used generally up to 4 to 5 years if properly cared for.

- Inspect ropes thoroughly before, during, and after use for cuts, frays, abrasion, mildew, and soft or worn spots.
- Never step on a rope or drag it on the ground unnecessarily.
- Avoid running rope over sharp or rough edges (pad if necessary).
- Keep ropes away from oil, acids, and other corrosive substances.
- Avoid running ropes across one another under tension (nylon to nylon contact will damage ropes).
- Do not leave ropes knotted or under tension longer than necessary.
- Clean in cool water, loosely coil, and hang to dry out of direct sunlight. Ultraviolet light rays harm synthetic fibers. When wet, hang rope to drip-dry on a rounded wooden peg, at room temperature (do not apply heat).

(4) ***Webbing and Slings.*** Loops of tubular webbing or cord, called slings or runners, are the simplest pieces of equipment and some of the most useful. The uses for these simple pieces are endless, and they are a critical link between the climber, the rope, carabiners, and anchors. Runners are usually made from either 9/16- or 1-inch tubular webbing and are either tied or sewn by a manufacturer.

b. **Carabiners**. The carabiner is one of the most versatile pieces of equipment available in the mountains. This simple piece of gear is the critical connection between the climber, his rope, and the protection attaching him to the mountain. New metal alloys are stronger to hold hard falls; and, they are lighter than steel, which

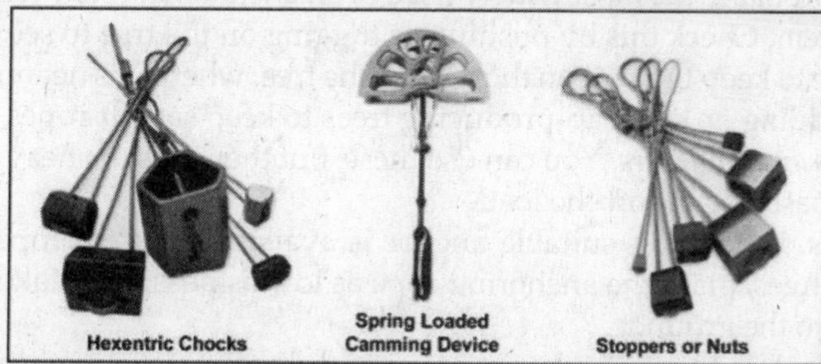

Figure 5-1. Examples of traditional (removable) protection used on rock

Figure 5-2. Examples of fixed (permanent or semi) protection used on rock

allows the Ranger to carry many at once. Consequently, steel carabiners are used less and less often. Basic carabiners come in several different shapes.

c. **Protection**. This is the generic term used to describe a piece of equipment, natural or artificial, that is used to construct an anchor. Protection, along with a climber, belayer, and climbing rope, forms the lifeline of the climbing team. The rope connects two climbers, and the protection connects them to the rock or ice. The two types of artificial protection are traditional (removable) and fixed (usually permanent) (Figures 5-1 and 5-2).

5-4. ANCHORS

Anchors form the base for all installations and roped mountaineering techniques. Anchors must be strong enough to support the entire weight of the load or of the impact placed upon them. Several pieces of artificial or natural protection may be incorporated together to make one multipoint anchor. Anchors are classified as artificial or natural:

a. **Artificial Anchors**. Artificial anchors are made from man-made materials. The most common ones use traditional or fixed protection (Figure 5-3).

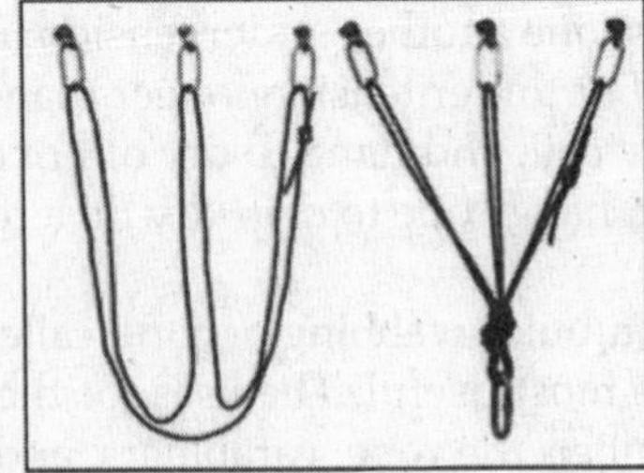

Figure 5-3. Construction of three-point, pre-equalized anchor with fixed artificial protection

b. **Natural Anchors**. Natural anchors are usually very strong and often simple to construct with little equipment. Trees, shrubs, and boulders are the most common anchors. All natural anchors require is a method of attaching a rope. Regardless of the type of natural anchor used, it must support the weight of the load.

(1) ***Trees***. These are probably the most widely used of all anchors. In rocky terrain, trees usually have a very shallow root system. Check this by pushing or tugging on the tree to see how well it is rooted. Anchor as low as possible to keep the pull on the base of the tree, where it is nearer its own anchor and therefore stronger. Use padding on soft, sap-producing trees to keep sap off ropes and slings.

(2) ***Rock Projections and Boulders***. You can use these, but they must be heavy enough, and they must have a stable enough base to support the load.

(3) ***Bushes and Shrubs***. If no other suitable anchor is available, route a rope around the bases of several bushes. As with trees, place the anchoring rope as low as possible. Make sure all vegetation is healthy and well rooted to the ground.

(4) ***Tensionless Anchor***. Use this to anchor rope on high-load installations such as bridging. The wraps of the rope around the anchor (Figure 5-4) absorb the tension, keeping it off the knot and carabiner. Tie this anchor with at least four wraps around the anchor. A smooth anchor, such as a pipe or rail, might require several more wraps. Wrap the rope from top to bottom. Place a fixed loop into the end of the rope, and attach it loosely back onto the rope with a carabiner.

Figure 5-4. Tensionless natural anchor

5-5. KNOTS

a. **Square Knot.** This joins two ropes of equal diameter (Figure 5-5). It has two interlocking bights; the running ends exit on the same side of the standing portion of the rope. Each tail is secured with an overhand knot on the standing end. When you dress the knot, leave at least a 4-inch tail on the working end.

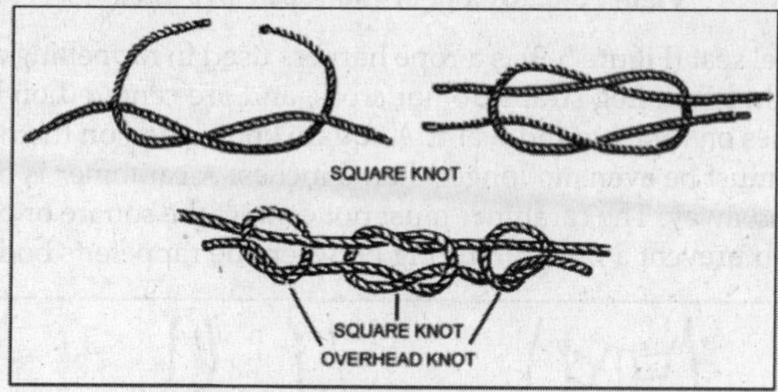

Figure 5-5. Square knot

b. **Round-Turn with Two Half Hitches.** This is a constant tension anchor knot (Figure 5-6). The rope forms a complete turn around the anchor point (thus the name round turn), with both ropes parallel and touching, but not crossing. Both half hitches are tightly dressed against the round turn, with the locking bar on top. When you dress the knot, leave at least a 4-inch tail on the working end.

Figure 5-6. Round-turn with two half-hitches

c. **End-of-the-Rope Clove Hitch.** The end-of-the-rope clove hitch (Figure 5-7) is an intermediate anchor knot that requires constant tension. Make two turns around the anchor. A locking bar runs diagonally from one side to the other. Leave no more than one rope width between turns of rope. Locking bar is opposite direction of pull. When you dress the knot, leave at least a 4-inch tail on the working end.

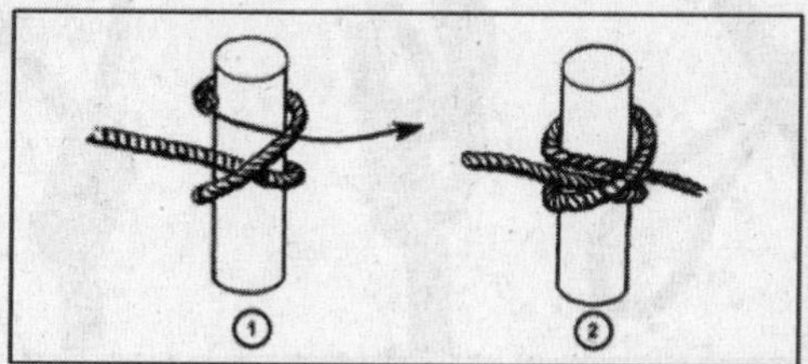

Figure 5-7. End-of-the-rope clove hitch

d. **Middle of the Rope Clove Hitch.** This knot (Figure 5-8) secures the middle of a rope to an anchor. The knot forms two turns around the anchor. A locking bar runs diagonally from one side to the other. Leave no more than one rope width between turns. Ensure the locking bar is opposite the direction of pull.

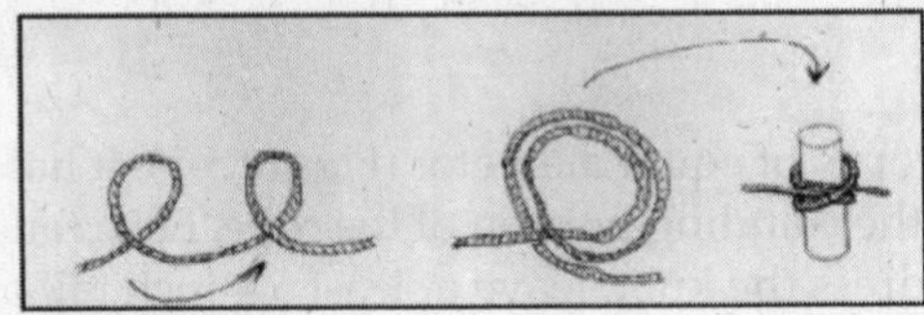

Figure 5-8, Middle-of-the-rope clove hitch

e. **Rappel Seat.** The rappel seat (Figure 5-9) is a rope harness used in rappelling and climbing, It can be tied for use with the left or right hand. Leg straps do not cross, and are centered on buttocks and tight. Leg straps form locking half hitches on rope around waist. A square knot is tied on the right hip and finished with two overhand knots. Tails must be even, no longer than 6 inches. A carabiner is inserted around all ropes, with the gate opening up and away. The carabiner must not contact the square or overhand knot. The rappel seat must be tight enough to prevent a fist from fitting between the rappeler's body and the harness.

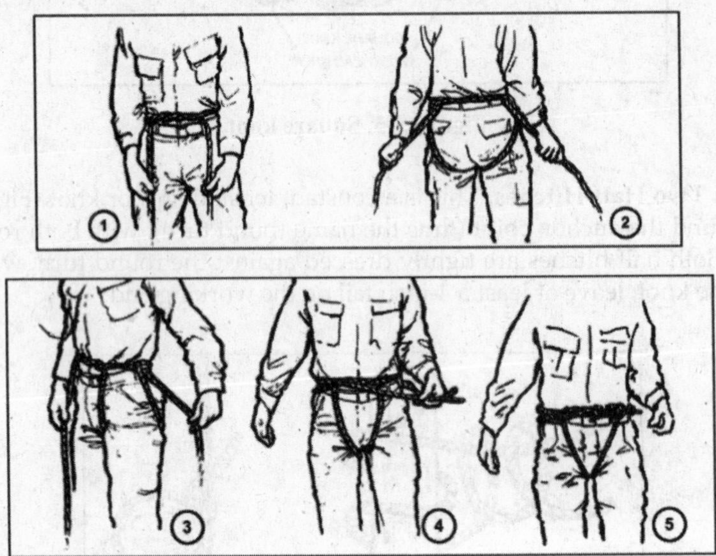

Figure 5-9. Rappel seat

f. **Double Figure Eight.** Use a Figure Eight loop knot (Figure 5-10) to form a fixed loop in the end of the rope. It can be tied at the end of the rope or anywhere along the length of the rope. Figure Eight loop knots are formed by two ropes parallel to each other in the shape of a Figure Eight, no twists are in the Figure Eight. Fixed loops are large enough to insert a carabiner. When you dress the knot, leave at least a 4-inch tall on working end.

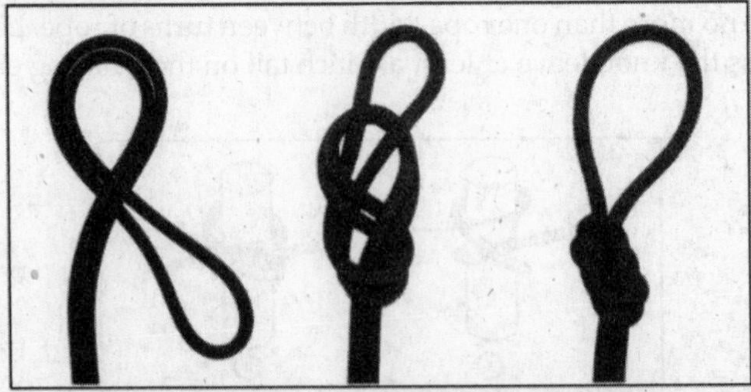

Figure 5-10. Double figure eight-loop knot

g. **Rerouted Figure Eight Knot.** This anchor knot also attaches a climber to a climbing rope. Form a Figure Eight in the rope, and pass the working end around an anchor. Reroute the end back through to form a double Figure Eight (Figure 5-11). Tie the knot with no twists. When you dress the knot, leave at least a 4-inch tail on the working end.

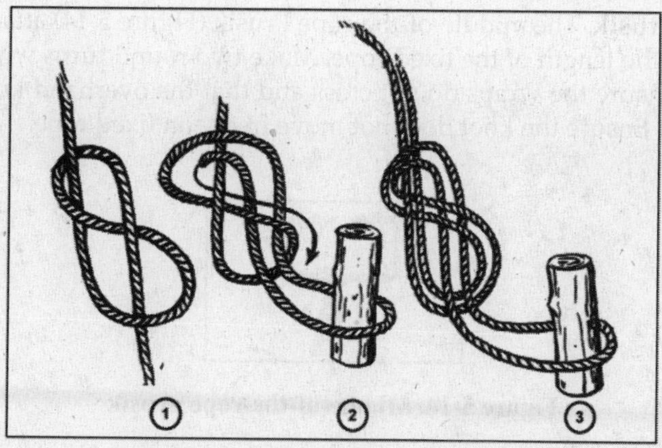

Figure 5-11. Rerouted figure eight knot

h. **Figure Eight Slip Knot**. The Figure Eight slip knot is used to form an adjustable bight in the middle of a rope. Knot is in the shape of a Figure Eight. Both ropes of the bight pass through the same loop of the Figure Eight. The bight is adjustable by means of a sliding section (Figure 5-12).

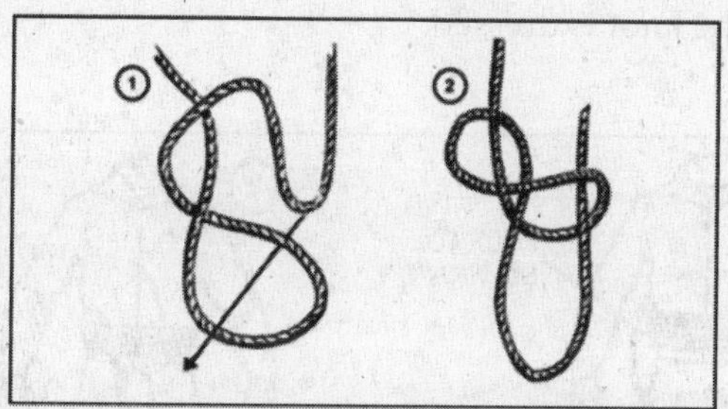

Figure 5-12. Figure eight slip knot

i. **End-of-the-Rope Prusik.** The End-of-the-Rope Prusik (Figure 5-13) attaches a movable rope to a fixed rope. The knot has two round turns, with a locking bar perpendicular to the standing end of the rope. Tie a bowline within 6 inches of the locking bar. When you dress the knot, leave at least a 4-inch tail on the working end.

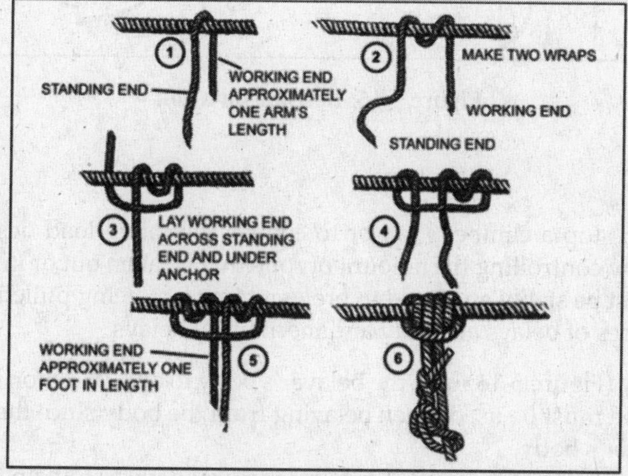

Figure 5-13. End-of-the-rope prusik

j. **Middle-of-the-Rope Prusik**. The middle-of-the-rope Prusik (Figure 5-14) attaches a movable rope to a fixed rope, anywhere along the length of the fixed rope. Make two round turns with a locking bar perpendicular to the standing end. Ensure the wraps do not cross and that the overhand knot is within 6 inches from the horizontal locking bar. Ensure the knot does not move freely on fixed rope.

Figure 5-14. Middle-of-the-rope prusik

k. **Bowline on a Coil**. This knot (Figure 5-15) secures a climber to the end of a climbing rope. Make at least four parallel wraps around the body, between the hipbone and lower set of ribs. Keep all coils free of clothing, touch and are tight enough to ensure that a fist cannot be inserted between the wraps and the body. Three distinct coils show through the bight of the bowline. The rope coming off the bottom of the coils is on the right side, forward of the hip and forms the bight and the overhand knot. The rope coming off the top of the coils is on the left side, forward of the hips and forms the third and final coil showing through the bight of the bowline. Bowline is centered on the gig line and secured with an overhand knot with a minimum of 4 inch tail remaining after the knot is dressed.

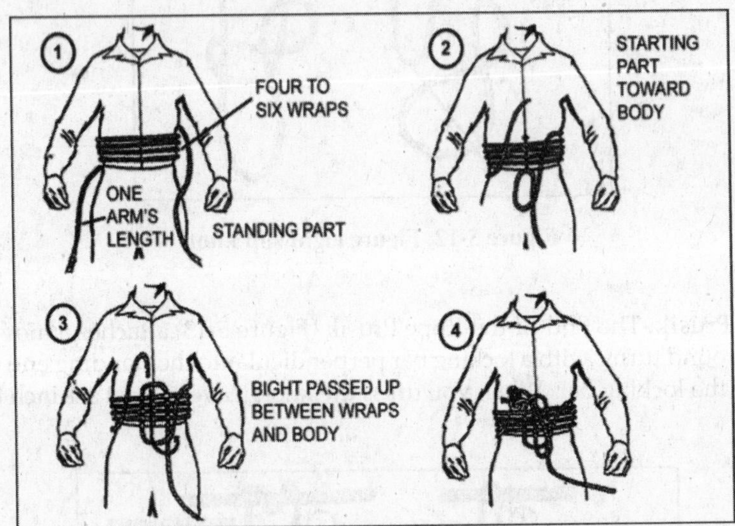

Figure 5-15. Bowline on a coil

5-6. BELAYS

Belaying is any action taken to stop a climber's fall or to control the rate a load descends. The belayer also helps manage the rope for a climber by controlling the amount of rope that is taken out or in, or by controlling a rappeller's rate of descent. The belayer must be stably anchored to prevent him from being pulled out of his position, and losing control of the rope. The two types of belays are body and mechanical belays.

a. **Body Belay.** This belay (Figure 5-16) uses the belayer's body to apply friction by routing the rope around the belayer's body. Caution must be used when belaying from the body since the entire weight of the load may be placed on the belayer's body.

b. **Mechanical Belay.** This belay (Figure 5-17) uses mechanical devices to help the belayer control the rope, as in rappelling. A variety of devices are used to construct a mechanical belay for mountaineering.

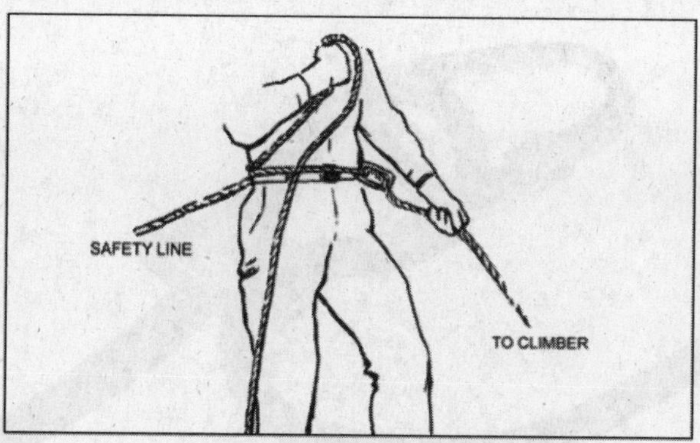

Figure 5-16. Body belay

Figure 5-17. Mechanical belay

(1) ***Munter Hitch.*** One of the most often used belays, the munter hitch (Figure 5-18), requires very little equipment. The rope is routed through a locking, pear-shaped carabiner, then back on itself. The belayer controls the rate of descent by manipulating the working end back on itself with the brake hand.

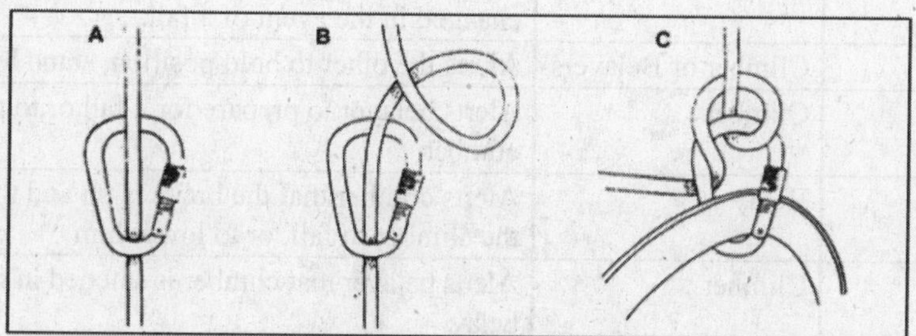

Figure 5-18. Munter hitch

(2) ***Air Traffic Controller.*** The ATC (air traffic controller) is a mechanical belay device (Figure 5-19) that locks down on itself when tension is applied in opposite directions. The belayer need apply very little force with his brake hand to control descent or arrest a fall.

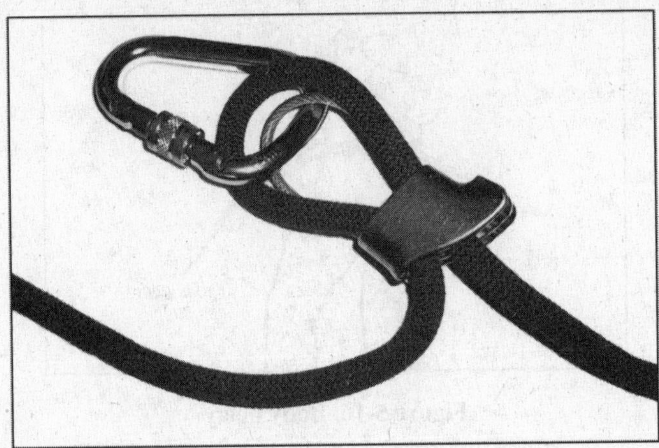

Figure 5-19. Air traffic controller

5-7. CLIMBING COMMANDS

Table 5-1 shows the sequence of commands used by climber and belayer.

Table 5-1. Sequence of climbing commands

Sequence	Command	Given by	Meaning
1.	BELAY ON, CLIMB	Belayer	Alerts climber that belay is on and climber may climb.
2.	CLIMBING	Climber	Alerts belayer that climber is climbing.
3.	UP-ROPE	Climber	Belayer, remove excess slack in the rope.
4.	BRAKE	Climber	Alerts belayer to immediately apply brake.
5.	FALLING	Climber	Alerts belayer that climber is falling and that the belayer should immediately apply the brake and prepare to arrest the fall.
6.	TENSION	Climber	Alerts belayer to remove all slack from climbing rope until rope is tight, then apply brake and hold position.
7.	SLACK	Climber	Alerts belayer to pull slack into the climbing rope (Belayer may have to assist)
8.	ROCK	Anyone	Alerts everyone that an object is about to fall near them. Belayer immediately applies brake.
9.	POINT	Climber	Alerts belayer that the direction of pull on the climbing rope has changed in the event of a fall.
10.	STAND-BY	Climber or Belayers	Alerts the other to hold position, stand by, I am not ready.
11.	DO YOU HAVE ME?	Climber	Alerts belayer to prepare for a fall or to prepare to lower the climber.
12.	I HAVE YOU	Belay	Alerts climber that the brake is on and the belayer is prepared for the climber to fall, or to lower him.
13.	OFF-BELAY	Climber	Alerts belayer that climber is safetied in or it is safe to come off belay.
14.	3-METERS	Belayer	Alerts climber to the amount of rope between climber and belayer (May be given in feet or meters)
15.	BELAY-OFF	Belayer	Alerts climber that belayer is off belay

5-8. ROPE INSTALLATIONS

Rope installations may be constructed by teams to assist units in negotiating natural and manmade obstacles, installation teams consist of a squad sized element, with 2 to 4 trained mountaineers. Installation teams deploy early and prepare the AO for safe, rapid movement by constructing various types of mountaineering installations. Following construction of an installation, the squad, or part of it, remains on site to secure and monitor the system, assist with the control of forces across it, and make adjustments or repairs during its use. After passage of the unit, the installation team may then disassemble the system and deploy to another area as needed.

a. **Fixed Rope Installations**. A fixed rope is anchored in place to help Rangers move over difficult terrain. Its simplest form is a rope tied off on the top of steep terrain. As terrain becomes steeper or more difficult, fixed rope systems may require intermediate anchors along the route. Planning considerations are as follows:
- Does the installation allow you to bypass the obstacle?
- (Tactical considerations) Can obstacle be secured from construction through negotiation, to disassembly?
- Is it in a safe and suitable location? Is it easy to negotiate? Does it avoid obstacles?
- Are natural and artificial anchors available?
- Is the area safe from falling rock and ice?

b. **Vertical Hauling Line**. This installation (Figure 5-20) is used to haul men and equipment up vertical or near vertical slopes. It is often used in conjunction with the fixed rope.

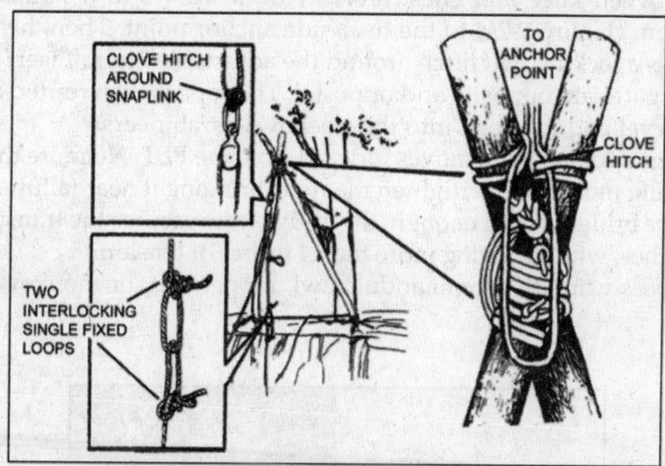

Figure 5-20. Vertical hauling line

(1) ***Planning Considerations.***
- Does the installation allow you to bypass the obstacle?
- (Tactical considerations) Can you secure the installation from construction through negotiation, to disassembly?
- Does it have good loading and off-loading platforms? Are the platforms natural and easily accessible? Do they provide a safe working area?
- Does it allow sufficient clearance for load? Is there enough space between the slope and the apex of the A-frame to allow easy on-loading and off-loading of troops and equipment?
- Does it have an A-Frame for artificial height?
- Does it allow you to haul line in order to move personnel and equipment up and down slope?
- Does the A frame have a pulley or locking carabiner to ease friction on hauling line?
- Does it have a knotted hand line to help Rangers up the installation?
- Does it allow for Rangers top and bottom to monitor safe operation?

(2) ***Equipment.***
- Three 120-foot (50m) static ropes.
- Three 15-foot sling ropes for constructing A-frame.
- Two A-frame poles, 7 to 9 feet long, 4 to 6 inches in diameter (load dependent).
- Nine carabiners.
- One pulley with steel locking carabiner.

c. **Bridges.** Rope bridges are employed in mountainous terrain to bridge linear obstacles such as streams or rivers where the force of flowing water may be too great or temperatures are too cold to conduct a wet crossing.

(1) ***Construction.*** The rope bridge is constructed using a static ropes. The max span that can be bridged is 50 percent of the ropes entire length for a dry crossing, 75 percent for a wet crossing. The ropes are anchored with an anchor knot on the far side of the obstacle, and are tied off at the near end with a transport tightening system. Rope Bridge Planning Considerations are as follows:
- Does the installation allow you to bypass the obstacle?
- (Tactical considerations) Can you secure the installation from construction through negotiation, to disassembly?
- Is it in the most suitable location such as a bend in the river? Is it easily secured?
- Does it have near and far-side anchors?
- Does it have good loading and off-loading platforms?

(2) ***Equipment (1-Rope Bridge).***
- One sling rope per-man.
- One steel locking carabineer.
- Two steel ovals.
- Two 120-foot static ropes.

(3) **Construction Steps**. The first Ranger swims the rope to the far side and ties a tensionless anchor (Figure 5-4) between knee and chest level, with at least 6 to 8 wraps. The BTC ties a transport tightening system (Figure 5-21) to the near side anchor point. Then, he ties a Figure Eight slipknot and incorporates a locking half hitch around the adjustable bight. Insert 2 steel oval carabineers into the bight so the gates are opposite and opposed. The rope is then routed around the near side anchor point at waist level and dropped into the steel oval carabineers.
- A three-Ranger pulling team moves forward from the PLT. No more than three men should tighten the rope. Using more can overtighten the rope, bringing it near failure.
- Once the rope bridge is tight enough, the bridge team secures the transport-tightening system using two half hitches, without losing more than 4 inches of tension.
- Personnel cross using the commando crawl, rappel seat, or monkey crawl method (Figures 5-22 thru 24).

Figure 5-21. Transport tightening system

Figure 5-22. Commando crawl method

Figure 5-23. Rappel seat (tyrolean traverse) method

Figure 5-24. Monkey crawl method

(4) ***Bridge Recovery.*** Once all but two Rangers have crossed the rope bridge, the bridge team commander (BTC) chooses either the wet or dry method to dismantle it. If he chooses the dry method, he should he should first anchor his tightening system with the transport knot.

- The BTC back-stacks all of the slack coming out of the transport knot, then ties a fixed loop and places a carabiner into the fixed loop.
- The next to last Ranger to cross attaches the carabiner to his rappel seat or harness, and then moves across the bridge using the Tyrolean traverse method.
- The BTC then removes all knots from the system. The far side remains anchored. The rope should now only pass around the near side anchor.
- A three-man pull team, assembled on the far side, takes the end brought across by the next to last Ranger and pulls the rope tight again and holds it.
- The BTC then attaches himself to the rope bridge and moves across.
- Once across, the BTC breaks down the far side anchor, removes the knots, and then pulls the rope across. If the BTC chooses a wet crossing, any method can be used to anchor the tightening system.
- All personnel cross except the BTC or the strongest swimmer.
- The BTC then removes all knots from the system.
- The BTC ties a fixed 100p, inserts a carabiner, and attaches it to his rappel seat or harness. He then manages the rope as the slack is pulled to the far side.
- The BTC then moves across the obstacle while being belayed from the far side.

d. **Suspension Traverse**. The suspension traverse is used to move personnel and equipment over rivers, ravines, chasms, and up or down a vertical obstacle. By combining the transport tightening system used during the Rope bridge, an A-Frame used for the Vertical haul Line (Figure 5-25), and belay techniques device, Units can construct a suspension traverse (Figures 5-26 and 5-27). Installation of a suspension traverse can be time-consuming and equipment-intensive. All personnel must be well trained and rehearsed in the procedures.

(1) **Construction**. The suspension traverse must be constructed using a static ropes. The max span that can be bridged is generally 75 percent length of the shortest rope. Planning considerations are the same as rope bridge and vertical haul line combined.

(2) *Equipment.*

- Three static installation ropes.
- Seven sling Ropes.

- Nine carabiners.
- One heavy duty double pulley.
- One locking carabiner.
- One canvas pad.

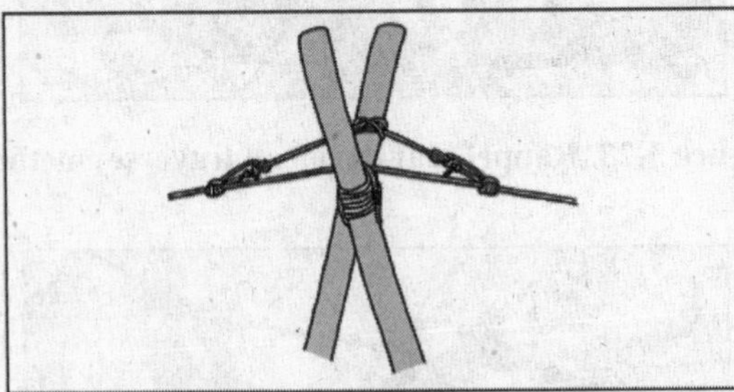

Figure 5-25. Anchoring the traverse rope to the a-frame

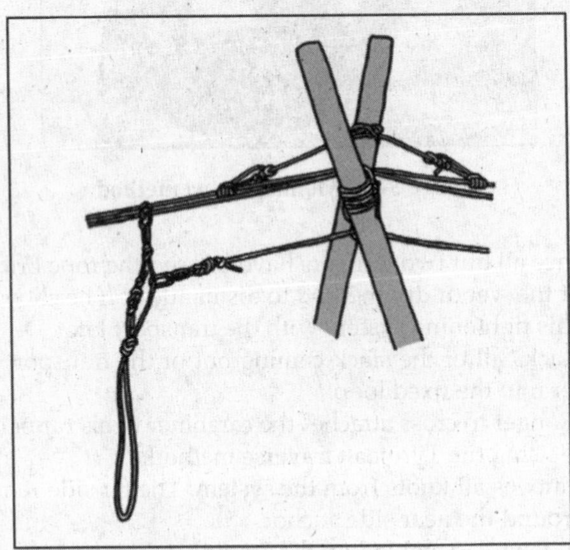

Figure 5-26. Carrying rope for use on a suspension traverse

Figure 5-27. Suspension traverse

5-9. RAPPELLING

Rappelling is a quick method of descent but can be extremely dangerous. These dangers include anchor failure, equipment failure, and individual error. Anchors in a mountainous environment should be selected carefully. Great care must be taken to load the anchor slowly and to ensure that no excessive stress is placed on the anchor. The best way to ensure this is to prohibit bounding rappels, and to use only walk-down rappels.

a. **Hasty and Body Rappels.** Hasty (Figure 5-28) and body rappels (Figure 5-29) are easier and faster than other methods, but should only be used on moderate pitches–never on vertical or overhanging terrain. Wear gloves to prevent rope burns.

Figure 5-28. Hasty rappel

Figure 5-29. Body rappel

b. **Seat-Hip Rappel**. The seat-hip rappel uses a mechanical rappel device that is inserted in a sling rope seat and is fastened to the rappeller to provide the necessary friction to remain in control. This method provides a faster and more controlled descent than any other method (Figure 5-30). There are several mechanical rappel devices (Figures 5-31 and 5-32) that can be used for the seat-hip rappel.

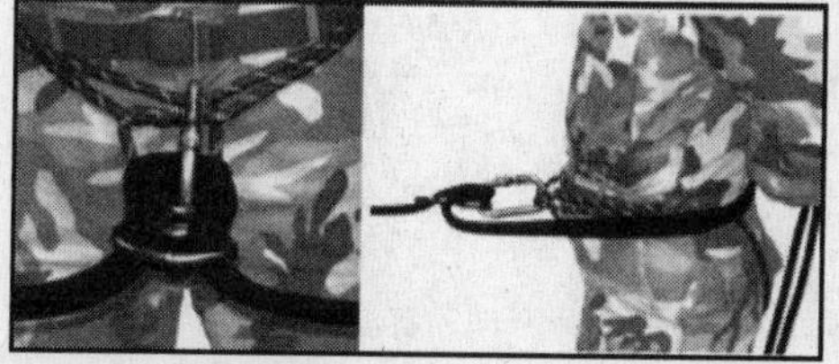

Figure 5-30. Figure eight descender

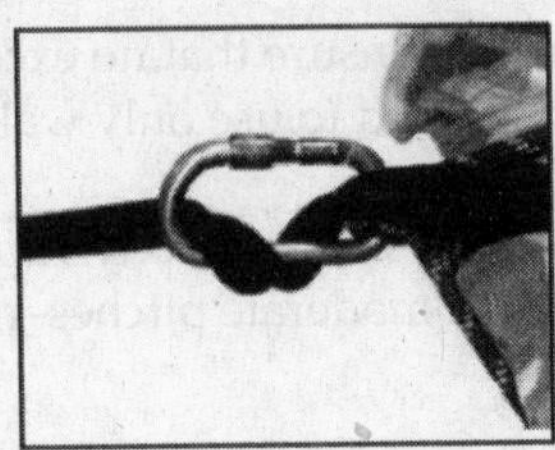

Figure 5-31. Carabiner wrap

Figure 5-32. Seat hip rappel with carabiner wrap descender

c. **Site Selection**. The selection of the rappel point depends on factors such as mission, cover, route, anchor points, and edge composition (loose or jagged rocks). There must be good anchors (primary and secondary). The anchor point should be above the rappeller's departure point. Suitable loading and off-loading platforms should be available.

- Each rappel point has primary and secondary anchors.
- Rappel point has equal tension between all anchor points.
- Double rope is used when possible.
- Ropes must reach the off loading platforms.
- Site has suitable on and off loading platforms.
- Personnel working near the edge are tied in.
- Select a smooth route free of loose rack and debris.

CHAPTER 6

Employment in Unconventional Warfare Conditions

Employment of SFODs in UW encompasses several of the seven phases of a U.S.-sponsored insurgency. The phases are preparation, initial contact, infiltration, organization, buildup, combat operations, and demobilization. Although each resistance movement is unique, U.S.-sponsored resistance organizations generally pass through all seven phases. The phases may not occur sequentially or receive the same degree of emphasis. They may occur concurrently or not at all, depending on the specific situation. This chapter covers infiltration through combat operations by addressing the following steps: infiltration, area assessment, development of the JSOA, development of a resistance organization, training the guerrilla force, combat operations, and combatting counterguerrilla operations.

Rules of Conduct:
1. There shall be no confiscation whatever from the poor peasantry.
2. If you borrow anything, return it.
3. eplace all articles you damage.
4. Pay fairly for everything that you purchase.
5. Be honest in all transactions with the peasants.
6. Be courteous and polite to the people and help them when you can.

Mao Tse-tung, 1928

INFILTRATION

6-1. Infiltration follows initial contact with the resistance organization or government in exile. Normally, OGAs conduct initial contact and make an assessment of the resistance potential. Part of the initial contact phase also involves making arrangements for reception and initial assistance of the infiltrating SFOD or pilot team. Successful infiltration into the JSOA requires detailed planning and preparation at the joint level. Several methods are considered based on METT-TC. Appendix F provides additional information.

AREA ASSESSMENT

6-2. The SFOD members and the commander begin an area assessment immediately after entry into the JSOA. This assessment is the collection of special information and serves as the commander's estimate of the situation. The area assessment is a continuous process that confirms, corrects, refutes, or adds to previous intelligence acquired before commitment. The area assessment also serves as a basis for changing premission operational and logistic plans. There are no fixed formulas for doing an area assessment. Each commander has to decide for himself what should be included and what conclusions may be drawn from the information he collects.

6-3. When making an area assessment, the SFOD commander considers all the major factors involved, including the enemy situation, security measures, and the many aspects of the civil component as defined by CASCOPE. The SFOD should only disseminate new intelligence information that differs significantly from the intelligence received before commitment. Area assessment is either initial or principal, depending on the urgency involved.

INITIAL ASSESSMENT

6-4. Initial assessment includes those requirements deemed essential to the pilot team or SFOD immediately following infiltration. The mission of the team is to assess designated areas to determine the feasibility of developing the resistance potential and to establish contact with indigenous leaders. These requirements must be satisfied as soon as possible after the team arrives in the AO. Much of this initial assessment may be transmitted in the initial entry report (IER) (ANGUS) or situation (CYRIL) report. Once the theater command or JSOTF has made a determination as to the feasibility of developing the area, additional SF elements may be infiltrated. The assessment team may remain with the operational element or be exfiltrated as directed.

PRINCIPAL ASSESSMENT

6-5. Principal assessment forms the basis for all other subsequent UW activities in the JSOA. It is a continuous operation and includes those efforts that support the continued planning and conduct of operations. It should be transmitted using the format planned during isolation. This format may be abbreviated by deleting information already confirmed. This report should include new or changed information.

AREA ASSESSMENT IN AN URBAN ENVIRONMENT

6-6. What makes urban guerrilla warfare so different from rural guerrilla warfare or conventional military contest is the presence of a large audience to the struggle. Unlike rural guerrillas, urban guerrillas cannot withdraw to some remote jungle where they are safe from observation and attack. They must be able to live in the midst of hundreds of witnesses and potential informers.

6-7. Appendix A provides guidance for the planning and conduct of UW in an urban environment. The appendix describes characteristics of cities and urban tactical operations, and provides an urban operations survey checklist. Users of Appendix A should already have had sufficient exposure to ASO and therefore amplifications and definitions of specific terms are unnecessary.

DEVELOPMENT OF THE JSOA

6-8. The organization and development of the JSOA or region involves early marshalling of the resistance command structure and the subsequent buildup of the resistance force. A well-organized JSOA allows close coordination between the SFOD and the resistance element. The SFOD gains a thorough knowledge of the AO through extensive area studies. These studies include history, economy, religion, infrastructure, ethnic groups, needs of the populace, customs, taboos, and other data that will affect the organization; C2; and selection of leaders within the resistance force.

OBJECTIVE

6-9. After infiltration, the major task facing the SFOD is to develop all resistance elements into an effective force able to achieve U.S. and the area commander's objectives. To the area command, the SFOD is the direct representative of the U.S. Government. The SFOD members must be diplomats as well as military advisers and establish a good working relationship with the resistance organization. This relationship develops from acceptance of U.S. sponsorship and operational guidance. The SFOD and guerrillas are united with a common goal against a common enemy.

DEVELOPMENT

6-10. Politics, ideology, topography, security, communications, and many other factors govern the shape, size, and ultimate organization of the JSOA or region. The operational areas of guerrilla forces must have clearly defined boundaries. These limits simplify coordination and C2 and reduce friction between adjacent units. The operational areas should conform to the existing spheres of influence of the established commanders. History demonstrates that areas with basic religious, ethnic, or political differences should not be included in the same area command.

6-11. JSOAs should not be larger than the communication and logistics capabilities can effectively support. JSOA is the largest territorial organization commanded by an overall area commander who is within enemy territory. The JSOA should include enough dense terrain for the operation, security, training, and administration of the guerrilla forces.

6-12. A country may be divided into several JSOAs based on administrative units or natural geographic boundaries. Administrative units include counties, districts, provinces, departments, and states. This system is satisfactory when guerrilla missions include sabotage, propaganda, and espionage conducted by small cellular units. One negative aspect of this method is that by following the present government's established unit of administration, the resistance is indirectly aiding the government's control and coordination efforts.

6-13. Countries divided by natural geographic boundaries are superior for military and overt operations on a large scale. Each major operational area should include difficult terrain or uncontrolled areas suitable for area complexes and guerrilla operations. Each JSOA and subordinate sector command may also include food-producing areas that will support the guerrilla force in the area. These considerations may only be ignored when logistics support from external sources is available regularly and on a very substantial scale.

6-14. The establishment of rapport between the SFOD and the resistance element is a vital first requirement for the SFOD. An effective working and command relationship helps develop a high degree of cooperation and influence over the resistance force. This influence is ensured when resistance leaders are receptive to the SFOD's suggestions to accomplish the mission. The command structure and the physical organization of the area are priority tasks of the SFOD. In some situations, the resistance organization may be well established, but in others, organizational structure may be totally lacking. In all cases, some improvement in physical area organization will probably be necessary. Tasks and requirements dictate the organization of the JSOA, but organization also depends on local customs and conditions more so than on any fixed set of rules.

GOVERNMENT-IN-EXILE

6-15. A government-in-exile does not exist in every UW situation. Where it does, the leader may be a "figure-head" for the resistance. He may be a deposed former leader of the country or a prominent person of society who commands the respect of his fellow citizens. A highly structured resistance organization might report to a national government-in-exile or, if one does not exist, to a shadow government in-country. The leader of the area command may declare himself the leader of a "shadow government." If the enemy government usurped power against the wishes of the people, the USG may instead recognize the government-in-exile as the official government of the country.

AREA COMMAND

6-16. An area command is a combined (indigenous and SF) command, control, communications, computers, and intelligence (C4I) structure that directs, controls, integrates, and supports all resistance activities in the JSOA or region. The size of the area command is dependent on METT-TC. The area commander is the resistance leader. Selected SFOD members serve as advisors to the area commander and his staff. Small and mobile, the HQ size is limited because of meager communication capabilities. Functions and forces must be decentralized due to the ever-present possibility of the area command being destroyed by enemy action. The area command, with the underground, auxiliary, and other support systems, should be organized prior to Phase II (Guerrilla Warfare). They all conduct centralized planning but give maximum latitude for decentralized execution to their subordinate sector commanders. This policy supports the utmost latitude allowing subordinate commanders to determine the "how to" in planning and executing their missions. Mutual confidence, cohesion, and trust must exist between the area commander, subordinate commanders, and the SFOD for each to be effective.

6-17. The area commander should be located where he can safely control the resistance movement and its activities. Flexibility, intelligence, mobility, and OPSEC are the keys to survival and success. The area commander or his designated representatives should make frequent visits to subordinate units, both for morale enhancement and to become acquainted with the local situation. Where personal visits are not possible, the commanders should communicate with each other frequently.

AREA COMMAND ELEMENTS

6-18. There are no rigid patterns for the structure and function of an area command. The area command is compartmented but should include representatives from all elements of the resistance movement. Regardless of the level of organization, the basic elements of the area command are the command group and the resistance forces. Figure 6-1 shows the JSOA command structure.

Command Group

6-19. The command group consists of political leaders or their representatives from the exiled or shadow government, the area commander as the resistance leader, the commander's staff, and key members of the SFOD.

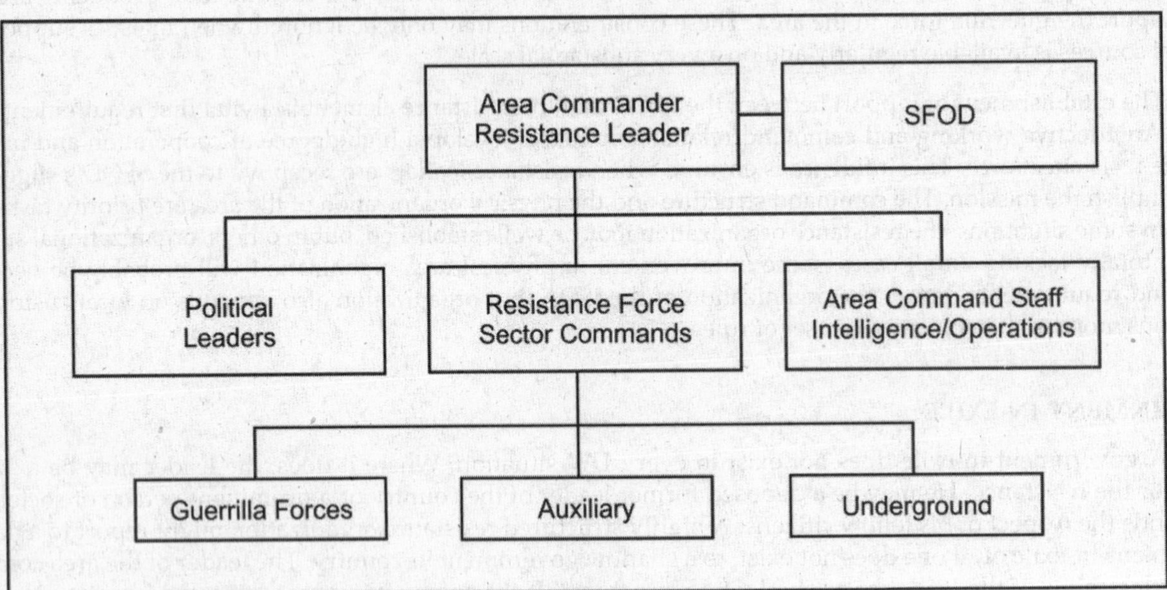

Figure 6-1. Area command structure

Resistance Forces

6-20. Sector commanders or resistance element leaders from each sector in the JSOA represent the resistance forces. Historically, U.S. UW doctrine has made a clear distinction among elements of the resistance movement—guerrilla forces, the auxiliary, and the underground. The composition and duties of these elements forming the resistance force will depend on factors unique to each JSOA and resistance organization.

AREA COMMAND MEETING

6-21. The area command meeting is the primary method of conducting business within an area command. The SFOD must thoroughly plan and rehearse its agenda for the meeting. Personnel must analyze information from the area study, operational area intelligence study, and area assessment to determine the main points for discussion. The meeting is not a confrontation between the area commander and the SFOD. Seating arrangements should integrate the area commander, his staff, and the SFOD among each other to form a large team. Planning considerations for the area command meeting include—

- Security measures.
- Key issues to be discussed.
- Personnel who should attend.
- Location of meeting site.
- Length of meeting.

6-22. METT-TC is the basis for an area command or sector meeting. Suitable locations for the site should be in a secure and isolated location, either rural or urban. When indigenous or enemy government-imposed population control measures are in effect, it may be easier for meetings to be held in rural or guerrilla-controlled territory. The initial meeting should be conducted as soon as possible after the SFOD infiltrates. During the meeting, SFOD members should—

- Establish personal and professional relationships with the resistance.
- Discuss guerrilla and SFOD abilities and limitations.
- Discuss procedures for developing the resistance cadre.
- Establish centralized planning and decentralized execution.
- Establish security measures and discuss threat activity.
- Discuss political boundaries, terrain features, targets, density of population, and other JSOA- and region-specific information.
- Establish positive U.S. influence with the resistance organization.
- Establish type and scope of combat operations.
- Organize the resistance infrastructure to survive in a nonpermissive environment.
- Organize cooperation between the resistance and local civilians.
- Establish necessary documentation, cover stories, and proper clothes.
- Discuss ROE.
- Emphasize unity of effort with open dialogue.
- Always plan for contingencies.

6-23. The SFOD advises and assists with security for the meeting in a similar manner to that of the area complex. Outer and inner security zones are formed. The outer security ring consists of observers strategically placed (determined by METT-TC) away from the meeting place. Members of the outer security zones observe avenues of approach and provide early warning. They may use handheld radios or telephones to provide early warning of enemy threats, which are passed using code words or messages. The inner security zones surround the meeting place itself and consist of enough personnel to allow for the escape of the resistance leadership in case of compromise. Before the meeting convenes, those present must decide on the actions to take in case of a compromise. They must consider escape plans and routes. A security element, usually members of the inner security zones, serves as a rear guard while key personnel, equipment, and documents are removed and quickly evacuated.

Intelligence Section

6-24. During the initial organization of an area command, the intelligence section of the staff is given special emphasis. Throughout all phases of the organization of a resistance force, the intelligence net is expanded progressively until the intelligence requirements for the area command HQ can be fulfilled. The functions of an area command intelligence section are to—

- Collect, record, evaluate, and interpret information of value to the guerrilla forces. It distributes the resulting intelligence to the area commander and staff and to higher and lower commands.
- Organize, supervise, and coordinate, together with the operations section, special intelligence teams (airfield surveillance, air warning, and coast watcher).
- Plan and supervise the procurement and distribution of maps, charts, photos, and other materiel for intelligence purposes.
- Recommend intelligence and counterintelligence (CI) policies.
- Collect and distribute information on evasion and recovery (E&R), to include instructions for downed aircrews, evaders, and escapees.
- Establish liaison with the intelligence staffs and lower commands.
- Provide intelligence personnel for duty at lower commands.
- Conduct training to carry out intelligence functions.

6-25. The intelligence section is organized into a forward and rear echelon to provide continuous operation when enemy pressure forces the area command HQ to move to alternate locations. When these moves are anticipated, the forward echelon sets up and begins operations in the prepared alternate site before the rear echelon moves. During large-scale overt operations, the forward echelon provides an intelligence section for an advance command post organized to direct the operations of two or more sector commands. A guerrilla area command must produce the intelligence needed for its own security and for local operations against the enemy. It must also gather the information required by higher HQ. Although supervised by the area command intelligence section, information collectors are decentralized as far as practicable to subordinate sector commands.

Sector Commands

6-26. Large area commands may establish subordinate sector commands. Sector command meetings are conducted after the initial area command meeting. Sectors are formed to simplify C4I operations and to provide a mechanism to promote centralized planning and decentralized execution. If the area command is subdivided into sector commands, its component units are the subordinate sector commands. The sector command is the command element of the resistance in a given sector. The same factors that define the boundaries of area complexes define the boundaries of sectors. The kinds and disposition of facilities within a sector are the same as those for an area complex. The sector command performs the same functions as the area command, except within the limits of its own boundaries. The component elements of a sector command are the functional components of a resistance movement.

AREA COMPLEX

6-27. An area complex is a clandestine, dispersed network of facilities to support resistance activities. It is a "liberated zone" designed to achieve security, control, dispersion, and flexibility. To support resistance activities, an area complex must include a security system, base camps, communications, logistics, medical facilities, supply caches, training areas, and escape and recovery mechanisms. The area complex may consist of friendly villages or towns under guerrilla military or political control.

6-28. According to Mao Tse-tung in *On Guerrilla Warfare*, a guerrilla base may be defined as an area, strategically located, in which the guerrillas can carry out their duties of training, self-preservation, and development. The ability to fight a war without a rear area is a fundamental characteristic of guerrilla action, but this does not mean that guerrillas can exist and function over a long period of time without the development of base areas. There is a difference between the terms base area and guerrilla base area. An area completely surrounded by territory occupied by the enemy is a "base area." On the other hand, a guerrilla base area includes those areas that can be controlled by guerrillas only while they physically occupy them.

6-29. Within the area complex, the resistance forces achieve security by—

- Establishing an effective intelligence net.
- Using the early warning with listening posts (LPs), observation posts (OPs), and security patrols.
- Practicing CI measures.
- Rehearsing withdrawals and CONPLANs.
- Employing mobility and flexibility.
- Using rapid dispersion techniques for personnel.
- Camouflaging and adhering to noise and light discipline.
- Organizing the active support of the civilian population.

6-30. The C2 base camp is in the heart of the area complex. Specially trained and equipped guerrilla forces control and defend this camp. A special guerrilla security detachment provides the internal protection for the area commander, his staff, and the SFOD. Key personnel, critical equipment, and sensitive information are based from there and may include the following:

- The area commander and staff.
- The SFOD and support personnel.
- Communication equipment.
- Controlled medical supplies and treatment facilities.
- Supply caches of weapons, ammunition, and explosives.

6-31. An area complex can be subdivided into two security zones: outer and inner (Figure 6-2). There are no clear-cut boundaries between zones, and security responsibilities can overlap. Each zone is the responsibility of a specific guerrilla element whose mission is to provide for the security and defense of the zone in the area complex to achieve total and overlapping security coverage.

Outer Security Zone

6-32. The outer security zone is vitally important to a guerrilla force. The local guerrilla forces and the civilian support infrastructure are organized and developed in the outer security zone. This area serves as the primary source of recruits for the guerrilla force. The outer zone also serves as the first line of in-depth security and defense for the area complex. Resistance elements in this area are responsible for providing the area command with timely and accurate information on enemy activities within the zone. Local guerrillas are the resistance element responsible for the zone's

Figure 6-2. Area complex security zones

control and defense. This element is also responsible for the conduct of operations within the zone. The local guerrilla forces organize, employ, and serve as part of the civilian support element. The civilian support element gathers current intelligence information and provides logistic, PSYOP, and operational support to the regular guerrilla forces and the area command. The initial screening, selection, and training of new resistance members takes place in this zone. The most promising and trusted recruits are then selected for membership in the regular or full-time guerrilla forces.

Inner Security Zone

6-33. The inner security zone encompasses the base camp of the regular or full-time guerrilla forces. These forces defend and control the zone and are constantly mobile within the area. The primary mission of the guerrilla forces operating in this zone is to temporarily delay any penetration made by the enemy. They watch trails and avenues of approach. They use OPs or LPs, fixed fighting positions, and pre-positioned obstacles such as bunkers and minefields to delay enemy forces. They employ harassment, ambushes, sniping, and other interdiction tactics and practice rapid withdrawal procedures. These tactics increase the in-depth defense of the area complex. They should also use command-detonated antivehicular and antipersonnel mines on a permanent basis. Guerrilla forces may place mines along probable enemy vehicular and personnel avenues of approach, such as trails, creeks, and riverbeds. The guerrillas must avoid, at all costs, becoming decisively engaged while carrying out their delaying and defensive mission. Civilians do not normally occupy the inner security zone; therefore, it may serve as an area of food cultivation for the guerrilla population.

GUERRILLA BASES

6-34. A guerrilla base is HQ for any size guerrilla force. A base may be temporary or permanent, depending on the guerrilla's stage of development. Guerrilla C4I, support, facilities, and operational units are located within the base. LOCs connect the base and facilities within the area complex. The installations and facilities found within a guerrilla base are the command posts, training areas or classrooms, a communications facility, and medical services. The occupants and facilities must be capable of rapid displacement with little or no prior warning. There is usually more than one guerrilla base within a sector or JSOA. They are in remote, inaccessible areas and their locations are revealed only on a need-to-know basis. Personnel must use passive and active security measures to provide base security, employing overhead cover, concealment, and escape routes. A mandatory requirement for a guerrilla base camp is a source of water. Wells may be dug where permanent bases are established. Ideally, there will be an abundance of water sources to choose from in the area. All base camps should have an alternate location for contingency use. In case the enemy overruns the base, all personnel should plan for and rehearse rapid withdrawals.

TYPES OF BASES

6-35. There are three types of guerrilla bases. In order of development, they are mobile, semipermanent, and permanent. Initially, all guerrilla base camps are mobile, and as the JSOA matures, semipermanent camps are constructed. When the JSOA matures enough to conduct battalion combat operations, the semipermanent camps become permanent. Normal occupation time is based on METT-TC.

Mobile

6-36. Full-time guerrillas and local guerrilla forces establish mobile bases. These bases are at the periphery of their zones of responsibility. Mobile bases are normally occupied for periods ranging from 1 to 7 days.

Semipermanent

6-37. HQ elements or sector commands establish semipermanent bases in the inner security zones. These bases are in areas that provide a tactical advantage for the guerrilla. Semipermanent bases are normally occupied for periods ranging from 1 to 2 weeks.

Permanent

6-38. This base is within the rear security zone of the area complex. The guerrilla command element, SFOD, and key installations and facilities are located here. Adequate training areas are established to support all the training activities. The guerrilla force protects the training areas, and an SFOD member, who is the subject-matter expert

(SME), monitors the training. When needed, personnel secure drop zones (DZs) and landing zones (LZs) to receive supplies and equipment. An SFOD member accounts for supplies. These DZs and LZs must be accessible to the appropriate aircraft and be a safe distance from the guerrilla base camp. Permanent bases may normally be occupied for periods ranging from 1 to 2 months.

BASE SECURITY MEASURES

6-39. The defense of any base includes strict adherence to camouflage, noise, and light discipline. Defense measures should also include inner security posts, LPs and OPs, security and tracking patrols, antipersonnel mines, and other obstacles to concentrate, impede, or stop the enemy (Figure 6-3). Personnel should plan contingencies for rapid withdrawal from the area before any enemy attack.

Figure 6-3. Permanent base security

Inner Security Posts

6-40. Inner security posts are normally established within 100 meters of the main body. The mission of the inner security posts is to delay a small reaction force that has penetrated the base perimeter and is closing in on the main body. This delay allows the main body to break out. During low visibility, inner security posts are closer, about 25 meters from the main body. A challenge and password system should be implemented.

Listening and Observation Posts

6-41. LPs and OPs are established in unit SOPs and based on observation and fields of fire, avenues of approach, key terrain, obstacles, and cover and concealment (OAKOC). At a minimum, LPs and OPs will be located on the most likely avenues of approach. They should be located on high and commanding ground surrounding the base, as per unit SOP. The mission of the posts is to detect and report in a timely manner enemy air and ground movement that threatens the guerrilla base. If the enemy is detected, post personnel may not fire on the enemy but radio a size, activity, location, unit, time, and equipment (SALUTE) report. This tactic saves giving away their position and possibly the position of the base. These posts are normally within 400 to 800 meters from the base.

Security and Tracking Patrols

6-42. Security and tracking patrols may be carried out at dawn and dusk to provide security and early warning for the base. Each patrol should carry a frequency modulated short-range radio, similar to an AN/PRC-77, enabling the patrol to relay information to the base in a timely manner. Patrols must search all areas, but give priority of search to the high ground surrounding the base and to creek and riverbeds in the area. Patrols also search roads and trails for tracks or signs of enemy presence. If there are friendly civilians in the area, they may be questioned regarding enemy activity. Civilians unfamiliar to the patrol may be a threat or sympathizer. Information provided by the friendly civilians is critical to the security of the guerrilla base camp. The mission of the security patrols is to detect signs or other indicators of enemy presence or activity. These indicators include—

- Tobacco, candy, gum, and food wrappers.
- Human excrement or other waste products.
- Tracks made by bare feet or boots on recently used trails.
- Broken branches and bent twigs suggesting direction of travel.
- Discarded rations, containers, and equipment.

6-43. Passive security measures that can be taken include camouflaging dwellings and hutches with vegetation. Personnel should change vegetation daily. They can also camouflage trails and erase tracks. Personnel should avoid smoke from cooking fires, especially during daylight hours, and maintain noise and light discipline at all times.

Antipersonnel Mines

6-44. SFODs may temporarily use antipersonnel mines along likely avenues of approach into the base. Creeks, riverbeds, and the surrounding elevations are good locations for placing antipersonnel mines. Personnel will warn the civilian population about the use of mines to preclude unnecessary civilian casualties. They may temporarily employ antipersonnel mines in the following areas not used by civilians:

- Near running water sources.
- Around fruit and shade trees.
- On little-used roads and trails.
- In and around abandoned fighting positions or around abandoned uninhabited dwellings.

6-45. Minefield reports should be submitted by the fastest secure means available and are classified Secret when complete. Exact format may be specified by local command SOP.

MISSION SUPPORT SITES

6-46. A mission support site (MSS) is a temporary operational and logistics base for guerrillas who are away from their main base camp for more than a few days. It extends the range of guerrillas in the JSOA by permitting them to travel long distances without support from their base camps. The guerrillas should not occupy them for more than 24 hours. Guerrillas should always reconnoiter and surveil the MSS before occupying it.

6-47. Personnel establish an MSS to support a specific mission and should not use it more than once. Using the MSS only once protects the force from setting up repeated patterns of movement. However, it may be used before and after a mission, based on METT-TC. The MSS may contain food, shelter, medical support, ammunition, demolitions, and other operational items. To preclude unnecessary noise and movement in and out of the MSS, auxiliary personnel may establish supply caches in the surrounding vicinity before the combat force arrives.

6-48. When selecting the location for an MSS, personnel must consider the following:

- Proximity to the objective.
- Level of enemy activity.
- Cover and concealment.
- Preplanned routes of withdrawal.
- Tribal or factional and religious issues.

METT-TC is very important when selecting the MSS. MSSs must not be near LZs, DZs, or any other sites of heightened activity.

DEVELOPMENT OF THE RESISTANCE ORGANIZATION

6-49. The primary technique or type of recruitment used in the early stages of a resistance movement is selective recruitment. As security is emphasized, recruitment is highly selective. Many tasks of the resistance force require no qualification for its recruits beyond a certain degree of intelligence and emotional stability. Since some activities require special qualifications, recruiters must look for individuals who can perform leadership duties, intelligence collection, and other special tasks. The screening process includes surveillance and background checks. The recruiters use the following methods to ensure loyalty: loyalty checks, oaths, and probationary periods. Once the resistance cadre is established and the resistance movement is successful, mass recruitment begins. Recruiters seek a base of support among large segments of the indigenous population. Auxiliary members are excellent recruiters because they can move easily through denied areas. The resistance movement must rely on mass support if it is to survive and expand (Figure 6-4). Recruiting techniques include appeals, coercion, and suggestion, as well as playing on an individual's feelings of governmental alienation.

6-50. Recruitment is difficult in the early phases of the operation and easier after the resistance establishes its credibility. If the resistance recruits too many civilians, enemy reprisals against the remainder of the community are very possible. The number of base camps and the quantity of supporting logistics stock limit the number of potential armed guerrilla recruits.

ADMINISTRATIVE PROCEDURES

6-51. As development of the resistance organization progresses, documentation and record keeping of mission functions is vital to maintaining a well-organized force. This information also enables the SFOD commander to conduct effective C2, pay, rewards, and eventually demobilization measures. The SFOD must establish administrative procedures early on to facilitate a well-organized guerrilla force. Appendix I addresses detailed administrative issues.

COMMANDERS

6-52. The most delicate part of an SFOD's duty is to ensure that competent indigenous personnel occupy key leadership positions. If leaders and staff members of the resistance organization do not appear qualified to fill positions held, the SFOD should try to increase their effectiveness. Increasing the effectiveness of these personnel will normally enhance the influence of the SFOD. The personality and characteristics of the area commander are extremely important. His ability must extend beyond military and technical fields. Successfully commanding a guerrilla force with all its diverse elements requires psychological and political skills. The area commander should have distinction among the civilian population and the confidence of his followers.

6-53. The area commander influences others to accomplish the mission by providing purpose, direction, and motivation. Purpose gives the guerrillas the reason why; direction shows what must be done; and motivation gives his guerrillas the will to do everything they are capable of to accomplish their mission.

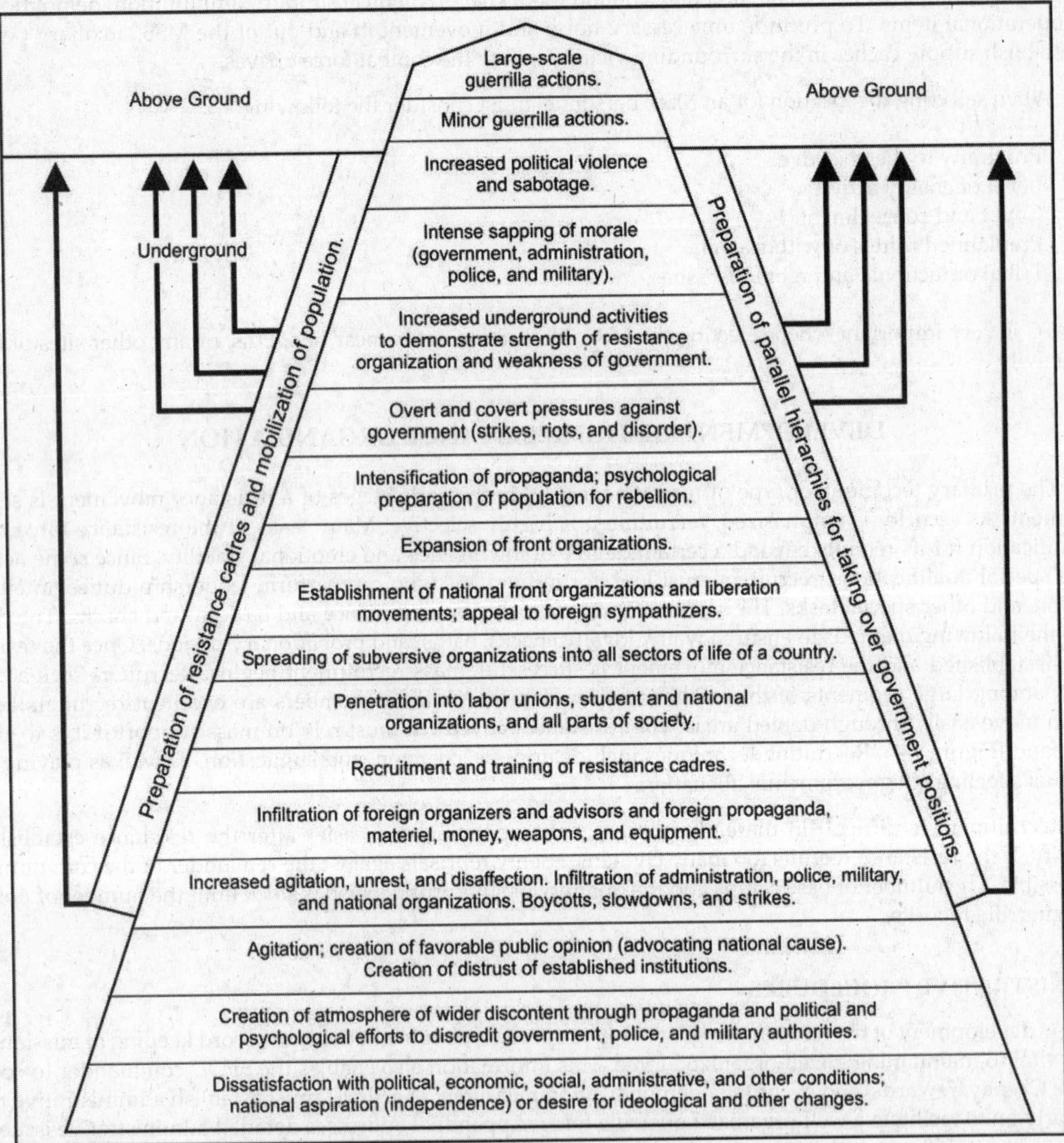

Figure 6-4. Building a resistance movement

6-54. A combat-tested leader demonstrates his tactical and technical proficiency and uses initiative to exploit opportunities for success. He accomplishes this process by taking calculated risks within the commander's intent. He leads by example (from the front) and not by fear and coercion. Successful leadership in combat enables a leader to—

- Never underestimate his enemy.
- Consider the civil component in all operations.

- Understand basic weapons and demolitions.
- Understand both conventional force and guerrilla tactics.
- Appreciate and understand the strategy of war.
- Respect and anticipate the objectives and campaign goals of conventional forces.
- Be able to task-organize himself and others.
- Be able to recognize and appoint good leaders.
- Improvise on short notice.
- Allow the use of initiative.
- Employ and exploit all types of intelligence-gathering opportunities.

6-55. Historically, the sector leaders have been recognized as commanders within their spheres of influence. In the organization of a command, every effort is made to assist and recognize a local guerrilla leader as the overall area commander. This concept must not be violated just because the local commander may lack the requisite military service or qualifications. If he can command the respect of the people and subordinate commanders in the area, the SFOD should tutor him in carrying out his area commander functions. Replacing locally developed leaders with area commanders from external (out-of-country) sources, even though the new area commanders are native-born, may create personal or political rivalries and alienate the area commanders already in existence. The recognition of commanders, especially the overall area commander, must not be arbitrary or hasty. Recognition should be based on a careful assessment of the existing political conditions and social attitudes within the JSOA. If a resistance movement has failed to develop due to serious personal rivalries or political differences, the concept of recognizing a popular local leader as the overall commander may in fact be violated. In this case, a leader who commands respect and can unify the efforts of the opposing factions is then appointed or infiltrated into the JSOA.

6-56. The local area commander is responsible for the organization, training, administration, and operations of guerrilla forces within his area. Specifically, the duties of the guerrilla area commander are operations of the forces under his command and coordination of operations between subordinate forces and allied forces. He continuously determines the resources, combat strength, dispositions, movements, and capabilities of the enemy that will affect completion of his mission. He also—

- Appoints or recognizes subordinate sector commanders.
- Prepares plans to accomplish assigned missions and contemplated missions.
- Prepares and assigns missions to subordinate sector commanders.
- Establishes adequate communication systems between the various forces of his command.
- Organizes and operates CI and intelligence nets.
- Plans security and defensive measures within the area command and the area complex.
- Guides general administrative policies.
- Establishes morale and welfare measures.
- Ensures the care and handling of all EPWs are IAW all the applicable Geneva Accords and Conventions.
- Plans, prepares, and employs PSYOP.
- Guides training for individuals and units.
- Requisitions and collects supplies from local sources.
- Requisitions supplies and equipment from outside the JSOA.
- Allocates and disburses equipment and supplies to subordinate sector commands.

6-57. The area commander ensures the reception, support, and protection of SFOD personnel in the JSOA. He accounts for key EPWs, prominent civilians, and for the rescue and exfiltration of downed aircrews. He is also responsible for the civilians in the area. Initially, his responsibilities are for the safety and welfare of those noncombatants within the JSOA. As the JSOA matures, he may actually supervise the organization of a civil administration capability among the populace using promising members of the resistance movement. The SFOD supports him in these requirements by employing CA assets, first as planners and advisors to the SFOD (including using reachback capabilities to CA specialists in rear areas or the continental United States [CONUS]), then as core advisor teams to fledgling civil administrators, and finally as fully staffed teams capable of providing support to civil administration. The organization and employment of these CA assets is based on U.S. policies and objectives in the JSOA and METT-TC.

ELEMENTS OF THE RESISTANCE

6-58. The resistance organization consists of three elements. They are the guerrilla force, the auxiliary, and the underground. The guerrilla force is the overt military or paramilitary arm. The auxiliary is the clandestine support element of the guerrilla force. The underground is a cellular organization that conducts clandestine subversion, sabotage, UAR, and intelligence collection activities.

GUERRILLA FORCE

6-59. Guerrillas are a decisive combat force. They conduct tactics, techniques, and procedures employed in the United States during the French and Indian Wars. They continued to have success during the American Revolution and during the American Civil War for both the Federal and Confederate troops. During World War II, a classic example of a decisive combat force was Merrill's Marauders and their use of raids, ambushes, and to a lesser extent, offensive and defensive maneuvers to defeat the Japanese in Burma.

6-60. The organization of a guerrilla force from the resistance movement or the reorganization of existing guerrilla forces into a combat command is a time-consuming process. The organization must follow a definite plan, phased and coordinated with the SFOB. Directives from outside the JSOA to the guerrilla area commanders prescribe the general COAs. Based on detailed reports and recommendations of the SFOD, the commander issues more specific orders much later to reach the desired organizational level. Then, the highly organized guerrilla force may be employed in overt combat operations.

6-61. Guerrilla forces are organized in a similar manner to conventional units. Since guerrilla operations normally do not exceed the equivalent of battalion-level operations, most guerrilla forces are organized only to that level. In the later stages of a successful UW situation, guerrilla forces conceivably could conduct coordinated regimental or higher operations against the enemy forces.

6-62. The progressive organization of a guerrilla force in an AO works in three general phases. These phases are not specific periods but normally overlap and merge into one another. The typical organization and functions of each phase are as follows.

Organization - Phase 1

6-63. In the first phase of organization, individuals band together under local leadership (Figure 6-5). Their main concern is survival. They have a basic need for shelter, food, water, and weapons. Appropriate terrain and friendly villages on the outer limits of enemy-controlled areas offer shelter. These small bands obtain food, water, and weapons locally. The activities of these small bands are limited to the organization and establishment of a support infrastructure within the local civilian population to obtain information, recruits, and logistic assistance. They may also conduct political work, small-scale attacks, and sabotage. The area commander locates his HQ where he can directly influence organization and operations in the most important sectors of his JSOA. His HQ is in a secure area where access is limited or uncontrolled by the enemy. The surrounding terrain should not favor large-scale, enemy-mounted, or dismounted operations. Logistic concerns and health conditions in the area are further considerations. Also, just in case, the area commander selects two or more alternate sites and prepares them for emergency use.

6-64. The area commander appoints a second-in-command and organizes a staff to accomplish military staff functions. The staff is kept small and mobile. It places special emphasis on the organization of the intelligence section. HQ units carry out the administrative functions. Based on advice from the SFOD, the area commander makes an estimate of the situation, formulates tentative organizational and operational plans, and issues directives to place them into effect. This effort should focus on—

- Division of the JSOA into sectors.
- Appointment of sector commanders.
- Assignment of missions to sector commanders.
- Organization in each sector: designation of units and authorized strengths.
- General operating principles and procedures.
- Communications system and responsibilities.

6-65. In areas that have no guerrilla forces or strong resistance movement, the area commander may appoint a sector commander for the exploitation and organization of the area. This support may consist of assigning cadre personnel for a sector commander's HQ, combat units to provide security, and a nucleus around which he may organize and expand his local forces. The area commander helps the sector commanders obtain the support of the indigenous population by visiting the sector and employing CA activities, such as HA, emergency services, military civic action (MCA), and support to civil administration. The effectiveness of CA activities may be enhanced by a strong public information campaign supported by PSYOP.

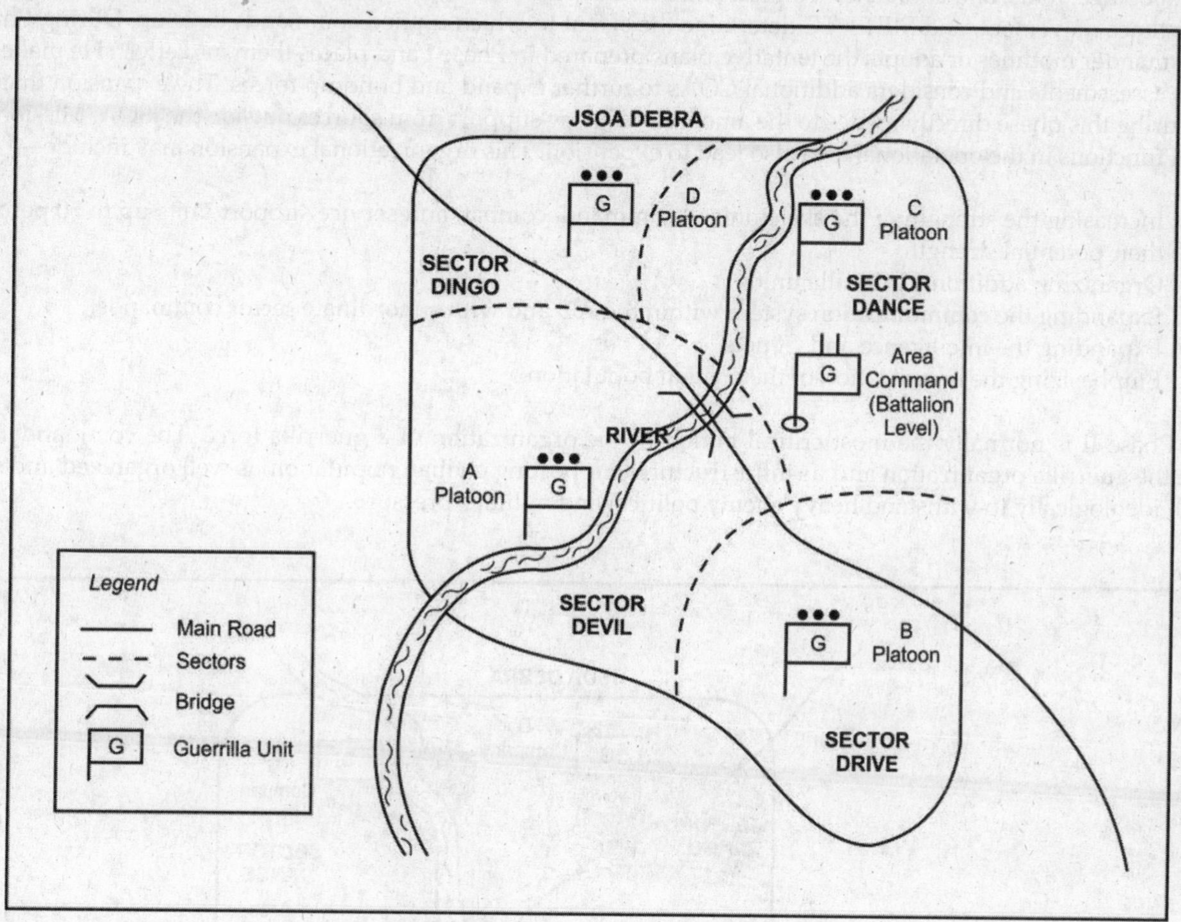

Figure 6-5. Typical phase i organization

6-66. In areas where many independent guerrilla forces exist, the area commander gives the appointed sector commander the necessary support to bring about unity of command. He gives this support through personal contact with the various local guerrilla leaders. The area commander may apply drastic measures to influence independent leaders and units that resist integration into the overall command. Withholding logistic support from outside the JSOA to those elements resisting integration is normally sufficient to encourage their willing compliance. The SFOD commander should be prepared to advise the area commander on the possible repercussions of the area commander's actions.

6-67. Normally, a skeleton organization is formed during Phase I. Also established are—

- A command HQ in each subordinate sector.
- A communication system linking the area command HQ with sector HQ.
- An extensive intelligence and CI net covering the entire JSOA. Establishment of this net is extremely important.

6-68. The overall strength of the command and the component units may be kept as low as one-third of the potential strength to be developed. Premature expansion and buildup of strength during this phase can cause undue strain on local resources, create hardships, and result in dissension among the civilian population.

Organization - Phase II

6-69. In the second phase of organization, the number and size of units increase (Figure 6-6). Small units unite under common leadership; volunteers, individual soldiers, or deserting army units further strengthen their ranks. When a tested local leader emerges as a commander, command and leadership improve. Personnel work diligently to establish contact with external support sources or with a sympathetic national government. These external support sources, along with battlefield recovery efforts, increase the quantity of war materiel. Greater enemy pressure results in widespread sabotage, raids, and ambushes. Political and administrative considerations, policies of the sponsor supporting the resistance movement, and METT-TC determine the extent to which unified commands develop. During Phase II, the commander modifies or adopts the tentative plans prepared in Phase I and places them into effect. He makes continuous assessments and considers additional COAs to further expand and build up forces. The expansion that takes place during this phase directly relates to the amount of logistic support from sources outside the JSOA. Missions and internal functions in the operational area also lead to expansion. This organizational expansion may include—

- Increasing the strength of the skeletonized command, combat, and service support units up to 50 percent of their potential strength.
- Organizing additional guerrilla units.
- Expanding the communication system within the AO and with subordinate sector commands.
- Expanding the intelligence and CI nets.
- Emphasizing the organization of the civilian population.

6-70. Phase II is normally the most critical period in the organization of a guerrilla force. The commander must ensure the guerrilla organization and its infrastructure (supporting civilian population) is well organized and strong enough ideologically to withstand heavy enemy political and military pressure.

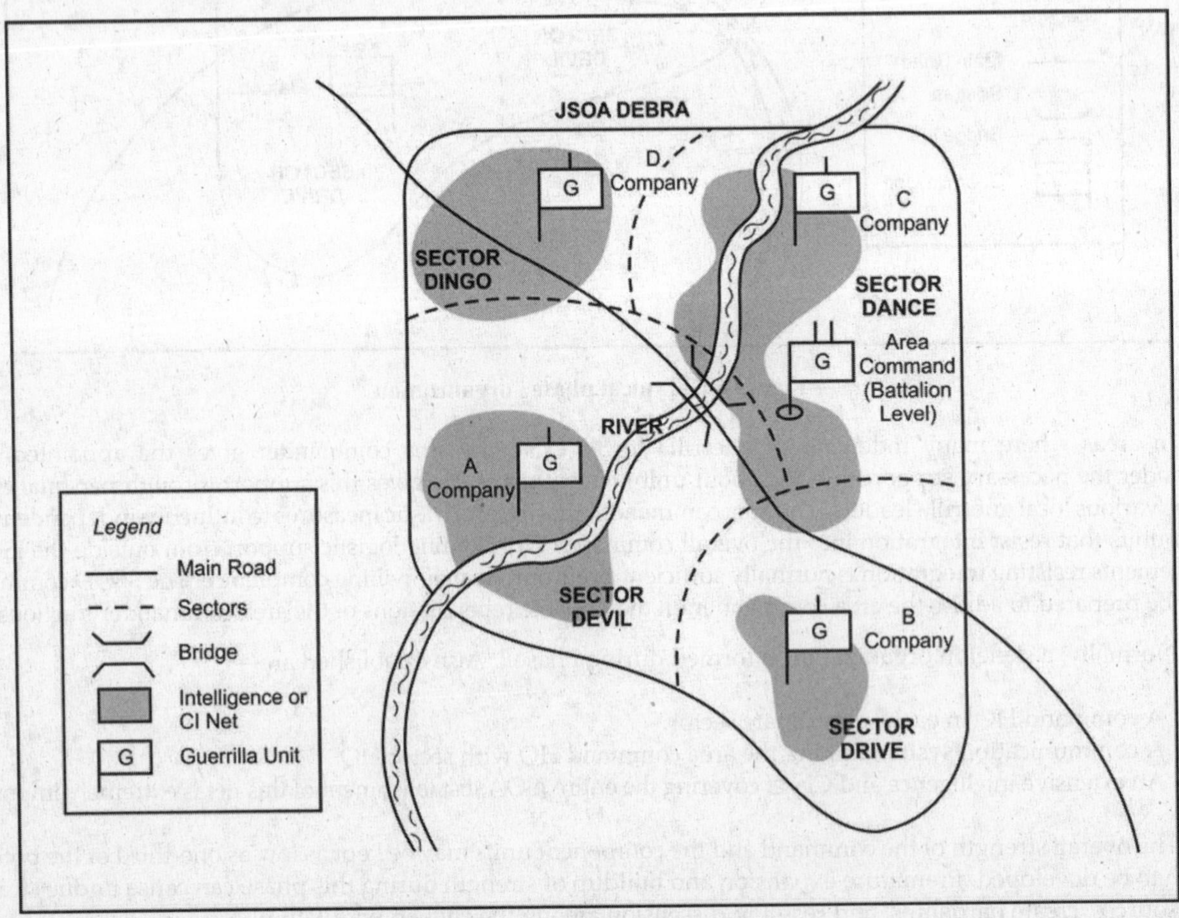

Figure 6-6. Typical phase ii organization

Organization - Phase III

6-71. During the third phase of organization (Figure 6-7), a unified command is established over some areas, often because of a strong and competent leader emerging as the recognized commander. Increased communication and liaison enhance control and coordination among the various guerrilla forces and external sources. Based on the mission assigned by higher HQ (input from the SFOD is a critical factor), the area commander makes an estimate of the situation and plans the mission. The decision to conduct an operation results in an OPLAN that states requirements for the area command staff, sector commands, and logistic elements. Portions of these tentative plans are then sent to subordinate commands. The subordinate commanders determine the area commander's intent and prepare their own plans accordingly. Also during Phase III, command personnel—

- Methodically develop and expand effective CI and intelligence nets.
- Observe and enforce strict OPSEC measures.

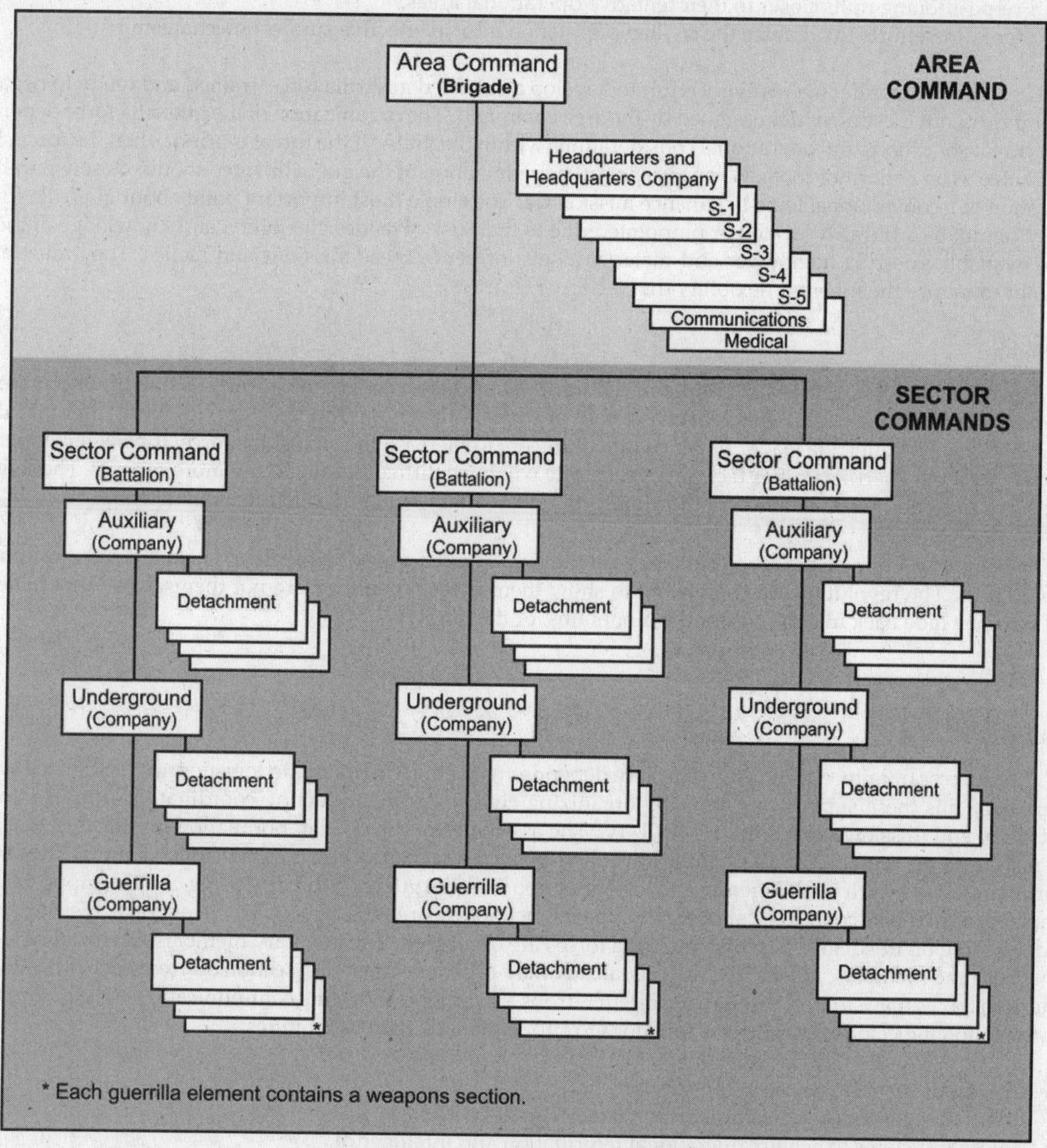

Figure 6-7. Typical phase iii organization

- Determine what control measures the enemy has imposed on the civilian population.
- Develop and implement programs of benefit to the populace (for example, developmental MCA projects), supported by PSYOP efforts to counter enemy propaganda and help elevate the morale of guerrillas and loyal civilians.
- Execute training and well-planned operations to improve the effectiveness of individuals and units.
- Infiltrate supplies from external sources to augment existing military equipment.

6-72. In addition, the guerrilla force, supported from an external source, develops a cohesive military establishment able to firmly defend and strike with substantial force at selected targets. General directives normally control guerrilla activities during this phase. Typical organizational expansion during Phase III may include—

- Building existing units up to authorized strength.
- Activating additional units.
- Pre-positioning units closer to their tentative operational areas.
- Increasing efforts to organize the civilian population into an effective support mechanism.

6-73. The joint commander makes every effort to develop a balanced guerrilla force, trained and ready to negate the threat and carry out these activities assigned by the area command. The organization of the guerrilla force depends on existing threat conditions and operational considerations within the JSOA. If the threat is armor, then the force should task-organize as an antiarmor force. When practical, the organization of the guerrilla force should closely parallel the organization of a conventional force to enhance mission C2. The single most important point about guerrilla forces is that they cannot be arbitrarily located or pinpointed due to their use of tactics, flexibility, and knowledge of the area. In turn, available guerrilla manpower and material assets influence these missions and tactics. They must also be careful not to reduce the inherent flexibility that the force requires.

Membership

6-74. The guerrilla force consists of people in different social classes and ethnic groups, some of whom are often antagonistic toward each other. They reflect a variety of educational and aptitude categories with different interests and inclinations. The guerrilla leader depends on volunteers to increase the size of his force. If he is incompetent or unpopular, or if the guerrillas suffer tactical reversals, he will have difficulties in getting more recruits. The following quote serves as a good representation of the underground, auxiliary, and guerrilla force relationship.

> The people are the sea; the revolutionaries are the fish. The sea supports the fish. It also hides them from predators. The revolutionaries only want to show themselves when they are not themselves vulnerable. Then they fade back into the sea, or the mountains, or the jungles.
>
> Mao Tse-tung

AUXILIARY

6-75. The success or failure of the guerrilla force depends on its ability to maintain logistic and intelligence support. The auxiliary fills these support functions by organizing civilians and conducting coordinated support efforts. Its organization and mission depend upon METT-TC. The assistance of the civilian population is critical to the success of the resistance movement. Auxiliary units have their own combat, support, and underground units. The auxiliary primarily provides security, intelligence, and logistic support for the guerrilla force by using civilian supporters of the resistance. The auxiliary conducts clandestine support functions by organizing people on a regional, district, or sector basis depending on the degree to which guerrilla forces are organized. The auxiliary members screen all new potential underground members. For OPSEC reasons, all auxiliary functions must first section off from each other and from the guerrilla forces they support through dead-letter drops and other clandestine communications. The guerrilla force needs the following clandestine support functions to supplement its own capabilities:

- Air, land, or maritime reception support.
- Internal systems for acquisition of supplies.
- Internal systems to acquire operational information and intelligence.

- Medical facilities for hospitalization, treatment, and rehabilitation of sick and wounded.
- CI systems to deter enemy penetration attempts.
- Outer zone security for early warning to guerrilla forces.
- Systems and procedures for recruitment of personnel.
- Compartmented communication systems for various support functions.
- Current information on terrain, weather, civilians, and local resources.
- Direct intelligence support, especially in the outer security zone of the guerrilla base camp.
- Deception operations support.
- Manufacture and maintenance of equipment.
- Transportation systems.

Organization

6-76. An auxiliary command committee organizes civilian sympathizers into subordinate elements or uses them individually. When possible, the committee organizes subordinates into a functionally compartmented structure (Figure 6-8, page 837). Historically, each subordinate auxiliary has had to perform several functions because of a shortage of loyal personnel.

6-77. The auxiliary normally organizes to coincide with or parallel the existing political system or administration. This system ensures that an auxiliary unit assists each community and the surrounding countryside.

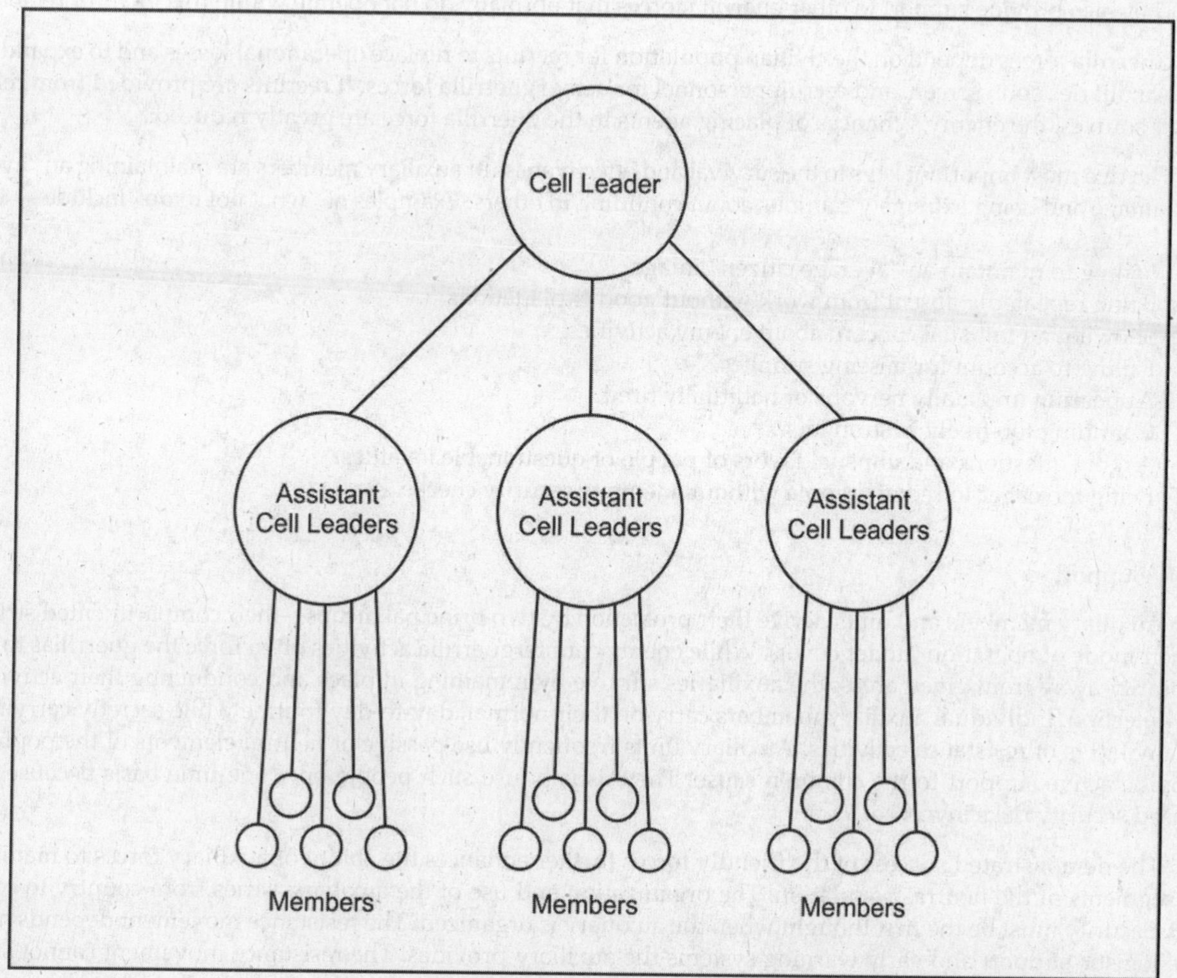

Figure 6-8. Auxiliary cell

6-78. Organization of auxiliary forces starts at any level or at several levels simultaneously. It is either centralized or decentralized. The auxiliary establishes commands at each administrative level; for example, at the regional, county, district, local community, or village level.

6-79. A command committee at each level controls and coordinates auxiliary activities within its AOR. In this respect, the committee resembles the command group and staff of a military unit. At the lowest level, one individual may perform two or three duties. Members of the command committee are assigned specific duties, such as—

- Security.
- Intelligence.
- Operations.
- Communications.
- Transportation.
- Supply.
- Recruiting.

Membership

6-80. Members of the auxiliary are people who maintain a permanent residence in the denied sector or AO and have identifiable and legitimate means of livelihood. The auxiliary members must appear in all respects to be "average citizens." They must be loyal to the resistance cause. People who are simply coerced or duped into supporting the resistance are not considered auxiliary members. Auxiliary components in a sector or AO are normally satellites of local guerrilla forces. They also provide support to other guerrilla forces that normally do not operate within this JSOA or region.

6-81. Guerrilla forces depend on the civilian population for recruits to replace operational losses and to expand their forces. Auxiliaries spot, screen, and recruit personnel for active guerrilla forces. If recruits are provided from reliable auxiliary sources, the enemy's chances of placing agents in the guerrilla force are greatly reduced.

6-82. The two most important keys to the survival and effectiveness of auxiliary members are maintaining an "average citizen" image and being extremely cautious about confiding in others. Examples of "what not to do" include—

- Failing to maintain an "average citizen" image.
- Being repeatedly absent from work without good explanations.
- Showing an unusual concern about enemy activities.
- Failing to account for missing supplies.
- Appearing unusually nervous or habitually tired.
- Confiding too freely in strangers.
- Asking questions and unusual favors of people of questionable loyalties.
- Being too eager to recruit people without adequate security checks.

Security Support

6-83. Auxiliary members and units derive their protection by two principal means—their compartmented structure and their mode of operation (under cover). While enemy counterguerrilla activities often force the guerrillas to move temporarily away from given areas, the auxiliaries survive by remaining in place and conducting their activities to avoid detection. Individual auxiliary members carry on their normal, day-to-day routine while secretly carrying out the many facets of resistance activities. Auxiliary units frequently use passive or neutral elements of the population to provide active support to the common cause. They usually use such people on a one-time basis because of the increased security risks involved.

6-84. The demonstrated success of the friendly forces further enhances the ability of auxiliary forces to manipulate large segments of the neutral population. The organization and use of the auxiliary varies from country to country or AO. Security must be the first thought when the auxiliary is organized. The resistance movement depends heavily on the logistic support and early warning systems the auxiliary provides. The resistance movement cannot survive without the support of its greatest asset—the civilian population.

6-85. Auxiliary members continue participating in the life of their community. To all appearances, they present no break from their daily routines and, at the same time, engage in resistance activities and operations. Such personnel are, in fact, leading double lives, and their success in the resistance depends on their ability to keep that side of their lives secret from all, including family and friends. The "farmer by day, supporter by night," commonly called a "part-time guerrilla," often is the forerunner to the full-time guerrilla.

6-86. The auxiliary leader assigns tasks to groups or individuals according to their capability, dependability, and the degree to which they are willing and able to participate. Those who unwittingly give support or are coerced into giving support are not considered auxiliaries. Personnel who sympathize strongly with the resistance movement but may be under surveillance by the enemy provide little value as auxiliary members. Other examples of personnel who might prove more dangerous than profitable are former political leaders or technicians employed by the enemy. Functions that require travel or transportation might be performed by such persons as foresters, farmers, fishermen, or transportation workers. In addition, these functions should, if possible, be covered by routine daily activities. Other duties, such as security and warning, require a valid reason for remaining at a given location over an extended period.

Intelligence Support

6-87. Auxiliary members can give considerable intelligence support due to their at-home status and their freedom of movement throughout the AO. The auxiliary organizes an extensive system of civilians who can keep enemy forces under surveillance and provide early warning of their movements. Individuals are selected because of advantageous locations that permit them to monitor the enemy.

6-88. When engaged in specific intelligence operations, select personnel and informants, because of their locations, can surveil virtually every overt enemy activity. The auxiliary also aids the area command CI effort by maintaining watch over transitory civilians, by screening recruits for guerrilla forces, and by monitoring refugees and other personnel not indigenous to the area. Due to their intimate knowledge of the civilian population, auxiliaries can identify attempts by enemy agents and local civilians sympathetic to the opposition or enemy forces in the area. They can also name those civilians whose loyalty to the resistance might be suspect. Auxiliary units collect information to support their own operations and those of the area command. This information provides direct intelligence support to guerrilla forces operating within the AOR.

6-89. Because the auxiliary members live and work among the civilian population at large, they can inconspicuously observe enemy movements and activities. They report sightings of interest to the guerrillas. Observers must have good reasons to justify their activities. Simply loitering in an area where the enemy is draws suspicion and causes the observer to be arrested and interrogated. The best justification for an observer's activities is that he or she works in the area. Examples are a sales clerk in a store near an enemy facility, a gas station operator in a gas station used by the enemy, a street cleaner near an enemy facility, and a farmer working in a field beside a road where enemy convoys are moving. The auxiliary can be sensitive to CI operations of the enemy, such as the attempt to infiltrate the guerrillas with recruits who are actually spies.

6-90. The area command controls auxiliary activities. The auxiliary members' responsibilities relate to their civilian occupations, such as construction workers with access to explosives and related supplies, doctors, medical assistants, pharmacists, hardware store managers, transportation workers, and communications technicians.

6-91. Also, civil service employees are excellent sources of information. Functions are compartmented so that if a member of the auxiliary is compromised, the information that he can reveal is limited and not time sensitive.

6-92. The auxiliary also provides the guerrillas goods and services that relate to their civilian occupations, it provides guerrilla recruiters with the names and addresses of prospective new guerrillas. It can also tell the guerrillas of homes and places in the community that favor the resistance and can give support.

Logistic Support

6-93. Most missions of the auxiliary support the guerrilla forces in its area. There are two methods—direct support or area command-directed support. Normally, the auxiliary provides direct support missions for the guerrilla forces in its area. The auxiliary supports guerrillas in all phases of logistic operations. The auxiliary—

- Provides transportation for supplies and equipment.
- Cares for the sick and wounded.
- Provides medical supplies.
- Arranges for doctors and other medical personnel.
- Collects food, clothing, and other supplies through a controlled system of levy, barter, or contribution.
- Sometimes provides essential services such as repair of clothing, shoes, and other items of equipment.
- Supplies personnel to help at reception sites.

6-94. The extent of the logistic support given by the auxiliary depends on the resources of the area, the degree of influence it exerts on the population, and enemy activities. When requisitioning support, the auxiliary must emphasize the righteousness of the resistance objectives and the commonality of resistance or population goals. The resistance depends on the goodwill of the population and the steady "I don't know" replies to enemy interrogators. In cases where the population acts only halfheartedly for the resistance, some civilians are willing to help by being observers, scouts, or messengers.

Home Guard

6-95. The home guard is the paramilitary arm of the auxiliary force. The various command committees control home guards. All auxiliary elements do not necessarily organize home guards. Home guards perform many missions for the auxiliary forces, such as tactical missions, guarding of caches, and training of recruits. Their degree of organization and training depends upon the extent of effective enemy control in the area.

Psychological Operations

6-96. A very important mission in which auxiliary units assist is PSYOP, which must be integrated and synchronized at all levels to achieve its full force-multiplier potential. The spreading of rumors, leaflets, and posters is timed with guerrilla tactical missions to deceive the enemy. The spreading of conveyed selected information usually involves little risk to the disseminator and is very difficult for the enemy to control.

Populace and Resources Control

6-97. The auxiliary employs populace and resources control (PRC) measures to minimize or eliminate black marketing and profiteering and to demonstrate to the enemy the power of the guerrilla movement. PRC consists of the following two distinct, but related, concepts:

- *Populace controls* provide security for the populace, mobilize human resources, deny personnel to the enemy, and detect and reduce the effectiveness of enemy agents. Populace control measures include curfews, movement restrictions, travel permits, registration cards, and resettlement of villagers. DC operations and noncombatant evacuation operations (NEO) are two special categories of populace control that require extensive planning and coordination among various military and nonmilitary organizations.
- *Resources controls* regulate the movement or consumption of materiel resources, mobilize materiel resources, and deny materiel to the enemy. Resources control measures include licensing, regulations or guidelines, checkpoints (for example, roadblocks), ration controls, amnesty programs, and inspection of facilities.

6-98. To perform PRC and give the enemy an impression of guerrilla power, the auxiliary establishes a legal control system to help prevent black marketing and profiteering. The auxiliary may use subtle coercion or other stricter means to control collaborators.

Evasion and Recovery

6-99. The auxiliary is ideally suited for the support of E&R mechanisms. Contact with, and control over, segments of the civilian population provide the area commander a secure means of aiding evaders.

6-100. The auxiliary members receive, conceal, and transport resistance personnel who are infiltrating into, or exfiltrating out of, the JSOA. They also receive and conceal guerrillas who have been wounded or separated from their units during hostilities.

Other Support Missions

6-101. The auxiliary may be called upon to perform several other guerrilla support missions, such as coordinating actions with the guerrillas against their targets. For example, the auxiliary may conduct minor acts of sabotage, such as cutting telephone lines, reversing street signs, giving false information, and obstructing troop movements. It may also support guerrilla missions by—

- Furnishing guides.
- Operating courier systems.
- Conducting active guerrilla-type operations on a limited basis.
- Raising funds.

UNDERGROUND

6-102. The underground supports the area command, auxiliary, and guerrilla force, based on METT-TC. These personnel commit sabotage, intelligence gathering, and acts of deception through the action arm, intelligence, supply, and personnel sections. Trainers develop a guerrilla METL after mission analysis and apply it to METT-TC.

Organization

6-103. The underground organizes into compartmented cells (Figures 6-9 and 6-10). It forms these cells within various political subdivisions of the sector or area, such as the U.S. equivalents of counties, towns, and neighborhoods. The underground environment may be urban or rural.

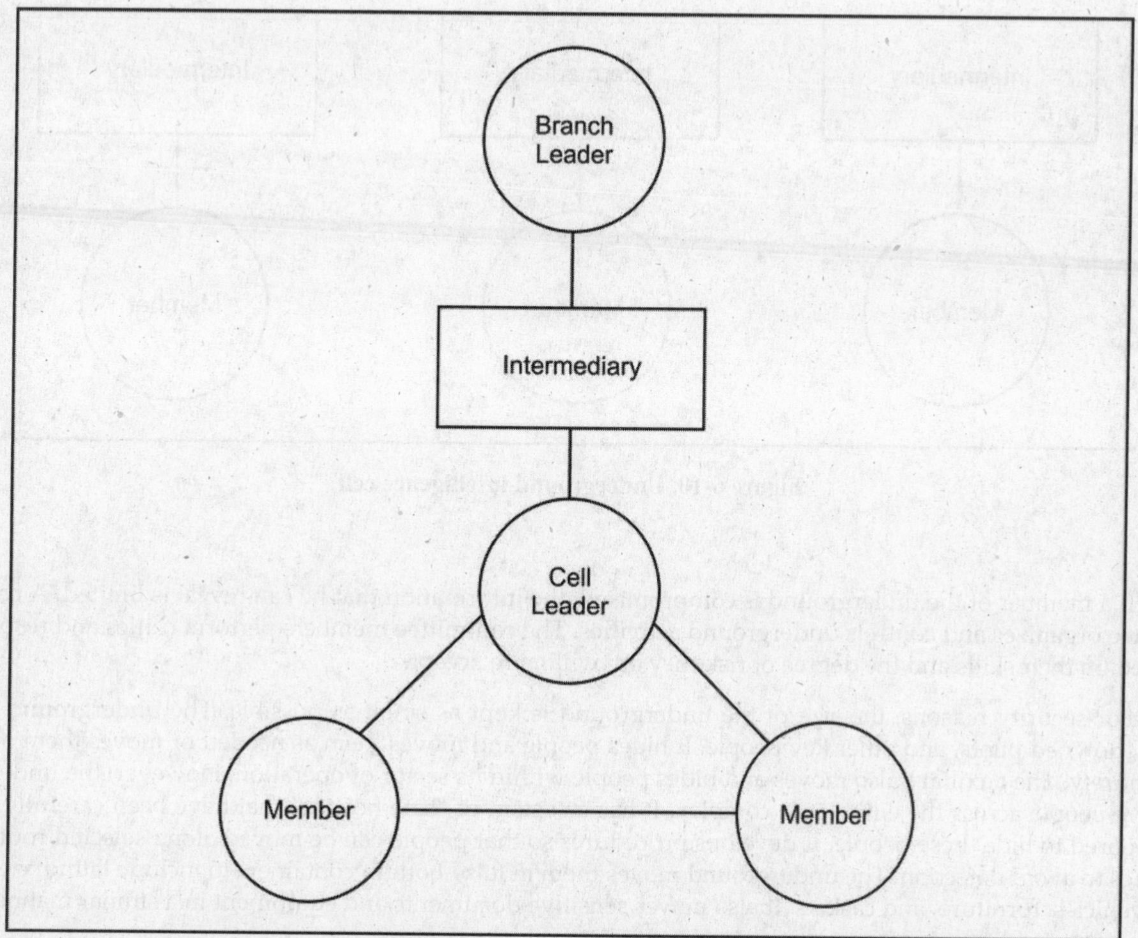

Figure 6-9. Underground operations cell

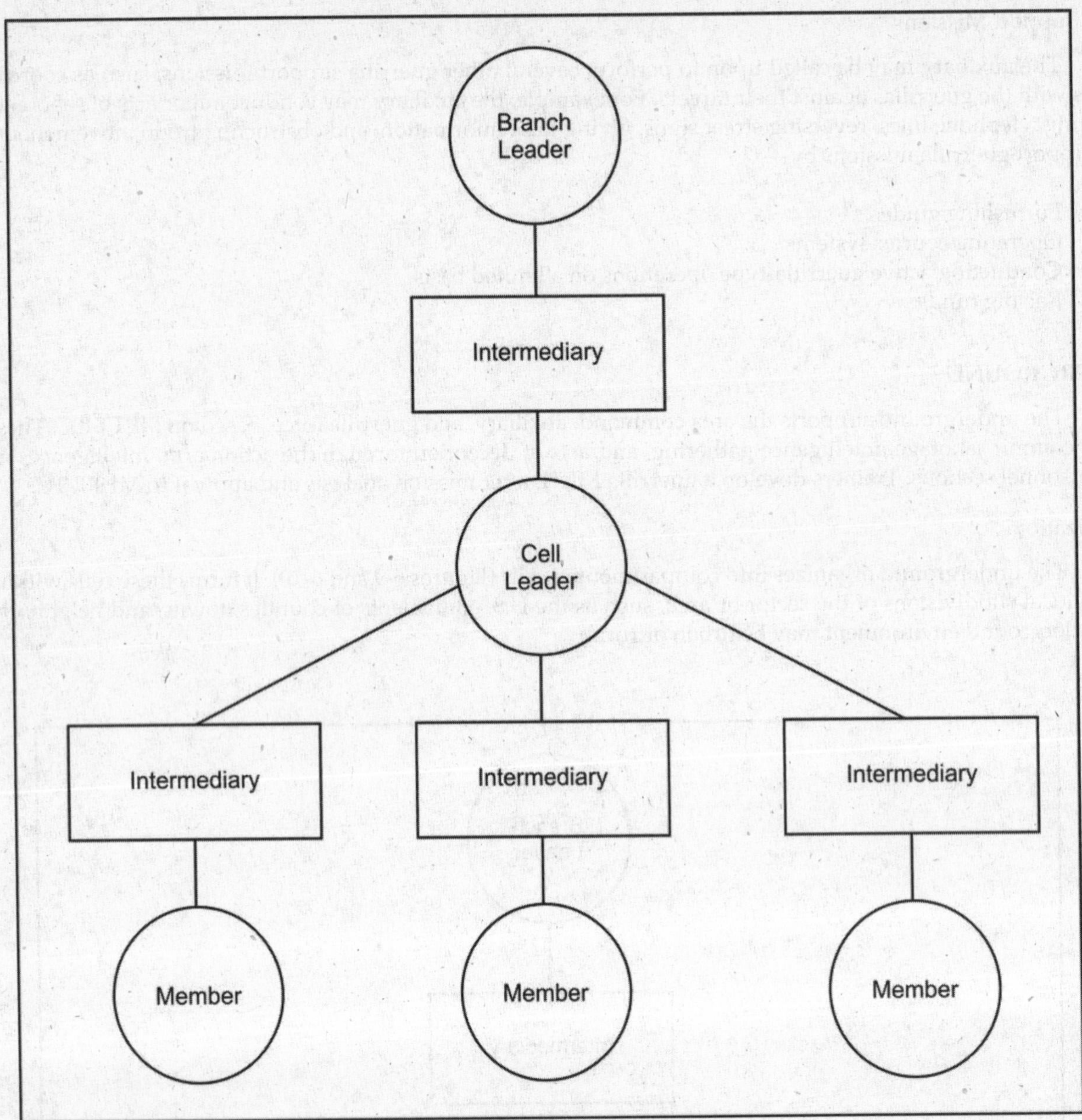

Figure 6-10. Underground intelligence cell

6-104. If a member of the underground is compromised, the information that he can reveal is limited. A command committee organizes and controls underground activities. The committee members perform duties and responsibilities based on their skills and the degree of risk they are willing to accept.

6-105. For security reasons, the size of the underground is kept as small as possible. The underground receives evaders, downed pilots, and other key people. It hides people and moves them as needed or moves them out of the JSOA entirely. The auxiliary also moves and hides people within its sector of operation. However, the underground can move people across the entire area complex. It has a system of "safe houses" that have been carefully selected and prepared to hide these people. It develops procedures so that people can be moved along selected routes at the best times to avoid detection. The underground moves them in false-bottom containers to include laundry carts, fish crates, vehicles, furniture, and caskets. It also moves sensitive documents and equipment in a similar manner.

6-106. To support other operations, particularly those involving the smuggling of personnel and materials, the underground commits acts of deception to steal bonafide documents (identification [ID] cards, passes, ration coupons, money, and passports) and use them under false pretenses. If the underground cannot obtain the bona fide documents, it prepares facsimiles.

Membership

6-107. The underground member needs to apply traditional behavior patterns to create a positive image. He is frequently prohibited from taking anything from the people without paying for it. He may even have to befriend certain segments of the population to influence them in support of the movement. He strives to conform to the normal behavior and daily activities of his neighborhood. By appearing conventional and inconspicuous, he makes it difficult for the security force to detect, identify, or find him. Without records or physical evidence, he is difficult to link to the organization. Contact and communications between members are key survival and critical points of subversive operations.

6-108. The underground normally contains more specialists and technicians than either the guerrilla or auxiliary components. Ideally, they are able to conduct combat operations in SR, DA, and UW. Also, they should possess the ability, experience, and equipment necessary to prepare all types of counterfeit documents and be able to produce counterfeit money.

6-109. To survive and be effective, a member of the underground must exhibit many positive personality traits necessary to endure hardship and he must be highly self-motivated. Among these traits, he must—

- Be technically and tactically proficient in combat skills, stealth, and self-discipline.
- Maintain and display an inconspicuous, "average citizen" image toward the enemy.
- Be very cautious about confiding in others. Secrecy and dedication to the cause come before any personal benefit, allowing for greater longevity.

Nature of Operations

6-110. Underground operations can be clandestine, covert, and overt. These operations have major similarities with those of both the guerrillas and the auxiliary. Some involve overt and violent actions and others are passive. The following paragraphs discuss the underground's relationship to other elements of the resistance.

6-111. Underground cells support the operations of the guerrillas and auxiliary (within their sector commands) with acts of deception, sabotage, and movement of personnel and equipment. Underground cells cooperate closely with other underground counterparts in their sectors and throughout the area complex. Cooperation enables successful movement of personnel and equipment in and out of the JSOA.

6-112. The guerrillas and auxiliary are more independent. Only in rare, coordinated operations does the underground work with its counterparts in other sectors.

6-113. The underground may commit acts of violence or sabotage to interdict enemy operations and movements.

6-114. The underground may publish a resistance newsletter or newspaper promoting the resistance cause among the civilian population. In countries with a controlled media system, a private publication of this nature will be of high interest. However, the underground must anticipate enemy reprisals for possession of the paper. Also, the enemy will probably search for the printing press. A defense against this threat is to print the paper outside the JSOA and smuggle it into the country, storing the supply in various locations.

6-115. The underground may engage in covert operations to disseminate embarrassing or incriminating information about the enemy or its officials. These revelations may inflame existing problems in sensitive areas and degrade the enemy's rapport with the civilian population or cause dissension in the enemy's ranks.

TRAINING THE RESISTANCE ORGANIZATION

6-116. A major part of the SFOD's mission is to plan, organize, conduct, and evaluate training of selected resistance cadre. This work prepares the SFOD to be trainers and force multipliers for the resistance organization. During premission planning, the SFOD develops a tentative training plan based on METT-TC. The SFOD members prepare the training plan, POI, and training aids in the indigenous language, if possible. They include sand tables with toy soldiers and vehicles as instruction aids. After commitment into the JSOA, SFOD members evaluate the present level of the resistance forces' training and update the initial training plan or modify it to ensure its effectiveness.

TRAINING PLAN

6-117. The training plan outlines how the SFOD will best accomplish its training objective. SFOD members develop the training plan in isolation based on an estimate of the training situation by the pilot team. Important factors in developing the training plan are mission, personnel, time, facilities, and organization for training. Other considerations are weather, climate, and the enemy situation.

MISSION

6-118. Based on operational directives from higher HQ, the SFOD determines the specific tasks, conditions, and standards the resistance forces must accomplish. If the resistance force has to conduct multiple missions, the SFOD must set up priorities for training. Because a guerrilla travels primarily on his feet, he must undergo rigorous physical training and numerous cross-country marches.

TIME

6-119. The available training time is a critical factor. The shorter the training time, the more time is taken to define the training objectives. SFOD personnel will lose training time because of operational requirements. They must include makeup training as an integral part of the training program.

FACILITIES

6-120. The SFOD will advise the area command and resistance force on selecting and establishing ranges, training areas, improvised classrooms, training aids, and other training facilities. Security is of prime importance. The SFOD locates ranges and training areas away from the base camp. It can make a small valley with aerial concealment or a man-made tunnel into single-lane ranges. Air and BB rifles are excellent alternate, inexpensive, training aids in lieu of full-caliber marksmanship training.

POLITICAL TRAINING

6-121. Politically or religiously extreme insurgents use frequent criticism and self-criticism sessions as a form of catharsis (venting). These sessions allow members to voice fears and problems and to hear from other members. An individual who is disillusioned with the resistance movement will find it difficult to conceal his true feelings in these sessions. He will become influenced by what his friends and comrades think of him. Ideologically oriented unit leaders are more cohesive and effective in their training. Cadres in each unit must set the "politically correct" example during these daily training sessions. They must continually reinforce rank-and-file members, assuring them that what they are doing is needed to carry out the will of the people. Such confidence will elevate morale and fighting spirit.

> Equal importance should be attached to the military and political aspects of the one-year consolidation and training program, which has just begun, and the two aspects should be integrated. At the start, stress should be placed on the political aspect, on improving relations between officers and men, enhancing internal unity and arousing a high level of enthusiasm among the masses of cadres and fighters. Only thus will the military consolidation and training proceed smoothly and attain better results.
>
> Mao Tse-tung, 1945

TRAINING THE GUERRILLA FORCE

6-122. SFOD members evaluate how well the guerrillas are trained through personal observations and inspections and the results of limited (easy) combat missions. Characteristics of the guerrilla force that may present obstacles to training include—

- A wide range of education and military experience.
- Different personal motivation for joining the force.
- Possible language and dialect barriers requiring training through interpreters.

TRAINING ORGANIZATION

6-123. The requirements for physical security in the JSOA dictate that guerrilla forces be dispersed over a wide area. Consequently, the system and organization for training are decentralized and "hands-on" training is emphasized. The SFOD must train the guerrilla cadre and later help this cadre in additional training and combat employment. Throughout the organization, development, and training phases of guerrilla activities, the guerrillas conduct limited combat operations. These actions support training, instill confidence, and test the readiness of the force. The goals of these combat operations are to—

- Attract additional recruits to the guerrilla force.
- Assist in gaining popular support from the civilian population.
- Allow the area command and SFOD an opportunity to evaluate the training.
- Increase the morale and esprit de corps of the guerrilla forces with initial successful combat operations.

TRAINING METHODS

6-124. The SFOD generally uses the three-tier concept for training. This concept is similar to the U.S. Army red, green, and amber training cycle. It allows for one-third of the guerrilla forces in training, one-third providing security for the training, and one-third providing support or doing small-scale operations. The three-tier concept accommodates the training of any size unit.

6-125. Generic POI development is the same anywhere. Trainers base all training (basic, advanced, and specialized) on METT-TC and the current combat skills of the guerrillas. They modify the training after contact with the guerrilla force. Appendix J outlines a generic guerrilla POI.

6-126. Trainers base all training (basic, advanced, and specialized) on METT-TC and the current combat skills of the guerrillas. They may modify the training after contact with the guerrilla force.

> As for the training courses, the main objective should still be to raise the level of technique in marksmanship, bayoneting, grenade-throwing and the like and the secondary objective should be to raise the level of tactics, while special emphasis should be laid on night operations.
>
> Mao Tse-tung, 1946

Basic Training

6-127. METT-TC determines the need for base camps within the JSOA. All guerrillas including the area command may receive basic training. Each base camp may conduct its basic training in sectors independent of the other two, or it may conduct a part of basic training and rotate to another camp for more training. Either the SFOD or guerrillas may rotate. The base camps may construct ranges and training areas for their use, or one base camp may construct a range and teach all marksmanship classes. Another base camp may construct training areas for raids, and the other may construct areas for ambushes and reconnaissance. The present combat abilities of the guerrillas and the threat determine how much basic training is needed.

6-128. Basic training contains subjects on small arms, first aid, land navigation, and political or PSYOP classes. The time allotted for training needs to be flexible—between 21 and 31 days, depending on the knowledge and abilities of the force.

Advanced Training

6-129. Each base camp conducts some advanced training or rotates to other base camps for additional training. This concept is similar to basic training, and the guerrillas or SFOD may rotate. Trainers can conduct medical and demolitions training in one base camp; communications and intelligence in another; and tactics, operations, and heavy weapons in the third. At the end of the advanced training period, the guerrillas or SFOD would rotate to another base camp for a new training cycle. For security reasons, all the engineer, communications, medical, and intelligence sergeants should not be in the same sector base camp at the same time.

6-130. Advanced training may last from 40 to 80 days. This phase consumes the most time, but it also pays the most dividends. Some subjects covered in greater depth include combat orders, machine guns, tactics, survival, and MOSs of medical, communications, weapons, and demolitions.

Specialized Training

6-131. Specialized training is broadly subdivided into elementary and advanced specialized training. Personnel and units assigned to the theater SF may have received elementary specialized training. If not, such training becomes a responsibility of the theater SF commander. Specialized training, elementary and advanced, is conducted by a training center operated by the theater SF.

6-132. Elementary specialized training consists of training individuals and teams to carry out their assigned functions. Intensive courses are conducted and include the following:

- Map reading and sketching.
- Patrolling.
- Close combat.
- Physical training.
- Fieldcraft.
- Tactics of both regular and guerrilla forces.
- Demolitions and techniques of sabotage.
- Use and care of weapons, including those of the enemy forces.
- First aid.
- Use of enemy and civilian motor transportation.
- Enemy organization and methods.
- Methods of organizing and training guerrillas.
- Security information.
- Methods of supply to guerrilla forces.

6-133. Advanced specialized training prepares qualified individuals and teams for specific missions in enemy territory. During this training, individuals are organized into the teams in which they will be employed. Thereafter the group trains, lives, and operates as a unit under simulated conditions of the area where they are to be employed. Special techniques, skills, and orientation are stressed to enable them to carry out their mission and to weld them into efficient, mobile, and self-sufficient teams. Parachute or amphibious training is given, depending on the contemplated means of entering enemy territory.

6-134. Besides the training outlined above, technical training is given to radio operators, medical technicians, demolition experts, and other specialists.

TRAINING STAFF AND AUXILIARY OR UNDERGROUND PERSONNEL

6-135. While the SFOD members are training the guerrilla force, the SFOD commander, ADC, and team sergeant are training the area command and staff, sector commander and staff, and selected members of the auxiliary or underground. The area commander and his staff may train in the same base camp with his guerrillas. Although the area command and auxiliary or underground may be trained anywhere in the JSOA, it should be compartmented for security reasons. FM 3-05.220 provides more information on training the auxiliary and underground in advanced SO techniques.

TRAINING THROUGH INTERPRETERS

6-136. Historically, SFOD members in a UW environment have been faced with a social and political power struggle when they tried to select an interpreter to work with them. The struggle has not always been to their advantage. The next few paragraphs discuss some tips on how to select an interpreter and avoid some of the often-repeated pitfalls.

Native Speaker

6-137. The ideal interpreter would be a native speaker from the AO who knows most of the area dialects. His speech, grammar, background, and social mannerisms should be understandable to the students. If he fits this ideal description, the students will listen to what he says, not how he says it. The students will understand the interpreter.

Social Status

6-138. An interpreter often is limited in his effectiveness with students if his social standing is considerably lower than that of his students. There may be significant differences among the students and the interpreter in military rank or memberships in ethnic or religious groups. When students are officers, it may be best to have an officer or civilian act as an interpreter. On the other hand, if students are enlisted personnel, an officer interpreter might intimidate the students and stifle class participation. An enlisted interpreter would be the best choice in this case. Most cultures recognize technical competence and international differences in military structure, so there should be no problem for the SFOD. Despite personal feelings on social status, the instructor's job is to train all students equally, not act as an agent of social reform in a foreign land. The instructor must accept local customs as a way of life.

English Fluency

6-139. If the SFOD instructor and interpreter can communicate with each other in English, the interpreter's command of English is adequate. The instructor can check the interpreter's level of "understanding" by asking him to paraphrase in English what the instructor has just said. If the interpreter restates the comments correctly, both are "reading off the same sheet of music."

Intelligence

6-140. The interpreter should be quick, alert, and responsive to changing conditions and situations. He must be able to grasp complex concepts and discuss them without confusion in a logical sequence. Education does not equate to intelligence, but better educated interpreters will be more effective due to experience and maturity.

Technical Ability

6-141. If the interpreter has technical training or experience in the instructor's subject area, he will be more effective since he will translate "meaning" as well as "words." A doctor could interpret for a medic, and former military personnel could interpret best for the weapons and intelligence sergeants.

Reliability

6-142. An instructor must be leery of any interpreter who arrives late for the class. Many cultures operate on a "flexible clock," where time is relatively unimportant. The interpreter must understand the concept of punctuality. Also, it is safe to assume that any interpreter's first loyalty is to his country, not to the United States. The security implications are clear; the instructor must be very cautious in explaining concepts to give the interpreter "a greater depth of understanding." Also, some interpreters, for political or personal reasons, may have a "hidden agenda" when they apply for the job.

Compatibility

6-143. The instructor must establish rapport with his interpreter early in their relationship and maintain compatibility throughout their joint effort. Mutual respect and understanding are essential to effective instruction. Some rapport-building subjects to discuss with the interpreter are history, geography, ethnic groups, political system, prominent political figures, monetary system, business, agriculture, exports, and hobbies. The SFOD member is building a friendship on a daily basis.

6-144. If several qualified interpreters are available, the instructor should select at least two. The exhausting nature of the job makes a half-day of active interpreting the maximum for peak efficiency. One interpreter, however skilled, will seldom be enough except for short-term courses conducted at a leisurely pace. If two or more interpreters are available, one of them can sit in the rear of the class and provide quality control of the instruction by crosschecking the active interpreter. Meanwhile, additional interpreters can conduct rehearsals, grade examinations, and evaluate the exercises. Mature judgment and a genuine concern that the students are learning important skills go a long way toward accomplishing the mission.

6-145. Good instructors will tactfully ask about their interpreters' background. With genuine concern, they ask about the interpreter's family, aspirations, career, and education. They can start with his home life; it's very important to him and is neutral territory. Instructors can follow up with a discussion of cultural traditions to find out more about him and the land he lives in.

6-146. The instructor should gain his interpreter's trust and confidence before embarking on sensitive issues such as sex, politics, and religion. He must approach these areas carefully and tactfully. They may be useful and revealing in the professional relationship between instructor and interpreter. Once this stage is reached, the two are well on their way to a valuable friendship and a firm, professional working relationship.

TRAINING THE INTERPRETERS

6-147. Very early on, the instructor conveys to the interpreter that he will always direct the training. However, he must stress how important the interpreter is as a link to the students. He can appeal to the interpreter's professional pride by describing how the quality and quantity of learning are dependent on his interpreting skills and his ability to function as a conduit between instructor and students. The instructor must also stress patriotism, that the defense of his country is directly related to his ability to transfer the instructor's knowledge to the students.

6-148. Because of cultural differences, interpreters may attempt to "save face" by concealing their lack of understanding. They may attempt to translate what they think the instructor "meant" without asking for a clarification. Disinformation and confusion result for the students. Ultimately, when the students realize they have been misled, they question the instructor's credibility, not the interpreter's. If the instructor has established rapport with his interpreter, he is in a better position to appeal to the interpreter's sense of duty, honor, and country. A mutual understanding allows for clarification when needed, leads to more accurate interpretation, and keeps the instructor informed of any student difficulties.

Conducting the Training

6-149. To prepare for teaching, the instructor must have initial lesson plans available for basic, advanced, and specialized training. He must also have on hand the available supporting documentation, such as FMs. When the class begins, the instructor should—

- Express the training objective in measurable performance terms.
- Outline the course content with methods of instruction and the various training aids to be demonstrated and then used by the students.
- Supply and circulate all class handout material when needed.
- Modify the training schedule to allow more time to train foreign students due to language and translation constraints.

6-150. A glossary of terms is a valuable aid for the instructor and the interpreter. Many English words and phrases do not translate literally into many foreign languages. Technical terms need to be clearly defined well ahead of class. A listing of the most common terms and their translated meaning will be a useful product.

6-151. The instructor presents bite-sized information tailored to the student audience. He talks directly to the students in a relaxed and confident manner. The interpreter watches the instructor carefully and emulates his style and delivery as he interprets for the students. During the translation, the instructor observes the interpreter to detect any problems. The interpreter will do some "editing" as a function of the interpreting process, but it is imperative that he transmits the instructor's meaning without additions or deletions. A well-coordinated effort is the key to success.

6-152. Although maximum improvisation must be used in all phases of operations, the following items accompanying deployed detachments may prove useful in conducting training:

- Grease pencils and colored chalk.
- Target cloth or ponchos (blackboard substitutes).

- Basic manuals on weapons generally found in the area (in the language of the country, if possible).
- Graphic training aids improvised from parachutes or other such material.

Student Questions

6-153. Whenever students have questions, the interpreter immediately relays them to the instructor for an answer. The students then realize the instructor, not the interpreter, is the SME and is in charge of the class. When a problem occurs, neither the instructor nor the interpreter corrects each other in front of the students. They must settle all differences in a professional manner.

6-154. Rapport is as important between student and instructor as it is between interpreter and instructor. When the interpreter and instructor treat the students as mature, valuable people capable of learning, rapport will build easily between the students and the instructor.

Communication

6-155. An instructor learns by experience that a way to communicate is through an interpreter. Use of profanity, slang, colloquialisms, and military jargon with students is harmful. Often, these expressions cannot be translated and do not come out with the desired meaning. If he must use a technical term or expression, the instructor makes sure the interpreter conveys the proper meaning in the indigenous language.

Transitional Phrases

6-156. Transitional phrases tend to confuse the learning process and waste valuable time. Expressions such as "for example" and "in most cases" or qualifiers such as "maybe" or "perhaps" are difficult to translate. Many native interpreters have learned much of their English from reading rather than hearing English spoken. The instructor keeps the class presentation as simple as possible, using short words and phrases.

Taboo Gestures

6-157. Social and cultural restrictions will manifest themselves during class. Gestures are learned behavior and vary from culture to culture. If the instructor doesn't know, he should ask the interpreter to relate the cultural taboos before class and avoid them. The instructor should know before class—

- When it is proper to stand, sit, or cross legs.
- If the index finger, chin, or eyes may be used for pointing.
- If nodding of the head means yes or no.

Manner of Speaking

6-158. The instructor should try to look at the students and talk directly to them, not the interpreter. He speaks slowly and clearly and repeats himself as needed. The instructor should not address the students in the third person through the interpreter. Instead, he should say something like, "I'm glad to be your instructor," and not "Tell them I'm glad to be their instructor."

6-159. The instructor must speak to the students as if they will understand every word he says. He must convey enthusiasm and use all of the gestures, movements, voice intonations, and inflections he would use for an English-speaking audience. The students will reflect the same amount of energy, interest, and enthusiasm that the instructor conveys to them. The instructor must not let the interpreter "sabotage" training with a less than animated delivery and presentation of the material.

6-160. When the interpreter is translating and the students are listening to get the full meaning of the translation, the instructor should do nothing that could be distracting. These distractions might be pacing the floor, writing on the blackboard, drinking water, or carrying on with other distracting activities.

6-161. The interpreter should be checked periodically to make sure the students understand the instructor's meaning. A cadre member, qualified in the native language, may observe and comment on the interpreter's knowledge, skills, and abilities. When the instructor has been misunderstood, the point needs to be made clear immediately. If further clarification is needed, the instructor should phrase the instruction differently and illustrate the point as necessary.

COMBAT EMPLOYMENT

6-162. North Vietnamese General Giap wrote in his hook, *The Military Art of Peoples War*, "We strike to win, strike only when success is certain; if it's not, then don't strike." This simple, straightforward idea for conducting combat operations is the key concept an SFOD advising guerrillas should never disregard.

OPERATIONS

6-163. The guerrilla force should carefully select, plan, and execute UW combat operations to ensure success with a minimum number of casualties. A combat defeat in the early stages of training demoralizes the guerrilla force. Combat operations should be commensurate with the status of training and equipment available to the resistance force. As training is completed and units are organized, guerrilla forces with SF assistance can plan and execute small-scale combat operations against "soft (easy) targets," an important confidence builder. Later, they progress to larger and more complex targets.

PRINCIPLES FOR SUCCESS

6-164. Successful UW combat operations depend on five principles. Those principles are speed of movement, surprise, low enemy morale, security, and collaboration with the local population.

Speed of Movement

6-165. To achieve speed, guerrillas practice rapid force concentration and rapid deployment from march formations. They also practice movements and attacks during periods of limited visibility, pursuit of disorganized enemy units with little time wasted on reorganization after an engagement, and fast withdrawals. Guerrillas use an MSS and travel light to increase their element of speed and surprise.

Surprise

6-166. To surprise the enemy, guerrillas plan to conduct and integrate deception operations into every UW mission.

Low Enemy Morale

6-167. Guerrillas take advantage of every opportunity to undermine enemy morale by including PSYOP.

Security

6-168. Guerrillas prepare the battlefield as far in advance as possible. Reconnaissance elements gather all available information on the terrain, installations, enemy units, and civilian activities. They also reconnoiter escape and withdrawal routes well in advance.

Collaboration With the Local Population

6-169. The auxiliary in the area provides the guerrillas information, transportation, supplies, hideouts, and guides familiar with the objective.

SECURITY WITHIN THE AREA OF OPERATIONS

6-170. The AO requires special security measures that apply particularly to insurgent forces. The survival of the insurgents depends upon constant vigilance on the part of every member of the organization, plus the ability to transmit warnings. Effective CI is also essential. Security measures must prevent losses by enemy action, ensure freedom of action, and minimize interruption of insurgent activities. Dependable security can be achieved by intensive training in security discipline, establishment of warning systems, and extensive CI.

Responsibility

6-171. The area commander is responsible for the overall security of the insurgent forces, although commanders of subordinate units must take individual measures for their own local protection. The chief of the security section of the area command controls all security operations, except CI. He prescribes necessary measures and coordinates those adopted by subordinate commanders. CI is the responsibility of the chief of the intelligence section of the area command. Again, subordinate commanders must establish local CI for their own security.

Factors Affecting Security

6-172. Security measures developed by the chief of the security section of the area command are affected by the following factors:

- Mission.
- Local situation of individual units.
- Physical characteristics of the AO.
- The enemy situation.
- Capabilities and limitations of the insurgent forces.
- Considerations affecting the civilian population.
- Operations of conventional and coalition forces.

6-173. During the early phases of insurgent warfare, the mission of insurgent forces will necessitate organization of a CI system alongside the intelligence system, development of a communications system that will facilitate warnings, and establishment of physical security for installations. Particular attention should be directed toward the enemy's state of internal security formations and their intelligence and communications systems.

6-174. Military actions against the enemy initiated during the early phases of operations should be planned and executed in such a way that they will not lead to wholesale enemy anti-insurgent activity, reprisals against the civilian population, or compromise of external logistical support in the latter stages of insurgent warfare. Operations are not curtailed for security reasons, because the established security system provides greater protection for the insurgents. Also, insurgent control over the area may rival the enemy's own influence.

Principles of Security

6-175. Dispersion. Insurgent forces avoid a large concentration of troops. Even though logistical conditions may permit large troop concentrations, commands should be broken down into smaller units and widely dispersed. The dispersion of forces facilitates concealment, mobility, and secrecy. Large forces may be concentrated to perform a specific operation, but on completion of the operation, they should again be quickly dispersed.

6-176. The principle of dispersion is applied to command, service, and technical installations. A large insurgent HQ, for example, is divided into several echelons and scattered over the area.

6-177. In the event of a well-conducted, large-scale enemy operation against the insurgent force, the area commander may find it necessary to order the division of units into smaller groups to achieve greater dispersion and facilitate escape from encirclement. This action should be taken only when all other means of evasive action are exhausted because such dispersion renders the force inoperative for a considerable period of time, lowers the morale of insurgents, and weakens the will of the civilians to resist. To assure successful reassembly of dispersed units, emergency plans must include alternate assembly areas.

6-178. Mobility. All insurgent installations and forces must have a high degree of mobility. Their evacuation plans must ensure that all traces of insurgent activity are eliminated before abandonment of the area.

6-179. Forces can maintain evacuation mobility by ensuring that equipment that must be moved can be disassembled into one-man loads. The area commander ensures suitable caches are provided for equipment that would reduce mobility, materiel that could provide intelligence for the enemy is destroyed, the area is policed, and signs of the route of withdrawal are eliminated.

Security of Information

6-180. Safeguarding Plans and Records. Information concerning insurgent operations is limited to those who need to know it. Only necessary copies are made or maintained. Each person is given only that information that is needed to accomplish his mission. Special efforts are made to restrict the amount of information given to individuals who are exposed to capture.

6-181. Administrative records are kept to a minimum, are cached, and the location made known only to a required few. Whenever possible, references to names and places are coded, and the key to the code is given on a need-to-know basis. Records that are no longer of value to operations or for future reports must be destroyed.

6-182. Security Discipline. Strict security discipline is necessary and all security measures must be rigidly enforced. Security instruction of personnel must be extensive. They must be impressed with the importance of not divulging information concerning insurgent activities to persons not requiring it. Individuals seeking such information must be reported to proper authorities.

6-183. Security violations are extremely serious and demand severe punishment. All cases involving a possible breach of security must be reported immediately.

6-184. The key to successful security of information, however, is the individual insurgent himself who must always be security-conscious. One careless individual can destroy the best security system devised.

6-185. Training. During the training phase, security consciousness must be stressed. Special emphasis should be placed on safeguarding documents, security of information, and resistance against interrogation.

Security of Movement

6-186. Security of movement can be provided only by an accurate knowledge of the enemy's location and strength. Intelligence regarding enemy disposition and activities is essential. The intelligence section of the area command, informed through its various nets, must provide this vital information for security of movement.

6-187. After the routes have been selected, the units must be briefed on enemy activity, primary and alternate routes, dispersal and reassembly areas along the way, and security measures to be observed en route. If the route leads through areas outside insurgent influence, auxiliary civilian organizations must provide security of movement for the insurgents.

Security of Installations

6-188. Most installations are located in isolated regions known as insurgent base of operations or guerrilla base. They are mobile and are secured by guards and warning systems. Alternate locations are prepared in advance so that any installation threatened by enemy action can be evacuated from the endangered base area to a more secure area. Location of these alternate areas is given to personnel only on a need-to-know basis.

6-189. Physical security of installations will include terrain CI. This may vary from simple deceptive measures, such as camouflage or destruction and reversal of road signs and mileposts, to the creation of physical barriers, such as roadblocks and demolition of roadbeds and bridges. The use of civilian guides to misdirect enemy troops (for example, into ambush) can also be effective.

Tri-Zonal Security System

6-190. A typical means of providing adequate security for the insurgent base area is a tri-zonal security system. This system provides the following series of warning nets:

- *Zone A* is the insurgent base area itself. It is secured by a regular guard system, but it largely depends for its safety upon advance warnings received by clandestine agents in Zone C, or posted observers in Zone B. If enemy action threatens, the insurgents move to another location before the arrival of enemy forces.
- *Zone B*, lying beyond the populated Zone C, is territory not well controlled by the enemy in which the insurgent forces can operate overtly. It is usually open, rugged terrain, and the warning system depends upon stationed observers, watching for enemy movements in the area.

- *Zone C*, the farthest from the insurgent base area, is usually well populated and is located inside enemy-controlled territory. Enemy security forces, police, and military units exercise relatively effective control, and the populace may be predominately hostile to the insurgents. At the same time, there are excellent and rapid LOCs, whereby clandestine agents are able to warn the insurgents quickly of enemy activity. This area is known as the clandestine zone and the functions of the warning system are the responsibility of the underground.

Security of Communications

6-191. Insurgent communications facilities are rigidly regulated by the SOI. These measures include restriction on what may be transmitted; the use of codes and ciphers; and means of concealment, deception, and authentication. Particular emphasis is placed on restricting time and number of radio transmissions to the absolute minimum.

Counterintelligence

6-192. Insurgent security depends not only on security measures taken to safeguard information, installations, and communications, but also on an active CI program to neutralize the enemy's intelligence system and especially to prevent the penetration of insurgent forces by enemy agents.

6-193. The intelligence section of the area command implements the CI program. Specially selected and trained CI personnel carefully screen all members of the insurgent organization and protect the insurgents from enemy infiltration. CI personnel also carry on an active campaign of deception, disseminating false information to mislead the enemy.

6-194. CI personnel must keep a constant check on the civilian population of the area through clandestine sources to ensure against the presence of enemy agents within their midst. Civilians upon whom the insurgents depend heavily for support may compromise the insurgent warfare effort as easily as a disloyal insurgent may.

6-195. False rumors and false information concerning insurgent strength, location, operations, training, and equipment can be disseminated by CI through clandestine nets. Facts may be distorted intentionally to minimize or exaggerate insurgent capabilities at any given time. Although such activities are handled within the intelligence section, they must be coordinated with the security section in order to prevent inadvertent violations of security.

Outlaw Bands

6-196. Outlaw bands, operating as insurgents, also endanger insurgent security by alienating the civilian population through their depredation. The area commander cannot tolerate outlaw bands, which are not willing to join the organized insurgent effort. Every effort must be made to persuade these bands to join forces. If all other methods fail, it may be necessary to conduct operations against these groups.

Reaction to Enemy Operations

6-197. Inexperienced insurgent commanders and troops are often inclined to move too soon and too frequently to escape enemy troops conducting anti-insurgent operations. Unnecessary movement caused by the presence of the enemy may expose insurgents to greater risks than remaining calm and concealed. Such moves disrupt operations and reduce security by dislodging previously established nets and exposing insurgents to enemy agents, informants, and collaborators.

DEFENSIVE OPERATIONS

6-198. Defensive operations are exceptional forms of combat for guerrilla forces. The guerrilla force may engage in defensive operations to—

- Prevent enemy penetration of guerrilla-controlled areas.
- Gain time for their forces to accomplish a specific mission.
- Assemble their main forces for counterattacks.

6-199. Guerrillas normally lack supporting fire: artillery, antitank weapons, and other weapons to face conventional forces. Historically, guerrillas have avoided a prolonged position type of defense. When committed, they modify the principles of defensive operations to best meet their needs and offset the difficulties. They are aware of their limitations. The guerrillas choose the terrain that gives them every possible advantage. They seek terrain that denies or restricts the enemy's use of armor and complicates his logistic support. In the guerrilla-position defense, they raid, ambush, and attack the enemy's LOCs, flanks, reserve units, and supporting arms and installations. The guerrillas provide camouflaged sniper fire on officers, radio operators, and other high-value targets. They mine or booby-trap approach and departure routes.

6-200. Guerrillas may resort to defensive operations to contain enemy forces in a position favorable for attacking their flanks or rear. They often begin or intensify diversionary actions in adjacent areas to distract the enemy. Guerrillas use skillful ruses to lure the attacking forces into dividing their troops or hold objectives pending the arrival of conventional or allied coalition forces.

OFFENSIVE OPERATIONS

6-201. The degree to which the offensive operations of guerrilla forces can be sustained depends, in the long run, on the base camp support available to them. When operating remotely from, or not with, conventional forces, the guerrilla forces establish and hold bases of their own. They locate their bases, if available, with a view to isolation and difficulty of approach by the opposing forces. They also consider strong defensive characteristics and closeness to neighboring supporting states. The bases should be organized for defense and tenaciously defended by trained, motivated forces.

RAIDS

6-202. A raid is a combat operation to attack a position or installation followed by a planned withdrawal. SF and guerrilla or area sector commanders must consider the nature of the terrain (METT-TC) and the combat efficiency of the raid force. Commanders base target selection on a decision matrix using CARVER. The SFOD assesses the criticality and recuperability of various targets during the area study. Accessibility and vulnerability are situation-dependent and these assessments must be supported by the most current area intelligence. CARVER factors are discussed in the following paragraphs.

6-203. *Criticality* is the importance of a system, subsystem, complex, or component. A target is critical when its destruction or damage has a significant impact on the output of the targeted system, subsystem, or complex, and, at the highest level, on the threat's ability to make or sustain war. Criticality depends on several factors:

- How rapidly will the impact of target destruction affect enemy operations?
- What percentage of output is curtailed by target damage?
- Is there an existence of substitutes for the output product or service?
- What is the number of targets and their position in the system or complex flow diagram?

6-204. *Accessibility* is the ease with which a target can be reached, either physically or by fire. A target is accessible when an action element can physically infiltrate the target, or if the target can be hit by direct or indirect fire. Accessibility varies with the infiltration and exfiltration, the survival and evasion and security situation en route to and at the target, and the need for barrier penetration, climbing, and so on, at the target. The use of standoff weapons should always be considered when evaluating accessibility. Survivability of the attacker is usually most closely correlated to a target's accessibility.

6-205. *Recuperability* is a measure of the time required to replace, repair, or bypass the destruction or damage inflicted on the target. Recuperability varies with the sources and ages of targeted components and with the availability of spare parts. The existence of economic embargoes and the technical resources of the enemy nation will influence recuperability.

6-206. *Vulnerability* is a measure of the ability of the action element to damage the target using available assets (both men and material). A target is vulnerable if the unit has the capability and expertise to successfully attack it. Vulnerability depends on the—

- Nature and construction of the target.
- Amount of damage required.
- Assets available (manpower, transportation, weapons, explosives, and equipment).

6-207. *Effect* is the positive or negative influence on the population as a result of the action taken. Effect considers public reaction in the vicinity of the target, but also considers the domestic and international reaction as well. Effects to consider include the following:

- Will reprisals against friendlies result?
- Will national PSYOP themes be reinforced or contradicted?
- Will exfiltration or evasion be helped or hurt? What will be the allied and domestic reaction?
- Will the enemy population be alienated from its government, or will it become more supportive of the government?

NOTE
Effect is often neutral at the tactical level.

6-208. *Recognizability* is the degree to which a target can be recognized under varying weather, light, and seasonal conditions without confusion with other targets or components. Factors that influence recognizability include the size and complexity of the target, the existence of distinctive target signatures, and the technical sophistication and training of the attackers.

6-209. Target selection factors may be used to construct a CARVER matrix. The matrix is a decision tool for rating the relative desirability of potential targets and for wisely allocating attack resources (Figure 6-11). To construct the matrix, analysts list the potential targets in the left column. For strategic-level analysis, analysts list the enemy's systems or subsystems (electric, power, rail). For tactical-level analysis, analysts list the complexes or components of the subsystems selected for attack by their higher HQ.

6-210. Next, analysts develop concrete criteria for evaluating each CARVER factor. For instance, time may be used to evaluate criticality. If loss of a component results in an immediate halt of output, then that component is very critical.

							Higher is Better
Potential Targets	**C**	**A**	**R**	**V**	**E**	**R**	**TOTAL**
Fuel Tanks	2	5	3	5	5	5	**25**
Fuel Pumps	3	4	3	5	5	4	**24**
Boilers	4	2	5	4	3	3	**21**
Turbines	4	2	5	4	3	3	**21**
Generators	2	3	3	4	4	5	**21**
Condensers	4	2	4	4	3	3	**20**
Feed Pumps	3	4	3	4	4	3	**21**
Circular Water Pumps	3	4	4	4	3	3	**21**

Figure 6-11. Sample CARVER matrix

If loss of the component results in a halt of output, but only after several days or weeks, then that component is less critical. Similarly, percentage of output curtailed might be used as the evaluation criterion.

6-211. Once the evaluation criteria have been established, analysts use a numerical rating system (for example, 1-to-5 or 1-to-10) to rank the CARVER factors for each potential target. In a 1-to-10 numbering system, a score of 10 would indicate a very desirable rating (from the attacker's point of view), and a score of 1 would reflect an undesirable rating. The evaluation criteria and numerical rating scheme shown are only included as examples. The analyst must tailor the criteria and rating scheme to suit the particular strategic or tactical situation and the particular targets being analyzed.

6-212. The area commander considers the possible adverse effects target destruction will have on future operations and the civilian population. Targets that will hinder or hurt the civilian population may be attacked only as a last resort. The goal is to diminish the enemy's military potential, not destroy the only footbridge in the area for civilians to go to work. However, an improperly timed operation may provoke enemy counteraction for which resistance units and the civilian population are unprepared. An unsuccessful guerrilla attack often may have disastrous effects on troop morale. Successful operations raise morale and increase prestige in the eyes of the civilians, making them more willing to provide support. PSYOP exploit the impact of successful raids. If a raid is unsuccessful, PSYOP personnel need to diminish the adverse effects on the friendly local indigenous force.

6-213. Although detailed, the plan for a raid must be practical and simple. The raid force commander plans activities so that the target is not alerted. He carefully considers time available, allowing enough time for assembly and movement. The best hours for the operation are between midnight and dawn when limited visibility ensures surprise. Personnel favor early dusk when knowledge of the installation is limited or other factors require tight control of the operation. A successful guerrilla withdrawal late in the day or at night makes close, coordinated pursuit by the enemy much more difficult.

6-214. The commander must strictly enforce OPSEC measures during planning. Only those personnel directly involved with the operation must be informed. Civilian sympathizers should never be informed of upcoming operations unless they provide support to the guerrilla forces. Personnel should carefully rehearse all raids and contingencies using real-time and full-size mock-ups. They must also select and rehearse an alternate plan and escape route for use in case of emergencies.

6-215. The raid unit must also plan for medical support. Reactive planning in the medical arena is predictably unsuccessful, resulting unnecessarily in loss of life or limb. Adequate and visible medical planning has considerable positive psychological effects on the raid force's morale. Personnel should plan to handle anticipated casualties with aid and litter teams at the objective, at planned rallying points (RPs), and in the base area. Considerations should include evacuation routes at all levels and priorities for evacuation, nonevacuation, and hospitalization. Personnel should coordinate with treatment facilities before a raid but not divulge the target or timing of the mission.

ORGANIZATION

6-216. The size of the raid force depends on METT-TC. The raid force may vary from a few personnel attacking a checkpoint to a battalion attacking a large supply depot. Regardless of size, the raid force consists of four basic elements: command, assault, security, and support with strategic placement of medical personnel within all elements.

Command Element

6-217. The raid force commander and key personnel normally make up this element. They provide general support to the raid, such as medical aidmen, radio operators and, if a fire support element is part of the raid, a forward observer. The command element is not normally assigned specific duties with any element. Personnel may work with any of the major elements of the raid force. The raid force commander locates himself where he may best control and influence the action.

Assault Element

6-218. Applying METT-TC, the assault element is specifically task organized by what is needed to accomplish the objective. If the raid objective is to attack and render unusable critical elements of a target system, such as a bridge or tunnel, the raid force assaults and demolishes the bridge or tunnel. If the target is enemy personnel, the raid force conducts its attack with a high proportion of automatic assault weapons, covered by mortar fire from the support element. Usually the assault element physically moves on or into the target. This method is the least preferred. A more preferred method is for the assault element to complete its task from a standoff distance. The assault element attacks using lasers, antitank weapons, and other heavy weapons.

Security Element

6-219. The security element supports the raid by securing withdrawal routes, providing early warning of enemy approach, blocking avenues of approach into the objective area, preventing enemy escape from the objective area, and acting as the rear guard for the withdrawing raid force. The size of the security element depends on the enemy's capability to intervene and disrupt the mission. If the threat has armor, then the element needs antiarmor weapons. Where the enemy is known to have aircraft, the security element employs antiaircraft weapons. As the assault element moves into position, the security element keeps the command group informed of all enemy activities, firing only if detected and on order from the command group. Once the assault begins, the security element prevents enemy entry into or escape from the objective area. As the raid force withdraws, the security element, enhanced by sniper teams, conducts a rearguard action to disrupt and ambush any enemy counterattacks and pursuits.

Support Element

6-220. The support element of the raid force conducts diversionary or coordinated attacks at several points on the target to help the assault element gain access to the target. It uses ambushes, roadblocks, and mortar fire on the threat. Support personnel also execute complementary tasks in eliminating guards, breaching and removing obstacles to the objective, and conducting diversionary or holding actions. They assist by providing fire support and acting as demolition teams to set charges and neutralize, destroy, or render parts of the target unusable. Historically, the support element has covered the withdrawal of the assault element from the immediate area of the objective, and then withdrawn on order or prearranged signal.

INTELLIGENCE AND RECONNAISSANCE

6-221. The raid force commander must have maximum intelligence on the target site, enemy reaction forces (including routes, strength, and avenues of approach), and the routine activities and attitudes of the indigenous population in the area. Intelligence and reconnaissance personnel conduct a premission survey of the routes to the target, locations for friendly support weapons, enemy defenses (to include key weapons, minefields, and weak points), critical nodes to be destroyed within the target site, and withdrawal routes. The raid force gains access to the target site itself. Civilian supporters may help in these attempts if they have a good cover for action. If tactically feasible, personnel may conduct surveillance of the target to learn last-minute requirements.

6-222. Intelligence and reconnaissance personnel conduct detailed intelligence gathering and leader reconnaissance before beginning the raid. They construct a basic SALUTE report to include the following:

- Strength and location of the threat and its combat effectiveness.
- The threat's armaments and its location.
- Reaction time, security, and protection.
- Positions of key and automatic weapons.

6-223. Intelligence gathering includes answers to the following questions:

- Are reserve threat troops in the vicinity?
- Are they waiting with armor or aircraft?
- What are their strength, time to reinforce, and communication abilities?
- Is the terrain accessible?
- Can it be blockaded or defended?
- What are the locations and capabilities of local inhabitants?
- What routes to and from the raid site provide cover, concealment, and security and simplify movement?

- Does the threat have armor or air support?
- Where should key support weapons—antitank, antiair, sniper teams, and machine guns—be placed?

6-224. Additionally, intelligence and reconnaissance personnel consult with supporting CA team members to consider the nonmilitary threats to the planned raid. They analyze the civilian component of the target area using CASCOPE. Typical questions are as follows:

- What civilian areas exist between the line of departure and the objective? What activities are employed in these areas?
- What civilian structures (permanent, semipermanent, or temporary) may be encountered along the route? What protection status is assigned to these structures?
- What civilian capabilities exist that could intercede or support the raid as part of a contingency? Is there a credible police capability?
- What organizations (host nation [HN], UN, NGO, multinational corporation, criminal, terrorist) exist in and around the objective area? What activities are they engaged in? What assistance might we obtain from them?
- What types of civilians might we encounter in and around the objective area? What general activities are they engaged in? What might be their reaction to contact with raid forces? What might be their reaction to combat operations?
- Are there any civilian events that may affect the conduct of the military operation, such as call to prayer or church services, festival celebrations, "rush hour" traffic, and planting or harvest season activities?

PARTICIPANT REHEARSALS

6-225. Raid participants conduct realistic, timely rehearsals for the operation using terrain similar to the target area whenever possible. Participants use sand tables, full-size mock-ups, sketches, and photographs, to assist in briefings. They practice immediate action drills (IADs) along with contingency and emergency actions. Guerrillas hold full-scale final rehearsals under conditions and visibility realistically expected in the objective area at the time of attack.

NIGHT RAIDS

6-226. The best time for a raid is during limited visibility. Darkness allows units to maneuver even closer to the enemy. Enemy reinforcements will have difficulty in moving to assist their troops under attack, and air assets will be at a disadvantage. However, maneuvering at night is more difficult to accomplish, and command, control, and communications (C3) are more difficult to maintain,

DAY RAIDS

6-227. Units conduct raids during daylight when the troops at the target location are lacking in security, morale, or discipline. A key question is whether they will get help from adjacent units, especially under adverse weather conditions of sandstorms, rain, or snowstorms.

FINAL INSPECTION

6-228. The raid force commander conducts a final inspection of personnel and equipment before moving to the objective area. He ensures weapons are test-fired, broken equipment is replaced, and the physical condition of each man is checked. He checks personal belongings to ensure that no incriminating documents are carried during the operation. This inspection assures the raid force commander that his unit is equipped and ready for a successful mission.

MOVEMENT

6-229. The raid force commander plans and conducts movement to the objective area so that the raid force's approach to the target is undetected (Figure 6-12). Movement may be by single or multiple routes. The preselected route or routes may end in assembly areas, one or more patrol bases, or MSSs, which enhance mission success. The raid force makes every effort to avoid contact with the enemy during movement. Upon reaching the objective rallying point (ORP), security and leader reconnaissance parties deploy and make final coordination before the assault force moves to the attack position.

Figure 6-12. Movement to and withdrawal from the objective area

ACTIONS IN THE OBJECTIVE AREA

6-230. Support elements move to their positions and eliminate sentries, breach or remove obstacles, and execute other tasks. The assault element quickly follows the select soldiers into the target area. Once the objective of the raid has been accomplished, the assault element and special troops withdraw, covered by fire support on preselected targets. If the attack is unsuccessful, the raid force ends the action to prevent undue loss of personnel, and the support elements withdraw according to plan. The assault and support elements assemble at one or more RPs, while the security elements cover the withdrawal according to plan.

WITHDRAWAL

6-231. The raid force commander designs withdrawal to achieve maximum deception against the enemy and minimum danger to the raid force. The various elements of the raid force withdraw on order, or at a prearranged time, but never the same way twice. The movement uses many doglegs over the previously reconnoitered routes to the base camp through a series of RPs. Should the enemy organize a close pursuit of the assault element, the security element (covering force) assists by fire and movement, harassing the enemy and slowing it down. Other elements of the raid force do not attempt to reach the initial rallying point (IRP) but, on their own initiative, lead the enemy away and attempt to lose them by evasive action in difficult terrain.

6-232. The raid force commander issues specific instructions concerning contingencies. The commander decides which COA to follow based on time and distance to be traveled, firepower or fire support, and the raid force's physical condition. The raid force then attempts to reestablish contact with the main force at other RPs or continues to the base camp as separate groups IAW METT-TC.

BATTALION (LARGE) RAIDS

6-233. When a target is large and well guarded, a much larger raid force conducts the mission to ensure a successful attack. Large raids involve the use of a battalion-sized unit. Conduct is similar to that of smaller raids, but C2 becomes more difficult as the force increases in size.

MOVEMENT TO THE OBJECTIVE AREA

6-234. Surprise is a priority in all raids but is more difficult to achieve during battalion operations. The number of troops to assemble and deploy requires additional MSSs farther from the target to preserve secrecy. Also, the force requires a longer route to the attack position. A large raid force usually moves by small components over multiple routes to an MSS, then to the objective (Figure 6-13).

CONTROL

6-235. Units need extensive radio communications equipment to coordinate C2 operations in an active electronic warfare (EW) environment. Effective coordination is difficult to achieve. Raid planners use pyrotechnics, audible signals, or runners to coordinate action at designated times. Even under optimum conditions, massing of the raid

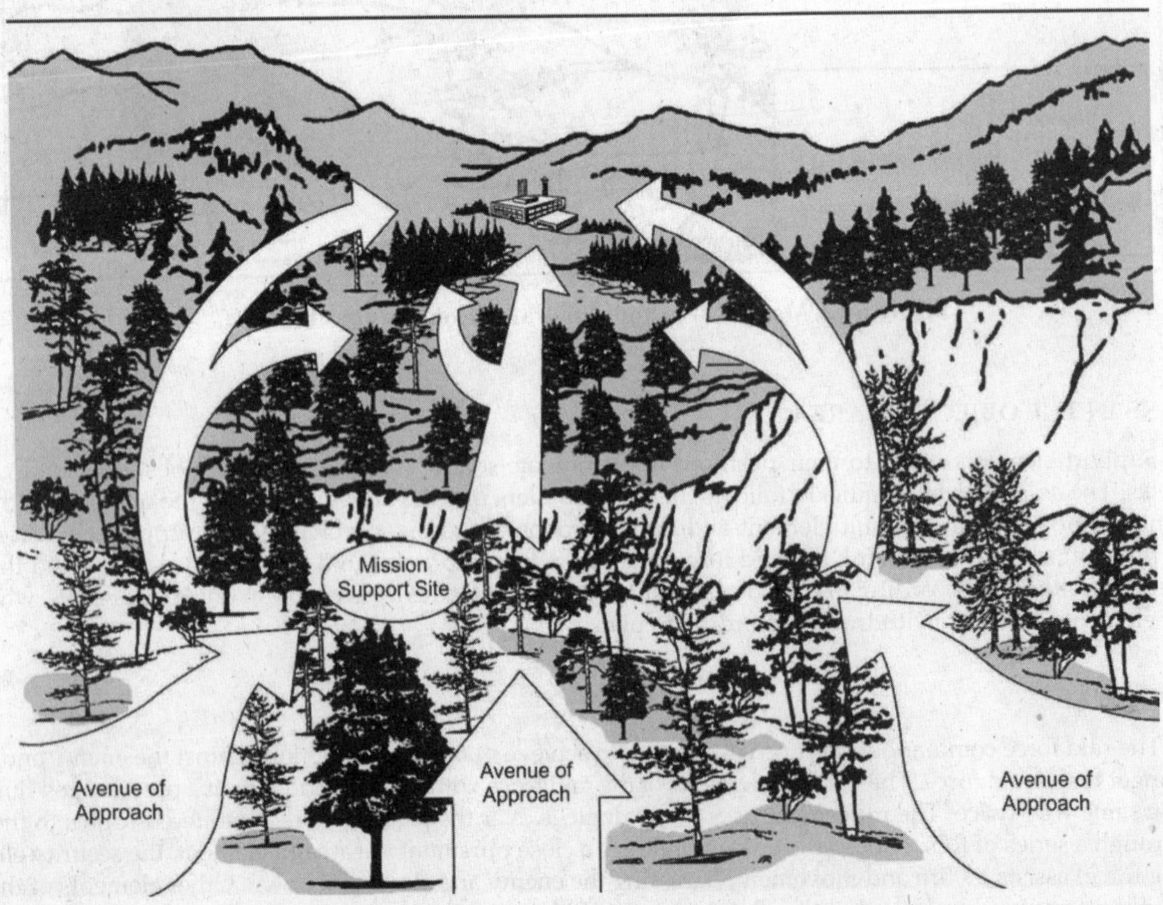

Figure 6-13. Movement to the objective area for a battalion raid

force at the objective is extremely difficult to control. Lights, armbands, or scarves enhance control. During planning, the raid force commander considers the complexity of the plan and the possibility of overall failure if subordinate elements do not arrive on time. He plans for these possible contingencies to ensure mission success.

TRAINING

6-236. Executing a large raid requires a high degree of training and discipline. Extensive rehearsals help prepare the force for the mission. In particular, commanders and staffs learn how to use large numbers of troops as a cohesive and coordinated fighting force.

FIRE SUPPORT

6-237. Raids usually require additional fire support. In the JSOA, such support may mean secretly caching ammunition in MSSs over a long period before the raid. Each member of the raiding force carries an extra mortar round, recoilless rocket round, or a can of machine gun ammunition.

TIMING

6-238. Timing is both crucial and much more difficult for a large raid. The time of the raid takes on increased importance because of the large number of personnel involved. More time is required to coordinate and move units, and the main action element usually needs more time to do its mission. As a result, larger raids require larger security elements to isolate the objective for longer time periods. The element moves to the objective during limited visibility, but due to fire support coordination requirements and the large number of personnel, the mission begins during early daylight hours.

WITHDRAWAL

6-239. Elements usually best withdraw from a large raid in small groups, over multiple routes, to deceive the enemy and discourage enemy pursuit. Dispersed withdrawal also denies a priority target to enemy air and fire support elements. The raid force commander considers the possibility of an alert and aggressive enemy counterattacking the dispersed elements of the force. He carefully weighs all METT-TC factors before deciding how, when, and where he will conduct his withdrawal.

AMBUSHES

6-240. The ambush is a surprise attack from a concealed position upon a moving or temporarily halted target. It is one of the oldest and most effective types of guerrilla tactics. An ambush is executed to reduce the enemy's overall combat effectiveness by destroying or harassing his soldiers and their will to win. An ambush may include an assault to close with and decisively engage the target, or the attack may be by direct or indirect fire to harass the enemy.

NOTE

The following article was originally serialized in *Red Thrust Star*, dated July and October 1995 and October 1996.

Afghanistan is not Europe, yet the Soviet Army that occupied Afghanistan in late December 1979 was trained to fight NATO on the northern European plain. Consequently, the Soviet Army had to reequip, reform and retrain on-site to fight the insurgent *mujahideen* [holy warrior] guerrillas. The Soviets were forced to revise their tactics and tactical methodologies in order to meet the demands of this very different war. One of the tactical areas which the Soviets thoroughly revised was the conduct of ambushes. The Soviets planned to use ambushes in the European theater, but they were primarily ambushes against attacking or withdrawing NATO armored columns. The Soviets constructed most of their ambushes around tanks and tank units. They planned to employ concealed individual tanks, tank platoons and tank companies along high-speed avenues of approach or withdrawal to engage the enemy from the flank and then to depart. Such ambushes were part of security zone defensive planning as well as planning for the deep battle and pursuit. The Soviets also trained their squad and platoon-sized reconnaissance elements to conduct dismounted ambushes to capture prisoners and documents. They employed a command element, a snatch group and a fire support group in these small-scale ambushes.

In Afghanistan, the *mujahideen* seldom used armored vehicles and seldom advanced along high-speed avenues of approach. Instead, they infiltrated light-infantry forces through some of the most inhospitable terrain on the planet to mass for an attack or ambush. The Soviets soon discovered that they had difficulty maintaining control of the limited road network, which constituted the Soviet lines of communication. The guerrillas constantly cut the roads and ambushed convoys carrying material from the Soviet Union to the base camps and cities in Afghanistan. The Soviet ability to maintain its presence in the country depended on its ability to keep the roads open and much of the Soviet combat was a fight for control of the road network. During the war, the guerrillas destroyed over 11,000 Soviet trucks (and reportedly even more Afghan trucks) through ambush. The Soviets learned from *mujahideen* ambushes and used the ambush to interdict the guerrilla supplies coming from Pakistan and Iran. The Soviets conducted ambushes mainly with reconnaissance and other special troops (airborne, air assault, spetsnaz and elements from the two separate motorized rifle brigades which were designed as counter-guerrilla forces). The composition and employment of ambush forces differed with the units involved and the part of Afghanistan in which they were employed.

DESTRUCTION

6-241. Destruction is the primary purpose of an ambush. The number of men killed, wounded, or captured and loss of equipment and supplies critically affect the enemy. Guerrillas benefit from the capture of equipment and supplies through battlefield recovery.

HARASSMENT

6-242. Frequent ambushes harass the enemy and force him to divert men from patrol operations to guard convoys, troop movements, and installations. When enemy patrols fail to accomplish their missions because they are ambushed, the enemy is deprived of the valuable contributions these patrols make to its combat effort. A series of successful guerrilla ambushes cause the enemy to be less aggressive and more defensive-minded. The enemy becomes apprehensive and overly cautious and reluctant to go on patrols, to move in convoys, or to move in small groups. The enemy wants to avoid night operations, is more subject to confusion and panic if ambushed, and is mentally defeated.

ELEMENT OF SURPRISE

6-243. Surprise allows the ambush force to seize control of any situation. The force achieves surprise by carefully planning, preparing, and executing the ambush. Guerrillas attack the targets when, where, and in a manner for which the enemy is least prepared.

COORDINATED FIRES

6-244. The ambush force commander positions and coordinates the use of all weapons, mines, and demolitions. He coordinates all fires, including artillery and mortars when available. Coordinated fire support ensures isolation of the kill zone. This isolation prevents enemy escape or reinforcement due to the large volume of accurate, concentrated fire.

CONTROL MEASURES

6-245. The ambush force commander maintains close control measures during the ambush operation. These control measures include provisions for—

- Early warning signals of target approach.
- Withholding fire until the target has moved into the killing zone.

- Opening, shifting, and halting fire at the proper time.
- Initiating proper actions if the ambush is prematurely detected.
- Timely and orderly withdrawal to a recognized RP.

CATEGORIES OF AMBUSHES

6-246. Ambushes have two general categories: point and area. A point ambush, whether independent or part of an area ambush, positions itself along the target's expected route of approach. It attacks a single kill zone. When there is not sufficient intelligence for a point ambush, the commander establishes an area ambush. An area ambush uses multiple point ambushes around a central kill zone.

6-247. These two variations succeed best in situations where routes of approach by relieving or reinforcing units are limited to those favorable for ambush by the guerrillas. Both variations were used extensively by the North Vietnamese guerrilla forces in Vietnam against U.S. forces in the Republic of Vietnam.

POINT AMBUSH

6-248. A point ambush, whether independent or part of an area ambush, is positioned along the target's expected route of approach. Formation is important because, to a great extent, it determines whether a point ambush can deliver the heavy volume of highly concentrated fire necessary to isolate, trap, and destroy the target.

6-249. The formation to be used is determined by carefully considering possible formations and the advantages and disadvantages of each in relation to terrain, conditions of visibility, forces, weapons and equipment, ease or difficulty of control, target to be attacked, and overall combat situation.

6-250. The following paragraphs discuss a few formations that have been developed for the deployment of point ambushes. Those discussed are named according to the general pattern formed on the ground by the deployment of the attack element.

Line Formation

6-251. The attack element is deployed generally parallel to the target's route of movement (road, trail, stream). This deployment positions the attack element parallel to the long axis of the killing zone and subjects the target to heavy flanking fire. The size of the target, which can be trapped in the killing zone, is limited by the area the attack element can effectively cover with a heavy volume of highly concentrated fire. The target is trapped in the killing zone by natural obstacles, mines (claymore, antivehicular, antipersonnel), demolitions, and direct and indirect fires (Figure 6-14). A disadvantage of the line formation is the chance that lateral dispersion of the target may be too great for effective coverage. Line formation is appropriate in close terrain that restricts target maneuver and in open terrain where one flank is restricted by mines, demolitions, mantraps, or sharpened stakes. Similar obstacles can be placed between the attack element and the killing zone to provide protection from the target's counterambush measures. When a destruction ambush is deployed in this manner, access lanes are left so that the target can be assaulted (Figure 6-15). The line formation can be effectively used by a rise from the ground ambush in terrain seemingly unsuitable for ambush. An advantage of the line formation is its relative ease of control under all conditions of visibility.

L Formation

6-252. The L-shaped formation is a variation of the line formation. The long side of the attack element is parallel to the killing zone and delivers flanking fire. The short side is at the end of and at right angles to the killing zone and delivers enfilading fire that finks with fire from the other leg. This formation is very flexible. It can be established on a straight stretch of a trail or stream (Figure 6-16), or a sharp bend in a trail or stream (Figure 6-17). When appropriate, fire from the short leg can be shifted to parallel the long leg if the target tries to assault or escape in the opposite direction. In addition, the short leg prevents escape in the direction of attack element and reinforcement from its direction (Figure 6-18).

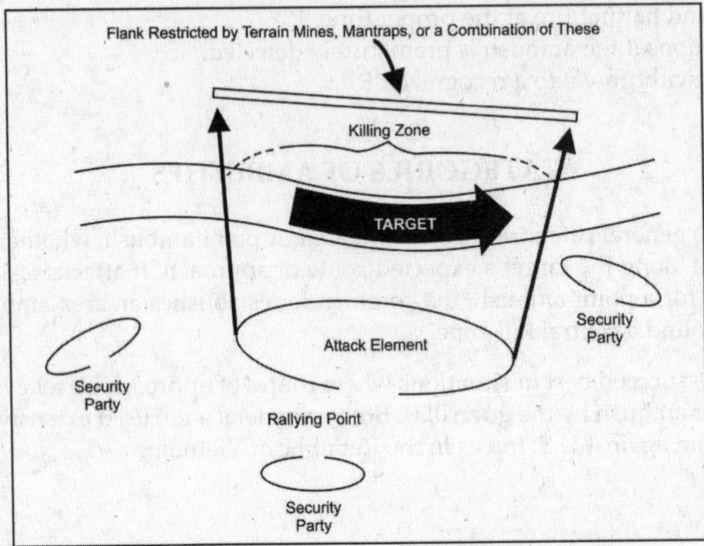

Figure 6-14. Line formation for harassing or destruction ambush

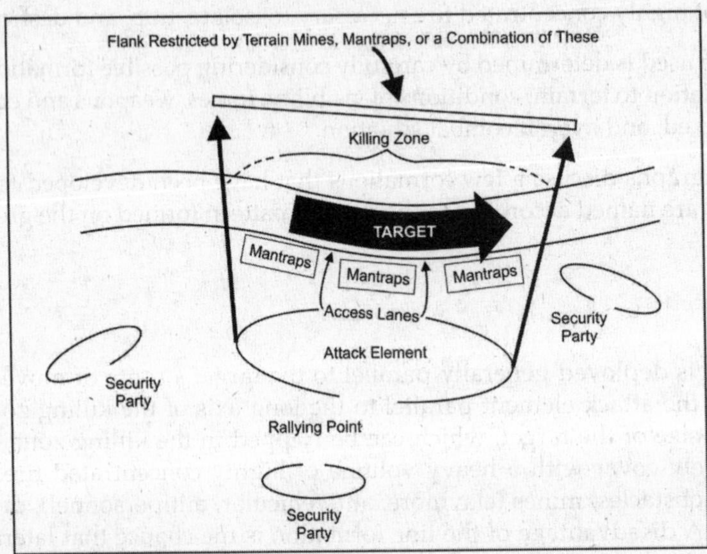

Figure 6-15. Line formation for destruction ambush

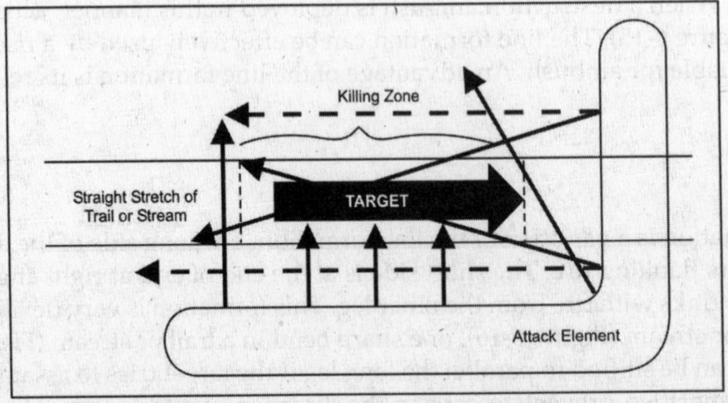

Figure 6-16. L formation for destruction ambush

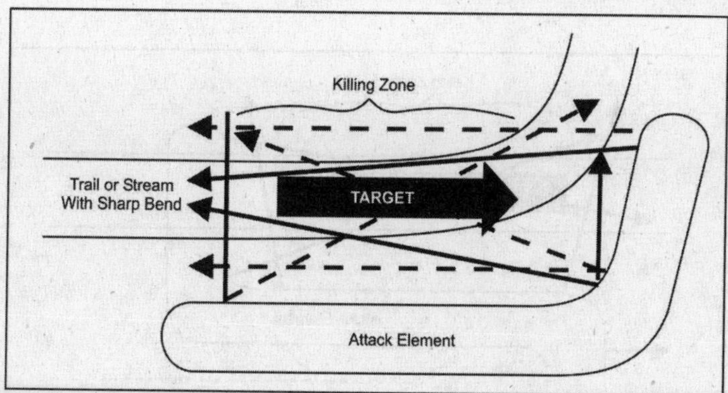

Figure 6-17. L formation for destruction ambush on bend of trail or stream

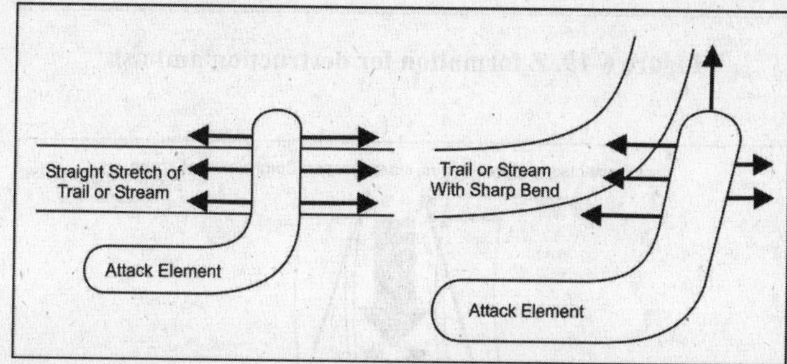

Figure 6-18. L formation where short leg of attack element prevents escape or reinforcement

Z Formation

6-253. The Z-shaped formation is another variation of the line formation. The attack force is deployed as in the L formation, but with an additional side so that the formation resembles the letter Z. The additional side (Figure 6-19) may serve to—

- Engage a force attempting to relieve or reinforce the target.
- Seal the end of the killing zone.
- Restrict a flank.
- Prevent envelopment.

T Formation

6-254. In the T-shaped formation, the attack element is deployed across and at right angles to the target's route of movement so that it and the target form the letter T. This formation can be used day or night to establish a purely harassing ambush and at night to establish an ambush to interdict movement through open, hard-to-seal areas (such as rice paddies).

6-255. A small group of persons can use the T formation to harass, slow, and disorganize a larger force. When the lead elements of the target are engaged, they will normally attempt to maneuver right or left to close with the ambush. Mines, mantraps, and other obstacles placed to the flanks of the killing zone slow the enemy's movements and permit the ambush patrol to deliver heavy fire and withdraw without becoming decisively engaged (Figure 6-20).

6-256. The attack element can also use the T formation to interdict small groups attempting night movement across open areas. For example, the attack element is deployed along a rice paddy dike with every second person facing in the opposite direction. The attack of a target approaching from either direction requires only that every second

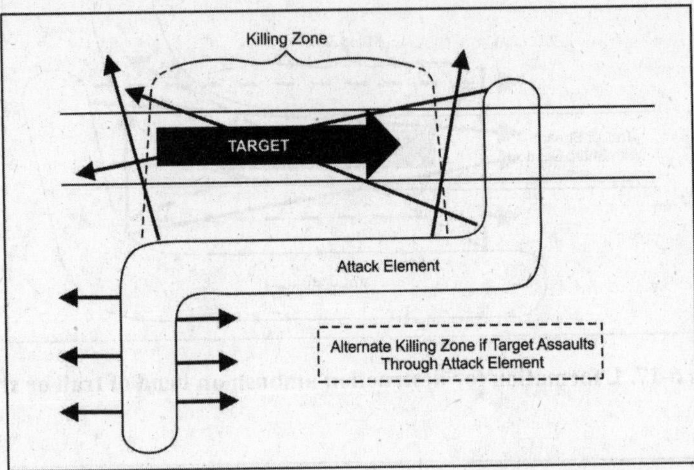

Figure 6-19. Z formation for destruction ambush

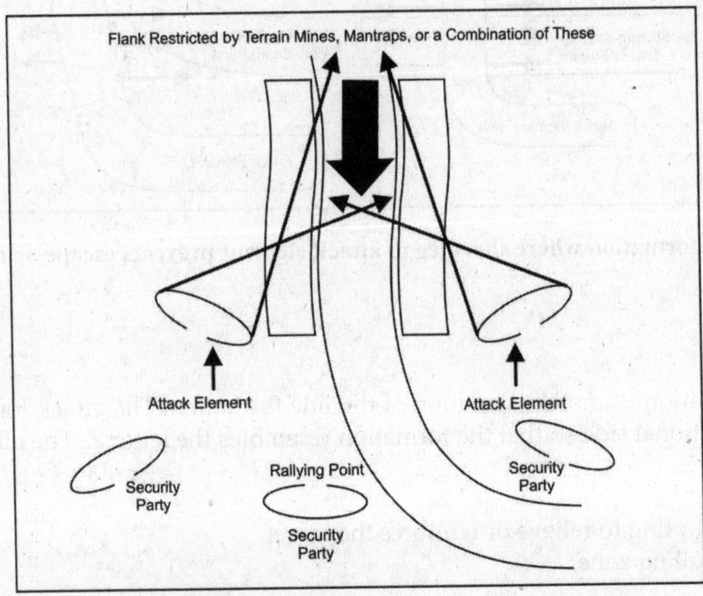

Figure 6-20. T formation for harassing ambush

person shift to the opposite side of the dike. Each person fires only to his front and only when the target is at very close range. Attack is by fire only and each person keeps the target under fire as long as it remains on his front. If the target attempts to escape in either direction along the dike, each man takes it under fire as it comes to his vicinity. The T formation is very effective at halting infiltration. But it has one chief disadvantage: while spread out, the ambush may engage a superior force. Use of this formation must, therefore, fit the local enemy situation (Figure 6-21).

V Formation

6-257. The V-shaped attack element is deployed along both sides of the target's route of movement so that it forms the letter V; care is taken to ensure that neither group (nor leg) fires into the other. This formation subjects the target to both enfilading and interlocking fire. The V formation is best suited for fairly open terrain but can also be used in the jungle. When established in the jungle, the legs of the V close in as the head elements of the target approach the apex of the V; the attack element then opens fire from close range. Here, even more than in open terrain, all movement and fire must be carefully coordinated and controlled to ensure that the fire of one leg does not endanger the other. The wider separation of elements makes this formation difficult to control, and there are fewer sites that favor its use. Its main advantage is that it is difficult for the target to detect the ambush until it has moved well into the killing zone (Figures 6-22 and 6-23).

Triangle Formation

6-258. This formation is a variation of the V and can be used in three different ways. One way is the closed triangle (Figure 6-24), in which the attack element is deployed in three groups or parties, positioned so that they form a triangle (or closed V). An automatic weapon is placed at each point of the triangle and positioned so that it can be shifted quickly to interlock with either of the others. Men are positioned so that their fields of fire overlap. Mortars may be

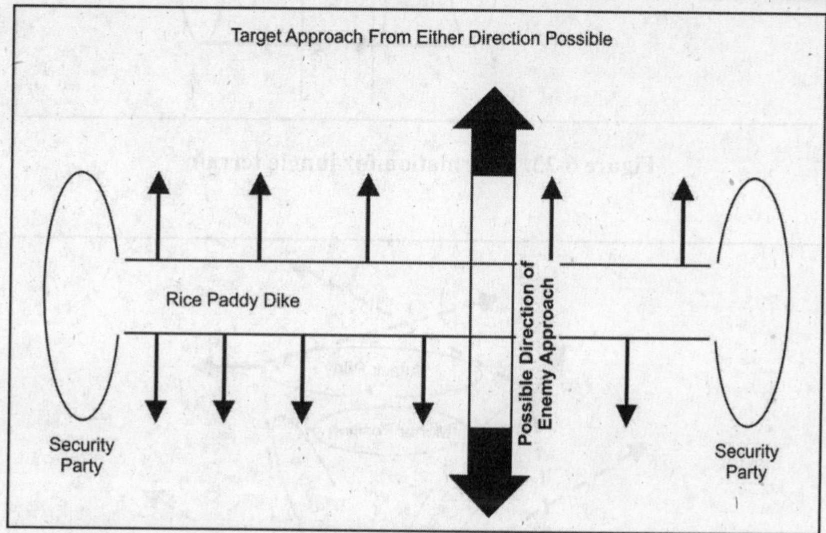

Figure 6-21. T formation for harassing ambush in rice paddy

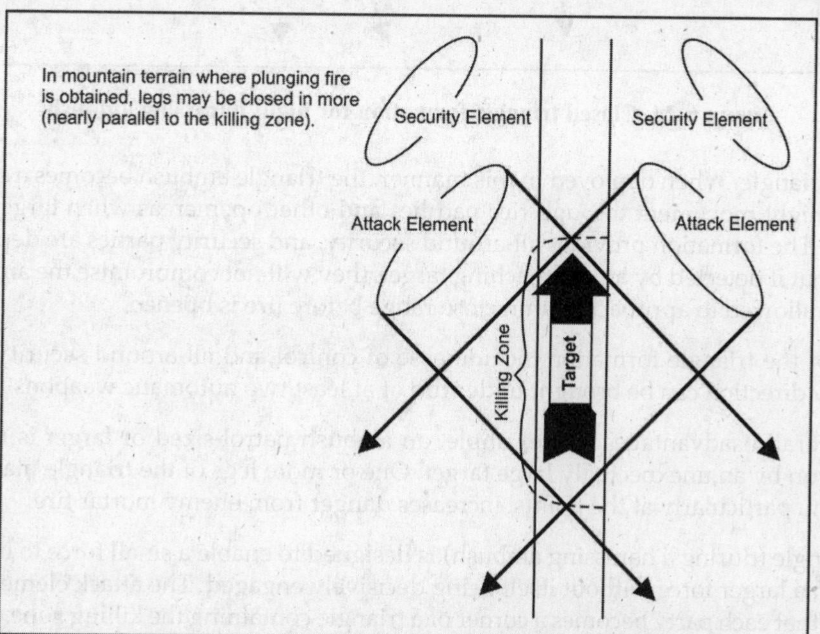

Figure 6-22. V formation for open mountain terrain

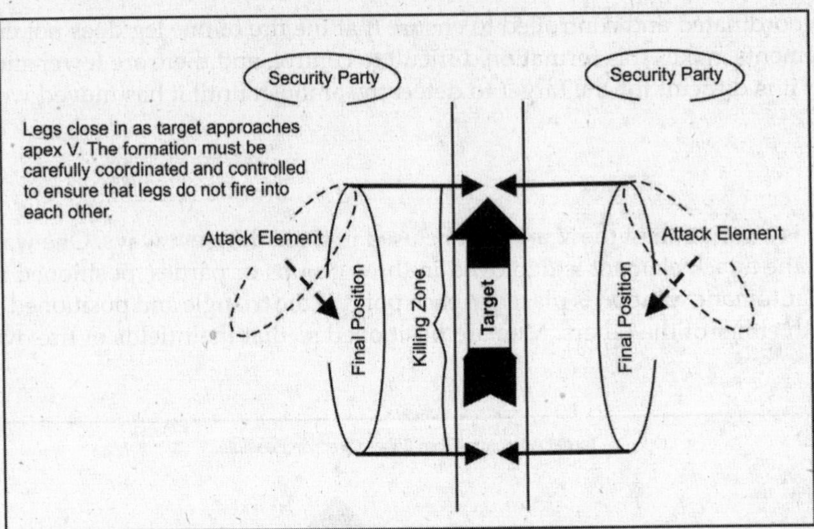

Figure 6-23. V formation for jungle terrain

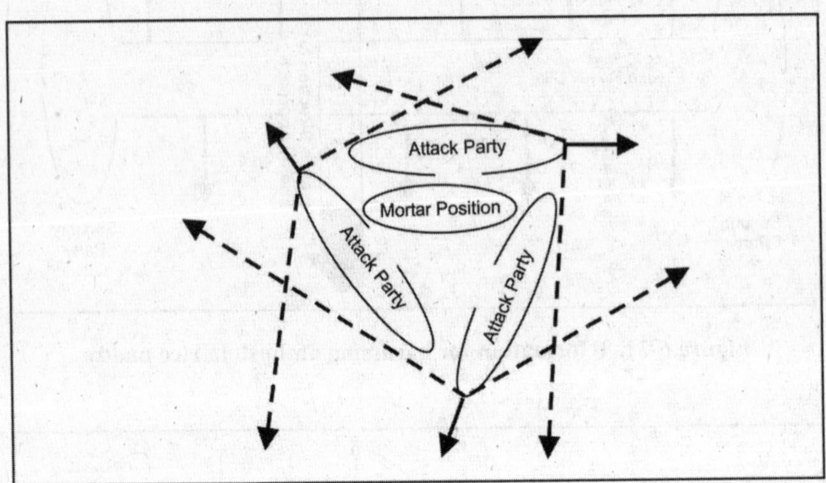

Figure 6-24. Closed triangle formation for night harassing ambush

positioned inside the triangle. When deployed in this manner, the triangle ambush becomes a small unit strongpoint. It is used to interdict night movement through rice paddies and other open areas when target approach is likely to be from any direction. The formation provides all-around security, and security parties are deployed only when they can be positioned so that if detected by an approaching target, they will not compromise the ambush. Attack is by fire only, and the target is allowed to approach within close range before fire is opened.

6-259. Advantages of the triangle formation include ease of control and all-around security. In addition, a target approaching from any direction can be brought under fire of at least two automatic weapons.

6-260. There are several disadvantages. For example, an ambush patrol-sized or larger is required to reduce the danger of being overrun by an unexpectedly large target. One or more legs of the triangle may come under enfilade fire. Lack of dispersion, particularly at the points, increases danger from enemy mortar fire.

6-261. The open triangle (during a harassing ambush) is designed to enable a small force to harass, slow, and inflict heavy casualties upon a larger force without itself being decisively engaged. The attack element is deployed in three parties, positioned so that each party becomes a corner of a triangle containing the killing zone. When the target enters the killing zone, the party to the target's front opens fire on the leading element. When the target counterattacks, the group withdraws and an assault party to the flank opens fire. When this party is attacked, the party opposite flank opens fire. This process is repeated until the target is pulled apart. Each party reoccupies its position, if possible, and continues to inflict the maximum damage possible without becoming decisively engaged (Figure 6-25).

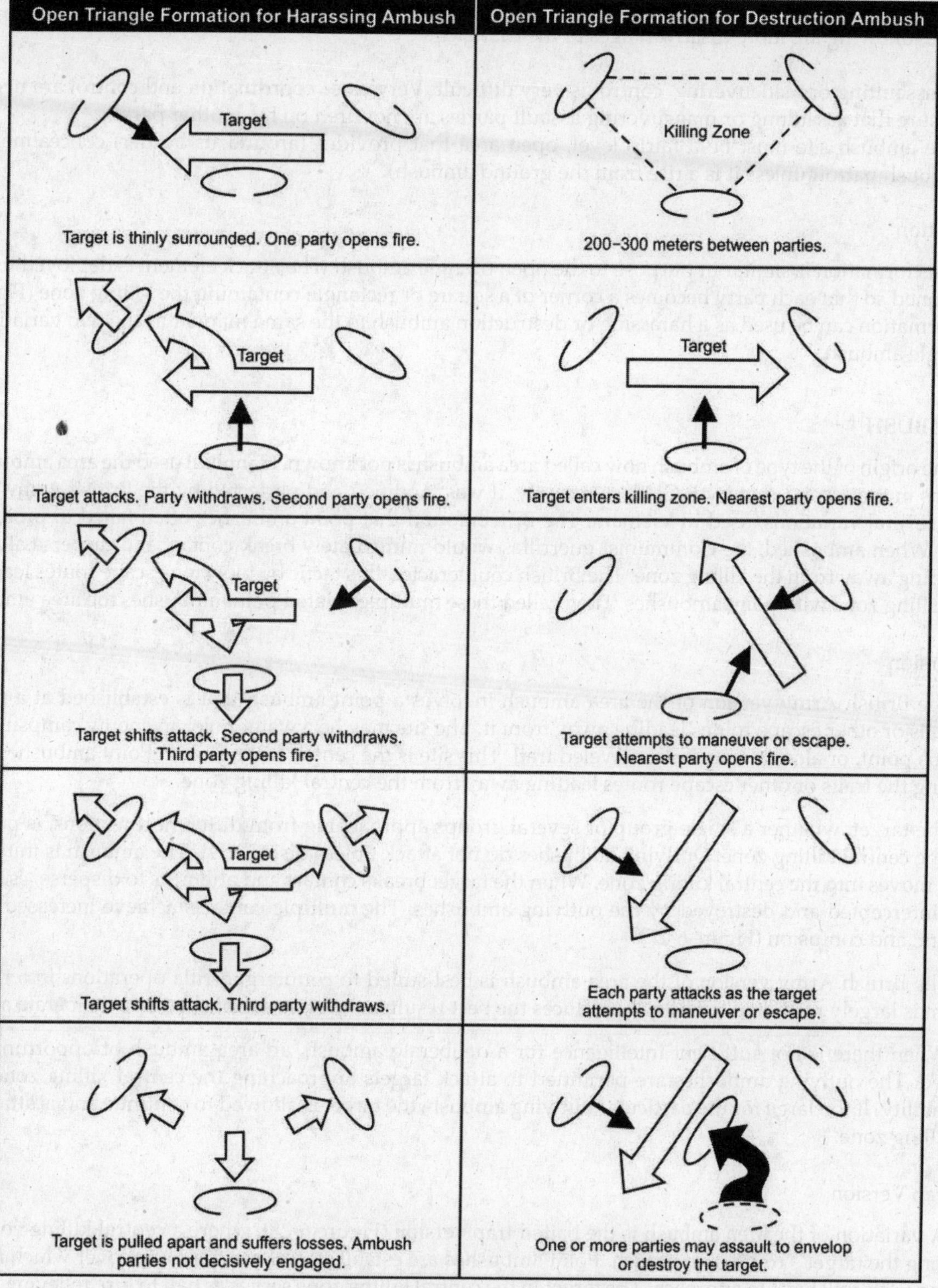

Figure 6-25. Open triangle formation

6-262. In an open triangle (during a destruction ambush), the attack element is again deployed in three parties, positioned so that each party is a point of the triangle, 200 to 300 meters apart. The killing zone is the area within the triangle. The target is allowed to enter the killing zone; the nearest party attacks by fire. As the target attempts to maneuver or withdraw, the other groups open fire. One or more assault parties, as directed assault or maneuver to envelop or destroy the target (Figure 6-25). As a destruction ambush, this formation is suitable for platoon-sized or larger forces. A unit smaller than a platoon would be in too great a danger of being overrun.

6-263. The following are more disadvantages of the triangle:

- In assaulting or maneuvering, control is very difficult. Very close coordination and control are necessary to ensure that assaulting or maneuvering assault parties are not fired on by another party.
- The ambush site must be a fairly level, open area that provides (around its border) concealment for the ambush patrol (unless it is a rise from the ground ambush).

Box Formation

6-264. This formation is similar in purpose to the open triangle ambush. The attack element is deployed in four parties, positioned so that each party becomes a corner of a square or rectangle containing the killing zone (Figure 6-26). The box formation can be used as a harassing or destruction ambush in the same manner as the two variations of the open triangle ambush.

AREA AMBUSH

6-265. The origin of the type of ambush now called area ambush is not known. Hannibal used the area ambush against the Romans in the second century B.C. More recently, it was modified and perfected by the British Army in Malaya and, with several variations, used in Vietnam. The British found that point ambushes often failed to produce heavy casualties. When ambushed, the Communist guerrillas would immediately break contact and disperse along escape routes leading away from the killing zone. The British counteracted this tactic by blocking escape routes leading away from the killing zone with point ambushes. They called these multiple-related point ambushes the area ambush.

British Version

6-266. The British Army version of the area ambush involves a point ambush that is established at a site having several trails or other escape routes leading away from it. The site may be a water hole, an enemy campsite, a known rendezvous point, or along a frequently traveled trail. This site is the central killing zone. Point ambushes are established along the trails or other escape routes leading away from the central killing zone.

6-267. The target, whether a single group or several groups approaching from different directions, is permitted to move to the central killing zone. Outlying ambushes do not attack unless discovered. The ambush is initiated when the target moves into the central killing zone. When the target breaks contact and attempts to disperse, escaping portions are intercepted and destroyed by the outlying ambushes. The multiple contacts achieve increased casualties, harassment, and confusion (Figure 6-27).

6-268. The British Army version of the area ambush is best suited to counterguerrilla operations in terrain where movement is largely restricted to trails. It produces the best results when it is established as a deliberate ambush.

6-269. When there is not sufficient intelligence for a deliberate ambush, an area ambush of opportunity may be established. The outlying ambushes are permitted to attack targets approaching the central killing zone, if within their capability. If too large for the particular outlying ambush, the target is allowed to continue and is attacked in the central killing zone.

Baited Trap Version

6-270. A variation of the area ambush is the baited trap version (Figure 6-28), where a central killing zone is established along the target's route of approach. Point ambushes are established along the routes over which relieving or reinforcing units will have to approach. The target in the central killing zone serves as bait to lure relieving or reinforcing units into the killing zones of the outlying ambushes. The outlying point ambushes need not be strong enough

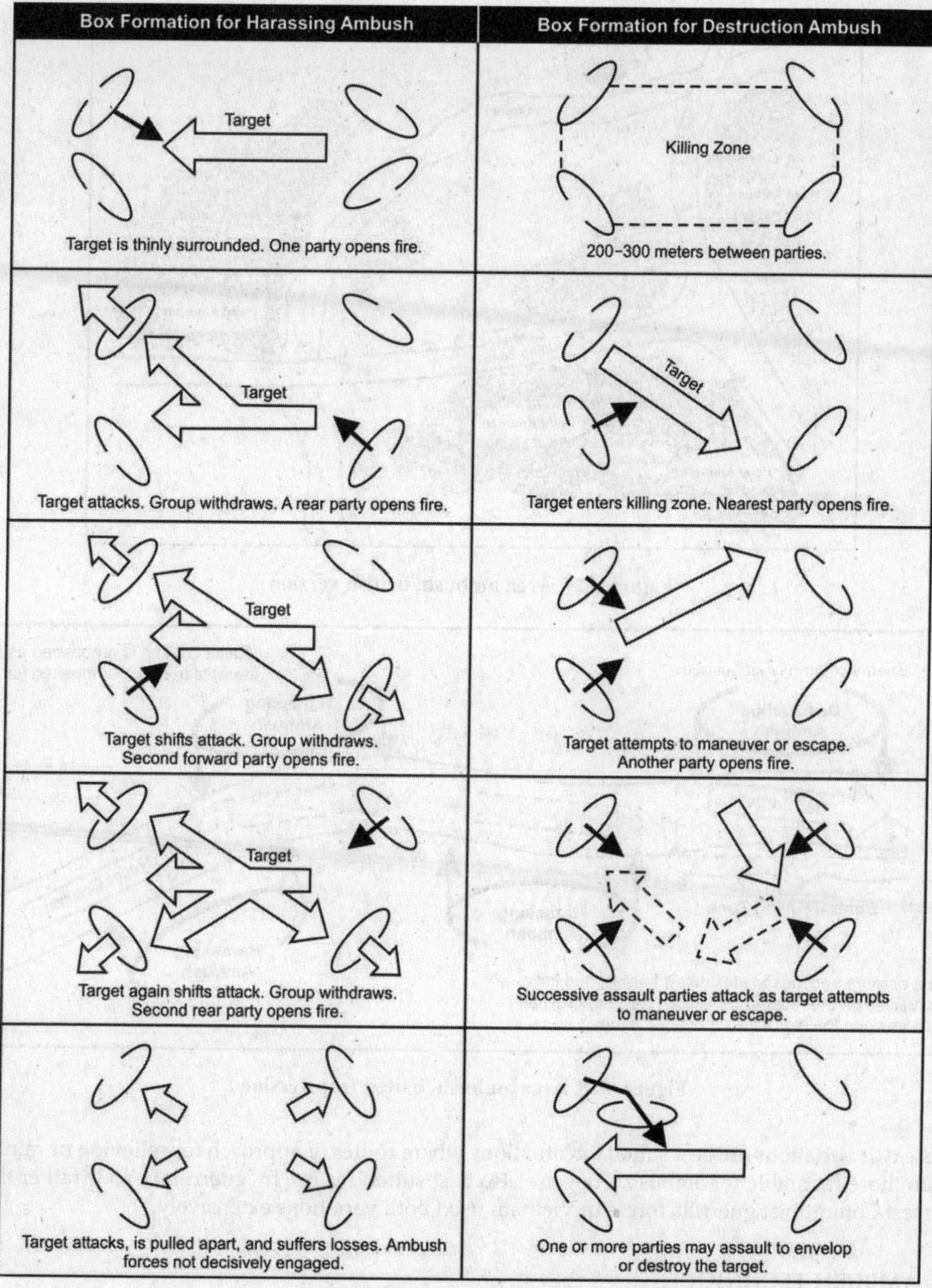

Figure 6-26. Box formation

to destroy their targets. They may be small, harassing ambushes that delay, disorganize, and eat away the target by successive contacts.

6-271. This version can be varied by using a fixed installation as bait to lure relieving or reinforcing units into the killing zone of one or more of the outlying ambushes. The installation replaces the central killing zone and is attacked. The attack may intend to overcome the installation or may be only a ruse.

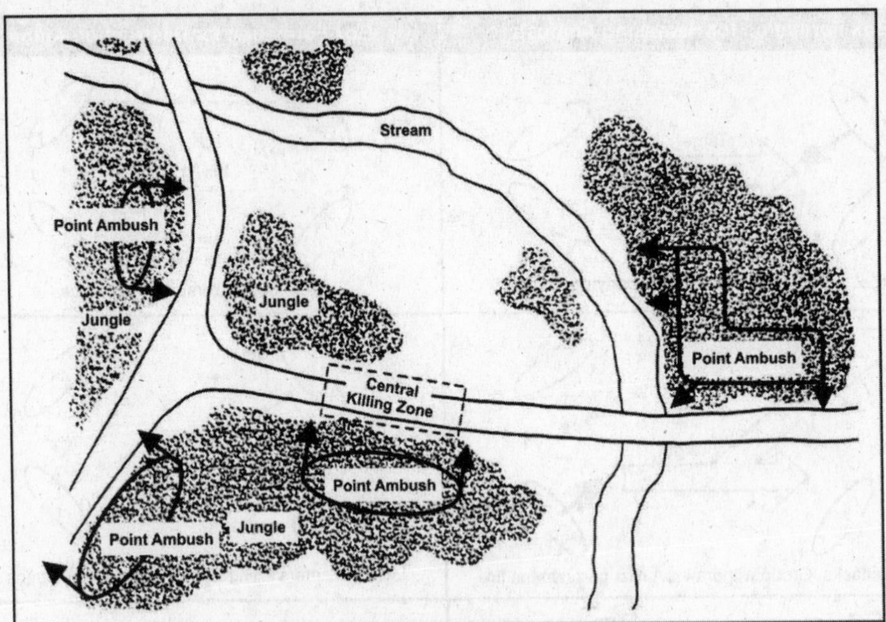

Figure 6-27. Area ambush, british version

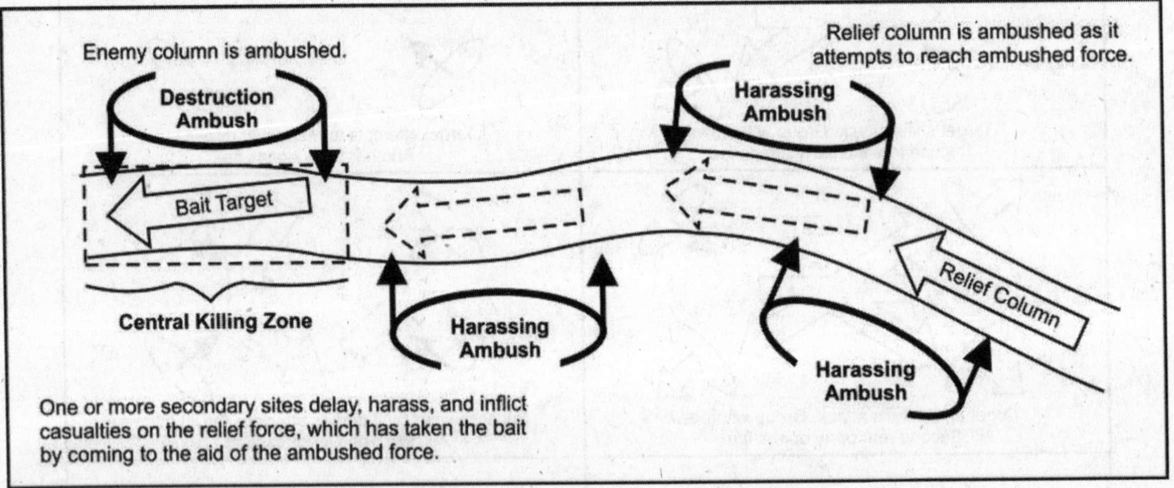

Figure 6-28. Area ambush, baited trap version

6-272. These two variations are best suited for situations where routes of approach for relieving or reinforcing units are limited to those favorable for ambush. They are also best suited for use by guerrilla forces, rather than counter-guerrilla forces. Communist guerrilla forces in Vietnam used both variations extensively.

UNUSUAL AMBUSH TECHNIQUES

6-273. The ambush techniques described above are so well known and widely used that they are considered standard. Other, less well known, less frequently used techniques are considered unusual. Two such techniques are described below.

Rise From the Ground Ambush

6-274. The attack element uses this type of ambush (Figure 6-29, page 873) in open areas that lack the good cover and concealment and other features normally desirable in a good ambush site. The attack element is deployed in the formation best suited to the overall situation. It is completely concealed in the spider-hole type of covered foxhole. Soil is carefully removed and positions expertly camouflaged.

6-275. When the ambush begins, the attack element throws back the covers and literally rises from the ground to attack. This ambush takes advantage of the tendency of patrols and other units to relax in areas that do not appear to favor ambush. The chief disadvantage is that the ambush patrol is very vulnerable if prematurely detected.

Demolition Ambush

6-276. Electrically detonated mines or demolition charges, or both, are positioned in an area (Figure 6-30) over which a target is expected to pass. This area may be a portion of a road or a trail, an open field, or any location that can be observed from a distance. Activating wires are run to a concealed observation point, which is sufficiently distant to ensure safety of the ambushers.

6-277. As large a force as desired or necessary can be used to mine the area. Two men remain to begin the ambush; others return to the unit. When a target enters the mined area (killing zone), the two men remaining detonate the explosives and withdraw immediately to avoid detection and pursuit.

SPECIAL AMBUSH SITUATIONS

6-278. The following techniques are not considered standard ambush scenarios and therefore require special considerations.

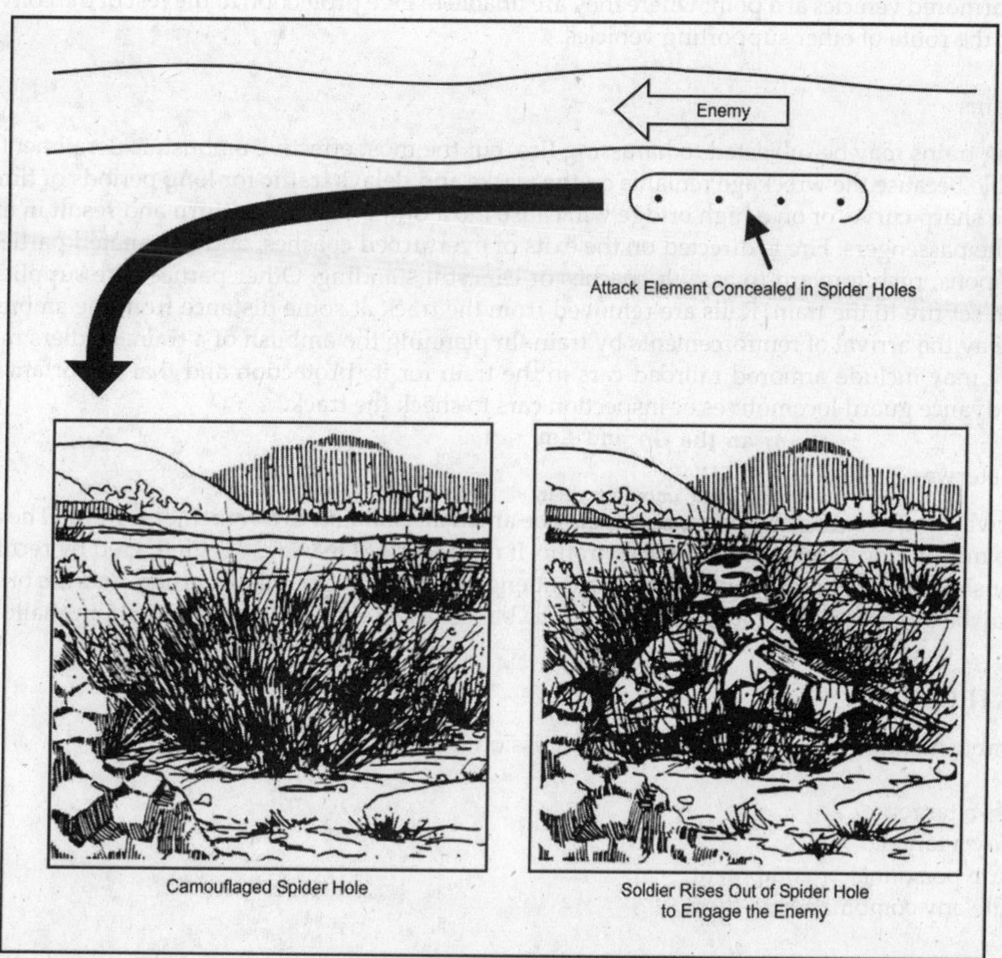

Figure 6-29. Unusual techniques, rise from the ground ambush

Figure 6-30. Unusual techniques, demolition ambush

Columns Protected by Armor

6-279. Attacks against columns protected by armored vehicles depend on the type and location of armored vehicles in a column and the weapons of the ambush patrol. If possible, armored vehicles are destroyed or disabled by fire of antitank weapons, landmines, Molotov cocktails, or by throwing hand grenades into open hatches. An effort is made to immobilize armored vehicles at a point where they are unable to give protection to the rest of the convoy and where they will block the route of other supporting vehicles.

Ambush of Trains

6-280. Moving trains may be subjected to harassing fire, but the most effective ambush is derailment. Train derailment is desirable because the wreckage remains on the tracks and delays traffic for long periods of time. Derailment on a grade, at a sharp curve, or on a high bridge will cause most of the cars to overturn and result in extensive casualties among the passengers. Fire is directed on the exits of overturned coaches, and designated parties, armed with automatic weapons, rush forward to assault coaches or cars still standing. Other parties take supplies from freight yards and then set fire to the train. Rails are removed from the track at some distance from the ambush site in each direction to delay the arrival of reinforcements by train. In planning the ambush of a train, soldiers must remember that the enemy may include armored railroad cars in the train for its protection and that important trains may be preceded by advance guard locomotives or inspection cars to check the track.

Ambush of Waterway Traffic

6-281. Waterway traffic, such as barges or ships, may be ambushed similar to a vehicular column. The ambush patrol may be able to mine the waterway and thus stop traffic. If mining is not feasible, fire delivered by recoilless weapons can damage or sink the craft. Fire should be directed at engine room spaces, the waterline, and the bridge. Recovery of supplies may be possible if the craft is beached on the banks of the waterway or grounded in shallow water.

AMBUSH PATROLS

6-282. An ambush patrol is a combat patrol whose mission is to—

- Harass a target.
- Destroy a target.
- Capture personnel or equipment.
- Execute any combination of these.

6-283. An ambush patrol is planned and prepared in the same general manner as other patrols; that is, by using patrol steps (troop leading procedures). Each step is explained below.

Planning and Preparation

6-284. Planners must first consider whether the ambush is to be a deliberate ambush or an ambush of opportunity. In a deliberate ambush, the greater amount of target intelligence available permits planning for every COA at the target. Plans for an ambush of opportunity must include consideration of the types of targets that may be ambushed, as well as varying situations. In both, plans must be flexible enough to allow modification, as appropriate, at the ambush site. When planning, the principles discussed below apply. All plans must be rehearsed in detail.

6-285. Simplicity. Every person must thoroughly understand what he is to do at every stage of the operation. In ambush more so than in other operations, failure of even one person to perform exactly as planned can cause failure.

6-286. Type of Ambush (point or area). Many factors affect the types of ambush. They include organization, the number of men required, the equipment and communications required, and all other aspects of the patrol.

6-287. Deployment. Each possible formation must be considered for its advantages and disadvantages.

6-288. Manner of Attack. An attack may be by fire only (harassing only) or may include an assault of the target (destruction ambush).

6-289. Size of Ambush Patrol. The patrol is tailored for its mission. Two men may be adequate for a harassing ambush. A destruction ambush may require the entire unit (squad, platoon, company).

6-290. Organization. An ambush patrol is organized in the same manner as other combat patrols to include a patrol HQ, an assault element, a support element, and a security element (Figure 6-31). The assault and support elements are the attack force; the security element is the security force. When appropriate, the attack force is further organized to provide a reserve force. When an ambush site is to be occupied for an extended period, double ambush patrols may be organized. One ambush patrol occupies the site while the other rests, eats, and tends to personal needs at the ORP or other concealed location. They alternate each 8 hours. If the waiting period is more than 24 hours, three ambush patrols are organized (Figure 6-32).

6-291. Equipment. The selection of accompanying equipment and supplies is based on the—

- Mission.
- Enemy threat.

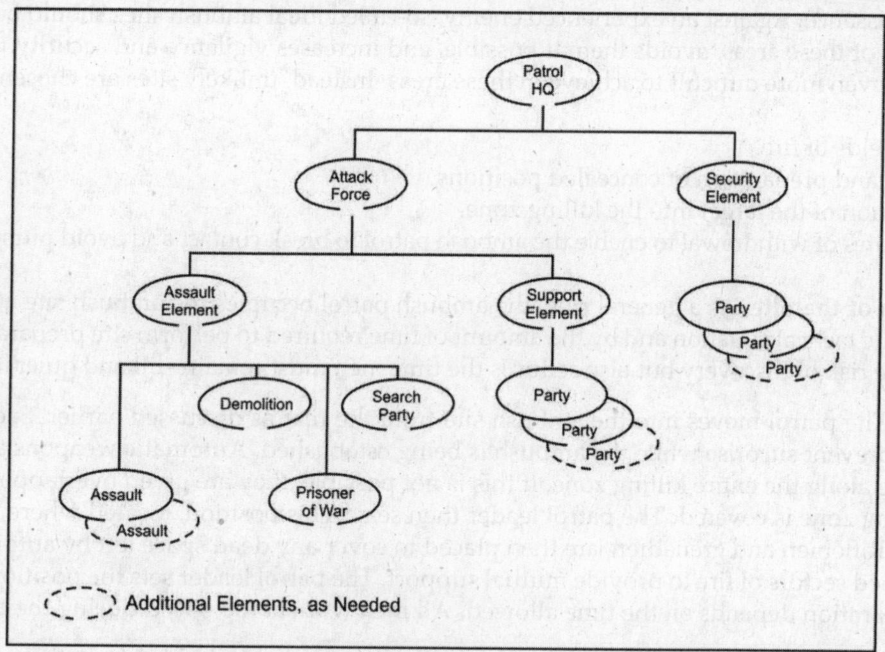

Figure 6-31. Organization of ambush patrols, example 1

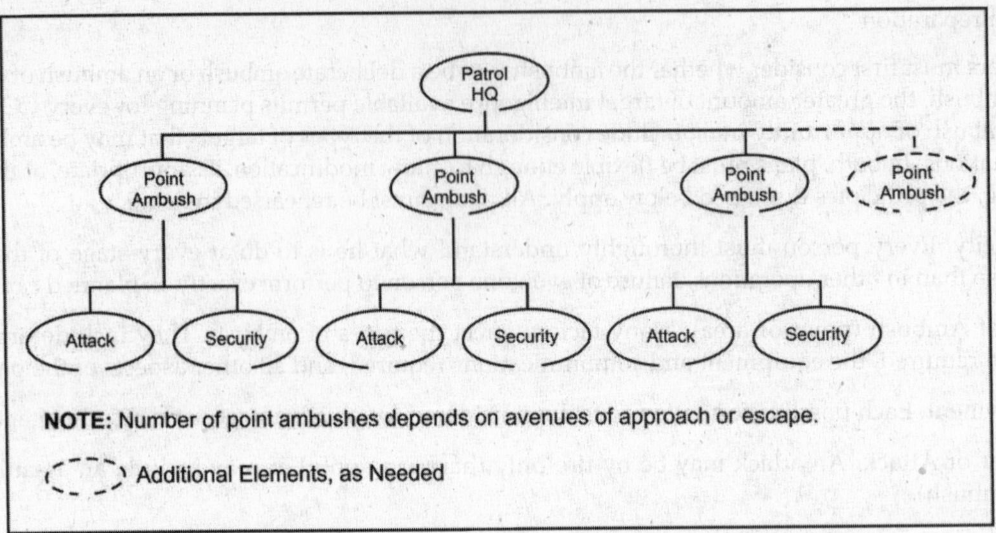

Figure 6-32. Organization of ambush patrols, example 2

- Size of the resistance force.
- Means of transportation.
- Distance and terrain.
- Weight and bulk of equipment.

6-292. **Routes.** A primary route is planned that will allow the patrol to enter the ambush site from the rear. The killing zone is not entered if entry can be avoided. If the killing zone must be entered to place mines or explosives, great care must be taken to remove any tracks and signs that might alert the target and compromise the ambush. If mines, mantraps, or explosives are to be placed on the far side, or if the appearance of the site from the target's viewpoint is to be checked, a wide detour around the killing zone is made. Here, too, great care must be taken to remove any traces that might reveal the ambush. An alternate route from the ambush site is planned, as in other patrols.

6-293. Site. Maps and aerial photographs are used to analyze the terrain. When possible, the patrol makes an on-the-ground reconnaissance. Against an experienced enemy, so-called ideal ambush sites should be avoided. An alert enemy is suspicious of these areas, avoids them if possible, and increases vigilance and security when they must be entered. Surprise is even more difficult to achieve in these areas. Instead, unlikely sites are chosen that offer—

- Favorable fields of fire.
- Occupation and preparation of concealed positions.
- Channelization of the target into the killing zone.
- Covered routes of withdrawal to enable the ambush patrol to break contact and avoid pursuit by effective fire.

6-294. **Occupation of the Site.** As a general rule, the ambush patrol occupies the ambush site at the latest possible time permitted by the tactical situation and by the amount of time required to perform site preparation required. This not only reduces the risk of discovery but also reduces the time men must remain still and quiet in position.

6-295. **Positions.** The patrol moves into the ambush site from the rear as discussed earlier. Security elements are positioned first to prevent surprise while the ambush is being established. Automatic weapons are then positioned so that each can fire along the entire killing zone. If this is not possible, they are given overlapping sectors of fire so that the entire killing zone is covered. The patrol leader then selects his position, located where he can tell when to begin the ambush. Riflemen and grenadiers are then placed to cover any dead space left by automatic weapons. All weapons are assigned sectors of fire to provide mutual support. The patrol leader sets the position preparation time. The degree of preparation depends on the time allowed. All men work at top speed during the allotted time.

6-296. **Camouflage.** Camouflage is of utmost importance. Each man must be hidden from the target. During preparation for the patrol, each man camouflages himself and his equipment and secures his equipment to prevent noise.

At the ambush site, positions are prepared with minimum change in the natural appearance of the site. All debris resulting from preparation of positions is concealed.

Execution

6-297. Effective C2 are essential to mission success. The patrol leader establishes the communications plan and control measures for execution. As the patrol leader makes contact, communications stand a good chance of breaking down. He must plan using the primary, alternate, contingency, and emergency (PACE) method. Rehearsals are conducted to ensure everyone knows and understands the following crucial points.

6-298. **Signals.** Three signals, often four, are needed to execute the ambush. Audible and visual signals, such as whistles and pyrotechnics, must be changed often to avoid establishing patterns. Too frequently, use of the same signals may result in their becoming known to the enemy. A target might recognize a signal and be able to react in time to avoid the full effects of the ambush. For example, if a white star cluster is habitually used to signal withdrawal in a night ambush, an alert enemy may fire one and cause premature withdrawal.

6-299. A signal by the security force to alert the patrol leader to the target's approach may be given by—

- Arm and hand signals.
- Radio (as a quiet voice message), by transmitting a prearranged number of taps, or by signaling with the push-to-talk switch.
- Field telephone, when there is no danger that wire between positions will compromise the ambush.

6-300. A signal to begin the ambush, given by the patrol leader or a designated individual, may be a shot or the detonation of mines or explosives. A signal for lifting or shifting fires, if the target is to be assaulted, may be given by voice command, whistles, or pyrotechnics. All fire must stop immediately so that the assault can be made before the target can react. A signal for withdrawal may also be by voice command, whistles, or pyrotechnics.

6-301. **Fire Discipline.** This is a key part of the ambush. Fire must be withheld until the signal is given, then immediately delivered in the heaviest, most accurate volume possible. Properly timed and delivered fires achieve surprise as well as destruction of the target. When the target is to be assaulted, the lifting or shifting of fires must be equally precise. Otherwise, the assault is delayed and the target has opportunity to recover and react.

6-302. **Withdrawal** to the **ORP**. The ORP is located far enough from the ambush site that it will not be overrun if the target attacks the ambush. Routes of withdrawal to the ORP are reconnoitered. Situation permitting, each person walks the route he is to use and picks out checkpoints. When the ambush is executed at night, each person must be able to follow his route in the dark.

6-303. On signal, the patrol quickly but quietly withdraws to the ORP, reorganizes, and begins its return march. If the ambush was not successful and the patrol is pursued, withdrawal may be by bounds. The last group may arm mines, previously placed along the withdrawal route, to further delay pursuit.

6-304. Contingency plans should include removal of the wounded, both friendly and hostile, under pursuit or at a more measured pace. Treatment location and moves from the target site to a rearward position must be flexible. Plans should also include insertion of medical assets within the assault element, as well as within the HQ. Security and support elements should be considered, depending on the mission.

MINES AND BOOBY TRAPS

6-305. Resistance forces may employ both mines and booby traps to enhance their combat operations. In areas occupied and protected by the enemy, the resistance should employ mines to impede, delay, and disrupt traffic using roads and trails. These actions cause the enemy to divert valuable forces to guard and clear those routes. The personnel and equipment patrolling the roads to detect and remove mines are prime targets for guerrilla mines and snipers. In congested areas where the enemy conducts offensive operations or patrol activities, the guerrillas should employ mines and mechanical booby traps. The mines and booby traps will inflict casualties, delay and channelize movement, and damage or destroy equipment. Mines should be deployed to reduce accidental injury of noncombatants. The resistance makes and uses military homemade mines. Most guerrilla mines are handmade, using duds, discarded ammunition, and materials thrown away by the enemy. Materials discarded as trash, such as improperly destroyed rations, ammunition, beer and soda cans, batteries, waterproof packing materials, and ammunition bandoleers, provide the resistance a valuable source of supply for mining and booby trap operations.

SNIPER OPERATIONS

6-306. Sniping as an interdiction technique has a very demoralizing effect on the enemy. Well-trained and properly used snipers can inflict many casualties. They can hinder or temporarily deny the use of certain routes or areas. Snipers also cause the enemy to use a disproportionate number of troops to clear and secure the area. They must have mission orders outlining priority targets to include key threat personnel. Snipers may cover an area that has been mined to prevent removal or breaching of the minefield. Snipers may be part of a raid or ambush to stop threat personnel from escaping the area under attack. They may also prevent or impede the enemy from reinforcing the objective. Besides their sniping mission, they may collect information for the area command or sector commands. All tactical plans can incorporate sniper missions. Provisions must be made for the sniper's rest and recuperation after continuous operations to prevent fatigue.

MAN-PORTABLE AIR DEFENSE SYSTEMS

6-307. The most recent and large-scale UW operation occurred in Afghanistan between the Soviet Union and the Afghanistan freedom fighter (Mujahideen). They were a formidable guerrilla force against Soviet airborne, air assault, Spetsnaz, and ground forces. Initially, the U.S. Army supplied the Mujahideen with Redeye missiles in the early 1980s but soon followed with improved man-portable air defense systems (MANPADS), the Stinger. With the new system the warhead did not have to get a direct hit; hitting close would cause an explosion.

6-308. The premier Soviet helicopter (HIND-D) has a dual-role capability as an air assault vehicle and a gunship platform. This helicopter was quickly rendered out of action with a well-placed hit on the transmission. The Stinger team easily found and exploited this weakness by aiming at and hitting the large red star behind the cockpit. The Soviets had to alter some of their basic tactical doctrine—use of vehicle-equipped ground forces in conjunction with either a helicopter (HELO) assault or gun run on suspected Mujahideen targets.

6-309. Using MANPADS in a UW role can have a significant tactical and operational impact. MANPADS are relatively new U.S. weapons, light and very mobile. They can be concealed easily for movement or cached for future operations. Most are relatively simple to operate. Guerrillas can quickly learn how to use them, as demonstrated very effectively in Afghanistan. They require little maintenance because the missile is self-contained. Personnel can use these systems in various ways, from the traditional defensive coverage to offensive tactics. Included are aerial ambushes, direct action or attacks on specific targets, and harassment attacks meant either to produce a psychological impact or to change enemy tactics. The degradation of the enemy's close air support pays great dividends, both tactically and psychologically, for the guerrilla.

Considerations

6-310. There are four employment considerations for MANPADS: mass, mix, mobility, and integration. Each of these considerations is discussed in the following paragraphs.

6-311. **Mass.** Units achieve mass employment by allocating enough MANPADS to defend an asset. Soldiers move all the available MANPADS to the key assets or operations that need them.

6-312. **Mix.** Mix results from using different types of weapons; that is, MANPADS and other weapons that may be effective against aircraft. Air defense operations are more effective when the guerrillas use a mix of weapons. This mix of weapons prevents almost any aircraft from countering the weakness of a solitary system with overlapping and concentrated fire. Although a guerrilla force is not likely to use ZSU-23-4s, Vulcans, and Hawks to any large extent, it will more than likely have some of the following or similar weapons systems available:

- ZSU-23s.
- RPG-7s.

- DSHKs.
- M2 HB caliber .50 machine guns.
- Redeyes.
- Stingers.
- Light machine guns and assault rifles.

6-313. **Mobility.** The guerrilla force must be able to move on short notice. Air defense assets must also be able to displace quickly in a UW environment.

6-314. **Integration.** Massing all air defense weapons in a common, coordinated effort provides integration. Units can integrate MANPADS with other weapons for the best effect based on terrain, enemy aerial tactics, and desired effect of the air defense operation, using METT-TC. Air defense personnel may use Stingers to force enemy aircraft to fly at lower altitudes. At lower altitudes, personnel can shoot down the enemy using massed heavy machine guns, rocket-propelled grenades (RPGs), and Stingers.

Employment

6-315. Defensive and offensive uses of MANPADS provide for a balanced defense, overlapping fires, weighted coverage, mutual support, and early engagement. Each use of MANPADS is described below.

6-316. **Balanced Defense.** Critical guerrilla assets may be subject to enemy attack as targets of opportunity. Since the attack can come from any direction, it is desirable to have equal firepower in all directions. The best COA is a balanced defense because the terrain may not favor a most probable avenue of approach by the enemy.

6-317. **Overlapping Fires.** Teams should position MANPADS 2 to 3 kilometers apart, and one team should overlap another. Other types of weapons should be mixed in to complement the MANPADS. This overlapping prevents the MANPADS team from being overwhelmed by multiple aircraft and increases the chances of their successful air defense against any enemy aircraft.

6-318. **Weighted Coverage.** Teams can weight a defense in circumstances where the terrain restricts low-level attacks to only particular avenues of approach. They can also weight a defense when intelligence has established that air attacks will come from a particular direction. Balance may be sacrificed with a weighted defense since most air defense weapons would be positioned to cover the probable direction of approach. The weighted defense then becomes the best COA.

6-319. **Mutual Support.** Support from another MANPADS team allows one to fire into the dead space of the other. If the terrain or situation will not allow covering each other's dead space, teams should make use of similar weapons to cover these areas using Stingers or Redeye missiles.

6-320. **Early Engagement.** Teams should position MANPADS and other similar systems well forward of the guerrilla force's main body or key facilities. This early engagement provides the best opportunity to identify and fix the enemy aircraft before they can attack the guerrillas.

Technical and Tactical Requirements

6-321. In addition to the principles and guidelines previously discussed, there are certain technical and tactical requirements that need to be considered before employing MANPADS. Among the questions are—

- What type of aircraft, ordnance, and electronic countermeasures (ECM) has the threat been using in the area?
- What aerial tactics have the enemy pilots been using in the area?

Terrain and Weather

6-322. Mountains and hills may present terrain-masking problems for MANPADS. Whenever possible, MANPADS teams should position along the commanding heights to detect and engage enemy aircraft effectively. Weather can also adversely affect MANPADS that need an infrared source to lock on. In addition, poor weather conditions, such as snow, fog, or rain, can obscure the gunner's vision.

Routes of Approach

6-323. There are two general categories of routes of approach: probable and forced. A probable route of approach is the one the enemy is most likely to use but to which he is not restricted. A pilot of an aircraft traveling at 500 knots and 150 meters above the ground can see little detail on the ground. He can, however, see large objects (highways, rivers, and buildings) and use them as aids to navigation. If these landmarks lead to key assets, they may be considered a sign of probable approach. A forced route of approach is the one an aircraft will be forced to use and with no options. The forced route will be to the advantage of the guerrilla because he knows the terrain and where he can hide to best engage the aircraft.

Map Analysis and Planning

6-324. Terrain analysis is necessary to find good observation points, fields of fire, routes of approach, and any terrain that may inhibit the full capabilities of MANPADS. The ideal planning range for MANPADS is 3 to 5 kilometers from the target. This positioning greatly enhances their survivability by optimizing the lock-on range to enemy aircraft.

Position Selection

6-325. When selecting positions for MANPADS, personnel should consider observation and fields of fire, communication position, physical security, cover and concealment, alternate positions, and safety considerations.

Offensive Operations

6-326. Aerial ambushes are similar to the ground "baited trap" ambush (Figure 6-33). If the enemy is known to reinforce outposts or ground units with air support, personnel select a target for a ground attack just to draw an aerial response from the enemy. Personnel also select a target that causes a probable or forced avenue of approach for the reinforcing aircraft. The guerrilla MANPADS teams, together with other air defense assets, are positioned at key points

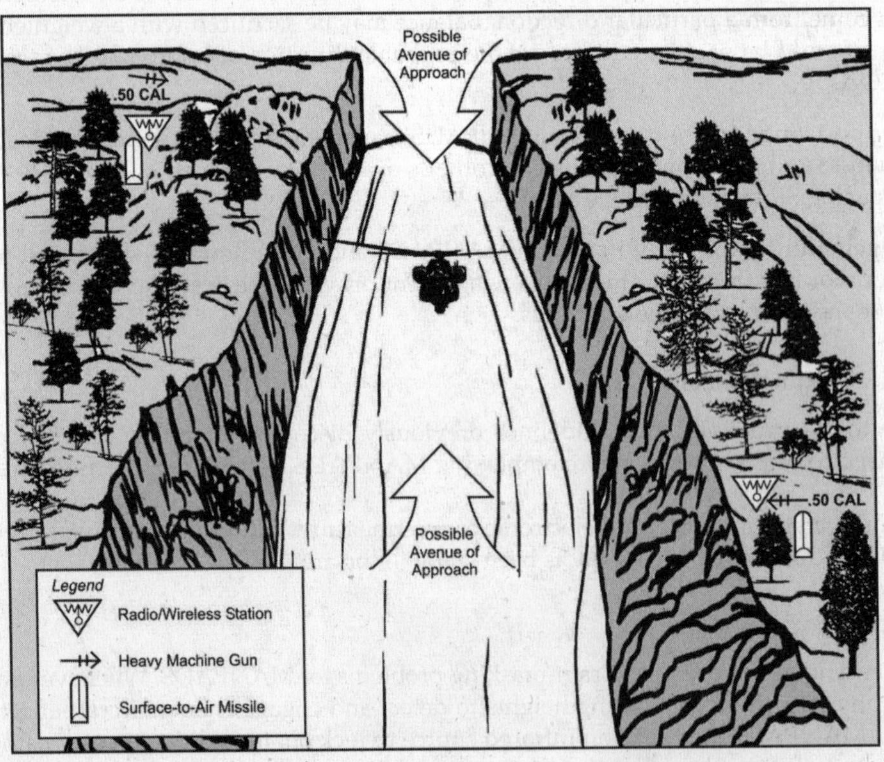

Figure 6-33. MANPADS in offensive operation, aerial ambush

along the aircraft's probable approach route. This pattern is very effective in mountainous terrain where valleys are the prime flight routes. An early warning post radios a timely, forewarning alert to prepare an ambush for the aircraft.

Direct Action

6-327. Units may use MANPADS in a DA role to take out a specific type of aircraft or aircraft with key personnel. This operation is most effective when employed around airfields. An aircraft is very vulnerable when taking off and, to a lesser extent, when landing. The concept is to use at least two MANPADS against the target. Personnel locate firing positions on a curve, 3 to 5 kilometers from the runway, within range and observation of the probable flight path of the aircraft. Personnel must study carefully the flight patterns to confirm this critical information. If the distance to the airfield is kept to 3 kilometers, a centralized positioning can cover flight routes either approaching or departing the airfield. With longer ranges and longer airfields, the MANPADS team must confirm the aircraft approach and takeoff direction and position the MANPADS toward that end of the airfield. The actual employment will depend heavily on the type of MANPADS available and the terrain around the target. When in doubt, personnel should use METT-TC.

Harassment

6-328. The harassment campaign focuses on disrupting the operational procedures of the airport and aircrews. The intended results are to force the pilots to lower their flight altitudes, making them more vulnerable to guerrilla ground fire. Harassment also forces the enemy to decrease its air reconnaissance and support effort.

Defensive Operations

6-329. In addition to the principles and guidelines of MANPADS employment discussed previously, defense planners must take other considerations into account. Personnel must establish air defense priorities first. Developing a priority list is a matter of assessing each asset to be defended. Air defense priorities include criticality, vulnerability, and recuperability.

6-330. Despite the type of defense used, the same principles, guidelines, and air defense priorities still apply. Among the types are stationary point, moving point, integrated, and pre-positioned defenses.

6-331. **Stationary Point.** The key to a stationary point defense is early engagement so that the enemy force cannot destroy the target. If the target is large, such as a series of facilities or units concentrated in a relatively small area, personnel should use a "star"-type defense. This type of defense makes use of interlocking fields of fire, bunkers, trenches, and concertina and tanglefoot wire along with mines and machine guns. Each leg of the star has central and alternate control capability to defend the base camp.

6-332. **Moving Point.** In the past, units have used this defense to defend march columns. In a UW environment, personnel and supplies may have to move in march columns. These columns consist of vehicles, carts, pack animals, bicycles, and personnel traveling on foot. Personnel use MANPADS to defend the columns by integration or pre-positioning.

6-333. **Integration.** If personnel decide to integrate MANPADS into the march column, they should deploy them evenly along the length of the column. This pattern ensures other weapon systems are tied in to complement the overall air defense plan. When only one MANPADS team of two men is available, both men should only be gunners. A single MANPADS should be placed in the column where it can provide the best air cover.

6-334. **Pre-Positioning.** Personnel pre-position MANPADS to defend a march column as it passes a critical point along the route. This method is preferred for defending a march column. Personnel use it when the distance to be traveled by the march column is relatively short. They also use it when air defense is required at only a few locations along the route. The MANPADS teams may join and integrate with the column after it passes the critical point (Figure 6-34). The MANPADS teams may each receive orders, positioning themselves at a given location. They are then given engagement instructions for a specific window of time. This plan allows both for maintaining OPSEC and receiving air defense coverage. Pre-positioned teams should be used only if the route to be used is relatively secure from enemy patrols (METT-TC) or current guerrilla intelligence reports reflect enemy patrols are minimal.

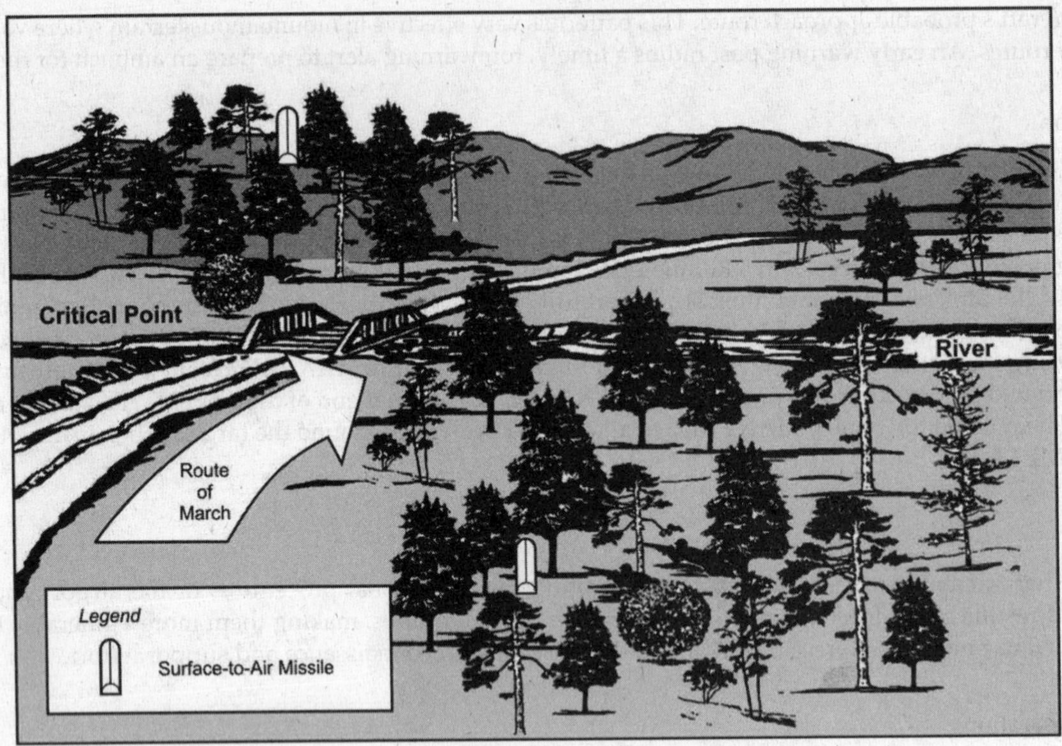

Figure 6-34. MANPADS pre-positioning at critical point defending a march column

SUPPORT AND SUSTAINMENT

6-335. UW missions cannot be accomplished without adequate support and sustainment. All units need food, clothing, water, medical, and personnel services sustainment. The types, quantity, and phasing of supplies influence the guerrillas, their capabilities and limitations, and the type of missions they undertake. Supplies and equipment made available to the guerrillas may influence their morale since each shipment represents encouragement and assurance of support from the outside world. Once a channel of supply is established, the guerrillas will continue to rely on that source for support. Appendix E and Appendix K provide additional information.

INDICATORS OF COUNTERGUERRILLA OPERATIONS

6-336. Tactical counterguerrilla operations are conducted to reduce the guerrilla threat or activity in the area. To effectively combat the enemy's counterguerrilla operations, soldiers must be familiar with the indicators of counterguerrilla operations, effective offensive and defensive tactics, and countertracking methods.

6-337. Security of the UW JSOA requires guerrilla intelligence measures to identify indications of impending counterguerrilla action, population control measures, and guerrilla reaction to enemy counterguerrilla actions. Some activities and conditions that may indicate impending enemy counterguerrilla actions are—

- Suitable weather.
- New enemy commander.
- Changes in battle situation elsewhere.
- Arrival of new enemy units with special training.
- Extension of enemy outposts, increased patrolling, and aerial reconnaissance.
- Increased enemy intelligence effort.
- Civilian pacification or control measures.
- Increased PSYOP against guerrillas.

6-338. Some measures that may be used to control the population of an area are—

- Mass registration.
- Curfews.
- Intensive propaganda.
- Compartmentation with cleared buffer zones.
- Informant nets.
- Party membership drives.
- Land and housing reform.
- Relocation of individuals, groups, and towns.
- Rationing of food and goods.

DEFENSIVE TACTICS

6-339. The existence or indication of counterguerrilla operations requires the SF and guerrilla force commanders to plan and use defensive tactics. Discussed below are some of the defensive tactics applicable against counterguerrilla operations.

Diversion Activities

6-340. A sudden increase in guerrilla activities or a shift of such activities to other areas assists in diverting enemy attention. For example, intensified operations against enemy LOCs and installations require the enemy to divert troops from counterguerrilla operations to security roles. Full use of underground and auxiliary capabilities assists in creating diversions.

Defense of Fixed Positions

6-341. The rules for a guerrilla defense of fixed positions are the same as those for conventional forces, except there are few supporting fires and counterattacks are generally not practicable. In conjunction with their position defense, elements of the guerrilla force conduct raids, ambushes, and attacks against the enemy's LOCs, flanks, reserve units, supporting arms, and installations. Routes of approach are mined and camouflaged snipers engage appropriate enemy targets. Diversionary actions by all elements of the resistance movement are increased in adjacent areas.

Delay and Harassment Activities

6-342. The objective of delay and harassment tactics is to make the attack so costly that the enemy eventually ends its operations. Defensive characteristics of the terrain are used to the maximum, mines and snipers are employed to harass the enemy, and ambushes are positioned to inflict maximum casualties and delay.

6-343. As the enemy overruns various strong points, the guerrilla force withdraws to successive defensive positions to again delay and harass. When the situation permits, the guerrilla force attacks the enemy's flanks, rear, and LOCs. If the enemy continues its offensive, the guerrilla forces should withdraw and leave the area. Under no circumstances should the guerrilla force become so engaged that it loses its freedom of action and permits enemy forces to encircle and destroy it.

Withdrawal

6-344. In preparing to meet enemy offensive action, the SF and guerrilla force commanders may decide to withdraw to another area not likely to be included in the enemy offensive. Key installations within a guerrilla base are moved to alternate bases, and essential records and supplies may be transferred to new locations. Less essential items will be destroyed or cached in dispersed locations. If the commander receives positive intelligence about the enemy's plans for a major counterguerrilla operation, he may decide to withdraw and leave his main base without delay.

6-345. When faced with an enemy offensive of overwhelming strength, the commander may disperse his force in either small units or as individuals to avoid destruction. This COA, however, renders the guerrilla force ineffective for an undetermined period of time and therefore should not be taken unless absolutely necessary.

COUNTERAMBUSH

6-346. The very nature of ambush—a surprise attack from a concealed position—places the ambushed unit at a disadvantage. Obviously, the best defense is to avoid being ambushed, but this is not always possible. A unit must, therefore, reduce its vulnerability to ambush and reduce the damage it will sustain if ambushed. These measures must be supplemented by measures to destroy or escape from an ambush.

Reduction of Vulnerability to Ambush

6-347. No single defensive measure or combination of measures can prevent or effectively counter all ambushes in all situations. The effectiveness of counterambush measures is directly related to the state of training of the unit and the leadership ability of its leader.

6-348. In avoiding ambush, dismounted units have an advantage over mounted units. They are less bound to the more obvious routes of movement, such as roads and trails (as in armored units). However, dismounted units are at a disadvantage when—

- Terrain, such as heavy jungle, restricts or prohibits cross-country movement.
- The need for speed requires movement on roads, trails, or waterways.

Preparation for Movement

6-349. In preparing for movement, the leader must use METT-TC and OAKOC. In doing so, he studies maps of the area and if possible, makes an aerial reconnaissance.

Map Reconnaissance

6-350. In studying maps of the terrain over which the leader will move his unit, the leader first checks the map's marginal data to determine reliability at the time the map was made. If reliability is not good, or if the map is old, he evaluates its reliability in light of all other information he can obtain. For example, a 20-year-old map may not show several nearby roads and trails! more recent building development in the area will not be shown. The leader considers the terrain in relation to all available information of known or suspected enemy positions and previous ambush sites. His map study includes evaluation of the terrain from the enemy's viewpoint: How would the enemy use this terrain? Where could the enemy position troops, installations, and ambushes?

Aerial Reconnaissance

6-351. If possible, the leader makes an aerial reconnaissance. The information gained from the aerial reconnaissance enables him to compare the map and terrain. He also obtains current and more complete information on roads, trails, man-made objects, type and density of vegetation, and seasonal condition of streams. An aerial reconnaissance reveals—

- Movement or lack of movement in an area (friendly, enemy, civilian).
- Indications of enemy activity. Smoke may indicate locations of campsites, patrols, or patrol bases. Freshly dug soil may indicate positions or ambush sites. Shadows may aid in identifying objects. Unusual shapes, sizes, shadows, shades, or colors may indicate faulty camouflage.

6-352. Despite its many advantages, aerial reconnaissance has limitations. Some examples include the following:

- Strength of bridges cannot be determined.
- Terrain surface may be misinterpreted.
- Mines and booby traps cannot be seen.
- Presence of aircraft may warn enemy.

ROUTE SELECTION

6-353. The factors the leader considers are the same whether he is selecting a route or studying a route he has been directed to follow. Each factor is discussed below.

Cover and Concealment

6-354. Cover and concealment are desirable, but a route with these features may obstruct movement. Terrain that provides a moving unit cover and concealment also provides the enemy increased opportunities for ambush. Identification of areas where ambushes may be concealed allows the leader to develop plans for clearing these areas. How the terrain affects *observation* and *fields of fire* available to the unit and to the enemy will influence the selection of and movement over a route, formations, rates of movement, and methods of control.

Key Terrain

6-355. Key terrain is an earth feature that has a controlling effect on the surrounding terrain. It must be identified and actions planned accordingly. If, for example, a hill provides observation and fields of fire on any part of a route, the leader must plan for taking the hill from the enemy or avoiding it altogether.

Obstacles

6-356. Obstacles may impede movement or limit maneuver along a route. They may also limit enemy action.

Current Intelligence

6-357. All available information is considered. This includes but is not limited to—

- Known, suspected, and previous ambush sites.
- Weather and light data.
- Reports of units or patrols that have recently operated in the area.
- Size, location, activity, and capabilities of guerrilla forces in the area.
- Attitude of the civilian population and the extent to which they can be expected to cooperate or interfere.

Counterintelligence

6-358. In counterguerrilla operations, in particular, a key feature of preparing for movement is denying the enemy information. A unit is especially vulnerable to ambush if the enemy knows the unit is to move, what time it is to move, where it is to go, the route it is to follow, and the weapons and equipment it is to carry. The efforts made to deny or delay enemy acquisition of this information comprise the CI plan. As a minimum, the plan restricts dissemination of information.

6-359. The leader gives out mission information only on a need-to-know basis. This procedure is especially important when the native personnel operating with the unit might possibly be planted informers. Once critical information is given, personnel are isolated so that nothing can be passed out. if it is likely that the enemy or enemy informers will observe the departure of a unit, deception plans should be used.

Communications

6-360. The leader plans how he will communicate with elements of his unit; with artillery, air, or other supporting units; and with higher HQ. On an extended move, a radio relay or a field-expedient antenna may be necessary. An aircraft might be used to help communicate with air, artillery support, or other units on the ground.

Fire Support

6-361. The leader plans artillery and mortar fires so they will deceive, harass, or destroy the enemy. They may be planned as scheduled or on-call fires.

6-362. Fires are planned—

- On key terrain features along the route. These can serve as navigational aids or to deceive, harass, or destroy the enemy.
- On known enemy positions.
- On known or suspected ambush sites.

- On the flanks of identified danger areas.
- Wherever a diversion appears desirable. For example, if the unit must pass near an identified enemy position, artillery or mortar fires on the position may distract the enemy and permit the unit to pass undetected.
- At intervals along the route, every 500 to 1000 meters for example. With fires so planned, the unit is never far from a plotted concentration from which a shift can be quickly made.

6-363. Coordination with the supporting unit includes—

- Route to be followed.
- Scheduled and on-call fires.
- Call signs and frequencies.
- Checkpoints, phase lines, and other control measures.
- Times of departure and return.

INTELLIGENCE

6-364. The unit must provide its own intelligence support. Members must be alert to report information and leaders must be able to evaluate the significance of this information in relation to the situation.

6-365. Obvious items from which intelligence may be gained are—

- Signs of passage of groups, such as crushed grass, broken branches, footprints, cigarette butts, or trash. These may reveal identity, size, direction of travel, and time of passage.
- Workers in fields, which may indicate absence of the enemy.
- Apparently normal activities in villages, which may indicate absence of the enemy.

6-366. Less obvious items from which negative information can be gained are the absence of—

- Workers in fields, which may indicate presence of the enemy.
- Children in the village, which may indicate they are being protected from impending action.
- Young men in the village, which may indicate the enemy controls the village.

6-367. Knowledge of enemy signaling devices is very helpful. Those listed below are some that were used by communist guerrillas in Vietnam.

- A farm cart moving at night shows one lantern to indicate that no government troops are on the road or trail behind. Two lanterns mean that government troops are close behind.
- A worker in the field stops to put on or take off his shirt. Either act can signal the approach of government troops. This is relayed to the insurgency.
- A villager, fishing, holds his pole out straight to signal all clear and up at an angle to signal that troops are approaching.

SECURITY

6-368. Security is obtained through organization for movement, manner of movement, and by every man keeping alert at all times. Some examples of these security measures are as follows:

- A two-man patrol can maintain security by organizing into a security team with sectors of responsibility.
- A larger unit can use any standard formation (file, column, V) and establish a reaction force. This reaction force can be positioned to the front, rear, or flanks of the main body so that it does not come under direct contact. Any unit of squad or larger, regardless of the formation used, should have security forces to the front, flanks, and rear.
- A dismounted unit moves by the same methods as a motorized patrol. These methods include continuous movement and traveling, traveling overwatch, and bounding overwatch formations.

COUNTERTRACKING

6-369. To be more effective in combatting counterguerrilla operations, soldiers should be familiar with countertracking techniques. If the person tracking the soldier is not an experienced tracker, some of the following techniques may throw him off.

Moving From a Thick Area to an Open Area

6-370. While moving in any given direction from a thick area to a more open area, soldiers walk past a large (10-inch diameter or larger) tree toward the open vegetation for five paces and then walk backward to the front of the tree and change direction 90 degrees. Soldiers must step carefully and leave as little sign as possible. If this is not the direction the soldiers want to travel, they must change direction again at another large tree in the same manner. The purpose is to draw the trackers into the open area where it is harder to track. This technique may lead the trackers to search in the wrong area before realizing they have lost the track.

6-371. When soldiers are being tracked by trained, persistent enemy trackers (those the soldiers are unable to lose because the trackers keep hearing or seeing them), the soldiers' best COA is to outrun or outdistance the trackers or double back and ambush them, depending on their strength compared to that of the soldiers.

Crossing a Road

6-372. Soldiers approach a trail from an angle and enter the trail in the direction they want to be followed, leaving considerable signs of their presence. After about 30 meters, soldiers walk backward to the point they entered the trail and exit in another direction leaving no sign. Soldiers move off on an angle opposite the one they entered the trail on for about 100 meters and change direction to their desired line of march.

Leaving Footprints

6-373. Soldiers walk backward over soft ground to leave reasonably clear footprints. They try not to leave every footprint clear and do not leave an impression of more than 1/4 inch deep. Soldiers continue this deception until they are on hard ground. They select the ground carefully to ensure that they have at least 20 to 30 meters of this deception. This technique should always be used when exiting a river or stream and can be used in conjunction with all other techniques as well. To add even further confusion to the following party, this tactic can be used several times to lay false trails before actually leaving the stream.

Crossing a Stream

6-374. When approaching a stream, soldiers approach at an angle in the same manner as a road. They move downstream for about 30 meters, backtrack, and move off into the intended direction. To delay the trackers, soldiers set up false tracks leaving footprints as described above.

6-375. Below are some additional tactics that soldiers can use to aid in eluding a following party:

- Stay in the stream for 100 to 200 meters.
- Keep in the center of the stream and in deep water.
- Watch (near the banks) for rocks or roots that are not covered with moss or vegetation, and leave the stream at this point.
- Walk out backward on soft ground.
- Walk up small, vegetation-covered tributaries and replace the vegetation, in its natural position.
- Walk downstream until coming to the main river, and then depart on a log or pre-positioned boat.
- Enter the stream, having first carried out the above tactic, then exit at the point of entry and make a large backward loop, crossing and checking it, and move off in a different direction.

> **NOTE**
>
> Using a stream as a deception technique is one of the best ways to slow down and lose a following party. The deception starts 100 meters from the stream and the successful completion of the tactic is to ensure that the following party does not know where to exit from the stream.

Camouflage Techniques

6-376. Walking backward to leave confusing footprints, brushing out trails, and moving over rocky ground or through streams are examples of camouflage techniques that may be used to confuse the tracker. Moving on hard surfaces or frequently traveled trails may also aid in eluding the tracker. Soldiers should avoid walking on moss-covered rocks as they can be easily displaced.

Techniques Used to Confuse Dogs

6-377. Enemy tracking teams may use dogs to aid in tracking the soldiers. Soldiers may confuse or delay dogs by—

- Scattering black or red pepper or, if authorized, a riot control agent (such as CS powder) along the route.
- Using silence-suppressed weapons against animals.

PART IV

Survive at All Costs

The Code of Conduct

ARTICLE I

I am an American, fighting in the forces which guard my country and our way of life. I am prepared to give my life in their defense.

ARTICLE II

I will never surrender of my own free will. If in command, I will never surrender the members of my command while they still have the means to resist.

ARTICLE III

If I am captured, I will continue to resist by all means available. I will make every effort to escape and aid others to escape. I will accept neither parole nor special favors from the enemy.

ARTICLE IV

If I become a prisoner of war, I will keep faith with my fellow prisoners. I will give no information or take part in any action which might be harmful to my comrades. If I am senior, I will take command. If not, I will obey the lawful orders of those appointed over me and will back them up in every way.

ARTICLE V

When questioned, should I become a prisoner of war, I am required to give name, rank, service number and date of birth. I will evade answering further questions to the utmost of my ability. I will make no oral or written statements disloyal to my country and its allies or harmful to their cause.

ARTICLE VI

I will never forget that I am an American, fighting for freedom, responsible for my actions, and dedicated to the principles which made my country free. I will trust in my God and in the United States of America.

Quick Checklist

DECIDE TO SURVIVE!

S - **S**ize up the situation, surroundings, physical condition, equipment.

U - **U**se all your senses

R - **R**emember where you are.

V - **V**anquish fear and panic.

I - **I**mprovise and improve.

V - **V**alue living.

A - **A**ct like the natives.

L - **L**ive by your wits.

1. IMMEDIATE ACTIONS

a. Assess immediate situation. *THINK BEFORE YOU ACT!*
b. Take action to protect yourself from nuclear, biological, or chemical hazards (Chapter IX).
c. Seek a concealed site.
d. Assess medical condition; treat as necessary (Chapter V).
e. Sanitize uniform of potentially compromising information.
f. Sanitize area; hide equipment you are leaving.
g. Apply personal camouflage.
h. Move away from concealed site, zigzag pattern recommended.
i. Use terrain to advantage, communication, and concealment.
j. Find a hole-up site.

2. HOLE-UP-SITE (CHAPTER I)

a. Reassess situation; treat injuries, then inventory equipment.
b. Review plan of action; establish priorities (Chapter VI).
c. Determine current location.
d. Improve camouflage.
e. Focus thoughts on task(s) at hand.
f. Execute plan of action. Stay flexible!

3. CONCEALMENT (CHAPTER I)

a. Select a place of concealment providing—
   (1) Adequate concealment, ground and air.
   (2) Safe distance from enemy positions and lines of communications (LOC).

(3) Listening and observation points.
(4) Multiple avenues of escape.
(5) Protection from the environment.
(6) Possible communications/signaling opportunities.

b. Stay alert, maintain security.
c. Drink water.

4. MOVEMENT (CHAPTERS I AND II)

a. Travel slowly and deliberately.
b. *DO NOT* leave evidence of travel; use noise and light discipline.
c. Stay away from LOC.
d. Stop, look, listen, and smell; take appropriate action(s).
e. Move from one concealed area to another.
f. Use evasion movement techniques (Chapter I).

5. COMMUNICATIONS AND SIGNALING (CHAPTER III)

a. Communicate as directed in applicable plans/orders, particularly when considering transmitting ***in the blind***.
b. Be prepared to use communications and signaling devices on short notice.
c. Use of communications and signaling devices may compromise position.

6. RECOVERY (CHAPTER IV)

a. Select site(s) IAW criteria in theater recovery plans.
b. Ensure site is free of hazards; secure personal gear.
c. Select best area for communications and signaling devices.
d. Observe site for proximity to enemy activity and LOC.
e. Follow recovery force instructions.

CHAPTER 1

Evasion

1. PLANNING

a. Review the quick reference checklist on the inside cover.
b. Guidelines for successful evasion include—
   (1) Keeping a positive attitude.
   (2) Using established procedures.
   (3) Following your evasion plan of action.
   (4) Being patient.
   (5) Drinking water (***DO NOT*** eat food without water).
   (6) Conserving strength for critical periods.
   (7) Resting and sleeping as much as possible.
   (8) Staying out of sight.
c. The following odors stand out and may give an evader away:
   (1) Scented soaps and shampoos.
   (2) Shaving cream, after-shave lotion, or other cosmetics.
   (3) Insect repellent (camouflage stick is least scented).
   (4) Gum and candy (smell is strong or sweet).
   (5) Tobacco (odor is unmistakable).
d. Where to go (initiate evasion plan of action):
   (1) Near a suitable area for recovery.
   (2) Selected area for evasion.
   (3) Neutral or friendly country or area.
   (4) Designated area for recovery.

2. CAMOUFLAGE

a. Basic principles:
   (1) Disturb the area as little as possible.
   (2) Avoid activity that reveals movement to the enemy.
   (3) Apply personal camouflage.
b. Camouflage patterns **(Figure 1-1)**:
   (1) Blotch pattern.
      (a) Temperate deciduous (leaf shedding) areas.
      (b) Desert areas (barren).
      (c) Snow (barren).
   (2) Slash pattern.
      (a) Coniferous areas (broad slashes).
      (b) Jungle areas (broad slashes).
      (c) Grass (narrow slashes).
   (3) Combination. May use blotched and slash together.
c. Personal camouflage application follows:
   (1) Face. Use dark colors on high spots and light colors on any remaining exposed areas. Use a hat, netting, or mask if available.
   (2) Ears. The insides and the backs should have **2** colors to break up outlines.
   (3) Head, neck, hands, and the under chin. Use scarf, collar, vegetation, netting, or coloration methods.

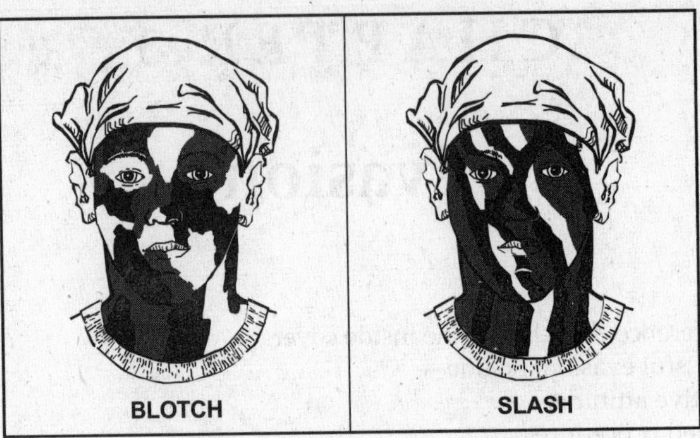

Figure 1-1. Camouflage patterns

(4) Light colored hair. Give special attention to conceal with a scarf or mosquito head net.

d. Position and movement camouflage follows:
   (1) Avoid unnecessary movement.
   (2) Take advantage of natural concealment:
      (a) Cut foliage fades and wilts, change regularly.
      (b) Change camouflage depending on the surroundings.
      (c) *DO NOT* select vegetation from same source.
      (d) Use stains from grasses, berries, dirt, and charcoal.
   (3) *DO NOT* over camouflage.
   (4) Remember when using shadows, they shift with the sun.
   (5) Never expose shiny objects (like a watch, glasses, or pens).
   (6) Ensure watch alarms and hourly chimes are turned off.
   (7) Remove unit patches, name tags, rank insignia, etc.
   (8) Break up the outline of the body, *"V"* of crotch/armpits.
   (9) Conduct observation from a prone and concealed position.

3. SHELTERS

a. Use camouflage and concealment.
b. Locate carefully—easy to remember acronym: ***BLISS.***

B - Blend
L - Low silhouette
I - Irregular shape
S - Small
S - Secluded location

(1) Choose an area—
   (a) Least likely to be searched (drainages, rough terrain, etc.) and blends with the environment.
   (b) With escape routes (*DO NOT* corner yourself).
   (c) With observable approaches.

(2) Locate entrances and exits in brush and along ridges, ditches, and rocks to keep from forming paths to site.

(3) Be wary of flash floods in ravines and canyons.
(4) Conceal with minimal to no preparation.
(5) Take the direction finding threat into account before transmitting from shelter.
(6) Ensure overhead concealment.

4. MOVEMENT

a. A moving object is easy to spot. If travel is necessary—
   (1) Mask with natural cover **(Figure 1-2)**.
   (2) Use the military crest.
   (3) Restrict to periods of low light, bad weather, wind, or reduced enemy activity.

Figure 1-2. Ground movement

   (4) Avoid silhouetting **(Figure 1-3)**.
   (5) At irregular intervals—
      (a) ***STOP*** at a point of concealment.
      (b) ***LOOK*** for signs of human or animal activity (smoke, tracks, roads, troops, vehicles, aircraft, wire, buildings, etc.). Watch for trip wires or booby traps and avoid leaving evidence of travel. Peripheral vision is more effective for recognizing movement at night and twilight.
      (c) ***LISTEN*** for vehicles, troops, aircraft, weapons, animals, etc.
      (d) ***SMELL*** for vehicles, troops, animals, fires, etc.
   (6) Employ noise discipline; check clothing and equipment for items that could make noise during movement and secure them.

b. Break up the human shape or recognizable lines.

c. Route selection requires detailed planning and special techniques (irregular route/zigzag) to camouflage evidence of travel.

Figure 1-3. Avoid silhouetting

d. Some techniques for concealing evidence of travel follows:
   (1) Avoid disturbing the vegetation above knee level.
   (2) ***DO NOT*** break branches, leaves, or grass.
   (3) Use a walking stick to part vegetation and push it back to its original position.
   (4) ***DO NOT*** grab small trees or brush. (This may scuff the bark or create movement that is easily spotted. In snow country, this creates a path of snowless vegetation revealing your route.)
   (5) Pick firm footing (carefully place the foot lightly but squarely on the surface to avoid slipping). ***TRY NOT TO—***
      (a) Overturn ground cover, rocks, and sticks.
      (b) Scuff bark on logs and sticks.
      (c) Make noise by breaking sticks. (Cloth wrapped around feet helps muffle this.)
      (d) Mangle grass and bushes that normally spring back.
   (6) Mask unavoidable tracks in soft footing by—
      (a) Placing tracks in the shadows of vegetation, downed logs, and snowdrifts.
      (b) Moving before and during precipitation allows tracks to fill in.
      (c) Traveling during windy periods.
      (d) Taking advantage of solid surfaces (logs, rocks, etc.) leaving less evidence of travel.
      (e) Patting out tracks lightly to speed their breakdown or make them look old.
   (7) Secure trash or loose equipment—hide or bury discarded items. (Trash or lost equipment identifies who lost it.)
   (8) Concentrate on defeating the handler if pursued by dogs.

e. Penetrate obstacles as follows:
   (1) Enter deep ditches feet first to avoid injury.
   (2) Go around chain-link and wire fences. Go under fence if unavoidable, crossing at damaged areas. ***DO NOT*** touch fence; look for electrical insulators or security devices.
   (3) Penetrate rail fences, passing under or between lower rails. If impractical, go over the top, presenting as low a silhouette as possible **(Figure 1-4).**
   (4) Cross roads after observation from concealment to determine enemy activity. Cross at points offering concealment such as bushes, shadows, bend in road, etc. Cross in a manner leaving your footprints parallel (cross step sideways) to the road. **(Figure 1-5).**
   (5) Use same method of observation for railroad tracks that was used for roads. Next, align body parallel to tracks with face down, cross tracks using a semi-pushup motion. Repeat for the second track. **(Figure 1-6).**

Figure 1-4. Rail fences

Figure 1-5. Road crossing

Figure 1-6. Railroad tracks

WARNING
If 3 rails exist, 1 may be electrified.

CHAPTER 2

Navigation

Assess the threat and apply appropriate evasion principles.

1. STAY OR MOVE CONSIDERATIONS

a. Stay with the vehicle/aircraft in a non-combat environment.
b. Leave only when—
   (1) Dictated by the threat.
   (2) Are certain of your location, have a known destination, and have the ability to get there.
   (3) Can reach water, food, shelter, and/or help.
   (4) Convinced rescue is not coming.
c. Consider the following if you decide to travel:
   (1) Follow the briefed evasion plan.
   (2) Determine which direction to travel and why.
   (3) Decide what equipment to take, cache, or destroy.
d. Leave information at your starting point (in a non-combat environment) that includes—
   (1) Destination.
   (2) Route of travel.
   (3) Personal condition.
   (4) Supplies available.
e. Consider the following for maps (in a combat environment):
   (1) ***DO NOT*** write on the map.
   (2) ***DO NOT*** soil the map by touching the destination.
   (3) ***DO NOT*** fold in a manner providing travel information.

NOTE
These actions may compromise information if captured.

2. NAVIGATION AND POSITION DETERMINATION

a. Determine your general location by—
   (1) Developing a working knowledge of the operational area.
      (a) Geographic checkpoints.
      (b) Man-made checkpoints.
      (c) Previous knowledge of operational area.
   (2) Using the ***Rate × Time = Distance*** formula.
   (3) Using information provided in the map legend.
   (4) Using prominent landmarks.
   (5) Visualizing map to determine position.
b. Determine cardinal directions (north, south, east, and west) by—
   (1) Using compass.

CAUTION

The following methods are *NOT* highly accurate and give only general cardinal direction.

(2) Using stick and shadow method to determine a true north-south line **(Figure 2-1)**.
(3) Remembering the sunrise/moonrise is in the east and sunset/moonset is in the west.
(4) Using a wristwatch to determine general cardinal direction **(Figure 2-2)**.
  (a) Digital watches. Visualize a clock face on the watch.
  (b) Northern Hemisphere. Point hour hand at the sun. South is halfway between the hour hand and 12 o'clock position.
  (c) Southern Hemisphere. Point the 12 o'clock position on your watch at the sun. North is halfway between the 12 o'clock position and the hour hand.
(5) Using a pocket navigator **(Figure 2-3)**—
  (a) Gather the following necessary materials:
  - Flat writing material (such as an MRE box).
  - 1-2 inch shadow tip device (a twig, nail, or match).
  - Pen or pencil.

  (b) Start construction at sunup; end construction at sundown. Do the following:
  - Attach shadow tip device in center of paper.
  - Secure navigator on flat surface (*DO NOT* move during set up period).
  - Mark tip of shadow every 30 minutes annotating the time.
  - Connect marks to form an arc.
  - Indicate north with a drawn arrow.

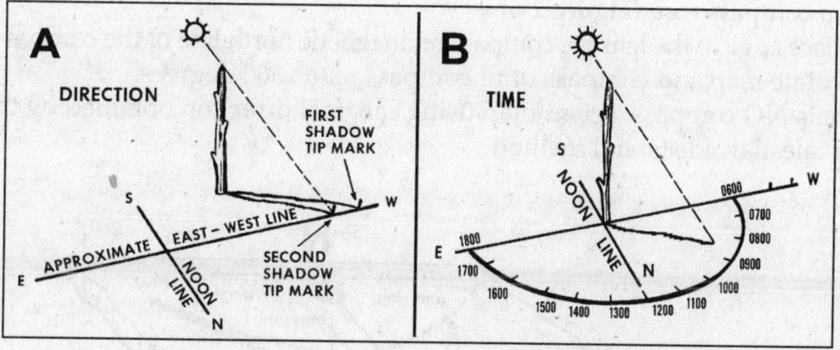

Figure 2-1. Stick and shadow method

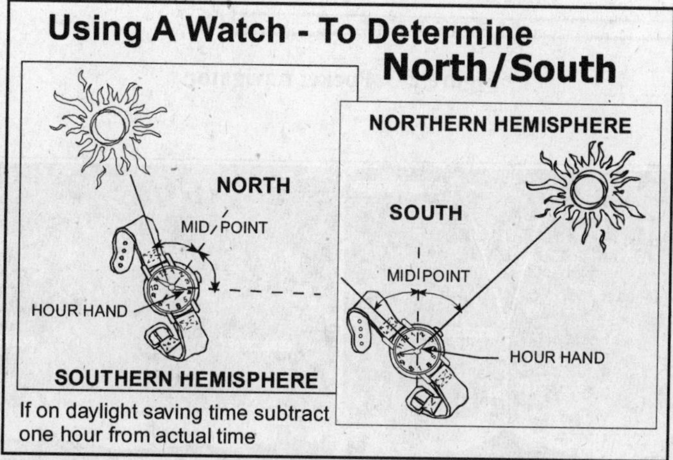

Figure 2-2. Direction using a watch

NOTE

The shortest line between base of shadow tip device and curved line is a north-south line.

(c) Do the following during travel:
- Hold navigator so the shadow aligns with mark of present time (drawn arrow now points to true north).

(d) Remember the navigator is current for approximately 1 week.

CAUTION

The Pocket Navigator is *NOT* recommended if evading.

(6) Using the stars **(Figure 2-4)** the—
(a) North Star is used to locate true north-south line.
(b) Southern Cross is used to locate true south-north line.

c. Orient the map by—
(1) Using a true north-south line **(Figure 2-5)**—
(a) Unfold map and place on a firm, flat, level nonmetallic surface.
(b) Align the compass on a true north-south line.
(c) Rotate map and compass until stationary index line aligns with the magnetic variation indicated in marginal information.
- Easterly (subtract variation from 360 degrees).
- Westerly (add variation to 360 degrees).

(2) Using a compass rose **(Figure 2-6)**—
(a) Place edge of the lensatic compass on magnetic north line of the compass rose closest to your location.
(b) Rotate map and compass until compass reads 360 degrees.

(3) If there is **NO** compass, orient map using cardinal direction obtained by the stick and shadow method or the celestial aids (stars) method.

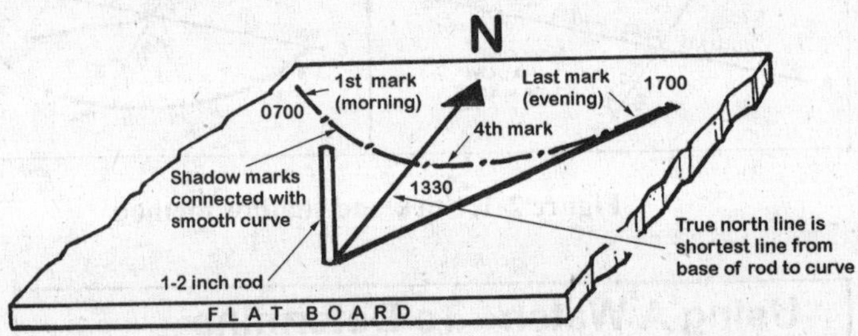

Figure 2-3. Pocket navigator

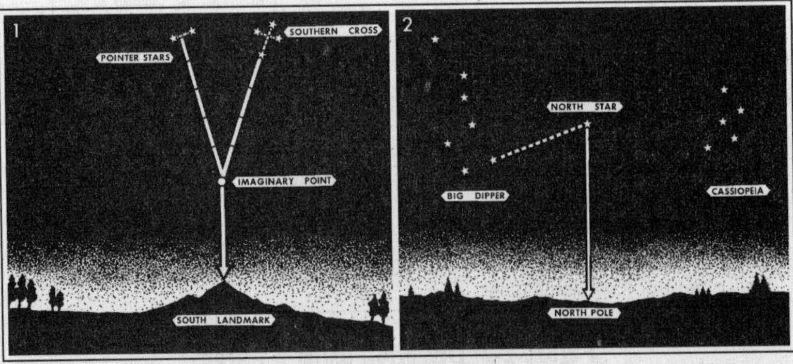

Figure 2-4. Stars

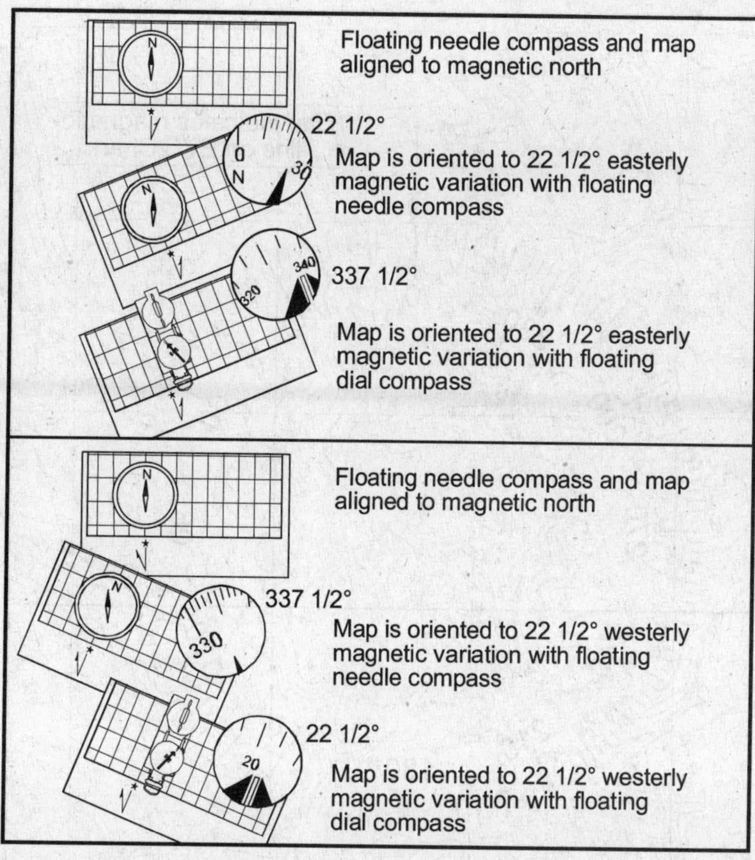

Figure 2-5. Orienting a map using a true north-south line

d. Determine specific location.
   (1) Global Positioning System (GPS).
      (a) ***DO NOT*** use GPS for primary navigation.
      (b) Use GPS to confirm your position ***ONLY***.
      (c) Select area providing maximum satellite reception.
      (d) Conserve GPS battery life.
   (2) Triangulation (resection) with a compass **(Figure 2-7)**.
      (a) Try to use **3** or more azimuths.
      (b) Positively identify a major land feature and determine a line of position (LOP).
      (c) Check map orientation each time compass is used.
      (d) Plot the LOP using a thin stick or blade of grass (combat) or pencil line (non-combat).
      (e) Repeat steps **(b)** through **(d)** for other LOPs.
e. Use the compass for night navigation by—
   (1) Setting up compass for night navigation **(Figure 2-8)**.
   (2) Aligning north-seeking arrow with luminous line and follow front of compass.
   (3) Using point-to-point navigation.
f. Route selection techniques follow:
   (1) Circumnavigation.
      (a) Find a prominent landmark on the opposite side of the obstacle.
      (b) Contour around obstacle to landmark.
      (c) Resume your route of travel.
   (2) Dogleg and 90 degree offset **(Figure 2-9)**.
   (3) Straight-line heading as follows:
      (a) Maintain heading until reaching destination.
      (b) Measure distance by counting the number of paces in a given course and convert to map units.

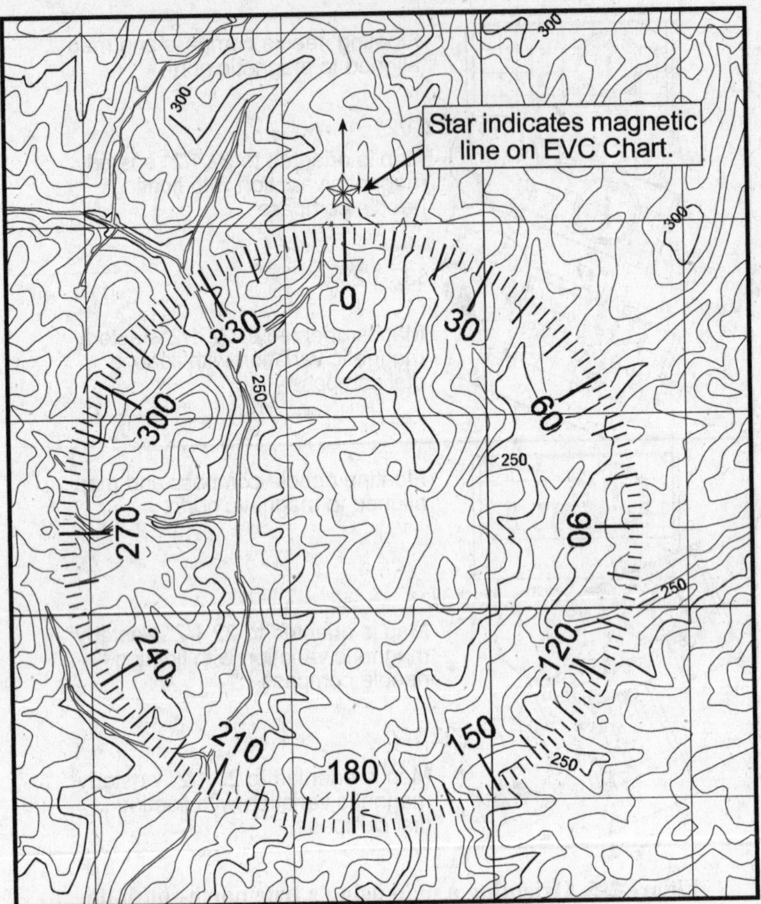

Figure 2-6. Map orientation with compass rose

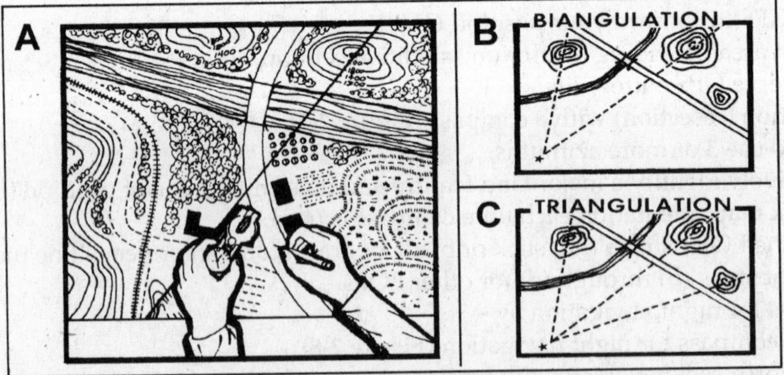

Figure 2-7. Triangulation

- One pace is the distance covered each time the same foot touches the ground.
- Distances measured by paces are approximate (example in open terrain, 900 paces per kilometer [average], or example in rough terrain, 1200 paces per kilometer [average]).

(c) Use pace count in conjunction with terrain evaluation and heading to determine location. An individual's pace varies because of factors such as steep terrain, day/night travel, or injured/uninjured condition. Adjust estimation of distance traveled against these factors to get relative accuracy when using a pace count.

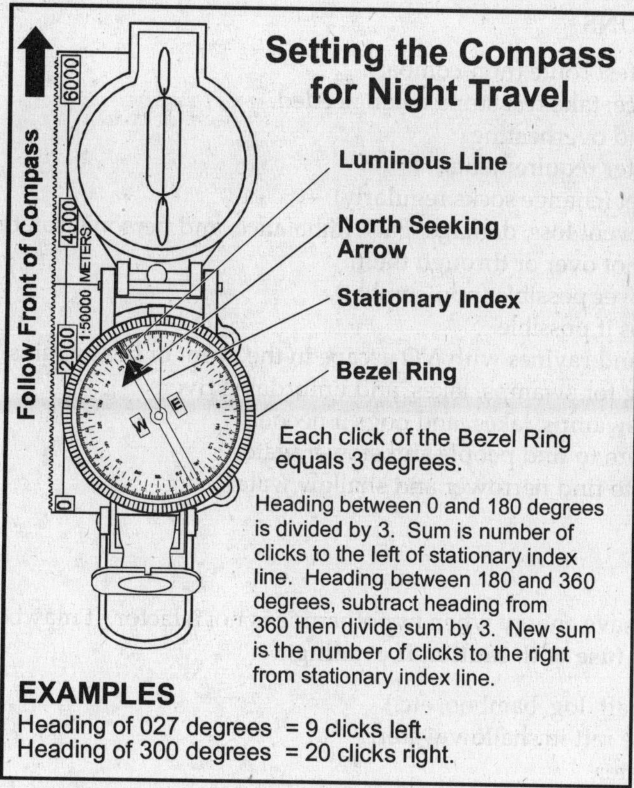

Figure 2-8. Compass night navigation setup

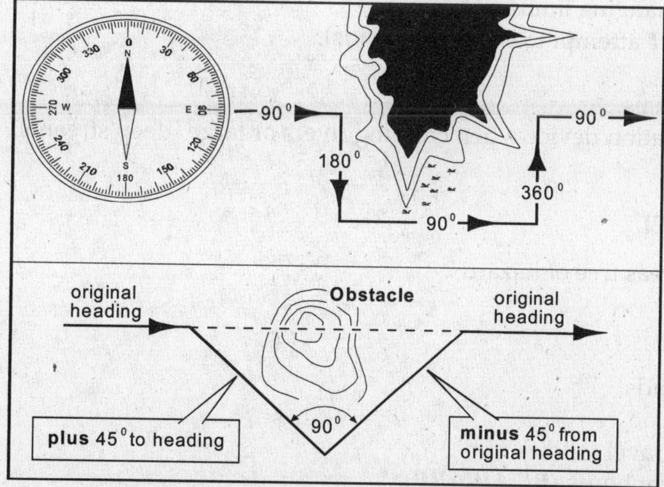

Figure 2-9. Dogleg and 90 degree offset

(4) Deliberate offset is—
  (a) Used when finding a point on a linear feature (that is, road or river).
  (b) Intentionally navigated to left or right of target so you know which way to turn at the linear feature.

(5) Point-to-point is same as straight line.
  (a) Pick out landmarks on the heading and walk the trail of least resistance to a point.
  (b) On reaching a point, establish another landmark and continue.

3. TRAVEL CONSIDERATIONS

a. Pick the easiest and safest route (non-combat).
b. Maintain a realistic pace; take rest stops when needed.
c. Avoid overdressing and overheating.
d. Consider food and water requirements.
e. Take special care of feet (change socks regularly).
f. Pack equipment to prevent loss, damage, pack imbalance, and personal safety.
g. Go **around** obstacles, not over or through them.
h. Travel on trails whenever possible (non-combat).
i. Travel in forested areas if possible.
j. Avoid creek bottoms and ravines with *NO* escape in the event of heavy rains.
k. Consider the following for swamps, lakes, and unfordable rivers:
   (1) Circumnavigate swamps, lakes, and bogs if needed.
   (2) Travel downstream to find people and slower water.
   (3) Travel upstream to find narrower and shallow water.

4. RIVER TRAVEL

River travel may be faster and save energy when hypothermia is not a factor. It may be a primary mode of travel and LOC in a tropical environment **(use with caution if evading)**.

a. Use flotation device (raft, log, bamboo, etc.).
b. Use a pole to move the raft in shallow water.
c. Use an oar in deep water.
d. Stay near inside edge of river bends (current speed is less).
e. Keep near shore.
f. Watch for the following ***DANGERS:***
   (1) Snags.
   (2) Sweepers (overhanging limbs and trees).
   (3) Rapids (*DO NOT* attempt to shoot the rapids).
   (4) Waterfalls.
   (5) Hazardous animals.
g. Consider using a flotation device when crossing rivers or large/deep streams.

5. ICE AND SNOW TRAVEL

Travel should be limited to areas free of hazards.

a. *DO NOT* travel in—
   (1) Blizzards.
   (2) Bitterly cold winds.
   (3) Poor visibility.
b. Obstacles to winter travel follow:
   (1) Reduced daylight hours *(BE AWARE)*.
   (2) Deep soft snow (if movement is necessary, make snowshoes **[Figure 2-10]**). Travel is easier in early morning or late afternoon near dusk when snow is frozen or crusted.
   (3) Avalanche prone areas to avoid:
      (a) Slopes 30-45 degrees or greater.
      (b) Trees without uphill branches (identifies prior avalanches).
      (c) Heavy snow loading on ridge tops.
   (4) If caught in an avalanche, do the following:
      (a) Backstroke to decrease burial depth.
      (b) Move hand around face to create air pocket as moving snow slows.

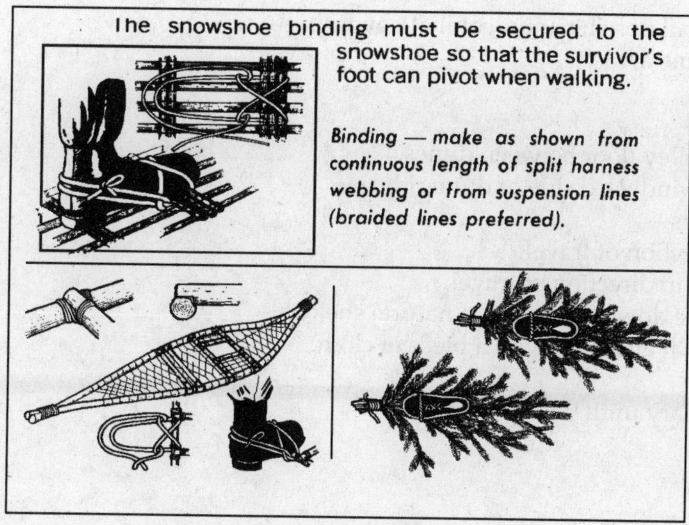

Figure 2-10. Improvised snowshoes

(5) Frozen water crossings.
  (a) Weak ice should be expected where—
  - Rivers are straight.
  - Objects protrude through ice.
  - Snow banks extend over the ice.
  - Rivers or streams come together.
  - Water vapor rising indicates open or warm areas.

  (b) Air pockets form when a frozen river loses volume.
  (c) When crossing frozen water, distribute your weight by laying flat, belly crawling, or using snowshoes.

c. Glacier travel is hazardous and should be avoided.

6. MOUNTAIN HAZARDS

a. Lightning. Avoid ridge tops during thunderstorms.
b. Avalanche. Avoid areas prone to avalanches.
c. Flash floods. Avoid low areas.

7. SUMMER HAZARDS (SEE PAGE 906; PARAGRAPH 3, *TRAVEL CONSIDERATIONS*, ITEMS H THROUGH K.)

(1) Dense brush.
  (a) Travel on trails when possible (non-combat).
  (b) Travel in forested areas if possible.
  (c) Avoid creek bottoms and ravines with no escape in the event of heavy rains.

(2) Swamps, lakes, and unfordable rivers.
  (a) Circumnavigate swamps, lakes, and bogs if needed.
  (b) Travel downstream to find people and slower water.
  (c) Travel upstream to find narrower and shallow water.

8. DRY CLIMATES

a. *DO NOT* travel unless certain of reaching the destination using the water supply available.
b. Travel at dawn or dusk on hot days.

c. Follow the easiest trail possible (non-combat), avoiding—
 (1) Deep sandy dune areas.
 (2) Rough terrain.
d. In sand dune areas—
 (1) Follow hard valley floor between dunes.
 (2) Travel on the windward side of dune ridges.
e. If a sandstorm occurs—
 (1) Mark your direction of travel.
 (2) Sit or lie down in direction of travel.
 (3) Try to get to the downwind side of natural shelter.
 (4) Cover the mouth and nose with a piece of cloth.
 (5) Protect the eyes.
 (6) Remain stationary until the storm is over.

9. TROPICAL CLIMATES

a. Travel only when it is light.
b. Avoid obstacles like thickets and swamps.
c. Part the vegetation to pass through. Avoid grabbing vegetation; it may have spines or thorns (**use gloves** if possible).
d. *DO NOT* climb over logs if you can go around them.
e. Find trails—
 (1) Where 2 streams meet.
 (2) Where a low pass goes over a range of hills.
f. While traveling trails—
 (1) Watch for disturbed areas on game trails; they may indicate a pitfall or trap.
 (2) Use a walking stick to probe for pitfalls or traps.
 (3) *DO NOT* sleep on the trail.
 (4) Exercise caution, the enemy uses the trails also.

10. OPEN SEAS

a. Using currents—
 (1) Deploy sea anchor **(Figure 2-11)**. Sea anchor may be adjusted to make use of existing currents.
 (2) Sit low in the raft.
 (3) Deflate the raft slightly so it rides lower in the water.
b. Using winds—
 (1) Pull in sea anchor.
 (2) Inflate raft so it rides higher.

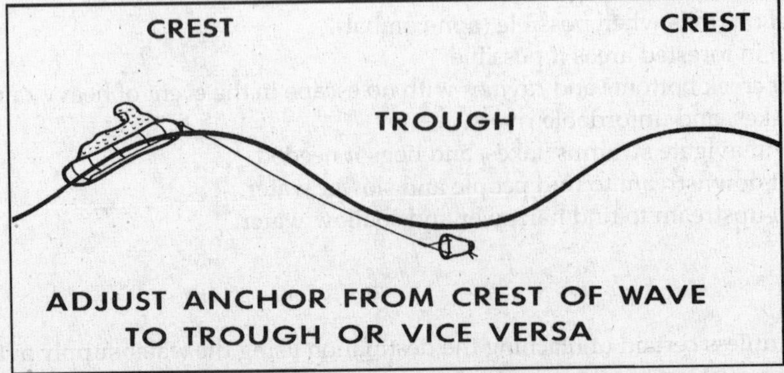

Figure 2-11. Sea anchor deployment

(3) Sit up in raft so body catches the wind.
(4) Construct a shade cover/sail **(Figure 2-12)**. (Sail aids in making landfall.)

c. Making landfall. Indications of land are—
(1) Fixed cumulus clouds in a clear sky or in a cloudy sky where all other clouds are moving.
(2) Greenish tint in the sky **(in the tropics)**.
(3) Lighter colored reflection on clouds (open water causes dark gray reflections) **(in the arctic)**.
(4) Lighter colored water (indicates shallow water).
(5) The odors and sounds.
(a) Odors from swamps and smoke.
(b) Roar of surf/bird cries coming from one direction.
(6) Directional flights of birds at dawn and at dusk.

d. Swimming ashore—
(1) Consider physical condition.
(2) Use a flotation aid.
(3) Secure all gear to body before reaching landfall.
(4) Remain in raft as long as possible.
(5) Use the sidestroke or breaststroke to conserve strength if thrown from raft.
(6) Wear footgear and at least **1** layer of clothing.
(7) Try to make landfall during the lull between the sets of waves (waves are generally in **sets** of **7**, from **smallest** to **largest**).
(8) In moderate surf.
(a) Swim forward on the back of a wave.
(b) Make a shallow dive just before the wave breaks to end the ride.
(9) In high surf.
(a) Swim shoreward in the trough between waves.
(b) When the seaward wave approaches, face it and submerge.
(c) After it passes, work shoreward in the next trough.
(10) If caught in the undertow of a large wave—
(a) Remain calm and swim to the surface.
(b) Lie as close to the surface as possible.
(c) Parallel shoreline and attempt landfall at a point further down shore.
(11) Select a landing point.
(a) Avoid places where waves explode upon rocks.
(b) Find a place where waves smoothly rush onto the rocks.

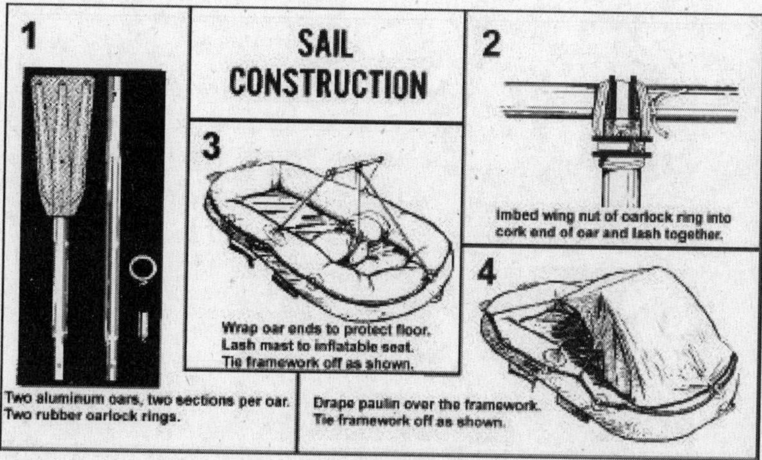

Figure 2-12. Shade/sail construction

(12) After selecting a landing site—
   (a) Face shoreward.
   (b) Assume a sitting position with feet 2 or 3 feet lower than head to absorb the shock of hitting submerged objects.

e. Rafting ashore—
   (1) Select landing point carefully.
   (2) Use caution landing when the sun is low and straight in front of you causing poor visibility.
   (3) Land on the lee (downwind) side of islands or point of land if possible.
   (4) Head for gaps in the surf line.
   (5) Penetrate surf by—
      (a) Taking down most shade/sails.
      (b) Using paddles to maintain control.
      (c) Deploying a sea anchor for stability.

CAUTION

DO NOT deploy a sea anchor if traveling through coral.

f. Making sea ice landings on large stable ice flows. Icebergs, small flows, and disintegrating flows are dangerous (**ice can cut a raft**).
   (1) Use paddles to avoid sharp edges.
   (2) Store raft away from the ice edge.
   (3) Keep raft inflated and ready for use.
   (4) Weight down/secure raft so it does not blow away.

CHAPTER 3

Radio Communications and Signaling

Inventory and review the operating instructions of all communications and signaling equipment.

1. RADIO COMMUNICATIONS (VOICE AND DATA)

a. Non-combat.
   (1) Ensure locator beacon is operational.
   (2) Follow standing plans for on/off operations to conserve battery use.
b. Combat.
   (1) Turn off locator beacon.
   (2) Keep it with you to supplement radio communications.
   (3) Follow plans/orders for on/off operations.
c. Make initial contact as soon as possible or as directed in applicable plans/orders.
d. If no immediate contact, then as directed in applicable plans/orders.
e. Locate spare radio and batteries (keep warm and dry).
f. Transmissions.
   (1) Use concealment sites (combat) that optimize line of site (LOS).
   (2) Face recovery asset.
   (3) Keep antenna perpendicular to intended receiver **(Figure 3-1)**.
   (4) ***DO NOT*** ground antenna (that is finger on antenna or attaching bolt, space blanket, vegetation, etc.).
   (5) Keep transmissions short (3-5 seconds maximum). Use data burst if available.
   (6) Move after each transmission (***ONLY*** in combat, if possible).
   (7) If transmitting in the blind, ensure a clear LOS towards the equator.
   (8) Use terrain masking to hinder enemy direction finding.
g. Listening (use reception times in applicable plans/orders or as directed by recovery forces).

2. SIGNALING

a. Pyrotechnic signals.
   (1) Prepare early (weather permitting).
   (2) Use as directed in applicable plans/orders or as directed by recovery forces.
   (3) Extend over raft's edge before activating.
b. Signal mirror **(Figure 3-2).**
   (1) Use as directed by recovery forces.
   (2) If no radio, use only with confirmed friendly forces.
   (3) Cover when not in use.

NOTE
Make a mirror from any shiny metal or glass.

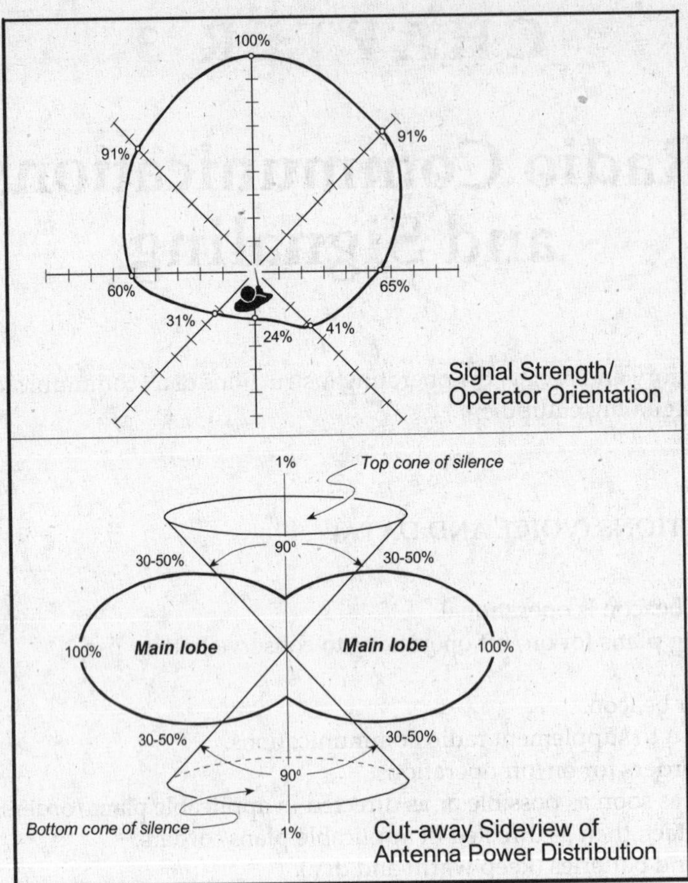

Figure 3-1. Radio transmission characteristics

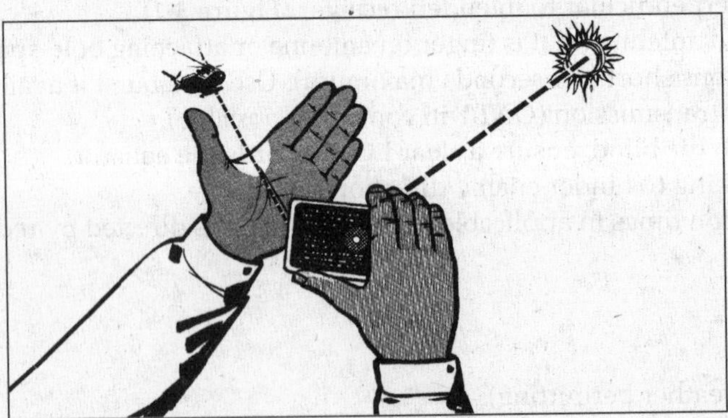

Figure 3-2. Sighting techniques

c. Strobe/IR lights.
   (1) Prepare early, consider filters and shields.
   (2) Use as directed by recovery forces.
   (3) Conserve battery life.

> **NOTE**
> Produces one residual flash when turned off.

d. Pattern signals (use as directed in applicable plans/orders).
   (1) Materials:
      (a) Manmade (space blanket, signal paulin, parachute).
      (b) Natural use materials that contrast the color and/or texture of the signaling area (rocks, brush, branches, stomped grass).
   (2) Location.
      (a) Maximize visibility from above.
      (b) Provide concealment from ground observation.
   (3) Size (large as possible) and ratio **(Figure 3-3)**.
   (4) Shape (maintain straight lines and sharp corners).
   (5) Contrast (use color and shadows).
   (6) Pattern signals **(Figure 3-4)**.

e. Sea dye marker.
   (1) ***DO NOT*** waste in rough seas or fast moving water.
   (2) Conserve unused dye by rewrapping.
   (3) May be used to color snow.

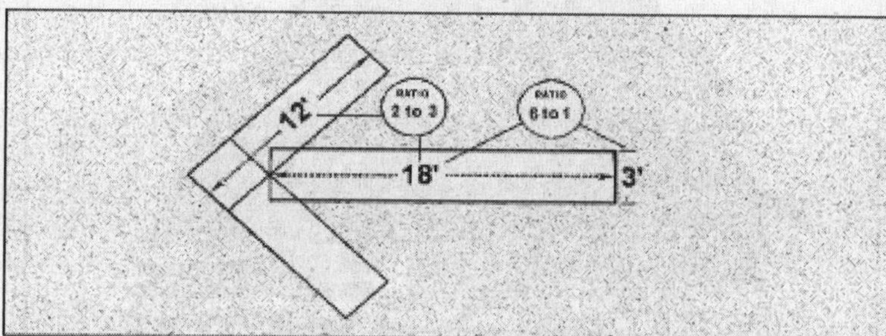

Figure 3-3. Size and ratio

NO.	MESSAGE	CODE SYMBOL
1	REQUIRE ASSISTANCE	V
2	REQUIRE MEDICAL ASSISTANCE	X
3	NO or NEGATIVE	N
4	YES or AFFIRMATIVE	Y
5	PROCEEDING IN THIS DIRECTION	↑

Figure 3-4. Signal key

f. Non-combat considerations:
   (1) Use a fire at night.
   (2) Use smoke for day (tires or petroleum products for dark smoke and green vegetation for light smoke). **(Figure 3-5)**
   (3) Use signal mirror to sweep horizon.
   (4) Use audio signals (that is, voice, whistle, and weapons fire).

Figure 3-5. Smoke generator

CHAPTER 4

Recovery

1. RESPONSIBILITIES

a. Establish radio contact with recovery forces (if possible).
b. Maintain communication with recovery forces until recovered.
c. Be prepared to authenticate as directed in applicable plans/orders.
d. Follow recovery force instructions, be prepared to report—
   (1) Enemy activity in the recovery area.
   (2) Recovery site characteristics (slope, obstacles, size, etc.).
   (3) Number in party/medical situation.
   (4) Signal devices available.
e. If no radio, a ground-to-air signal may be your only means to effect recovery.

2. SITE SELECTION

a. Locate area for landing pick-up, if practical (approximately 150 feet diameter, free of obstructions, flat and level).
b. Assess evidence of human activity at/near the site (in combat).
c. Locate several concealment sites around area (in combat).
d. Plan several tactical entry and exit routes (in combat).

3. SITE PREPARATION

a. Pack and secure all equipment.
b. Prepare signaling devices (use as directed or as briefed).
c. Mentally review recovery methods (aircraft, ground, boat, etc.).

4. RECOVERY PROCEDURES

a. Assist recovery force in identifying your position.
b. Stay concealed until recovery is imminent (in combat).
c. For a landing/ground recovery—
   (1) Assume a non-threatening posture.
   (2) Secure weapons and avoid quick movement.
   (3) *DO NOT* approach recovery vehicle until instructed.
   (4) Beware of rotors/propellers when approaching recovery vehicle, especially on sloping or uneven terrain. Secure loose equipment that could be caught in rotors/propellers.
d. For **hoist** recovery devices (**Figures 4-1 and 4-2**)—
   (1) Use eye protection, if available (glasses or helmet visor).
   (2) Allow metal on device to contact the surface before touching to avoid injury from static discharge.
   (3) Sit or kneel for stability while donning device.
   (4) Put safety strap under armpits.
   (5) Ensure cable is in front of you.
   (6) Keep hands clear of all hardware and connectors.
   (7) *DO NOT* become entangled in cable.

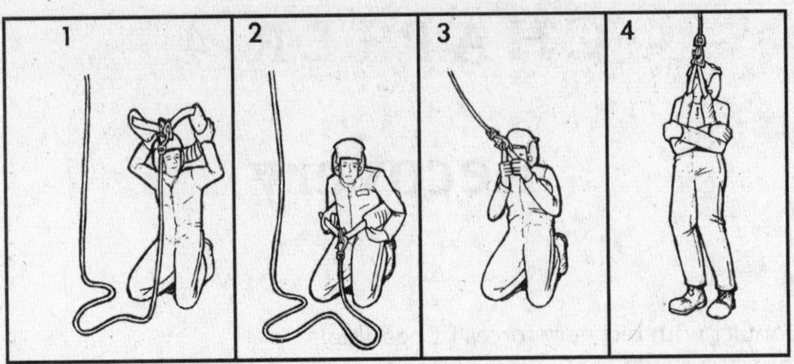

Figure 4-1. Rescue strap

Figure 4-2. Forest penetrator

(8) Use a thumbs up, vigorous cable shake, or radio call to signal you are ready.

(9) Drag feet on the ground to decrease oscillation.

(10) ***DO NOT*** assist during hoist or when pulled into the rescue vehicle. Follow crewmember instructions.

e. For **nonhoist** recovery (rope or unfamiliar equipment)—

(1) Create a ***"fixed loop"*** big enough to place under armpits (**Figure 4-3**).

(2) Follow the procedures in "**d**" above.

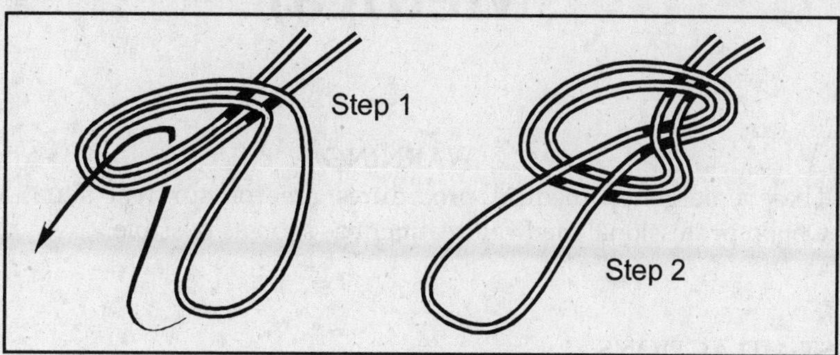

Figure 4-3. Fixed loop

CHAPTER 5

Medical

WARNING
These emergency medical procedures are for survival situations. Obtain professional medical treatment as soon as possible.

1. IMMEDIATE FIRST AID ACTIONS

Remember the *ABCs* of Emergency Care:
*A*irway *B*reathing *C*irculation

a. Determine responsiveness as follows:
   (1) If unconscious, arouse by shaking gently and shouting.
   (2) If no response—
      (a) Keep head and neck aligned with body.
      (b) Roll victims onto their backs.
      (c) Open the airway by lifting the chin **(Figure 5-1)**.
      (d) Look, listen, and feel for air exchange.
   (3) If victim is not breathing—
      (a) Check for a clear airway; remove any blockage.
      (b) Cover victim's mouth with your own.
      (c) Pinch victim's nostrils closed.
      (d) Fill victim's lungs with **2** slow breaths.

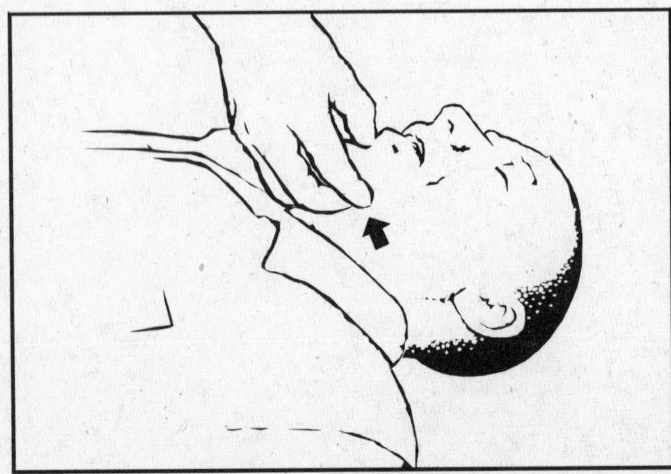

Figure 5-1. Chin lift

(e) If breaths are blocked, reposition airway; try again.
(f) If breaths still blocked, give **5** abdominal thrusts:
- Straddle the victim.
- Place a fist between breastbone and belly button.
- Thrust upward to expel air from stomach.

(g) Sweep with finger to clear mouth.
(h) Try **2** slow breaths again.
(i) If the airway is still blocked, continue **(c)** through **(f)** until successful or exhausted.
(j) With open airway, start mouth to mouth breathing:
- Give **1** breath every 5 seconds.
- Check for chest rise each time.

(4) If victim is unconscious, but breathing—
(a) Keep head and neck aligned with body.
(b) Roll victim on side (drains the mouth and prevents the tongue from blocking airway).
(5) If breathing difficulty is caused by chest trauma, refer to **page 921, paragraph 1d, *Treat Chest Injuries.***

CAUTION

DO NOT remove an impaled object unless it interferes with the airway. You may cause more tissue damage and increase bleeding. For travel, you may shorten and secure the object.

b. Control bleeding as follows:
(1) Apply a pressure dressing **(Figure 5-2)**.
(2) If ***STILL*** bleeding—
(a) Use direct pressure over the wound.
(b) Elevate the wounded area above the heart.
(3) If ***STILL*** bleeding—
(a) Use a pressure point between the injury and the heart **(Figure 5-3)**.
(b) Maintain pressure for 6 to 10 minutes before checking to see if bleeding has stopped.
(4) If a limb wound is ***STILL*** bleeding—

CAUTION

Use of a tourniquet is a ***LAST RESORT*** measure. Use ***ONLY*** when severe, uncontrolled bleeding will cause loss of life. Recognize that long-term use of a tourniquet may cause loss of limb.

(a) Apply tourniquet (TK) band just above bleeding site on limb. A band at least 3 inches (7.5 cm) or wider is best.
(b) Follow steps illustrated in **Figure 5-4**.
(c) Use a stick at least 6 inches (15 cm) long.
(d) Tighten only enough to stop arterial bleeding.
(e) Mark a *TK* on the forehead with the time applied.
(f) ***DO NOT*** cover the tourniquet.

CAUTION

The following directions apply ***ONLY*** in survival situations where rescue is ***UNLIKELY*** and ***NO*** medical aid is available.

(g) If rescue or medical aid is not available for over 2 hours, an attempt to ***SLOWLY*** loosen the tourniquet may be made 20 minutes after application. Before loosening—
- Ensure pressure dressing is in place.
- Ensure bleeding has stopped.
- Loosen tourniquet ***SLOWLY*** to restore circulation.
- Leave loosened tourniquet in position in case bleeding resumes.

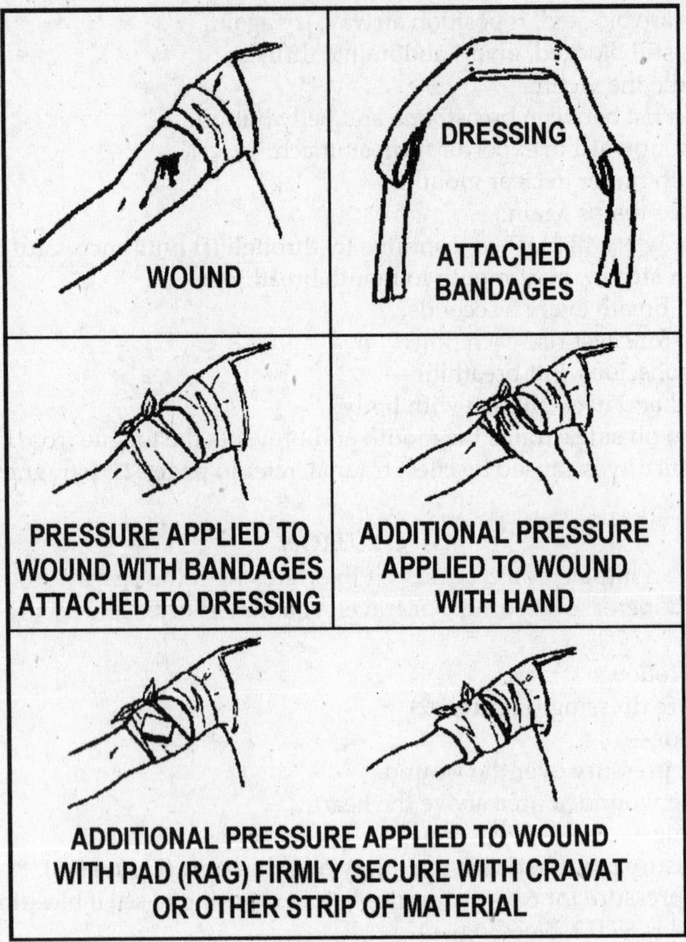

Figure 5-2. Application of a pressure dressing

c. Treat shock. (Shock is difficult to identify or treat under field conditions. It may be present with or without visible injury.)
   (1) Identify by one or more of the following:
      (a) Pale, cool, and sweaty skin.
      (b) Fast breathing and a weak, fast pulse.
      (c) Anxiety or mental confusion.
      (d) Decreased urine output.
   (2) Maintain circulation.
   (3) Treat underlying injury.
   (4) Maintain normal body temperature.
      (a) Remove wet clothing.
      (b) Give warm fluids.
         - *DO NOT* give fluids to an unconscious victim.
         - *DO NOT* give fluids if they cause victim to gag.
      (c) Insulate from ground.
      (d) Shelter from the elements.
   (5) Place conscious victim on back.
   (6) Place very weak or unconscious victim on side, this will—
      (a) Allow mouth to drain.
      (b) Prevent tongue from blocking airway.

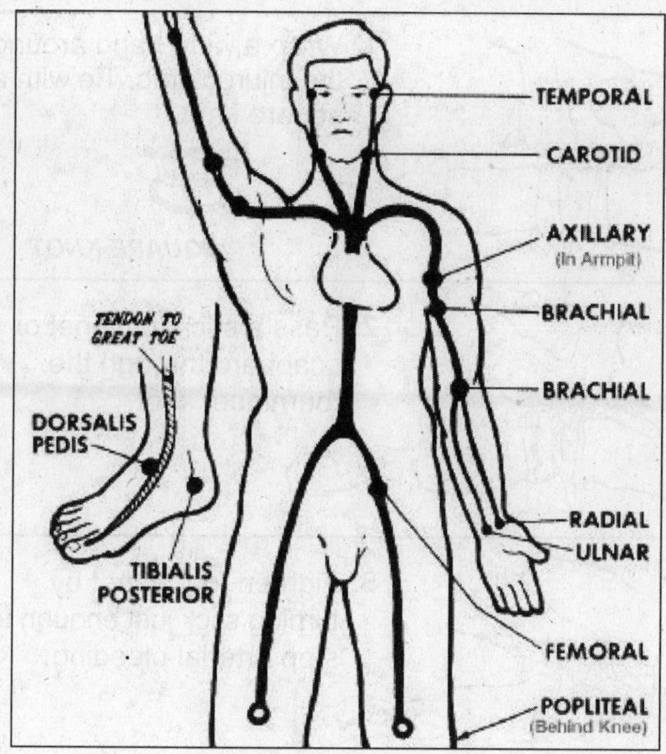

Figure 5-3. Pressure points

d. Treat chest injuries.
   (1) Sucking chest wound. This occurs when chest wall is penetrated; may cause victim to gasp for breath; may cause sucking sound; may create bloody froth as air escapes the chest.
      (a) ***Immediately*** seal wound with hand or airtight material.
      (b) Tape airtight material over wound on ***3 sides only*** **(Figure 5-5)** to allow air to escape from the wound but not to enter.
      (c) Monitor breathing and check dressing.
      (d) Lift untapped side of dressing as victim ***exhales*** to allow trapped air to escape, as necessary.
   (2) Flail chest. Results from blunt trauma when *3* or ***more*** ribs are broken in *2* or more places. The flail segment is the broken area that moves in a direction opposite to the rest of chest during breathing.
      (a) Stabilize the flail segment as follows:
         - Place rolled-up clothing or bulky pad over site.
         - Tape pad to site.
         - ***DO NOT*** wrap tape around chest.
      (b) Have victim keep segment still with hand pressure.
      (c) Roll victim onto side of flail segment injury (as other injuries allow).
   (3) Fractured ribs.
      (a) Encourage deep breathing (painful, but necessary to prevent the possible development of pneumonia).
      (b) ***DO NOT*** constrict breathing by taping ribs.

e. Treat fractures, sprains, and dislocations.
   (1) Control bleeding.
   (2) Remove watches, jewelry, and constrictive clothing.
   (3) If fracture penetrates the skin—
      (a) Clean wound by gentle irrigation with water.
      (b) Apply dressing over wound.
   (4) Position limb as normally as possible.

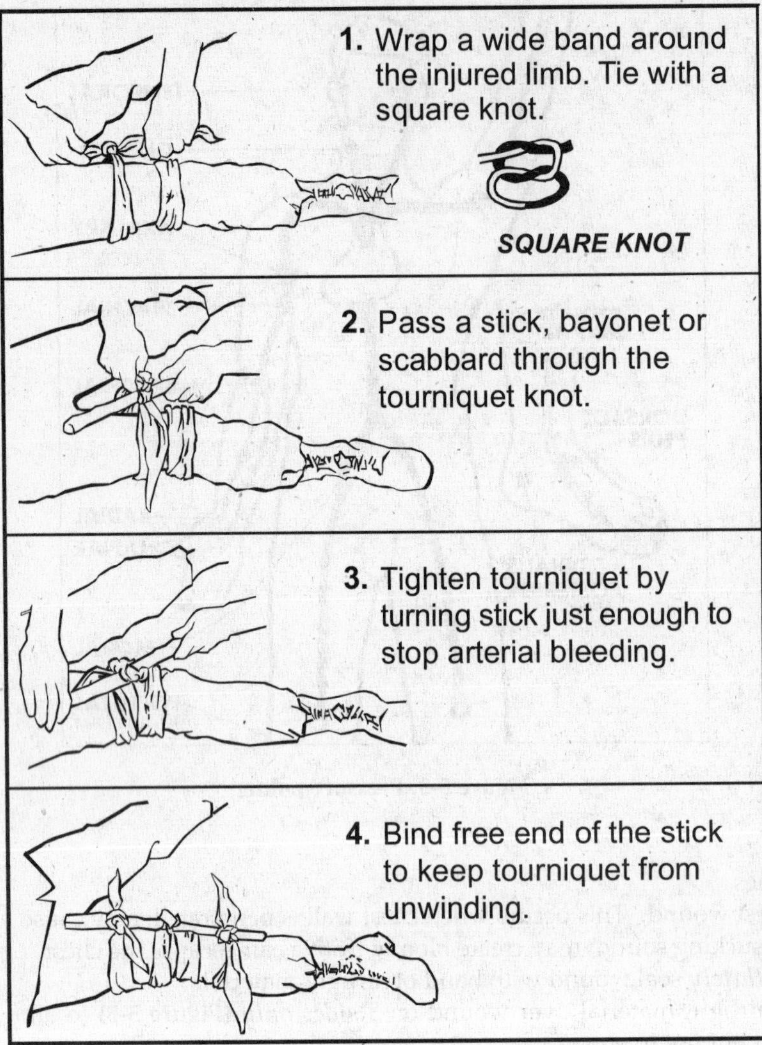

Figure 5-4. Application of a tourniquet

(5) Splint in position found (if ***unable*** to straighten limb).

(6) Improvise a splint with available materials:

(a) Sticks or straight, stiff materials from equipment.

(b) Body parts (for example, opposite leg, arm-to-chest).

(7) Attach with strips of cloth, parachute cord, etc.

(8) Keep the fractured bones from moving by immobilizing the joints on both sides of the fracture. If fracture is in a joint, immobilize the bones on both sides of the joint.

CAUTION

Splint fingers in a slightly flexed position, *NOT* in straight position. Hand should look like it is grasping an apple.

(9) Use ***RICES*** treatment for 72 hours.

(a) Rest.

(b) Ice.

(c) Compression.

(d) Elevation.

(e) Stabilization.

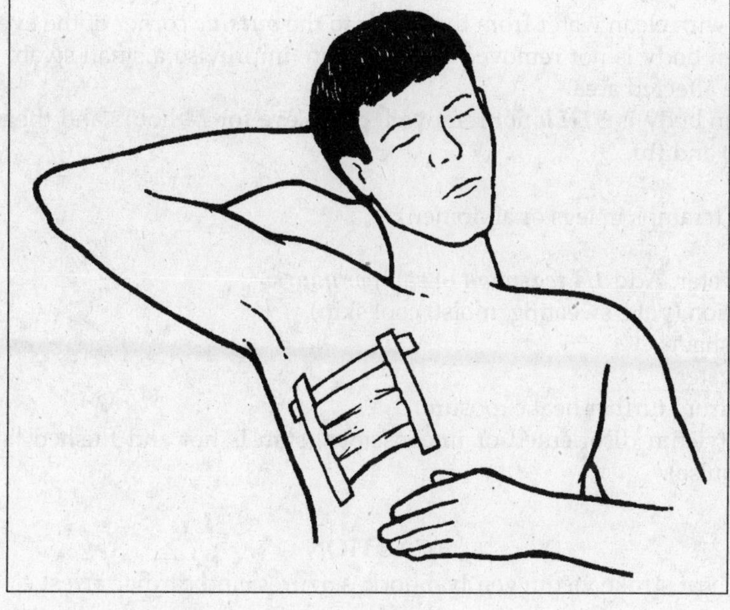

Figure 5-5. Sucking chest wound dressing

(10) Apply cold to acute injuries.
(11) Use 15 to 20 minute periods of cold application.
 (a) ***DO NOT*** use continuous cold therapy.
 (b) Repeat 3 to 4 times per day.
 (c) Avoid cooling that can cause frostbite or hypothermia.
(12) Wrap with a compression bandage after cold therapy.
(13) Elevate injured area above heart level to reduce swelling.
(14) Check periodically for a pulse beyond the injury site.
(15) Loosen bandage or reapply splint if no pulse is felt or if swelling occurs because bandage is too tight.

2. COMMON INJURIES AND ILLNESSES

a. Burns.
 (1) Cool the burned area with water.
  (a) Use immersion or cool compresses.
  (b) Avoid aggressive cooling with ice or frigid water.
 (2) Remove watches, jewelry, constrictive clothing.
 (3) ***DO NOT*** remove embedded, charred material that will cause burned areas to bleed.
 (4) Cover with sterile dressings.
 (5) ***DO NOT*** use lotion or grease.
 (6) Avoid moving or rubbing the burned part.
 (7) Drink ***extra*** water to compensate for increased fluid loss from burns. (Add ***1/4 teaspoon*** of ***salt*** [if available] to ***each quart*** of ***water***.)
 (8) Change dressings when soaked or dirty.

b. Eye injuries.
 (1) Sun/snow blindness (gritty, burning sensation, and possible reduction in vision caused by sun exposure).
  (a) Prevent with improvised goggles. **(See Chapter 6, page 931, Figure 6-2.)**
  (b) Treat by patching affected eye(s).
   - Check after 12 hours.
   - Replace patch for another 12 hours if not healed.
  (c) Use cool compresses to reduce pain.

(2) Foreign body in eye.
(a) Irrigate with clean water from the ***inside*** to the ***outside*** corner of the eye.
(b) If foreign body is not removed by irrigation, improvise a small swab. Moisten and wipe gently over the affected area.
(c) If foreign body is ***STILL*** not removed, patch eye for 24 hours and then reattempt removal using steps **(a)** and **(b).**

c. Heat injury.
(1) Heat cramps (cramps in legs or abdomen).
(a) Rest.
(b) Drink water. Add ***1/4 teaspoon*** of salt ***per quart.***
(2) Heat exhaustion (pale, sweating, moist, cool skin).
(a) Rest in shade.
(b) Drink water.
(c) Protect from further heat exposure.
(3) Heat stroke (victim disoriented or unconscious, skin is hot and flushed [sweating **may** or **may not** occur], fast pulse).

CAUTION

Handle heat stroke victim gently. Shock, seizures, and cardiac arrest can occur.

(a) Cool as rapidly as possible (saturate clothing with water and fan the victim). Remember to cool the groin and armpit areas. (Avoid overcooling.)
(b) Maintain airway, breathing, and circulation.

d. Cold injuries:
(1) Frostnip and frostbite—
(a) Are progressive injuries.
- Ears, nose, fingers, and toes are affected first.
- Areas will feel cold and may tingle leading to—
  - Numbness that progresses to—
    - Waxy appearance with stiff skin that cannot glide freely over a joint.

(b) Frostnipped areas rewarm with body heat. If body heat ***WILL NOT*** rewarm area in 15 to 20 minutes, then frostbite is present.
(c) Frostbitten areas are deeply frozen and require medical treatment.

CAUTION

In frostbite, repeated freezing and thawing causes severe pain and increases damage to the tissue. ***DO NOT*** rub frozen tissue. ***DO NOT*** thaw frozen tissue.

(2) Hypothermia—
(a) Is a progressive injury.
- Intense shivering with impaired ability to perform complex tasks leads to—
  - Violent shivering, difficulty speaking, sluggish thinking go to—
    - Muscular rigidity with blue, puffy skin; jerky movements go to—
      - Coma, respiratory and cardiac failure.

(b) Protect victim from the environment as follows:
- Remove wet clothing.
- Put on dry clothing (if available).
- Prevent further heat loss.
  - Cover top of head.
  - Insulate from above and below.
- Warm with blankets, sleeping bags, or shelter.
- Warm central areas before extremities.

- Place heat packs in groin, armpits, and around neck.
- Avoid causing burns to skin.

CAUTION

Handle hypothermia victim gently. Avoid overly rapid rewarming which may cause cardiac arrest. Rewarming of victim with skin-to-skin contact by volunteer(s) inside of a sleeping bag is a survival technique but can cause internal temperatures of all to drop.

e. Skin tissue damage.
  (1) Immersion injuries. Skin becomes wrinkled as in ***dishpan hands***.
    (a) Avoid walking on affected feet.
    (b) Pat dry; ***DO NOT*** rub. Skin tissue will be sensitive.
    (c) Dry socks and shoes. Keep feet protected.
    (d) Loosen boots, cuffs, etc., to improve circulation.
    (e) Keep area dry, warm, and open to air.
    (f) ***DO NOT*** apply creams or ointments.
  (2) Saltwater sores.
    (a) Change body positions frequently.
    (b) Keep sores dry.
    (c) Use antiseptic (if available).
    (d) ***DO NOT*** open or squeeze sores.
f. Snakebite.

CAUTION

This snakebite treatment recommendation is for situations where medical aid and specialized equipment are not available.

  (1) Nonpoisonous. Clean and bandage wound.
  (2) Poisonous.
    (a) Remove constricting items.
    (b) Minimize activity.
    (c) ***DO NOT*** cut the bite site; ***DO NOT*** use your mouth to create suction.
    (d) Clean bite with soap and water; cover with a dressing.
    (e) Overwrap the bite site with a tight (elastic) bandage **(Figure 5-6)**. The intent is to slow capillary and venous blood flow but not arterial flow. Check for pulse below the overwrap.
    (f) Splint bitten extremity to prevent motion.
    (g) Treat for shock **(page 926, paragraph 1c)**.
    (h) Position extremity below level of heart.
    (i) Construct shelter if necessary (let the victim rest).
    (j) For conscious victims, force fluids.
g. Marine life.
  (1) Stings.
    (a) Flush wound with salt water (fresh water stimulates toxin release).
    (b) Remove jewelry and watches.
    (c) Remove tentacles and gently scrape or shave skin.
    (d) Apply a steroid cream (if available).
    (e) ***DO NOT*** rub area with sand.
    (f) Treat for shock; artificial respiration may be required **(page 926, paragraph 1a)**.
    (g) ***DO NOT*** use urine to flush or treat wounds.
  (2) Punctures.
    (a) Immerse affected part in hot water or apply hot compresses for 30-60 minutes (as hot as victim can tolerate).

(b) Cover with clean dressing.
(c) Treat for shock as needed.

h. Skin irritants (includes poison oak and poison ivy).
(1) Wash with large amounts of water. Use soap (if available).
(2) Keep covered to prevent scratching.

i. Infection.
(1) Keep wound clean.
(2) Use iodine tablet solution or diluted betadine to prevent or treat infection.
(3) Change bandages as needed.

j. Dysentery and diarrhea.
(1) Drink *extra* water.
(2) Use a liquid diet.
(3) Eat charcoal. Make a paste by mixing fine charcoal particles with water. (It may relieve symptoms by absorbing toxins.)

k. Constipation (can be expected in survival situations).
(1) ***DO NOT*** take laxatives.
(2) Exercise.
(3) Drink **extra** water.

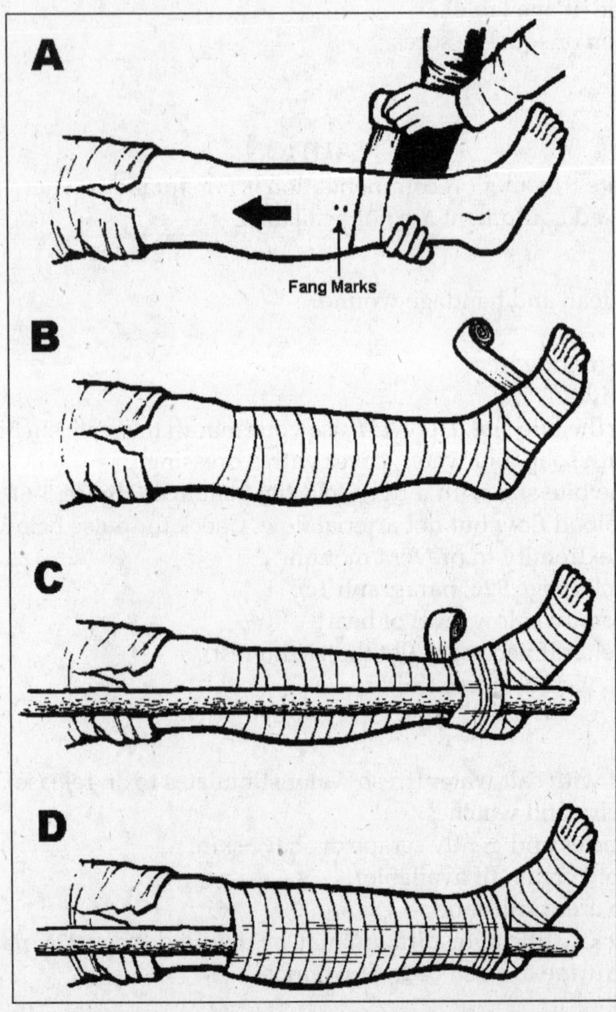

Figure 5-6. Compression bandage for snake bite

3. PLANT MEDICINE

a. Tannin.
   (1) Medical uses. Burns, diarrhea, dysentery, skin problems, and parasites. Tannin solution prevents infection and aids healing.
   (2) Sources. Found in the outer bark of all trees, acorns, banana plants, common plantain, strawberry leaves, and blackberry stems.
   (3) Preparation.
      (a) Place crushed outer bark, acorns, or leaves in water.
      (b) Leach out the tannin by soaking or boiling.
         - Increase tannin content by longer soaking time.
         - Replace depleted material with fresh bark/plants.
   (4) Treatments.
      (a) Burns.
         - Moisten bandage with cooled tannin tea.
         - Apply compress to burned area.
         - Pour cooled tea on burned areas to ease pain.
      (b) Diarrhea, dysentery, and worms. Drink strong tea solution (may promote voiding of worms).
      (c) Skin problems (dry rashes and fungal infections). Apply cool compresses or soak affected part to relieve itching and promote healing.
      (d) Lice and insect bites. Wash affected areas with tea to ease itching.

b. Salicin/salicylic acid.
   (1) Medical uses. Aches, colds, fever, inflammation, pain, sprains, and sore throat (aspirin-like qualities).
   (2) Sources. Willow and aspen trees **(Figure 5-7)**.
   (3) Preparation.
      (a) Gather twigs, buds, or cambium layer (soft, moist layer between the outer bark and the wood) of willow or aspen.
      (b) Prepare tea as described in paragraph **3a(3)**.
      (c) Make poultice.
         - Crush the plant or stems.
         - Make a pulpy mass.
   (4) Treatments.
      (a) Chew on twigs, buds, or cambium for symptom relief.
      (b) Drink tea for colds and sore throat.
      (c) Use warm, moist poultice for aches and sprains.
         - Apply pulpy mass over injury.
         - Hold in place with a dressing.

c. Common plantain.
   (1) Medical uses. Itching, wounds, abrasions, stings, diarrhea, and dysentery.
   (2) Source. There are over 200 plantain species with similar medicinal properties. The common plantain is shown in **Figure 5-7**.
   (3) Preparation.
      (a) Brew tea from seeds.
      (b) Brew tea from leaves.
      (c) Make poultice of leaves.
   (4) Treatments.
      (a) Drink tea made from seeds for diarrhea or dysentery.
      (b) Drink tea made from leaves for vitamin and minerals.
      (c) Use poultice to treat cuts, sores, burns, and stings.

d. Papain.
   (1) Medical uses. Digestive aid, meat tenderizer, and a food source.
   (2) Source. Fruit of the papaya tree **(Figure 5-7)**.
   (3) Preparation.
      (a) Make cuts in **unripe** fruit.

(b) Gather milky white sap for its papain content.
(c) Avoid getting sap in eyes or wounds.

(4) Treatments.
(a) Use sap to tenderize tough meat.
(b) Eat **ripe** fruit for food, vitamins, and minerals.

e. Common Cattail.

(1) Medical uses. Wounds, sores, boils, inflammations, burns, and an excellent food source.
(2) Source. Cattail plant found in marshes **(Figure 5-7)**.
(3) Preparation.
(a) Pound roots into a pulpy mass for a poultice.
(b) Cook and eat green bloom spikes.
(c) Collect yellow pollen for flour substitute.
(d) Peel and eat tender shoots (raw or cooked).

(4) Treatments.
(a) Apply poultice to affected area.
(b) Use plant for food, vitamins, and minerals.

4. HEALTH AND HYGIENE

a. Stay clean (daily regimen).

(1) Minimize infection by washing. (Use white ashes, sand, or loamy soil as soap substitutes.)
(2) Comb and clean debris from hair.
(3) Cleanse mouth and brush teeth.
(a) Use hardwood twig as toothbrush (fray it by chewing on one end then use as brush).
(b) Use single strand of an inner core string from parachute cord for dental floss.
(c) Use clean finger to stimulate gum tissues by rubbing.
(d) Gargle with salt water to help prevent sore throat and aid in cleaning teeth and gums.

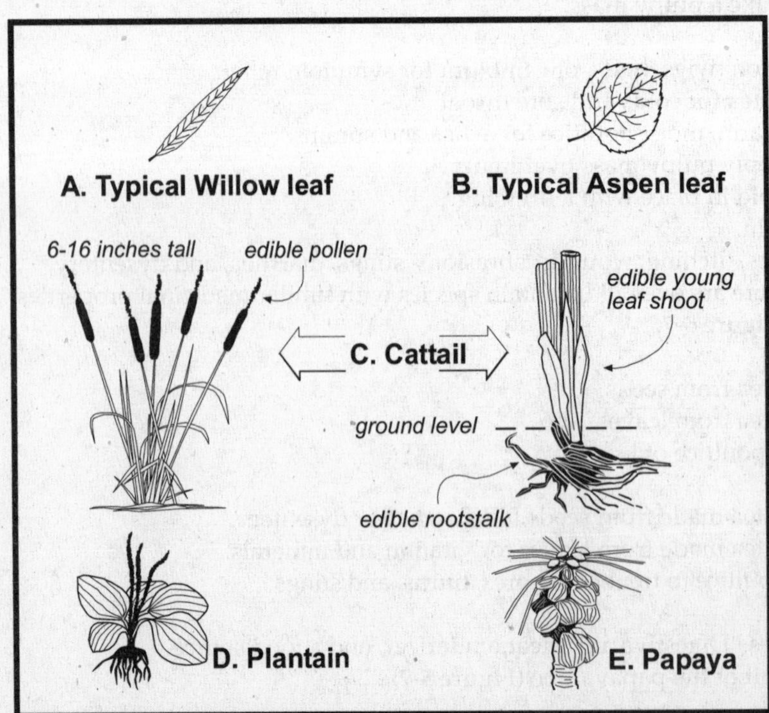

Figure 5-7. Useful plants

(4) Clean and protect feet.
   (a) Change and wash socks
   (b) Wash, dry, and massage.
   (c) Check frequently for blisters and red areas.
   (d) Use adhesive tape/mole skin to prevent damage.

b. Exercise daily.

c. Prevent and control parasites.
   (1) Check body for lice, fleas, ticks, etc.
      (a) Check body regularly.
      (b) Pick off insects and eggs (***DO NOT*** crush).
   (2) Wash clothing and use repellents.
   (3) Use smoke to fumigate clothing and equipment.

5. RULES FOR AVOIDING ILLNESS

a. Purify all water obtained from natural sources by using iodine tablets, bleach, or boiling for 5 minutes.
b. Locate latrines 200 feet from water and away from shelter.
c. Wash hands before preparing food or water.
d. Clean all eating utensils after each meal.
e. Prevent insect bites by using repellent, netting, and clothing.
f. Dry wet clothing as soon as possible.
g. Eat varied diet.
h. Try to get 7-8 hours sleep per day.

CHAPTER 6

Personal Protection

1. PRIORITIES

a. Evaluate available resources and situation, then accomplish individual tasks accordingly.
b. First 24 hours in order of situational needs—
   (1) Construct survival shelter according to selection criteria.
   (2) Procure water.
   (3) Establish multiple survival signals.
   (4) Build Fire.
c. Second 24 hours in order of situational needs—
   (1) Construct necessary tools and weapons.
   (2) Procure food.

2. CARE AND USE OF CLOTHING

a. Never discard clothing.
b. Wear loose and layered clothing.
   (1) Tight clothing restricts blood flow regulating body temperature.
   (2) Layers create more dead air space.
c. Keep entire body covered to prevent sunburn and dehydration in hot climates. When fully clothed, the majority of body heat escapes through the head and neck areas.
d. Avoid overheating.
   (1) Remove layers of clothing before strenuous activities.
   (2) Use a hat to regulate body heat.
   (3) Wear a hat when in direct sunlight (in hot environment).
e. Dampen clothing when on the ocean in hot weather.
   (1) Use salt water, ***NOT*** drinking water.
   (2) Dry clothing before dark to prevent hypothermia.
f. Keep clothing dry to maintain its insulation qualities (dry damp clothing in the sun or by a fire).
g. If you fall into the water in the winter—
   (1) Build fire.
   (2) Remove wet clothing and rewarm by fire.
   (3) Finish drying clothing by fire.
h. If no fire is available—
   (1) Remove clothing and get into sleeping bag (if available).
   (2) Allow wet clothes to freeze.
   (3) Break ice out of clothing.
i. Keep clothing clean (dirt reduces its insulation qualities). Examine clothing frequently for damage.
   (1) ***DO NOT*** sit or lie directly on the ground.
   (2) Wash clothing whenever possible.
   (3) Repair when necessary by using—
      (a) Needle and thread.
      (b) Safety pins.
      (c) Tape.
j. Improvised foot protection **(Figure 6-1)**.
   (1) Cut **2** to **4** layers of cloth into a 30-inch square.
   (2) Fold into a triangle.

(3) Center foot on triangle with toes toward corner.
(4) Fold front over the toes.
(5) Fold side corners, one at a time, over the instep.
(6) Secure by rope, vines, tape, etc., or tuck into other layers of material.

3. OTHER PROTECTIVE EQUIPMENT

a. Sleeping bag.
(1) Fluff before use, ***especially*** at foot of bag.
(2) Air and dry daily to remove body moisture.
(3) Improvise with available material, dry grass, leaves, dry moss, etc.

b. Sun and snow goggles **(Figure 6-2)**.
(1) Wear in bright sun or snow conditions.
(2) Improvise by cutting small horizontal slits in webbing, bark, or similar materials.

c. Gaiters **(Figure 6-3)**. Used to protect from sand, snow, insects, and scratches (wrap material around lower leg and top of boots).

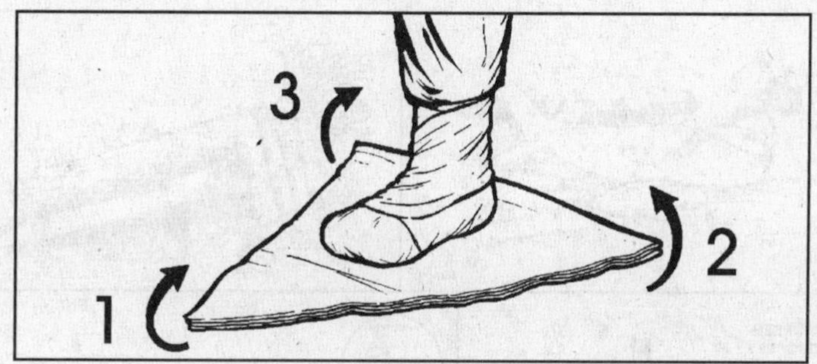

Figure 6-1 Improvised foot wear

Figure 6-2. Sun and snow goggles

Figure 6-3. Gaiters

4. SHELTERS

Evasion considerations apply.

a. Site selection.
  (1) Near signal and recovery site.
  (2) Available food and water.
  (3) Avoid natural hazards:
    (a) Dead standing trees.
    (b) Drainage and dry river beds except in combat areas.
    (c) Avalanche areas.
  (4) Location large and level enough to lie down in.

b. Types.
  (1) Immediate shelters. Find shelter needing minimal improvements **(Figure 6-4)**.
  (2) General shelter. Temperate climates require any shelter that gives protection from wind and rain.
  (3) Thermal A Frame, Snow Trench, Snow Cave. **(Figures 6-5 through 6-7)**. Cold climates require an enclosed, insulated shelter.

Figure 6-4. Immediate shelters

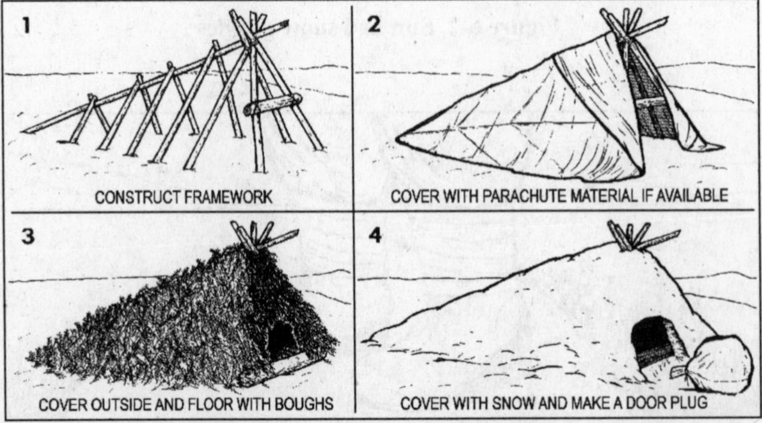

Figure 6-5. Thermal a frame

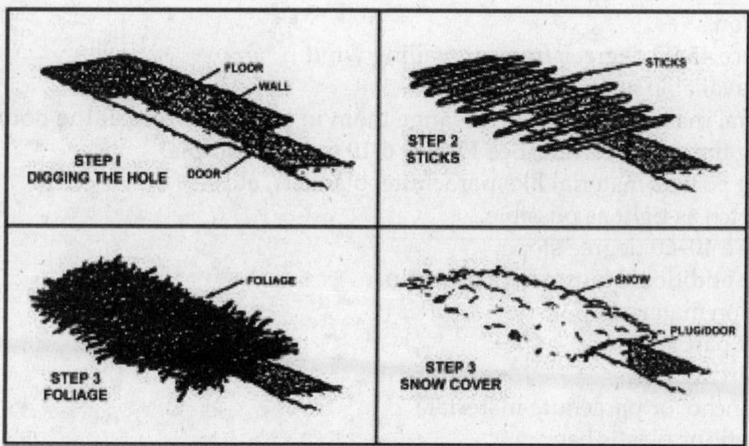

Figure 6-6. Snow trench

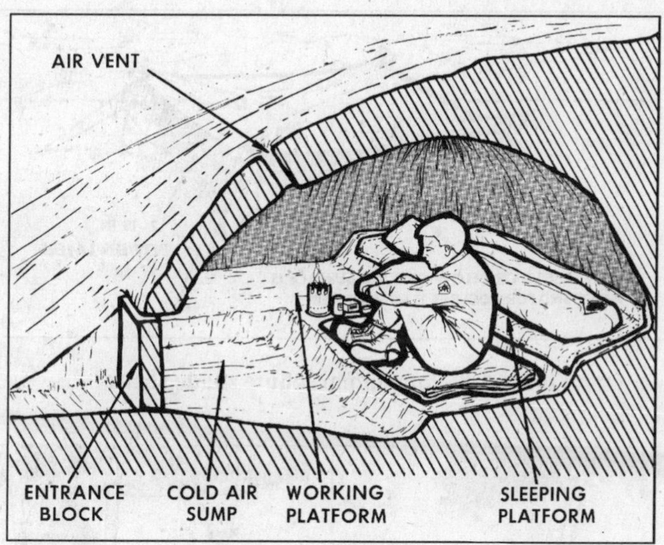

Figure 6-7. Snow cave

(a) Snow is the most abundant insulating material.

(b) Air vent is required to prevent carbon monoxide poisoning when using an open flame inside enclosed shelters.

> **NOTE**
>
> As a general rule, unless you can see your breath, your snow shelter is too warm and should be cooled down to preclude melting and dripping.

(4) Shade shelter. Hot climates require a shade shelter to protect from ultraviolet rays **(Figure 6-8)**.

(a) To reduce the surface temperature, the shelter floor should be elevated or dug down (approximately 18 inches).

(b) For thermal protection, a minimum of **2** layers of material suspended 12-18 inches above the head is required. White is the best color to reflect heat (inner most layer should be of darker material).

(5) Elevated platform shelter **(Figure 6-9)**. Tropical / wet climates require enclosed, elevated shelter for protection from dampness and insects.

c. Shelter construction.
   (1) Have entrance 45-90 degrees from prevailing wind.
   (2) Cover with available material.
      (a) If natural materials are used, arrange them in layers starting at the bottom with each layer overlapping the previous one. See **Figure 6-10** for an example.
      (b) If using porous material like parachute, blankets, etc.—
         - Stretch as tight as possible.
         - Use a 40–60 degree slope.
         - Use additional layers in heavy rain.

d. Shelter construction materials:
   (1) Raft and raft parts.
   (2) Vehicle or aircraft parts.
   (3) Blankets, poncho, or parachute material.
   (4) Sheet of plastic or plastic bag.
   (5) Bark peeled off dead trees.
   (6) Boughs, broad leaves, dry moss.

Figure 6-8. Poncho/parachute shade shelter

Figure 6-9. Elevated platform shelter

Figure 6-10. Shingle method

(7) Grass and sod.
(8) Snow.
(9) Sand and rocks.

e. Bed construction. Construct a bed to protect from cold, damp, ground using—
(1) Raft or foam rubber from vehicle seats.
(2) Boughs, leaves, or dry moss.

5. FIRES

CAUTION
Weigh hazards and risks of detection against the need for a fire.

a. Evasion considerations:
(1) Use trees or other sources to dissipate smoke.
(2) Use fires at dusk, dawn, or during inclement weather.
(3) Use fires at times when the local populace is cooking.

b. Fire building. The 3 essential elements for starting a fire are heat, fuel, and oxygen.
(1) Heat sources:
(a) Matches or lighter.
(b) Flint and steel (experiment with various rocks and metals until a good spark is produced).
(c) Sparks from batteries.
(d) Concentrated sunlight (use magnifying glass or flashlight reflectors).
(e) Pyrotechnics, such as flares **(last resort)**, etc.
(f) Friction method **(Figure 6-11)**. Without prior training, this method is difficult to master and requires a lot of time to build the device.

NOTE
If possible, carry a fire-starting device with you.

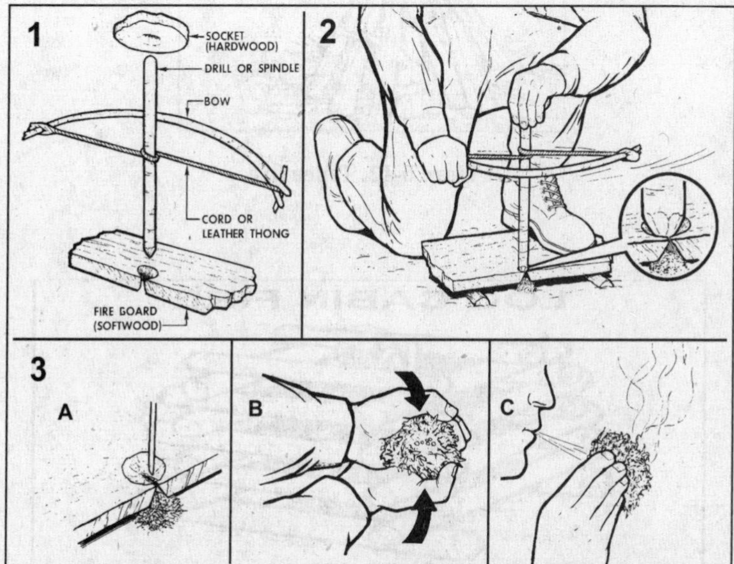

Figure 6-11. Friction method

(2) Fuel is divided into **3** categories: tinder, kindling, and fuel. (Gather large amounts of each category before igniting the fire.)

(a) **Tinder.** Tinder must be very finely shaved or shredded to provide a low combustion point and fluffed to allow oxygen to flow through. (To get tinder to burn hotter and longer, saturate with Vaseline, Chapstick, insect repellant, aircraft fuel, etc.) Examples of tinder include—

- Cotton.
- Candle (shred the wick, not the wax).
- Plastic spoon, fork, or knife.
- Foam rubber.
- Dry bark.
- Dry grasses.
- Gun powder.
- Pitch.
- Petroleum products.

(b) **Kindling.** Kindling must be small enough to ignite from the small flame of the tinder. Gradually add larger kindling until arriving at the size of fuel to burn.

(c) **Fuel.** Examples of fuel include—

- Dry hardwood (removing bark reduces smoke).
- Bamboo (open chambers to prevent explosion).
- Dry dung.

c. Types. Fires are built to meet specific needs or uses.

(1) Tepee fire **(Figure 6-12)**. Use the tepee fire to produce a concentrated heat source for cooking, lighting, or signaling.

(2) Log cabin fire **(Figure 6-13)**. Use the log cabin fire to produce large amounts of light and heat, to dry out wet wood, and provide coals for cooking, etc.

(3) Sod fire and reflector **(Figure 6-14)**. Use fire reflectors to get the most warmth from a fire. Build fires against rocks or logs.

Figure 6-12. Tepee fire

Figure 6-13. Log cabin or pyramid fires

CAUTION

DO NOT use porous rocks or riverbed rock—they may explode when healed.

(4) Dakota fire hole **(Figure 6-15)**. Use the Dakota fire hole for high winds or evasion situations.
(5) Improvised stoves **(Figure 6-16)**. These are very efficient.

Figure 6-14. Sod fire and reflector

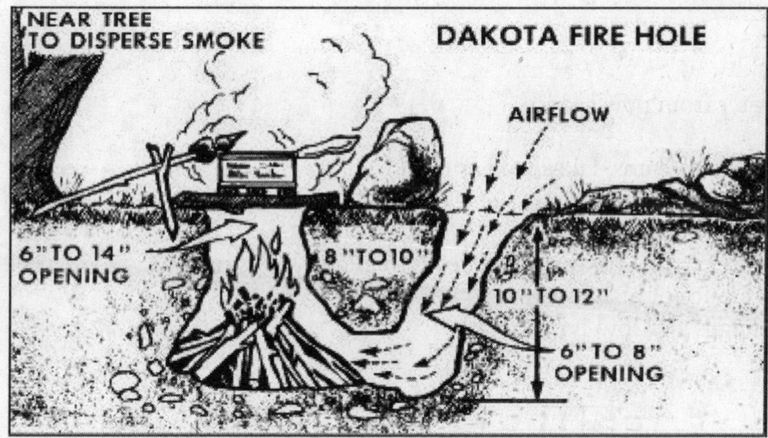

Figure 6-15. Dakota fire hole

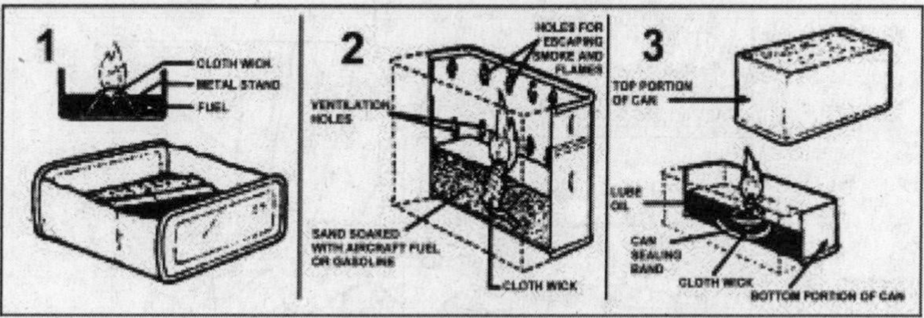

Figure 6-16. Improvised stove

CHAPTER 7

Water

1. WATER REQUIREMENTS

Drink **extra** water. Minimum 2 quarts per day to maintain fluid level. Exertion, heat, injury, or an illness increases water loss.

> **NOTE**
> Pale yellow urine indicates adequate hydration.

2. WATER PROCUREMENT

a. *DO NOT* drink—
   (1) Urine.
   (2) Fish juices.
   (3) Blood.
   (4) Sea water.
   (5) Alcohol.
   (6) Melted water from new sea ice.

b. Water sources:
   (1) Surface water (streams, lakes, and springs).
   (2) Precipitation (rain, snow, dew, sleet) **(Figure 7-1)**.
   (3) Subsurface (wells and cisterns).
   (4) Ground water (when no surface water is available) **(Figure 7-2)**.
      (a) Abundance of lush green vegetation.
      (b) Drainages and low-lying areas.

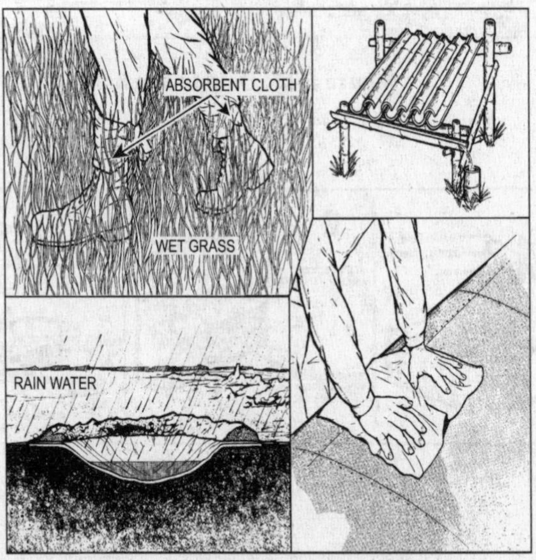

Figure 7-1. Water procurement

(c) *"V"* intersecting game trails often point to water.
(d) Presence of swarming insects indicates water is near.
(e) Bird flight in the early morning or late afternoon might indicate the direction to water.

(5) Snow or ice.
(a) ***DO NOT*** eat ice or snow.
- Lowers body temperature.
- Induces dehydration.
- Causes minor cold injury to lips and mouth.

(b) Melt with fire.
- Stir frequently to prevent damaging container.
- Speed the process by adding hot rocks or water.

(c) Melt with body heat.
- Use waterproof container.
- Place between layers of clothing.
- *DO NOT* **place next to the skin.**

(d) Use a water generator **(Figure 7-3)**.

(6) Open seas.
(a) Water available in survival kits.
(b) Precipitation.
- Drink as much as possible.
- Catch rain in spray shields and life raft covers.
- Collect dew off raft.

(c) Old sea ice or icebergs **(Table 7-1)**.

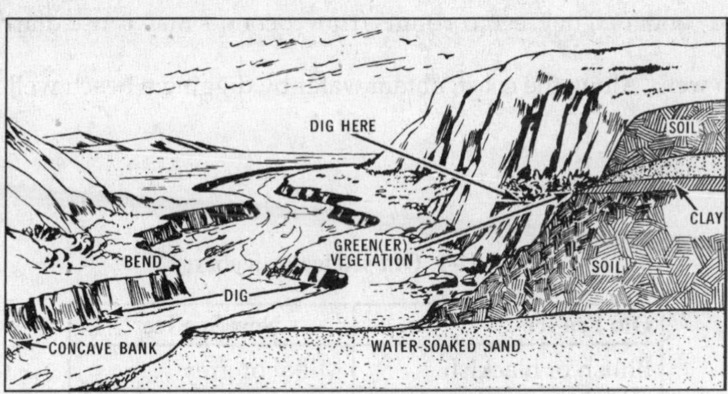

Figure 7-2. Water indicators

Figure 7-3. Water generator

(7) Tropical areas.
   (a) All open sources previously mentioned.
   (b) Vegetation.
   - Plants with hollow sections can collect moisture.
   - Leaning Tree. Cloth absorbs rain running down tree and drips into container **(Figure 7-4)**.
   - Banana plants.
   - Water trees (avoid milky sap).
     - Tap before dark. Let sap stop running and harden during the daytime.
     - Produce most water at night.
     - For evasion situations, bore into the roots and collect water.
   - Vines **(Figure 7-5A)**.
     - Cut bark (*DO NOT* use milky sap).
     - If juice is clear and water like, cut as large a piece of vine as possible (cut the top first).
     - Pour into hand to check smell, color, and taste to determine if drinkable.
     - *DO NOT* touch vine to lips.
     - When water flow stops, cut off 6 inches of opposite end, water will flow again.
   - Old bamboo.
     - Shake and listen for water.
     - Bore hole at bottom of section to obtain water.
     - Cut out entire section to carry with you.
     - Filter and purify.
   - Green bamboo **(Figure 7-5B)**.

CAUTION

Liquid contained in green coconuts (**ripe** coconuts may cause diarrhea).

   - Beach well. Along the coast, obtain water by digging a beach well **(Figure 7-6)**.

(8) Dry areas.
   (a) Solar still **(Figure 7-7)**.
   (b) Vegetation bag **(Figure 7-8)**.

Table VII-1. Old sea ice or icebergs

Old Sea Ice	New Sea Ice
Bluish or blackish	Milky or grey
Shatters easily	Does not break easily
Rounded corners	Sharp edges
Tastes relatively salt-free	Tastes extremely salty

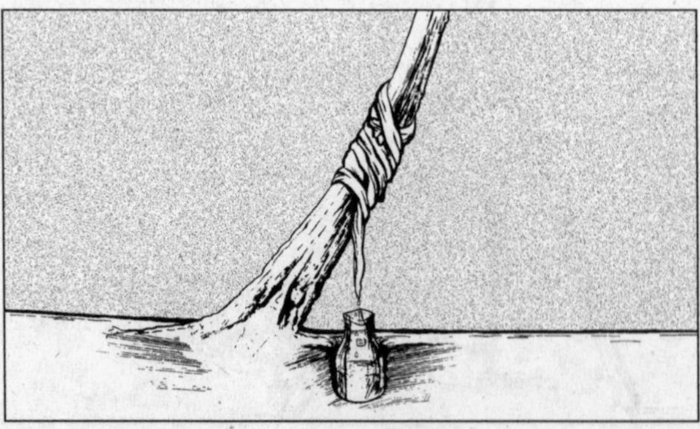

Figure 7-4. Leaning tree

(c) Transpiration bag **(Figure 7-9)**.
- Water bag must be clear.
- Water will taste like the plant smells.

(d) Seepage basin **(Figure 7-10)**.

CAUTION
DO NOT use poisonous/toxic plants in vegetation/ transpiration bags.

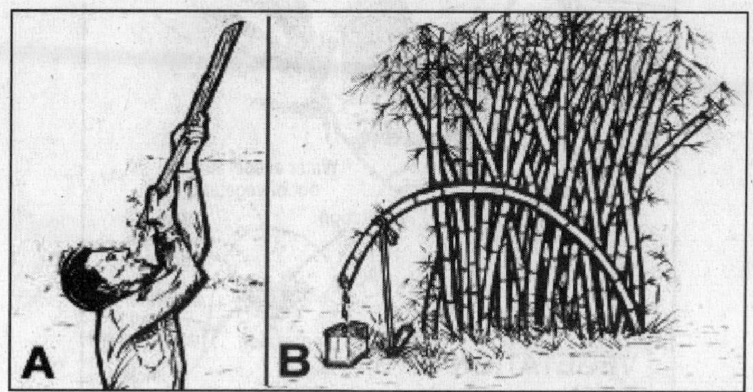

Figure 7-5 A and B. Water vines and green bamboo

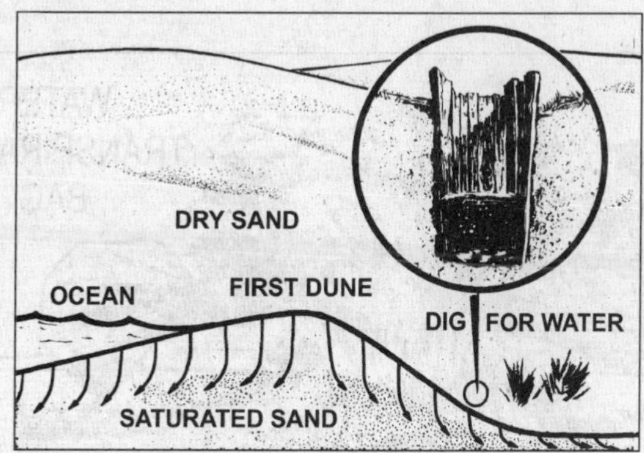

Figure 7-6. Beach well

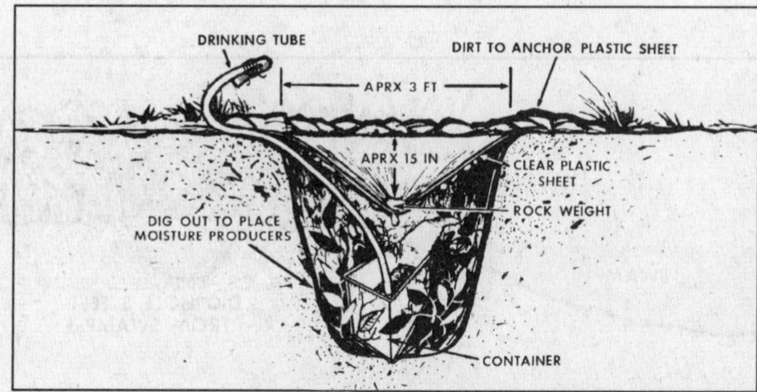

Figure 7-7. Solar still

3. WATER PREPARATION AND STORAGE

a. Filtration. Filter through porous material (sand/charcoal).
b. Purification.
   (1) Water from live plants requires no further treatment.
   (2) Purify all other water.

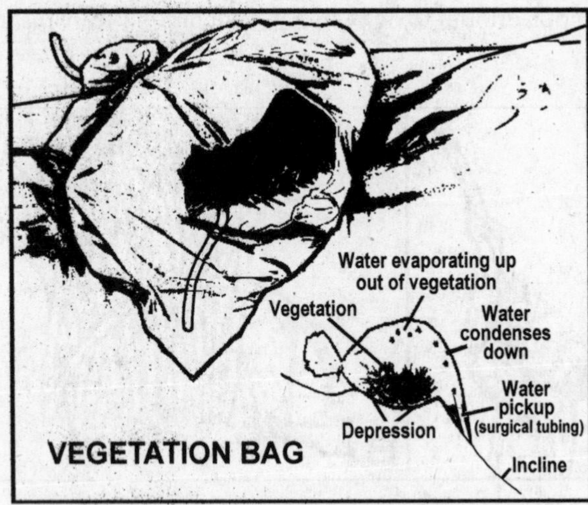

Figure 7-8. Vegetation bag

Figure 7-9. Transpiration bag

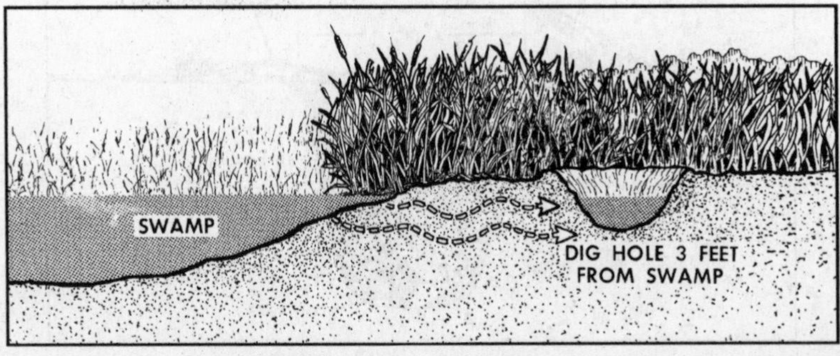

Figure 7-10. Seepage basin

(a) Boil at least 1 minute.
(b) Pour from one container to another to improve taste to aerate.
(c) Water purification tablets. Follow instructions on package.

c. Potable Water.
(1) If water cannot be purified, obtain water from a clear, cold, clean, and fast running source (if possible).
(2) Put in clear container and expose to the sun's ultraviolet rays to kill bacteria.

d. Storage. To prevent contamination, use a clean, covered or sealed container.
(1) Trash bag.
(2) Prophylactic.
(3) Section of bamboo.
(4) Flotation gear.

CHAPTER 8

Food

1. FOOD PROCUREMENT

a. Sources and location.
   (1) Mammals can be found where—
      (a) Trails lead to watering, feeding, and bedding areas.
      (b) Droppings or tracks look fresh.
   (2) Birds can be found by—
      (a) Observing the direction of flight in the early morning and late afternoon (leads to feeding, watering, and roosting areas).
      (b) Listening for bird noises (indication of nesting areas).
   (3) Fish and other marine life locations **(Figure 8-1)**.
   (4) Reptiles and amphibians are found almost worldwide.
   (5) Insects are found—
      (a) In dead logs and stumps.
      (b) At ant and termite mounds.
      (c) On ponds, lakes, and slow moving streams.

b. Procurement techniques.
   (1) Snares—
      (a) Work while unattended.
      (b) Location:
         - Trails leading to water, feeding, and bedding areas.
         - Mouth of dens **(Figure 8-2)**.
      (c) Construction of simple loop snare.
         - Use materials that will not break under the strain of holding an animal.
         - Use a figure 8 (locking loop) if wire is used **(Figure 8-3)**.
            - Once tightened, the wire locks in place, preventing reopening, and the animal's escape.
         - To construct a squirrel pole **(Figure 8-4)** use simple loop snares.

Figure 8-1. Fishing locations

- Make noose opening slightly larger than the animal's head (**3-finger** width for squirrels, **fist-sized** for rabbits).

(d) Placement of snares (set as many as possible).
- Avoid disturbing the area.
- Use funneling (natural or improvised) **(Figure 8-5)**.

(2) Noose stick (easier and safer to use than the hands).

(3) Twist stick **(Figure 8-6)**.

(a) Insert forked stick into a den until something soft is met.

(b) Twist the stick, binding the animal's hide in the fork.

(c) Remove the animal from the den.

(d) Be ready to **kill** the animal; **it may be dangerous**.

Figure 8-2. Snare placement

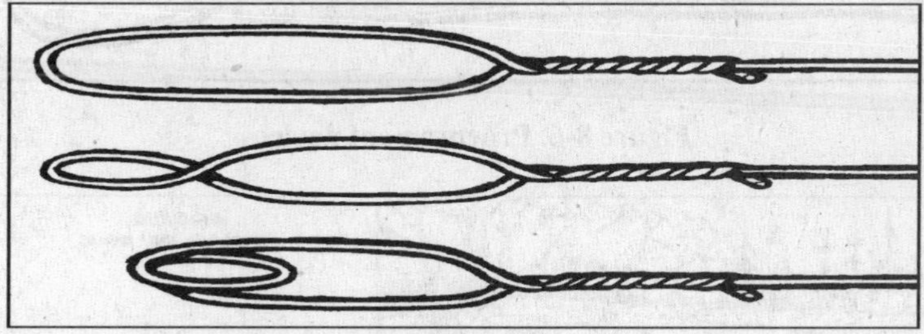

Figure 8-3. Locking loop

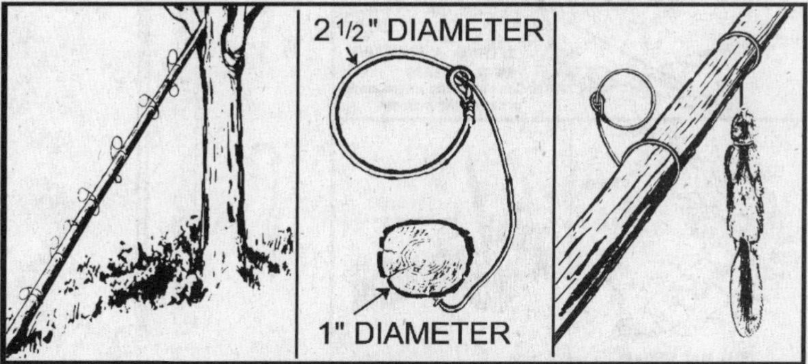

Figure 8-4. Squirrel pole

(4) Hunting and fishing devices. (See **Figure 8-7** for fishing procurement methods.)
  (a) Club or rock.
  (b) Spear.
  (c) Slingshot.
  (d) Pole, line, and hook.
  (e) Net.
  (f) Trap.

Figure 8-5. Funneling

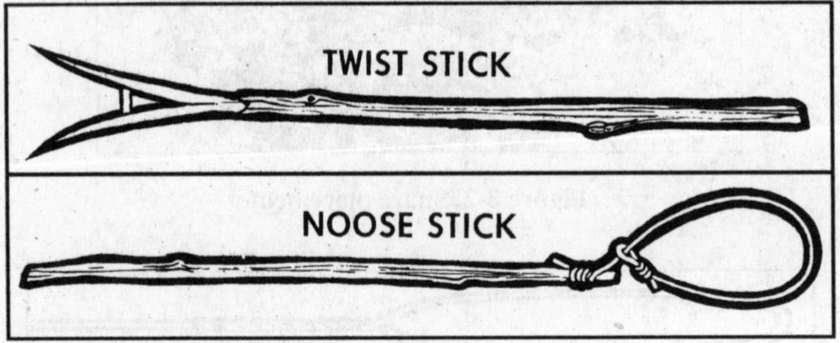

Figure 8-6. Procurement devices

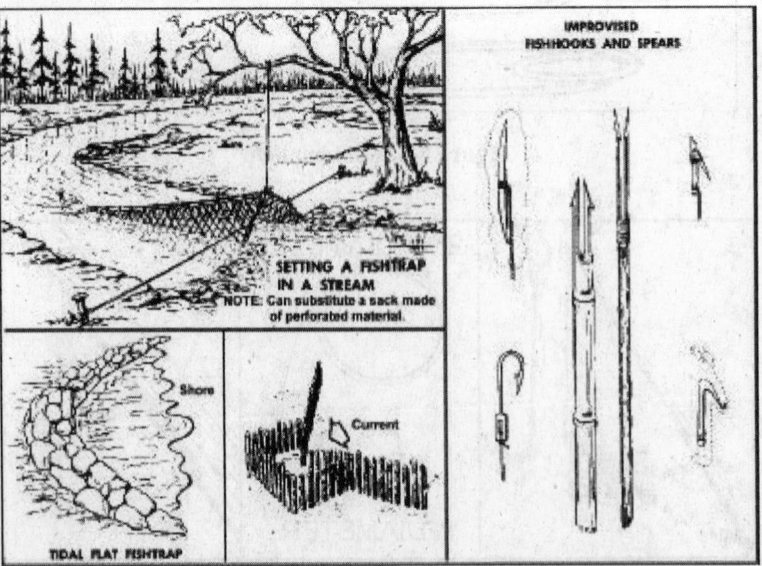

Figure 8-7. Procurement methods

(5) Precautions:
   (a) Wear shoes to protect the feet when wading in water.
   (b) Avoid reaching into dark holes.
   (c) **Kill** animals before handling. Animals in distress may attract the enemy.
   (d) ***DO NOT*** secure fishing lines to yourself or the raft.
   (e) **Kill** fish before bringing them into the raft.
   (f) ***DO NOT*** eat fish with—
      - Spines.
      - Unpleasant odor.
      - Pale, slimy gills.
      - Sunken eyes.
      - Flabby skin.
      - Flesh that remains dented when pressed.
   (g) ***DO NOT*** eat fish eggs or liver (entrails).
   (h) Avoid all crustaceans above the high tide mark.
   (i) Avoid cone-shaped shells **(Figure 8-8).**
   (j) Avoid hairy insects; the hairs could cause irritation or infection.
   (k) Avoid poisonous insects, for example:
      - Centipedes.
      - Scorpions.
      - Poisonous spiders.
   (l) Avoid disease carrying insects, such as—
      - Flies.
      - Mosquitoes.
      - Ticks.

c. Plant Foods. ***Before using the following guide use your evasion chart to identify edible plants:***

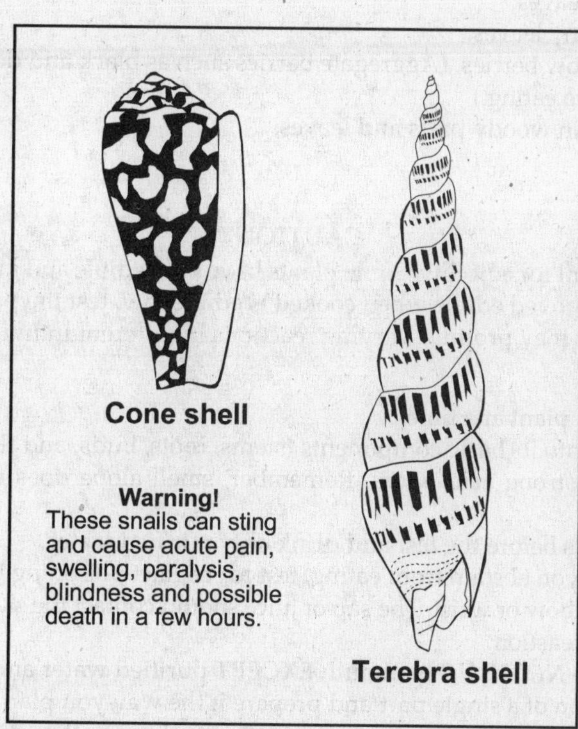

Figure 8-8. Cone-shaped shells of venomous snails

NOTE

If you cannot positively identity an edible plant and choose to try an unknown plant, these guidelines may help determine edibility.

(1) Selection criteria.
   (a) Before testing for edibility, ensure there are enough plants to make testing worth your time and effort. Each part of a plant (roots, leaves, stems, bark, etc.) requires more than 24 hours to test. ***DO NOT*** waste time testing a plant that is not abundant.
   (b) Test only 1 part of **1** plant at a time.
   (c) Remember that eating large portions of plant food on an empty stomach may cause diarrhea, nausea, or cramps. ***Two*** good examples are ***green apples*** and ***wild onions.*** Even after testing food and finding it safe, eat in moderation.
(2) Avoid plants with the following characteristics:

NOTE

Using these guidelines in selecting plants for food may eliminate some edible plants; however, these guidelines will help prevent choosing potentially toxic plants.

   (a) Milky sap (dandelion has milky sap but is safe to eat and easily recognizable).
   (b) Spines, fine hairs, and thorns (skin irritants/contact dermatitis). ***Prickly pear*** and ***thistles*** are exceptions. ***Bracken fern fiddleheads*** also violate this guideline.
   (c) Mushrooms and fungus.
   (d) Umbrella shaped flowers (hemlock is eliminated).
   (e) Bulbs (***only*** onions smell like onions).
   (f) Grain heads with pink, purplish, or black spurs.
   (g) Beans, bulbs, or seeds inside pods.
   (h) Old or wilted leaves.
   (i) Plants with shiny leaves.
   (j) White and yellow berries. (Aggregate berries such as black and dewberries are always edible, test all others before eating.)
   (k) Almond scent in woody parts and leaves.

d. Test procedures.

CAUTION

Test all parts of the plant for edibility. Some plants have both edible and inedible parts. **NEVER ASSUME** a part that proved edible when cooked is edible raw, test the part raw before eating. The same part or plant may produce varying reactions in different individuals.

(1) Test only **1** part of a plant at a time.
(2) Separate the plant into its basic components (stems, roots, buds, and flowers).
(3) Smell the food for strong acid odors. Remember, smell alone does not indicate a plant is edible or inedible.
(4) ***DO NOT*** eat 8 hours before the test and drink only purified water.
(5) During the 8 hours you abstain from eating, test for contact poisoning by placing a piece of the plant on the inside of your elbow or wrist. The sap or juice should contact the skin. Usually 15 minutes is enough time to allow for a reaction.
(6) During testing, take ***NOTHING*** by mouth **EXCEPT** purified water and the plant you are testing.
(7) Select a small portion of a single part and prepare it the way you plan to eat it.
(8) Before placing the prepared plant in your mouth, touch a small portion (a pinch) to the outer surface of your lip to test for burning or itching.

(9) If after 3 minutes there is no reaction on your lip, place the plant on your tongue and hold it for 15 minutes.

(10) If there is no reaction, thoroughly chew a pinch and hold it in your mouth for 15 minutes ***(DO NOT SWALLOW)***. If any ill effects occur, rinse out your mouth with water.

(11) If nothing abnormal occurs, swallow the food and wait 8 hours. If **any ill effects** occur during this period, **induce** vomiting and drink a water and charcoal mixture.

(12) If no ill effects occur, eat ¼ **cup** of the same plant prepared the same way. Wait another 8 hours. If no ill effects occur, the plant part as prepared is safe for eating.

CAUTION

1. Ripe tropical fruits should be peeled and eaten raw. Softness, rather than color, is the best indicator of ripeness. Cook unripe fruits and discard seeds and skin.
2. Cook underground portions when possible to reduce bacterial contamination and ease digestion of their generally high starch content.
3. During evasion, you may not be able to cook. Concentrate your efforts on leafy green plants, ripe fruits, and above ground ripe vegetables not requiring significant preparation.

2. FOOD PREPARATION

Animal food gives the greatest food value per pound.

a. Butchering and skinning.

(1) Mammals.

(a) Remove the skin and save for other uses.

(b) One cut skinning of small game **(Figure 8-9)**.

- Open the abdominal cavity.
- Avoid rupturing the intestines.
- Remove the intestines.
- Save inner organs (heart, liver, and kidneys) and all meaty parts of the skull, brain, tongue, and eyes.

(c) Wash when ready to use.

(d) If preserving the meat, remove it from the bones.

(e) Unused or inedible organs and entrails may be used as bait for other game.

(2) Frogs and snakes.

(a) Skin.

(b) Discard skin, head with 2 inches of body, and internal organs.

(3) Fish.

(a) Scale (if necessary) and gut fish soon after it is caught.

(b) Insert knifepoint into anus of fish and cut open the belly.

Figure 8-9. Small game skinning

(c) Remove entrails.
(d) Remove gills to prevent spoilage.
(4) Birds.
(a) Gut soon after killing.
(b) Protect from flies.
(c) Skin or pluck them.
(d) Skin scavengers and sea birds.
(5) Insects.
(a) Remove all hard portions such as the legs of grasshoppers or crickets. (The rest is edible.)
(b) Recommend cooking grasshopper-size insects.

CAUTION
Dead insects spoil rapidly, ***DO NOT*** save.

(6) Fruits, berries, and most nuts can be eaten raw.
b. Cooking.

CAUTION
To kill parasites, thoroughly cook all wild game, freshwater fish, clams, mussels, snails, crawfish, and scavenger birds. Saltwater fish may be eaten raw.

(1) Boiling (most nutritious method of cooking—drink the broth).
(a) Make metal cooking containers from ration cans.
(b) Drop heated rocks into containers to boil water or cook food.
(2) Baking.
(a) Wrap in leaves or pack in mud.
(b) Bury food in dirt under coals of fire.
(3) Leaching. Some nuts (acorns) must be leached to remove the bitter taste of tannin. Use one of the following leaching methods:
(a) First method:
- Soaking and pouring the water off.
- Crushing and pouring water through. Cold water should be tried first; however, boiling water is sometimes best.
- Discarding water.

(b) Second method:
- Boil, pour off water, and taste the plant.
- If bitter, repeat process until palatable.

(4) Roasting.
(a) Shake shelled nuts in a container with hot coals.
(b) Roast thinly sliced meat and insects over a candle.

3. FOOD PRESERVATION

b. Keeping an animal alive.
c. Refrigerating.
(1) Long term.
(a) Food buried in snow maintains a temperature of approximately 32 degrees F.
(b) Frozen food will not decompose (freeze in meal-size portions).
(2) Short term.
(a) Food wrapped in waterproof material and placed in a stream remains cool in summer months.
(b) Earth below the surface, particularly in shady areas or along streams, is cooler than the surface.
(c) Wrap food in absorbent material such as cotton and re-wet as the water evaporates.

c. Drying and smoking removes moisture and preserves food.
   (1) Use salt to improve flavor and promote drying.
   (2) Cut or pound meat into thin strips.
   (3) Remove fat.
   (4) ***DO NOT*** use pitch woods such as fir or pine; they produce soot giving the meat an undesirable taste.

d. Protecting meat from animals and insects.
   (1) Wrapping food.
      (a) Use clean material.
      (b) Wrap pieces individually.
      (c) Ensure all corners of the wrapping are insect proof.
      (d) Wrap soft fruits and berries in leaves or moss.
   (2) Hanging meat.
      (a) Hang meat in the shade.
      (b) Cover during daylight hours to protect from insects.
   (3) Packing meat on the trail.
      (a) Wrap before flies appear in the morning.
      (b) Place meat in fabric or clothing for insulation.
      (c) Place meat inside the pack for carrying. Soft material acts as insulation helping keep the meat cool.
      (d) Carry shellfish, crabs, and shrimp in wet seaweed.

e. ***DO NOT*** store food in the shelter; it attracts unwanted animals.

CHAPTER 9

Induced Conditions

(Nuclear, Biological, and Chemical Considerations)

1. NUCLEAR CONDITIONS

> **CAUTION**
> Radiation protection depends on time of exposure, distance from the source, and shielding.

a. Protection.
  (1) **FIND PROTECTIVE SHELTER IMMEDIATELY!**
  (2) Gather all equipment for survival (time permitting).
  (3) Avoid detection and capture.
    (a) Seek existing shelter that may be improved (**Figure 9-1**).
    (b) If no shelter is available, dig a trench or foxhole as follows:
      - Dig trench deep enough for protection, then enlarge for comfort (**Figure 9-2**).
      - Cover with available material.
  (4) Radiation shielding efficienceis (**Figure 9-3**).
  (5) Leave contaminated equipment and clothing near shelter for retrieval after radioactive decay.
  (6) Lie down, keep warm, sleep, and rest.

b. Substance:
  (1) Water. Allow no more than 30 minutes exposure on **3d** day for water procurement.
    (a) Water sources (in order of preference):
      - Springs, wells, or underground sources are **safest**.
      - Water in pipes/containers in abandoned buildings.

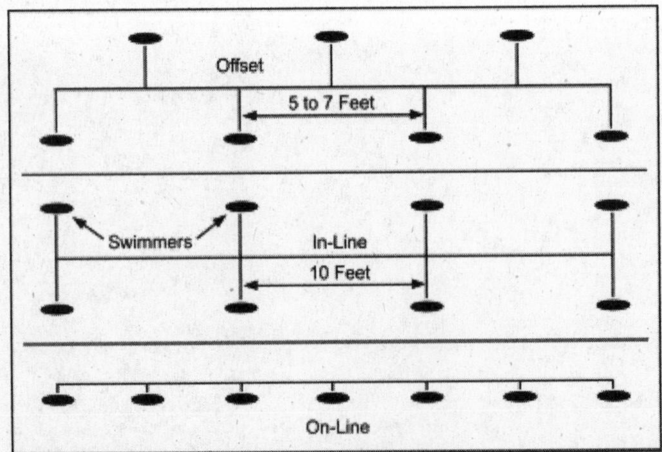

Figure 9-1. Immediate action shelter

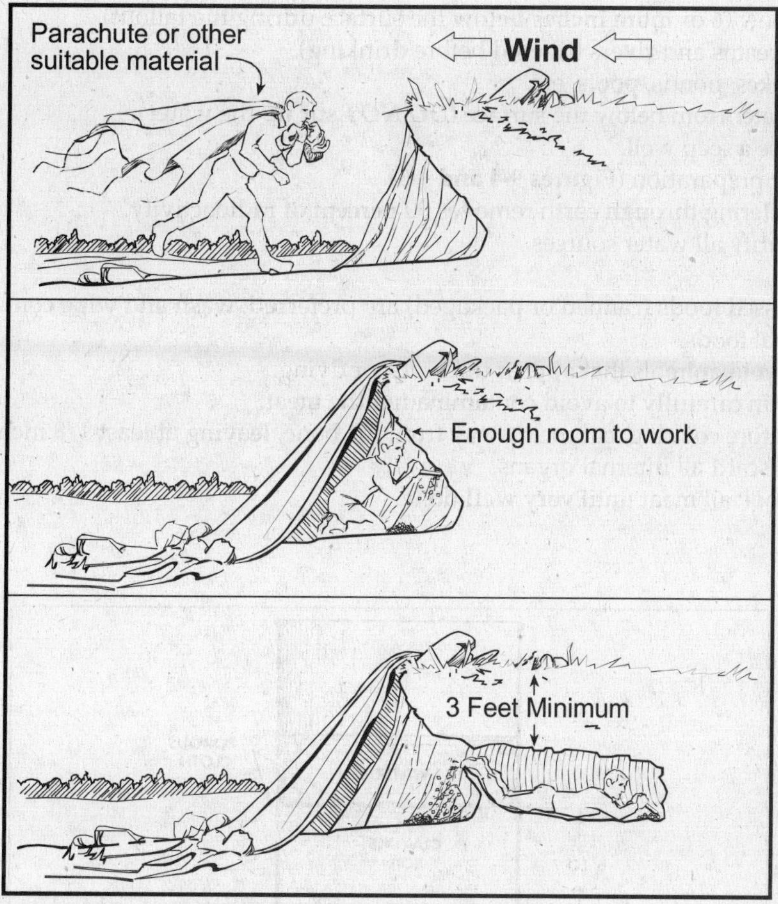

Figure 9-2. Improvised shelter

NUCLEAR EXPLOSIONS: Fall flat. Cover exposed body parts. Present minimal profile to direction of blast. ***DO NOT** look at fireball!* Remain prone until blast effects are over.

SHELTER: Pick, as soon as possible, 5 minutes unsheltered is maximum!

Priority:
(1) Cave or tunnel covered with 3 or more feet of earth.
(2) Storm/storage cellars
(3) Culverts.
(4) Basements.
(5) Abandoned stone/mud buildings.
(6) Foxhole 4 feet deep (remove topsoil within 2 feet radius of foxhole lip).

RADIATION SHIELDING EFFICIENCIES

Iron/Steel	.7 inches	**Cinder Block**	5.3 inches
Brick	2.0 inches	**Ice**	6.8 inches
Concrete	2.2 inches	**Wood (Soft)**	8.8 inches
Earth	3.3 inches	**Snow**	20.3 inches

One thickness reduces received radiation dose by 1/2.
Additional thickness added to any amount of thickness reduces received radiation dose by 1/2.

SHELTER SURVIVAL: Keep contaminated materials out of shelter.
Good Weather: Bury contaminated clothing outside of shelter (recover later).
Bad Weather: Shake strongly or beat with branches. Rinse and /or shake wet clothing. ***DO NOT** wring out!*

PERSONAL HYGIENE: Wash entire body with soap and *any* water; give close attention to fingernails and hairy parts.
No Water: Wipe all exposed skin surfaces with clean cloth or uncontaminated soil. Fallout/dusty conditions--keep entire body covered. Keep handkerchief/cloth over mouth and nose. Improvise goggles. ***DO NOT** smoke!*

DAILY RADIATION TIME TABLE for NO RATE METER

4-6	Complete isolation	**9-12**	2-4 hours exposure per day
3-7	Brief exposure (30 minutes maximum)	**13**	Normal movement.
8	Brief exposure (1 hour maximum)		

Figure 9-3. Radiation shielding efficiencies

- Snow (6 or **more inches below** the surface during the fallout).
- Streams and rivers (filtered before drinking).
- Lakes, ponds, pools, etc.
- Water from below the surface (***DO NOT*** stir up the water).
- Use a seep well.

(b) Water preparation (**Figures 9-4 and 9-5**).

- Filtering through earth removes 99 percent of radioactivity.
- Purify all water sources.

(2) Food.

(a) Processed foods (canned or packaged) are preferred; wash and wipe containers before use.

(b) Animal foods.

- Avoid animals that appear to be sick or dying.
- Skin carefully to avoid contaminating the meat.
- Before cooking, cut meat away from the bone, leaving at least 1/8 inch of meat on the bone.
- Discard all internal organs.
- Cook all meat until **very well** done.

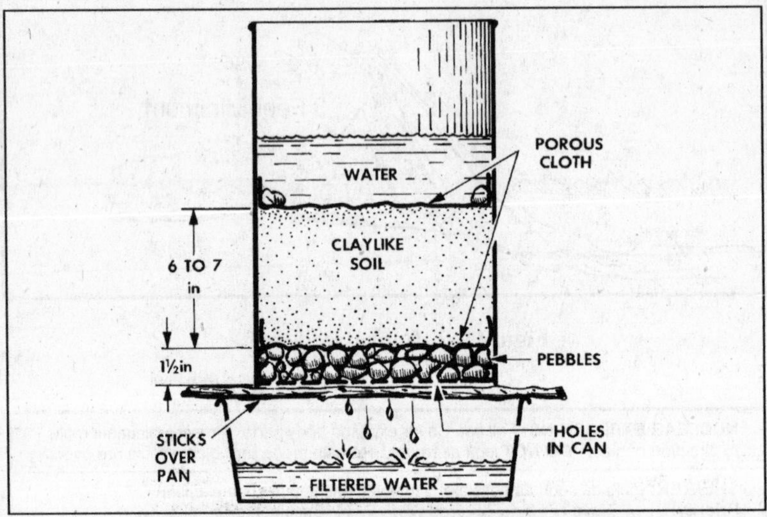

Figure 9-4. Filtration systems, filtering water

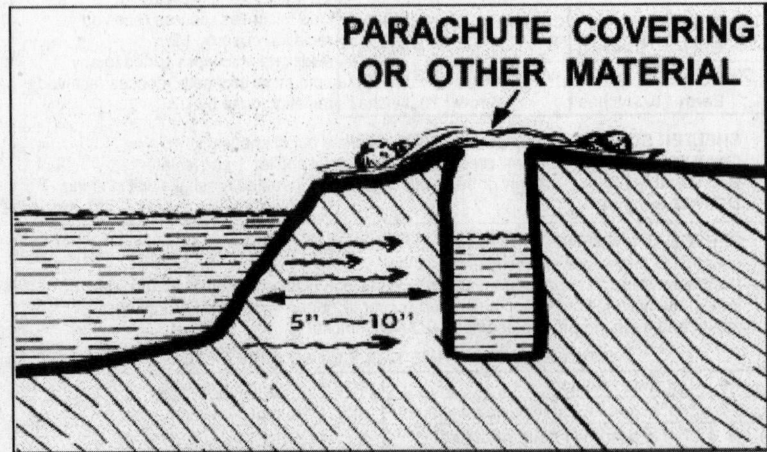

Figure 9-5. Filtration systems, settling water

(c) Avoid.
- Aquatic food sources (use only in extreme emergencies because of high concentration of radiation).
- Shells of all eggs (contents will be safe to eat).
- Milk from animals.

(d) Plant foods (in order of preference).
- Plants whose edible portions grow underground (for example, potatoes, turnips, carrots, etc.). Wash and remove skin.
- Edible portions growing above ground that can be washed and peeled or skinned (bananas, apples, etc.).
- Smooth skinned vegetables, fruits, or above ground plants that are not easily peeled or washed.

c. Self-aid:

(1) General rules:
(a) Prevent exposure to contaminants.
(b) Use personal hygiene practices and remove body waste from shelter.
(c) Rest, avoid fatigue.
(d) Drink liquids.

(2) Wounds.
(a) Clean affected area.
(b) Use antibacterial ointment or cleaning solution.
(c) Cover with clean dressing.
(d) Watch for signs of infection.

(3) Burns.
(a) Clean affected area.
(b) Cover with clean dressing.

(4) Radiation sickness (nausea, weakness, fatigue, vomiting, diarrhea, loss of hair, radiation burns).
(a) Time is required to overcome.
(b) Rest.
(c) Drink fluids.
(d) Maintain food intake.
(e) Prevent additional exposure.

2. BIOLOGICAL CONDITIONS

a. Clues which may alert you to a biological attack follow:
(1) Enemy aircraft dropping objects or spraying.
(2) Breakable containers or unusual bombs, particularly those bursting with little or no blast, and muffled explosions.
(3) Smoke or mist of unknown origin.
(4) Unusual substances on the ground or vegetation; sick looking plants or crops.

b. Protection from biological agents follow:
(1) Use protective equipment.
(2) Bathe as soon as the situation permits.
(3) Wash hair and body thoroughly with soap and water.
(4) Clean thoroughly under fingernails.
(5) Clean teeth, gums, tongue, and roof of mouth frequently.

c. Survival tips for biological conditions follow:
(1) Keep your body and living area clean.
(2) Stay alert for clues of biological attack.
(3) Keep nose, mouth, and skin covered.
(4) Keep food and water protected. Bottled or canned foods are safe if sealed. If in doubt, boil food and water for 10 minutes.
(5) Construct shelter in a clear area, away from vegetation, with entrance 90 degrees to the prevailing wind.
(6) If traveling, travel crosswind or upwind (taking advantage of terrain to stay away from depressions).

3. CHEMICAL CONDITIONS

a. Detecting.
   (1) Smell. Many agents have little or no odor.
   (2) Sight. Many agents are colorless:
      (a) Color. Yellow, orange, or red smoke or mist.
      (b) Liquid. Oily, dark patches on leaves, ground, etc.
      (c) Gas. Some agents appear as a mist immediately after shell burst.
      (d) Solid. Most solid state agents have some color.
   (3) Sound. Muffled explosions are possible indications of chemical agent bombs.
   (4) Feel. Irritation to the nose, eyes, or skin and/or moisture on the skin are danger signs.
   (5) Taste. Strange taste in food or water indicates contamination.
   (6) General indications. Tears, difficult breathing, choking, itching, coughing, dizziness.
   (7) Wildlife. Presence of sick or dying animals.

b. Protection against chemical agents follows:
   (1) Use protective equipment.
   (2) Avoid contaminated areas.
      (a) Exit contaminated area by moving crosswind.
      (b) Select routes on high ground.
      (c) Avoid cellars, ditches, trenches, gullies, valleys, etc.
      (d) Avoid woods, tall grasses, and bushes as they tend to hold chemical agent vapors.
      (e) Decontaminate body and equipment as soon as possible by—
         - Removing. Pinch-blotting.
         - Neutralizing. Warm water.
         - Destroying. Burying.

c. Self-aid in chemically contaminated areas.
   (1) If a chemical defense ensemble is available—
      (a) Use all protective equipment.
      (b) Follow antidote directions when needed.
   (2) If a chemical defense ensemble is not available—
      (a) Remove or tear away contaminated clothing.
      (b) Rinse contaminated areas with water.
      (c) Improvise a breathing filter using materials available (T-shirt, handkerchief, fabric, etc.).

d. Tips for the survivor:
   (1) *DO NOT* use wood from a contaminated area for fire.
   (2) Look for signs of chemical agents around water sources before procurement (oil spots, foreign odors, dead fish, or animals).
   (3) Keep food and water protected.
   (4) *DO NOT* use plants for food or water in contaminated areas.

APPENDIX A

The Will to Survive

ARTICLE VI CODE OF CONDUCT
I will never forget that I am an American fighting for freedom, responsible for my actions, and dedicated to the principles which made my country free. I will trust in my God and in the United States of America.

1. PSYCHOLOGY OF SURVIVAL

a. Preparation—
   (1) Know your capabilities and limitations.
   (2) Keep a positive attitude.
   (3) Develop a realistic plan.
   (4) Anticipate fears.
   (5) Combat psychological stress by—
      (a) Recognizing and anticipating existing *stressors* (injury, death, fatigue, illness, environment, hunger, isolation).
      (b) Attributing normal reactions to existing *stressors* (fear, anxiety, guilt, boredom, depression, anger).
      (c) Identifying signals of distress created by *stressors* (indecision, withdrawal, forgetfulness, carelessness, and propensity to make mistakes).

b. Strengthen your will to survive with—
   (1) The Code of Conduct.
   (2) Pledge of Allegiance.
   (3) Faith in America.
   (4) Patriotic songs.
   (5) Thoughts of return to family and friends.

c. Group dynamics of survival include—
   (1) Leadership, good organization, and cohesiveness promote high morale:
      (a) Preventing panic.
      (b) Creating strength and trust in one another.
      (c) Favoring persistency in overcoming failure.
      (d) Facilitating formulation of group goals.
   (2) Taking care of your buddy.
   (3) Working as a team.
   (4) Reassuring and encouraging each other.
   (5) Influencing factors are—
      (a) Enforcing the chain of command.
      (b) Organizing according to individual capabilities.
      (c) Accepting suggestions and criticism.

2. SPIRITUAL CONSIDERATIONS

a. Collect your thoughts and emotions.
b. Identify your personal beliefs.
c. Use self-control.

d. Meditate.
e. Remember past inner sources to help you overcome adversity.
f. Pray for your God's help, strength, wisdom, and rescue.
   (1) Talk to your God.
   (2) Give thanks that God is with you.
   (3) Ask for God's help.
   (4) Pray for protection and a positive outcome.
g. Remember scripture, verses, or hymns; repeat them to yourself and to your God.
h. Worship without aid of written scripture, clergy, or others.
i. Forgive—
   (1) Yourself for what you have done or said that was wrong.
   (2) Those who have failed you.
j. Praise God and give thanks because—
   (1) God is bigger than your circumstances.
   (2) God will see you through (no matter what happens).
   (3) Hope comes from a belief in heaven and/or an after-life.
k. Trust.
   (1) Faith and trust in your God.
   (2) Love for family and self.
   (3) Never lose hope.
   (4) Never give up.
l. With other survivors—
   (1) Identify or appoint a religious lay leader.
   (2) Discuss what is important to you.
   (3) Share scriptures and songs.
   (4) Pray for each other.
   (5) Try to have worship services.
   (6) Write down scriptures and songs that you remember.
   (7) Encourage each other while waiting for rescue, remember—
      (a) Your God loves you.
      (b) Praise your God.

3. ATHEISM.

a. The Pentagon lacks the imagination to give advice to, or acknowledge persons who do not believe in a God.
b. The Pentagon's only official position on atheism and atheists is that "there are no atheists in foxholes."
c. If you are an atheist, your team members will fully expect you to become a co-religionist, and will resent you if you do not at least feign interest in their brand of_____.
d. Many of your team members fully expect you to die for their right to hound you and prevent your professional advancement unless and until you believe in their God.
e. Many atheists exit foxholes.